Great Lives from History

The Middle Ages

477 - 1453

Volume 2
Kōken-Jan Žižka
Indexes

Editor
Shelley Wolbrink
Drury University

Editor, First Edition
Frank N. Magill

SALEM PRESS
Pasadena, California   Hackensack, New Jersey

Cover photos: Library of Congress

∞ The paper used in these volumes conforms to the American National Standard for Permanence of Paper for Printed Library Materials, Z39.48-1992 (R1997).

Some of the essays in this work originally appeared in the following Salem Press sets: *Dictionary of World Biography* (1998-1999, edited by Frank N. Magill) and *Great Lives from History* (1987-1995, edited by Frank N. Magill).

Library of Congress Cataloging-in-Publication Data

Great lives from history. The Middle Ages, 477-1453 / editor, Shelley Wolbrink.— 1st ed.
p. cm.
Includes bibliographical references and index.
ISBN 1-58765-164-5 (set : alk. paper) — ISBN 1-58765-165-3 (v. 1 : alk. paper) — ISBN 1-58765-166-1 (v. 2 : alk. paper)
1. Biography—Middle Ages, 500-1500. 2. Middle Ages—History. I. Wolbrink, Shelley.
CT114.G74 2005
920′.009′02—dc22

2004016696

First Printing

PRINTED IN THE UNITED STATES OF AMERICA

Contents

Key to Pronunciation

Many of the names of personages covered in *Great Lives from History: The Middle Ages, 477-1453* may be unfamiliar to students and general readers. For these unfamiliar names, guides to pronunciation have been provided upon first mention of the names in the text. These guidelines do not purport to achieve the subtleties of the languages in question but will offer readers a rough equivalent of how English speakers may approximate the proper pronunciation.

Vowel Sounds

Symbol	**Spelled (Pronounced)**
a	answer (AN-suhr), laugh (laf), sample (SAM-puhl), that (that)
ah	father (FAH-thur), hospital (HAHS-pih-tuhl)
aw	awful (AW-fuhl), caught (kawt)
ay	blaze (blayz), fade (fayd), waiter (WAYT-ur), weigh (way)
eh	bed (behd), head (hehd), said (sehd)
ee	believe (bee-LEEV), cedar (SEE-dur), leader (LEED-ur), liter (LEE-tur)
ew	boot (bewt), lose (lewz)
i	buy (bi), height (hit), lie (li), surprise (sur-PRIZ)
ih	bitter (BIH-tur), pill (pihl)
o	cotton (KO-tuhn), hot (hot)
oh	below (bee-LOH), coat (koht), note (noht), wholesome (HOHL-suhm)
oo	good (good), look (look)
ow	couch (kowch), how (how)
oy	boy (boy), coin (koyn)
uh	about (uh-BOWT), butter (BUH-tuhr), enough (ee-NUHF), other (UH-thur)

Consonant Sounds

Symbol	**Spelled (Pronounced)**
ch	beach (beech), chimp (chihmp)
g	beg (behg), disguise (dihs-GIZ), get (geht)
j	digit (DIH-juht), edge (ehj), jet (jeht)
k	cat (kat), kitten (KIH-tuhn), hex (hehks)
s	cellar (SEHL-ur), save (sayv), scent (sehnt)
sh	champagne (sham-PAYN), issue (IH-shew), shop (shop)
ur	birth (burth), disturb (dihs-TURB), earth (urth), letter (LEH-tur)
y	useful (YEWS-fuhl), young (yuhng)
z	business (BIHZ-nehs), zest (zehst)
zh	vision (VIH-zhuhn)

Complete List of Contents

Volume I

Volume 2

List of Maps and Tables

Eastern Hemisphere c. 800 C.E.

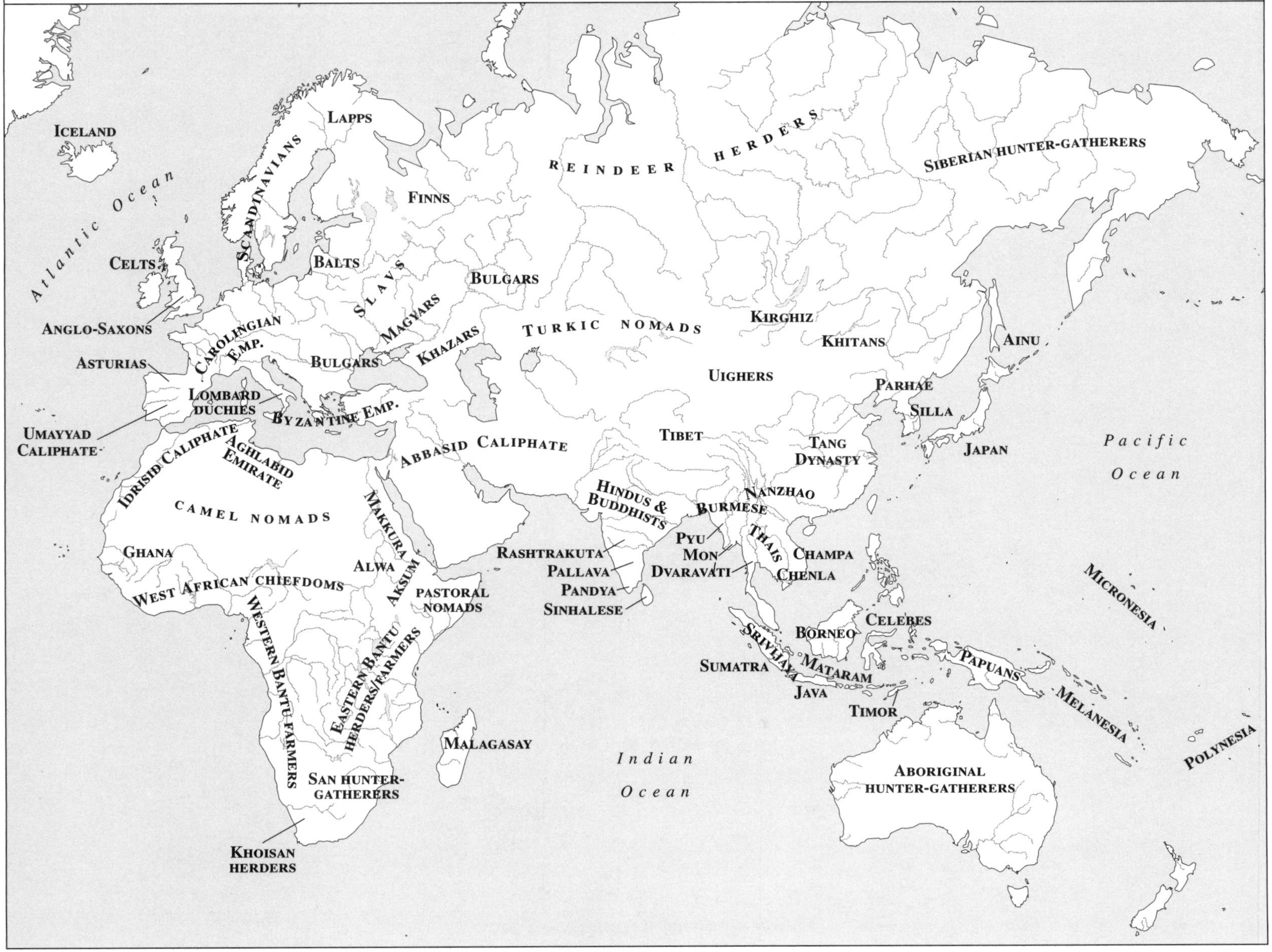

Eastern Hemisphere c. 1000

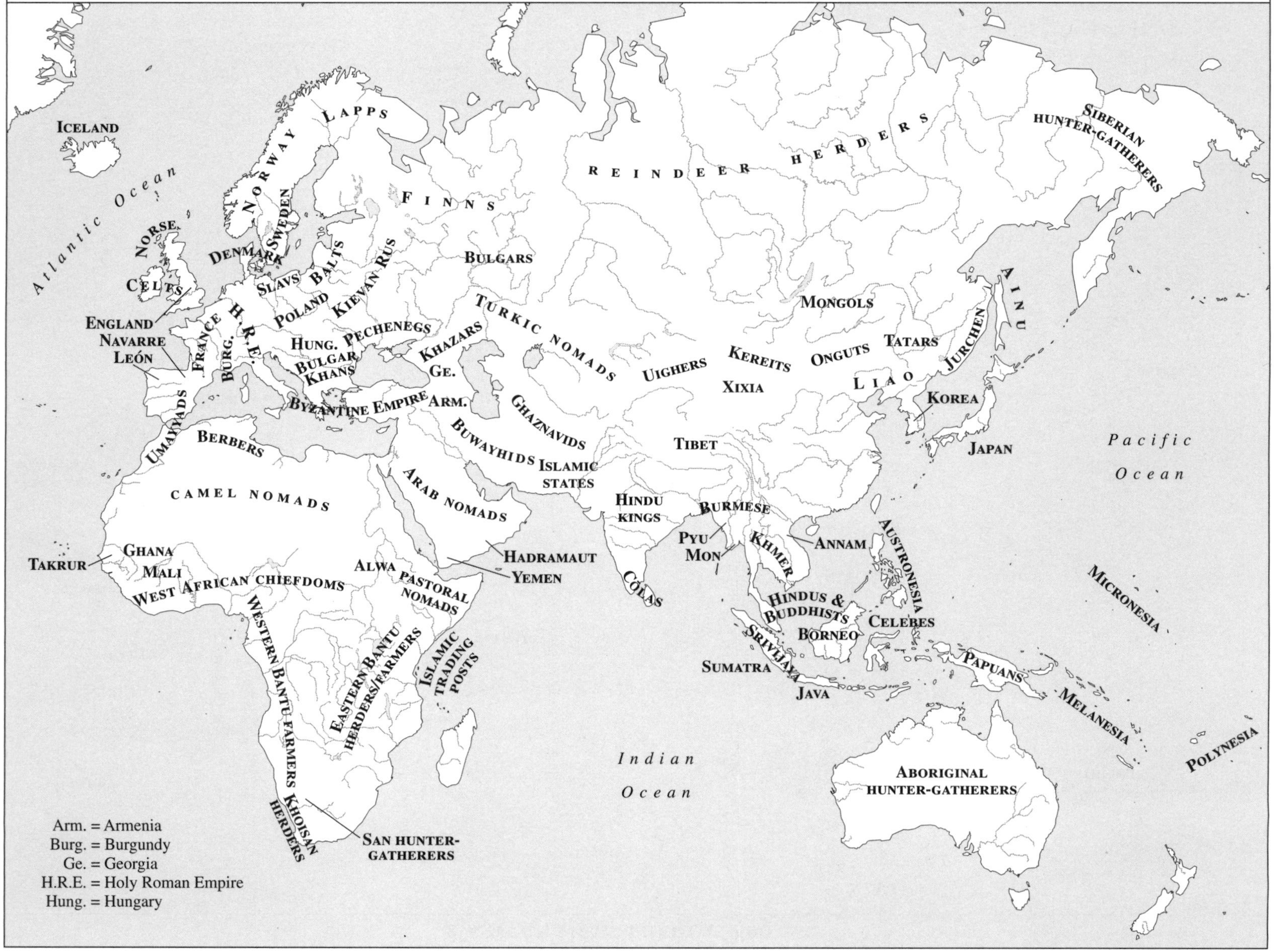

Arm. = Armenia
Burg. = Burgundy
Ge. = Georgia
H.R.E. = Holy Roman Empire
Hung. = Hungary

Eastern Hemisphere, 1279

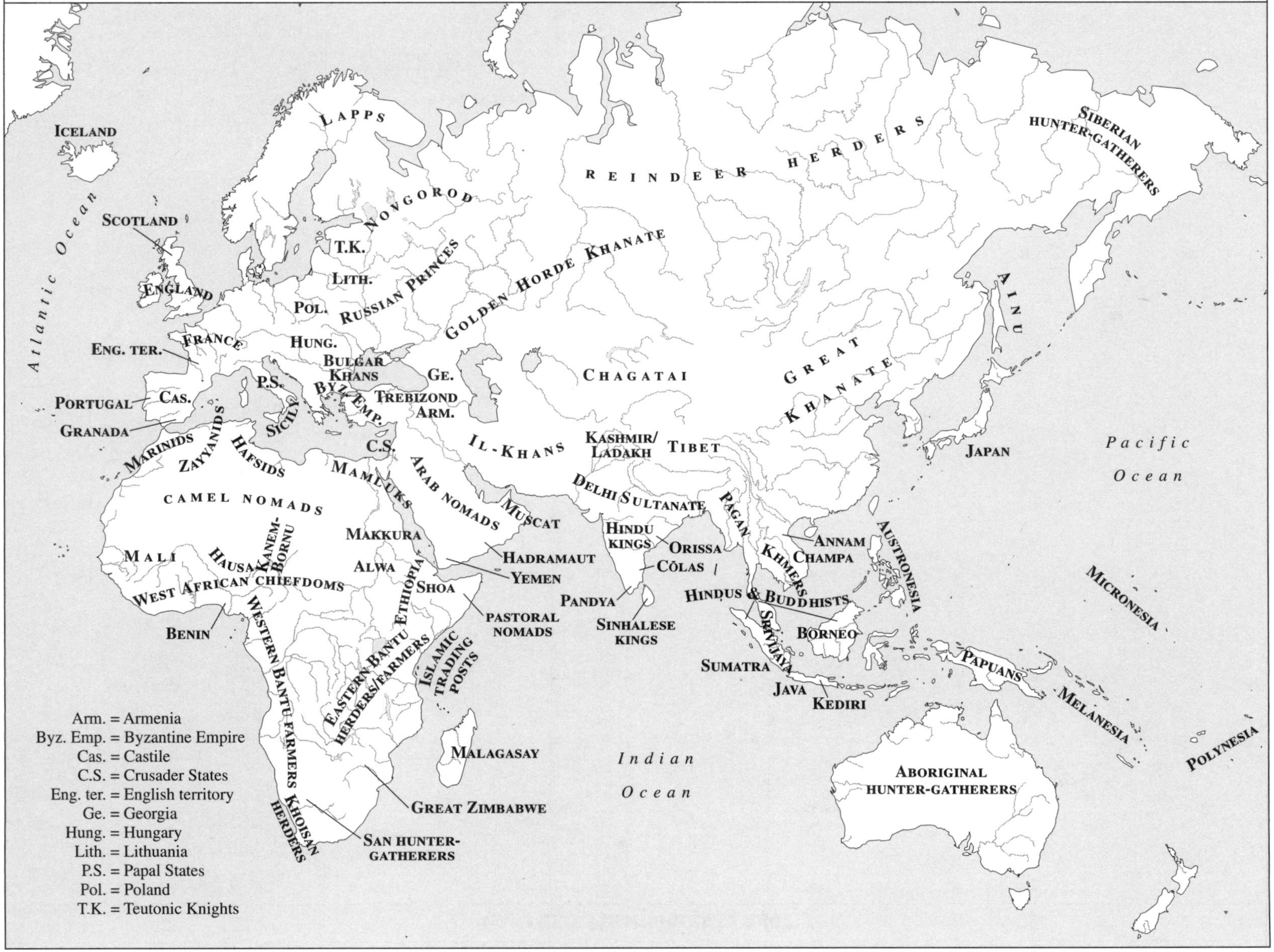

Eastern Hemisphere, 1492

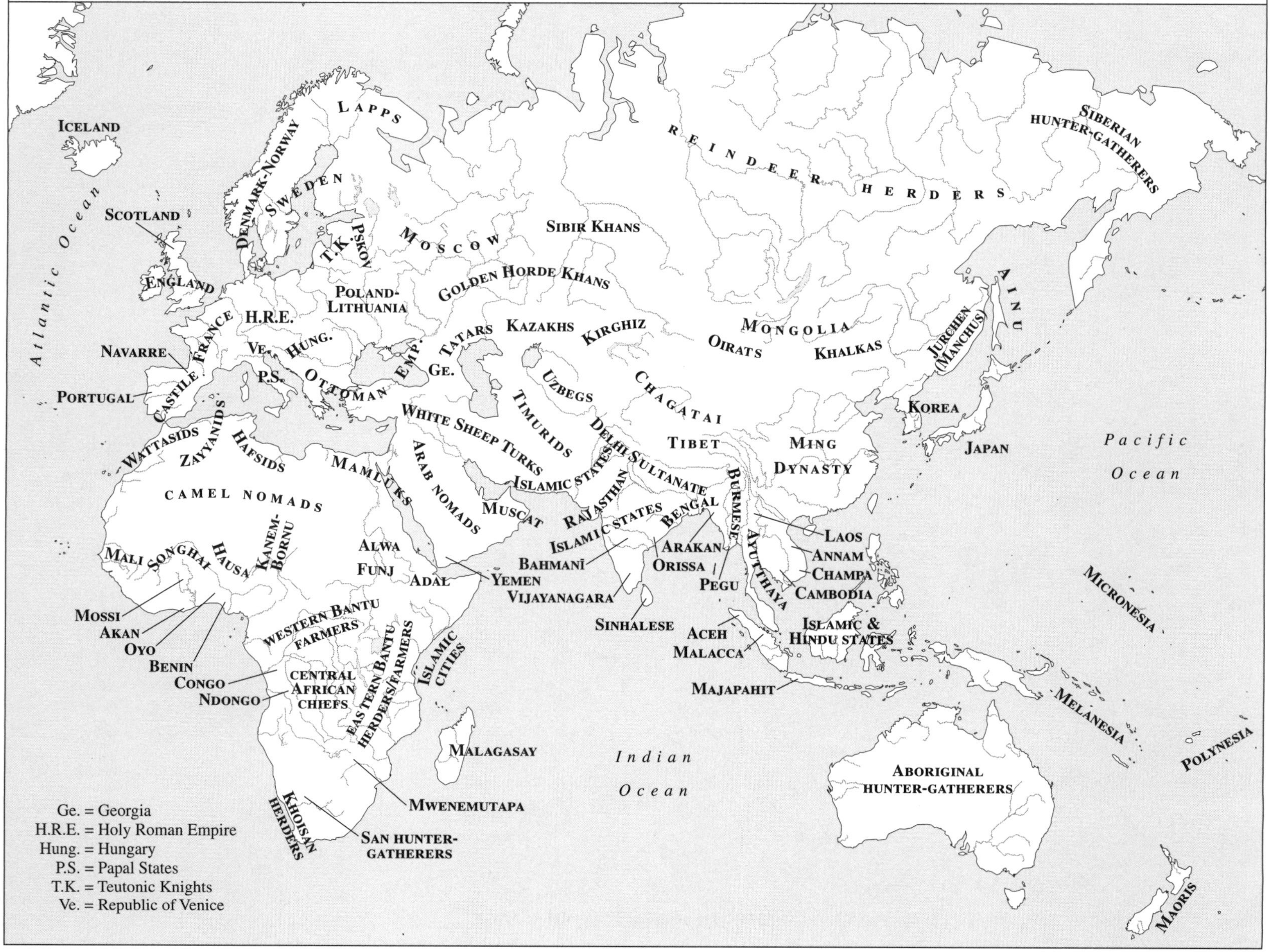

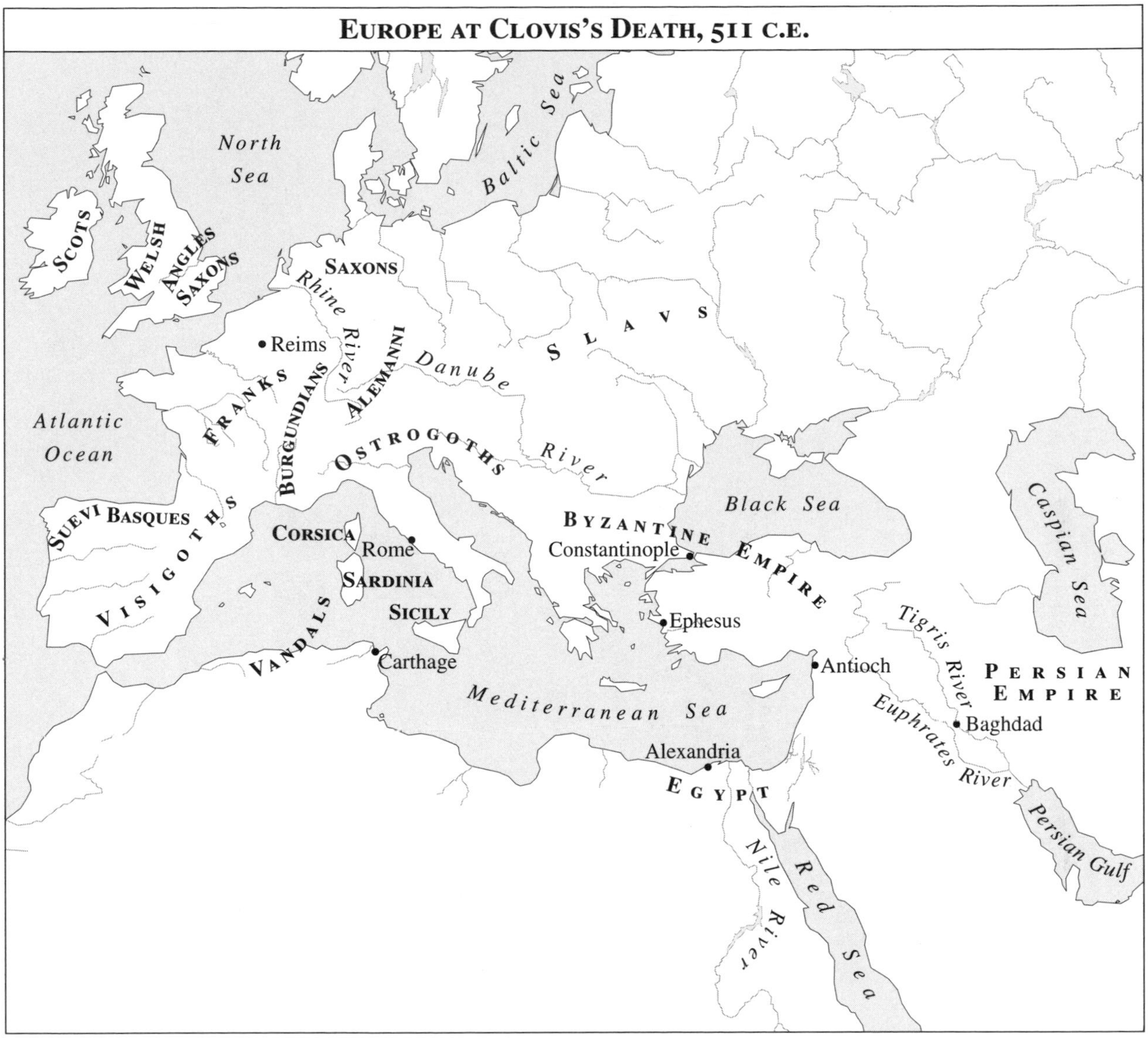
EUROPE AT CLOVIS'S DEATH, 511 C.E.
North Sea
Baltic Sea
SCOTS
WELSH
ANGLES
SAXONS
SAXONS
Rhine River
Reims
ALEMANNI
Danube River
SLAVS
FRANKS
BURGUNDIANS
Atlantic Ocean
OSTROGOTHS
Black Sea
Caspian Sea
SUEVI
BASQUES
VISIGOTHS
CORSICA
Rome
SARDINIA
SICILY
BYZANTINE EMPIRE
Constantinople
Ephesus
VANDALS
Carthage
Antioch
Tigris River
PERSIAN EMPIRE
Mediterranean Sea
Euphrates River
Baghdad
Alexandria
EGYPT
Persian Gulf
Nile River
Red Sea

BYZANTINE EMPIRE AT JUSTINIAN'S DEATH, 565 C.E.

Carolingian Empire, 768-814 C.E.

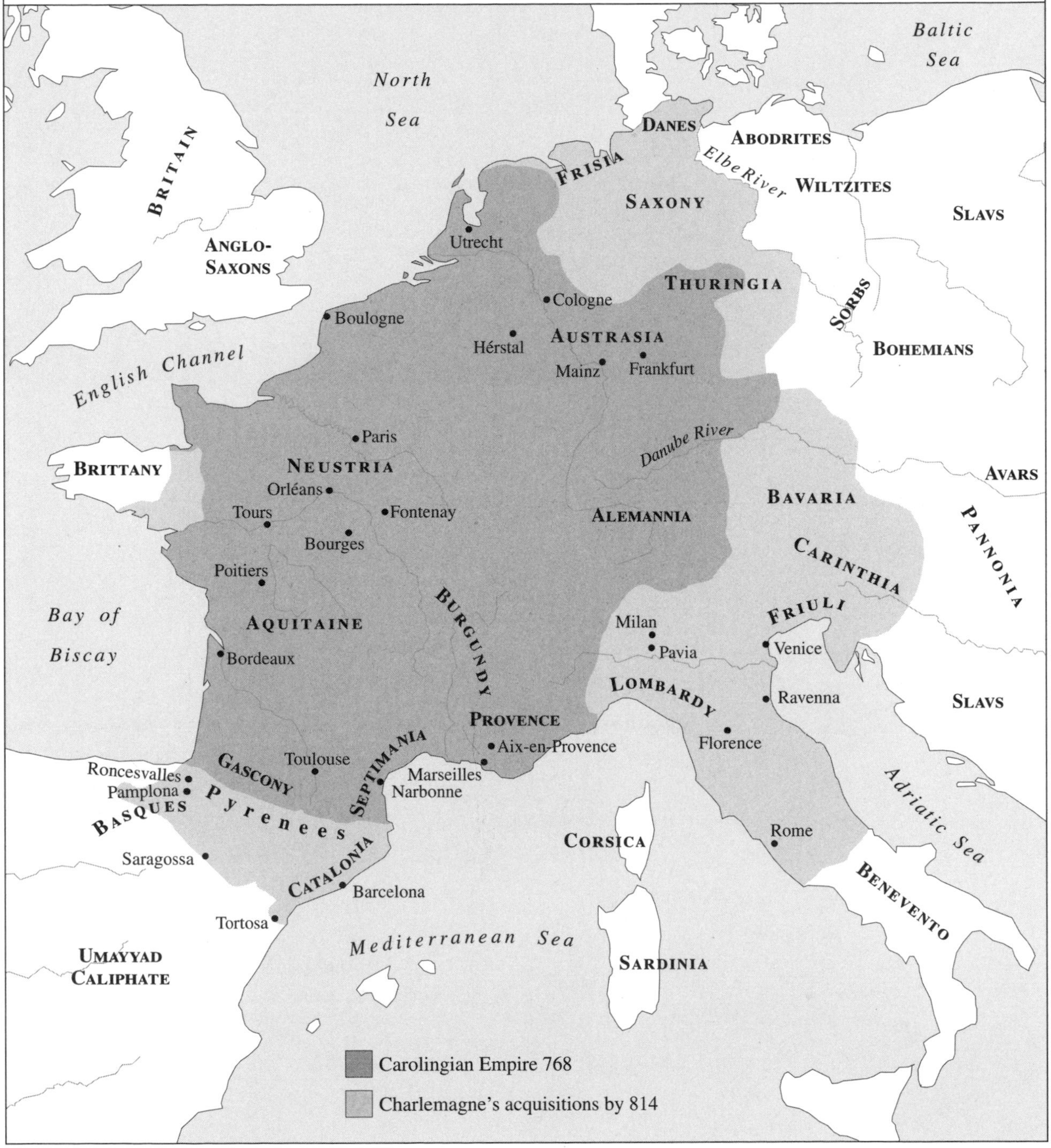
North Sea
Baltic Sea
Britain
Anglo-Saxons
Danes
Abodrites
Frisia
Elbe River
Wiltzites
Saxony
Slavs
Utrecht
Thuringia
Cologne
Sorbs
Boulogne
Hérstal
Austrasia
Bohemians
Mainz
Frankfurt
English Channel
Paris
Danube River
Brittany
Neustria
Avars
Orléans
Bavaria
Tours
Fontenay
Alemannia
Pannonia
Bourges
Carinthia
Poitiers
Burgundy
Bay of Biscay
Aquitaine
Friuli
Milan
Pavia
Venice
Bordeaux
Lombardy
Ravenna
Slavs
Provence
Florence
Septimania
Aix-en-Provence
Toulouse
Roncesvalles
Gascony
Marseilles
Pamplona
Narbonne
Adriatic Sea
Pyrenees
Basques
Corsica
Rome
Saragossa
Catalonia
Benevento
Barcelona
Tortosa
Mediterranean Sea
Umayyad Caliphate
Sardinia
Carolingian Empire 768
Charlemagne's acquisitions by 814

HOLY ROMAN EMPIRE C. 1190

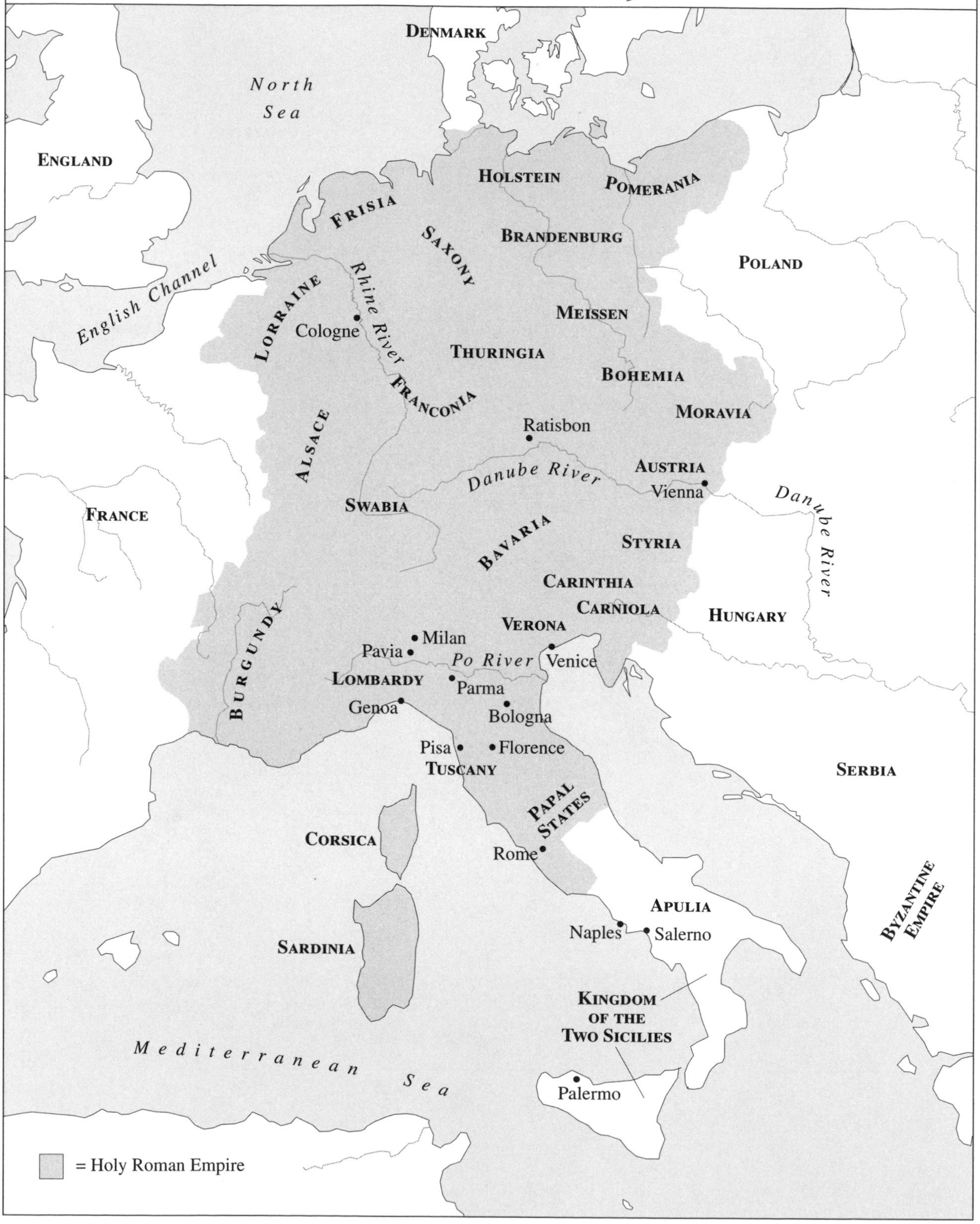

DENMARK
North Sea
ENGLAND
HOLSTEIN
POMERANIA
FRISIA
SAXONY
BRANDENBURG
POLAND
English Channel
LORRAINE
Rhine River
Cologne
MEISSEN
THURINGIA
BOHEMIA
FRANCONIA
MORAVIA
ALSACE
Ratisbon
AUSTRIA
Danube River
Vienna
FRANCE
SWABIA
Danube River
BAVARIA
STYRIA
CARINTHIA
CARNIOLA
HUNGARY
BURGUNDY
VERONA
Milan
Pavia
Po River
Venice
LOMBARDY
Parma
Genoa
Bologna
Pisa
Florence
TUSCANY
SERBIA
PAPAL STATES
CORSICA
Rome
BYZANTINE EMPIRE
APULIA
Naples
Salerno
SARDINIA
KINGDOM OF THE TWO SICILIES
Mediterranean Sea
Palermo
= Holy Roman Empire

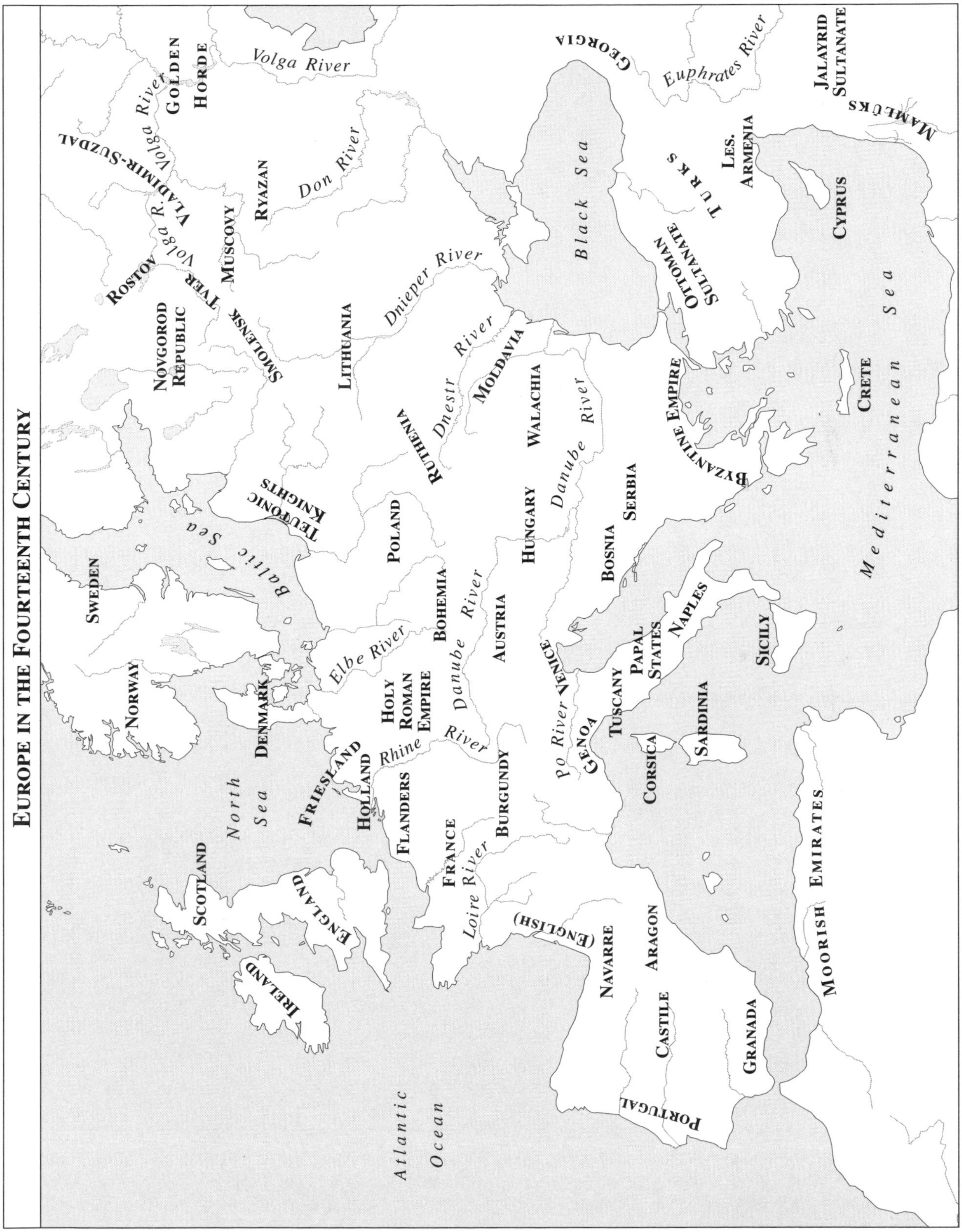
EUROPE IN THE FOURTEENTH CENTURY
Atlantic Ocean
North Sea
Baltic Sea
Black Sea
Mediterranean Sea
Volga River
Volga R.
Don River
Dnieper River
Dnestr River
Danube River
Elbe River
Rhine River
Po River
Loire River
Euphrates River
GOLDEN HORDE
VLADIMIR-SUZDAL
RYAZAN
MUSCOVY
ROSTOV
TVER
NOVGOROD REPUBLIC
SMOLENSK
LITHUANIA
TEUTONIC KNIGHTS
POLAND
RUTHENIA
MOLDAVIA
WALACHIA
HUNGARY
BOHEMIA
AUSTRIA
HOLY ROMAN EMPIRE
SWEDEN
NORWAY
DENMARK
FRIESLAND
HOLLAND
FLANDERS
FRANCE
BURGUNDY
SCOTLAND
ENGLAND
IRELAND
(ENGLISH)
NAVARRE
ARAGON
CASTILE
PORTUGAL
GRANADA
MOORISH EMIRATES
VENICE
GENOA
TUSCANY
PAPAL STATES
CORSICA
SARDINIA
NAPLES
SICILY
BOSNIA
SERBIA
BYZANTINE EMPIRE
OTTOMAN SULTANATE
TURKS
LES. ARMENIA
GEORGIA
CYPRUS
CRETE
MAMLUKS
JALAYRID SULTANATE

Africa c. 1000–1500

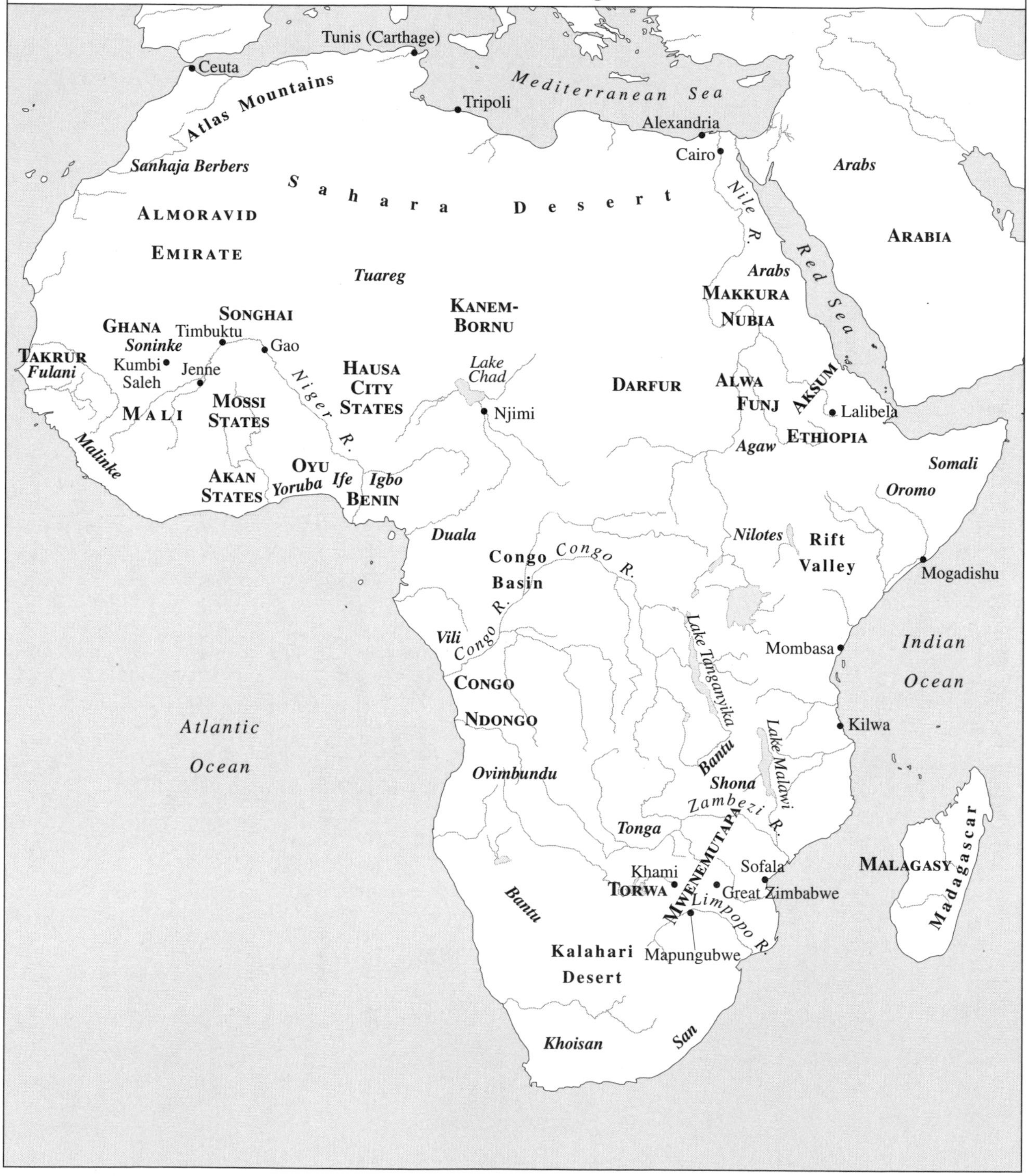
Tunis (Carthage)
Ceuta
Atlas Mountains
Mediterranean Sea
Tripoli
Alexandria
Cairo
Sanhaja Berbers
Arabs
Sahara Desert
Nile R.
Almoravid Emirate
Arabia
Red Sea
Tuareg
Arabs
Makkura Nubia
Kanem-Bornu
Songhai
Ghana
Soninke
Timbuktu
Gao
Takrur
Fulani
Kumbi Saleh
Jenne
Niger R.
Hausa City States
Lake Chad
Darfur
Alwa
Funj
Aksum
Lalibela
Mali
Mossi States
Njimi
Ethiopia
Agaw
Malinke
Somali
Akan States
Oyu
Yoruba
Ife
Igbo
Benin
Oromo
Duala
Nilotes
Rift Valley
Congo Basin
Congo R.
Mogadishu
Vili
Congo R.
Lake Tanganyika
Mombasa
Indian Ocean
Congo
Ndongo
Lake Malawi
Kilwa
Atlantic Ocean
Bantu
Ovimbundu
Shona
Zambezi R.
Tonga
Mwenemutapa
Sofala
Malagasy
Madagascar
Khami
Torwa
Great Zimbabwe
Bantu
Limpopo R.
Kalahari Desert
Mapungubwe
Khoisan
San

THE AMERICAS TO C. 1500

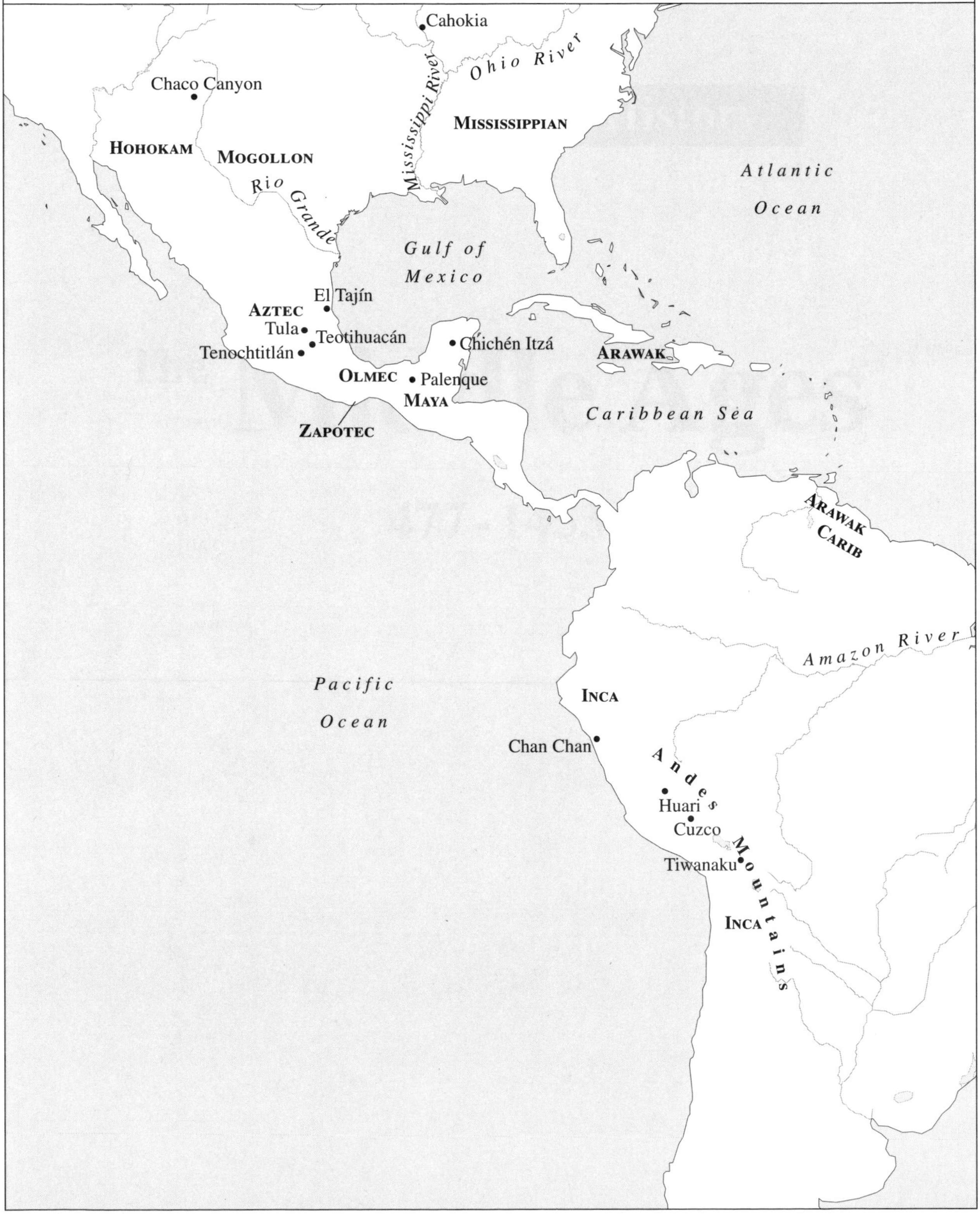
Cahokia
Ohio River
Chaco Canyon
Mississippi River
MISSISSIPPIAN
HOHOKAM
MOGOLLON
Rio Grande
Atlantic Ocean
Gulf of Mexico
El Tajín
AZTEC
Tula
Teotihuacán
Tenochtitlán
Chichén Itzá
ARAWAK
OLMEC
Palenque
MAYA
ZAPOTEC
Caribbean Sea
ARAWAK
CARIB
Amazon River
Pacific Ocean
INCA
Chan Chan
Andes Mountains
Huari
Cuzco
Tiwanaku
INCA

KŌKEN

Japanese empress (r. 749-758, r. 764-770)

The last of the female monarchs of early Japan, Kōken was an ardent sponsor of Buddhism. Her two reigns are characterized by increased state patronage of Buddhist temples, as evidenced by the immensely expensive construction of the bronze Great Buddha statue in Nara's Tōdaiji.

BORN: 718; Nara, Japan
DIED: 770; Nara, Japan
ALSO KNOWN AS: Shōtoku Tennō; Kōken Tennō; Princess Abe
AREA OF ACHIEVEMENT: Government and politics

EARLY LIFE

Kōken (koh-kehn), the woman who would occupy the throne of Japan twice over the course of the Nara period (710-784), was born to the future emperor Shōmu (r. 724-749) and Lady Asuka. Princess Abe, as she was known before ascending the throne, was uniquely qualified in the eyes of her contemporaries at court to become empress one day because she boasted an impressive bloodline. On her father's side, her grandfather was Emperor Mommu (r. 697-707); her great-grandmother, Empress Gemmei (r. 707-715), had been instrumental in the construction of Nara, the grandest capital Japan had ever known. At the time of Princess Abe's birth, her aunt occupied the throne as Empress Genshō (r. 715-724), and at the age of six, the princess saw her father become Emperor Shōmu. Her mother, Lady Asuka, was the daughter of Fujiwara Fubito, the powerful founder of the Fujiwara clan. It was Fubito who established the custom of selecting the principal consorts of the emperor exclusively from the Fujiwara family.

According to the official chronicles compiled at the behest of Empresses Gemmei and Genshō, the *Kojiki* (712 C.E.; *Records of Ancient Matters*, 1883; best known as *Kojiki*) and the *Nihon shoki* (compiled 720 C.E.; *Nihongi: Chronicles of Japan from the Earliest Times to A.D. 697*, 1896; best known as *Nihon shoki*), the imperial family was directly descended from the sun goddess Amaterasu. The chronicles record that this goddess had entrusted the Japanese archipelago into the care of her great-great-grandson, the emperor Jimmu, in 660 B.C.E., and that ever since, Japan had been ruled by Jimmu's line alone. The imperial institution and the dynasty itself were thus products of a claim made on the basis of religious concepts rooted in Shintō, Japan's native religion.

In reality, the imperial dynasty was about two hundred years old by the time of Kōken's birth (the first historical emperor was Kimmei, r. 539-571). The early years of the dynasty had seen the introduction of Buddhism and the establishment of a political and administrative system based on the Chinese model. Since the reign of Suiko (r. 593-628), Buddhism had been considered an important part of the life of the imperial court. Patronage of temples had become nothing short of an obligation for the aristocratic families who intended to remain part of the courtly culture. The move of the capital to Nara in 710 was probably influenced by the fact that several major temples already had been erected there.

There was an inherent contradiction in basing the integrity of the imperial dynasty on a set of native myths while relying on foreign inspirations (in particular Buddhism and Confucianism) for the functioning of the court as an institution and for the ordering of the polity. Emperors routinely promoted Buddhism while serving as high priests of the politically most important religion, Shintō. This conflict was apparent throughout the Nara period, but it would be especially noticeable in the events involving Kōken's two reigns as empress.

Several historical precedents existed for women occupying the throne. Before Kōken, five women had ruled as empresses regnant, one of them ruling twice. However, they had all been compromise candidates promoted to forestall succession disputes and, with one exception, had all been widows of previous emperors. Kōken's case would be remarkably different.

Her father ascended the throne as Emperor Shōmu in 724, after his aunt, Empress Genshō, abdicated in his favor. Five years later, he elevated his consort Lady Asuka, Kōken's mother, to the position of empress. Lady Asuka was of Fujiwara stock, and thus her promotion was designed to enhance the standing of this powerful clan. Up to that point, only women of the imperial bloodline had been elevated to that position. Emperors had routinely married their paternal half sisters or cousins, as such endogamous arrangements were considered permissible and even desirable to strengthen the coherence of the dynasty. The former Lady Asuka, now Empress Kōmyō, set out to make a name for herself as an ardent supporter of Buddhism. She also had a tremendous influence on her daughter, whose education she oversaw. She might also have had a hand in suggesting that her firstborn daughter be the first woman in Japanese history to be installed as

KUBLAI KHAN

Mongol ruler (r. 1260-1294)

As a Mongol general and the great khan, Kublai helped conquer and came to rule over an empire that encompassed most of Eurasia. He founded the Yuan Dynasty of China and brought the Mongols to the peak of their power and influence.

BORN: 1215; Mongolia
DIED: 1294; Dadu (now Beijing), China
ALSO KNOWN AS: Khubilai Khan; Kubla Khan
AREAS OF ACHIEVEMENT: Warfare and conquest, government and politics

EARLY LIFE

Kublai Khan (kew-bli kahn) was born somewhere in the Mongol heartland, but the exact site cannot be agreed on by scholars. He was the son of Tolui and the grandson of Temüjin, who had become Genghis Khan, the founder of the Mongol Empire. Kublai's three surviving brothers were Mangu, Hülagü, and Arigböge. At the time of Genghis Khan's death, Kublai was only twelve years old, but he was already an accomplished horseman; as he matured, he gained a reputation as a warrior of great personal courage.

In 1251, Mangu succeeded his cousin Güyük (r. 1246-1248) as great khan of the Mongol Empire. Güyük had succeeded his father, Ogatai (r. 1229-1241), who previously had succeeded his father, Genghis Khan (r. 1206-1227). Kublai served his older brother successfully as a general and led military campaigns for him in South China against the forces of the collapsing Song Dynasty (960-1279). Kublai added Sichuan, Yunnan, and Hukawng (now in Myanmar) to Mangu's domains, and one of Kublai's commanders initiated the invasion of Vietnam. During his part in the conquest of the Song, Kublai gradually came under the influence of Chinese civilization. Under Mangu, the Mongol Empire also expanded southwestward into Persia, Mesopotamia, and Syria.

When word of Mangu's death in 1259 reached Kublai in China, he quickly concluded a truce with his Song adversaries and returned to the Mongol capital of Karakorum. On May 6, 1260, Kublai had himself proclaimed great khan of the Mongol Empire. Kublai's right to succeed was severely challenged by his youngest brother, Arigböge, and a four-year civil war ensued between the two, culminating in 1264 with the triumph of Kublai Khan.

LIFE'S WORK

Not surprisingly, the great khan Kublai took a view of China that was somewhat different from that of his predecessors. In 1264, he moved his capital from Karakorum in Mongolia to Khanbalik (known to the Chinese as Dadu, now Beijing) in North China. He initiated new action in 1267 to complete the conquest of the Song Dynasty in South China in 1279. Kublai proclaimed his dynasty the Yuan (origin) Dynasty in 1271 and ascended the dragon throne of China, thus establishing himself and his heirs as the legitimate successors to the Song Dynasty until 1368. By 1279, he had accomplished something that the Song had failed to do—the unification of China under one ruler. Moreover, in less than one hundred years, Kublai and his Mongol predecessors had established an empire larger than that which it had taken the Romans four hundred years to assemble a millennium earlier.

In 1276, Kublai's authority was challenged in the west by Kaidu, khan of Transoxiana and Kashgaria (Chinese Turkistan), and the struggle that followed did not end un-

Drawing of Kublai Khan patterned on a Chinese engraving. (Library of Congress)

til a decade after Kublai's death. Meanwhile, Kublai Khan's armies subjugated Burma and Indochina in the 1280's but failed in their invasions of Japan through Korea in 1274 and again in 1281 (in part because of typhoons, the *kamikaze* or "divine wind," in the Sea of Japan) and in their invasion of Java in 1293. The Mongol Empire was not a naval power, and its armies did not fare well in the tropics. Kublai also abandoned the further conquest of Europe with the destruction of Kievan Rus as too troublesome, costly, and generally unrewarding.

China was the jewel of his empire (which eventually encompassed 80 percent of Eurasia), and Kublai tried to keep it free of war. The Sinicizing of Kublai continued after he became emperor; eventually, he even accepted conversion to Buddhism, yet was tolerant toward all religions and philosophies except Daoism. Kublai had his heirs educated as Chinese; he also established the right of succession only for his descendants. The new Mongol "square character" alphabet used during the Yuan Dynasty was designed by the Tibetan lama Pagspa for Kublai; Pagspa also governed Tibet for him. Kublai Khan introduced the use of Chinese paper money for the whole Mongol Empire and created a more unified monetary system from 1282 to 1287. This reform led directly not only to the stimulation and expansion of commercial activity across the Mongol Empire but also to inflation, when the new paper currency ceased to be backed effectively by or convertible to hard money.

Kublai Khan's reign also was characterized by extensive patronage of the arts and learning and by an ambitious program of public works, including the construction of an extensive network of roads and the rebuilding and extension of the Grand Canal between Beijing and Hangzhou. A new law code for China was promulgated in 1291. To the Chinese, Kublai Khan was known as the emperor Shizu, the ablest and most enlightened of the Yuan rulers. He established a luxurious court, including a fabled summer retreat at Shangdu (Samuel Taylor Coleridge's "Xanadu"). Yet he and his Mongols were never beloved by their Chinese subjects and were always viewed as alien overlords by them.

To enable the culturally inferior and greatly outnumbered Mongols to maintain control over China, Kublai Khan readily employed foreigners over native Chinese as administrators and advisers and also kept the top offices in Mongol hands. He was tolerant of Christianity, and among his subjects there were many followers of the Nestorian church. Kublai also admitted and allowed himself to be advised by Roman Catholics, the most famous of these being the Polos from the Republic of Venice.

Major Rulers of the Yuan Dynasty, 1279-1368

Reign	*Ruler*
1279-1294	Kublai Khan (Shizu)
1294-1307	Temür Oljeitu (Chengzong)
1308-1311	Khaishan (Wuzong)
1311-1320	Ayurbarwada (Renzong)
1321-1323	Shidelbala (Yingzong)
1323-1328	Yesun Temür (Taiding)
1328-1329	Tugh Temür (Wenzong Tianshundi)
1329	Tugh Khoshila (Mingzong)
1329-1332	Tugh Temür (Wenzong)
1333-1368	Toghon Temür (Shundi)

Between 1262 and 1266, two merchant brothers, Niccolò Polo and Maffeo Polo, journeyed across Eurasia to the seat of the great khan in search of trade. They arrived back in Venice with desired merchandise from the East as well as an invitation from the great khan for Christian missionaries to come to China and a request for an alliance with the Christian West and its Crusaders against Islamic Egypt. This tolerance of Christianity and apparent but unfulfilled promise of a joint crusade against Islam probably was responsible for the linking of Kublai Khan to the medieval Christian Prester John legends.

Under the protection of a solid gold pass (*paisa*) of safe conduct from Kublai Khan himself, the Polo brothers set off for China in 1275, this time accompanied by Niccolò's son Marco. They did not arrive in Europe until 1295. During these years at Kublai's court, they served him as advisers, administrators, and ambassadors. Their adventures were many, and they came to experience much of his vast but somewhat shaky empire. Marco Polo's account of his travels and experiences, *Divisament dou monde* (fourteenth century; *The Travels of Marco Polo*, 1579), is an invaluable European source on Kublai Khan and the Mongol Empire.

By the time of the Polos' return to Venice, Kublai's control had weakened so much that he could no longer guarantee their safety via the overland route they had originally traveled some seventeen years before. Consequently, they departed China by sea for the Middle East. In 1294, Kublai Khan died in Khanbalik (known to the Chinese as Dadu; now Beijing). He was succeeded by his grandson Temür (Chengzong; r. 1294-1307). In 1368, the last Mongol emperor of China, Shundi, was overthrown and left Beijing for Mongolia. The Mongol Yuan

Dynasty was replaced by the Chinese Ming Dynasty (1368-1644), and the remaining Mongols were driven out of or absorbed by a resurgent Chinese civilization.

SIGNIFICANCE

Kublai Khan created one of the largest empires in the history of the world; at the heart of the Mongol Empire under Kublai Khan was China. The Mongols reached the greatest extent of their power and influence under Mangu and his brother Kublai, but how unified their "state" was certainly is open to question.

Under Kublai, there were no more than three million Mongols to control a domain stretching over 80 percent of Eurasia, consisting of many thousands of square miles and containing numerous diverse peoples. By necessity, this empire had to be decentralized and relied heavily on Mongol-supported local administrators. It did this effectively for about two centuries. At the same time, the Mongols were forced to discriminate ruthlessly against the often culturally superior peoples they came to control. This practice was no more apparent than in the Yuan Dynasty's rule over China, enforced by a rigid caste system separating the rulers from the ruled. Despite such rigidity, even Kublai, the most effective of the Yuan emperors, had trouble maintaining control.

In the final analysis, the Mongols were spread too thin over their great empire, and their initial military-technological advantage was not sufficient to make up for their numerical and cultural inferiority to those whom they had conquered. Gradually, the Mongols were absorbed or overthrown by their conquered peoples. Hence, although Kublai Khan's military and political achievements were significant, they also were fleeting.

—*Dennis Reinhartz*

FURTHER READING

Benson, Douglas S. *The Mongol Campaigns in Asia: A Summary History of Mongolian Warfare with the Governments of Eastern and Western Asia in the Thirteenth Century.* Chicago: Author, 1991. A detailed military and diplomatic history of the Mongolian Empire in which Kublai Khan is seen as a major figure. Contains maps and illustrations.

Dīn, Rashīd al-. *The Successors of the Genghis Khan.* Translated by John Andrew Doyle. New York: Columbia University Press, 1971. This book is the classic contemporary Islamic account of the Mongol Empire from the death of the Genghis Khan through the reign of Temür Khan, grandson of Kublai Khan. The largest chapter is reserved for the life and achievements of Kublai Khan.

Larner, John. *Marco Polo and the Discovery of the World.* New Haven, Conn.: Yale University Press, 1999. A discussion of the Polo family, Marco's relationship with Rustichello, the making of the book, and the explorer's influence. Contains maps of the fifteenth century. Bibliography and index.

Marshall, Robert. *Storm from the East: Genghis Khan to Khubilai Khan.* Berkeley: University of California Press, 1993. A popular history of the Mongol Empire, from its beginning to the invasion of Europe and later China, to its ultimate fall. Contains dynastic tables, illustrations, maps, bibliography, and index.

Nicolle, David. *The Mongol Warlords: Genghis Khan, Kublai Khan, Hülegü, Tamerlane.* Poole, England: Firebird, 1990. An examination of the major Mongol rulers. Bibliographies and index.

Onon, Urgunge, trans. *The Secret History of the Mongols: The Life and Times of Chinggis Khan.* Rev. ed. Richmond, England: Curzon, 2001. A literal and annotated translation of a work written only a generation after Genghis Khan's death.

Polo, Marco. *The Travels of Marco Polo.* Translated by Ronald Latham. 1958. Reprint. New York: Penguin Books, 1996. One of the best translations into English of Marco's book. Contains a brief but good introduction by the translator.

Rossabi, Morris. *Khubilai Khan: His Life and Times.* Berkeley: University of California Press, 1988. A readable yet comprehensive biography, of interest to both the scholar and the layperson. Includes notes, a glossary of Chinese characters, extensive bibliographies of works in Western languages and works in Oriental languages, and an index. Illustrated.

Roux, Jean-Paul. *Genghis Khan and the Mongol Empire.* New York: Harry N. Abrams, 2003. An examination of Genghis Khan and the empire that he created.

SEE ALSO: Genghis Khan; Marco Polo; William of Rubrouck.

RELATED ARTICLES in *Great Events from History: The Middle Ages, 477-1453*: 1115: Foundation of the Jin Dynasty; 1271-1295: Travels of Marco Polo; 1275: Nestorian Archbishopric Is Founded in Beijing; 1368: Establishment of the Ming Dynasty; 1381-1405: Tamerlane's Conquests; 1405-1433: Zheng He's Naval Expeditions.

LADY ALICE KYTELER

Anglo-Irish noblewoman

Kyteler was one of the first persons accused of being a witch in the early years of the medieval witch-hunts, or witch craze. Her trial marked the symbolic start of an onslaught of witch-hunts that did not subside until three centuries later.

BORN: 1280; Kilkenny, Ireland
DIED: After 1324; England
ALSO KNOWN AS: Dame Alice Kyteler; Lady Alice Kettle; Alice Kyteller; Alice le Kyteler
AREAS OF ACHIEVEMENT: Religion and theology, government and politics

EARLY LIFE

Alice Kyteler (KIHT-luhr) was raised in a wealthy Anglo-Irish family in Kilkenny, Ireland, and was part of Kilkenny's minor nobility. There are few records on Kyteler before her trial for witchcraft in 1324, other than listings in marriage registers. However, something of her earlier life can be reconstructed from the testimony given about her at her trial and by a few legal records.

Kyteler was married four times, the first marriage to William Outlaw, a rich banker. His marriage to Kyteler indicates the high social status of her family. Outlaw was dead by 1302, although not before he and Kyteler had a son, also named William. They may also have had a daughter, as there is a record of a Rose Outlaw. Her husband's death left Kyteler and her son very wealthy. Although she would marry three more times, Kyteler apparently did not have more children; her son, William, became the focus of her life. William followed in his father's footsteps, becoming a moneylender.

In 1302, Kyteler married her second husband, Adam le Blond, another moneylender and a friend of her first husband. In that same year, Alice and Adam were accused of homicide, although there is no record of whom they were accused of killing. They were also accused by relatives of Kyteler and by a seneschal (a steward or representative of the king) of theft; all charges were eventually dismissed for lack of legal foundation. The seneschal was Arnold le Poer, presumably a relative of her fourth husband. It is clear that by the time of her second marriage Kyteler was already distrusted by her distant relatives and neighbors and that there was already some jealousy about her and her son's wealth. Also, her connection to money lending placed Kyteler into one of the most despised professions in the fourteenth century. She would prove an easy target for accusations of malfeasance.

By 1311, Adam le Blond was also dead and had left all his property to his stepson William, although he had children from a previous marriage. In 1316, Kyteler married for a third time, this time to Richard de Valle, a landowner who died the same year of their marriage. Kyteler successfully sued de Valle's children (a second set of stepchildren) for a portion of his estate, further increasing her wealth. By 1324, Kyteler had married a fourth man, John le Poer, who had been a witness on her behalf when she and her second husband, Adam le Blond, had been accused of homicide and theft.

LIFE'S WORK

In 1324, John le Poer was bedridden with a wasting sickness of an unknown nature. According to the trial record, John was told by a house servant that the cause of his illness was poison given to him by his wife. In the late Middle Ages, it was common to associate poisoning with witchcraft, and apparently John became suspicious about his wife's activities. According to a later account of the trial, written in the sixteenth century by the English chronicler Raphael Holinshed, he seized Alice's keys and searched her personal belongings. There he found two disturbing items: a sacramental wafer with the name of the devil stamped on it rather than that of Jesus Christ and a vial of ointment. John believed his wife used the ointment to grease a staff she used to travel about at will (a precursor to the belief that witches used broomsticks to fly), and the wafer was viewed as a sign of her diabolism, or Satanism.

John's suspicions about Alice, which he reported to the bishop of Ossory, Richard de Ledrede, were supported by her stepchildren's claims that she had killed her former husbands, their fathers. In inheriting money and property from each of her three previous husbands, Kyteler had disinherited these stepchildren. Furthermore, Kyteler made it clear that she intended to pass all her property on to her own son, William. Thus, in accusing Kyteler of witchcraft, the stepchildren were also protesting their own disinheritance. When she was eventually convicted of witchcraft, all of Kyteler's goods were seized and then open to claiming by her stepchildren.

In 1324, Ledrede brought formal charges of practicing witchcraft against Kyteler and eleven of her friends, family, and staff. Included among the accused were her son, William, her maid Petronilla of Meath, and Petronilla's daughter. Kyteler would eventually be convicted of *malificium* (harmful magic) and of copulating with a demon named Robin, or Son of Art.

Petronilla was tortured under church laws that allowed forcible examination of suspected heretics. Under torture, she confessed that Kyteler had been a skillful witch who had taught her the dark craft. She went into great detail about how Kyteler and her fellow witches had acquired their power and had renounced the church. Although Kyteler was the primary focus of the trial, she and her son were not tortured. Their wealth and influence in the town probably helped protect them.

Petronilla confessed that she had arranged meetings for her mistress and Robin, Kyteler's supposed demon lover. Petronilla admitted that she had witnessed Kyteler and Robin copulating (in daylight, which Ledrede found significant as it was highly inappropriate behavior for that time). Petronilla stated that sometimes Robin appeared as a black dog or a large cat, sometimes as a small black man, and sometimes with two male companions. Petronilla claimed that since Kyteler credited Robin for her wealth, this showed that Kyteler was trafficking with demons for profit, leading to an accusation of diabolism as well as witchcraft.

Kyteler was also accused of using ointments and potions made from the clothing of unbaptized dead infants and parts of dead bodies (hair and nails mostly), and from cocks and peacocks at crossroads. Kyteler and her sect were said to have forsworn their faith in Christ and to have refused to attend Mass or give confession for set periods of time (usually a month, but sometimes as long as a year) whenever they sought out demons for power. Petronilla accused her mistress of sweeping or raking the streets of Kilkenny after sundown (when folk belief held it was dangerous to sweep) toward her son's door, chanting a wish that all the wealth of Kilkenny end up at his door.

At first, Kyteler confessed and agreed to pay a fine and renounce her witchcraft. Two of her fellow accused, Petronilla and another woman, were burned alive. Petronilla was first whipped publicly six times. Several of the other accused were excommunicated and had to make public statements of guilt. William Outlaw was absolved after agreeing to make public penance and to replace the church roof. Notably, William agreed to admit only to having aided heretics, not to being one himself. After she made her confession, Ledrede accused Kyteler of relapsing to witchcraft, an accusation to which she made a plea of innocence to the bishop of Dublin. Kyteler accused Ledrede of defaming her character. While awaiting a final judgment, she fled to England with one of the daughters of Petronilla. Nothing more is known of Kyteler's fate.

The trial of Kyteler, Petronilla, and the others of their supposed sect was driven by the enthusiasm of Ledrede. Ledrede had been given the bishopric of Ossory by Pope John XXII, who would remain a patron of the bishop throughout his career. Both men shared an obsession with heresy. Ledrede, an English Franciscan, had been in France during the infamous trial for heresy of the Templars.

One of Ledrede's first acts as bishop had been to purge his court of heretics in 1318, and he wrote a treatise that warned that many Christians were transgressing with demons. Long before Kyteler was brought before him by her husband and stepchildren, Ledrede was an enthusiastic witch-hunter; Kyteler's trial allowed him a platform from which to promote his theories about Satanism and heresy.

Ledrede also used the trial to advocate the power of the Eucharist. He was convinced that there was an active community of heretics in his diocese, and he was determined to eradicate them. He was also extremely unpopular with the civic authorities of Kilkenny, including Arnold le Poer, the seneschal. Although le Poer had once accused Kyteler of crimes, in the witch trial he argued on her behalf. One of the reasons Ledrede was unpopular was his national origin; le Poer called him an English interloper and accused him of being paranoid about heresy.

SIGNIFICANCE

The time period in which the witchcraft trial against Kyteler took place and the nature of the accusations against her make Kyteler and her life significant: She stood accused of being a witch in one of the first true witchcraft trials in Europe. The better-known witch craze, in which thousands of women and men were accused and executed for witchcraft, did not begin until a century after Kyteler's trial. However, Kyteler's trial set the stage for all the standard accusations and fears about *malificium*. The specifics of her trial—such as copulation with demons, use of unbaptized infants, and animal sacrifice—became common motifs in later trials. Political, personal, and financial motivations also led to many of the later witch-hunts.

—Candace Gregory

FURTHER READING

Cohn, Norman. *Europe's Inner Demons: An Inquiry Inspired by the Great Witch-Hunt*. New York: Basic

Books, 1975. Focuses on the psychological aspects of the witch-hunts and on how ideas of sorcery and witchcraft from ancient times through the Middle Ages melded into the idea of witches.

Davidson, L. S., and J. O. Ward, eds. *The Sorcery Trial of Alice Kyteler: A Contemporary Account (1324)*. Binghamton: Center for Medieval and Early Renaissance Studies, State University of New York at Binghamton, 1993. An account of the trial by Ledrede with supplemental texts and an excellent introduction.

Heinemann, Evelyn. *Witches: A Psychoanalytic Exploration of the Killing of Women*. New York: Free Association Books, 2000. Argues for a psychoanalytic and historical approach to the study of witch-hunts in general.

Kieckhefer, Richard. *European Witch Trials: Their Foundations in Popular and Learned Culture, 1300-1500*. Berkeley: University of California Press, 1976. The definitive study of how the witch-hunts began and how the trials were conducted.

Kors, Alan Charles, and Edward Peters, eds. *Witchcraft in Europe, 400-1700: A Documentary History*. 1972. Rev. ed. Philadelphia: University of Pennsylvania Press, 2001. An extensive collection of original sources on the role of Christianity and the Papacy in prosecuting witchcraft and sorcery; the nature of evil, and inquisitions, persecutions, and trials; and an introduction addressing the "problem of European witchcraft."

Russell, Jeffrey Burton. *The Devil, Heresy, and Witchcraft in the Middle Ages*. Boston: Brill, 1998. Places the witch-hunts in the context of the history of heresy and dissent in the Middle Ages.

Sergeant, Philip W. *Witches and Warlocks*. Yorkshire, England: EP, 1974. A detailed account of the Kyteler case.

Thurston, Robert W. *Witch, Wicce, Mother Goose: The Rise and Fall of the Witch Hunts in Europe and North America*. New York: Longman, 2001. One of the best studies of the witch-hunts. Includes a detailed analysis of the Kyteler case and its place in the history of persecutions of witches in Europe.

Wright, Thomas, ed. *A Contemporary Narrative of the Proceedings Against Dame Alice Kyteler: Persecuted for Sorcery in 1324*. 1843. Reprint. New York: AMS Press, 1968. Translation of the original Latin account of the trial, with some supporting documents.

SEE ALSO: Pietro d'Abano; Peter Abelard; Saint Dominic; Fredegunde; Jan Hus; Innocent III; Joan of Arc; Margery Kempe; William of Ockham; Saint Patrick; Marguerite Porete; John Wyclif.

RELATED ARTICLES in *Great Events from History: The Middle Ages, 477-1453*: 1233: Papal Inquisition; 1250-1300: Homosexuality Criminalized and Subject to Death Penalty; July 2, 1324: Lady Alice Kyteler Is Found Guilty of Witchcraft; May 4-8, 1429: Joan of Arc's Relief of Orléans.

LALIBELA

King of Ethiopia (r. c. 1181-c. 1221)

The most illustrious of the Ethiopian rulers to emerge after the fall of the ancient kingdom of Aksum, Lalibela restored the power of the Ethiopian states, consolidated the Christian sphere of influence, and undertook the construction of the extraordinary rock-hewn churches at Roha.

BORN: c. mid-twelfth century; Roha, Lasta (now in Ethiopia)
DIED: c. 1221; in Roha, Lasta
ALSO KNOWN AS: Gebre Mesqal
AREAS OF ACHIEVEMENT: Government and politics, architecture

EARLY LIFE

Lalibela (lah-lee-BEHL-ah) was born of a prominent family related to the Zagwe Dynasty, which ascended the Ethiopian throne after the collapse of the Christian kingdom of Aksum. The first Zagwe king, Mara Tekle Haimanot, rose to power in 1137 after overthrowing Dil Naʿad, the last Aksumite king. The Zagwe rulers moved the seat of imperial power to their home district of Bugna in Lasta Province. Lalibela's father, Jan Seyoum, was the brother of the reigning monarch and was governor of the important district of Bugna, which served as the base of power for the Zagwe rulers.

The young Lalibela is said to have studied in some of the most famous monasteries in Ethiopia, including at Mertula Mariam in Gojam Province. He is said to have been a profound scholar and a devoted Christian at a young age. Although not supported by credible sources, the hagiographic tradition reports that he made a pilgrimage to Jerusalem, where he received much of the inspiration for his later achievements. On completing his education, Lalibela was married to Masqal Kebra, who later played a prominent role in the religious life of the country and is one of the few women canonized as a saint by the Ethiopian Orthodox Church.

On returning to his birthplace in Lasta, Lalibela found himself at odds with his brother Harbe, who by then had taken the Zagwe throne. Fearing for his safety, Lalibela fled to the outlying regions of the empire and began to mobilize support against his brother. He appears to have succeeded in building a broadly based alliance among the discontented elements of the empire. Realizing the futility of further struggle, Harbe is said to have voluntarily abdicated the throne in favor of his brother.

LIFE'S WORK

Lalibela ascended the throne around 1181 and soon emerged as the most legendary of the Ethiopian kings. The Ethiopian state witnessed considerable imperial expansion and remarkable literary and architectural revival under his rule. He carried out successful campaigns designed to consolidate imperial control over northern Ethiopia, including the highlands of what is today Eritrea. He subdued the still predominantly non-Christian regions of the upper Blue Nile in the west and pushed the frontiers of the Christian kingdom as far as the Awash River in the south and to the edge of the Ethiopian Plateau in the east. The military colonies and monasteries established in the outer areas of these newly acquired regions facilitated a rapid process of assimilation. This in turn contributed significantly to the political and cultural homogenization of the Ethiopian state, which already had begun during the Aksumite period in the first millennium C.E.

At a period when Muslim forces had defeated the Latin Crusaders in the Middle East and Islam was making formidable strides elsewhere in northeast Africa, Lalibela spearheaded a multifaceted movement that was designed to reinvigorate the Ethiopian Orthodox Church and to enhance its spiritual, literary, and architectural tradition.

Lalibela ended the long period of stagnation that had characterized Ethiopian foreign trade since the rise of Muslim hegemony in the Red Sea region in the eighth century. Although Ethiopia had lost most of its Red Sea coastal outlets, including the ports of Adulis and the Dahlak Islands, Lalibela sought alternative routes to the south. The port of Zeila (now in Somaliland) in the east was conveniently located to service much of the Ethiopian state, whose orientation had decisively shifted southward after the collapse of the Aksumite kingdom. Commercial contacts with Egypt and the Yemen were resumed during this period.

Lalibela also pursued an active foreign policy that was designed to end the country's isolation, including the development of good relations with Sultan Saladin in order to ensure the continuity of relations between the Ethiopian Church and the Egyptian Coptic Church (from which Ethiopia received its bishops). There is evidence that Lalibela sent at least two missions to Cairo in 1200 and 1209. The cordial relations he established with Saladin appear to have helped in easing the pressure on the

Coptic Christians in Egypt and in protecting Ethiopian Christians in Jerusalem. Saladin is said to have given lands in Jerusalem to Ethiopian Christians.

Stories of Lalibela's accomplishments at home as well as the active foreign policy he pursued seem to have reached Europe to some degree. This vague information may have provided the inspiration for the spread of the myth of the so-called Prester John, the legendary Christian monarch in the east who was believed to be a bulwark against Muslim expansion and was expected to liberate the Holy Land from the hands of the Muslims.

Lalibela is remembered not only for his remarkable achievements as an empire builder but also for building the grand complex of monolithic rock-hewn churches at Roha (renamed Lalibela after his death) in the rugged terrain of Lasta Province. These monuments were said to replicate Jerusalem and the Holy Land that was lost to the Christian world when Saladin recaptured it from the Crusaders in 1187. The eleven edifices attributed to Lalibela are all sculpted inside and out from solid volcanic rock and are interconnected by a maze of long underground tunnels and passages. The eleven churches are called Bete Medhane Alem, Bete Mariam, Bete Michael, Bete Mesqal, Bete Amanuel, Bete Marqorewos, Bete Libanos, Bete Gabriel, Bete Giorgis, Bete Denagil, and Bete Golgotha. Each building is architecturally unique and sumptuously decorated with a variety of paintings. Some of the buildings have immense columns.

The most impressive and the largest of this complex is the Bete Medhane Alem (the Church of Our Savior), which measures 33.5 meters (110 feet) long by 23.5 meters (77 feet) wide and 11 meters (36 feet) high. It has 32 external colonnades on all four sides. The other fascinating structure is the Bete Giorgis (Church of Saint George), which is built in the shape of a cross from a great block of rock and stands in the midst of a trench that is 12 meters (nearly 40 feet) deep.

These architectural wonders have fascinated many visitors throughout the ages. Francisco Alvarez, a Jesuit priest and a member of the Portuguese mission to Ethiopia who visited the site in the 1520's, wrote in his book *Verdadeira informação das terras do preste João das Indias* (1540; *Narrative of the Portuguese Embassy to Abyssinia During the Years 1520-1527*, 1881; best known as *The Prester John of the Indies*, 1961) that the likes of such buildings "cannot, as it appears to me, be found in the world." He further remarked, "I weary of writing more about these buildings, because it seems to me that I shall not be believed if I write more."

Ethiopian legend claims that Lalibela was miraculously flown to Jerusalem, where Christ appeared to him and instructed him to build a second Jerusalem in Ethiopia. Ethiopian Orthodox Christians consider the site as the new Holy Land that was intended to replace as a pilgrimage center the real Jerusalem, which was lost to the Muslims. King Lalibela himself is canonized by the Ethiopian Church. The *Gadla Lalibela* (the hagiography of Lalibela) claims that visiting these churches is like seeing the face of Christ. Several landmarks in the area are given biblical names. The local stream that flows through the site is named the Jordan River (after the original Jordan River) and the nearby mountain is called Mount Tabor (again, like the original). There is also a place called the Court of Judgment to symbolize the site where the decision to crucify Christ was made. One of the eleven churches that house the tomb of Lalibela is called Golgotha (the Holy Sepulcher).

Lalibela's monuments have served as a source of inspiration and hope for Ethiopian Christians over the course of the last eight centuries. Thousands of Ethiopians make the pilgrimage to Lalibela every year. After the Church of Saint Mary of Zion in Aksum, which supposedly houses the Ark of the Covenant, Lalibela is regarded as the most sacred site in Ethiopia.

In spite of these accomplishments, Lalibela was unable to overcome the weakness he had inherited from his predecessors. Zagwe hold over the Ethiopian empire had always remained precarious. Zagwe rulers were unable to remove the stigma that they were usurpers who had snatched power from the lawful rulers of the Aksumite line. Although they were the greatest patrons of the Ethiopian Church and produced three kings who were canon-

The Zagwe Dynasty

Reign	*Ruler*
c. 1137-1152	Mara Tekle Haimanot
c. 1152-1181	Yimrehane-Kristos
c. 1181-1221	Lalibela
c. 1221-1260	Naᶜakuto Laᶜab
c. 1260-1270	Yitbarek (Yetbarek)
1270	Solomonid Dynasty begins; reign of Yekuno Amlak

Note: The evidence for the succession of Zagwe rulers is debated by scholars; here, the regnal dates reflect primarily the order of succession and vary widely among sources.

century. A considerable portion of Landini's three-part ballate are texted only in the upper voice; the two lower voices move in an instrumental fashion. This particular three-voice texture was so widely used in fourteenth century France that the term "French ballade style" has been widely adopted to describe it when it occurs elsewhere. Also, some of Landini's three-part compositions reveal the use of polytextuality and isorhythm, both popular practices frequently found in the fourteenth century French motet. Nevertheless, Landini's use of the French techniques should not be overemphasized. Even when it occurs, he remains true to his heritage, with the emphasis always on the vocality of the melodic line.

Landini has also been associated with a type of cadence that was quite popular with French and Italian composers of the fourteenth and fifteenth centuries. This particular cadence was an ornamented version of one commonly used in the thirteenth century in which, step-by-step, the bottom voice moved down from what in modern terminology would be described as the second scale degree to the tonic, the middle voice would move upward from the fourth scale degree to the fifth, and the upper voice would move from the seventh scale degree to the tonic. The important feature of this thirteenth century cadence was the linear movement upward of the upper two voices in parallel fourths while the lowest voice moved downward.

The fourteenth century ornamentation of this cadence occurred in the uppermost voice. The seventh scale degree would descend by step to the sixth scale degree and then skip up the interval of a third to the tonic; the overall movement is still upward. The rhythmic patterns applied to the movement of the upper voice could vary. Because of Landini's frequent use of the ornamented cadence formula, it is often referred to as "the Landini sixth."

Francesco Landini died in Florence on September 2, 1397. He was buried in the church of San Lorenzo, where he had long served as organist. His tombstone depicts him with his portative organ.

SIGNIFICANCE

Landini, famous during his own lifetime as a composer and as an outstanding performer, was also known for his literary accomplishments. Filippo Villani, a noted Florentine chronicler, included him in his book on famous Florentine personages, telling of Landini's having been crowned with a laurel wreath in Venice by the king of Cyprus for having won a poetry contest. The composer is known to have exchanged verses with Franco Sacchetti, the Florentine poet whose texts Landini had set to music. He is also known for the extended Latin poem he wrote in support of William of Ockham's philosophical position.

Landini's fame as a composer and performer reached such proportions that, in addition to his given name, he was called and recognized by names referring to both his affliction and his instrument of choice: Francesco Cieco (Francesco the blind) and Francesco degli Organi (Francesco of the organs).

Landini held an important position as a fourteenth century Italian composer. Although some of his music reflected French influence, he maintained the vitality of the Italian tradition in the late fourteenth century. With his death, Italian music yielded to northern domination; it was not to flourish again until the sixteenth century.

—*Michael Hernon*

FURTHER READING

D'Accone, Frank. "Music and Musicians at the Florentine Monastery of Santa Trinita, 1360-1363." *Quadrivium* 12 (1971): 131-151. An interesting account of old church records discovered by D'Accone that document Landini's service as organist at the monastery of Santa Trinita in the early 1360's and his subsequent service at the church of San Lorenzo from 1365 until his death in 1397.

Ellinwood, Leonard. "The Fourteenth Century in Italy." In *The New Oxford History of Music*, edited by Egon Wellesz. Vol. 3. 1966. Reprint. London: Oxford University Press, 1986. A good, concise overview of the primary sources, forms, and composers of fourteenth century Italy. Contains some information about Landini.

_______. "Francesco Landini and His Music." *Musical Quarterly* 22 (1936): 190-216. Remains one of the important sources of information about Landini in spite of its age. The article contains important biographical information and an extended discussion of his compositional output. There are seven selected compositions by Landini at the end of the article that have been transcribed into modern notation.

Fischer, Kurt von. "Francesco Landini." In *New Grove Dictionary of Music and Musicians*, edited by Stanley Sadie. 2d ed. Vol. 10. New York: Grove, 2001. The author provides a thorough discussion of Landini and his music. The article is divided into three sections that discuss his life, extant musical compositions, and musical style. A list of his extant compositions, with short commentary, is provided, along with a lengthy bibliography.

_______. "On the Technique, Origin, and Evolution of

Italian Trecento Music." *Musical Quarterly* 47 (1961): 41-57. Provides a brief survey of compositional techniques employed by Italian composers of the fourteenth century. While several composers are discussed, the treatment of Landini is more extensive.

_______. "Text Underlay in Landini's Ballet for Three Voices." *Current Musicology* 45/47 (1990): 179-197. Landini is seen as one of the most important contributors to the Italian ballata for three voices with textless contratenor.

Hoppin, Richard H. *Medieval Music*. New York: W. W. Norton, 1978. Provides an excellent survey of medieval music from chant up to music of the early fifteenth century. One chapter is devoted to the Italian *ars nova* and contains considerable information about Landini.

Pirrotta, Nino. *Music and Culture in Italy from the Middle Ages to the Baroque: A Collection of Essays*. Cambridge, Mass.: Harvard University Press, 1984. Contains a series of twenty-two essays on Italian music. The book is interdisciplinary in nature and provides a wealth of information about Italian music and Italian culture in general.

Schachter, Carl. "Landini's Treatment of Consonance and Dissonance." In *The Music Forum*, edited by William Mitchell and Felix Saltzer. Vol. 2. New York: Columbia University Press, 1970. A careful and thorough analysis of how Landini used consonance and dissonance in his compositions. Schachter provides numerous musical excerpts from Landini's works to support his contentions.

See also: William of Ockham.

Related articles in *Great Events from History: The Middle Ages, 477-1453*: c. 1310-1350: William of Ockham Attacks Thomist Ideas; May 20, 1347-October 8, 1354: Cola di Rienzo Leads Popular Uprising in Rome.

Saint László I

Polish-born king of Hungary (r. 1077-1095)

By means of legislative reforms, diplomacy, and military bravura, László attained for Hungary both internal security and, with the annexation of Croatia, a new, more active role in the affairs of the world.

Born: June 27, 1040; Poland
Died: July 29, 1095; Nitra, Slovakia
Also known as: Ladislas I; Saint Ladislas; Ladislaus I
Areas of achievement: Government and politics, religion and theology, military

Early Life

Saint László (LAHS-lo) was the second of three sons born to Hungarian king-to-be Béla I (r. 1060-1063), who at the time still lived in exile in Poland. Béla had fled Hungary, along with his brothers Andrew and Levente, shortly before the end of the great Stephen I's reign, when it was learned that their father, Vászoly, had been arrested for his part in an alleged pagan conspiracy and tortured to death. (His eyes were removed, and his ears were filled with molten lead.) Béla sought refuge at the court of the Polish king Mieszko II (r. 1025-1034) and eventually married the prince's daughter, Richeza. This marriage produced three sons, Géza, László, and Lambert.

László's early life is shrouded in mystery. Essentially all that is known of it is that he spent his boyhood years at the court of his uncle, King Casimir I of Poland (r. 1034-1037, 1040-1058). In that atmosphere, imbued as it was with the spirit of the Christian renaissance, László apparently was reared to be a devout Christian. Eventually, in 1046, Béla and his brothers were summoned home by the growing legions weary of the rule of Stephen's nephew and handpicked successor, Peter. When Andrew I (r. 1046-1060), who had married his son Salamon to the daughter of Holy Roman Emperor Henry III (r. 1046-1056), decided on his only child as his successor, Béla, who was the rightful heir to the crown, revolted. In the ensuing struggle, Béla's forces defeated those of Andrew, who died in battle. Béla thus succeeded his brother, but was himself assassinated in 1063, presumably by backers of Salamon.

Civil war was averted only through the intervention of the priests and nobles. In exchange for their oath to Salamon, Géza and László were appointed duces (*herceg*), or leaders, of Nitra and Bihor counties respectively. It was during this period that László distinguished himself as a soldier. In 1068, a horde of Cumans, on their way home after raiding Hungary, were intercepted by the united front of László, Géza, and Salamon and were ut-

New York: Arno Press, 1977. Gives a fairly lengthy and readable account of László's reign in the chapter titled "The Christian Kingdom in the Middle Ages." Bibliography, index, list of kings of Hungary, and genealogical tables.

Kosztolnyik, Z. J. *Five Eleventh Century Hungarian Kings: Their Policies and Their Relations with Rome*. Boulder, Colo.: East European Quarterly, 1981. A heavily documented study of the Hungarian kings from Stephen to László. Features a bibliographical essay and an index.

_______. *Hungary Under the Early Árpáds, 890's to 1063*. Boulder, Colo.: East European Monographs, 2002. A historical survey of the House of Árpád. Discusses the early years of the Magyars, their migrations and settlement patterns, military campaigns, and more. Genealogical tables, maps, bibliography, index.

Lázár, István. *Hungary: A Brief History*. Translated by Albert Tezla. 6th ed. Budapest: Corvina Press, 2001. Presents a brief but concise history of Hungary, from its beginnings during the days of Árpád through the present day. Maps, index.

Sinor, Denis. *History of Hungary*. 1959. Reprint. Westport, Conn.: Greenwood Press, 1976. The brief account of László in this primer on Hungarian history is colorful and vivid. Has both an index and a chronology of events.

Vámbéry, Armin. *Hungary in Ancient, Medieval, and Modern Times*. 1886. Reprint. Freeport, N.Y.: Books for Libraries Press, 1972. In this venerable but rather dated work on Hungarian history, the reign of László is briefly treated in the chapter "The Kings of the House of Árpád." Includes an index and illustrations.

Yolland, Arthur B. *Hungary*. New York: Frederick A. Stokes, 1917. This work includes an entire chapter on László titled "St. Ladislas and His Age." Bibliography, index, appendix, photographs, and maps.

Zarek, Otto. *The History of Hungary*. London: Selwyn and Blount, 1939. The chapter on László and his successor Kálmán is brief but informative. The text is supplemented by many study aids, including a map, an index, a bibliography, and a table of place-names in Hungarian, German, Slavonic, and Romanian (with a phonetic guide to pronunciation).

SEE ALSO: Árpád; Gregory VII; Henry IV (of Germany); János Hunyadi; Stephen I.

RELATED ARTICLES in *Great Events from History: The Middle Ages, 477-1453*: c. 850: Development of the Slavic Alphabet; 890's: Magyars Invade Italy, Saxony, and Bavaria; 893: Beginning of Bulgaria's Golden Age; August 10, 955: Otto I Defeats the Magyars; 1040-1055: Expansion of the Seljuk Turks; June 28, 1389: Turkish Conquest of Serbia.

LEIF ERIKSSON

Norwegian explorer

Though probably not the first European to encounter North America, Leif made the first deliberate exploration of the North American continent and provided the main stimulus for later, unsuccessful attempts at permanent settlement.

BORN: c. 970; Iceland, possibly in Haukadal
DIED: c. 1035; probably near Julianehaab, Greenland
AREA OF ACHIEVEMENT: Exploration

EARLY LIFE

Very little is known of the early life of Leif Eriksson (layv EHR-ihk-suhn). He was the son of Erik the Red (Erik Thorvaldson) and Thjodhild, and he seems to have had two brothers, Thorvald and Thorstein, and one sister, Freydis. His father's career, however, is well-known. Erik was born in Norway but was forced to flee from there as a result of "some killings." He settled first at Drangar in Iceland but then moved to Haukadal. At that time, though land was still readily available in Iceland, the country had been known for more than a century and intensively settled for perhaps eighty years; there were many powerful and well-established families in all the areas where Erik attempted to settle.

In Haukadal, he became involved in several conflicts, killing at least two of his neighbors, Eyjolf the Sow and Hrafn the Dueler. He was driven out, tried to make his home elsewhere, killed another neighbor in an argument over timber, and was then—not unreasonably—outlawed together with his family.

Erik then made the momentous decision to try to find an unsettled land. Seafarers blown off course had reported land to the west of Iceland, and in 982, Erik sailed, together with his family, to find it. He landed in Greenland near what is now Julianehaab and spent three years

Leif Eriksson. (Library of Congress)

exploring the country. In 985, he returned to Iceland, and in 986, he set sail again with twenty-five ships to found a permanent settlement in Greenland. Only fourteen of the ships arrived, with perhaps four hundred people, but this landing formed the basis for the later colonization of the eastern, middle, and western settlements of Greenland, which lasted until changing climate and Eskimo hostility exterminated the colonies, probably in the early 1500's.

Nevertheless, this colonizing move had transformed Erik from a hunted outlaw in a land severely afflicted by famine to the undisputed head of a new nation, the patriarch of a land with reasonable grazing (in the more temperate climate of the late tenth century) and unparalleled hunting, trapping, and fishing opportunities. It seems reasonable to suppose that the total change of lifestyle also made an impression on his children, including Leif, who may have wondered if they too could not become great men or great women by similar daring seamanship.

LIFE'S WORK

To reconstruct Leif's life, two Icelandic sagas are indispensable: *Groehnlendinga saga* (c. 1390; *The Greenlanders' Saga*, 1893) and *Eiríks saga rauda* (c. 1263; *The Saga of Erik the Red*, 1841), the latter existing in two different versions. These sagas do not tell quite the same tale, but reasons for their deviations can often be seen. According to *The Greenlanders' Saga*, which was composed much earlier than its late fourteenth century transcription date, America was originally sighted not by Leif but by Bjarni Herjolfsson, who had been blown off course on his way to Greenland. Bjarni refused, however, to land at any of the three places he sighted (to the disgust of his crew) and finally made his way to his father's farm, located about fifty miles from the farm Erik and Leif had established at Brattahlith. Bjarni's sightings caused much discussion, and some time later, probably around the year 1000, Leif came to him and bought his ship—presumably thinking that if the ship had reached this strange destination once, it could do so again. Leif hoped to get his father, now a man of fifty or more, to lead the expedition, because of his famous good luck, but on his way to the ship, Erik fell off his horse, hurt himself, and refused to go any farther. It was not his fate to discover more new lands, he said. He would leave that to his son.

The Greenlanders' Saga then relates that Leif and his men came in succession to countries they called Hellu-

LEO IX

Pope (1049-1054)

Leo IX was one of the most important of the medieval popes. Coming to the Papacy after a long period of papal and religious decline, during an era when the authority of the Holy Roman Emperors was at its most influential, Leo instituted a number of significant reforms within the Church that had profound results not only for the Roman church in the West and the Orthodox church in the East but also for the Holy Roman Empire and other kingdoms in Europe.

BORN: June 21, 1002; Egisheim, Alsace (now in France)
DIED: April 19, 1054; Rome (now in Italy)
ALSO KNOWN AS: Bruno of Egisheim
AREAS OF ACHIEVEMENT: Religion and theology, church reform

EARLY LIFE

Leo IX was born Bruno of Egisheim, son of Hugo, count of Egisheim. The family was related to Conrad II, the Holy Roman Emperor. His parents were very religious, and Bruno was destined from an early age to enter the Church. The higher offices in the Church were generally reserved for members of aristocratic families, and Bruno was educated at a school for upper-class boys in Toul, an establishment noted for its atmosphere of piety and its reforming sympathies. After his schooling, he served as a deputy to Herman, the bishop of Toul, and led the military vassals of the bishop into battle alongside the emperor (a common action by members of the clergy in that strife-torn era). Herman died in 1026, and Bruno was chosen as the new bishop of Toul, although he was only in his mid-twenties and might instead have had a successful secular career serving the emperor. Toul was a poor diocese and not an obvious choice for an ambitious cleric. Bruno was consecrated bishop in 1027.

Rampant corruption plagued the Western church in the tenth and eleventh centuries; the monastic establishments and their regular clergy, as well as various elements in the secular clergy, from the Papacy down to the village priest, had succumbed to it. There were two major abuses within the Church, and both had widespread ramifications. Simony, or the buying and selling of church offices, was rife, and there was doubt whether a clergyman tainted with simony could validly perform the sacraments on which salvation depended. The second major abuse was that of Nicolaism, a name of unknown origin that came to stand for various types of sexual incontinence among the clergy. Requirements that all clergymen be celibate were widely disregarded, and many clerics had wives, mistresses, and children.

In addition, it was a violent age, and even the Church was not immune. During the eleventh century, many clergymen, including popes, were murdered, often by their fellow clergy. There were demands for reform, both from within the Church and from secular society. Some improvement had slowly occurred, often stemming from the example set first by the monastery of Cluny, in France, founded in 910, but also by other monasteries in northern Europe.

Bruno was never a monk, but he was a strong admirer of Saint Benedict of Nursia, the founder of Western monasticism in the sixth century, and many of his closest advisers were monks. Bruno was a reforming bishop in Toul, and he concentrated particularly on ending abuses in the various monastic houses. He was also active militarily in defending his diocese from threatened invasion. Bruno was a loyal vassal to his relative the Holy Roman Emperor and a staunch defender of the empire. An able diplomat, he traveled to Rome on many occasions. Even though Toul was not a prominent diocese, Bruno became widely known, not only in the empire but also in other kingdoms, in ecclesiastical as well as political and military spheres.

LIFE'S WORK

In 1048, Pope Damasus II died after serving as the bishop of Rome, or pope, for only twenty-three days; it was widely rumored that his death was caused by poison. The selection of the new pope depended on the wishes of the Holy Roman Emperor, Henry III, for by the eleventh century, the emperors had become not only secular rulers of the empire, which extended from the Germanies into Italy, but also the effective arbiters of the Church. In practice, the emperors not only chose the high officials of the Church but also invested their choices with the signs of the office, the bishop's staff and ring. The Church had periodically fought against the involvement of laymen such as the emperors in the selection of bishops, abbots, and other clergy, and various church councils had passed resolutions against the practice of lay investiture. In the feudal age, however, the needs of secular society became intertwined with those of the Church; powerful kings, emperors, and other laypeople would not allow the Church to choose its own officials unilaterally. Too much was at stake, including the possession of land, which translated into wealth and political and military power. Because of the lands they held, counts and dukes had to be loyal vassals to their lords, and in the opinion of most kings and emperors, so must bishops and abbots.

Emperor Henry III chose the new pope at Worms. His selection was his relative, Bruno of Toul. Henry was a powerful ruler of both church and state who believed himself to have been chosen by God to rule; it is doubtful that he saw himself as subordinate to the pope, even in many areas of religion. He had already chosen two previous popes. Bruno was perhaps an obvious choice, given his family connection and his already wide reputation, but even Henry could not know just how significant his selection was to become. Under Bruno, who took the name Leo in honor of Leo the Great, the Papacy became a major center of reform. The movement had not begun at Rome, but with Leo, the Papacy became the driving force for reform for the next two centuries. Although the effective choice had already taken place at Worms, an election at Rome was the norm; thus, in late 1048, Leo left Toul for the Eternal City. He took with him other high-ranking clergymen, including the monk Hildebrand, who, as Pope Gregory VII, would later carry many of Leo's reforms to fruition. Early accounts of his life have Leo entering Rome barefoot, as a simple pilgrim, and being received ecstatically by the Roman populace. His papacy had begun.

Although the reform of abuses in the Church had already started, Leo gave focus and direction to the reform impetus. Because of his experience as bishop and diplomat, his intellectual capabilities, his knowledge of the problems faced by the Church in the eleventh century, and his vision of what the power of the Papacy might accomplish, Leo was ideally suited to change the Church. To do so, however, he could not remain in Rome. His own preference may have been to travel widely, and given the state of the Church and the nature of medieval society, it was impossible that the curtailment of the various abuses could be enforced without the actual physical presence of the pope where the problems were manifest. In any event, Leo was a peripatetic pope. He held many councils and synods during his reign, some in Rome but many others in Italy, France, Hungary, and the Holy Roman Empire. He preached particularly against simony and clerical incontinence, held up the canon law of the Church as the legal justification for the reforms, and, citing his authority as pope, demanded obedience. Accused and recalcitrant bishops and other church officials were summoned to Rome and in many cases were excommunicated and removed from office.

As a reformer, Leo was concerned with more than the spiritual state of the Church. As bishop of Toul he had been involved in various diplomatic, political, and military affairs, and those interests continued when he became pope. Given the character of medieval society, the Church could not be merely an institution that dealt in spiritual and otherworldly matters; since at least the mid-eighth century, the Church had also been a temporal Italian state. At times the Papal States were under the influence and control of the Holy Roman Emperor; Henry III intervened widely in Italian affairs. At other times the states of the Church had to rely on their own resources—military, diplomatic, political, and economic—to survive and prosper in a violent age. It was perhaps unfortunate that the church had become a state, but it was a reality that Leo accepted.

The political and military threat to the temporal powers of the Church during Leo's reign occurred in southern Italy. Beginning before 1020, numerous bands from the duchy of Normandy in northern France had begun to loot and wage war in Sicily and southern Italy. The Normans were Christians, but much of the history of the medieval world was the story of Christians waging war on other Christians, often brutally. Leo and others complained about the ruthlessness of the Normans, but there were

Pope Leo IX. (Library of Congress)

also political considerations. The Church and the Holy Roman Empire had an interest in the region, as did the Byzantine Empire, which had had a toehold in southern Italy for many centuries. The Norman influx upset those established power relationships.

Henry III was at that time involved with his claims to Hungary and thus gave little support to his kinsman Leo. When, after many diplomatic exchanges, warnings, and broken promises, Leo decided to wage a holy war against the Normans, he lacked sufficient resources. He had his own vassals and the support of a number of Italian princes, but without the military might of the Holy Roman Empire, Leo's forces were no match for the Normans. Before Leo had hardly begun his campaign he was defeated in a bloody battle at Civitate, a village in central Italy, in 1053, and was forced to surrender. He was treated with honor and respect by the Normans, but if he was not broken in spirit, his physical capabilities had begun to wane. For the next several months, he remained in Benevento, and he returned to Rome only in the spring of 1054.

At Benevento, Leo set into motion one of the most momentous and symbolic events of the Middle Ages. In fact if not in theory, the Christian world was not ruled by a single church. In the West, over many centuries, the bishops of Rome and the Papacy had emerged as the central focus of religious faith and practice. The Papacy had argued successfully that the popes were the apostolic successors to the first bishop of Rome, Peter, who himself had been given the keys to the heavenly kingdom by Jesus Christ. Added to this Petrine Theory, as it is known, was the Donation of Constantine, an eighth century forgery that purported to give the Papacy all of the Western lands after Constantine had abandoned them to found his city of Constantinople in the early fourth century. This document was discovered to be a forgery only in the fifteenth century, and in earlier times, church officials such as Leo were sincerely convinced of its accuracy.

Yet in Constantinople, in the Byzantine Empire, the Papacy's claims had never been totally accepted. Patriarchs of Constantinople, spiritual leaders of the largest city in Christendom and the wealthy and powerful Byzantine Empire, had often been reluctant to follow the lead of the Roman bishops. In the eyes of Eastern leaders, the West was more barbarous and less cultured than the East. Different historical experiences and cultural traditions, different religious practices, different languages—Greek in the East, Latin in the West—all combined to create friction and disagreements. Theologically, East and West quarreled over the issue of clerical celibacy and the so-called *Filioque* doctrine that had evolved in the West (possibly in the seventh century) and that described the Holy Spirit as coming not only from God the Father but also from Jesus Christ the Son. That was a change from the creedal language agreed on in 381, which had defined the Holy Spirit as coming only from God the Father. Through the centuries, then, Rome and Constantinople had coexisted only in an uneasy truce.

With the approval and guidance of Leo, an embassy was sent to Constantinople under the papal legate, Cardinal Humbert. Leo's temporal aim was to gain assistance from the Eastern emperor against the Normans; he also hoped, however, to attain the more far-reaching goal of uniting the Eastern and Western churches under papal leadership. Earlier popes and patriarchs had been unwilling to push their respective claims; thus, Leo's delegation, with its assertion of Western authority and supremacy and its criticism of Eastern abuses and heresies, was a new departure. It did not accomplish what Leo intended. His delegation did not receive the expected submission from the patriarch, Michael Cerularius; instead, Humbert excommunicated Michael in a dramatic confrontation. In turn, Leo's delegates were excommunicated by the Eastern church. The attempt to unite the two churches resulted instead in opening a gulf between the Roman church and the Eastern Orthodox church that has proved permanent.

Significance

Leo IX died on April 19, 1054, three months before the acts of excommunication took place in Constantinople. He had returned to Rome only a month earlier. Leo was buried in Rome; he was canonized in 1087. The reform program he had instituted as pope was continued by his successors, many of whom had been his advisers. Preeminent among them was Hildebrand, who, as Gregory VII, became pope in 1073.

The entire body of reform and the era itself would later bear Gregory's name; still, Gregory's conflict with Holy Roman Emperor Henry IV over lay investiture and his claim to papal supremacy in general were but the logical outcome of the seeds planted during the pontificate of Leo IX. Leo reigned as pope for only five years, but his reign was a watershed in the history of the Papacy, in the reform of the institutional Church, in the relations between the Church and the secular powers, and in the growth of the papal monarchy. Commentators then and since have criticized Leo for his military activities while pope and for creating the long-lasting estrangement between the Roman and Orthodox churches, but his commitment to the moral and spiritual reform of the Church and the broader society cannot be in doubt.

—*Eugene S. Larson*

Further Reading

Barraclough, Geoffrey. *The Origins of Modern Germany.* Oxford: Basil Blackwell, 1972. This study is the classic account of the rise of Germany from the era of Charlemagne. The author sees Leo as a key figure in resisting the claim of the Holy Roman Emperors that they had been chosen by God to rule not only the state but also the church, a concept known as theocratic kingship or imperial theocracy.

Douglas, David C. *The Norman Achievement, 1050-1100.* Berkeley: University of California Press, 1969. Douglas, biographer of William the Conqueror, here describes the impact of the Normans throughout Europe, from Normandy and England to Sicily and Italy. His discussion of Leo and the Battle of Civitate particularly stresses Leo's call for a holy war or crusade against the Normans, a concept that would come to fruition in the Crusades to recapture the Holy Land from the Muslims.

Knowles, David, and Dimitri Obolensky. *The Middle Ages.* New York: McGraw-Hill, 1968. This work is the second volume in a five-volume history of the Catholic church. The authors single out Leo for considerable discussion and in the broader context of the history of the Church note that "for the first time for almost two centuries a pope of ability, energy and spirituality was in office."

Mann, Horace K. *The Lives of the Popes in the Middle Ages: Volume 6, 1049-1130.* 2d ed. London: Kegan Paul, Trench, Trübner, 1925. Mann's account of Leo, which extends to almost two hundred pages, is one of the few extensive biographies in English of Leo's life and works. The treatment of Leo is extremely sympathetic. The volume includes, in translation, almost all the medieval sources regarding the pope and thus is indispensable.

Parisse, Michel, ed. *La Vie du Pape Léon IX: Brunon, évêque de Toul.* Translated by Monique Goullet. Paris: Belles Lettres, 1997. A French translation of the biography attributed to Wibertus or Cardinal Humbert, contemporaries of Leo. Bibliography, indexes.

Runciman, Steven. *The Eastern Schism.* New York: Oxford University Press, 1955. This study is a well-written narrative of the conflict between the Papacy and the Eastern Orthodox church during the eleventh and twelfth centuries. Runciman states that many persons and events bear responsibility for the Schism of 1054 but particularly singles out Cardinal Humbert for exacerbating an already difficult situation.

Southern, R. W. *Western Society and the Church in the Middle Ages.* Grand Rapids, Mich.: Wm. B. Eerdmans, 1970. This volume in the Pelican History of the Church is a succinct but comprehensive history of the Church during medieval times. It briefly but adequately puts Leo and such issues as the dispute with Constantinople into the historical and scholarly context.

Ullmann, Walter. *The Growth of Papal Government in the Middle Ages.* 3d ed. London: Methuen, 1970. The author, who has written numerous books on the medieval Church, discusses the significance of Leo in the emergence of the Papacy as a rival to the Holy Roman Empire, and notes particularly the importance of the Donation of Constantine for Leo in his dispute with the Patriarch of Constantinople.

Williams, Schafer, ed. *The Gregorian Epoch: Reformation, Revolution, Reaction?* Boston: D. C. Heath, 1964. This is a volume in the Problems in European Civilization series and includes fourteen different selections by historians from the mid-nineteenth century to the 1960's. As the title suggests, the articles concentrate on the reforms associated with Gregory VII, but many of the issues discussed relate to the years of Leo's pontificate.

See also: Saint Benedict of Nursia; Gregory VII; Henry III.

Related articles in *Great Events from History: The Middle Ages, 477-1453*: 1054: Beginning of the Rome-Constantinople Schism; 1440: Donation of Constantine Is Exposed.

Leonardo of Pisa

Italian mathematician

Leonardo provided Western Europe with the earliest and most heralded Latin account of the Hindu-Arabic number system and its computational methods. He contributed substantially to the acceptance of the Arabic algebraic system and created a revolutionary mathematical technique known as the Fibonacci sequence.

Born: c. 1170; Pisa (now in Italy)
Died: c. 1240; Pisa
Also known as: Leonardo Fibonacci (given name); Leonardo Pisano
Area of achievement: Mathematics

Early Life

Leonardo of Pisa was born Leonardo Fibonacci, the surname meaning "son of Bonaccio." Although very little is known about his life beyond the few facts gleaned from his mathematical writings, his father, Guglielmo, was a successful merchant who was the chief magistrate of the community of Pisan merchants in the North African port of Bugia (now Bejaïa, Algeria). As a young boy, he joined his father there and began the study of mathematics in this culturally diverse environment.

Desiring his son to be a successful merchant or commercial agent, Guglielmo sent Leonardo to study with a Muslim master who introduced him to the intricacies of Arabic mathematics, especially al-Khwārizmī's *Kītab al-jabr wa al-muqābalah* (algebra; c. 820) and the practical value of the Hindu-Arabic numeral system represented by the nine Indian figures (1, 11, 111, 4, 5, 6, 7, 8, 9), the fourth through the ninth symbols representing the first letters of the Hindu names for these integers. As he grew older, he traveled around the Mediterranean area, especially Egypt, Syria, Greece, Sicily, and Provence; visited the dominant commercial centers; acquired knowledge of the arithmetical systems used by hundreds of merchants; and mastered the theoretical subtleties of Greek and Arabic mathematics, chiefly those of Plato of Tivoli, Savasorda, Euclid, Archimedes, Hero of Alexandria, and Diophantus. He even resided for a time at the court of Frederick II, the Holy Roman Emperor, where he engaged in scientific speculations with Frederick and his court philosophers, the most notable being Michael Scot, to whom Leonardo dedicated one of his works.

In his later years, Leonardo probably served Pisa administratively as an examiner of municipal accounts. This commercial expertise, however, was always secondary to his lifelong passion for mathematics.

Life's Work

The rapid improvements that marked the history of Western mathematics in the thirteenth century, particularly in the fields of arithmetic and algebra, were largely a result of the genius of Leonardo, although a second mathematician of originality, Jordanus Nemorarius, made significant contributions, especially to the theory of numbers and to mechanics. Yet Jordanus showed no trace of Arabic influence. Developing the Greco-Roman arithmetical tradition of Nicomachus and Boethius, he habitually used letters for generalizing proofs in arithmetical problems, an awkward method that Leonardo could avoid because of his employment of Arabic numbers.

Leonardo's pioneering achievements in mathematics began in 1202, when he wrote his first work, *Liber abaci* (English translation, 2002). Even though the title, which means "book of the abacus," is a misnomer because Leonardo eschewed Roman numerals and the methods of the abacus, the work became the earliest in the West to extol the superiority of the nine-numeral Arabic system of numbers when used in conjunction with the zero. When the *Liber abaci* first appeared, Arabic numerals were known to only a few European philosophers through the Latin translations of al-Khwārizmī's ninth century treatise. Leonardo understood fully the advantages of this system for mathematical operations. He displayed the system brilliantly in this edition and in a second, revised edition of 1228 dedicated to Michael Scot, the emperor's chief scholar, and provided more rigorous demonstrations than in any previous or contemporary work. Leonardo realized that the great merit of this system was that it contained the symbol for zero and that any number could be represented simply by arranging digits in order, the value of a digit being shown by its distance from zero or from the first digit on the left.

Predominantly theoretical in nature, the *Liber abaci* was also valuable for its commercial arithmetic, which covered such operations as profit margins, barter, money changing, conversions of weights and measures, partnerships, and interest. After his death, Italian merchants generally adopted Leonardo's Arabic system of numeration, and his book remained the standard in Europe for more than two centuries.

Besides popularizing a new system of numerals

throughout the West, the *Liber abaci* was revolutionary for two reasons. First, it introduced Arabic algebra to European civilization. Leonardo's algebra was rhetorical, but it was unique because of its employment of geometrical methods in its descriptions. He dealt primarily with the extraction of square and cube roots, progressions, indeterminate analysis (an equation with two or more unknowns for which the solution must be in rational numbers, whole numbers or common fractions), false assumptions (when a problem is worked out by incorrect data, then corrected by proportion), the rules of three and five (methods of finding proportions), the solution of equations of the third degree, and other algebraic and geometrical operations.

Of even greater importance was Leonardo's famous sequence of numbers known before the nineteenth century as the Series of Lamé but now called correctly the Fibonacci sequence. In answer to the problem of how many pairs of rabbits could be produced from a single pair if each pair produced a new pair each month and every new pair became productive from the second month onward (supposing that no pair died), he devised the recurrent, or recursive, series of 1, 1, 2, 3, 5, 8, 13, 21, 34, 55, 89, 144, 233, and so on. In this number sequence, in which the relation between two or more successive terms can be expressed by a formula, each term is equal to the sum of the two preceding ones. In the nineteenth century, the series proved of immense value in the study of divisibility, prime numbers, and Mersenne numbers. In the modern world, the Fibonacci sequence is used in botany for determining the patterns of natural growth.

In addition to the *Liber abaci*, Leonardo wrote three other significant works. In 1220, his *Practica geometriae* (practice of geometry) presented theorems based principally on two of Euclid's works. It applied algebra to the solution of geometrical problems, a radically innovative technique for thirteenth century Europe. In 1225, two smaller works appeared, the *Flos* (prime) and the *Liber quadratorum* (*The Book of Squares*, 1987). More original than the *Liber abaci*, they were devoted to questions involving quadratic and cubic equations, in addition to several refinements to his earlier algebraic discourses. *The Book of Squares* may be considered Leonardo's masterpiece. Although the *Liber abaci* made his reputation, *The Book of Squares* made him the most important contributor to number theory until Pierre de Fermat, the celebrated seventeenth century French mathematician who was instrumental in early experimentation aimed at determining the exact length of a quadrant of Earth's meridian, the scientific basis of the metric system of weights and measures.

Significance

The impact of Leonardo on future generations was enormous. His pioneering achievements helped spread Arabic numeration and Arabic algebra throughout the West. Popular diffusion followed in the form of almanacs, calendars, and literary and poetic productions. Merchants accepted his new system—the Italians first and other Europeans by the end of the sixteenth century. Even as early as the second half of the thirteenth century, lectures in the universities incorporated the new numbering system. His use of geometry in algebraic problems and, conversely, his use of algebra in solving geometric problems ushered in a new era in these disciplines. In time, the Fibonacci sequence revolutionized many divergent scientific fields. Last, aside from their scientific merit, his works were of tremendous cultural influence, particularly as they relate to metrology and to the major economic conditions of his time. In short, Leonardo was the greatest Christian mathematician of the Middle Ages. The mathematical renaissance in the West dates from him.

—Ronald Edward Zupko

Further Reading

Crombie, A. C. *Augustine to Galileo: The History of Science, A.D. 400-1650*. 1953. Reprint. Cambridge, Mass.: Harvard University Press, 1979. Includes much discussion of Leonardo's influence on mathematics and number theory prior to the scientific revolution.

_______. *Medieval and Early Modern Science*. 2 vols. 1959. Reprint. Cambridge, Mass.: Harvard University Press, 1961. Excellent descriptive bibliographies in both volumes, with coverage of Leonardo's precursors, his impact on popularizing Arabic numerals, and his contributions to later medieval mathematics.

Fibonacci, Leonardo. *Fibonacci's "Liber abaci": A Translation into Modern English of Leonardo Pisano's Book of Calculation*. New York: Springer, 2002. Notes on the translation provide information on Leonardo and his work. Bibliography.

Gies, Joseph, and Frances Gies. *Leonard of Pisa and the New Mathematics of the Middle Ages*. Gainesville, Ga.: New Classics Library, 1969. Contains a summary of Leonardo's life, a general survey of his works, and a brief overview of the history of numerical notation.

eral ideas from memory images in the imagination so that it can be made into an actual intellect. The Active Intellect allows the material intellect to form images and ideas. It gives the material intellect an understanding of separate ideas and how they all relate to one another. Thus, human reason and the rational capacity of humans must reside in the Active Intellect. The Active Intellect is the divine force. Levi ben Gershom acknowledged that the Active Intellect can think for itself, and it acts with the aid of an instrument that is natural warmth, to which it gives a soul.

Levi ben Gershom also conflicted with Orthodox Jews with regard to his views on the afterlife. He alleged that human souls have two components: a material part and an intellect. These components make it possible for people to think, understand, and learn from their experiences. Levi ben Gershom was also concerned with prognostication. He deduced that there are three ways in which people can know the future: dreams, divination, and prophecy. He believed, however, that prognostication itself comprises a twofold aspect. Future events can be determined from the order of the heavenly bodies and by foretelling. The Active Intellect also takes part in the latter half of this two-pronged explanation of prognostication. The Active Intellect knows these events that are predicted in dreams, divination, and prophecy. This intellect then gives this knowledge to humans. The level of prophecy is higher in an individual whose intellect is more developed and perfected.

Where Levi ben Gershom conflicted most with traditional Jews was on the issue of Jewish chosenness. He did not believe that the Jews were God's chosen people. A simple question that he asked set off a spark: How can the Jewish people be God's chosen people if God is an impersonal being with limited powers? Additionally, how can there be a chosen people if God does not directly get involved in human and world affairs? Contemporary scholars know that Levi ben Gershom did have some relationship with Christian theologians and thinkers, but it is not clear to what extent the Catholic Church influenced him. One of the major issues that the Church refuted was the idea that the Jews were God's chosen people.

SIGNIFICANCE

Levi ben Gershom became a controversial figure after his death. He was sometimes vilified in academic circles, especially among Orthodox Jews, because of the intellectual positions that he maintained. There were many traditional Jewish scholars who disagreed with the unorthodox views that he expressed in works such as *The Wars of the Lord*. Many conservative Jewish philosophers began to attack his writings. There was a period of time when interest in Levi ben Gershom's writings waned because of these literary attacks.

Recent scholars have rediscovered the value of Levi ben Gershom's insights. He advocated that life on earth has meaning and that terrestrial events have order. Astrology, he believed, was the way to uncover that meaning. He is seen today as one of the greatest intellectuals of medieval times and, in terms of scholarship, he is considered second only to Maimonides, his great predecessor. He is rightfully portrayed as an insightful, genuine philosopher whose ideas transcended his time and the writings of his contemporaries.

—*David Treviño*

FURTHER READING

Eisen, Robert. *Gersonides on Providence, Covenant, and the Chosen People: A Study in Medieval Jewish Philosophy and Biblical Commentary.* Albany: State University of New York Press, 1995. A study into Levi ben Gershom's biblical interpretations of the Jews and their relations with God.

Husik, Isaac. *A History of Mediaeval Jewish Thought.* New York: Meridian Books, 1960. A general work on the predominant Jewish philosophers during the Middle Ages. The section on Levi ben Gershom is thorough and well-researched.

Hyman, Arthur. *Essays in Medieval Jewish and Islamic Philosophy: Studies from the Publications of the American Academy for Jewish Research.* New York: KTAV, 1977. A very enticing work that compares the religious and secular writings of significant Jewish and Islamic philosophers during the Middle Ages.

Levi ben Gershom. *The Wars of the Lord: Book One: The Immortality of the Soul.* Translated by Seymour Feldman. Philadelphia: Jewish Publication Society, 1984. In addition to highlighting Levi ben Gershom's beliefs, the translator's lengthy introduction captures the essence of Levi ben Gershom's life and works.

_______. *The Wars of the Lord: Book Two, Book Three, and Book Four.* Translated by Seymour Feldman. Philadelphia: Jewish Publication Society, 1987. This is the second analysis of Levi ben Gershom's *The Wars of the Lord*, with notes by the translator.

Nadler, Steven. "Gersonides on Providence: A Jewish Chapter in the History of the General Will." *Journal of the History of Ideas* 62, no. 1 (January, 2001). Argues that the concept of general will—divine purpose and effect—appears in the fourteenth century writings of Levi ben Gershom and thus did not originate during the seventeenth century, as previously believed.

Sirat, Colette. *A History of Jewish Philosophy in the Middle Ages*. London: Cambridge University Press, 1985. A general study of Jewish religious and secular thought and belief in the centuries constituting the Middle Ages.

SEE ALSO: Pietro d'Abano; Averroës; Avicenna; al-Ghazzālī; Ibn Gabirol; Judah ha-Levi; Moses Maimonides; Moses de León; Naḥmanides.

RELATED ARTICLES in *Great Events from History: The Middle Ages, 477-1453*: c. 1150: Moors Transmit Classical Philosophy and Medicine to Europe; 1190: Moses Maimonides Writes *The Guide of the Perplexed*; c. 1275: The *Zohar* Is Transcribed.

LI BO
Chinese poet

Li Bo's clever, sensuous, and mystical verse has led many to consider him China's foremost lyric poet.

BORN: 701; Chinese Turkistan (now in China)
DIED: 762; Sichuan Province, China
ALSO KNOWN AS: Li Po (Wade-Giles); Li Bai (Pinyin), Li Pai (Wade-Giles); Li Taibo (Pinyin), Li T'ai-po (Wade-Giles)
AREA OF ACHIEVEMENT: Literature

EARLY LIFE

According to tradition, the ancestors of Li Bo (lee boh) had been exiled to the remote area of northwestern China (Chinese Turkistan) now known as the Xinjiang Uygur Autonomous Region early in the seventh century. When he was about five, his father, a small businessman whose income was supplemented by his wife's work as a washerwoman, successfully petitioned the authorities for permission to move his family to the city of Zhang Ming in Sichuan Province, a more civilized, if still decidedly provincial, community.

During their exile, Li Bo's ancestors had intermarried with the Mongolian peoples of the northwest frontier, as a result of which he was taller and sturdier than the average Chinese, and his wide mouth and bulging eyes were also commented on in several contemporary descriptions. Li Bo's unusual background was reflected in his schooling, for he concentrated on the study of esoteric religious and literary works rather than the prescribed Confucian classics, although he certainly read and was familiar with the latter. He became deeply interested in Daoism, a more mystical and romantic philosophy than the thoroughly practical Confucianism that dominated Chinese society at the time, and received a diploma from the Daoist master Gai Dianshi (Kao Tien-shih) in recognition of these studies. In 720, his exceptional scholastic abilities were recognized by the governor of his province, who predicted that he would become a famous poet.

After a turbulent adolescence, during which he fell in with a group of roughnecks devoted to sword fighting, Li Bo became interested in more contemplative pursuits. Between the ages of twenty and twenty-four, he lived as a recluse with a fellow student of Daoism in a remote part of Sichuan Province, there acquiring even more of a reputation for wisdom and literary ability. Now emotionally as well as intellectually mature, he resolved to broaden his horizons by seeing what the world outside his native province had to offer.

LIFE'S WORK

Li Bo began his travels by exploring those areas of China through which the Yangtze River passed. In the central province of Hubei, he met and married Xu Xinshi (Hsu Hsin-shih), the granddaughter of a retired prime minister, in 727. Although they had several children and Xu Xinshi seems to have been a model wife, Li's wanderlust was evidently untamed. He continued to ramble about the country, sometimes with his wife and sometimes not, visiting other poets and scholars and becoming something of a legend among his fellow intellectuals. In 735, while traveling in the northern province of Shanxi, he saved the life of the soldier Guo Ziyi (Kuo Tzu-i), who would later be pleased to return the favor when he rose to high political rank. A short time after this, Li Bo is mentioned in accounts of a celebrated group of hard-drinking men of letters, the "Six Idlers of the Bamboo Brook," who resided in the northeastern province of Shandong.

While engaged in his travels across the length and breadth of China, Li had begun to write the deceptively simple lyrics that posterity would consider among the finest achievements in Chinese verse. The majority of his work cannot be accurately dated, but since both his life-

Thirteenth century portrait of Li Bo by Chinese artist Liang Chick. (Courtesy of E. P. Dutton)

style and his literary accomplishments remained relatively constant throughout his career, determining dates is not as important as it might be for a less precocious writer.

His early interest in Daoism was one of the most significant influences on his poetry, one that has sometimes been insufficiently appreciated by Western commentators. Laozi (Lao-tzu; 604-sixth century B.C.E.) and Zhuangzi (Chuang-tzu; c. 365-290 B.C.E.), respectively the founder and the chief apostle of this philosophy, emphasized the necessity of living in harmony with the Dao, or Way, giving up the trivial concerns of conventional social life and cultivating the virtues of simplicity and directness. Withdrawal from the world was encouraged, and at their most extreme, Li's verses take an almost sinful pride in their creator's capacity for achieving the heights of heavenly bliss:

> You ask what my soul does away in the sky,
> I inwardly smile but cannot reply;
> Like the peach-blossom carried away by the stream,
> I soar to a world of which you cannot dream.

As the poet grew older, however, these early expressions of mystical communion with inexpressible realities gave way to more down-to-earth recipes for pleasuring the soul. Just as modern-day readers buy self-help books far more frequently than the classic works of religion and philosophy, so did the people of Li Bo's day seek practical formulas for attaining peace of mind. Thus, when Daoist recluses discovered that the drinking of wine offered a close approximation of the mental states reached through serious meditation, alcohol soon became a respectable as well as popular means of attuning the senses to the subtle harmony of nature's underlying unities.

Li first impressed his fellow countrymen as a singer of the praises of wine, and even centuries later, he is a kind of unofficial patron saint of serious drinkers. Unlike those who drink to forget, however, Li and the recluses, musicians, poets, and vagabonds among whom he spent much of his life drank to heighten their appreciation of beauty and to loosen their tongues in the description of it. One of his most famous poems, a celebration of wine, asserts that "in life, when you are happy, you must drink your joy to the last drop." It is in this context of the celebration of good fortune, rather than the drowning of sorrows, that his advocacy of intoxication should be understood.

This kind of joyful imbibing often figures in the various versions of how Li Bo came to meet the reigning emperor, Xuanzong (Hsüan-tsung, r. 712-756), and although the exact circumstances remain a matter of conjecture, it is known that by 742, Li Bo had become a favorite of this Daoist-oriented ruler. It is claimed that the emperor was once so taken with a poem praising the accomplishments of his government that he broke tradition by serving Li food with his own hands. On another occasion, the poet impressed him by dashing off a piece when obviously very drunk. The most famous poem he wrote at court, "Jing bing diao" ("A Song of Pure Happiness"), was inspired by the emperor's beautiful concubine Yang Guifei (Yang Kuei-fei):

> Her robe is a cloud, her face a flower;
> Her balcony, glimmering with the bright spring dew,
> Is either the tip of earth's Jade Mountain
> Or a moon-edged roof of paradise.

Li seems, however, to have offended either a powerful member of the court or perhaps even the emperor himself; in 744, ordered to leave the capital, he resumed his earlier pattern of wandering about the kingdom. Shortly thereafter, he met the younger poet Du Fu, and for a period of two or three years, they traveled together, studying at remote Daoist monasteries and exchanging ideas about poetry. Du Fu seems to have functioned as a calming influence on his friend; he encouraged Li to write down his verses rather than simply declaim them to an admiring circle of drinking companions. Because the two were almost polar opposites in terms of poetry as well as personality, the friendship between them came to be held up as a symbol of how artistic ideals can transcend individual differences.

After parting from Du, Li continued on his roaming life, spending most of his time in the southern and western provinces of Jiangxi and Jiangsu. In 756, he unthinkingly accepted an invitation to the court of a prince who was using the opportunity afforded by the rebellion of the Tatar general An Lushan to assert his own dynastic claims. When this prince's armies were defeated in 757, Li was imprisoned; he gained release only after his old friend Guo Ziyi, now the new emperor's minister of war, interceded on his behalf.

This experience was, in a way, a practical demonstration of the dangers of ignoring Daoist precepts about withdrawing from the world, and during the five years of life that remained to him, Li avoided any intrigues of this sort. He also seems to have been reconciled with his wife and children and lived a contented and—because he was still in some political disgrace—quiet life. After he died in 762, even old friends such as Du Fu did not hear the news until several years later. His death, according to legend, was an appropriate one for a lover of wine: Drunk in his boat on a beautiful evening, he leaned far over the side to admire his reflection in the water, fell overboard, and drowned. In a culture in which the manner of death was just as important as behavior in life, Li Bo's passing ensured that he would achieve immortality as both legend and literary genius.

SIGNIFICANCE

Li Bo's poetry has been highly valued for its consummate grace and original choice of words. He wrote during a period when one of China's most revered dynasties, the Tang (T'ang; 618-907), was at the apex of its power and prestige, and his verses seemed to catch the spirit of a self-confident and somewhat hedonistic age. He had, after all, been an intimate of the emperor himself, a fact that continued to fascinate succeeding generations as they preserved the many stories of the poet's brash behavior toward his sovereign.

Li Bo was a sworn enemy of the mindless conformity to sterile traditions that is always a danger in highly stratified societies, but it was the pursuit of pleasure, not some quixotic and suicidal act of rebellion, that marked both his life and his work. In verses that were the literary equivalent of Daoism's injunctions to accept the universe rather than strive to change it, he sang the delights of wine, women, and song in spontaneous language that appealed to nobles and ne'er-do-wells alike.

Li Bo is one of the great romantic figures of Chinese literature, a poet whose adventurous and idiosyncratic life seems perfectly encapsulated in his direct and unhackneyed verses. The facility with which he wrote of mundane pleasures, gently grieved over their transience, and explored the possibilities of mystical communion with transcendent reality is just as attractive today as it was during his own time. Few readers of Chinese literature have remained immune to his charm.

—*Paul Stuewe*

FURTHER READING

Cooper, Arthur, comp. and trans. *Li Po and Tu Fu: Poems Selected and Translated with an Introduction and Notes*. Harmondsworth, England: Penguin Books, 1973. The translations are generally excellent, and the extensive background material on the history of Chinese poetry and literature is helpful. Li's connection with Du Fu is usefully discussed.

Li Bo. *Banished Immortal: Visions of Li T'ai-po*. Translated by Sam Hamill. Fredonia, N.Y.: White Pine Press, 1987. A collection of translations of poetry by Li Bo.

_______. *Li Pai: Two Hundred Selected Poems*. Translated by Rewi Alley. 1980. Reprint. Hong Kong: Joint Publishing, 1987. A selection of poetry by Li Bo.

_______. *The Selected Poems of Li Po*. Translated by David Hinton. New York: New Directions, 1996. A translation of Li Bo's poems. Includes some analysis.

Pine, Red, trans. *Poems of the Masters: China's Classic Anthology of T'ang and Sung Dynasty Verse*. Port Townsend, Wash.: Copper Canyon Press, 2003. A collection of poetry from the Tang and Song Dynasties that includes the work of Li Bo. Indexes.

Seaton, J. P., and James Cryer, trans. *Bright Moon, Perching Bird: Poems by Li Po and Tu Fu*. Scranton, Pa.: Harper & Row, 1987. This work, part of the Wesleyan Poetry in Translation series, features the works of Li Bo and Du Fu, two Tang poets. Provides some information on Tang Dynasty poetry.

Seth, Vikram, trans. *Three Chinese Poets: Translations of Poems by Wang Wei, Li Bai, and Du Fu*. Boston: Faber and Faber, 1992. A collection of poems by Li Bo, Wang Wei, and Du Fu. Commentary provides useful information.

Waley, Arthur. *The Poetry and Career of Li Po*. 1950. Reprint. London: G. Allen & Unwin, 1979. A still-useful introduction, although Waley's obsession with what he considers the immoral aspects of Li's character sometimes prejudices his judgment of the poetry. Includes many translations.

SEE ALSO: Du Fu; Li Qingzhao; Ouyang Xiu; Sima Guang; Su Dongpo; Wang Anshi; Wang Wei.

RELATED ARTICLES in *Great Events from History: The Middle Ages, 477-1453*: 618: Founding of the Tang Dynasty; 755-763: Rebellion of An Lushan; 960: Founding of the Song Dynasty; 960-1279: Scholar-Official Class Flourishes Under Song Dynasty.

LI QINGZHAO

Chinese poet

The greatest woman lyricist in the history of classical Chinese literature, Li Qingzhao made use of everyday language to explore the subtleties of human emotions. Her simple yet elegant style shaped the poetic expressions of the Southern Song Dynasty and inspired many lyricists.

BORN: 1084; Jinan, Shandong Province, China
DIED: c. 1155; Hangzhou, Zhejiang Province, China
ALSO KNOWN AS: Li Ch'ing-chao (Wade-Giles)
AREA OF ACHIEVEMENT: Literature

EARLY LIFE

Li Qingzhao (lee cheeng-jahoh) was born the oldest child of a family that was very fond of literature. Her father, Li Gefei (Li Ke-fei), was a renowned essayist; her mother, who came from a politically distinguished family, was also known for having literary talent. From 1086 to 1093, her father assumed a teaching position at the Imperial Academy in the capital, Kaifeng, and engaged himself in composing literary works while fulfilling his scholarly obligations. This position provided him with ample opportunity to work at home. During those seven years, Li learned from her parents much about classical Chinese literature as well as the art of literary composition. Except for a short interruption in 1094, when her father was assigned to a provincial position, Li's education at home continued well into her mid-teens.

The earliest extant works by Li, two poems of the same title, "Wuxi zhongxing song shi" ("On Paean to Revival, Inscribed on the Cliff of Wuxi"), were composed at the age of sixteen. These two poems were written in order that they might rhyme with a poem of the same title by Zhang Lei (Chang Lei), a famous poet in the Song Dynasty (960-1279). Taking exception to Zhang Lei's traditional stance, which celebrates the restoration of the central government during the reign of Emperor Suzong (Su-tsung) in the Tang Dynasty (618-907), Li was critical of those writers who forgot and overlooked the corruption and rebellion that preceded this restoration. The fact that Li was able to compose a poem that rhymed with the work of such a renowned poet at a time when women were discouraged from participating in men's social gatherings—occasions that formed the basis of such poems—indicates the degree of recognition accorded her by her contemporaries. The efflorescence of her creativity, however, did not begin until after her marriage, which occurred in 1101.

LIFE'S WORK

Li Qingzhao's marriage to Zhao Mingcheng (Chao Ming-ch'eng) inspired her to compose many lyrics of enduring fame in the history of Chinese literature. The third son of Zhao Tingzhi, a censor who later became the premier during the reign of Emperor Huizong (Hui-tsung, r. 1101-1125), Zhao Mingcheng was studying at the Imperial Academy at the time of his marriage to Li. Although the marriage was arranged by their parents, as was the custom in China, it proved to be a happy one for Li. She began to compose lyrics celebrating the joy of their union. As exhibited in the works at this stage—for example, "Jianzi mulanhua" ("The Magnolia Flower") and "Yu jia ao" ("Tune: A Fisherman's Honor")—Li in her married life was a charming yet somewhat coquettish woman who was well aware of her own beauty. She not only often compared herself to a flower but also intended to rival the beauty of a flower—all to attract her husband's attention. Because of his studies at the Imperial Academy, her husband could return home only on the first and fifteenth days of each month. Consequently, her works of this time also contain melancholy expressions, lamenting her husband's absence. In such lyrics as "Xiaochongshan" ("Tune: Manifold Little Hills") and "Cui huayin" ("Tipsy in the Flowers' Shade"), Li often refers to late spring and expresses sadness that her husband is unable to share the splendid season with her. Generally, the beautiful natural scenery described in her poetry becomes an emblem of her own beauty, which awaits appreciation.

In the second year of her marriage, a power struggle broke out at the imperial court, an event that greatly affected Li's life. Disliked by the new emperor, her father was expelled from his position as vice minister of rituals and was assigned to a provincial position. In an attempt to rescue her father, Li wrote a poem of petition to her father-in-law, Zhao Tingzhi. The poem moved many people but apparently did not save her father, who served the term of five years in confinement. While Li's father fell into disfavor with the emperor, her father-in-law rose to power and soon became the vice premier. During the redistribution of political power, her father-in-law was engaged in a struggle for political domination with the premier, Cai Jing (Ts'ai Ching), the notorious leader of the New Party. When Zhao finally became the premier, Li wrote and dedicated a poem to him, calling his attention to the inherent danger of becoming an overtly powerful figure. In the midst of this political upheaval, Zhao Mingcheng entered public service. His official career, however, ended abruptly four years later on the death of his father. As Li expected, after Zhao Tingzhi's death in 1107, the reinstated Cai seized the opportunity to vent his anger on Zhao's family.

To avoid persecution, Li Qingzhao and her husband moved back to his hometown in the countryside, Qingzhou, and remained there for ten years. Living in a state of seclusion, Li greatly enjoyed her life with her husband. During these years, she helped her husband with the composition of *Jin shi lu* (a record of bronze and stone vessels), a valuable reference book on Chinese antiquities. Her poetic career continued in the meantime. Because her life at this time was pleasant and peaceful, many of her works were aesthetic studies on the beauty of various flowers—cassia, chrysanthemums, lilacs, and plum blossoms. Lacking depth of human emotion or symbolic significance, these poems, such as "Tanpo wan xisha" ("Cassia Flowers, to a New Version of the Silk Washing Brook") and "Zhegu tian" ("Partridge Sky"), are essentially impressionistic sketches with limited aesthetic merit.

A great change, however, occurred when Li was in her forties—a change that enabled her to perfect her art of lyricism. In 1126, several years after her husband resumed his official career, nomads from the northeast of China invaded the capital and captured emperors Huizong and Qinzong (Ch'in-tsung, r. 1125-1126). As a result of this invasion, her husband assumed a new position in the south the following year. Having to prepare to move their belongings, Li stayed behind and did not join him until the next year. Four months or so after she left Qingzhou to join her husband, their house, along with many rich collections, was burned to the ground by a rebellious troop. A year after she joined her husband in the south, her husband was again transferred and compelled to go to his prefecture, Jiankang (Chien-k'ang), by himself. In August of 1129, three months after he became the prefect of Jiankang, Zhao died. The ceaseless warring and the constant separation from and eventual death of her husband made Li particularly aware of the transience of this world. Rather than celebrating the beauty of flowers and the joy of springtime, she expressed the sorrows of separation, loneliness, and death. Because of the depth of feeling, the elegance of language, and the great musicality of her lyrics, many of her works—"Wuling chun" ("Spring at Wuling"), "Sheng sheng man" ("A Sad Song to a Slow Tune"), and "Gu yan er" ("On Plum Blossoms, to the Tune of a Little Wild Goose") among them—circulated widely among her contemporaries and became quite popular during her time.

The latter half of 1129 witnessed not only the death of her husband but also another invasion of the nomads. To flee from the enemy, Li followed the central government, wandering from one place to another. Because of her suffering during the war as well as her need for a companion, she married again in 1132. The second marriage, lasting only about three months, ended in disaster. During the following two decades, Li led a relatively quiet life, occasionally contributing verses to the royal family when they celebrated various festivals. Like many of her contemporaries, she became a Buddhist after much suffering. As a result of her belief, her works at the last stage of her life no longer exhibited bitter grief but rather took the form of serene reminiscences of her past life. The theme of transience often manifests itself in her contemplations of the past and present. As indicated by the titles of some of her last works, "Joy of Tranquillity" and "Forever Encountering Mirth," Li accepted the end of her life with serenity.

SIGNIFICANCE

In the long, splendid history of Chinese poetry—an area traditionally dominated by men—only Li Qingzhao distinguished herself as a woman of great achievement. Shortly after their appearance, her lyrics became the representative voice of the Chinese woman confined to her house for most of her life. Many poets before Li had attempted to represent a woman's psyche in their poetry, but none was her equal in capturing the nuances of a woman's inner life. Her portrayal of a woman's joy and sorrow is equally applicable to the experience of men to the extent that it often comes to represent the joys and sorrows inherent in the human condition. Li's works not only were popular among the common people but also were greatly admired by the literati. Ever since the appearance of the first anthology of poetry, *Shijing* (compiled fifth century B.C.E.; *The Book of Songs*, 1937), many poets who were also officials had assumed the mask of a woman to express their feelings toward their sovereigns. They regarded their relationship to their sovereigns as that of a wife to her husband. In this respect, Li's lyrical voice agreed with the sensibility of the officials, who often experienced sorrow, though of a different kind, in their relationship to their lords. Consequently, men and women, both educated and uneducated, found solace in Li's work.

In the history of Chinese poetry, Li's achievements lie not so much in the nature of her themes—love, loneliness, separation, and death—as in the manner in which she treats her subjects. Her masterly use of colloquial language, the creation of striking imagery, and the subtle structure of her lyrics place her firmly in a position of enduring literary significance. Because of the popularity of her works, her lyrical style became the model for many later poets and significantly influenced the development of Chinese lyricism, especially those lyrics composed during the time of the Southern Song Dynasty. Apart from being a renowned poet, Li was an accomplished scholar. Completed by her years after her husband's death, *Jin shi lu* exhibits Li's talent for outstanding scholarship. This highly admired work considerably enhanced other scholars' understanding of the development of ancient Chinese culture.

—*Vincent Yang*

FURTHER READING

Chang, Kang-i Sun, and Haun Saussy, eds. *Women Writers of Traditional China: An Anthology of Poetry and Criticism*. Stanford, Calif.: Stanford University Press, 1999. Part 1 of this anthology contains the poets' works, divided by dynasty, and part 2 contains criticism. Biographies of the poets, including Li Qingzhao, are included. Bibliography and index.

Hu, P'ing-ch'ing. *Li Ch'ing-chao*. New York: Twayne, 1966. This critical study on Li Qingzhao treats both her life and her works in great detail and provides one with a clear sense of her achievements. Most of her famous poems are translated in a lucid, though sometimes prosaic, style.

Li Qingzhao. *As Though Dreaming: The Tz'u of Pure Jade*. Translated by Lenore Mayhew and William McNaughton. Berkeley, Calif.: Serendipity Books, 1977. A collection of Li Qingzhao's poetry.

_______. *Li Ch'ing-chao: Complete Poems*. Translated and edited by Kenneth Rexroth and Ling Chung. New York: New Directions, 1979. A collection of Li Qingzhao's poetry, with critical notes and a biography.

_______. *Plum Blossom: Poems of Li Qingzhao*. Translated by James Cryer. Chapel Hill, N.C.: Carolina Wren Press, 1984. A translation of poetry by Li Qingzhao, with illustrations.

Rexroth, Kenneth, and Ling Chung, eds. *Women Poets of China*. Rev. ed. New York: New Directions, 1990. This collection of works by women poets of China, which first was published in the 1970's, contains works by Li Qingzhao and other notable poets.

Yang, Vincent. "Vision of Reconciliation: A Textual Reading of Some Lines of Li Qing-zhao." *Journal of the Chinese Language Teachers Association* 19 (1984): 10-32. This essay is a close reading of four representative poems by Li Qingzhao. Focusing on the imagery and structure of the poems, the author attempts to show Li's art of lyricism. At the end, the particular nature of her imagination is illustrated through her use of poetic techniques. The analysis is an application of Western literary criticism to Chinese poetry.

SEE ALSO: Du Fu; Li Bo; Ouyang Xiu; Sima Guang; Su Dongpo; Wang Anshi; Wang Wei.

RELATED ARTICLES in *Great Events from History: The Middle Ages, 477-1453*: 960: Founding of the Song Dynasty; 960-1279: Scholar-Official Class Flourishes Under Song Dynasty; c. 1000: Footbinding Develops in Chinese Society; 1069-1072: Wang Anshi Introduces Bureaucratic Reforms.

PIETRO LORENZETTI AND AMBROGIO LORENZETTI

Italian painters

The Lorenzetti brothers recognized the problems of depicting three-dimensional space on a two-dimensional surface. Although they did not fully solve the problems of perspective, their experiments with space provided a necessary stage for the development of Italian Renaissance painting.

PIETRO LORENZETTI

BORN: c. 1280; probably Siena, Republic of Siena (now in Italy)
DIED: 1348; Siena, Republic of Siena

AMBROGIO LORENZETTI

BORN: c. 1290; Siena, Republic of Siena (now in Italy)
DIED: 1348; Siena, Republic of Siena
AREA OF ACHIEVEMENT: Art

EARLY LIVES

As Pietro Lorenzetti (PYAY-troh loh-raynt-SAYT-tee) and Ambrogio Lorenzetti (ahm-BROH-joh loh-raynt-SAYT-tee) lived and worked in a period during which the lives of artists were not considered important, biographical information is based on a few public records, existing paintings (some of which are damaged and many of which are neither signed nor dated), and guesswork. For example, in 1306 the Sienese government paid 110 lire for a painting intended for the Palazzo Pubblico to a "Petruccio di Lorenzo." Because Petruccio is a diminutive form of Pietro, most historians have concluded that the recipient was in fact Pietro Lorenzetti and that he was a relatively young man in 1306. To receive payment directly, however, the artist had, by Sienese law, to be at least twenty-five years old. Therefore, 1280 is generally given as the approximate date of Pietro's birth.

Unfortunately, no similar documentation has been found in relation to Ambrogio's birth date. Consensus that the two men were brothers is based on an inscription from a public hospital that has long since been torn down. On the facade of the Sienese hospital was a series of frescoes depicting the various stages in the life of Mary, the mother of Jesus. These frescoes, dated 1335, listed Pietro and Ambrogio as the two artists and also identified the artists as brothers. Because Pietro's name appeared first, it is assumed that Pietro was older.

Pietro's earliest work that can be dated with certainty is a panel for the altarpiece in the Church of the Pieve in Arezzo, a town in central Italy. On April 17, 1320, Pietro signed a contract for the composition, which is not one painting but nineteen. The central portion is a Madonna and Child with pictures of various saints in the side panels and an Annunciation immediately above the Madonna and Child.

This work illustrates one of Pietro's chief concerns, the emotional state of his figures. In the central portion, the Christ Child gazes happily at his mother, and the saints, each of whom is encased in a separate archway, turn toward one another, almost as though they were in conversation. In the Annunciation panel, Mary's eyes are locked into Gabriel's as the young Virgin, awestruck by the news of her impending pregnancy, clutches at her throat. Some historians have theorized that the model for the bearded Saint Luke may have been the artist himself, a portrait signature common among later artists. Another trademark of Pietro that is evident in the Arezzo panel is the interest in spatial relationships. Although the figures seem flat by High Renaissance standards, Pietro employs the techniques of modeling and overlapping.

The only dated evidence of Ambrogio's early work is also a Madonna and Child. Painted in 1319 for Vico l'Abate, a small church just outside Florence, Ambrogio's panel depicts a stiff Virgin staring straight ahead. Although she is seated, Mary seems to have no lap. On the other hand, the baby seems much more realistic. His tender gaze almost manages to focus on his mother's face, while the toes on his left foot curl backward in a touchingly realistic gesture that stands as an Ambrogioian signature. After painting the *Vico l'Abate Madonna*, Ambrogio may have remained in Florence for several years, as the next document related to him, dated 1321, indicates that creditors in Florence seized a suit of clothes belonging to the artist for payment of a debt that he owed.

LIVES' WORK

The work that marks the transition into Pietro's mature style is an altarpiece of 1329. This work for the Carmelite Church in Siena contains a Crucifixion, another Madonna and Child surrounded by saints, and a narrative sequence depicting scenes from the history of the Carmelite order. The figures in the main part of the altarpiece are not very interesting, because the crucified Christ could almost as easily be lying on a flat table as hanging from a cross, the crowned Virgin is stiff and joyless, and the Christ Child is weightless. On the other hand, the narrative scenes on the predella panels at the base of the altarpiece illustrate Pietro's experimentation with perspective through the use of diagonal lines and proportion.

For the Church of Saint Francis in Assisi, Pietro worked on a funeral chapel for the Cardinals Napoleone and Giovanni Orsini. The huge altarpiece is arranged on two levels. The central level contains figures of various saints with scenes from their lives. Above is a Passion cycle composed of eleven scenes from the last days of Christ, including the Crucifixion and the Ascension. Below the main level was originally a predella containing thirteen scenes—the major portion of which is now in the Uffizi in Florence, while two small panels are in Berlin. Much of the work is thought to have been done by students of Pietro, but the master's hand is evident in the later scenes from the Passion cycle, especially the powerful *Descent from the Cross*. In this scene, the angular body of Christ is being lifted off the cross by his friends. Mary tenderly cradles the head of her son as their left eyes almost touch. Particularly interesting is the state of Christ's body, which, through line and modeling, is depicted in the early stages of rigor mortis.

Because Mary was considered the patron saint of Siena, the Sienese took a special interest in the Virgin. The Cathedral of Siena commissioned a whole cycle of altarpieces depicting the life of Mary. Pietro's contribution, the *Birth of the Virgin*, signed and dated in 1342, is the artist's latest work for which documentation exists. This painting, which has been moved to the Opera del Duomo in Siena, depicts Saint Anne, Mary's mother, lying on her bed with its checkered bedspread while the baby Virgin is being bathed. The *Birth of the Virgin* is important for two reasons. One innovation is the secular setting for a religious subject. In addition to the aforementioned checkered bedspread, the water pitcher and basin, trunk, and blankets are all objects that could be found in a middle-class Sienese household. Another innovation is the use of space. The diagonals in both the bedspread and the rug seem to disappear in a single vanishing point, a technique that was to be used by artists for the next one hundred years to give the appearance of three-dimensional space. Also, the frame of the triptych and the architecture in Anne's house are the same style and shape, so that the two appear to be part of the same system. The result is that the viewer seems to be looking not at a picture but through a window into the saint's bedroom.

Ambrogio, a more introspective artist than Pietro, is generally considered the more talented of the two brothers. Around 1330, Ambrogio completed work on an altarpiece at Massa Marittima, a town to the south and west of Siena. This work, a *Maestà*, or "Madonna in Majesty," emphasizes Mary's position as queen of Heaven. A *Maestà* differs from a simple "Madonna Enthroned" because of the larger, more complicated design with the Madonna and Child being accompanied by a host of angels, prophets, and saints. Two other Sienese artists who are roughly contemporary with Ambrogio, Duccio di Buoninsegna and Simone Martini, also painted *Maestàs*. In contrast to Duccio's and Martini's figures, those of Ambrogio seem to be more energetic and less somber, and the supporting characters are more emotionally involved with the Madonna and Child. Also, in a marked improvement over the stiffness of the *Vico l'Abate Madonna*, the Virgin gazes tenderly into the child's eyes while the child, curling the toes on his right foot, clutches at Mary's collar.

Although most of Ambrogio's paintings and frescoes concerned religious subjects, the work for which the artist is most famous is political in nature. Apparently in competition with his brother, Ambrogio won the commission for a fresco series entitled *Good and Bad Government* for the Sala della Pace in the Palazzo Pubblico of Siena. This signed work, dated 1338-1339, is monumental. Covering three walls of the chamber, it depicts good and bad government allegorically and the effects of each type of government in both town and country realistically. Ambrogio chose the better-lighted wall for the allegory of Good Government. Of all the figures, the semireclining Peace is the most often reproduced, because the body's casual stance and enfolding drapery show a strong classical influence on which Renaissance artists were to build.

It is, however, the section called "The Effect of Good Government in the Country" that is the most innovative. The first large-scale landscape since classical times, it is a panorama of the countryside surrounding Siena. Citizens are climbing up the hillside toward the cathedral, fields are being plowed, grain is being harvested, and peasants are bringing their meats and produce into the city. This portrayal of humankind in command of nature rather than the other way around marks an important stage in the concept of humankind's relation to the universe. Floating above the scene is an allegorical figure named Securitas, whose semiclad figure marks another innovation in artistic thinking. The notion that the human body should be an object of joy and celebration rather than a source of shame, while only hinted at here, would be explored in detail by artists of the Renaissance.

In 1342, at the same time that his brother was painting

the *Birth of the Virgin* in the cathedral in Siena, Ambrogio was painting the *Presentation in the Temple*. In this altarpiece, all the adults are depicted as separated and distinct individuals of varying ages, and the Christ Child is a real baby instead of a small adult. The thin, straight hair frames oversized eyes, while the baby sucks his finger. Even more interesting is the setting of this work, supposedly a medieval cathedral, whose immense space is suggested by the use of diagonal perspective, a system in which farther objects are higher on the picture plane than nearer objects and are aligned along an oblique axis.

SIGNIFICANCE

Of necessity, Pietro and Ambrogio both concentrated on religious subjects. Tracing their many versions of the Madonna and Child is instructive, as both evolved from painting stiff, frontal Virgins to depicting tender, naturalistic mothers. Ambrogio from the first was more successful in capturing the essence of a baby and toward the end of his career was creating almost realistic infants.

Ironically, both brothers' highest achievements occurred when they moved away from religious subjects, perhaps because they felt more free to experiment. Pietro's *Birth of the Virgin* succeeds primarily because of the addition of everyday details whose arrangement contributes to the appearance of space on the picture plane. Ambrogio's sensuous Peace and Securitas in the *Good and Bad Government* frescoes would have been unthinkable in a religious context.

Of the eight different ways of achieving perspective, the brothers experimented with at least five. Even so, Pietro's most successful use of perspective, the *Birth of the Virgin*, seems stiff, crowded, and crudely executed by Renaissance standards. Although Ambrogio's *Presentation in the Temple* presents the architectural space very convincingly, the figures are too large for the space they inhabit. As a result, to those who are accustomed to viewing work by High Renaissance artists, it is easy to dismiss the achievements of the Lorenzettis. Yet it is the concepts and experiments of Pietro and Ambrogio and other pre-Renaissance artists that laid the groundwork for their successors.

—*Sandra Hanby Harris*

FURTHER READING

Becherucci, Luisa. "Lorenzetti." In *Encyclopedia of World Art*. New York: McGraw-Hill, 1964. Gives an exhaustive, chronological history of the dated works by both Ambrogio and Pietro Lorenzetti as well as every known detail relating to their personal lives in a clear, readable manner. Includes an extensive bibliography.

Cannon, Joanna, and André Vauchez. *Margherita of Cortona and the Lorenzetti: Sienese Art and the Cult of a Holy Woman in Medieval Tuscany.* University Park: Pennsylvania State University Press, 1999. Details the relationship between the Margherita Cycle and the Lorenzetti brothers while providing much information about the brothers and their works. Illustrations, bibliography, and index.

Frugoni, Chiara. *Pietro and Ambrogio Lorenzetti*. Florence: Scala, 1998. Part of the Great Masters of Art series, this volume examines the lives and works of the Lorenzetti brothers. Bibliography and index.

Leuchovius, Deborah. "Notes on Ambrogio Lorenzetti's Allegory of Good Government. *Rutgers Art Review* 3 (January, 1982): 29-35. Examines Ambrogio's mural on good government and its political symbolism.

Rowley, George. *Ambrogio Lorenzetti*. 2 vols. Princeton, N.J.: Princeton University Press, 1958. Contains a detailed analysis of the stylistic features of Ambrogio's work and traces the artist's development through his dated as well as his undated works. A highly controversial commentary, partially because Rowley seeks to assign many works thought to be by Ambrogio's hand to that of other artists. Includes an excellent bibliography and helpful chronology.

Starn, Randolph. *Ambrogio Lorenzetti: The Palazzo Pubblico, Siena*. New York: George Brazilier, 1994. Examines the fresco Ambrogio did for the Palazzo Pubblico in Siena and looks at the relationship between politics and art. Contains illustrations.

Vasari, Giorgio. *The Lives of the Painters, Sculptors, and Architects*. Reprint. New York: Alfred A. Knopf, 1996. Vasari, a sixteenth century Italian painter and architect, wrote one of the earliest biographies of Italian artists. Contains a complimentary account of the work of Ambrogio but does not mention Pietro. Although known to include many inaccuracies, this work provides many useful details about painting that have either disappeared or disintegrated.

SEE ALSO: Fra Angelico; Cimabue; Donatello; Duccio di Buoninsegna; Lorenzo Ghiberti; Giotto; Simone Martini; Masaccio; Andrea Orcagna.

RELATED ARTICLE in *Great Events from History: The Middle Ages, 477-1453*: c. 1410-1440: Florentine School of Art Emerges.

LOUIS THE GERMAN

King of Germany (r. 843-876)

As the ruler who founded the kingdom that later became known as Germany, Louis, while supporting the idea of the unity of the Carolingian Empire, protected his kingdom from the covetousness of his relatives, patronized the Church, and defended his lands from numerous attacks by such peoples as the Vikings, Hungarians, Bohemians, Moravians, and Slavs.

BORN: c. 804; possibly Aquitaine (now in France)
DIED: August 28, 876; Frankfurt (now in Germany)
ALSO KNOWN AS: Louis II the German; Ludwig II der Deutsche; Ludwig der Deutsche
AREA OF ACHIEVEMENT: Government and politics

EARLY LIFE

Louis the German was the third son of Louis the Pious and Ermengard. His father, the third son of Charlemagne, would become sole ruler of the Carolingian Empire in 814. His mother was the daughter of a government official, Count Ingram. Probably Louis spent most of his early years at the courts of his father and grandfather. When Charlemagne died, Louis the Pious had to make numerous arrangements for the governance of the empire. The new emperor granted the rule of Bavaria and Aquitaine to his two eldest legitimate sons, Lothair and Pépin, respectively. Because of his youth, Louis continued to live in his father's household.

Three years later, Louis the Pious issued the Ordinatio Imperii of 817, in which he proclaimed the disposition of the empire for the remainder of his reign as well as after his death. Louis received Bavaria, which Lothair had ruled since 814. On the death of the emperor, Louis's share of the empire was to be increased to include Carinthia and the Bohemian, Slavic, and Avar marches. Lothair would act as coemperor and succeed their father as sole emperor, who would then maintain a loose supervision over the kingdoms ruled by his Carolingian relatives. In the future, the various Carolingian kingdoms were to be passed on without further subdivision. Thus, Louis the Pious was able to preserve the unity of the empire while conforming to the Frankish practice of dividing a man's patrimony equally among his sons.

From 817 to early 832, Louis acted as a loyal son and his father's lieutenant. At eighteen, he commanded a flank of the expedition that Louis the Pious mounted against Brittany in 824. Beginning in 825, Louis actively governed Bavaria while annually returning to France to attend his father's court. Some of his attention was spent on wars against the Slavs in 825 and the Bulgars in 828 that accomplished little. In 827, Louis married Emma, a daughter of Count Welf, who was also the father of Judith of Bavaria. Nine years earlier, the emperor had married Judith, by whom he had a son, Charles the Bald, in 823. During the summer of 829, Louis the Pious took two actions that produced dissension in both the royal family and the government. He granted some lands to Charles, his youngest son, and replaced a number of his governmental officials. The result was a revolt led by the displaced ministers, who seized control of the government and gained the support of Lothair and Pépin. Despite being under house arrest, Louis the Pious arranged an understanding with Pépin and Louis and in October, 830, reclaimed control of the empire's government.

From 829 until 843, the rule of the empire would be contested by Louis the Pious's sons and elements of the empire's governmental bureaucracy. On recovering the government, the emperor sent Lothair to Italy and rewarded Pépin, Louis, and Charles with more lands. To Louis's lands were added Thuringia, Saxony, Frisia, Flanders, Brabant, Hainault, most of Austrasia, and part of Neustria. On the emperor's death, the three brothers would be allowed to act independently of one another, to aid one another in defense of the empire's borders and the Roman church, and to ignore Lothair, who would rule in Italy. Furthermore, the emperor expected his three younger sons to remain loyal or he would punish them by removing lands from their rule. Distrust had become so great on all sides, however, that the remaining decade of the emperor's life was to see continual plotting and intermittent rebellions by his three older sons.

LIFE'S WORK

From 832 onward, Louis the German followed a policy of protecting his German lands while occasionally acting as a mediator in family disputes. During the 830's, Louis often found himself in opposition to his father's plans and particularly to those concerning Charles. After Pépin began a revolt late in 831, Louis made plans to invade Alamannia, an area recently given to Charles that contained a number of Welf estates, in early 832. When the emperor entered Bavaria in May, Louis sought and obtained a pardon. The spring of 833 saw an attempt by Lothair, Pépin, and Louis to seize the empire's government from their father. Supported by Pope Gregory IV and various imperial ministers, the three brothers confronted their father at Rothfield. With his followers slipping away, the emperor surrendered. Lothair was declared sole emperor, and Louis the German returned to Bavaria in the late summer.

When Lothair tried to harass his father into becoming a monk, Louis, somewhat distressed by this, and Pépin marched on Paris, where Lothair and their father were. Lothair fled, leaving Louis the Pious to reclaim the emperorship in early March, 834. Then, in October, 837, the emperor gave to Charles the territories between the Seine and Meuse Rivers in northeast France, lands that had been held at different times by Lothair and Louis the German. In late 838, after a meeting with Lothair and two with the emperor, Louis the German declared war against his father; this war continued until his father's death in June, 840. In the spring of 839, Louis the Pious again divided the empire; this time it was evenly split between Lothair and Charles, while Louis the German was allowed only the rule of Bavaria.

With the emperor's death, Lothair continued the war against his brother Louis, who faced a Saxon revolt at the same time. Unable to arrange an accord with Lothair, Charles reluctantly joined Louis. On June 25, 841, at Fontenoy, they defeated Lothair, who was again defeated in September. To protect themselves and defeat Lothair, at Strasbourg on February 14, 842, Louis and Charles exchanged the famous Strasbourg oaths that bound them together in a defensive alliance against Lothair. By operating together, Louis and Charles forced Lothair to open negotiations. At a meeting near Mâcon on June 15, the three brothers agreed to divide the empire into three equal parts. A year of further discussions among their representatives produced the Treaty of Verdun in August, 843. By this treaty, Louis retained the Germanic territories east of the Rhine plus three counties to the west of it and the whole of Alamannia; Charles kept the French kingdom; and Lothair held Italy, plus a corridor of counties between his brothers' kingdoms, as well as continuing his use of the title of emperor. The political unity of the Carolingian Empire had come to an end.

With the passage of time, the Treaty of Verdun became the cornerstone of the kingdom of Germany. Louis's immediate concerns were the protection of his borders from the Vikings and various peoples to the east, the maintenance of the Church, and future relations with his brothers. For the most part, the wars against the Bohemians, Moravians, and Slavs were successful. The Vikings, however, remained a threat to both Germany and the rest of the Carolingian lands, despite Louis's efforts to keep them at bay. Within Germany, Louis supported the Church by means of numerous grants, received the support of his clergy, and endorsed its efforts to convert the neighboring pagan peoples. Nevertheless, it was the clergy of Aquitaine in the 850's and those of northeastern France between 858 and 860 who thwarted the attempts of segments of the Aquitanian and French populations to replace Charles the Bald with Louis.

During the dozen years between the settlement at Verdun and the death of Lothair in 855, relations among the three brothers were precarious. At Meerssen in March, 847, the brothers agreed to cooperate against external threats and in sorting out internal problems that were common to the kingdoms. Yet the distrust among them, especially between Charles and Lothair, clouded the arrangement. After attempts in 849 and 850 to patch up differences, the brothers in May, 851, again at Meerssen, came to a consensus. As relations between Lothair and Charles improved, Louis began to drift away from them. Early in 855, Louis sent his eldest son, Louis the Younger, to assist the Aquitanians in a revolt against Charles. The rebellion's failure and a mediation undertaken by Lothair restored peace. Lothair then died, leaving a complex division of his lands that would dominate the rest of his brother Louis's life.

Lothair had divided his kingdom equally among his

Engraving of Louis the German. (Hulton|Archive at Getty Images)

THE CAROLINGIAN KINGS

Reign	*Ruler*
687-714	Pépin II of Heristal (mayor of Austrasia/Neustria)
714-719	Plectrude (regent for Theudoald)
719-741	CHARLES MARTEL (the Hammer; mayor of Austrasia/Neustria)
747-768	Pépin III the Short (mayor of Neustria 741, king of all Franks 747)
768-814	CHARLEMAGNE (king of Franks 768, emperor 800)
814-840	Louis the Pious (king of Aquitaine, emperor)
840-855	Lothair I (emperor)
843	Treaty of Verdun divides Carolingian Empire into East Franks (Germany), West Franks (essentially France), and a southern and middle kingdom roughly corresponding to Provence, Burgundy, and Lorraine)
843-876	LOUIS II THE GERMAN (king of Germany)
843-877	CHARLES II THE BALD (king of Neustria 843, emperor 875)
855-875	Louis II (emperor)
877-879	Louis II (king of France)
879-882	Louis III (king of France)
879-884	Carloman (king of France)
884-887	Charles III the Fat (king of France, emperor 881)
887-898	Odo (Eudes; king of France)
887-899	Arnulf (king of Germany 887, emperor 896)
891-894	Guy of Spoleto (Wido, Guido; emperor)
892-898	Lambert of Spoleto (emperor)
893-923	Charles III the Simple (king of France)
915-924	Berengar I of Friuli (emperor)
923-929?	Robert I (king of France)
929-936	Rudolf (king of France)
936-954	Louis IV (king of France; Hugh the Great in power)
954-986	Lothair (king of France; Hugh Capet in power 956)
986-987	Louis V (king of France)

Note: The Carolingians ruled different parts of the Frankish kingdom, which accounts for overlapping regnal dates in this table. The term "emperor" refers to rule over what eventually came to be known as the Holy Roman Empire.

three sons, Emperor Louis II in Italy, Charles, king of Provence, and Lothair II, king of Lotharingia, all of whom would have no legitimate sons. Because of the weaknesses of their small kingdoms, Lothair's sons found themselves somewhat at the mercy of their two uncles. A party to a barren marriage and directly caught between the large kingdoms of Louis the German and Charles the Bald, Lothair II tried to divorce his wife and marry his mistress. Actions by his uncles and the Papacy blocked these efforts, thereby virtually ensuring that Lothair's kingdom would fall at his death to his two uncles. Louis the German was ill when Lothair II died in August, 869, and so could not forestall Charles the Bald's seizure of Lotharingia. A year later to the day, August 8, 870, faced with the possibility of an attack by Louis the German, Charles agreed to honor an arrangement the two had made in 869 to partition Lotharingia. By this Treaty of Meerssen, the kingdom was split from north to south along a line that would be disputed again and again in future centuries. Because Emperor Louis II had only a female heir, the possibility of obtaining the emperorship came to interest his two uncles. Engelberga, Louis II's wife, favored Louis the German's ambitions in this regard, while Popes Hadrian III and John VIII sided with Charles the Bald. Although Engelberga claimed after her husband's death that his wish was for Carloman, Louis the German's eldest son, to have the emperorship, Charles the Bald, combining diplomacy and fighting skill, outmaneuvered his brother's armies and raced to Rome in late 875. As Pope John crowned Charles emperor on Christmas Day, Louis the German with his son Louis the Younger was leading a fruitless invasion into

France. The French magnates remained loyal to Charles, so Louis the German had to abandon his attack and return to Germany. After Charles and Pope John solidified the new emperor's hold on Italy, on August 28, 876, they dispatched an embassy to meet with Louis the German. On that day, however, Louis had died at Frankfurt. Immediately Charles tried to negate the 870 Treaty of Meerssen by seizing Lorraine, only to be decisively defeated by Louis the Younger.

SIGNIFICANCE

On balance, Louis the German achieved success as a medieval king. As a warrior, he had protected his lands from external threats from the east as well as from his brothers, Lothair and Charles the Bald. Louis overcame the several internal rebellions led by his sons in the early 860's, along with the occasional one by a magnate, with his position strengthened further. His reputation as a good ruler is evidenced by the willingness of various French magnates to seek him out as a king for both Aquitaine and France. His generosity to the German church resulted in its clergy's continual support of their king, even at times against the wishes of the Papacy, which often involved itself in ecclesiastical affairs north of the Alps.

Of Louis the German's private life, little is known. Indications are that he spent his youth in the household of Louis the Pious and possibly that of Charlemagne. How this experience developed his character is not clear, but through much of his life, Louis the German defended the concept of a unified empire, an idea supported in both households. Although Louis had no illegitimate children, as both Charlemagne and Louis the Pious had had, he did follow a common Carolingian policy regarding marriages of daughters. All three of his surviving daughters, Hildegard, Ermengard, and Bertha, were placed in nunneries and died unmarried. He allowed his sons at first to maintain relationships with mistresses; later they married the daughters of counts. His own death followed so quickly on that of Emma in January, 876, that one cannot be sure if he might have remarried.

Louis the German's greatest accomplishment was the founding of a kingdom, Germany, that would survive as a separate entity. He provided it with three future kings, the youngest of whom, Charles the Fat, would become an emperor as well. By the time Louis's line died out in 911, the concept of a German kingdom separate from the rest of the old Carolingian Empire was strong enough that the German magnates chose to remain distinct from troubled France and selected a German duke as their king.

—*Kenneth G. Madison*

FURTHER READING

Cabaniss, Allen, trans. *Son of Charlemagne: A Contemporary Life of Louis the Pious*. Syracuse, N.Y.: Syracuse University Press, 1961. Cabaniss has translated the ninth century *Vita Hludovici*, written by an anonymous author, probably of Louis the Pious's household. This history provides considerable information about the emperor's relations with all of his sons, including Louis the German. With it and Nithard's account (below), the reader may develop a good picture of Louis the German's early life.

Deanesly, Margaret. *A History of Early Medieval Europe from 476 to 911*. 1956. 2d ed. London: Methuen, 1960. Deanesly's study provides an excellent introduction to the Carolingian period and the basic outline of Louis the German's activities.

Eyck, Frank. *Religion and Politics in German History: From the Beginnings to the French Revolution*. New York: St. Martin's Press, 1998. An analysis of how Germanic peoples preserved links with classical civilization through their ability to assimilate other cultures and peoples, from their alliances with eighth century popes through the Reformation and Counter-Reformation. The initial bond between the Germanic rulers and popes turned to conflict as the Papacy gained power. Tables, maps, bibliography, index.

Gibson, Margaret, and Janet Nelson, eds. *Charles the Bald: Court and Kingdom*. Oxford: British Archaeological Reports, 1981. This is a collection of twenty-one papers presented at a colloquium held in London in 1979, covering a wide range of subjects beyond Charles the Bald.

Halphen, Louis. *Charlemagne and the Carolingian Empire*. Translated by Giselle de Nie. Amsterdam: North-Holland, 1977. Originally published in French in 1947, Halphen's book is the basic work available in English on the ninth century. It details Louis the German's relationships with his father and brothers and as such is the starting point for anyone interested in the first German king.

Jeep, John M., et al., eds. *Medieval Germany: An Encyclopedia*. New York: Garland, 2001. An A-Z encyclopedia that addresses all aspects of the German- and Dutch-speaking medieval world from 500 to 1500. Entries include individuals, events, and broad topics such as feudalism and pregnancy. Bibliographical references, index.

Moore, Robert Ian. *The First European Revolution, c. 970-1215*. Malden, Mass.: Blackwell, 2000. According to the publisher, "a radical reassessment of

Europe from the late tenth to the early thirteenth centuries [arguing that] the period witnessed the first true 'revolution' in European society," supported by transformation of the economy, family life, political power structures, and the rise of the non-Mediterranean cities. Bibliography, index.

Nelson, Janet L. *Politics and Ritual in Early Medieval Europe*. London: Hambledon Press, 1986. This collection of seventeen articles published since 1967 illustrates the complexity of the scholarship required to understand the world of Louis the German, who repeatedly is mentioned in its pages. Nelson is especially good on the institution of kingship and the narrative sources of the ninth century.

Nithard. "Histories." In *Carolingian Chronicles*. Translated by Bernhard Walter Scholz with Barbara Rogers. Ann Arbor: University of Michigan Press, 1970. Here is the basic source for the struggle between Louis the German and his brothers from 840 to 843. Reading it provides the reader with the flavor of the troubles that dogged the brothers through most of their lives.

SEE ALSO: Basil the Macedonian; Charlemagne; Charles the Bald; Nicholas the Great; Rabanus Maurus.

RELATED ARTICLES in *Great Events from History: The Middle Ages, 477-1453*: June 7, 793: Norse Raid Lindisfarne Monastery; 843: Treaty of Verdun; 850-950: Viking Era.

LOUIS IX

King of France (r. 1226-1270)

Louis IX reformed and centralized the French government and judiciary and increased the prestige of the royal house of France through his saintly life. In his international policy, he worked consistently for the twin goals of peace within Christendom and redemption of the Holy Land, participating in two Crusades.

BORN: April 25, 1214; Poissy, France
DIED: August 25, 1270; near Tunis (now in Tunisia)
ALSO KNOWN AS: Saint Louis
AREAS OF ACHIEVEMENT: Government and politics, religion and theology

EARLY LIFE

Louis (LEW-ee) was born at Poissy, near Paris, the son of the crown prince of France, Louis the Lion. His grandfather, Philip II Augustus, a contemporary of Richard I (Richard the Lion-Hearted), was still vigorous and ruled until Louis was nine years old. In 1214, the year of Louis's birth, Philip won at Bouvines over King John of England and annexed the French territories of the English royal family. Louis's mother, Blanche of Castile, a niece of John, had a claim to the English throne that led to an unsuccessful invasion of England by her husband in 1216. Blanche and Louis had twelve children, of whom nine survived infancy.

At the death of Philip II in 1223, Louis the Lion succeeded to the throne as Louis VIII and pursued vigorous policies of expansion of crown territories and repression of heretics. He died suddenly on November 8, 1226, on returning from a successful crusade against Albigensian heretics in southern France. Queen Blanche, regent through the terms of his will, arranged for the immediate coronation of her twelve-year-old son as King Louis IX.

The early years of the regency were marked by attacks from all sides. The great nobles of the realm often owed feudal allegiance to the crowns of both England and France and were likely to play one against the other. They were also tempted to replace the boy king with one of their own number. Hugh, count of La Marche, stepfather to Henry III of England, and Peter of Dreux or Peter Mauclerc, count of Brittany, actually invited Henry III to invade France but were unable to provide sufficient troops and supplies and eventually surrendered to the royal forces. Blanche succeeded in holding even the most vulnerable territories for her son.

Louis IX led his first military campaign at the age of fourteen and was soon recognized as an able and inspiring commander. By the time he married Marguerite of Provence in 1234, the worst of the domestic uprisings were over, and the realm of France settled into a period of peace. Along with her concerns of government, Blanche had devoted herself to the religious education of her children. Louis developed into a particularly devout man and maintained a close attachment to his mother. (Relations between Blanche and her daughter-in-law were notoriously poor.) The young Louis is described as tall and slender, blond, and with the face of an angel. He was firm in his character and endowed with humor and intelligence.

Life's Work

No formal date is given for the end of Blanche's regency. She continued as royal counselor and regent in Louis' absence until her death in 1252. Gradually, Louis assumed more responsibility for government. His understanding of Christian monarchy demanded a high standard of personal virtue and continual effort to make salvation a possibility for all of his subjects. To that end, he pursued peace and justice in his kingdom. Under Louis IX, the royal government began to regularize and expand its role in administration and the judiciary. Originally, the king had ruled only within those territories that were his by feudal succession. Louis ruled a greatly expanded area through the gains made by Philip II and Louis VIII; as he extended the limits of his judicial power to these areas, he also assumed the same power in territories held by the great lords who owed him feudal allegiance. This process was a gradual one. Military considerations forwarded centralization, as did Louis's growing popularity.

Engraving of a kneeling Louis IX of France. (Library of Congress)

Louis IX was an exceptionally devoted Christian, practicing charity in unostentatious sincerity. He contributed liberally to cloistered religious orders and participated in the heavy manual labor of building the Cistercian monastery Royaumont. His unassailable piety allowed him to maintain the temporal rights of the French nation against the worldly power of the Catholic Church. He supported French bishops in their resistance to the papal practice of appointing Italians to open positions in the French church, opposed the bishops when they demanded that he use royal authority to enforce decrees of excommunication, and insisted on the maintenance or expansion of his own jurisdiction in contested areas.

Louis inherited a system of *baillis* and *sénéchaux*, royal administrators sent to govern the regions of France, to administer justice, to assist in military levies, and otherwise to represent the Crown. Louis regularized and reformed this governmental system, making administrative posts merit appointments and guarding against corruption by sending out a body of traveling *enquêteurs*, auditors and inquisitors who went to each region and investigated complaints.

Louis was deeply involved in the judicial system and is pictured by chroniclers such as Jean de Joinville as giving personal justice while seated under a huge oak tree near his castle at Vincennes. Because the laws were not codified, a judgment in any matter depended on regional tradition. Louis formed his decisions with a knowledge of feudal tradition, Roman and canon law, and his own vigorous common sense. He applied these decisions throughout his expanded realm. Many feudal nobles were incensed when he outlawed the practice of trial by combat. He did not hesitate to call the highest nobles to account and in many cases reversed decisions made in the courts of his royal brothers or the nobles.

Louis IX faced an unstable world. England and France had been at war for decades. The Holy Roman Empire was in disarray; Frederick II of Sicily had been handpicked to rule by Pope Innocent III, but conflicts had arisen, and even though Frederick recovered Jerusalem in 1229, Pope Gregory IX excommunicated him and preached a crusade against him. Hordes of Mongols were beating at the gates of Europe. A succession of crusades were preached by the popes of these times—crusades to rescue the Holy Land (Jerusalem fell again in 1244) and crusades against heretics within Europe.

Louis went on two Crusades himself, the Seventh (1248-1254) and the Eighth (1270). His endeavors to remain on good terms with Frederick II as well as with the Papacy reflect his desire for Christian peace and his need of aid from both sources for the prosecution of his Crusades. He was able to arrange a stable truce with Henry III of England before leaving France in 1248. On his return, he worked for the establishment of a formal peace with England and succeeded with the Treaty of Paris of 1259.

At the beginning of Louis's reign, the abbey of Royaumont was built as a memorial to his father. He took great interest in the process. He also presided over the translation of the remains of his royal ancestors to the royal necropolis of Saint-Denis. In 1239, Louis acquired several relics of Christ's Passion, including the Crown of Thorns, and he began the construction of the Sainte Chapelle next to the royal residence on the Île de la Cité in Paris to house them. In all these things, Louis responded to his own sense of religious fervor and his role as anointed leader of his people. Following his recovery from a serious illness in 1244, he determined to go on a Crusade. His departure with the flower of French nobility in 1248 was seen as a special grace.

Louis's Crusade (the Seventh Crusade) began with elaborate preparations, provisions stockpiled during a period of years, the building of a French Mediterranean port at Aigues-Mortes, and a general settling in order of all temporal concerns. Queen Marguerite accompanied her husband and bore three children while on Crusade. The city of Damietta in Egypt was the first target; it fell almost without a fight, and she remained there, holding the city. In 1250, Louis and his men were captured as they retreated in disarray from the city of Mansourah. Near death from dysentery, Louis refused to leave his troops and insisted on staying with them until every survivor was ransomed. Damietta was part of the payment. Louis remained in the east, fortifying the Christian kingdoms of Outremer. Only the death of Queen Blanche in November, 1252, succeeded in calling him home. The news reached Louis in Sidon during the summer of 1253; he arrived in Paris in early September, 1254. The Crusade, in spite of early good luck, was a fiasco fatal to many, including Louis's favorite brother, Robert of Artois, and nearly cost the king his life.

Louis's long absence damaged France less than it might have, thanks to Blanche's able regency, but disorders had arisen, and Louis set to work to clean house. He was a humbled man, conscious of the failure of his Crusade and seeking a renewal of his own spiritual life through redoubled asceticism and penitence. From his first moments back in France, he began to plan a return trip to the east, and his efforts to amend any disorder may be seen as tending toward this goal. While in Syria, he had been distressed to see that the libraries for Islamic scholars were superior to those available to Christians in France. On his return, he assembled a royal library, copied as many manuscripts as possible, and gathered what would be the beginning of the French National Library. He encouraged the University of Paris and favored the establishment of the Sorbonne by his counselor Robert de Sorbon. He gathered the greatest biblical scholars of his day and delighted in their debates. Thomas Aquinas dined at his table. The years between the Crusades were also devoted to the pleasant duties of education and marriage of his children, the last of whom was born in 1260.

The Treaty of Paris with Henry III of England dates from this time of

THE CAPETIANS

Reign	*Ruler*
987-996	Hugh Capet
996-1031	Robert II the Pious
1031-1060	Henry I
1060-1108	Philip I the Fair
1108-1137	Louis VI the Fat
1137-1179	LOUIS VII THE YOUNGER (with ELEANOR OF AQUITAINE, r. 1137-1180)
1179-1223	PHILIP II AUGUSTUS
1223-1226	Louis VIII the Lion
1223-1252	BLANCHE OF CASTILE (both queen and regent)
1226-1270	LOUIS IX (Saint Louis)
1271-1285	Philip III the Bold
1285-1314	PHILIP IV THE FAIR
1314-1316	Louis X the Stubborn
1316	Philip, brother of Louis X (regent before birth of John I and during his short life)
1316	John I the Posthumous
1316-1322	Philip V the Tall
1322-1328	Charles IV the Fair

peace and order. This treaty, unpopular on both sides of the Channel, ended Plantagenet claims to French lands, at the price of large money grants from Louis IX to Henry III. Louis made Henry the gift of several parcels of land from his own properties and accepted Henry's feudal homage, making him a peer of France. Louis was also called on by the English barons to arbitrate their disputes with Henry III. In January, 1264, he gave an award, the Mise of Amiens, which upheld Henry on almost every point. The barons ignored it, and by August, 1264, Henry had relinquished almost all the concessions made to him in the Treaty of Paris for money to use in civil war against his barons.

The death of Frederick II in 1250 left the Holy Roman Empire in complete disarray. Charles of Anjou, Louis IX's brother, became king of Sicily by papal invitation and ruled from 1266 to 1285. His influence may have guided Louis's plans for his second Crusade (the Eighth Crusade). In spite of the king's frail health, Louis and his sons sailed from Aigues-Mortes in early July, 1270. Louis's first Crusade had attacked Egypt. This Crusade was directed against Tunis, directly across the Mediterranean from Charles's Sicily. The heat and unsanitary conditions led to an almost immediate outbreak of severe dysentery among the French. Louis's son, John Tristan, born at Damietta in 1250, died on August 3, 1270. Louis himself died on August 25. His remains were returned to France by his heir, Philip III, and entombed at Saint-Denis in May, 1271. Almost immediately after his funeral, his tomb was credited with miracles. His canonization was celebrated in 1297.

Significance

Louis IX's great genius and great folly was to incarnate the thirteenth century ideal of kingship. Even his faults, such as his anti-Semitism, were consistent with his desire to further the salvation of his people. He was extremely generous to converts, but the unconverted Jew or heretic was a danger to wavering Christians. His Crusades were disasters on a worldly level, costing many lives and resources, yet they served to give a focus to Louis's reforms and reorganization in France. As a simple nobleman would set the affairs of his estate in order before going on crusade, so the king did for his kingdom.

Louis saw the performance of government at all levels as a reflection of his personal performance as monarch. This view gave a special resonance to his administrative reforms. In 1254, the Great Ordinance was promulgated, formulating and regularizing the higher standards of justice and tighter royal control in the courts that Louis sought throughout his reign. Crown officials were publicly sworn to accept a severely practical code of ethics and stringent auditing. His Treaty of Paris of 1259 was not a simple political gesture but an idealistic personal one. His intent in making generous personal concessions to Henry III was to ensure friendship between their children and to gain Henry's personal loyalty to him as feudal lord. In his most idealistic actions, Louis was also most immediately personal. It was his embodiment of the medieval Christian ideal that made Louis the focus of French national spirit and mystic prestige for the crown of France for centuries to come.

—*Anne W. Sienkewicz*

Further Reading

Cartlidge, Cherese. *The Crusades: Failed Holy Wars.* San Diego, Calif.: Lucent Books, 2002. Provides a history of the Crusades from the perspective of the Europeans, Byzantines, Muslims, and Jews. The author argues that the Crusaders were overly cruel and violent and ultimately were focused on riches instead of religion.

Dahmus, Joseph. *Seven Medieval Kings.* Garden City, N.Y.: Doubleday, 1967. This book presents Louis as one of seven outstanding monarchs spanning the period of the Middle Ages. Louis's character and achievements are placed in historical perspective.

Fawtier, Robert. *The Capetian Kings of France: Monarchy and Nation, 987-1328.* Translated by Lionel Butler and R. J. Adam. London: Macmillan, 1960. This is a standard work on France under the Capetian Dynasty, to which Louis belonged, and includes a substantial section dedicated to him and France under his rule.

Hallam, Elizabeth M, and Judith Everard. *Capetian France, 987-1328.* 2d ed. New York: Longman, 2001. This excellent and scholarly book is firmly grounded on the most basic and practical aspects of the Capetian era. Chapter 5, "Louis IX: The Consolidation of Royal Power, 1226-1270," directly discusses Louis. The book as a whole places Louis within the context of his ancestors and descendants. Includes maps, genealogical tables, and a bibliography.

Joinville, Jean de. *The Life of Saint Louis.* London: Sheed and Ward, 1955. This basic primary work, a memoir by a friend and crusading companion of Louis, was written in the author's old age for Louis's grandson. It is often referred to by writers on the period and is the source for many personal anecdotes that succeed in revealing the more human side of Louis.

Jordan, William Chester. *Louis IX and the Challenge of*

the Crusade: A Study in Rulership*. 1979. Reprint. Princeton, N.J.: Princeton University Press, 2000. This study concentrates on the development of Louis's character and his philosophy of rulership through his preparation for and involvement in his crusades. The text unites psychological analysis with detailed economic and political data. Includes maps, illustrations, appendices, and an extensive bibliography.

Labarge, Margaret Wade. *Saint Louis: Louis IX, Most Christian King of France*. Boston: Little, Brown, 1968. This complete, readable, and well-documented biography of Louis presents maps, illustrations, a table of dates, a chart of family relationships, an annotated list of sources, and a general bibliography.

Lloyd, Simon. "The Crusades of Saint Louis." *History Today* 47, no. 5 (May, 1997): 37-43. The author presents a clearly written overview of Louis's legacy and achievements, especially his devotion to the Crusades. Includes several photographs.

Pernoud, Régine. *Blanche of Castile*. Translated by Henry Noel. London: Collins, 1975. This biography of Louis's mother, Blanche, illuminates his family background, childhood, and early reign. The author supplies family charts, illustrations, and a bibliography.

See also: Saint Albertus Magnus; Baybars I; Blanche of Castile; Hubert de Burgh; Giovanni da Pian del Carpini; Frederick II; Gregory IX; Henry III; Innocent III; King John; Simon de Montfort; Philip II; Richard I; Thomas Aquinas; Vincent of Beauvais; William of Rubrouck; William of Saint-Amour.

Related articles in *Great Events from History: The Middle Ages, 477-1453*: 987: Hugh Capet Is Elected to the French Throne; 1127-1130: Creation of the Kingdom of Sicily; 1209-1229: Albigensian Crusade; July 27, 1214: Battle of Bouvines; 1227-1230: Frederick II Leads the Sixth Crusade; 1258: Provisions of Oxford Are Established; c. 1265-1273: Thomas Aquinas Compiles the *Summa Theologica*; 1290-1306: Jews Are Expelled from England, France, and Southern Italy.

Saint Ludmilla

Duchess of Bohemia

Ludmilla converted from paganism to Christianity and set out to Christianize the duchy she ruled with her husband, Duke Bořivoj. Ludmilla also educated her grandson, Wenceslas, whose reign and martyrdom led to the full establishment of Christianity in Bohemia and later throughout the surrounding region.

Born: c. 860; Mielnik, Bohemia (now in the Czech Republic)
Died: September 15, 921; Tetin, near Beraun, Bohemia (now in the Czech Republic)
Also known as: Ludmila
Areas of achievement: Religion and theology, government and politics

Early Life

Details about the life of Ludmilla (loot-MIHL-ah) are scarce. She is not as well-known as the Western European saint Joan of Arc, and she remains most widely recognized in the Czech Republic only. Some extended studies of her life have been published, but they have not been translated from the Czech language.

As a young Slavic princess, Ludmilla married Duke Bořivoj, a member of the royal Přemyslid Dynasty of Bohemia. According to legend, the founder of the dynasty was a plowman who in the eighth century chose a Bohemian princess named Libussa to be his wife. Although little is known about the plowman and the princess, their immediate descendants united Bohemia's warring tribes into a single duchy. By the ninth century the dukedom was ruled by Ludmilla's husband, Bořivoj, the first Přemysl sovereign to have his life recorded. He established Prague Castle as the family seat.

Life's Work

In 871, Saint Methodius (c. 825-884), a missionary to the Slavs, converted Ludmilla and Bořivoj to Christianity and baptized them. Although most accounts depicting their rejection of paganism stress the heroic stance they took, one story differs dramatically. In this version, Saint Methodius assured the ambitious Duke Bořivoj that once he accepted Christianity "his enemies would be made his footstool." Whatever the original motivation, Ludmilla and Bořivoj soon turned into dynamic defenders of the faith. Instead of subduing their enemies, though, their advocacy of Christianity led to an insurrection among the pagan fanatics, including powerful families in Bohemia who were determined to hold on to their old ways. As a consequence, these elements drove the fervent converts out of Bohemia, but they were soon recalled and reigned for seven more years.

The duke and duchess had two sons, Spitignev and Wratislaw. After Bořivoj stepped down and retired with Ludmilla to their castle in Tetin, he turned the dukedom over to Spitignev, who died two years later. The younger son, Wratislaw, then assumed power in 915. He had entered into an unfortunate marriage with Drahomíra, known as "the disheveled one." She was the daughter of the chief of the Veletians, a Slav tribe from the nearby region called Lusatia, which later became part of Germany. While pretending to be a Christian, she actually favored paganism and conspired against the spread of Christianity in Bohemia. The new duke and duchess had twin sons, Wenceslas (c. 907-929) and Boleslav I (d. 967), sometimes called Boleslav I the Cruel. The year of their births in the castle of Stochov near Prague is said to be between 907 and 910. Even though the castle no longer stands, the site has become a destination for religious pilgrims. According to tradition, Ludmilla planted the oak tree that still grows on the site in honor of Wenceslas's birth. It is believed that she ordered the baby Wenceslas's nurses to nourish the sapling with his bath water, which helped the tree grow strong and to flourish over the centuries.

The aging and widowed Ludmilla arranged so that she could raise Wenceslas. At the Tetin castle near Prague, Ludmilla devoted herself to molding the young Wenceslas's character into a model of virtue. According to one record, "she undertook, with the utmost care, to form his heart to the love of God." Paul, who served as Ludmilla's personal chaplain, baptized Wenceslas when he was an infant. A disciple of Saint Methodius, Paul subsequently labored with Ludmilla to secure her grandson in the Christian faith and to educate him so that he would develop into a just and intelligent ruler. Their efforts must have been successful, for it is recorded that by his early teens, Wenceslas was not only admirably devout but also "understood Latin as if he were a bishop and read Slavonic with ease."

Ludmilla likely regarded the duty of educating the young Wenceslas as her most important one. Probably not educated herself, she would have left the teaching to her faithful chaplain and would have focused her full attention on her grandson's spiritual development. Living at the seat of power all of her life, Ludmilla was probably well-versed in the ways of the world and would have grasped fully the particulars of political intrigue. She was undoubtedly troubled by the conflicts between Christians and non-Christians that were flaring up under her daughter-in-law's misguided rule. She saw her protégé Wenceslas as the one who could set Bohemia on the right path toward casting off paganism and embracing Christianity.

The agreement that permitted Ludmilla's custody of Wenceslas lasted until the death of the young man's father, who was killed fighting against the Magyars, a tribe from the area of Siberia that settled in the ninth century in what is now Hungary. After determining that Wenceslas—who was about thirteen at the time of Wratislaw's demise—was too young to rule, his scheming mother, Drahomíra, took over as regent. Drahomíra refused to allow Wenceslas to see his grandmother, fearful that Ludmilla would plot to overthrow her. Drahomíra's suspicions of Ludmilla's intentions were probably well-founded.

Resentful and fearful of Ludmilla's continued influence over Wenceslas, Drahomíra took action. It is generally believed that she arranged for the hiring of assassins to break into the castle at Tetin and murder Ludmilla. Tradition has it that the duchess was at prayer when Drahomíra's agents strangled Ludmilla with her own veil.

As punishment for her apparent role in the murder, Drahomíra was sent into exile. When Wenceslas assumed power at the age of eighteen, he allowed his mother to return to Bohemia. Wenceslas's service as duke of Bohemia comprises another story, but he fulfilled his grandmother's expectations during an impressive reign that ended with his murder in 929.

Tradition tells us that Ludmilla's death did not diminish her influence, for many miracles took place over her tomb following her martyrdom and her manifestation as a saint. In a hypocritical twist, Drahomíra ordered a church, named Saint Michael's, built in Tetin to mark the site of Ludmilla's death. Drahomíra was buried in this church. Wenceslas later moved his grandmother's remains to a church in Prague named for Saint Vitus, where her relics are still venerated. Saint Ludmilla's Feast Day falls on September 16.

Significance

Ludmilla, with Duke Bořivoj, Christianized Bohemia. The libretto that Emil Frída (also known as Jaroslav Vrchlicky; 1853-1912) wrote for Czech composer Antonín Dvořák's (1841-1904) oratorio *Saint Ludmila* (1886) celebrates the conversion of the duchess, who pleads in one of her recitatives,

> The true God, I long to find Him.
> . . . I am firmly resolved
> To know the truth, and falsehood flee;
> In meekness bow before the sacred Cross.

Her long and pious life fulfilled this resolution. After she died a martyr's death, she continued to spread the truth and conquer falsehood as thousands over the centuries have venerated her.

Ludmilla made her second vital contribution by educating Wenceslas and ensuring that he was firmly grounded in the Christian faith. Her training of him turned him into a stern but fair ruler who carried out his grandparents' desire to spread Christianity throughout Bohemia. Although Wenceslas has emerged over the centuries as a more widely recognized saint—partly through the Christmas song "Good King Wenceslas"—he remains inextricably bound to Ludmilla, his loving mentor and spiritual guide.

Finally, Ludmilla's significance extends beyond religion into the national arena. When Dvořák set out to compose the oratorio celebrating Saint Ludmilla, he intended to depict her as a player in monumental scenes from Czech history, scenes that would give the nation self-confidence and reveal the greatness of the Czech historical tradition. A British publisher had commissioned the oratorio for the Leeds Festival in 1886. For Dvořák, the invitation to participate in one of England's great musical events provided an opportunity to compose a purely Czech oratorio that would place his country's music and history in an international milieu. With these objectives in mind, he conceived of *Saint Ludmila* as being more nationalistic in character than religious. Although Frída's libretto, which stresses the antitheses of the pagan and Christian worlds, did not at all fulfill Dvořák's intentions, the composer accepted it, determined to let his music alone turn Ludmilla into a pivotal figure in Czech history.

Dvořák saw Ludmilla as a distinctive personage in his country's tradition. First she had long served as a patron saint, which in its fullest definition means advocate, protector, and defender. Equally important to Dvořák, she had emerged as the mother of the nation. In her dual roles as patron and as mother, Saint Ludmilla has witnessed and overseen a torrent of historical events in her corner of the world during the past thousand or so years, but she has survived it all. With the resurgence of Catholicism in the post-communist era, Saint Ludmilla along with her grandson Saint Wenceslas reign once more.

—*Robert L. Ross*

Further Reading

Demetz, Peter. *Prague in Black and Gold: Scenes from the Life of a European City*. New York: Hill and Wang, 1997. Traces the history of Prague from its beginning to the present and combines myths about the city with historical facts. Includes details on the period in which Ludmilla lived.

Dvořák, Antonín. *Saint Ludmila: An Oratorio*. London: Novello, Ewer, 1968. Contains Emil Frída's complete libretto (in English translation) for *Saint Ludmila*. Provides an introduction to the work that explains Dvořák's approach to the story of Ludmilla.

The Encyclopedia of Catholic Saints. Philadelphia: Chilton Books, 1966. A twelve-volume work arranged according to dates of the saints' feast days. Provides general information on saints worldwide. Illustrations.

Rosenwein, Barbara H. *A Short History of the Middle Ages*. Orchard Park, N.Y.: Broadview Press, 2002. A readable and succinct overview of medieval history and the development of Europe from 300 to 1500, including material on the former kingdom of Bohemia.

Ryan, Patrick J. "Rival Brothers." *America* 169 (September 18, 1993). Discusses the story of Ludmilla's family, in particular the rivalry between Wenceslas and Boleslav. Applies the story to the post-communist Czech Republic, stressing that the lives of Ludmilla and Wenceslas serve as models in the present pursuit of peace and justice.

Sayer, Derek. *The Coasts of Bohemia*. Princeton, N.J.: Princeton University Press, 1998. Examines the kingdom of Bohemia, now the Czech Republic, from medieval to modern times, and stresses the country's important position in Central Europe. Interweaves discussions of Czech art, literature, music, and cultural traditions into the text.

See also: Anna, Princess of the Byzantine Empire; Saint Clotilda; Clovis; Saint Cyril and Saint Methodius; Jan Hus; Joan of Arc; Otto I.

Related articles in *Great Events from History: The Middle Ages, 477-1453*: 496: Baptism of Clovis; 735: Christianity Is Introduced into Germany; c. 850: Development of the Slavic Alphabet; 890's: Magyars Invade Italy, Saxony, and Bavaria; c. 960: Jews Settle in Bohemia; 1414-1418: Council of Constance; July 6, 1415: Martyrdom of Jan Hus.

Raymond Lull

Catalan mystic, scholar, and teacher

Lull devised a unique and influential Neoplatonic and non-Scholastic philosophy, founded a school of Arabic, composed Arabic books, corresponded with Islamic savants in North Africa, and helped create the Catalan language. Friend of rulers, prelates, and the powerful, he wandered the courts of Europe, advocating for his many enterprises.

Born: c. 1235; Palma de Mallorca, Majorca (now in Spain)

Died: Early 1316; Tunis, Majorca, or on a voyage to Majorca

Also known as: Raymond Lully; Ramon Llull; Ramon Lullus; Raymond Lullus; Ramon Lull; Doctor Illuminatus

Areas of achievement: Literature, philosophy, religion and theology

Early Life

Raymond Lull (Ramon Llull in his native Catalan) was born to a Crusader who had helped conquer Islamic Majorca island some three years before. Like most youngsters of his affluent class, he apparently received a gentleman's education in the vernacular but called himself "illiterate" in the learned Latin. As was fashionable, he became a troubadour composer and gave himself to a life of womanizing and trivialities. A disputed report makes the boy Lull a page at the court of James I the Conqueror, the ruler of the various realms confederated around Catalonia and Aragon; he held the post of majordomo, or head of household, at the subordinate court of the conqueror's son, James II of Majorca. Lull's marriage to Blanca Picany in 1257 gave him a son, Domènec, and a daughter, Magdalena, though he continued to live a dissolute life.

In later years, he confided many details of his life to monks of Vauvert in Paris, from which a fascinating *vita coetanea* (contemporary life) was composed in 1311. In it Lull tells of five apparitions of the crucified Christ in 1263 that frightened and then converted him to a life of religious fervor at age thirty.

Lull's Majorca was a cosmopolitan center of western Mediterranean trade and culture, with a third of its population still Muslim, with a large Jewish community, and with merchant colonies and an immigrant society from many countries. It was natural for Lull to focus on converting Muslims and to learn Arabic. Leaving a fund to support his abandoned family, he set about acquiring a formal education in Latin, while adopting the coarse cloth and mendicant lifestyle of a wandering holy man. During nine years of intensive study on Majorca, he learned Latin and Arabic passably well, and studied the Qurʾān, the Talmud, and the Bible as well as the works of Plato, Aristotle, and the standard European authors. A book written by a disciple six years after his death shows Lull as a thin, serene figure, his bald head capped and his beard unusually long.

Life's Work

Lull was both a meditative thinker and a man of restless action. The two personas were fused: action in the service of his contemplative vision. His active life can be followed in his constant travels during thirty years, until his death at the end of a journey. During these travels, he wrote an average of nine or ten books a year. Some of these works were treatises or booklets, but seven ran to 150,000 words, three to 250,000, one to 400,000, and one to nearly a million. During his studies, Lull had made a compendium in Arabic of al-Ghazzālī's logic; more significant, he also wrote in Arabic *Libre de contemplació* (1273; *Book of Contemplation*, 1985). *Book of Contemplation* is an encyclopedic summa of mysticism; some scholars think it his greatest work. At the end of his studies, during two sessions of intense contemplation on Mount Randa on Majorca, he received a cosmic illumination and then a vision of a Christlike shepherd, which set the direction of his future thought and books. As a guest at La Real Abbey, he now composed the first version of his celebrated work on the ultimate constitution of reality and its symbolic expression in systems, which he called *Ars compendiosa inveniendi veritatem* (c. 1274; a brief art of finding truth). Later he devised a machine with crank and revolving wheel to demonstrate his art graphically as propositions revolved in circles, squares, and triangles.

Acclaim for his books led James II of Majorca to invite Lull to his court at Montpellier in 1274-1275. Lull persuaded the king to endow a center or priory on Majorca called Miramar, where relays of thirteen Franciscan friars would learn Arabic for missionary work, a foundation Pope John XXI confirmed in 1276. Lull seems to have spent the next decade writing on Majorca, though older scholars have him traveling widely in Europe and Africa. The fourteen books finished on the island include *Libre de l'ordre de cavalleria* (1279; *The Book of the Order of Chivalry*, 1484), *Doctrina pueril* (1274-1276; teaching of children), *Libre del gentil e dels tres savis* (1274-1276; *The Book of the Gentile and Three Wise Men*, 1985), and works on law, medicine, logic, theology, and angels. At Montpellier in 1283, he wrote his novel *Blanquerna* (English translation, 1925), named after its hero, and two more books on his art. At Rome in 1287 seeking papal multiplication of language schools, Lull discovered that the pope had died; he therefore journeyed to Paris to lecture on his art at the university, to visit Philip IV the Fair, and to write his novel *Libre de meravalles* (1288-1289; *Felix: Or, Book of Wonders*, 1985) and five other works. Back at Montpellier, perhaps after a side trip to Rome, he lectured and wrote on his art. A brief residence in Genoa allowed him to translate the latest work on his art into Arabic, before pleading again at the papal court for schools and for a crusade; *Libre de passage* (1292; book of passage), his petition to Pope Nicholas IV, and his treatise on converting infidels date from this Roman stay of 1292.

Though his chronology is sometimes difficult to establish, Lull seems to have announced at Genoa his intention to preach to the Muslims in Tunis, but out of cowardice, he refused to sail. The resultant popular scorn induced a grave psychosomatic illness. Stirred by two visions, he tried unsuccessfully to enter the Dominican order and then became a Franciscan external affiliate or layman-tertiary. He did voyage to Tunis in 1293, where his preaching on the Trinitarian Art to Muslim savants caused the Ḥafṣid sultan Abū Hafs to imprison and then to expel him. At the Franco-Angevin court of Naples, Lull lectured on the art, preaching also to the Muslim colony of nearby Lucera and conferring with the new pope, Celestine V, at Naples, in 1294-1295. Lull fitted in a trip to Barcelona and to Majorca, where he dedicated a philosophical work to his son; later, he returned in 1295 to Rome, where he presented two books to the latest pope, Boniface VIII. Stopping at Genoa to compose several books, Lull visited James II at Montpellier and traveled on for a prolonged stay lecturing at the University of Paris from 1297 to 1299. At Paris he consulted with Philip IV and composed thirteen of his most important works—on topics ranging from theology, mathematics, and astronomy to love, proverbs, and encouragement for the Venetian prisoners of war (including Marco Polo) at Genoa.

Staying at the court of James II of Aragon at Barcelona in 1299, Lull wrote two books and preached by royal permission to subject Muslims and Jews. In 1300-1301, he preached to Majorca's Muslims and wrote seven books. At the news that the Mongol khan Maḥmūd Ghāzān was conquering Syria, Lull embarked for Cyprus, intending to oppose him; once arrived, Lull found that the rumor was false. He visited Henry II of Cyprus, hoping that the king would send him to preach to the local Muslims and to the ruler of Islamic Egypt. Lull wrote two books on Cyprus, including his *Rhetorica nova* (1301; *Ramón Llull's New Rhetoric*, 1994). Illness and an attempt by two assistants to poison him frustrated his efforts on the island. He visited Cilician Armenia, writing a book there on belief in God (1302). Perhaps after a trip to Jerusalem, he wrote *Mil proverbis* (1302; thousand proverbs) at sea on his way back to Italy. From 1303 to 1305, he worked alternately in Genoa and Montpellier, producing at Montpellier fifteen of the nineteen books written by him during this period.

At the court of James II of Aragon at Barcelona in 1305, Lull composed *Liber de Trinitate et Incarnatione* and *Liber praedicationis contra judeos*. In 1306, he worked at the University of Paris as well as at the court of Pope Clement V at Lyon. Back on Majorca, he took ship for Islamic Bougie, where he preached in the center of town and barely escaped being stoned. Jailed for six months and scheduled for execution, he wrote in Arabic a Christian-Muslim dialogue. Later, expelled, shipwrecked, and nearly drowned off Pisa, he took advantage of his recuperation in that city to finish his greatest work, *Ars generalis ultima* (1305-1308; last general art). At Pisa, he composed a total of eight books, including one on memory, and tried to persuade the city council to found a crusading military order. He visited Genoa and Pope Clement V at Avignon, before settling down at Montpellier to write eighteen books during 1308-1309. While lecturing at the University of Paris in 1310-1311, he produced thirty-five books, many against the work of the philosopher Averroës.

When the ecumenical council met at Vienne in France in 1311-1312, Lull appeared before it to argue successfully for a statute mandating chairs of Asian languages at the major universities. He also urged consolidation of the military orders for more effective crusading. The suppression of the Knights Templar in 1312 was the result. Back at Montpellier briefly in May, 1312, to write a book on angels, he continued on to Majorca, writing there seventeen books and making his will. He spent the year from spring, 1313, to spring, 1314, at the Messina court of his supporter Frederick III of Sicily, where thirty-seven books were published. He was in Tunis again in 1314-1315 and produced twenty-six more works, mostly small in size. Lull died before March, 1316, at Tunis, Majorca, or aboard ship on the way to Tunis.

SIGNIFICANCE

Lull was the first European to write on philosophy in the vernacular. Since his goal was to unify the three faiths of Abraham (Judaism, Christianity, and Islam), revelation and mysticism were prime components of his philosophy as well as the reason for his writing and debating in Arabic. He joined elements of Islamic and Jewish learning to Christian thought, especially to the tradition of Augustinian Neoplatonism. Fundamentally syncretistic rather than innovative, his conceptual and stylistic patterns are puzzlingly complex. Lull is also the first great name in Catalan prose, and his *Blanquerna* is the first European novel on a contemporary theme. Audacious and immensely vigorous, he traveled tirelessly around the western Mediterranean as a propagandist and reformer. His writings are astonishing for their variety and number. The ten large volumes of the modern Mainz edition hold only 50 of his 280 works. Lull is famous as a mystic and a poet; he even has reputations as an occultist and a martyr. Attempting to organize all knowledge, his art mechanizes logic and thought processes into what Anthony Bonner calls "an extraordinary network of systems" in symbolic computation, foreshadowing computer science.

For centuries after his death, theologians and philosophers were divided over his writings. In 1376, the inquisitor Nicholas Eymerich condemned one hundred Lullian "errors," and Pope Gregory XI condemned twenty of Lull's books; Pope Martin V reversed this condemnation in 1416. Jean de Gerson battled Lull's great influence at Paris and around 1400 had his art banned from the Sorbonne. Nevertheless, Lullism continued to excite academics and mystics. Lull enjoyed a transcendental influence in the Renaissance, especially on Heinrich Cornelius Agrippa, Cardinal Bessarion, Giordano Bruno, Nicholas of Cusa, Lefèvre d'Étaples, and Giovanni Pico della Mirandola. A chair was founded in Lull's name at the Renaissance university of Alcalá in 1508, and Philip II of Spain projected a Lullian academy in 1582. Lull's *The Book of the Order of Chivalry* was one of the first books published by William Caxton when printing came to England. Sir Francis Bacon, René Descartes, François Rabelais, and Jonathan Swift mocked Lull, but Gottfried Leibniz was deeply influenced by him. Though never canonized, the layman Lull was allowed a limited cultus (cult) within the Franciscan order, with his feast day on July 3 confirmed in 1858 by Pope Pius IX.

—*Robert I. Burns*

FURTHER READING

Bonner, Anthony, ed. and trans. *Selected Works of Ramón Llull, 1232-1316*. 2 vols. Princeton, N.J.: Princeton University Press, 1985. The first one hundred pages of introduction provide an excellent short biography, including Lull's own semiautobiography. Introductions, before each of the seven works (including two on Lull's art), add considerable information. Includes a revised catalog of Lull's works, by date and place, as well as a bibliography and an index.

Evans, G. R. *Fifty Key Medieval Thinkers*. New York: Routledge, 2002. Succinct biographies of important thinkers—mainly theologians and philosophers—of the Middle Ages, including Lull. Also provides a bibliography and an index.

Hillgarth, Jocelyn N. *Ramón Lull and Lullism in Fourteenth-Century France*. Oxford, England: Clarendon Press, 1971. Though concerned with Paris as the most important center of Lullism after Lull's death, the author also offers an excellent short biography of Lull in English. Includes a detailed chronology, bibliography, index, and twelve illustrations of Lull's life.

_______. *The Spanish Kingdoms, 1250-1216*. 2 vols. Oxford, England: Clarendon Press, 1976-1978. Besides giving full background on Lull's times, this text provides a long chapter comparing Lull with contemporary Spanish literary figures such as King Alfonso X.

Johnston, Mark D. *The Evangelical Rhetoric of Ramón Llull: Lay Learning and Piety in the Christian West Around 1300*. New York: Oxford University Press, 1996. Discusses Lull's "art of arts," beauty in language, order, and virtue and propriety in speaking. Includes an extensive bibliography and an index.

_______. *The Spiritual Logic of Ramón Llull*. Oxford, England: Clarendon Press, 1987. A philosophical survey of Lull's logic in its fundamentals and development. Argues that Lull adapted his Scholastic predecessors so that his art was applied in a unique way to logic and so that it could be a program both of thought and of argumentation. Concludes that Lull was not a philosophical genius, as most scholars think, but one of the greatest moral teachers. Includes a brief biography.

Llull, Ramón. *Doctor Illuminatus: A Ramón Llull Reader*. Edited and translated by Anthony Bonner. Princeton, N.J.: Princeton University Press, 1993. An abridged version of Bonner's 1985 edition of *Selected Works of Ramón Llull*. Includes maps and other illustrations, a bibliography, and an index.

Menocal, Maria Rosa, Raymond P. Scheindlin, and Michael Sells, eds. *The Literature of Al-Andalus*. New York: Cambridge University Press, 2000. Part of the Cambridge History of Arabic Literature series, provides a biographical look at Lull's work in the context of Muslim Spain.

Peers, Edgar Allison. *Ramón Lull: A Biography.* New York: Macmillan, 1929. A still-useful full-length biography in traditional biographical format.

Vega, Amador. *Ramón Llull and the Secret of Life*. Translated by James W. Heisig. New York: Crossroad, 2003. A look at Lull's religious and spiritual philosophy. Discusses language and alchemy, contemplation, formation, conversion, wonder, and more. Includes a bibliography and an index.

SEE ALSO: Peter Abelard; Saint Anselm; Boethius; Saint Bonaventure; Boniface VIII; John Duns Scotus; Saint Isidore of Seville; Alexander Neckam; Thomas Aquinas.

RELATED ARTICLES in *Great Events from History: The Middle Ages, 477-1453*: c. 1120: Order of the Knights Templar Is Founded; April 16, 1209: Founding of the Franciscans; c. 1250: Improvements in Shipbuilding and Navigation.

Ma Yuan
Chinese painter

Together with his somewhat younger contemporary, Xia Gui, Ma Yuan formed the Ma-Xia school of Chinese painting. In some ways, the school served as the prototype for Chinese landscape painting and heavily influenced both Chinese and Japanese painters.

Born: c. 1165; He Zhong, Shanxi Province, China
Died: c. 1225; Hangzhou, Zhejiang Province, China
Also known as: Ma Yüan (Wade-Giles); Qinshan (Pinyin), Ch'in-shan (Wade-Giles); He Zhong (Pinyin), Ho Chung (Wade-Giles); One-Cornered Ma
Area of achievement: Art

Early Life
Ma Yuan (mah yew-ahn) belonged to what was probably the most prolific and distinguished family of painter-scholars in Chinese history. Altogether, seven members of his family served the Northern and Southern Song imperial families. This service lasted from the time of Yuan's great-grandfather Ma Fen in the late eleventh century, to that of his son Ma Lin in the mid-thirteenth century. Besides Yuan, the Ma artists included his great-grandfather, Fen; his grandfather, Xiongzu; Shirong, his father; Gongxian, an uncle; Kui, his brother; and his son Lin. Each of them received accolades from the imperial court, but unquestionably Ma Yuan became the most famous, and his legacy was the most profound.

Despite the acclaim that surrounded the Ma painters, little is known about their personal lives, and exact dates for their professional careers are generally missing. In part, the absence of such information reflects the turbulence of the times in which they lived. Ma Fen painted at a time when the Chinese rulers of the Northern Song Dynasty (Sung; 960-1127) were conspiring with a Tungusic people, the Jurchen, to end the Khitan control over northern China. Although this alliance did manage to displace the Khitans in 1126, the subsequent rupture between the Song and the Jurchen resulted in a further loss of territory and a rather ignominious Chinese retreat to the south. The imperial court abandoned the capital, Gaifeng, and moved to Hangzhou at the mouth of the Zhe estuary in the Yangtze area. Although Hangzhou became the most beautiful of Chinese capitals, the sting of losing northern China to "barbarians" marked the Southern Song era (1127-1279) in Chinese eyes as less than respectable. One Chinese critic, for example, has said that Ma's "incomplete" paintings were a reflection of a "divided and less than complete empire."

During Ma Yuan's lifetime, the Southern Song was in even further military retreat, a time when Genghis Khan was forming the Mongol nation and setting it on the path toward world conquest. The Mongols would become the first foreigners in Chinese history to conquer all China, and the Southern Song would bear the stigma of being the first dynasty to have lost all China to a "barbarian" conqueror.

Despite the Southern Song's so-called military weakness, a point that many Western scholars claim has been exaggerated by Chinese historians, the dynasty was a glorious and sophisticated one. During the late twelfth and early thirteenth centuries, Hangzhou was probably the most cosmopolitan city in the world, and the imperial Chinese court surrounded itself with scholars, historians, poets, and painters. Neo-Confucianism flourished, and poetry and prose of great excellence abounded. The wealthy lived luxurious and generally tranquil lives.

It was in such a milieu that Ma Yuan worked. No doubt he was highly literate and something of a scholar, as were most of the court dignitaries of that period. If the reign of the Southern Song was not known as a great military period of Chinese history, it was certainly one of the most enlightened in terms of scholarship and governmental support of artists. Thus, Ma Yuan received numerous awards, such as the Golden Girdle, and was artist-in-attendance at the imperial court.

The earliest suggested painting by Ma Yuan purportedly dates from the reign of Gaozong (Kao-tsung; r. 1127-1162), although such an early date is unlikely. At the latest, Ma was said to have still been artist-in-attendance during the reign of Lizong (Li-tsung; r. 1225-1264). Certainly he was very active during the reign of Ningzong (Ning-tsung; r. 1195-1224), receiving as he did the patronage of the empress Yang and her family. This patronage is verified by several seals bearing the empress Yang's name, together with inscriptions on Ma Yuan's paintings. These inscriptions not only offer some of the very few concrete dates connected to Ma Yuan but also corroborate the generally held view that Ma's career was principally that of a court painter.

Life's Work
Ma Yuan's paintings offer a glimpse of court life in Hangzhou. Many of the works attributed to him depict fa-

vorite aristocratic pastimes, such as nighttime entertainment in a villa or scenes from the panoramic West Lake. However, Ma Yuan was much more than a reflection of the grandeur of the Song court. Consciously or not, he began a style unique to him and his younger contemporary, Xia Gui, which would make his career a watershed in the history of Chinese art.

In addition to his nicknames Qinshan (Ch'in-shan) and He Zhong (Ho Chung; the latter indicating that he was from He Zhong, Shanxi Province), Ma was also known as "One-Cornered Ma." The latter name reveals the innovative aspects of Ma's career. "One corner" refers to a tendency in many of Ma's works to emphasize one corner of a scene. This was described by some Chinese critics as "leaning to one corner," or being, therefore, incomplete.

Ma's one-corner emphasis may have been a reflection of Daoist beliefs concerning the illusory nature of appearances; certainly, mood and imagination are more important in his art than is detailed reproduction. Critics and detractors of Ma Yuan's style and paintings often refer to his lyric and poetic qualities. Empty spaces are, in his works, opportunities for the viewer's imagination to soar.

Ma's one-cornered style calls to mind the approach of the great Daoist historian of the Early Han Dynasty, Sima Qian (145-86 B.C.E.), who often narrated a biography of a particular subject from the narrow perspective of the subject himself and left other perspectives to the biographies of the subject's contemporaries. In a sense, this too was a one-cornered approach. One final explanation for Ma's style is that, as part of China was occupied by a "barbarian" state, the Jurchen Jin Dynasty (1115-1234), the Southern Song constituted only a corner of the true Chinese empire and was, therefore, incomplete.

Regardless of whether Ma's peculiar quirk was a political statement or a philosophical expression, the result resembles the work of a photographer who consciously blurs all but the focal point of a shot. In Ma Yuan, this technique was executed with great subtlety, and it endowed his paintings with an almost eerie sense of transience.

Not all aspects of Ma Yuan's style were original. Like Xia Gui, Ma often used what has been described as the ax-stroke method of depicting rocky mountains. This technique, which is generally attributed to the great Northern Song painter Li Tang (Li T'ang), has been described as "hacking out the angular facets of rocks with the side of the brush." Sharp contours can be seen elsewhere in Ma Yuan's works, and critics have referred to his "exact severity" and use of a "squeezed brush" to define leaves. Furthermore, the seemingly restless movement of water in many of his works is often said to be typical of the fighting-water technique. Although precedents for all but the one-cornered style can be found, the combinations that Ma used emerge as singularly his.

His works, often in the form of fans, album leaves, and (less frequently) scrolls, painted in ink with traces of color, can be found in numerous museums around the world. In the United States, paintings by Ma Yuan and very close Ming copies of his work are located in the Cincinnati Art Museum, the Cleveland Museum of Art, the Fogg Museum, and the Freer Gallery. Many more of his works hang in Japanese galleries. The reason for this is his great popularity during the Ashikaga period (Muromachi; 1336-1573) in Japan. Unfortunately, it is also a consequence of Japanese collectors' helping themselves during their country's wartime occupation of China. In China, the majority of Ma's works available for viewing are in either the Beijing or the Taipei palace museums. A major problem for those wishing to examine his art lies in the fact that forgeries and imitations are common, and not a few of the paintings bearing his name were done by his students or by later admirers. With a few exceptions, however, art experts have been able to distinguish the genuine works from imitations with considerable confidence.

SIGNIFICANCE

The impact of Ma Yuan on subsequent Chinese painting was slow in developing. In some measure, this was a result of Chinese art critics' characterizing Ma and Xia Gui as belonging to the Northern school of painting at a time when the Southern school was considered to be the proper school for China's literati. Such distinctions were social as much as they were aesthetic; the professional court painters were criticized in contrast to the literati, who pursued painting strictly as a gentlemanly hobby. Furthermore, the Ma-Xia school was sometimes derided as being an academic school whose style was easily learned. During the Ming Dynasty (1368-1644), however, interest in Ma Yuan and appreciation of his worth began to develop.

Even before the Ming resurrection of the Ma-Xia school, the Japanese had begun to admire these two painters and their school. Because the paintings were not yet highly collectible and therefore could be acquired without great difficulty, the Japanese brought back numerous fine examples of both painters, particularly during the shogunates of Yoshimitsu (1358-1408) and Yoshimasa (1435-1490) of the Ashikaga period. The

Ma-Xia school has remained popular in Japan to this day. Moreover, in recent years Western critics have come to consider Ma Yuan and Xia Gui as the best of the Chinese landscape painters. An interesting development is that Chinese critics may be taking their cue from Japan and the West in elevating Ma to the highest echelon of China's artistic pantheon.

—*Hilel B. Salomon*

FURTHER READING

Barnhart, Richard M., et al. *Three Thousand Years of Chinese Painting*. New Haven, Conn.: Yale University Press, 1997. The chapter "The Five Dynasties and the Song Period (907-1279)" discusses the Ma-Xia painters. This oversize book includes beautiful color plates and a helpful glossary.

Cahill, James. *Chinese Painting*. New York: Rizzoli International, 1977. Contains a chapter devoted to Ma Yuan, Xia Gui, and Ma Lin, with examples of their work.

_______. *An Index of Early Chinese Painters and Paintings: T'ang, Sung, and Yuan*. Berkeley: University of California Press, 1980. Contains a lengthy list of paintings attributed to Xia Gui that are located in museums and private collections.

Edwards, Richard. "Ma Yuan." In *Sung Biographies*, edited by Herbert Franke. Wiesbaden, West Germany: Franz Steiner, 1976. The most detailed discussion of Ma Yuan in English, with an excellent discussion of Ma's impact on Chinese art.

Fong, Wen C., and James Watt. *Possessing the Past: Treasures from the National Palace Museum, Taipei*. New York: The Metropolitan Museum of Art, 1996. Informative discussions of the Ma-Xia school and its artists, especially in the chapter on the Imperial Painting Academy of the Song Dynasty. Beautifully illustrated with examples of paintings by the Ma-Xia artists.

Lee, Sherman. *Chinese Landscape Painting*. 1954. Reprint. Cleveland, Ohio: Cleveland Museum of Art, 1962. Contains examples of Xia's art, together with a brief critique of his technique.

Loehr, Max. *The Great Painters of China*. New York: Harper and Row, 1980. Contains a very brief sketch of Xia Gui's life and an excellent discussion of his technique. Also has several photographs of Xia's paintings.

Sullivan, Michael. *The Arts of China*. 4th ed. Berkeley: University of California Press, 1999. Contains a brief passage about Ma Yuan and Xia Gui with examples of their work.

SEE ALSO: Xia Gui; Yan Liben.

RELATED ARTICLE in *Great Events from History: The Middle Ages, 477-1453*: c. 1190-1279: Ma-Xia School of Painting Flourishes.

GUILLAUME DE MACHAUT

French poet, musician, and composer

Generally acclaimed as the most important figure of the French ars nova, *Machaut was among the first to compose polyphonic settings of the fixed forms of medieval poetry (ballade, rondeau, virelay), to write songs for four voices, and to compose an integrated setting of the entire Ordinary of the Mass.*

BORN: c. 1300; Machault, near Reims, France
DIED: Possibly April, 1377; Reims, France
AREAS OF ACHIEVEMENT: Music, literature

EARLY LIFE

Guillaume de Machaut (gee-yohm deh mah-shoh) was born most likely in the village of Machault in the Champagne region of France, not far from the cathedral city of Reims. Some music historians surmise that he may have been born in Reims itself, but as practically nothing is known of his early life, such speculations remain mere guesses; one scholar, however, has traced the existence of a Wuillaume Machaux—who may have been the poet's father—at Reims around 1310. The little information available indicates that Machaut was educated by clerics in an ecclesiastical venue, probably in Paris and Reims, and that he eventually earned a master of arts degree, although he never took holy orders.

Sometime around 1323, Machaut joined the entourage of John of Luxembourg, the blind king of Bohemia, a well-admired ruler and exemplar of chivalry and courtesy and a lover of war and the battlefield. For the next several years, Machaut's life involved constant travel—primarily because John involved himself in various military campaigns, although much of the travel was simply for entertainment—to places such as France, Lithuania,

Poland, Prussia, and Silesia. One of Machaut's earliest known works, *Bone pastor Guillerme* (1324; good shepherd William), a Latin motet celebrating the installation of Guillaume de Trie as the new archbishop of Reims, was written during his early years in King John's service. Another work, *Le Jugement dou Roy de Behaingne* (*The Judgment of the King of Bohemia*, 1984), although undated, was almost certainly written during the years Machaut spent with John. As clerk, personal secretary, and general assistant to King John, Machaut frequently benefited from the king's influence on Popes John XXII and Benedict XII: In 1330, he was named canon at Verdun; in 1332, he became canon at Arras; and in 1337, he was awarded a more desirable canonicate in Reims. Machaut appears to have settled in Reims in the late 1330's, leaving that city only to accompany King John on occasional journeys. After the king's heroic suicide in the Battle of Crécy in 1346, Machaut continued his association with the royal family through King John's daughter, Bonne of Luxembourg, who later became the wife of John II of France. He also maintained close ties with other nobles, among them Charles of Navarre, Jean de France, the future Charles V of France, and Amadeus VI of Savoy.

LIFE'S WORK

Although Machaut remained linked with the royal courts of Europe, he spent the rest of his life as a canon at Reims Cathedral, having relinquished his other canonicates. Evidence points to the probability that the Reims canons—who were either tonsured clerics, as Machaut probably was, or priests who had taken holy orders—functioned as choristers for cathedral services. As churchmen, they were bound by innumerable rules of behavior and dress: They were required to dine together at the refectory on certain days of the week as well as certain holy days, they had to reside within the city walls of Reims, and they had to sing a minimum of thirty-two masses during the year. Although this restrictive and semicloistered life in a cathedral city was markedly different from the exciting years of foreign travel with King John, it provided Machaut with both the time and the artistic environment in which to write poetry and compose music.

Machaut's *Remède de Fortune* (the remedy of fortune; English translation, 1988)—a long poem generally considered an early work, although it is difficult to assign specific dates to much of Machaut's output—is a didactic narrative in which a lover passionately delineates the physical and moral beauty of the lady he adores and asserts that his love for her has instilled in him all the virtues. A collection of examples of both the lyric forms he favored (ballade, lay, rondeau, and virelay) and older forms (*complainte* and chanson *royale*) which he used only in this work, the *Remède de Fortune* is something of an anthology of fourteenth century lyric forms. Many of the individual forms look back to trouvère (court poet) compositions of the thirteenth century with their occasional reliance on the old rhythmic modes and stanzaic forms and in their three-voice structure, which suggests French polyphony of the age preceding that of Machaut; the ballades, however, have four voices—a decided innovation—although the fourth voice may have been intended as an alternate to one of the other three.

La Fonteinne amoureuse (written between 1360 and 1362; *The Fountain of Love*, 1993) has attracted critical attention for its treatment of the story of Paris of Troy and his judgment of the three goddesses. In this poem, the narrator overhears a young nobleman lamenting his unrequited love. The two men discuss at length the fountain of love from which the nobleman has drunk, and then they fall asleep. They both dream that Venus appears and recounts Paris's story and then produces the lady whom the nobleman loves. The lovers exchange rings, the dream fades, and the two men awaken. On the nobleman's finger is the lady's ring, and he vows to spend his life serving Venus and building a temple in her honor. Although this poem has traditionally been seen as a flattering portrait of Jean de France on the eve of his marriage, recent scholarship refutes that theory by indicating that the poem is, in reality, a critical look at the results of a nobleman's devoting himself to love instead of to the responsibilities of his position as a member of the nobility.

Around 1364, Machaut completed his *La Messe de Nostre Dame* (*Machaut's Mass*, 1990), a complex work and the first complete surviving polyphonic setting of the Ordinary of the Mass. In the following century, such settings would become common, but in Machaut's day, his achievement was monumental. The mass is in four voices and without instrumentation, although in its performance an organ may have doubled the tenor part in some sections. Machaut broke from the custom of his predecessors in using more ornamentation and contrary motion between voices, ensuring that the text was emphasized and therefore heard. Pope John XXII, who had been responsible for Machaut's comfortable position at Reims, had in his bull of 1324-1325 required that the text of the Mass be clearly heard and not submerged in the music.

Machaut's most interesting and most famous work is probably *Le Livre dou Voir-Dit* (1365; *The Book of the*

True Poem, 1998), a nine-thousand-line romance that features different meters, forty-six letters in prose, and several lyric poems, some of them set to music. The work is particularly interesting to medieval scholars because it supplies much biographical information about Machaut, not only concrete facts but also commentary on his psychological state during specific incidents. In the piece, Machaut, then in his sixties, describes in some detail his love affair with a seventeen-year-old noble lady whose identity has long occupied scholarly interest. Initially thought to be Agnes d'Evreux, sister of Charles the Bad of Navarre, Toute-belle (Machaut's name for his lover) is now generally held to be Peronne d'Unchair, dame of Armentieres, a wealthy heiress from Machaut's home province of Champagne. *The Book of the True Poem* contains one of the famous correspondences of literary history in its series of letters between the narrator and the young lady, who insists that he publicize their affair in songs and poems, some of them supposedly of her own composing. It is clear from the letters that the lady enjoys the notoriety of her affair with a celebrated poet, as she alternately teases her elderly lover and chides him for being afraid to visit her. Machaut's narrator is a decided departure from the typical courtly lover in that he describes himself as aged, gouty, blind in one eye, and undignified. Such a lover would become common in later narrative poetry, much of it influenced by Machaut's works.

As a composer, Machaut produced a body of work that is larger than that of any other fourteenth century musician and noteworthy for its range of form and style. Early in his career he had concentrated on traditional forms such as the motet, but he became more and more interested in secular song and polyphony, combining the two traditions in his ballades and rondeaux, many of which were incorporated into his long narrative poems, such as *Remède de Fortune* and *The Book of the True Poem*.

In his later years, Machaut seems to have devoted his time to supervising the production of his works in elaborately illuminated and very expensive manuscripts for some of his royal patrons, among them Amadeus of Savoy and Jean de France. Machaut died sometime in 1377 in Reims, where he had produced so much of his best work.

Significance

As master of Reims, Machaut enjoyed fame and prestige during his lifetime and remained a major figure for some time after his death. His real contribution, however, lies in his influence on other, later poets, not only in France but also in England. Not a true innovator (the fixed forms he favored had evolved in the work of others), he took the literary heritage in which he had been educated and adapted and reworked it, thus creating a synthesis of past and present. In one way or another, Machaut was indirectly responsible for several of the major developments in the verse narrative of the Middle Ages; his corpus of work includes early examples of the judgment poem, the poem of complaint against Fortune, the consolation poem, the Marguerite poem, the poem containing classical exempla, and the poem with an elderly man as narrator. He helped to introduce into lyric verse some elements—the woman's point of view, the psychology of dreams, the combination of allegory and autobiography—that would become commonplaces in the poetry of later eras. Yet many of his works represent nearly perfect manifestations of older genres that fell into disfavor soon after his death; among these are the lay, virelay, motet, and *dit amoreus*.

Le Dit dou Vergier (translated as part of the collection *The Fountain of Love . . . and Two Other Love Vision Poems*, 1993) is generally considered, on the basis of its style and allusions, to be Machaut's first long narrative poem. In the Prologue, Machaut describes his theory of poetry: Because poetry is language ornamented with rhyme and meter, it is allied to both music and rhetoric; its function should be lyrical, allegorical, didactic, and personal. Machaut clearly believed that poetry and music belonged together. Eustache Deschamps, the self-proclaimed disciple of Machaut (probably his nephew), re-elaborated Machaut's ideas in his *L'Art de dictier* (1392, art of the composer; English translation, 1994), in which he illustrated the interrelationship of music and poetry and the idea of poetry as song.

Praised by many medieval poets in various countries, Machaut was a major influence on Jean Froissart, Christine de Pizan, and certainly Geoffrey Chaucer, whose *The Book of the Duchess* (c. 1370) clearly derives in part from at least seven of Machaut's narrative poems, as well as from a few motets and at least one lay.

—*E. D. Huntley*

Further Reading

Brownlee, Kevin. *Poetic Identity in Guillaume de Machaut*. Madison: University of Wisconsin Press, 1984. An in-depth analysis of Machaut's prologue and his seven long narrative love poems, with special attention to Machaut's development of a distinct poetic identity. Includes informative notes to each chapter and a select bibliography.

Butterfield, Ardis. *Poetry and Music in Medieval France: From Jean Renart to Guillaume de Machaut*. New York: Cambridge University Press, 2002. Explores the world of poets, musicians, and composers in the time of Machaut, looking at song and the written record, song and performance, song and poetry, and sources of song. Includes an extensive bibliography and an index.

Caldwell, John. *Medieval Music*. Bloomington: Indiana University Press, 1978. A straightforward historical overview of Western music from about 950 to 1400. A chapter on fourteenth century French music provides a good introduction to Machaut's musical milieu and devotes several pages to a detailed discussion of Machaut's work, especially his handling of polyphony.

Calin, William. *A Poet at the Fountain: Essays on the Narrative Verse of Guillaume de Machaut*. Lexington: University Press of Kentucky, 1974. A series of essays examining the narrative verse of Machaut.

Cosman, Madeleine Pellner, and Bruce Chandler. *Machaut's World: Science and Art in the Fourteenth Century*. New York: New York Academy of Sciences, 1978. A collection of essays covering such topics as scientific thought, paper manufacturing, and Gothic architecture, all in the context of the fourteenth century that Machaut knew. The most valuable group of essays specifically discusses Machaut as a poet in the modern sense of the word, rather than as simply a poet-composer.

Davis, Steven. "Guillaume de Machaut, Chaucer's *Book of the Duchess*, and the Chaucer Tradition." *Chaucer Review* 36, no. 4 (2002). Discusses Machaut's influence on Chaucer, especially in Chaucer's writing of *The Book of the Duchess*.

De Looze, Laurence. *Pseudo-autobiography in the Fourteenth Century: Juan Ruiz, Guillaume de Machaut, Jean Froissart, and Geoffrey Chaucer*. Gainesville: University Press of Florida, 1997. Looks at Machaut in the context of autobiographical writings by his contemporaries in the Middle Ages.

Ehrhart, Margaret J. *The Judgment of the Trojan Prince Paris in Medieval Literature*. Philadelphia: University of Pennsylvania Press, 1987. A study of several medieval versions of the story of the Trojan prince Paris, his judgment of the rival goddesses, and the consequences of that judgment. Included in the study is a detailed analysis of Machaut's *La Fonteinne amoureuse*.

Huot, Sylvia. "Guillaume de Machaut and the Consolation of Poetry." *Modern Philology* 100, no. 2 (November, 2002): 169-196. A scholarly presentation of Machaut's work that argues that his literary work is modeled on that of the poet Boethius, but Machaut's writing uses a female allegory for Hope and consolation instead of Boethius's philosophy as consolation.

Robertson, Anne Walters. *Guillaume de Machaut and Reims: Context and Meaning in His Musical Works*. New York: Cambridge University Press, 2002. Historical look at the connections between Machaut's work and the influences of Reims. Includes an extensive bibliography and an index.

Wilkins, Nigel. Introduction to *La Louange des Dames*, by Guillaume de Machaut. New York: Barnes and Noble Books, 1973. Precedes a collection of Machaut's lyric poetry and musical settings. This introductory material, which is in English, contains valuable information on Machaut, including a good short biography, a bibliography of selected secondary sources, a chronology of Machaut's works and manuscript sources, and brief essays on Machaut's lyrics and his poetic form.

SEE ALSO: Adam de la Halle; Boethius; Cædmon; Guido Cavalcanti; Alain Chartier; Geoffrey Chaucer; Chrétien de Troyes; Christine de Pizan; Dhuoda; John Dunstable; Eleanor of Aquitaine; Jean Froissart; Gottfried von Strassburg; Hartmann von Aue; Francesco Landini; Marie de France; Johannes de Muris; Pérotin; Philippe de Vitry; Walther von der Vogelweide.

RELATED ARTICLES in *Great Events from History: The Middle Ages, 477-1453*: c. 1100: Rise of Courtly Love; August 26, 1346: Battle of Crécy; 1373-1410: Jean Froissart Compiles His *Chronicles*.

Maḥmūd of Ghazna

Muslim sultan of Ghazna (r. 997-1030)

Maḥmūd of Ghazna conquered and ruled over much of what is now Afghanistan, Eastern Iran, and Pakistan, and is known as the first Muslim sultan to plunder large areas of what is now India.

Born: c. 971; Ghazna, Central Asia (now Ghaznī, Afghanistan)
Died: 1030; Ghazna
Also known as: Maḥmūd of Ghaznin
Areas of achievement: Warfare and conquest, military

Early Life

Maḥmūd (MAWK-muhd) of Ghazna (GAWZ-naw) was born in the declining years of the Sāmānid Dynasty, based in Bukhara (now in Uzbekistan). Although the Sāmānid rulers asserted the value of Persian culture and language, they often relied on military conscripts from the Turkic tribes to their east.

Maḥmūd's father, Subüktigin, a former captured slave of Turkic descent who converted from Buddhism to Islam, eventually rose to the rank of general in the service of Alptigin, a Turkic provincial administrator for the Sāmānids. During a period of turmoil over succession to the Sāmānid throne, Alptigin and his general moved their forces to the south of the kingdom and established themselves in Ghazna in 962, but Alptigin died soon thereafter. Eventually, Subüktigin, whose continued military skill and personal dignity inspired the admiration of the nobility in Ghazna, was chosen to rule the city-state, which was nominally still part of the fading Sāmānid realm. His son Maḥmūd, only seven at the time, was almost immediately given administrative authorities. Maḥmūd had been trained in combat skills and had also been tutored in Islamic scripture, literature, and politics. He began to accompanying his father on military campaigns to defend and expand the territory of Ghazna, and he distinguished himself in battles against the Hindu ruler Jaipal—who ruled much of the neighboring Punjab region—and, later, against the governor of Khorāsān (now Eastern Iran), who rebelled against the Sāmānid authority.

Life's Work

As a reward for crushing the rebels in a decisive battle near Herāt (now in northwest Afghanistan), in 994, the Sāmānid ruler appointed Maḥmūd as the new governor of Khorāsān province, resulting in a significant expansion of his father Subüktigin's power. However, when Subüktigin died in 997, Maḥmūd became involved in a succession struggle of his own against his younger brother Ismāʿīl, who had been given the authority to rule their Ghazna homeland. Maḥmūd quickly defeated Ismāʿīl, and after imprisoning him, became, at age thirty, the ruler of an expanded Ghazna. In the meantime, a new Sāmānid ruler had given Maḥmūd's recently acquired Khorāsān province to the general Begtuzun, who imprisoned, blinded, and overthrew the new monarch. Begtuzun was defeated by Maḥmūd, who maintained his father's traditional loyalty to the Sāmānids in spite of the disappointment he had just experienced. Soon, however, in 999, the last major claimant to the remnants of the Sāmānid kingdom was conquered by the Ilak Khan of Kashghar, his neighbor to the east, and Maḥmūd became the emperor of a vast area covering much of central Asia and eastern Iran.

This very real political and material power was soon recognized by a respected authority in the Muslim world, the caliph in Baghdad, who gave Maḥmūd honorific titles and sent him a robe. Chronicles of the era mark this time as the official replacement of the Sāmānid Dynasty by Maḥmūd's Ghaznavid Dynasty (977-1186). A new phase in the career of Sultan Maḥmūd began, as he increasingly directed his campaigns to the south. He was able to use the legitimacy conferred on him by the caliph to rationalize his wars of conquest and plunder as "holy wars" against "heretics" (mostly Ismāʿīlī and other Shīʿite residents of these areas, whose interpretations of Islam differed from those of the caliphs in Baghdad), and "infidels" (Hindus, Buddhists, and other non-Muslim groups). A pattern emerged as he started a series of invasions of the Indian subcontinent. These invasions, which amounted to seventeen by the end of his reign, usually took place during the winter months. He alternated these invasions by defending attacks on his empire and from intrigues within.

Maḥmūd's first two invasions of the subcontinent constituted a renewal of his father's war with Jaipal, the raja (prince or chief) of the Punjab region (between northwest India and eastern Pakistan). In 1000, Maḥmūd captured some forts along his southern frontier, and in 1001, he returned, approaching the town of Peshawar with a huge army. Jaipal responded with an even larger army, but Maḥmūd defeated them and captured Jaipal, who, after paying ransom, immolated himself on a funeral pyre, following Rājput custom. Before his death, however, Jaipal

THE GHAZNAVID DYNASTY, 977-1186

Reign	*Ruler*
977-997	Subüktigin (Sāmānid governor)
997	Ismāʿīl
997-1030	MAḤMŪD OF GHAZNA
1001-1024	Invasions of India
1030-1031	Muḥammad
1031-1040	Masʿūd I
1040-1041	Muḥammad (second rule)
1041-1048	Mawdūd
1048	Masʿūd II
1048-1049	ʿAlī
1049-1052	ʿAbd al-Rashīd
1052-1059	Farrukhzād
1059-1099	Ibrāhīm
1099-1115	Masʿūd III
1115-1116	Shīrzād
1116-1117	Malik Arslan Shāh
1117	Seljuk occupation
1117-1150	Bahrām Shāh
1150-c. 1152	Ghūrid occupation
c. 1152-1157	Bahrām
1157-1160	Khusraw Shāh in Lahore
1160-1186	Khusraw Malik
1186	Ghūrid conquest

named his son Anandpal the new ruler, thus extending the old conflict into the next generation on both sides.

In 1004, Maḥmūd crossed the Indus River to attack the raja of Bhatiya (now Bhera, north Punjab), an independent city-state on the Jhelum River. After a ferocious battle lasting four days, Sultan Maḥmūd led a decisive charge into the defenders' ranks, and the raja killed himself in retreat from the city. On the way back to Ghazna, Maḥmūd, whose forces and supplies had been reduced, was attacked by the ruler of Multan. This ruler and many of his subjects were Ismāʿīlī Muslims, followers of the Carmathian beliefs, and therefore fierce enemies of the ʿAbbāsid caliph who had blessed Maḥmūd's activities. In 1005, Maḥmūd planned an expedition to avenge the previous years' attack and promote his own more orthodox branch of Islam. Anandpal came to Dāʿūd's aid, but was defeated, and Dāʿūd purchased peace with treasure and the promise to follow Sunni Muslim orthodoxy. Maḥmūd wanted to maintain Ghaznavid authority in the area and appointed Jaipal's grandson Sukhpal, a new convert to Islam, governor of the area before returning north.

This arrangement was short-lived. Sukhpal recanted, allying himself with his uncle Anandpal. Under Anandpal's leadership, the kingdoms of Northern and Central India, supported enthusiastically by their subjects, joined forces against the invader. After fighting a serious threat from his former ally Ilak Khan in Khorāsān, Maḥmūd returned in 1008 to fight the hosts assembled against him. An epic battle ensued, and Maḥmūd's army appeared to be losing, when a stroke of luck aided his victory: Anandpal's war elephant was startled by an explosion, became disoriented, plunged away from the battle, and carried the leader along. The allied Indian forces and rulers, who before the external threat emerged had been warring against each other, assumed Anandpal had deserted them, and the coalition collapsed in chaos. After Maḥmūd plundered the undefended Hindu temple at Nagarkot (Kangra) in the foothills of the Himalayas, Anandpal bargained for peace, thereby exposing his neighbors to Maḥmūd's power. Maḥmūd returned to Ghazna with treasure and slaves, continuing to build an army that included many members of the very Hindu and non-Sunni Muslim populations that he was supposedly converting. They were allowed to practice their own religions, and the Hindu Tilak became a trusted general in the service of Maḥmūd's son Masʿūd. To some extent, this was a continuation of the pattern of upward social mobility through military ranks that had resulted in Maḥmūd's own father's rise from captured slave to monarch. For such people, however, the price of survival and advancement was total obedience, including participation in attacks on their own cultures.

Maḥmūd continued to make deep but temporary incursions into India every few years, but annexed areas on his own borders. When Anandpal died, Maḥmūd fought against his grandson Nidar Bhim and eventually formed a permanent government in Lahore. He was frustrated in attempts to invade the mountainous region of Kashmir. However, in 1018, he swept across the plain along the Jamuna River and subdued the cities of Mahaban, Bulandshahr, and Mathura. His next-to-last campaign in India (1024-1026) was perhaps the most dramatic and risky. On the coast of Gujarat, where the Krishna River joins the Indian Ocean, was the great Śiva temple of Somnath, a site of ancient symbolic importance and held sacred by Hindus, who brought offerings from great distances. Maḥmūd had heard stories of the wealth of the temple. He traveled there by crossing the desert and swampland at great speed, and then attacked the city. After a desperate struggle of several days, he entered the temple and took the treasure, which is said to have surpassed the wealth of any other kingdom of his time. During his return, his forces were attacked by the Jats (Indo-

Aryans) of Multan, and his last invasion (1027) was to punish and enslave them.

His final years were spent fighting the Seljuk Turks to the west of his kingdom. During his reign, he had transferred a good part of the wealth of the northern subcontinent to Ghazna and spent lavishly on architecture, art, schools, and mosques until it became one of the most impressive capitals of the Islamic world. The culture of the court was largely inspired by his Sāmānid predecessors of northeastern Persia. The Persian poet Firdusi spent twenty-five years completing *Shahnamah* (c. 1010; the book of kings), an epic poem that glorified Maḥmūd and Persian history. Although Firdusi suffered mistreatment at court because of his Shīʿite religious beliefs, his poem is regarded as a classic of Persian literature. Another important scholar in the court of Maḥmūd was al-Bīrūnī, active in the fields of history, mathematics, languages, logic, and astronomy. He came to Ghazna before 1017 and learned Sanskrit from the Hindu pandits (wise men) of the court. His most famous work is *Kitāb-ul-Hind*, a detailed study of Hindu life and philosophy based on his personal observations and reading of Sanskrit texts. Al-Bīrūnī continued to serve in the court of Masʿūd after Maḥmūd's death in 1030.

Maḥmūd's personal qualities made up a complex mixture of ambition, tempered by practicality and bravery, tempered by caution. He often joined in on battles, which inspired his soldiers and exposed him to danger, and he accumulated battle wounds along with his treasure and slaves. He enjoyed drinking wine and sometimes fought with his own men over female slaves. However, military and political affairs were primary, and he hid his true feelings from those around him. Occasionally, some vulnerabilities emerged: he was self-conscious about his pockmarked face, and when he was dying of a consumptive illness, he is reported to have wept over a display of his many treasures.

Significance

Although he was credited by the caliphate of his day and by some later writers as a champion of Islam and as a destroyer of idols, Maḥmūd's personal goals appear to have been primarily political dominance, self-preservation, and the accumulation of wealth. His raids into the Indian subcontinent and destruction of Hindu temples provided a model for later invaders of Central Asia and a warning for subsequent generations of defenders. His administration continued to promote the use of the Persian language in elite circles of Central Asia, thus providing an alternative to Arabic in the Islamic world and helping to stimulate the development of Urdu and other languages of the northern subcontinent. In terms of ideology, his reign represented a continued shift away from the egalitarian spirit of early Islam and asserted the secular monarchy as an absolute power, in spite of his nominal allegiance to the caliphate.

—*John E. Myers*

Further Reading

Adams, W. H. Davenport. "Maḥmūd the Sultan." In *Warriors of the Crescent*. New York: Appleton, 1892. The substantial chapter on Maḥmūd includes interactions with other historical figures.

Flood, Finbarr Barry. "Between Cult and Culture: Bamiyan, Islamic Iconoclasm, and the Museum." *Art Bulletin* 84, no. 4 (December, 2002). Argues that the looting of the Somnath temple by Maḥmūd was part of a complex history, one that stands in stark contrast to the traditional argument that Maḥmūd's act was indicative of a Muslim iconophobia (fear of icons) against South Asian iconophilia (love of icons). Footnotes, photographs.

Habib, Mohammad. *Sultan Maḥmūd of Ghaznin*. 2d ed. Delhi: S. Chand, 1967. This well-written biography provides an overview of not only Maḥmūd's life but also the cultural and political context of the time in which he lived, including major developments in the centuries immediately before and after.

Meisami, Julie Scott. *Persian Historiography to the End of the Twelfth Century*. Edinburgh: Edinburgh University Press, 1999. Explores the writing of Persian-Iranian history during the time of the Sāmānid, Ghaznavid, and Seljuk dynasties. Also discusses Firdusi's *Shahnamah* as historical prose. Maps, bibliography, index.

Nazim, Muhammad. *The Life and Times of Sultan Maḥmūd of Ghazna*. Lahore, Pakistan: Khalil, 1971. A very detailed account, including a chapter on the sultan's political administrative structures, and appendices with Persian language sources. Map, bibliography, index.

Thapar, Romila. *Narratives and the Making of History*. New York: Oxford University Press, 2000. Includes a chapter that focuses on what many regard the most symbolic act of Maḥmūd's career: his destruction of the Hindu idol in the famous temple at Somnath. The author deconstructs various interpretations of the event. Bibliography, index.

Utbi, Abdul Nasr Muhammad bin Muhammad al Jabbar al. *Kitāb-i-Yamini*. Translated by James Reynolds.

1858. Reprint. Lahore, Pakistan: Qausain, 1975. The contemporary account of Maḥmūd's court historian, carefully translated, with copious notes.

SEE ALSO: Alp Arslan; al-Bīrūnī; Firdusi; Niẓām al-Mulk.

RELATED ARTICLES in *Great Events from History: The Middle Ages, 477-1453*: 834: Gypsies Expelled from Persia; 956: Oğhuz Turks Migrate to Transoxiana; 997-1030: Reign of Maḥmūd of Ghazna; 1010: Firdusi Composes the *Shahnamah*; 1040-1055: Expansion of the Seljuk Turks; 1193: Turkish Raiders Destroy Buddhist University at Nalanda; 1206-1210: Quṭ al-Dīn Aybak Establishes the Delhi Sultanate; 1299: ʿAlāʾ-ud-Dīn Muḥammad Khaljī Conquers Gujarat.

MOSES MAIMONIDES

Jewish scholar and philosopher

Maimonides was and remains one of the most influential Jewish philosophers in history. He classified Jewish law, life, and observance, as defined in the Torah, Mishnah, and Talmud; interpreted the philosophical bases of Judaism in the light of Aristotelian thought; established the early foundations of psychotherapy by combining study of medicine and psychology; and influences both Jewish and Christian thinking to this day.

BORN: March 30, 1135; Córdoba (now in Spain)
DIED: December 13, 1204; Cairo, Egypt
ALSO KNOWN AS: Moses ben Maimon (birth name); Abū ʿImrān Mūsa ibn Maymūn ibn ʿUbayd Allāh
AREAS OF ACHIEVEMENT: Religion and theology, philosophy, medicine

EARLY LIFE

Moses Maimonides (MOH-zehz mi-MAHN-uh-deez) was a child of destiny, recognized as such by the family and society into which he was born. His birth as son of the renowned Maimon ben Joseph was regarded as so important that the day, hour, and minute were recorded, as well as the fact that it occurred on the eve of Passover, which fell on the Sabbath. The young Maimonides (sometimes referred to as the Second Moses) was extraordinarily sensitive to his religious and intellectual heritage and to an awareness of his destiny—to be a leader of his people. As a result of this precocity, the child spent no time playing or attending to his physical health, lest such activities interfere with his life's mission.

Although Maimonides' boyhood and physical characteristics are not recorded, biographical accounts place much emphasis on his intellectual development. His major teacher was his father, who was a Talmudic scholar, a member of the Rabbinical Council, *dayan* (judge) of Córdoba (a position held for generations in the family), and an acknowledged scholar and writer in the areas of Bible exposition, Talmudic commentary, astronomy, and mathematics. The young boy's knowledge expanded from other sources as well: Jewish scholars, his relatively untroubled interactions with the life and scholars of the Spanish and Arab communities of Córdoba, and countless hours reading the manuscripts in his father's library. In turn, Maimonides, entrusted with the education of his younger brother, David, began to develop his classification skills as he transmitted his own knowledge to the younger boy.

When Maimonides was thirteen, the religiously fanatical Almohad faction captured Córdoba. Jews and Christians were initially forced to choose between apostasy and death but later were allowed the third option of emigration. Historical sources are unclear as to how long Maimonides' family remained in Córdoba, in what other cities they lived, or whether they formally converted or professed belief in the other monotheistic religion while continuing to practice Judaism. In their writings, both Maimonides and his father addressed the difficulties of living as a Jew and the minimum expectations afforded the still-practicing Jew in a hostile environment. Clearly, between 1148 and 1160, when the family settled in Fez in Morocco, Maimonides, in addition to his other activities, was collecting data for the three great works of his career.

In Fez, Maimonides studied medicine, read extensively, and wrote while his father and brother established a thriving jewelry business. While ostensibly involved with the Arabic community, the family remained faithfully Jewish. This period of accommodation with Muslim leaders and thought was broken by the prominence given to Maimonides' *Iggereth Hashemad* (c. 1162; letter concerning apostasy), which reassured the many Jews who were similarly accommodating to their environment. Because this leadership position thrust on Maimonides threatened the family's security, they emigrated to Palestine in 1165. After remaining five months in Acre, the family settled in Egypt, living first in Alexandria and then in Cairo.

During the family's stay in Alexandria, Maimonides' father died, and his brother David drowned. David's death was particularly grievous, as Maimonides wrote: "For a full year I lay on my couch, stricken with fever and despair." At the age of thirty, Maimonides began to support himself and David's wife and children financially by putting to use the medical career for which he had prepared during his years in Fez. Embarking on his dual career of Jewish scholarship and medicine, Maimonides made notable contributions that remain relevant and significant to the present day. His personal life remains obscure, but his letters indicate that his first wife died young. He remarried in 1184 and fathered both a girl and a boy, Abraham, who later followed in his father's path of scholarship and leadership. In fact, ten generations of the Maimonides family followed as leaders of the Cairo community.

LIFE'S WORK

Maimonides' twofold scholarly approach throughout his life was to examine existent knowledge in a field through classification followed by integration. In clear and succinct form, he would then publish the results, which had a major impact as each succeeding generation continued to find new, contemporaneous, and ever-relevant meanings in his writings.

The achievements of Maimonides, one of history's "men for all seasons," are broad and deep. He has been equally influential in four areas: religion, philosophy, psychology, and medicine. In the fields of religion and religious thought, Maimonides made his significant impact primarily through two major works: *Siraj* (1168; *The Illumination*) and *Mishneh Torah* (1180; *The Code of Maimonides*, 1927-1965). The first was written in Arabic, the second in Hebrew. *Siraj* is a commentary on the Mishnah, the early compilation of Jewish law. Maimonides' intent in this work was to clarify for Jews the complex discussion of law of which the Mishnah is composed and to provide an understandable framework of guidelines for living a life satisfactory to God. Probably the most important section of *The Illumination* is the statement of Maimonides' articles of faith, the basic principles of Judaism, which include the existence of a Creator, the unity of Deity, the incorporeality of God, the external nature of God, the worship and adoration of God alone, the existence of prophecy, the greatness of Moses as a prophet, the gift of the law to Moses by God on Sinai, the immutability of the law, the knowledge by God of the acts of humans, reward for the righteous and punishment for the wicked, the coming of the Messiah, and the resurrection of the dead.

The Code of Maimonides continues the explanation of Jewish law with a codification by subject of the content of the massive Talmud in fourteen books, each representing one area of Jewish law. The work begins with a statement of purpose, followed by book 1 on God and humans. It ends with a poetic longing for the Messianic Age, when "the earth will be filled with the knowledge of God as the waters cover the sea."

Maimonides' contributions to religion and religious thought overlap his contributions in philosophy. His major philosophical contribution, however, is *Dalālat al-ḥaʾirīn* (1190; *The Guide of the Perplexed*, 1881), in which he addresses and reconciles the rationalist Aristotelian philosophy with Jewish beliefs and faith. His treatments of philosophical constructs include discussions of God, Creation, prophecy, the nature of evil, Divine Providence, and the nature of humans and moral virtue.

Moses Maimonides. (The New York Academy of Medicine)

More than his other writings, *The Guide of the Perplexed* has become part of mainstream philosophy of all society rather than remaining unique to Judaism. One reason for its generalized significance may be that it represents the beginnings of psychotherapy. In the section on the nature of humans and moral virtue, Maimonides defines a life satisfactory to God as one that approaches happiness through development of intellect and control of appetites by morality, referring especially to control of the sexual drive. This work also represents a bridge between Maimonides' contribution in the second area, philosophy, and his major contributions to both the third and fourth areas, psychology and medicine.

In the study of medicine, Maimonides' significant contribution was in his clear, textbook descriptions of major areas of the discipline he describes metaphorically as one of the "strange women [in addition to his betrothed, the Torah] whom I first took into my house as her handmaids [and who have] become rivals and absorb a portion of my time." Maimonides' medical writings date between 1180 and 1200 and include most notably *A Physician's Prayer* (*The Medical Aphorisms of Moses Maimonides*, 1970, 1972), an encyclopedia, a glossary of drug names, treatises on asthma and poisons and their cures, and *Physiology and Psychology of Married Life*.

SIGNIFICANCE

Maimonides' contributions span and integrate history. His contributions begin with his scholarship in religion and religious thought that explores concepts and events from Creation to the giving of the Torah, to the canonization of prophetic thought in the Mishnah and the Talmud. His scholarship then moves to philosophical contributions that integrate the Jewish world of antiquity with the Greek world of Aristotle and with the Arabic worlds of Spain and Egypt of the twelfth century. In his contributions to psychology and medicine, Maimonides foreshadows modern practices in healing and Freudian thought.

History shaped Maimonides' insights as he codified and synthesized Jewish literature. In turn, Maimonides guided the insights of his contemporaries and those of succeeding generations as he responded to the realities of medieval Spain and the traditions of Aristotle, developing a new blend of faith and rationalistic thought. He influenced the thought of succeeding scholars by providing new religious, philosophical, psychological, and medical foundations on which to build the concept of a good life.

—June H. Schlessinger and Bernard Schlessinger

FURTHER READING

Amundsen, Darrel W., ed. *Medicine, Society, and Faith in the Ancient and Medieval Worlds*. Baltimore: Johns Hopkins University Press, 1996. Covers the connections between medicine and religious faith, canon law on medical practice, medical ethics, and more.

Arbel, Ilil. *Maimonides: A Spiritual Biography*. New York: Crossroad, 2001. A brief biographical introduction to Maimonides as a rabbi and Jewish philosopher. Includes a bibliography and an index.

Bratton, Fred. *Maimonides: Medieval Modernist*. Boston: Beacon Press, 1967. Acquaints the Christian world with the life and works of Maimonides from the viewpoint of a Christian. This easy-to-follow text places Maimonides in perspective in the environment of medieval Spain and evaluates the scholar's writings in relation to their impact on the Jewish-Christian worlds and European thought.

Cohen, Robert S., and Hillel Levine, eds. *Maimonides and the Sciences*. Boston: Kluwer Academic, 2000. A survey of Maimonides' Aristotelianism, naturalism, "repudiation of astrology," epistemology, and science of language. Includes a bibliography and an index.

Katchen, Aaron L. *Christian Hebraists and Dutch Rabbis: Seventeenth Century Apologetics and the Study of Maimonides' "Mishneh Torah."* Cambridge, Mass.: Harvard University Press, 1984. Concentrates on seventeenth century Holland, in which the *Mishneh Torah* began to be translated and distributed widely. Included are an extensive bibliography and indexes to biblical passages from specific works, to specific titles from the Mishnah, to the Babylonian Talmud, to the Midrashic literature, and to other general literature.

Katz, Steven T., ed. *Maimonides: Selected Essays*. New York: Arno Press, 1980. Part of the Jewish Philosophy, Mysticism, and the History of Ideas series, this volume contains reprints of fourteen essays in four languages. Together, the essays represent the best of pre-World War II scholarship on Maimonides' writings.

Kreisel, Howard. *Maimonides' Political Thought: Studies in Ethics, Law, and the Human Ideal*. Albany: State University of New York Press, 1999. A discussion of Maimonides' legal and political ideas, including those on the intellect, the idea of "the good," ethics, and the "love and fear of god." Includes an extensive bibliography and an index.

Maimonides, Moses. *Rambam: Readings in the Philosophy of Moses Maimonides*. Translated by Lenn Evan Goodman. New York: Viking Press, 1976. This careful translation and commentary on Maimonides' *The Guide of the Perplexed* and *Eight Chapters* (part of the commentary on the Mishnah) is also valuable for its long and helpful general introduction and for its annotated bibliography.

Neusner, Jacob, ed. *Collected Essays on Philosophy and on Judaism*. 3 vols. Lanham, Md.: University Press of America, 2003. Vol. 1 discusses Maimonides and Greek philosophy. Part of the Studies in Judaism series.

Roth, Leon. *Spinoza, Descartes, and Maimonides*. New York: Russell and Russell, 1963. An excellent exposition of the thinking of Maimonides, especially in his *The Guide of the Perplexed*, in relation to the writings of Baruch Spinoza. Although the book supposedly focuses on Spinoza, the author notes strongly that Maimonides influenced not only Spinoza but also "the course of European speculation," from Saint Albertus Magnus and Thomas Aquinas to G. W. F. Hegel.

Seeskin, Kenneth. *Searching for a Distant God: The Legacy of Maimonides*. New York: Oxford University Press, 2000. Discusses the far-reaching influence of Maimonides' work in religious philosophy. Chapters cover "the urge to philosophize," monotheism, monotheism and freedom, creation, and more. Includes a bibliography and an index.

Yellin, David, and Israel Abrahams. *Maimonides: His Life and Works*. 1903. 3d ed. New York: Hermon Press, 1972. A complete treatment of the life of Maimonides. Noteworthy are the still-valuable selected bibliography of books by and about Maimonides in English, the extensive notes, and the genealogical table of Maimonides' descendants through four generations.

See also: Saint Albertus Magnus; Arnold of Villanova; Averroës; Ibn Gabirol; Levi ben Gershom; Moses de León; Naḥmanides; Thomas Aquinas.

Related articles in *Great Events from History: The Middle Ages, 477-1453*: c. 950: Court of Córdoba Flourishes in Spain; c. 1150: Moors Transmit Classical Philosophy and Medicine to Europe; 1190: Moses Maimonides Writes *The Guide of the Perplexed*; c. 1265-1273: Thomas Aquinas Compiles the *Summa Theologica*; c. 1275: The *Zohar* Is Transcribed; 1290-1306: Jews Are Expelled from England, France, and Southern Italy.

Margaret of Denmark, Norway, and Sweden

Danish-born queen of Denmark, Norway, and Sweden (1376-1412)

Margaret was the first to unite Scandinavia (through the Kalmar Union) under one sovereign ruler and the first ruling queen of Denmark, Norway, and Sweden.

Born: 1353; Søborg, Denmark
Died: October 28, 1412; Flensburg, Denmark
Also known as: Margaret I
Area of achievement: Government and politics

Early Life

Born in 1353, Margaret was the younger daughter of King Valdemar IV Atterdag of Denmark and Queen Hedevig (the sister of the duke of Slesvig). Betrothed at the age of six to Hákon VI of Norway, born in 1340, she became his wife in 1363, when she was ten and he twenty-three.

She did not go to the court at Akershus until she was sixteen, however, but spent her early married years in Norway in the household of Märta, the married daughter of the Swedish Saint Brigit, a mystic visionary and the founder of a monastic order. At Märta's house, Margaret must have heard daily of political happenings in all the Scandinavian kingdoms, for Brigit was somewhat of a celebrity, better known than any other Scandinavian citizen. Her children similarly were well traveled, educated, and cosmopolitan. Margaret in her later life worked tirelessly for Brigit's canonization, accomplished in 1391.

Margaret's son Olaf was born in 1370, when she was seventeen, a year after she joined Hákon at the Norwegian court. When Olaf was five, Valdemar IV Atterdag died. Then only twenty-two, Margaret persuaded the council of state to elect Olaf king with herself as regent, even though her sister's son Albert of Mecklenburg was the logical heir as son of the elder daughter. The Danish council did not like the Germans, however, and had many quarrels with the Prussian nobility. War with Mecklenburg and Holstein followed, but Albert was defeated. On the death of her husband, Hákon, in 1380, Margaret managed to secure Olaf's election as king of Norway (he was only ten years old), again with herself as regent. By this time, she was only twenty-seven years old.

Some background should be remembered for fourteenth century Scandinavia. Denmark, Norway, and Sweden had been isolated from the rest of Europe for a thousand years, developing a culture of their own, free from the influences of both Rome and the Teutonic cultures of Germany. They had produced one of the world's great literatures (that of the Nordic sagas), and women had a social position they had nowhere else. Scandinavians practiced rotation of crops, invented their own system of writing (runes), and discovered new lands in the West. Feudalism came to these cultures very late, and the system that developed in Scandinavia had no serfdom, no lifetime service to an overlord. Instead, all three countries were unified kingdoms from early in their history; military service was owed to the monarch not by the person but by the district. Laws had more than a local application, because the whole of each kingdom was united and easily connected by water transportation.

Margaret of Denmark, Norway, and Sweden. (R. S. Peale and J. A. Hill)

The fourteenth century, however, was disastrous for Scandinavia. The cities of the Hanseatic League (an assembly of German trading towns), as well as the various northern German states such as Holstein and Mecklenburg, conquered much of the wealthiest Scandinavian territory—Skåne (in Sweden), the islands of Bornholm and Gotland, the Baltic states, and Slesvig (part of the Jutland peninsula).

Worse, the Black Death was particularly difficult for sparsely populated Norway and Sweden. Brought to Bergen by ship in 1349, the plague killed one-third to one-half of the population before the end of the century. By 1400, there were only sixty of the more than three hundred noble families remaining in Norway. Farms lay in ruin, crops were neither planted nor harvested, the clergy death rate left parishes without religious leadership, and famine and poverty were everywhere. A letter exists from young Queen Margaret written to Håkon in 1370, in which she begs for basic provisions for herself and the servants.

> You must know, my lord, that I and my servants suffer and are in dire need for lack of food and drink, so that neither they nor I get the necessities. And so I beg you that you will find some way out so that things may improve and that those who are with me shall not leave me on account of hunger.

Members of the royalty were often in straitened circumstances for years. Håkon's mother, Queen Blanche, for example, left at her death only some linens for bed and table, a few spices, and "a few table knives and four silver spoons."

Margaret's father, Valdemar IV Atterdag, was called "another day" because of his characteristic expression and the "new day" he brought in for Denmark. After twelve years without a king, under the chaos of the rule of the German dukes, he reunified the country, bought back lost land (such as Gotland), and made favorable treaties with Hanseatic cities such as Lübeck. Margaret continued his policies and strengthened the monarchy.

LIFE'S WORK

Margaret's great achievement was the uniting of all Scandinavia under one sovereign. Olaf died suddenly at the age of seventeen in 1387. With no clear heir, only Margaret remained—and no woman had ever been queen. Nevertheless, in preference to Albert of Mecklenburg, she was chosen "all-powerful lady and mistress," regent of Denmark and Norway, with the right to name her successor.

In Norway, a disaffected faction reported that Olaf was not dead. The impostor claimed the crown and gained followers by revealing information that only Olaf and Margaret could know. Margaret hurried to Norway and proved that the impostor was the son of Olaf's nurse by showing that he did not have a large wart on his back, Olaf's birthmark. The false Olaf was tortured and burned at the stake.

Soon Margaret named her grandnephew Erik of Pomerania as her successor; both the Norwegian and the Danish clergy and nobility agreed with this move. In Sweden, the nobles opposing King Albert, led by Birger, Brigit's son and Märta's brother, called on Margaret for assistance. She accepted on the condition that she be made queen of Sweden. Albert had insulted Margaret, calling her "a king without breeches" and the "abbot's concubine," as well as claiming both Denmark and Norway for himself. He also sent her a hone to sharpen her needles, swearing not to put on his nightcap until she surrendered.

The battle lines were drawn for civil war in Sweden. In September, 1388, the Battle of Falköping was fought, with about twelve thousand men on each side. Both sides incurred great losses, but in the end, Margaret's forces were victorious; both Albert and his son Erik were captured. When the prisoners were brought before her, she had Albert fitted for a paper nightcap that was 17 meters (19 yards) long, proportioned to his verbal offenses. He was imprisoned in Skåne for seven years. Margaret was now the undisputed queen of Sweden as well as of Norway and Denmark.

Sweden, too, accepted Erik of Pomerania, and in 1397 Kalmar, Sweden, was the site for a gala coronation ceremony. Erik was crowned king of all the Scandinavian countries by the archbishops of Uppsala and Lund. At the same time, Margaret called together a large group of nobles and clergy from all three countries, and together they drafted an arrangement for a closer union of the three governments. The resulting document had three articles. The first provided that the three kingdoms should have the same king, to be chosen successively by each of the kingdoms. The second article decreed that the monarch divide his time equally among the three kingdoms. The third article directed that each kingdom should continue its own laws, customs, and councils, but that foreign alliances concluded with one country would be binding on all three, that all must aid the others in time of war, and that banishment or treason in one country would be treated the same way in all.

Nevertheless, the document, called the Kalmar Union, is inconsistent. The six parchment copies called for do not exist; they seem never in fact to have been drawn. The single copy extant is on paper, not parchment, and has only ten seals, instead of the requisite seventeen. These wax seals are stamped on the paper, rather than attached to the document. Perhaps this copy is a draft, and the others were never agreed on or made. There are no Norwegian seals at all, and only three Danish ones. Scholars continue to debate the issue, wondering who exactly was opposed to the union and for what reasons. Despite these problems, the union existed de facto for the lifetimes of Margaret and Erik, and the union of Denmark and Norway continued until 1814.

Margaret continued to consolidate and strengthen her power. She kept close, personal contact with all levels of government in the three kingdoms and was an indefatigable traveler, spending more time away from Denmark than at home. She appointed administrators and bishops, having them serve away from their home countries in order to strengthen their personal loyalty to her. The

MONARCHS OF DENMARK, NORWAY, AND SWEDEN, 1375-1523

Reign	*Ruler*
1375-1387	Olaf (V of Denmark, of Norway)
1376-1412	MARGARET I OF DENMARK, NORWAY, AND SWEDEN
1380	Unification of Denmark and Norway
1397	Kalmar Union (joins Norway, Denmark, and Sweden)
1412-1439	Eric (VII of Denmark, III of Norway, XIII of Sweden)
1439-1448	Christopher (III of Denmark)
1448-1481	Christian I of Oldenburg
1481-1513	Hans/John (II of Sweden)
1513-1523	Christian II
1523	Gustavus I Vasa founds independent Swedish line

Danehof, or Danish Assembly, was never called, since she made decisions personally. She continued to win back the Danish lands lost to German states, through battle, treaty, or outright purchase. She negotiated marriage contracts to strengthen alliances, first Erik's marriage to Philippa, daughter of Henry IV of England, and later a marriage treaty with Bavaria. Nevertheless, she remained steadfastly neutral in the bloody wars between England and France and in other European conflicts.

Margaret transformed the coinage, minting coins of pure silver rather than of copper, thus strengthening the Crown's economic position. Even though she had inherited heavy debts from her father, after 1385 her economic situation was markedly improved when she regained the Swedish castles in Skåne. Earlier, she had had to borrow from the bishop of Roskilde; now, she was able to make large donations of money and property to the Church. According to some scholars, these gifts were cleverly arranged, however, so that the property reverted to the Crown after a certain income had accrued. In any event, she was well loved for her generosity to religious establishments such as the motherhouse of the Brigittine order at Vadstena, Sweden.

Margaret's last years were especially concerned with the perennial problem of regaining lost Danish territory in Slesvig. In 1412, not yet sixty years old, she died suddenly, probably of the plague, on board her ship in Flensburg harbor in Slesvig after she had been welcomed into the city and negotiations had begun.

SIGNIFICANCE

Called the "Semiramis of the North" after the queen of Babylon, Margaret was one of the strongest monarchs of the three kingdoms. She had a gift for avoiding strife and persuading factions to come to terms under her strong leadership. She managed to influence public opinion in controversial matters, such as heavy taxes and the appointment of Germans to administrative posts. Tactful but assertive, she could be charming even while ruthless. She was restrained and lovable, knowing how to keep both the Church and the nobility happy. She used her considerable resources to strengthen the kingdoms by means of alliances and contributions and kept clear of expensive foreign wars.

Margaret's achievement at a time when all Scandinavia was being threatened by German cultural and economic domination was to unite the kingdoms and not only hold back the Germans but also regain lands lost to the south. At the time of her death, the Scandinavian Union was by far the most powerful force in the Baltic; it was also the second largest accumulation of European territory under a single sovereign. It is not too much to say that she almost single-handedly kept Scandinavia independent at a time when the kingdoms could easily have been made subservient to various German states.

—*Margaret McFadden*

FURTHER READING

Andersson, Ingvar. *A History of Sweden*. 2d ed. Translated by Carolyn Hannay and Alan Blair. New York: Praeger, 1970. The chapter titled "The Union of Kalmar" deals with the subject from the Swedish perspective, giving much detail about the controversy surrounding the document.

Derry, T. K. *A History of Scandinavia*. Minneapolis: University of Minnesota Press, 1979. This work is particularly good on social and cultural history. Chapter 3 deals with Margaret and the Kalmar Union and gives a contextual discussion on life in the Middle Ages. Includes maps, genealogical tables, and a helpful time line of parallel events in the Scandinavian countries. Excellent bibliography.

Duggan, Anne J., ed. *Queens and Queenship in Medieval Europe*. Rochester, N.Y.: Boydell Press, 1997. Papers from a conference that explore the reigns of several queens of the European Middle Ages, with a chapter on the queens of Scandinavia. Includes a bibliography and an index.

Jochens, Jenny M. "Denmark." In *Dictionary of the Middle Ages*. Vol. 4. New York: Scribner, 1984. This helpful article gives a historical overview of Denmark in the medieval period, focusing on political history and connections between the Scandinavian countries. A bibliographical essay surveys scholarly work in English and Scandinavian languages.

Larsen, Karen. *A History of Norway*. 1948. Reprint. Princeton, N.J.: Princeton University Press, 1974. A good source on Norway, this study is particularly helpful on the social-historical context. Chapters 9 and 10 cover the years of Margaret's reign, evaluating her somewhat negatively from the Norwegian perspective. Good bibliography.

Scott, Franklin D. "Margareta and the Union of Kalmar." In *Sweden: The Nation's History*. Carbondale: Southern Illinois University Press, 1988. Discusses Margaret and the Kalmar Union as seen by Sweden. Includes maps, bibliography, and index.

_______. "A Saint and a Queen: Two Indomitable Figures of the Fourteenth Century." In *Scandinavian Studies*, edited by Carl F. Bayerschmidt and Erik J.

Friis. Seattle: University of Washington Press, 1965. One of the few scholarly articles on Margaret available in English. Discusses Margaret and Saint Brigit, focusing on the international and Scandinavian values that each espoused and the many connections between the two women.

Sinding, Paul C. *History of Scandinavia: From the Early Times of the Norsemen and Vikings to the Present Day*. 9th ed. New York: Author, 1867. This study has more detailed information on Margaret, in chapters 2 and 3, than do most other texts. Each chapter begins with an outline, making it easy to find topics.

See also: Saint Brigit; Henry IV (of England); Valdemar II.

Related articles in *Great Events from History: The Middle Ages, 477-1453*: c. 1150-1200: Rise of the Hansa Merchant Union; 1347-1352: Invasion of the Black Death in Europe; June 17, 1397: Kalmar Union Is Formed.

Marie de France

French poet

The earliest known French woman poet, Marie de France is still admired for her narrative and poetic skill and for her psychological insight.

Born: c. 1150; Île de France
Died: c. 1215; England?
Area of achievement: Literature

Early Life

Marie de France's (mah-ree deh frahns) identity is still a matter of conjecture. Her name is known because in an epilogue to *Fables* (after 1170; English translation, 1983) she said, "My name is Marie, and I come from France." It has been pointed out that during the twelfth century, "France" was actually the Île de France, the area within the rivers around Paris, as opposed, for example, to Normandy. The phrase "from France" and other evidence indicate that she was not living in France when she composed her works; it is fairly clear that she was in England, and that the king to whom she dedicated *Lais* (c. 1167; *Lays of Marie de France and Other French Legends*, 1911, better known as *The Lays*) was Henry II of England.

Marie de France was almost certainly a member of the nobility. She was well read and knew English and Latin as well as her native French. She was influenced by Ovid, and she claimed to have taken her fables from those of Alfred the Great; regardless of whether she actually did, she was familiar with earlier English literature. Beyond this, conjecture begins. Scholars have suggested that she might have been the abbess of Reading, a noble lady in Herefordshire, or a countess. Some evidence exists that she could have been the abbess of Shaftesbury, King Henry's illegitimate half sister, the daughter of Geoffrey Plantagenet. There has been much speculation as to the identity of the "Count William" to whom *Fables* is dedicated, but because the name was so popular at Henry's court, that clue has not been helpful. At any rate, because her work does not include any borrowings from the influential Chrétien de Troyes, it is assumed that her first poems, the *lais* (lays), were composed in the latter part of the 1160's.

Because so little is known about her life, her personality must be deduced from her work. She is a member of the privileged classes, compassionate toward her inferiors but impatient with their attempts to rise above their proper station. Highly intelligent, she is gifted also with the common sense evident in her second work, *Fables*, and with the insight into human nature, which can be seen in *The Lays*.

Life's Work

Marie de France's first work was a group of twelve *lais*, or narrative poems retold from stories, many of Celtic origin, which she had probably heard sung by Breton bards. Generally they are either set in Brittany or attributed to a Breton source. Marie de France formulated her own structure for these poems: a prologue, the story, and an epilogue, all in octosyllabic couplets. *The Lays* vary in length from one hundred to one thousand lines. Their theme is the power of love, which sometimes shapes lives for good, sometimes for bad. The stories include temptation, infidelity, treachery, seduction, betrayal, frustration, imprisonment, suffering, and death, as well as fidelity, forgiveness, and reunion. In addition to the thematic unity, the stories are unified by the voice of the poet, a realist who reveals the subtle differences among her characters, despite the similarity of the intensity of their passions.

MAJOR WORKS BY MARIE DE FRANCE

Date	Work
c. 1167	*Lais* (*The Lays*)
After 1170	*Ysopet* (*Fables*)
1208-1215	*Espurgatoire Saint Patriz*

The Lays have been divided between those that are realistic and those that draw on folklore or in some way include supernatural elements. Sometimes the realistic stories end sadly, sometimes happily. "La Fraisne," for example, ends with a young girl's reunion with the mother who had abandoned her; "Milun," with the marriage of the lovers and their reunion with their son. "Chaitivel" and "Les Dous Amanz," on the other hand, end in bitterness and death.

Interestingly, adulterous loves are treated sympathetically in some stories and unsympathetically in others. "Chievrefueil" is a touching story of a brief, idyllic tryst between the queen of Cornwall and her banished Tristan. In "Laostic," too, the sympathy is with the lovers, not with the old husband. The scheming lovers in "Équitan" on the other hand are scalded to death. In "Eliduc," the faithful mate, in this case the wife, is the sympathetic character. Nobly desiring her husband's happiness, she retires to a convent so that he can be with the princess he loves. Later, both Eliduc and his new wife follow the first wife's lead and give up human love for divine.

Although the supernatural tales will support some interesting symbolic or allegorical analyses, on the surface they deal with the same problems and passions as the realistic lays. The hero of "Bisclavret" is a werewolf with a wife just as treacherous as the wife in "Équitan," and as the faithful mate, he is rewarded. True love, however, is not necessarily marital love. In three other lays, the supernatural forces are on the side of true love. In "Guigemar," a magic boat brings a lover to a lady whose husband has locked her up; in "Yonec," a lover comes to an imprisoned wife as a falcon and even fathers a child, who grows up to kill the cruel husband. In "Lanvel," it is a supernatural lady who rescues her knight and carries him off to Avalon, where Guinevere cannot endanger his life with false accusations. Whether realistic or supernatural, the poems of *The Lays* were particularly significant; instead of the artificial patterns of courtly love, they dramatized the play of overpowering passions that could persist through suffering, absence, and death. If there was danger in such emotions, there was also sometimes grandeur.

Marie de France's next work, *Fables*, was quite different in tone. Whether her source was really Alfred the Great, as she claimed, or some other writer in the tradition of Aesop, Marie de France made the materials her own, much as she had done with the Breton lays. Her collection consists of 102 fables, ranging in length from eight lines to more than one hundred. Like *The Lays*, the tales are told in octosyllabic rhymed couplets. There is a standard format: After a general statement, the story is told, and the poem concludes with a moral.

While the romantic *lais* had been limited to love among the upper classes, *Fables* dealt with every social class. Nevertheless, Marie de France emphasized the importance of hierarchy, as in fable 15, when an ass mimics the dog by jumping on his master. The moral is that one should stay in one's own station. In fable 38, a flea thanks a camel for a ride to his destination and even offers to return a favor. Like the flea, the poet said, when the poor get close to the rich, they overestimate their own importance.

On the other hand, Marie de France gave practical advice to all levels of society, as in fable 47, in which she warned that one should be careful in legal matters, or in fable 74, in which she showed the way that the arrogant bring about their own downfall. Her compassion for victims of injustice is evident in fable 4, in which a dog sues a sheep and by his clever lies deprives the innocent sheep first of his wool and then of his life. Most of the fables, however, are not so pessimistic. Their very structure suggests that humans can learn to live more wisely as well as more safely. If humans use their reason, they will understand that society is a whole, functioning properly only when every element in it is treated justly. Fable 27 is the story of the man who refused to give his stomach some food, only to discover that neither his hands nor his feet could perform their proper functioning without the help of the organ he had despised.

Marie de France's final work was *Espurgatoire Saint Patriz* (English translation, 1894), which has been dated as being begun in 1208 and finished in 1215. Written in the same couplet form as her other works, *Espurgatoire Saint Patriz* is based on a Latin work written by an English monk, Henry of Salisbury, whose popularity is demonstrated by the fact that Marie de France's version is only one of seven that appeared during the period. In taking an Irish knight through Purgatory, this kind of story anticipates Dante's *La divina commedia* (c. 1320; *The Divine Comedy*, 1802). As her final work, it illustrates the intellectual depth and versatility that place her among the finest poets of the twelfth century.

SIGNIFICANCE

Despite the paucity of biographical details about Marie de France, her fame as a writer has never diminished since her lifetime, when, as one of her contemporaries attested, *The Lays* brought her popular success. That *Fables* also was popular is evidenced by the fact that it is preserved in no less than twenty-three manuscripts.

It would be difficult to overestimate Marie de France's influence on later writers. From the thirteenth to the fifteenth centuries, *Fables* was translated or adapted frequently. In fact, as Mary Lou Martin pointed out, for several centuries it was *Fables* for which she was best known. She is also credited with inventing or refining the *lai* form, however, and although her poems in that genre were the models for all the later lays, critics believe that her poems were never surpassed by those of her successors. With the development of Romanticism in the late eighteenth century, writers such as Johann Wolfgang von Goethe rediscovered *The Lays*; they are now generally considered Marie de France's most significant production. Certainly they are emphasized by today's critics, who find a depth of symbolic meaning beneath their deceptively simple surface.

Marie de France should be remembered as the first woman writing in French whose name is now known. Her importance, however, is not merely historical. Because of her knowledge of human nature, her skill in storytelling, and her poetic genius, she deserves recognition not only as an early woman writer but also as one of the finest poets, woman or man, of the medieval period.

—Rosemary M. Canfield Reisman

FURTHER READING

Bloch, R. Howard. *The Anonymous Marie de France.* Chicago: University of Chicago Press, 2003. Argues that Marie de France was a writer of profound importance and significance, a "Joyce of the twelfth century." Includes notes and an index.

Crosland, Margaret. *Women of Iron and Velvet: French Women Writers After George Sand.* New York: Taplinger, 1976. Despite the seeming limits of the title, in the second chapter the author discusses Marie de France from a feminist perspective, thus providing a different view of her importance.

Damon, S. Foster. "Marie de France: Psychologist of Courtly Love." *PMLA* 44 (Spring, 1929): 968-996. An outstanding study of the subject, structured as a systematic analysis of the similarities and differences among the characters in the various *lais*.

Donovan, Mortimer J. *The Breton Lay: A Guide to Varieties.* Notre Dame, Ind.: University of Notre Dame Press, 1969. Includes an initial chapter on Marie de France, which is followed by other chapters detailing the later development of the lay form. Contains useful plot summaries of *The Lays*.

Ferrante, Joan M. *Woman as Image in Medieval Literature: From the Twelfth Century to Dante.* New York: Columbia University Press, 1975. Argues that Marie de France's lays, in which an imprisoned woman invents or calls forth an ideal lover, indicate the power of the female imagination.

Ferrante, Joan M., et al., eds. *In Pursuit of Perfection: Courtly Love in Medieval Literature.* Port Washington, N.Y.: Kennikat Press, 1975. Discussion of Marie de France in this book is brief, but the author includes an argument that "Eliduc" represents Marie de France's rejection of the tradition of courtly love. The various essays provide a good, general background for the study of medieval literature on love.

Holmes, Urban Tigner, Jr. *A History of Old French Literature: From the Origins to 1300.* Rev. ed. New York: Russell and Russell, 1962. One of the authoritative books on medieval literature. An assessment of the merits of various opinions, helping the reader make sound judgments.

Larsen, Anne R., and Colette H. Winn, eds. *Writings by Pre-Revolutionary French Women: From Marie de France to Elizabeth Vigée-Le Brun.* New York: Garland, 2000. Translations of Marie de France's "Chievrefueil," "Laostic," and "Bisclavret."

Martin, Mary Lou. *The Fables of Marie de France: An English Translation.* Birmingham, Ala.: Summa, 1984. The translator's fine introduction to this book provides an interesting thematic analysis of the fables as well as a discussion of their literary reputation.

SEE ALSO: Boethius; Cædmon; Guido Cavalcanti; Charles d'Orléans; Alain Chartier; Geoffrey Chaucer; Chrétien de Troyes; Christine de Pizan; Dante; Eleanor of Aquitaine; Firdusi; Guillaume de Machaut.

RELATED ARTICLES in *Great Events from History: The Middle Ages, 477-1453*: c. 1100: Rise of Courtly Love; c. 1306-1320: Dante Writes *The Divine Comedy.*

SIMONE MARTINI
Italian artist

Martini, the first painter to be knighted, expanded on the French Gothic style through his innovative painting techniques and sophisticated use of color, techniques that highlighted, in part, expressivity, emotionality, and three-dimensionality.

BORN: c. 1284; Siena, Republic of Siena (now in Italy)
DIED: 1344; Avignon, Provence, France
AREA OF ACHIEVEMENT: Art

EARLY LIFE

Simone Martini was born in a section of Siena known as San Egidio. Little is known about his parents, but it is believed that he had a brother, Donato, who was also his student. It is probable that Martini spent the first years of his life in Siena and received his early training in the studio of Duccio di Buoninsegna, the master painter of the city. Yet no record of Martini's early training has been found, and historians know little of his life before 1315. In that year, Martini produced a masterpiece, the Siena *Maestà*, a work so advanced in technique and so important politically—it was placed in the council chamber of the Palazzo Pubblico (city hall) in Siena—that it has fostered an ongoing search for Martini's apprenticeship works. Art historians suspect that several other works, including *Christ Blessing* and *Saint John the Evangelist*, also date from that period.

Other attempts have been made to locate Martini's presumed lost earlier works by tracing his connection with Duccio. Four years earlier, in 1311, Duccio had painted a *Maestà* of his own in the cathedral and naturally expected to receive the commission for city hall. Still others, because of the unusual French Gothic style of Martini's paintings, have sought in vain to find evidence that he spent his early life in France. It is generally agreed that the Italian historian Giorgio Vasari is in error in assigning Martini's training to the school of Giotto in Siena; Vasari's claim that Martini was the pupil of his father-in-law Memmo di Filippuccio is also believed to be false.

When Martini was thirty-three, he was invited to the Angevin court of Naples, where he was granted a yearly payment of fifty ounces of gold and where, on July 23, 1317, he was knighted, the first painter in history to be so honored.

LIFE'S WORK

Martini lived at a time when the Byzantine style flourished in Italy under the guidance of the master painters Giotto (of Florence) and Duccio (of Siena). Because Siena and Florence were flourishing cities with rapid economic growth, they became cultural centers as well, attracting writers and artists eager to engage the budding ideals of the Italian Renaissance. Florence, the larger and more progressive city, became a tourist and industrial center. It was known particularly for its modeling and enormous art productivity. Siena, locked deep in the Tuscan hills without natural resources, was not suited for industry but survived on banking and trade. For years, the Sienese were the pope's bankers, a fact that may have helped Martini establish contacts outside his isolated city. In the world of art, Siena became known for its decorative detail and its daring, innovative style.

The so-called Sienese school, of which Martini was a leading figure, thrived for more than 150 years. Few of the early Sienese paintings survive, but one of the earliest is a dossal dated 1215, heavily wrought with a gold-covered surface, called *Blessing Christ and Six Scenes*. Then came the work of such well-known artists as Nicola Pisano, Guido da Siena, Giotto, Duccio, Martini, the Lorenzetti brothers (Pietro and Ambrogio), and Barna of Siena. Following this great flourishing of painters, the Siena school became suddenly, mysteriously quiet.

The influence of the two leading painters of the time, Giotto and Duccio, can be seen clearly in Martini's art. From Giotto, he derived a sort of Gothic freedom; from Duccio, he learned structural technique. Martini's work represents a rather radical shift from the Greco-Roman-Byzantine style from which all painters were struggling to free themselves (a shift neither of the two other painters could achieve) toward a newly emerging, humanistic style. His art, therefore, is a struggle of its own, an attempt to break loose from the restrictions of the physical canvas into a visual essence of being. He was at the same time trying to wean himself from the power of his early teacher Duccio, straining to achieve an independent, vibrant style.

Martini's earliest known painting, the great *Maestà* fresco in the Siena city hall, incorporates both the Gothic and the humanistic. The Gothic style is characterized by greater emphasis on curved lines, the use of nature as subject matter, and a heightening of motion and emotion in art. Martini was able to achieve this style by carving out wider spaces between his objects and by rendering a closer focus on reality. For example, in Duccio's *Maestà* the main panel is packed with angels and saints to the point of overcrowding, but Martini's *Maestà* loosens up the spacing. Using a blue background, which also gives an impression of open space, Martini pared down the massive throne and set a Gothic queen squarely in the seat under a Gothic canopy, instead of the vague, abstract character used by Duccio. Yet it is in the mastery of the musical lines, its rhythms, its flowing grace, and its light undulations and modulations that Martini's paintings achieve a distinctive Gothic movement and feeling.

Art historians are somewhat puzzled as to how Martini developed his style. Some critics claim that he obtained his taste for the Gothic and the Oriental from Giotto. Others argue that he analyzed imported cloth, jewelry, furniture, and art in Siena trade centers. Both views are certainly plausible. Because Martini was in such demand from commissions and traveled widely, he gained a broad, empirical, cultural base for his art.

In addition to his Gothic style, Martini is noted for highlighting his paintings in a manner that makes his subjects appear three-dimensional. The effect is the creation of a sensuous outer beauty with an inner mysticism. Such an effect comes partly from his own expansive range of human feeling, partly from the awakening of the period to humanistic sympathies, and partly from his later contact with the Humanist poet Petrarch. The rediscovery of sensibilities and of beauty in life engendered in Martini a search for more responsive artistic subjects. The *dolce stil nuovo* (sweet new style; used in reference to Dante's style) was a vital issue of the period, in both the visual and verbal arts, and Martini was at the forefront of the search for a visual language to express it.

As a result of his spreading fame, Martini was summoned to the French Angevin court of Naples to be knighted by King Robert of Anjou. The most noted work attributed to his four-year stay in Naples is the altarpiece showing King Robert being crowned by his brother Louis, who gave up the right to the crown in order to be canonized in 1317. In the *Saint Louis of Toulouse* painting, he again employs early Gothic forms instead of the heavier Byzantine forms, in this case a truncated gable that recurs in other paintings. This work also introduces, perhaps for the first time in Italy, a five-part *predella* exhibiting scenes from the life of Saint Louis.

In 1319, Martini moved to Pisa, where he composed the large polyptych for the Dominican church dedicated to Saint Catherine and from there to the small town of Orvieto, where he painted another polyptych for the Dominican order. The inner trefoiled units of these two polyptychs show an interesting evolution of Martini's style from the Romanesque oval shape in the Pisa work (1319) to the more Gothic ogival shape in the Orvieto work (early 1320's). Here, too, the Christ child, unlike the earlier Byzantine models, stands with curled hair on his mother's knee, more in the style of Gothic sculpture. Finally, his preference for the clearer and brighter enamel-like colors acts to free up more space than do Duccio's subdued hues.

In 1321, Martini returned to his home in Siena and repaired his damaged *Maestà* while composing several other works now lost, including the famous *Madonna* (1321) for the chapel in the Palazzo Pubblico. During this period, Martini began collaborating with the painter Lippo Memmi. By 1324, the partnership was already close, for in that year Martini married Giovanna, the sister of Lippo Memmi and the daughter of painter Memmo di Filipuccio. According to Petrarch, Martini was not a handsome man, but his wife loved him dearly and remained his companion for the rest of his life.

From 1324 to 1340, Martini is known to have been in and around the three cities of Assisi, Florence, and Siena (all fairly close together). Evidence points to several lost portraits he must have painted of castles and towns under the control of the Sienese. In an eight-year span (from 1328 to 1336), he painted some of his greatest works, in-

Simone Martini. (Library of Congress)

cluding the two best of his career: the large *Guidoriccio da Fogliano* fresco (1328) and the *Annunciation* painting (1333) in the Cathedral of Siena, but most of the remaining works are missing. Internal evidence in these later paintings appears to show that his brother-in-law's conservative style acted as a brake on Martini's style, since the more creative and energetic Gothic spirit seemed to erupt when Martini worked alone.

Martini is known to have bought a house in Siena in 1340. In that same year, he departed for the French city of Avignon, where he spent the last four years of his life. This city probably appealed to Martini because it was a commercial as well as a religious center of power. While there, Martini formed a close friendship with Petrarch, composing a miniature portrait (now lost) of the famous Laura of Petrarch's poems, in exchange for which Petrarch immortalized Martini's name in two sonnets. In addition to the Laura portrait, Martini composed for Petrarch an illuminated title page for one of his manuscripts.

What is most significant about this phase is that Martini was for art what the new literary voices in Italy at the time (Petrarch, Giovanni Boccaccio, Dante) were to literature. Since Martini had more than a passing interest in the freeing of art from the highly Romanesque mannerism, he and Petrarch would have had much in common. Martini's paintings of the period are more volumetric and palpable, calling for a greater attention to human sensibility.

SIGNIFICANCE

It is unclear whether the Black Death ended the Sienese school or the school died of artistic inbreeding resulting in inertia. What is clear is that Martini's exploitation of the Gothic style at a time when art thirsted for new ideas, his slight traces of Oriental flavor, his freeing of color tones, his vivid figures, and his sensitivity to humanistic values all served to doom the highly stylized Byzantine art and to usher in a more expressive style. Through perspective, color, and design, Martini created new ways to use space, and his approach to realism broke the shackles of the Romanesque style. That he was at the forefront of this striving toward a loftier representation of humankind in all the arts shows both his importance as an artist and his acute awareness of the direction painting needed to go at that time in history.

Martini's designs and his iconography show a sophisticated artistry far beyond the expectations of fourteenth century theory. His brilliant style was to have a major impact on the history of Italian painting for the next hundred years. His influence can be seen in the full, clear faces depicted in the work of his brother-in-law Lippo Memmi, and other, little-known artists such as Lippo Vanni and Bartolo di Fredi carried on Martini's tradition in a mediocre fashion. Although the Sienese influence was felt in Hungary, France, and Bohemia, the dazzling styles of Duccio, Martini, and the Lorenzetti brothers eventually died out, except in the works of Barna of Siena, who alone advanced the art beyond that of his predecessors.

—*Ernest R. Pinson*

FURTHER READING

Cole, Bruce. *Sienese Painting: From Its Origins to the Fifteenth Century.* New York: Harper and Row, 1980. Contains excellent, succinct material on Martini. A well-written work, it covers the Sienese school from its beginnings in 1215 to 1450.

Dini, Giuletta Chelazzi, Alessandro Angelini, and Bernardina Sani. *Sienese Painting: From Duccio to the Birth of the Baroque.* New York: H. N. Abrams, 1998. Surveys the history of painting in Siena from Duccio's and Martini's time to the Baroque period. Includes illustrations, some in color, and a bibliography and index.

Moran, Gordan, and M. Mallory. *Guido Riccio: A Guide to the Controversy for Tourists, Scholars, Students, Art Librarians.* Siena, Italy: Edizioni Notizie d'Arte, 2000. Discusses the ongoing scholarly debate about attributing the famous mural at Palazzo Pubblico to Martini.

Paccagnini, Giovanni. *Simone Martini.* London: Heinemann, 1957. An excellent, complete work in English on Martini's life and works. The reproduced prints of paintings are large, and there are generous historical and critical notes. This book is essential to any study of Martini.

Vasari, Giorgio. *Lives of the Most Eminent Painters, Sculptors, and Architects.* Translated by Gaston Du C. De Vere. 3 vols. New York: Abrams, 1979. Besides legal documents and art prints, this work, originally published in English between 1850 and 1907, is the earliest source of material on Martini's life. It is the most comprehensive study of Martini prior to the twentieth century, and it provides specific details not gathered from analysis of paintings or from legal documents.

Vavalà, Evelyn Sandberg. *Sienese Studies: The Development of the School of Painting of Siena.* Florence: L. S. Olschki, 1953. One of the earliest surveys of the Sienese school of painters, this volume begins with the oldest known paintings of Siena and provides a chapter on each of the Sienese artists.

Weigelt, Curt H. *Sienese Painting of the Trecento*. 1930. Reprint. New York: Hacker Art Books, 1974. One of the better books on the Sienese school of painters. Contains one chapter on Martini and provides much material on the Gothic influence. Includes a bibliography.

White, John. *Art and Architecture in Italy, 1250-1400*. 3d ed. New Haven, Conn.: Yale University Press, 1993. This study of the period before and including the early Renaissance provides a chapter on Martini and covers painting, architecture, and sculpture set against a social and historical backdrop. Includes an excellent selection of illustrations of paintings and drawings, an extensive bibliography, and an index.

SEE ALSO: Fra Angelico; Arnolfo di Cambio; Giovanni Boccaccio; Filippo Brunelleschi; Cimabue; Dante; Donatello; Duccio di Buoninsegna; Jan van Eyck and Hubert van Eyck; Lorenzo Ghiberti; Giotto; Pietro Lorenzetti and Ambrogio Lorenzetti; Masaccio; Andrea Orcagna; Petrarch; Nicola Pisano and Giovanni Pisano; Jean Pucelle; Claus Sluter; Rogier van der Weyden.

RELATED ARTICLES in *Great Events from History: The Middle Ages, 477-1453*: c. 950: Court of Córdoba Flourishes in Spain; c. 1150-1200: Development of Gothic Architecture; 1347-1352: Invasion of the Black Death in Europe; c. 1410-1440: Florentine School of Art Emerges.

MASACCIO

Italian painter

During a brief career, Masaccio became one of the major creators of the new Renaissance style of painting. His innovations utilizing perspective created a standard of realism admired and imitated by subsequent generations of artists.

BORN: December 21, 1401; Castel San Giovanni, Republic of Florence (now San Giovanni Valdarno, Italy)
DIED: 1428; Rome, Papal States (now in Italy)
ALSO KNOWN AS: Tommaso di Giovanni di Simone Guidi (given name)
AREA OF ACHIEVEMENT: Art

EARLY LIFE

In contrast to the lives of such prominent Renaissance artists as Leonardo da Vinci and Michelangelo, little is known concerning the life of the Florentine painter Masaccio (mah-ZAHT-choh), who managed during his brief life to revolutionize the world of painting. He was born Tommaso di Giovanni di Simone Guidi in the small Tuscan town of Castel San Giovanni on Saint Thomas's Day, December 21, 1401.

His grandfather had settled in San Giovanni in the 1380's and established himself as a successful furniture maker. Masaccio's parents, Giovanni di Mone Cassai and Monna Iacopa di Martinozzo, were only twenty and nineteen when their first son was born; they still lived with his grandfather. Masaccio was a nickname derived from Tommaso, meaning "hulking Tom" or "slovenly Tom." In 1406, his parents had another son, Giovanni, who also became an artist and was nicknamed "Lo Scheggia," meaning "the splinter" or "chip." In the same year, Masaccio's father died, and his mother soon remarried. Her second husband was an elderly pharmacist named Tedesco.

The next sixteen years of Masaccio's life are essentially a mystery. Coming from a prosperous family of artisans, he no doubt enjoyed a comfortable childhood. The first specific records of him after 1406 date from January, 1422, when he enrolled in the Florentine guild of physicians and apothecaries, which then included artists in its membership. It remains uncertain under whom he trained, the old theory that he studied under the artist Masolino having been convincingly disproved. He possibly learned some basics about painting from one of the artisans who decorated the painted chests produced in his grandfather's shop. It is also uncertain exactly when Masaccio left San Giovanni for the greater opportunities afforded by Florence. He may have studied there with the painter Mariotto di Cristofano, the husband of one of his stepsisters.

The Florence that became the adolescent Masaccio's new home was then one of the most vibrant and important cities in Europe, on the threshold of its greatest century. One of the chief ways the city fathers expressed their pride in Florence's increasing prominence was by commissioning painters, sculptors, and architects to produce works of art for the city. Masaccio arrived in Florence at exactly the time when monumental artistic projects were making the city the leading artistic center of Europe.

Though the identity of Masaccio's teachers remains a mystery, his revolutionary style was undoubtedly influenced by three key individuals: Giotto, Florence's greatest painter of the previous century; Donatello, the contemporary master sculptor; and Filippo Brunelleschi, the inventive architect and artist. By his early twenties, Masaccio had absorbed the simple dignity of Giotto's composition and solid naturalism of Donatello's sculptures and applied them to Brunelleschi's new laws of linear perspective, so that he was ready to produce some of the most influential paintings and frescoes of the century.

Life's Work

The young Florentine genius enjoyed an active career of less than a decade before his premature death. His earliest known work, a triptych discovered in the obscure Church of San Giovenale in the valley of the Valdarno in 1961, consisted of a Madonna and Child flanked by four saints, a very traditional subject. Already, however, Masaccio was showing signs of a new naturalism and inventiveness in this work. The Christ child was originally completely nude and depicted eating grapes, an iconographical innovation referring to the Eucharist. The triptych's figures clearly mirrored those of Giotto a century earlier and showed a skilled use of foreshortening and light.

Another early work, dating from approximately 1423, was his *Madonna and Child with Saint Anne and Angels*, an altarpiece painted for the Church of Sant'Ambrogio in Florence. Evidently part of this work was painted by Masolino, although scholars disagree on the exact division of work between the two.

One of the few works of Masaccio that can be dated definitively is another altarpiece, a polyptych done for the Church of Santa Maria del Carmine in Pisa. The work was commissioned for a chapel, and Masaccio received eighty florins for his undertaking. The polyptych was dismantled in the eighteenth century and the various pieces scattered. Scholars have subsequently identified eleven of these, and they are now housed in museums in London, Berlin, Naples, Pisa, and Vienna. The only surviving description of the entire work is found in Giorgio Vasari's history. For his centerpiece of the Pisa polyptych, Masaccio again painted the *Madonna and Child.* Surrounding them are four small angels, two of them playing lutes. Another key panel features a dramatic crucifixion scene notable for its rather bulky rendition of Christ and its moving Mary Magdalene. Surviving pieces from the work's predella include a visitation by the Magi and scenes from the lives of various saints.

Masaccio. (Library of Congress)

Works such as the Pisa altarpiece undoubtedly added to the growing reputation of the young painter. Contemporary records reveal little about the details of his life in Florence during this period. The number of known works he produced demonstrates that he was rarely without work and thus reasonably secure financially. Tax returns from July, 1427, indicate that he was living in a house rented for ten florins a year. His younger brother and widowed mother were living with him. He also rented part of a workshop for an additional two florins a year. Donatello and Brunelleschi were among his close friends. Writing more than a century after Masaccio's death, Vasari characterized him as an affable, absent-minded individual unconcerned with worldly goods and careless about his dress.

By the mid-1420's, several key elements combined to produce Masaccio's distinctive style. In obvious rebellion against the delicacy of the International Gothic favored by such successful contemporary Florentine artists as Gentile da Fabriano, Masaccio emphasized solid, monumental figures accompanied by somber and simple backgrounds. His careful study of the human form and the effect of light produced works of revolutionary realism. Although color was not unimportant to him, Masaccio was more clearly dedicated to form. His figures emerged as unique individuals rather than faceless stereotypes. Instead of the elaborate brocades habitually used in International Gothic, Masaccio's biblical figures wore simple, heavy cloaks. Above all, the new laws of perspective enabled the young master to produce works that put his figures in believable space rather than having them float aimlessly against solid gold backgrounds.

The outstanding examples of Masaccio's style are found in his frescoes located in the Brancacci Chapel in the Florentine Church of Santa Maria del Carmine. The exact date of his work there remains unclear, as does the name of the patron, although it was undoubtedly a member of the influential mercantile Brancacci family. Some of the chapel's frescoes were the work of Masolino, who had earlier collaborated with the young artist on the altarpiece for the Church of Sant'Ambrogio. It remains uncertain whether the two worked together in the chapel or whether Masolino began the project and then abandoned it to Masaccio when he left for another commission in Hungary. The chapel remained unfinished at the time of Masaccio's death and was completed only in the 1480's by a third artist, Filippino Lippi.

Scholars generally attribute six of the major scenes and part of another to Masaccio. One of these includes *The Expulsion from Paradise*, a moving work showing Adam and Eve being driven from the Garden of Eden. The figures, depicted against a bleak landscape, almost resemble freestanding sculpture in the new tradition of Donatello. Masaccio's masterful use of atmospheric perspective and emotional expression infuses the scene with drama.

The majority of Masaccio's Brancacci chapel frescoes, though, depict various scenes from the life of Saint Peter, a rare iconographical theme in Florence during this period. By far the most famous of these, and generally regarded as his masterpiece, is *The Tribute Money*. Inspired by the biblical story found in Matthew 17:24-27, the fresco is a simultaneous narrative in three parts. In the center section, a tax collector confronts Christ and his apostles and demands tribute. On the left, Saint Peter obeys Christ's injunction to cast forth his hook and take a coin out of the mouth of the first fish he catches; on the left, Saint Peter pays the tribute to the tax collector. This fresco was perhaps inspired by a new tax imposed by the Florentine government in 1427. Whatever the inspiration, the figures in *The Tribute Money*, as well as in Masaccio's other frescoes in the chapel, exhibit a convincing realism and individuality.

Masaccio's most unconventional fresco is located in the Church of Santa Maria Novella in Florence. The famous *Holy Trinity with the Virgin and Saint John*, most commonly dated to 1425, again shows his creative genius. It depicts the Trinity within an architectural framework inspired by Brunelleschi, expertly creating an illusion of depth through the barrel vaulted ceiling. To accompany the Trinity, Masaccio painted figures of Mary and John and below them full-size portraits of the donor and his wife. Their identities remain uncertain although it is possible that they were members of the Lenzi family. For the first time, the donors are portrayed on the same scale as the divine figures, a significant innovation. Long covered by a sixteenth century altar, *Holy Trinity with the Virgin and Saint John* was not rediscovered until 1861. When it was cleaned in 1952, restorers discovered a skeleton painted below the donors. Such memento mori were rare in Florence's artistic tradition.

In addition to the previously discussed works, Masaccio produced several others that have been destroyed. These included a "Consecration" fresco for the Carmine Cloisters in Pisa, a fresco of Saint Ives and his wards for Florence's Church of the Badia in 1627, and a Saint Paul fresco for that city's Church of the Carmine. Vasari mentions that Masaccio painted several portraits of eminent Florentines, but these remain lost or have not survived.

Sometime in 1428, the young artist abandoned work on the Brancacci Chapel and left Florence for Rome. The reason remains unclear, although it was possibly a response to a summons from his friend Masolino, who was then in the city. Before the end of the year, Masaccio died, so suddenly and unexpectedly that rumors spread that he had been poisoned. His friend Brunelleschi summarized the impact of the twenty-seven-year-old genius's demise when he remarked that the art world had suffered a most grievous loss.

Significance

The paintings of Masaccio had an influence on the formation of the Renaissance style equal to the contemporary accomplishments in sculpture by Donatello and in architecture by Brunelleschi. The young Florentine was thus one of the three pivotal influences in establishing Florentine ascendancy in the art world during the fifteenth century, a most remarkable achievement considering the brevity of his career.

His handful of surviving frescoes inspired generations of painters who studied them for their masterful skill in making the human figure come alive. Such prominent artists as Fra Filippo Lippi, Sandro Botticelli, Andrea del Verrocchio, Leonardo da Vinci, Michelangelo, and Raphael all found inspiration for aspects of their style in the work of Masaccio. All made the pilgrimage to the tiny Brancacci Chapel to study his masterly modeling of the human figure.

Influenced by the earlier works of Giotto, as well as by classical sculpture, Masaccio created a brilliant new standard for painting that effectively abandoned medieval two-dimensionality and instead explored the possibilities for realism provided by atmospheric and linear perspective. Masaccio's figures emerged as real individuals, full of emotion and dignity. They symbolized the self-confidence of the Renaissance epoch dawning in Florence and served as models for countless later Renaissance works. The Brancacci Chapel frescoes established artistic standards that endured virtually unchallenged until the nineteenth century. Although the details of his life remain obscure and largely undocumented, Masaccio's importance in art history remains firmly entrenched. Few other painters, if any, have managed to transform the course of painting so decisively in such a short time.

—*Tom L. Auffenberg*

FURTHER READING

Ahl, Diane Cole, ed. *The Cambridge Companion to Masaccio*. New York: Cambridge University Press, 2002. A comprehensive look at Masaccio and his works as well as fifteenth century art in Florence. Bibliography and index.

Casazza, Ornella. *Masaccio and the Brancacci Chapel*. New York: Riverside Book Company, 1990. An examination of the Brancacci Chapel frescoes created by Masaccio. Bibliography and index.

Fremantle, Richard. *Masaccio*. New York: Smithmark, 1998. A catalog of the artist's works along with criticism and interpretation. Illustrations and bibliography.

Goffen, Rona, ed. *Masaccio's Trinity*. New York: Cambridge University Press, 1998. A collection of essays on Masaccio's portrayal of the Trinity that relates his work to the times in which it was produced and examines the techniques used. Index.

Guillaud, Maruice. *Frescoes by Masaccio in the Brancacci Chapel: Along with the Frescoes by Masolino and Filippino Lippi*. New York: Guillaud Edition, 1991. Examines the frescoes in the Brancacci Chapel done by Masaccio and those finished by Masolino and Filippino Lippi. Contains 44 leaves of plates, chiefly color.

Joannides, Paul. *Masaccio and Masolino: A Complete Catalogue*. New York: H. N. Abrams, 1993. A complete catalog of the works of Masaccio and Masolino. Contains illustrations, a bibliography, and index.

Strehike, Brandon, and Cecilia Frosinini, eds. *The Panel Paintings of Masolino and Masaccio: The Role of Technique*. Milan: Five Continents, 2002. An examination of panel paintings with an emphasis on the techniques employed by Masolino and Masaccio.

Vasari, Giorgio. *The Lives of the Artists*. Edited by William Gaunt. Reprint. New York: Alfred A. Knopf, 1996. First published in 1550 and substantially expanded in 1568, Vasari's collection of biographies of famous Renaissance architects, sculptors, and painters provides the earliest secondary information about the life and career of Masaccio. He established many historical traditions about Masaccio and described some of his works that have subsequently been destroyed or lost. Some of his statements have been disproved by modern art historians.

SEE ALSO: Filippo Brunelleschi; Donatello; Giotto.

RELATED ARTICLE in *Great Events from History: The Middle Ages, 477-1453*: c. 1410-1440: Florentine School of Art Emerges.

AL-MASʿŪDĪ
Arab historian and geographer

Al-Masʿūdī, called the Herodotus of the Arabs, traveled extensively and gathered enormous quantities of information on poorly known lands. His work helped set the tone for future Arabic scholarship.

BORN: c. 890; probably Baghdad (now in Iraq)
DIED: 956; Al-Fusṭāt (now Cairo, Egypt)
ALSO KNOWN AS: Abū al-Ḥasyn ʿAlī ibn Ḥusain al-Masʿūdī Masʿūdī
AREAS OF ACHIEVEMENT: Historiography, geography, exploration

EARLY LIFE

Al-Masʿūdī (ahl-mahs-eh-DEE) came from an Arab family in Baghdad that claimed descent from one of the early companions of the Prophet Muḥammad, though some sources erroneously describe him as of North African origin. His educational background is unknown, but his career reflects a catholic and almost insatiable thirst for knowledge.

By the standards of the tenth century, al-Masʿūdī was a peerless traveler and explorer whose feats surpass those of Marco Polo more than three centuries later. He began his travels as a young man, visiting Iran, including the cities of Kermān and Istakhr, around 915. Subsequently, he fell in with a group of merchants bound for India and Ceylon. Later, al-Masʿūdī seems to have found his way as far as southern China. On his return from China, he made a reconnaissance of the East African coast as far as Madagascar, then visited Oman and other parts of southern Arabia. There followed a visit to Iran, particularly the region of the Elburz Mountains, south of the Caspian Sea.

On yet another journey, al-Masʿūdī visited the Levant. He examined various ruins in Antioch and reported on relics in the possession of a Christian church in Tiberias in 943. Two years later, he returned to Syria, settling there for most of the remainder of his life. From Syria, he paid several extended visits to Egypt. Although it is uncertain whether he traveled there, al-Masʿūdī's writing also demonstrates detailed knowledge of the lands of North Africa.

Al-Masʿūdī's written work is characterized by his adherence to the rationalist Mutazilite school of Islamic thought. The Mutazilites, who applied logical analysis to fundamental questions of human existence and religious law, combined an intellectual disposition with a preference for vocal activism.

LIFE'S WORK

Regrettably, much of al-Masʿūdī's literary work has been lost, so that in modern times it is known only by the references of others and from his own summaries in extant material. Only a single volume remains extant, for example, out of perhaps thirty that constituted al-Masʿūdī's monumental attempt to write a history of the world. The surviving volume covers the myth of creation and geographical background as well as the legendary history of early Egypt.

The major work of al-Masʿūdī which has survived is *Murūj al-dhahab wa maʿādin al-jawāhir* (947; partial translation as *Meadows of Gold and Mines of Gems*, 1841). Apparently, there was a considerably larger, revised 956 edition of this work, but it is not extant. Al-Masʿūdī laid out his philosophy of history and the natural world in *Kitāb al-Tanbīh wa al-Ishrāf* (book of indications and revisions), a summary of his life's work.

In his books, al-Masʿūdī presents a remarkable variety of information. His material on peoples and conditions on the periphery of the Islamic world is of vital importance, as modern knowledge of this aspect of Islamic history is extremely scanty. For modern scholars, however, al-Masʿūdī's style and critical commentary leave something to be desired. His presentation jumps from subject to subject, without following a consistent system. Al-Masʿūdī made little attempt to distinguish among his sources or to obtain original versions of information, as, for example, the eleventh century geographer and historian al-Bīrūnī was careful to do. He treated a sailor's anecdote or a folktale in the same way as he did a map or a manuscript.

On the other hand, al-Masʿūdī's uncritical approach doubtless led to the preservation of material, much of it useful, which would not have found its way into the work of a more conventional scholar. Al-Masʿūdī expressed none of the condescension one sometimes finds in other writings of the time for non-Muslim authorities; he displays as much enthusiasm for learning what lay outside Islam as he does for Islamic teaching. The broad scope of his investigations was without precedent.

The juxtaposition of sources of varying authority in al-Masʿūdī's work is enough to raise skeptical questions in the minds of modern readers. In discussing the geography of the Indian Ocean, for example, he first presents the "official" version, heavily dependent on erroneous ideas borrowed from Ptolemy and other Hellenistic writers, who regarded the sea as largely landlocked and accessible only through a few narrow entrances. Al-Masʿūdī then lays out contrary—and more accurate—information about the Indian Ocean drawn from sailors' tales and from his own experience, indicative of the vastness of the ocean and the cultural diversity of the countries surrounding it. He also presents the orthodox notion of his time that the Caspian Sea and the Aral Sea were connected, followed by an account of his own explorations that revealed that they are separate bodies of water.

Al-Masʿūdī departed from established form in presenting his information in a loosely topical manner, organized around ethnic groups, dynasties, and the reigns of important rulers instead of the year-by-year chronicle method typical of the time. In this respect, he anticipated the famed fourteenth century Islamic historian Ibn Khaldūn, whose work, in turn, represents a major step toward modern historical scholarship.

A noteworthy feature of al-Masʿūdī's observations of nature is his attention to geologic forces that shape the environment. Although his comments sprang mostly from intuition, they were often prescient of modern scientific theory. He wrote, for example, of physical forces changing what once was seabed into dry land and of the nature of volcanic activity.

Significance

Al-Masʿūdī deserves to be included among the major Arabic historians, despite the loss of most of his work. His career marks the introduction of a new intellectual curiosity in Islam, one that sought knowledge for its own sake and paid scant attention to the boundaries between Islam and the rest of the world. His fascination with geographical elements in history and human affairs would be taken up by many later Arabic scholars.

Western historians have suggested that al-Masʿūdī's intellectual disposition reflects the development of Hellenistic influence in Islamic scholarship, foreshadowing the pervasive Greek character in nontheological Islamic writing in the eleventh and twelfth centuries, particularly in Mediterranean lands. He has been compared both to Herodotus of the fifth century B.C.E. and to the first century C.E. Roman geographer and historian Pliny the Elder. Lack of knowledge about al-Masʿūdī's training and education makes such judgments problematic, but there can be no doubt that his work is in many respects prototypical of what was to come in Islam.

—*Ronald W. Davis*

Further Reading

Ahmad, S. Maqbul. "Al-Masʿūdī's Contribution to Medieval Arab Geography." *Islamic Culture* 27/28 (1953/1954): 61-77, 275-286. This detailed account of al-Masʿūdī's life and work suggests that he was somewhat defensive about scholarship. Points out that Ptolemy was also indiscriminate about sources; al-Masʿūdī may have tried to justify his eclectic sources in terms of ancient predecessors. He rejected most astronomical sources because of their reliance on astrology. Describes al-Masʿūdī as a "roads and countries" scholar, heavily descriptive, less enamored with traditional cosmography.

_______. "Travels of Abuʿl Ḥasan ʿAlī B. al-Husain al-Masʿūdī." *Islamic Culture* 28 (1954): 509-524. Summarizes al-Masʿūdī's travels, based on his own accounts. Speculates that all travel inferences cannot be taken for granted and that some information may have been gleaned at second hand, even though the geographer's writings do not say so explicitly.

Ahmad, S. Maqbul, and A. Rahman, eds. *Al-Masʿūdī: Millenary Commemoration Volume*. Aligarh, India: Indian Society for the History of Science, 1960. These essays examine the career of al-Masʿūdī after one thousand years. Every major aspect of his thought and writing is covered, including his sources, his geographical and scientific ideas, his use of poetry and other devices, and his knowledge of the peoples of Western Europe. Several essays also discuss how al-Masʿūdī's writings have been used as resources for modern scholars in various fields. Bibliography.

Donner, Fred M. *Narratives of Islamic Origins: The Beginnings of Islamic Historical Writing*. Princeton, N.J.: Darwin Press, 1998. A study of the early years (around the seventh century) of Islamic historiography. Extensive bibliography, index.

Khalidi, Tarif. *Arabic Historical Thought in the Classical Period*. New York: Cambridge University Press, 1994. Traces the history of Muslim historiography, especially its focus on the documentation of scholars, scholarship, and learned society. Quotes historians and historical texts of the time period. Bibliography, index.

_______. "Masʿūdī's Lost Works: A Reconstruction of Their Content." *Journal of the American Oriental Society* 94 (1974): 35-41. Discusses the growing realization among scholars of al-Masʿūdī's importance. His historical works were produced apparently after a long period of reflection on law, philosophy, science, and theology. He relied on scientific explanations for historical schema, anticipating the methods of Ibn Khaldūn.

Modi, Sir Jivanji Jamshedji. "Macoudi on Volcanoes." *Journal of the Bombay Branch of the Royal Asiatic Society* 22 (1908): 135-142. Shows that al-Masʿūdī's descriptions and notions of volcanic activity are broadly similar to ancient ideas of Hell and to myths derived from the fantastic shapes perceived in vapor clouds. Al-Masʿūdī also displays intuition about the concentration of volcanoes in certain geographical areas and reports the volcanic activity of Java and Sumatra.

Robinson, Chase F. *Islamic Historiography.* New York: Cambridge University Press, 2003. An introduction to the writing of history in Arabic, with a focus on the sociopolitical functions of historiography from the eighth to the sixteenth century. Written especially for those with little or no background in Islamic history or in Arabic. Bibliography, index.

SEE ALSO: al-Bīrūnī; Ibn Khaldūn; Marco Polo; al-Ṭabarī; Yaqut.

RELATED ARTICLES in *Great Events from History: The Middle Ages, 477-1453*: 872-973: Publication of *The History of al-Ṭabarī*; 1271-1295: Travels of Marco Polo; 1377: Ibn Khaldūn Completes His *Muqaddimah.*

MATILDA OF CANOSSA

Italian noblewoman

One of the most powerful women in medieval history in her own right, Matilda played key roles in supporting papal authority and claims both before and during the Investiture Controversy.

BORN: 1046; probably in Lucca, Tuscany (now in Italy)
DIED: July 24, 1115; Bondeno, near Mantua (now in Italy)
ALSO KNOWN AS: Matilda of Tuscany; Mathilde; the Great Countess
AREA OF ACHIEVEMENT: Government and politics

EARLY LIFE

Matilda (muh-TIHL-duh) of Canossa was born into a family that had served the Holy Roman Empire in Italy for several generations. Canossa was a hilltop castle in southern Lombardy. Her great-grandfather Azzo of Canossa pleased Emperor Otto the Great so much that he gave Azzo the title of count and marquis over Modena, Reggio, and parts of southern Lombardy. Azzo's son, Tedaldo, remained in imperial good graces, as did Boniface, Tedaldo's son. When the marquis of Tuscany, Rainieri, defied the authority of the emperor, and Boniface aided his lord, Boniface received control of Tuscany and the titles duke and marquis of Tuscany, first recorded in 1031. In the Tuscan cities, such as Florence, Arezzo, and Lucca, the duke personally held the position of count, exerting a very direct feudal control.

Holy Roman Emperor Henry III grew wary of having such a powerful vassal in distant Italy. Boniface's lands stretched across Italy from the Ligurian coast to the Adriatic Sea, and from Bergamo in the north to Siena in the south. Tensions were clearly visible to contemporaries, and Henry may have had a hand in Boniface's death while hunting in 1052. Boniface had married a daughter of the imperial duke of Lorraine, Beatrice, who brought important German lands with her as dowry. She was steeped in the high culture of the day and developed at Canossa a court renowned for its splendor and learning.

Matilda was born into this court and inheritance. She became heiress after her only brother's death in 1055. Beatrice, certainly to protect her children, married Godfrey of Lorraine shortly after Boniface's death. At the same ceremony in Mantua, the couple affianced Matilda and Godfrey's rather older son, Godfrey the Hunchback. Henry was enraged at this double-coupling of two of his more powerful vassals, and Matilda, still a child, found herself at the center of a major controversy.

Matilda was well educated for a woman of her day and is noted for her unusual martial training under Arduino della Palude. She could handle the weapons of the day and even had two sets of armor made for her. It is recorded that she rode at the head of her troops at times. She could handle four languages—the medieval forms of Latin, French, Italian, and German—and collected manuscripts. During her long reign, she also showed considerable skill as an administrator, which she doubtless acquired as a young woman and on the job.

LIFE'S WORK

The Godfreys' revolt against Henry was sharp but short-lived, and Beatrice and her husband attended the royal coronation of the very young Henry IV in 1056. Four years later the family became entangled in papal politics.

Pope Stephen IX, a leading reformer at the papal court and brother of the elder Godfrey, died suddenly in March, 1059. One portion of the cardinals elected the bishop of Velletri, who was acceptable to reformers but not their first choice. Other reformers held off until December, when they elected the bishop of Florence, himself from Lorraine. The reformers played their cards well and got both the imperial party in Germany and the people of Rome—well bribed—to support their Nicholas II and the deposing of the very short-reigned antipope, Benedict X. No less than Godfrey of Lorraine and Tuscany escorted Nicholas into Rome. This pope spent much of his time in Florence, and Matilda may well have gained her intense affection for the reform papacy directly from him. When Nicholas died, the reformer-bishop Anselm of Lucca replaced him, taking the name Alexander II in September, 1061. However, this election, too, was contested, and Godfrey again played a vital role in physically protecting the reform-party pope against, in this case, the empress-regent's party. Young Henry IV, born in 1050, grew to manhood under Alexander, and he quickly came to realize that "reform" meant lessening imperial control over the church in imperial lands. Pope and young German king clashed with increasing frequency.

Portrait of Matilda of Canossa, from a manuscript poem in the Vatican Library. (Frederick Ungar Publishing Co.)

The elder Godfrey died in 1069, and Matilda took the reins of her vast territories. She married her fiancé, Godfrey, sometime between 1069 and 1071. Their only child died shortly after birth. In 1073, Alexander died, and the Tuscan-born powerhouse behind Church reform, Hildebrand, was acclaimed pope in Rome in April, 1073. He took the name Gregory VII. Disaffection among the German lords against the young king was a constant theme in the German part of the empire, but Godfrey decided to serve his lord, estranging himself physically and politically from Matilda, who steadfastly supported the pope in any controversy with the emperor. Beatrice, on whom Matilda had relied for much, died in 1076.

At the beginning of the same year, Henry IV made his move against Pope Gregory. The reformers had been especially troubled by nonclerical appointments to important church offices such as bishoprics. The king and emperor-elect insisted on retaining that power, especially on the grounds that many German bishops were also, by their offices, his feudal vassals. This disagreement, known as the Investiture Controversy, swept up the era's best legal minds and fueled the revival and study of Roman law. Matilda's patronage of the Law School at Bologna and of the great jurist Irnerius were based in her interest in these matters.

In March, 1075, Gregory published *Dictatus papae*, a far-reaching set of papal claims that went so far as to recognize a pope's right to depose an emperor. The following January, at an imperial council held at Worms, Henry's supporters laid out a series of legal charges and declared the pope deposed. Gregory was confronted with these charges and the decree and promptly excommunicated Henry and anathemized his clerical followers. Gregory then explained his position and actions to the German feudal lords; these lords, not well-disposed to Henry to begin with, decided that Henry had one year from the excommunication to have the sentence lifted or they would no longer recognize his authority as a Christian ruler.

Late in the year, Henry, with few material or financial resources, headed south to plead his case in Rome. Gregory for his part was heading north to rally the German lords. Because Henry had supporters in Lombardy—many Lombard bishops had met at Piacenza and supported the deposing of Gregory—Matilda arranged an escort for the sixty-year-old pope. On news of Henry's descent south, the party decided to spend the winter at Canossa. Matilda hosted not only Gregory and his entourage but also the steady stream of Henry's bishops and abbots who had changed their minds and were seeking reconciliation with the Church. Those who found the pope at Canossa were locked in dank, cold cells and fed only some bread and water, until Gregory was convinced of their repentance. As Henry and his party approached, they stopped short: He feared that the pope would not lift the sanction. He sent envoys who failed to move Gregory, so he enlisted Matilda's aid; according to tradition, she agreed only after the abject ruler begged for her help from his knees. Henry consented to don penitential clothing and fast from sunrise to sunset—not long in the dead of winter—placing himself outside the castle gate at Canossa. On the fourth day, Gregory relented and released Henry from the excommunication. Henry quickly returned to Germany. The pope planned to follow, but Matilda convinced him otherwise, and she continued to host him.

Soon Henry was in a stronger position than ever, and Matilda began to feel the pressure of a new force in Italian politics: the emergence of urban communes in Lombardy and Tuscany. By the early 1080's, the former "capital" of Lucca was in constant revolt, led by antireform clergy and liberty-seeking town councillors and supported by the emperor. Florence had already replaced Lucca as the center of Tuscan administration. Henry returned to Italy in 1080. Sweeping through Matilda's territories, he bought the support of many towns with special privileges and harassed her supporters. By 1084, with her army defeated and towns in revolt, she had no resources to aid Gregory, whom Henry had imprisoned in the papal fortress of Castel Sant'Angelo. As Gregory watched, Henry installed his new antipope, Clement III, whom he would recognize until Clement's death in 1100. The Norman ruler of much of southern Italy, Robert Guiscard, rescued the pope, who died in exile.

In 1087, Robert of Normandy, estranged son of William the Conqueror, sought the hand of Matilda in marriage. He failed, but in 1089, Welf (Guelph) of Bavaria married Matilda, who, at forty-three, was about twice his age. The Bavarian family was one of Henry's biggest problems, and newly elected pope Urban II urged this marriage on her. Henry rapidly seized all of Matilda's possessions in Germany and moved into Italy again. Mantua fell after a year, and Ferrara immediately. Henry supported a revolt in Liguria, the area surrounding Genoa. Holed up in her castle of Carpineta, Matilda held out as her advisers and vassals pleaded with her to drop her alliance to Urban and recognize Clement. For his part, Henry relished the revenge he was obtaining for the humiliation at Canossa, and he targeted that stronghold particularly. By a neat stratagem, however, she brought her forces up behind his and defeated them, humiliating him yet again.

During her last two decades, the movement toward urban autonomy gained speed and was co-opted by Henry IV's successor, who was happy to sell privileges and rights. Her reactions to this movement seem to indicate that she did not understand these trends. Without an heir who would acquire either feudal or allodial possessions, she apparently lacked the concern she might otherwise have had. From their perspective, cities such as Florence loved Matilda for her *lese faire* attitude. In fact, the Papacy had been her heir, but after her death near Mantua in 1115, the emperor claimed everything as his. This exacerbated papal-imperial tensions in northern Italy and presented many opportunities for the thriving city-states of Lombardy and Tuscany to stake out their own power bases by playing each side off the other.

Significance

Matilda's support of the papal side in the Investiture Controversy from the mid-eleventh century until nearly its denouement in 1122 with the Concordat of Worms helped ensure that imperial power did not merely swamp the reformers' movement and subsume the Church into the state as happened in the Byzantine Empire. Though other powers such as the French and the southern Italian Normans did their part, Matilda literally stood between the emperor and pope.

Insofar as she did not stifle the beginnings of communal autonomy in Lombardy and Tuscany, she helped ensure that it would advance. Pisa emerged as a sea power and both Florence and Siena laid the foundations for their future power. Her struggles with the imperial party opened the door further for the negotiations that further weakened imperial power over these budding economic centers.

—Joseph P. Byrne

Further Reading

Blumenthal, Uta-Renate. *The Investiture Controversy: Church and Monarchy from the Ninth to the Twelfth Century.* Philadelphia: University of Pennsylvania Press, 1988. Standard work in English on the controversy.

Duff, Nora. *Matilda of Tuscany: La gran donna d'Italia.* New York: E. P. Dutton, 1910. Full biography of Matilda; draws on original sources and establishes the political context of her role in papal/imperial affairs.
Jones, Philip. *The Italian City-State: From Commune to Signoria.* New York: Oxford University Press, 1997. The ambiguity of Matilda's will allowed the first flourishing of communal independence in Lombardy and Tuscany.
McCash, June Hall, ed. *The Cultural Patronage of Medieval Women.* Athens: University of Georgia Press, 1996. Matilda appears in this collection of articles as the major figure in church and cultural patronage of her day in northern Italy.
Tellenbach, Gerd. *Church, State, and Christian Society at the Time of the Investiture Contest.* Buffalo, N.Y.: University of Toronto Press, 1991. Treatment of the intellectual and theological issues that shaped Matilda's positions, though she does not appear in this work at all.

SEE ALSO: Gregory VII; Henry IV (of Germany); Otto I; Urban II; William the Conqueror.
RELATED ARTICLES in *Great Events from History: The Middle Ages, 477-1453*: November 27, 1095: Pope Urban II Calls the First Crusade; 1127-1130: Creation of the Kingdom of Sicily.

MECHTHILD VON MAGDEBURG

German mystic and writer

The mystic Mechthild was the first woman to write in her native German, rather than in Latin, as she described God's revelations to her.

BORN: c. 1210; Saxony (now in Germany)
DIED: c. 1297; Helfta, near Eislebern (now in Germany)
ALSO KNOWN AS: Mechthild of Magdeburg; Mechtild
AREAS OF ACHIEVEMENT: Literature, religion and theology

EARLY LIFE

All biographical information about Mechthild von Magdeburg (MEHK-tihld vahn MAHG-duh-burk) comes from her own writings. She was probably from a noble family of Saxony. She records that when she was only twelve years of age, she was greeted by the Holy Ghost; although she was not schooled in theology, she knew that God was speaking to her. From that time onward, she states, the greeting was repeated daily and she became very conscious of God's presence. Mechthild continued to experience frequent visions and interior messages from God. Instead of following the ordinary course of marrying, she listened to God's direction and made a different decision.

Around 1230, inspired by her revelations, Mechthild left her home to become a Beguine at Magdeburg. The Beguines were lay women from the upper classes who led lives of chastity and poverty but who did not belong to a religious community or order. Although the movement was predominantly one of women, men known as Beghards also lived in this manner. The Beguines were one of the few if not the only medieval religious movement not inspired or guided by men.

During the thirteenth century, the Beguines flourished in Belgium and parts of Germany. Some Beguines maintained their own homes; others, Mechthild among them, lived a communal life of prayer, almsgiving, penance, and service. Although Beguines did not take religious vows, they lived a monastic life. Many of their beguinages, or common houses, became centers of intense mystical experience. They were also places of study, writing, translation of texts, and copying of other texts for use by the faithful. The Beguine movement continues today in Belgium.

One of the practices of the Beguines was the use of the vernacular (or native language), rather than Latin, for Bible reading. This significant departure from custom earned them intense criticism by church personnel. The Beguines were also criticized because they would not become a formal religious community, probably because this status would have restricted them in their many services among the poor. They were condemned by the Council of Vienna in 1311, but this condemnation seems to have had relatively little influence.

The Beguines' use of the vernacular quite probably influenced Mechthild's decision to record her visions in her own Low German, a first for that time.

During her time as a Beguine, Mechthild, guided by a Dominican confessor and spiritual director, began to write an account of her visions and revelations. Although at first her confessor was skeptical, he was eventually convinced of Mechthild's sincerity and placed her under obedience to continue her writing. Writing in her native Low German, Mechthild set herself to work, completing six of the seven books of revelations. She completed the work much later, after she left the Beguines. Mechthild claims that God gave the work its title: *Das fliessende Licht der Gottheit* (*The Revelations of Mechthild of Magdeburg, 1210-1297: Or, The Flowing Light of the Godhead*, 1953; best known as *The Flowing Light of the Godhead*, 1998). Divine light is indeed the central image in the work, and Mechthild was ever moving toward that light.

Life's Work

Mechthild's life's work consists of the single piece cited above, the early portions of which she completed during her time as a Beguine. Her writings and other comments provoked opposition, partly because of her choice to write in Low German, partly because of her audacious claims of God's intimacy with her, and partly because of her strong denunciations of the vices of clergy in general and the clergy of Magdeburg in particular. Evidently guided by God's revelations, Mechthild named several ecclestiastical abuses; her accusations made her the target of negative criticism. It is thought that her noble birth gave her the freedom to describe abuses without fear of recrimination.

Although Mechthild sought no recognition, her visions eventually became known; these, together with her naming of clerical abuses, brought her unremitting attention from the many who came to the Beguines seeking religious counsel. Unable to live her spiritual life in peace, sometime after 1270 Mechthild sought refuge, joining the Cistercian nuns at Helfta in order to find seclusion and support. The Cistercians were strictly cloistered, and with them Mechthild was able to find the peace and seclusion she sought. It is thought that her confessor urged this move, probably to shelter Mechthild but also to protect the Beguine community.

Mechthild's move was to prove deeply beneficial. The saintly abbess, Gertrud of Hakeborn (1231-1291; not to be confused with Saint Gertrude, 1256-1302), received her at Helfta and encouraged her to continue writing. Although Mechthild was older than many of the nuns, they received her as a peer. As time passed, they realized that she was favored by God and revered her as one chosen for divine grace. Although it is not known whether Mechthild became a member of the Cistercians, she lived among them until her death. Because of her several skirmishes with ecclesiastical authorities when she was with the Beguines, Mechthild's health suffered; in her later years she was blind and greatly weakened by illness.

The Flowing Light of the Godhead, Mechthild's single masterpiece, is not a cohesive work so much as a collection of visions, teachings, exhortations, experiences, bits of dialogue, and scriptural commentary. The work bears strong resemblance to other literary pieces of the time, particularly folk songs, lyrical poetry, and drama. The use of Low German lends a homey touch to Mechthild's writing; she uses common figures of speech and her own local idiom. She combines poetry and prose with ease, although in general the work contains more poetry than prose. In recording the experiences of her own soul with God, Mechthild describes the spiritual journey both in general and in detail. She moves from a deep desire for God to a more mature appreciation of God's presence within her heart; as she grows in the spiritual life, her love intensifies. She believes that God's love for her grows as well.

Mechthild's writings indicate that she experienced both visions (that is, she "saw" God and several of the saints) and auditory messages (that is, she "heard" inner voices speaking to her). Because she was not writing for the edification of other readers, it can be assumed that she is narrating with complete sincerity. She professes a deep longing for God's presence and experiences intense sadness when this longing is not fulfilled. She describes God as having the same longing for the human heart.

Because Mechthild was a highly intuitive and poetic writer, it is not possible to analyze her work. She wrote with great feeling, often speaking of her great ache to be with God. In her work, she speaks extensively of the mystery of suffering, particularly the sufferings of Jesus Christ but also the suffering of the souls in Purgatory and the condemned souls in Hell. She writes as though she is describing actual visions or interior experiences, but it is not possible to tell when she is narrating and when she is creating. It may be that this distinction did not exist for Mechthild. She was, it is generally concluded, a true mystic; her sense of the divine was strong and real, and she wrote about it with a sense of the limitations of language.

In many ways, Mechthild reflects the spiritual climate of her time. Grim and detailed in her depiction of the sufferings of those who offend God, she uses the conventional flames, pestilence, sounds, smells, and other horrors in describing Hell. Although she believes that God is a God of love, she is more concerned with focusing on God's justice and wrath. She goes so far as to claim that the souls in the lowest part of Purgatory may not be saved, a claim condemned by the Catholic Church in

1520. This claim was probably motivated by her deep distress at the notion of sin, even the lesser or venial sins for which the purgation of Purgatory is appropriate.

Part of the richness of Mechthild's writing comes from the fact that she wrote for her confessor alone, without any aim of teaching others. Her writing is personal and has a simplicity that more formal works lack; readers of her work come away with the feeling that they have overheard her dialogues with God.

Mechthild's conception of Purgatory and Hell is believed by some to be the basis for Dante's description of the same scenes in his *La divina commedia* (c. 1320; *The Divine Comedy*, 1802). Although it is not possible to prove this influence, it is striking that cantos 27-33 of the second book of Dante's work, on Purgatory, are very similar—some say identical—to Mechthild's descriptions in *The Flowing Light of the Godhead*. It should also be noted that three-part descriptions of Hell and Purgatory are not uncommon. If Dante had access to Mechthild's work, it would most likely have been a translation from the German into Italian, something highly unlikely, not impossible, but virtually impossible to document.

Although no original manuscript of Mechthild's work is known to exist, the work was published after her death and went through several translations. She was relatively unknown until the mid-nineteenth century, when renewed interest in the medieval mystics, Mechthild among them, caused her works to be reprinted. In later years, she was often included in collections of spiritual writings by women, where she is frequently compared with Julian of Norwich and Hildegard von Bingen. Although she is now regularly included in collections of spiritual writings, there seems to have been no cult or following (as in the case with many persons reputed to be mystics and visionaries), nor has there been any movement to declare her a saint.

SIGNIFICANCE

Mechthild of Magdeburg, writing at the command of her confessor, produced the first major mystical work in Low German. She occupies a firm place among the medieval mystics and remains important both for her spirituality and as a pioneer of German literature, because of her use of the vernacular in a time when this practice was not ordinarily sanctioned. As scholars continue to explore spiritual works written by women, Mechthild's place in that canon becomes even more secure.

—*Katherine Hanley*

FURTHER READING

Anderson, Elizabeth A. *The Voices of Mechthild of Magdeburg*. Oxford, England: Peter Lang, 2000. Considers the voices of Mechthild as prophet and mystic in *The Flowing Light of the Godhead*. Quotations from Mechthild are in both Middle German and Anderson's English translation. Notes summarize secondary studies; bibliography.

Dronke, Peter. *The Medieval Lyric*. New York: Harper and Row, 1968. Dronke includes Mechthild in his analysis of themes and concepts in the medieval lyric.

Flinders, Carol Lee. *Enduring Grace: Living Portraits of Seven Women Mystics*. San Francisco: Harper, 1993. One of the most readable and insightful treatments of Mechthild's work; good analysis of recurring themes in the seven writers.

Tobin, Frank. *Mechthild von Magdeburg: A Medieval Mystic in Modern Eyes*. Columbia, S.C.: Camden House, 1995. A full-length study of Mechthild, including a survey of critical literature that has appeared since her rediscovery in the mid-nineteenth century. The single most helpful treatment of Mechthilde, her life, and her writing.

Underhill, Evelyn. *Mysticism: The Nature and Development of Spiritual Consciousness*. 1911. Reprint. London: Methuen, 1962. Although nearly a century old, this work remains the classic study of mysticism. Mechthild is mentioned numerous times as Underhill discusses various types of mysticism, mystical revelations, and related topics. Helpful for the reader unfamiliar with mysticism and the terms used in discussing it.

Zehringer, William C. "Mechthild of Magdeburg's Spiritual Pilgrimage." *Review for Religious* (May/June, 2001): 277-284. Explores the spirituality and theology of Mechthild's writing. According to the author's note, the article is adapted from a chapter of a book in progress.

SEE ALSO: Beatrice of Nazareth; Hildegard von Bingen; Julian of Norwich; Marguerite Porete.

RELATED ARTICLES in *Great Events from History: The Middle Ages, 477-1453*: March 21, 1098: Foundation of the Cistercian Order; 1136: Hildegard von Bingen Becomes Abbess; c. 1306-1320: Dante Writes *The Divine Comedy*.

Mehmed II

Sultan of Ottoman Empire (r. 1451-1481)

As sultan of the Ottoman Empire, Mehmed II commanded armies that captured Constantinople, and under his rule control of the Balkans and Anatolia in substantial portions was extended as the Ottoman state became one of the most important powers of early modern times.

Born: March 30, 1432; Adrianople, Ottoman Empire (now Edirne, Turkey)
Died: May 3, 1481; Hunkârçayırı, near Maltepe, Ottoman Empire (now in Turkey)
Also known as: Mehmed Fatih (Mehmed the Conqueror)
Areas of achievement: Government and politics, military, warfare and conquest

Early Life

Although it is known that, as a prince of the Ottoman Empire, Mehmed (meh-MEHT) was the son of Murad II, the sixth sultan, the identity of the boy's mother has not been established with certainty. It would appear that she was one of the sultan's slave girls, and she may have been from a non-Muslim family in the Balkans. Mehmed was born in Adrianople, the Ottoman capital of that time. At about the age of two, he was sent to a special court at Amasya, in north central Anatolia; later, he was taken to Manisa, near İzmir, where he was educated by tutors who subsequently gained distinction in the academic profession or as government ministers.

For reasons that still remain obscure, and notwithstanding Ottoman reverses of this period during fighting in Europe, in August, 1444, Murad abdicated in favor of Mehmed. A coalition of Christian powers had been formed, under the leadership of Hungary's János Hunyadi, which was also promoted by the Byzantine Empire, the Papacy, and Venice, in an effort to present a common front against the Ottoman state. After attending to conflicts in Asia, and even with his son nominally ruler, Murad returned at the head of a large army, and a major defeat was inflicted on their opponents at Varna, in Bulgaria, on November 10, 1444. While this major battle served notice to European governments that the Ottomans could not easily be dislodged from the Balkans, other engagements followed; though the position of George Branković, the despot of Serbia, remained problematical, the renowned Skanderbeg (George Kastrioti) of Albania had commenced resistance to the Ottomans. In May, 1446, Murad returned to the throne in the wake of a janissary revolt. Another important battle was fought in October, 1448, at Kosovo in Serbia; while Murad commanded Ottoman troops, Mehmed also took part in actual fighting as Hungarian and other armies were put to flight.

For Mehmed, family concerns arose at a relatively early age. His first son, who later was to become his successor as Bayezid II, was born to him by Gülbahar, a slave girl, in December, 1447, or January, 1448. In 1450, Mehmed's second and favorite son, Mustafa, was born, though the identity of Mustafa's mother remains unclear. Subsequently a marriage with a woman from a suitable social station was arranged when Mehmed took Sitt Hatun, from a noted family of central Anatolia, as his wife. Mehmed also became the father of six other children, some of whom were born from liaisons or marriages that were concluded after he came to power. Although during Murad's second reign Mehmed may have continued to regard himself as the rightful sultan, a reconciliation of sorts would appear to have taken place; yet Murad died of apoplexy rather unexpectedly. On February 18, 1451, Mehmed ascended to the throne in Adrianople. While in the past Ottoman rulers, including Murad, had eliminated family members for political reasons, Mehmed had two of his brothers executed and sanctioned the practice of fratricide by which, for nearly two centuries, sultans summarily were to remove potential rivals from any struggle for supreme power.

Life's Work

At the outset of his second reign, Mehmed II attended to a flurry of unrest in Anatolia and stirrings of discontent among the janissaries before turning to military planning, which was centered on a single consuming ambition. The Byzantine Empire had maintained a prolonged and precarious existence even though Constantinople was surrounded by territories under Ottoman control; by virtue of its double line of walled fortifications and its position at the edge of the Bosporus, the imperial city remained difficult of access to armies in the field. While the Byzantine emperor Constantine XI Palaeologus had threatened to support a different claimant to the Ottoman throne, a trade agreement with Venice had been renewed, at the request of Çandarli Halil, the grand vizier, and a treaty was negotiated with Hungary. Though Halil advised against precipitous action, it had become evident that the beleaguered city could expect little European assistance. Mehmed commenced preliminary operations with the construction of a major fortress north of Constantinople. A sympathetic Hungarian gunsmith known as Urban helped to cast cannon of a size larger than any that previously had been used. In the face of an Ottoman blockade, Byzantine forces received few reinforcements, apart from a Genoese contingent from Chios; some Venetian and Genoese fighting men already had been stationed nearby. The Ottomans possessed an immense numerical advantage, with possibly eighty thousand men under arms, as opposed to about nine thousand defenders.

The siege began on April 6, 1453, and, following repeated bombardments, Mehmed resolved finally to storm the city. On May 29, after some sharp fighting at many points, Ottoman troops entered Constantinople through a gate to the north and subdued their opponents in short order. Apparently Constantine died at this time. For his military prowess, Mehmed acquired the nickname Fatih, or the Conqueror. The city was pillaged briefly, and some prominent men, including Çandarli Halil, were executed. Afterward, to encourage the restoration and development of the new Ottoman capital, which became known as Istanbul, the sultan allowed many original inhabitants to return to their homes. Further settlers, both Muslims and Christians, were recruited from Asia and Europe. As a mark of his toleration for religious communities within the Ottoman Empire, Mehmed recognized Gennadius II Scholarios, a churchman who had opposed union with the Catholics, as the Greek Orthodox patriarch; a Jewish grand rabbi and an Armenian patriarch also were accepted as representatives of their faiths in Mehmed's capital.

Mehmed II. (Library of Congress)

Subsequent military endeavors revealed the broad sweep of Mehmed's ambitions and the extent of Ottoman power on two continents. Although in 1456 Ottoman forces failed to take Belgrade after a siege of six weeks when Hunyadi's forces intervened successfully against them, the Hungarian commander died later that year, and shortly thereafter George Branković of Serbia also died. In 1459, the Ottomans annexed what remained of the southern Slavic area, while in 1463 most of Bosnia was occupied as well. During other expeditions, Ottoman forces captured Athens in 1456, and during the next four years much of the Morea (in Greece) was overrun. Some setbacks that were suffered by Mehmed's armies did not have lasting effects. A campaign into Walachia to enforce a previous tributary relationship, against the infamous Vlad Ţepeş (the Impaler, who was also the historical prototype for the famous horror figure Dracula), resulted in a grisly massacre of Ottoman soldiers. Yet, under pressure from Mehmed, Vlad was deposed in 1462, and when he returned to power much later he met with death in battle.

In Asia Minor, Ottoman forces secured the submission of Trebizond, the last Greek kingdom of the Byzantine era, in 1461. Subsequently a particularly dangerous threat arose when Uzun Ḥasan, ruler of the Turkmen Ak Koyunlu Dynasty that had become established in western Iran, attempted to displace Mehmed's authority in central Anatolia. An entire Ottoman army was mobilized, and, when Mehmed led his troops in person, a convincing victory was obtained at Bashkent near Erzincan, on August 11, 1473. Ottoman control of the area northwest of the Euphrates River thus was consolidated. An important success for Ottoman policy on the northern coast of the Black Sea came in 1475, when the Tatar khanate of the Crimea acknowledged Mehmed's suzerainty. Political complications at several points in the Balkans had led to a prolonged war with Venice, between 1463 and 1479, and during much of his later reign Mehmed was also involved in undertakings of several sorts in Europe. Although the redoubtable Skanderbeg, who was allied with the Venetians, had resisted Ottoman incursions until shortly before his death in 1468, eventually the fortress of Krujë surrendered to Mehmed himself in 1478, and Ottoman forces held most of Albania. In the end, Venice was compelled to make peace on relatively harsh terms. Mehmed evidently was not entirely appeased, and in 1480 an Ottoman army obtained a foothold in Italy by capturing Otranto; a landing at Rhodes, in the eastern Mediterranean, was repelled, however, by the Knights of Saint John.

THE OTTOMAN SULTANS THROUGH THE BYZANTINE CONQUEST, C. 1281-1453

Reign	*Sultan*
c. 1281/88-1326	OSMAN (ʿOSMĀN) I
1326-1362	Orhān I
1362-1389	Murad I
1389-1402	Bayezid I
1402-1421	Mehmed I
1421-1444	Murad II
1444-1446	MEHMED II
1446-1451	Murad II (second rule)
1451-1481	MEHMED II (second rule)
1453	Fall of Constantinople, end of the Byzantine Empire

While Mehmed frequently accompanied his armies during their campaigns, his administrative work brought many reforms, some of which provoked an adverse reaction after his death. His conception of power was along strictly autocratic lines, and often he did not attend meetings of the Divan, or council of state. Where he did delegate authority, he exercised some care in maintaining distinctions among offices that were subordinate to his. Mehmed also directed the codification of laws, which were promulgated on his authority and were meant to serve regulatory purposes alongside Qurʾānic law. Fiscal policies were far-reaching but high-handed. Mehmed instituted the sale of private monopolies in essential goods to augment government revenues; some private estates and religious foundations were confiscated as state lands. Commercial relations with other countries were promoted even as Mehmed had customs duties increased. One of the most widely resented of Mehmed's measures, however, was the repeated reduction in the silver content of Ottoman coinage.

In other respects, Mehmed has been regarded as having had an urbane and cosmopolitan outlook. He was a patron of literary men, including Persian poets, and he composed a collection of verse in his own right. In addition to supervising the conversion of Byzantium's most famous church into the Hagia Sophia mosque, he left further architectural monuments, of which the Faith mosque in Istanbul was perhaps the most notable. He had an interest in the visual arts that overcame any religious objections to such forms of representation, and he supported the production of medals and paintings by which his appearance has become known. The most famous portraits of Mehmed, by Sinan Bey, a Turkish artist, and by Gentile Bellini, a Venetian master whom Mehmed commissioned to paint his likeness, show broad, angular features with the eyes set in a stern fixed gaze; a large curved nose was set above thin, taut lips and a small, slightly receding chin. A brown or reddish mustache and full beard suggested somewhat more of an imperious bearing. Sinan's work also depicts Mehmed as having some tendency toward corpulence, which reputedly affected the sultan during his later years. Indeed, when Mehmed died, on May 3, 1481, at a place about 15 miles (25 kilometers) east of Istanbul, the effects of gout were cited as a cause. Some suspicion has existed, however, that he was poisoned.

SIGNIFICANCE

The interpretations that have generally been advanced of Mehmed II's character and aims are of several sorts. While his importance in the expansion of Ottoman power has invariably been acknowledged, some have maintained that he intended essentially to extend his authority over an area roughly corresponding to that of the Byzantine Empire from a much earlier period. It has further been contended, though with some notable exaggerations, that older Byzantine practices served as the model for some of the measures that were implemented during his reign. Other views have emphasized the Turkic elements in his methods of rule and have noted that continuity among Ottoman rulers was stressed in the official court historiography of Mehmed's period. It has been maintained as well that, because primacy with respect to other Islamic states was asserted in many of Mehmed's pronouncements, he regarded his efforts as the fulfillment of aspirations that were at once both religious and political. The conception of Mehmed as a Renaissance ruler who was at home in several cultural milieus, while alluring to certain writers, has been sharply criticized as neglecting the priority he typically assigned to military matters. On the other hand, the notion that Mehmed was unusually cruel and vindictive, or inordinately devoted to conquest as an end in itself, has been challenged by those who would argue, with some justice, that the Ottoman ruler was probably no more severe than other commanders of his age. In all, it would appear that, very much in the way that Ottoman traditions combined political and cultural elements from several sources, the achievements of Mehmed may have arisen from aims and ideas that reflected his various purposes.

—*John R. Broadus*

FURTHER READING

Babinger, Franz Carl Heinrich. *Mehmed the Conqueror and His Time*. Edited by William C. Hickman. Translated by Ralph Manheim. Princeton, N.J.: Princeton University Press, 1978. This imposing work by an important modern scholar is by far the most significant Western study of Mehmed's statecraft. Provides references that summarize scholarly views and research findings. Bibliography, index.

Ducas. *Decline and Fall of Byzantium to the Ottoman Turks*. Translated by Harry J. Magoulias. Detroit, Mich.: Wayne State University Press, 1975. A well-informed Greek writer produced this chronicle of which the most useful and detailed portions deal with events from the time of Murad until 1462. In spite of a tendency to criticize Mehmed harshly, the author provides some shrewd insights about political developments of this period. Bibliography.

Freely, John. *Istanbul: The Imperial City*. New York: Viking, 1996. Explores the history of the city now known as Istanbul, from the seventh century B.C.E. through the fall of the Ottoman Empire in the early twentieth century. Includes chapters on the city when it was known as Constantinople and its fall during Mehmed's time. Illustrations, spelling and pronunciation guide, bibliography, index.

Gueriguian, John L. "Amirdovlat, Mehmed II, and the Nascent Armenian Community of Constantinople." *Armenian Review* 39, no. 2 (1986): 27-48. Some interesting and little-known facts about one of Mehmed's personal physicians are presented here alongside speculation about Mehmed's physical and psychological condition.

Inalcik, Halil. "The Policy of Mehmed II Toward the Greek Population of Istanbul and the Byzantine Buildings of the City." *Dumbarton Oaks Papers* 23/24 (1969/1970): 231-249. In a solid scholarly study, the author demonstrates the extent of Mehmed's efforts to promote recovery and urban development after the siege of 1453.

Kritovoulos. *History of Mehmed the Conqueror*. Translated by Charles T. Riggs. Princeton, N.J.: Princeton University Press, 1954. The divided sympathies of a Greek writer who became the governor of Imbros under Mehmed are expressed in this narration of events from 1451 until 1467. The work was dedicated to Mehmed and praises him highly in places, but delivers lamentations for the fate of peoples in formerly Byzantine lands. Illustrations.

Michałowicz, Konstanty. *Memoirs of a Janissary*. Translated by Benjamin Stolz. Ann Arbor: Department of Slavic Languages and Literatures, University of Michigan, 1975. The experiences of a Southern Slav who was taken prisoner and accompanied Mehmed's armies were set down in this account, which is of particular value for the period between the fall of Constantinople and the Bosnian campaign of 1463. Text transcribed from a Czech manuscript, with the translation on facing pages. Bibliography, index.

Raby, Julian. "Pride and Prejudice: Mehmed the Conqueror and the Italian Portrait Medal." *Studies in the History of Art* 21 (1987): 171-194. A noted art historian herein provides some interesting evidence, drawn partly from Venetian archives, about Mehmed's interest in portraiture during various stages of his career.

Runciman, Steven. *The Fall of Constantinople, 1453*. New York: Cambridge University Press, 1990. This study by a distinguished Byzantinist, originally published in 1965, is probably the standard work in English on the famous siege. Attention to scholarly detail does not impede the retelling of enthralling and tragic episodes from the last days of the city's resistance to the Ottomans. Illustrations, maps, bibliography, index.

Sicker, Michael. *The Islamic World in Ascendancy: From the Arab Conquests to the Siege of Vienna*. Westport, Conn.: Praeger, 2000. Presents a history of the rise and expansion of the Islamic empire, including the conquests of Mehmed. Concludes with a chapter on the end of the ascendancy. Bibliography, index.

Tursun Beg. *The History of Mehmed the Conqueror*.

Edited and translated by Halil Inalcik and Rhoads Murphey. Chicago: Bibliotheca Islamica, 1978. The work of an important Ottoman writer is presented here in a summary translation followed by a facsimile of an original Turkish manuscript. The author, who participated in a number of Mehmed's campaigns, comments in places on the harsher qualities of Mehmed's character in an account meant partly as instruction for Mehmed's successor. Bibliography, index.

SEE ALSO: Hārūn al-Rashīd; János Hunyadi; Justinian I; Osman I; Tamerlane.

RELATED ARTICLES in *Great Events from History: The Middle Ages, 477-1453*: 532-537: Building of Hagia Sophia; 1040-1055: Expansion of the Seljuk Turks; 1077: Seljuk Dynasty Is Founded; 1273: Sufi Order of Mawlawīyah Is Established; 1442-1456: János Hunyadi Defends Hungary Against the Ottomans; May 29, 1453: Fall of Constantinople.

MELISENDE

Queen of Jerusalem (r. 1131-1153)

Melisende was a powerful ruling and cultural figure of the Latin Crusader kingdom of Jerusalem. She served as a patron of the arts, architecture, and the Christian Church at a time when it was rare for a woman to do so.

BORN: 1105; Edessa, Anatolia (now Urfa, Turkey)
DIED: September 11, 1161; Jerusalem (now in Israel)
AREAS OF ACHIEVEMENT: Government and politics, architecture, patronage of the arts, religion and theology

EARLY LIFE

Melisende (mehl-ih-SEHND-ah) was the firstborn daughter of an Armenian princess, Morphia of Melitene, and a European noble who fought in the First Crusade, Baldwin of Le Bourgh, the count of Edessa. While living in Edessa, the couple had three daughters: Melisende, Alice (b. 1106), and Hodierna (b. 1115).

Growing to the age of fourteen in Edessa, Melisende was influenced by high standards of education, the eastern way of life, and her mother's orthodox form of Christianity. At that time it was common for young noblewomen to be married in their early teens. However, unexpected circumstances put Melisende's future on hold. In 1118, while her father was making pilgrimage to Jerusalem, his cousin, the first Crusader king, Baldwin I, died. After the funeral, the nobility selected her father as King Baldwin II (r. 1118-1131).

Women had not played a prominent role among Crusader rulers up to this time. However, Baldwin II delayed his coronation for eighteen months until Morphia and her three daughters could move to Jerusalem. Together they were crowned on Christmas Day, 1119. Baldwin's hopes likely were for a male heir, but the following year Morphia gave birth to a fourth daughter, Joveta.

While Melisende was still a teenager, a young man, Hugh of LePuiset, arrived in Jerusalem. Since Hugh's late father had been a cousin of Baldwin II, he was taken into the royal court of Jerusalem, where he and Melisende developed a close relationship. Eventually he was given the title count of Jaffa, and, as the closest male relative of the king, he assumed a high degree of influence.

There is no evidence that Morphia took an active role in government in Jerusalem. However, when the king was taken captive by Muslim forces in 1123-1124, it was Morphia who brought about his release. She first hired Armenians, who infiltrated the garrison, and then traveled to Syria to negotiate his release, even handing over her youngest daughter as hostage until ransom could be paid.

In 1128, about the time of Morphia's death, Baldwin began to look to Melisende to continue the reign, offering her a number of responsibilities. A grant to the Holy Sepulchre in 1129 was made in her name. She signed charters with the inscription *filia Regis et regni Hierosolimitani haeres* (daughter of the king and heir to the kingdom of Jerusalem).

Melisende's younger sister Alice was already providing the model of a strong woman leader. In 1126, Alice had married Bohemond II, the prince of Antioch (r. 1126-1130), and found herself well liked by the local Orthodox population. Her daughter Constance was born two years later. Then, in 1130, Bohemond was killed in battle. Instead of waiting for her father to appoint a regent, Alice assumed the regency herself, initiating contacts with the Muslim prince Zangī for support. However, Baldwin intervened, appointing Count Jocelin of Edessa regent and banishing his daughter to Latakia. When Jocelin soon died, the leadership of Antioch allowed the regency to stand vacant, with Alice exerting influence from a distance.

However, Frankish property laws would not permit Melisende to rule Jerusalem by herself. Also, women were excluded from the military leadership critical in the Crusader kingdom. Baldwin therefore sent a delegation to France to find her a suitable husband. Fulk V, count of Anjou, a forty-year-old widower with two grown children, was selected with the endorsement of King Louis VI of France and Pope Honorius II.

According to William of Tyre, the chief chronicler of this period, there were questions whether Melisende accepted the arranged marriage. Nevertheless, they were married in May, 1129. Fulk immediately joined his father-in-law in a conquest of Damascus. In 1130, Melisende bore a son, Baldwin III, and in 1135 another son, Amalric I. Both would serve as Latin Crusader kings.

When Baldwin II grew ill, he transfered power to Fulk and Melisende. He took off the crown and moved to the Church of the Holy Sepulchre, where he lived his final days as a monk.

JERUSALEM: CRUSADER KINGS AND QUEENS, 1095-1291

Reign	*Ruler*
1095-1099	First Crusade
1099-1100	Godfrey of Boulogne (or Bouillon)
1100-1118	Baldwin I of Boulogne
1118-1131	Baldwin II of Le Bourg
1131-1153	MELISENDE
1131-1143	Fulk V of Anjou
1143-1162	Baldwin III
1147-1149	Second Crusade
1162-1174	Amalric I
1174-1183	Baldwin IV the Leper
1185-1186	Baldwin V
1185-1190	Sibylla
1186-1192	Guy of Lusignan
1189-1192	Third Crusade
1190-1192	Conrad of Montferrat
1192-1197	Henry of Champagne
1192-1205	Isabella I
1197-1205	Amalric II
1202-1204	Fourth Crusade
1205-1210	Maria of Montferrat (regent)
1210-1225	John of Brienne
1210-1228	Isabella (Yolanda) II
1217-1221	Fifth Crusade
1225-1228	FREDERICK II
1227-1230	Sixth Crusade
1228-1254	Conrad IV Hohenstaufen
1244	Fall of Jerusalem
1248-1254	Seventh (or Sixth) Crusade
1254-1268	Conradin Hohenstaufen
1268-1284	Hugh III
1268-1284	Charles of Anjou (rival)
1270	Eighth (or Seventh) Crusade
1284-1285	John I
1285-1306	Henry I of Jerusalem (II of Cyprus)
1291	Fall of Acre to the Mamluks

LIFE'S WORK

The coronation of Fulk and Melisende took place on Holy Cross day, September 14, 1131. Tensions soon developed between the couple. Her father had envisioned a joint rule that would guarantee the place of inheritance to his young grandson. However, Fulk did everything to limit Melisende's power, with all official acts for the first five years coming only in his name. The nobility in Jerusalem quickly sympathized with Melisende, viewing Fulk's efforts as a power grab. When he attempted to gain control over Antioch, Alice publicly opposed him and reclaimed the regency in an alliance with the popular patriarch.

Jerusalem was divided between partisans of Fulk and partisans of Melisende, with her second cousin Hugh emerging as her strongest supporter. By 1134, a full rebellion erupted. Rumors filled the city of Jerusalem of an illicit affair between Melisende and Hugh—accepted as factual by many. Yet others note the church consistently backed Melisende throughout this struggle. The rumors were probable attempts by Fulk to discredit the queen. Things came to a head when Hugh was accused of treason and then challenged to a duel, but instead of agreeing to a duel, he sought refuge among Muslims in Ascalon. The patriarch of Jerusalem sought terms of peace that would have exiled Hugh for three years in Italy. While waiting for his ship, Hugh was stabbed in the back during a game of dice. Most people believed that King Fulk immediately put the assassin to death to silence him from implicating the king. The tide turned against Fulk, and he feared for his life.

Eventually, Fulk made a most favorable settlement with Melisende. Shortly thereafter she bore him a second son. According to William of Tyre, Fulk "never tried to initiate anything, even in trivial matters, without her foreknowledge." This is documented in six surviving acts from this period made in both their names.

The influence of Melisende extended to Antioch, where she negotiated the return of her sister Alice to the city. Officially, Alice ruled by herself from 1135 to 1136. A strange twist occurred when Raymond of Poitiers, prince of Antioch (r. 1136-1149), arrived and asked for her hand in marriage. Instead, he kidnapped Alice's eight-year-old daughter Constance and was married to her by the new patriarch Radulph. Alice was again banished to Latakia, while Raymond and Constance ruled Antioch.

Fulk's death in a hunting accident in the fall of 1143 gave Melisende another chance to rule. She was designated regent for thirteen-year-old Baldwin III. On Christmas Day, 1143, they were crowned as corulers in the Church of the Holy Sepulchre. William of Tyre described the ritual as an anointing, a significant act because it imitated the coronation of David and the Old Testament kings and suggested rule by divine right. In reality, Melisende controlled the government. William of Tyre reported on her abilities in glowing terms, writing,

> Melisende, the king's mother, was a woman of great wisdom who had much experience in all kinds of secular matters. She had risen so far above the normal status of women that she dared to undertake important measures. It was her ambition to emulate the magnificence of the greatest and noblest princes and to show herself in no wise inferior to them. Since her son was as yet under age, she ruled the kingdom and administered the government with such skillful care that she may be said to truly have equaled her ancestors in that respect. As long as her son was willing to be governed by her counsel, the people enjoyed a highly desirable state of tranquility, and the affairs of the realm moved on prosperously.

In 1145, when Baldwin reached a legitimate ruling age, Melisende downplayed the celebration and instead began to maneuver him out of every place of influence. For the next seven years his name was omitted from official acts.

Although she was not permitted to lead the army, Melisende chose her cousin Manasses of Hierges as constable and closest adviser. In 1144, they sent an army to Edessa to assist Jocelin. When this proved unsuccessful, she wrote Bernard of Clairvaux to call for a second Crusade. In 1148, Melisende traveled to Acre (now in Israel) to receive King Louis VII of France and advised him to attack Damascus, a city under control of eastern Christians. When the Crusade appeared a failure, the criticism mounted.

Baldwin was especially put off by the haughty attitude of Manasses and rallied many of the nobles of Jerusalem against him. In 1152, he made an official complaint to the high court that his mother had excluded him from his rightful rule. Baldwin decided that he would be crowned king on Easter Day. Melisende requested a second coronation for herself, but Baldwin excluded his mother and appeared in public as a secretly crowned king. Baldwin's next step was to request that the kingdom be divided in two, so that Melisende could continue ruling in Jerusalem and he would rule the north. This created a dilemma for the leading nobles, who recognized both Melisende's experience as an efficient administrator and Baldwin's inherited right to rule. The matter was determined by force when Baldwin's army invaded Jerusalem and besieged Melisende in the Tower of David.

Melisende retired from Jerusalem and retained only the city of Nablus. However, rather than retire from public life, she traveled to Tripoli, where she advised her niece Constance. Constance remained sole ruler of Antioch from the death of her husband, Raymond of Poitiers, in 1149 to her remarriage to the Crusader Reginald of Châtillon in 1153. Melisende also offered counsel to her own sister Hodierna, concerning both her strained marriage with Count Raymond II of Tripoli and Hodierna's becoming regent of Tripoli following his death.

Realizing that his mother still exerted influence in the north where the Muslim sultan Nureddin (d. 1174) was growing in power, Baldwin reconciled himself to her. From 1153, she served as Baldwin's closest adviser and shared in many of his public acts. In 1157, when Baldwin was campaigning in Antioch, she undertook her own military attack and recovered a fortress beyond the Jordan. On November 30, 1160, Melisende suffered a stroke, which limited her abilities until her death.

SIGNIFICANCE

Melisende's most lasting contribution was to the art and architecture of Jerusalem. She initiated extensive work on both the Church of the Nativity in Bethlehem and the Church of the Holy Sepulchre in Jerusalem. In 1149—about fifty years after the arrival of the first Crusaders—she presided over the ceremonies dedicating the remodeled Church. Second Crusaders remarked on the magnificent paved streets and the vaulted roofs of the city, which are still visible in the Old City *suq* (marketplace) today.

Melisende's youngest sister, Joveta, took monastic vows at a convent just inside the city walls, at what is now called Stephen's Gate. There the queen built the Church of Saint Anne, which is still considered one of the most impressive Crusader structures in Jerusalem. Later she obtained land in Bethany (now in Jordan) to establish and endow the convent of St. Lazarus, where Joveta later became abbess. Her final project was a new structure for the Tomb of the Virgin in the Valley of Josaphat, where her mother had been buried. Melisende, too, chose to be buried in a chamber still visible inside this structure. The queen's name is also connected with the Melisende Psalter, a beautifully illustrated text with an ivory cover. Created in 1135, it was a gift from her husband, Fulk.

—*Fred Strickert*

FURTHER READING

Boas, Adrian J. *Crusader Archaeology: The Material Culture of the Latin East.* New York: Routledge, 1999. Explores the material culture of the early Crusades in Jerusalem and surrounding rural areas, with chapters on defense structures, ecclesiastical architecture, fine arts, arts and crafts, building techniques and materials, and burial. Bibliography, index.

Folda, Jaroslav. *The Art of the Crusaders in the Holy Land, 1098-1187.* New York: Cambridge University Press, 1995. An illustrated look at the history of the art of the first three Crusades, with chapters on the influences of Melisende, Fulk, and the Baldwins. Includes a discussion of historical writing about Crusader art and the artistic context of the First Crusaders. Maps, bibliography, and index.

Hamilton, Bernard. "Women in the Crusader States: The Queens of Jerusalem." In *Medieval Women*, edited by Derek Baker. Oxford, England: Blackwell, 1978. A study focusing on the role of women who governed Jerusalem during the Crusades.

Riley-Smith, Jonathan, ed. *The Oxford History of the Crusades.* New York: Oxford University Press, 1999. An illustrated history that shows the artistic and architectural legacy of Melisende. Bibliography, index.

Runciman, Steven. *The Kingdom of Jerusalem and the Frankish East, 1100-1187.* Vol. 2 in *A History of the Crusades.* New York: Cambridge University Press, 1951-1958. One of the most detailed resources on the Crusader era, by a respected British scholar. Illustrations, maps, and a genealogical table.

William of Tyre. *A History of Deeds Done Beyond the Sea.* 1941. Reprint. New York: Octagon Books, 1976. Provides a contemporary account of the era, written shortly after Melisende's death. Bibliography, index.

SEE ALSO: Saint Bernard of Clairvaux; Saladin.

RELATED ARTICLES in *Great Events from History: The Middle Ages, 477-1453*: 1009: Destruction of the Church of the Holy Sepulchre; November 1, 1092-June 15, 1094: El Cid Conquers Valencia; November 27, 1095: Pope Urban II Calls the First Crusade; 1147-1149: Second Crusade.

MI FEI

Chinese calligrapher

An accomplished calligrapher and the paragon of Chinese artist-connoisseurs, Mi Fei played a pivotal role in the transmission of the classical tradition of Chinese calligraphy.

BORN: 1052; Xiangyang, Hubei Province, China
DIED: 1107; Huaiyang, Jiangsu Province, China
ALSO KNOWN AS: Mi Fu; Yuanzhang (Pinyin), Yüanchang (Wade-Giles); Xiangyang (Pinyin), Hsiangyang (Wade-Giles); Haiyue Waishi (Pinyin), Haiyüeh Wai-shih (Wade-Giles); Midian; Mi the Eccentric
AREA OF ACHIEVEMENT: Art

EARLY LIFE

Mi Fei (mee fay) did not come from a distinguished family tradition, but he was reared on the palace grounds, as his mother served as a palace lady of the empress and wife of Emperor Yingzong (Ying-tsung; r. 1064-1067).

Together with Su Dongpo (Su Tung-p'o; 1036-1101), Huang Tingqian (Huang T'ing-chien; 1045-1105), and Cai Xiang (Ts'ai Hsiang; 1012-1067), Mi Fei is known as one of the four great masters of calligraphy of the Song Dynasty (Sung; 960-1279). He was a gifted artist with deep perceptions and passionate sensitivity. He possessed an irrepressible urge to rise above stuffy conventions and had a tendency to protest against accepted practices. Outspoken and unbridled, Mi Fei liked to wear loosely fitted robes with sweeping sleeves, in the style popular during the Tang Dynasty (T'ang; 618-907), and he had an idiosyncratic fixation on cleanliness, refusing to share towels and utensils with even his closest associates. Furthermore, he had a passion, if not an obsession, for grotesquely shaped rocks, before which—according to tradition—he would even prostrate himself and worship. It is therefore not at all surprising that Mi Fei acquired the nickname Midian, or Mi the Eccentric.

LIFE'S WORK

Mi Fei was a collector, art critic, connoisseur, painter, and calligrapher. He was appointed a collator in the Imperial Library at the age of twenty and subsequently served for two decades in minor official posts in the southern provinces. His home on the palace grounds and successive travels in the south afforded him ample opportunity to cultivate social contacts and to study many calligraphic works in private collections. He completed his first book on classical calligraphic works, *Bao zhang dai fang lu* (records of searches for precious scrolls), in 1086. He was widely acclaimed as a leading calligrapher in 1088, at the age of thirty-six, when he wrote his famous *Shu su tie* (calligraphy on coarse Sichuan silk).

In 1092, Mi Fei was appointed subprefect in Yungjiu, Henan; he was then close to the capital, Kaifeng, where famed collectors and dealers were easily accessible. According to his necrology, in 1103 he was given the title doctor of the imperial sacrifices (*taichang boshi*) for his calligraphic skills. Mi Fei reached the pinnacle of his official career in 1105, when he was invited to become doctor of calligraphy and painting (*shuhua boshi*) and, shortly thereafter, assistant division chief of the board of rites (*libu yuanwailang*). He was given an audience with Emperor Huizong (Hui-tsung; r. 1101-1125), to whom he presented his own handwritten copy of the "Thousand-Character Essay" following the foremost example of pre-Tang standard script (*kaishu*).

Mi Fei maintained close contacts with some of the outstanding intellectuals of his time. At the age of thirty-two, he was fortunate enough to make the acquaintance of Su Dongpo. Su Dongpo was a towering figure in an influential circle of scholar-officials, and he considered Mi Fei his protégé. He encouraged Mi Fei to begin a serious study of calligraphic works of the masters of the Eastern Jin Dynasty (Chin; 317-420 C.E.), particularly those of Wang Xizhi (Wang Hsi-chih; c. 307-379) and Wang Xianzhi (Wang Hsien-chih; 344-386). Mi Fei equipped himself with a boat that he named *Shuhua fang* (boat of calligraphy and painting) and sailed it up and down the waterways in southeastern China, eagerly participating in the privileged social game of collecting and trading art objects.

A unique combination of connoisseur and artist is immediately discernible in Mi Fei. For him, connoisseurship and artistic skills complemented each other—one was the *sine qua non* of the other. This view is particularly understandable in the cultural climate of which Mi Fei was a part, for nearly all the original brushwork art of the classical period was lost and copying the works of the early masters was an integral part of practicing calligraphy. Copies of the originals, or copies of the copies, served as the primary source of information for the study of early masterpieces. One could depend only on the expert judgment of the connoisseurs, who might have viewed more originals and better copies.

Mi Fei had diligently practiced the art of calligraphy since his early childhood. He copied most laboriously works of masters of the Eastern Jin Dynasty—works he regarded as stylistic prototypes, embodying the highest standards of fine calligraphy. Few artists, in fact, have ever engaged in such a prolonged and fruitful study of the works of their predecessors. Mi Fei became known for his extraordinary ability to copy faithfully works of early masters down to the minutest details. He frequently borrowed masterworks from his associates and copied them meticulously. His skill reached such perfection that even some of the most discerning connoisseurs were confounded and could not differentiate his copies from the originals. Through his ardent and creative absorption of the skills and artistic spirit embodied in the works of earlier masters, Mi Fei achieved an unprecedented level of brush mastery. His calligraphic works demonstrate a refreshing style and a distinctive cultivated air.

Mi Fei's critical writings are widely regarded as the foremost source of information for the history of calligraphic work before the Song Dynasty. He transmitted an image of the Jin masters' art through his personal interpretations. Although Mi Fei's writings lacked systematic integrity, he presented himself forcefully and methodically. He scrutinized an enormous volume of painting and calligraphic pieces and offered candid (though often cantankerous) and trenchant comments in the form of discussions. Although Mi Fei wrote on the history of calligraphy and painting, connoisseurship of ink stones and paper, techniques of scroll mounting, and the use of seals, those observations on calligraphy have had the most lasting influence.

According to Mi Fei, extensive and continuous stylistic explorations within the classical tradition are paramount: They are directly beneficial to the development of the theoretical proficiency required of an artist. This proficiency helps facilitate the formation of the artist's personal style. In addition, Mi Fei regarded the development of calligraphy as a social phenomenon, not to be dictated by the particular style of an individual. He wrote most frequently in running script (*xingshu*), most popular during the Song. This style combines the legibility of standard script with the creative freedom of cursive. Mi Fei also left behind specimens written in the traditional seal (*zhuanshu*) and clerical (*lishu*) styles. In fact, a wide spectrum of styles and a variety of shapes and strokes are found in his oeuvre. His brush strokes seem to have been made in rhythmic bursts; they display restless energy and effortlessness. Fluidity and spontaneity characterize his work. Artistic creation, according to Mi Fei, must demonstrate quintessential artistic qualities such as *chaoyi* (transcendence), *pingdan* (plain tranquillity), and *tianren* (natural perfection). This view decisively and profoundly influenced many artists in China after him.

Although his calligraphic works are better known than his paintings, Mi Fei's landscapes did give rise to a new school of painting, known as the Mi school. His creative inner impulse led him to break with accepted conventions. It is said that in his landscape paintings he abandoned drawn lines altogether in favor of blobs of splashed ink, thus giving more vitality to his creations. The term "Mi mountains" (*Mijiashan*) refers to the landscapes of Mi Fei and his son Mi Yuren (Mi Yu-jen), who was an accomplished artist in his own right.

SIGNIFICANCE

Calligraphy was the art form most widely practiced in traditional China. Everyone who aspired to enter into officialdom was expected to be a proficient calligrapher. Exquisite and refined calligraphy was regarded by the Chinese as their supreme artistic and, simultaneously, moral achievement. That brushwork mirrored the personality and the moral character of the artist was a concept accepted since the early Han Dynasty (206 B.C.E.-220 C.E.). For the Chinese, calligraphy is an effective means through which one cultivates inner strength and morality. Thus, in China, Mi Fei—calligrapher, art historian, and connoisseur *par excellence*—is immortalized for his artistic eminence.

—*San-pao Li*

FURTHER READING

Gao, Jianping. *The Expressive Act in Chinese Art: From Calligraphy to Painting*. Stockholm: Almqvist & Wiksell International, 1996. An examination of the place of calligraphy and painting in Chinese art. Bibliography and index.

Ledderose, Lothar. *Mi Fu and the Classical Tradition of Chinese Calligraphy*. Princeton, N.J.: Princeton University Press, 1979. This scholarly, comprehensive, and detailed study of Mi Fei discusses the pivotal role he played in the transmission of the classical tradition of the Jin masters' art. The author traces the evolutionary patterns in the history of Chinese calligraphy through a study of the methods Mi Fei used to investigate the past. Mi Fei's historical and aesthetic concepts are carefully examined. Numerous illustrations help enliven the author's skillful discussions.

Mi Fei. *Mi Fu on Ink-Stones*. Translated by R. H. van Gulik. Peking: H. Vetch, 1938. A translation of one of Mi Fei's works, although on ink stones rather than on calligraphy.

Sturman, Peter Charles. *Mi Fu: Style and the Art of Calligraphy in Northern Song China*. New Haven, Conn.: Yale University Press, 1997. A treatment of the calligrapher that deals largely with his artistic style and his legacy. Bibliography and index.

Sullivan, Michael. *The Three Perfections: Chinese Painting, Poetry, and Calligraphy*. Rev. ed. New York: George Braziller, 1999. A general examination of calligraphy and its relation to the other arts of painting and poetry in China. Bibliography.

SEE ALSO: Ma Yuan; Ouyang Xiu; Wang Wei; Xia Gui; Yan Liben.

RELATED ARTICLES in *Great Events from History: The Middle Ages, 477-1453*: 907-960: Period of Five Dynasties and Ten Kingdoms; 960: Founding of the Song Dynasty; 960-1279: Scholar-Official Class Flourishes Under Song Dynasty; c. 1190-1279: Ma-Xia School of Painting Flourishes.

MINAMOTO YORITOMO

Japanese shogun (1192-1199)

Yoritomo led the Minamoto (Genji) clan when it defeated the Taira (Heike) and established the Kamakura shogunate, beginning seven centuries of feudal rule in Japan.

BORN: 1147; Kyoto, Japan

DIED: February 9, 1199; Kamakura, Japan

AREAS OF ACHIEVEMENT: Government and politics, warfare and conquest

EARLY LIFE

Minamoto Yoritomo (mee-nah-moh-toh yoh-ree-toh-moh) rose to prominence as a leader of provincial warriors in eastern Japan. The circumstances of his birth were central to his career. He was the son of Minamoto Yoshitomo (1123-1160) and a court lady, the daughter of Fujiwara Sukenori, and had eight brothers or half brothers. Little is known of Yoritomo's first twelve years except that he lived in Kyoto (he would later demonstrate that he was comfortable with courtiers in his regime).

Yoshitomo was a ninth generation descendent of Emperor Seiwa (r. 858-876) and the leader of the dominant branch of the Minamoto (Genji) clan—long called the "tooth and claws of the Fujiwara" for helping the dominant court family intimidate rivals and put down rebellions. However, such service was often repaid by court promotion of the rival Taira (Heike) clan, also of royal blood, to check the Minamoto. The court's dangerous game of using warriors for political muscle proved costly when two factions called warriors to the capital in 1156. The resulting Hōgen disturbance consisted of only one modest battle, won by Minamoto Yoshitomo, although many losers were Minamoto. The winning side, which supported Emperor Go-Shirakawa, elevated Taira Kiyomori (1118-1181) to high office while slighting Yoshitomo, who had sided with Kiyomori, and enraged Yoshitomo by demanding capital punishment (unused for 350 years) for fifty warriors on the losing side, mainly Minamoto family members, including Yoshitomo's father and brother.

In 1159, Yoshitomo and disgruntled Fujiwara family members unsuccessfully attempted a coup (Heiji disturbance); he and his two oldest sons were killed. Thirteen-year-old Yoritomo, his oldest surviving son, was exiled to Izu. Hōjō Tokimasa (1138-1215), his second warden there, later allowed Yoritomo to wed his daughter Masako and then became his loyal vassal.

LIFE'S WORK

Over the next two decades, Kiyomori gained dictatorial control of the state, placing scores of Taira in high offices, marrying his daughter Tokuko to Emperor Takakura (r. 1168-1180) and making their two-year-old son Emperor Antoku (r. 1180-1185). Kiyomori's arrogance provoked rebellion by a passed-over prince, Mochihito, and an aging Minamoto courtier, Yorimasa, initiating the Gempei War (1180-1185). They soon died, but in Izu, Yoritomo, now thirty-two, took up Mochihito's call to expel the Taira. Yoritomo had difficulty recruiting kinsmen; in his first battle, his overwhelmingly outnumbered force was crushed, and he narrowly escaped capture (Ishibashiyama; August 23, 1180). However, after establishing a permanent base in Kamakura, he increased his force dramatically by persuading many erstwhile opponents to join him and by offering protection and confirmation of property rights to warriors who became his vassals. By the time he faced Taira loyalists again, at Fujigawa, Suruga Province (November 20, 1180), he had a huge force, which the fearful Taira fled without fully engaging. It was his last Gempei battle. Yoritomo turned his army back to Kanto, where he forced reluctant Minamoto lords to join him.

Widespread famine and plague brought a hiatus in the war, during which Yoritomo solidified his control by creating the office of samurai (*samurai dokoro*; November, 1180). The initial organ of the feudal government that he would establish, the office of samurai curbed warrior lawlessness, particularly confiscation of land, and became the entity though which he organized his warriors.

The virtual truce ended in April, 1183, when the Taira moved into Chubu to attack Yoritomo's cousin Minamoto (Kiso) Yoshinaka (1154-1184) and feckless uncle Minamoto Yukiie. Yoshinaka, a daring and resourceful warrior, controlled five provinces and, though he had supported Yoritomo in 1180, in reality represented a third potent military force with Yoritomo and the Taira. Yoshinaka rushed to meet his attackers, crushing their larger force at Kurikara Pass, Toyama, then driving them from Kyoto. There he received an imperial mandate to pursue them but delayed, wary of Yoritomo, whom retired emperor Go-Shirakawa was secretly contacting. Yoshinaka's unruly troops became unwelcome. First denied authorization to attack Yoritomo, the impulsive Yoshinaka stormed Go-Shirakawa's residence, beheading scores of his supporters. Yoshinaka then offered to ally with the Taira against Yoritomo but was rebuffed.

Finally granted the authorization he sought, Yoshinaka was even elevated to the highest military office, shogun. In response, Yoritomo ordered his half brothers Noriyori and Yoshitsune (1159-1189) to march on Kyoto. Yoshinaka weakened his position by sending some of his troops against Yukiie, who had deserted him, then divided the remainder between the Seta and Uji approaches to the capital. Yoshitsune broke though Uji and entered Kyoto. Yoshinaka died trying to flee Noriyori's Seta force. The victors quickly moved west against the Taira base at Ichinotani. Yoshitsune, with seventy men, boldly scaled the Hiyodori Impasse to its north and charged down a steep ravine, befuddling the startled defenders. Suffering one thousand slain and nine chieftains captured, the Taira fled to Shikoku (March, 1184).

It was six months before the Genji pursued their advantage, apart from soliciting converts in Shikoku and Kyushu. In August, Yoritomo sent an army under Noriyori west, but timidity and logistical problems bogged him down. In November, 1184, Yoritomo established two more governmental organs, the office of administration (*kumonjo*, later renamed *mandokoro*), headed by Ōe Hiromoto, and the judicial board (*monchūjo*), headed by Miyoshi Yasunobu. These men were experienced Kyoto scholar-administrators and contributed much to the success of the emerging *bakufu* (tent government) Yoritomo was creating, whose core institutions were now in place.

Meanwhile, a rift developed between Yoritomo and Yoshitsune. Yoritomo, evidently jealous of his brother's military brilliance and fearing a potential rival, failed to recommend him for court honors after Ichinotani, even though Noriyori and four others far less deserving were given governorships. Yoshitsune then accepted appointments (palace guard, imperial police) from Go-Shirakawa, which angered Yoritomo, who had prohibited such appointments without his recommendation. If Go-Shirakawa hoped to divide the brothers, he succeeded but with appalling consequences for the court.

Nevertheless, Noriyori's ineptness forced Yoritomo to give a new command to Yoshitsune. Once again, he

Scene depicting Minamoto Yoritomo, seated on left, and his brother Yoshitsune. (F. R. Niglutsch)

displayed daring and strategic brilliance. Crossing to Shikoku with only 150 men in a storm that had damaged most of his ships, Yoshitsune made a forced march through the night to the stronghold of Yashima, burning villages as he approached to appear to be a larger force (March 22, 1185). The frightened Taira embarked before guessing the truth, then sailed west. With new allies, Yoshitsune assembled a large naval force. A month later (April 25), he engaged the Taira in the Kyushu-Honshu straits at Dannoura. Awaiting a tidal change, he closed on the Taira ships, his archers targeting sailors to facilitate boarding Taira ships. Many chiefs and Kiyomori's emperor-grandson, Antoku, died in the battle, the Taira's final defeat.

Yoshitsune's brilliant generalship left Yoritomo supreme. However, the latter, fearful of potential rivals and willing to credit his slanderous vassal Kajiwara Kagetoke's reports, ordered Yoshitsune to Kamakura, then refused him entry, ignored his plea of loyalty, and sent him back to Kyoto—soon to be followed by an assassin. The latter bungled, driving Yoshitsune closer to the court and Yukiie, whom Yoritomo also wished to eliminate. Go-Shirakawa authorized the two to take up arms against Yoritomo, but their plan to establish bases in Kyushu and Shikoku ended when a storm destroyed their vessels. Yukiie was captured and executed six months later. Yoshitsune eluded authorities in the capital area for many more months, then made his way north to Hiraizumi and the protection of Fujiwara Hidehira.

Yoritomo punished the court, demanding dismissal of those who supported the mandate to attack him, the establishment of a ten-man advisory council appointed by him, and the appointment of Fujiwara Kanezane, long his intimate, as imperial adviser. Kanezane's approval was required of all court decrees, and he informed Yoritomo of court activities. Yoritomo also gained from the court the power to appoint provincial constables (*shugo*) and military estate stewards (*jitō*), and to impose a 2 percent "emergency military tax" on previously untaxed manors (*shōen*)—ostensibly to deal with the public menace constituted by the fugitive Yoshitsune. The *shugo* managed the *bakufu*'s *jitō* in each province; the latter, who were supported by the *shōen* they oversaw, extended Kamakura's power to the local level throughout the country—though appointment of both official was gradual. Hōjō Tokimasa's presence in Kyoto with troops had encouraged acceptance of these demands. Thus, Yoritomo exploited Yoshitsune's recent alliance with the court (which, obviously, he had created), to eliminate its autonomy and enhance the power of the *bakufu*.

Major Emperors of the Kamakura Period (1185-1333) and Kemmu Restoration (1333-1336)

Reign	*Ruler*
1183-1198	Go-Toba
1198-1210	Tsuchimikado
1210-1221	Jintoku
1221	Chukyo
1221-1232	Go-Horikawa
1232-1242	Shijō
1242-1246	Go-Saga
1246-1260	Go-Fukakusa
1260-1274	Kameyama
1274-1287	Go-Uda
1287-1298	Fushimi
1298-1301	Go-Fushimi
1301-1308	Go-Nijō
1308-1318	Hanazonō
1318-1339	Go-Daigo

Yoritomo exploited in yet another way the existence of the "renegade" Yoshitsune. Yoshitsune's protector in Ōshū, Fujiwara Hidehira, died in October, 1187. Throughout the following year Yoritomo pressed Hidehira's heir Yasuhira, via court orders, to give up Yoshitsune, and finally obtained court permission to attack Ōshū. Fearful, Yasuhira attacked Yoshitsune, coerced his suicide (June 15, 1189), and sent his head to Kamakura in a lacquer box of sake. Undeterred, Yoritomo overran Ōshū with a huge army, eliminating the last sizable force that might oppose him. In the west, recent converts had been called on to demonstate their loyalty by joining the campaign. Hence, his grip on the entire country was strengthened.

The death of Go-Shirakawa in 1192 left Kanezane unchallenged at court. He persuaded the boy-emperor Go-Toba (1183-1198) to grant Yoritomo what Go-Shirakawa had long denied: the title of *shōgun* (generalissimo; August, 1190). Thus, the regime Yoritomo set up in Kamakura became the shogunate, an institution that would endure for seven centuries.

The honor did not make Yoritomo less distrustful. The following year, he had Noriyori executed on trumped-up charges. His cruelty had already strained his domestic relations. When Yoshinaka turned against him, Yoritomo had Yoshinaka's twelve-year-old son—held as a hostage and betrothed to Yoritomo's six-year-old daughter Ohime—executed. The girl and her mother, Masako,

Major Leaders of the Kamakura Shogunate, 1192-1333

Reign	Shogun
1192-1199	MINAMOTO YORITOMO
1202-1203	Minamoto Yoriie
1203-1219	Minamoto Sanetomo
1226-1244	Kujo Yoritsune
1244-1252	Kujo Yoritsugu
1252-1266	Prince Munetaka
1266-1289	Prince Koreyasu
1289-1308	Prince Hisaaki
1308-1333	Prince Morikuni

were outraged, and the fearless Masako forced Yoritomo to have the boy's killer executed. Yoritomo later hoped to make Ohime an imperial consort, but she died at the age of twenty.

Although he dominated his age, the cause of Yoritomo's death at about age fifty-two is not known. His foresight, judgment, ability to attract able men to his service, and relentless drive to enlarge his power shaped Japan's history. However, there was nothing noble about him. He made a great show of religious piety and sought court mandates whenever possible to give his actions an aura of legitimacy, but he was ruthless, with slight regard for human life. He earned his countrymen's respect but not their love. His deplorable treatment of Yoshitsune is remembered as well as anything else he did.

As for the epic struggle with the Taira that defined his life, his death brought a great irony. He had killed all his male relatives save his two young sons, far less able than himself. His father-in-law Hōjō Tokimasa took over as shogunal regent, also heading the *mandokoro*, *samurai dokoro*, and council of office, and would be succeeded by his son. Both of Yoritomo's sons were murdered, and eventually (1254), princes served as figurehead shoguns, while the Hōjō, one of the ablest political families in Japanese history, ran the country. The Hōjō were a branch of the Taira clan.

Significance

The centralized political system Japan borrowed from China in the seventh century had fatally atrophied by the twelfth. Whereas Taira Kiyomori had established a short-lived dictatorship based on usurpation of outmoded institutions, Yoritomo built a new political system in Kamakura based on feudal command. It imposed discipline on the warrior class, gave them fair treatment though its legal institutions, and provided them financial support through *jitō* appointments and estates confiscated from the Taira. Thus reunified and strengthened, Japan was able to repulse the Mongol invasions of 1274 and 1281, and, although the shogunate was transferred to Kyoto when the Hōjō were defeated in 1333, and to Edo in 1600, it would endure until 1867.

—R. Craig Philips

Further Reading

Mass, Jeffrey P. *Warrior Government in Early Medieval Japan: A Study of the Kamakura Bakufu, Shugo, and Jitō*. New Haven, Conn.: Yale University Press, 1974. A good review of the development of warrior rule in Japan.

_______. *Yoritomo and the Founding of the First Bakufu*. Stanford, Calif.: Stanford University Press, 1999. A revisionist work that emphasizes the conservative elements in Yoritomo's government and the limited implementation in his lifetime of the reforms associated with him.

Sansom, George. *A History of Japan to 1334*. Vol. 1. Stanford, Calif.: Stanford University Press, 1958. One of the most respected histories of Japan.

Shinoda, Minoru. *The Founding of the Kamakura Shogunate, 1180-1185, with Selected Translations from the Azuma Kagami*. New York: Columbia University Press, 1960. Excellent study of the political and military developments that brought Yoritomo control of Japan.

Sugawara Makoto. "Bushidō." *The East* 16-19 (1980-1983). Interesting, very detailed narrative, based on traditional histories.

See also: Ashikaga Takauji; Fujiwara Michinaga; Taira Kiyomori.

Related articles in *Great Events from History: The Middle Ages, 477-1453*: 792: Rise of the Samurai; 858: Rise of the Fujiwara Family; 1156-1192: Minamoto Yoritomo Becomes Shogun; 1219-1333: Hōjō Family Dominates Shoguns, Rules Japan; 1336-1392: Yoshino Civil Wars.

SIMON DE MONTFORT

English political leader

Simon de Montfort was a passionate, adventurous, and self-confident medieval nobleman who emerged as the leader of a group of English barons intent on curbing abuses of power by King Henry III. He dramatically changed the relationship between king and Parliament in ways critical to the development of that institution as a force to limit and monitor the royal prerogative.

BORN: c. 1208; Montfort, Île-de-France, France
DIED: August 4, 1265; Evesham, Worcestershire, England
ALSO KNOWN AS: Simon V de Montfort; earl of Leicester
AREA OF ACHIEVEMENT: Government and politics

EARLY LIFE

No surviving document records the birth date or place of Simon de Montfort (MAHNT-furt), but historians believe that he was born around 1208. He was the fourth son in a family of four sons and three daughters. His father, Simon IV de Montfort, was an ambitious Norman nobleman who became famous for answering Pope Innocent III's call for a crusade against the Albigensian-Waldensian heretics in southern France. Simon V was born sometime during that long, bitter, and infamous campaign. Simon's mother, Alice, was the daughter of the powerful noble Bouchard V, Sire de Montmorenci. She was a vigorous and pious woman who accompanied her husband on the crusade to help and encourage him. Simon IV had inherited the earldom of Leicester through his mother, who was the sister of the childless Robert IV de Beaumont, fourth earl of Leicester. Simon IV, however, had been too preoccupied with the crusade to take possession of the earldom. Then, in 1207, King John of England confiscated all the English holdings of those Norman lords loyal to King Philip II of France because Philip had declared several of John's northern French provinces forfeit during a dispute.

Nothing is known directly of Simon's youth, but from his later life it is obvious that he was well educated and well trained for war. He was fluent in Latin, French, and English, and he was a friend of the leading educated Englishmen of his day. He clearly also possessed courage, intelligence, and great tactical ability, or he could not have risen from a landless fourth son of a French noble family to the most powerful aristocrat in England and leader of the Barons' Cause. Although no portrait or likeness of him has survived, he was reported to have been tall, handsome, and possessed of a commanding presence and a magnetic personality.

On the death of his father, Simon's eldest brother, Amaury VI, inherited the family lands and titles, but there was a conflict of interest between his French inheritance and claims to the earldom of Leicester. Rather than leave the English claim dormant, he signed it over to Simon, who went to England in 1230 to ask the new king, Henry III, to restore the earldom. Henry III was sufficiently impressed to award him a modest annual income from the royal treasury until the restoration could be arranged, which took two years. With that ancient and respected title came other honors and privileges, including the office of steward of England and adviser to the king as a member of the royal court. Besides merely ceremonial functions, the position of steward included responsibility for the just administration of English law, including the removal of evil counselors from the king's service and preparation for their trial before the next Parliament. The new earl of Leicester took these responsibilities more seriously than was the custom, and he later made them part of the basis of his actions in the Barons' Cause.

At court, Simon met the king's sister Eleanor. She was a widow and a postulant for holy orders, but she had not yet taken the nun's veil when she and Simon met, and they fell in love. Henry III and Leicester were on good terms at this point, and the king permitted them to be married, on January 7, 1238. Simon and Eleanor had six children—Henry, Simon VI, Guy, Richard, Amaury, and Eleanor—and were both strong and imperious personalities. While they are reported to have quarreled from time to time, there were also many indications that they were thoroughly devoted to each other.

LIFE'S WORK

Not much is known of Simon in the years after he acquired his earldom. There is occasional mention of him performing his ceremonial duties as steward and other assignments for Henry III. As someone who was frequently at court, however, Simon must have been aware of the English lords' growing disaffection for Henry III. There were three major complaints: The king did not consult with his English nobles on the governing of England or offer them offices in the central government, but surrounded himself with nobles from his holdings in France as advisers and state officials; the king spent lavishly on his court, family, friends, and grandiose foreign

Engraving of Simon V de Montfort unseated from his horse before the gates of Toulouse. (F. R. Niglutsch)

policy and was constantly squeezing his English vassals for more money; the king was arbitrary, willful, and capricious, and his paranoia toward the English lords on numerous occasions erupted into violent verbal assaults that were undignified for him and humiliating to the nobles. Some, including Simon, also complained that he was too deferential to the pope in Rome. In 1234, 1236, 1237, and 1244, there were major troubles over one or more of these problems. Twice, Parliament forced Henry III to dismiss his French counselors, but he would bring them back as soon as Parliament disbanded. Once Henry III took refuge in the Tower of London.

In August of 1239, Henry directed one of his verbal outbursts at Simon, who was so enraged that he left for France and then went on to Palestine to join the remnants of the Sixth Crusade. Other than fighting with the forces that obtained the release of his older brother Amaury VI, Simon was not involved in any notable military exploits. He returned to France in early 1242 to find Henry III there summoning his knights and nobles and planning to retake the French provinces lost to the king of France by his father, King John. Simon agreed to join the king's forces in return for a grant of money. The English were beaten back that summer, however, and by spring, 1243, Henry III had spent so much money while in winter quarters in Bordeaux that he was forced to accept the offer of King Louis IX of France to sign a five-year truce, which later was renewed or extended until 1259.

The breach between Simon and Henry III seemed healed. Over the next five years, Simon received numerous land and money grants from Henry III and undertook several important missions for him. In 1244, Simon was involved with a party of English nobles in one of their periodic confrontations with the king over his French counselors and seemingly endless need for more money. Even with the king's capitulation, Simon managed to remain on good terms with both the king and Parliament. In 1248, Henry III asked Simon to restore order to Gascony, one of the king's remaining French provinces, which was torn by factionalism and civil strife. Simon agreed but stipulated that Henry III give him absolute control of the province and its revenues for seven years, supply him with fifty knights at Henry III's expense, and protect Gascony from neighboring kingdoms for the duration. After Simon energetically put down several rebellions and exacted stern penalties, a number of Gascon nobles complained to Henry III in 1251 and brought charges of brutality against Simon in an attempt to rid themselves of him. Henry III, in one of his fickle turns against Simon, conducted a five-week trial of Simon's administration of the province. Although angered and humiliated by the king's actions, Simon defended himself well and was unanimously acquitted of all charges.

Capriciously, Henry III then pardoned all rebels and gave their lands back, which undermined all that Simon had accomplished. Henry III then went to Gascony himself, only to be met with the largest force yet raised by the Gascon rebels, forcing him to bring over his own army and use the same tactics as Simon had used in order to pacify the province. After that incident, King Henry III seems to have recovered from his unreasonable fear of Simon and once again trusted the earl with various assignments.

The amity between Henry III and Simon, however, did not last. In 1253, the pope entangled Henry III in Rome's century-old quarrel with the Hohenstaufen dynasty of the Holy Roman Empire and southern Italy by offering the crown of the kingdom of Sicily to Edmund, Henry III's second son. In order to accept, however, Edmund needed to assume the Papacy's huge debt, incurred in its military efforts to seize the kingdom from the Hohenstaufens, and to mount an expensive major military operation to defeat Manfred, who was the able bastard son of the late emperor and regent in Sicily for the new emperor, Conrad IV. At about the same time, Henry III arranged the election of his brother, Richard of Cornwall, to Holy Roman Emperor, another expensive policy. By 1258, Henry III's Sicilian policy had become a ruinous and expensive trap. His English lords were unwilling to continue contributing soldiers and money, and the pope threatened excommunication if Henry III reneged. In desperation, the king agreed to the nobles' plan of establishing a council of twenty-four, twelve chosen by Henry III and twelve by the nobles, to meet in Oxford and consider how to reorder the government so that it served the best interests of the whole community of the realm. The phrase "the whole community of the realm" had been adopted by Simon and the other barons as a definition of what constituted the legitimate use of royal authority. Simon was an active participant in the party of nobles that made these demands and one of the twelve whom they chose to meet at Oxford. The result of their work was known as the Provisions of Oxford, 1258.

The Provisions of Oxford required a minimum of three formal meetings of Parliament per year, gave the great lords the authority to appoint the principal officers of state, and established a Council of Fifteen to conduct the king's business on a regular daily basis. In theory, the king was left nearly powerless, but in fact he was indispensable because all decisions were in his name and required his agreement or signature. (This loophole was a great weakness of the Barons' Cause and eventually was exploited by Henry III.) The king was allowed to conclude the negotiations for a treaty with Louis IX concerning a number of matters outstanding between them, especially the surrender of any claim to those French provinces lost by his father, King John, and England's undisputed title to Gascony and other holdings in southern France. Henry III left England for Paris immediately after agreeing to the Provisions of Oxford, and he remained there until April of 1260, assisted from time to time by Simon.

While Henry III was in France, the English barons removed from office and exiled from court the king's, and even the queen's, French friends and relatives. Henry III failed to call the required meetings of Parliament and council, a maneuver he seems to have thought would both weaken the position of the nobles opposing him and rally supporters. Simon and the others responded by calling Parliament on their own, the most revolutionary move the barons ever made. What Henry III found most offensive, however, was the subversion of his eldest son and heir, Prince Edward, to the Barons' Cause by Simon. Henry III never forgave Simon, and it caused the final break between them.

When Henry III finally returned from France, the barons found him determined to resist their reforms. The Sicilian venture was over, and Louis IX had given Henry III a generous financial settlement that temporarily freed him from financial dependence on the barons. He brought a number of French nobles with him as advisers, thus outraging the English barons. Henry III refused to see Prince Edward until he ended his alliance with the barons, which weakened their position. He also made charges against Simon. By April of 1261, Henry III had convinced Pope Alexander IV to release him from his vows to uphold the Provisions of Oxford and all the resultant statutes and ordinances. In February, 1262, the new pope, Urban IV, confirmed Henry III's release from all oaths, and Simon, disgusted with the dissension and lack of resolve within the nobles' ranks, went into exile in France. King Henry III followed early in 1262 to attempt to put Simon on trial for treason. Realizing that the king had learned nothing and that they could now only submit or rebel, the remaining barons reorganized while Henry III was in France, called on Simon to return to lead them, and took up arms in the spring of 1263.

The nation divided for a civil war. Many of the important nobles, most of the lesser nobility, and large numbers from the lower classes supported Simon and the rebellious barons. In six weeks, Simon defeated and imprisoned the leaders of the opposition in a series of minor engagements. Yet at a meeting of Parliament in September of 1263 to reinstate the Provisions of Oxford, the barons' party broke up in factionalism caused by the distribution of royal favors. With both sides roughly equal in strength and the barons weakened by dissension, Simon agreed to Henry III's suggestion to submit the matter to arbitration by Louis IX. The French king was renowned for his justice, but he could not be expected to rule against the royal cause. In his decision, the Mise of Amiens, given January 24, 1264, Louis IX voided the Provisions of Oxford and all the other achievements of the barons. Once again, the barons could either fight or submit.

Simon, who had fallen from his horse and fractured his leg, had remained in England during the arbitration sessions in France. When word of the Mise of Amiens reached him, he rallied the forces of the Barons' Cause by announcing that he would go down fighting. Nobles and commoners flocked to him in support, and at the Battle of Lewes, on May 7, 1264, Simon won a resounding victory over the main Royalist force, taking Henry III, Prince Edward, and Richard of Cornwall prisoner. For the next fifteen months, Simon was the de facto ruler of England. In the Mise of Lewes, Henry III agreed to swear to uphold the Magna Carta, the Charter of the Forest, and the Provisions of Oxford. He also agreed to cut his expenses and live on the income from his own domains, to provide full amnesty for Simon and the other leaders of the Barons' Cause, and to give Prince Edward as hostage until a final and full agreement could be reached.

After taking control of all important strongholds and seeing to the needs of local government, Simon called a meeting of Parliament for January, 1265. The elections for this parliament were so unique that it has been called the Great Parliament. Each county or shire was to elect two knights, and each town or borough was to elect two burghers. Knights had been included twice previously, but only to vote money for the king. In 1265, they were asked for advice on the reorganization of the government. The burghers had never been invited before. Simon was attempting to broaden the base of the Barons' Cause and give substance to the idea that the central government should concern itself with the interests and needs of the whole community of the realm, not only the great lords and prelates. In doing so through an assembly of elected representatives, Simon set a major precedent for the evolution of the modern Parliament.

To rule temporarily, Simon established a triumvirate of the bishop of Chichester, the earl of Gloucester, and himself to govern England in the king's name. There was also a baronial council that would meet periodically and, less frequently, meetings of Parliament for major decisions. The flaw in the system was the lack of any means to resolve disagreements that divided the leadership. Simon thought that he could produce consensus through the force of his own dynamic leadership, but to be certain, he placed his sons and wife in charge of key strongholds and military units.

To convert the victory at Lewes into a permanent settlement that all sides could accept, Simon established a council of arbitrators, with two members selected by the French king, two by the triumvirate, and the papal legate of England as a tiebreaker. The only real achievement of this group was to neutralize the French and buy time. The papal legate was hostile to the barons because they had ended the payments to the pope for the Sicilian campaign and supported the English prelates and clergy who desired greater freedom from Rome. Other hostile factions included Henry III's queen, Eleanor of Provence, who remained in France to raise money and troops to free him, sneaking knights across the Channel to England when she could. These forces were to join those English knights and great lords who, while they may not have liked Henry III, could not accept the affront to the royal dignity that the reforms of Simon and his followers were instituting.

In the spring of 1265, Leicester and Gilbert de Clare, the earl of Gloucester, quarreled, principally over the favored treatment of Simon's sons and the manner in which they had been abusing their positions in order to enrich themselves. Gloucester's fiefs lay close to Simon's and the Welsh border. Simon had made an alliance with Llewelyn ap Gruffydd, the dominant Welsh prince. After his quarrel with Simon, Gloucester allied with the marcher lords, whose territories made up the Welsh border and whose special responsibility to England's king was to contain the Welsh and expand the march territory into Wales whenever possible. Gloucester induced the marcher lords to invade Simon's earldom in retaliation for his alliance with Llewelyn. To save his lands, Simon and two of his sons took to the field. Meanwhile, the French knights whom Henry III's queen had been assembling slipped into England by way of South Wales and maneuvered around behind Simon. With Gloucester's connivance, Prince Edward escaped from Simon and rallied the royal forces to trap Simon, cutting him off from reinforcements. Two of Leicester's other sons, Simon V and Amaury, who were in charge of a military force near London, bungled the operation to relieve Simon. They lingered along the way to gather booty and then were captured. Simon nearly succeeded in breaking through the encircling Royalist forces by himself, but on August 3, 1265, at Evesham, he was surrounded. When he learned of his sons' capture, he chose to fight and die there rather than return to London to finish his life as a prisoner in the Tower of London or be executed. The Battle of Evesham took place the next morning and was quickly over after Simon's Welsh allies deserted him. Simon's son Henry died with him, but Guy was only wounded. When Simon fell, his body was horribly mutilated and dismembered. This outrageous violation of the code of chivalry undoubtedly contributed significantly to making a martyr of Simon. The legend of Simon as the champion of freedom and the lesser classes of Englishmen, which soon traveled the length and breadth of England, made him more dangerous to the royal cause than he ever was alive. Some two hundred miracles were claimed to have occurred at his tomb in the years immediately after his death, and many poems and folk ballads were composed in his honor.

SIGNIFICANCE

Simon de Montfort lived and made major contributions in a crucial era in English constitutional history. A central problem of medieval political theory was how to translate into workable political institutions the principle that the king was limited in authority by the law of the land. Magna Carta had stated the principle in 1215, but it took the English centuries to institutionalize it.

In the reign of Henry III, third in a line of inept kings, the English nobility was transformed from a cooperative and supportive feudal class into one that was increasingly nationalistic, alienated from the royal court, critical, and distrustful of the king's power. Simon was the single most important architect of that transformation. He emerged first as a major participant in and then as the guiding intelligence and leader of the dissident movement. In the Provisions of Oxford, he helped give form to the idea that the king must govern for the benefit of the whole community of the realm. When the king reneged on the Provisions of Oxford, Simon rallied the barons, won the Battle of Lewes, instituted reforms in the legal system, called a new-style parliament, and governed England. Simon established the critical precedent that the whole community of the realm was best served by a broad-based parliament that included representatives from the lesser nobility and burghers and that did more than merely approve new taxes. After the Battle of Evesham, neither Henry III nor his successor, Edward I, could undo Simon's accomplishments.

Simon's legend as a champion of liberty survived in English folklore and in the new adversarial relationship between Parliament and king. Simon is justly remembered by a statue before the entrance of the House of Commons as one of the remarkable Englishmen who were responsible for the development of Parliament.

—*Richard L. Hillard*

FURTHER READING

Bémont, Charles. *Simon de Montfort, Earl of Leicester, 1208-1265*. Translated by E. F. Jacob. 1930. Reprint. Westport, Conn.: Greenwood Press, 1974. A thorough and scholarly biography (the original French was published in 1884) that is still a useful resource.

Hollister, Charles Warren. *The Making of England, 55 B.C. to 1399*. 4th ed. Lexington, Mass.: D. C. Heath, 1983. The first volume of a four-volume general history of England. Provides an excellent, well-researched survey of English history for the general reader. Includes a brief discussion of Simon and the Barons' Cause.

Jacob, E. F. *Studies in the Period of Baronial Reform and Rebellion, 1258-1267*. Oxford, England: Clarendon Press, 1925. Dated but still an in-depth, well-researched study of the Barons' Cause.

Joliffe, John Edward Austin. *The Constitutional History of Medieval England: From the English Settlement to 1485*. 4th ed. New York: W. W. Norton, 1961. A very thorough and scholarly treatment that covers the contributions of Simon and the development of Parliament, written clearly enough for the general reader. Combines narrative with a brilliant interpretive style.

Labarge, Margaret Wade. *Simon de Montfort*. London: Eyre and Spottiswoode, 1962. An excellent, well-researched biography of Simon, including the background to the life and times of the earl.

Milson, S. F. C. *The Legal Framework of English Feudalism*. Cambridge, England: Cambridge University Press, 1976. A thorough examination of the legal aspects of the feudal system for those wishing an in-depth account. Mentions Simon and the Barons' Cause only in passing.

Myers, A. R. *Parliaments and Estates in Europe to 1789*. London: Thames and Hudson, 1975. For the general reader, covering the evolution of legislatures as a phenomenon of Western civilization, from their feudal origins to the start of the French Revolution.

Powicke, Frederick Maurice. *King Henry III and the Lord Edward: The Community of the Realm in the Thirteenth Century*. 2 vols. Oxford, England: Clarendon Press, 1947. Concentrates on the reigns of Henry III and Edward I and the development of the concept of

the community of the realm as an idea to limit royal prerogative.
Treharne, Reginald F. *The Baronial Plan of Reform, 1258-1263*. 1932. Reprint. Manchester, England: Manchester University Press, 1971. Traces in depth the history of the Barons' War, emphasizing its political and constitutional aspects.
_______. *Simon de Montfort and Baronial Reform: Thirteenth-Century Essays*. Edited by E. B. Fryde. London: Hambleton Press, 1968. The principal concentration of these essays is on the period 1258-1264, Henry's crisis years.
Valente, Claire. *The Theory and Practice of Revolt in Medieval England*. Burlington, Vt.: Ashgate, 2003. Addresses in its opening chapter the study of revolts and also discusses theories of resistance, the Magna Carta, and the concept of the community of the realm.
Weiler, Björn K. U., ed. *England and Europe in the Reign of Henry III (1216-1272)*. Burlington, Vt.: Ashgate, 2002. Looks at Henry's reign as it affected England and the Continent.

SEE ALSO: Edward I; Henry III; King John; Louis IX.
RELATED ARTICLES in *Great Events from History: The Middle Ages, 477-1453*: June 15, 1215: Signing of the Magna Carta; 1258: Provisions of Oxford Are Established.

MOSES DE LEÓN
Jewish rabbi, scholar, and philosopher

Through his lifework, the Zohar, *Moses de León exercised the greatest influence on Judaic religious thought after the Talmud and the Bible.*

BORN: 1250; probably León (now in Spain)
DIED: 1305; Arévalo (now in Spain)
ALSO KNOWN AS: Moses ben Shem Tov de León (full name)
AREAS OF ACHIEVEMENT: Religion and theology, philosophy, literature

EARLY LIFE

Moses de León (moh-says day lay-ohn) was an itinerant scholar who spent the greater part of his life wandering from town to town in his native province of Castile. Although few concrete personal details are known of these years, his writings reflect the social and religious unrest of his times. In the thirteenth century, Spain was still divided, Muslim and Christian, with Christian Spain slowly but steadily gaining the upper hand. Large numbers of Jews were Christian subjects either as a consequence of the Reconquest or because they were forced to flee Muslim Spain during the increasingly violent persecutions of the Almoravids and the Almohads, who had entered Spain in the eleventh and twelfth centuries and tolerated no religious dissension even among their own people. During the era of the *taifas*, the previous Arab rulers, before the arrival of the fanatical newcomers, the Jewish communities had been prominent and respected, and Jewish intellectuals had blossomed in the civilized cosmopolitan atmosphere of al-Andalus (Andalusia). In fact, the Iberian peninsula, both Christian and Muslim, produced some of the greatest philosophers of Jewish history.

The most famous and most controversial of the religious thinkers was Moses Maimonides (d. 1204) of Córdoba, who interpreted basic Judaic religious beliefs and traditions in the light of Aristotelian rationalism. His *Dalālat al-ḥaʾirīn* (1190; *The Guide of the Perplexed*, 1881) became one of the cornerstones of medieval Jewish philosophy and, through its Latin translations, influenced the writings of men of many divergent beliefs, not least among them Thomas Aquinas. As conditions in the Jewish communities began to worsen, however, for many there was cold comfort in pristine rational arguments. Earlier, in the name of faith and revealed truth, many Jewish traditionalists, scandalized, had attacked Maimonides' teachings as a form of heresy. Now their protests were united with the yearnings of a beleaguered people who needed something in which to believe.

Both groups found a source of strength in the uniquely Jewish mystical expression of the Kabbalah. The tradition of the Kabbalah, which literally means "received," traces its roots back to Abraham, but the term came to mean the mystical beliefs and practices that entered Europe through Italy from Palestine and Babylonia in the twelfth and thirteenth centuries. There were originally two great schools of Kabbalistic thought in Germany and the Provençal region of France, but the movement reached its zenith in Spain in the Jewish communities of Barcelona, Burgos, Gerona, and Toledo. Here the new theosophy merged with an intellectual Judaic tradition well into its golden age and refined its characteristic admixture of Gnostic and Neoplatonic elements.

The basic tenet of the Kabbalah is that the visible world is merely a reflection of a greater unseen world; the two worlds are interdependent, their influences flowing back and forth. An action in one will cause an equal repercussion in the other. Glimpses of this hidden reality could be read, for example, in every word, name, number, and syllable of the Torah, if one knew the code. This reading was the task and obligation of the Kabbalistic masters who could interpret these mysteries of spiritual revelation. Moses de León was one of the teachers of the Kabbalah who spread its doctrines during his travels through Castile and through his writings. In *Shoshan Edoth* (*The Rose of Testimony*) and *Sepher ha-Rimmon* (*The Book of the Pomegranate*), he attempted a mystical Kabbalistic treatment of the Ten Commandments. He seems to have used Guadalajara as his home base until around 1292, when he finally settled in Ávila. The rabbi then dedicated the rest of his life to the reworking and circulation of the manuscripts of the work that was to become the bible of Kabbalistic thought, the *Sepher ha-Zohar* (the book of splendor; usually called simply the *Zohar*).

LIFE'S WORK

The *Zohar* was the overriding preoccupation and great accomplishment of de León. It is not one work, but rather a miscellanea, written partly in Aramaic and partly in Hebrew, of biblical interpretation, mystic theology, prophecy, and moral and ethical teaching generally expounded by well-known rabbinical philosophers. The most famous and most quoted passages constitute a commentary on the Pentateuch, the first five books of the Bible. A summary of the prevalent Kabbalistic concepts of its time, the *Zohar*, with a vocabulary and set of correspondences all its own, sets out to reveal not only the mystical significance underlying all Judaic theology and edicts but also the hidden relevance of all material creation. The human is acclaimed as the unifier, the conjunction of the visual and spiritual worlds. By the end of the Middle Ages, the *Zohar*, with its appeal to faith and the heart, passionate at times in its lyrical beauty, had captured thousands in its mystical web. Paradoxically, however, the man whose crowning achievement it was, disclaimed the honor.

De León never accepted authorship of the *Zohar*. Instead, he circulated the manuscripts, ostensibly as a type of editor, and attributed their actual writing to Rabbi Simon bar Yohai, a famous Hebrew sage who lived in Palestine in the second century. Pursued by victorious Romans, bar Yohai hid in a cave for thirteen years, legend asserting that he spent the time mastering the secrets of the universe. When questioned as to how he obtained the document, de León revealed that the mystic Naḥmanides (1194-1270), a fellow Kabbalist of great prestige, had discovered the work in Palestine and, shortly before his death, had sent it to the Spanish rabbi. Although there was much discussion over de León's claims, his account of events was never seriously doubted during his lifetime, with one exception. Isaac de Acre, a close friend of Naḥmanides, but who surprisingly had never heard of such a manuscript, demanded that de León swear to its authenticity. De León did so and promised to show him the original, but died on the way to Ávila. Isaac, however, did not give up. He continued the journey and enlisted the aid of prominent Jewish leaders in Ávila. One of these, Joseph of Ávila, promised de León's widow, who was in great financial distress, a great sum of money and even a marriage between his son and her daughter if she told the truth concerning the authorship of the *Zohar*. She finally admitted that her husband had written the entire work himself without any outside references, recently discovered or not.

That is the position taken by most modern scholars. There are, indeed, glaring anachronisms in the work. For example, bar Yohai, who himself appears as one of the characters, mentions other rabbis who died centuries after. Also, the Aramaic dialect in which the *Zohar* was partially written was seldom used by the Jewish writers of the second century (the time period to which de León attributed the work), who preferred Hebrew. Although there are a few proponents for an unknown ninth or tenth century Palestinian Kabbalist as author, it is generally agreed that de León, a poverty-stricken, virtually unknown wanderer, wrote the *Zohar* and attributed it to the legendary bar Yohai in order to endow his work with importance and prestige.

Self-protection may also have been a principal motive. During the thirteenth century, the Jews in Spain not only faced Muslim and Christian persecution but also were divided in bitter social strife within their own communities. There was widespread hatred and resentment of the dominant Jewish courtier class. It was believed that while they had enjoyed influence and power in the Castilian court, they not only had forgotten their own people but also had manipulated them for their own and their Christian masters' political ends. One of the aims of the Kabbalist movement from the very beginning had been the elevation of religious and moral conduct and standards together with the overthrow of the wealthy aristocracy. The *Zohar*, therefore, is not simply a mystical treatise, but contains a bitter attack against the rich and the religious leaders who looked the other way and failed to chastise their influential patrons. The rabbinical scholars in the *Zohar* were meant to exemplify the conduct and theology of the true religious man and provided de León with camouflage for his acid criticism. His arguments were reinforced by the vivid memory of the execution of several important Jewish courtiers in 1280-1281. They were not mourned by many in the Jewish communities.

The *Zohar*, therefore, was widely accepted as a guide to proper Jewish behavior. In addition, with its glorious visions of the coming of the Messiah and the resurrection and vindication of his true followers, it gave spiritual comfort amid suffering; as the intensity of the persecutions increased, so did the importance of the *Zohar*, its influence reaching its zenith after the final, terrible expulsion of the Jews from Spain in 1492. The exiles spread the ideals of their beloved *Zohar* throughout the world. The chief center of Kabbalist thought became, fittingly, Safed in Palestine, close to the burial place of Simon bar Yohai. By the sixteenth century, the *Zohar* and its Kabbalistic teachings held sway in Judaic religious philosophy as important scholars such as Isaac ben Solomon Luria (1534-1572) interpreted and refined its tenets and practices. Its influence started to wane only with the coming of the Enlightenment and the emergence of a new generation of rationalists. Nevertheless, the Kabbalah did greatly inspire the powerful Hasidic movement of the eighteenth century, which still has thousands of adherents. The Hasidic appeal to strength of faith and purity of heart is pure *Zohar*.

The understanding of the Kabbalah, however, has suffered a progressive deterioration throughout the centuries as the underlying significance of its philosophy and terminology has been forgotten or misused. The name itself has become synonymous with superstition and magic as an aura of pseudoreligious, medieval occultism has encircled it. Sequences of its numbers and letters are evoked in magical incantations, and its symbols are worn to ward off evil spirits. Therefore, it is not surprising that the Kabbalah and its textbook, the *Zohar*, have been furiously attacked by contemporary Jewish scholars. Zoharic concepts, with their pagan and Gnostic elements, have come to represent, in the opinion of many, all that should be alien to progressive Jewish thought. It has not helped that Christian scholars, entranced by its mystical insights and unaware of its source, have used de León's vindication of Judaism to strengthen such Christian articles of faith as the explanation of the Trinity and the identification of Jesus Christ with the biblical Messiah. De León wished to write a guide for the strong in faith. He realized that his concepts and terminology were complex, but even he could not have understood their ramifications.

Significance

De León compiled a controversial work whose influence has been profound and varied throughout the centuries. At times, his teachings have been used in ways that would have horrified him. Itself an attack on declining religious values and practice, the *Zohar* has become for some a handbook of occult lore and ritual. This view, however, in no way negates its religious and historical importance. The *Zohar* is not only a reflection of prevalent Judaic mystical thought; it provides valuable insights into the background and philosophy behind the mystical fervor that swept through all faiths in the twelfth and thirteenth centuries. In many ways, it is startlingly similar to Christian apocalyptic literature, and the wandering Judaic sages portrayed in its pages could, with a slight change of name, be taken for Franciscan mendicant friars. More important, in its portraits and indictment of the conduct of the wealthy, the powerful, and the apostate, it illustrated the social and moral climate in which a movement such as the Kabbalah could be born and gain momentum.

The *Zohar* also stands as a symbol. The exiled Spanish Jews cherished it as a living link in the spiritual chain of their heritage, which had been so cruelly broken in 1492. Other Jews, in empathy, seeing this self-identification of the Sephardim with the *Zohar*, came also to regard the book as a tribute to the tenacity of faith. The great work of an exiled people seemed expressly made for a religion that saw itself in continual exile.

An ardent Kabbalist, de León believed himself to be capable of interpreting the hidden signification underlying all material objects. In his philosophy, the *Zohar* not only attempted to decipher these meanings but also was in itself a further cipher in the chain of correspondences between the higher and lower worlds. He could not have foreseen how later readers would find so many different codes and meanings.

—Charlene E. Suscavage

Further Reading

Anidjar, Gil. *"Our Place in al-Andalus": Kabbalah, Philosophy, Literature in Arab Jewish Letters*. Stanford, Calif.: Stanford University Press, 2002. Analyzes the history of the Kabbalah, the *Zohar*, and Judaism in Andalusian Spain, also during the time of de León's compilation of the *Zohar.*

Baer, Yitzhak. *From the Age of Reconquest to the Fourteenth Century.* Vol. 1 in *A History of the Jews in Christian Spain.* 2 vols. Translated by Louis Schoffman. Philadelphia: Jewish Publication Society of America, 1992. Traces century by century the deteriorating social conditions in the medieval Jewish communities that influenced the rise of the Kabbalah.

Berg, Rav Philip S. *The Essential Zohar: The Source of Kabbalistic Wisdom.* New York: Bell Tower, 2002. A practical, contemporary interpretation of the *Zohar* by a well-known Kabbalist, written for the general reader.

Cahn, Zvi. *The Philosophy of Judaism: The Development of Jewish Thought Throughout the Ages, the Bible, the Talmud, the Jewish Philosophers, and the Cabala, Until the Present Time.* New York: Macmillan, 1962. Contains a chapter on Moses de León and discusses the problem of authorship of the *Zohar.*

Caplan, Samuel, and Harold U. Ribalow, eds. *The Great Jewish Books and Their Influence on History.* New York: Horizon Press, 1952. Contains a discussion of the reasons behind the growth of Zohartic thought, emphasizing not only historical factors but also the beauty and power of the text itself, using selections from the original as illustrations.

Epstein, Isidore. *Judaism: A Historical Presentation.* Baltimore: Penguin Books, 1966. Concise information and clear explanations of prevailing Judaic philosophical trends during the Middle Ages, many of which have Spanish origins.

Margolies, Morris B. *Twenty Twenty: Jewish Visionaries Through Two Thousand Years.* Northvale, N.J.: Jason Aronson, 2000. Provides biographies of leading visionaries in the Jewish tradition, including de León and Maimonides. Includes bibliography and index.

Moses de León. *The Zohar.* Translated by Harry Sperling and Maurice Simon. 5 vols. London: Soncino Press, 1931-1934. A complete and faithful English translation.

O'Callaghan, Joseph F. *A History of Medieval Spain.* Ithaca, N.Y.: Cornell University Press, 1975. Detailed description of Spain as the philosophic battleground between the proponents of Maimonides' rationalism and the mystical, "irrational" tenets of the *Zohar.*

See also: Ibn Gabirol; Moses Maimonides; Naḥmanides; Thomas Aquinas.

Related article in *Great Events from History: The Middle Ages, 477-1453*: c. 1275: The *Zohar* Is Transcribed.

Muḥammad

The Prophet, founder of Islam

Through Muḥammad, the Qur'ān was recited and propagated as the revealed word of Allāh, and through his teachings and leadership, Islam was established as a religious system and a way of life that has possessed extraordinary influence and persuasive powers in many parts of the world.

Born: c. 570; Mecca, Arabia (now in Saudi Arabia)
Died: June 8, 632; Medina, Arabia (now in Saudi Arabia)
Also known as: Abū al-Qāsim Muḥammad ibn ʿAbd Allāh (full name)
Areas of achievement: Religion and theology, government and politics

Early Life

Muḥammad (moh-HAH-mehd) was the only child of his parents' marriage. His father, ʿAbd Allāh ibn ʿAbd al-Muṭṭalib, from the tribe of Quraysh, was a merchant who transported goods on camel caravans along routes into Syria and Palestine. The boy's mother, Āminah bint Wahb, was from another clan of the same tribe. Muḥammad was probably born in the city of Mecca, which at that time was important as a commercial outpost as well as a religious center. At about that time, or shortly thereafter, his father died. The family's means were so modest, according to one account, that apart from personal possessions they were left with little more than five camels and a few sheep. Muḥammad's mother died when he was about six years old; he was then reared in turn by a grandfather and an uncle.

Relatively little is known with certainty about his early years. It would seem that for quite some time, he lived in relative poverty. It is probable, however, that his intelligence and tact gained some recognition for him among local traders. When he was about twenty-five, he married Khadīja (c. 554-619), a wealthy widow with several children. According to tradition, though she was about fifteen years older than he, four daughters were born to them, as well as sons who died in early childhood. Throughout their life together, he was devoted to her.

Muḥammad was subject to periods of introspection and abstraction, and at times he would meditate alone among the hills and caves north of Mecca. His own recollections and the verses recorded as the holy writ of Islam furnished an account of the divine inspiration that he maintained had appointed his destiny for him. Probably during the year 610, he received some definite indications of the mission he was to assume.

One day, Muḥammad heard a voice from on high declare that he was the messenger of Allāh. Subsequent revelations seemed to confirm this calling. Further manifestations appeared, sometimes in the form of visions, and as forms could be discerned more clearly, Muḥammad came to believe that the powerful being appearing to him was the archangel Gabriel (Jibril). An encounter that took place on what was later called "the night of destiny" began with the mighty spirit calling on him to recite; inquiring about what he should recite, Muḥammad struggled three times with the great being before uttering the lines that would be placed at the very beginning of the Qurʾān.

By this time, because of the intensity of his mystical experiences, Muḥammad determined to consult others. He confided in his wife, and she referred him to one of her cousins, an elderly religious scholar; he suggested that Muḥammad had received guidance of the sort that had been instrumental in the development of Judaism and Christianity. Other revelations, at times accompanied by images of an angel, seemed to confirm further Muḥammad's growing conviction that he had been chosen to convey Allāh's tidings to the world. Increasingly, he was given to recitations that would eventually be incorporated in the Qurʾān (though not always in chronological sequence). As the means of transmission seemingly became more regular and certain, Muḥammad also felt moved to convey his message to those around him.

At that time, several different gods and goddesses were worshiped in Arabia; one of them resembled the Allāh of Muḥammad's prophecies. In Mecca, a celebrated black stone shrine, known from its shape as the Kabah, or Cube, served as the centerpiece for religious practices. In the beginning, there were relatively few converts to Muḥammad's message that there was only one God, who would not countenance idolatry. Khadīja and others in the Prophet's household were the first to accept the new faith; also prominent among the early Muslims was Abū Bakr, a moderately successful local merchant whose dauntless loyalty and resolute good sense were to prove invaluable in many ways.

Others who accepted Islam included some younger members of influential clans, men from outlying families or tribes, and former slaves. Most local people, however, preferred to remain with their ancestral beliefs; some of them claimed that Muḥammad was mad or possessed by spirits. Wealthy citizens were no doubt put off by his statements condemning distinctions of riches and poverty.

In about 615, some Muslims emigrated for a time to Abyssinia (now Ethiopia), in the hope that there they might find a more congenial reception. It was probably during this period that Muḥammad delivered some of the ringing denunciations of unbelief that were subsequently recorded in the Qurʾān; graphic descriptions of Hell probably were meant to illustrate the fate of those who rejected him. Still, though there was little overt persecution beyond throwing stones and casting thorns in the Prophet's path, the Meccans by and large rejected the new religion; indeed, for some time a boycott was organized against the small Muslim community. Muḥammad's fortunes as a religious leader seemed to have reached their nadir; in 619, he was further saddened by the death of his wife and of his uncle Abū Ṭālib, who had encouraged his efforts without actually embracing Islam.

LIFE'S WORK

Somewhat more favorable prospects presented themselves in other Arabian cities. Although little progress was made in Taif, southeast of Mecca, Muḥammad had reason to believe that Medina (Yathrib) would prove more receptive to his preaching. In 622, the celebrated emigration or departure (*hijrah*) took place: Muḥammad and many of his disciples removed themselves to Medina. The year 622 later was adopted as the beginning of the Muslim calendar. In Medina, Muḥammad confronted many problems essentially of a political order; a compact he reached with residents of the city recognized the interests of the Muslims as a separate group and established that his authority as the messenger of Allāh would be binding for the settlement of their disputes.

Military expeditions also became important to the new Muslim polity, and raids were mounted to harass Meccan caravans. The first outbreak of major violence, which occurred near Nakhlah, between Mecca and Taif, took place during a month that Arabian tradition had held holy. The Muslims insisted that combating unbelief served a greater good than the observance of time-honored truce periods. In 624, in a major battle fought at Badr, southwest of Medina, a party of Muslims defeated a larger force of their opponents; relatively few men were killed on either side, but the Meccans lost their commander.

Engagements of this sort undoubtedly had the effect of strengthening solidarity and morale among the various groups that had embraced Islam. The doctrine of *jihad*, or war for the faith, arose during this period. Some setbacks were encountered; north of Medina, at Uhud, in March, 625, the Prophet for the first time took part personally in combat; he was struck by a stone and wounded, and he may have killed one of his opponents. The Muslims were compelled to retreat, however, when their adversaries launched a successful flank attack. Ḥamzah ibn ʿAbd al-Muṭṭalib, the Prophet's uncle, was acclaimed a martyr for the faith after he was killed by an enemy's javelin. Their pagan opponents attempted to follow up their victory with a full-scale expedition against Medina. Although they raised an army of about ten thousand men, they were unable to penetrate the entrenchments Muḥammad's forces had dug about the city. In the spring of 627, after some desultory skirmishes, the Meccans abandoned their siege, leaving the Muslims victorious in the Campaign of the Ditch (al-Khandaq).

Some portions of the Qurʾān were revealed during Muḥammad's sojourn in Medina; many of these verses are notable for their striking imagery and resonant tone. It would appear that the Prophet was acutely sensitive to comments from others about the literary quality of his teachings. In keeping with Muḥammad's position within the Muslim community, many passages established legislative norms that were taken as binding on believers. Sumptuary regulations and the prohibition of wine were among the obligations imposed on the faithful. For those who were able, the giving of alms was also enjoined. Many matters affecting marriage and divorce were also subject to religious law; it is possible that the permission for men to take four wives derived from concern for women who had been left widowed after the Battle of Uhud.

The eschatology formulated by Muḥammad bore some resemblance to those of previous faiths but was distinctive and original on many points. The Last Judgment, which is to come suddenly and in the midst of cosmic upheaval, is vividly depicted in some of the earlier revelations. The Resurrection, when the living are to be spirited away while the dead will be summoned from their graves, is to be followed by a reckoning when the book of each person's life is opened. Some later lines supply detailed descriptions of the afterlife; others speak of the presence of angels. The Prophet warned against the intrigues of Satan (Shaytan, or Iblis), who was portrayed as an angel who fell from grace and ever after has been devising temptations to lure people from the straight path; he has lesser servants at his beck and call, who also lay traps for unwary mortals.

Clearly, many of Muḥammad's teachings reflect Jewish and Christian doctrines; indeed, some later verses make reference to Moses, King David, and Jesus, all of whom were venerated as predecessors of the Prophet. It seems likely, however, that Muḥammad's knowledge of other scriptures was incomplete; some of his ideas may have been suggested by oral accounts that had circulated in various forms. In other ways, Islamic beliefs diverged from those of Judaism and Christianity. Muḥammad rebuffed requests that he provide signs or other evidence of miraculous powers; he maintained that Allāh, who alone could act in such ways, would do so only when it accorded with the divine purpose. Muḥammad's criticisms of Christian beliefs later came to figure prominently in Muslim polemics; he asserted, for example, that the doctrine of the Trinity was not compatible with faith in one God. According to the Qurʾān, Muḥammad was the last and the seal of the prophets; his teachings were universal in character and were meant to be received by all humankind. (In Medina, Muḥammad was dismayed and perplexed when local Jewish groups rejected the message of Islam; some of them were expelled from the area and, when it was feared that others might assist Meccan forces, in 627, the tribe of Banū Qurayza was summarily eliminated.)

Surviving descriptions of Muḥammad's manner and bearing suggest that he was a man of impressive dignity. He had a broad and powerful torso, thick black hair, a long beard, and a hooked nose. His eyes were very dark and piercing. Although he had a pleasant smile, he tended to laugh infrequently. It is said that he retained a youthful appearance even in his later years. His personal life became a matter for subsequent speculation, and his character and motivations were questioned, but it seems likely that some of the criticisms concerning his relations with women were misplaced. By the end of his life, Muḥammad had nine wives. Among them were ʿĀʾishah bint Abū Bakr, who reputedly was his favorite, and Zaynab bint Jaḥsh, a maternal cousin; a concubine, Mariyah the Copt, was the mother of the only child born to the Prophet's household during these later years, but their son, Ibrāhīm, died during his second year. Some later critics charged that the Prophet was driven by sensual impulses, but there is little evidence to support this accusation. It would appear that some of Muḥammad's marriages were undertaken in order to forge alliances with key clan leaders. Jealousy did sometimes erupt among Muḥammad's wives, despite his practice of staying one day with each of them in turn.

After the Muslims had successfully withstood the siege of Medina, Muḥammad seized on certain diplomatic stratagems that displayed political foresight and adroit statesmanship. Outlying tribes, impressed by the stalwart example of the Islamic community in Medina, began to accept the new faith. In March, 628, Muḥammad embarked on what ostensibly was a pilgrimage to Mecca. On the way, at al-Hudaybiya, he and his men halted to negotiate a truce whose terms seemed quite unfavorable to the Muslims. This apparent setback, however, produced a period of peace that allowed the forces of Islam to gather their strength. During the next year, when, in keeping with this agreement, about two thousand Muslims entered the city as pilgrims, it would appear that the Meccans were daunted by their numbers; certain key Meccans even converted. In November, 629, a quarrel that arose over one of the tribes that had aligned itself with the Muslims provided an occasion for Muḥammad to abrogate the peace of al-Hudaybiya; an army of ten thousand men was assembled, and in January, 630, they marched into Mecca, which yielded after very little fighting. The Prophet solemnly proclaimed an end to the practice of idolatry; a general amnesty was also announced. Excepting four men who were sentenced to death, even those regarded as criminals or long-standing enemies were pardoned.

Shortly thereafter, the most dangerous Bedouin tribe that still opposed the Prophet in the Hejaz was vanquished at Hunayn, to the east of Mecca. The Arab Islamic state had already become a force to be reckoned with; Muḥammad had sent embassies to the Byzantine emperor, the king of Persia, and other heads of state. Although for the time being efforts to expand beyond Arabia met with little success, the Muslims held sway in the Prophet's homeland. Muḥammad spent most of the time that remained to him in Medina; in March, 632, he made his last pilgrimage to Mecca, where he uttered what has been regarded as his final revelation. On his return, he was affected briefly by an illness; without designating a successor he died, apparently rather peacefully, in Medina on June 8, 632.

SIGNIFICANCE

Despite its small and inauspicious beginnings, the faith Muḥammad taught eventually came to be accepted in many parts of the world. In the unsettled conditions that prevailed during the early seventh century, Arabia was ready to receive the teachings of Islam; the Muslim faith, with its austere monotheism and its specific moral guidelines, answered clear spiritual needs. Islam provided a way of life that applied to many spheres of human activity, for Muḥammad's prophecy extended to legislation and guidance of the community as well as to strictly spiritual matters.

Some commentators, particularly from Western countries, have given particular attention to Muḥammad's military endeavors and his many marriages, but the traits that recommended him most to the faithful were his sincerity, his simple eloquence, and his skill and insight in attending to his community. Also striking was the essential humility that, in keeping with his faith in one God, restrained him from claiming that he was more than the messenger by whom Allāh's word was made known. While by some standards his life fell short of the perfection to which religious leaders are called, Muḥammad's intense devotion and masterful leadership set a compelling example by which his essential aims were realized. In so doing, he secured wide acceptance of the Allāh of his revelations.

—*John R. Broadus*

FURTHER READING

Andrae, Tor. *Moḥammed: The Man and His Faith*. Translated by Theophil Menzel. 1936. Reprint. Salem, N.H.: Ayer, 1989. A brief but informative study that discusses the life and character of the Prophet. Summarizes religious revelations and teachings and examines the sources of his theological inspiration. Concludes with a sympathetic evaluation of Muḥammad's personality in relation to comparable figures from other religions.

Cook, Michael. *Muḥammad*. Oxford: Oxford University Press, 1996. This brief survey considers the various problems of Islamic doctrine that arose during the Prophet's lifetime. Bibliography.

Glubb, John Bagot. *The Life and Times of Muḥammad*. 1970. Reprint. New York: Cooper Square Press, 2001. This sympathetic work by a British writer, who for some time was the commander of the Arab Legion in Jordan, is of interest partly for its depiction of Arabian life and customs and for its reconstruction of desert battles. Bibliography, index.

Green, Joey, ed. *Jesus and Muḥammad: The Parallel Sayings*. Berkeley, Calif.: Seastone, 2003. This text presents quotations from the New Testament and the Qurʾān that demonstrate similarities between Christianity's core values and the tenets of Islam. Topics include love, God, *jihad*, faith, wisdom, law, and charity. Bibliography and an index of quotations.

Haykal, Muḥammad Husayn. *The Life of Muḥammad*. Translated by Ismail Ragi A. al-Faruqi. Indianapolis, Ind.: North American Trust, 1976. An Islamic treatment of the Prophet that provides a full and detailed account of Muḥammad's work. Bibliography, index.

Ibn Hisham, ʿAbd al-Malik. *The Life of Muḥammad: A Translation of Isḥāq's "Sirat rasul Allāh."* Translated by Alfred Guillaume. London: Oxford University Press, 1955. This version of a biographical chronicle from a traditionist of the second century after Muḥammad shows how the Prophet's life was perceived by early Muslims. Highly regarded by scholars.

Ibn Kathīr. *The Life of the Prophet Muḥammad*. Translated by Trevor Le Gassick. Reading, England: Garnet, 2000. Translation of the classic text *al-Sira al-Nabawiyya* by a prominent fourteenth century Islamic theologian and historian. Events ordered chronologically and drawn from contemporary sources. Part of the Great Books of Islamic Civilization series. Bibliography, index.

Khan, Muḥammad Zafrulla. *Muḥammad: Seal of the Prophets*. Boston: Routledge and Kegan Paul, 1980. A full and sympathetic study. The interpretation advanced here, that Muḥammad was an exemplar of religious piety, may have its roots in the author's affiliation with the Ahmadiyah movement, which has heterodox missionary inclinations. Bibliography, index.

Rogerson, Barnaby. *The Prophet Muḥammad: A Biography*. London: Little, Brown, 2003. Presents a biographical account of the life of Muḥammad. Chapters discuss his early life, the cities of Mecca and Medina, Arabia, his first revelations, and more. Bibliography, index.

Wadud, Amina. *Qurʾān and Woman: Rereading the Sacred Text from a Woman's Perspective*. 2d ed. New York: Oxford University Press, 1999. The author's unique reading of the Qurʾān sheds light on the role of women and relations between women and men presented in the book of Islam. Chapters explore the biases of earlier interpretations and its effects on tradition and Islamic culture and society, equality between men and women, and more. Includes a list of women mentioned in the Qurʾān, a bibliography, and an index.

Watt, W. Montgomery. *Muḥammad at Mecca*. 1953. Reprint. New York: Clarendon Press, 1972. Explores Muḥammad's early years, his first revelations, and the origins of the Qurʾān. Bibliography.

_______. *Muḥammad at Medina*. 1956. Reprint. New York: Clarendon Press, 1981. The author discusses the political and theological implications that accompanied the rise of Islam. Bibliographical footnotes, index.

SEE ALSO: al-Ḥasan al-Baṣrī; Khadīja; al-Ṭabarī; ʿUmar I.

RELATED ARTICLES in *Great Events from History: The Middle Ages, 477-1453*: c. 610-632: Muḥammad Receives Revelations; 630-711: Islam Expands Throughout North Africa; 637-657: Islam Expands Throughout the Middle East; October 10, 680: Martyrdom of Prophet's Grandson Ḥusayn; 780: Beginning of the Harem System; 872-973: Publication of *The History of al-Ṭabarī*.

MURASAKI SHIKIBU
Japanese writer

The foremost writer of the Heian period, Murasaki created The Tale of Genji, *one of the greatest works in Japanese literature and the world's earliest novel, defining in it the aesthetic sensibility of the aristocratic courtier class whose lives and culture her writings reflected.*

BORN: c. 978; Kyoto, Japan
DIED: c. 1030; Kyoto, Japan
ALSO KNOWN AS: Tō Shikibu
AREA OF ACHIEVEMENT: Literature

EARLY LIFE

Murasaki Shikibu (mew-rah-sah-kee shee-kee-bew) began her life in the late tenth century when the Fujiwara family dominated politics at the capital of Kyoto. Controlling the posts of chancellor and regent, the Fujiwara permitted the emperors to reign but not rule. Moreover, the Fujiwara influenced the succession to the throne by marrying their daughters into the imperial line. Fujiwara Michinaga, the most powerful family member in the middle of the Heian period (794-1185), married four of his daughters to emperors and was the grandfather of three emperors.

Fujiwara no Tametoki (b. c. 945) was a member of a cadet branch of this clan. A low-ranking member of the court bureaucracy, he was adept in the Chinese Confucian classics and poetry—talents he inherited from his father and grandfather, who were literary figures in their own right. Eventually, through the assistance of Michinaga, his powerful kinsman, Tametoki rose to a post in the bureau of ceremonials (*shikibu-shō*). He married a daughter of Fujiwara no Tamenobu, and about 978, they had a daughter.

This daughter's real name is unknown, but history has come to know her as Murasaki Shikibu. Because surnames were uncommon, women frequently were known by names derived from a brother's or father's official post. *Shikibu*, her father's title, became part of her name and *Murasaki* (violet or purple) perhaps was derived from the color of the wisteria flower, whose Chinese character made up the first syllable of the name Fujiwara (wisteria plain). Some sources call her Tō Shikibu, *tō* being another way of reading the first part of Fujiwara.

Heian women were expected to be educated at home in calligraphy, playing the koto, embroidery, painting, and other feminine arts. Men, on the other hand, were to learn the Chinese classics and the histories in preparation for official careers. Murasaki, however, received a broad education in both the feminine arts and the traditional Chinese classics. In fact, she was better at composition in Chinese than her brother Nobunori. She often delighted her father by quoting from the Chinese histories, composing poems in imitation of Chinese masters, and displaying a command of literature that normally would have been expected only of boys. She also was well versed in Japanese literary genres and Buddhist writings.

In addition, Murasaki was proficient at *kana* writing. The Japanese, lacking a written script for their language, had borrowed the Chinese system about the time that Buddhism was introduced from the continent (via Korea) in the sixth century. Unfortunately, the Chinese characters, linked as they were to the monosyllabic Chinese syntax, were awkward for expressing the very different polysyllabic Japanese language. As a result, the Japanese eventually used the cursive, written form of certain Chinese graphs for sound value alone. This new syllabary, called *hiragana*, was used with *katakana* (a script, also derived from Chinese characters, reserved for writing foreign words) and *kanji* (Chinese characters). Thus, *kana* blended three different systems into one written language.

Writing thus became less intimidating; in addition, Japanese ideas could be liberated from Chinese models wedded to the foreign script. Men, however, looked down on using the easy *kana* syllabaries, preferring to use characters alone in imitating Chinese genres. Women, who were not expected to know Chinese, were given free rein to write in *kana*, and they experimented with new literary forms to express uniquely Japanese sentiments. In fact, the Heian period marked the emergence of an original Japanese literature liberated from Chinese stereotypes; much of it was produced by talented women such as Murasaki.

When Murasaki's father was assigned to the post of governor of Echizen, she accompanied him in 996 and evidently spent several years in the provinces. In 999, Murasaki returned to Kyoto to marry Fujiwara no Nobutaka, a man nearly her father's age. Although her husband had had children by three other women and had a reputation for high-handedness when he was the provincial governor of Yamashiro, their marriage was nevertheless a happy one. In 1001, Murasaki gave birth to a daughter, Kenshi, who would become a poet as well. Soon after, Murasaki's husband died in an epidemic.

LIFE'S WORK

Perhaps seeking consolation for her husband's death, Murasaki turned to writing. About 1002, she started work on a tale (*monogatari*) about the romantic escapades of a fictitious character: a handsome, talented son born to an emperor by a low-ranking consort. The hero's name was Genji (the shining one) and the work was called *Genji monogatari* (c. 1004; *The Tale of Genji*, 1925-1933).

Highly cultured and living among the aristocratic class, Murasaki drew on her own experiences, which were augmented by her profound knowledge of human nature, to capture in this story the ambience of Heian life. It is said that her penchant for gossip and her curiosity may have given her access to privileged information about real court personalities, which then became the stuff of her tale; some even suggest that she had an affair with Michinaga. However, such theories do not do justice to her truly creative ability.

Around 1005, Murasaki was brought to court by Michinaga to serve as a tutor and companion to his daughter Shōshi, the nineteen-year-old consort to the Emperor Ichijō (r. 986-1011). Chapters of *The Tale of Genji* were read at court, and the young emperor once complimented Murasaki on her literary erudition.

Murasaki also kept a diary, *Murasaki Shikibu nikki* (eleventh century; *Murasaki Shikibu: Her Diary and Poetic Memoirs*, 1982) and some poetic memoirs (*kashū*), works that surprisingly reveal little about herself. In one telling remark, though, Murasaki recorded that fellow ladies-in-waiting resented her aloofness. She denied that she was conceited and considered herself a misunderstood, gentle person victimized by court gossip. Her novel was being written not as a self-serving display of her learning but, as she has Genji say at one point, because she "was moved by things, both good and bad," and wanted "to commit [them] to writing and make it known to other people—even to those of later generations."

While in imperial service, she enriched her impressions of aristocratic life at court and eventually produced more than fifty chapters incorporating, in a fictitious way, what she was observing at first hand. Her Genji epitomized the idealized Heian aristocrat. Adept at all the genteel arts, he romanced a bevy of women by being a cultured lover in a world sensitized to beauty. Included among Genji's many paramours was one to whom he returned frequently—the Lady Murasaki, a sensitive, gentle character perhaps personifying qualities for which the author hoped that she herself would be remembered.

On the surface a book about romantic and sexual love, *The Tale of Genji* is in reality a complex, almost psychological, exploration of human emotions and relationships. Plot development is minimal, and time references are muted. Karmic retribution and a sense of impermanence seem to bracket the amorous trysts of Genji, making the work a reflective analysis of the human predicament. As the story darkens in its final chapters (one theory holds that they were completed by someone other than Murasaki), the author herself seems to retreat from the glitter of the court, fatalistically preparing for her own end.

MAJOR EMPERORS OF THE HEIAN PERIOD, 794-1185

Reign	*Ruler*
781-806	Kammu
806-809	Heizei
809-823	Saga
823-833	Junna
833-850	Nimmyō
850-858	Montoku
858-876	Seiwa
876-884	Yōzei
884-887	Kōkō
887-897	Uda
897-930	Daigo
930-946	Suzaku
946-967	Murakami
967-969	Reizei
969-984	En'yu
984-986	Kazan
986-1011	Ichijō
1011-1016	Sanjō
1016-1036	Go-Ichijō
1036-1045	Go-Suzaku
1045-1068	Go-Reizei
1068-1073	Go-Sanjō
1073-1087	Shirakawa (cloistered, 1086-1129)
1087-1107	Horikawa
1107-1123	Toba (cloistered, 1129-1156)
1123-1142	Sutoku
1142-1155	Konoe
1155-1158	Go-Shirakawa (cloistered, 1158-1192)
1158-1165	Nijō
1165-1168	Rokujō
1168-1180	Takakura
1180-1185	Antoku

It is not known how Murasaki ended her days. Reportedly she retired to a Buddhist nunnery to reflect on the impermanence of the material world, just as many of the characters of *The Tale of Genji* did. She may have died in her mid-thirties, although some historians say that she lived on to 1025 or 1030. Tradition has it that a certain grave in Kyoto is the site of her burial.

SIGNIFICANCE

The Heian period was a singular time in Japanese literary history, one in which women writers dominated all genres. Murasaki Shikibu's contribution was to define the ideal of the cultivated aristocrat—Genji—living and loving in the effete, rarefied world of courtiers. The Heian sensibility of *mono no aware* (the pity of things), a feeling that Murasaki vividly depicted in her prose and poetry, permeated this milieu, evoking melancholy enjoyment of ephemeral pleasures; her writings would preserve for generations of readers the pleasure of eavesdropping on an age unsurpassed in cultural richness. Her characters and their emotional responses to one another provided the inspiration for picture scrolls (*e-maki*), Nō dramas, puppet plays, Kabuki theater, and other art forms celebrating the aesthetic sensitivity that Murasaki codified in Japanese literature.

—*William M. Zanella*

FURTHER READING

Bowring, Richard. *Murasaki Shikibu: Her Diary and Poetic Memoirs*. Princeton, N.J.: Princeton University Press, 1982. Chapter 1 is an up-to-date, concise summary of what Western and Japanese scholars know about Murasaki's life. Reproduces scenes from *The Tale of Genji* picture scroll. Includes a bibliography, mostly of Japanese works.

Keene, Donald. *Landscapes and Portraits: Appreciations of Japanese Culture*. Palo Alto, Calif.: Kodansha International, 1971. Reprints Keene's 1967 essay, "Feminine Sensibility in the Heian Era," which explores the emergence of women writers and the *kana* writing system. Murasaki and *The Tale of Genji* are analyzed as part of this phenomenon. Includes illustrations and a bibliography.

Morris, Ivan. *The World of the Shining Prince: Court Life in Ancient Japan*. 1964. Reprint. New York: Kodansha International, 1994. Morris's study is the best interpretative work on the historical and cultural milieu of *The Tale of Genji*. Chapter 9 is an excellent biographical account of Murasaki. Includes a complete glossary listing historical figures in Murasaki's life.

Murasaki Shikibu. *The Diary of Lady Murasaki*. Translated by Richard Bowring. New York: Penguin, 1996. A good translation of Muraskai's other writings. Includes poetry, nonfiction, and a personal look into Lady Murasaki's life. Includes bibliographical references.

_______. *The Tale of Genji*. Translated by Edward G. Seidensticker. 1976. Reprint. New York: Knopf, 1992. In the second major English translation of *The Tale of Genji*, Seidensticker produced a translation that more closely reflected the original than did Arthur Waley's translation.

_______. *The Tale of Genji*. Translated by Royall Tyler. 2 vols. New York: Viking, 2001. A detailed yet poetic translation of the famous tale by a modern scholar.

_______. *The Tale of Genji by Lady Murasaki*. Translated by Arthur Waley. New York: Houghton Mifflin, 1925-1933. 6 vols. Waley's translation of *The Tale of Genji*, a relatively poetic, "free" translation, introduced the work to a Western audience.

Puette, William J. *Guide to "The Tale of Genji" by Murasaki Shikibu*. Rutland, Vt.: Charles E. Tuttle, 1983. Includes a useful précis plot of *The Tale of Genji*, supplemented by background chapters on topics relevant to understanding the novel. Chapter 4 gives a brief biography of Murasaki. Good bibliography.

Seidensticker, Edward G. "Eminent Women Writers of the Court: Murasaki Shikibu and Sei Shōnagon." In *Great Historical Figures of Japan*, edited by Hyoe Murakami and Thomas J. Harper. Tokyo: Japan Cultural Institute, 1978. This authoritative essay by a respected translator of *The Tale of Genji* compares and contrasts the lives and literary works of Murasaki and her court rival.

SEE ALSO: Fujiwara Michinaga; Nijō; Sei Shōnagon.

RELATED ARTICLES in *Great Events from History: The Middle Ages, 477-1453*: March 9, 712, and July 1, 720: Writing of *Kojiki* and *Nihon Shoki*; 794-1185: Heian Period; c. 800: *Kana* Syllabary Is Developed; 858: Rise of the Fujiwara Family; c. 1001: Sei Shōnagon Completes *The Pillow Book*; c. 1004: Murasaki Shikibu Writes *The Tale of Genji*.

Johannes de Muris

French music theorist

Muris was a leading proponent of the notational reform of music in early fourteenth century Europe, a time marked by Church authority even in matters of music and that also witnessed the persistence of secular rather than spiritual music and the start of a "new art" advocating more rhythmic complexity in music.

Born: c. 1300; Lisieux diocese, Normandy (now in France)
Died: c. 1351; probably in or near Paris, France
Also known as: John of Meurs; Jehan des Murs; Jean de Muris
Area of achievement: Music

Early Life

Johannes de Muris (yoh-HAHN-ehs deh MOOR-ihs) has been most widely known by the Latinized version of his name, leaving open to speculation his country of origin and the original spelling of his name. Modern scholarship has established that he was not Swiss or English, as has been speculated, but French and that the French version of his name is Jehan des Murs.

The French music theorist, mathematician, and astronomer was born in Normandy in the diocese of Lisieux. Although nothing is known about his childhood or background, much is known about the activities and accomplishments of his adult life. This is a result in part of the contemporary discovery of a manuscript, located in El Escorial library near Madrid, Spain, that contains a number of biographical annotations. Most of these are believed to be in Muris's own handwriting.

Muris is known to have been a student in Paris, where he pursued an education in astronomy and mathematics. His earliest extant writings are from this period and may be dated as early as 1317. A Vienna manuscript, the earliest dated manuscript attributed to him (although the date may be erroneous), finds Muris working on a calendar in an attempt to determine the date of Easter. Although there are far more than one hundred extant manuscripts attributed to him, the authenticity of many remains in question.

Muris wrote on astronomical, mathematical, and musical topics, but it is his writings on music that are the most significant and for which he is best known. Of the five musical treatises attributed to him, *Ars novae musicae* (the art of new music, 1321) and *Musica speculativa secundum Boetium* (1323) are generally regarded as the most important. The mathematical treatise entitled *Opus quadripartitum numerorum* (1343), which was written two decades later than either of the two musical treatises cited above, remains one of his best-known nonmusical writings.

Muris completed his studies sometime in the early 1320's. He is generally believed to have taught at the University of Paris shortly thereafter. During those early days as a student and teacher in Paris, he became friends with Philippe de Vitry, the other major French theorist of the early fourteenth century; both men advocated fundamental changes in music.

Life's Work

The first of Muris's treatises on music may be his most important. This work, entitled *Ars novae musicae*, may have been written as early as 1319, when Muris was still a student in Paris. Clearly, musicians, and certainly theorists, were aware that they were breaking new ground; this awareness is reflected in Muris's title, *Ars novae musicae*, and in Vitry's title, *Ars nova* (1320; English translation, 1961). *Ars novae musicae*, itself controversial, was born in an era of controversy, instability, and change.

Although the thirteenth century had been a period of relative stability, with the Church enjoying a position of authority not only in religious matters but in affairs of state as well, that began to change in the fourteenth century. The early years of the century witnessed the challenge of papal authority, ultimately resulting in the relocation of the Papacy to Avignon from 1305 to 1378, a period known as the Avignon Papacy or the Babylonian Captivity of the Church. The ensuing years until 1417 were little better; occasionally, there were as many as three different men claiming the papacy at the same time. Confusion in leadership, emerging and newly redefined limitations of authority for church and state, as well as corrupt and immoral clergy led to a general disillusionment with the Church.

Religious instability was accompanied by economic decline, wars, the Black Death (which decimated more than one-third of the population of Europe), and civil turmoil. Although all these events did not occur at once, a new environment was created that precipitated a dramatic change in the arts; this change was reflected in music. French composers of the fourteenth century created more secular music than sacred music, and much of it reflected a heightened interest in intellectual games that frequently manifested itself in rhythmic intricacies. The trend toward greater rhythmic complexity, which had begun in the late thirteenth century, placed demands on the older Franconian notational system that it could not accommodate.

Ars novae musicae, along with Vitry's *Ars nova*, is one of the important early fourteenth century treatises advocating notational reform. Muris's work, which may predate Vitry's, addressed one of the hotly debated musical issues of the day, advocating acceptance of duple division of the note value on an equal basis with the traditional triple division of note values. Muris's logically argued yet restrained presentation, which could be described as a masterpiece in diplomacy, raised considerable concern among those who supported the "old art."

Most notable among those who vigorously opposed the new art was Jacques de Liège, who produced a treatise circa 1325 to 1330 entitled *Speculum musicae*; in it, he defended the old art. In addition, the writings of Muris and Vitry prompted a papal bull issued by Pope John XXII in 1324 in which the innovations of the new school were condemned. Nevertheless, the conservatives could not stem the change, and their objections were largely ignored.

Even the emphasis of Muris's treatise reflects the changing times, as is clear when Muris's work is compared with a treatise by a conservative theorist from the same era. For example, de Liège's *Speculum musicae*, which, ironically, was mistakenly attributed to Muris at one time, follows a standard format. It may be broken into two basic divisions, material that falls into the realm of the speculative and philosophical and material that is concerned with practical matters and their application. Most of de Liège's treatise is focused on the speculative material, which is typical of a medieval work. Muris's treatise, however, while broken into the same two divisions, treats the speculative material in an obligatory fashion and moves quickly to the second division, *musica practica*, to deal with substantive issues that affect working musicians. The new focus of Muris's treatise is indicative of the change that was beginning to occur in writing about music in the fourteenth century.

The other musical treatise for which Muris is best known is *Musica speculativa secundum Boetium*, which was written around 1323, while he was in Paris. In it, Muris explains selected passages taken from the writings of Boethius, who was the most famous and influential writer on music in the early Middle Ages. Muris again combines mathematics and music in an explanation of musical proportions. The treatise also contains a section on the division of the monochord, a device consisting of a single string stretched over a long, wooden resonator with a movable bridge that allowed the vibrating string length to be varied. The monochord was very popular in antiquity and the Middle Ages for the demonstration of acoustic principles as they related to music.

Other music treatises attributed to Muris are *Quaestiones super partes musicae* (c. 1322), *Libellus cantus mensurabilis* (c. 1340), and *Ars contrapuncti secundem Johannes de Muris* (c. 1340).

Scholars have dated Muris's death as no earlier than 1351 because of a letter thought to have been written by him congratulating Vitry on his appointment as bishop of Meaux in that year. Although his death is generally accepted as around 1351, the authenticity and date of the letter itself remain in question. Muris is believed to have died in or near Paris.

SIGNIFICANCE

Although Muris is best known for two of his five treatises on music, it should be remembered that these were the works of a young man whose primary interest was in mathematics and astronomy. Muris produced a number of works on astronomy and mathematics during his lifetime, but they have not attracted the same attention in their respective disciplines as have his treatises on music. Nevertheless, he must have enjoyed a certain reputation in the scientific community; he was invited to Avignon by Pope Clement VI in 1344 for a conference on calendar reform. Later, in collaboration with a Firminus de Bellaville, who had also been invited to the conference, Muris presented the pope with a recommendation for reforming the calendar, although it was not implemented.

Muris is not believed to have been a composer because no compositions are mentioned in his writings and none has been attributed to him. Nevertheless, he was held in high esteem as a theorist by his contemporaries and also in subsequent generations. After his death, his reputation eclipsed even that of Vitry. Muris's writings on music became an important part of the university curriculum in the fourteenth and fifteenth centuries, rivaling the authority of Boethius's works. As Muris's fame grew, so did the legend of his accomplishments. The creation of certain note values was even attributed to him in the sixteenth century.

—*Michael Hernon*

FURTHER READING

Butterfield, Ardis. *Poetry and Music in Medieval France: From Jean Renart to Guillaume de Machaut*. New

York: Cambridge University Press, 2002. Explores the world of poets, musicians, and composers in the time of Muris, exploring topics such as song combined with performance and poetry, and the sources of songs. Includes an extensive bibliography and an index.

Carpenter, Nan Cooke. *Music in the Medieval and Renaissance Universities*. Norman: University of Oklahoma Press, 1958. Looks at the academic study of music during the Middle Ages and Renaissance. The work contains biographical information on Muris, discussion of his writings on music, and information about his posthumous impact on university curricula.

Faulkner, Quentin. *Wiser than Despair: The Evolution of Ideas in the Relationship of Music and the Christian Church*. Westport, Conn.: Greenwood Press, 1996. A study of the Church's powerful influence on the making of music, including in medieval Europe. Includes a chapter called "Ecclesiastical Authority in Theory and Practice," and provides a bibliography and an index.

Gallo, F. Alberto. *Music of the Middle Ages II*. New York: Cambridge University Press, 1985. This volume contains an excellent treatment of the music of fourteenth century France. Included is a brief breakdown of Muris's *Ars novae musicae*. Also discusses the old art versus the new art.

Gushee, Lawrence. "Johannes de Muris." In *New Grove Dictionary of Music and Musicians*, edited by Stanley Sadie. 6th ed. Vol. 9. London: Macmillan, 1980. A comprehensive source on the life and works of Muris, his musical and nonmusical writings, and the influence of his writings. Includes an excellent bibliography.

_______. "New Sources for the Bibliography of Johannes de Murs." *Journal of the American Musicological Society* 22, no. 1 (1969): 3-26. Looks at a Spanish manuscript that contains older but still valuable biographical information about Muris.

Hoppin, Richard. *Medieval Music*. New York: W. W. Norton, 1978. While only brief references are made to Muris, the book provides an excellent survey of medieval music from chant to music of the early fifteenth century. One chapter, devoted to the new art, discusses the musical innovations of the fourteenth century.

Karpinski, Louis. "The *Quadripartitum numerorum* of John of Meurs." *Bibliotheca Mathematica* 13 (1912-1913): 99-114. A detailed and highly technical discussion of Muris's famous mathematical treatise.

Lang, Paul Henry. *Music in Western Civilization*. New York: W. W. Norton, 1941. An authoritative work on the history of music and its role in Western culture. Most appropriate for readers with a basic knowledge of music history.

Reaney, Gilbert. "Ars Nova in France." In *Ars Nova and the Renaissance 1300-1540*. Vol. 3 in *The New Oxford History of Music*, edited by Egon Wellesz. London: Oxford University Press, 1966. An excellent overview of the musical forms and composers of fourteenth century France. Contains some information about Muris and a good discussion of the notational innovations of the fourteenth century.

Thorndike, Lynn. "John de Murs and the Conjunction of 1345." In *A History of Magic and Experimental Science*. Vol. 3. New York: Macmillan, 1923-1941. An excellent source concerning the scientific activities, accomplishments, and writings of Muris. Some biographical material is included.

SEE ALSO: Adam de la Halle; Boethius; Guido Cavalcanti; John Dunstable; Guido d'Arezzo; Hildegard von Bingen; Hrosvitha; Francesco Landini; Guillaume de Machaut; Pérotin; Philippe de Vitry.

RELATED ARTICLES in *Great Events from History: The Middle Ages, 477-1453*: 1305-1417: Avignon Papacy and the Great Schism; 1347-1352: Invasion of the Black Death in Europe.

Mansa Mūsā

King of Mali (r. 1312-1337)

Mūsā was the ruler of the empire of Mali, the dominant political and cultural force in West Africa in the fourteenth century and a major influence in the development of an Islamic intellectual and religious environment in the region.

Born: c. 1280; probably Niani, Mali
Died: 1337; Niani, Mali
Also known as: Kankan
Area of achievement: Government and politics

Early Life

Mansa Mūsā (MAN-sah MOO-sah) was a member of the powerful Keita clan, whose members ruled the West African empire of Mali from around 1250 until some two centuries later. According to the Muslim historian Ibn Khaldūn, Mūsā was the ninth ruler of Mali and a grandnephew of its founder, Sundiata. ("Mansa" is an honorific title analogous to "highness" or "excellency" in Europe.)

Almost nothing is known about Mūsā's childhood, since the various chronicles that mention him are little more than dynastic narratives. It is reasonable to suppose that he was educated as a Muslim, a matter of importance in assessing his later achievements. Mali was the first large Islamic polity in West Africa, and the Keita Dynasty was generally Islamized by Mūsā's time. There is considerable disagreement over whether Sundiata, the founder of the line, was a Muslim; he is usually depicted as a pagan sorcerer-king. For a time, the use of Arabic names for the Keita rulers was observed only indifferently, but by Mūsā's reign, the practice was firmly established.

Life's Work

Historians generally identify Mūsā's reign with the height of Malian prestige and cultural achievement. This tendency is, in part, a result of the fact that much more is known about Mūsā than about others of his clan. Ibn Khaldūn covers Mali, particularly the career of Mūsā, extensively, despite the empire's position on the edge of the Islamic world, and the historian is effusive in his praise. Shortly after Mūsā's death, the accomplished traveler Ibn Baṭṭūṭah made his way to Mali and passed on a detailed and positive account of its culture. Mūsā also made himself more accessible to posterity by undertaking the *hajj*, the pilgrimage to Mecca, together with an enormous entourage. In 1324-1325, his party passed through Cairo, where he was interviewed by Egyptian government secretaries, and in 1338, some of these interviews were recorded by al-ʿUmarī, whose work still survives.

Evidence suggests that Mūsā was a devout Muslim, in contrast to the rather nominal piety of some of his predecessors. Although he was the third ruler of the Keita Dynasty to undertake the *hajj*, the first two did not take Arabic names, and one of them died en route under mysterious circumstances. Mūsā appears to represent the growing Islamic influence in Mali, but local traditions about him also imply that pagan religious and political elements resented this development and on occasion may have resisted it.

Mūsā was the builder of a strong and growing empire, rather than the caretaker of a kingdom in its golden age, as some popular accounts suggest. Even during his pilgrimage, Malian armies were active, and the capture of the enormous Songhai principality of Gao, east of the great bend of the Niger River, may have forced the king to end his travels early and hasten back to Mali. By the end of Mūsā's reign, Mali extended from the Atlantic coast, near modern Senegal, close to the borders of contemporary Nigeria in the east and far into the Sahara Desert in the north. Only the forest fringe of the West African coast from Liberia to Benin remained outside direct Malian authority. Some historians describe Mali as substantially larger than all Europe. Though probably accurate as far as area is concerned, these estimates imply a far larger population than actually existed. A fairer comparison of the size and population of Mali would be to the Inca Empire in South America.

Mali's livelihood derived principally from the export of gold across the Sahara to entrepôts on the Mediterranean, where it was purchased by European merchants. The trade itself began as early as Roman times, but during Mali's period of development and greatest strength, it expanded by at least an order of magnitude. In the thirteenth and fourteenth centuries, many European governments, pressed by expanding economies and currency demands, returned to minting gold coins after a hiatus of many centuries. The frantic demand for gold drove prices up and encouraged the systematization of gold production in Mali. Under Mūsā and other Malian kings, the gold trade became a state monopoly, and the revenue doubtless was critical to the ability of the empire to expand and consolidate in Mūsā's time. In this sense, Mūsā and the Keita clan were as much a part of the medieval economic surge in the Mediterranean world as any European family of bankers or princes.

It was in religion and culture, however, that Mūsā may have had his greatest impact. He actively encouraged the spread of Islam and the development of Islamic institutions. His efforts included a campaign for the construction of mosques throughout his domain. Among the intellectuals who accompanied Mūsā back to Mali after his pilgrimage was Abū Isḥāq al-Sahili, possibly the most outstanding architect of medieval Islam. His varied talents included not only architecture and city planning but also poetry and music, and they indicate the richness of Islamic culture with which Mūsā seeded his kingdom. Abū Isḥāq perfected techniques of mosque construction using West African materials, including the difficult task of building minarets out of mud brick. Some of his mosques still stand in the cities of modern Mali.

Mūsā also encouraged the development of systematic study and education. At the Sankore mosque in the fabled city of Timbuktu, near the northernmost part of the Niger's course, theologians, geographers, mathematicians, historians, and scientists gathered into a community that continued to publish until well into the eighteenth century. Just as Christian thinkers collected around cathedrals and thus began the European university tradition, Muslim intellectuals congregated around mosques, and Sankore was one of the best. Its fame spread as far as Egypt and Morocco. Professors summoned to teach in Timbuktu from some of the intellectual hotbeds of Islam often became the students of the Timbuktu scholars rather than their instructors.

Significance

Mansa Mūsā probably died in 1337. Under his rule, Mali had achieved a level of wealth and international prestige never before experienced in West Africa. It carried on diplomatic relations with Egypt, North African kingdoms, and other African states, and occasionally came to the notice of Europeans. Malian administrative and economic elaboration was crucial to driving the forces of medieval European expansion, trade, and capital accumulation. Thanks to Mūsā's determination, Islam was able to sink its roots deeply into West African culture.

There was, however, a tragic element in Mansa Mūsā's story. His was a tempestuous family; no firm rules of succession could be established. Mūsā himself may have come to the throne in circumstances of intrigue: He told the Egyptians a story that his predecessor had disappeared on an ocean voyage. Owing in part to this dynastic instability, much of the cultural efflorescence under Mūsā did not survive.

Nor did a substantial amount of his contrived Islamic influence. Underneath the struggles for power in Mali and the Keita clan lay a network of pagan priests and other royal families who regarded Islam as an adversary. Later, the Songhai broke away from Mali and eventually overwhelmed it. They were more disposed to paganism, and in the Songhai period, many elements of Islamic culture and influence in West Africa vanished or were seriously diminished. Many later historians, more familiar with recent African history than with the medieval period, consequently undervalued the influence of Islam in West African history.

The greatest irony of Mūsā's career is something he himself could not have known. When his pilgrimage entourage arrived in Cairo in 1324, it brought so much gold that it dumbfounded local observers. In obedience to Muslim piety, the pilgrims distributed incredible amounts of wealth throughout Egypt, so much that some medieval historians believe that the gold standard in the eastern Mediterranean nearly collapsed. Inevitably, news of this phenomenon traveled along the commercial intelligence network in the Mediterranean, until it reached the famous guild of Jewish cartographers in the Balearic Islands.

By 1375, Mūsā's likeness was appearing on European maps of West Africa, where previously there had been only fabulous beasts to conceal Europe's ignorance of the region. On those maps, Mūsā was shown seated on a throne of gold. It was the beginning of the end. Almost at the same time as the pagan Songhai began to run amok, Portuguese mariners began probing their way down the African coast, electrified by tales of unbelievable wealth: Mali was doomed.

—*Ronald W. Davis*

Further Reading

Bell, Nawal Morcos. "The Age of Mansa Mūsa in Mali: Problems in Succession and Chronology." *International Journal of African Historical Studies* 5 (1972): 221-234. A summary of problems in Keita dynastic structure and chronology. Concludes that scholars have relied too heavily on Ibn Khaldūn's assurances of legitimate succession and that it was really an ad hoc affair without clearly established rules.

Bovill, E. W. *The Golden Trade of the Moors*. London: Oxford University Press, 1968. A description of Mūsā's era, emphasizing his contributions to the cultural and intellectual life of the empire.

Burns, Khephra. *Mansa Mūsa: The Lion of Mali*. Illustrated by Leo and Diane Dillon. San Diego: Harcourt, 2001. Designed for young readers, a fictional account of Mansa Mūsā's wanderings as a boy.

Davidson, Basil, ed. *The African Past: Chronicle from Antiquity to Modern Times*. Boston: Little, Brown, 1964. A translation of selected descriptions of Mūsā in Cairo during the pilgrimage to Mecca, and a portion of Ibn Baṭṭūṭah's account of Mali. Also see Davidson's *The Lost Cities of Africa* (Boston: Little, Brown, 1959).

Levtzion, Nehemia. "The Thirteenth- and Fourteenth-Century Kings of Mali." *Journal of African History* 4 (1963): 341-354. Summarizes the history of the Keita Dynasty, more or less according to Ibn Khaldūn. Describes how Mūsā usually received favorable treatment from chroniclers because he was a Muslim and shows how nearly every achievement in the history of Mali has been associated with his reign. Also see Levtzion's *Ancient Ghana and Mali* (London: Methuen, 1973).

Palumbo, Joe. *Mansa Mūsa, African King of Gold: A Unit of Study for Grades 7-9*. Los Angeles: National Center for History in the Schools, University of California, Los Angeles, 1991. A teacher's guide to preparing a unit on Mansa Mūsā.

Trimingham, J. Spencer. *A History of Islam in West Africa*. London: Oxford University Press, 1962. An extensive treatment of the empire of Mali, constructed both from the work of major Arab geographers and chroniclers and from Arabic-language sources written by contemporaneous West African scholars.

SEE ALSO: ʿAbd al-Malik; Ibn Baṭṭūṭah; Ibn Khaldūn; al-Idrīsī; Damia al-Kāhina; Lalibela; Sundiata; Ṭāriq ibn-Ziyād.

RELATED ARTICLES in *Great Events from History: The Middle Ages, 477-1453*: 1230's-1255: Reign of Sundiata of Mali; 1324-1325: Mansa Mūsā's Pilgrimage to Mecca Sparks Interest in Mali Empire.

NAḤMANIDES
Jewish scholar and physician

A creative and original scholar whose work synthesized many of the intellectual trends of his time, Naḥmanides mediated disputes within the Jewish world and was compelled to defend Jewish beliefs in a disputation with a Dominican friar in 1263. He spent the final years of his life in Palestine.

BORN: 1194; Gerona, Catalonia (now in Spain)
DIED: 1270; Acre, Palestine
ALSO KNOWN AS: Nachmanides; Moses ben Naḥman (full name); Ramban (acronym for *R*abbi *M*oses *b*en *N*aḥman); Moses Gerondi, Rabbenu ("Our" Rabbi Moses of Gerona); Bonastrug de Porta (Spanish name)
AREAS OF ACHIEVEMENT: Religion and theology, philosophy, education, medicine

EARLY LIFE

Naḥmanides (Nahkh-MAHN-ih-dees) was born into a prominent scholarly family in Gerona, Catalonia, a major Jewish center in northeastern Spain, and he lived there most of his life as a teacher and community leader. Thirteenth century Catalonia had been reconquered by Christian forces from Muslim rule, and it was an important commercial center and cultural crossroads, particularly for the Jewish community. Its population included survivors of Muslim persecutions in southern Spain and North Africa and refugees from expulsions in northern France, along with a native Jewish community of considerable antiquity with close ties to the Jews of Provence. These diverse elements created a complex religious and intellectual milieu of competing traditions, including the philosophical rationalism and scientific approach of the Jews of Muslim lands, the strict talmudism and pietism of northern Europe, mystical teachings from Provence, and the pragmatic traditionalism of the indigenous Spanish-Jewish community.

All these trends are evident in the scholarship of Naḥmanides. While little is known about his early education, he apparently studied in Provence and Évreux, France, as well as in his native Gerona. Naḥmanides was also trained as a physician, and he earned his living, in part, through his medical practice.

LIFE'S WORK

As a scholar and head of a yeshiva (Jewish academy for talmudic study) in Gerona, Naḥmanides produced a diverse and important body of writings, including commentaries on the Hebrew Bible and the Babylonian Talmud. His stature as an outstanding teacher and leader drew him into several public disputes, both within and beyond the Jewish community. These included his involvement in the controversy over the writings of Jewish philosopher Moses Maimonides (1135-1204) in the 1230's and his participation in a forced debate with a Christian friar in the 1260's.

Contention over the legal and philosophical writings of Maimonides was an ongoing feature of Jewish life in thirteenth century Provence and Spain, beginning even during Maimonides' lifetime. Controversial issues included the comprehensive ambitions of Maimonides' legal code, the *Mishneh Torah* (1180; *The Code of Maimonides*, 1927-1965); his apparent rejection of the doctrine of bodily resurrection in his major philosophical work, *Dalālat al-ḥaʾirīn* (1190; *Guide of the Perplexed*, 1881); and general disagreement over the role that philosophy and other branches of secular learning should play in Jewish intellectual life. The disputes in which Naḥmanides played a role began in Montpellier in southern France over assertions that some Jews, influenced by Maimonides' philosophical approach, were rejecting the precepts of Jewish law and interpreting biblical and talmudic texts allegorically. The "anti-Maimunists" took their accusations to the rabbis of northern France who prohibited reading the writings of Maimonides on pain of excommunication; the supporters of Maimonides' work in Provence responded with a counterban, excommunicating their opponents. Both parties sought adherents in Spain. Naḥmanides allied himself with the traditionalists who saw the writings of Maimonides as a potential danger to Jewish piety and observance. Nevertheless, Naḥmanides recognized the very different cultural contexts of northern France, where secular studies and philosophy had no role in traditional Jewish learning, and of Spain, where Jews had long considered scientific and philosophical studies an essential part of a full education.

Naḥmanides attempted to mediate the dispute in a way that would preserve the larger Jewish community from the threats of both rampant rationalism and a catastrophic schism, while at the same time he wanted to protect Maimonides' colossal contribution to Jewish learning. He appealed to both sides to moderate their extreme language and proposed the adoption of an educational program that would incorporate the progressive study of secular subjects side by side with traditional Jewish sources, which would vary based on the age and location of students. Unfortunately, Naḥmanides' attempt to find a middle ground was not successful as extremists on both sides seized control of the debate. This phase of the quarrel ended with the public burning of Maimonides' major writings in 1233, the same year the French anti-Maimunists apparently encouraged the involvement of representatives of the Inquisitorial branch of the Roman Catholic Church, which was already actively expunging the Christian Catharist heresy in Provence.

In 1263, some thirty years after his unsuccessful efforts to mediate the controversy over Maimonides' writings, Naḥmanides, as the recognized leader of Catalan Jewry, was forced by King James I of Aragon (r. 1214-1276) to participate in a public disputation with a Dominican friar, a Jewish convert to Christianity who had taken the name Pablo Christiani. However, Naḥmanides agreed to do so only if the king would guarantee he could speak freely. The purpose of the debate, orchestrated by members of the Dominican order, was conversionary, based on the expectation that the force of Christian arguments in refuting Jewish claims would be sufficient to convince Jews of the errors of their ways and lead to their baptisms. Beginning in the thirteenth century, such disputations, together with sermons to which Jews were periodically compelled to listen, became increasingly common stratagems to convert Jews to Christianity.

The debate at Barcelona, held in the presence of royal officials, noblemen, church dignitaries, and Jewish leaders, lasted for four days. It was not a free and open exchange of views but a carefully orchestrated encounter limited to the question of whether or not rabbinic sources stated that the messiah had already come. Pablo offered rabbinic stories in which the messiah was an active participant, and Naḥmanides was compelled either to disprove or accept them, although without in any way questioning the truths of Christianity or offending the Christians present. A striking and innovative feature of this approach was its use of rabbinic literature against the Jewish faith, an approach that was possible because Pablo had been educated in talmudic studies prior to his conversion. Thus, Naḥmanides was doubly on the defensive; any refutations of apparent talmudic "truths" could call the entire rabbinic framework of medieval Judaism into question.

Two reports of the disputation survive. The rather terse Latin version describes the debate from a Christian point of view, ending in a resounding victory for Pablo and the discomfiture of Naḥmanides. The detailed Hebrew account by Naḥmanides, on the other hand, recounts in great detail Naḥmanides' rebuttal of Pablo's claims and the definitive defeat of the Christian challenger. A significant feature of Naḥmanides' version is the distinction he establishes between the legal literature (*halakhah*) of the Talmud and its narrative passages (*aggadah*). Naḥmanides argued that whereas the *halakhah* is considered a part of divine revelation and binding on all Jews, the *aggadah* (or *midrash*) should be seen as exemplary literature, similar to the content of a sermon, and need not be taken literally. In arguing that rabbinic legends were simply meant as homilies and consolation texts, Naḥmanides was able to discount the legends by implying that the messiah had actually appeared in particular times and places. However, Naḥmanides diverged quite significantly from traditional Jewish views of the divine origin of all of rabbinic writings by making such qualitative differentiations among talmudic texts.

Scholars accept that it is impossible to reconstruct a precise version of what occurred at the debate because both extant narratives were written after the fact for partisan audiences. What is certain is that when Naḥmanides published his written account of the disputation in 1265, members of the Dominican order accused him of insulting the Christian faith and complained to both King James and to Pope Clement IV, demanding he be put on trial and punished. Although the king, who had a cordial and profitable relationship with the Catalan Jewish community, was inclined to protect the Jewish leader, it seems likely that fears of ecclesiastical prosecution impelled the elderly Naḥmanides to fulfil his long cherished aspiration of leaving Spain for Palestine, where he spent the rest of his life, first in Jerusalem and then in Acre where he died in 1270.

Naḥmanides was a prolific scholar. Among his many legal works, his *novellae* (legal innovations) on the Talmud are considered high points of Jewish religious creativity in Spain. They drew on earlier Spanish-Jewish talmudic scholarship, characterized by its elucidation of the *halakhah* for practical purposes, and they also introduced the methodology of the northern French analytic tradition of talmudic argumentation for its own sake, until Naḥmanides' time little known in Spain. Naḥmanides' works also incorporated the teachings of Provence, thus creating a threefold Spanish, French, and Provençal synthesis distinguished by its wealth of sources, clear and lucid style, and logical structure. Naḥmanides was also a biblical exegete; among other exegetical works he completed an extensive and influential commentary on the Torah (the first five books of the Hebrew Bible) in his last years in Palestine. This commentary includes Naḥmanides' conviction that the Torah, as the word of God, is the source of all knowledge, future as well as past; his exegesis is also noted for its incorporation of many elements from the Kabbalah, Jewish mystical tradition.

Like many Spanish Jews, Naḥmanides felt strongly the pain of living in exile in a foreign land and longed to return to the land of Israel; he taught that only in Israel was it possible to fully observe the commandments. He also understood the necessity of offering comfort to the Jews of Spain by emphasizing the truth of Jewish messianic beliefs and the certainty of their ultimate fulfillment. In his thirteenth century eschatological work, *Sefer ha-Geʾulah* (*The Book of Redemption*, 1978), Naḥmanides affirmed that the promised redemption of the Jewish people from exile and the advent of the messiah, a human king descended from King David who would reestablish a Jewish kingdom, were based on solid and certain biblical promises.

SIGNIFICANCE

As a scholar, Naḥmanides enriched Spanish-Jewish intellectual life and literature by incorporating the talmudic dialectics of northern France and the mysticism of Provence into his many legal writings and his influential biblical commentaries. As a community leader, he sought to offer a moderate response to the attack on the writings of Maimonides that would guard against the growth of religious skepticism while maintaining the valuable contributions of philosophy and the secular sciences. His coerced participation in the Barcelona disputation of 1263, and its aftermath, altered the course of his final years, leading to his settlement in Palestine to avoid being persecuted by the Church. In a broader way, these events also presaged the increasingly perilous situation of Jewish life in Spain in the centuries to come.

—Judith R. Baskin

FURTHER READING

Baer, Yitzhak. *A History of the Jews in Christian Spain*. 2 vols. Philadelphia: Jewish Publication Society, 1961. The standard history of this period provides a great deal of information about Naḥmanides' life and contributions in a larger historical and cultural context.

Chavel, Charles. *Ramban: His Life and Teachings*. New York: Feldheim, 1960. This biography by the editor and translator of many of Naḥmanides' writings, describes Naḥmanides' familial and educational background and details his scholarly oeuvre and major aspects of his thought.

Chazan, Robert. *Barcelona and Beyond: The Disputation of 1263 and Its Aftermath*. Berkeley: University of California Press, 1992. An analytical study of the famous disputation in the larger context of the Christian assault on Jews and Jewish beliefs in the later Middle Ages.

Henoch, Chaim. J. *Ramban: Philosopher and Kabbalist: On the Basis of His Exegesis of the Mitzvoth*. Northvale, N.J.: Jason Aronson, 1998. This volume evaluates Naḥmanides within the larger Jewish intellectual milieu of thirteenth century Spain and also demonstrates the significant extent to which Jewish mystical teachings permeated all of his writings, including his biblical exegesis and legal studies.

Idel, Moshe. "Naḥmanides: Kabbalah, Halakhah, and Spiritual Leadership." In *Jewish Mystical Leaders in the Thirteenth Century*, edited by Moshe Idel and Mortimer Ostow. Northvale, N.J.: Jason Aronson, 1998. A detailed exposition by a major scholar of Jewish mysticism of Naḥmanides' central role in the spread of the Kabbalah in Europe, a signal contribution that the author believes has been underestimated and misunderstood.

Margolies, Morris B. *Twenty Twenty: Jewish Visionaries Through Two Thousand Years*. Northvale, N.J.: Jason Aronson, 2000. Provides biographies of leading visionaries in the Jewish tradition, including Naḥmanides and Maimonides. Also provides a bibliography and index.

Twersky, Isadore, ed. *Rabbi Moses Naḥmanides (Ramban): Explorations in His Religious and Literary Virtuosity*. Cambridge, Mass.: Harvard University Press, 1983. An introduction (by the editor) and five scholarly essays on various aspects of Naḥmanides' writings.

SEE ALSO: Averroës; Ibn Gabirol; Levi ben Gershom; Moses Maimonides; Moses de León.

RELATED ARTICLES in *Great Events from History: The Middle Ages, 477-1453*: 1190: Moses Maimonides Writes *The Guide of the Perplexed*; 1233: Papal Inquisition; c. 1275: The *Zohar* Is Transcribed; 1290-1306: Jews Are Expelled from England, France, and Southern Italy.

Alexander Neckam

English monk and scholar

Neckam typified the broadening humanistic interests of the twelfth century through his writing and teaching in areas including grammar, science, and theology.

Born: September 8, 1157; St. Albans, Hertfordshire, England

Died: Probably March 31, 1217; Kempsey, Worcestershire, England

Also known as: Alexander Necham; Alexander Nequam

Areas of achievement: Religion and theology, monasticism

Early Life

Little is known about the family of Alexander Neckam except that his mother, Hodierna, was probably nurse to Richard the Lion-Hearted, the future king of England, who was also born in 1157. He began his education at the monastery school of St. Albans. His pleasant memories of the school as well as its high reputation suggest that his early education fostered the abilities that were to produce his later literary achievements.

He continued his education in Paris, which, in the second half of the twelfth century, was the preeminent European intellectual center in the liberal arts and theology. Neckam was associated with the school of Petit Pont, which the logician Adam of Petit Pont made famous for its subtle disputation in the mid-twelfth century. Neckam's studies also included theology, medicine, and canon and civil law. He probably taught as a master and also began writing during his years in Paris. Although they contain no definitive date of composition, several of his works fit well into probable interests connected with his studies in Paris. The *Commentary on Martianus Capellus* (c. 1177-1190) deals primarily with mythology based on the standard treatise on the liberal arts by this late antique author. The *Novus avianus* (c. 1177-1190; new aviary) and *Novus Esopus* (c. 1177-1190; new Aesop) contain bird and animal fables that probably represent exercises in his ability to write on set themes. *De nominibus utensilium* (c. 1177-1190; on the names of utensils) is characteristic of elementary school instruction: It is a list of words taken from all facets of everyday life, from household furnishings to ships and sailing, put together in sentences whose purpose was to teach boys the Latin equivalents of these words. Its basic idea comes from a treatise on more difficult words by Adam of Petit Pont.

Life's Work

When Neckam returned to England around 1182, he spent about twenty years as a teacher. First, he was a master at Dunstable, a school under the control of St. Albans monastery. After about a year, he obtained a teaching position at the St. Albans school during the abbacy of Warin (1183-1195). Variations on a story based on his name—*nequam*, meaning worthless, naughty, or bad in Latin—are connected with his assumption of the position at St. Albans. According to the thirteenth century account of Matthew Paris, Abbot Warin summoned him with a wordplay on his name: "Si bonus es venias; si nequam nequaquam" (if you are a good man, come; if worthless, by no means). In other versions, the abbot gives this response to Neckam's petition to become a monk at St. Albans.

During the 1190's, Neckam taught at Oxford University. Although he is considered the first Scholastic theologian at Oxford, only a few traces of his teaching or lectures can be detected in his later writings. About fifty sermons, mainly from his Oxford period, survive. They are addressed to a variety of audiences, including scholars, laymen, and monks. Their form is simple, and they make only sparing use of the compositional techniques, rhetorical devices, and exempla that became characteristic of the developed sermon of the thirteenth century.

Neckam considered the monastic vocation the highest calling in life, and he fulfilled this ideal by entering the Augustinian abbey of Cirencester in Gloucestershire between 1197 and 1202. He became abbot in 1213. As an Augustinian canon, his learning and experience were called into service for both ecclesiastical and royal business. In 1212-1213, at the time of the interdict, he took part in royal affairs. In 1213, for example, King John ordered him to inquire into royal rights in the priory of Kenilworth. On several occasions, he was an ecclesiastical judge and a papal judge delegate. In 1215, he left England to attend the Fourth Lateran Council, and he returned in 1216. He died in March of 1217 at Kempsey, a manor of the bishop of Worcester, and was buried in Worcester Cathedral.

Most of the literary production on which Neckam's reputation rests comes from his later life when he was a canon at the abbey of Cirencester. In some of his writings, he continued his interests in grammar. The *Sacerdos ad altare* (c. 1200-1210), whose title of convenience comes from the first words of the treatise, is similar to the earlier *De nominibus utensilium* in its presentation of words put together into sentences with lengthy glosses on points of grammar following each section. The types of words, however, are different because they represent a higher social and intellectual level with an emphasis on priests and their vestments, the church and monastery with furnishings, the royal court, and the student and his reading list. This course of study is of particular interest because it gives some insight into the curriculum of the schools at Paris in the late twelfth century.

The *Corrogationes Promethei* (c. 1200-1204) is the primary source of Neckam's grammatical teaching. The meaning of the title, "collections of Prometheus," is uncertain. It may refer to one medieval view of Prometheus, the brother of Atlas, as instructing men in the arts; thus, the work would be a collection for a basic education in the arts that began with grammar. The first part concerns the art of grammar, including figures of speech, construction of sentences, accents, and orthography, with much material based on Arelius Donatus and Priscian, the main Roman authors of grammatical texts that were used in the Middle Ages. The second part glosses difficult words or passages from the Bible.

Science was another area of intellectual inquiry to which Neckam made an important contribution. Although many of his works contain scattered pieces of scientific information, two of his writings are devoted primarily to scientific questions. The *De naturis rerum* (on the natures of things), written before 1205, is the earliest and most extensive. Neckam considered it a moral treatise, and moral or spiritual interpretations follow the descriptions of natural phenomena. The subjects he discusses, however, represent the state of knowledge of natural sciences in England in the late twelfth century. He begins with creation and the firmament, discussing astronomy, including eclipses and the marks on the moon. The remainder of *De naturis rerum* is structured according to the elements. He begins with air and some of its properties as seen in the theory of the vacuum. He also catalogs birds that inhabit the air. Similarly, he discusses some properties of water followed by aquatic creatures. For the earth, he begins with minerals, then vegetables, and finally ends with animals, culminating with humanity.

The *Laus sapiente divine* (c. 1213; praise of divine wisdom) was composed just before he became abbot of Cirencester; in the last year of his life, the *Suppletio defectum* (1216), which is a supplement of lacking material, was added to it. The *Laus sapiente divine* is, in some ways, a versified form of the *De naturis rerum.* Its organization into ten distinctions differs, however, and the omission of many stories and more extensive treatment of some subjects, such as an enumeration of the stars and the theory of the elements, make it an equally interesting source for Neckam's scientific views. The *Suppletio defectum,* also in verse, is divided into two sections. The first, dealing with birds, animals, and plants, covers material familiar from his other writings. The second section, on problems about humankind as well as astronomy, introduces some new information.

Because he was a cleric and canon educated at Paris, a substantial portion of Neckam's writings concerns theological matters. Most are commentaries on books or passages in the Bible in the older monastic form consisting of lengthy discussions explaining the four senses of

Alexander Neckam. (Library of Congress)

Scripture: literal or historical, allegorical, tropological, and anagogical. These works include the *Solatium fidelis animae* (after 1197; consolation of the faithful soul), a moralized interpretation of the days of creation; the *Commentary on Ecclesiastes*, which the two books of *De naturis rerum* introduce; the *Commentary on the Song of Songs* (before 1213), which emphasizes the relationship between Christ and the Virgin; the *Commentary on Proverbs* (before 1213); and the *Tractatus super mulierem fortem* (after 1213; treatise on strong women), which comments on Proverbs 31:10-31 in honor of Mary Magdalene, the Virgin, and the Church. The newer scholastic commentary of the schools appears in his *Gloss on the Psalter* (after 1197), which follows the scholastic reading of text and gloss on the Bible and the second part of the *Corrogationes Promethei*, which utilizes the scholastic *distinctio* on the meaning of biblical words. He expounds his theological views in the four books of the *Speculum speculationum* (before 1213; mirror of speculations), which is notable for his discussion of grace and free will in the fourth book. Also surviving in parts or excerpted collections (*florilegia*) are several hymns and minor works such as the *Laus beatissime virginis* (after 1197; praise of the most blessed Virgin).

SIGNIFICANCE

Neckam is significant because in both his career and his writings he represents a transition from the developing schools and humanistic learning of the twelfth century to the expanded sources, new methods of teaching, and scientific interests of the later Middle Ages. In education, he was among the first authors of basic and practical descriptive vocabularies for primary instruction in Latin, although his grammatical glosses remained close to traditional expositions of Donatus and Priscian. Although he was instrumental in introducing Scholastic disputation in his Oxford teaching, his sermons and theological writings generally followed more traditional forms. For related theological and scientific problems, he demonstrated an early awareness of a broader corpus of the writings of Aristotle, whom he highly praised as great and most acute. Nevertheless, although various citations in his scientific writings point to some familiarity with Aristotle's works on natural science, Neckam relied most heavily on the more widely known Aristotelian treatises on logic. Also, while he evidenced interest in scientific observation and gave perhaps the earliest references to the compass and to glass mirrors, he repeated much information, often fabulous, from older authors such as Isidore of Seville. Through his prolific writings in many fields, his teaching at several educational levels, and his active participation in monastic life as well as royal and ecclesiastical service, Neckam was important in transmitting and transforming the widening intellectual interests of the twelfth century into their scholastic form of the late medieval period.

—*Karen K. Gould*

FURTHER READING

Davenport, Anne A. "The Catholics, the Cathars, and the Concept of Infinity in the Thirteenth Century." *Journal of the History of Science in Society* 88, no. 2 (June, 1997): 263. This substantial essay (thirty-three pages) focuses on the work of Neckam and Richard Fishacre, another thirteenth century theologian, with an eye to the social and political implications of the controversy between Cathar heretics and Catholics.

Gaselee, Stephen. "Natural Science in England at the End of the Twelfth Century." *Proceedings of the Royal Institution of Great Britain* 29, no. 3 (1937): 397-417. This piece contains a brief biography of Neckam. It remains one of the fullest descriptions of the contents of Neckam's *De naturis rerum*.

Haskins, Charles Homer. *Studies in the History of Mediaeval Science*. Cambridge, Mass.: Harvard University Press, 1924. Chapter 28 ascribes the *Sacerdos ad altare* to Alexander Neckam. It provides a transcription of the section on a student reading list.

Holmes, Urban Tigner. *Daily Living in the Twelfth Century, Based on the Observations of Alexander Neckam in London and Paris*. Madison: University of Wisconsin Press, 1952. Based on Neckam's writings, an account of what Neckam experienced during his time in Paris, with a focus on such aspects of daily life as his student quarters, food, and the medieval city of Paris, novelistically presented. Beautifully illustrated.

Hunt, R. W. *The Schools and the Cloister: The Life and Writings of Alexander Nequam, 1157-1217*. Edited and revised by Margaret Gibson. Oxford, England: Clarendon Press, 1984. This book is a biography of Neckam with a discussion of all of his writings. It contains a complete list of the writings, in chronological order, giving all known manuscript sources and printed editions. It also has thorough bibliographical references to other works about Neckam.

Russell, Josiah C. "Alexander Neckam in England." *English Historical Review* 47 (1932): 260-268. Discusses the documentation for Neckam's life and career in England. An appendix contains emendations to M. Esposito's list of Neckam's works.

Thorndike, Lynn. *A History of Magic and Experimental Science*. Vol. 2. New York: Macmillan, 1923. One chapter discusses Neckam's life and learning, concentrating on his scientific writings and their contribution to scientific knowledge.

SEE ALSO: Richard I.

RELATED ARTICLE in *Great Events from History: The Middle Ages, 477-1453*: c. 1250: Improvements in Shipbuilding and Navigation.

NEST VERCH RHYS AP TEWDWR

Princess of Wales

Nest was the mother of many influential individuals, through her marriages and through her numerous liaisons, and was the subject of an infamous abduction that triggered political power struggles and won her notoriety as the "Helen of Wales."

BORN: c. 1080; probably Deheubarth, Wales
DIED: c. 1136; place unknown
ALSO KNOWN AS: Nest ferch Rhys ap Tewdwr; Nesta; Helen of Wales; Nest of Deheubarth; Nest of Pembroke
AREA OF ACHIEVEMENT: Government and politics

EARLY LIFE

Although little is known of her early life, Nest verch Rhys ap Tewdwr (nehst vhurk ris ahp TEH-ew-dur) was born into a position of privilege, as the eldest of the three children of the most powerful figure in southern Wales. Nest was the daughter of Rhys ap Tewdwr, who in 1075 claimed the kingdom of Deheubarth, which then comprised much of southern Wales. In 1081, Rhys ap Tewdwr secured his position as sole ruler of Deheubarth by winning the Battle of Mynydd Carn and then making an alliance with William the Conqueror (r. 1066-1087) of England. Nest's mother, Gwladus, was herself from a powerful family, being the daughter of Rhiwallon ap Cynfyn, who ruled the realm of Powys, in north Wales. No medieval sources offer details about the date or location of Nest's birth.

Throughout the period of her youth, Nest would surely have been brought up in a culturally Welsh royal household, for Rhys ap Tewdwr managed to hold off the advance of Anglo-Norman colonization that had been ravaging the more northerly realms of Wales. The new English king, William II (r. 1087-1100), appears to have respected his father's alliance with the house of Deheubarth, since the English did not attempt large-scale colonization of the realm until after the death of Rhys ap Tewdwr, who was killed in 1093 by Anglo-Norman invaders in southeast Wales, near Aberhonddu (modern Brecon). That Nest's father was an individual of immense stature is reflected in both Welsh and English chronicle sources, which claim that Rhys ap Tewdwr's death marked the fall of kingship by the native Welsh, as opposed to the encroaching Normans.

Rhys ap Tewdwr's death created a power vacuum that both Welsh and English forces struggled to fill. Whereas Nest had spent her youth in a stable realm under firm Welsh control, her much younger brothers were both victimized by the unstable political situation triggered by their father's death: Gruffydd ap Rhys ap Tewdwr, heir to the throne of Deheubarth, had to flee to Ireland, while Nest's youngest brother, Hywel, was captured by Arnulf, the earl of Pembroke. Although details about Nest's activities in the years immediately following the death of Rhys ap Tewdwr are not known, she surely lived in some fear that she might follow her brothers in becoming a victim of the political ambitions of the numerous Normans and Welsh seeking to gain ascendancy in Deheubarth.

LIFE'S WORK

It is clear that Nest's status as a princess outlived the death of her father, as Gerald of Windsor is said to have married her, around 1095, in order to consolidate his political position in the region. Gerald was an Anglo-Norman settler who became the first constable of the strategic castle at Pembroke in 1097, in southwest Wales, and who also held lands that included nearby Carew. Gerald could thus shelter Nest in the shifting and violent region that Deheubarth had become since the death of her father. Nest's marriage with Gerald triggered a feud with the ruler of the realm of Powys, Cadwgan ap Bleddyn, who felt threatened by the alliance of an Anglo-Norman landlord with the erstwhile princess. However, Gerald, as an officer of the powerful king of England, Henry I (r. 1100-1135), ensured that he and Nest could enjoy relative domestic security.

Indeed, Nest would go on to have five children by her husband Gerald of Windsor: three sons (David, William, and Maurice) and two daughters (Gwladus and Angharad). Gerald acquired a strong enough power base to conquer, by 1115, the region of Emlyn, in the realm of Dyfed, in west-central Wales. That Gerald and Nest enjoyed a prosperous marriage can be measured by the fact that all their children survived to become individuals of influence: David Fitzgerald would become archdeacon of Ceredigion and, in 1148, bishop of St. David's, while William and Maurice would follow in their father's footsteps as major landlords and military powers in southern Wales. Nest and Gerald's daughters would each marry Anglo-Norman settlers who held positions of power in southwest Wales: Gwladus married Tancard, the constable of the castle of Haverford, while Angharad was betrothed to William de Barri, who would follow his father as lord of Manorbier.

Although no physical description of Nest survives, she clearly struck her contemporaries as a woman of great beauty. Nest's beauty attracted many suitors, and she proved to be far from faithful in her marriage to Gerald. Shortly after her marriage, Nest became the mistress of Henry I and had a son by him, Henry Fitzhenry, sometime before 1109. Henry Fitzhenry would later lose his life as part of Henry II's (r. 1154-1189) 1157 invasion of Anglesey, in north Wales, while his sons, Meiler and Robert, would be part of the 1170 Anglo-Norman conquest of Ireland. Nest was also the mother of William Fitzhai, sometime before 1116, possibly by Hait, who is listed as the sheriff of Pembroke in 1130. William would go on to become the lord of St. Clears, in southwest Wales.

Nest's most famous suitor, however, was Owain ap Cadwgan, who is said to have been drawn to visit Nest, in 1109, after having heard stories of her remarkable beauty at a Christmas feast in the courts of Ceredigion, in the western part of his father's realm, Powys. Although Owain was Nest's second cousin (through his great-grandmother, Angharad, daughter of Maredudd ap Owain, who was Nest's great-great-aunt), he and his father, Cadwgan ap Bleddyn, had been hostile to the territorially ambitious Gerald of Windsor. However, there was at the time enough peace between the parties to allow Owain to satisfy his desire to see Nest, and so he paid her a visit at Gerald's castle in Emlyn, called Cenarth Bychan. (Cilgerran is usually proposed as the site of this unidentified castle, although Cardigan has also been suggested.) The praises of Nest's beauty were for Owain clearly confirmed by this visit, for he soon began planning the abduction that would cement Nest's fame as the "Helen of Wales."

Later in 1109, Owain and fifteen companions conducted a surprise attack on Cenarth Bychan, setting fire to the castle's buildings and terrorizing its residents with battle cries. Gerald, who fled from the raid through a privy, is reported to have done so on the advice of Nest. After destroying the undefended castle, Owain took possession of Nest and her children, as well as an unnamed, illegitimate child of Gerald's, bringing them all back to his land of Ceredigion. Although some scholars have speculated that Nest played a willing role in the events, the earliest surviving version of the anonymous chronicle source, *Brut y Tywysogion* (wr. c. 681-1282; *The Chronicle of the Princes*, 1860), makes clear that Nest believed that Owain had come, not for her, but to kill Gerald, and is equally clear in stating that Owain raped Nest, before abducting her to his homeland.

Owain's abduction of Nest triggered open hostilities not only with Gerald of Windsor, but also with his feudal lord, Henry I, who had fathered a child by Nest. Cadwgan, fearing an invasion, was not able to convince his son to return Nest. Nest, however, convinced Owain—whom, the chronicle implies, Nest had by then accepted willingly as her lover—to return her children to Gerald. Meanwhile, Henry I began plans for retaliation, using Richard of Beaumais, bishop of London, to convince Ithel and Madog ap Rhiryd, who were related to Owain as members of the ruling house of Powys, to invade Ceredigion and destroy Cadwgan and his now outlawed son. Ithel and Madog ravaged their lands, killing or driving out all those loyal to Cadwgan and Owain, who themselves managed to escape the slaughter (with Owain fleeing to Ireland and Cadwgan hiding in his realm of Powys).

Although the chronicles are silent about Nest's fate during this tumultuous period, she was presumably returned to her husband later in 1109. The supporters of Owain who fled to Dyfed, in southwestern Wales, faced the vengeance of Gerald of Windsor, who held sway there; however, Walter, the chief justice of Gloucester, is reported to have dissuaded Gerald from executing all of these men. Owain's abduction of Nest proved disastrous both for his supporters and for his father, who was dispossessed of Ceredigion, which Henry I granted to Ithel and Madog (though Cadwgan was later given back his lands). Gerald continued to exact vengeance on Owain and those loyal to him, despite the fact that Owain had regained royal favor by 1115. Although he and Owain were both fighting against the rebels involved in the Deheubarth rising led by Nest's brother, Gruffydd ap Rhys, Gerald and a contingent of Fleming mercenaries killed Owain in 1116, at Ystrad Rwnws (near modern Carmarthen).

Although little is known of Nest's life after 1109, some scholars have speculated that Nest may have outlived her husband and entered into a second, yet unrecorded marriage. As the date of Gerald of Windsor's death is not known (he is last mentioned in chronicle sources in 1116), Nest's last known child, Robert Fitzstephen, may indeed have been the product of marriage with Stephen, who is listed as the constable of the castle of Cardigan in 1136. Robert Fitzstephen would go on to succeed his father at Cardigan and acquire new lands in Cemais, in southwest Wales. Although no source names the time and place of Nest's death, she may well have spent her last years at Cardigan, under Stephen's protection.

SIGNIFICANCE

Nest left a profound mark on the political history of twelfth century Wales. Through her status as the daughter of the powerful Welsh king, Rhys ap Tewdwr, she aided her husband Gerald of Windsor in maintaining his base of power in southwest Wales, allowing him to conquer the region of Emlyn, of which their son, William Fitzgerald, would in turn become lord. Her notorious abduction by Owain ap Cadwgan triggered an invasion of Ceredigion, which brought about sweeping changes in the power structure of the realm of Powys.

Perhaps Nest's greatest legacy lies in the influence of her numerous children and grandchildren. Not only did her son David become a bishop, but her remaining sons became key players in wars in Wales, while William Fitzgerald, Robert Fitzstephen, and Nest's grandchildren, by both Angharad and Henry Fitzroy, became key figures in the Anglo-Norman conquest of Ireland that was launched in 1169. Among Nest's numerous grandchildren that influenced the history of both Wales and Anglo-Norman England, perhaps the most notable is Angharad's son, Gerald of Wales (also known as Giraldus Cambrensis), who would become one of the most influential of all British historians.

—*Randy P. Schiff*

FURTHER READING

Davies, John. *The Making of Wales*. Herndon, Va.: Sutton, 1996. A general survey of the history of Wales, useful for its assessment of the impact of Anglo-Norman settlement in Nest's Wales. Features numerous maps and photographs.

Davies, R. R. *The Age of Conquest: Wales, 1063-1415*. New York: Oxford University Press, 2000. Presents a history of Wales and the influence of the Normans. Illustrations, extensive bibliography, and index.

_______. *Conquest, Coexistence, and Change: Wales, 1063-1415*. New York: Oxford University Press, 1987. A general survey of the political and military history of medieval Wales, especially valuable for its discussion of Anglo-Norman colonization as a background for Nest's era. Features many useful maps and genealogical tables.

Lloyd, J. E. *A History of Wales from the Earliest Times to the Edwardian Conquest*. 2 vols. 1911. Reprint. London: Longmans, 1967. In this influential general survey of medieval Wales, the author brings together much of the chronicle evidence for the details of Nest's marriage, liaisons, and abduction, and provides genealogical tables for all the ruling houses of Wales.

Turvey, Roger. *The Welsh Princes: The Native Rulers of Wales, 1063-1283*. London: Longman, 2002. A general study of the ruling class into which Nest was born, offering insight into the sociocultural background of the Welsh elite, both before and after Anglo-Norman settlement.

SEE ALSO: Gwenllian verch Gruffydd; Henry I; Henry II; William the Conqueror.

RELATED ARTICLES in *Great Events from History: The Middle Ages, 477-1453*: October 14, 1066: Battle of Hastings; 1169-1172: Normans Invade Ireland.

NGO QUYEN

Vietnamese king (r. 939-944)

Ngo Quyen's victory on the Bach-dang River against Chinese forces in 938 ended ten centuries of Chinese domination and restored Vietnamese independence.

BORN: c. 898; Western Red River Delta, Kingdom of Nam Viet (now in Son Tay Province, Vietnam)

DIED: 944; Duong Lam, Kingdom of Nam Viet (now in Vietnam)

AREAS OF ACHIEVEMENT: Warfare and conquest, military, government and politics

EARLY LIFE

According to Vietnamese folklore, Ngo Quyen (NGOH kee-EHN) was given his name, Quyen, which means authority and power, because three black moles were discovered on his back when he was born. These moles were regarded as a sign of future greatness. He became known for his physical strength, wisdom, and bravery and was considered an expert in the martial arts at an early age.

Quyen's father, Ngo Man, was a provincial magistrate in Phong. The young Ngo grew up at a time of immense changes in Vietnam. After almost a millennium of political control by China, the fall of the Tang Dynasty (T'ang; 608-907) fostered a period of political fragmentation within China known as the Five Dynasties and Ten Kingdoms period (907-960). Vietnam took advantage of this Chinese disunity to strengthen its power.

After the Vietnamese displaced the Tang governor of the region, they elected a local chieftain, Khuc Thua Du. This leader passed the rule to his son, who in turn sent his son to the area. When officials attempted to reestablish Chinese authority, they were ousted by a former general of Khuc Thua Du named Duong Dien Nghe.

Ngo Quyen became a general under Duong Dien Nghe. Not only did Nghe place Quyen in charge of Ai Province, but he also gave him one of his daughters in marriage. Quyen was regarded as a loyal subordinate and effective commander. Nghe was assassinated in 937 by one of his officers, Kieu Cong Tien, who attempted to reexert Chinese influence in the area. Both to avenge the death of his friend and to maintain indigenous control, Quyen mobilized an army and soon killed Tien. In doing so, Quyen naturally became the leader of the Vietnamese forces.

LIFE'S WORK

By 938, Ngo Quyen had become a battle-hardened veteran of many military conflicts. His skills would be necessary against Chinese forces, who sent an expedition south to quash resistance. Led by Liu Hongcao (Liu Hung-ts'ao), the Chinese planned to travel on the Bach-dang River and place army personnel in the Giao region.

Anticipating the Chinese move, Ngo Quyen devised an ingenious and devastating strategy. He had his men place iron-tipped wooden poles in the bed of the river just below the surface. Quyen then had his forces provoke a fight with the Chinese and retreat down river. As Liu Hongcao's boats chased the Vietnamese, the tide receded and the stakes trapped the Chinese vessels. During Quyen's counterstrike, more than half the Chinese drowned, and most of their boats were destroyed. The remaining Chinese forces retreated.

The Battle of Bach-dang River ushered in a new period in Vietnamese history. Besides ending one thousand years of foreign dominance, the nationalist feelings that followed the military victory led Vietnam to proclaim its independence. The hero of the battle, Ngo Quyen, took the title of king in 939.

During his short reign, Ngo Quyen was credited with a number of achievements. First, he established the kingdom of Nam Viet. Though there is no record of how Quyen's court was organized, there is evidence of the development of ceremonies and costumes, designation of mandarinates, and an emphasis on maintaining a strong military to defend the central government. Second, he set up a capital at Co-loa, site of the ancient capital of Thuc in the Au Lac kingdom, which ruled the country long before Chinese domination. This decision showed Quyen's knowledge of Vietnamese history and willingness to form a new national identity. Third, this period became known as the Ngo Dynasty because of the achievements and legacy of its leader.

On the other hand, Ngo Quyen's short reign had its share of problems. Royal control was never consolidated. State leaders built their power locally without developing loyalty to the throne. Finally, it was clear that Ngo's kingdom still sought to emulate certain Chinese customs, which produced isolation between the throne and Vietnamese society in later years. Although the dynasty that Ngo Quyen founded would last until 965, his death in 944 precipitated a period of strife. Local warlords vied with Quyen's descendants for control. Meanwhile, Ngo family squabbles weakened its position. A sharing of power by two Ngo brothers produced two kings ruling simultaneously, an arrangement that fell apart after fifteen years.

In 965, a new leader and dynasty emerged under Dinh Bo Linh, a former mercenary soldier who unified the divisive states. Proclaiming himself emperor, Linh renamed the country Dai Co Viet. After placating China, he received recognition of his position, something China refused to offer during the Ngo Dynasty.

VIETNAM: INDEPENDENT GOVERNMENTS, 10TH-20TH CENTURIES

Dates	*Government*
939-965	Ngo Dynasty (NGO QUYEN, founder)
968-980	Dinh Dynasty
980-1009	Le Dynasty
1009-1225	Ly Dynasty
1225-1400	Tran Dynasty
1400-1407	Ho Dynasty
1428-1789	Later Le Dynasty
1790-1802	Chinese occupation
1802-1859	Nguyen Dynasty
1859-1954	French colonization
1940-1945	Japanese occupation
1945	Independence from Japan
1954	Independence from France, division into North and South Vietnam
1975	Reunification of North and South Vietnam, establishment of Socialist Republic of Vietnam

SIGNIFICANCE

Not only was Ngo Quyen a national hero in his own time but also his legacy is clearly seen in the evolution of Vietnam. First, ensuing dynasties followed the same goals identified during his reign: to prevent internal competition, to protect areas against Chinese invasion, and to acquire land to the south so as to expand the population. Second, except for two brief periods totaling thirty years, Vietnam retained its independence until French colonization of the country in the mid-nineteenth century. Third, subsequent rulers largely retained the capital that Quyen established—albeit under different names—where modern-day Hanoi is located.

Ngo Quyen deserves his place alongside Le Loi and Nguyen Anh, who vanquished the Chinese in 1428 and 1802, respectively, and Ho Chi Minh as one of the architects of Vietnamese independence. The military and political precedents that he set were acknowledged by the Socialist Republic of Vietnam in October, 1999, when a commemorative stamp was issued in his honor depicting the victory in the 938 Battle of Bach-dang River.

—*Samuel B. Hoff*

FURTHER READING

Bain, Chester A. *The Roots of a Conflict*. Englewood Cliffs: Prentice-Hall, 1967. Comprehensive history of Vietnam through the mid-1950's.

Gettleman, Marvin E. *Vietnam: History, Documents, and Opinions on a Major World Crisis*. New York: New American Library, 1970. Contains a chapter on Vietnamese history.

Hall, D. G. E. *A History of South-East Asia*. London: Macmillan Education, 1988. Includes a section on the history of Vietnam.

Hess, Gary R. *Vietnam and the United States: Origins and Legacy of War.* New York: Twayne, 1998. Offers a short history of the development of Vietnam.

Taylor, Keith Weller. *The Birth of Vietnam*. Berkeley: University of California Press, 1983. Traces the evolution of Vietnam from the beginning of recorded history in the third century B.C.E. to the tenth century.

Tucker, Spencer C. *The Encyclopedia of the Vietnam War: A Political, Social, and Military History*. New York: Oxford University Press, 2000. Contains an entry on Ngo Quyen, including citations leading to Vietnamese studies on Ngo.

SEE ALSO: Taizong; Wu Hou.

RELATED ARTICLES in *Great Events from History: The Middle Ages, 477-1453*: 618: Founding of the Tang Dynasty; 690-705: Reign of Empress Wu; 907-960: Period of Five Dynasties and Ten Kingdoms; 939-944: Reign of Ngo Quyen; 982: Le Dai Hanh Invades Champa; 1323-1326: Champa Wins Independence from Dai Viet; 1428: Le Loi Establishes Later Le Dynasty.

NICHIREN
Japanese monk

Through extraordinary dedication, Nichiren founded the Lotus sect of Buddhism, which, in turn, gave rise to a fervent Japanese nationalism.

BORN: March 30, 1222; Kominato, Japan
DIED: November 14, 1282; Sochu-ji Temple, Ikegami, Japan
ALSO KNOWN AS: Zennichi; Zennichi-maru (given name); Zenshōbō Renchō
AREA OF ACHIEVEMENT: Religion and theology

EARLY LIFE

Japanese sources trace the lineage of Nichiren (nee-chee-rehn), one of the most famous of Japan's Buddhist leaders, to the Fujiwara family of early Japan. Feudal power struggles, exile, and dispossession reduced Nichiren's family to humble circumstances. Born to Shigetada, a fisherman, Nichiren was first named Zennichi-maru; Nichiren (lotus of the sun) is a Buddhist name that he adopted later as a monk—*nichi*, the sun, symbolizes Japan, and *ren*, the lotus, is the primary Buddhist symbol.

For ten years, Nichiren conscientiously studied Buddhism as a monk of the prominent Tendai sect centered at Mount Hiei, near Kyoto. He came to believe that he alone could help the Japanese people and save the nation.

LIFE'S WORK

In 1253, Nichiren began a turbulent ministry marked by confrontation with various governmental authorities. He propagated a new doctrine believed to have been preached by the historic Buddha, Siddhārtha Gautama, in his later career, a doctrine centered mainly on the Mahāyāna Buddhist sutra *Saddharma-pundarika*. He referred to himself as a reincarnation of the bodhisattva Vishish-ṭachāritra, an ancient disciple of the Buddha.

Early in his career, Nichiren became convinced that he would establish the true sect of Buddhism, a sect that would dominate the world from a holy see in Japan. This sect was known as the Lotus sect of Buddhism, and Nichiren's role in history is inseparable from the rise and continuing influence of this doctrine.

Nichiren's life and work, although rooted in traditional Japanese society, heralded an entirely new spirit of nationalism and religious intolerance. Although most great religious leaders came from southern Japan, Nichiren came from the eastern provinces. His religion was permeated with a patriotic fervor and bore a strong, independent spirit—an offensive, temperamental disposition characteristic of the eastern samurai warriors of medieval Japan.

Just as the rise of Protestantism in early modern Europe is understandable only against the background of the dominant Catholic church, so Nichiren's form of Buddhism must be understood in relation to the other sects that dominated Japanese history. Some of these sects had fallen into corrupt practices and were scorned by the populace, and much of Nichiren's career was marked by vitriolic criticism of them. For example, Nichiren criticized the Tendai sect, of which he himself was a member. This sect was popular among the elite of Japan and stressed ornate ritualism and "high church" ceremonies. Nichiren also railed against the most popular sect, Amidaism, or the Pure Land (Jōdo) sect, which emphasized simple salvation by faith and complete trust in Amida Buddha. Pure Land Buddhism was popular with the poor and downtrodden, to whom it gave comfort for the battle of life and consolation in the hour of death. While the older forms of Buddhism were weakening, the Pure Land sect had matured during the great strife and chaos of a country in perpetual civil war and would compete with the Nichiren sect as the dominant belief.

All Japan's traditional Buddhist sects, except that of Nichiren, had counterparts in China. The Zen sect, for example, appealed to the samurai class, with its simple and direct approach to salvation and emphasis on intellectual effort, self-reliance, and meditation. Buddhist sects were generally pacifist by nature and not exclusive. However, Nichiren's new sect was seen as an unorthodox doctrine, hostile to other forms of Buddhism and given to militant, intolerant attitudes and behavior. This was the first sect of Japanese origin, a new doctrine whose time had come among a people prepared for its distinctive claims.

Nichiren and his adherents held that truth and salvation were to be found only in the *Lotus Sutra*, and an important part of their ritual was the repeated utterance of the mystic words *Namu myōhō renge kyō*, meaning "homage to the wonderful law of the *Lotus Sutra*." This new doctrine, like most new types of protestant Buddhism that emerged in medieval Japan, was characterized by a highly dogmatic form of teaching. It offered a message similar to the messages of some Western religions, placing much emphasis on the "last days" and stressing a preparation for the advent of a savior. During this dark period of Japanese history, Nichiren and others emphasized the idea of *mappo*, or the "end of the holy Buddhist law." Some historians speculate that this idea emerged from the pessimism of a degenerate era of feudal Japan characterized by misery, epidemics, and internecine warfare. Others challenge this notion and call attention to the eastern provinces of Japan, where the warrior clans were characterized by a vigorous creative spirit and a mood of confidence.

Whatever the case, Nichiren emerged with a new apocalyptic creed. This idea of a savior is not a central theme in traditional Buddhism, but there is mention in early Buddhist texts of a savior, Maitreya Buddha, who was to come in the dark ages. The apocalyptic characteristics of his doctrine distinguish Nichiren's brand of Buddhism from various popular religions that emerged during his era.

Nichiren declared that he was a reincarnated bodhisattva who had come forth specifically to preach a singular truth that the "latter day of the Buddhist law" was to give way to a new era of salvation. This promise of a new era was the cardinal feature of the Lotus sect. His birth and mission, Nichiren maintained, were clearly described in the twelfth and thirteenth chapters of the *Hokke* scripture.

The general spiritual aspects of Nichiren's teachings are fairly close to traditional Buddhism. The sect's uniqueness was its emphasis on the role of the *Lotus Sutra* as the means of spiritually unifying the world and establishing peace. Nichiren preached and wrote often about peace, although he himself was very quarrelsome in his manner. He once admitted that he was the most uncompromising man in Japan, and he used strong language to condemn other Buddhist leaders; his sermons and invective against them were marked by such epithets as "devil," "liar," and "fiend."

Nichiren used the same strong language against the military government (*bakufu*) at Kamakura. His antagonism made him many enemies, and he was exiled for a time and subsequently released in 1263, only to return with renewed criticism of rival religions and government officials.

Nichiren's mission must also be seen in the context of a special crisis that faced Japan—a Mongol invasion. Nichiren distressed the high officers of the government by sharply criticizing their handling of the crisis and castigating them for lack of foresight and courage. The adherents of other Buddhist sects that he had attacked then plotted against him, and he was condemned for treason. Sentenced to death, Nichiren gained a stay of execution on the very site in which he was to be beheaded. The details of this incident are not clear, but Nichiren disciples interpret his evasion of death as a miracle.

In exile for three years on the island of Sado (1271-1274), Nichiren studied and meditated, perfected his doctrinal interpretation, and reached the conclusion that he was the savior about whom much had been said.

There were samurai warriors who admired Nichiren's courage and facilitated his return to the capital in 1274, on the eve of the Mongol invasion. Government officials attempted to resolve their confrontation with this influential monk, but he was uncompromising. Until his death in Sochuji at Ikegami in 1282, he demanded that the government condemn all other sects as apostate, suppress their heresies, and unite Japan under the *Hokke* religion. Nichiren did have a more charitable side to his personality, apparent as he went among his poor followers. During his lifetime, however, the main body of his believers were the samurai warriors, attracted by his militant, crusading spirit.

Apart from his charismatic character, Nichiren was an eccentric scholar with a keen mind and a vigorous style, the author of religious treatises of great literary excellence. It is in this connection that Nichiren made an additional contribution, in the realm of Japanese national consciousness, that emerged only after his death. His influence here was probably even more significant than his founding of the religion that bears his name. Japan was the first nation in Asia, indeed the first non-Western nation, to experience the phenomenon of nationalism, and Nichiren contributed to this important development. This is best seen in his treatise *Risshō ankoku ron* (1260; *On the Establishment of the Orthodox Teaching and the Peace of the Nation*, 1980), which stressed the national crisis and maintained that only by espousing Nichiren Buddhism could the nation be saved.

His vision was actually broader than the country of Japan, for he claimed that his doctrine had universal validity, that his truths would emerge from Japan to be propagated throughout the world. He had visions of a universal Buddhist church, with a holy see located in Japan. This nationalistic aspect of religion was unique to Japan.

Nichiren left an indelible mark on the religious history of Japan. Indeed, while some religions have had a limited appeal and impact on the life of a nation, Nichiren's religion has had a lasting appeal to the Japanese, many of whom have seen themselves as special and belonging to a nation that somehow has a mission in the world. No religion has done as much as Nichiren Buddhism to identify Buddhism with the national life of a country. Also, no other sect of Buddhism has been so characterized by an apocalyptic mysticism as that of Nichiren.

Following Nichiren's death in 1282, the perpetuation of his particular brand of Buddhism was left in the hands of six disciples, and there was considerable sectarian conflict among rival factions that continued for centuries. The main headquarters of the dominant sect continued at Mount Minobu, with a rival branch of the religion located nearby. Fairly reliable reports indicate that, after World War II, the Nichiren sect numbered some 10 million adherents, with more than five thousand temples, while the rival sect numbered 300,000 adherents with two hundred temples.

SIGNIFICANCE

Nichiren's life was a series of crises, and his religion was a crisis-born, militant sect. It is generally seen as the culmination of a process of Japanization of the Buddhism introduced from China and Korea, and it bore the seeds of nationalism.

Nichiren's brand of Buddhism is not to be dismissed as past history, for in the 1930's, there appeared a Buddhist renaissance inspired by the Nichiren sect. The movement was quickly eclipsed when it came into conflict with Japan's military leaders on the eve of World War II. Following the war, however, the religion re-emerged and produced a remarkable revival, becoming the most rapidly growing religion in Japan in the 1950's. The religion was again characterized by Nichiren's deep-rooted doctrine and militant conviction. Soka Gakkai, as this revivalistic, intolerant religion was called, claimed to be the wave of the future for the Japanese people and the world. It gained millions of adherents, mainly among workers and less-educated people and, by 1955, had even influenced the political arena: Vigorous campaigns were waged to elect its representatives to the national assembly of Japan. This marriage between religion and politics harks back to Nichiren himself, who asserted that religion and national life were inseparable.

—*Paul Hyer*

FURTHER READING

Anesaki, Masaharu. *Nichiren: The Buddhist Prophet*. Cambridge, Mass.: Harvard University Press, 1916. This classic study on Nichiren was written by a recognized authority on Japanese history. Illustrated with maps.

Christensen, J. A. *Nichiren: Leader of Buddhist Reformation in Japan*. Fremont, Calif.: Jain, 2001. A look at the life of Nichiren, originally published in 1981 by the Buddhist Order of America.

Eliot, Charles N. E. *Japanese Buddhism*. New York: Barnes and Noble Books, 1959. A standard treatment of the Buddhist world from which Nichiren emerged.

Nichiren. *Nichiren: Selected Writings*. Translated by Laurel R. Rood. Honolulu: University of Hawaii Press, 1980. A selection of important primary writings by the prophet himself. Includes a lengthy bibliography and a helpful index.

Sansom, George B. *Japan: A Short Cultural History*. Stanford, Calif.: Stanford University Press, 1978. A standard work by a British scholar and diplomat that gives the historical context of Nichiren's career.

SEE ALSO: Kōbō Daishi.

RELATED ARTICLES in *Great Events from History: The Middle Ages, 477-1453*: 538-552: Buddhism Arrives in Japan; 792: Rise of the Samurai; 1156-1192: Minamoto Yoritomo Becomes Shogun; 1175: Hōnen Shōnin Founds Pure Land Buddhism; 1204: Genghis Khan Founds Mongol Empire.

NICHOLAS OF AUTRECOURT
French philosopher

Nicholas's thought on certainty and uncertainty in knowledge anticipated some of the discoveries of the eighteenth century Scottish philosopher David Hume and later rationalists and empiricists. He contributed to the end of high Scholastic thought by proposing a form of radical nominalism critical of the Aristotelian notions of substance and causation.

BORN: c. 1300; Autrecourt, near Verdun, France
DIED: After 1350; probably Metz, Lorraine, France
ALSO KNOWN AS: Nicolaus de Autricuria
AREAS OF ACHIEVEMENT: Philosophy, religion and theology

EARLY LIFE

Nicholas of Autrecourt (oh-truh-cohr) was born in the French diocese of Verdun, a region that was also the birthplace of two other iconoclastic contemporaries, James of Metz and John of Mirecourt. Of Nicholas's early youth, little is known, though he apparently proved himself a bright boy, matriculating at the University of Paris and living as a fellow of the Sorbonne between 1320 and 1327.

During the time Nicholas was a student, the University of Paris was, intellectually, an especially exhilarating place. Change was in the air. By the fourteenth century, the seams of the much-patched fabric of Scholastic synthesis had begun to unravel rapidly because the internal oppositions between Christian theology and Aristotelian metaphysics and Aristotelian logic were becoming more and more obvious.

The criticism of Scholasticism that resulted from the need to resolve these oppositions was not, however, an entirely new creation. It was an outgrowth of the logical methods of Scholasticism itself. Thus when William of Ockham personally carried his nominalistic philosophy to France to answer the charge of heretical and erroneous opinions before the papal commission at Avignon in 1324, he was greeted by the professors of the University of Paris as a fellow laborer. It is impossible to discount the influence of both the rise of nominalism and the Parisian intellectual atmosphere on Nicholas's intellectual development, even though Nicholas's philosophy cannot, in any proper sense, be considered a form of Ockhamism.

Shortly after completing his studies in 1327, Nicholas received his licentiate in theology and the degrees of master of arts and bachelor of theology and laws. Appropriately equipped, he embarked on an academic career at his alma mater. His tenure at the University of Paris, which lasted from 1327 to 1340, represents the period of his greatest accomplishment.

LIFE'S WORK

It was during his tenure as an academic that Nicholas wrote the controversial works that helped shape the intellectual scene of the fourteenth century. Unfortunately, the fragmentary nature of the surviving corpus makes it impossible to describe the full scope of his thought. Of Nicholas's commentaries on the writings of Aristotle and Peter Lombard, all that survives comes from the replies of Jean Buridan in his commentaries on Aristotle's *Physica* (c. 335-323 B.C.E.; *Physics*, 1812) and *Metaphysica* (c. 335-323 B.C.E.; *Metaphysics*, 1801) and those of Thomas of Strassburg in his commentary on Peter Lombard's *Sententiarum libri IV* (1148-1151; *The Books of Opinions of Peter Lombard*, 1970; better known as *Sentences*). The only surviving Nicholatian texts are two complete letters and fragments of five others written to Bernard of Arezzo, an almost complete letter to Egidius, an answer to a theological question, and a philosophical treatise entitled *Exigit ordo* (*The Universal Treatise of Nicholas of Autrecourt*, 1971). All were written before 1340, the *Exigit ordo* apparently being the last. Only the two complete letters have been translated into English in their entirety. It is on the basis of this motley collection of works that any reconstruction of the main themes of Nicholas's philosophy proceeds.

Nicholas's philosophical starting point is the logical principle of noncontradiction: A thing cannot be and not be something at the same time. All arguments formed to arrive at truth that do not follow from the principle of noncontradiction are merely probable. Only deductive arguments that presuppose this principle are absolutely certain.

Nicholas distinguishes two kinds of certainty that characterize different forms of experience: the certainty of faith and the certainty of evidence. The certainty of faith is guaranteed by God's grace, is subjective, and is thus beyond the criticism of philosophers. One who has it finds it supernaturally indubitable, and nothing more can be said; it is its own proof. The second variety of certainty is the proper province of philosophers. It is called the certainty of evidence and is characterized by admitting no degrees. Either the evidence produces certainty or it does not. Nicholas does maintain that the certainty of evidence comes in two varieties: the certainty of evidence about simple things and the certainty of evidence about complex things. By the former, Nicholas means the certainty of inner perception or experience; by the latter, he means the certainty of propositions. The principle of noncontradiction can be used to test both varieties.

In some of his writings, Nicholas provides demonstrations as to how the criterion of noncontradiction can be applied to simple and complex judgments. In the case of perception (simple certainty), he argues the impossibility of separating judgments of existence associated with perception from the perceptions themselves. In other words, to perceive a color and to be aware that one is perceiving a color are inseparable acts. To maintain that one perceives a color and that one is not, at the same time, conscious of perceiving a color is a contradiction. From this Nicholas draws the inference that everyone perceives his or her own existence. To maintain that the perception of existence is possible without a consciousness of that existence is a contradiction; to maintain this is to assert that there can be a perception without something doing the perceiving.

In the case of complex things (or propositions), Nicholas provides a number of analogous arguments that show that the certainty of propositions, too, depends on the principle of noncontradiction. If it were possible to be certain about a proposition that was not dependent on the principle of noncontradiction, then this act would be tantamount to saying that one could be certain about a proposition that could be either true or false, or—more subtly—that one could be certain about a proposition that appears true and yet is possibly false. Yet certainty does not allow the possibility of falsehood. The only recourse, then, is to rest the judgment of propositions on a principle that guarantees that certainty is achieved only when conclusions are reached that cannot fail to be true or about which there is no possibility of falsehood. The principle of noncontradiction alone meets this requirement.

Nicholas characterizes certain propositional knowledge as that variety that modern logical positivists term "tautologous." When Nicholas asserts that "A is P and therefore it is not the case that A is not P," he construes that relationship not in the manner of medieval Aristotelians, who thought of it either as the relation between a substance and another higher genera or as the relation between a substance and its accident. Rather, he construes that relationship in the manner of some modern logicians who see the relationship between A and P as being simply that between an object and one of the predicates that make it what it is. According to Nicholas, there is no substance underlying the perceptions of the object.

Because the Aristotelian substance is beyond the five senses, it can never be an object of a perception. Nor can it be an object entertained in a proposition, because propositions depend on the five senses to flesh out their content. The Scholastic discussions of substance, accidents, and efficient causation were mere babble to Nicholas. In their place, he substitutes a kind of phenomenalistic Democritean atomism. The only realities are atoms of quality that in momentary confluence present themselves as things; the only real things are the perceptible combinations of these qualities.

It is possible to have certainty about the judgment of perception associated with these things, but this certainty lasts only as long as the things are present. Certainty is momentary and cannot be extended to judgments about the past or future behavior of things. The existence of a thing at one time cannot be inferred from the existence of another thing at another time, because neither can be put into a relation of identity or of part to whole. One's only recourse is to count up the number of conjunctions and decide the probability of their occurring together in sequence. Moreover, if that is the best one can do for perceptible things, then it is impossible to talk about the causal relations that hold between nonperceptible things such as substances, because probable demonstrations require, at the very least, perceptible things. Because an Aristotelian substance is not perceptible and because only correlations, not perceptible relations, can be found between perceptible things, it is impossible to establish a probable correlation between a substance and a perceptible thing or a substance and another substance.

With arguments such as these, Nicholas was able to challenge some of the most cherished thinking of the accepted Aristotelian metaphysics. Of all of his criticisms, the most devastating were his critiques of the Scholastic proofs of God's existence. Because these proofs relied heavily on the Aristotelian notions of substance, cause, and accident, Nicholas was able to demonstrate that even a probable proof making use of these notions was impossible. The irony of Nicholas's critique is that he used the most fundamental principle of Aristotelian logic: the principle of noncontradiction.

The controversy surrounding the audacity, brilliance, and rigor of Nicholas's philosophy spread across France like a brushfire. By 1338, his prominence as an academic had become so great that he was made a canon of the cathedral at Metz and given a prebend's stall. This honor did not come with a condition of residency but was a comfortable stipend that allowed Nicholas to pursue advanced study. This he did in comfort, until 1339, when a decree was issued by the faculty of arts accusing students and some of the faculty of insubordination as evidenced by their study of nominalistic philosophy and the meeting of secret nominalistic conclaves. This decree was followed, in December of 1340, by further, more severe decrees against Ockhamism as well as a request from Pope Benedict XII that Nicholas and other Parisian professors critical of Scholastic Aristotelianism appear before the Papal Curia at Avignon. The first papal inquiry was postponed because Benedict died shortly after issuing his summons, but on May 19, 1342, Pope Clement VI reopened the inquiry by appointing a commission of Inquisition under the directorship of William, Cardinal Curty.

Before this commission, Nicholas defended himself with great skill and subtlety. He made it clear that his thought was proposed with the intention of fruitful discussion alone, that his philosophy was designed to reveal the weaknesses of the Scholastic synthesis so that these might be remedied; it was not designed to pull the Scholastic edifice down. He also pointed out that at no time had he denied any of the dogmatic declarations of the Church and urged that when one of his probable arguments stood in contradiction to dogma, the argument should be understood as false. Cardinal Curty, for the most part, remained unmoved. He termed Nicholas's counterarguments "foxy excuses" and produced a list of sixty condemned propositions.

Uncertain of his fate, Nicholas fled from Avignon and went briefly into hiding, probably in the court of Ludwig of Bavaria. In 1346, he was summoned to Paris to recant the condemned propositions, to burn his writings, and to be stripped of his academic credentials. On November 25, 1347, after recanting his philosophy and being discharged from the faculty of the University of Paris, Nicholas watched as his collected works were publicly burned.

Although disgraced in the eyes of the Church, Nicholas lived the rest of his life in its bosom. In 1350, he was made a deacon at the cathedral of Metz, and in the document recording this event is found the final mystery in this controversialist's life: He is described as possessing the licentiate in sacred theology, a license that ought to have been taken from him when he was discredited. It is possible that the authorization to teach sacred theology was officially restored by the Church sometime after his public recantation, or perhaps this mention was merely an act of charity on the part of the clerics at Metz, who had always appreciated Nicholas's brilliance. About the remainder of his life, little is known.

Significance

It is difficult to measure the direct influence Nicholas of Autrecourt had on Western theological and philosophical development since no Nicholatian school survived the conflagration of 1347. Nicholas is most important not for the direct force he exercised in shaping Western thought but for his part in the rise of nominalistic philosophy that characterized the fourteenth century and that was the herald of empirical natural philosophy, the death of the Aristotelian metaphysic, and the birth of the Reformation.

Even so, Nicholas's philosophy did directly shape the fashion in which more traditional theologians and philosophers, such as Jean Buridan and Thomas of Strassburg, read and interpreted Aristotle and their more immediate predecessors. Moreover, in many respects, Nicholas's thought was modern, and in fact, quite prescient. In accepting the law of noncontradiction as the cornerstone of certainty, he anticipated the thought of the rationalists and their *more geometrico*. In his insistence on the primacy of perception and the certainty associated with judgments of perception, he anticipated later empiricists. In arguing that causation could be established as probable at best, he anticipated some of the arguments of skeptical philosopher David Hume.

Finally, perhaps the most significant thing about the career of Nicholas of Autrecourt was his intellectual honesty. Using logic like a sharp scalpel, he ruthlessly cut away many of the contradictions living in the body Scholastic. The audacity of his intellectual project provides an example for anyone who finds the formulaic repetition of tired old answers unsatisfying.

—*Thomas Ryba*

Further Reading

Copleston, Frederick C. *Late Medieval and Renaissance Philosophy.* Vol. 3 in *A History of Philosophy.* New York: Image Books, 1963. One of the most thorough contemporary histories of philosophy written in English. Volume 3 provides an extensive, but very compact, exposition of Nicholas's life, arguments, and influence within the context of fourteenth century nominalism. The end of this volume contains notes referring to the Latin sources and a multilanguage bibliography.

_______. *Medieval Philosophy.* New York: Harper and Bros., 1963. A pointed summary of the history of medieval philosophy. More general and accessible than the volumes in *A History of Philosophy*, it provides a brief overview of the period, discussing only Nicholas's general significance to philosophy. It contains a brief bibliography of French and English works.

Hyman, Arthur, and James J. Walsh, eds. *Philosophy in the Middle Ages: The Christian, Islamic, and Jewish Traditions*. 2d ed. Indianapolis, Ind.: Hackett, 1983. An 805-page text that provides English translations of the first and second letters of Nicholas to Bernard of Arezzo. Also provides a brief but detailed biography of Nicholas and some comments on his importance. Includes a short bibliography.

Nicholas of Autrecourt. *Nicholas of Autrecourt: His Correspondence with Master Giles and Bernard of Arezzo, a Critical Edition from the Two Parisian Manuscripts*. Introduction, translation, explanatory notes, and indexes by L. M. de Rijk. New York: E. J. Brill, 1994. Provides Nicholas's correspondence in Latin and English with two of his fourteenth century contemporaries.

Sihvola, Juha, ed. *Ancient Scepticism and the Sceptical Tradition*. Helsinki, Finland: Societas Philosophica Fennica, 2000. Surveys the work of philosophy, including that of Nicholas, in the tradition of skepticism, the belief in suspended judgment, and the doctrine of uncertainty in knowledge. Includes a bibliography.

Thijssen, J. M. M. H. *Censure and Heresy at the University of Paris, 1200-1400*. Philadelphia: University of Pennsylvania Press, 1998. A look at the intersections between the medieval Church, education, academic freedom, and heresy, with a chapter devoted to Nicholas's tenure at the University of Paris.

Weinberg, Julius R. *Nicholas of Autrecourt: A Study in Fourteenth Century Thought*. Princeton, N.J.: Princeton University Press, 1948. A seminal work on Nicholas's thought that contains chapters on the theories of evidence, probability, change, and causation as well as a bibliography of the standard works.

_______. *A Short History of Medieval Philosophy*. Princeton, N.J.: Princeton University Press, 1969. This work contains a chapter on the criticism characteristic of nominalism. Provides lucid summaries of Nicholas's logical arguments in abbreviated form. Includes a bibliography.

SEE ALSO: Peter Abelard; Jean Buridan; William of Ockham.

RELATED ARTICLES in *Great Events from History: The Middle Ages, 477-1453*: c. 950: Court of Córdoba Flourishes in Spain; 1100-1300: European Universities Emerge; c. 1150: Moors Transmit Classical Philosophy and Medicine to Europe; 1305-1417: Avignon Papacy and the Great Schism; c. 1310-1350: William of Ockham Attacks Thomist Ideas.

NICHOLAS THE GREAT

Italian pope (858-867)

Nicholas strengthened the power of the Papacy by actively promoting the primacy of the Holy See in all Church matters and in secular cases of moral consequence.

BORN: c. 819-822; Rome (now in Italy)
DIED: November 13, 867; Rome
ALSO KNOWN AS: Saint Nicholas I
AREA OF ACHIEVEMENT: Religion and theology

EARLY LIFE

Nicholas the Great was born to a noble family in Rome. His father was Theodorius, a man of great learning, who served as a regionary notary and worked for Pope Leo IV. No facts are extant about Nicholas's mother. As a youngster, Nicholas was serious, intelligent, and eager to learn, traits he inherited from his father and which Theodorius encouraged in the boy. Nicholas was always a good student; he became well read in both secular and theological writings. The clergy at Rome anticipated a bright future for the young scholar.

In 845, Pope Sergius II called Nicholas to serve him as a subdeacon and a member of the Curia at the Lateran palace. Nicholas was made a deacon by Sergius's successor, Pope Leo IV, and during the reign of Benedict III, Nicholas became a highly valued adviser to the Holy See. Benedict was extraordinarily fond of Nicholas as a personal companion and respected his counsel. Benedict died on April 17, 858; Nicholas is said to have wept openly and profusely at the funeral.

Nicholas's success as a scholar and adviser for almost fifteen years in Rome also brought him to the attention of Emperor Louis II, who befriended him. When a successor was being considered after Benedict's death, Louis remained in Rome and pressed for Nicholas's acceptance by the balloting clergy. On April 22, 858, Nicholas was elected to the papacy. His formal installation took place on April 24, 858. Nicholas is thought to have been the first pope to be fitted with a gem-encrusted secular crown at his consecration the following October, although no records exist to confirm this fact positively.

Nicholas's rise to the papacy resulted from several factors, all involving his personal attributes. He was a handsome man with fine facial features and a graceful bearing, winning laymen and clergy alike to his favor. He was very learned but at the same time modest, and he also had a reputation as an eloquent speaker. When Nicholas held to a principle, he did so faithfully and with more courage and commitment than did most men. He was also sincere, just, and honest in his dealings with all, whether of noble or humble rank.

Nicholas would have to call on all of these traits to aid him through a short but difficult papacy. He reigned for nine years, at a time when anarchy threatened Western Europe. The descendants of Charlemagne had divided his empire into three sections. These rulers often quarreled among themselves; they had unruly offspring as well. This civil discontent also made for some anarchic acts by the clergy. Some corrupt bishops held small kingdoms of their own, where they ruled over both civil and spiritual issues. Others came under the influence of powerful civil leaders. Some ambitious and undisciplined clergy took goods and property from their parishioners and guided these people ineffectively, if at all. When Nicholas became pope, the issues created by such disobedience and strife fell to him to resolve.

Nicholas the Great. (Library of Congress)

LIFE'S WORK

Nicholas's papacy is marked by three major crises that occurred almost simultaneously with one another. The first crisis involved his disciplining of corrupt and ambitious clergymen. Nicholas came into conflict with the powerful, independent Archbishop Hincmar of Reims. Hincmar had dismissed a member of the clergy for being an unworthy administrator; that bishop, Rothad of Soissons, appealed to Pope Nicholas, complaining that Hincmar had judged him unfairly. Nicholas, as defined in canon law, was the spiritual authority to whom all bishops were to appeal when they were in conflict with their archbishops. Hincmar had deposed Rothad at a synod in 862, after which time that bishop was imprisoned. Nicholas overturned the decision of this synod because at the time that it met, Rothad had already begun an appeal to Rome. Hincmar was forced to abide by the pope's pronouncement and reinstate Rothad at Soissons during Christmas week of 864.

In a similar case of a tyrannical church leader, Nicholas came into conflict with Bishop John of Ravenna. John had begun to confiscate lands in his area, even some belonging to the Holy See. In addition, Nicholas learned that John made exorbitant demands on his congregation for his housing, food, and entertainment. John also had dismissed any clergymen who disagreed with his method of administration. Nicholas sent warnings to the bishop to end his misconduct, but they were ignored. Nicholas intervened and went to Ravenna personally to restore property to its rightful owners. In November of 861, John came to Rome to beg the pope's pardon; Nicholas reinstated him as bishop, with the stipulation that John personally report annually to Rome on his activities.

The second area in which Nicholas had to intervene for the sake of justice was in royal marriages in Europe. The most famous case of Nicholas's defending an oppressed, defenseless spouse came in the two marriages of King Lothair II, a Frankish ruler. Lothair had taken a wife, Waldrada, in 855 in what was then a Germanic traditional ceremony but not a Church-sanctioned marriage. Waldrada, a noblewoman from Lorraine, had three children by Lothair. In 857, the king married Theutberga, the daughter of Count Bosco of Burgundy, in the Church;

this marriage was a politically feasible union, but it produced no children. In 860, Lothair decided to return to Waldrada. The Frankish archbishops whom Lothair requested to dissolve his marriage to Theutberga readily complied with their civil ruler. Nicholas, after Theutberga made an appeal to him, intervened and declared Lothair's marriage to her to be the only valid union. Emperor Louis II marched on Rome with his imperial army to protest what he believed was an unfair decision about Lothair's choice of wife. Nicholas retreated inside the buildings of Saint Peter's to fast and pray, while Louis's troops angrily smashed up religious processions in the Roman streets. Finally, after two days, both men agreed to discuss the case. Possibly, this meeting was mediated by Louis's wife. The result of the discussion was that Theutberga would remain Lothair's legitimate wife and that he was to cease living with or meeting with Waldrada. Nicholas was so eager to see full justice done in this case that in October, 863, he called to Rome the two archbishops who had supported Lothair in his renunciation of Theutberga. These two Frankish archbishops, Günther of Cologne and Theutgard of Trier, were deposed by Nicholas and replaced. Nicholas also excommunicated Waldrada and her principal supporters.

These conflicts concerning corrupt and ambitious church officials and immoral imperial marriages are relatively minor in comparison with the one great crisis that Nicholas faced in his papacy. For several reasons, including cultural differences between Rome and Constantinople and the personal ambitions of a learned Constantinopolitan layman, Nicholas's papacy was marred by a serious schism between the Western and the Eastern churches.

At Constantinople, Emperor Michael III had an adviser named Bardas who lived an immoral personal life; Bardas had left his wife to live with his son's young widow. When ordered by the patriarch, Ignatius, to return to his wife, Bardas refused. After that incident, Ignatius did not allow the adulterer to receive Communion at Mass on the Feast of the Epiphany in 857. When the emperor saw how his favored adviser was being treated, he dismissed Ignatius in late 858. Michael replaced Ignatius with Photius, a learned Greek layman and his imperial secretary; in less than a week, Photius was consecrated through all the various stages of the clergy, from lector to priest. Then, on December 25, 858, he assumed the office of patriarch. Protests arose from angered supporters of Ignatius, who was in exile at Terebinthos. Michael announced that Ignatius had resigned his office, but historical evidence does not exist to prove that claim. One particularly vocal supporter of Ignatius, the monk Theognostos, traveled to Rome, where he lodged an appeal with Pope Nicholas to intervene on Ignatius's behalf.

As an investigation into this incident at Constantinople began, Nicholas declared that no one was yet to recognize Photius because his case had to be reviewed. When Photius wrote a courteous letter to Nicholas requesting that he be sanctioned as the patriarch, the pope answered by sending two legates to Constantinople to study the situation. The two trusted legates that Nicholas sent on this delicate mission, Radoald of Porto and Zachary of Agnani, immediately had trouble in the Byzantine city. They were pressured by Photius and the emperor to vote at a council held on the patriarchal dispute. Nicholas had sent these two clergymen only to investigate and to report back to him; they were not authorized to represent him in any voting assembly. This Council of Constantinople, convened in late 861, voted to accept Photius as the legitimate patriarch.

When the two legates returned to Rome in 862, Nicholas immediately deposed them, their votes, and the decision of the Council of Constantinople. Nicholas then convened his own Council of Rome in early 863, at which Photius was threatened with excommunication if he did not restore Ignatius to the patriarchy. When Photius learned of this decision and ignored it, the split between the Eastern and the Western churches grew wider.

In August of 867, Photius conducted a council of his own, at which time he declared Nicholas to be deposed and excommunicated. On September 24, 867, Michael was assassinated; his successor, Emperor Basil, reinstated Ignatius to the See of Constantinople on November 26, 867, and Photius was deposed. Pope Nicholas did not live to hear of these events; he died on November 13, 867. Each November 13, the Roman Catholic church celebrates the Feast of Saint Nicholas in honor of the canonized pope.

SIGNIFICANCE

Nicholas the Great was a persistent and courageous fighter for the rights of all oppressed people. His actions in defending parishioners from corrupt clergymen and betrayed spouses from cruel husbands clearly show how uncompromising he was in the pursuit of justice. Nicholas also gained a reputation throughout Europe as a friend to the poor. He established an innovative program by which all the poor of Rome were fed on a regular schedule. Anyone blind or disabled had a daily meal sent to him. The able-bodied reported to the Lateran palace once a week to receive a food ration. Nicholas even devised a special token to be carried by each person to remind him on which day of the week to report for food.

This pope was also a very organized and eloquent letter writer. On his ascension, he had appointed Anastasius the Librarian his personal secretary. Nicholas's choice of such a highly literate man proved valuable, especially when the pope's health failed. Nicholas, in his last years of life, was frequently incapacitated by a painful illness and also from general exhaustion from his zealous attention to his numerous duties. In such instances, Anastasius helped the weakened pope to draft his typically long letters.

Nicholas sent missionaries to Scandinavia to convert people there to Christianity. He was also chiefly responsible for the conversion of Bulgaria in the time of King Boris I. Boris had been baptized by the clergy at Constantinople, with Michael as his godfather. When Boris became disappointed with what he believed was the Eastern Church's lack of enthusiasm and of useful aid in their missionary efforts in Bulgaria, he turned to Nicholas for advice. Nicholas immediately sent to Boris two bishops and a very lengthy, meticulously detailed letter. This letter, known as *Responsa Nicolai ad Consulta Bulgarorum* (866), answers the 106 questions that Boris had concerning Christianity and his role as a Christian ruler. Nicholas responded to these questions with precise answers and in terminology Boris could understand. Theologians to this day praise Nicholas's response to Boris as one of the greatest documents in papal history.

Nicholas was also responsible for a great secular achievement during his time in office. He was able to unite Western Europe by providing a strong central authority for all church matters. Europe in the mid-800's lacked cohesion, consisting of several small, bickering kingdoms. Nicholas continually kept Rome at the forefront of European life, both in religious and in civil matters. When King Boris requested that a code of civil laws be sent to him, it was Latin laws Nicholas sent.

Pope Nicholas's greatest lasting achievement was his maintaining and strengthening the supreme authority of the Roman See. When arrogant and independent clergymen attempted to rule their parishioners with no input from Rome, Nicholas swiftly ended their autonomy. He reserved for himself and future popes the right to intercede in any church affairs gone wrong. Nicholas was one of the most powerful, beneficent, and active popes of the Middle Ages.

—*Patricia E. Sweeney*

FURTHER READING

Cavarnos, Constantine. *Saint Photios the Great: Philosopher and Theologian*. Belmont, Mass.: Institute for Byzantine and Modern Greek Studies, 1998. A collection of monographs delivered in 1987 at the Library of Hellenic College/Holy Cross Creek Orthodox School of Theology on Photius, Nicholas the Great's counterpoint. Bibliography and index.

Coppa, Frank J., ed. *Encyclopedia of the Vatican and Papacy*. Westport, Conn.: Greenwood Press, 1999. An encylopedia of the popes. Lists antipopes and ecumenical councils. Bibliography and index.

Duffy, Eamon. *Saints and Sinners: A History of the Popes*. 2d ed. New Haven, Conn.: Yale University Press, 2001. A general history of the popes, with information on Nicholas the Great.

Dvornik, Francis. *The Photian Schism: History and Legend*. 1948. Reprint. New York: Cambridge University Press, 1970. A leading authority describes the events leading to and widening the schism between Nicholas and Photius. This book serves two purposes: to dispel the myths about how the schism occurred and to replace these myths with accurate historical evidence about it. An extremely well-documented and scholarly study.

Levillain, Philippe, ed. *The Papacy: An Encyclopedia*. New York: Routledge, 2002. A dictionary of the Papacy that covers the medieval years. Bibliography and index.

Ullmann, Walter. *A Short History of the Papacy in the Middle Ages*. 1972. Reprint. New York: Routledge, 2003. This book contains a substantial section of bibliographical notes giving Ullmann's sources for each chapter. He points out the long-term significance of Nicholas's solutions to the various crises he faced. Much space is devoted to a discussion of the conflict between Nicholas and Photius and the strategies that each man employed in dealing with the other.

SEE ALSO: Boris I of Bulgaria; Charlemagne; Saint Cyril and Saint Methodius; Gregory VII; Ratramnus.

RELATED ARTICLES in *Great Events from History: The Middle Ages, 477-1453*: 726-843: Iconoclastic Controversy; 864: Boris Converts to Christianity; 893: Beginning of Bulgaria's Golden Age.

Nicholas V
Italian pope (1447-1455)

Nicholas V restored church unity by ending the schism between the Papacy and the conciliar party in Basel. He initiated serious efforts at church reform, helped bring peace to Italy, and sponsored architectural and literary projects in Rome.

Born: November 15, 1397; Sarzana, Republic of Genoa (now in Italy)
Died: March 24, 1455; Rome (now in Italy)
Also known as: Tommaso Parentucelli (given name)
Areas of achievement: Diplomacy, church reform, patronage of the arts

Early Life

Tommaso Parentucelli, the future Pope Nicholas V, was born a physician's son at Sarzana in the Republic of Genoa. Orphaned early, he was forced in his youth to withdraw from the University of Bologna to earn a living as a tutor in Florence. There he met Humanist scholars and artists who enhanced his interest in the classical studies then gaining popularity among the educated classes of northern Italy. In 1419, he was able to return to complete a doctorate in theology. The impressive academic record and serious demeanor of the young priest caught the eye of Niccolò Albergati, the bishop of Bologna, who offered him a position as his assistant. This association, which lasted twenty years, provided Parentucelli with a valuable apprenticeship in church politics.

He accompanied Albergati on many trips, within Italy and beyond. He visited the papal court under Martin V, the first pontiff to reign unchallenged in Rome in more than a century. Parentucelli used every opportunity on his travels to acquire the classical manuscripts that had become his passion. Then, in 1439, his skills in settling a dispute with Greek churchmen at the Florence Council so impressed Pope Eugene IV that, on Albergati's death in 1443, the pope named Parentucelli to succeed him as bishop of Bologna.

In late 1446, the pope elevated Parentucelli to the cardinalate for his performance as papal diplomat among the German princes. Finally, when Eugene died in March, 1447, Parentucelli was elected his successor by the College of Cardinals. He had been only four years a bishop and less than four months a cardinal, but his spirituality and conciliatory temperament seemed most to have recommended him as a compromise candidate. He took the papal name Nicholas V in honor of his patron Niccolò Albergati. The new pope was a small, homely man of delicate constitution, but he had a driving sense of purpose to confront the problems inherited from Eugene.

The Roman church was in crisis. The Council of Basel, convened half a generation before, continued to reject papal authority, recognizing only its own creation, the antipope Felix V. In Germany, most princes remained either hostile to Rome or neutral in the papal-conciliar struggle. They found effective political leverage in the mutual antagonism of pope and council. In addition, the Church suffered across Europe from scandals and corruptions that went largely unchecked. Simony and concubinage were rife among the clergy, while exotic superstitions beguiled many among the general populace. Some secular lords ruthlessly exploited church property and appointments in their lands. In Italy, the major city-states seemed incapable of peaceful coexistence. Also, the last years of Eugene IV's troubled pontificate had left Rome and the Papal States dangerously vulnerable and in a state of decay. The papal treasury was empty. The extent to which Nicholas met such challenges and the means that he chose would define his place in papal history.

Life's Work

Nicholas intensified at once the negotiations with the German princes begun by Eugene IV. Within a year, the new pope had reached a milestone agreement with Austrian emperor Frederick III and most of the princes. The Concordat of Vienna of February, 1448, conceded official imperial recognition of Nicholas V as head of the Church and acknowledged specified papal rights to church revenues and appointments in Germany. In return, the pope accepted certain limits to his taxing and investiture privileges in the German church.

By recognizing the Austrian state as an equal in political negotiations, the pope probably surrendered in the long term more than he received. Yet the Concordat of Vienna in effect sounded the death knell of the Basel Council. With the crumbling of its last major political support, the council declared itself dissolved in April, 1449. Nicholas, the skilled diplomat, had already persuaded the antipope Felix to abdicate in exchange for a generous pension and the official rank of cardinal-bishop, second in honor only to Nicholas himself. All spiritual penalties were annulled, and most conciliarists were reconciled with Rome. On the model of the Vienna agreement, the pope proceeded to individual understand-ings with the kings of Portugal, Castile, and Poland, as well as with lesser princes.

To celebrate the restored unity of the Western church, Pope Nicholas declared 1450 a jubilee year in which Christians everywhere were invited to Rome. They were offered the spiritual benefits of a rich indulgence (a release from penalties for sins) and the opportunity to visit the sacred places there. The donations of the thousands of pilgrims who swarmed to the papal city filled church coffers to overflowing, which provided Nicholas with the financial means to pursue other major policies.

First, to confront the spiritual neglect, corruption, and schism plaguing the Church at large, the pope in 1450 dispatched a number of cardinal-legates. They were instructed to bring the jubilee indulgence to those unable to come to Rome and, above all, to reform in the name of the Papacy such spiritual deformities as they found. Prominent were the missions to France, northern Italy, and the German empire, including Bohemia.

Most extensive of all was the reform legation through the Germanies of Cardinal Nicholas of Cusa; however, the pope's conciliatory style served more to undermine Nicholas of Cusa's efforts than to reinforce them. The legate found his decrees against the most serious abuses, such as the cult of bleeding hosts, modified or rescinded by a pontiff fearful of offending German princes and prelates so recently partisans or sympathizers of the Basel Council. Nicholas of Cusa's legation, the last major reform attempt within the German church before Martin Luther, came to little. The other missions achieved only marginal success.

In providing for the security of Rome and the Papal States, however, Nicholas proved strikingly successful. Recognizing that peace and order at home were the essential preconditions to substantive actions elsewhere, he moved energetically in a number of directions. He built new walls around the city, then dismissed the disruptive mercenaries who had controlled Rome for nearly a decade. They were replaced by strategically located fortifications, manned by new troops under officers chosen for their loyalty and competence. Nicholas imposed similar changes in the Papal States, appointing new governors, usually drawn from the local population. Finally, he granted effective self-government to the city of Rome, conceding rights of taxation and of appointment to civil office to influential local nobles. In such ways, Nicholas peacefully defused the sometimes-furious resentment that the Roman aristocracy had felt toward his predecessor.

With these considerable political and ecclesiastical achievements realized over the first four years of his pontificate, the pope turned full attention to still another realm, the cultural and intellectual. It is for his achievements here that Nicholas would be called the first "Renaissance pope." Nicholas had once commented that, after God, his greatest love lay in buildings and books. Because of the jubilee donations, he now had the funds to pursue his passions.

It was to proclaim in more visible ways the return of greatness and dignity to the papal city that Nicholas commissioned a sweeping program of architectural construction and renovation. He built new bridges and aqueducts and completed the repair of more than forty dilapidated churches. Most impressive, Nicholas put together an elaborate plan for a project of urban renewal that would encompass both the renovation and the new construction of buildings in the Borgo region adjacent to the Vatican palace and within the palace itself.

In the neoclassical style of the designs, including porticoed streets, round towers, triumphal arches, lush gardens, and fountains, there is evident the close influence of the renowned architect Leon Battista Alberti. Although Nicholas was able to complete only the refurbishing of the Vatican Palace, his plan provided the general framework for future projects, including the completion in the early sixteenth century of the new Saint Peter's Basilica. Fra Angelico and Piero della Francesca were among the painters commissioned by Nicholas to decorate various Vatican buildings, including the walls of his private chapel.

Nicholas also regarded himself as the patron of all who laid claim to Humanist achievement, and he delighted in the company of scholars. He spared no expense in making the papal court a lively center of the new learning and literature. For example, distinguished Humanists such as Lorenzo Valla and Poggio were amply compensated for translating the Greek classics of Homer and Thucydides, among others, into a fluid Latin for Western readers.

Nicholas was determined as well to restock a papal library that had in the previous century been dispersed beyond recovery by the upheavals of papal exile and schism. He searched for rare manuscripts, had copies made of others, and donated his private collection. Nicholas left some 1,150 manuscripts, both Latin and Greek, patristic as well as classical. He thereby laid the original foundations of the Vatican library, one of the cultural treasures of Western civilization. After 1453, the pope's health deteriorated rapidly, marked by recurring and agonizing attacks of gout. To the end, he remained actively engaged in his various endeavors. He was buried in Saint

Peter's Basilica, close to the tomb of his predecessor, Eugene IV.

Significance

The pontificate of Nicholas V constitutes something of a turning point in papal history. His diplomatic successes in ending the conciliar threat, regaining the allegiance of the German princes, and bringing peace to much of Italy portended at least a partial recovery of papal authority and prestige. Further, as a Christian Humanist scholar, bibliophile, and patron of the arts, Nicholas enjoyed considerable success in making Rome for a time the center of art, architecture, and literature in the West. He provided a major stimulus to cultural distinction on the model of the classical past.

The greatest disappointment of his pontificate was the failure after the first few years to carry forward the ambitious program of church reform that he had launched. Particularly discouraging to him was the cold response of the Western states to his plea for a crusade to liberate the Byzantine Empire from the Ottoman Turks.

Yet the reign of Nicholas was, overall, a time of peace, prosperity, and promise after generations of conflict and upheaval in the Church. As the peacemaker pope, Nicholas sought to use all the weapons of papal diplomacy and Renaissance culture he could mobilize to signal the restoration of an unchallenged papal monarchy in Rome and the revived glory of the Western church.

—*Donald D. Sullivan*

Further Reading

Burroughs, Charles. *From Signs to Design: Environmental Process and Reform in Early Renaissance Rome.* Cambridge, Mass.: The Massachusetts Institute of Technology Press, 1991. Burroughs discusses Nicholas's years as pope and his reputation as a great patron of architecture and city planning. He examines the notion of urbanism in response to Carroll Westfall's work on the pope's patronage.

Creighton, Mandell. *The Italian Princes, 1464-1518.* Vol. 3 in *History of the Papacy During the Period of the Reformation.* London: Longmans, Green, 1882. Based largely on published sources of the time. The balanced, even-handed treatment has withstood well the test of subsequent scholarship. Especially enlightening on Nicholas' relations with the Basel Council and with the German Empire, as well as the discussion of the Papacy in its Italian setting.

Pastor, Ludwig von. *History of the Popes from the Close of the Middle Ages.* Vol. 2. Edited and translated by F. I. Antrobus. St. Louis: Herder Book, 1892. The most detailed study in English of the full range of Nicholas's activities, including his achievements in cultural patronage, political negotiations, and especially in the extensive reform mission of papal legates in the German empire and neighboring lands. Pastor, among the first scholars granted access to the secret Vatican archives, bases his account largely on manuscript evidence.

Stieber, Joachim W. *Pope Eugenius IV, the Council of Basel and the Secular and Ecclesiastical Authorities in the Empire: The Conflict over Supreme Authority and Power in the Church.* Leiden, the Netherlands: E. J. Brill, 1978. Shows how Nicholas, over the crucial first two years of his pontificate, continued closely certain policies of his predecessor, Eugene IV. Above all, he sought through major concessions to enlist the support of Europe's secular powers against a conciliar party that sought to reduce the Papacy under the authority of general church councils. In a valuable appendix, Stieber provides a thorough discussion of the main documentary sources for Nicholas's pontificate.

Stinger, Charles L. *The Renaissance in Rome.* 1985. Reprint. Bloomington: Indiana University Press, 1998. Provides in separate segments a clear overview of the main facets of Nicholas's cultural activities. New preface by author. Updates Pastor's standard position not only that Nicholas was the first true Renaissance pope but also that his pontificate represents a major turning point in the recovery of the Papacy.

Venchi, Innocenzo, et al. *Fra Angelico and the Chapel of Nicholas V.* Vatican City State: Edizioni Musei Vaticani, 1999. Examines Fra Angelico's work on the Capella di Niccoló V in Vatican City. Illustrated with photographs by Alessandro Bracchetti.

Vespasiano da Bisticci, Florentino. *Renaissance Princes, Popes, and Prelates.* Translated by William George and Emily Waters, with an introduction by Myron P. Gilmore. New York: Harper & Row, 1963. Contains a lively and very readable short biography of Nicholas by a close friend, the Humanist bibliographer Vespasiano. While the account is invariably laudatory, it offers personal details that provide a vivid sense of the pope's personality.

Westfall, Carroll W. *In This Most Perfect Paradise: Alberti, Nicholas V, and the Invention of Conscious Urban Planning in Rome, 1447-1455.* University Park: Pennsylvania State University Press, 1974. Contends that Nicholas's vast scheme of renovation for the city of Rome began with the architect Alberti's concept of urban renewal. Westfall suggests that Alberti's general designs were adapted by others to specific projects. In the collaboration of pope and architect, Westfall sees a remarkable breakthrough toward a conscious and comprehensive urban design.

See also: Fra Angelico; William of Ockham; Poggio; Lorenzo Valla.

Related article in *Great Events from History: The Middle Ages, 477-1453*: c. 1410-1440: Florentine School of Art Emerges.

Nijō

Japanese writer and poet

Nijō, a court lady, excelled in poetry and in playing the biwa, a stringed musical instrument. She became a Buddhist nun and traveled throughout the country, writing poetry and meeting many government and religious leaders. Toward the end of her life, she wrote a memoir that is one of the most remarkable literary works of Japan's medieval era.

Born: 1258; Heian-kyō (now Kyoto), Japan
Died: After 1306; place unknown
Also known as: Lady Nijō; Gofukakusa-in no Nijō; Sanjō; Nakanoin Masatada no Musume
Area of achievement: Literature

Early Life

Nijō (nee joh) was born in a dynamic, if uncertain, time of political intrigue, increasing commerce, and new ideas. In the late 1100's, the imperial government had been overrun by military families. Thereafter, Japan operated with dual governments, an imperial one in Kyoto and a military one some distance away, in Kamakura. Also at this time, many new Buddhist movements were flourishing in Japan.

Nijō's parents had a close relationship with Emperor Go-Fukakusa (r. 1246-1260), whose reign ended while he was still a teenager, when he was forced to abdicate in deference to his younger brother, Emperor Kameyama (r. 1260-1274), whom his father preferred. He maintained considerable power, however, in his retirement through a well-established system of abdicated, or cloistered, emperors preserving entrenched centers of political power and wealth. Nijō's mother had provided, scholars believe, the special service of introducing Go-Fukakusa to sexual relations before he took his primary wife. Her family, the Shijō branch of the Fujiwara, were politically influential and were also known as literati and poets. Nijō's mother died in the summer of 1259, the year following Nijō's birth.

Nijō's father, a relatively well-connected member of the influential Koga family that was also known for its poets and scholars of poetry, was clearly devoted to his daughter. He looked carefully after her future until his early death in 1272. Because of his influence and the special relationship Nijō's mother had to Go-Fukakusa, Nijō was invited at the age of four by Go-Fukakusa to live at the palace. She was registered by her father as the adopted daughter of a grand minister (a legal relationship something like a godfather). This status kept open the possibility that someday she might become an imperial consort or perhaps an empress. It was a reasonable hope, except that her father passed away the same year Go-Fukakusa took her, with her father's consent, as a companion. This new relationship was initiated without the thirteen-year-old being forewarned. In the memoir, Nijō writes of listening bitterly as her father offered breakfast to the emperor on the morning after the emperor has been allowed into her bedchamber for the first time. She thinks, though exactly of which man it is not clear, "I never wish to see him again; I yearn for it to be yesterday."

Life's Work

The first three of the five parts of the memoir written by Nijō, *Towazugatari* (wr. c. 1306; *The Confessions of Lady Nijō*, 1973) narrate her life at court. The description of her difficult and ultimately indefensible position at the palace as the abdicated emperor's companion is one of the most revealing autobiographical accounts of love from early Japan. The final two parts of her memoir describe her travels, which were extensive for her time, when travel was both demanding and perilous. Nijō loved daringly, took Buddhism seriously, and traveled far more widely than was usual for a woman. She was a woman of energy, intelligence, and insight. She has been called the female Saigyō after one of the most famous and loved of all Japanese poets, Priest Saigyō, because of her deep commitment to Buddhism, her poetic ability, and her extensive journeys.

The last date in Nijō's memoir is 1306. It was probably written soon after that, based on notes taken over the years. In her memoir, therefore, she recalls her life from the perspective of an aristocratic woman in her fifties who left the imperial court to become a Buddhist nun. What is known of her derives almost entirely from her fictionalized memoir. One can imagine that she continued her extensive religious travels and perhaps participated in a limited number of poetry events; unfortunately, there are no historical records pertaining to the years postdating 1306 that could substantiate such speculation.

Though later she was driven coldly from court at the jealous request of Go-Fukakusa's primary wife and though Nijō's conversion to Buddhism strikes the reader as sincere, her relationship with Go-Fukakusa is the memoir's organizing framework. It is difficult to doubt that she loved him when reading of her attendance at his funeral (from afar as she is no longer an official part of the imperial court) and how she ran after the funeral procession shoeless until she no longer could keep up with it.

It is more difficult to say exactly, however, what the nature of their relationship was. Go-Fukakusa, at least as depicted in the memoir, clearly had a cruel streak. On the first two nights with Nijō, he allows her to refuse his amorous advances, but on the third night, he forces himself on her, tearing her clothes. In 1274, when Nijō is just sixteen, he tells her to "prove her love" by helping him seduce another woman. Three years later, he forces her to sleep with Kanehira, powerful regent to the boy-emperor of the time (Go-Uda, r. 1274-1287), grand minister, and man of about fifty. Go-Fukakusa is described as listening from the next room. His brother and rival Kameyama also requests that Nijō be allowed to sleep between them. Go-Fukakusa refuses this, but Kameyama is able to take Nijō away while Go-Fukakusa slumbers.

In this manner, the memoir vividly provides details of the complex mixture of romantic disappointment, disparagement, passion, and attachment that was the twenty-three-year relationship between Go-Fukakusa and Nijō. This relationship begins when he arrives unannounced in her bedroom and proceeds to her father's dying words that she should consider herself disowned if she ever leaves Go-Fukakusa, to the infant death of their only child, to Go-Fukakusa's bending to the will of his wife and ordering Nijō's service at court terminated, to their furtive meetings after this, and to her peering into his death room. It is a stunning portrayal of one couple's complicated and not always easy to understand love; for example, the reader is surprised by her sudden declaration of longing for Go-Fukakusa the morning after he roughly makes her his lover.

Go-Fukakusa was not the only man Nijō loved. Interwoven with his dominating presence are two others codenamed "Snowy Dawn" and "Predawn Moon." The first, scholars have determined, was Saionji Sanekane, whose family for about two generations had exercised profound influence on the imperial court. By Sanekane's time, this influence had extended to the military government in Kamakura. Sanekane was a key figure in striking a balance between the rival retired emperors Go-Fukakusa and Kameyama in their bid before the military government for the designation of crown prince between their children. Sanekane's two daughters would become consorts to Kameyama and Go-Fukakusa's son, Emperor Fushimi (r. 1287-1298). It is with Sanekane, who moved dangerously between major political factions, that Nijō entangled her fate, even from the early days of her relationship with Go-Fukakusa at age thirteen. They parented a girl in 1274, but the birth was necessarily secret and the child given up for adoption, with Sanekane separating child from mother the moment the umbilical cord was cut.

"Predawn Moon" was probably Priest-Prince Shōjo, abbot of Ninna Temple and half-brother of Go-Fukakusa. Nijō had two boys by him; heart-wrenchingly, the second child was born after his death in 1281.

Amid these lovers—both sought out by and pressed on her—Nijō struggles, attempting to negotiate with the limited resources allowed her the unpredictable waters of the politics of governmental and imperial women's quarters. At one point when Go-Fukakusa and Shōjo are talking easily with one another and she flees the room, only to run into Sanekane in the hallway, who complains that she has no time for him, she writes despairingly, "I had no place left for myself." That became a reality in 1283, when, at the age of twenty-five, she was forced from court. The order was delivered by letter via her grandfather and simply stated that she was to leave the palace permanently that night. That evening, she served Go-Fukakusa briefly one last time, with his only remark being, "And how is it? Will you be leaving tonight?"

When the reader begins the fourth part of her memoir, Nijō is already a nun. There is no description of any momentous decision to take tonsure; it is a given, as her father once said, that if she is to lose Go-Fukakusa, this will be the moral choice. In fact, however, one senses the preeminence of Buddhism even during the long and detailed chapters describing her life at court. Lay life, as she depicts it, is fundamentally a life of endless anxiety. The memoir speaks less of a conversion to Buddhism than an evaluation of her personal fate through the lens of Buddhist values. She humbly and quite frankly notes how she again and again is motivated and compromised by romantic desire and, just as unreservedly, reveals her only partial adherence to Buddhist wisdom.

Religious feelings of guilt, devotion, and compassion run deep in her story, especially in her pilgrimage years. Guilt guides her thoughts, for example, when she tries to hide from her dying father the fact that she is pregnant, because, according to Buddhist teaching, if her father learned that he could soon enjoy a grandchild, his spirit might be unwilling to let go of worldly attachments, something that would not further his spiritual well-being. She wonders, too, if the death of her son by Go-Fukakusa the same year she gives birth to a daughter by Sanekane is caused by the adulterous nature of that relationship.

Her devotion to Buddhism is evident in her arduous pilgrimages, copying of scriptures, and many prayers. It is no more poignantly illustrated, though, than her decision to make an offering to Buddha of the last remaining, cherished possessions given to her by her now deceased parents, an offering on behalf of Go-Fukakusa's soul and, of course, that of her mother and father. The gradual development of her compassion can be seen best, perhaps, in how she describes those whom she meets on her travels and her interest in their personal troubles. Traveling broadens her world and the circle of people about whom she takes times to think.

Nijō's poetry was widely anthologized, and she performed the *biwa* (a stringed instrument) with critical acclaim at many formal occasions. A pair of poems from near the end of her memoir are representative of the conflict she experienced between her increasing devotion to Buddhism and her continued mourning for the men whom she cherished. When she made an offering of the last possession of Go-Fukakusa's that she owned, an embroidered robe he had given her and on which they had no doubt slept and which she continued to use, she wrote:

> It is such an anguish,
> thinking that from today
> I will see it no more—
> this keepsake, this
> bedrobe, well worn.

She follows this poem immediately, without explanation, with another that evokes the memory of the also deceased "Predawn Moon," perhaps her most cherished lover:

> Awakened, and at pillowside lingers
> the predawn moon's rays.
> The river's rush accompanies my wail of tears.

And this, too, is followed, again without transition, of her hearing that another, though less welcome, lover, Emperor Kameyama, had passed away. In Nijō's delicately narrated memoir, the appeal and suffering associated with romantic love, on one hand, and values of Buddhist compassion with its transcendent view beyond lay life, on the other, are complexly interwoven.

SIGNIFICANCE

Nijō's romantic involvement with the two competing abdicated emperors and the politician who was key in determining which of the imperial lines would find favor with the ruling military government surely colored the character and ultimate shape of that brotherly rivalry. However, because her only child by Go-Fukakusa died in infancy, her impact on the political situation was limited to private affairs of which little is known.

Nijō's memoir is a rich historical resource and is often quoted by the court history *Masukagami* (1368-1375; *The Clear Mirror: A Chronicle of the Japanese Court During the Kamakura Period, 1185-1333*; 1998). However, its influence on self-reflective literature is greatest. In her day, that genre was the quasifictional autobiography and was written primarily by aristocratic women. Later, the self-reflective protagonist approach would reappear in full form in the post-World War II genre of I novels (*shishōsetsu*), a tradition with enormous impact on modern Japanese fiction.

The rediscovery in 1940 of *Towazugatari* is one of the great events of modern Japanese literary scholarship because of the memoir's descriptive richness of medieval Japan and superior literary qualities.

—*John R. Wallace*

FURTHER READING

Childs, Margaret H. "The Value of Vulnerability: Sexual Coercion and the Nature of Love in Japanese Court Literature." *The Journal of Asian Studies* 58, no. 4 (November, 1999): 1059-1079. Discusses strategies female fictional characters deployed for resisting and influencing male romantic interest.

The Clear Mirror: A Chronicle of the Japanese Court During the Kamakura Period, 1185-1333. Translated by George W. Perkins. Stanford, Calif.: Stanford University Press, 1998. A full translation of the preeminent historical narrative written shortly after the death of Nijō. Describes in detail the imperial court of which she was a part.

McCullough, Helen Craig, comp. and ed. *Classical Japanese Prose: An Anthology*. Stanford, Calif.: Stanford

University Press, 1990. Includes a partial translation of *Towazugatari*, other early Japanese women's memoirs, and other relevant literary texts.

Mass, Jeffrey P., ed. *The Origins of Japan's Medieval World: Courtiers, Clerics, Warriors, and Peasants in the Fourteenth Century.* Stanford, Calif.: Stanford University Press, 1997. Essays exploring with great credibility the history of the century in which Nijō lived; its research is based on a wide variety of documents of the time.

Nijō. *The Confessions of Lady Nijō*. Translated by Karen Brazell. Stanford, Calif.: Stanford University Press, 1973. A complete translation, with introduction, of *Towazugatari*.

Stevenson, Barbara, and Cynthia Ho, eds. *Crossing the Bridge: Comparative Essays on Medieval European and Heian Japanese Women Writers*. New York: Palgrave, 2000. A collection of essays that compares the lives and literary approaches of leading women writers in classical and medieval Europe and Japan.

SEE ALSO: Murasaki Shikibu; Sei Shōnagon.

RELATED ARTICLES in *Great Events from History: The Middle Ages, 477-1453*: 794-1185: Heian Period; c. 800: *Kana* Syllabary Is Developed; 858: Rise of the Fujiwara Family; c. 1001: Sei Shōnagon Completes *The Pillow Book*; c. 1004: Murasaki Shikibu Writes *The Tale of Genji*.

NIẒĀM AL-MULK

Iranian government administrator

The vizier, or principal minister, of the second and third Seljuk rulers of Iran, Niẓām was the virtual architect of the Seljuk Empire in the Middle East, which he administered for thirty years between 1063 and 1092. His The Book of Government *became a classic text of medieval Muslim statecraft.*

BORN: 1018 or 1019; Ṭūs, Khorāsān (now in Iran)
DIED: October 14, 1092; near Nahāvand, Persia (now in Iran)
ALSO KNOWN AS: Abū ʿAlī Ḥasan ibn ʿAlīAbū ʿAlī
AREA OF ACHIEVEMENT: Government and politics

EARLY LIFE

Niẓām al-Mulk (nee-ZAH-mewl-MEWLK) was born in or near the city of Ṭūs, near modern Mashhad, in the northeastern Iranian province of Khorāsān. He is invariably referred to not by his full name but as Niẓām al-Mulk (regulator of the state), a title given to him by the Seljuk sultan Alp Arslan. His father belonged to the ancient class known as *dihqans*, landowning gentry of Iranian stock who, at least in Khorāsān, had survived the Arab conquest of the seventh century by demonstrating their usefulness to the invaders as local officials and tax collectors, roles that they continued to play for centuries. Niẓām al-Mulk's father was a middle-ranking official in the service of the Ghaznavid sultans Maḥmūd of Ghazna (r. 997-1030) and Masʿud I (r. 1031-1041), and Niẓām al-Mulk's mature views on what constituted an ideal system of administration must have been colored by what he knew firsthand of Ghaznavid rule, as well as by what he had heard of Sāmānid rule in tenth century Bukhara. He himself received an excellent formal education, probably in Nishapur, after which he too entered Ghaznavid service.

When the Ghaznavids were forced to abandon their territories in eastern Iran to the Seljuk Turks (c. 1040), Niẓām al-Mulk transferred to the service of the Seljuks and was employed in a secretarial capacity by the new governor of Balkh, in northern Afghanistan. The governor's superior was the Seljuk sultan's brother, Chaghrï Beg, who was quick to recognize the superior abilities of the young official. On his deathbed, Chaghrï Beg is said to have strongly recommended Niẓām al-Mulk to the attention of his son, Alp Arslan, who took him into his household and eventually appointed him to the post of vizier—in effect, his man of business and general factotum.

Under the rule of their first sultan, Toghrïl Beg (r. 1040-1063), the Seljuks, originally Turkish nomads from the Central Asian steppes, became masters of a Middle Eastern empire extending from the Mediterranean eastward to the Pamirs, with its center of power on the Iranian plateau. It was to be the historic role of Niẓām al-Mulk to condition these steppe warriors to the norms of traditional Irano-Islamic statecraft and to erect an institutional framework by which to administer their far-flung conquests.

When Sultan Toghrïl Beg died in 1063, there was uncertainty over the succession, and the late sultan's vizier, al-Kunduri, endeavored to prevent the accession of Toghrïl Beg's eldest nephew, Alp Arslan, by advancing the claims of Alp Arslan's younger brother, Sulaimān. In the intrigues that followed, Niẓām al-Mulk seems to have played a major role in bringing about Alp Arslan's accession, as well as in effecting al-Kunduri's removal, imprisonment, and eventual murder. Before his death, al-Kunduri is said to have sent the following warning to Niẓām al-Mulk:

> You have introduced a reprehensible innovation and an ugly practice into the world by executing a minister and by your treachery and deceit, and you have not fully considered what the end of it all will be. I fear that this evil and blameworthy practice will rebound on the heads of your own children and descendants.

Niẓām al-Mulk and several of his sons and grandsons did suffer violent deaths.

Meanwhile, with Alp Arslan now sultan (r. 1063-1072 or 1073), Niẓām al-Mulk became vizier of the Seljuk Empire, head of the civil administration, the sultan's chief counselor, and, for all practical purposes, his deputy. After Alp Arslan's death, Niẓām continued to serve as the vizier of Alp Arslan's son, Malik-Shāh (r. 1073-1092), and to such an extent was he perceived to be the presiding genius of the Seljuk Empire that the Arab historian Ibn al-Athīr (1160-1233) long afterward described the thirty years during which Alp Arslan and Malik-Shāh reigned (and which was, in fact, the golden age of Seljuk rule) as *al-dawlah al-Niẓamiyah*, the age of Niẓām al-Mulk.

LIFE'S WORK

As vizier, Niẓām al-Mulk was responsible for the entire administration of the civil affairs of the empire, including the collection of revenue and its disbursement. He was the head of the bureaucracy, and all matters relating to the *diwan* (chancery) were in his charge. As the personal representative and closest adviser of the sovereign, he was also a member of the *dargah* (the sultan's court).

The duties of viziers were rarely precisely defined. While many viziers were not involved in military matters, Niẓām al-Mulk is known to have campaigned with his master and also to have conducted independent military operations. His involvement in military affairs necessitated the maintenance of good working relations with the great Turkish emirs, or commanders. This involved diplomatic skills of a high order, since the emirs were generally disinclined to take orders from non-Turkish bureaucrats. As vizier, Niẓām al-Mulk also maintained close contacts with the leading *ʿulama*, the Muslim clerics. The highest judicial appointments for the Shariʿa (religious law) and *mazalim* (equity and arbitration) courts were awarded to members of the *ʿulama*, appointments that, no doubt, would have required Niẓām's prior approval. He was also responsible for the distribution of government funds allocated for the support of pious scholars, religious endowments, and education, as well as for alms.

In addition to the day-to-day running of the administration, Niẓām al-Mulk seems to have exercised a general oversight with regard to relations with other states and also with regard to cultural policy and propaganda. He contributed markedly to the revival of Sunni Islam that characterized the eleventh and twelfth centuries. Before the arrival of the Seljuks in the Middle East, the political fortunes and spiritual vitality of Sunni Islam had been at a very low ebb. Its central institution, the ʿAbbāsid caliphate of Baghdad, had long been in decline. In fact, since 945, the caliphs had been virtual captives of a line of Buyid emirs who had made themselves masters of Baghdad. As Shīʿites, the Iranian Buyids displayed scant respect for the orthodox "commander of the faithful," as the caliph was officially styled. This period of decline had come to a close in 1055, when Toghrïl Beg had occupied Baghdad and released the caliphs from ninety years of thralldom to the Buyids, although at the cost of making them clients of the all-powerful Seljuk sultan. Nevertheless, the Seljuks were seriously committed to restoring the spiritual authority of the caliphate, through which their own de facto rule could be conveniently legitimized. It was the achievement of Niẓām al-Mulk that he was able to harness the raw power of the Seljuks on behalf of both an orthodox religious revival and a restoration of hallowed Iranian traditions of statecraft and autocracy.

The institutional decline of the ʿAbbāsid caliphate reflected a deeper spiritual malaise prevailing throughout much of the Islamic world, of which deep sectarian fissures constituted both cause and effect. At the beginning of the eleventh century, Egypt, much of North Africa, Hejaz, Palestine, and Syria were under the rule of a rival, heterodox caliphate, that of the Shīʿite Fāṭimids. The Fāṭimids dispatched *dāʿīs* (missionaries) throughout the provinces still nominally loyal to the ʿAbbāsids to spread revolutionary millennial doctrines that threatened the very foundations of the orthodox Sunni political and social order. Linked with the Fāṭimids were the so-called Assassins, members of the Ismāʿīlī sect of the Nizaris, with their strongholds in the Alburz Mountains of northern Iran, as well as in the mountains of Syria and Lebanon. Niẓām al-Mulk regarded these latter as the most formidable adversaries of the renovated political order, of which he saw himself as the architect.

It was to counter such dangerous heterodoxy that he embarked on the policy of founding well-endowed madrasas, or theological colleges (known as Nizamiyas in honor of their founder), in such major urban centers as Baghdad, Isfahan, Neyshabur, and Herāt. The purpose of these colleges, with their scholarships for needy students, their learned faculties, and their excellent libraries, was to graduate well-educated orthodox *ʿulama*, jurists and bureaucrats who would provide a new administrative elite for the Seljuk Empire. The curriculum varied from college to college, but generally it included study of the Qurʾān, the traditions of the Prophet (Hadith), Muslim jurisprudence (*fikh*), Qurʾānic exegesis (*tafsir*), and theology (*kalam*), as well as grammar and prosody, belles lettres, and, in some cases, mathematics and medicine. There has been keen scholarly debate regarding the origins of the madrasa as an educational institution, as well as the innovative role of Niẓām al-Mulk himself, but whatever his objectives in founding his Nizamiyas, it is unlikely that they made much direct impact on contemporary methods or modes of administration. What is beyond question is that, from the time of Niẓām al-Mulk, the madrasa became a ubiquitous feature of urban life throughout the Muslim world.

It may be supposed that throughout the reign of Alp Arslan, Niẓām al-Mulk acted as the sultan's representative, well aware that he owed everything to his master's confidence and favor. With Malik-Shāh, the relationship was rather different. Niẓām al-Mulk acted as the experienced, worldly wise mentor counseling a youthful, impetuous ward. It was a role that Malik-Shāh did not appreciate. With the passing of the years, the sultan grew increasingly suspicious and resentful of his vizier's enormous authority. Moreover, like most viziers before and after him, Niẓām al-Mulk was unable to resist the temptation of gathering excessive wealth and power for both himself and his extended family. Probably, he believed that he could secure his position and be certain that his orders were being carried out only if he surrounded himself with relatives and protégés, appointing them to key positions in the central administration or those of the provinces. Such nepotism bred corruption and the abuse of power and multiplied the vizier's enemies. As the years passed, Malik-Shāh came to wonder whether he was still master in his own house. When Jamāl al-Dīn, Niẓām al-Mulk's eldest son, brutally murdered a member of the sultan's household, Malik-Shāh gave orders for the criminal to be secretly poisoned, but he still did not move openly against his old servant.

In the end, it was the sultan's favorite wife, Terkhen-Khatun, who would play a major part in Niẓām al-Mulk's downfall. Terkhen-Khatun was determined to ensure the succession of her son, Maḥmūd, while the vizier supported the candidacy of Berk-Yaruq, the sultan's older son by another wife. Thus, Niẓām al-Mulk and Terkhen-Khatun were set on a collision course. The eventual outcome was the vizier's dismissal and his replacement by Terkhen-Khatun's nominee, Tāj al-Mulk.

Niẓām al-Mulk, however, seems to have remained in the sultan's entourage, despite his disgrace. While traveling with the sultan from Isfahan to Baghdad, not long afterward, he was stabbed to death by an assailant near Nahavand on October 14, 1092. The general assumption was that his murderer had acted on behalf of the Ismāʿīlīs, whom Niẓām al-Mulk had vigorously persecuted, but suspicion also pointed to the sultan, who may have found the presence of his old minister an embarrassment, and to his supplanter, Tāj al-Mulk, who was murdered by Niẓām al-Mulk's servants a few months later. Malik-Shāh himself died of a fever less than a month after the death of his great minister. With the removal of Niẓām al-Mulk's guiding hand, the Seljuk Empire entered a period of internal strife and struggles for the succession, presaging its eventual dismemberment.

SIGNIFICANCE

Niẓām al-Mulk enjoys the posthumous reputation of a model statesman and of being the man who provided the administrative framework by means of which the Seljuks could exercise their Middle Eastern hegemony. Within the Persian literary tradition, he is the ideal of the sage minister, the counselor of kings. In reality, his position at the pinnacle of power can never have been wholly secure. His master could dismiss him at a moment's notice. His executive actions must often have provoked resentment on the part of members of the ruling house and of the great emirs. Within the bureaucracy itself, aspiring subordinates and rivals awaited the opportunity to profit by his mistakes.

In the final analysis, Niẓām al-Mulk's enduring legacy is not the imperial structure that crumbled so soon after his death, but his single surviving literary undertaking. This work is the *Siyāsat-nāma* (c. 1091; *The Book of Government: Or, Rules for Kings*, 1960), written not long before his death to instruct Malik-Shāh in the art of kingship. Written in a plain, unadorned style and divided into fifty sections, it addresses such matters as the duties and conduct of the ruler, the organization and management of the sultan's household, the recruitment and training of slaves, the control of the army and the bureaucracy, and the evils of innovation, especially in religion. Predictably, it is strongly anti-Shīʿite, but above all, it is a work deeply imbued with nostalgic devotion for the traditions and glories of ancient Iran, as befits a writer who was the embodiment of the Irano-Islamic cultural heritage and of an enduring political philosophy rooted in realpolitik and autocracy. The British Iranologist Edward G. Browne described it as "one of the most remarkable and instructive prose works which Persian literature can boast."

A standing monument to Niẓām al-Mulk's fame is the fine prayer hall he had built in the congregational mosque of Isfahan, which is still standing. Memorials of a different kind were his numerous descendants. A number of sons and grandsons served as viziers to later Seljuk sultans, but most perished violently; not one displayed any great talent. Niẓām al-Mulk himself emerges from the contemporary sources as a harsh, pragmatic realist who does not seem to have inspired the flattering anecdotes attached to the reputations of some medieval Muslim statesmen. A twelfth century belletrist tersely noted that Niẓām had no regard for poets, he himself having no skill at the art, and cared little for mystics or men of religion. The record points to a man endowed with great practical abilities and possessing both an enormous appetite for power and all the skills and ruthlessness needed for wielding it.

—*Gavin R. G. Hambly*

Further Reading

Bosworth, C. E. "The Political and Dynastic History of the Iranian World (A.D. 1000-1217)." In *The Cambridge History of Iran*, vol. 5, edited by J. A. Boyle. Cambridge, England: Cambridge University Press, 1968. This chapter provides a masterly and very detailed review of the Seljuk period in which Niẓām al-Mulk played so conspicuous a part.

Bowen, H. C. "The *Sar-gudhasht-i sayyidnā*, the 'Tale of the Three Schoolfellows,' and the *Wasaya* of the Nizām al-Mulk." *Journal of the Royal Asiatic Society* (1931): 771-782. This interesting article examines some of the late and spurious legends that have collected around the name of Niẓām al-Mulk.

Browne, Edward G. *A Literary History of Persia*. 1926. 4 vols. Reprint. Cambridge, England: Cambridge University Press, 1969. This is still the standard account of classical Persian literature, into which is woven a historical narrative that places authors' lives and works in their contemporary settings. Vol. 2 contains rather extensive discussions of various aspects of the career and writing of Niẓām al-Mulk.

Klausner, Carla L. *The Seljuk Vizierate: A Study of Civil Administration, 1055-1194*. Cambridge, Mass.: Harvard University Press, 1973. This monograph provides important background material and discussion on Niẓām al-Mulk's career as the most famous vizier of the Seljuk sultans. Bibliography, index.

Lambton, Ann K. S. "The Dilemma of Government in Islamic Persia: The *Siyāsat-nāma* of Nizām al-Mulk." *Iran: Journal of the British Institute of Persian Studies* 22 (1984): 55-66. This article is essential for understanding Niẓām al-Mulk's ideas concerning government and for a more general examination of medieval Islamic political thought.

_______. "The Internal Structure of the Saljuq Empire." In *The Cambridge History of Iran*, vol. 5, edited by J. A. Boyle. Cambridge, England: Cambridge University Press, 1968. This is still the best account of the political and administrative institutions of the Seljuk Empire, which were largely molded and then dominated for so long by Niẓām al-Mulk.

Makdisi, G. "Muslim Institutions of Learning in Eleventh-Century Baghdad." *Bulletin of the School of Oriental and African Studies* 24 (1961): 1-56. A most interesting discussion of the rise of the madrasa, providing useful background information on Niẓām al-Mulk's educational policy.

Niẓām al-Mulk. *The Book of Government: Or, Rules for Kings*. Translated by Hubert Darke. Richmond, Surrey, England: Curzon Press, 2002. This polished translation of the *Siyāsat-nāma* is essential reading for an understanding of both Niẓām al-Mulk and the workings of government during the Seljuk period. Bibliography, index.

Tibawi, A. L. "Origin and Character of al-Madrasah." *Bulletin of the School of Oriental and African Studies* 25 (1962): 225-238. As a response to Makdisi's article (listed above), this essay provides the student with useful insights into a significant area of scholarly debate.

See also: Alp Arslan; Maḥmūd of Ghazna; Omar Khayyám.

Related articles in *Great Events from History: The Middle Ages, 477-1453*: c. 950-1100: Rise of Madrasas; 969-1171: Reign of the Fāṭimids; 998-1030: Reign of Maḥmūd of Ghazna; 11th century: Expansion of Sunni Islam in North Africa and Iberia; 1040-1055: Expansion of the Seljuk Turks; 1077: Seljuk Dynasty Is Founded.

WILLIAM OF OCKHAM
English philosopher

The most original and perhaps least understood of the late medieval philosophers, Ockham exercised a pervasive influence over his contemporaries and other thinkers for at least two centuries. He held that intuition was the only form of knowledge and that God could be approached only through faith and revelation, not through the "proofs" of natural reason. Misconstrued, Ockham's nominalism had serious implications for the Church's teachings on the Eucharist.

BORN: c. 1285; Surrey, England
DIED: 1347 or 1349; Munich, Bavaria (now in Germany)
ALSO KNOWN AS: William of Occam; Doctor Invincibilis; Venerabilis Inceptor
AREAS OF ACHIEVEMENT: Philosophy, religion and theology

EARLY LIFE

Nothing is known of the parentage or childhood of William of Ockham (AHK-uhm), except that he entered the Franciscan order before he was fourteen and received his early education at the Franciscan house at Southwark. In 1303, he was ordained a subdeacon by Archbishop Winchelsey and thereafter went to Oxford University, where he obtained the baccalaureate. He taught at Oxford, lecturing on Peter Lombard's *Sententiarum libri IV* (1148-1151; *The Books of Opinions of Peter Lombard*, 1970; better known as *Sentences*), while at the same time writing the first version of his celebrated commentary on *Sentences*, titled *Anglici super quatuor libros sententiarum subtilissimae quaestiones earumdemque decisiones* (c. 1322), as well as works on logic. Around 1321, he left Oxford to return to the Franciscans in Southwark, where he taught philosophy, but there is no evidence for the tradition that he went to the University of Paris and there met Marsilius of Padua.

The decade that ended in 1324 was perhaps the most productive of his entire life. In terms of originality and sheer intellectual brilliance, Ockham's was one of those minds that come early to fruition. In addition, he had a gift for rapid and prolific writing. This was the period when he revised (not for the last time) his commentaries on *Sentences*, wrote several commentaries on Aristotle, and completed the *Summa logicae* (1322; *Ockham's Theory of Terms: Part I of the "Summa logicae,"* 1974, and *Ockham's Theory of Propositions: Part II of the "Summa logicae,"* 1980). He also wrote most of the *Quodlibeta septem* (1322-1327; *Quodlibetal Questions*, 1991), an undertaking of remarkable maturity, embodying a vast amount of reading and reflection within the Scholastic tradition. Yet despite his later, and posthumous, reputation as the philosopher who dissolved the Thomist-Aristotelian synthesis, Ockham, during his years in England, was essentially a mainstream thinker: original, controversial, but not necessarily dangerous. His ideas circulated widely among fellow teachers and students, and for a young man he enjoyed a formidable reputation. Some of his statements were later questioned by opponents, and eventually accusations against his teaching reached the Papal Curia, but his excommunication in 1328 had nothing to do with his academic career in England. He raised issues of major intellectual concern to contemporaries, but he did not attack the Church or its teachings, or rail against clerical wealth and corruption. A typical English representative of his order, he did not (so far as is known) adopt the radical line of the Spiritual Franciscans with regard to the *vita apostolica* (apostolic life), and he was uninfluenced (and was perhaps uninterested in) the Joachimite writings in favor with the Italian Fraticelli. He was involved neither in clerical politics nor in calls for reform, and he was certainly no self-proclaimed iconoclast.

Yet in 1323, Ockham was accused of error by John Lutterell, a former chancellor of Oxford University, who was eager to curry favor at the papal court, and so he was compelled to set off for Avignon, then the residence of the pope, in order to defend himself from the charges laid against him. Avignon was to be his home for the next four years, and while he may have suffered from some loss of freedom, he continued writing and revising his earlier works. Meanwhile, a commission appointed to examine his writings met during 1324-1325 and identified fifty-one propositions deserving of further scrutiny. Although it detected many errors, however, it found no evidence of heresy. In 1326, the commission began a second inquiry, perhaps as a direct result of papal prompting, and this time uncovered ten heretical propositions. The papers were then passed to the famous Inquisitor Jacques Fournier (the future Benedict XII, 1334-1342), but apparently no further steps were taken prior to Ockham's flight from Avignon in 1328. It is not difficult to imagine, however, the frustration and uncertainty engendered during Ockham's stay in Avignon. As the famous medievalist David Knowles put it,

> The brilliant young man had the mortifying experience of waiting on the delays and debates of his judges, with his high hopes dashed, and in the demoralizing surroundings of a city of luxury and intrigue, where the atmosphere was rendered permanently electric by the irascible octogenarian autocrat Pope John XXII, an untiring generator of storm and lightning.

Life's Work

The year 1328 marked a virtual bifurcation in Ockham's career. Before that year, he had been an academic, a teacher of theology and logic. Thereafter, he became a committed and forceful polemicist, the champion of the Spiritual Franciscans, the implacable opponent of Pope John XXII (1316-1334), whom he came to regard as a heretic, and a propagandist for the Holy Roman Emperor, Ludwig IV of Bavaria (r. 1314-1347), the pope's bitter foe.

The event that provided the catalyst for the change in Ockham's life was the arrival in Avignon of Michael of Cesena, minister general of the Franciscans, who had been summoned there by the pope to answer charges relating to apostolic poverty. The Spiritual Franciscans had long held that neither Jesus nor his apostles had owned any personal belongings, and that Saint Francis of Assisi had intended a similar evangelical poverty for his followers. Meanwhile, the success of the Franciscan movement had resulted in the order becoming the recipient of great wealth. This development the Spiritual Franciscans abhorred, just as they abhorred the all-too-visible wealth of the Church and the worldly and luxurious lifestyles of many clerics. Their radical idealism, therefore, constituted a profound challenge to the Church as an institution, and it was not a challenge that the Church could afford to disregard. The debate had gone on for years, but Nicholas III (r. 1277-1280), deeply sympathetic to Franciscan idealism, had sought a compromise, by which the Church administered the property of the Franciscans on their behalf, thereby enabling them to maintain their founder's commitment to a life of apostolic poverty. This compromise had been refined during the pontificate of Clement V (1305-1314).

John XXII, however, stirred up a hornet's nest of opposition when, in December, 1322, he issued the bull, or edict, *Ad conditorem canonum*, in which he handed back to the Franciscans the property that, since the time of Nicholas III, had been held in trust for them. Less than a year later, in a second bull, *Cum inter nonnullos* (1323), John pronounced that it was heresy to teach the doctrine of Christ's absolute poverty and followed in November, 1324, with the bull *Quia quorundam*, in which he asserted his absolute authority to rule in such matters without reference to the pronouncements of his predecessors. Hitherto, Michael of Cesena had been a moderate, endeavoring to hold the middle ground within the Franciscan order and maintain a continuous dialogue with the Curia. John, however, was outraged by Franciscan intransigence, and he summoned Michael and a learned Franciscan canonist, Bonagratia of Bergamo, to answer for their flock.

Once in Avignon, and in considerable danger from John's anger, Michael of Cesena discovered that one of the most celebrated of Franciscan scholars was a fellow resident in the town, and he therefore commanded Ockham, as his subordinate, to review the various papal pronouncements on apostolic poverty from the point of view of a theologian. Hitherto, Ockham relates in a letter, he had deliberately avoided looking into these issues, fearful of what he might find, but ordered by his superior to examine the various bulls, he found in them statements that he later described as erroneous, foolish, ridiculous, fantastic, insane, defamatory, and worst of all, heretical. From this time forward, he was filled with horror at the thought that the pope himself had become a heretic, and in consequence could no longer command the allegiance of the Church, views that came to be shared by Michael of Cesena and Bonagratia of Bergamo. On the night of May 28, 1328, the three men fled from Avignon, traveling down the Rhône to Aigues Mortes, where an imperial galley was waiting to transport them to Pisa. There they were well received by Ludwig and his entourage, which included the Italian author of the *Defensor pacis* (wr. 1320-1324), Marsilius of Padua, like Ludwig himself, a bitter foe of John XXII. Ludwig's quarrel with the pope went back to his election in 1314 by the German princes, which John had refused to recognize, but the disagreement had escalated when Ludwig had marched on Rome earlier in the year, had been crowned before the Roman people by a layman, Sciarra Colonna (the same who, a quarter of a century earlier, had assaulted Boniface VIII on behalf of the king of France), and had then formally announced the deposition of John XXII and his replacement by a Franciscan antipope, Nicholas V. At Pisa, the emperor was fresh from his triumphs in Rome. It was said (but the tradition may not be authentic) that on entering Ludwig's presence, Ockham declared, "Defend me with your sword, and I shall support you with my pen." Regardless of whether this statement was uttered, Ockham lived for the next two decades under the emperor's protection in Munich.

From 1328 until his death, Ockham's writings were, in the broadest sense, political, personally attacking John XXII and his successor, Benedict XII, raising fundamental issues with regard to the governance of the Church, and vigorously upholding the rights of lay rulers. His very first polemic, *Opus nonaginta dierum*, written between 1330 and 1332, was a defense of Michael of Cesena, whose views had been condemned by John XXII in his bull *Quia vir reprobus* (November, 1329), and a refutation, sentence by sentence, of John's pronouncements on the question of evangelical poverty. The subject matter of this work is diverse, ranging from the nature of property and its usage to the authority of the pope. Throughout the work it is clear that Ockham is acutely aware that a pope fallen into heresy must drag all Christendom down with him unless remedies are applied.

Far more ambitious is the *Dialogus* (c. 1334), a work conceived in the form of a discussion between master and pupil, of which the first part was probably begun in 1333 and completed toward the end of 1334 (by which time John XXII had been succeeded by Benedict XII), followed by a second and, in 1337 or 1338 (some have placed it as late as 1346), by an unfinished third part. Heresy is the principal theme of the *Dialogus*. This is perhaps Ockham's most original political work, and it is marked by his characteristic concern for the precise meaning of words, for definitions, and for painstaking analysis.

It is not always clear where Ockham is taking his readers in the *Dialogus*. The direction becomes clearer in three later works of political philosophy. In the *Octo quaestiones de potestate papae* (1340-1342), which may have been written at the emperor's behest, he resuscitates the classic debate regarding the sources and extent of the authority of pope and emperor, and their relations with each other—issues that are also central to the *Breviloquium* (1341-1342) and the *De imperatorum et pontificum potestate* (1347). Yet Ockham also addressed more immediate issues of his times. Thus, in the *An princeps pro suo succursu*, written on behalf of Edward III of England (probably late in 1338), he upholds the right of the English king to tax his clergy in times of national crisis. Similarly, in the *Consultatio de causa matrimoniali*, written prior to February, 1342, and presumably on Ludwig's orders, Ockham takes up the problem of consanguinity, which seems to stand in the way of the marriage of Ludwig's son, Ludwig of Brandenburg, to Margaret, the heiress of the Tirol, arguing that in such a case the emperor possesses the authority to grant a dispensation. A further problem, however, was that Margaret was already married to someone else. To deal with this situation, Marsilius of Padua was called in to argue in his *Defensor minor* that in cases of a husband's impotence (as this one was said to be) the emperor had the authority to grant a divorce. In the light of Ludwig's poisonous relations with successive popes, there was not the slightest possibility of obtaining either a papal divorce or a papal dispensation with regard to consanguinity, and so the emperor turned to the two great luminaries of his court, Ockham and Marsilius, to legitimate a course of action on which he had set his heart. The "marriage" was celebrated on February 10, 1342.

That same year, Michael of Cesena died. He had long been stripped of his position as minister general, but he had remained the vicar of that minority of Franciscans who had broken permanently with Avignon. Thereafter, Ockham served as vicar until, in 1348, he sent the seal to Minister General William Farinier, perhaps in the course of negotiations for a reconciliation with the Church, from which Ockham had been excommunicated since 1328. It is uncertain whether it was Ockham himself or the Curia or perhaps Farinier who took the initiative. In any case, his position had become dangerously exposed since Emperor Ludwig's death in 1347 and the accession of Charles IV of Bohemia, a favorite with Avignon. Benedict XII had died in 1342, and his successor, Clement VI (1342-1352), a suave, Francophile diplomat, may well have been disposed to bring about the public reconciliation of a notorious heretic, who was also the most influential scholar of the age. Whether Ockham was reconciled before his death is a matter for speculation, but there has survived a form of submission drawn up by Clement, which was passed on to Farinier, presumably for transmission to Ockham. In it, there is no mention of those charges that had first brought him from England to Avignon a quarter of a century earlier, but Ockham was required to disassociate himself entirely from the opinions of the late excommunicants, Michael of Cesena and the emperor Ludwig; he was to deny utterly that the emperor possessed the authority to make or unmake popes; and he was to declare himself faithful to the official teachings of the Church. It does not sound like a very onerous recantation.

Whether the document ever reached Ockham's hands, whether there was ever a formal reconciliation, or whether Ockham died before the arrangements could be completed will never be known. He died in 1347 or 1349, probably in the course of the ravages of the Black Death, and tradition has it that he was buried in the Franciscan church in Munich, implying that he was no longer an excommunicant.

Significance

Ockham was the most powerful and perhaps the most original mind of the later Middle Ages. "No later reformer," wrote E. F. Jacob, thinking ahead to the age of Martin Luther, "is uninfluenced by his ideas," and David Knowles described him as "one of the half-dozen British philosophers who have profoundly influenced the thought of western Europe." Yet scholars have found it difficult to categorize Ockham, some regarding him as the apex of the medieval Scholastic achievement, others viewing him as the great skeptic whose dialectic helped to dissolve the Thomist-Aristotelian synthesis of the thirteenth century.

He is also a prime example of the "unfinished" thinker, whose tremendous intellectual activity as a young man virtually came to an end when he involved himself in the affairs of popes and emperors and the writing of propaganda. It is impossible now to conceive of what he might have written, or in what direction he might have taken contemporary thought, had he not abandoned teaching for polemics after 1328. Before judging him too harshly for the loss to philosophy, however, it is well to remember that to a man of Ockham's time, the issue of apostolic poverty and the terrible conviction that the head of the Church had lapsed into heresy were matters of such urgency as to outweigh entirely the claims of scholarship and the schools.

Today, "Ockham's razor" remains perhaps the most widely known vestige of the philosopher's thought in the popular mind: The phrase refers to the scientific principle that the simplest or least complex theory among competing theories—that which requires the fewest assumptions, in other words—is to be preferred to alternative explanations for unfamiliar phenomena.

—*Gavin R. G. Hambly*

Further Reading

Klocker, Harry R. *William of Ockham and the Divine Freedom*. 2d ed. Milwaukee, Wis.: Marquette University Press, 1996. A condensed overview of Ockham's concepts of efficient causality, final causality, knowledge of the self and God, and the divine ideas. Bibliography and index.

Leff, Gordon. *The Dissolution of the Medieval Outlook: An Essay on Intellectual and Spiritual Change in the Fourteenth Century*. New York: Harper and Row, 1976. This overview provides essential context for the study of Ockham's thought.

_______. *William of Ockham: The Metamorphosis of Scholastic Discourse*. Manchester, England: Manchester University Press, 1975. A magisterial work that the author presents as a retraction of much of his earlier writing on Ockham.

McGrade, Arthur S. *The Political Thought of William of Ockham: Personal and Institutional Principles*. New York: Cambridge University Press, 2002. Indispensable for serious study, this work considers Ockham as a man so disturbed by the threat to fundamental Christian and human rights of such figures as Pope John XXII that he was willing to take radical action to overhaul traditional political thought.

Maurer, Armand A. *The Philosophy of William of Ockham: In the Light of Its Principles*. Toronto: Pontifical Institute of Mediaeval Studies, 1999. The fruit of four decades of research, this study addresses Ockham in three parts that cover his basic philosophy about logic and reality, the reality of God and divine attributes, and the concept of Creation from the angels to the physical universe and finally the human being.

Moody, Earnest A. *The Logic of William of Ockham*. New York: Sheed and Ward, 1935. Still useful for an understanding of Ockham's logic.

Ockham, William of. *Guillelmi de Ockham Opera Politica*. Edited by H. S. Offler et al. 3 vols. Manchester, England: Manchester University Press, 1940, 1956, 1963. This is a definitive edition of the political writings.

_______. *Predestination, God's Foreknowledge, and Future Contingencies*. Translated by Marilyn McCord Adams and Norman Kretzmann. New York: Appleton-Century-Crofts, 1969. An accessible translation of the *Tractatus de praedstinatione et de praescientia Dei et de futuris contingentibus*, with related extracts from Ockham's commentary on *Sentences*, from his commentary on Aristotle's *De interpretatione*, and from the *Summa logicae*.

See also: Jean Buridan; Edward III; Saint Francis of Assisi; Francesco Landini; Nicholas of Autrecourt; William of Auvergne; William of Auxerre.

Related articles in *Great Events from History: The Middle Ages, 477-1453*: November 18, 1302: Boniface VII Issues the Bull *Unam Sanctam*; 1305-1417: Avignon Papacy and the Great Schism; c. 1310-1350: William of Ockham Attacks Thomist Ideas.

Odoacer

First barbarian king of Italy (r. 476-493)

Although of uncertain ethnic background, Odoacer forged a powerful war band, deposed the last Western Roman emperor, and established the first German kingdom in an area that had been part of the Roman Empire.

Born: c. 435; Central Europe

Died: About March 15, 493; Ravenna (now in Italy)

Also known as: Odovacar; Odovakar

Areas of achievement: Government and politics, warfare and conquest

Early Life

Odoacer (oh-doh-AY-suhr) was born in central Europe north of the Danube River. His father was Edeco (sometimes spelled Edica or Edecon), a Hun who served under the infamous Attila. The Huns broke up following the death of Attila in 453, and Edeco, who had married into a German tribe, the Scirae, returned to their land north of the Danube and became a Scirian prince. Evidence of Odoacer's mixed parentage includes the fact that "Edeco" seems to be a name of Hunnic origin, while "Odoacer" is Germanic. Odoacer is sometimes referred to as a Heruclian or a Rugian, other Germanic tribes who contributed men to Odoacer's war band. The best summary of Odoacer's ethnic composition is that he was a Danubian-Hunnic-German.

In 469, Edeco was most likely killed when the Ostrogoths (East Goths) defeated the Scirae in Pannonia, a Roman province south of the Danube. One of his two sons, Hunulf (Onulf), survived the battle and entered the service of the Eastern Roman emperor in Constantinople. Odoacer, the other son, had not been a part of the campaign. As early as 460, he was the leader of a mixed war band composed of Huns, Germans, Goths, and Romans. The war band first operated as itinerant thieves in Pannonia and Noricum to the west. In 461, Odoacer, then about twenty-six years old, was on his way to Italy in search of fame and fortune. He stopped in Noricum to visit the imprisoned Saint Severinus. He was described as having been very tall and fur-clad during the visit. Severinus told Odoacer to go to Italy, where he would become a great man.

Arriving in Italy, Odoacer and most of his war band joined the imperial guard in Rome. In 472, they were part of an invasion of Rome led by Ricimer, the grandson of a Visigoth king, who had been trying to rule Italy from Milan as a rival of the emperor in Rome. Ricimer captured Rome and executed the emperor, who had been sent from the Eastern capital at Constantinople; Ricimer died five weeks later, leaving a power struggle in Rome. In 474, Zeno, the new Eastern emperor, appointed Julius Nepos to rule in the west. However, Nepos was deposed in 475 and fled across the Adriatic Sea to Dalmatia. The power struggle resumed, and the result was the end of the Western Empire in 476.

Life's Work

Odoacer stood ready to participate in the power struggle. Also ready was Orestes, a Roman and a friend of Edeco who had been a Hunnic subject under Attila and who had joined Ricimer in the siege of Rome in 472. Orestes rose rapidly to the position of master of soldiers, or commander in chief, of the Roman army, and it was he who deposed Nepos in 475 and installed his young son, Romulus Augustulus, as the Western emperor in Ravenna. The actual government of the Western Empire had been moved to Ravenna in 402 by Emperor Honorius to provide better protection against barbarian invasions. Orestes made himself regent for his son, but his fortunes were soon to collapse.

Odoacer and his war band had been quietly supporting the interests of Orestes, who had promised them a third of Italy for their support. When they reminded Orestes of the promise, however, they were ignored. Odoacer stepped forward and promised his war band that if they would help him depose both Romulus Augustulus and Orestes, he would give them their promised territory. The men agreed, and the result was war between Odoacer and his late father's friend in the climactic year of 476.

Odoacer won several quick victories, forcing Orestes to seek refuge in the city of Ticinum-Pavia. Odoacer attacked and captured the city, and Orestes was put to death. In Ravenna, Paulus, the brother of Orestes, was captured and killed, and the young emperor, Romulus Augustulus, was deposed; he was sent with a pension to live in the palace of Lucullus near Naples. Subsequently, the historical record falls silent on the fate of the last Western Roman emperor.

Odoacer's men proclaimed him king. Whether he was the principal king of Italy or merely one king among several is unclear. Historians debate whether his reign ended or continued the Western Roman Empire. Odoacer gave his men their land in the vicinity of their garrisons. Although humiliating to the once proud Romans, this action was less devastating because Italy had been depopulated and many estates vacated as a result of the wars and invasions of the fifth century.

Odoacer persuaded the senate to send a delegation on behalf of Romulus Augustulus to the Eastern Roman capital at Constantinople. The delegates were instructed to then ask Zeno, the Eastern emperor, to appoint Odoacer as a viceroy with the title of patrician. After some hesitation, Zeno granted the request.

Historians since Edward Gibbon (*The History of the Decline and Fall of the Roman Empire*, 1776-1788) have debated the uneasy relationship between Zeno and Odoacer. In spite of his show of humility, Odoacer seemed to believe that he ruled Italy by right of conquest and not by delegation of authority from Zeno, from whom he now wanted recognition as an "allied power" of the Eastern Empire. Zeno refused but still hoped to use Odoacer to advance his own interests. The first break between the two men occurred after Odoacer's failure to obey Zeno's order to restore Julius Nepos to the Western throne.

Odoacer's growing independence can be best seen in his foreign policy, which was based primarily on agreements with other German kingdoms in the former Western Empire. He first signed an agreement with Gaiseric, the Vandal king in north Africa, that gave control of Sicily to Odoacer in return for an annual tribute paid to Gaiseric. In 477, he made peace with the Visigoth (West Goth) king, Euric, who was establishing control in Spain. By this agreement, Odoacer gave up claim to a coastal strip of southern Gaul (France) from the Rhone River to the Alps.

In 480, Odoacer crossed the Adriatic Sea to occupy Dalmatia, supposedly to avenge the recent murder of Julius Nepos, the deposed Western emperor. His attempt to move north into Pannonia-Savia, then under Ostrogoth control, was not completely successful.

By 486, the uneasy relationship between Odoacer and Zeno was unraveling. Zeno encouraged Feletheus, king of the Rugians in Noricum, to attack Odoacer. However, in a preemptive strike, Odoacer crushed the Rugians and sent the spoils to Zeno. Feletheus and his Ostrogoth wife were put to death. In 488, an attempt by Frideric, the son of Feletheus, to regain Noricum was crushed by Hunuf, the brother of Odoacer, who had left the service of the Eastern Empire and joined Odoacer. In 489, Zeno classified Odoacer as a usurper and sent Theodoric, the Ostrogoth king, to Italy to dethrone him. In response, Odoacer appointed his son, Thela (Ocla), to the throne of the Western Empire. Yet Odoacer did not proclaim himself an independent ruler, as both Gaiseric and Euric had done.

Intending to make Italy his permanent home, Theodoric marched in with about 100,000 Ostrogoths, including 20,000 warriors. After quick conquests of Verona and Milan, he tried an unsuccessful surprise attack on Ravenna, after which he took refuge in Ticinum-Pavia. Odoacer took the offensive and recaptured Milan, but his fortunes were soon reversed. Alaric II, a Visigoth from Toulouse (France), in a rare display of Gothic unity, brought an army to relieve Theodoric. Odoacer was forced to retreat to the Adda River, where he suffered a decisive defeat in August, 490, and was forced to return to Ravenna.

Odoacer. (Hulton|Archive at Getty Images)

BARBARIAN KINGS OF ITALY, 476-553

Reign	*Ruler*
476-493	ODOACER
493-526	Theodoric
526-534	Athalaric
534-536	Theodatus (Theodahad)
536-540	Vitiges (Witiges)
540-541	Theodobald (Heldebadus)
541	Eraric
541-552	Totila
552-553	Teias

For the next two years, Theodoric sought to establish an effective siege of the well-defended Ravenna. In July, 491, Odoacer fought his last major battle, a failed attempt to break the siege. By August, 492, Ravenna was cut off by land and by sea. In February, 493, Bishop John of Ravenna negotiated an agreement that allowed Theodoric to enter Ravenna and for Theodoric and Odoacer to rule Italy jointly. On March 5, 493, Theodoric entered Ravenna.

About ten days later, a banquet was held to commemorate the agreement. At the end of the meal, two of Theodoric's men grabbed Odoacer's hands while Theodoric thrust his sword through the body of his longtime enemy. Odoacer's wife was starved to death, his brother was killed in a church, and his followers were killed on the spot wherever they were found. His son was exiled to France but was killed later trying to reconquer Italy. The motive for this cold-blooded murder and massacre, in addition to rivalry for control of Italy, might have been Odoacer's killing of the Rugian leader, Feletheus, and his Ostrogoth wife, who apparently was related to Theodoric.

SIGNIFICANCE

Although he came from a barbarian background and although he was apparently illiterate, Odoacer ruled Italy for more than sixteen years with amazing wisdom and stability. He did not visualize himself as ending the Western Roman Empire. Even when his relationship with the Eastern emperor deteriorated, he never considered his territory anything other than a part of the Roman Empire. Odoacer never claimed the title of emperor, instead adopting the idea of *imitatio imperii* (image of the emperor). He never assumed the right of legislation, and he never had a coin struck in his honor, as was the custom of Roman emperors. He preserved and enhanced the Roman imperial system whereby the emperors had governed large areas through special agents. Odoacer also made use of, and increased the power of, the Roman senate.

Odoacer and his contemporaries were never entirely able to surmount their barbarian backgrounds, but they had great respect for Roman civilization. This is evidenced by the different standards of treatment they meted out to the Romans under their control as compared with their treatment of fellow barbarians. Odoacer was also deeply impressed by Christianity, although the Arian Christianity to which he was exposed was not the orthodox version that soon became the Roman Catholic Church. Odoacer's personal conduct seems to have been little affected by either Roman civilization or Christianity, but had he been able to rule more peacefully and for a longer period, his contributions to Western civilization might have been much greater.

—*Glenn L. Swygart*

FURTHER READING

Eyck, Frank. *Religion and Politics in German History: From the Beginnings to the French Revolution*. New York: St. Martin's Press, 1998. An analysis of how Germanic peoples preserved links with classical civilization through their ability to assimilate other cultures and peoples, from their alliances with eighth century popes through the Reformation and Counter-Reformation. The initial bond between the Germanic rulers and popes turned to conflict as the Papacy gained power. Tables, maps, bibliography, index.

Gibbon, Edward. *The Decline and Fall of the Roman Empire*. Abridged by D. M. Low. New York: Harcourt, Brace, 1960. The classic history of Roman decline. Includes five chapters on the barbarian invasions of Italy in the fifth century that culminated in Odoacer's removal of the last Western emperor in 476. Two additional chapters cover general conditions of the period and the rule of Theodoric.

Goffart, Walter. *Barbarians and Romans*. Princeton, N.J.: Princeton University Press, 1980. Covers the years 418 to 584. Deals primarily with the process of accommodation between the Romans and their barbarian invaders. Chapter 2 covers the land allotments in Italy given to Odoacer's war band and later to Theodoric. Also discusses the blending of cultures. Five appendices provide background for the period.

La Rocca, Cristina, ed. *Italy in the Early Middle Ages, 476-1000*. New York: Oxford University Press, 2002. Ten chapters by historians and archaeologists integrate new archaeological findings to examine Italy's regional diversities, rural and urban landscapes, organization of public and private power, ecclesiastical institutions, manuscript production, and more. Starts with the fall of Rome and Odoacer. Illustrations, maps, bibliography, index.

Randers-Pehrson, Justine Davis. *Barbarians and Romans: The Birth Struggle of Europe, A.D. 400-700.* Norman: University of Oklahoma Press, 1983. Has several chapters covering the fifth century barbarian invasions of the Western Empire. Includes coverage of the struggle between Odoacer and Theodoric. Also has photographs, both color and black and white, of numerous artifacts and historic sites related to Romans and barbarians of the period.

Thompson, E. A. *Romans and Barbarians: The Decline of the Western Empire.* Madison: University of Wisconsin Press, 1982. Includes a chapter devoted to the events surrounding the year 476 and contains maps that help trace the territorial changes taking place in the Western Empire. Also discusses later invasions of Italy by the Eastern Empire and by the Lombards.

Wickham, Chris. *Early Medieval Italy: Central Power and Local Society, 400-1000.* Ann Arbor: University of Michigan Press, 1989. A social and archaeological history of early medieval Italy covering the time of Odoacer, which has been adopted by many college courses in medieval history. Illustrations, maps, bibliography, Index.

Wolfrum, Herwig. *History of the Goths.* Translated by Thomas Dunlap. Berkeley: University of California Press, 1988. Good background for the German and Gothic invasions of Italy. Gives a detailed account of Odoacer's conflict with Theodoric, including a discussion of Theodoric's motives for his murder of Odoacer.

SEE ALSO: Amalasuntha; Saint Benedict of Nursia; Boethius; Cassiodorus; Clovis; Justinian I; Theodora; Theodoric the Great.

RELATED ARTICLES in *Great Events from History: The Middle Ages, 477-1453*: 484: White Huns Raid India; 496: Baptism of Clovis; 524: Imprisonment and Death of Boethius; 568-571: Lombard Conquest of Italy.

SAINT OLAF

King of Norway (r. 1016-1028)

By consolidating and unifying Norway under a strong Christian monarchy, Olaf established his country's first national government and permanently influenced the political and religious development of his land.

BORN: c. 995; west of the Oslo fjord, Norway
DIED: July 29, 1030; Stiklestad, Norway
ALSO KNOWN AS: Olaf Haraldsson; Olaf II
AREAS OF ACHIEVEMENT: Government and politics, religion and theology

EARLY LIFE

Olaf Haraldsson was the great-great-grandson of King Harald Fairhair, the legendary warrior chief and first king (r. 872-930) in southeastern Norway. Olaf's father, Harald Grenske, was a regional king in southeastern Norway and died while Olaf was still an infant. His mother, Áasta (Astrid), daughter of a prominent man in the Uplands, was remarried to Sigurd Syr, a regional king in Ringerike.

An anecdote concerning Olaf's childhood, related by the Icelandic historian Snorri Sturluson in *Heimskringla* (c. 1230-1235; *The Heimskringla: Or, Chronicle of the Kings of Norway*, 1844), reveals something of the boy's disposition and of his attitude toward his stepfather, Sigurd, an unpretentious, mild-mannered farmer. One day King Sigurd asked Olaf to go to the stable and saddle a horse for him. Olaf returned, leading a large goat saddled with the king's harness. Olaf not only thought the menial task unworthy of a chieftain and warrior but also repudiated the unmartial life of his stepfather by suggesting that this animal was as suitable for a farmer-king as horses are for other riders. From an early age, Olaf showed an unswerving desire to become a warrior and demonstrated contempt for any lesser life. He was hot-tempered, imperious, and proud of his birth.

Although the Viking Age was coming to an end and Olaf himself was to be the last great Viking chief, Viking expeditions were still taking place during Olaf's boyhood, and experience as a Viking was still considered a suitable education for a young man of the chieftain class. Thus, at age twelve and in the company of experienced men, Olaf participated in raids off the shores of the Baltic Sea, in Jutland, and in Frisia. From age fourteen to nineteen, Olaf remained in Western Europe, mainly in the service of a king—a fact that suggests that the Viking era was indeed passing and the era of wars between states had begun. In the service of King Ethelred II, the Unready, of England (r. 978-1013 and 1014-1016), Olaf helped to repel the Danish invasions of England from 1009 to 1014. Earlier, he had fought on the side of the Danes against the English while serving King Sweyn Forkbeard, but it is clear that Olaf's alliance was with the English and with Ethelred, who became his protector. The influence of the English on Olaf was to prove substantial, and it was probably while in Ethelred's service in Rouen, Normandy, that he was converted to Christianity and baptized in 1013. By the age of nineteen, Olaf had gained wide political and military training, considerable eminence as a warrior and a leader, great wealth through large tribute payments, and a knowledge of European systems of government. By the age of twenty, through skill and some luck, he had gained the throne of Norway.

It is unclear exactly when Olaf decided to conquer Norway. His political fortunes in England worsened when King Ethelred died and Canute (the Great) of Denmark (son of King Sweyn Forkbeard) established his rule in England. Olaf was very conscious of his royal ancestry and his right to the throne, however, and it is reasonable to assume he had some idea of the desirability of a unified Norwegian kingdom. Olaf's namesake and kinsman, King Olaf I (r. 995-1000) had briefly unified the country and had attempted through hardhanded methods to impose Christianity on the land, but after his death in the Battle of Svolder in 1000, rule of Norway passed to Erik and Sweyn, the earls of Lade, in part as representatives of the Danish and Swedish crowns. The unity and independence of Norway had thus been lost, and much of the country had reverted to paganism.

In 1015, Olaf and 120 followers set sail for Norway, not in Viking warships but in two merchant vessels. Olaf clearly expected to win the throne with the help of forces raised within the country itself. In Norway, there were many regional kings (such as Olaf's stepfather), each ruling his own little "province." They owed allegiance to a foreign crown and paid tribute, but they were allowed to run their own domestic affairs as they saw fit. The arbitrariness of their rule and the growing differences in wealth and distinction among their subjects were grievances that Olaf was able to exploit. Promising freedom from the tyranny and exactions of local kings, Olaf won the support of the yeoman. He used the prestige of his ancestry and the wealth he had acquired to win many others to his side. He manipulated national sentiment against the Danish and Swedish overlords to lead a rebellion. Finally, he employed his military proficiency and won a decisive naval battle against Earl Sweyn and established himself as King Olaf II.

Life's Work

Olaf II is remembered as the first effective king of all Norway, a great lawgiver, a zealous Christian missionary, and eventually Norway's patron saint. Certainly there is little in Olaf's early life to suggest that he would become a national saint. Neither his career as ruthless Viking warrior nor his character hints of the saintly. Such varying descriptions of Olaf exist that it is difficult to discern his true nature. One physical characteristic, however, is clear from his nickname, which was variously Olaf the Big, Olaf the Stout, and, as one of his enemies called him, Olaf the Fat. Although he was a large man and possibly inclined toward corpulence, his swiftness and agility as a warrior belies the stereotype, and Snorri records that he was capable of great asceticism. In some verses supposedly written by Olaf, he accuses himself of being too susceptible to the charms of women. Icelandic poets as late as the fifteenth century allude to his many amours, one of whom produced an illegitimate son, Magnús, who succeeded his father as king. Still, his life also gives evidence of the gradual subduing of paganism, both within Norway and within himself.

Some modern historians doubt that Olaf was as devout a Christian as medieval historians stated in their writings, which were somewhat hagiographic in tone. Olaf's devotion to Christianity undoubtedly had practical as well as spiritual motivations. Norway had been Christian in name since the time of Olaf I, but following his death a pagan reaction set in. Olaf, while in England, possibly perceived that national unity through an established church was a politically astute strategy. He undoubtedly intended to establish a state church similar to what he had observed in England, for he brought numerous bishops and priests from England. Certainly Christianity could not be established without law and permanent organization. Olaf abolished the system of petty kings and established the authority of priests to administer the many churches he had built throughout Norway and to regulate the lives of the people according to fundamental Christian principles. The Church was given authority to regulate marriages, fasts, and feast days, and to abolish pagan practices. Many of the laws in the Kristenret (the name given to Saint Olaf's code of laws) appeared revolutionary to the heathen, for it stated that parents no longer had the right to rid themselves of unwanted children through exposure; that a man would be permitted only one wife, to whom he must be faithful; and that the worship of house gods was forbidden. Other ideas, such as the Sabbath as a holy day of rest even for thralls, or the concept of a fast day even for those who could afford to eat and drink abundantly, were also disturbing and viewed by many pagans as unwarranted intrusions into private life. Thus, many of Olaf's laws were met with fierce resistance, and accordingly, Olaf, despite his desire to treat his people according to principles of mercy and peace, used increasingly harsh methods to enforce the code of laws. He mutilated obdurate heathens and deprived them of their property, and during the last phase of his reign he resorted to burning villages and executing men. Yet Olaf was also capable of great restraint and even of magnanimity in dealing with his enemies, and he was known for his evenhanded treatment of all people, in spite of rank.

Olaf reigned for twelve relatively peaceful years, during which time he established the first national government in Norway and continued his systematic efforts to establish Christianity throughout the land, particularly in the north and in the interior, where resistance was greatest. A foreign war, however, brought about his downfall.

King Canute, who ruled both England and Denmark, began a plan to reclaim Norway. He sent money and gifts to the deposed petty kings and promised to restore their freedom and authority, which Olaf had taken away. Through his emissaries, he also agitated the many individuals who resented the new faith that had been thrust on them and all those who found Olaf's strict rule to be too harsh, as well as those who hoped to gain greater independence under a more distant king. Realizing that an erosion of support for him was taking place among his people, Olaf entered into an alliance with the Swedish king, and together they made a precipitous, ill-conceived attack on Canute in Denmark, presumably before he could attack them. The attack failed and instead initiated Canute's conquest of Norway in 1028. Olaf, knowing he had been betrayed by his country folk, fled to Russia, where he was entertained by King Jaroslav and Queen Ingigerd (to whom Olaf had once been engaged). King Jaroslav offered him authority and dominions in Russia, but Olaf desired only that it might be God's will for him to return to Norway. In 1030, he left his son Magnús at the Russian court and returned to Norway by way of Sweden. The king of Sweden supplied him with four hundred men and authorized him to call for volunteers. Olaf marched through dense forest to Norway, where other kinsmen joined him, mainly ruffians and robbers. According to some accounts, Olaf rejected all heathen volunteers who refused baptism; according to other accounts, Olaf went into battle with three thousand men, Christians on his right and heathens on his left.

King Canute appointed Kálf Árnason, Olaf's former friend, to command the defense of Norway. The opposing armies met at Stiklestad at midday in brilliant sunshine, but after an hour the sky turned red, the sun was obscured, and the battlefield became dark as night. Olaf's army, greatly outnumbered, fought on bravely, but Olaf was wounded. He was leaning against a boulder and calling on God for help when he received his deathblow, probably from Kálf Árnason. In addition to an eclipse of the sun, other miracles were recorded on this day within a few hours of Olaf's death—wounds were healed and sight was restored to a blind man by contact with Olaf's blood. When Olaf's body was exhumed a year after burial and found to be incorrupt, he was proclaimed a saint. In 1041, the Church officially declared his sainthood, and his remains were placed above the high altar of St. Clement's Church, where many more miracles reportedly occurred. The cult of Saint Olaf spread rapidly, and miracles relating to Saint Olaf were reported in places as distant as Constantinople and the British Isles. Churches were dedicated to Saint Olaf throughout Western Europe, and a painting of him appeared in the Nativity Church in Bethlehem around 1170.

The unusual circumstances of Olaf's death and the events that followed it help to explain how Olaf became a saint within a few years of his death. Neither Olaf's followers nor his detractors could help but associate his death with the death of Christ on Calvary. Another factor was the increasing discontent with the rulers that Canute installed in Norway following Olaf's defeat and death. Sweyn, son of Canute, was still a child when appointed regent, and power was therefore transferred to his tyrannical mother, Álfífa. The harsh laws, increased taxes, and precedence given to Danes in Norway (in court, the witness of one Dane was regarded as the equivalent of ten Norwegians) roused the people to fury and caused them to view Olaf as a martyr and a champion of national liberty. Ironically, Olaf's enemies led the expedition to Russia to bring back Olaf's ten-year-old son, Magnús, to be king. Additional factors in the reversal of opinion about Olaf II may have been the self-interest of leading aristocrats in establishing a shrine to Saint Olaf, which would attract pilgrims from many lands, and the desire of church prelates for eminence.

The most enigmatic aspect of Olaf's sainthood remains Olaf himself. There is much disagreement and controversy about his personality and his life, especially about the way he could embody Christian principles (humility, forgiveness, and nonviolence) yet at times reveal an almost instinctive cruelty and arrogance. He was a missionary king, continuing the work of Olaf I in bringing lost souls to salvation (even against their will). He was a Viking, punitive, shrewd, and ruthless when necessary. Snorri stated that Olaf, while in exile at the Russian court, became increasingly engrossed in prayer and contemplated traveling to Jerusalem to take monastic vows. According to Snorri, Olaf relinquished all desire to rule for the sake of power and wished only to be an instrument of God's will. A dream told him to regain the kingdom. As Olaf drew near his last battle, many signs of sanctity were seen, among them Olaf's immersion in prayers and fasting and his selfless concern for the souls of his men.

Significance

In art, Saint Olaf is always depicted holding a battle-ax with a dragon under his foot, representing the heathendom he destroyed. Gradually, it became customary to depict a face on the dragon resembling the king's own, suggesting that it was also Olaf's own heathen nature that he trampled underfoot. Undoubtedly, by consolidating and strengthening the monarchy in Norway, by upholding law and order, by attempting to be both just and strict, and by promoting passage of laws consistent with Christian principles, King Olaf II was a great civilizing force in a dark time. His martyr's death and subsequent canonization established the concept of Norway as a unified Christian nation under the rule of a single Christian monarch. Thus he is known as the "Eternal King" of Norway.

—*Karen A. Kildahl*

Further Reading

Fassler, Margot E., and Rebecca A. Baltzer, eds. *The Divine Office in the Latin Middle Ages: Methodology and Source Studies, Regional Developments, Hagiography.* New York: Oxford University Press, 2000. Explores the Divine Office—the daily worship services other than Mass that were central to the Middle Ages and its saints—and includes a chapter on Olaf's transformation from Viking to saint. Extensive bibliography and index.

Gjerset, Knut. *History of the Norwegian People.* 1932. Reprint. New York: AMS Press, 1969. A complete history of Olaf's rise and fall, and detailed accounts of the social, political, and economic conditions in the land of the time.

Larsen, Karen. *A History of Norway.* 1948. Reprint. Princeton, N.J.: Princeton University Press, 1974. A good general account of Norway's history and one of the most readable. Provides a brief overview of Olaf's development and one of the most sympathetic accounts of his life. Includes a brief bibliography.

McKitterick, Rosamond, ed. *The New Cambridge Medieval History.* 7 vols. New York: Cambridge University Press, 2000. Volume 5 examines the period of the Middle Ages from about 1198 to about 1300 and includes a section on "Scandinavia and the Baltic Frontier," with essays discussing the region's kingdoms and military orders. Reference made to Saint Olaf (Olav) and many contemporaries.

Roesdahl, Else. *The Vikings.* 2d ed. Translated by Susan M. Margeson and Kirsten Williams. New York: Penguin Books, 1998. Provides a solid, meticulous survey of Viking expansion. Includes maps, illustrations, an extensive bibliography, and index.

Snorri Sturluson. *Heimskringla: History of the Kings of Norway.* 1964. Reprint. Translated by Lee M. Hollander. Austin: University of Texas Press, 1991. A history of the kings of Norway from the quasi-mythic origins of the dynasty to the year 1177 by the thirteenth century Icelandic poet. Provides the text of "Saint Olaf's Saga" ("Oláfs saga Helga"), one of Snorri's greatest literary achievements and a major if controversial source about Olaf II. Includes an introduction and copious notes.

Turville-Petre, Gabriel. *The Heroic Age of Scandinavia.* London: Hutchinson's University Library, 1951. An introductory history of the Norsemen to the year 1030. A chapter devoted to Olaf II emphasizes that the cult and legends of Olaf II have eclipsed the historical figure. Includes a discussion of the confusion about the date of Olaf's death (which does not coincide with the solar eclipse). Brief bibliography.

Undset, Sigrid. *Saga of Saints.* 1934. Reprint. Translated by E. C. Ramsden. Freeport, N.Y.: Books for Libraries Press, 1968. A chapter on Olaf offers interesting insights into the differences between pagan and Christian values and practices. An uncritical presentation of the many legends and miracles surrounding Olaf.

See also: Canute the Great; Ethelred II, the Unready; Olaf I; Snorri Sturluson.

Related articles in *Great Events from History: The Middle Ages, 477-1453*: 850-950: Viking Era; 1016: Canute Conquers England.

Olaf I

King of Norway (r. 995-1000)

Olaf's reign as king brought about a temporary unification and Christianization of Norway, and his exploits later made him a national hero and legend for his people.

Born: c. 968; in the area of the Oslo fjord, Norway
Died: September 9, 1000; Svolder, probably near Rügen in the Baltic (now in Germany)
Also known as: Olaf Tryggvason (birth name)
Areas of achievement: Military, religion and theology, government and politics

Early Life

Olaf Tryggvason, named after his grandfather, was a great grandson of Harald Fairhair, who had made himself king of most of Norway (r. 872-930). Fairhair, who had at least four wives, had numerous descendants who sought to rule his domain after his death. The country was rife with conflict, and in the midst of this turmoil, Olaf was born. His father, Tryggve Olafson, king of a small portion of Norway, was killed around the time of Olaf's birth. The attackers were sons of Eric Bloodaxe, whom Fairhair had designated as his legitimate heir. Olaf's mother, Astrid, left the Oslo fjord area with her young son to escape those who had killed her husband. She did not fear for her daughters, but her son was the heir to Tryggve's domain. Consequently, Olaf, if he lived, could one day challenge the sons of Eric Bloodaxe.

Astrid took Olaf and went to live with her relatives among the Swedish Vikings in Russia. Her brother was a powerful man in the service of King Vladimir I, whose court was in Novgorod. The saga accounts of Olaf's being sold into slavery while crossing the Baltic with his mother are almost certainly fictional.

Olaf was reared among the Vikings in Russia as a warrior and an athlete. Maturing physically at a young age, he grew large and strong. He was ambidextrous; not only could he throw a spear with either hand, he could launch spears with both hands simultaneously. He was known for his ability to juggle three swords, and reputedly more. His athletic prowess was widely acclaimed. An example of his agility was his alleged ability to walk on the oars outside his boat while his crew rowed.

Besides possessing immense physical strength, Olaf was reputed to be one of the most handsome, playful, and forgiving of men, yet the gruesome side of the Viking character was also evident in him. He tormented his foes and on various occasions burned them, let wild hounds devour them, or threw them from high mountains.

Kings of Norway, 680-1387

Reign	*Ruler*
680-710	Olaf the Tree Hewer
710-750	Halfdan I
750-780	Oystein (Eystein) I
780-800	Halfdan II White Legs
800-810	Gudrod the Magnificent
810-840	Olaf Geirstade
840-863	Halfdan III the Black
863-872	Civil War
872-930/33	Harald I Fairhair
933-934	Erik I Bloodaxe
934-961	Hákon I the Good
961-970	Harold II Grayfell
970-995	Earl (Jarl) Hákon
995-1000	Olaf I Tryggvason
1000-1015	Erik I
1016-1028	Saint Olaf II Haraldsson
1028-1035	Canute the Great
1035-1047	Magnus I the Good
1047-1066	Harald III Hardrada
1066-1069	Magnus II
1069-1093	Olaf III the Peaceful
1093-1103	Magnus III the Barefoot
1103-1122	Oystein (Eystein) II
1103-1130	Sigurd I the Crusader
1130-1135	Magnus IV the Blinded
1130-1136	Harald IV Gillechrist
1136-1155	Sigurd II
1136-1161	Inge I
1142-1157	Oystein (Eystein) III
1161-1162	Hákon II
1163-1184	Magnus V
1184-1202	Sverre Sigurdsson
1202-1204	Hákon III
1204-1217	Inge II
1217-1263	Hákon IV
1263-1281	Magnus VI
1281-1299	Erik II Magnusson
1299-1319	Hákon V
1320-1343	Magnus VII (II of Sweden)
1343-1380	Hákon VI
1376-1387	Olaf IV (V of Denmark)
1380	Unification of Norway and Denmark

Life's Work

Separating the actual life of Olaf from the myth and legend that surround him is quite difficult. Though his life was a favorite subject of medieval historians and poets, almost two centuries passed after his death before the first saga about him was compiled. Skaldic poetry provides much of the information about Olaf, but few of these poems have survived in their entirety. Nevertheless, it is clear that Olaf left Russia to pursue opportunities further west. If he was ever to regain his ancestral territory in Norway, he needed to acquire wealth, fame, and an army of his own. As a Viking chieftain, he participated in raids along the Baltic coast, the Netherlands, and Ireland and eventually in Danish invasions of England.

Whether or not Olaf participated in the 991 Danish attack on England, he profited from the inability of England's King Ethelred II, the Unready. In alliance with Sweyn Forkbeard, a son of the king of Denmark, Olaf helped lead a large-scale raid on southern England in 994; the nursery rhyme "London bridge is falling down" may have originated from this assault. Although driven off in their attempt to seize London, they pillaged the countryside. Desperate, Ethelred finally responded by bribing them with a payment, or Danegeld, of sixteen thousand pounds of silver. Sweyn returned to Denmark with his share. Olaf, however, after taking English hostages to his ships to ensure his own safety, decided to let an English bishop baptize him. When Olaf accepted Christianity, none other than King Ethelred was his sponsor. The *Anglo-Saxon Chronicle* (compiled c. 890 to c. 1150; English translation, 1953) asserts that when Olaf was confirmed, he vowed never to return to England with hostile intent. This vow, whether he made it or not, was fulfilled, for he never returned.

Along with his newly acquired wealth and faith, Olaf took his ships and veteran warriors to Norway to reclaim his father's territory. He returned to Norway aware that the time might be ripe to seize control of Trøndelag. Haakon Sigurdsson, earl of Lade, ruled that territory. Haakon was not a king, but he governed central Norway on behalf of the Danish king. The free farmers, usually called "bonders," were the backbone of Norwegian society. They did not fight to prevent foreign rule, and some actually preferred rule by a foreign king because a distant ruler made it easier to avoid taxes. Apparently, Haakon's support had declined among the people because of his treatment of female subjects. Whatever the causes of unrest, Haakon's overthrow coincided closely with Olaf's arrival.

Stepping into the void in Trøndelag, Olaf asserted control over Haakon's territory as the local population initially welcomed him. He acquired the territory in the Oslo fjord his father once held, as well as lands in western and southwestern Norway. In the last two areas, the personal ties of his step-brother and mother were important. The demands of being a king were many, and Olaf met the challenge of consolidating the realm of his kingship. During his reign, he was almost entirely on the offensive, maintaining or expanding his control.

Olaf was the first effective missionary king in Norway. He rapidly baptized most of the people on the eastern and western coasts, but his methods met strong resistance in the pagan strongholds of Trøndelag and north Norway. Yet whether he was a genuine Crusader for Christianity or was using the religion to bring more territory under his control is difficult to determine. For years, many Norse traders were "temporary Christians" while in Christian lands, reverting to paganism when they left. The Christian lands tended to be more populous and better armed than the pagan Norse lands. An international religion, Christianity offered the prospect of economic and strategic ties.

To help subdue the defiant people in Trøndelag, Olaf founded the city of Nidaros in the middle of Trøndelag's fertile farmlands in 997. Olaf established his capital in the new city. Located on the Nid River in an easily defensible position, the site may have reminded him of either London or Dublin. Now known as Trondheim, the city boasts Scandinavia's grandest medieval cathedral.

Olaf's zest and energy were sufficient to win his subjects' respect, ensure obedience to his mass baptisms, and make him a popular king. Yet his kingdom was not a national unit but merely the land he conquered and owned, limited in scope and unstable in nature. The people's intrinsic loyalty was to family rather than any national grouping. As their settlements were isolated among the fjords, residents were inclined to consider anyone not from their locality as a foreigner.

Olaf gained his kingdom by sea power, and without sea power his kingdom was doomed. At Trondheim, therefore, he ordered construction of new ships for his fleet. The *Long Serpent* was his most famous ship, considered one of the greatest ships in the north. Leif Eriksson, son of Erik the Red, came to the city to trade while this ship was being built. Olaf met Leif, converted him to Christianity, and encouraged him to take a priest with him when he returned to Greenland in the spring. Leif ventured into North America before his travels were finished.

For such a handsome and prominent man, Olaf apparently had excessive trouble with women. The sagas tell of several different marriages and thwarted romantic encounters. Perhaps Olaf's most detrimental encounter was with a woman he did not marry. Sigrid the Proud, the queen of Sweden, was a recent widow whom Olaf wanted to marry. The queen was a good political match, and she seemed willing. According to the sagas, however, when he insisted that Sigrid become Christian, she refused. After he insulted her, she replied that his words could well cause his death. Marrying the king of Denmark, she urged him and her son, now Sweden's king, to go to war against Olaf.

The sagas vividly describe Olaf's final battle at Svolder in 1000. The exact location remains uncertain, but the naval battle probably took place in the Baltic. He faced his former comrade Sweyn Forkbeard, now Denmark's king, who joined forces with the king of Sweden and the Norwegian earl Erik, son of Earl Haakon. Even if they were not motivated by Sigrid's anger, Olaf's opponents certainly coveted the various territories under his control. Though outnumbered, Olaf was determined to fight. Defeated at sea, he jumped overboard, refusing to be captured alive. Afterward, rumors lingered that he had managed to swim away to safety, but he was never seen in Norway again. His reign as king had lasted only five years.

Sculpture of King Olaf I. (Hulton|Archive at Getty Images)

SIGNIFICANCE

Though Olaf died in his thirties, his legend has persisted for more than one thousand years. He was perhaps the quintessential Viking, and his life and kingship, influenced by Christianity, marked the beginning of the end of the Viking era. His namesake and distant relative Olaf II, later Saint Olaf, completed the transition. Not only is Olaf I credited with bringing Christianity to Norway, but some credit him with the conversion of Iceland, the Faroe and the Orkney Islands, the Shetland Islands, and Greenland; however, such claims embellish Olaf's record too much. At any rate, his conversion was one of the sword, not the soul, and he did not establish an institutional church to maintain the faith of those he converted.

In the short term after Olaf's death, it was as if he had never existed. Left defenseless after his defeat, his kingdom was divided between his conquerors. The southern provinces went to Denmark. The Swedish king took the southeast lands, central and southern Trøndelag. Erik and Sweyn, sons of Haakon, ruled the rest of Norway for fifteen years, allowing it to lapse into pagan practices. Yet the earls of Lade ultimately lost the battle for control of Norway to Harald Fairhair's descendants.

An Icelandic poet who happened to be Olaf's godson wrote that Olaf's death left the northern lands empty and dull. A fierce warrior and destroyer of heathen sanctuaries, he hastened the pace of the western Scandinavians' assimilation of the culture and faith of Christianity. He owed his accomplishments to his ability to obtain and keep many supporters. While some followed him out of admiration and friendship, others complied out of fear. In the more mundane tasks of establishing efficient and effective governmental administration, however, Olaf was neither interested nor successful.

—John M. Pederson

FURTHER READING

Foote, Peter G., and David M. Wilson. *The Viking Achievement: The Society and Culture of Early Medieval Scandinavia*. London: Sidgwick and Jackson, 1980. Describes the society and culture of medieval Scandinavia during the Viking Age in Norway, Denmark, Sweden, and Iceland. Gives an understanding of daily life before, during, and after Olaf's time.

Franklin, Simon, and Jonathan Shepard. *The Emergence of Rus, 750-1200*. New York: Longman, 1996. A comprehensive work on the Viking eastward expansion. Maps, extensive bibliography, list of genealogies, and excellent index.

Gibson, Charles. *The Two Olafs of Norway with a Cross on Their Shields*. London: Dobson, 1968. Following the basic stories of the sagas, this historical novel discusses the lives of Olaf I and Saint Olaf, and gives background discussion of earlier pagan Viking kings of Norway.

Howard, Ian. *Swein Forkbeard's Invasions and the Danish Conquest of England, 991-1017*. Rochester, N.Y.: Boydell and Brewer, 2003. Discusses propaganda and legend surrounding, and possible explanations for, the Danish invasions of England during Olaf's time.

Larsen, Karen. *A History of Norway.* 1948. Reprint. Princeton, N.J.: Princeton University Press, 1974. Provides a general history of Norway from the Vikings to modern times. Discusses Olaf and his contemporaries.

Roesdahl, Else. *The Vikings*. 2d ed. Translated by Susan M. Margeson and Kirsten Williams. New York: Penguin Books, 1998. Provides a solid, meticulous survey of Viking expansion in the east. Includes maps, illustrations, an extensive bibliography, and index.

Snorri Sturluson. *From the Sagas of the Norse Kings*. Oslo: Dreyer, 1967. A selected compilation of the essence of the great sagas of the Norse kings. Edited to reduce the use of old Norse names and terms. The most extensive selections pertain to Olaf I and Saint Olaf.

Wernik, Robert. *The Vikings*. Volume 7. *The Seafarers*. Alexandria, Va.: Time-Life Books, 1979. A still-popular account of the Viking era, with many pictures and illustrations. Contains several references to Olaf, including a discussion of the construction of the *Long Serpent*.

SEE ALSO: Canute the Great; Ethelred II, the Unready; Leif Eriksson; Margaret of Denmark, Norway, and Sweden; Saint Olaf; Rurik; Snorri Sturluson; Valdemar II; Vladimir I.

RELATED ARTICLES in *Great Events from History: The Middle Ages, 477-1453*: 850-950: Viking Era; 988: Baptism of Vladimir I; 11th-12th centuries: First European-Native American Contact; 1016: Canute Conquers England; June 17, 1397: Kalmar Union Is Formed.

SAINT OLGA

Princess of Rus (r. 945-964)

Olga was the first of the Rus ruling elite known to have converted to Christianity and among the first Rus saints of the Orthodox Church. She served as regent after her husband's death and was instrumental in setting up tributary and trading systems that helped unite the Kievan Rus state.

BORN: 890; Pskov, Rus (now in Russia)
DIED: 969; Kiev, Kievan Rus (now in Ukraine)
ALSO KNOWN AS: Helga
AREAS OF ACHIEVEMENT: Religion and theology, government and politics

EARLY LIFE

Little is known of the early life of Olga (OHL-gah). According to tradition, she was born in Pskov, a city in which the main bridge over the Velikaia River in Pskov is still named for her, and there is a cross on the nearby riverbank called Olga's Cross. Her name probably comes from the Scandinavian Helga, and there is some confusion in the historiography as to her origin. Some historians argue she was of Slavic stock and took a Scandinavian name when she married into the Varangian (Viking) clan that ruled Rus (now Belarus, Ukraine, and Russia) in 903, but others contend that she came from among the Scandinavians who settled in northwestern Rus in the ninth and tenth centuries.

Olga is first mentioned in "Povest vremennykh let" (compiled c. 1113; *The Russian Primary Chronicle*, 1930), the earliest Russian history, compiled in Kiev. The chronicle states that in 903, she came to Kiev to marry Igor (r. 912-945). According to the *Stepennaia Kniga* (a genealogical account of the ruling dynasty compiled by Metropolitan Makarii at the court of Russian czar Ivan the Terrible, r. 1547-1584, in the sixteenth century), Igor met Olga while he was fishing along the Velikaia River in Pskov. Seeing a fish on the other side of the river, he called over a boat to carry him to the other side. Once in the boat, Igor noticed that the boatman was, in fact, a maiden (Olga), who was "very young, beautiful, and brave" and he was smitten by her appearance as "his passions were kindled and he uttered shameless words to her."

LIFE'S WORK

Little is known of Olga's life, even during Igor's reign. The chronicles focus on Igor's attack on Constantinople in 945 and his commercial treaty with the Byzantines that ended the war. Provisions in that treaty allowed the Christians to ratify the treaty by swearing an oath at the Church of St. Elias in Kiev, indicating that a significant number of Christians inhabited Rus. The chronicle then tells how Igor died that same year while attempting to collect excessive tribute from the Derevlian tribe living northwest of Kiev along the Usa River, a tributary of the Pripet. According to the chronicle, his men were jealous of the retainers of Sveinald, the commander of the guard in Kiev, who were better dressed and armed. They asked Igor to go to the Derevlian land after the tribute was collected and gather additional tribute. After attacking the Derevlians, Igor sent his retinue back to Kiev, while he returned to raid the Derevlians yet again. Hearing of his return, the Derevlians ambushed and killed Igor. They then sent word to Olga that her husband was dead and that she should thus marry their prince, Mal.

Olga reappears in the chronicle with a cunning reply to the Derevlians, one concealing the terrible vengeance she intended for her husband's killers. When the twenty best men of the Derevlians sailed down the Dnieper River and arrived at Kiev, she told them she wished to honor them by showing her subservience, and hence told them that when her retainers arrived the next morning to fetch them, they were to reject all offers to walk or ride to her castle and instead demand that the Kievans carry them up the hill in their boat to Olga. When they arrived, the Derevlian envoys were dropped into a ditch dug in the courtyard and buried alive. She then sent word to the Derevlian land that if they wanted her to marry their prince, the princes themselves ought to come to Kiev. When they arrived, she told them to bathe before she would see them and then had them locked in the bathhouse and burned alive. She then sent a message to the Derevlians' main city, Iskorosten, and told them to make large quantities of honey and mead for a funeral feast she wished to hold at her husband's tomb. When the Derevlians were drunk, her retainers slaughtered them. Returning to Kiev, she raised an army that put the Derevlian army to flight and besieged the remaining Derevlians in Iskorosten. The siege lasted a year before Olga came up with a plan to take the city. She asked for three pigeons and three sparrows from each house and on receiving them, handed them out to her soldiers and told them to tie a piece of sulfur wrapped in a cloth to each bird and, as night fell, set them free. They flew back to their nests in the city and burned it to the ground. The surviving Derevlians were killed, enslaved, or forced to pay a heavy tribute.

This elaborate story of the sack of Iskorosten is similar to accounts of sieges carried out by Genghis Khan, Hardraada (Harold III), Robert Guiscard, and others. However, the accounts of the vengeance Olga wrought on the Derevlians are probably not historically accurate; rather, they are hagiographic devices representing her behavior after baptism, demonstrating how Christianity tempered her pagan barbarism.

Olga's cleverness is also shown in the story of her baptism, which *The Russian Primary Chronicle* dates to around 957. In that year, she is said to have traveled to Constantinople, where Emperor Constantine VII Porphyrogenitus (r. 913-959) found her "very fair of countenance and wise as well," and wanted to marry her. Learning of his wishes, she told him that she could not marry him because she was pagan, and that if he wanted her baptized, he would have to do it himself. The emperor, with the patriarch's assistance, baptized her, and the patriarch himself instructed her in the faith and praised her because she "loved the light, and quit the darkness." When Constantine again suggested marriage, she told him that it was no longer possible because she was now his goddaughter. The tale again shows her cleverness as well as her quick grasp of Christian precepts. It, too, is probably apocryphal because the emperor was, first of all, already married—his wife, Helen, apparently served as Olga's godmother, since Olga was christened Helen. However, the chronicle notes that she was named after "the ancient Empress, mother of Constantine the Great" (r. 306-337). In addition, Constantine Porphyrogenitus, one of the most educated and erudite of the Byzantine emperors, would certainly have been aware of the Church's prohibition on marriage between a godparent and godchild. Furthermore, Byzantine sources contradict the Russian chronicle; an account in Constantine's own *De ceremoniis aulae Byzantinae* gives the year of Olga's visit to Constantinople as 957 and notes that she was already a Christian when she arrived in the city.

Olga is also credited with establishing law, building towns and trading posts, establishing hunting preserves, and setting tribute in Rus. In addition to the heavy tribute she exacted from the Derevlians, she is said to have established laws in the Derevlian land and to have set up trading posts and hunting preserves there. She also traveled to Novgorod in northwestern Rus to collect tribute and to establish trading posts along the Msta River and collect tribute along the Luga River. The chronicle, com-

RULERS OF KIEVAN RUS, C. 862-1167

Reign	*Ruler*
c. 862-879	RURIK
879-912	Oleg
912-945	Igor
945-964	SAINT OLGA (regent)
964-972	Svyatoslav I
972-980	Yaropolk
980-1015	VLADIMIR I (with ANNA)
1015-1019	Sviatopolk I
1019-1054	Yaroslav
1054-1073	Iziaslav
1073-1076	Svyatoslav II
1076-1078	Iziaslav (restored)
1078-1093	Vsevolod
1093-1113	Sviatopolk II
1113-1125	Vladimir II Monomakh
1125-1132	Mstislav
1132-1139	Yaropolk
1139-1146	Vyacheslav
1146-1154	Iziaslav
1149-1157	Yuri I Dolgoruky
1154-1167	Rostislav

pleted in 1116, notes that "Her hunting grounds, boundary posts, towns and trading posts still exist throughout the whole region, while her sleigh stands in Pskov to this day." It also notes that her fowling preserves along the Dnieper and Desna Rivers and her village of Ol'zhich still existed into the twelfth century.

Olga also served as regent for her son, Svyatoslav, during his minority because he was only a child of two at the time of his father's death in 945. The chronicle's discussion of her collection of tribute and establishment of trading posts demonstrates her activities as regent. Presumably, she also governed the country during Svyatoslav's frequent absences from Kiev after he attained his majority in 964.

A quintessential warrior, Svyatoslav campaigned against the Jewish-led khanate of Khazaria on the lower reaches of the Volga and Don Rivers in 963 (the khanate was eventually destroyed by the Russians in 968), sacked Bulgar-on-the-Volga near what is now Kazan in 965, and invaded Danubian Bulgaria in 967. While he was campaigning in Bulgaria in 968, the Petchenegs, a tribe inhabiting the Pontic steppe, besieged Kiev and forced Svyatoslav to return and break the siege (in part to rescue his mother and sons). He then made it known that he wished to move his capital to Bulgaria because of the many goods that flowed through the country to Constantinople. His mother begged him not to go until after her death; she died three days later at the age of 79, having forbidden the Rus from holding a pagan funeral feast for her. Instead, a priest celebrated a Christian funeral. Svyatoslav then returned to Bulgaria but was defeated in a series of battles by the Byzantine emperor John I Tzimisces (r. 969-976), and was forced to sue for peace and to withdraw in July, 971. En route back to Kiev, Svyatoslav was ambushed and killed by the Petchenegs while fording the cataracts on the Dnieper River south of the city, having never accepted Christianity.

Although she was the first of the ruling elite to convert, she was not able to convince her own son, Svyatoslav, to become Christian: *The Russian Primary Chronicle* explains that, "when any man wished to be baptized, he was not hindered, only mocked." Thus Svyatoslav told his mother that he could not accept Christianity by himself because his retinue would laugh at him. In spite of this failure in her personal life, the chronicle notes that Olga "prayed night and day for her son and for the people."

SIGNIFICANCE

Olga is praised for laying the groundwork for the ultimate Christianization of Rus under her grandson, Vladimir (r. 980-1015). Western European sources indicate that in 959 Olga sent a request to the Holy Roman Emperor Otto I (r. 962-973) and asked for priests to help convert Rus. Two German monks were consecrated bishops for Rus: the first, consecrated in 960, died in 961 while still in Germany; the second, Adalbert of St. Maxim's Monastery in Trier, had gone to Kiev, but he was not accepted, so he returned to Germany in 962.

The description of Olga's death in *The Russian Primary Chronicle* is followed by a glorification of her for being among the first Rus converts to Christianity. She is called "the wisest of women" and is further praised because "she shone like the moon at night, and she was radiant among the infidels like a pearl in the mire." Whereas the chronicler recognized her sanctity, and Grand Prince Vladimir had her body re-interred in a church in the early eleventh century, she was probably not formally canonized until the fourteenth century, and is the third Rus saint to be venerated by the Orthodox Church (after her great grandsons, Boris and Gleb, martyred in 1015). Her feast day is July 11, and she is known as "equal to the apostles" because of her efforts to convert Rus.

—*Michael C. Paul*

FURTHER READING

Cross, Samuel Hazzard, and Olgerd P. Sherbowitz-Wetzor, ed. and trans. *The Russian Primary Chronicles, Laurentian Text.* Cambridge, Mass.: Medieval Academy of America, 1973. An English translation of the first Russian chronicle compiled in Kiev in the early twelfth century, traditionally by the monk and chronicler Nestor but probably by several authors.

Labunka, Miroslav. "Religious Centers and Their Missions to Kievan Rus: From Ol'ga to Volodimir." *Harvard Ukrainian Studies* 12/13 (1988-1989): 159-193. Discusses early efforts to Christianize Russia (Rus) up to the official baptism in 988.

Lenhoff, Gail. *Early Russian Hagiography: The Lives of Prince Fedor the Black.* Wiesbaden, Germany: Harrassowitz, 1997. A discussion of early Russian saintly veneration, with some discussion of the saintly cult surrounding Olga.

Vernadsky, George. *Kievan Russia.* New Haven, Conn.: Yale University Press, 1976. A very readable work on the earliest period of Russian history, from the ninth to the mid-thirteenth century.

SEE ALSO: Saint Alexander Nevsky; Anna, Princess of the Byzantine Empire; Otto I; Rurik; Vladimir I.

RELATED ARTICLES in *Great Events from History: The Middle Ages, 477-1453*: c. 850: Development of the Slavic Alphabet; 850-950: Viking Era; 864: Boris Converts to Christianity; 988: Baptism of Vladimir I; July 15, 1240: Alexander Nevsky Defends Novgorod from Swedish Invaders.

OMAR KHAYYÁM

Persian mathematician and poet

Khayyám was a leading medieval mathematician and the author of Persian quatrains made famous through the English poet Edward FitzGerald's 1859 study, The Rubáiyát of Omar Khayyám.

BORN: May 18, 1048?; Nishapur, Persia (now in Iran)
DIED: December 4, 1123?; Nishapur
AREAS OF ACHIEVEMENT: Mathematics, literature

EARLY LIFE

Omar Khayyám (OH-mahr ki-YAHM) was born in all likelihood in Nishapur, then a major city in the northeastern corner of Iran. At his birth, a new Turkish dynasty from Central Asia called the Seljuks was in the process of establishing control over the whole Iranian plateau. In 1055, when their leader, Toghrïl Beg, entered Baghdad, the Seljuks became masters of the Muslim caliphate and empire. Of Omar's family and education, few specifics are known. His given name indicates that he was a Sunni Muslim, for his namesake was the famous second caliph under whose reign (634-644) the dramatic Islamic expansion throughout the Middle East and beyond had begun. The name Khayyám means "tentmaker," possibly designating the occupation of his forebears. Omar received a good education, including study of Arabic, the Qur'ān, the various religious sciences, mathematics, astronomy, astrology, and literature.

At Toghrïl Beg's death, his nephew Alp Arslan succeeded to the Seljuk throne, in part through the machinations of Niẓām al-Mulk (1019-1092), also from Nishapur, who was to serve the Seljuks for more than thirty years as a vizier (government administrator). Alp Arslan (r. 1063 to 1072 or 1073) was succeeded by his son Malik-Shāh, who ruled to 1092.

During this period of rule, Khayyám studied first in Nishapur, then in Balkh, a major eastern city in what is now Afghanistan. From there, he went farther northeast to Samarqand (now in Uzbekistan). There, under the patronage of the chief local magistrate, he wrote a treatise in Arabic on algebra, classifying types of cubic equations and presenting systematic solutions to them. Recognized by historians of science and mathematics as a significant study, it is the most important of Khayyám's extant works (which comprise about ten short treatises). None of them, however, offers glimpses into Khayyám's personality, except to affirm his importance as a mathematician and astronomer whose published views were politically and religiously orthodox.

From Samarqand, Khayyám proceeded to Bukhara and was probably still in the royal court there when peace was concluded between the Qarakhanids and the Seljuks in 1073 or 1074. At this time, he probably entered the service of Malik-Shāh, who had become Seljuk sultan in 1072.

LIFE'S WORK

Two of Malik-Shāh's projects on which Khayyám presumably worked were the construction of an astronomy observatory in the Seljuk capital at Eşfahān in 1074 and the reform of the Persian solar calendar. Called *maleki* after the monarch, the new calendar proved more accurate than the Gregorian system centuries later.

Khayyám was one of Malik-Shāh's favorite courtiers, but after the latter's death Khayyám apparently never again held important positions under subsequent Seljuk rulers. In the mid-1090's, he made the *hajj* (pilgrimage) to Mecca and then returned to private life and teaching in Nishapur. It is known that Khayyám was in Balkh in 1112 or 1113. Several years later, he was in Marv, where a Seljuk ruler had summoned him to forecast the weather for a hunting expedition. After 1118, the year of Sanjar's accession, no record exists of any work by Khayyám. He died in his early eighties.

Some of the meager information available today regarding Khayyám was recorded by an acquaintance called Nizāmī ʿArūzī (fl. 1110-1161) in a book called *Chahár Maqála* (c. 1155; English translation, 1899). Nizāmī tells of visiting Khayyám's grave site in 1135 or 1136. Surprisingly, given Khayyám's reputation as a poet, the anecdotes regarding him appear in Nizāmī's "Third Discourse: On Astrologers," and no mention of him is made in the "Second Discourse: On Poets." In other words, though in the West Omar Khayyám is known for his poetry, no evidence in Persian suggests that he was a professional court poet or that he ever was more involved with poetry than through the occasional, perhaps extemporaneous, composition of quatrains (*rubai* or *robai*, plural *rubáiyát*). Because the quatrains first attributed to Khayyám are thematically of a piece and are distinct from panegyric, love, and Sufi quatrains, they can be usefully designated as "Khayyamic" even if authorship of many individual quatrains is impossible to determine definitively.

The following three quatrains are among the most typical and earliest to be attributed to the historical figure of Omar Khayyám:

> There was a drop of water, it merged with the sea.
> There was a speck of dirt, it merged with the earth.
> Your coming into the world is what?
> A fly appearing and disappearing.
>
> Drink wine: the universe means your demise,
> intends the death of your pure life and mine.
> Be seated on the grass and drink bright wine,
> for here will blooms bloom from your dust and mine.
>
> This ancient caravanserai called the world,
> home of the multicolored steed of night and day,
> is where a hundred Jamshids feasted and
> a hundred Bahrams ruled in splendor, and left.

In the centuries following Khayyám's death, increasing numbers of quatrains attributed to him appeared in manuscripts. Several of these manuscripts came to the attention of Edward FitzGerald (1809-1883), a serious student of Persian, who found them particularly appealing. His study of them inspired him to compose *The Rubáiyát of Omar Khayyám*, the first edition of which consisted of 75 quatrains and appeared in 1859. A second edition, expanded to 110 quatrains, appeared in 1868. The third edition in 1872 and the fourth in 1879 contained 101 quatrains, and the latter is the standard text. By FitzGerald's death, his work had begun to receive favorable critical attention, but its extraordinary fame, making it the single most popular poem of the Victorian Age, did not commence until later. A comparison of *The Rubáiyát of Omar Khayyám* with the Khayyamic Persian quatrains that FitzGerald had read and studied reveals that the themes, tone, and imagery of his poem are very close to those in the Persian quatrains, but that FitzGerald's poem is not a translation in any sense. It was the worldwide popularity of *The Rubáiyát of Omar Khayyám* that drew scholarly attention in Iran to Khayyám as a poet, so that he now is recognized as a leading figure in the Persian literary pantheon, along with Firdusi (between 932 and 941-between 1020 and 1025), Jalāl al-Dīn Rūmī (1207-1273), Saʿdi (1200-1291), and Hafiz (c. 1320-1389 or 1390).

SIGNIFICANCE

The Persian quatrains attributed to Omar Khayyám express the point of view of a rationalist intellectual who sees no reason to believe in a human soul or an afterlife (as in the first quatrain quoted above). The speaker would like to live a springtime garden life, but his continuing awareness of his own mortality and his inability to find answers in either science or religion lead him to a modified *carpe diem* stance: In this far-from-perfect world, in which human beings do not have a decent chance at happiness, one should nevertheless endeavor to make the best of things (as in the second quatrain quoted above). Some slight consolation is offered in appreciating the fact that human beings have faced this situation from the beginning of time (as in the third quatrain quoted above).

In the orthodox Seljuk age, Khayyamic quatrains constituted a bold, individualistic voicing of skepticism. Because literary Iranians throughout history have admired individualists and free spirits, Omar Khayyám has been mythologized into a figure quite different from what the known facts about his biography imply. For example, he was a hero and inspiration to Sadegh Hedayat (1903-1951), Iran's most acclaimed twentieth century author, in whose novel *Buf-i kur* (1936; *The Blind Owl*, 1957) are palpable Khayyamic echoes.

Regardless of the historical facts, the view of Hedayat and many others is that Khayyám bucked the tide of religious orthodoxy and dared to say what many secular-minded people believe: that religion, science, and government fail to give an adequate explanation of the mystery of the individual lives of human beings.

—*Michael Craig Hillmann*

FURTHER READING

Bloom, Harold, ed. *Edward FitzGerald's "The Rubáiyát of Omar Khayyám."* Philadelphia: Chelsea House, 2004. Presents an introduction to FitzGerald's infamous study and chapters that consider the "fin de siècle cult" of FitzGerald's work, comparisons with poets such as Tennyson, "forgetting" Fitzgerald's study, and more. Bibliography, index.

Boyle, J. A. "Omar Khayyám: Astronomer, Mathematician, and Poet." In *The Cambridge History of Iran*, edited by R. N. Frye. Vol. 4. Cambridge, England: Cambridge University Press, 1975. A succinct and careful review of the known facts about Khayyám's life, concluding with a brief review of the dispute over Khayyám's attitude toward Sufism, with which he presumably had little affinity.

Dashti, Ali. *In Search of Omar Khayyám*. Translated by L. P. Elwell-Sutton. London: Allen and Unwin, 1971. A very reliable study of Khayyám, which includes a review of his age and the known facts of his life, a collection of seventy-five quatrains that the author argues can be attributed with some confidence to Khayyám, and a sympathetic and sensitive identification of themes in the poems.

FitzGerald, Edward. *The Rubáiyát of Omar Khayyám*. 4th ed. London: Bernard Quaritch, 1879. This is the last edition the author saw to press and thus the official, final version of the poem.

Gray, Erik. "Forgetting FitzGerald's Rubáiyát." *Studies in English Literature, 1500-1900* 41, no. 4 (Autumn, 2001). Argues that the notion of "forgetting" or remembering "imperfectly" marks FitzGerald's poetic study as an important text in the context of Victorian poetry and in continuing literary work.

Heron-Allen, Edward. *Edward FitzGerald's "Rubáiyát of Omar Khayyám" with Their Original Persian Sources*. Boston: L. C. Page, 1899. A study of FitzGerald's stanzas paralleled with the Persian texts of possible sources, demonstrating that, although FitzGerald was inspired by Khayyamic and other Persian quatrains, *The Rubáiyát of Omar Khayyám* is an original English poem and not a translation.

Hillmann, Michael C. "Perennial Iranian Skepticism." In *Iranian Culture: A Persianist View*. Lanham, Md.: University Press of America, 1988. A treatment of the significance to Iranian culture today of the ideas expressed in Khayyamic quatrains, which are compared to FitzGerald's poem. Comprehensive bibliography.

Kennedy, E. S. "The Exact Sciences in Iran Under the Saljuqs and Mongols." In *The Cambridge History of Iran*, edited by J. A. Boyle. Vol. 5. Cambridge, England: Cambridge University Press, 1968. Surveys the foundations of mathematics, algebra, trigonometry, planetary theory, observational astronomy, mathematical geography, specific gravity determination, and rainbow theory, with a discussion of Khayyám's contribution to polynomial equations and his possible contribution to observational astronomy.

Khayyám, Omar. *The Algebra of Omar Khayyám*. Translated by Daoud S. Kasir. 1931. Reprint. New York: AMS Press, 1972. A great history of mathematics and Khayyám's most important extant work, prefaced with a discussion of the state of algebra before his time and Khayyám's methods and significance. Bibliography.

Nasr, Seyyed Hossein. *The Islamic Intellectual Tradition in Persia*. Edited by Mehdi Amin Razavi. Richmond, Surrey, England: Curzon Press, 1996. Presents a chapter exploring Omar as a philosopher, poet, and scientist. Bibliography, index.

Ozdural, Alpay. "A Mathematical Sonata for Architecture: Omar Khayyám and the Friday Mosque of Isfahan." *Technology and Culture* 39, no. 4 (October, 1998). Explores the possibility that Omar, with his theories on ornamental geometry and the triangle, was the designer of the North Dome Chamber (or Great Mosque), built in 1088-1089, in Eşfahān, Iran. Includes technical language and geometrical drawings.

Rashed, Rushdei, and Bijan Vahabzadeh. *Omar Khayyám: The Mathematician*. New York: Bibliotheca Persica Press, 2000. An exploration of Omar's work in mathematics. Part of the Persian Heritage series. Bibliography, index.

SEE ALSO: Abul Wefa; Alhazen; Alp Arslan; Roger Bacon; al-Battānī; al-Bīrūnī; Firdusi; Hafiz; al-Jāḥiẓ; al-Khwārizmī; Jalāl al-Dīn Rūmī; Saʿdi.

RELATED ARTICLES in *Great Events from History: The Middle Ages, 477-1453*: 595-665: Invention of Decimals and Negative Numbers; 1010: Firdusi Composes the *Shahnamah*; 1040-1055: Expansion of the Seljuk Turks; 1077: Seljuk Dynasty Is Founded; c. 1100: Arabic Numerals Are Introduced into Europe.

ANDREA ORCAGNA
Italian artist and architect

In paintings and in sculptural and architectural projects combining religious intensity with naturalism, Orcagna extended the expressive range of Italian art in the mid-fourteenth century.

BORN: c. 1308; Florence (now in Italy)
DIED: c. 1368; Florence
ALSO KNOWN AS: Andrea di Cione (given name)
AREA OF ACHIEVEMENT: Art

EARLY LIFE

Little is known of the early life of Andrea Orcagna (ahn-DRAY-uh ohr-KAHN-yah); even the date of his birth is conjectural. In *Le vite de' più eccellenti architetti, pittori, et scultori italiani* (1549-1550; *Lives of the Most Eminent Painters, Sculptors, and Architects*, 1850-1907), Giorgio Vasari states that Orcagna lived to the age of sixty. This fact, together with the reasonable assumption that he died in 1368, is the only basis for claiming 1308 as the year of his birth.

The name "Orcagna" is derived from "Arcagnuolo"; the artist's actual name was Andrea di Cione, and it is known that his three brothers were also artists: Nardo, probably older than Andrea, and two younger brothers, Matteo and Jacopo. While still a child, according to Vasari, Orcagna began to study sculpture under Andrea Pisano and only after some years took up drawing and painting. Orcagna had achieved some recognition as a painter by 1346, but it was not until 1352 that he became a member of the Florentine stonemason's guild responsible for works of sculpture; thus Vasari's claim may be incorrect. The uncertainty is not a matter of very great importance, however, because Orcagna's career, like those of many artists of his time, was based on a variety of artistic endeavors, including the practice of architecture as well as of painting and sculpture.

Orcagna was born in an era when the practice of the visual arts was still based more on traditions of craftsmanship than on the exploration of individual artists. It was seldom thought necessary by contemporary writers to research and record the details of the lives of even those artists who emerged from the background of the workshops. Few such accounts survive, and much biographical detail is circumstantial. In Orcagna's case, for example, it is known that he was married only from a 1371 reference to his widow; the same document serves as the only dated evidence of his death.

LIFE'S WORK

Orcagna's career is documented only between 1343 and 1368. By 1347, he was associated with his brother Nardo, sharing a workshop with him and probably participating in his commissions for paintings. Orcagna's reputation grew rapidly in the early 1350's, leading to major commissions in Florence, Orvieto, and Siena. In 1354 he was commissioned by the wealthy Strozzi family to paint an altarpiece for the family chapel in the church of Santa Maria Novella in Florence. The work, which was completed in 1357, is *Christ Conferring Authority on Saints Peter and Thomas Aquinas*. It is a panel painting executed in tempera, a medium that lends itself to precise shapes, deliberate design, and strong colors. In these characteristics, it is a somewhat conservative departure from the successful norms established by Orcagna's great predecessor, Giotto, whom he knew during the latter part of Giotto's life. Giotto's life's work was almost wholly concerned with painting in the fresco medium, which is more successfully employed to render objects as volumes rather than as shapes and which gives a greater sense of atmosphere as well as harmony of color. These differences in technique relate to differences in artistic objective. Giotto's aim was to humanize the religious content of Christianity, particularly the legend of Saint Francis, in paintings possessing a sense of great physical reality. Orcagna's purpose, more than a generation later, was to reemphasize the institutional authority of the Church by rendering religious topics in a majestically austere style. In the Strozzi altarpiece, the resurgent Dominican order is, in effect, given a vote of confidence over the less-orthodox Franciscan order—the painting depicts Christ enthroned, bestowing a book on Saint Thomas Aquinas (the second patron of the order after Saint Dominic) while giving the keys of Paradise to Saint Peter, the symbol of the Church of Rome.

For the years 1355, 1356, and 1357, the records of the Florentine church Or San Michele show Orcagna as the capomaestro, or superintendent, of work on a kind of chapel within the arcade of an adjacent grain market. Known as the Tabernacle, it is an ornate structure decorated with a wealth of carving, enclosing a painting of an enthroned Madonna and Child by Orcagna's near-contemporary, Bernardo Daddi. Planning and execution of the Tabernacle called on Orcagna's varied skills in architecture, sculpture, and even goldsmithing. One authority has called it delightful and sumptuous; another compares its decoration to spun sugar and questions Orcagna's reputation as an architect, which rests solely on this one surviving, documented example. It is clear, in any case, that Orcagna attempted to blend elements from disparate architectural and sculptural traditions, probably as much in response to demands of his patrons as to his own artistic objectives.

In 1357, Orcagna was employed in the work on the cathedral of Florence, Santa Maria del Fiore; in 1358, he went to Orvieto, where he served as capomaestro until 1362. From 1360 to 1362 his work on the decoration of the Orvieto façade, consisting of a rose window and mosaics, was done in collaboration with his brother Matteo, who remained in Orvieto while Andrea returned to Florence to carry on other work. The last recorded work by Orcagna, finished in June, 1368, was a Madonna for Or San Michele, now lost. Two months later, he fell ill and presumably died shortly thereafter; a commission for a triptych on the subject of Saint Matthew was turned over to his brother Jacopo for completion.

SIGNIFICANCE

Orcagna was not the leading Italian artist of the fourteenth century, an honor that unquestionably belongs to Giotto. Also held in precedence to Orcagna are Duccio di Buoninsegna, Simone Martini, the brothers Pietro and Ambrogio Lorenzetti, and others. In the realm of Florentine painting, however, possibly only Maso di Banco could be judged to rank with Orcagna, and Maso's painting lies largely within Giotto's sphere of influence. Orcagna inherited the moral seriousness of Giotto and Maso but found it necessary to depart from the sense of equilibrium that characterizes the art of Giotto and his immediate followers. Orcagna's dramatic feeling for active religious faith is different from the simplicity and humanism of Giotto and seems to reflect a sense of spiritual discipline that corresponds to the contemporary preaching of the Dominicans.

There can be little doubt that the nature of the times in which he lived influenced Orcagna's art. In addition to political uncertainty during the early 1340's, there were significant Florentine bankruptcies in 1343 and 1345, followed by a famine in 1346 in Tuscany, the region that includes Florence and Siena. Then, in 1348, a calamitous plague struck in June. The Black Death, as it was called, was thought by many to be a punishment from God; the Dominicans capitalized on this fear by claiming that the order knew the secret of protecting the city from a recurrence of the plague. Much of the populace reacted to the material stresses of the times with increased devotion, but some responded with religious indifference; a tension between the two forms of reaction lent increased importance to the Church, its hierarchy and its rituals, and to the art that supported them. In response to the needs of the Church as well as to his own spiritual inclinations, Orcagna's art assumed a powerful, dedicated character that distinguishes it from the work of less receptive and adventurous artists.

To some degree, one must speculate on the matter of Orcagna's individual achievement in relation to the work of others who might have collaborated with him, including his brothers Nardo and Jacopo; Nardo, in particular, was an artist of great sensitivity. As in the case of many artists of the Gothic period and before, it is best to temper the concept of individual genius with an appreciation of the nature of collective endeavor and of shared artistic traits. Yet even accounting for these factors, Orcagna stands out as a strong figure in the midst of many remarkable artists emerging from the workshops of early and mid-fourteenth century Italy.

—*Clyde S. McConnell*

FURTHER READING

Hartt, Frederick, and David G. Wilkins. *History of Italian Renaissance Art: Painting, Sculpture, Architecture*. 5th ed. New York: H. N. Abrams, 2003. This large volume, the standard survey of this period of the history of art, is both readable and profusely illustrated and offers an authoritative bibliography.

Meiss, Millard. *Painting in Florence and Siena After the Black Death: The Arts, Religion, and Society in the Mid-Fourteenth Century*. 1964. Reprint. Princeton, N. J.: Princeton University Press, 1978. This classic of art scholarship, detailed yet readable, places Orcagna, along with several other artists, in the social and historical context of mid-fourteenth century Italy. The book's small black-and-white illustrations, though essential to understanding the author's arguments, are unlikely to communicate the full power of the works discussed.

Paoletti, John T., and Gary M. Radke. *Art in Renaissance Italy*. 2d ed. Upper Saddle River, N.J.: Harry N. Abrams, 2002. An examination of art in Italy during the Renaissance, when Orcagna was active. Bibliography and index.

Understanding Art: A Reference Guide to Painting, Sculpture, and Architecture in the Romanesque, Gothic, Renaissance, and Baroque Periods. 2 vols. Armonk, N.Y.: Sharpe Reference, 2000. A reference work on art that sheds light on Orcagna's art as well as that of his predecessors, contemporaries, and later artists. Illustrations, bibliography, and index.

Vasari, Giorgio. *Vasari's Lives of the Artists: Biographies of the Most Eminent Architects, Painters, and Sculptors of Italy*. Reprint. New York: Alfred A. Knopf, 1996. Vasari, a sixteenth century painter, wrote his book "not to acquire praise as a writer but to revive the memory of those who adorned these professions." First published in 1550, the work is more colorful than it is useful, since scholarship has overtaken virtually all of Vasari's information; nevertheless, each page of this classic document enlivens its subject as no other source does.

SEE ALSO: Fra Angelico; Cimabue; Duccio di Buoninsegna; Saint Francis of Assisi; Lorenzo Ghiberti; Giotto; Pietro Lorenzetti and Ambrogio Lorenzetti; Simone Martini; Masaccio; Andrea Pisano; Thomas Aquinas.

RELATED ARTICLES in *Great Events from History: The Middle Ages, 477-1453*: 1305-1417: Avignon Papacy and the Great Schism; c. 1320: Origins of the Bubonic Plague; 1347-1352: Invasion of the Black Death in Europe; c. 1410-1440: Florentine School of Art Emerges.

OSMAN I

Turkish military leader

Under Osman's patient and steady leadership, the influence and territorial extent of his principality expanded until it arose as a regional power, which, as the Ottoman Empire, ultimately became one of the great powers of the early modern world.

BORN: c. 1258; Söğüt, Ottoman Empire (now in Turkey)

DIED: 1326; Söğüt

ALSO KNOWN AS: Osman Ghāzī

AREAS OF ACHIEVEMENT: Government and politics, warfare and conquest, military

EARLY LIFE

When Osman (ahs-MAHN), the son of Ertuğrul, was born in northwestern Anatolia at Söğüt, much of the surrounding area was held by Turkish tribes that had moved into that region in the wake of widespread political upheaval. The Seljuk sultanate, which had displaced Byzantine power, increasingly began to weaken under Mongol pressure from the east, and separate march lords arose in border areas. Ertuğrul, as a leading noble, was granted lands about 90 miles (150 kilometers) southeast of Constantinople in return for his service as a commander on behalf of the Seljuk sultan. Some Turkish materials maintain that Ertuğrul and his associates were from the Kayı, one of the Oğuz tribes that had earlier played a major role in the settlement of Asia Minor. Relatively little is known specifically about Osman's youth. One explanation of his given name has cited an Arabic form, ʿUthmān, which would seem to signify an early acquaintance with Islam; another version has suggested that it was taken from the Turkish name Ataman. Osman succeeded his father in 1281 or 1288; some have speculated that as an octogenarian, Ertuğrul yielded power before his death.

Various quaint tales have been recounted about Osman's early life. It is known that for advice he turned to Edebali, who was respected as a wise and venerable old man. There probably is as much legend as fact to the account that Osman had a dream showing great rivers of the world outlined against a tree, which Edebali interpreted as a sign that his achievements would bring great and lasting renown on his house. Other claims that Osman's fame as the founder of a mighty dynasty was foretold in portents from his own time may well have been the concoctions of later annalists. As the sheikh of a dervish order, Edebali may have exercised some spiritual influence on Osman; some accounts maintain that he urged the Qur'ān on Osman as a condition of marrying his daughter. Osman had two wives, and among the nine children born to his household were Alāeddin, who became an important administrator, and Orhan, his eventual successor.

Depiction of Osman proclaiming the Muslim faith. (F. R. Niglutsch)

Life's Work

After he assumed power, Osman began a series of military campaigns that gradually cleared a path for the growth of his state. In the process, Turkish as well as Greek opponents had to be confronted. His first conquest of note was achieved in 1288, when he drove the neighboring Germiyan tribe from Karacahisar, to the south of his birthplace. At about that time he also wrested İnegöl, to the west, from Greek lords. Osman's armies captured outposts such as Bilecik and Körprühisar, which lay northwest of Söğüt in the direction of Nicaea (İznik). When Turkmen chieftains to the north relented in their raids on Byzantine positions, Osman's troops began to operate in that region as well. Some sources suggest that Osman conspired to murder his uncle (or cousin) Dündar, whom he may have regarded as a potential rival within his own ranks. Osman began to assert personal sovereignty by having his name read in the *hutbe*, or religious invocation, which customarily was delivered during Friday services. By 1299, Osman was sufficiently powerful to be able to terminate payments to Seljuk rulers or their Mongol suzerains. It seems more likely, however, that some form of tribute was disbursed during the early fourteenth century until this practice was discontinued after his death.

By this time, Osman's warriors were in a position to disrupt access along routes leading from Constantinople to inland cities; further raids were also mounted across the frontier. A decisive engagement came about when a Byzantine force, determined to check Turkish incursions, embarked on an expedition that marked the first effort on the part of the central government to meet the challenge of Ottoman power. At Bapheus (Koyunhisar), near Nicomedia (İzmit), on July 27, 1302, an army of about two thousand men met a Turkish force later estimated at about five thousand troops. Osman's men, who excelled in cavalry tactics, carried out a series of charges that broke through the lines of their heavily armored adversaries. They were prevented from turning this action into a rout only by the stalwart defense of Slavic mercenaries in the Byzantines' rear guard. Thereafter, Osman was left in a position to consolidate his gains. Although some action was necessary to repel Tatar irruptions in lands to the south, major objectives involved the reduction of Byzantine resistance in areas where Ottoman forces could dominate the countryside. By 1308, several fortresses were captured that brought Osman's armies within range of Prousa (Bursa), northwest of Mount Olympus, or Uludağ. Moreover, Ottoman units had already reached the Black Sea and by this time also ranged as far as the Sea of Marmara. An arc was thus drawn about that corner of Anatolia to hem in Byzantine holdings on their southern and eastern frontiers. Subsequently, Osman remained steadfast in his determination to subdue his opponents by landward expansion leading to the encirclement of local strongholds.

The nature of government under Osman has been represented in several ways, and it may well have been that there were some variations in the practices that he employed. Osman himself has been described as having swarthy features, with dark hair and a dark beard; he had long arms and was well built. He was reputed to have been a good horseman. When centuries later his portrait was made to show him as the first of his dynasty, he was depicted seated on his throne, a regal figure with a solemn and pensive demeanor. Throughout his rule, Osman was known as bey (provincial governor); the title of sultan came into use only during the late fourteenth century. While for a time he had resided in Karacahisar, after about twelve years Osman made Yenişehir his capital, possibly because of its location on a line south of Nicaea and east of Prousa. The extent to which Islamic conceptions of war and administration were important for early Ottoman institutions has been disputed. Different approaches indeed may have been used as Osman and his staff increasingly had to deal with diverse peoples in their vicinity. While in time later historians, both Ottoman and Western, often contended that the new state owed its expansion to the practice of *ghāza*, or war for the faith, divisions along religious lines may not have been so sharply drawn as was the case during subsequent periods of struggle. The nucleus of Osman's army was composed of Turkish warriors who had settled in western Anatolia with their leaders.

Disorders and internecine conflict in other parts of Asia Minor probably led to the flight of Turkmen bands, which tended increasingly to settle on the frontier; some of them may have joined Osman's forces. When news of Osman's feats was received in other Muslim lands, men from adjoining areas also enrolled themselves in his armies. The distinction between religious warfare and raids into outlying Byzantine lands, however, may not have been very great, and for that matter villagers involved in local turmoil may have elected to support the Ottomans. Fiscal exactions on the part of Greek authorities quite possibly hastened this process. Some townspeople may also have valued the relative security provided by Ottoman rule. There is also evidence that in some cases lands were obtained by purchase or through marriages involving the families of local seigneurs. Some materials refer to the service of Greek Orthodox Christians with Osman's army. While many of them apparently embraced their commander's Muslim faith, forced conversion was not carried out as a matter of policy among conquered peoples at large. A certain number of renegades rose to important positions in the service of the Ottoman state. One of them, who became known as Köse Mihal, was from a prominent Greek family. After he was captured during an early raid, he became one of Osman's advisers on military matters. Moreover, while political authority was exercised on a local level through Osman's family, particularly his sons, who governed particular cities and towns, religious preferences were not always decisive on more basic concerns. It is known that at times Osman intervened to prevent Christians from being treated unfairly by Muslim merchants, and he also opposed the wholesale depredation of villages in Bithynia.

Apart from the outcome of military undertakings, not much is known about the last years of Osman's rule. In 1317, his son Orhan captured Atranos (Orhaneli), southwest of Mount Olympus. The Ottomans increasingly began to mobilize large armies to provide a show of strength that might daunt beleaguered Byzantine garrisons. A report from about 1330 maintained that the Ottomans could put about forty thousand men into the field. Although this estimate may have been exaggerated, it has been taken as indicative of the growing strength of Ottoman forces during that period. In 1321, the maritime city of Mudanya, 45 miles (70 kilometers) from Constantinople, was taken, and

THE OTTOMAN SULTANS THROUGH THE BYZANTINE CONQUEST, C. 1281-1453

Reign	*Sultan*
1281/88-1326	OSMAN (ʿOsmān) I
1326-1362	Orhan I
1362-1389	Murad I
1389-1402	Bayezid I
1402-1421	Mehmed I
1421-1444	Murad II
1444-1446	MEHMED II
1446-1451	Murad II (second rule)
1451-1481	MEHMED II (second rule)
1453	Fall of Constantinople, end of the Byzantine Empire

thus a logistical connection that was vital for the defense of Prousa was severed. While Ottoman armies also encircled Nicaea, preparing for its eventual capture under Orhan in 1331, want and deprivation gradually began to weaken the Byzantine defenders further south. The capture of Prousa, which as Bursa in its turn became the capital of the Ottoman state, was accomplished finally with minimum fighting. When it yielded, on April 6, 1326, Osman evidently had been inactive for some time; it is recorded that he received word from Orhan of the city's fall while he was on his deathbed. The source of his final illness has been described as an infirmity of the limbs. He had returned to Söğüt, and when he died later that year, he left his son an enlarged and strategically situated state with a growing military tradition that had already proved its capacity to endure struggle and conflict.

SIGNIFICANCE

During the generations that followed, Ottoman power was established in other parts of Anatolia, and by the late fourteenth century significant conquests had been achieved in the Balkan peninsula as well. After certain setbacks, notably in the wake of Tamerlane's incursions into Asia Minor, sultans of the fifteenth century proceeded to subdue other lands in Europe and Asia.

In 1453, Constantinople fell to the Ottomans, while elsewhere further expansion was carried out. Once the Ottoman Empire had become a great power, with its own distinctive ethos and means of government, historians began to trace the origins of the Ottoman state and in many instances attempted to find lofty antecedents and edifying principles in the acts of past rulers. In an early form, this tendency appeared in writers such as the poet-historian Ahmedi (1334?-1413). Other chronicles, such as those of Aşıkpaşazâde (1400-after 1484) and Neşri (d. c. 1520), which also formed the basis for later historical studies, depicted religious themes and doctrines of holy war in ways meant to stress the elements of continuity they contended had existed throughout Ottoman history.

Moreover, genealogical claims were added whereby the house of Osman was asserted to have descended from Noah and other illustrious figures. Occasionally, other legends were incorporated into historical writings. As a result, quite apart from obvious overstatements and embellishments, many of the ideals and principles of the ascendant Ottoman state were also attributed to Osman and his immediate successors. Traditions of this sort came to be regarded as part of Osman's heritage, and the epithet *gazi* often accompanied his name.

Even during the waning years of the Ottoman Empire, such conceptions were widely accepted. During the first part of the twentieth century, some modifications were introduced, but the importance of religious warfare for the early Ottoman state was propounded in studies that otherwise showed more critical assessments of the sources and evidence that were available. Other scholars, however, have pointed to latitudinarian aspects of politics in frontier areas. Economic and demographic issues, in a broader context, have also been considered significant.

There is still much that remains murky about Osman's life and work, and many details will perhaps remain beyond the realm of historical knowledge. The importance of his accomplishments, however, remains evident: By the unswerving and methodical pursuit of his objectives, Osman elevated his state to a position of consequence alongside other principalities, and his methods of rule facilitated the transition from Byzantine to Ottoman administration in a vital portion of Asia Minor. Although the success of his endeavors also depended on the lassitude of Byzantine government, and certainly he and his successors benefited from the fragmentation of political authority that affected much of the area, the combination of resolute persistence in military efforts and pragmatic administration of internal concerns was essential in Osman's role as the founder of the state that came to bear his name.

—*John R. Broadus*

FURTHER READING

Acun, Fatma. "A Portrait of the Ottoman Cities." *Muslim World* 92, nos. 3-4 (Fall, 2002). A comprehensive and detailed historical survey of the cities of the Ottoman Empire, beginning in medieval times. Argues that the Ottomans administered their empire in a flexible manner, incorporating local customs in government and in architecture. Discusses Turkish settlement in Anatolia, Osman's birthplace, starting in the eleventh century.

Cahen, Claude. *Pre-Ottoman Turkey: A General Survey of the Material and Spiritual Culture and History, c. 1071-1330.* Translated by J. Jones-Williams. New York: Taplinger, 1968. As an essential contribution to modern understanding of early Turkish states in Anatolia, this study considers political developments alongside an analysis of the social problems that affected the formation of the Seljuk sultanate and later principalities. The author, a noted French specialist, does not deal particularly with matters of personality or biography; rather, his work is useful in pointing to the broader historical forces that led to the eventual emergence of the Ottoman Empire.

Gibbons, Herbert Adams. *The Foundation of the Ottoman Empire: A History of the Osmanlis up to the Death of Bayezid I (1300-1403)*. New York: Century, 1916. This work is one of the more useful older studies of Ottoman history. Subsequent research has modified some conclusions, supplied details where formerly these were lacking, and turned away from the author's conceptions about early national and dynastic alignments. Nevertheless, as a narrative account this effort still warrants consideration. Osman's life and rule are discussed in the first chapter. Extensive bibliography.

Goodwin, Jason. *Lords of the Horizons: A History of the Ottoman Empire*. New York: Picador, 2003. A history of the Ottoman Turks beginning in 1288. Looks at the empire's artistic achievements, the first use of the cannon in the seizure of Constantinople, religious tolerance and the empire's longevity, harems, and more. Illustrations, maps, bibliography, index.

Inalcik, Halil. *The Ottoman Empire: The Classical Age, 1300-1600*. Translated by Norman Itzkowitz and Colin Imber. London: Phoenix Press, 2000. An important survey by a prominent modern scholar, this work is useful largely for its treatment of Ottoman institutions as they developed during the heyday of the empire. Although historical events are discussed in a cursory fashion, economic relations and the structure of government are considered in specific terms where fundamental patterns of administration are concerned. Bibliography, index.

_______. "The Question of the Emergence of the Ottoman State." *International Journal of Turkish Studies* 2 (1981): 71-79. A useful and important, though brief, restatement of historical theories regarding the Ottomans' position with respect to neighboring states; some emphasis is placed on population movements and military factors where they affected political developments.

Jennings, Ronald C. "Some Thoughts on the Gazi-Thesis." *Wiener Zeitschrift für die Kunde des Morgenlandes* 76 (1986): 151-161. This article considers problems with the theory of holy war as a factor promoting early Ottoman conquests. The author comments favorably on arguments that evidence from later times has been taken too readily as applicable also to the period of Osman and his immediate successors.

Lindner, Rudi Paul. *Nomads and Ottomans in Medieval Anatolia*. Bloomington: Research for Inner Asian Studies, Indiana University, 1983. A number of primary materials and anthropological studies have been used in this important work of scholarship and interpretation. In considering ways in which previous explanations for the Ottoman ascendancy have been inadequate, the author contends that often enough Muslim and Christian peoples worked together, and thus warfare for the faith was not always an inseparable part of Ottoman ideology.

Runciman, Steven. *The Fall of Constantinople, 1453*. New York: Cambridge University Press, 1990. This study by a distinguished Byzantinist, originally published in 1965, is probably the standard work in English on the famous siege. Attention to scholarly detail does not impede the retelling of enthralling and tragic episodes from the last days of the city's resistance to the Ottomans. Illustrations, maps, bibliography, index.

Wittek, Paul. *The Rise of the Ottoman Empire*. 1938. Reprint. New York: B. Franklin, 1971. This brief study, which concisely summarizes many of the conclusions reached by an influential scholar, is significant as an exposition of the thesis that religious warfare supplied major impetus in the advance of Turkish states on the frontiers of the Byzantine Empire. Bibliography.

SEE ALSO: Alp Arslan; Maḥmūd of Ghazna; Mehmed II; Tamerlane.

RELATED ARTICLES in *Great Events from History: The Middle Ages, 477-1453*: 1040-1055: Expansion of the Seljuk Turks; August 26, 1071: Battle of Manzikert; 1077: Seljuk Dynasty Is Founded; 1189-1192: Third Crusade; 1204: Knights of the Fourth Crusade Capture Constantinople; 1273: Sufi Order of Mawlawīyah Is Established; May 29, 1453: Fall of Constantinople.

OTTO I

King of Germany (r. 936-973) and Holy Roman Emperor (r. 962-973)

Otto's decisive victory over the Magyars shaped the fate of Europe. His coronation as emperor determined the course of German policy for centuries to come. Internally, he overcame tribalism by putting central administration in the unifying hands of the Church.

BORN: November 23, 912; Saxony (now in Germany)
DIED: May 7, 973; Memleben, Thuringia (now in Germany)
ALSO KNOWN AS: Otto the Great
AREA OF ACHIEVEMENT: Government and politics

EARLY LIFE

In 912, when Otto (AH-toh) was born the first son of Matilda, second but first legitimate wife of his father, Henry, the latter was still duke of Saxony, and the idea of a powerful central kingship in Germany was a rather remote one. Real power was held by the dukes of the various tribes, and the title king of Germany did not wield much more than ceremonial influence. It would be up to Otto to seek a change. When his father was elected king in 919 after the death of Conrad I, the last Franconian king from the line of Charlemagne, Henry I relied on his might as duke of Saxony and did not require more than ceremonial homage to his royal position from his largely independent ducal colleagues.

Nevertheless, Henry I seemed to have planned more for his successor. Against the wishes of his wife, who favored Otto's younger son Henry, who had been born when his father was already king, Henry I promoted Otto as heir apparent and succeeded in winning for him the hand of an English princess. In 930, Otto married Edith, whose dowry, the town of Magdeburg, would play an important role in Otto's later politics.

Henry I had prepared the German nobility to elect Otto I at a council in Erfurt on his death. Accordingly, a splendid coronation ceremony took place at the chapel of Aachen on August 7, 936. There, the nobles swore Otto an oath of fealty, and three archbishops anointed the king and his wife and crowned Otto on the marble chair that had belonged to Charlemagne. A contemporary illustration of the banquet that followed shows the king with his crown; he has long blond hair, a beard, and an open, intelligent face, and he is sitting elevated at a table where the four dukes of the kingdom are waiting on him, each holding an instrument signifying his ceremonial office of chamberlain, steward, cupbearer, and marshal. It is worth noting that Otto wears ceremonial Franconian clothes, not Saxonian clothes; thus, the illustration shows Otto's awareness of a new status in an office that had its own regal tradition.

LIFE'S WORK

The splendor of the coronation and the demonstration of unity and loyalty of dukes and nobles soon wore off and left Otto with a series of rebellions at home and increasing danger at the boundaries of his kingdom. In the south, the Magyars were barely held at bay, and in the east the Slavs were pressing against the eastern marches; there, Otto relied on the military prowess of his margraves Herman Billung and Count Gero. Because of Otto's grants of land to Count Gero, his own half brother Thankmar, a bastard son of Henry I from his first, annulled marriage, felt slighted and joined Duke Eberhard of Franconia in an open rebellion against the king. Thus, hardly two years after his accession, Otto faced the first challenge to exercise the rights of his royal position.

Initial combat brought victory for Otto when Thankmar fell and Eberhard submitted to the king. In 939, however, his younger brother Henry, whom Otto had installed in Bavaria and who had been captured by the rebels, switched to the side of his captors. Suddenly, the rebellion gathered momentum. Eberhard turned coat again, the French king supported the insurgents, and Giselbert of Lotharingia and even the archbishop of Mainz closed ranks against Otto. In this precarious position, Otto was saved by a clever attack on the disjointed rebels. A strike by two of his warlords brought the death of Eberhard and the drowning of Giselbert in the Rhine River. Thereafter, the rebellion faltered, and Otto forgave his brother, only to have Henry try to assassinate him in 941. Again, Otto showed largesse when his brother approached him, penitent, on Christmas Day in the cathedral in Frankfurt. From that point onward, Henry proved loyal and valuable, and he obtained the duchy of Bavaria in 947.

After these early struggles to bring the quarrelsome and independent-minded German nobles in line, Otto tried to achieve control of the duchies through a series of dynastic marriages of his Saxon princes and princesses. To counteract the accumulation of hereditary privileges by the nobles, the king relied on ecclesiastical administrators and officers, who could have no legal offspring, to govern his royal holdings.

Yet Otto used the Church for more than interior administration. In the east, his biggest project was the establishment of the archbishopric of Magdeburg, which would serve as a base from which the land between the Rivers Elbe and Oder could be pacified. This territory had long been dominated by the Slavs, whose belligerence presented a constant danger to the Saxonian lands. (Against the resistance of the archbishop of Mainz, who feared a diminution of his own power, Otto finally succeeded in creating the new archdiocese in 968.)

In 951, when his authority had grown so much that even the prince of Bohemia paid tribute to him, Otto had begun to turn his attention to Italy. An occasion to march southward arose with the reception of a distress call from Princess Adelaide of Burgundy, whom Berengar of Ivrea had imprisoned for her refusal to marry his son. Otto, a widower since 946, chased away Berengar, crowned himself king of the Lombards, and married Adelaide in Padua. Many contemporaries believed that they would soon see the imperial crown on Otto's head, and indeed, in 952, Otto was recognized as king of Italy.

Rome, however, did not welcome Otto, and at home his son Liudolf rebelled, fearing the influence and potential offspring of his new stepmother. Immediately, Otto marched north to discover a huge rebellion, which humiliated him. His battles with the insurgents were indecisive at best, but a new attack by the Magyars brought public opinion against the rebels. Under public pressure from the nobles, the uprising faltered, and Liudolf had to submit to his father early in 955.

Finally able to collect and command a great army, Otto attacked the invaders at their camp by the city of Augsburg. The ensuing Battle of the Lechfeld (955) was a complete victory for the Germans. Never again would the Magyars threaten Europe; instead, they gave up their existence as nomadic plunderers and settled to live peacefully in their homelands in Hungary.

Six years after his great victory, Otto followed the custom of appointing his heir as coregent and saw Otto II, his six-year-old son by Adelaide, elected and crowned king of Germany. Having regulated his succession, Otto received a call for help from Pope John XII, a rather worldly youth who found himself threatened by Berengar. That was Otto's chance to obtain the imperial crown for himself and thus to fashion himself after the great Charlemagne, who had been the last real emperor. On February 2, 962, after a successful arrival in Rome, Otto was crowned emperor of the Holy Roman Empire of the German Nation, marking the beginning of a tradition for the German kings that would last almost a millennium—until the rise of Napoleon Bonaparte, who formally abolished the title in 1802.

Otto I. (Library of Congress)

A few days after his coronation, Otto signed a mutual treaty, the Privilegium Ottonianum, which bestowed land on the Papacy (the grant consisted of territories that were yet to be conquered) in exchange for the emperor's right to ratify papal elections. Theoretically, the popes were placed under imperial control, but in reality the Romans readily deposed officeholders whom they found objectionable. This practice began almost immediately after Otto engineered the deposition of John XII for committing treason with Berengar; the imperial nominee for the succession was himself deposed, then reinstated, but he died soon after. Otto's next choice, John XIII, was chased away by the Romans, who elected an antipope. To protect his candidate, Otto had to spend the years from 966 to 972 in Italy.

During this time, Otto also tried to contact the Byzantine Empire, which at first showed only arrogance to the German upstarts. After a new ruler came to power in the East, Otto's diplomatic mission succeeded, and he obtained the hand of the gifted princess Theophano for his son Otto II, who married her in 972.

At the height of his power, Otto I returned to Germany to hold a great assembly of his court at Quedlinburg in Saxony on March 23, 973. This time, the ceremonies were less perfunctory and reflected the real power of the person venerated as king and emperor. After a reign of thirty-seven years, at age sixty, Otto died a few weeks later in the adjacent town of Memleben and was put to rest beside his first wife, Edith.

Saxon Kings of Germany, 919-1024

Reign	*King*
919	Henry I the Fowler (Saxon, not crowned)
936-973	Otto I
973-983	Otto II
983-1002	Otto III
1002-1024	Henry II the Saint
1024	Franconian/Salian line begins (Conrad II)

Significance

Otto the Great was the first king of Germany to consolidate real power and authority for the kingship and give a clearer sense of national unity to the tribes of Germany. His defeat of the Magyars secured the boundaries of the later empire in the southeast, and his expansion to the Oder River created a stable area for German settlement, the limits of which would mark the eastern frontier for a long time.

Otto's grasping of the imperial throne gave his kingship additional prestige and influence over the rich cities of northern Italy, but it also allowed for direct German involvement in Roman and Italian politics, which had the potential to strain the resources and muddle the interests of the German rulers and their people. Further, Otto's coronation laid the foundation for a mutual dependency and rivalry between emperor and pope; in a crippling struggle for power, both sides would vie for control over each other, with the pope claiming superiority over the emperor because of his ultimate spiritual authority and the latter adamantly refusing the pope's meddling in imperial affairs. Similarly, Otto's reliance on the clergy to administer his kingdom in order to weaken local power would prove to be a double-edged sword, lending unity to the empire at the price of ecclesiastical (and, consequently, Romish) power in Germany.

Culturally, Otto's reign brought Germany in touch with the almost forgotten legacy of the great Mediterranean cultures of antiquity and led to a general intellectual flourishing that has been called the "Ottonian renaissance." The fine arts thrived, some monasteries became true centers of academic life, and the written documents of the era show sophistication of learning.

—*R. C. Lutz*

Further Reading

Eyck, Frank. *Religion and Politics in German History: From the Beginnings to the French Revolution*. New York: St. Martin's Press, 1998. An analysis of how Germanic peoples preserved links with classical civilization through their ability to assimilate other cultures and peoples, from their alliances with eighth century popes through the Reformation and Counter-Reformation. The initial bond between the Germanic rulers and popes turned to conflict as the Papacy gained power. Tables, maps, bibliography, index.

Fleckenstein, Josef. *Early Medieval Germany*. Translated by Bernard S. Smith. New York: North Holland, 1978. Apart from providing an excellent portrayal of life in Germany around Otto's time, this work provides solid information on Otto's life and puts his achievements and struggles in the larger context of German history.

Haight, Anne Lyon, ed. *Hroswitha of Gandersheim: Her Life, Time, Works, and a Comprehensive Bibliography*. New York: Hroswitha Club, 1965. Contains translations of this medieval chronicler's works. Hroswitha's contemporary account of Otto's reign reads well and is an invaluable source for further studies.

Henderson, Ernest F. *History of Germany in the Middle Ages*. Reprint. New York: Haskell House, 1968. Chapters 8 and 9 offer an informed, readable account of Otto's rule as king and emperor and present his achievements in a larger historic context. Although this work was written in 1894, it is still a useful historical source.

Hill, Boyd H., Jr. *Medieval Monarchy in Action*. New York: Barnes and Noble Books, 1972. The introduction to this collection of translations of selected documents of the period has an informed chapter on Otto I that provides a precise overview of his reign.

_______. *The Rise of the First Reich*. New York: John Wiley and Sons, 1969. A collection of translations of contemporary sources, such as Widukind's chronicles and the writings of Liudprand of Cremona on Otto. Fourteen plates of medieval art works and a map of

Germany give the reader an illustrated view of Otto's era.

Jeep, John M., et al., eds. *Medieval Germany: An Encyclopedia.* New York: Garland, 2001. An A-Z encyclopedia that addresses all aspects of the German- and Dutch-speaking medieval world from 500 to 1500. Entries include individuals, events, and broad topics such as feudalism and pregnancy. Bibliographical references, index.

Liudprand, Bishop of Cremona. *The Embassy to Constantinople and Other Writings.* Translated by F. A. Wright, edited by John Julius Norwich. 1930. Reprint. Rutland, Vt.: Charles E. Tuttle, 1993. Liudprand's contemporary writings on Otto provide a rare glimpse into his world from a medieval perspective.

Moore, Robert Ian. *The First European Revolution, c. 970-1215.* Malden, Mass.: Blackwell, 2000. According to the publisher, "a radical reassessment of Europe from the late tenth to the early thirteenth centuries [arguing that] the period witnessed the first true 'revolution' in European society," supported by transformation of the economy, family life, political power structures, and the rise of the non-Mediterranean cities. Bibliography, index.

SEE ALSO: Charlemagne; Henry II the Saint; Hrosvitha; Matilda of Canossa; Saint Olga; Sylvester II.

RELATED ARTICLES in *Great Events from History: The Middle Ages, 477-1453*: c. 950: Court of Córdoba Flourishes in Spain; August 10, 955: Otto I Defeats the Magyars.

OUYANG XIU

Chinese writer and philosopher

A political figure and innovative writer of prose and poetry, Ouyang Xiu substantially shaped the Confucian tradition that dominated China for almost a thousand years.

BORN: 1007; Mianyang (now in Sichuan Province), China

DIED: 1072; Yingzhou (now in Anhui Province), China

ALSO KNOWN AS: Ou-yang Hsiu (Wade-Giles)

AREAS OF ACHIEVEMENT: Literature, philosophy

EARLY LIFE

The father of Ouyang Xiu (oh-yahng shew) held an office in the Chinese civil service system. When Ouyang Xiu was a very young child, his father died. His mother undertook his education. As he grew to young adulthood, the Chinese society of the Song Dynasty (Sung; 960-1279) was undergoing marked change. The previous dynasty, the Tang (T'ang; 618-907), had been dominated by aristocratic families and influenced by the military. During this period, however, the economy had expanded rapidly, and the gentry, steeped in Confucian learning, were becoming more powerful. To increase their influence, they sought to regularize the civil service system, entrance to which was gained increasingly through a series of examinations in Confucian writings. Because Confucian learning was a step to political power, writing style and the careful selection of classical models in prose and poetry were of utmost importance. The model style of the late Tang and early Song, known as "parallel prose," had grown rigid and formalistic, enforcing conventions of length, grammar, and diction on writers.

Ouyang Xiu, studying alone, discovered the works of an influential Tang period writer, Han Yu (Han Yü; 768-824). Believing Han Yu's style, *guwen* (ancient style), to be a much better vehicle for expressing ideas than parallel prose, Ouyang began to practice it. Because he wrote in the unconventional *guwen* style, he failed his first two attempts at the examinations, in 1023 and 1027. The resourceful young man thereupon presented an established scholar, Yan Shu (Yen Shu), with samples of his writings in the *guwen* style. Yan Shu was so impressed that he began to sponsor Ouyang, who rose rapidly, gaining his doctorate in 1030 with very high marks.

LIFE'S WORK

Ouyang Xiu began his career as a prefectural level (county) judge from 1031 to 1034 in Luoyang, formerly the capital city. Confucian bureaucrats led lives of studied leisure, with minimal official duties. They vied in writing poetry and prose and engaged in rounds of banquets. Ouyang wrote many *ci* (songs), poems meant to be sung to popular tunes. His *ci* were lively songs of love and romance, often performed by the singing girls who attended the fetes. During this period, Ouyang married, but his wife died in childbirth.

In 1034, his reputation as a writer came to the attention of the court. He was promoted to the position of collator of texts at the capital, Kaifeng, where he compiled an annotated catalog of the Imperial Libraries. He increasingly distinguished himself as a prose writer in both the *guwen* style and the wooden parallel style in which court documents were still written. He remarried, but he lost his second wife to childbirth in 1035.

Ouyang was drawn into a battle between conservatives and reformers, triggered by an official, Fan Zhongyan (Fan Chung-yen), who attempted to make the court and the emperor more responsible to the opinions of the Confucian bureaucrats. The Confucian political system had many merits, such as the great stability and continuity that it provided Chinese society, but it also had many defects. The system was, like Confucianism itself, rigidly hierarchical, based on differences in gender, age, education, and social status. It was difficult to challenge established authority, and political quarrels often involved vituperative personal attacks. In the increasingly bitter conflict between reformers and conservatives, Ouyang's patron, Fan Zhongyan, was demoted. Ouyang courageously came to Fan's defense and was exiled in 1036, as he had expected. In 1037, Ouyang married his third wife, with whom he would live the rest of his days.

Posted to a remote region of Hubei Province, Ouyang wrote a history of the Five Dynasties Period (907-960) between the Tang and Song Dynasties, *Xin wudai shi* (1036; a new history of the Five Dynasties), which eventually became part of the official corpus of dynastic histories, an unusual honor for a work that was not produced under court direction. Confucians value historical studies as the highest form of intellectual work, believing that history reveals models for human behavior.

The tide at court turned in favor of the reformers, and in 1040, Ouyang Xiu was invited back, under the patronage of Fan Zhongyan, but he declined. Henceforth he came to be known as a man who would not trade on friendship for personal advantage, a rare stand within the Confucian world. He was soon recalled to his former post as collator of texts. By 1042, the reformers were dominant, and Ouyang became policy critic, then drafting official, both influential posts.

Ouyang's powerful writing and reputation as an independent thinker made him a key figure in the reform program, but clique fighting sharpened. When Fan Zhongyan was accused in 1043 of forming a "faction," for which there was no place in the Confucian system, Ouyang wrote a remarkable essay on partisanship in which he argued that it was proper for gentlemen to ally to express positions on political issues. The essay became a classic political statement and was denounced by authoritarian emperors as late as the eighteenth century.

The iconoclastic reformers were very vulnerable, and soon their fortunes declined again; many were sent into exile. Ouyang was attacked on moral grounds, perhaps because of his reputation as the *bon vivant* author of romantic songs. In 1045, he was accused of having sexual relations with his sister's stepchild, a very serious charge in the family-centered Confucian culture. Although acquitted, he was again exiled, to Yingzhou, where he served in a series of prefectural governorships. One of the values for which Ouyang was later remembered was his insistence that gentlemen, though in exile, should not be bitter but rather should cultivate their inner essence and live productive and carefree lives. He lived out these values in Yingzhou.

Ouyang's mother died in 1052. Although he could have returned to court shortly thereafter, he withdrew for the full two years of formal mourning sometimes practiced at the death of a parent. His mother occupies a special place in Confucian legend, along with the mother of the great philosopher Mencius (c. 372-c. 289 B.C.E.), who also educated her son under adverse circumstances.

During this exile, Ouyang's reputation grew. His *shi* (poems), though they were valued for their adherence to classical tradition, had a carefree and lighthearted air that was rare in previous poetry. Their serenity, achieved through Confucian self-cultivation, continued to be influential in later generations. He also compiled an important catalog of archaeological artifacts. Ouyang was very happy during this period, doing the things that he loved, which included hosting literary gatherings at his Old Drunkard's Pavilion, where abundant wine was poured by witty and attractive singing girls. In 1054, however, he was recalled to court.

At court, Ouyang produced another history, *Xin Tang shu* (1060; the new Tang history). In 1057, he conducted the doctoral examinations, insisting that they be written in *guwen* and be judged on their substance rather than their adherence to classical forms. In 1059, he wrote one of the most beautiful pieces in Chinese literature, "The Sounds of Autumn," a *fu* (rhapsodic prose poem). The *fu*, like parallel prose, was a classical form that had grown stiff and formal. Ouyang Xiu and his protégé Su Dongpo (1036-1101) managed to revivify the genre.

Ouyang Xiu next served as prefect of Kaifeng, as policy critic, and as assistant chief minister, his highest office. He now counseled gradual reforms to avoid the backlash fatal to his earlier efforts. He was instrumental in promoting a period of benevolent rule under two emperors between 1060 and 1066. Problems arose at court, however, and in 1067, enemies charged that Ouyang had committed incest with his daughter-in-law.

Although the ensuing investigation cleared him, Ouyang, now sixty years old, resigned. He was appointed to a post near his estates in Yingzhou. In 1069, another former protégé, the statesman-poet Wang Anshi (1021-1086), undertook a doomed program of radical reforms. Criticizing the program as ill-advised, Ouyang repeatedly requested permission to resign. Finally, in 1071, it was granted. He returned to his estate in Yingzhou, but he did not long enjoy his freedom, for in the summer of 1072, he died of unknown causes.

SIGNIFICANCE

Ouyang Xiu made a lasting mark in many areas of human endeavor. As the "literary master" of the Song period, his prose and poetry became models for later generations. He contributed major works in history and archaeology, and his methods for writing genealogies became the standard in China. He was a much sought-after writer of epitaphs, one of the highest Confucian literary pursuits. His prose and poetry have been translated into the world's major languages and may be found in standard anthologies. While achieving these heights, he also had an important political career.

Like many universal minds, Ouyang was not to be the greatest name of his generation in any one field. His friends Su Dongpo and Mei Yaoqian (Mei Yao-ch'ien; 1002-1062) surpassed him in writing poetry, his political rival Sima Guang (Ssu-ma Kuang; 1019-1086) bested him in writing history. Nevertheless, because of the breadth of his abilities and his optimistic and lighthearted attitude, coupled with intense self-cultivation, it was Ouyang Xiu who became a model scholar, political figure, and Confucian gentleman for generations of Chinese.

—*Jeffrey G. Barlow*

FURTHER READING

Egan, Ronald C. *The Literary Works of Ou-yang Hsiu (1007-1072).* Cambridge, England: Cambridge University Press, 1984. Includes a good critical introduction to Song literature. An excellent analysis of the writings of Ouyang Xiu, with much biographical information. The appendices include translations of some of his prose pieces, and his poetry is reproduced throughout.

Lai, Monica, and T. C. Lai. *Rhapsodic Essays from the Chinese.* Hong Kong: Kelly and Walsh, 1979. This work reproduces six essays in the *fu* form, including Ouyang Xiu's famous piece "The Sounds of Autumn." The work includes reproductions of paintings depicting Ouyang writing the piece, as well as facsimiles of the original in his calligraphy and a printed contemporary edition. It also includes another important *fu*, "The Red Cliff," written by Su Dongpo.

Liu, James T. *Ou-Yang Hsiu: An Eleventh-Century Neo-Confucianist.* Stanford, Calif.: Stanford University Press, 1967. The classic study of Ouyang Xiu, with more attention to biography and political life than in the work of Egan, listed above. Based on a wide reading of classical and modern Chinese sources. Liu should be considered the foremost biographer of Ouyang.

Ouyang, Xiu. *Love and Time: Poems of Ou-yang Hsiu.* Edited and translated by J. P. Seaton. Port Townsend, Wash.: Copper Canyon Press, 1989. A collection of Ouyang Xiu's poems, translated into English.

Pine, Red, trans. *Poems of the Masters: China's Classic Anthology of T'ang and Sung Dynasty Verse.* Port Townsend, Wash.: Copper Canyon Press, 2003. A collection of poetry from the Tang and Song Dynasties that contains the works of Ouyang Xiu, among others. Indexes.

SEE ALSO: Du Fu; Li Bo; Li Qingzhao; Sima Guang; Su Dongpo; Wang Anshi; Wang Wei.

RELATED ARTICLES in *Great Events from History: The Middle Ages, 477-1453*: 618: Founding of the Tang Dynasty; 907-960: Period of Five Dynasties and Ten Kingdoms; 960: Founding of the Song Dynasty; 960-1279: Scholar-Official Class Flourishes Under Song Dynasty; 1069-1072: Wang Anshi Introduces Bureaucratic Reforms.

SAINT PATRICK
Irish patron saint

Saint Patrick is a semilegendary figure who served as a missionary bishop to Ireland and converted large numbers of pagans to Christianity. He is the patron saint of Ireland.

BORN: Probably between 418 and 422; Britain (now possibly in England, Scotland, or Wales)
DIED: March 17, 493; Saul, Ireland
ALSO KNOWN AS: Maewyn Succat (given name); Succat (given name); Patricius (Latin name)
AREA OF ACHIEVEMENT: Religion and theology

EARLY LIFE

It is difficult to be certain about specific details and dates in Saint Patrick's life. The main sources for information are his very brief autobiography entitled *Confessio* (c. 489; *Confession*, 1918); the *Epistola ad milites Corotici* (471; *Letter to the Soldiers of Coroticus*, 1918), in which he excommunicated Coroticus, an Irish tyrant who had killed several Irish converts to Christianity; and a fanciful seventh century biography by Muirchu.

The first part of Muirchu's *Vita Sancti Patricii* (seventh century; *Life of St. Patrick*, 1920) is based almost exclusively on Saint Patrick's *Confession*; for this reason, historians have tried to rely almost exclusively on Saint Patrick's autobiography in an effort to establish the major details of his life. However, Saint Patrick did not always include detailed information about specific dates and events. His main concern in writing *Confession* was to leave a record of his spiritual transformation from a young man uninterested in Christianity into an active missionary.

Saint Patrick was born probably between 418 and 422 somewhere in Britain. In his *Confession*, written in Latin, he wrote that his hometown was "Bannaventa Burniae," but no one has ever been able to identify this village. His father was a deacon named Calpurnius, and his grandfather was a priest named Potitus. At that time, celibacy was not required of priests in the Catholic Church, but Saint Patrick did not reveal his mother's name. In *Confession*, Saint Patrick wrote of his indifference to religion during his early years, and he spoke also of a terrible sin that he had committed at the age of fifteen. He never explained the nature of this sin, but it still disturbed him years later when he wrote his autobiography. When he was sixteen years old, Saint Patrick was seized by marauders and taken into slavery in western Ireland. He was sold to a landowner in County Mayo. During his six years of slavery, he became a believing Christian. In *Confession*, he described his amazing escape. He left Mayo, walked on foot across Ireland, and escaped by boat to either Britain or Gaul (now France). There he was once again enslaved, but he had a series of dreams that he interpreted as meaning that God would free him from slavery so that he could return to Ireland as a missionary. After his second escape from slavery, he studied in England and became a priest. In his *Confession*, he states that when certain "senior" clergymen learned of the sin he committed at the age of fifteen, he was criticized, and another priest was appointed the bishop of Ireland, a position that Patrick would, nevertheless, eventually assume.

LIFE'S WORK

Although there is still some disagreement among historians, it is now generally assumed that Saint Patrick began his missionary work as the bishop of Ireland in 456. It is believed that he remained in Ireland until his death or until shortly before his death (when he may have retired to a monastery in England) on March 17, 493. In *Confession*, Saint Patrick reveals himself to be a modest priest devoted to converting pagans to Christianity and to the spiritual guidance of new Christians in Ireland.

Muirchu and other biographers of Saint Patrick told imaginative tales about Patrick's missionary work in Ireland. They claimed that Saint Patrick proved the superiority of Christianity over paganism by defeating pagan magicians in a wrestling contest. They also asserted that, just as Christ had fasted and prayed in the mountains for forty days, so, too, had Saint Patrick climbed Croagh Patrick, a mountain in County Connaught, where he spent forty days in prayer and direct communication with God. These legends are still popular in Ireland, and each July thousands of pilgrims climb Croagh Patrick and pray in the small chapel located at the top. However, it is not necessary to believe in such legends to recognize the significance of Saint Patrick's central role in spreading Christianity throughout Ireland.

Ireland (or Hibernia, as it was known during Roman times) was outside the boundaries of the Roman Empire. Although earlier missionaries had made great efforts to proselytize those living under Roman domination, similar efforts had not been made outside the Roman Empire. Saint Patrick's major contribution to the spread of Christianity was his determination to consecrate his life to bringing the word of God to people living in countries that had been long neglected by Rome.

In 431, Pope Celestine appointed Palladius the first bishop of Ireland, but he specified that Palladius was to serve as bishop to the "Irish who believe in Christ." This remark suggests quite clearly that the mission of Palladius was to serve as spiritual leader to Christians in Ireland and not to undertake missionary work. Between Palladius's appointment in 431 and Patrick's nomination twenty-five years later, another bishop had continued the pastoral work of Palladius. The name of this bishop is unknown.

Saint Patrick broke with tradition because he targeted those who were not Christian. He realized that many to whom he spoke were hostile toward Christianity. He could not coerce them to convert, as the Roman Empire had attempted after Christianity had become the state religion during the fourth century. Instead, he had to persuade men and women that they should abandon their gods and accept Christianity. Because he had lived in Ireland as a slave, he knew the local language and had no difficulty communicating in Celtic, the only language spoken by the vast majority of people in Ireland at that time. He accommodated Christianity to local traditions so that new converts would not feel threatened.

Depiction of Saint Patrick banishing the snakes from Ireland. (Library of Congress)

He quickly realized that he needed the help of local priests so that new converts would remain faithful to their new religion. In *Confession*, he wrote at great length of the joy he experienced each time he persuaded a pagan to accept Christianity. He did not limit his activity to one region of Ireland. He traveled extensively, and his personal missionary efforts definitely extended from the area around Dublin to as far north as Armagh and as far west as the Atlantic coast in counties Clare and Connemara. He may not have reached the southwestern and southeastern regions of Ireland, but priests whom he had ordained soon spread Christianity throughout the island.

Converting so many pagans to Christianity was a massive undertaking. Historians now believe that Christian dioceses in Britain contributed significantly to support Patrick's efforts. He did not want the Irish to believe that he was exploiting them for his own benefit. In his *Confession*, he states clearly that he refused to accept any money from them. Although celibacy was not yet required of priests, Saint Patrick never married, and he states that he returned gifts that recent converts had given him. He strove to be a spiritual leader with whom all could identify. He demonstrated great personal courage. In one area, a local chieftain threatened to kill him, but Saint Patrick persuaded the chieftain to allow him to pay the chieftain's sons to serve as his traveling companions. After just two weeks, he states, he had converted these men to Christianity. In his *Confession*, he explains that his personal experience with poverty and slavery helped him to appreciate the dignity of all whom he encountered in Ireland. He was as proud of his conversions of family members of chieftains as he was of his conversions of impoverished peasants.

After Patrick had been working for fifteen years as a missionary in Ireland, a chieftain named Coroticus, whom he had converted to Christianity, abducted several converts and planned to sell them into slavery. Several people resisted, and Coroticus killed them. In his *Letter to the Soldiers of Coroticus*, Saint Patrick not only excommunicated Coroticus but also instructed his soldiers that they need no longer obey him, because his orders were incompatible with Christ's teaching concerning the dignity of human life. Saint Patrick showed complete disregard for the very real threat that Coroticus might attempt to kill him. His personal courage, high ethical standards, and his unrelenting efforts to spread Christianity throughout Ireland endeared him to people from all social classes.

Significance

More than fifteen hundred years after his death, Saint Patrick remains a revered figure in Ireland and elsewhere in the Catholic world. Before his arrival in Ireland in 456, there had been no systematic effort on the part of Christian missionaries to convert people who lived in countries that had not been influenced by Greco-Roman culture. Saint Patrick believed that Christianity would become a universal religion only if Christians reached out with respect and understanding to people from very different cultures. He was successful in his efforts to convert the Irish to Christianity largely because he spoke their language, respected their traditions, and did not attempt to impose his cultural values on them; instead, he simply tried to share religious values with them. He thus helped to broaden the scope of Christianity.

For the Irish, who have endured centuries of political domination and religious persecution, Saint Patrick represents a dignified man who discovered, through his own suffering, the essential dignity of each individual. Saint Patrick humbled himself to serve others, demonstrated inner courage, and remained faithful to his essential beliefs despite violent opposition from those opposed to him. Saint Patrick helped generations of Irish men and women cope with poverty, religious persecution, and economic adversity.

—*Edmund J. Campion*

Further Reading

Bieler, Ludwig. *Studies on the Life and Legend of St. Patrick.* Edited by Richard Sharpe. London: Variorum, 1986. Contains nineteen essays that examine early biographies of Saint Patrick and describe the creation of the numerous legends connected with him. Bibliography, index.

Carney, James. *The Problem of St. Patrick.* Dublin: Dublin Institute for Advanced Studies, 1973. Contains a solid historical study of what is known about Saint Patrick's life. The author distinguishes carefully between fact and fiction. Bibliography.

Davies, Oliver, trans. *Celtic Spirituality.* New York: Paulist Press, 1999. A very useful sourcebook with a good historical introduction. Bibliography, index.

De Paor, Liam, trans. *Saint Patrick's World: The Christian Culture of Ireland's Apostolic Age.* Notre Dame, Ind.: University of Notre Dame Press, 1993. Explores, through contemporary sources, Christianity in Ireland during the time of Saint Patrick and discusses his writings, including the *Epistola ad milites Corotici*. Bibliography, index.

Fletcher, Richard *The Barbarian Conversion: From Paganism to Christianity.* Berkeley: University of California Press, 1999. A comprehensive study of the history of the development of Christianity in pagan Europe. Illustrations, bibliography, index.

Gogarty, Oliver St. John. *I Follow Saint Patrick.* 1938. New ed. London: Constable, 1950. A lyrical book by an important Irish poet and physician who describes quite eloquently why Saint Patrick is still so highly revered by the Irish, both in Ireland and in exile. Maps.

McCaffrey, Carmel, and Leo Eaton. *In Search of Ancient Ireland: The Origins of the Irish, from Neolithic Times to the Coming of the English.* Chicago: New Amsterdam Books, 2002. A history of Ireland that includes discussion of Saint Patrick, Celtic spirituality, sainthood, and monasteries. Illustrations, maps, bibliography, index.

MacMullen, Ramsay. *Christianity and Paganism in the Fourth to Eighth Centuries.* New Haven, Conn.: Yale University Press, 1997. Surveys the relationship between paganism and the Christian world through the sixth century. Illustrations, bibliography, index.

O'Donoghue, Noel D. *Aristocracy of Soul: Patrick of Ireland.* Wilmington, Del.: Michael Glazier, 1987. Examines spiritual and theological aspects of Saint Patrick's *Confession* and contains an excellent English translation of the *Confession.*

Proudfoot, Alice Boyd, ed. *Patrick: Sixteen Centuries with Ireland's Patron Saint.* New York: Macmillan, 1983. Provides an excellent selection of literary and artistic works that evoke various aspects of the Saint Patrick legends and describe the evolving meaning of his life for generations of Irish writers.

Staunton, Michael. *The Illustrated Story of Christian Ireland: From St. Patrick to the Peace Process.* Dublin:

Emerald Press, 2001. Discusses Ireland before Christianity and the lives of Irish saints, including Saint Patrick and Saint Brigit. Bibliography, index.

Thompson, E. A. *Who Was Saint Patrick?* New York: St. Martin's Press, 1985. Contains a reliable historical study of Saint Patrick's life as it is revealed in his *Confessio* and *Epistola ad milites Corotici*. Includes a solid bibliography of important historical studies and an index.

SEE ALSO: Anna, Princess of the Byzantine Empire; Saint Bede the Venerable; Saint Boniface; Saint Brigit; Saint Clotilda; Gregory the Great; Olaf I.

RELATED ARTICLES in *Great Events from History: The Middle Ages, 477-1453*: 590-604: Reforms of Pope Gregory the Great; 596-597: See of Canterbury Is Established; 731: Bede Writes *Ecclesiastical History of the English People*.

PAUL OF AEGINA

Byzantine physician and writer

Paul of Aegina was a celebrated Byzantine physician, surgeon, and medical writer. His Epitome *summarized nearly all medical knowledge of his time and had a profound influence on Western European, Arabic, and Persian medicine. His treatment of surgery is the best summary of ancient surgery that has survived.*

BORN: c. 625; Aegina, Greece
DIED: c. 690; place unknown
ALSO KNOWN AS: Paulus Aegineta (Latin name)
AREA OF ACHIEVEMENT: Medicine

EARLY LIFE

Little is known of the life and career of Paul of Aegina (ih-JI-nuh). He was born on the Greek island of Aegina in the Saronic Gulf near Athens in the early seventh century. As a young man, he studied at Alexandria in Egypt. At this time, the eastern Mediterranean world was dominated by the Byzantine Empire, which came into existence in 395, when the Roman Empire was divided in two. Centered in the great city of Constantinople, named after the emperor Constantine in 330, the Eastern Roman Empire gradually developed a separate identity. Enjoying geographic and economic advantages over the Western Roman Empire, it survived after the fall of Rome in the west. No one thought of it as a new empire but rather as a continuation of the Roman Empire on a reduced scale.

Alexandria had long enjoyed a reputation as one of the chief centers of learning in the Mediterranean. It was renowned as a center of medical study, particularly the study of anatomy. Late antiquity witnessed a gradual decline in the quality of learning in all fields, but the schools of medicine continued to function at Alexandria well into the Byzantine period, even if their finest days were past. Hence Alexandria continued to attract young medical students, as it had for centuries. Paul seems to have practiced medicine in Alexandria, where he may even have taught, but how long he remained is not known. In 640, the city fell to the Muslims, ending, for all intents and purposes, Alexandria's prominence as a center of science and medicine. Whether Paul remained there after the conquest, and if so how long, are unknown.

According to a later Arab source, Paul had special experience in women's diseases and enjoyed considerable success in their treatment. Midwives are said often to have sought his aid regarding difficult cases and to have received from him much useful advice. For that reason he was given the title of *alqawabeli*, or "the birth-helper." He wrote on pediatrics and obstetrics and in fact summarized nearly everything that was known at the end of antiquity on these subjects. He does not, however, seem to have specialized in these areas to the exclusion of others, for his writings reveal wide experience in medicine and surgery generally.

LIFE'S WORK

Byzantine medicine fell heir to nearly a thousand years of Greek medical development. Greek medicine, after reaching its zenith in the work of Galen in the second century, began a long period of decline and ossification. In late antiquity, medical writers increasingly abandoned firsthand medical investigation in favor of compiling encyclopedic compendia of medical knowledge in which the great medical writers of the past, whose works were regarded as too extensive to be manageable, were summarized and abridged. Hence much of the earlier Greek medical heritage was passed down to subsequent generations in the form of medical encyclopedias. In the fourth century, Oribasius, the court physician to Emperor Julian, compiled a large medical encyclopedia in seventy books. This practice of systematic compilation was continued by Byzantine physicians such as Aëtius of Amida and Alexander of Tralles in the sixth century. Paul of Aegina, who had Oribasius's work at his disposal, believed that it was too long to be used by most ordinary physicians and so compiled his own abridgment of it, *Epitome medicae libri septum* (*The Seven Books of Paulus Aegineta*, 1844-1877, commonly known as the *Epitome*).

In the preface to his *Epitome*, Paul disclaims originality, saying that he has compiled the work from previous authors except for a few things that he has employed of his own. He includes material chiefly from Oribasius, but also information from other distinguished medical writers. His statement that earlier writers had said all that there was to say on medicine has been taken to indicate Paul's recognition of the low state of medicine in his own day. In fact, however, it is probably no more than a conventional expression of piety to the great medical writers of the past.

Book 1 of the *Epitome* deals with hygiene and regimen. Paul accepts Greek humoral pathology, discusses the temperaments, and recommends dietary therapeutics for different seasons and ages. Book 2 is devoted to fevers, which are symptomatic of acute or chronic diseases, and to the discussion of the value of the pulse (of which Paul classifies sixty-two varieties), urine, and sputum as indications of disease. In book 3, Paul deals with topical afflictions. He begins at the top of the head (with afflictions of the hair) and proceeds downward to the toenails. Included are discussions of diseases of the kidneys, liver, and uterus. Book 4 treats diseases of the skin (such as leprosy and cancer) as well as intestinal worms. Book 5 deals with toxicology and describes the treatment of stings and bites of venomous animals. Book 6 is devoted to general surgery and book 7 to simple and compound medicines (Paul includes some six hundred plants and ninety minerals).

In the *Epitome*, there are 242 sections that deal with virtually every aspect of medicine and represent a summary of medical knowledge in Paul's day. While relying heavily on Oribasius, Paul also drew on Galen, Soranus, Aëtius, and Dioscorides, sometimes reproducing them word for word. Yet Paul was no mere copyist. He was critical, providing correctives where necessary. On one occasion, having given the Hippocratic opinion on a particular condition, he added the warning, "Time, however, has demonstrated that this procedure is inadvisable."

Book 6 of the *Epitome* contains the best short treatment of ancient surgery that survives. The book is divided into two sections that deal respectively with manual operations and the treatment of fractures and dislocations. Altogether, Paul provides detailed descriptions of more than 120 operations. In general, he describes surgery only on the surface of the body or in its orifices (such as nasal or genital passages), where surgical instruments can be easily inserted. Paul describes lithotomy (surgical removal of bladder stones), trephination (removal of a bone disc from the skull), removal of tonsils, and amputation of the breast. Also included are surgical techniques for tracheotomies, catheterization, and removal of hemorrhoids. The method that he recommends for excision of tonsils remained virtually unchanged in practice for centuries. Paul describes as well venesection, cupping, and the use of ligation for bleeding vessels. Book 6 also contains one of the most detailed treatments of ancient ophthalmic surgery extant. Paul records procedures for removal of cataracts, and his treatment of trachoma is especially good for the age in which it was written. His account of military surgery is similarly comprehensive. Paul's treatment of surgery shows him to have been probably the greatest surgeon of his day. Although his accounts of surgical procedures were for the most part derived from the works of earlier medical writers, he reproduced them with clarity and precision. He did not hesitate to reject established procedures when he thought it necessary. Thus, in his treatment of fractures, he sometimes contradicts Hippocratic teaching in favor of what he regards as sounder procedures (for example, he recommends the immediate reduction of dislocations).

Among other aspects of medicine treated by Paul are pediatrics (he includes discussion of dentition, convulsions, and constipation), lung diseases, and difficult labor. He provides one of the earliest descriptions in medical literature of lead poisoning. There are also descriptions of encephalitis, apoplexy, and epilepsy. In his discussion of insanity, there are excellent clinical observations as well as sound recommendations for treatment. Paul also gives the first description of hygienic rules for travelers, which became very popular in the Middle Ages.

Significance

Paul was the last great physician and surgeon of the early Byzantine period. Following his death near the end of the seventh century, there was little original work done in medicine; few influential Byzantine physicians are known until the eleventh century. Although Paul reflects the tendency of late Roman and Byzantine physicians to substitute the collected wisdom of earlier Greek writers for experimentation and independent judgment, he rose above his contemporaries in rejecting traditional procedures and therapeutics where they conflicted with his personal experience. Since the time of Aulus Cornelius Celsus (c. 25 B.C.E.-c. 50 C.E.), it appears that in technical skill Roman and Byzantine surgeons had made considerable advancement. Paul's treatment of surgery represents the culmination of advances made by Greek surgeons. The progress, however, ended with him: There was no one after Paul who equaled him. Hence, he became the authoritative writer on surgery for later Byzantine physicians—which had negative as well as positive ramifications. In describing the operation for hernia, for example, Paul recommended that the testicle be removed; as a result of his authority, this unfortunate procedure continued to be practiced until the sixteenth century. His treatment of surgery was long used as a textbook at the University of Paris. In the sixteenth century, his works were translated into Latin and quoted extensively by medical writers. His discussion of surgery was extracted by Hieronymus Fabricius ab Aquapendente (the teacher of William Harvey) in his work on surgery published in 1592.

Paul's reputation was at least as great among Muslim physicians as it was among European Christians. Arab and Persian physicians quoted him frequently and regarded him as an authoritative Greek writer on medicine. The famous Persian physician al-Rāzī borrowed heavily from Paul's surgery. Abū al-Qāsim (1013-1106), the great Muslim surgeon, based his well-known treatise, *al-Taṣrīf liman ʿajaz ʿan al-Taʾālīf*, on the surgical writings of Paul. Inasmuch as Abū al-Qasim remained the leading authority on surgery until the thirteenth century, Paul of Aegina continued to influence surgery in the Muslim world nearly as long as he did in the West.

—*Gary B. Ferngren*

Further Reading

Biller, Peter, and Joseph Ziegler, eds. *Religion and Medicine in the Middle Ages*. Rochester, N.Y.: York Medieval Press, 2001. An examination of medicine in medieval times with an emphasis on religion and the Catholic Church's influence. Bibliography and index.

French, R. K. *Medicine Before Science: The Rational and Learned Doctor from the Middle Ages to the Enlightenment*. New York: Cambridge University Press, 2003. An examination of the role of physicians in the Middle Ages. Bibliography and index.

Garcia Ballester, Luis. *Galen and Galenism: Theory and Medical Practice from Antiquity to the European Renaissance*. Burlington, Vt.: Ashgate, 2002. A study of Galen and how his beliefs on medicine affected later physicians such as Paul of Aegina.

McVaugh, Michael R., and Nancy G. Siraisi, eds. *Renaissance Medical Learning: Evolution of a Tradition*. Philadelphia: History of Science Society, 1991. A look at how medicine was learned during the early Renaissance. Bibliography and index.

Paul of Aegina. *The Seven Books of Paulus Aegineta*. Translated by Francis Adams. 3 vols. London: Sydenham Society, 1844-1847. An excellent translation into English of the *Epitome* prefaced by a good introduction on Paul of Aegina and his influence on later medicine.

Scarborough, John, ed. *Symposium on Byzantine Medicine*. Washington, D.C.: Dumbarton Oaks, 1984. A collection of papers by specialists that deal with virtually every aspect of Byzantine medicine.

SEE ALSO: Pietro d'Abano; Alhazen; Avicenna; Jacqueline Félicie; Guy de Chauliac; Moses Maimonides; al-Rāzī; Trotula.

RELATED ARTICLES in *Great Events from History: The Middle Ages, 477-1453*: 809: First Islamic Public Hospital; c. 1010-1015: Avicenna Writes His *Canon of Medicine*; c. 1150: Moors Transmit Classical Philosophy and Medicine to Europe.

JOHN PECHAM

Archbishop of Canterbury (1279-1292)

Pecham was a scholar whose writings ranged from Augustinian theology to optics. As archbishop of Canterbury he vigorously sought to remove abuses and to maintain the Church's independence from lay interference, resulting in confrontations with the king as well as with his own bishops and abbots.

BORN: c. 1230; probably Patcham, Sussex, England
DIED: December 8, 1292; Mortlake, Canterbury, England
ALSO KNOWN AS: John Peccham; Johannes Peckham
AREA OF ACHIEVEMENT: Religion and theology, church reform

EARLY LIFE

John Pecham (PEHCH-uhm) was born sometime around 1230, probably in Patcham, near modern Brighton. Nothing is known of his ancestry, but he received his early education from the monks of Lewes Priory, after which he proceeded to Oxford University. There, he read for the degree of master of arts, joined the Franciscan order, and was influenced by the great scholar Adam Marsh. Oxford during the thirteenth century hosted a brilliant band of Franciscan thinkers and teachers, and it was surely in the Franciscan house there that the seeds of Pecham's future commitment to scholastic philosophy, scientific enquiry, and the Franciscan life of preaching and apostolic poverty were sown.

In 1250, he moved from Oxford to Paris, where he studied theology (Saint Bonaventure was among his teachers) and eventually obtained his doctorate, perhaps around 1269. For nearly twenty years, he studied, lectured, and wrote in what was then the intellectual capital of Christendom. He entered with enthusiasm into the famous disputations of the schools, debating among others the English Dominican Robert Kilwardby, and he played a notable part in defending the Mendicant orders against their detractors among the secular clergy. He won the esteem of the queen of France, Margaret of Provence, and came to know personally the great Saint Thomas Aquinas. By the time he left Paris, he was regarded as one of the leading scholars of the age.

In 1270, he returned to Oxford as regent master of theology, and again he clashed in debate with Kilwardby, now provincial prior of the Dominicans. Kilwardby, however, left Oxford in 1272, having been chosen by Gregory X (1271-1276) as the archbishop of Canterbury. Meanwhile, in 1275 or 1276, Pecham was elected provincial prior of the English Franciscans, on whose behalf he attended a general council of the order in Padua, traveling the entire way on foot in order to obey the order's rule against riding. By now, so great was his fame that Nicholas III (1277-1280) summoned him to Rome to become *lector sacri palatii* (lecturer in the school attached to the papal palace). He was the first holder of the appointment, and his public lectures aroused such enthusiasm that they were attended by cardinals and bishops.

Whether in Paris, Oxford, or Rome, Pecham had been writing extensively on subjects ranging from theology to mathematics and physics. His commentaries on the Scriptures and on Peter Lombard's *Sententiarum libri IV* (1148-1151; *The Books of Opinions of Peter Lombard*, 1970; better known as *Sentences*) and his collections of *quaestiones* (a genre of theological literature in the form of questions and answers) were devoured by contemporary students. His *Perspectiva communis*, on optics, and his *Tractatus de sphera* placed him firmly within that tradition of scientific inquiry for which the Oxford Franciscans were then renowned. Among so considerable a body of academic texts, his religious poem "Philomela, praevia," formerly attributed to Saint Bonaventure, stands somewhat apart, as do several other poems of which he may have been the author.

In 1278, Canterbury fell vacant, for Kilwardby had been summoned to Rome and a cardinalate. As had happened prior to Kilwardby's nomination as archbishop, Edward I (1272-1307) strongly urged the claims of his trusted counselor, Robert Burnell, bishop of Bath and Wells, but once again the pope rejected the suggestion out of hand. Instead, Nicholas III named Pecham (much against his will, it is said) and consecrated him in February, 1279. On his way across France, Pecham had a meeting with Edward at Amiens, where the latter was in conference with Philip III. Whatever resentment the king felt regarding the rejection of his candidate, he received his new archbishop in a friendly manner, and when Pecham was enthroned in Canterbury cathedral in October, 1279, Edward was present.

LIFE'S WORK

Pecham lived at a time when the Papacy claimed an absolute supremacy over all temporal rulers as the embodiment of a universal monarchy divinely ordained. With such a claim Pecham was in complete sympathy. It would have been strange had he felt otherwise. The Mendicant orders were the spiritual shock-troops of the thirteenth century Papacy, and although the Spiritual Franciscans were soon to become alienated from the Curia, Pecham does not seem to have been influenced by their teachings. He was, nevertheless, wholly committed to the Franciscan ideal of apostolic poverty, and both his everyday life as a friar and his public stand as primate of England bear out David Knowles's observation that "the English Minors, though showing little inclination towards the eremitical life of the Italian Spirituals . . . were, as a body, more united than any other province in their resolve to preserve the first purity of the rule." In any case, he never feared a fight, and as archbishop he upheld the Mendicants against the secular clergy, just as he defended the Church as a whole from lay interference and championed the authority of Rome against the particularism of the *Ecclesia Anglicana*. Clearly, Nicholas III had known well what he was doing when he chose Pecham for Canterbury. As Knowles writes of Pecham, "Contrary to what might have been expected from a lifelong student and teacher, he appears as a man of prompt decision, great practical ability and grasp of detail. He never feared to take the initiative in action, nor did he shrink from conflict."

Pecham's first action on arriving in England was to summon a provincial council to meet at Reading in July, 1279. Such councils had been prescribed annually by the Lateran Council of 1215, but they were comparatively rare in England. It seems likely, therefore, that Nicholas III had specifically instructed Pecham to initiate regular councils. At Reading, Pecham reissued the canons of the four previous councils that had been held during the thirteenth century, laying stress on those of 1268, in particular. To these some additions were made, especially with respect to the sin of pluralism (that is, a cleric being in possession of two or more benefices simultaneously). Pluralism was very common throughout the English church, and the issue was one that was bound to place the archbishop in direct conflict with some of his own suffragans.

Pecham then had Magna Carta read out and gave orders that new copies were to be posted in every cathedral and collegiate church. Finally, he had the Church's canons on the subject of excommunication read to the assembly, with instructions that these were to be explained by the parish priests to their congregations every week in order that everyone should be familiar with the consequences of disregarding spiritual authority. The Reading agenda was an implicit criticism of the government and its officials, who had shown themselves hostile to the rights and liberties of the Church. Thus, it was a challenge, and as such it was taken up in the parliament that met in Westminster at Michaelmas of that same year. This was the parliament that passed the statute of Mortmain, forbidding the transfer of land to the Church without regard for the existence of prior rights and obligations. It was not an assembly favorably disposed toward ecclesiastical pretensions. Pecham was compelled to withdraw three of the canons of excommunication proclaimed at Reading and to rescind his instructions with regard to Magna Carta. Not long afterward, in January, 1280, the king exacted from the clergy a tax of one-fifteenth for three years. Edward had won the first round, but Pecham was not easily quelled.

In 1280, the archbishop resolved to exercise his rights of visitation over the Royal Peculiars, royal chapels that enjoyed exemption from episcopal jurisdiction. In Pecham's eyes, this was an intolerable anomaly and so, in the spring of 1280, he embarked on a visitation of the diocese of Coventry and Lichfield, where several were located. Not surprisingly, he uncovered rampant pluralism. He also met with resistance. As a result, he proceeded with suits against the deans and canons of the royal chapels of Derby, Shrewsbury, and Tettenhall and excommunicated the dean and canons of Wolverhampton. He was coming close to trespassing on royal preserves. Following Reading and the matter of the Royal Peculiars, strong undercurrents of tension between Pecham and the government surfaced whenever issues arose that, in Pecham's opinion, touched on the honor or the rights of the Church. It is not altogether surprising, therefore, that, still unchastened, he summoned a provincial council to Lambeth in October, 1281, to reaffirm his position on excommunication and other contentious matters. This time, however, as Sir Maurice Powicke puts it, Edward

> wisely refrained from reprisals. Probably he had taken the archbishop's measure and realized both the value of his good-will and the advantages of a conciliatory attitude towards clerical grievances. After all, in any particular issue, the last word lay with the Crown.

With regard to his administration as metropolitan, Pecham's financial situation was exceptionally trying. This state of affairs was a result of the actions of his predecessor, Kilwardby. Setting out for Rome in 1278, Kilwardby had become involved with an appeal by the entire English clergy against the proceedings of the resident papal nuncio. Kilwardby needed large sums of money; thus, before leaving, he had transferred to the king the annual rents and income from the Canterbury estates in return for a lump sum of cash, which he had taken with him to Rome, together with some of his cathedral's vestments and ornaments, and all the registers and judicial records. Because of this, the Lambeth Palace records today begin with the tenure of Pecham. Kilwardby had left the archiepiscopal household virtually penniless, but Pecham had financial troubles of his own. As a friar who had no personal possessions, he had been forced to borrow heavily in Rome to pay for his consecration and the journey to England, where, he discovered on arrival, there was nothing with which to pay the debt he had incurred. In consequence, he was to be haunted throughout his administration by lack of funds and the difficulties of paying creditors. On the positive side, his need taught him to become a practical and frugal manager of the Canterbury estates.

The only Franciscan and the last friar to become archbishop of Canterbury, Pecham was not particularly well disposed toward the high ecclesiastics with whom he had to deal, many of whom, while possessing outstanding qualifications and real ability, were unashamed pluralists. Additionally, though his own life was humble enough, he set great store on the dignity of his office. As a result, he quarreled almost immediately with the new archbishop of York, William Wickwane (1275-1285), over matters of precedence, although the pope had expressly ordered him not to. In 1284, there was a similar contretemps with the bishop of St. David's, Thomas Bek. Pecham's confrontations with those whom he regarded as pluralists were acrimonious, as in the case of Anthony Bek, the future bishop of Durham, and John Kirkby, the royal treasurer. Even fiercer was the quarrel with Thomas de Cantilupe (1218?-1282), the aristocratic bishop of Hereford.

Pecham's visitations did not stop with the secular clergy but were also extended to the regulars, and he was said to have been especially ill-disposed toward the Benedictines. There is no doubt that he strictly investigated the great monastic houses of Glastonbury, Reading, and Christ Church, Canterbury. Pecham's relations with the abbot of Westminster were particularly cool, and in 1290, as a result of a quarrel between the Westminster monks and the Franciscans, he placed the abbey under an interdict. If Pecham tended to be hostile to the monks, his attitude reflected that of the Mendicant orders as a whole. By contrast, he was a warm supporter of the Dominicans, the Carmelites, and the Austin friars, while showing the greatest favor to his brother Franciscans, to whom he granted the right to hear confessions and give absolution.

In his later years, he became embroiled in an unprofitable squabble with the Dominicans, having in 1284 formally condemned certain erroneous doctrines taught in the schools at Oxford, with which the Dominicans were identified. In so doing, he seemed to be casting aspersions on the teachings of his old master, Aquinas. A vicious pamphlet war followed and so great a storm was raised that Pecham felt compelled to write to several cardinals in Rome to defend himself.

His last years were marked by failing health. He died at Mortlake on December 8, 1292, after a long illness, and was buried in Canterbury Cathedral.

SIGNIFICANCE

Pecham possessed the quintessential virtues of the Franciscans. He was austere and devout, dedicated to the *vita apostolica* (apostolic life) and the saving of souls prescribed by the order's founder. Also in the tradition of the thirteenth century Mendicants, he was a man of formidable intellect and wide learning, which ranged from biblical exegesis to the wonders of creation. He would perhaps have been happier had he been able to pass his entire life within strictly academic circles, and there is clearly a bifurcation between the scholar's life, which he lived prior to 1279, and his later years as archbishop. Pecham's fourteen years at Canterbury were not an unqualified success. That he was forceful and sincere in his dedication to reform cannot be doubted, and even his enemies acknowledged his personal honesty. Yet he was too angular and argumentative, alienating laymen and churchmen alike, king, barons, bishops, and abbots.

At his best, however, Pecham embodied some of the strongest currents in the spiritual life of his century, in his commitment to apostolic poverty and the Franciscan ideal, to preaching and learning, and to the service of the Papal Curia. Ironically, both during his life and posthumously, he was always more admired and better appreciated in Paris and Rome than in his own country.

—*Gavin R. G. Hambly*

FURTHER READING

Cross, F. L., and E. A. Livingstone. *Oxford Dictionary of the Christian Church*. 3d ed. New York: Oxford University Press, 1997. Along with Hook's *Lives*, one of the few standard sources on the archbishops of Canterbury.

Douie, Decima L. *Archbishop Pecham*. Oxford, England: Clarendon Press, 1952. An outstanding, full-length study of Pecham, and one of the best biographies of a medieval prelate.

Hook, Walter Farquhar. *Lives of the Archbishops of Canterbury.* 12 vols. London: R. Bentley, 1860-1876. The venerable and still authoritative compendium archiving the biographies of the archbishops since Anglo-Saxon times.

Johnstone, Hilda. "Archbishop Pecham and the Council of Lambeth of 1281." In *Essays in Medieval History Presented to Thomas Frederick Tout*, edited by A. G. Little and F. M. Powicke. Manchester, England: Manchester University Press, 1925. An essay covering one of the central episodes in Pecham's career as archbishop.

Knowles, M.D. "Some Aspects of the Career of Archbishop Pecham." *English Historical Review* 57 (1942): 1-18, 178-201. An absorbing account of Pecham's scholarly activities, placing him squarely within the intellectual setting of his age.

Pecham, John. *John Pecham and the Science of Optics.* Edited by David C. Lindberg. Madison: University of Wisconsin Press, 1970. An edition and translation of Pecham's *Perspective Communis.*

Powicke, Frederick M. *The Thirteenth Century, 1216-1307.* Oxford, England: Clarendon Press, 1953. Chapter 10 contains an excellent overview of the state of the English church, with Pecham very much at center stage.

Rossignol. *Rossignol: An Edition and Translation.* Edited by J. L. Baird and John R. Kane. Kent, Ohio: Kent State University Press, 1978. Pecham's poem "Philomela, praevia" is translated into English and discussed in relation to its genre.

Sharp, Dorothea E. *Franciscan Philosophy at Oxford in the Thirteenth Century.* Oxford, England: Clarendon Press, 1930. Discusses the Franciscan roots of Pecham's scholarship.

Smith, Jeremiah J. *The Attitude of John Pecham Toward Monastic Houses Under His Jurisdiction.* Washington, D.C.: Catholic University of America Press, 1949. A study of one aspect of Pecham's archiepiscopal administration.

Witney, Kenneth. *The Survey of Archbishop Pecham's Kentish Manors, 1283-85.* Maidstone, England: Kent Archaeological Society, 2000. A translation of the fifteenth century Latin copy in the Canterbury Cathedral Library of the full survey, supplemented by a translation of the Kentish section of a thirteenth century summary of the survey.

SEE ALSO: Alhazen; Saint Bonaventure; Thomas Aquinas.

RELATED ARTICLES in *Great Events from History: The Middle Ages, 477-1453*: April 16, 1209: Founding of the Franciscans; June 15, 1215: Signing of the Magna Carta; November 11-30, 1215: Fourth Lateran Council; November 18, 1302: Boniface VII Issues the Bull *Unam Sanctam*; 1305-1417: Avignon Papacy and the Great Schism; c. 1310-1350: William of Ockham Attacks Thomist Ideas.

PETRUS PEREGRINUS DE MARICOURT

French writer and inventor

Petrus was the author of the first Western scientific treatise on the principles of magnetism. His practical inventions included a floating compass and a pivoted compass, both of which were used for finding the meridian and the azimuths of heavenly bodies.

BORN: Early thirteenth century; place unknown
DIED: Thirteenth century; place unknown
ALSO KNOWN AS: Peter of Maricourt; Pierre le Pélerin de Maricourt
AREAS OF ACHIEVEMENT: Physics, engineering, literature, geography, astronomy, science and technology

EARLY LIFE

Very little is known about the life of Petrus Peregrinus de Maricourt (PEE-truhs pehr-eh-GRI-nuhs deh MAHR-ih-coort), a name that means Peter the Pilgrim of Maricourt. What is known comes from two sources: Peregrinus's *Epistola Petri Peregrini de Maricourt ad Sygerum de Foucaucourt, militem, de magnete* (*Epistle of Petrus Peregrinus de Maricourt, to Sygerus of Foucaucourt, Soldier, Concerning the Magnet*, 1902), completed on August 8, 1269, at Lucera, and references in Roger Bacon's treatise *Opus tertium* (c. 1266; English translation, 1912).

The surname "de Maricourt" indicates that Peregrinus hailed from Méhaircourt, a village in Picardy (an old province in northern France); whether he was born at Méhaircourt or simply lived there is not known. Given his extensive education, it is clear that he was of noble birth. The appellation "Peregrinus" has been a matter of controversy. As "Peregrinus" was an honorary title given to people who had made pilgrimages to the Holy Sepulcher in Jerusalem or who had participated in a crusade, it was formerly conjectured that Peregrinus was a Knight Templar or was a member of one of Louis IX's Crusades in the thirteenth century. It is now recognized that "Peregrinus" was also bestowed on anyone who fought in an officially sanctioned Crusade outside the Holy Land. Thus, Peregrinus probably received his appellation from his service at the siege of Lucera, where he apparently wrote his work on magnetism.

Frederick II, the Holy Roman Emperor of Germany who was excommunicated three times in his life by the Papacy, had established early in the thirteenth century the town of Lucera in southern Italy as a colony and place of refuge for Saracens. Three times between 1255 and 1269, this town, guarded by Saracens and supported by the German emperor, was attacked by the forces of Charles I of Anjou, king of Italy. As the Papacy had declared these assaults official Crusades, Peregrinus received his title "Peregrinus" from his activity in Charles's final siege of the city in 1268-1269. Given his keen interest in mechanical devices, it seems likely that Peregrinus served as an engineer: Perhaps he constructed machines for breaching walls or hurling objects.

Other information on Peregrinus's life comes from Roger Bacon. In Bacon's *Opus tertium* (chapter 11), Peregrinus is referred to as one of the two "perfect mathematicians" and a *magister*, that is, someone who had earned a master of arts degree, perhaps at the University of Paris. In chapter 13, Bacon describes Peregrinus as the greatest experimental scientist of his time and one completely skilled in alchemy, warfare, agriculture, and the theory and use of all technical arts.

Life's Work

Although Peregrinus had planned to write a treatise on mirrors and may in fact have composed one on the composition of an astrolabe (a manuscript on such a topic bears his name in the title), his fame rests on the work on magnetism. The work is divided into two parts, theoretical and practical. The first, consisting of ten chapters, is devoted to the properties and effects of magnets and the principles of magnetism; the second discusses the construction of three instruments utilizing magnets (two compasses and a perpetual motion machine).

After an introductory chapter stating the purpose of his work, Peregrinus sets forth the qualifications of the scientist. Peregrinus insists that theory and speculation alone are insufficient; one must be good at manual experimentation, for only then can errors, undetected by abstract thinking and mathematics, be corrected. Chapter 3 contains a discussion of the properties of a good lodestone (natural magnet). It should look ironlike, slightly bluish, and pale. It should be heavy, homogeneous in material, and possessing "virtue," or the power to attract the greatest amount of iron. Thus, in the latter instance, Peregrinus considered the extent of magnetic strength (perhaps the lifting power of the stone) to be of crucial importance.

Chapter 4 is critical to the history of magnetism, for here is the earliest account of magnetic polarity and the methods for fixing the north and south poles. The poles of the lodestone are analogous to the celestial poles. In this respect, Peregrinus followed medieval thinking. According to the cosmology of the Middle Ages, Earth was the center of the universe, fixed and immobile; around it lay ten heavens, all of which, except the outermost, where God resided, rotated about their common center. The rotation of the heavens was on an axis, the ends of which formed the north and south celestial poles. Peregrinus believed that the celestial poles attracted the magnet; it was only later that scientists, beginning with William Gilbert in 1600, thought of Earth as having its own magnetic poles.

The theory of the celestial poles led Peregrinus to form two methods of distinguishing the poles of a lodestone. The first method involves a lodestone that has been polished into a spherical shape. A needle or piece of iron is placed on the stone's surface; a line is then drawn in the direction of the needle, dividing the sphere in half. If this procedure is performed repeatedly, all the lines (meridians) will converge at two points—the poles. This conclusion represents an astounding piece of scientific experimentation: The poles of a spherical magnet are recognized and the magnetic meridians located.

The second method was also revolutionary. Peregrinus insisted that the poles can also be detected without drawing meridians—simply by noting the greatest attraction of a needle by the magnetic force. Peregrinus suggested that a needle of iron, 5 or 7.5 centimeters long (about 2 or 3 inches), if moved around a lodestone, would locate the polar point, the place where the needle stands the most erect. What Peregrinus observed is the action of the magnetic field of force: At the poles the needles stand erect, and at other points, they are more or less inclined.

The next step was to determine which pole is north and which is south (chapter 5). Here Peregrinus set forth the fundamental law of magnetic polarity. If the magnet is placed in a wooden cup and the cup into a large vessel of water, then the north pole of the lodestone will point toward the north celestial pole and the south pole of the lodestone to the celestial south pole. Even if one forcibly turns the magnet away in a new direction, it will return to its true alignment. Next, the effect of one lodestone on another was demonstrated. The north pole of a lodestone, when brought close to the south pole of a second lodestone, will cause the latter to try to adhere to it; the same will happen if the south pole of the one is moved to the other's north pole. If the reverse is done, however—that is, if like poles are brought into close proximity—then the poles "flee" each other. Thus Peregrinus established the law of attraction and repulsion. Peregrinus then made a further startling discovery: If a magnet is broken into two, each part will act like a magnet and have its own north and south poles; moreover, the opposite poles of the magnets will unite if brought together, thus making again a unified magnet. Peregrinus's work was the first theory of persistence of polarity in the separate parts of a magnet.

Peregrinus next showed the action of a magnet on iron: A needle when touched by the north pole of the magnet will turn to the south celestial pole and vice versa. Thus, the south pole of the needle will be attracted to the north pole of the magnet and repelled by the south pole; the north pole of the needle will be attracted to the south pole of the magnet and repelled by the north pole. Polarity, however, can be reversed by touching the north pole of the needle with the north pole of the magnet, causing the needle's north pole to be converted into a south pole. This observation of reversal of magnetic polarity was centuries ahead of its time.

Peregrinus finished part 1 of his work with a discussion of the cause of the virtue (attractive power) of the lodestone. He rejected the then commonly held view that mines of magnetic stone in the northern region of the world caused a magnet to be oriented on a north-south line. Instead, the poles of a magnet are influenced by the celestial poles.

Peregrinus also refuted the idea that the Pole Star was at the true north; rather, it was Polaris that rotated around that point. It should be noted, however, that Peregrinus was not aware of declination, that is, the fact that the compass needle does not point due north but at a small angle that varies from place to place. This effect had long been observed by the Chinese and is mentioned in an eleventh century work by Shen Gua (Shen Kua). The discovery in Europe of the declination was formerly attributed to Christopher Columbus during his voyage of 1492 or even to Sebastian Cabot during his voyage to Labrador in 1497-1498; current scholars, however, recognize that European mariners knew of declination long before this.

The chapter closes with a description of a perpetual motion machine with pivoted spherical magnets. The magnet, made with fixed pivots at its poles so that it could freely rotate, would follow the motion of the celestial poles and so rotate. This theory was possible, one must remember, because Peregrinus believed that Earth was motionless and the celestial heavens rotated around it.

Part 2 is very important for the history of the compass. The Chinese had known about the magnet's properties of pointing north-south and had employed it for geomancy; yet they did not apply this knowledge to the construction of a mariner's compass until the twelfth century. At about the same time, references to the mariner's compass appeared in Western literature; whether the compass was introduced from the East by Arab or European sailors or was independently developed is not known. This early compass was a water compass. A needle or piece of iron, after being placed on a magnetic stone, was floated on wood in a vessel of water; it would turn until it pointed in the direction of north. Hardly a sophisticated piece of equipment, this early compass gave only a directional heading and did not permit any bearings.

Peregrinus made tremendous improvements on this water compass by constructing two compasses—a dry compass and a wet one. The latter consisted of an oval magnet inside a bowl or wooden case and floated on water inside a large vessel. The rim of the vessel was marked into four quadrants by the four cardinal points of the compass. Each quadrant was subdivided into ninety equal parts, or degrees. On top of the container that had the magnet inside it, Peregrinus placed a light bar of wood, with an upright pin at each end. This device allowed the navigator to determine not only the direction of the ship but also the azimuth of any heavenly body (sun, moon, or star). The innovation, in other words, was a combination of a compass needle and nautical astrolabe that was capable of steering a vessel on any given course.

Peregrinus proceeded to invent a pivoted compass. In place of the floating bowl and the vessel of water, a circular compass container was constructed with a transparent lid of glass or quartz. The top of the container was divided into the same ninety parts per quadrant as in the floating compass; then, a movable pivot rule with upright pins at each end was fastened on top of the lid. An axis of brass or silver was then fastened below the lid and the bottom of the vessel. Two needles—one of iron, the other of brass or silver—were inserted at right angles through the axis. The iron needle was then magnetized by a lodestone so that it would point north and south. The lid of the vessel was then turned until its north-south points were in line with those of the needle. Azimuthal readings could then be made by rotating the pivot rule to the heavenly body sought. Others later improved this compass by adding the compass card, that is, the thirty-two points of the compass affixed to the compass's pointing needle.

Peregrinus closes his treatise with yet another attempt at perpetual motion by magnetic power. He conceived of a wheel of silver with a series of iron teeth. A magnet was to be placed at the end of a radial arm within the ring and close to the teeth. Peregrinus believed that any one tooth of the wheel would be attracted to the north pole of the magnet. Because of its attraction to the north pole, the tooth would gain enough momentum to move onto the magnet's south pole. Here it would be repelled by the south pole, whose momentum would force that tooth beyond the magnet. The next tooth is attracted to the north pole of the magnet, and so on. This alternating attraction and repulsion of the teeth would cause the wheel, to which the teeth are attached, to move in perpetual motion.

In summary, Peregrinus found and differentiated the poles of a magnet. He then formulated the laws of magnetic repulsion and attraction and discussed the strength of the magnetic force field by the amount of inclination of an iron needle when brought into close contact with a magnet at various points. He knew that the Pole Star was not at the true north and, therefore, did not affect the magnet. He knew also about reversal of magnetic polarity. Peregrinus applied this knowledge to practical inventions.

Significance

Peregrinus's pivoted and floating compasses allowed the determination of the meridian and the azimuths of heavenly bodies and were the first to have the fiducial line and a division of 360 degrees. He suggested the conversion of magnetic energy into mechanical energy by a perpetual motion machine.

Peregrinus's "letter" on magnetism is the first scientific work on the subject. His work exerted considerable influence on later writers and was drawn on extensively by William Gilbert, who laid the foundation of magnetic science in 1600 in his *De magnete, magneticisque corporibus, et de magnete tellure* (1600; *On the Magnet, Magnetic Bodies Also, and on the Great Magnet the Earth*, 1860).

—*Steven M. Oberhelman*

Further Reading

Aczel, Amir D. *The Riddle of the Compass: The Invention That Changed the World*. New York: Harcourt, 2001. A brief but detailed and thorough account of the invention of the compass. Also discusses the history of navigation up to the fifteenth century.

Benjamin, Park. *History of Electricity*. 1898. Reprint. New York: Arno Press, 1975. One of the most extensive discussions in English of Peregrinus's life and work. The style is a bit trying, but this work explains very well the ideas expressed in Peregrinus's treatise. Includes bibliography and index.

Gilbert, William. *On the Magnet*. New York: Basic Books, 1958. A reprinted edition of Gilbert's foundational text on magnetic science.

Grant, Edward. "Petrus Peregrinus." In *Dictionary of Scientific Biography*, edited by Charles C. Gillispie. Vol. 10. New York: Scribner, 1974. A definitive treatment of Peregrinus. Contains an invaluable bibliography.

Harradon, H. D. "Some Early Contributions to the History of Geomagnetism-I." *Journal of Terrestrial Magnetism and Atmospheric Electricity* 48 (1943): 3-17. Contains a brief discussion of Peregrinus's life and work, followed by a translation of the letter. (This journal is now named the *Journal of Geophysical Research*.)

Mottelay, Paul Fleury. *Bibliographical History of Electricity and Magnetism, Chronologically Arranged*. 1922. Reprint. New York: Arno Press, 1955. Contains a summation of the letter, with a bibliography on Peregrinus and the manuscripts and editions of the letter.

Peregrinus of Maricourt, Petrus. *Epistle of Petrus Peregrinus of Maricourt, to Sygerus of Foucaucourt, Soldier, Concerning the Magnet*. Translated by Silvanus P. Thompson. London: Chiswick Press, 1902. The translator includes a good introduction to Peregrinus's life and theories on magnetism.

Sarton, George. *From Rabbi Ben Ezra to Roger Bacon*. Vol. 2 in *Introduction to the History of Science*. Huntington, N.Y.: R. E. Krieger, 1975. Short but very helpful biography of Peregrinus, and a summation of the contents of the letter.

Stern, David P. "Demystifying Magnetism." *The World and I* 15, no. 10 (October, 2000). A brief, readable article on William Gilbert's magnetic science, a science that was greatly influenced by Peregrinus.

Thompson, Silvanus P. "Petrus Peregrinus de Maricourt and His *Epistola de magnete*." *Proceedings of the British Academy* 2 (1905-1906): 377-408. Extensive discussion of Peregrinus's life, his work, and his impact.

SEE ALSO: Abul Wefa; Saint Albertus Magnus; Alhazen; Āryabhaṭa the Elder; Roger Bacon; al-Battānī; al-Bīrūnī; Brahmagupta; Jean Buridan; Frederick II; al-Khwārizmī; Leonardo of Pisa; Levi ben Gershom; Louis IX; Omar Khayyám.

RELATED ARTICLES in *Great Events from History: The Middle Ages, 477-1453*: 595-665: Invention of Decimals and Negative Numbers; 7th-8th centuries: Maya Build Astronomical Observatory at Palenque; April or May, 711: Ṭārik Crosses into Spain; c. 950: Court of Córdoba Flourishes in Spain; c. 1100: Arabic Numerals Are Introduced into Europe; c. 1120: Order of the Knights Templar Is Founded; 1227-1230: Frederick II Leads the Sixth Crusade; 1248-1254: Failure of the Seventh Crusade; 1328-1350: Flowering of Late Medieval Physics.

PÉROTIN

French composer

Pérotin was a pioneer in the evolution of harmony as a principle of Western music. He transformed the nature of early music by first introducing three- and four-voice textures into church music, by developing polyphonic forms with semichordal sequences, and by adapting liturgical forms to secular purposes.

BORN: 1155-1160; possibly Paris, France
DIED: 1200-1205; probably Paris, France
ALSO KNOWN AS: Perotinus
AREA OF ACHIEVEMENT: Music

EARLY LIFE

Almost nothing is known about the life of Pérotin (pay-roh-tan), which in itself reveals the lack of personal esteem accorded artists during the Middle Ages. There is one existing contemporary reference to him, significantly in a treatise on twelfth century composers attributed to a writer designated Anonymous IV. That text associates Pérotin with the then recently built Cathedral of Notre Dame, first begun in 1163; since he cannot be identified as any of the registered principal musicians of the cathedral, the cantors and succentors, he is assumed to have been a choirmaster, though he could have been an organist. The treatise does attribute to him, however, specific compositions by title and others by type.

The named compositions are convincingly dated 1198-1200; the others seem to have been written a bit earlier. His association in the text with the earlier composer Léonin suggests that Pérotin may have begun working under his tutelage, suggesting a possible birth date. Because nothing in his music reflects the changes that took place in music and society after 1203, it is convenient to assume that his death occurred around that time. This date seems more likely because his music was not only admired but also widely copied and distributed, surviving in several different widely separated manuscripts. Had he written after 1203, his work would have been preserved. All attempts to determine more information about the man and his life have failed. Pérotin lives on in his music and in the general information known about life in twelfth century Paris.

LIFE'S WORK

Because Pérotin's music is in some ways almost as obscure as his life, it is easy to discount his significance. His music is really accessible only to specialists, and specialists often are so mired in minutiae that they lose sight of the larger implications of their enthusiasms. Thus few scholars will say that Pérotin was one of the most important composers in Western music, although in many ways he can be considered the father of harmony; since harmonic texture and sequence is the major distinguishing quality of Western music, Pérotin was indeed of consequence.

Along with his predecessor Léonin, Pérotin was connected with innovations in music associated with the Cathedral of Notre Dame. Earlier in the twelfth century, composers centered at the Abbey of St. Martial at Limoges in south-central France had developed a new kind of two-part music called florid, melismatic, or Saint Martial organum. Although not the first type of multipart, multivoice music, it was distinct in having the upper voice improvise a free plainchant melody over drawn-out single notes in the lower, like drones. This lower line had originally been a melody itself; now that became unrecognizable. Thus, a new, nonmelodic aspect became added to the texture of music.

Léonin made the first significant changes to this style, developing a form known as Notre Dame organum, though he also worked in the equally important, related form of descant. Much of his work is preserved in the *Magnus liber organi* (c. 1170; great book of organum), a liturgical cycle of two-part settings for vespers and matins, as well as alleluias and graduals for the Mass. *Magnus liber organi* is the first identified volume of compositions by one master; its importance is attested by its preservation in several manuscripts in Italy, Germany, and Spain, as well as in France. Léonin introduced two new features in his work. One involved composing alternating sections of two-part polyphony and choral unison chant; this alternation becomes the principal formal structure. The second novelty is within the polyphony itself: The upper, "melody" part becomes flexible and semi-improvisatory, seeming to reach climaxes almost accidentally.

Léonin's organum looks and sounds much like chant superimposed on drone, something like unornamented bagpipe music. His descant is much different. Here the lower part moves more quickly, though in equally measured tones; the upper voice moves even faster now in a distinctly rhythmic pattern, almost as if dancing after swaying in the chant of the organum. When combined with organum in this way, the descant sections were called clausulae; they contrasted with the organum sections also in reaching distinct and definite final cadences.

Pérotin continued, expanded, and also transcended these practices. He adopted the basic formal style invented by Léonin but regularized it by establishing more precise rhythms and using clausulae more frequently. The lower part of the organum becomes less dronelike, more rhythmically regular and more melodic. In this respect Pérotin laid the foundation for the later thirteenth century motet, which became the major musical form of the succeeding three centuries. More important, he developed organum in a completely different way by adding first a third and then a fourth voice, creating an entirely new texture in music.

In terms of linear structure, Pérotin's triple and quadruple organum resemble Léonin's—both have alternating sections of slower, more sustained and faster, more rhythmic material, though Pérotin is always more rhythmic and melodic. Yet the difference in horizontal structure, or overlayering, is almost breathtaking. The upper voices dance, intertwine, cross, and resolve over the moving bottom line. Each line is distinct, moving on its own, but all play against the others. Something completely new happens in the process. The accepted intervals for voice doubling in organum were octaves, fifths, and (rarely) fourths. One of the perhaps unexpected results of multiplying upper voices is the regular emergence of thirds; the combination produces for the first time in Western music what sounds like a sequence of chords. These do not yet work together to form a chordal progression to resolution, but they establish the basis for this later formulation. Pérotin himself is still working with the tonal modes of medieval plainsong, so this kind of progression is unthinkable in his work, but the germ of the idea is there.

This foreshadowing is only part of his glory. Another part resides in the new sounds he creates. His music creates shifting webs of sonority and dissonance, in which the voices weave around one another in an unfolding maze centered on the stable lower part, much like mists floating above a mountain valley. A completely different source of beauty arises from Pérotin's practice of reflecting the vowel patterns of the text in the melodies and rhythms to which he sets them. In this he anticipates the text imaging of later composers, though few of them match him in subtlety and delicacy.

Pérotin also invented and popularized another, simpler polyphonic form known as conductus. Conductus seems to have originated in separating clausulae from organum and substituting secular (though still sacred) verses for the original hymn and sequence texts. These new verses were then reset so that all voices moved in nearly equal rhythms. This music, written for two, three, or four voices within a fairly restricted range, rested on cadences of fifths and unisons; since thirds occurred frequently and instrumental doublings were common, the effect was quasichordal, prefiguring later harmonic hymn settings. This type, known as conductus style, was extended to other forms, including completely secular ones.

Compared to Léonin's clausulae, conductus became a considerably expanded form; unlike it, the texts for conductus were commonly set syllabically. Eventually conductus even absorbed certain clausulae—which proved easily detachable from organum—and used them as contrasting melismas, textless and rhythmically varied, within its own structure. These contrasting passages—called caudae—gave conductus a structure parallel to that of organum, though the texts were treated quite distinctly.

One further difference had a major effect on the future of music: Pérotin began composing a new melody for the lower part rather than adopting an ecclesiastical chant. Thus he became the first composer to devise both the melodic and the harmonic aspects of polyphonic compositions.

SIGNIFICANCE

Pérotin's final achievement was in laying the foundations of the motet, linked earlier to his practice in organum. In fact, his work in both organum and conductus foreshadowed and tended toward the motet; it is not at all surprising that the motet should supersede both in the history of music. No existing motets have been ascribed to Pérotin, but this lack should not be allowed to obscure his significance in this regard. In that preprint age, the identification of composers in manuscripts was haphazard and casual; it is not incidental that the best-known composer until the sixteenth century is Anonymous. Further, secular music was then far from the serious business it later became. For centuries to come a composer would be identified primarily by his religious and liturgical work. Pérotin can be singled out as the most prolific composer of descant clausulae of the early thirteenth century, and these clausulae are barely distinguishable from motets. Thus he is the true father of motets, and hence of formal Western music.

He is equally important for ecclesiastical music. His organum, for example, established the prevailing manner of presenting the Mass for the following 150 years—in itself a remarkable achievement. Even more remarkable is the recognition that when Guillaume de Machaut introduced innovations in Mass settings, the musical form he used was still the organum of Pérotin. Yet beyond that fact lies Pérotin's almost miraculous anticipation of chordal harmony, since Western music eventually chose to focus almost exclusively on that as a medium of musical expressiveness. In fact, since he worked long before Western composers decided to concentrate on the major-minor axis of tonality, his modal quasichords explore harmonic areas left inaccessible to composers before the twentieth century. Listening to him opens the ear to untrodden regions of sound.

—*James L. Livingston*

FURTHER READING

Caldwell, John. *Medieval Music*. Bloomington: Indiana University Press, 1978. This study attempts to synthesize reconstructions of Pérotin's music. Includes an extensive bibliography.

Grout, Donald Jay, and Claude V. Palisca. *A History of Western Music*. 6th ed. New York: Norton, 2001. An excellent attempt to place Pérotin in the evolution of Western music. Includes extensive examples and bibliography.

LaRue, Jan, ed. *Aspects of Medieval and Renaissance Music: A Birthday Offering to Gustave Reese*. New York: W. W. Norton, 1966. Contains much information about the nature and forms of medieval music and its background and includes an excellent biographical sketch.

Sanders, Ernest H. *French and English Polyphony of the Thirteenth and Fourteenth Centuries: Style and Notation*. Brookfield, Vt.: Ashgate, 1998. A study that focuses on musical polyphony and the motet in Pérotin's time and considers the dating of Pérotin's works.

Treitler, Leo. *With Voice and Pen: Coming to Know Medieval Song and How It Was Made*. New York: Oxford University Press, 2003. A collection surveying the history of vocal music and its literary aspects in the Middle Ages. Discusses the organum of Notre Dame, the structure of the alleluia, the chant, the history of music writing, music and poetry, and more. Includes a bibliography and index.

Waite, William G. *The Rhythm of Twelfth-Century Polyphony: Its Theory and Practice*. 1954. Reprint. Westport, Conn.: Greenwood Press, 1973. Much more than the title suggests, this work is primarily an attempt to decipher medieval manuscript musical notation in order to reconstruct actual musical practice. Contains detailed analyses of the various forms practiced by Pérotin.

SEE ALSO: Adam de la Halle; John Dunstable; Francesco Landini; Guillaume de Machaut; Johannes de Muris; Philippe de Vitry.

RELATED ARTICLE in *Great Events from History: The Middle Ages, 477-1453*: c. 1100: Rise of Courtly Love.

PETRARCH
Italian poet and scholar

Petrarch's scholarship stimulated a revival of interest in classical studies, and his vernacular poetry created a veritable Petrarchan school of sonneteers.

BORN: July 20, 1304; Arezzo, Tuscany (now in Italy)
DIED: July 18, 1374; Arquà, Carrara (now in Italy)
ALSO KNOWN AS: Francesco Petrarca (full name)
AREA OF ACHIEVEMENT: Literature

EARLY LIFE

The father of Petrarch (PEH-trahrk), Pietro di Parenzo—more commonly known as Ser Petracco—was, like Dante, a member of the White Guelph Party in Florence. Following the victory of the Black Guelphs, he was levied a heavy fine and sentenced to the loss of a hand. He fled with his wife, Eletta Canigiani, to Arezzo in October of 1302, and there, on July 20, 1304, Francesco Petrarca was born. The following year, Petrarch and his mother moved to Incisa, where his brother, Gherardo, was born in 1307.

Because Incisa was under Florentine rule, Pietro could visit his wife and children only surreptitiously, so in 1311 the family moved again, this time to Pisa. There Petrarch saw for the first and only time that other famous Florentine exile, Dante. Apparently it was at Pisa, too, that Petrarch began his studies under yet another exile, Convenevole da Prato. In 1312, the family again relocated, settling in Carpentras, France, northeast of Avignon, to be close to the papal seat. Many years later, Petrarch wrote to Guido Sette, recalling his life in the French village: "Do you remember those four years? What happiness we had, what security, what peace at home, what freedom in the town, what quietness and silence in the country!" Sette, who became archbishop of Genoa, was to be a lifelong friend and correspondent.

In 1316, Petrarch was sent to the University of Montpellier to study law, the family profession. He was already showing far more interest in the classics than in legal matters; according to his own account, his father discovered his Latin library and threw all but two books, one by Vergil and one by Cicero, into the fire, sparing this pair only because of his son's pleas. Like so many other of Petrarch's autobiographical accounts, this anecdote seems too pat to be true, for throughout his life Petrarch took Vergil and Cicero as his models, seeking to surpass the one in poetry, the other in prose. While Petrarch was still at Montpellier, his mother died; the event called forth his earliest surviving poem, a moving Latin elegy of thirty-eight hexameter lines, one for each year of her life.

To complete his legal studies, Petrarch was sent to the University of Bologna in 1320, the most celebrated law school in Europe. Again, Petrarch showed more interest in Latin literature than in law, recording in February, 1325, his purchase of Saint Augustine's *De civitate Dei* (413-427; *The City of God*, 1610); this copy is now at the University of Padua. His father's hostility to classical studies seems to have vanished, if it ever existed, for from Paris he brought his son that compendium of medieval learning, Saint Isidore of Seville's *Etymologiae* (late sixth century to early seventh century). The acquisition of the volume by Augustine also belies Petrarch's claim that in his youth he read only secular works.

The death of his father in April, 1326, freed Petrarch to pursue his own interests. He returned to Avignon and studied literature. In his *Posteritati* (1370-1372; *Epistle to Posterity*, 1966), he describes himself as having been a good-looking youth, with bright eyes and a medium complexion. He had two illegitimate children—a son, Giovanni, born in 1337, and a daughter, Francesca, born six years later—and sustained many enduring friendships throughout his life.

LIFE'S WORK

About a year after his return from Bologna, Petrarch had one of the most important encounters of his life. As he wrote in 1348 in his copy of Vergil that served as a diary,

> Laura, illustrious through her own virtues, and long famed through my verses, first appeared to my eyes in my youth, in the year of our Lord 1327, on the sixth day of April, in the church of Saint Clare in Avignon, at matins.

Virtually all of his vernacular poetry was to revolve around this woman: The verses of the *Rerum vulgarium fragmenta* (1470, also known as *Canzoniere; Rhymes*, 1976) celebrate his love for her both during her life and after her death; the various *Trionfi* (1470; *Tryumphs*, 1565, best known as *Triumphs*, 1962) reveal her power over Petrarch, Cupid, mortality, and even time itself.

Petrarch's father had left his two sons enough money to free them from the need to work, but by 1330 the peculations of feckless executors and dishonest servants forced the young men to seek some occupation. Because Petrarch despised law and hated medicine, as he would make clear in a later diatribe against the profession (*In-*

vective contra medicum, 1352-1355), he took minor religious orders, and, in the autumn of 1330, he entered the household of Cardinal Giovanni Colonna. Subsequently, he received various benefices, among them the canonries of Lombez, Pisa, Parma, Padua, and Monselice. Neither pluralism nor nonresidency troubled him; he treated these posts as sinecures, though he was willing to trade them for less lucrative offices to oblige his friends. Though at various times throughout his life he was offered papal secretaryships and even bishoprics, he always refused, preferring the freedom to read and write over power and money.

During the early 1330's, he traveled widely and added to his library. A list of his favorite books, compiled in 1333 (*Libri mei peculiares*), already contained some fifty entries, about twenty of them by Cicero and Seneca. A 1346 letter to Giovanni dell' Incisa makes clear his sentiment: "I am possessed by one insatiable passion, which I cannot restrain—nor would I if I could. . . . I cannot get enough books."

Among the Ciceronian works he may have owned was *De gloria*, of which no copy is now extant. He certainly owned the *Pro Archia* (62 B.C.E.), which he found in Liège in 1333; the discovery added an important speech to the known canon, and this defense of poetry treated a subject of lifelong interest to Petrarch himself. Sometime before 1337, his collecting led to his preparing the first scholarly edition of Livy's history of Rome, *Ab urbe condita libri* (26 B.C.E.-15 C.E.; *The History of Rome*, 1600). Originally composed of 142 books arranged in groups of ten (called decades), by the Middle Ages this monumental work had been scattered. During his travels, Petrarch had found manuscripts in Chartres and Verona, and he recognized that they belonged together. His own transcript, now in the British Museum, united the first, third, and fourth decades to create the most complete copy then known. Moreover, his philological knowledge allowed him to complete certain gaps and choose the best among various readings. His text served as the basis of subsequent editions, and his comments remain useful to scholars of the Roman historian.

Engraving of Petrarch. (Library of Congress)

In these years, he was writing lyrics, sonnets, and canzoni in Italian, as well as a comedy, *Philologia*, now lost. About one hundred of these vernacular poems were to be incorporated into the 366 that constitute the final version of the *Canzoniere*. His Latin works of the period are fewer, but he did address an appeal to Pope Benedict XII to return to Rome. Throughout his life, he regarded the Eternal City as the only fit place for the seat of the Papacy and the Holy Roman Emperor, and he repeatedly urged popes and kings to return there.

His own visit to Rome in 1337 marked a milestone in his life, for thereafter he devoted an increasing amount of effort to Latin compositions. He began *De viris illustribus* (1351-1353; reorganized as *Quorundam virorum illustrium epithoma*), a biographical compendium of classical and more recent figures; in 1338 or 1339, he started work on *Africa* (1396; English translation, 1977), an epic about Scipio Africanus. The former was his attempt to create a historical work to rival Livy's, while with the latter he hoped to imitate, indeed surpass, Vergil's *Aeneid* (c. 29-19 B.C.E.; English translation, 1553). Neither work was ever finished, but both circulated in manuscript during his lifetime and earned for him much fame. Indeed, by September, 1340, his reputation was such that both the University of Paris and the Roman senate invited him to be crowned poet laureate.

Petrarch rejected the medieval Scholasticism that the university represented, and he regarded Rome as the true center of culture. On April 8, 1341, he was crowned with a laurel wreath in the senatorial palace on the Capitoline, where he delivered a speech praising poetry. While in

MAJOR WORKS BY PETRARCH

Date	*Work*
wr. 1325-1366	*Rerum familiarium libri* (also as *Books on Personal Matters*)
1341	*Collatio laureationes* (*Coronation Oath*)
1343-1345	*Rerum memorandum libri*
1346	*De vita solitaria* (*The Life of Solitude*)
1353-1358	*Secretum meum*, or *De secreto conflictu curarum mearum* (*My Secret*)
1359-1360	*Sine nomine* (*Book Without a Name*)
wr. 1361-1374	*Senilium rerum libri* (*Letters of Old Age*)
1363	*Epistolae metricae* (*Metrical Letters*)
1364	*Bucolicum carmen* (*Eclogues*)
1364-1366	*Rerum familiarium libri xxiv* (*Books on Personal Matters*)
1366	*De remediis utriusque fortunae* (*On Remedies for Good and Bad Fortunes*)
1367	*De sui ipsius et multorum ignorantia* (*On His Own Ignorance and That of Many*)
1370-1372	*Posteritati* (*Epistle to Posterity*)
1396	*Africa*
1470	*Rerum vulgarium fragmenta* (also as *Canzoniere* or *Rhymes*)
1470	*Trionfi* (*Triumphs*)

Rome, he began his collection of antique coins, which he treasured not for their monetary value but for their historical information.

He was now living in the country in Vaucluse, not far from Avignon but still removed from crowds and the papal court. Perhaps, again, he was imitating such classical models as Horace, who had retired to his Sabine farm, or his beloved Cicero at Tusculum. Certainly he was the first person since antiquity to retreat from the city to write. He seems genuinely to have loved nature, choosing to live in rural seclusion whenever possible. In a poetic epistle to Giacomo Colonna he wrote, "How delightful it is to imbibe the silence of the deep forest." Elsewhere he speaks of rising at midnight to wander in the moonlit landscape, and in his introspective *Secretum meum* (or *De secreto conflictu curarum mearum*, 1353-1358; *My Secret*, 1911), a supposed dialogue between Augustinus (Saint Augustine) and Franciscus (Petrarch) that defends the pursuit of secular literature and scholarship, Augustinus speaks of the days when, "lying upon the grass in the meadows, you [that is, Petrarch] listened to the murmur of the stream as it broke over the pebbles: Now, sitting on the bare hills, you measured freely the plain extended at your feet."

Petrarch's aversion to Avignon was certainly sincere. In one of his metrical epistles he complains of "The uproar that resounds within the walls/ Of the straitened city, where the very ground/ Cannot contain the crowds, nor the very sky/ Contain the clamor." He hated the intrigues of the papal court, and in his *Sine nomine* (1359-1360; *Book Without a Name*, 1973), so called because he deleted the names of the addressees, he described Avignon as a place

> in which no piety, no charity, and no faith dwell; where pride, envy, debauchery, and avarice reign with all their arts; where the worst man is promoted and the munificent robber is exalted and the just man is trampled on; where honesty is called foolishness and cunning is called wisdom; where God is mocked, the sesterce [money] is adored, the laws are trodden under foot, and the good are scorned.

Much as he loved the seclusion of Vaucluse, he frequently traveled through northern Italy on papal missions, and in 1344, he bought and refurbished a house in Parma, apparently with the intention of remaining permanently. He would leave France for good in 1353, and in his letters as well as in *Invectiva contra eum qui maledixit Italiae* (1373) and in poems such as "Italia mia" ("My Italy"), he revealed himself as a true Italian patriot. His residence in Parma was short-lived; in December, 1344, the marquess of Mantua and the Visconti brothers of Milan laid siege to the city. Petrarch fled the fighting on February 23, 1345, and traveled to Modena, Bologna, and Verona.

In Verona, he found a volume of letters from Cicero to his brothers Quintus and Brutus and to the literary patron and critic Atticus. This discovery marked yet another of

Petrarch's contributions to the world's knowledge of the Roman orator, and it led directly to Petrarch's decision to preserve and collect his own letters in the twenty-four books of *Rerum familiarium libri* (wr. 1325-1366; English translation, 1975-1985, also known as *Books on Personal Matters*) and the eighteen of *Senilium rerum libri* (wr. 1361-1374; *Letters of Old Age*, 1966).

Back in Vaucluse, he wrote the first draft of *De vita solitaria* (1346; *The Life of Solitude*, 1924), praising the country life, and began his *Bucolicum carmen* (1364; *Eclogues*, 1974), writing four of the twelve eclogues of this collection modeled on Vergil's pastorals. A visit to his brother at Montrieux, where Gherardo had entered the Carthusian monastery in 1343, prompted *De otio religioso* (1376), a celebration of monasticism. Although Petrarch's writings before this date were not exclusively secular, these works suggest a deepening interest in religion.

In 1348, Petrarch was again living in Parma, where he learned of Laura's death. In response to this news, he wrote three more eclogues, two dealing with the Black Plague that had killed Laura and a third specifically treating her death. He also began the third of his six *Triumphs*, the triumph of Death, with Laura once more the theme.

Following several years of travel between France and Italy, Petrarch settled in Milan in 1353, residing there until 1361. There he completed his *De remediis utriusque fortunae* (1366; *Physicke Against Fortune*, 1597; also as *On Remedies for Good and Bad Fortunes*, 1966). He explained its contents in a letter to Guido Sette:

> All philosophers, all experience, and truth itself agree in this: that in times of adversity . . . the one remedy is patience . . . and that in times of prosperity the one remedy is moderation. I have had it in mind, of late, to write at some length about both these remedies, and now have I done so.

In his dedicatory preface, Petrarch notes that of good fortune and bad, the former is the more dangerous.

During this period, Petrarch undertook various missions for the Visconti brothers. In 1354, he attempted to effect peace with the doge of Venice and Genoa, and when that effort failed, he was sent to Emperor Charles IV to enlist his support against the Venetians. Another embassy took him to France to welcome King John back from English captivity; the king was so impressed with Petrarch that he tried to dissuade him from returning to Italy. Emperor Charles IV had also wanted Petrarch to remain with him in Prague, but Petrarch's Italian patriotism impelled him to reply, "In the whole world there is nothing under heaven that can be compared to Italy, in respect either to the gifts of nature or to human worth."

Through his scholarship he was, however, able to serve the emperor. Duke Rudolf IV of Austria was claiming autonomy from the Holy Roman Empire because of certain privileges he claimed that his country had been granted in patents by Julius Caesar and Nero. Charles sent the documents to Petrarch, who exposed them as forgeries.

In 1362, Petrarch moved to Venice, offering to bequeath his extensive collection of books to the city in return for a house during his lifetime. Although the proposal eventually fell through, it marks the first attempt to establish a public library for "those ingenious and noble men . . . who may delight in such things." Again, one sees that Petrarch was well ahead of his age.

After several years of moving between Venice, Pavia, Milan, and Padua, he settled in Padua in 1368, before moving in 1370 to rural Arquà, about ten miles to the southwest, where he spent the remainder of his life in the care of his daughter. Until his death on July 18, 1374, he continued to revise his earlier works and to add new ones, such as the last of the *Triumphs* and a Latin translation of the story of Griselda by his friend Giovanni Boccaccio.

SIGNIFICANCE

In his *Epistle to Posterity*, Petrarch writes, "Perhaps you will have heard something of me." Posterity has, indeed. Rodolphus Agricola, the Dutch Humanist who was Petrarch's first biographer, claimed that Petrarch initiated the study of classical literature, and Boccaccio told him that "because of your example, many within and perhaps without Italy are cultivating studies neglected for centuries." His interest in classical antiquity led to the recovery of many previously lost or obscure works, thus aiding in the modern study of Cicero, Sextus Propertius, and the ancient geographer Pomponius Mela.

Petrarch claimed, "I never liked this present age. . . . I am alive now, yet I would rather have been born at some other time." One assumes he would have preferred the age of Cicero. Certainly, it was as a classicist that he hoped to earn his reputation. In 1359, he rejected Boccaccio's suspicions that he (Petrarch) harbored any jealousy toward Dante:

> I ask you, is it likely that I should envy a man who devoted his whole life to things to which I gave myself only in the first flush of youth; so that what for him was, if not the only, certainly the most important branch of literary art, has for me been only a pastime and relaxation and a first exercise in the rudiments of my craft.

This dismissal of the *Canzoniere*, which he disparagingly called *Rerum vulgarium fragmenta*, is disingenuous, for he continued to add to these vernacular poems and polish them throughout his life. However Petrarch may have felt about these works, posterity has regarded them as his major literary achievement. These poems have been translated into more than a dozen languages and influenced the poets of the French Pléiade, the English Renaissance, and Italy. Among the progeny of this first sonnet cycle in the West are Sir Philip Sidney's *Astrophel and Stella* (1591), Edmund Spenser's *Amoretti* (1595), and William Shakespeare's *Sonnets* (1609).

Even as a classicist, Petrarch was more modern than he allowed, for he adapted rather than imitated classical models. His eclogues treat contemporary themes; his epic *Africa* sought to portray Scipio as a fusion of classical heroism and Christian saintliness; his unfinished *Rerum memorandum libri* (1343-1345) classifies the deeds and writings of the ancients under the four cardinal Christian virtues of Prudence, Justice, Fortitude, and Temperance. He was thus the first of the Christian Humanists, as he was the first Humanist to study Greek (though he made little progress in the language), the first modern historian, and, as he repeatedly reveals in his letters, the first person to analyze himself so carefully. In sum, Petrarch may be called the first modern man.

—*Joseph Rosenblum*

FURTHER READING

Bergin, Thomas G. *Petrarch.* New York: Twayne, 1970. A critical biography by a leading translator of Petrarch's Latin writings. Covers the life and works, with detailed discussions of the *Canzoniere* and the *Triumphs.*

Fubini, Riccardo. *Humanism and Secularization: From Petrarch to Valla.* Durham, N.C.: Duke University Press, 2003. An examination of Humanism and its relationship with Petrarch, Bracciolini, and Poggio. Bibliography and index.

Jones, Frederic J. *The Structure of Petrarch's "Canzionere": A Chronological, Psychological, and Stylistic Analysis.* Rochester, N.Y.: Boydell and Brewer, 1995. An analysis of Petrarch's poetry, particularly his *Canzionere.* Bibliography and indexes.

Kennedy, William J. *The Site of Petrarchism: Early Modern National Sentiment in Italy, France, and England.* Baltimore: Johns Hopkins University Press, 2003. An examination of Petrarch's nationalism as it manifested itself in literature and its effect. Bibliography and index.

Mann, Nicholas. *Petrarch.* New York: Oxford University Press, 1984. This brief book talks about Petrarch's writings as a lifelong effort to create and explain a self. Includes a useful bibliography of primary and secondary sources.

Mazzotta, Giuseppe. *The Worlds of Petrarch.* Durham, N.C.: Duke University Press, 1993. A critical look at the poetry and other works of Petrarch, including the *Canzionere.* Also examines his Humanism. Bibliography and index.

Quillen, Carol E. *Rereading the Renaissance: Petrarch, Augustine, and the Language of Humanism.* Ann Arbor: University of Michigan Press, 1998. Examines Petrarch as a reader and writer as well as his correspondence in relation to Humanism. Also looks at Saint Augustine. Bibliography and index.

SEE ALSO: Giovanni Boccaccio; Leonardo Bruni; Geoffrey Chaucer; Dante; Jean Froissart; Giotto; Simone Martini; Cola di Rienzo; Philippe de Vitry.

RELATED ARTICLES in *Great Events from History: The Middle Ages, 477-1453*: c. 1100: Rise of Courtly Love; 1305-1417: Avignon Papacy and the Great Schism; c. 1350-1400: Petrarch and Boccaccio Recover Classical Texts; 1387-1400: Chaucer Writes *The Canterbury Tales.*

PHILIP THE GOOD
Duke of Burgundy

Despite his failure to build a unified state between France and the German states, Philip created sound administrative policies throughout his territories and established one of the most brilliant and cultured courts in Europe.

BORN: July 31, 1396; Dijon, Burgundy (now in France)
DIED: June 15, 1467; Bruges, Flanders (now Brugge, Belgium)
ALSO KNOWN AS: Philip III
AREAS OF ACHIEVEMENT: Patronage of the arts, government and politics

EARLY LIFE

Philip the Good was the third of four Valois dukes of Burgundy and the ablest among them. He was born in the ducal capital of Burgundy, the son of Duke John the Fearless and Margaret of Bavaria. Reared in wealthy circumstances, he was fascinated by the courtly manners of chivalry and ambitious for the future of Burgundy.

He succeeded to his inheritance on September 10, 1419, at the brutal assassination of his father by agents of the heir to the French throne. In 1409, Philip married Michelle of France, daughter of Charles VI and sister to Catherine, the wife of Henry V of England. Philip was involved with both countries as a result of the Hundred Years' War and always conscious of the fact that the duchy of Burgundy had been exploited by the French crown until the days of his grandfather, Philip the Bold.

Because of Philip's interest in art and patronage of artists, as well as his desire to publicize the history of his territory by encouraging official chroniclers, there are portraits and writings that form a clear picture of the duke. He was described as being of medium stature with proportionate weight, slim in arms and legs. His biographer wrote that he was bony rather than fleshy and had a dark complexion with brown hair. His eyebrows were thick above gray eyes and his nose was somewhat long.

In personality, he was said to have been proud, sensitive, and temperate. He had a fear of drunkenness and was abstemious in food and drink. His rather large brood of illegitimate children—numbered at eleven by modern scholarship, more by his contemporaries—indicated that his sexual appetite was not governed by the same moderation.

Although he had a quick temper, he did not hold grudges, and a sincere apology usually sufficed to clear the air after differences with his associates. As a youth he was fond of sports, riding, fencing, jousting, and hunting. He loved reading and tried to read, or be read to, each day. He had inherited a remarkable library of nine hundred volumes; by the end of his reign it had grown to include four times that number.

After his father's assassination, Philip dressed in black, although his simple clothing was of rich material and he had a penchant for fine jewels. He loved to hear music but was not very musical himself. Less superstitious than most of his contemporaries, he disliked flattery but demanded much of his courtiers.

LIFE'S WORK

The basis of Philip's inheritance was the duchy of Burgundy, roughly equivalent to a sizable portion of southeastern France on a modern map. It had been a holding of the French crown but was given to Philip the Bold, fourth son of John II of France, in 1364. It was a reward from the king to a son who had been captured with him at the Battle of Poitiers in 1356 and who had shared his father's captivity in England.

Although not originally intended, the duchy became virtually independent of the French crown thereafter. Territories of Flanders, Nevers, Artois, and Rethel (all portions of modern northern France and Belgium) were added by 1380. Philip's first marriage brought him additional French territory, and during his reign, he added more, namely Namur, Hainaut, Brabant, Holland, Zeeland, and Luxembourg. These territories incorporated much of modern Belgium, the Netherlands, and Luxembourg.

Philip's goal was a firm union of these lands, which he acquired by force of arms, marriage contracts, negotiation, and purchase. The difficulty lay in the fact that they were scattered possessions. Not only were they separated geographically but also they had no linguistic or cultural unity. In spite of the obvious, the duke sought to unify the administrative apparatus, especially the financial chambers. Although he had some success, effective union never was a reality. He was spurred on by his knowledge that the Carolingian Empire had been divided into three parts by the Treaty of Verdun (843). Lothair had been granted a middle kingdom, which Philip believed might be recreated if he could gain the duchy of Lotharingia from the German emperor. In this he was to be disappointed. Yet he passed on to his heir the dream of such a state.

His relationship with the leaders of many of his wealthy cities was often stormy. From the 1430's to the 1450's, great cities such as Antwerp, Ghent, and Bruges rose in rebellion. These and other communes had developed autonomous control of internal affairs, and the merchant leadership resisted the centralizing efforts of ducal government, while accepting the overall hegemony of the Burgundian power structure.

Efforts toward political union did not deter the duke from spending excessive energy and monies in creating the most lavish court of his age. He was more successful in achieving this goal. His patronage of art brought such names as Hans Memlinc, Rogier van der Weyden, and Jan van Eyck to his court. He encouraged the illumination of manuscripts, which included exquisite miniature painting at the capitals. Tapestries also became art forms of remarkable size and workmanship, sometimes illustrating legends of ancient history as well as contemporary scenes.

Artisans of every kind filled the cities. The gigantic caldron built to heat six thousand gallons of water for the court baths was the talk of Europe. In Dijon, walls were smoothed for murals, a superior tile was developed for roofs, and cloths of the richest material were developed for the prevailing fashions (which were carefully preserved in artists' portraits).

Education was encouraged, and chroniclers such as Georges Chastellain and Olivier de La Marche kept careful records, investigating past history as well as glorifying the House of Burgundy. The search for and the copying of books became an end in itself. Perhaps the duke's perception in choosing qualified men to carry out his governmental and cultural pursuits made much of the work possible. Philip the Good was adept at delegating authority. His chancellor, Nicholas Rolin of Auten, served him loyally for thirty-nine years.

As a psychological effort to strengthen the position and reputation of the Burgundian dukes, nothing was more successful than Philip's establishment of the chivalric order known as the Order of the Golden Fleece. It was established in Bruges on July 10, 1430, at Philip's

Engraving of Philip the Good being presented with a translation of the Chronicles of Jacques de Guyse. (Library of Congress)

marriage to his third wife, Isabel of Portugal. It was a chivalric order much like the Order of the Garter in England, extended as a signal honor to a chosen few.

The symbol of the Golden Fleece represented the victory of the mythological Jason over his challengers. Churchmen would have preferred a biblical victor, but wool was a commodity on which the manufacturing towns of Flanders had built a great industry. By dedicating the order to the Virgin, Philip believed that the pagan symbol did not threaten Christianity. The rules of the order demanded loyalty and service of its members, and it is probable that Duke Philip envisioned it as a nucleus for a crusading movement to wrest the property of Christians and the Holy Land from Turkish hands. He also hoped that it would establish a link between noblemen from all parts of his holdings, a link that would increase the possibility for internal union.

The first meeting of the order was held on November 22, 1431, at Lille. There, the sixty-six statutes that established the order were read, and the number of members increased to thirty-one. Saint Andrew, patron of Burgundy, was named sponsor. The Papacy confirmed the order and its goal by three bulls and praised its founder. Standards for admission were based on proven military accomplishment, courage, honor, and devotion to Christian precepts. Treachery, immorality, cowardice, or unbecoming conduct were grounds for expulsion.

To celebrate the order, elaborate and beautiful pageants were created around tournaments. The tournaments, frowned on by the Church as dangerous, became famous throughout Europe. The feasts that attended them were served in splendor by liveried servants in a hall where the labors of Hercules were depicted in priceless tapestries. The duke's order became a highly coveted honor, and its value in bringing attention to him and his family was significant.

Philip survived serious illnesses in 1465 and again in 1466. It was said that he maintained his faculties until his death at seventy in 1467. He was succeeded by his son, Charles, the last of the Valois dukes of Burgundy.

Philip the Good faced insurmountable problems as he proceeded with his grandiose plans for a unified Burgundian state. While his internal problems were legion, the role of his disparate duchy in international affairs was an even greater problem. The wealth of his territories was well known. England and France, in the throes of struggling national statehood, were very much aware of the role of Burgundy.

Following the assassination of his father, Philip was an ally of the French for a period of time. He was to share the regency of France with John, duke of Bedford, brother of Henry V of England, after the latter's successful conquest of French forces. Yet Philip refused that responsibility, fearing the growth of English power on the Continent. A wool-producing country, England was interested in its commercial connections to the provinces of Burgundy, where artisans and merchants were masters of woolen manufacture. Therefore, Philip had to be wary of both countries, and he became more aloof in his dealings with them as his reign progressed.

For a period of time Philip had serious concerns as a dynast about producing an heir. His first wife, Michelle of Valois, whom he married in 1409, died childless in 1422. His second wife, Bonne of Artois, also died childless. Finally, Isabel of Portugal, whom he married in 1430, gave birth to the son and heir so necessary for Philip. While Philip did not hesitate to recognize his illegitimate sons and employ them in various ways to serve his state, his legitimate son Charles was his successor.

Significance

The lasting contribution of Philip the Good resulted from his patronage of artists whose works still hang in museums from Spain to Vienna, and from his desire for the House of Burgundy to be chronicled in song and history. The illuminated manuscripts from his court, now collected in Brussels, are a reminder of his love of beauty and craftsmanship.

His chivalric tendencies, concretized in court etiquette, influenced every European court for centuries. They became, especially in the latter part of his reign, the greater part of his interest. The effort to increase his territories and to improve his administration also flagged as time went by. A modern biographer has said that one of his problems was that he lived too long.

He bequeathed to his son, the last of the Valois dukes of Burgundy, a failing political structure, handicapped by an increasingly cumbersome administration. The heads of the territories he valued had developed varying degrees of distrust, even hatred, for the ducal power. Perhaps Philip was too medieval for the new, Renaissance concepts of national statehood, but his appreciation of civility and beauty have earned for him an important place in European cultural history.

—*Anne R. Vizzier*

Further Reading

Cartellieri, Otto. *The Court of Burgundy.* Translated by Malcolm Letts. 1929. Reprint. New York: Barnes and Noble Books, 1972. A work that is the result of twenty years of research on the Burgundian court. Well-chosen plates add to its usefulness, as well as a detailed genealogical chart. Includes chapter notes but no index.

Clark, Gregory T. *Made in Flanders: The Master of the Ghent Privileges and Manuscript Painting in the Southern Netherlands in the Time of Philip the Good.* Turnhout, Belgium: Brepols, 2000. Surveys illuminated manuscript painting in Flanders. Includes some colored illustrations.

Fowler, Kenneth A. *The Age of Plantagenet and Valois: The Struggle for Supremacy, 1328-1498.* New York: Putnam, 1967. A very basic text on the subject of the Hundred Years' War whose value lies mainly in its splendid plates, which include portraits, weapons, armors, clothing, buildings, and interiors.

Seward, Desmond. *A Brief History of the Hundred Years' War: The English in France, 1337-1453.* London: Robinson, 2003. A valuable adjunct to an understanding of the complicated period of struggle between France and England, with attention to the Burgundian faction. A clear, historical overview of a most difficult subject. Includes illustrations and maps.

Taylor, Aline S. *Isabel of Burgundy.* Lanham, Md.: Madison Books, 2001. Explores the life of Philip's third wife, Isabel, an important and powerful figure in medieval history and in the domestic and foreign affairs of Burgundy. Isabel served as an authority and negotiator for France during Philip's absences.

Tyler, William R. *Dijon and the Valois Dukes of Burgundy.* Norman: University of Oklahoma Press, 1971. Primarily a social history, this important book helps the reader gain a sense of the wealth and level of expenditure that made Burgundy known throughout the Continent. Includes excellent descriptions of life at court, art, feasts, and tournaments. Contains a short selected bibliography, chronological summary, and family chart.

Vaughan, Richard. *Philip the Good: The Apogee of Burgundy, 1419-1467.* Rochester, N.Y.: Boydell and Brewer, 2002. The author, a preeminent authority on the history of Valois Burgundy, presents a highly detailed study of the reign of the third duke. Part of the History of Valois Burgundy series. Includes a bibliography and index.

_______. *Valois Burgundy.* Hamden, Conn.: Archon Books, 1975. This volume, an overview of the territories and their four rulers, is clearly written, with sufficient maps to make the territorial problems intelligible. Includes a bibliography and index.

See also: Jan van Eyck and Hubert van Eyck; Jean Froissart; Henry V; Jean Pucelle; Rogier van der Weyden.

Related articles in *Great Events from History: The Middle Ages, 477-1453*: 843: Treaty of Verdun; c. 1100: Rise of Courtly Love; 1337-1453: Hundred Years' War; 1373-1410: Jean Froissart Compiles His *Chronicles*.

Philip II

King of France (r. 1179-1223)

Philip II, the strongest of the Capetian kings of France, greatly expanded the royal domain and created an efficient system of political administration.

Born: August 21, 1165; Paris, France
Died: July 14, 1223; Mantes, France
Also known as: Philip Augustus; Philippe Auguste
Area of achievement: Government and politics

Early Life

Philip II was born the son of King Louis VII and Adela of Champagne. Because he was Louis's only son, his birth was received with great enthusiasm and hailed as the beginning of a new era. In his youth, however, Philip suffered from poor health and timorousness, which alarmed the king so much that in 1179 he made a pilgrimage to Saint Thomas Becket's shrine in Canterbury. Philip recovered and apparently grew up a strong, well-built young man, though his health declined again after the Third Crusade. He returned with little hair, was extremely nervous, and had good vision in one eye only.

On November 1, 1179, Philip, continuing an old Capetian custom, was crowned at Reims to ensure the succession. Although he was only fourteen years of age, it was a fortuitous move, for King Louis would die shortly thereafter. The youth was plunged almost immediately into a morass of political problems, for his maternal uncles, William, archbishop of Reims, and the counts of Champagne, Blois, and Sancerre sought an opportunity to control the new king. Philip, like his grandfather Louis VI, was stubborn and determined to send a message to the nobility that he would rule as well as reign. Thus, on April 28, 1180, Philip married Isabella of Hainaut, daughter of Baldwin V, count of Hainaut, and niece of Philip of Alsace, count of Flanders; this marriage gave him control over the queen's dowry of Artois and an interest in other family lands. He succeeded in avoiding domination by his wife's family as well. Two months after his marriage, Philip formed an alliance with King Henry II of England that effectively alienated the counts of Champagne and Flanders. By the time of his father's death on September 18, 1180, Philip was in firm control of the monarchy.

Life's Work

Philip's alliance with Henry drove his disaffected vassals together and precipitated a great revolt. The breach was widened in 1182, when Isabella, countess of Flanders and wife of Philip of Alsace, died, leaving Vermandois, Amiénois, and Valois to her sister Eleanor, countess of Beaumont. Because both the king and Philip of Alsace claimed these important lands, the rebellion continued until the two sides reached an agreement in 1186. For his part, the king received the county and city of Amiens, sixty-five castles, the county of Montdidier, and a portion of Vermandois.

At the expense of relatives and truculent nobles, Philip had begun to enlarge the royal domain. The most important story of his reign, however, was the struggle with the house of Anjou to recover French Continental possessions. The Angevin kings had come through the years to rule Normandy, Anjou, Aquitaine, Maine, and Touraine—in sum, most of western and southern France. Although Henry II was Philip's vassal for these lands, clearly the English king was the dominant force in the relationship. Because Philip was no match for Henry on the field of battle, he elected to continue the policy of intrigue begun by his father, Louis VII, with Henry's discontented sons.

There was relative peace between the two sides until 1186-1187, when Richard, Henry's eldest surviving son, failed to keep his promise to marry Alice, Philip's sister. Richard I, called the Lion-Hearted and considered the most able warrior of his day, had little interest in a woman rumored to have been his father's mistress. At any rate, when Henry refused to return either Alice or her dowry, the French Vexin (a region between central Normandy and the royal domain around Paris), Philip declared war and marched into Berry. As he had done in the past, Philip sought to foment discord in the Angevin house. In November, 1188, Richard threw his support to Philip

Engraving patterned on a sculpture of Philip II. (Hulton|Archive at Getty Images)

and rendered homage for the Continental fiefs at Bonmoulins. The alliance proved successful, and in July of the following year, Henry submitted near Tours. According to the Treaty of Colombières, Richard was recognized as Henry's successor, while Philip received Auvergne and other territorial concessions. Henry died two days later after learning that John, his favorite, had also turned against him.

For the moment, Richard and Philip were friends, but it soon became obvious that Philip had traded one formidable opponent for another. In 1190, the two kings joined forces and sailed from Europe on the Third Crusade. Philip's mother, Adela, and his uncle, the archbishop of Reims, were appointed regents in his absence. In Messina, Italy, Richard and Philip quarreled and parted company. Richard, it would seem, had once again refused to marry Alice and, instead, had taken Berengaria of Navarre to be his queen. That necessitated a revision of their earlier agreement. According to the Treaty of Messina in 1191, Richard would retain the French Vexin, unless he died without issue, in exchange for Alice, the town of Gisors, and ten thousand marks.

After the settlement, Philip went on to Palestine, where he was eventually rejoined by Richard in the siege of Acre. Philip remained long enough to take the city, and then, supposedly for reasons of illness, he decided to return to France. More likely, his departure was hastened by mounting differences with Richard and political concerns at home. Philip of Alsace, count of Flanders, had died on the Crusade, and Philip was eager to assert his wife's claim to the count's lands. Philip was also determined—though it would be a violation of feudal and canon law—to take advantage of Richard's absence from Europe to attack Angevin holdings in France. When Richard learned that Philip and John, his younger brother, were plotting against him, he left Palestine and attempted to dash incognito across Europe. He was recognized and captured by Leopold V, duke of Austria, and, at the insistence of Philip, was turned over to Emperor Henry VI to be held for ransom. With Richard out of the way, Philip attacked the Vexin and made plans to invade Normandy. His success, however, was short-lived. In 1194, Richard was released, and thereafter he initiated a series of wars that resulted in the eventual recapture of all lost lands.

Twenty years into his reign, Philip had gained little in his struggle with the Angevins. Moreover, he had become embroiled in a major dispute with the Papacy. In 1193, Philip formed an alliance with Canute VI, king of Denmark, in preparation for an invasion of England. As part of the agreement, Philip, whose first wife had died in 1190, was to marry the Danish king's sister Ingeborg. Almost immediately, Philip developed an aversion to his new bride and tried to have the marriage annulled on grounds of consanguinity. Matters went from bad to worse when, in 1196, Philip took another wife. Eventually Ingeborg's party referred the matter to Pope Innocent III, who placed France under an interdict in 1200. In July of that year, Philip's third wife died, but the rift with the Church continued until 1213, when Philip, preoccupied with more important political considerations, took back his estranged queen.

Although the Ingeborg affair proved distracting and injurious, there were encouraging developments on another front. In 1199, Richard met an untimely death and was succeeded by Philip's fellow conspirator, John. Although John was a better king and administrator than his brother, he was an inept general. He also had a rival claimant for the throne in his nephew Arthur, duke of Brittany and count of Anjou, a division Philip was quick to exploit. All that was needed was an excuse. The opportunity presented itself in August, 1200, when John married Isabella of Angouleme, who was betrothed to Hugh of Lusignan, count of La Marche. The angry count waged a brief, unsuccessful war against John before referring the matter to Philip's court. John, accordingly, was summoned to answer for his crime, and when he failed to appear, Philip and Arthur prepared for war. In the ensuing struggle, Arthur was captured, imprisoned, and executed, probably on John's orders. Arthur's outraged Breton and Angevin vassals then threw their full support behind Philip. By 1205, Philip had taken control of Normandy, Maine, Anjou, Touraine, and portions of Poitou. Yet John would not concede defeat and was soon at work lining up new allies. The most important of these was his nephew, Otto IV, the Holy Roman Emperor. In 1214, the coalition invaded Philip's dominions, but suffered a crushing defeat at the Battle of Bouvines, which put an end forever to John's hopes of reclaiming the lost French lands.

By 1214, Philip's most important battles with the English, his nobles, and the Church were over. He had increased the size and wealth of the French royal domain to such extent that it was necessary to revamp the archaic Capetian system of administration. Royal agents, called bailiffs and seneschals, drawn from the middle class and paid a salary, were sent into the various counties and duchies to collect the king's revenue, administer justice, and occasionally command armies in defense of the realm. In this way, Philip built up an efficient and powerful administrative bureaucracy composed of men whose first loyalty was to the king.

Philip's last years were fairly tranquil. He apparently felt comfortable enough with his conquests and administrative arrangements to eschew the coronation of his son and heir, Louis VIII, in his lifetime, a departure from the Capetian practice of the past two centuries. Nor would he lend anything more than token support to Louis's invasion of England in 1216. As his health failed, Philip's chief concerns were spiritual, namely, the Albigensian crusade and the defense of the Holy Land. Philip died at Mantes on July 14, 1223.

SIGNIFICANCE

The first two centuries of Capetian rule were relatively uneventful. Although the great nobles of the realm recognized the king as their feudal overlord, the king's actual authority did not extend much beyond the Île de France, or Paris and its environs. Some gains were made under Louis VI and Louis VII, but when Philip II assumed power in 1180, he was still surrounded by the great magnates of the realm. Over the next forty years, through marriage, political alliances, and war, Philip would more than triple the size of the French royal domain. The additional land and revenue, in turn, necessitated a revision of existing administrative agencies, giving France a more centralized government.

There can be little doubt, then, that Philip was the greatest of the Capetian monarchs. Yet he has received less attention than some of the other historical giants of the era, and he has been judged more harshly. Critics point out that he was cruel and treacherous and that he accomplished little while Henry and Richard were alive. His supporters, on the other hand, argue that while he had little interest in education and the arts, he was intelligent, generous, and a great supporter of the Church. He reigned longer than Henry II and was a more accomplished king than Richard. When he died in 1223, his empire was still intact.

—*Larry W. Usilton*

FURTHER READING

Baldwin, John W. *The Government of Philip Augustus.* Berkeley: University of California Press, 1986. A lengthy study of Philip's administration, with detailed footnotes and appendices. Should appeal mainly to an advanced reader.

Bradbury, Jim. *Philip Augustus: King of France, 1180-1223.* New York: Longman, 1998. Part of the Medieval World series, this biographical study explores Philip's life in the context of the Battle of Bouvines, Church history, and French history in general.

Burl, Aubrey. *God's Heretics: The Albigensian Crusade.* Stroud, England: Sutton, 2002. Explores the crusade, ordered by Pope Innocent III, including Philip's role. Argues that the massacre was the first act of genocide in Europe.

Davis, R. H. C. *A History of Medieval Europe: From Constantine to Saint Louis.* 2d ed. New York: Longman, 1988. A general history of the area from the fourth through the thirteenth centuries. A brief section is devoted principally to Philip's attempts to expand the royal domain at the expense of his barons and the English. Very good for the beginning student.

Dunbabin, Jean. *France in the Making, 843-1180.* 2d ed. New York: Oxford University Press, 2000. A thorough political history of France under the Capetians. Includes an extensive bibliography and an index.

Fawtier, Robert. *The Capetian Kings of France: Monarchy and Nation, 987-1328.* Reprint. London: Macmillan, 1962. Perhaps the best study of the Capetian line from beginning (987) to end (1328). Philip receives much attention throughout.

Hallam, Elizabeth M, and Judith Everard. *Capetian France, 987-1328.* 2d ed. New York: Longman, 2001. A 480-page history of the Capetian Dynasty for both students and other scholars. Maps, genealogies, and detailed, extensive bibliographies enhance the book's value.

Luchaire, Achille. *Social France at the Time of Philip Augustus.* 1912. Reprint. New York: Harper and Row, 1967. A good work that, although not primarily concerned with Philip, yields valuable background information about the Church, nobility, and peasantry during his day.

Powicke, F. M. "The Reigns of Philip Augustus and Louis VIII of France." In *The Cambridge Medieval History*, edited by H. M. Gwatkin and J. P. Whitney. Vol. 6. Cambridge, England: Cambridge University Press, 1911-1936. A chapter from an excellent multivolume survey for all readers of the period. One of the best brief studies of Philip's reign, by an eminent British historian. Provides valuable information on Philip's character, marriages, and political struggles.

Tierney, Brian, and Sidney Painter. *Western Europe in the Middle Ages, 300-1475.* 5th ed. New York: McGraw-Hill, 1992. One of the better surveys of the period. Contains an excellent chapter on the feudal monarchies of England, France, and the empire. Provides a good overview of Philip's career. An excellent introductory work.

SEE ALSO: Saint Thomas Becket; Hubert de Burgh; Eleanor of Aquitaine; Henry II; Innocent III; King John; Louis IX; Richard I.

RELATED ARTICLES in *Great Events from History: The Middle Ages, 477-1453*: 987: Hugh Capet Is Elected to the French Throne; 1154-1204: Angevin Empire Is Established; 1189-1192: Third Crusade; 1209-1229: Albigensian Crusade; July 27, 1214: Battle of Bouvines.

PHILIP IV THE FAIR
King of France (r. 1285-1314)

As king, Philip steadfastly created a strong monarchy in France. He developed a bureaucracy that allowed for firmer central control of raising revenues in the kingdom. His efforts, by accelerating the departure from a feudal form of government, began to modernize the French state.

BORN: 1268; Fontainebleau, France
DIED: November 29, 1314; Fontainebleau
AREA OF ACHIEVEMENT: Government and politics

EARLY LIFE

Philip IV, known as "the Fair" because of his supposedly handsome and stately appearance, was born at the royal castle of Fontainebleau, southeast of Paris. The second son of the weak king Philip III—who succeeded the holy and revered Louis IX—and Isabella of France, young Philip endured a difficult childhood. When he was three years old, his mother died, and in 1274, his father remarried, taking Marie of Brabant as his second wife. Marie, probably hoping to see her own children rather than her stepchildren become the heirs of the French throne, shunned Philip and his older brother Louis. Prince Louis died in 1276, making Philip the next in line to the throne.

Although Philip III did not have a particularly close relationship to his son and heir, the king did provide Philip with an education befitting a royal prince. The king arranged for the famous scholar Giles of Rome to instruct his young son. Giles's clerk, Guillaume d'Ercuis, however, was tasked with teaching Prince Philip. Guillaume provided the prince not only with the basics of reading and writing but also with the warmth and close companionship he lacked after his mother's death. At his father's court, Philip also learned about aristocratic life and the business side of government, with its bureaucrats, foreign diplomats, favor-seekers, and feudal barons, whose every demand had to be considered and answered in order to preserve their loyalty and support.

On August 28, 1284, Philip III arranged a brilliant marriage for his son, betrothing him to Jeanne, the heiress to the kingdom of Navarre and the county of Champagne. This marriage arrangement was particularly important because it brought the extremely valuable and strategically located county of Champagne into the lands held directly by the king, thereby providing the Crown with a plentiful income as well as a solid foothold in vulnerable eastern France. Philip was a most devoted husband, who, unlike many other monarchs in medieval Europe, seems truly to have loved the spouse who was provided for him. After his wife's death in 1305, Philip did not remarry.

Shortly after his son's marriage, Philip III became involved in a papal crusade against Pedro, king of Aragon, who had attacked Philip's uncle King Charles I of Sicily, a vassal of the pope. While on this disastrous mission to conquer Aragon, King Philip became ill, and he died on October 5, 1285. Philip, his heir, became the new king of France later in the month on receiving the news of his father's death. He inherited a poorly waged war, a massive financial burden, and an Aragonese enemy.

LIFE'S WORK

The suddenness with which Philip the Fair ascended the French throne was emphasized by his immediate departure from his predecessor's interests, concerns, and method of government. Abandoning the papally ordered crusade against Aragon, the young king directed his attention toward selecting new advisers and reordering the bureaucratic machinery of his kingdom. Unlike his father, Philip IV strongly desired to make the kingdom of France independent of papal or Church influence, control, or interference. Philip believed that his subjects' political concerns were more important than those of the pope and that whatever was good for the kingdom would necessarily be favorable for the Church.

Although the new king was a pious man who supported the Church financially within his kingdom, he also knew, as one of his biographers put it, the importance of the "religion of monarchy." This powerful ideology established the king as the most powerful individual within the kingdom, deserving absolute obedience, and permitted him to act autonomously. Philip demonstrated his devotion to this "religion" throughout his reign by strengthening the power of the royal administration, asserting his sovereignty over all subjects, noble and nonnoble alike, in his realm, and engaging in struggles with external powers, such as the English king Edward I and Pope Boniface VIII, who encroached on his territories or rights.

Because the French monarchy under the Capetian Dynasty had emerged as a feudal state, the majority of governmental business was undertaken not by the king but by his personal vassals, who resided in the various regions of the realm and loyally provided military and governmental service for their lord. Thus, Paris, the royal

THE CAPETIANS

Reign	*Ruler*
987-996	Hugh Capet
996-1031	Robert II the Pious
1031-1060	Henry I
1060-1108	Philip I the Fair
1108-1137	Louis VI the Fat
1137-1179	LOUIS VII THE YOUNGER (with ELEANOR OF AQUITAINE, r. 1137-1180)
1179-1223	PHILIP II AUGUSTUS
1223-1226	Louis VIII the Lion
1223-1252	BLANCHE OF CASTILE (both queen and regent)
1226-1270	LOUIS IX (Saint Louis)
1271-1285	Philip III the Bold
1285-1314	PHILIP IV THE FAIR
1314-1316	Louis X the Stubborn
1316	Philip, brother of Louis X (regent before birth of John I and during his short life)
1316	John I the Posthumous
1316-1322	Philip V the Tall
1322-1328	Charles IV the Fair

capital, was not yet the seat of royal power in the thirteenth century, and vassals, who had pledged to be loyal to the king, provided legal, military, and administrative service as they saw fit in the king's absence. To maintain itself as the protector and defender of the French people, the French monarchy, under the guidance of Philip IV, created a new bureaucratic order and uniformity.

As the amount and complexity of legal business in the realm increased in the late thirteenth century, it became increasingly obvious that the king's courts needed to be reorganized. The Parlement, which had initially been an outgrowth of the royal council that heard certain types of important legal cases, was routinely engulfed in work. Under Philip, the court was divided into several lesser courts that held inquests, received petitions for equity cases, heard cases based on the written law used in southern France, or pronounced judgments in suits. The king also relied heavily on a corps of officers to supervise affairs and administer justice in local jurisdictions.

In addition to this reorganization of the court, Philip's reign witnessed a reorganization of royal finances and the development of effective mechanisms for accounting, auditing, and disbursing royal funds and tax revenues by the chamber of accounts. To manage the large bureaucracy needed to rule the kingdom, Philip depended on a small, permanent royal council—instead of the large council made up of most of the leading aristocrats and prelates of the kingdom. This smaller body was made up of full-time civil servants who could travel with the king throughout his realm and act decisively when called on. With this large, complex, and powerful army of bureaucrats, Philip was better prepared to know the state of his kingdom and to rule his subjects than his predecessors, who had depended on their occasionally cantankerous feudal vassals to assist them in the task of governing.

Philip IV's strong assertion of royal power within France is a theme that can be noted throughout his twenty-nine-year reign. From the early years, when Philip cast aside his father's advisers and policies in favor of his own, to the middle years, when he tangled with the most powerful vassal, Edward I, duke of Aquitaine and king of England, to the final weeks of his life, when he taxed his subjects heavily and ignited an aristocratic rebellion, the king appeared determined to shape both his reign and his nation. Unwilling to be a passive observer, the workhorse king played an active role in policy making, participating in the meetings of the small royal council, drafting letters and pronouncements, and issuing orders to his civil servants.

Although Philip insisted on assuming this dominant role in French politics, he also portrayed himself as the protector of his subjects. When Edward encroached on the rights of the French and attacked La Rochelle in 1294, Philip summoned him to appear before the Parlement. When Edward refused to appear as a king suspected of wrongdoing in Philip's court, Philip seized the duchy of Aquitaine and declared war against his English vassal. For several years, the two kings fought in an inconclusive war. Only in 1302, when Edward's ally, the count of Flanders, inflicted a stunning defeat on Philip's large army at Courtrai, was peace restored.

To finance the war, Philip levied several onerous taxes on the French, regardless of their rank. In the final years of the war, the subjects demanded that they be allowed to give their consent to such extraordinary levies. Philip, always anxious to be seen as a good monarch, obliged them by assembling representatives from various localities to approve taxes and, in 1302, by convoking the Estates

General, to endorse the principles of regular royal taxation during wartime. By pursuing his legal claims against the rebellious Duke Edward, plunging the realm into a protracted war to protect his royal powers, and establishing regular taxation to support the royal government and armies, Philip demonstrated not only his desire to rule France firmly but also his sovereign power over his subjects as their king.

Philip's pressing financial need, created by the prolonged war against Edward, contributed to his famous clash with Boniface VIII. In this conflict, the king claimed that as king of all subjects, laypersons as well as the clergy, he had the right to tax everyone in order to defend the realm against enemies. The pope strenuously resisted Philip's effort to tax churchmen. Boniface decreed that it was illegal for a monarch to do so, and, in 1302, he threatened to excommunicate the king and release all of his subjects from their obligation to be loyal to him.

Unwilling to allow Boniface VIII to dictate to him, Philip turned on the pope. He effectively declared that the pope could not interfere with what the king regarded as the internal affairs of the kingdom. He condemned the pope for his actions and threats, spreading propaganda throughout the kingdom about the pope's unjustified actions and raising questions about the pope's legitimacy and moral conduct. Shortly before he was due to be banned from the Church, Philip ordered a small band of soldiers to arrest the pope at his residence in Italy. With the arrest, Boniface had no choice but to capitulate. By this extreme political statement, Philip clearly established that the king of France was the sole ruler of every French person and that, in order to preserve his autonomy, he would not surrender to the orders and threats of the pope.

SIGNIFICANCE

When Philip IV the Fair died in November, 1314, France was in turmoil. His heir, Louis X, inherited a kingdom riddled with rebellions, as noblemen across the northern half of the realm resisted the payment of yet another round of burdensome royal taxes. This uprising, however, revealed the successes Philip had achieved. A king noted for his steeliness, Philip created during his long reign a mature kingdom, established on principles of firm royal government and furnished with the courts, professional bureaucrats, institutions, and accepted procedures necessary for maintaining a cohesive nation. It was this very royal strength that the rebels condemned in 1314, as they felt the Crown's grip tighten on what they perceived as their own rights and privileges.

Some years before, when the exasperated bishop of Pamiers reflected on the character of the French king, he wrote, "The king stares at men fixedly, without uttering a word. . . . He is not a man, not a beast, he is a graven image." This owl-like monarch, who struck the perfect pose of a determined ruler and did not hesitate to impose his will on subjects and enemies alike, had introduced his realm to effective government between 1285 and 1314. Moreover, the image that the king presented to the bishop reflects the awesomeness that he had cultivated. His subjects, enemies, officers, and fellow monarchs revered the royal majesty as respectful worshipers who acknowledged and trembled before the royal might he wielded. It is not the effective administration of the realm alone for which Philip the Fair deserves credit, but also his creation and practice of the "religion of monarchy."

—David M. Bessen

FURTHER READING

Barzel, Yoram, and Edgar Kiser. "Taxation and Voting Rights in Medieval England and France." *Rationality and Society* 14, no. 4 (November, 2002). Explores the history of taxation and voting rights and their complex relationship during the reign of Philip and others. A scholarly, technical discussion.

Fawtier, Robert. *The Capetian Kings of France: Monarchy and Nation, 987-1328*. Reprint. London: Macmillan, 1962. A survey of the first dynasty that ruled France that provides a picture of the needs and growth of the French monarchy, culminating in the reorganization under Philip.

Hallam, Elizabeth M, and Judith Everard. *Capetian France, 987-1328*. 2d ed. New York: Longman, 2001. A 480-page history of the Capetian Dynasty for both students and other scholars. Maps, genealogies, and detailed, extensive bibliographies enhance the book's value.

Lynch, Joseph H. *The Medieval Church: A Brief History*. New York: Longman, 1992. Surveys the history of the Church during the Middle Ages and includes a chapter on Philip and Boniface in the context of the Avignon Papacy. Also offers a bibliography and index.

Perroy, Edouard. *The Hundred Years' War*. Translated by D. C. Douglas. New York: Capricorn Books, 1965. A very good survey of the late medieval conflict between the kings of England and France. The early chapters are devoted to explaining the origins of the struggle, especially during the reign of Philip.

Petit-Dutaillis, Charles. *The Feudal Monarchy in France and England: From the Tenth to the Thirteenth Cen-*

tury. 1936. Reprint. New York: AMS Press, 1983. A useful book for understanding the concept of the feudal state and how it differed from the bureaucratic state created by kings such as Philip.

Strayer, Joseph R. "Philip the Fair: A 'Constitutional' King." In *Medieval Statecraft and the Perspectives of History: Essays by Joseph R. Strayer*, edited by John F. Benton and Thomas N. Bisson. Princeton, N.J.: Princeton University Press, 1971. In this brief work, the author not only outlines the perceptions of monarchy that Philip had but also indicates how Philip implemented his ideas about the function of the king in France.

_______. *The Reign of Philip the Fair*. Princeton, N.J.: Princeton University Press, 1980. Although not a chronological biography of the king, this book examines how Philip totally reformed the government of France by changing the personnel of government, relying more on professional bureaucrats for the business of rule, and reorganizing the administration of the realm.

Wood, Charles T., ed. *Philip the Fair and Boniface VIII: State Versus Papacy*. New York: Holt, Rinehart and Winston, 1967. This small volume contains many of the primary documents and historical interpretations of the famous struggle between pope and king.

SEE ALSO: Boniface VIII; Edward I; Isabella of France; Louis IX; Marguerite Porete.

RELATED ARTICLES in *Great Events from History: The Middle Ages, 477-1453*: 1295: Model Parliament; 1305-1417: Avignon Papacy and the Great Schism.

PHILIPPA OF HAINAUT

French-born queen of England (r. 1327-1369)

Philippa of Hainaut won the hearts of the English subjects of King Edward III, helped him keep the peace, and served as regent during his absences from England. Queen's College at Oxford University in England is named for Philippa.

BORN: c. 1312; Bois-de-Valenciennes, France
DIED: August 15, 1369; Windsor, Berkshire, England
ALSO KNOWN AS: Philippa of Hainault
AREA OF ACHIEVEMENT: Government and politics

EARLY LIFE

Philippa of Hainaut (fil-EE-pah uhv HAY-naut) came from royal stock. Her father, William the Good, was count of Hainaut and Holland. Her mother was Jeanne de Valois, granddaughter of King Philip III of France. Philippa first met Edward, her future husband, when his mother, Queen Isabella of France, wife of King Edward II, fled to France with Edward, heir apparent to the British throne, where they first met Philippa.

Isabella's marriage to King Edward II was collapsing, and she had been fully aware of the widespread rumors of the king's homosexuality. She had taken a lover, Roger Mortimer, who influenced her considerably. Edward II was a weak king, overly concerned with appearances and possessions, and his subjects became increasingly concerned about his ineptitude. Isabella's fleeing to Paris with her son Edward III in 1326 led her to fear that some of the king's minions would track them down and attempt to return Edward III, then fourteen, to England by force. To thwart this threat, Isabella sought refuge with her cousin Jeanne, wife of William the Good and mother of Philippa, at her rural palace in Bois-de-Valenciennes. Jeanne and her husband had four daughters and one son.

Isabella and Edward were welcomed in Valenciennes and were encouraged to remain as long as they wished. Jeanne urged her children to amuse their royal guest Edward while Isabella concentrated on resolving her political dilemma. Edward was shy and withdrawn, except with Philippa, who was the only one among the children with whom he felt at ease. The two grew close in the week that Edward spent at Valenciennes. On leaving, Edward kissed Philippa, who cried uncontrollably at the prospect of his departure. Edward was equally moved. Before she left Valenciennes, Isabella, observing the compatibility of Edward and Philippa, rejoiced and committed Edward to marrying Philippa on his ascent to the throne. She had been plotting an invasion of England and realized that a union of her son with the count of Hainaut's daughter might well help her to obtain assistance, both financial and military, to implement her plans for an invasion.

Isabella received the assistance she desired. On September 23, 1326, her army and a cadre of seven hundred volunteers from Hainaut landed at Harwich, where they were met by friendly forces that included Henry of Lancaster, Thomas of Norfolk, and many of the most celebrated people of East Anglia, all bent on forcing Edward II's abdication. Edward II fled to the Tower of London, then attempted to escape to Ireland, but he eventually was captured, and on January 25, 1327, he capitulated, agreeing that Edward III would succeed him.

Edward II abdicated on January 29, 1327. His son's coronation occurred at Westminster Abbey on February 1, 1327. The new king had turned fourteen the preceding November. Early in April, his ambassadors journeyed to Valenciennes to broker his marriage to Philippa. This union was blocked temporarily when Pope John XXII, disturbed by the tactics used to depose Edward II, denied the dispensation required because Edward and Philippa were distant cousins, placing them within the third degree of consanguinity. Only after Edward personally petitioned the pope for a dispensation did John XXII provide it.

In October, 1327, the proxy union between Philippa and Edward was performed at Valenciennes by the bishop of Lichfield, who brought with him the news of Edward II's death. The king was first thought to have died from natural causes, but later his death was declared a murder caused by the insertion of hot irons into the former king's intestines.

Edward III, now occupied with leading royal forces against the Scots, narrowly escaped death when the Scottish forces attacked his encampment, advancing as far as Edward's tent before they were repulsed. In January, 1328, however, Philippa and Edward were married again, this time in a more traditional royal ceremony at York.

Life's Work

When Philippa first arrived in England in 1327 with her retinue, Edward could not meet her because he was involved in his battle against the Scots. He charged the constable of Dover with welcoming Philippa and making her comfortable. As Philippa traveled through the counties south of London, the populace, relieved to have a new king, received her enthusiastically.

As her entourage approached villages along the way, Philippa, despite bitter cold weather, insisted on leaving her carriage and riding through each small town on a saddle horse so that she could interact with people, who already regarded Edward III as an idol. His bride was accorded similar status. She delighted Edward's subjects by insisting on stopping at Canterbury on the way to London to worship at Saint Thomas Becket's tomb.

When Philippa arrived in London on the morning of Christmas Eve, 1327, London's church bells clanged their welcome. An array of dignitaries awaited her at the north end of London Bridge. During her stay in London, Philippa won the hearts of everyone she met.

Eager to join her husband, she left London after three days, but her arrival was celebrated for many days after her departure. So bad was the weather that the carriages carrying Philippa's retainers and wedding gifts were bogged down in mud. The procession did not arrive in York, where Edward awaited, until the end of January, 1328.

A royal wedding ceremony was held the next day. Because Lent was about to begin, Edward and Philippa could not take a honeymoon. The Church forbade sexual intercourse during the forty days of Lent. Finally, when Lent ended, the couple embarked on a leisurely trip through Lincoln and Northampton, arriving at their destination, Woodstock, early in June.

Edward had been dominated since birth by his scheming mother. When Edward became king, Isabella and her paramour, Roger Mortimer, attempted to control him completely. Isabella frequently snubbed Philippa. She delayed Philippa's coronation because she considered herself the legitimate queen of England.

Philippa was appalled when Isabella arranged for the marriage of her seven-year-old daughter, Joan, to five-year-old David, son of the Scotsman Robert Bruce, in an effort to broker an alliance between England and Scotland. She ordered Edward to travel north to participate in the marriage rites. At the last minute, however, openly defying his mother, he refused to attend the wedding, going only as far as Northampton. Philippa had discerned Isabella's deviousness and was made miserable by it. Edward now sought a way to escape his mother's domination, and Philippa gave him her full support and encouragement in these efforts.

Mortimer contrived to have Parliament meet in Winchester, where he laid a trap for Lancaster, Norfolk, and Kent. He insisted that Edward attend, but Edward agreed to do so only if Philippa came along. In the end, the detestable Mortimer destroyed Lancaster and Norfolk and had York, Edward's uncle, beheaded, forcing Edward's reluctant approval of the execution. Philippa, still in her teens, was present with Edward at the Parliament in Winchester when these appalling events occurred. Philippa became aware that Isabella was declining mentally and was moving toward an ever-consuming insanity.

The major obligation of most queens is to produce an heir and a "spare" so that the line of ascendancy will be preserved. Philippa was slow to become pregnant, but shortly after Edward returned from France, she was expecting. Edward was determined that Philippa would be queen of England before her first child's birth. At his insistence, and contrary to Isabella's wishes, Philippa's coronation took place in Westminster Abbey on March 4, 1330.

Following the ceremony, Philippa went to Woodstock to await the birth of her child, Edward, born on June 15, 1330. Her husband went with her and stayed beside her until their child was born. Parliament was forced to meet at Woodstock to accommodate the king. Philippa gave birth to seven sons and five daughters between her eighteenth and forty-third years.

When Edward, at seventeen years old, saw his first child, he resolved to escape the stranglehold Isabella and Mortimer had on him. He acted decisively by capturing Mortimer, having him tried, convicted, and transported to London, where he was hanged. Isabella's insanity was now advanced, but Philippa, inherently gentle and generous, saw to it that she was well cared for. Edward could reign without his mother's direct influence.

Edward and Philippa had a virtually perfect marriage that lasted until Philippa's death on August 15, 1369. Philippa often accompanied Edward to battle. She was present in 1333 when the English defeated the Scots decisively at the Battle of Neville's Cross. She also accompanied the king on his expedition to Flanders between 1338 and 1340.

Philippa served as regent when it was necessary for Edward, at one point king of both England and France, to be away. Although she had little desire to influence government, she intervened in 1347 when Edward threatened to have six burghers of Calais executed. Her intervention saved their lives.

If Philippa had any failing, it was her extravagance. Her generosity regularly caused her expenditures that exceeded the royal income, resulting in huge debts. At one point, when Philippa and her children were in Ghent, Edward had to return to England to raise money. His creditors insisted that Philippa and the children remain in Ghent as security for the debts the royal family had incurred there.

SIGNIFICANCE

Philippa was among the most conciliatory queens England ever knew. Her subjects revered her as few public figures are revered. She raised her family well, and five of her sons—including Edward, the so-called Black Prince, and John of Gaunt—had notable political careers. Her daughters were bright, vital women. Four of them preceded Philippa in death. The loss of her daughter Joan, who died on her honeymoon at age fifteen, caused Philippa to lose her spirit.

Perhaps foreseeing her own death, Philippa engaged Alice Perrers as her personal servant, probably in 1366. It has been suggested that Philippa chose Alice because she thought Alice would be a reasonable substitute for her in Edward's life after her demise. Actually, Alice did become Edward's mistress, although their intimate relationship seemingly did not begin until after Philippa died.

—*R. Baird Shuman*

FURTHER READING

Allmand, Christopher. *War, Government and Power in Late Medieval France*. Liverpool, England: Liverpool University Press, 2000. Despite its seeming focus only on war and government, this book discusses the literary culture of the court of Hainaut, including Philippa and her secretary Jean Froissart.

Bothwell, J. S., ed. *The Age of Edward III*. York, England: York Medieval Press, 2001. Several of the eleven contributions to this collection touch on Philippa. The fullest discussion is found in Bennett's chapter, "Isabelle of France, Anglo-French Diplomacy and Cultural Exchange in the late 1350's."

Crawford, Anne. *The Letters of the Queens of England, 1066-1547*. Dover, N.H.: A. Sutton, 1994. Includes a chapter that addresses the letters and correspondence of Philippa.

Froissart, Jean. *Chronicles. Selected, Translated, and Edited by Geoffrey Brereton*. Baltimore: Penguin Books, 1968. These chronicles, compiled by Philippa's personal secretary from 1362 until her death in 1369, contain valuable insights into the life of the queen and court.

Kay, George F. *Lady of the Sun: The Life and Times of Alice Perrers*. New York: Barnes and Noble Books, 1966. This account of the life of Philippa's personal servant who became Edward III's mistress also contains a succinct overview of Philippa's life. Chapters 3 and 4 are particularly relevant.

McKisack, May. *The Fourteenth Century: 1307-1399*. Oxford, England: Clarendon Press, 1959. This comprehensive study of the fourteenth century and of the effects of the Hundred Years' War on the reign of Edward III contains valuable insights into the political role Philippa played as queen of England.

Sedgwick, Anne Douglas. *Philippa*. Boston: Houghton Mifflin, 1930. A dated but still compelling full-scale treatment of Philippa's life.

SEE ALSO: Robert Bruce; David II; Edward II; Edward III; Jean Froissart; Isabella of France.

RELATED ARTICLES in *Great Events from History: The Middle Ages, 477-1453*: 1337-1453: Hundred Years' War; 1373-1410: Jean Froissart Compiles His *Chronicles*.

ANDREA PISANO
Italian scuptor

Bronze, unknown as a medium for sculpture in Florence before the 1330's, was brought to that city by Pisano, who made an important contribution to art with his baptistery door, which was to be the example to be matched and supremely surpassed during the Florentine Renaissance.

BORN: c. 1270-1290; Pontedera, near Pisa (now in Italy)
DIED: c. 1348; probably Orvieto, Papal States (now in Italy)
ALSO KNOWN AS: Andrea da Pontedera
AREA OF ACHIEVEMENT: Art

EARLY LIFE

Nothing certain is known of the early life of Andrea Pisano (ahn-DRAY-uh pee-SAHN-oh). His first appearance as a public figure does not occur until 1330, when he received the most important commission of his artistic career. The fine detail and design of his bronze sculptures suggest that he may have had training as a goldsmith. He may also have been trained by Giovanni Pisano, who was a sculptor who had, in turn, been trained by his father Nicola Pisano. The Pisanos, father and son, were natives of Pisa and made important contributions to the development of bronze sculpture in the thirteenth and fourteenth centuries, but they were not related to Andrea Pisano, whose real name is, in fact, Andrea da Pontedera. The fact that he was generally called Pisano and emerges as a worker in bronze, a speciality of Pisan artists, suggests a Pisan connection.

In 1330, he gained the prestigious contract for a set of doors on the baptistery of the cathedral in Florence. Some reputation must have helped to capture this grand opportunity. It is likely that a competition took place, and it is known that Pisano's wax model for the doors had to be redone. He must have been known for prior work of some quality, but nothing has been so identified, and his work in Florence was to be the major source of his modest fame.

LIFE'S WORK

The baptistery is a separate building to the west of the cathedral in Florence. It may have been started as early as the fifth century and was probably annexed through the centuries. Local craft guilds took on themselves the responsibility for major religious buildings, and it was the Guild of Cloth Importers that sponsored the work on the baptistery. In 1329, it was decided that a set of bronze doors should be added to the south face of this octagonal, white-and-green marble building. The obvious subject for decoration of the door was the life of John the Baptist, and the upper series of the twenty-eight panels that Pisano designed for the door took John as their subject, and the lower set depicted Christian virtues. The individual scenes were enclosed by a border of Gothic design.

Both technically and aesthetically, Pisano's door was a great success and provided the example and impetus for the later, even finer work of Lorenzo Ghiberti on two further doors, which were initiated at the beginning of the fifteenth century.

The use of bronze, an extremely expensive material, had died out after the fall of the Roman Empire, and very few examples of Greek and Roman bronze have survived, given its frangible nature and the obvious temptation to melt it down for other uses. The example of Nicola Pisano and Giovanni Pisano in successfully bringing bronze back into the realm of religious sculpture was to mark the beginning of a renewed, flexible use of the metal that Andrea Pisano's baptistery door instituted in Florence. It would be in Florence, in particular, where the use of bronze was to have a glorious future and where so much of the greatest art of the early Renaissance would be produced, after Pisano, by artists such as Ghiberti and Donatello.

However, Pisano brought something else to Florence. The earlier Pisanos, working with bronze in several cities throughout northern Italy, had also shown in their design an interest in adding to their Gothic roots the more realistic, more sensuous influences of classical sculpture, as well as delicate rhythms of French Gothic design. Giovanni, in particular, had strong connections to northern Gothic artists and seems to have had some considerable influence on Pisano. Working in the last century of the Gothic period, the Pisanos, and Andrea, in their wake, manifested the return to the celebration of the human body that had been central to classical art and was to reach elegant and celebratory expression in the early years of the Italian Renaissance.

Pisano is not, in fact, a Renaissance artist. He was a late Italian Gothic artist who manipulated with considerable success not only his heritage of medieval ideas and preconceptions but also other influences that come together for the first time in his own work. The restrained, flat style of Gothic art is present in the baptistery sculpture, and his use of space is unadventurous, but the compositions and modeling have a reality about them that suggests greater things to come. The influence of Giotto, the most important "link" figure between late Gothic and early Renaissance art, is also apparent in the harmonious juxtapositions, the sense of space in the panels. That is not surprising because Giotto was responsible for the adjacent campanile. An added dimension of Pisano's work on the panels is his use of drapery, gracefully reminiscent of French Gothic influences that he may have picked up from Giovanni Pisano.

The Giotto influence is even more pronounced in Andrea Pisano's own work on the campanile, where he was responsible for a series of reliefs, decorating the lower stories of the tower. There is some opinion that Giotto may have had a hand in the design of these scenes. Whatever the truth may be, it is obvious that the tender sonority and grace of these scenes, as well as the similar aura surrounding a series of marble figures that Pisano carved for niches on the tower, are examples of Giotto's effect on Pisano, who was to succeed him as the supervisor of the campanile project when Giotto died in 1337.

Pisano remained in Florence until 1343 and may have left then simply because of the financial difficulties of that time, which forced the guilds to cut back on their social and religious projects. He seems to have returned to Pisa initially, but he soon moved to Orvieto, where he became the overseer of works at the cathedral. By this time his son, Nino Pisano, who was also a sculptor and would succeed him as overseer at the cathedral, was working with him. Andrea Pisano probably was a victim of the Black Death, which struck at the end of the 1330's. There seems to be little work after the Florence period that can be identified as that of Pisano, so it is to those two projects, the baptistery and the campanile, that his reputation is attached.

SIGNIFICANCE

Pisano's contribution to the history of art is a minor one, but it is not insignificant, in terms of either technique or aesthetic theory. His baptistery work was in itself proof positive of the potential for bronze as a legitimate medium for the new Humanism, and a close study of the technical mastery that he displayed in dealing with the John the Baptist theme reveals a capacity for the subtle manipulation of this difficult metal.

If he was less successful than Ghiberti in infusing psychological subtlety and dramatic breadth into the panels, it is important to remember how far he did go, how much emotional power he did express in his work. Ghiberti comes at the beginning of a new age, a new sensibility, and it has often been suggested that the Renaissance can be dated from the moment at which he presented his design for the second portal of the baptistery in 1401.

Yet the Renaissance did not suddenly spring fully formed from the work of Ghiberti; it had been brewing slowly, sometimes painfully, throughout the preceding century. In sculpture, particularly in bronze sculpture, the Renaissance can be seen working its way out of the aging Gothic sensibility in the work of the Pisanos. Nicola knew that the old ways, the static, flattened, restrained designs of the Gothic, however graced by northern influences, were not sufficient for him, and he was constantly circling the idea that the classical, heathen world holds the answer in its glorification of the human form. He passed that idea on to his son, and it passed, in turn, into the work of Andrea Pisano.

Andrea Pisano was, in short, that peculiar kind of artist who comes at the end of one tradition and who may easily fail if he does not possess, as Pisano did, the rare gift for assimilation and absorption of new ideas and the capacity to express the conjunction of the old and new in ways that not only make for art of outstanding quality but also for an example that will lead the greater artists of the new mode.

When Pisano was asked to design the first door for the baptistery, there was not an artisan in town who could work with bronze. It was necessary to import a bell caster from Venice to work with the artist. When Pisano left town, years later, the tradition was there in proof, in the great door and in his work on the campanile panels. Some years later, again with the financial support of the guild, the great sculptor Ghiberti followed the example set by Pisano and carried the bronze sculpture into the glories of the Renaissance.

—*Charles H. Pullen*

FURTHER READING

Avery, Charles. *Florentine Renaissance Sculpture*. London: John Murray, 1982. A great aid to the untrained reader, beginning step-by-step with a group of chapters that move out of the late Gothic period into the Renaissance. Very good at putting the ubiquitous Pisanos in the right order in time, contribution, and influence. With generous illustration.

Moskowitz, Anita Fiderer. *The Sculpture of Andrea and Nino Pisano*. New York: Cambridge University Press, 1986. An examination of the sculpture created by Andrea Pisano and his son. Contains 350 illustrations, bibliography, and index.

Paolucci, Antonio. *The Origins of Renaissance Art: The Baptistry Doors, Florence*. New York: George Braziller, 1996. An examination of the bronze doors prepared at the Battistero di San Giovanni in Florence and of the works of Pisano and Lorenzo Ghiberti. Illustrations.

Pope-Hennessy, John. *Italian Gothic Sculpture*. 3 vols. 4th ed. London: Phaidon Press, 1996. Pisano makes sense only if he can be seen clearly as both a precursor of the Renaissance and as a late Gothic artist. Pope-Hennessy is one of the finest, most elegant commentators on both elements of Pisano's gift.

See also: Donatello; Lorenzo Ghiberti; Giotto; Nicola Pisano and Giovanni Pisano.

Related articles in *Great Events from History: The Middle Ages, 477-1453*: c. 1320: Origins of the Bubonic Plague; 1347-1352: Invasion of the Black Death in Europe; c. 1410-1440: Florentine School of Art Emerges.

Nicola Pisano and Giovanni Pisano

Italian sculptors

By synthesizing Gothic and classical influences, Nicola Pisano and Giovanni Pisano created sculptural styles that are considered proto-Renaissance in their concern with expanded form and space and humanized narrative scenes.

Nicola Pisano

Born: c. 1220; probably Apulia (now in Italy)
Died: Between 1278 and 1284; Pisa (now in Italy)
Also known as: Nicolas de Apulia

Giovanni Pisano

Born: c. 1250; Pisa (now in Italy)
Died: Between 1314 and 1318; probably Siena, Republic of Siena (now in Italy)
Area of achievement: Art

Early Lives

Although the earliest known work of Nicola Pisano (nee-KAW-lah pee-SAHN-oh) is the signed and dated pulpit for the baptistery of Pisa of 1260, the style and skill demonstrated there are clearly the work of a mature artist. His history and career before 1260, however, are largely a matter of conjecture based on a few late documents and observable influences on the style of his known works. On the basis of two documents dated 1266 that refer to him as "Nicolas de Apulia," it is thought that he was probably born in southern Italy around 1220. This theory is supported by the strong influence of classical sculpture seen in the marble reliefs of the Pisa pulpit, an influence that suggests a familiarity with the classicized art encouraged in the south during the reign of Frederick II. Nicola may also have passed through Rome while making his way north.

By 1258, Nicola had established himself as an artist in Pisa. Because his son Giovanni is documented as having been born in Pisa, possibly as early as 1248, Nicola most likely arrived in that city around mid-century. Attributions of works whose dates precede that of the Pisa pulpit have been made, but none is certain. A visit to France by Nicola in the 1250's has been suggested, based on stylistic and iconographic details of the Pisa pulpit, but such a trip is not accepted by all scholars.

Giovanni Pisano was trained as a sculptor by his father. Nicola's contract for a pulpit in the Siena cathedral names Giovanni as a junior member of the studio by 1265. From this evidence, his birth date is placed around 1250. Inscriptions on two of Giovanni's own works mention his place of birth as being Pisa.

Besides the Siena pulpit, it is known that Giovanni assisted his father on the Fontana Maggiore (great fountain) in Perugia and probably on the exterior, second-story sculpture of the Pisan baptistery. The emphatic Gothicism of his mature style can be identified in parts of these earlier commissions, and portions of them have been attributed to his hand. It has been suggested that his knowledge of French Gothic art was acquired during a trip to France between 1270 and 1276, but the evidence for such a visit is strictly stylistic. Alternatively, it is possible that he learned of the French style through a study of portable artworks such as ivory carvings and manuscript illuminations.

Lives' Work

Nicola Pisano's pulpit for the baptistery of Pisa demonstrates that in 1260 he was working in a heavily classicized style. The classical influence can be seen in his handling of draperies, the sculpting of bodies and heads, the emphasis on the human form, the technical virtuosity, and the sense of classical reserve that permeates the reliefs and statuettes. Specific sources for some of the figures can be found among ancient Greek, Roman, and Etruscan works. Nicola's classicism was neither debased nor pastichelike but extended to the structure of the pulpit itself, the interest in space and form, and the depiction of narrative scenes as human dramas. The Pisa pulpit also reflects other influences, including Italian Romanesque sculpture, Italo-Byzantine painting, and French Gothicism.

The pulpit at Pisa marked a distinct development beyond the Romanesque style prevalent in Italy at the time, a style characterized by flattened forms, shallow cutting, schematic draperies, and little illusion of three-dimensional space. Nicola's talent, however, was not static. Within a few years of the completion of the Pisa pulpit, the French Gothic style began to influence his work heavily. This development can be seen in his next major commission, a pulpit for the cathedral in Siena, completed in 1268. In the relief sculpture and statuettes for this work, Nicola continued his emphasis on volumetric human form and retained an innate classicism, but he exploited the expressive and emotional possibilities inherent in the more fluid naturalism of the Gothic.

Nicola's reputation rests on the achievement of these two pulpits, but he was involved in other commissions as well. He designed the tomb of Saint Dominic in San Domenico Maggiore at Bologna, the execution of which fell to his studio, most notably to Arnolfo di Cambio. In 1273, he built, or reconstructed, the altar dedicated to Saint James in the cathedral at Pistoia. In 1278, he completed work on the Fontana Maggiore in Perugia. He may also have been involved in architectural designs, in particular the arcade and sculpture on the second story of the baptistery in Pisa. There is no mention of him after 1278, and in 1284 he is documented as deceased.

By the time of his father's death, Giovanni Pisano had become one of the most prominent artists in Italy. Sometime after March, 1284, he renounced his Pisan citizenship and became a citizen of Siena, where he worked as an architect and sculptor on the cathedral. By 1290, he is documented as capomaestro (supervisor of works) at the cathedral, a position that he retained until 1296. During this period, he designed a façade for the cathedral, and the lower portion may have been completed according to his plan. He also created sculptures of human and animal figures to decorate the façade. These statues are notable for their plasticity and movement. The figures were conceived with their designated positions on the façade in mind. Proportional distortions were imposed that would be optically resolved when viewed from below at a distance. The poses were planned to complement one another for a unified compositional effect. The figures reveal an expressive intensity that became the hallmark of Giovanni's style.

Giovanni departed Siena under accusations of fiscal irregularities at the cathedral works. By 1297, he was back in Pisa as capomaestro of that town's cathedral works, but he retained his Sienese citizenship and property. In 1301, he completed a pulpit for the Church of San Andrea in Pistoia. The next year, he began a pulpit for the Cathedral of Pisa that was completed in 1310. The sculpted portions of these two pulpits reveal an extreme expressive style and compositions marked by rhythmic patterns and advanced spatial considerations. Deep carving and protruding forms serve to deny the planar surface of the marble panel. In the Pisa pulpit, he once again composed the work with the spectator's viewpoint in mind. Throughout the narrative reliefs of both pulpits, Giovanni manipulated naturalism for expressive purposes but managed to avoid overt distortion.

The supports for the Pisa pulpit include large sculpted figures whose style shows a retreat from the strong Gothic expressiveness of the earlier relief panels. A modifying restraint is evident, quite possibly the result of contact with the works of the early fourteenth century Florentine painter Giotto. This more composed style is also evident in one of Giovanni's freestanding Madonnas, created about 1305 for the altar of the Arena Chapel in Padua. The same chapel contains Giotto's greatest fresco cycle, painted between 1304 and 1312. Although Giovanni's Madonna is clearly derived from French Gothic types, the emphasis on more subtle expression and dignified massing heralds a new artistic age.

Giovanni's last known work was a monument to Margaret of Luxembourg in San Francesco di Castelletto at Genoa, undertaken in 1312. It was commissioned by the Hohenstaufen emperor Henry VII, a recent ally of Pisa, in honor of his wife, who had died in Genoa that year. Despite its current disassembled state, the central figure group of Margaret being awakened by two angels displays a subtle poignancy unique to Italian Gothic sculpture.

Documents show that Giovanni was still alive in 1314 but dead by 1318. He was buried in Siena.

SIGNIFICANCE

Nicola Pisano and Giovanni Pisano are two late medieval Italian sculptors whose works reflect influences, intentions, and explorations that mark them as forerunners of the Italian Renaissance. Nicola's first style demonstrated strongly classical tendencies that were later subordinated to the expressive naturalism of Gothicism. Giovanni's sculpture was more consistently Gothic, but, like his father, he manipulated the Gothic idiom in the interest of naturalism, especially in the exploration of integrated, spatial compositions made up of volumetric forms. Along with the sculptor Arnolfo di Cambio, Nicola and Giovanni Pisano were largely responsible for freeing Italian sculpture from its long subordination to architecture. Their careers also mark the beginning of a noticeable evolution in the status of artists, and their signing of their works symbolically separates them from the anonymous craftsperson-sculptors of the Middle Ages. Both artists stand at the threshold of a new era of art, one that emphasized the personal, human qualities of images and narratives over didactic, symbolic concepts. The Pisanos' compositional and interpretive innovations influenced the pictorial explorations of fourteenth century Italian artists. Along with the fourteenth century painters Giotto and Duccio di Buoninsegna, Nicola and Giovanni Pisano are considered the principal late medieval Italian artists whose works were proto-Renaissance in style.

—*Madeline Cirillo Archer*

FURTHER READING

Ayrton, Michael. *Giovanni Pisano, Sculptor.* New York: Weybright and Talley, 1969. A lavish monograph written from an artist's perspective. Introduction by the sculptor Henry Moore. More than three hundred photographs reproduce all the known and attributed works, with many detail shots. Diagrams, bibliography, and catalog notes on the plates. Also includes information on and photographs of Nicola Pisano's work.

Crichton, G. H., and E. R. Crichton. *Nicola Pisano and the Revival of Sculpture in Italy.* Cambridge, England: Cambridge University Press, 1938. An early monograph, but still useful. Includes an extensive discussion of stylistic influences. Places Nicola within a historical and art historical context. An appendix lists and quotes the documents related to the birthplace controversy.

Dodsworth, Barbara W. *The Arca di San Domenico.* New York: Peter Lang, 1995. An examination of the work done by Nicola Pisano on the Arca di San Domenico in Bologna, Italy. Illustrated, with bibliography.

Moskowitz, Anita Fiderer. *Nicola Pisano's Arca di San Domenico and Its Legacy.* University Park: Pennsylvania State University Press, 1994. An analysis of Nicola Pisano's Arca di San Domenico in Bologna and its influence. Illustrations, bibliography, and index

Pope-Hennessy, John. *Italian Gothic Sculpture.* Vol. 1 in *An Introduction to Italian Sculpture.* 4th ed. London: Phaidon Press, 1996. A standard study of the period. The text provides excellent stylistic perspectives on the artists' careers. Includes photographic reproductions, biographical data, catalog entries, and a selective bibliography for Nicola and Giovanni Pisano and other sculptors of the late medieval period in Italy.

White, John. *Art and Architecture in Italy: 1250-1400.* 3d ed. New Haven, Conn: Yale University Press, 1993. A basic reference on late medieval Italian art. Contains chapters on Nicola Pisano and Giovanni Pisano that discuss all of their principal works as well as some undocumented attributions. Includes photographic reproductions, notes, and brief bibliography.

SEE ALSO: Arnolfo di Cambio; Duccio di Buoninsegna; Frederick II; Giotto; Andrea Pisano.

RELATED ARTICLE in *Great Events from History: The Middle Ages, 477-1453*: c. 1410-1440: Florentine School of Art Emerges.

Poggio

Italian scholar

Through his tireless efforts, Poggio discovered and copied manuscripts of classical Latin authors that had been lost for centuries and that, if not for him, might have remained lost forever.

Born: February 11, 1380; Terranuova, near Arezzo, Tuscany, Republic of Florence (now in Italy)
Died: October 30, 1459; Florence
Also known as: Gian Francesco Poggio Bracciolini (full name)
Area of achievement: Literature

Early Life

Gian Francesco Poggio Bracciolini, better known as Poggio (PAWD-joh), received his earliest education in Arezzo, but at the age of sixteen or seventeen moved to Florence to complete his studies and train for the profession of notary. He was taught Latin by John of Ravenna and may have been a student in Greek under Manuel Chrysoloras, although this is disputable because Poggio never gained mastery of Greek. Because he was from a poor family, Poggio copied manuscripts for the book trade to support himself in these endeavors in Florence.

Poggio's knowledge of Latin caught the attention of Coluccio Salutati, a student of Petrarch and Florence's first Humanist chancellor. It was probably at this time that Salutati nurtured in the young Poggio a love for the classics and the determination to search for lost manuscripts. Also at this time, Poggio met and became a close friend of Niccolò Niccoli, a wealthy Florentine with whom he shared a lifelong passion for classical artifacts and classical manuscripts. These two men, along with Leonardo Bruni, Ambrogio Traversari, and Leon Battista Alberti, carried on the intellectual movement begun by Petrarch in the late 1300's and continued by Salutati in the early 1400's.

In 1403, Poggio entered the Papal Curia as a *scriptor* (scribe). He soon advanced to the post of apostolic secretary and, except for an unhappy interlude from 1418 to 1422, when he served Henry Beaufort, bishop of Winchester, in England, spent the next fifty years in service to five different popes.

During the early years of his career in the Curia, Poggio developed the Humanist style of writing. The letters of this hand, simpler and rounder in formation and easier to read than Gothic, directly imitated the Carolingian script of the eleventh century. The earliest example of Humanist script is in a manuscript of Cicero's letters to Titus Pomponius Atticus in Poggio's own hand and dated 1408.

Life's Work

Poggio's main interest throughout his lifetime was in the area of classical studies—including archaeology, architecture, coins, epigraphy, and statues, as well as manuscripts. On entering Rome for the first time in 1403, Poggio was struck by the decay of the once-noble city. He was the first to use a truly scientific approach to the study of the city's ruins. Comparing the sights with descriptions from Livy, Marcus Vitruvius Pollio, and Sextus Julius Frontinus, Poggio was able to catalog in part the remains of ancient Rome. He accurately assigned to the Republican era a bridge, an arch, a tomb, and a temple. Among the buildings dating to the Empire, he described several temples, two theaters (including the theater of Pompey the Great), the Colosseum, the Column of Trajan, and the mausoleums of the emperors Augustus and Hadrian. His treatise, *De varietate fortunae* (1431-1438; on the vicissitude of fortune), is the most important document for the physical state of Rome in the fifteenth century. Many artifacts that he discovered on his travels were used to decorate his villa outside Florence.

Poggio's most significant contribution to classical scholarship came in the area of ancient manuscripts. It is reported that as early as 1407 Poggio was in the monastery of Monte Cassino looking for lost texts. The Council of Constance in 1414-1418, however, opened up the monastic libraries of the transalpine countries to Italian scholars. The council meetings, designed to establish one single pope in Rome, afforded the apostolic secretary much leisure time in which to explore the monasteries in search of ancient Latin manuscripts.

From 1415 to 1417, Poggio made his most important and most numerous discoveries in the monasteries of France, Germany, and Switzerland. In 1415, at Cluny, Poggio unearthed two previously unknown orations of Cicero. At Saint Gall the next year came his astounding discovery of the entire *Institutio oratoria* (c. 95 C.E.; *On the Education of an Orator*, 1856; better known as *Institutio oratoria*) by Quintilian, which had previously been known only from a mutilated copy found in Florence by Petrarch in 1350. In the same expedition, Poggio also found most of the first half of Gaius Valerius Flaccus's *Argonautica* (c. 90 C.E.) and a ninth century manuscript of Asconius Pedianus's commentaries on

Cicero's orations. On other trips in 1417, he unearthed Sextus Pompeius Festus's *De significatu verborum* (second or third century C.E.), Lucretius's *De rerum natura* (c. 60 B.C.E.; *On the Nature of Things*, 1682), Marcus Manilius's *Astronomica* (c. 14-27 C.E.), Silius Italicus's *Punica* (first century C.E.), Ammianus Marcellinus's *Res gestae* (c. 378 C.E.), Apicius's *De re coquinaria* (late fourth century C.E.; *The Roman Cookery Book*, 1817), and Statius's *Silvae* (c. 91-95 C.E.). Also in 1417, Poggio found a manuscript of Cicero's oration on behalf of Caecina, a Roman general.

After his reinstatement as secretary in the Papal Curia in 1423, Poggio brought to light manuscripts of Sextus Julius Frontinus's *De aquaeductibus* (c. 97 C.E.) and Firmicus Maternus's *Matheseos libri* (c. 354 C.E.). Other ancient authors rediscovered by Poggio included Columella, Vitruvius Pollio, Nonius Marcellus, Marcus Valerius Probus, and Eutyches. In Poggio's mind, the end justified the means, and he was not above stealing to appropriate manuscripts, as he makes clear in his letters.

Poggio is not without his critics in the area of manuscripts. The seeker of lost texts was not especially careful with his discoveries after he had copied them, and many of his manuscripts disappeared shortly after they were found. Manilius's *Argonautica* was copied, then the original was lost. Asconius Pedianus is only preserved in copies made from the manuscript found by Poggio. The codex of Gaius Valerius Flaccus disappeared shortly after it was copied, and Cicero's work on the comedian Quintius Roscius is known only from an apograph of the recovered text. This carelessness has caused great anguish, even anger, among modern paleographers and textual critics who are more interested in the contents of ninth century texts than they are in Poggio's fifteenth century copy.

Poggio's own writings reveal a multitude of interests and range from moral dialogues to indecent satires on clergy and friars. Two of his more important moral essays are *De avaritia* (1428-1429; on greed) and *De varietate fortunae*. *Facetiae* (1438-1452; *The Fables of Poge the Florentyn*, 1484, 1879) paints humorous, often obscene, vignettes of priests, monks, and rival Humanists. Of most historical value are Poggio's letters, published in three separate works. Addressed to 172 correspondents, the nearly six hundred epistles reveal not only Poggio's own life but also the activities of a number of popes and various rulers throughout Europe, and especially in Italy.

In 1435, at the age of fifty-five, Poggio married the eighteen-year-old Vaggia Buondelmonti. He seems to have been quite happy with his wellborn bride, even though the marriage forced him to forsake his mistress, with whom he had had fourteen children. In 1453, he left the papal court to become chancellor of Florence and devoted the rest of his life to continuing Leonardo Bruni's *Historiarum, Florentini populi* (c. 1415; history of the Florentine republic). Poggio died in 1459 and was buried in the Church of Santa Croce, where a statue by the artist Donatello commemorates him.

Significance

Poggio's contribution to classical studies is threefold. His development of the Humanist script, which was refined by the succeeding generation of scribes, became the prototype for the Roman font when the art of printing was introduced into Italy from Germany. The Roman type, which was easier to read, gradually supplanted the Gothic. Because of Poggio's calligraphic efforts, books became more legible. His collection of Latin inscrip-

Poggio. (Library of Congress)

tions, which he compiled in 1429, evolved over centuries into the modern *Corpus inscriptionum Latinarum*, an ongoing reference work listing all known Latin inscriptions. This reference work provides Latin linguists, Roman historians, Latin philologists, and other scholars with crucial information about early, even pre-Republican, Rome.

Poggio's most lasting achievements, however, lie in the area of manuscript recovery. Petrarch, initiating the intellectual movement called Humanism, had begun the efforts to find and copy ancient texts, and his work had been carried on by Giovanni Boccaccio. In the next generation, Salutati, who espoused the same philosophy of the importance of the classics, continued their work. In addition, he transmitted his beliefs to a number of his most gifted students, Poggio among them.

Poggio, however, eclipsed both predecessors and contemporaries in the amount and importance of his discoveries. In continuing activities begun by Petrarch, he was advancing the Humanist movement, but, more important, he preserved for posterity classical works that might have disappeared forever. Although succeeding centuries have produced far fewer revelations of ancient manuscripts, scholars continue to devote their lives to searching for lost texts. It is in part because of Poggio's successes that they do so.

—*Joan E. Carr*

Further Reading

Bracciolini, Poggio. *Two Renaissance Book Hunters: The Letters of Poggius Bracciolini to Nicolaus de Niccolis*. Edited by Phyllis Walter Goodhart Gordon. 1974. Reprint. New York: Columbia University Press, 1991. This English translation of the Latin reveals Poggio's excitement and problems at finding and copying old manuscripts. The introduction chronicles Poggio's life. Includes copious notes and an extensive bibliography.

Fubini, Riccardo. *Humanism and Secularization: From Petrarch to Valla*. Durham, N.C.: Duke University Press, 2003. An examination of Poggio, including the influence received from Petrarch. Bibliography and index.

Kajanto, Iiro. *Poggio Bracciolini and Classicism: A Study in Early Italian Humanism*. Helsinki: Suomalainen Tiedeakatemia, 1987. Analysis and criticism of the life and works of Poggio, especially as they relate to Humanism. Bibliography.

Salemi, Joseph S., trans. "Selections from the *Facetiae* of Poggio Bracciolini." *Allegorica* 8 (1983): 77-183. Published in a bilingual format, this study is a translation of forty of Poggio's fables, as well as the introduction and conclusion. Provides insight into Poggio's cynical view toward most of humanity. The footnotes are helpful. Illustrated.

Trinkhaus, Charles. *The Scope of Renaissance Humanism*. Ann Arbor: University of Michigan Press, 1983. Contains a careful survey of Humanists, how they interacted, and what they contributed.

See also: Giovanni Boccaccio; Leonardo Bruni; Donatello; Nicholas V; Petrarch.

Related article in *Great Events from History: The Middle Ages, 477-1453*: c. 1350-1400: Petrarch and Boccaccio Recover Classical Texts.

MARCO POLO

Italian explorer

Through his Asian travels and his book recording them, Marco Polo encouraged a medieval period of intercultural communication, Western knowledge of other lands, and eventually the Western period of exploration and expansion.

BORN: c. 1254; Venice? (now in Italy)
DIED: January 8, 1324; Venice
AREA OF ACHIEVEMENT: Exploration

EARLY LIFE

Despite his enduring fame, very little is known about the personal life of Marco Polo. It is known that he was born into a leading Venetian family of merchants. He also lived during a propitious time in world history, when the height of Venice's influence as a city-state coincided with the greatest extent of Mongol conquest of Asia. Ruled by Kublai Khan, the Mongol Empire stretched all the way from China to Russia and the Levant. The Mongols also threatened other parts of Europe, particularly Poland and Hungary, inspiring fear everywhere by their bloodthirsty advances. However, their ruthless methods brought a measure of stability to the lands they controlled, opening up trade routes such as the famous Silk Road. Eventually, the Mongols discovered that it was more profitable to collect tribute from people than to kill them outright, and this policy also stimulated trade.

Into this favorable atmosphere ventured a number of European traders, including the family of Marco Polo. The Polos had long-established ties in the Levant and around the Black Sea; for example, they owned property in Constantinople, and Marco's uncle, for whom he was named, had a home in Sudak in the Crimea. From Sudak, around 1260, another uncle, Maffeo, and Marco's father, Niccolò, made a trading visit into Mongol territory, the land of the Golden Horde (Russia), ruled by Berke Khan. While they were there, a war broke out between Berke and the khan of the Levant, blocking their return home. Thus Niccolò and Maffeo traveled deeper into Mongol territory, moving southeastward to Bukhara, which was ruled by a third khan. While waiting there, they met an emissary traveling farther eastward who invited them to accompany him to the court of the great khan, Kublai, in Cathay (modern China). In Cathay, Kublai Khan gave the Polos a friendly reception, appointed them his emissaries to the pope, and ensured their safe travel back to Europe: They were to return to Cathay with one hundred learned men who could instruct the Mongols in the Christian religion and the liberal arts.

In 1269, Niccolò Polo and Maffeo Polo finally arrived back in Venice, where Niccolò found that his wife had died during his absence. Their son, Marco, then about fifteen years old, had been only six or younger when his father left home; thus Marco was reared primarily by his mother and the extended Polo family—and the streets of Venice. After his mother's death, Marco had probably begun to think of himself as something of a orphan. Then his father and uncle suddenly reappeared, as if from the dead, after nine years of travel in far-off, romantic lands. These experiences were the formative influences on young Marco, and one can see their effects mirrored in his character: a combination of sensitivity and toughness, independence and loyalty, motivated by an eagerness for adventure, a love of stories, and a desire to please or impress.

LIFE'S WORK

In 1268, Pope Clement IV died, and a two- or three-year delay while another pope was being elected gave young Marco time to mature and to absorb the tales of his father and uncle. Marco was seventeen years old when he, his father, and his uncle finally set out for the court of Kublai Khan. They were accompanied not by one hundred wise men but by two Dominican friars, and the two good friars turned back at the first sign of adversity, another local war in the Levant. Aside from the pope's messages, the only spiritual gift Europe was able to furnish the great Kublai Khan was oil from the lamp burning at Jesus Christ's supposed tomb in Jerusalem. Yet, in a sense, young Marco, the only new person in the Polos' party, was himself a fitting representative of the spirit of European civilization on the eve of the Renaissance, and the lack of one hundred learned Europeans guaranteed that he would catch the eye of the khan, who was curious about "Latins."

On the way to the khan's court, Marco had the opportunity to complete his education. The journey took three and a half years by horseback through some of the world's most rugged terrain, including snowy mountain ranges, such as the Pamirs, and parching deserts, such as the Gobi. Marco and his party encountered such hazards as wild beasts and brigands; they also met with beautiful women, in whom young Marco took a special interest. The group traveled through numerous countries and cul-

Engraving of Marco Polo patterned on a Venetian mosaic. (Library of Congress)

tures, noting the food, dress, and religions unique to each. In particular, under the khan's protection the Polos were able to observe a large portion of the Islamic world at close range, as few if any European Christians had. (Unfortunately, Marco's anti-Muslim prejudices, a European legacy of the Crusades, marred his observations.) By the time they reached the khan's court in Khanbalik (modern Peking), Marco had become a hardened traveler. He had also received a unique education and had been initiated into manhood.

Kublai Khan greeted the Polos warmly and invited them to stay on in his court. Here, if Marco's account is to be believed, the Polos became great favorites of the khan, and Kublai eventually made Marco one of his most trusted emissaries. On these points, Marco has been accused of gross exaggeration, and the actual status of the Polos at the court of the khan is much disputed. If at first it appears unlikely that Kublai would make young Marco an emissary, on examination this seems quite reasonable. For political reasons, the khan was in the habit of appointing foreigners to administer conquered lands, particularly China, where the tenacity of the Chinese bureaucracy was legendary (and eventually contributed to the breakup of the Mongol Empire). The khan could also observe for himself that young Marco was a good candidate: eager, sturdy, knowledgeable, well traveled, and apt (Marco quickly assimilated Mongol culture and became proficient in four languages, of which three were probably Mongol, Turkish, and Persian). Finally, Marco reported back so successfully from his first mission—informing the khan not only on business details but also on colorful customs and other interesting trivia—that his further appointment was confirmed. The journeys specifically mentioned in Marco's book, involving travel across China and a sea voyage to India, suggest that the khan did indeed trust him with some of the most difficult missions.

The Polos stayed on for seventeen years, another indication of how valued they were in the khan's court. Marco, his father, and his uncle not only survived—itself an achievement amid the political hazards of the time—but also prospered. Apparently, the elder Polos carried on their trading while Marco was performing his missions; yet seventeen years is a long time to trade without returning home to family and friends. According to Marco, because the khan held them in such high regard, he would not let them return home, but as the khan aged, the Polos began to fear what would happen after his death. Finally an opportunity to leave presented itself when trusted emissaries were needed to accompany a Mongol princess on a wedding voyage by sea to Persia, where she was promised to the local khan. The Polos sailed from Cathay with a fleet of fourteen ships and a wedding party of six hundred people, not counting the sailors. Only a few members of the wedding entourage survived the journey of almost two years, but luckily the survivors included the Polos and the princess. Fortunately, too, the Polos duly delivered the princess not to the old khan of Persia, who had meanwhile died, but to his son.

From Persia, the Polos made their way back to Venice. They were robbed as soon as they got into Christian territory, but they still managed to reach home, in 1295, with plenty of rich goods. According to Giovanni Battista Ramusio, one of the early editors of Marco's book, the Polos strode into Venice looking like ragged Mongols. Having thought them dead, their relatives at first did not recognize them, then were astounded, and subsequently were disgusted by their shabby appearance. Yet, according to Ramusio, the scorn changed to delight when the returned travelers invited everyone to a homecoming banquet, ripped apart their old clothes, and let all the hidden jewels clatter to the table.

The rest of the world might have learned little about the Polos' travels if fate had not intervened in Marco's life. In his early forties, Marco was not yet ready to settle down. Perhaps he was restless for further adventure, or perhaps he felt obliged to fulfill his civic duties to his native city-state. In any event, he became involved in naval warfare between the Venetians and their trading rivals, the Genoese, and was captured. In 1298, the great traveler across Asia and emissary of the khan found himself rotting in a prison in Genoa—an experience that could have ended tragically but instead took a lucky turn. In prison Marco met a man named Rustichello (or Rusticiano), from Pisa, who was a writer of romances. To pass the time, Marco dictated his observations about Asia to Rustichello, who, in writing them down, probably employed the Italianized Old French that was the language of his romances. (Old French had gained currency as the language of medieval romances during the Crusades.)

Their book was soon in circulation because Marco remained in prison only a year or so, very likely gaining his freedom when the Venetians and Genoese made peace in 1299. After his prison experience, Marco was content to lead a quiet life in Venice with his family and bask in his almost instant literary fame. He married Donata Badoer, a member of the Venetian aristocracy, and they had three daughters—Fantina, Bellela, and Moreta—all of whom eventually grew up to marry nobles. Thus Marco seems to have spent the last part of his life moving in Venetian aristocratic circles. After living what was then a long life, Marco died in 1324, roughly seventy years of age. In his will he left most of his modest wealth to his three daughters, a legacy that included goods that he had brought back from Asia. His will also set free a Tatar slave, Peter, who had remained with him since his return from the court of the great khan.

Significance

The book that Marco and Rustichello wrote in prison in the fourteenth century was titled *Divisament dou monde* (literally, description of the world), although in Italian it is usually called *Il milione* (the million), and it is usually translated into English as *The Travels of Marco Polo* (1579). The original title is more indicative of its contents than this English title, which is somewhat deceptive, because after its prologue, the book is actually a cultural geography instead of a travelogue or an autobiography.

The book was immediately popular. Numerous copies were made and circulated (this was the age before printing), including translations into other dialects and languages. Some copyists were priests or monks who, threatened by descriptions of other religions and the great khan's notable religious tolerance, made discreet emendations. These changes may in part account for the emphasis on Christian miracles in the book's early sections and even for its anti-Muslim sentiments. The numerous manuscripts with their many variants have created a monumental textual problem for modern editors of the work, since Marco and Rustichello's original manuscript has disappeared.

Modern readers might be surprised by the book's impact in Marco's time and for centuries afterward, but to readers of the early fourteenth century, descriptions of Asia were as fantastic as descriptions of outer space are today. Unfortunately many people then tended to read it as though it were science fiction or fantasy, perhaps in part because of its romantic style (including Rustichello's embellishments). The title *Il milione*, whose origin is obscure, could refer to the number of lies the book supposedly contains. (Some readers considered Marco Polo merely a notorious liar.) Yet, allowing for textual uncertainties, modern commentators have judged the book to be remarkably accurate; thus, it was a valuable source for those readers who took it seriously. For centuries, it was the main source of Western information about Asia, and it exercised a tremendous influence on the Western age of exploration (Christopher Columbus carried a well-marked copy with him). It has also continued to influence the Western imagination—inspiring plays, novels, and films, as well as unrestrained scholarly speculation about Marco's life and travels. In short, Marco Polo has become a symbol of Western man venturing forth.

Yet in large part the meaning of Marco Polo's experience has been misinterpreted. His sojourn in the East has too often been seen as the first probe of Western man into unknown territory, with Marco as a kind of spy or intelligence gatherer identifying the locations of the richest spoils, the first example of Western man as conquerer (a viewpoint that is shamefully ethnocentric). Although he did influence the Western age of exploration, conquest, and colonization, this was hardly his intent. Instead, Marco can best be seen as an exponent of intercultural communication who lived during a period when communication between East and West opened up for a brief time.

—*Harold Branam*

Further Reading

Calvino, Italo. *Invisible Cities*. Translated by William Weaver. 1974. Reprint. San Francisco: Arion Press, 1999. Originally published in 1972 as *Le città invisibili*, this postmodernist novel by one of Italy's leading writers is a fascinating example of an imaginative work inspired by Marco Polo. Consists of conversations between Marco Polo and Kublai Khan and Marco's descriptions of imaginary cities.

Larner, John. *Marco Polo and the Discovery of the World*. New Haven, Conn.: Yale University Press, 1999. A discussion of the Polo family, Marco's relationship with Rustichello, the making of the book, and the explorer's influence. Contains maps of the fifteenth century. Bibliography and index.

Polo, Marco. *The Travels of Marco Polo*. Translated by Ronald Latham. 1958. Reprint. New York: Penguin Books, 1996. One of the best translations into English of Marco's book. Contains a brief but good introduction by the translator.

Wood, Frances. *Did Marco Polo Go to China?* Boulder, Colo.: Westview Press, 1996. Wood argues that Marco Polo may not have made the fabulous journey described in his book. Wood claims that the details of that work could have been taken from the works of other travelers and that Polo's narrated tale could have been embellished by the ghost writer who transcribed it. Wood neglects to say where Polo could have been if not in China.

See also: Pietro d'Abano; Giovanni da Pian del Carpini; Genghis Khan; Kublai Khan; Raymond Lull; al-Masʿūdī; William of Rubrouck.

Related articles in *Great Events from History: The Middle Ages, 477-1453*: c. 1145: Prester John Myth Sweeps Across Europe; 1204: Genghis Khan Founds Mongol Empire; 1271-1295: Travels of Marco Polo; 1415-1460: Prince Henry the Navigator Promotes Portuguese Exploration.

Marguerite Porete

French writer and mystic

A religious mystic burned as a heretic, Marguerite Porete wrote a book of spiritual contemplation and mysticism called The Mirror of Simple Souls. *The book was written not in Latin but in the vernacular, and, despite Church condemnation, it secretly circulated for centuries, attracting readers until at least the early seventeenth century.*

Born: c. 1255-1280; probably the region of Hainaut (now in Belgium)

Died: June 1, 1310; Paris, France

Also known as: Marguerite de Porret/Poiret; Marguerite of Hainaut

Areas of achievement: Religion and theology, literature

Early Life

Despite a great deal of scholarly research, no historian has been able to learn many details concerning the early life of Marguerite Porete (po-reht). However, her book and the records of her trial for heresy tell us some details. Porete's writing suggests that she was well educated in both religious works and the courtly literary tradition. Because of her education and because her book disparages the crudeness of peasants and merchants, some scholars think that she might have been raised in an aristocratic family.

The Inquisition classified Porete as a Beguine (probably from a Flemish word meaning "to pray"). The Beguines were composed of a variety of pious laywomen in northwestern Europe. The movement was organized in Flanders by Marie d'Oignies in the twelfth century, and it spread into northern France, Belgium, the Netherlands, and Germany. However, Porete never called herself a Beguine, and it is not certain that she formally belonged to the organization. Beguines lived a life of holiness without connection to an official, formal order, and they did not take perpetual vows. Living alone or with families, they devoted themselves to prayer, poverty, chastity, and charitable works. They wore an austere garb and lived by begging and doing menial work. For women not wishing to marry or enter a monastery, joining the sisterhood was one of the few life-options available.

Because Beguines were mostly unsupervised, it was common for members to develop heterodox or even heretical notions. Many members were women who did not hesitate to attack the materialistic values and corruption of the Church, attacks that greatly displeased the clergy. In Porete's day, many people suspected that Beguines and Beghards, a corresponding association of men, were guilty of immorality and heresy. The two groups were frequently confused with the secret Free Spirit sect, whose members were rumored to practice sexual promiscuity without any sense of guilt.

Sometimes the term Beguine was used loosely to refer to an unmarried woman who practiced an ascetic lifestyle. Porete mentioned in her book that Beguines were among her severe critics. Given her strong religious inclinations, it would have appeared natural for her to be drawn into the sisterhood. Perhaps she was a solitary itinerant Beguine who expounded her message to anyone willing to listen. Certainly Porete's persecutors believed that she was affiliated with the movement, which was detested in conservative circles. The inquisitors were ready to make an example of a Beguine with heterodox ideas.

LIFE'S WORK

In the early 1300's, Porete was apparently living in the region around Valenciennes, a French town on the Schelde River near the border with Belgium. It is not known exactly when she wrote *Le Miroir des âmes simples* (*The Mirror of Simple Souls*, 1927), but it was sometime before 1306, the year in which the bishop of Cambrai ordered it publicly burned and prohibited its use under threat of excommunication. If the book had appeared only in Latin, it possibly would have been ignored. However, literary works in vernacular languages, like *The Mirror of Simple Souls*, found a large and growing readership.

The Mirror of Simple Souls, written for a spiritual elite rather than average Christians, articulates a religious viewpoint usually called mysticism, the belief that a person might attain direct spiritual union with God. The book poetically synthesized mystical ideas that were found in many previous writings, such as those of Pseudo-Dionysius, Joachim of Fiore, several women mystics, and the Franciscan Spirituals. It is written in the format of a play with dialogues, a form earlier used by Boethius. The allegorical characters include Soul, Love, Reason, Desire, Truth, and Discretion.

Committed to the values of faith and love, Porete had little use for strict reason. She expressed contempt for academic theologians because she believed they were incapable of understanding divine truth and spirituality. She asserted that only a person with an inspired and childlike soul could achieve the divine illumination necessary to understand such concepts. According to her scheme, the maturing person's soul (or spirit) passes through seven states until it finally enters a state of perfection and becomes "annihilated" as a separate entity, just as a river empties into an ocean. An annihilated soul would actually become godlike while the person is still alive.

For Porete, love is the essence of God, and it is also the essence of the annihilated soul. Thus, she writes that an annihilated soul "is God by condition of love." Her view of love is always highly abstract and relates primarily to contemplation rather than practice. She does not define love by reference to either altruistic behavior or erotic sexuality.

Porete never directly contradicted Catholic dogma, but she often made nonliteral and metaphorical interpretations of concepts such as the Trinity. She simply ignored those beliefs and practices not relevant to her mysticism and pantheism. For Porete, pantheism meant that the spirit of God was found everywhere, not just within the Church. Her pantheism implied that the Church was not necessarily the final authority in religious matters. Disparaging "Holy Church the Little," which was governed by reason, she taught that annihilated souls belonged to "Holy Church the Great," which was governed by divine love.

Although some modern theologians argue that her book was not actually heretical, her views on freedom were clearly inconsistent with medieval orthodoxy. Because she was convinced that *The Mirror of Simple Souls* was inspired by the Holy Spirit, she was simply unwilling to conform her teachings to the demands of bishops and councils. Unfortunately for her, and many others, this was the age of Pope Boniface VIII's bull *Unam sanctam* (one holy catholic and apostolic church, 1302), which strongly affirmed the necessity of obedience to the clerical hierarchy in matters of religious doctrine.

The authorities were especially disturbed by Porete's tendency toward antinomianism, the doctrine that an enlightened soul can ignore the laws of the Church and of the state. "Virtues, I take leave of you forever," she wrote. "I was never more free, except as departed from you." To orthodox ears, such statements seemed to advocate the radical libertinism of the Free Spirit heresy. Yet no one accused Porete of sinful behavior. She was probably simply emphasizing that the spiritual elite would be virtuous without the need for external rules. She did not deny that conventional rules are necessary for persons lacking spiritual maturity. Porete's ambiguous rhetoric, however, was always susceptible to any number of different interpretations.

Other ideas in *The Mirror of Simple Souls* displeased the orthodox clergy. Porete denigrated outward religious practices, including the sacraments. Likewise, she expressed little concern about future judgment and the afterlife. In fact, she wrote that by participating in the worship of God, she was already in Paradise, which was "nothing other than seeing god."

Ignoring the bishop of Cambrai's condemnation of 1306, Porete persisted in her missionary activities. She even dared to send copies of *The Mirror of Simple Souls* to prominent members of the clergy. The bishop of Cambrai again threatened her with severe punishment, as did the inquisitor of Lorraine. Undeterred, she extended her work to Paris, where *The Mirror of Simple Souls* attracted the attention of the notoriously harsh inquisitor general of France, the Dominican master William of Paris, who was also the personal confessor of King Philip IV the Fair. At this time King Philip was preparing for war with neighboring kingdoms, he was in the process of destroying the Knights Templars, and he was also involved in a power struggle with the Papacy. Given these conflicts, Philip and his close associates were determined to act as vigorous defenders of the orthodox faith.

In late 1308, William had Porete arrested and imprisoned in Paris. About the same time, he also ordered the arrest of Guiard de Cressonessart, a mystical Beghard who was accused of defending Porete and of denying the authority of the pope. The two prisoners were ordered to appear before the Inquisition court. Both refused to swear an oath, and they were kept in inquisitorial dungeons for the next year and a half. To decide their fates, William convoked a panel of five law professors and eleven theologians from the University of Paris.

On April 3, the panel judged unanimously that Porete's book was heretical and that the two defendants should be handed over to the government for execution unless they retracted. Guiard retracted and was sentenced to life imprisonment. Porete, however, refused to renounce her unorthodox doctrines. On May 31, 1310, William formally declared her a relapsed heretic and then turned her over to secular authorities. The next day, she was burned at the stake before a huge crowd at the Place de Grève (now l'Hôtel de Ville). This was a busy period for the Inquisition. Outside Paris that same month, at least fifty-four Templars were condemned to the flames as heretics.

Following Porete's execution, controversy surrounding *The Mirror of Simple Souls* did not end. In 1312, the ecumenical council of Vienne condemned eight alleged errors of *The Mirror of Simple Souls* and also denounced the "faithless women commonly known as Beguines." Yet, *The Mirror of Simple Souls* continued to circulate clandestinely, and during the next two centuries it was translated several times into English, Latin, and Italian. The Inquisition frequently confiscated the book, but it kept reappearing. Several church councils reaffirmed its heretical status. At least forty copies existed in the sixteenth century.

Significance

The movement of late medieval mysticism had an enormous influence on many thinkers, and Porete's *The Mirror of Simple Souls* was a relatively significant part of that movement. Meister Eckhart, the most famous of the German mystics, expressed ideas similar to those in *The Mirror of Simple Souls*. He was in Paris soon after Porete's execution, and he personally knew some of the theologians who condemned her book. If he read it, he unquestionably found reinforcement for his own work. During the next four centuries, numerous persons of mystical temperament, including Marguerite of Navarre, expressed admiration for *The Mirror of Simple Souls*. Some of the Lollards, Mennonites, and early Quakers were probably among its readers.

—*Thomas Tandy Lewis*

Further Reading

Babinsky, Ellen L. "Christological Transformation in *The Mirror of Souls*, by Marguerite Porete." *Theology Today* 60, no. 1 (April, 2003): 34-48. Argues that Porete's goal in *The Mirror of Simple Souls* is the reader's spiritual transformation. Christology is the theological interpretation of the life and work of Christ.

Brunn, Emilie, and Georgette Epiney-Burgard. *Women Mystics in Medieval Europe*. New York: Paragon House, 1989. Following an introduction to mysticism and the Beguines, the book gives excellent descriptions of five mystic writers, including Porete, Hildegard von Bingen, Mechthild von Magdeburg, Beatrice of Nazareth, and Hadewijch of Antwerp.

Conn, Marie A. *Noble Daughters: Unheralded Women in Western Christianity, Thirteenth to Eighteenth Centuries*. Westport, Conn.: Greenwood Press, 2000. Looks at the history of women mystics and religious devotees, including the Beguines, from the time of Porete through the eighteenth century.

Dronke, Peter. *Women Writers of the Middle Ages: A Critical Study of Texts from Perpetua to Marguerite Porete*. New York: Cambridge University Press, 1984. A survey of feminist perspectives from the third to the beginning of the fourteenth century, with impressionist comments on Porete and other writers.

Holywood, Amy. *The Soul as Virgin Wife: Mechthild of Magdeburg, Marguerite Porete, and Meister Eckhart.* Notre Dame, Ind.: University of Notre Dame Press, 2001. This book emphasizes the feminist perspectives of Mechthild and Porete, and argues that their writings directly influenced Eckhart's ideas about divine love.

Lea, Henry Charles. *A History of the Inquisition in the Middle Ages.* New York: Macmillan, 1962. A standard work that includes a good summary of Porete's trial and the full text of her condemnation by the Inquisition.

Lerner, Robert. *The Heresy of the Free Spirit in the Later Middle Ages.* Berkeley: University of California Press, 1972. A fascinating book arguing that Church authorities exaggerated the libertinism of the Free Spirits and even more the Beguines and Beghards.

McGinn, Bernard, ed. *Meister Eckhart and the Beguine Mystics: Hadewijch of Brabant, Mechthild of Magdeburg, and Marguerite Porete.* New York: Continuum, 1996. This book, edited by an outstanding scholar in the field, argues that Eckhart's spiritual vision owed much to Porete and other women mystics.

Porete, Marguerite. *The Mirror of Simple Souls.* Translated by Ellen Babinsky. New York: Paulist Press, 1993. A readable translation with an interesting and scholarly sixty-one page introduction to Porete's ideas and their historical context.

Robinson, Joanne Maguire. *Nobility and Annihilation in Marguerite Porete's "Mirror of Simple Souls."* Albany: State University of New York Press, 2001. A scholarly monograph that focuses on Porete's doctrine of the soul's annihilation.

SEE ALSO: Beatrice of Nazareth; Boethius; Saint Brigit; Christina of Markyate; Hildegard von Bingen; Joachim of Fiore; Joan of Arc; Julian of Norwich; Margery Kempe; Lady Alice Kyteler; Mechthild von Magdeburg; Philip IV the Fair; John Wyclif.

RELATED ARTICLES in *Great Events from History: The Middle Ages, 477-1453*: c. 1120: Order of the Knights Templar Is Founded; c. 1175: Waldensian Excommunications Usher in Protestant Movement; November 11-30, 1215: Fourth Lateran Council; 1233: Papal Inquisition; November 18, 1302: Boniface VII Issues the Bull *Unam Sanctam*; July 2, 1324: Lady Alice Kyteler Is Found Guilty of Witchcraft; 1377-1378: Condemnation of John Wyclif.

PRISCIAN

Byzantine scholar

Priscian's Institutiones grammaticae *preserved and abridged several earlier works of classical Latin grammar in a form so useful that it was copied and annotated and became the standard work in its genre until the end of the Middle Ages.*

BORN: Fifth century; Caesarea, Mauretania (now Cherchell, Algeria)
DIED: Sixth century; Constantinople, Byzantine Empire (now Istanbul, Turkey)
ALSO KNOWN AS: Priscianus Caesariensis (full Latin name)
AREAS OF ACHIEVEMENT: Linguistics, literature

EARLY LIFE

Few details are known about the life of Priscian (PRIHSH-ee-uhn). He was a native of the Vandal kingdom in North Africa and at some time before 503 moved his residence to Constantinople, capital of the Eastern Roman Empire. His presence in Constantinople is attested by the Ostrogothic writer and public official Cassiodorus (c. 490-c. 585), who asserts that in his own time, Priscian was a teacher of Latin grammar there. From Priscian's words in his *De laude imperatoris Anastasii* (sixth century; *Priscian of Caesarea's De Laude Anastasii Imperatoris*, 1991) it is clear that he disliked barbarians, such as the Ostrogoths, who ruled Italy from about 489 to 568: "My hope is that both Romes may be obedient to you [Anastasius] alone."

It is possible that the Symmachus to whom Priscian dedicated three minor works was the same man who was put to death with his son-in-law Boethius for plotting against the Ostrogothic king Theodoric the Great (c. 454-526) in 524; if so, that would provide additional motivation for Priscian's political leanings and distaste for the Goths. Judging from the fact that in his panegyric Priscian makes no mention of Anastasius's war against the Persians from 503 to 505, it is likely that he wrote it before the war. In addition, since his chief book on grammar was revised or copied by his pupil, Theodorus, "in the consulship of Olybrius" in 526, it is possible that

Priscian was dead by that year. Theodorus's copy is the original of all the extant manuscripts of Priscian's *Institutiones grammaticae* (526; grammatical foundations), in eighteen books.

LIFE'S WORK

Eleven writings are attributed to Priscian. Their order of composition is not known and only estimates of their dates can be made. Priscian's most important work is clearly his *Institutiones grammaticae*. He certainly completed this large work, now formatted in two volumes, before 526, when it was copied by Theodorus. In its dedication to one "Julianus, consul and patrician," Priscian states that he has translated from the Greek treatises of the grammarian Apollonius Dyscolus (fl. second century) and his son, the language scholar Aelius Herodianus (fl. second century). Priscian chose his sources well, for Apollonius has been called "the father of scientific grammar," and Herodianus continued his father's work. They lived in Alexandria and Rome serving the emperors Antoninus Pius and Marcus Aurelius, respectively. Priscian follows Apollonius closely in his treatment of pronouns, adverbs, conjunctions, and syntax, as can be determined from the extant parts of the latter's work. Apollonius's most original contribution to grammatical studies was in the area of syntax. Nevertheless, Priscian believed his own book to be brief compared to the "spacious scrolls" of Apollonius or the "sea" of Herodianus. Indeed, the success of Priscian's *Institutiones grammaticae* may derive from its relative brevity.

A valuable feature in Priscian's grammatical work is his inclusion of copious quotations from both Greek and Latin authors to exemplify particular grammatical principles. Thus, he preserved much that would otherwise have been lost: precious passages of Quintus Ennius, Marcus Pacuvius, Accius, Cato the Censor, and Marcus Terentius Varro. Most often quoted are Cicero and Sallust, but other Latin writers such as Plautus, Terence, Vergil, Horace, Ovid, Lucan, Statius, Persius, and Juvenal also appear. Priscian's Greek examples come chiefly from Homer, Plato, Isocrates, and Demosthenes. In the first sixteen books of the *Institutiones grammaticae*, often called *Priscianus major* (the great Priscian), he concentrates on grammar itself; the last two books, *Priscianus minor* (the little Priscian), are devoted to syntax. Here Priscian was more original because there existed fewer works on syntax from which to borrow. In one manuscript, the last two books are referred to as a distinct book called *De constructione* (on constructions). A table of contents would include book 1, on the letters and their sounds; book 2, on syllables, words, sentences, and nouns; book 3, on comparatives, superlatives, and diminutives; book 4, on interrelated forms such as verbals and participles used as nouns; book 5, on the gender, number, and case of nouns; book 6, on the endings of the nominative case and the formation of the genitive case; book 7, on the remaining cases—dative, accusative, and ablative; books 8, 9, and 10, on verbs—the general rules for their conjugations and especially the formation of the perfect tense of the four conjugations; books 11 through 16, each devoted to one of the parts of speech—participles, pronouns, prepositions, adverbs, interjections, and conjunctions; and books 17 and 18, on syntax (word order, construction of sentences).

During the Middle Ages, each branch of the *trivium* (grammar, logic, and rhetoric) and *quadrivium* (arithmetic, geometry, astronomy, and music) had its own "classic" textbook. For grammar, two treatises of Aelius Donatus (fl. fourth century) known as the *Ars minor* (English translation, 1926) and *Ars maior* (elementary and advanced grammar), which formed the *Ars grammatica* (English introduction to work, 1982), were used as textbooks in elementary schools through the Middle Ages. The more advanced *Institutiones grammaticae* of Priscian served as the classic text in the universities. His minor works include a treatise on the initial lines of the twelve books of Vergil's *Aeneid* (c. 29-19 B.C.E.; English translation, 1553), important as an illustration of the exercises demanded of schoolchildren in Priscian's day, and treatises on accents, on the declensions of nouns, and on the meters of the playwright Terence (fl. second century B.C.E.) (dedicated to Symmachus). Priscian wrote a prose treatise on the symbols used to denote numbers and on weights and measures (*De figuris et nominibus numerorum, et de normis et ponderibus*), also dedicated to Symmachus. In addition, he wrote a poem devoted entirely to weights and measures (*De ponderibus et mensuris carmina*), which is incomplete. Of the extant 162 lines, fifty-five concern weights, the rest the standards of measure for fruits and liquids.

His free translation of the *Progymnasmata* (preparatory rhetorical exercises, or, first steps in rhetoric; partial English translation, 2003), written by the Greek Hermogenes of Tarsus in the second century, is significant because with it Priscian supplemented his own grammar and brought to the Latin Middle Ages the elements of Greek rhetorical theory. His translation, *Praeexercitamina rhetorica*, comprised the last section of Hermogenes's major work on rhetoric. The section *De laude* (on panegyrics) contains examples and suggestions for extolling almost anything, from the sport of hunting to horses, doves, and trees. Priscian's use of mythological material ignores the intellectual struggle then dividing Christianity and paganism. This work too was dedicated to Symmachus.

The panegyric in honor of Emperor Anastasius has been dated about 503. It contains 334 iambic and hexameter lines. In about the year 100, the panegyric, or praise for a ruler, had been introduced into rhetoric as a genre separate from persuasive and judicial oratory. Priscian's panegyric may have served as his classroom model. Priscian's poem *De sideribus* (on the stars) contains about two hundred lines and is a simple and dry naming of stars and planets. He also produced a poetic free translation of the *Oikumenes periegesis* (second or third century; English translation, 1697) by Dionysius Periegetes (fl. second or third century), a geographer of the early Roman Empire. Priscian's version, called *De situ* or *Descriptio orbis terrarum*, was probably intended for the instruction of pupils.

Significance

The list of scholars throughout the Middle Ages who studied, quoted, or copied Priscian reads like a Who's Who of medieval intellectual history. Indeed, the modern reader may find it difficult to understand the durability of Priscian's influence over the field of grammatical studies. It should be remembered that, while language is constantly changing, grammar, the underlying structure of language, changes slowly. In addition, reverence for the correctness of past usage kept Priscian's book from early obsolescence.

Priscian was one of the sources used by his younger contemporary Flavius Magnus Aurelius in the latter's *De orthographia* (on spelling). The English scholars Aldhelm (c. 639-709) and Saint Bede the Venerable (672 or 673-735) quoted Priscian, indicating that a manuscript of the *Institutiones grammaticae* had reached England by their day. English scholar Alcuin (735-804) names Priscian among the authors available in the York library, and the substance of his second dialogue on grammar is borrowed from Priscian. As headmaster of Charlemagne's Palatine school at Aachen, Alcuin relied on Priscian among the other stock authors, including Donatus, Cassiodorus, Saint Bede the Venerable, Saint Isidore of Seville, and Phocas. Alcuin's pupil Rabanus Maurus (c. 780-856) made a copy of Priscian's *Institutiones grammaticae* and introduced it into Germany at the monastery of Fulda, whose library he founded. Servatus Lupus of Ferrieres, Rabanus's pupil, quoted frequently from Priscian in his letters on literary and grammatical matters. His own disciple Remigius wrote commentaries on Priscian while teaching at Auxerre, Reims, and Paris. Meanwhile, Priscian's work was favored among Irish scholars in monastic centers, where an interest in Greek was kept alive. Irish poet and scholar Sedulius Scottus (fl. c. 848-c. 860 or 874?) and possibly Irish-born theologian and philosopher John Scotus Erigena (c. 810-c. 877) wrote commentaries on Priscian's grammatical foundations. At least three (of more than one thousand extant) of Priscian's manuscripts are written in the Irish minuscule script of the ninth century, including that which came to Saint Gall around 860.

Between the times of Alcuin and Peter Abelard (1079-1142), Donatus and Priscian continued to be the principal grammar authorities followed by scholars. From the twelfth century on, however, the emphasis on theology, philosophy, and natural history at the University of Paris brought about significant changes, and literature and grammar were reduced in importance. The new authorities for grammar were the scholars at that university who continued to produce commentaries on or abridgments of Priscian. As late as 1141, Theodoric, chancellor of the school at Chartres, wrote a treatise on the seven liberal arts, liberally quoting Donatus and Priscian for his section on grammar.

It was during the thirteenth century that Priscian gradually lost the place of honor to his commentators, Petrus Helius, professor at Paris about 1142, and Robert Kilwardby, archbishop of Canterbury from 1272 to 1279. In that period of changing curricula, some scholars regretted the neglect of the study of authors such as Homer, Claudian, Persius, Donatus, and Priscian. One such person was John of Garland, an English scholar at Paris, who wrote fourteen books on Latin grammar. Another was Henri d' Andeli, a master at Rouen whose poem *The Battle of the Seven Arts* (1259) depicts a war between the authors on the side of grammar and those defending logic (Plato and Aristotle). In one episode, Priscian is made to hold his own in combat with Aristotle. In the fourteenth century, Priscian was superseded by the modern compilations of Alexander de Villa Dei, author of a hexameter poem on syntax, grammar, and the figures of speech, called *Doctrinale puerorum* (c. late twelfth century), which drew largely from Priscian. Another who was preferred to Priscian was Evrard of Béthune (fl. c. 1212), who also presented a grammar, called *Graecismus* (c. late twelfth century), in verse format. Presumably, their use of verse as a memory aid was a key to their success.

Besides the rise of logic and other arts, which started to claim precedence over grammar in the schools, another reason must be noted for the demise of grammar and the eclipse of Priscian. Throughout the Middle Ages, Latin was still a living language in the Church and the schools, undergoing the dynamic changes common to living languages. New vocabulary, however, included technical terms and the names of things unknown to antiquity. As Latin departed more and more from classical Latin, the huge and precise grammatical foundations of Priscian became less useful. On the southwest doorway of Chartres Cathedral, which is decorated with personifications of the seven arts and their leading representatives, Grammar and Priscian are found together. The two are also identified in the representation of the Seven Earthly Sciences in the chapter house of Santa Maria Novella Church in Florence. The Renaissance thus paid its homage to Priscian, greatest of all Latin grammarians.

—*Daniel C. Scavone*

FURTHER READING

Cameron, A. D. E. "Priscian's *De laude Anastasii*." *Greek, Roman, and Byzantine Studies* 15 (1974). Discussion of the date and circumstances of Priscian's panegyric to Emperor Anastasius. Concludes that the events not mentioned in the work provide evidence that it must have been written before 503.

Curtius, Ernst Robert. *European Literature and the Latin Middle Ages*. Translated by Willard R. Trask. 1952. Reprint. Princeton, N.J.: Princeton University Press, 1990. A modest treatment that provides excellent information on Priscian's later influence. Includes a bibliography.

Koerner, E. F. K., and R. E. Asher, eds. *Concise History of the Language Sciences: From the Sumerians to the Cognitivists*. New York: Pergamon, 1995. A history of linguistics, with a chapter on Priscian and Latin grammar. Includes a bibliography and an index.

Lanham, Carol Dana, ed. *Latin Grammar and Rhetoric: From Classical Theory to Medieval Practice*. New York: Continuum, 2002. A history of Latin rhetoric and grammar in the time of Priscian. Includes discussion of Saint Bede and Cassiodorus, among others. Bibliography and index.

Sandys, John Edwin. *From the Sixth Century B.C. to the End of the Middle Ages*. Vol. 1 in *A History of Classical Scholarship*. 1903. Reprint. New York: Hafner, 1967. Encyclopedic coverage of writing on grammar from Greece and Rome through Priscian to the fourteenth century.

Wilson, Henry A. "Priscianus Caesariensis (Priscian of Caesarea)." In *A Dictionary of Christian Biography, Literature, Sects, and Doctrines*, edited by William Smith. Vol. 4. New York: Kraus, 1967. A thorough treatment of Priscian and his writings. Reprinted from the original edition of 1840.

SEE ALSO: Peter Abelard; Alcuin; Saint Bede the Venerable; Boethius; Cassiodorus; Charlemagne; Saint Isidore of Seville; Alexander Neckam; Rabanus Maurus; Theodoric the Great.

RELATED ARTICLES in *Great Events from History: The Middle Ages, 477-1453*: 731: Bede Writes *Ecclesiastical History of the English People*; 781: Alcuin Becomes Adviser to Charlemagne; c. 1025: Scholars at Chartres Revive Interest in the Classics.

MICHAEL PSELLUS
Byzantine philosopher and historian

Psellus infused both Byzantine state theory and Orthodox theology with a revived classical tradition, while preserving a history of the personalities and events of his time.

BORN: 1018; Nicomedia, Byzantine Empire (now İzmit, Turkey)
DIED: c. 1078; Constantinople, Byzantine Empire (now Istanbul, Turkey)
ALSO KNOWN AS: Constantine Psellus
AREAS OF ACHIEVEMENT: Philosophy, historiography, religion and theology, government and politics

EARLY LIFE

Constantine Psellus (PSEHL-uhs), who took the name Michael only when he withdrew to a monastery in 1054, was born into a family with imperial connections but only modest means. The coemperors at the time were the elderly brothers Basil II (r. 976-1025) and Constantine VIII (r. 976-1028). Psellus's own family is poorly known. Although nothing is recorded about his father, his mother, Theodote, was the subject of one of Psellus's seven extant elegies. In addition to introducing her son to the Orthodox faith and the study of Scripture, she secured the Platonist John Mauropus, later the archbishop of Euchaita, as his tutor. Under Mauropus's influence, Psellus made several lifelong friends: Constantine X Ducas, Constantine Leichudes, and John Xiphilinus. These friends would later assist one another amid the intrigues of the Byzantine court.

Before Psellus reached the age of sixteen, his education in rhetoric had progressed far enough to bring him into the imperial circle. At the court, the youth regularly saw "and on one occasion actually talked with" the elderly emperor, Romanus III (r. 1028-1034). Psellus also attended the imperial funeral; in writing of this period, he would describe himself as one who "had not yet grown a beard" and was just beginning the study of the classical poets.

Psellus's studies were extensive: He memorized Homer's *Iliad* (c. 750 B.C.E.; English translation, 1611), and the frequency with which various phrases from the *Odyssey* (c. 725 B.C.E.; English translation, 1614) were used in his later writing demonstrates his educational base. He also knew the works of Greek and Latin historians and debated constantly the distinction between true history and panegyric or scandalmongering. Astrology, auguries, soothsaying, and magic practices used for sexual potency ("arts" accepted at the imperial court) as well as arithmetic, geometry, music, and astronomy received his attention. He learned enough medicine to practice. Finally, he read enough on military strategy and equipment of war to go into the field.

Because of his family's financial difficulties, which included the need to provide a dowry for his elder sister, Psellus was forced to curtail his education for a time. He briefly became a tax collector and judicial clerk in Philadelphia, before resuming his studies at the age of twenty-five. Although he was married, nothing is known about his wife. In his own works, he refers to the loss of his beloved daughter, Styliane.

Once back at his studies, Psellus trained his tongue with rhetoric, shaped his mind with philosophy, and integrated the two so that he might give voice eloquently to the art of reasoning. This oratorical ability would take him directly into the service of Emperor Constantine IX (r. 1042-1055).

LIFE'S WORK

The death in relatively quick succession of three aged emperors—Basil II, Constantine VIII, and Constantine's son-in-law, Romanus III—left in control Constantine's daughters, Zoë (978-1050) and Theodora (980-1056), who both, by imperial law, held the title of augusta. Romanus, while married to Zoë, in his old age had preferred a mistress; Zoë was left to engage in an affair with a younger court official. She secured the crown for her lover, whom she married; he reigned as Michael IV from 1034 to December 10, 1041. Although he died prematurely, in anticipation of his death, a nephew was adopted to establish the succession. When this heir took control as Michael V (r. 1041-1042) and exiled Zoë, the populace revolted and Theodora had him executed. Alexis, the patriarch, then permitted a violation of Church and state law so that the empress Zoë could marry a third time; she chose Constantine IX, who was one of the last members of the ancient family of Monomachi. Constantine, who became coruler with the sisters, brought directly into his service Michael Cerularius as patriarch, Constantine Leichudes as president of the senate, and Constantine Psellus as secretary.

Psellus relates that under Michael V he had been "initiated into the ceremonies of entry into the imperial presence." He witnessed, from the outer porch of the imperial palace, the uprising of the people on behalf of Theodora.

Psellus had no difficulty surviving the short interlude when the *gynaikonitis* (women's quarters) served as the imperial council chamber and the two empresses continued the business of administration. According to his later account, however, "they confused the trifles of the harem with important matters of state."

A major event in the reign of Constantine IX was the establishment of faculties of law and philosophy for an imperial university at Constantinople in 1045. The faculty of law was to be headed by a salaried *nomophylax* (law professor), which was assigned to John Xiphilinus. There was also established a chair of philosophy for Psellus. Only the barest hint of these events appears in *Chronographia*, apparently written after 1071 (English translation, 1953), and the dimensions of his scholarship must be deduced from the orations and treatises that have survived. Latin had been the language of Old Rome; New Rome had lost its use. It was being revived in the late tenth century, however, and Romanus III could speak it. The study of law required it, and Psellus gave some time to its study.

As a rhetorical philosopher, Psellus was a master of words and the boundaries of their meaning. He saw everything in terms of Orthodox theology and the mysteries of Scripture. Military victories were accomplished by "the Mother of the Word" carried into battle as the "ikon of the Savior's Mother." Although religious subjects raised many unresolved questions, his mastery of words prevented any accusation of heresy against him as he taught the relationship of classical philosophy to Christian faith.

Psellus perceived that certain Platonic allegories and Aristotelian doctrines related to dialectic or proof by syllogism had received no proper explication. His own studies led him from the teachings of Plato and Aristotle through those of the Neoplatonists Plotinus, Porphyry, and Iamblichus to the writings of Proclus in the fifth century. In his studies, he found a mean between material nature and pure ideas, which he proceeded to synthesize in the manner of geometrical proofs so that he could give logical demonstration in elegant oration. He carried these studies full circle back to "the mystery of our Christian religion"; thus, its dualities—of human and divine nature, of finite and infinite time, and of faith capable of proof yet divinely inspired—could receive the same logical, elegant demonstration.

He produced commentaries on the Song of Songs, on Plato's doctrine of ideas, on *Timaeos* (360-347 B.C.E.; *Timaeus*, 1793) and *Phaedros* (388-368 B.C.E.; *Phaedrus*, 1792), and on Aristotle's *De interpretatione* (*On Interpretation*) and *Categories* (collectively known as *Organon*, 335-323 B.C.E.; English translation, 1812). He paraphrased the *Iliad* and studied Homer's poems allegorically. Two composites gathered up his broadly defined "scientific" thinking: In the "Dialogue on the Operation of the Daimons," considered his literary masterpiece, he opposed a variety of heretical movements; "On Teaching Miscellany" was written for his young pupil, the future Michael VII Ducas. This latter work began in Orthodox fashion with Christian propositional dogmatics, but it climaxed with Neoplatonic interpretations of reality.

Psellus also wrote on Athenian judicial terminology and the topography of Athens, as well as on the "character" of Church fathers Gregory of Nazianzus and John Chrysostom. Some five hundred letters remain extant, filling out glimpses of his time and personality.

Zoë died in 1050 at age seventy-two. Constantine IX reigned on, but he appeared to have switched loyalties from Psellus and his friends—learned, self-made men—back to their opponents of the old aristocracy and the military establishment. Constantine Leichudes and John Xiphilinus turned to the Church and underwent monastic tonsuration. Psellus followed their example, receiving the monastic name Michael before retiring to the monastery on Mount Olympus.

When Constantine IX died in 1055 without leaving an heir, power passed again to the empress Theodora. Having never married, she chose no man as a coruler, but she required the rhetorical and literary services of Psellus. Even early in the reign of Constantine IX, Psellus had been consulted by the empress in dispatching confidential letters and conducting other private business. Such services may have contributed to his departure; they certainly brought him back to power.

Theodora's reign did not last. Her death in 1056 at the age of seventy-six precipitated a search for a successor. Michael VI (called "the Aged") was at best a temporary choice (r. 1056-1057), although Psellus continued to support him. All interests—those of the people, the senate, and the army—had to be satisfied by any selection. The army acclaimed Isaac Comnenus in 1057 (r. 1057-1059); a battle with the emperor's men followed shortly thereafter at Hades, near Nicaea. After Isaac's victory, Psellus led an embassy of three, including Theodorus Alopus and Constantine Leichudes, which negotiated the transfer of power. Isaac was proclaimed emperor by the populace in September of that year, and Michael VI abdicated, intending to die in peace. As a result of their efforts, Constantine Leichudes became patriarch and

Psellus was honored as the president of the senate. Despite (or because of) his success, however, Isaac fell ill; to preserve the fragile peace, he was tonsured by the new patriarch and went to live in a monastery. Constantine X Ducas (r. 1059-1067), Psellus's other longtime friend, was chosen by Isaac (on his apparent deathbed) as the new emperor.

In 1064, John Xiphilinus was forced to leave his abbacy to become the new patriarch, while Psellus functioned as prime minister. Psellus stayed on under Constantine X's wife, Eudocia, who ruled briefly with her two young sons until she remarried. When Constantine's successor was captured at the Battle of Manzikert in 1071, Eudocia's older son, Michael, became emperor as Michael VII Ducas (r. 1067-1078). He was the product of Psellus's teaching, and a contemporary chronicler, John Scylitzes, condemned the philosopher for having made Michael unfit to rule.

Psellus finished *Chronographia* with a panegyric to Michael VII and his family. The history abruptly ends with a comment on the role of Divine Providence, stating that the dictates of Fortune for even the most important men are reversed. The chronicler Attaleiates simply records the death in 1078 of "Michael, monk and *hypertimos*" (most honorable).

Significance

Psellus began his *Chronographia* with a discussion of the reign of Basil II to link it to the earlier historian Leo the Deacon. Psellus's work was later overlapped, supplemented, copied, or continued by numerous others. Psellus explicitly rejected the chronicle form, saying that unlike Thucydides, he had neither numbered his work by Olympiads nor divided it into seasons.

John Italus, one of his students and his successor to the chair of philosophy, was tried for heresy, having too fully revived the ancient notions of the soul and its transmigration, as well as of the eternalness of matter and ideas. An anonymous satire of the twelfth century contrasts Psellus's favorable reception by philosophers in the underworld with that given to Italus. Because of the energy he spent on the re-creation of the university in Constantinople, Psellus came to be viewed as a harbinger of the Renaissance, and renewed study of him has continued. Not all of his works in manuscript have been published, however, and only a few have been translated.

The schism of Eastern and Western churches of 1054, between Constantinople and Rome, left no mark on *Chronographia*, though a treatise written by Psellus against the Latin theologians survives. His denunciation in late 1058 of the patriarch Michael Cerularius, who was subsequently removed by the emperor, was not unrelated to the events of the schism. Yet its force was blunted within a few months by the necessity for Psellus to give a laudatory oration at Cerularius's funeral.

This species of elegy, like his speeches of imperial panegyric, clearly illustrates how in his public conduct Psellus was a man of his time, with the ability to survive, accommodate himself, be of service with increasing influence, and provide criticism of the past in each new administration. Psellus thought highly of himself, as is clear from *Chronographia*, and he was genuinely convinced that he was well regarded by the many rulers under whom he served.

—*Clyde Curry Smith*

Further Reading

Hussey, Joan M. *Church and Learning in the Byzantine Empire, 867-1185*. 1937. Reprint. New York: Russell and Russell, 1963. The context and function of both university and monastery in the Byzantine Empire, in particular the life of Psellus, are treated thoroughly.

_______, ed. *The Byzantine Empire*. Vol. 4 in *The Cambridge Medieval History*. New York: Cambridge University Press, 1967. While Psellus is cited intermittently, the sections included on his scholarship and literary achievements are particularly valuable, and the bibliography is prodigious.

Ierodiakonou, Katerina, ed. *Byzantine Philosophy and Its Ancient Sources*. New York: Oxford University Press, 2002. Discusses philosophical thought in the time of Psellus, who is the subject of two chapters. Includes a section on research in Byzantine philosophy, a bibliography, an index of places, and an index of names.

Kaldellis, Anthony. *The Argument of Psellos' Chronographia*. Boston: Brill, 1999. A study of Psellus's philosophy and his studies on religion in *Chronographia*. Includes a bibliography and index.

Pelikan, Jaroslav. *The Spirit of Eastern Christendom (600-1700)*. Vol. 2 in *The Christian Tradition: A History of the Development of Doctrine*. Chicago: University of Chicago Press, 1974. Perceives Psellus as the central figure among the eleventh century Orthodox theologians who rose to the defense of classical philosophy within a Christian Hellenism.

Psellus, Michael. *Fourteen Byzantine Rulers: The Chronographia*. Translated by Edgar R. A. Sewter. 1966. Rev. ed. New York: Penguin Books, 1982. The only major work by Psellus translated into English, *Chronographia* provides his character sketches, in varying length and degree of partisanship, of the imperial figures, both male and female, from Basil II to Michael VII.

Runciman, Steven. *The Eastern Schism.* 1955. Reprint. New York: AMS Press, 1983. The schism's relative lack of mention in Psellus's writings makes this historical discussion important, especially that on the role of the patriarchs of Constantinople with whom Psellus was closely associated.

Vasiliev, A. A. *History of the Byzantine Empire, 324-1453.* 2 vols. 2d rev. ed. Madison: University of Wisconsin Press, 1964. With extensive notes and bibliography, this account of the Eastern Roman state discusses political, dynastic, social, literary, scholarly, and artistic events and achievements. Chapter 6 covers the time and life of Psellus, though his impact appears throughout other discussions.

SEE ALSO: Anna Comnena; Jean Froissart.

RELATED ARTICLES in *Great Events from History: The Middle Ages, 477-1453*: 976-1025: Reign of Basil II; 1054: Beginning of the Rome-Constantinople Schism; August 26, 1071: Battle of Manzikert; 1373-1410: Jean Froissart Compiles His *Chronicles*.

JEAN PUCELLE
French painter

Jean Pucelle's manuscript illuminations depicted—for the first time by a painter in northern Europe—coherent, three-dimensional spatial settings. The emotional interaction of figures in his work influenced the direction of artistic developments in northern European painting in the late Middle Ages and the early Renaissance.

BORN: c. 1290; Paris or northern France
DIED: 1334; Paris, France
ALSO KNOWN AS: Jehan Pucelle
AREA OF ACHIEVEMENT: Art

EARLY LIFE

Although more documents can be connected with Jean Pucelle (zhahn pew-sehl) than with most medieval artists in northern Europe, they reveal comparatively little information about his personal life. Because he begins to appear in documents with an important commission—indicating that he was a mature artist—in 1319, his birth probably occurred around the end of the thirteenth century. One characteristic feature of his illumination is the lively quality of border ornament, which shows close observation of nature and inventive, often humorous grotesques. These stylistic traits, which were particularly developed in north French illumination, may point to a birthplace in this region.

It is likely that he was trained in the traditional medieval manner as an apprentice to one or more artists—probably in Paris, which was a major artistic center in the Gothic period. Another possible influence on Pucelle's formative background was the intellectual milieu of the University of Paris, one of the main universities in the later Middle Ages. As a center for theological studies, its faculty was primarily drawn from the mendicant orders of Dominicans and Franciscans. Most of the manuscripts that Pucelle illuminated were for either Dominican or Franciscan usage. In addition, Pucelle's complex and original iconographic programs, accompanied in *The Belleville Breviary* (1323-1326) by a written explanation most likely composed by the artist, suggest that Pucelle was both literate and receptive to intellectual currents in theology.

LIFE'S WORK

Pucelle was primarily an illuminator of manuscripts. The first documented reference to his work as an artist, however, is a payment listed in the 1319-1324 accounts of the Confraternity of St. Jacques-aux-Pèlerins in Paris for the design of the group's great seal. The importance of this confraternity's membership demonstrates Pucelle's high standing as an artist. It also shows that the range of his artistic endeavors extended beyond manuscript illumination to include various aspects of design in other media.

Pucelle's manuscript illumination, on which his artistic reputation is based, is generally divided into two phases: early works dating around 1320 and mature works done from about 1323 until his death in 1334. The Italian influences in the illumination of his mature period suggest that a trip to Italy intervened between these two stages. The early works, especially *The Breviary of Blanche of France* (c. 1320) and *The Hours of Jeanne of Savoy* (c. 1320), show several important characteristics of Pucelle's illumination. Both manuscripts, which were intended for young women of the French nobility, are an indication of Pucelle's continued patronage by members of the French royal family. The illumination, executed by several artists, demonstrates how Pucelle often collaborated with other illuminators. Also, the style of Pucelle's painting in these manuscripts shows connections with Parisian illuminators of the early fourteenth century. At the same time, however, his miniatures evidence new interest in modeled figures painted in lighter color tonalities, spatial effects, and inventive border drolleries.

Miniatures in Pucelle's manuscripts from around 1323 on give indications of inspiration from Italian art of the early Trecento. From study of the *Maestà* altarpiece by Duccio di Buoninsegna in the Cathedral of Siena, painted between 1308 and 1311, Pucelle was attracted to the depiction of three-dimensional spatial settings and emotional interaction of figures in narrative scenes. In *The Hours of Jeanne d'Evreux*, the Virgin of the Annunciation stands within a room while the angel approaches through an antechamber in a composition very similar to *The Annunciation of the Death of the Virgin* from the *Maestà*. In Pucelle's *The Entombment* in this book of hours, the Virgin embracing Christ's body and the lamenting figure of Mary Magdalene behind the tomb repeat poses from the *Maestà*'s depiction. Similarly, emotional scenes combined with sculptural plasticity of figures show Pucelle's adaptation of aspects of Giovanni Pisano's sculptured pulpit at the church of San Andrea in Pistoia, completed in 1301: The grisaille painting technique of *The Hours of Jeanne d'Evreux* gives the painted figures a sculpturesque solidity. Other manuscripts with illuminations by Pucelle continue these Italian-inspired visual interests. A miniature in *The Miracles of Notre Dame* (executed before 1334), for example, depicts a Tuscan fortress much like the Palazzo Vecchio in Florence. The varied types of artistic borrowing, from three-dimensional spatial settings to iconographic motifs, suggest that Pucelle's knowledge of Italian art was based on firsthand observation.

Documentary evidence connects Pucelle with three illuminated manuscripts that represent the artistic achievement of his mature painting. *The Hours of Jeanne d'Evreux* is a small book of hours done for Jeanne d'Evreux, the wife of Charles IV, between her marriage in 1325 and her husband's death in 1328. This manuscript has been identified with a book of hours described in a codicil to Jeanne d'Evreux's testament in 1371 as being illuminated by Pucelle. It was willed to her nephew, Charles V, and is mentioned in an inventory of his private collection of treasures at Vincennes. Finally, it was owned by Charles V's brother, the great bibliophile Jean, duke of Berry; it appears in inventories of his library in the early fifteenth century described as "Heures de Pucelle" (hours by Pucelle). The Billyng Bible, copied by an English scribe named Robert Billyng, contains a colophon that dates the manuscript's completion in 1327 and names Jean Pucelle, Anciau de Cens, and Jaquet Maci as illuminators. *The Belleville Breviary* was first owned by Jeanne de Belleville. Liturgical evidence from this Dominican breviary, including the absence of the office of Saint Thomas Aquinas—which the Dominicans adopted in 1326—dates the manuscript between 1323 and 1326. It contains marginal records of payment by Pucelle to other illuminators and decorators. Two other manuscripts have been attributed on stylistic grounds to the last years of Pucelle's career, *The Breviary of Jeanne d'Evreux* and *The Miracles of Notre Dame*. Other manuscripts are associated with Pucelle's shop.

The primary characteristics of Pucelle's illumination are depicting figures in unified, often three-dimensional spatial settings; portraying the psychological reactions of figures in narrative scenes; and presenting abstract theological concepts through visual iconography. *The Hours of Jeanne d'Evreux*, which is considered a masterwork done entirely by Pucelle, shows many of these artistic features. The three-dimensional enclosure in which the Annunciation takes place shows the depiction of spatial surroundings. In other miniatures, figures are tightly grouped, but the grisaille painting technique in shades of gray heightens the impression of plastically rendered forms. Many of the miniatures, especially in the Passion cycle, depict strong emotional reactions as seen when the Virgin swoons at the Crucifixion. In addition, the borders are enlivened with *bas-de-page* scenes that, as in the Annunciation to the Shepherds, extend the theme of the miniature. The crouching figures that support the architectural frames of some miniatures as well as the drolleries and grotesques that emerge from line endings reflect the observation of nature and lively humor characteristic of northern sculpture and illumination. *The Belleville Breviary* is especially outstanding for its complex iconographic program. Although parts of its illumination are now missing, the written exposition of the iconography prefaced to the manuscript along with surviving portions permit reconstruction of a program that includes Old Testament prophets revealing a prophecy as a New Testament article of faith in the calendar, three full-page miniatures that complete and expand on these relationships between Old and New Testaments, and in the Psalter, the idea of Virtues overcoming Vices, all culminating in the Last Judgment.

In most manuscripts associated with Pucelle, some variations in style and quality of illumination show that he usually worked with other miniaturists and decorators. The illumination of the Billyng Bible, for example, generally displays more conservative and traditional stylistic and compositional features, although it is contemporary with the aesthetically innovative hours of Jeanne d'Evreux. While such collaboration was a typical practice in Gothic manuscript illumination, it raises questions about Pucelle's artistic movement. Some view him as the head of a workshop, planning iconographic and illustrative elements and executing major parts of the illumination. Another interpretation suggests that he was one of several independent illuminators working on commission for a Parisian stationer. Regardless of the amount of his personal painting in any single manuscript with which he is connected, however, at his death in 1334, Pucelle had participated in, and probably directed the illumination of, many of the most outstanding French manuscripts of the first half of the fourteenth century.

SIGNIFICANCE

While further study will continue to clarify Pucelle's precise artistic role in the manuscripts with which his name is associated, his connection with these prominent artistic works shows him to have been a major innovating force in northern European art of the fourteenth century. By merging qualities of Italian and northern painting and sculpture, his illumination introduced new aesthetic concerns. His narrative scenes show a psychological interaction of figures with heightened emotion. The borders and expanded *bas-de-page* scenes in many of his manuscripts are enlivened with a naturalism and keen observation characteristic of northern Gothic art. His personal iconographic invention, particularly evident in *The Belleville Breviary*, demonstrates his intellectual grasp of theological concepts. Throughout his illumination, these creative artistic ideas are presented with an exquisite refinement characteristic of the Parisian court style.

As a recognition of his achievement as an artist, Pucelle's illumination continued to influence developments in French painting into the early fifteenth century. His immediate successor, the illuminator Jean le Noir, repeated Pucelle's compositional innovations with some modifications throughout a career that extended from the 1330's to the 1370's. Pucelle's stylistic interests influenced late fourteenth century painters, as seen, for example, in *Parement de Narbonne*, which also adopts the grisaille technique. The identification of manuscripts illuminated by Pucelle in *Jeanne d'Evreux's Testament* and in the duke of Berry's inventories, unusual during this period, also attests this artist's continued reputation. The quality, creativity, and influence of his illumination make Jean Pucelle one of the most significant artists of the later Middle Ages.

—*Karen K. Gould*

FURTHER READING

Avril, François. *Manuscript Painting at the Court of France: The Fourteenth Century, 1310-1380*. New York: George Braziller, 1978. A survey of Parisian fourteenth century illumination with a good discussion of Pucelle and his relation to French manuscript painting throughout this century. Excellent color plates and a good bibliography. No index.

Deuchler, Florens. "Jean Pucelle—Facts and Fictions." *Bulletin of the Metropolitan Museum of Art* 29 (1971): 253-256. Reviews the evidence about Pucelle's life and the attribution of works to this artist. This article is skeptical about the relationship of documentary evidence to firm attribution of *The Hours of Jeanne d'Evreux* to Pucelle.

Ferber, Stanley. "Jean Pucelle and Giovanni Pisano." *Art Bulletin* 66 (1984): 65-72. This article presents the case that Pucelle must have studied the sculptured pulpit by Pisano at Pistoia. A good overview of the evidence supporting a trip by Pucelle to Italy and the relationships of Pucelle's illumination to Italian early Trecento art.

Hamburger, Jeffrey. "The Waddesdon Psalter and the Shop of Jean Pucelle." *Zeitschrift für Kunstgeschichte* 44 (1981): 243-257. A discussion of the Waddesdon Psalter that contains some illumination by Pucelle and other miniature painting by a collaborator in a style close to Pucelle's. The article raises issues about the nature of Pucelle's workshop.

Meiss, Millard. *French Painting in the Time of Jean de Berry: The Late Fourteenth Century and the Patronage of the Duke*. 2 vols. London: Phaidon, 1967. Pucelle's work as an illuminator is discussed in the context of the background for French manuscript painting of the late fourteenth century. The book shows Pucelle's influence throughout the century.

Morand, Kathleen. *Jean Pucelle*. Oxford, England: Clarendon Press, 1962. This monograph covers Pucelle's life and career as an illuminator. Because it was published before the discovery of the date of Pucelle's death, some of the later manuscripts attributed to Pucelle in this book are now seen as works by his followers.

_______. "Jean Pucelle: A Re-examination of the Evidence." *Burlington Magazine* 103 (1961): 206-211. Analyzes in detail the documentary evidence connecting Pucelle with the Billyng Bible, *The Belleville Breviary*, and *The Hours of Jeanne d'Evreux*. It supports the interpretation of Jean Pucelle as illuminator of *The Hours of Jeanne d'Evreux*.

Nordenfalk, Carl. "Maître Honoré and Maître Pucelle." *Apollo* 89 (1964): 356-364. In part a review of Morand's monograph on Pucelle. As a review essay, it adds perceptive observations and interpretations of Pucelle's illumination.

Panofsky, Erwin. *Early Netherlandish Painting*. 2 vols. Cambridge, Mass.: Harvard University Press, 1953. Although this book concentrates on northern Renaissance painting of the fifteenth century, Pucelle's illumination is discussed from the standpoint of his contribution as an innovator of and precursor to the northern Renaissance style.

Randall, Lilian M. C. "Games and the Passion in Pucelle's *Hours of Jeanne d'Evreux*." *Speculum* 47 (1972): 246-257. Explains the meaning and relevance of several of the *bas-de-page* scenes to the iconographic program of the miniature cycle in *The Hours of Jeanne d'Evreux*.

Sandler, Lucy Freeman. "Jean Pucelle and the Lost Miniatures of *The Belleville Breviary*." *Art Bulletin* 66 (1984): 73-96. Reconstructs the three lost full-page miniatures from the important and unusual iconographic cycle illustrating *The Belleville Breviary*. It provides an edition and translation of the text prefaced to the manuscript that explains this iconographic program.

SEE ALSO: Fra Angelico; Arnolfo di Cambio; Cimabue; Donatello; Duccio di Buoninsegna; Jan van Eyck and Hubert van Eyck; Giotto; Pietro Lorenzetti and Ambrogio Lorenzetti; Simone Martini; Masaccio; Andrea Orcagna; Nicola Pisano and Giovanni Pisano; Rogier van der Weyden.

RELATED ARTICLES in *Great Events from History: The Middle Ages, 477-1453*: c. 950: Court of Córdoba Flourishes in Spain; 1100-1300: European Universities Emerge; April 16, 1209: Founding of the Franciscans; c. 1410-1440: Florentine School of Art Emerges.

Rabanus Maurus

Frankish theologian and scholar

As one of the leading scholars of the ninth century Carolingian revival of learning, Rabanus introduced generations of medieval students to the wisdom of the Bible and the church fathers and to the practical skills they would need as priests and monks. As abbot of Fulda and later as archbishop of Mainz, he played a leading role in church governance at a time when the leaders of the Church helped to shape society.

Born: c. 780; Mainz (now in Germany)
Died: February 4, 856; Winkel, Rhineland (now in Germany)
Also known as: Hrabanus; Rhabanus Magnentius
Areas of achievement: Religion and theology, monasticism, education, scholarship

Early Life

Very little is known about the early life of Rabanus Maurus (rah-BAHN-uhs MAW-ruhs). He was apparently born to an aristocratic Frankish family. He became a monk at the monastery of Fulda, where he was ordained a deacon in 801. Young monks who showed intellectual promise often were sent to other monasteries for additional reading and study under the tutelage of famous masters. Rabanus was sent to study with Alcuin, an Anglo-Saxon scholar who was a close friend and adviser of Charlemagne. Alcuin was one of the leading figures in Charlemagne's attempt to improve intellectual, cultural, and spiritual life in the Frankish kingdom. As abbot of the monastery of St. Martin in Tours, Alcuin established Tours as an important intellectual center and trained an entire generation of future abbots, bishops, and scholars there. Rabanus was especially close to his mentor. It was Alcuin who gave him the name Maurus, which was the name of the most beloved disciple of Benedict of Nursia, the founder of Benedictine monasticism. Rabanus was Alcuin's Maurus.

After Alcuin's death in 804, Rabanus Maurus returned to Fulda. He was ordained a priest in 814 and named master of Fulda's monastic school in 819. When the abbot died in 822, Rabanus succeeded to that office and added the duties of an administrator of an important monastery to his work as a scholar. In 847, he became archbishop of Mainz.

Life's Work

Rabanus was born at an important moment in the political and cultural history of Western Europe. Charlemagne had become king of the Franks in 768, and on Christmas Day in the year 800, he was crowned emperor by the pope. Charlemagne's empire was an ambitious experiment. Charlemagne, who died in 814, and his son, Louis the Pious, who reigned from 814 to his death in 840, tried to maintain political unity in a Europe that had been fragmented ever since the decline of the Roman Empire in the West during the fourth and fifth centuries. Family rivalries and attempts by the military aristocracy to usurp royal power always threatened political stability and unity.

Charlemagne and his successors were not merely fighters and politicians. With the aid of their ecclesiastical advisers, men such as Alcuin, they broadened the role of the ruler to include in it the moral and spiritual regeneration of society. The interest of Frankish leaders in education and culture was part of a practical program to improve society by inculcating Christian practices and principles in the Frankish people.

The bishops and abbots of cathedrals and monasteries throughout Francia were the point men in the effort to reform society. Often the loyalties of church leaders such as Rabanus were compromised. As monks, they pursued lives of contemplation and distance from the world, an ideal difficult to achieve when kings and emperors sought their help and advice. As bishops, they tried to manage the responsibilities of their provinces and to supervise the clergy and people while sometimes called on to choose sides in dynastic disputes by committing the moral and fiscal resources of their bishoprics to one side or the other.

Rabanus's career started off simply enough at Fulda when he composed a series of poems entitled *De laudibus sanctae crucis* (in praise of the Holy Cross), which he dedicated to Louis the Pious. The poems were a great success, for they revived the classical practice of joining text to pictures. Rabanus's "figural poems," copied over the design of the Cross or over a full-length drawing of the emperor holding the Cross in his hand, delighted both mind and eye. While still a master at Fulda, Rabanus wrote *De institutione clericorum* (c. 810; on the training of clergy). The book was dedicated to Archbishop Haistulf of Mainz but owed its inspiration to Rabanus's students, who wanted him to put his lectures into written form. *De institutione clericorum* is a manual that covers all the topics a priest needed to know in the ninth century before beginning his ecclesiastical duties.

Its various chapters range widely over the books of the Bible, vestments, rituals, festivals, ceremonies, church hierarchy, and many other topics.

His next work, *De computo* (on computation), dates from 820, when Rabanus responded to the plea of a monk named Macharius to explain the very technical subjects of determining dates and numerical reckoning. In the absence of a uniform calendar, it was critical that the clergy be able to determine when feast days were to take place. *De computo* considered various calendar systems; defined seconds, minutes, hours, days, weeks, months, and years; and even broached astronomical topics, since fixing dates depended on the positions of the celestial bodies.

The last work Rabanus wrote before he became abbot of Fulda was a commentary on the biblical book of Matthew. His interest in explaining the Bible was a natural outgrowth of his function as a teacher. Students of the Bible in the Middle Ages needed commentaries to help them understand the many difficult terms used to describe biblical people, animals, plants, places, money, clothing, and rituals. Readers also had to know something about the historical contexts of the various books. Mostly they had to be helped to understand the mystical and sacred meaning that was believed to lie behind the literal meaning of the biblical text. Rabanus was a skilled expositor not because he was clever and original but because he had mastered much of the work of earlier authors and could synthesize it effectively for his own audience. His success at explaining Matthew led to requests throughout his life to comment on other books of the Bible. Soon he had produced commentaries on almost all the books of both the Old and New Testaments.

When he became abbot of Fulda in 822, Rabanus became deeply involved in managing the estates of the monastery, which apparently had been neglected by his predecessors. Fulda was a rich monastery and controlled properties scattered all over the eastern, Germanic part of the Carolingian Empire. Rabanus's first literary work of his abbacy indirectly concerned the landed wealth of his monastery. Gottschalk, a monk of Fulda who had been given to the monastery as a child by his father, wished to be released from his monastic vows. Gottschalk argued that the practice of giving children to monasteries, or oblation, was invalid because children could not freely assent to their vows. More was at stake in Gottschalk's challenge than the life of one monk. Parents often gave grants of land to the monastery in order to help support the abbey that sheltered their children. If Gottschalk succeeded in overturning the practice of oblation, he would thereby threaten not only the sanctity of vows but also the landed wealth of the monasteries. Rabanus's *De oblatione puerorum* (on the oblation of boys), written in 829 at the request of Louis the Pious, represented a stout defense of oblation. Gottschalk was defeated at subsequent church councils in his attempt to renounce his vows, and child oblation continued as a practice in the medieval Church until the twelfth century.

Rabanus's next work, *De reverentia filiorum erga patres* (834; on the reverence of sons for their fathers), was also inspired by controversy. Louis's sons had revolted against him when it appeared to them that the emperor was diminishing their power for the benefit of a son born of a second marriage. Rabanus's essay defended Louis and sought to remind his sons of their obligation of filial piety toward their father. Though Louis was restored to power, the revolt deeply troubled a society that professed Christian values and tried to implement them even in the political arena. Rabanus's *De virtutibus et vitiis* (on virtues and vices) is a product of the 830's and represents the abbot's attempt to call Carolingian society back to moral principles of behavior.

When Louis died in 840, a brutal struggle for power and for the rights of succession broke out among his sons. Rabanus supported the eldest son, Lothair. The choice

Rabanus Maurus. (Library of Congress)

was unfortunate, since by 842, Lothair was defeated by his brother, Louis the German. Rabanus, who by this time was sixty years old and in poor health, retired from his abbacy, probably fearing that his advocacy of Lothair would bring harm to his beloved monastery. He removed himself to Petersberg, close by Fulda, and continued his scholarly and pedagogical activities. His monumental *De rerum naturis* (840's; on the nature of things) belongs to this period. This work was an encyclopedic survey of all the things one had to know in order to interpret Scripture. It was modeled on the *Etymologiae* (late sixth or early seventh century; partial translation in *An Encyclopedist of the Dark Ages*, 1912) of Saint Isidore of Seville and owed much to it. Yet Rabanus's purpose was different because his work, in addition to providing factual information, was concerned with revealing the mystical significance of things.

Rabanus's retreat from public life was short-lived. When he responded to Louis the German's request to prepare a biblical commentary, the volume Rabanus produced was a visible sign that the estrangement between monk and king had come to an end. After Archbishop Otgar of Mainz died in 847, Rabanus, undoubtedly with the king's support, became the new archbishop. Rabanus threw himself with his usual energy into the administrative tasks of his new responsibilities. He presided over a number of important church councils, supported Louis and Louis's son, Lothair II, and all the while continued to write.

Among the major works from this period is the *Martyrologium* (martyrology). This book lists the saints whose feast days were celebrated throughout the year and provides brief historical notes about each one. Even as he approached the end of his life, Rabanus was concerned to write books that were useful in the practice of the Christian religion. In this vein, he also prepared two penitentials, books that listed sins and prescribed the appropriate penance for each; a collection of sermons; and *De sacris ordinibus, sacramentis divinis, et vestimentis sacerdotalibus* (850's; on sacred orders, the divine sacraments, and priestly vestments). His last work was probably the *Tractatus de anima* (treatise on the soul), to which he appended excerpts from the military manual of the Roman author Vegetius as a useful gift to Lothair.

SIGNIFICANCE

Despite a busy and sometimes tumultuous public life, Rabanus Maurus was a prolific scholar whose works helped to transmit the learning of earlier Christian authors to a new audience of Frankish Christians in the ninth century. Rabanus's learning and skills as an author helped to train the priests and monks who attempted to implement the Carolingian vision of a Christian society.

Rabanus wrote most of his works at the request of students, fellow bishops, abbots, kings, and emperors. Although he often modestly remarked in the prefaces to his works "I did what I could," his blending of a broad range of earlier authors, some of whom contradicted one another, into a pedagogically effective format was a considerable achievement. Rabanus did not try to be original in fields where traditional truths were more to be authenticated and explained than to be superseded by new insights. Nevertheless, his compilations were, in effect, new works that presented their readers with insights from many texts.

His works were copied many times over in the Middle Ages and continued to be influential even into the age of the printing press, when most of them were published for the first time. Dante placed Rabanus in Paradise with other medieval scholars in his *La divina commedia* (c. 1320; *The Divine Comedy*, 1802). Many modern writers, perhaps with only minor exaggeration, have dubbed Rabanus Maurus the *praeceptor Germaniae*, the teacher of Germany.

—*John J. Contreni*

FURTHER READING

Duckett, Eleanor Shipley. *Carolingian Portraits: A Study in the Ninth Century*. Ann Arbor: University of Michigan Press, 1962. Rabanus is not the subject of one of Duckett's portraits, but she does provide chapters on Lupus of Ferrières and Walafrid Strabo, two Carolingian scholars who studied with the great master. This book succeeds in providing some of the flavor of Carolingian intellectual life.

Eyck, Frank. *Religion and Politics in German History: From the Beginnings to the French Revolution*. New York: St. Martin's Press, 1998. An analysis of how Germanic peoples preserved links with classical civilization through their ability to assimilate other cultures and peoples, from their alliances with eighth century popes through the Reformation and Counter-Reformation. The initial bond between the Germanic rulers and popes turned to conflict as the Papacy gained power. Tables, maps, bibliography, index.

Laistner, M. L. W. *Thought and Letters in Western Europe, A.D. 500 to 900*. 2d ed. Ithaca, N.Y.: Cornell University Press, 1957. This work is a good introduction to the Carolingian renaissance and to the world of literature and scholarship in which Rabanus moved.

Laistner emphasizes the influence of the classical literary heritage on medieval thought and literature.
Le Berrurier, Diane O. *The Pictorial Sources of Mythological and Scientific Illustrations in Hrabanus Maurus' "De rerum naturis."* New York: Garland, 1978. This reprint of the author's fine arts thesis examines the sources and significance of imagery in Rabanus's magnum opus. Illustrations, bibliography.
McCulloh, John. Introduction to *Rabani Mauri "Martyrologium."* Turnhout, Belgium: Brepols, 1979. This is the best discussion of Rabanus's life and work available in English. Although parts of it are directed to the edition of the martyrology that McCulloh edited for this volume, readers will benefit from McCulloh's discussion of Rabanus's career and his useful bibliography.
McKitterick, Rosamond. *The Frankish Kingdoms Under the Carolingians, 751-987.* White Plains, N.Y.: Longman, 1983. This is the best general account of Carolingian history available in English. It is particularly good on the Carolingian reform program and on the close links between intellectual life and politics.
Raby, F. J. E. *A History of Christian-Latin Poetry.* Rev. ed. London: Oxford University Press, 1957. This is a general, handbook discussion of medieval poetry. The section on Rabanus is slight but important.
Stevens, Wesley M. "*Compotistica et astronomica* in the Fulda School." In *Saints, Scholars, and Heroes: Studies in Medieval Culture in Honor of Charles W. Jones.* 2 vols. Collegeville, Minn.: St. John's University Press, 1979. This is a fine study of the art of *computus* and also of the Fulda school.
_______. Introduction to *Rabani Mauri "De computo."* Turnhout, Belgium: Brepols, 1979. This introduction to Stevens's edition of the Latin text of Rabanus's *De computo* contains much valuable information as well as a bibliography.

SEE ALSO: Alcuin; Charlemagne; Saint Isidore of Seville; Louis the German; Priscian.
RELATED ARTICLES in *Great Events from History: The Middle Ages, 477-1453*: 754: Coronation of Pépin the Short; 781: Alcuin Becomes Adviser to Charlemagne.

RĀBIᶜAH AL-ᶜADAWIYAH
Muslim Sufi mystic and saint

Often called the first Muslim saint, Rābiᶜah al-ᶜAdawiyah developed the idea of selfless love within the Sufi tradition. She stressed worship for the sake of love of God over ritual as well as worship over the attempt to ensure entry into paradise.

BORN: c. 717; Basra (now in Iraq)
DIED: 801; Basra
ALSO KNOWN AS: Rābiᶜa al-ᶜAdawiyya; Rābiᶜa al-ᶜAdawiyyah; Rābiᶜa al-ᶜQaysiyya; Rābiᶜa al-ᶜBasriyya; Rābiᶜah of Basra
AREAS OF ACHIEVEMENT: Religion and theology, literature

EARLY LIFE

Almost all information about the early life of Rābiᶜah al-ᶜAdawiyah (RAH-biah al-Ah-dah-WI-yah) is legendary in nature. According to these stories, Rābiᶜah was from one of the lowest classes in society—either a slave or a very poor servant. Some hold that she was stolen from her family as a young child and enslaved. Margaret Smith, a twentieth century biographer of Rābiᶜah, presents her as a freed slave from the al-ᶜAtik, a tribe of Qays bin ᶜAdi. Her various second names thus derive from her tribal origin (al-ᶜAdawiyah and al-Qaysiyya) and her birthplace of Basra (al-Basriyya).

Farīd al-Dīn ᶜAṭṭār, who lived some four centuries after Rābiᶜah, relates several stories of miracles surrounding her birth in his biography of the saint. One of these includes the Prophet Muḥammad appearing to Rābiᶜah's father (who was despondent over his poverty and inability to provide for another child). As her father slept, Muḥammad told him that his daughter would be a renowned saint whose intercession would be sought by many. According to ᶜAṭṭār, Rābiᶜah was orphaned, and when famine in Basra separated her and her three sisters, she was kidnapped and sold into slavery.

ᶜAṭṭār relates that shortly afterward, while working for her master, a stranger came to Rābiᶜah. As tradition demanded that the stranger not see her unveiled, Rābiᶜah sought to flee, but fell and dislocated her wrist in the process. According to this biography, the girl bowed her head and prayed, and said that despite all her hardships she wanted only to know whether God was satisfied with her. According to this account, Rābiᶜah then heard a voice reply that on judgment day she would be of such status with God that all would envy her.

Rābiʿah then began fasting each day. One night, her master woke from his sleep and heard Rābiʿah praying. According to one account, she was praying that what she wanted most was to follow God, but her status as a slave made her subject to another master. On uttering these words, a lamp appeared over Rābiʿah's head, and the light from the lamp illuminated the entire house. Her master interpreted this as the light of Rābiʿah's saintliness and then freed her. After being freed, Rābiʿah retreated into the desert, where she focused on spirituality and religion, renounced worldly pleasures, and lived a life of extreme asceticism.

LIFE'S WORK

Except for the year of her death and her writings, virtually all that is known about Rābiʿah is legendary in nature. Therefore, it is not possible to give a chronological account of her life. It is known that Rābiʿah eventually returned to Basra, where she attracted numerous followers. These disciples came to her house to hear her teach, to pray and study with her, and to ask her advice. Rābiʿah became of the best-known Sufi figures of her time.

Sufism, which originated in the eighth century, is the word used to describe Islamic mysticism. It derives from the Arabic term *sūf*, or wool, the material from which were made the robes of the early mystics. The wool robes indicated their avoidance of luxury. Broadly speaking, Sufism represents attempts to expand the frontiers of religion beyond ritual and to search for spiritual truth. It is a tradition based on the lives of the Prophet and it emphasizes an ascetic lifestyle and embraces simplicity. The Sufi emphasis on renunciation of the material world for the spiritual includes an emphasis on (though not a requirement of) celibacy, eschewing material possessions, and renouncing money and things not earned by one's own labor or critical to one's daily needs. Early Sufism reacted against the time's dominant culture and its emphasis on wealth, social position, and sexuality. In other words, Sufism can be interpreted as a form of dissent and resistance to government and orthodox religion. Likewise, Sufism provided poor or slave women such as Rābiʿah with a means to escape their subordinate position and to become independent and valued.

Legends often link Rābiʿah with another noted Sufi, al-Ḥasan al-Baṣrī, who died in 728 and therefore likely never met Rābiʿah (although one legend, discussed below, does show that al-Ḥasan imagined meeting her). The legends surrounding both Rābiʿah and al-Ḥasan are instructive, though, as they emphasize Rābiʿah's importance within the Sufi community and her extreme piety. The legends are also effective vehicles for relating Rābiʿah's teachings. Al-Ḥasan was known for his frequent weeping about his sins and the sins of others. According to legend, al-Ḥasan feared God's judgment and never laughed or joked. His code of piety included never allowing himself to be alone with women, for it might pose too much temptation. Yet in one commonly cited story, al-Ḥasan said, "I passed one whole night and day with Rābiʿah speaking of the Way and the Truth, and it never passed through my mind that I was a man nor did it occur to her that she was a woman, and at the end when I looked at her I saw myself as bankrupt and Rābiʿah as truly sincere." This story of al-Ḥasan's experience with Rābiʿah transcends gender and the traditional male fear of sexual temptation; it also emphasizes the exceptional nature of Rābiʿah's intellectual abilities and religious understanding, even in comparison to one of the most renowned mystics of the period. Such stories about Rābiʿah that refute the widespread notion of sexuality as the dominant force in male-female relations are common.

Another anecdote relates al-Ḥasan's refusal to attend any gathering where Rābiʿah was not included. A later story tells of al-Ḥasan's proposal of marriage to Rābiʿah, who turns him down, explaining that she has four questions concerning Judgment Day to ponder and therefore no time to concern herself with a husband, who would surely divert her from these important issues. This was typical of her response to the many men who sought her hand in marriage—all of whom she refused, saying she belonged only to God.

Rābiʿah's refusals of marriage and her independence and autonomy were uncommon for most women of her society at the time. Sufi women tended to have more independence and latitude in such matters than orthodox women, though Sufi tradition is not without its own history of male dominance and the belief that women are inherently dangerous and tempting. Nevertheless, Sufi tradition includes stories like those of Rābiʿah, which emphasize a more positive view of women.

Many stories also emphasize Rābiʿah's superior abilities when compared to her male colleagues. One such tale again pairs Rābiʿah with al-Ḥasan, who tosses his carpet onto a body of water, sits on it, and asks Rābiʿah to join him. Understanding that al-Ḥasan is attempting to impress onlookers with his abilities, Rābiʿah responds by tossing her carpet into the air, flying up to it, and perching on it, inviting al-Ḥasan to come up to her where people can see them better. When he does not respond, knowing that he has been outdone, Rābiᶜah comments that both their actions were trivial and that the real work of God is beyond such things. This story thus illustrates Rābiᶜah's disdain for trivial acts designed to impress, and her belief that real faith lies much deeper.

Another oft-repeated story highlights a similar point in Rābiᶜah's teachings, emphasizing the meaningless nature of ritual. A prominent religious figure of the time, Ibrāhīm ibn Adham, set out for Mecca to perform the required pilgrimage. Along the way, he stopped at every prayer location he encountered. Ibrāhīm took fourteen years to get to Mecca because he prayed at every site. When he arrived, he did not see the Kaaba (the cubical building Muslims ritualistically circle on foot during the *hajj*, or pilgrimage, and toward which Muslims face while praying). Instead, he heard a voice inform him that the Kaaba had risen up and gone forth to meet a woman on her way to Mecca. This woman was Rābiᶜah, who returned with the Kaaba and explained to an astounded, jealous, and offended Ibrāhīm that while Ibrāhīm had been occupied with ritual and external prayer, she had eschewed ritual and focused on internal prayer. Not only does this anecdote highlight the importance of inner belief, it also shows how a woman can exceed a man in religious devotion and understanding.

Perhaps the most important saying attributed to Rābiᶜah is the following: "I am going to light a fire in paradise and pour water in hell so that both veils may completely disappear from the pilgrims and their purpose may be sure. Thus the servants of God may see Him, without any object of hope or motive of fear." This saying illustrates her idea of divine love—that one should love God sincerely, without ulterior motives.

Rābiᶜah was also a noted poet, as were many Sufis. In her poetry, Rābiᶜah expresses her passionate love of God, a love so consuming that she was known to have said that it left no room in her heart even for the love of the Prophet Muḥammad. Although Rābiᶜah also had a reputation as a miracle worker, a reputation strengthened by later biographers, she herself did not enjoy being thought of as a miracle worker and she discouraged others from naming her a source of miracles.

Rābiᶜah died in 801. Although the date of her birth is not known, it is said that she was extremely aged when she died, perhaps eighty or older. As Margaret Smith argued in her biography of Rābiᶜah, as a Sufi whose life had been spent in sincere belief and passionate expression of her love for God, Rābiᶜah must have welcomed death as a means of uniting at last with her beloved.

Significance

Rābiᶜah al-ᶜAdawiyah is important as a religious figure, a saint said to be endowed with miraculous powers, a poet whose verse expressed her love for God, and a role model and teacher to her disciples. Perhaps most significantly, she developed the doctrine of divine love, which had a permanent influence on Sufi thinking and practice. With the development of this doctrine, love became a central theme of Sufism.

Rābiᶜah is also an important figure as a woman, exemplifying independence, autonomy, and the religious achievement of women within the Islamic tradition. Rābiᶜah's life and work took place within the more liberal Sufi tradition, liberal compared to orthodox Islam of the ninth century. Yet, even within this context, Rābiᶜah's life was extraordinary.

Rābiᶜah's teachings, beliefs, poetry, and life show an emphasis on asceticism, meditation, the ability of men and women to transcend imposed and restrictive gender roles, a consuming love of God, sincere worship, and a desire for union with the divine.

—*Amy J. Johnson*

Further Reading

Abrahamov, Binyamin. *Divine Love in Islamic Mysticism: The Teachings of al-Ghazālī and al-Dabbāgh.* New York: RoutledgeCurzon, 2003. A study of the ideas of divine love in Sufism and in the mysticism of eleventh-twelfth century theologian al-Ghazzālī. Extensive bibliography and an index.

Ahmed, Leila. *Women and Gender in Islam.* New Haven, Conn.: Yale University Press, 1992. This book discusses the changing roles and norms of Muslim women throughout history. Although the author's discussion of Rābiᶜah is relatively brief, the work is valuable in tracing the development of gender roles in Islamic history.

Denny, Frederick Mathewson. *An Introduction to Islam.* New York: Macmillan, 1994. This book discusses the religion of Islam and its history, including Islamic mysticism and various types of Sufi orders.

El Sakkakini, Widad. *First Among Sufis: The Life and Thought of Rābiᶜa al-ᶜAdawiyya, the Woman Saint of Basra.* Translated by Nabil Safwat. London: Octagon Press, 1982. This brief biography of Rābiᶜah is a very accessible account of her life and her teachings. Includes an introduction by the writer Doris Lessing.

Esposito, John, ed. *The Oxford History of Islam.* New York: Oxford University Press, 1999. Good general book on the history of Islam and its role in political expansion. Information about Sufism, including its

relationship to various governments, is discussed throughout the text.
Helminski, Camille Adams, comp. *Women of Sufism: A Hidden Treasure: Writings and Stories of Mystic Poets, Scholars and Saints*. Boston: Shambhala, 2003. A rich collection of primary sources on and by Sufi women. The compiler introduces each of the writings and places them in historical context. Entries on Rābiʿah and Khadīja, the first convert to Islam and a wife of the Prophet Muḥammad. Bibliography.
Roded, Ruth, ed. *Women in Islam and the Middle East: A Reader.* New York: I. B. Tauris, 1999. Provides a collection of original sources on women in Islam in the Middle East, from the Middle Ages through the twentieth century. Looks at devout women in Sufism; the legal, cultural, political, religious, and domestic contexts of women's experience; the foundations of Islam; selective quotation of the Prophet's words; and more. Bibliography, index.
Sells, Michael A., ed. and trans. *Early Islamic Mysticism: Sufi, Qurʾān, Mirʿaj, Poetic, and Theological Writings*. New York: Paulist Press, 1996. Explores the sources of Islamic mysticism, with a chapter on Rābiʿah and a chronology of major figures in the development of Sufism. Bibliography, index.
Smith, Margaret. *Muslim Women Mystics: The Life and Work of Rābiʿa and Other Women Mystics in Islam.* Boston: Oneworld, 2001. A good companion to Smith's standard biography of Rābiʿah. Covers the life of Rābiʿah, her teachings and writings, and other women mystics in Islam. Chapters discuss asceticism and prayer, celibacy, monastic life, women saints, love, hope, fear, and more. Also provides a survey of sources, a bibliography, and an index.
_______. *Rābiʿa the Mystic and Her Fellow Saints in Islam.* 1928. Reprint. London: Cambridge University Press, 1984. Smith's biography of Rābiʿah is the standard work on the saint. Although the prose may at times seem old-fashioned to readers, this biography is extremely valuable for the author's use of centuries-old Arabic and Persian texts.

See also: Blessed Angela of Foligno; al-Ashʿarī; Beatrice of Nazareth; al-Ghazzālī; al-Ḥallāj; al-Ḥasan al-Baṣrī; Joan of Arc; Jalāl al-Dīn Rūmī.
Related articles in *Great Events from History: The Middle Ages, 477-1453*: 637-657: Islam Expands Throughout the Middle East; March 21, 1098: Foundation of the Cistercian Order; 1273: Sufi Order of Mawlawīyah Is Established.

Rāmānuja

Indian philosopher

Rāmānuja expounded a theistic interpretation of Vedānta philosophy and led the Śrī Vaiṣṇavas community in its formative period.

Born: c. 1017; Śrīperumbūdūr, near Madras, southern India
Died: 1137; Śrīraṇgam, southern India
Area of achievement: Religion and theology

Early Life

The dates of the life of Rāmānuja (rah-MAHN-ewj-uh) are somewhat controversial, because the 120-year life-span attributed to him by Śrī Vaiṣṇavas tradition seems exceptionally long; it is also possible that he was born some sixty years later than the traditional date. Particularly noteworthy about the time and place of his life, however, is that most of the region of Tamil Nadu in southern India was at this time a single powerful state, the Cōla kingdom. Śrīraṅgam, which would figure so prominently in Rāmānuja's life, was at the center of a prosperous, highly organized state, the rulers of which often lavishly supported the various religious traditions within their realm.

Rāmānuja was born into a Brahman family—apparently Smārtas Brahmans—who had inclinations toward Vishnu (Viṣṇu) worship but were not members of the Śrī Vaiṣṇavas sect. Traditionally, males of his family were scholars of the Vedic texts and rituals. Rāmānuja was married early in his life, then went to study with Yādavaprakāśa, a local scholar of the Upaniṣads and Vedānta. Disagreements with his teacher's interpretations of the sacred texts, combined with his increasing interest in the devotional practices of the Śrī Vaiṣṇavas sect, finally led to a decisive break with his teacher and to Rāmānuja's initiation into the sect.

The last great leader of the Śrī Vaiṣṇavas community, Yāmuna, had died immediately before Rāmānuja's initiation, denying Rāmānuja the opportunity of serving and being instructed by the living master of the tradition.

Still, Rāmānuja regarded himself as Yāmuna's disciple and was acclaimed as Yāmuna's successor by devotees in the Śrī Vaiṣṇavas center of Śrīraṅgam.

Detailed instruction in Śrī Vaiṣṇavas doctrine followed Rāmānuja's initiation; this instruction was provided in Rāmānuja's home by a devotee named Periya Nambi. After six months, Rāmānuja's wife quarreled with Nambi's wife regarding their relative status in the caste system; although all of them were Brahman, Rāmānuja's wife believed that Nambi and his wife were members of a subcaste lower in status and that contact with them was polluting. Nambi and his wife left Rāmānuja's home, terminating his instruction. Rāmānuja was so infuriated with his wife's behavior that he sent her back to her parents and shortly thereafter became an ascetic. This incident illustrates Rāmānuja's attitude that the social order of caste hierarchy was less important than the spiritual rank of devotees within the Śrī Vaiṣṇavas community.

Life's Work

After becoming an ascetic, Rāmānuja lived in a small monastery he had established near the temple in Kanci. Several of Rāmānuja's younger relatives and other Brahmans came to him for instruction, were initiated into the Śrī Vaiṣṇavas community, and became Rāmānuja's disciples. Among these disciples was his former teacher, Yādavaprakāśa, who composed a manual of rules for ascetics of the Śrī Vaiṣṇavas community at Rāmānuja's request, a work that still exists.

Soon the devotees in Śrīraṅgam heard of these developments and asked Rāmānuja to assume leadership of the community and administration of the temple at Śrīraṅgam. He did so, and during the next few years, he thoroughly reorganized the administration of the temple. Because the worship of the lay followers of Śrī Vaiṣṇavism centered on the temple, its administration was a matter of great concern to the whole community. Rāmānuja was able to introduce new procedures and new temple personnel without alienating members of the prior regime.

These reforms were accomplished even though several temple officers were displaced and disciples of Rāmānuja (some of whom were his relatives) who came from a different group of Brahmans and from a different area were given positions. Rāmānuja's changes necessitated the peaceful coexistence not only of different subcastes of Brahmans but also of Brahmans and non-Brahmans, for many different groups helped administer the temple. The relatively liberal attitude toward status distinctions based on caste within the Śrī Vaiṣṇavas community is a striking feature of Rāmānuja's tenure as the community's leader.

Because Rāmānuja had not had the opportunity of being taught by Yāmuna, the previous master of the tradition, he sought out five of Yāmuna's disciples to transmit some portion of the master's teachings. Receiving from one the secret meaning of the sacred mantra, Rāmānuja then publicly revealed the teaching to a group of Śrī Vaiṣṇavas. He justified violating the prohibition against publicizing this doctrine on the grounds that even if he was damned for doing so, others would be saved by his action. Śrī Vaiṣṇavas tell this story because it illustrates vividly Rāmānuja's compassion for his fellow devotees and his desire to spread the teachings of the doctrine, with all of their saving power, to a wider audience.

Nine works have been attributed to Rāmānuja. Three of these works are commentaries on the *Vedānta-sūtras*, the best known and longest of which is the *Śrībhāṣya*; the shorter ones are entitled *Vedātadīpa* and *Vedāntasāra*. Also attributed to Rāmānuja is a commentary on the *Bhagavadgītā* (c. 200 B.C.E.-200 C.E.; *The Bhagavad Gita*, 1785). Perhaps his earliest work is a summary statement of his philosophical position entitled *Vedārthasaṃgraha*. (These writings have all been translated widely and are best known by their original titles.)

The other four works traditionally ascribed to Rāmānuja are devotional in mood and somewhat different in content from the works above; for this reason, some modern scholars have questioned whether Rāmānuja actually composed them. One work is a ritual manual to be used in one's daily worship. The other three are prose hymns in praise of Vishnu. Śrī Vaiṣṇavas have preserved these nine works, which have become the basis of the distinctive theology and practice of their community.

Rāmānuja accepted the traditional Hindu concept of reincarnation and the law of karma, which determines the nature of one's rebirth based on one's actions in one's previous life. For Rāmānuja, ultimate reality is God, a personal lord who reveals himself to those who acknowledge their dependence on him. The traditional Vedānta is concerned with knowledge of ultimate reality as the means of attaining emancipation from the cycle of rebirth. Rāmānuja's interpretation of Vedānta incorporates knowledge of ultimate reality with the performance of one's ritual duties and social duties as secondary means of attaining liberation, but the primary means is devotion (*bhakti*). Devotion in the Śrī Vaiṣṇavas community is a recollection of the attributes of God with an attitude of love, so that the devotee feels the presence of God constantly and vividly. Most *bhakti* traditions regard this devotion as the means to the attainment of God's presence; for Rāmānuja, the devotee who feels a need for God's presence discovers that God needs the loving devotion of his devotee as well. *Bhakti* in Śrī Vaiṣṇavism is thus the mutual participation of God and his devotees.

Rāmānuja traveled through much of India, taking the doctrines and practices of the Śrī Vaiṣṇavas sect to all who would listen. His influence was particularly strong in southern India, where many converts were won. Late in his life, however, Rāmānuja was forced to flee from Śrīraṅgam when a newly installed king demanded that he declare obeisance to Śiva (Shiva). Rāmānuja fled north to the Hoysaḷa kingdom, where he was free to practice Śrī Vaiṣṇavism. After the death of the fanatical king of Cōla, Rāmānuja was able to return to Śrīraṅgam and spend his remaining years peacefully in the company of many disciples.

SIGNIFICANCE

Rāmānuja emerged as the leader of the small Śrī Vaiṣṇavas community between the eleventh and twelfth centuries and was instrumental in transforming this sect into one of the largest devotional religious movements in India. Rāmānuja's leadership was twofold: He was both the chief administrative officer of the Śrīraṅgam temple and the authoritative teacher of the community of devotees for whom Śrīraṅgam was the center.

Since the twelfth century, Rāmānuja has been seen as the most important teacher and leader of the Śrī Vaiṣṇavas community. In fact, Rāmānuja has been regarded by his followers as the means by which salvation was to be attained. Through the teachings that he enunciated and by worshipping at the temple that he reorganized and supervised, the blessed state was attainable. Rāmānuja was thus regarded as the mediator between Vishnu (God) and his community of devotees.

Rāmānuja's leadership established Śrī Vaiṣṇavism as a dynamic and growing tradition in southern India. His reforms of the temple's administrative procedures and the example of his own life served to integrate Brahmans and non-Brahmans within one religious community. Subsequent leaders of Śrī Vaiṣṇavism have followed the procedures for temple administration that Rāmānuja instituted and have relied on his writings as the official doctrines of the sect.

One of the most significant aspects of Rāmānuja's thought is that it provided a theistic interpretation of Vedānta in opposition to Śaṅkara's monism, which was very much the dominant interpretation. In so doing, Rāmānuja contributed to the establishment of devotional theism as acceptable to even the most orthodox Brahmans. Devotional theism has become the most popular kind of worship in India, in part because of Rāmānuja's intellectual and organizational skills.

—*Bruce M. Sullivan*

FURTHER READING

Bartley, C. J. *The Theology of Rāmānuja: Realism and Religion*. London: RoutledgeCurzon, 2002. A look at the religious beliefs of Rāmānuja. Bibliography and index.

Lakshamma, G. *The Impact of Rāmānuja's Teaching on Life and Conditions in Society*. Delhi: Sundeep Prakashan, 1990. An examination of the life of Rāmānuja and his impact on his society. Bibliography.

Lipner, Julius. *The Face of Truth: A Study of Meaning and Metaphysics in the Vedantic Theology of Rāmānuja*. Houndsmills, Basingstoke, Hampshire, England: Macmillan, 1986. Analysis of Rāmānuja's Vedantic religious views. Index and bibliography.

Lott, Eric J. *God and the Universe in the Vedantic Theology of Rāmānuja*. New York: Barnes and Noble, 1980. This work is a clear and concise study of the religious thought of Rāmānuja, with particular attention to his doctrines regarding God and humanity's relationship to God. For Rāmānuja, the soul is dependent on God much as the body is dependent on the soul which it contains. Bibliography.

Rangarajan, Haripriya. *Rāmānuja Sampradāya in Gujarat: A Historical Perspective*. Bombay: Somaiya Publications, 1996. An examination of Rāmānuja and Śrī Vaiṣṇavism in Gujarat. Bibliography and index.

Srinivasa Chari, S. M. *The Philosophy of the Upaniśads: A Study Based on the Evaluation of the Comments of Śaṇkara, Rāmānuja, and Madhva*. New Delhi: Munshiram Manoharial, 2002. An examination of the Upaniśads that looks at the comments of Rāmānuja. Bibliogrpahy and index.

Vineeth, Vadakethala F. *Self and Salvation in Hinduism and Christianty: An Inter-religious Approach*. New Delhi: Intercultural Publications, 1997. A study that looks at the philosophy of self and salvation of Rāmānuja and Paul Tillich (1886-1965). Bibliography and index.

SEE ALSO: Śaṅkara.

RELATED ARTICLES in *Great Events from History: The Middle Ages, 477-1453*: 788-850: Śaṇkara Expounds Advaita Vedānta; c. 985-1014: Reign of Rājarāja I.

Ratramnus

French writer and abbot

Ratramnus was one of the leading theological writers of the first Eucharistic controversy, and his treatise on the subject has been cited in subsequent occurrences of that debate.

Born: Early ninth century; near Amiens (now in France)
Died: c. 868; Corbie, West Frankish Kingdom (now in France)
Areas of achievement: Literature, religion and theology

Early Life

Little is known concerning the life of Ratramnus (ruh-TRAM-nuhs) except that he entered the Benedictine abbey of Corbie in about 825, was ordained a priest, involved himself in the doctrinal controversies of his time through his writings, and died about 868. All that is known of him comes from his own writings.

The abbey of Corbie, where Ratramnus spent his entire adult life, was located near Amiens in northern France. It had been founded in the seventh century by the Frankish king Chlothar III and his mother Bathilda and was set up under the Benedictine rule by a monk of Luxeil. By the ninth century, Corbie was held in high regard by scholars because of its scriptoria, library, and school. As a center for the study of the liberal arts, Corbie, like a number of other Carolingian monasteries, served as a bridge between the learning of the ancient world and the modern period in European history. Some of the earliest documents written in the Carolingian script were prepared there by monks assigned the task of copying Roman and patristic manuscripts.

The writings of Ratramnus indicate that he was an extremely well-read scholar, one who was held in high regard by his contemporaries, such as the bishops Hildegard of Meaux and Odo of Beauvais and the theologians Gottschalk of Orbais and Lupus of Ferrara. Pope Nicholas the Great called on him to write a treatise in defense of the primacy of the bishop of Rome. In addition, the Frankish king Charles the Bald on two occasions petitioned him to write tracts on doctrinal matters. Yet, were it not for his first treatise, *De corpore et sanguine Domini* (*Concerning the Body and Blood of the Lord*, 1549), written sometime between 844 and 850, Ratramnus would probably not be remembered, since he left no disciple to keep his memory alive.

Life's Work

Ratramnus was drawn into the first Eucharistic controversy in the history of the Church when he was called on sometime between 844 and 850 by Charles the Bald to prepare a treatise on Eucharistic doctrine. Charles had already received a book on that subject written by Saint Paschasius Radbertus, abbot of Corbie, but because Charles disliked the abbot—grave political differences existed between them—it is likely that the king desired a treatise on the subject that would be significantly different. The choice of Ratramnus for this task indicates that he already had a reputation as a scholar and that his view on the Eucharist was known to be at variance with that held by his abbot.

Paschasius, a pupil of Saint Adalhard and Saint Wala, former abbots of Corbie, claimed that his treatise *De corpore et sanguine Domini* was based on the writings of many of the Greek and Roman church fathers, including Saint Ambrose, Saint John Chrysostom, Saint Jerome, Saint Augustine, and Gregory the Great. In his work, Paschasius considered two questions concerning the Eucharist: First, does the sacrament contain something hidden, which can be known only by faith, or is the whole reality present? Second, is the body of Christ that was born of the Virgin Mary and suffered and died on the Cross the same body that is received in the Eucharist by the faithful? According to Paschasius, there is a strict identity between the historical body and the Eucharistic body of Christ.

> And therefore, O man, whenever you drink this cup or eat this bread, you should keep in mind that you are not drinking any other blood than the one that was poured out for you and for all for the forgiveness of sins, and that this is no other flesh than the one that was given up for you and for all and that hung on the Cross.

Paschasius believed that the substance of the bread and wine was changed into the actual body and blood of Christ although the elements retained the outward appearance as bread and wine. The presence of the historical body of Christ at many places at the same time in the Eucharist is explained by a creative act on the part of God on each occasion. The presence of Christ's body and blood in the Eucharist is an objective reality; thus, even someone who received them in an unworthy manner would still receive the true body and blood of the Lord.

Ratramnus, in his treatise of the same title as that of Paschasius, attacked the latter's position by making a distinction between the words *figura* and *veritas*. *Figura* denotes something that is set forth under a veil, as when Christ speaks of himself as the bread or the vine or the door. The word *veritas*, however, means the showing of a thing unveiled or as it really is, as when it is said that Christ was born of a virgin. The bread and wine exhibit one thing to the senses but present something altogether different to the minds of the faithful. Thus, there is no material miracle in the Eucharist; the elements are the same outwardly as before, but inwardly they are Christ's body and blood. In their bodily nature, the elements are, even after consecration, bread and wine, but in power and spiritual efficacy they are the mysteries of the body and blood of Christ.

In addressing the second question as to the relationship between the historical and the Eucharistic body of Christ, Ratramnus argued that though there was a resemblance between the bodies, they were not identical as Paschasius had said. Although the historical body could properly be called "the real flesh of Christ," the Eucharistic body was "the sacrament of the real flesh." Existing between these two bodies was a difference "as great as that which exists between a pledge and the thing for which it is pledged, between an image and the thing of which it is an image, appearance and reality." The believer does receive the body and blood of Christ in the Eucharist but not as a historical and empirical reality. In maintaining this position on the Eucharist, Ratramnus could claim a long tradition that could be traced back to Augustine, while Paschasius was more clearly indebted to Ambrose.

In addition to his major writing on the Eucharistic questions, Ratramnus wrote several other treatises at the request of friends and influential men. In 849-850, he wrote an essay *De praedestinatione* (on predestination), dedicated to Charles the Bald but written in defense of his friend Gottschalk, who was under attack for his views by Hincmar, bishop of Reims. In 853, Ratramnus wrote *De nativitate Christi* (concerning the birth of Christ). In this controversy, he once again had Paschasius as an opponent. The abbot had written a work in which he not only defended the idea of the virgin birth of Christ but also argued that Christ had not been born like other men, that his birth had taken place without the sorrow or pain that were the consequences of the curse placed on Eve for her sin. Ratramnus, while agreeing that Mary was "virgin before giving birth, virgin while giving birth, virgin after giving birth," nevertheless insisted that Christ's birth was like that of other men, for to say otherwise was a threat to Christ's true humanity, and it was theologically necessary that Christ be both God and human.

In 863, at the request of Odo, bishop of Beauvais, Ratramnus wrote an essay in which he challenged the heretical view of a monk who claimed that there existed a single spirit that was shared by all humans. His final treatise was written in 867 at the request of Pope Nicholas I. Entitled *Contra graecorum opposita* (against the opposition of the Greeks), it was one of several written on the subject by Frankish clergymen, but it was by far the fullest and most logically argued. In this work, Ratramnus defended the claims of the bishop of Rome to primacy over the whole Church against the rival claims of the patriarch of Constantinople. With this work, the pen of Ratramnus was stilled by death, which came around the year 868, although there was no eulogy to record the precise date.

SIGNIFICANCE

Despite the high regard of his contemporaries, had it not been for his role in the Eucharistic controversy, Ratramnus would likely have been forgotten soon after his death. During the next two centuries, his book on the Eucharist received only sporadic attention, while that of Paschasius won great favor among the influential thinkers of that time. In the middle of the eleventh century, another Eucharistic controversy erupted when Berengar, head of the school of Tours, promoted the Eucharistic views of Ratramnus although erroneously attributing the book containing them to John Scotus Erigena. Ratramnus's book was condemned and destroyed under the name of Erigena at the synod held in Vercelli in 1050.

With the definition of the doctrine of transubstantiation at the Fourth Lateran Council in 1215, which in general affirmed the Eucharistic position of Paschasius, it might be thought that Ratramnus's treatise would have been relegated to oblivion. In the course of the Reformation, however, many of the reformers (with the notable exception of Martin Luther) embraced the ideas of Ratramnus as anticipations of their own Eucharistic views. His book was printed for the first time in 1549 and was widely circulated in Protestant circles; in 1559, the censors of the Council of Trent placed it on the Index of proscribed books. By the twentieth century, a number of Catholic theologians had concluded that Ratramnus was not clearly heretical in his views and may indeed have been closer in his Eucharistic views to Augustine than had been traditionally thought.

—Paul E. Gill

FURTHER READING

Bynum, Caroline Walker. "The Blood of Christ in the Later Middle Ages." *Church History* 71, no. 4 (December, 2002): 685-715. The author discusses "blood piety" in the Eucharistic tradition in Europe and also argues that there is "an asymmetry between the body and blood symbols themselves" in this same tradition.

Fahey, John F. *The Eucharistic Teaching of Ratramn of Corbie*. Mundelein, Ill.: Saint Mary of the Lake Seminary, 1951. A text devoted exclusively to the Eucharistic views of Ratramnus. Contains a very useful historical introduction. Supports the view that Ratramnus may have been closer to the orthodox view of the Eucharist than traditionally thought. Extensive bibliography.

Harnack, Adolph. *History of Dogma*. Edited by Alexander Balmain Bruce. Vols. 5 and 6. New York: Dover, 1961. This translation of the classic German work, written between 1886 and 1890, is extremely useful but rather esoteric. Provides an excellent background to the writing of Ratramnus. Bibliography.

Morrison, Karl F. *Tradition and Authority in the Western Church, 300-1140*. Princeton, N.J.: Princeton University Press, 1969. Valuable for explaining the political and religious climate existing in the Frankish kingdoms at the time Ratramnus was writing. Extensive bibliography.

Pelikan, Jaroslav. *The Growth of Medieval Theology, 600-1300*. Vol. 3 in *The Christian Tradition: A History of the Development of Doctrine*. Chicago: University of Chicago Press, 1978. This work has become the standard for the exposition of Christian doctrine. All of Ratramnus's writings are discussed and evaluated. Draws extensively on primary sources. Excellent bibliography.

Radding, Charles M., and Francis Newton. *Theology, Rhetoric, and Politics in the Eucharistic Controversy, 1078-1079: Alberic of Monte Cassino Against Berengar of Tours*. New York: Columbia University Press, 2003. Discusses the Eucharistic controversy of the eleventh century in which Ratramnus's work was reintroduced and promoted by Berengar. Includes bibliography and index.

SEE ALSO: Charles the Bald; Gregory the Great; Nicholas the Great; William of Ockham.

RELATED ARTICLES in *Great Events from History: The Middle Ages, 477-1453*: November 11-30, 1215: Fourth Lateran Council; c. 1310-1350: William of Ockham Attacks Thomist Ideas; 1377-1378: Condemnation of John Wyclif.

RAYMOND OF PEÑAFORT

Spanish religious scholar

Raymond of Peñafort compiled the decretals (the official code of Church law) promulgated by Pope Gregory IX in 1234 and wrote a penitential handbook for priests, Summa de casibus poenitentiae, *used throughout the Middle Ages.*

BORN: c. 1175; Peñafort, near Villafranca del Panadés, Catalonia (now in Spain)
DIED: January 6, 1275; Barcelona, Catalonia
AREA OF ACHIEVEMENT: Religion and theology

EARLY LIFE

Raymond was born into the Spanish noble family of Peñafort (payn-yah-FOHRT), whose castle was on a high rock above the village of Villafranca del Panadés, not far from Barcelona. It is probable that he was educated in the school of the Cathedral of the Holy Cross in Barcelona, the city to which he kept returning and in which he spent the last part of his life. He was evidently a brilliant student, for he is said to have begun teaching philosophy in Barcelona at the age of twenty (which might have been as early as 1195). Both here and later, in Bologna, Raymond shared his learning out of love and charged nothing for his services as a teacher.

Around the year 1210, Raymond joined with a canon of the cathedral at Barcelona, Peter the Red, and journeyed to Bologna to study canon law. After six to eight years of study there, he was recognized as a master of canon law, and from 1218 to 1221, he taught in Bologna. Again refusing payment from his students, he was given a salary by grateful citizens of Bologna. During this period he wrote his first treatise in canon law, *Summa juris canonici* (1218-1221; a summation of canon law), only part of which is preserved in a unique manuscript.

LIFE'S WORK

The turning point in Raymond's life came when he was persuaded by the bishop of Barcelona to return to Barcelona to help in the founding of a convent of the newly established Dominican order (also known as the Order of Preachers) by being the teacher for the friars in Barcelona. Raymond was earnest in his service to God and to the Church, and within a short time, he had been made canon and then provost of the Cathedral of the Holy Cross. Yet he was not content to be merely on the periphery of the Dominican order, and on Good Friday, 1222, Raymond became a Dominican friar, and for the rest of his life he was associated with the convent of Saint Catherine in Barcelona.

From 1222 to 1229, Raymond concerned himself with various activities having to do with counteracting the presence of the Moors and the Islamic religion in Spain. In about 1223, he helped found (with Peter Nolasco) the Order of Our Lady of Ransom (the Mercedarians), an organization dedicated to the rescue and rehabilitation of Christians held prisoner by the Muslims. From 1227 to 1229, he was the chief assistant to John of Abbeville, papal legate, who was in charge of restoring ecclesiastical discipline in Spain according to the principles laid down at the Fourth Lateran Council of 1215. It was Raymond's task to go into towns before the legate and prepare them for his message. Raymond also joined with the legate in preaching a crusade against the Moors, and in 1229, he was appointed directly by Gregory IX to enlist warriors for the Crusade in the towns of Narbonne and Arles. Also in this year, Raymond had his first direct involvement with James I the Conqueror, a champion of the Crusade; Raymond was ecclesiastical judge in an investigation concerning the king's marriage and the legitimacy of the rights of succession of his eldest son. Raymond's relationship with the king, although sometimes stormy, was to endure for the rest of his life.

Notwithstanding all these activities, Raymond found time during this period to write the most popular of his treatises, *Summa de casibus poenitentiae* (1222-1229; summary of cases of penitence). It was a handbook for priests that went beyond the usual matching of sins with appropriate penances; it provided a systematic discussion of problems of Christian conscience and (in accordance with Raymond's expertise in canon law) also dealt with appropriate Church practices in regard to particular sins. The first three books treated, respectively, sins against God, sins against other people, and miscellaneous questions of Church discipline and canon law. The fourth book, on marriage (added in 1235), was largely a redaction of the *Summa de matrimonio* (c. 1214; summary of matrimony) by Tancred. Raymond's work was circulated both in its entirety and in condensed form throughout the later Middle Ages. One of the best-known restatements of it was in portions of "The Parson's Tale," actually a sermon on penitence (c. 1395) in Geoffrey Chaucer's *The Canterbury Tales* (1387-1400).

When Raymond's assignment with the papal legate in Spain was completed, Gregory IX, greatly impressed with Raymond's abilities, called him to Rome in 1230 and appointed him his personal confessor; quickly added to this honor were the offices of chaplain and penitentiary, the latter function giving Raymond the opportunity to render decisions on canon law on behalf of the pope. As the pope's confessor, Raymond is said to have imposed penances on Gregory that required him to give special attention to the petitions of the poor. Raymond was often addressed by Pope Gregory as Father of the Poor, and he was styled by a contemporary as Promoter of the Petitions of the Poor. There was, however, a severe side to Raymond, shown perhaps most obviously in his work while in the papal court to establish the Inquisition in the region of Aragon in Spain, using his influence with James I.

Raymond's most significant accomplishment in the service of Gregory was to draw up a condensation of canon law from the time of Gratian (whose *Decretum* of 1150 had formed the core of canon law for the last eighty years), up to and including the first part of Gregory's papacy. Gregory's purpose was for Raymond to edit, condense, and catalog these laws to produce a comprehensive, indexed digest of the accepted rules for Church governance. The completed work of Raymond was authorized and promulgated in 1234 under the papal bull *Rex pacificus*; this landmark codification of canon law came to be known as the *Decretals* of Gregory IX and remained a key part of canon law in the Roman Catholic Church until the modern overall revision in 1917.

Pope Gregory wished to install Raymond as bishop of Tarragona in 1235, but Raymond begged to be released from this appointment, and, indeed, he became ill at the prospect. He was allowed to return to Spain in 1236, after complying with Gregory's insistence that he at least nominate someone else to fill the vacant bishopric. He was not allowed to rest for long in his beloved Barcelona; in 1238, he was elected the third master general of the Dominican order. Although he served in this post for only two years (once again managing to get himself relieved of it), his talents for codifying and reorganization were once more exercised in revising the rules of the order. Testifying to the effectiveness of his revision was the longevity of the Raymundian Code for the Dominicans, which was not superseded until 1924.

After Raymond resigned his post, he returned to Barcelona, and there is no record of his leaving Spain again, although he might have done so in order to found a Dominican convent among the Moors in Tunis in northern Africa. He also founded a Dominican house in the midst of Moors in Murcia, in southeastern Spain. The last thirty-five years of his life were dedicated to the conversion of Moors and Jews in Spain. To this end, he established the teaching of Arabic and Hebrew in several Dominican convents, continued his work to rescue Christian prisoners through the Mercedarians, and encouraged Thomas Aquinas to write a treatise directed at persuading pagans of the truth of the doctrines of Christianity. It seems that Raymond was also instrumental during this period of his life in establishing the Inquisition in Catalonia. His name is associated with a guidebook for inquisitors drawn up under Esparrago, bishop of Tarragona, in 1241.

SIGNIFICANCE

Raymond is surprisingly little known for one who lived so long and was continually active. Even his two most influential writings (the *Decretals* of Gregory IX and the *Summa de casibus poenitentiae*) did not bring him fame. Raymond was evidently self-effacing and preferred to work behind the scenes. These qualities of character are seen in his refusal to take fees for his teaching, his faithful service to his superiors, and his eagerness to avoid appointment to prominent offices. Yet in spite of his relative anonymity, his life had a tremendous influence: His revisions and compilations of canon law for Gregory IX and for the Dominican order lived into the twentieth century; his writings on penitence were widely circulated and were used by Chaucer; his efforts toward the conversion of the Jews and Moors in Spain were a catalyst for the study of Hebrew and Arabic by Dominicans; and he was the instigator of one of the important writings of Thomas Aquinas. The continuing respect in which he was held by his contemporaries was evidenced by his being visited in his last illness by two kings, James I and Alfonso of Castile. Raymond's holiness of life, as well as his service to the Church, was recognized in his canonization in 1601.

—*Elton D. Higgs*

FURTHER READING

Jasper, Detlev, and Horst Fuhrmann. *Papal Letters in the Early Middle Ages: History of Medieval Canon Law.* Washington, D.C.: Catholic University of America Press, 2001. Collection includes two separate sections, Jasper's "The Beginnings of the Decretal Tradition" and Fuhrmann's "The Pseudo-Isidorian Forgeries," on papal law (decretals) during the time of Raymond and Pope Gregory. Includes a bibliography and indexes of papal letters and manuscripts.

Kuttner, Stephan. "The Barcelona Edition of St. Raymond's First Treatise on Canon Law." *Seminar* 8 (1950): 52-67. A review by an authority on Raymond's works of a printed edition of the unique fragmentary manuscript of the *Summa juris canonici*. Gives a brief summary of Raymond's other important writings.

_______. "Raymond of Peñafort as Editor: The 'Decretales' and 'Constitutiones' of Gregory IX." *Bulletin of Medieval Canon Law* 12 (1982): 65-80. Examines the method by which Raymond revised and edited the materials at his disposal for his major canonical work. Shows the extent to which Raymond exercised his own judgment and drew on uncirculated letters from Gregory in his final compendium.

Pennington, Kenneth. "Summae on Raymond de Pennafort's 'Summa de Casibus' in the Bayerische Staatsbibliothek, Munich." *Traditio* 27 (1971): 471-480. A survey of thirteenth and fourteenth century adaptations and summaries of Raymond's work on penitential principles. Shows the popularity of this work.

Richardson, H. G. "Tancred, Raymond, and Bracton." *English Historical Review* 59 (1944): 376-384. Treats the interrelationship of the writings of the three authors. Little specifically about Raymond.

Schwertner, Thomas M. *Saint Raymond of Pennafort.* Edited by C. M. Antony. Milwaukee, Wis.: Bruce, 1935. A complete English-language biography of Raymond. The author is a Dominican, and some of his material comes from miracles of Raymond attested in the document of canonization. His other major source is the Latin *Raymundiana*, a collection of early accounts of Raymond's life.

Somerville, Robert, and Bruce C. Brasington, trans. and comps. *Prefaces to Canon Law Books in Latin Christianity: Selected Translations, 500-1245.* New Haven, Conn.: Yale University Press, 1998. A collection of prefaces from Christian canon law books, including Raymond's preface to the decretals of Gregory IX.

SEE ALSO: Alfonso X; Henry de Bracton; Geoffrey Chaucer; Saint Dominic; Gregory IX; James I the Conqueror; Tancred; Thomas Aquinas.

RELATED ARTICLES in *Great Events from History: The Middle Ages, 477-1453*: November 11-30, 1215: Fourth Lateran Council; 1227-1230: Frederick II Leads the Sixth Crusade; 1233: Papal Inquisition; c. 1265-1273: Thomas Aquinas Compiles the *Summa Theologica*; 1387-1400: Chaucer Writes *The Canterbury Tales*.

al-Rāzī

Persian physician and philosopher

The most original thinker and the keenest clinical observer of all the medieval Muslim physicians, al-Rāzī produced the first clinical account of smallpox and measles as well as a twenty-four-volume compendium of medical knowledge. He also set new standards for medical ethics, the clinical observation of disease, and the testing of medical treatment.

Born: 864; Rayy, Persia (now in Iran)
Died: c. 925; Rayy, Persia
Also known as: Rhazes (Latin name); Abū Bakr Muḥammad ibn Zakariyā al-Rāzī (full name)
Areas of achievement: Medicine, philosophy

Early Life

There is little information about the life of al-Rāzī (ahl-RAH-zee). He was born in Rayy, a few miles from what is now Tehran, administered a hospital in that town as well as in Baghdad, and died in his hometown about 925. In his youth, music was his chief interest; he played the lute and studied voice. On reaching adulthood, he rejected this pursuit, however, asserting that music produced by grown men lacked charm. He then turned to the study of philosophy, a lifelong interest, and developed decidedly egalitarian views, a keen interest in ethics, and a profoundly questioning stance toward received dogmas, both religious and scientific. In his thirties, he began to pursue medical studies and a career as a physician.

His interest in medicine reportedly arose after a visit to a sick home in Baghdad, where he was so moved by the suffering of the sick and maimed patients that he determined to devote the rest of his life to alleviating human misery through the practice of medicine. Exactly where he acquired his medical training is unknown, although it was most likely in Baghdad, where he lived from 902 to 907. At that time, the city was the leading center of learning in the Middle East and contained fully equipped hospitals, well-stocked libraries, and a sound tradition of research. Successive ʿAbbāsid caliphs, from al-Manṣūr (r. 754-775) and Hārūn al-Rashīd (r. 786-809) to al-Maʾmūn (r. 813-833), had generously endowed institutes for the study of ancient Greek arts and sciences as well as those of Persia and India. Some scholars suggest that al-Rāzī, who spent most of his life in Iran, probably studied medicine at the University of Jondisabur, a Sāsānid-founded institution, which remained a major medical center in the medieval Muslim East.

Life's Work

Al-Rāzī, an outstanding clinician and a brilliant diagnostician and medical practitioner, was probably the most learned and original of all the medieval Muslim physicians. His scientific and philosophical writings total some 113 major and 28 minor works, of which 12 discuss alchemy. While chief physician and master teacher of the hospital in Rayy, he produced the ten-volume encyclopedia *Kitāb al-ṭibb al-Manṣūrī* (c. 915), named for his patron Manṣūr ibn Isḥāq al-Samānī of Sijistān; a Latin translation, *Liber Almansoris*, was first published in Milan in the 1580's. Al-Rāzī was invariably described as a generous and gracious man with a large head, full beard, and imposing presence. His lectures, which attracted full-capacity crowds of students, were organized so that his senior students handled all questions they could answer, deferring to him only those issues beyond their knowledge.

Early in his career, he earned a reputation as an effective and compassionate healer, which resulted in his appointment in 918 by the ʿAbbāsid caliph al-Muqtadir as physician in chief of the great hospital at Baghdad. In choosing a new site for this main hospital, al-Rāzī is said to have had pieces of meat hung in different quarters of Baghdad, finally selecting the spot where the meat was slowest to decompose, which he deemed the area with the healthiest air. As a result of his compassion for the sick and his contributions to medical ethics, al-Rāzī is justifiably compared to Hippocrates. In his Baghdad hospital, he provided patients with music, storytelling, recitations of the Qurʾān, and separate convalescent quarters. He not only treated poor patients free of charge but also supported them with his own funds during their convalescence at home. He emphasized a holistic approach to treating illness—that the mind as well as the body must be treated—but above all insisted that the art of healing must rest on a scientific basis. In his c. 919 treatise on medical ethics, al-Rāzī warns physicians that laypersons think doctors know all and can diagnose a problem with a simple examination. He laments that frustrated patients turn to quacks who may alleviate some symptoms but not effect a cure. Al-Rāzī advises reputable physicians not to despair or promise cures but to use their critical judgment, apply tested treatments to appropriate cases, and be thoroughly familiar with the available medical literature.

Al-Rāzī, like Hippocrates, based his diagnoses on observation of the course of a disease. In administering treatments, he paid serious attention to dietetics and hygienic measures in conjunction with the use of closely monitored drug therapy. His fine powers of observation and detailed clinical descriptions are evident in his best-known monograph, *al-Jadarī wa al-Ḥasbah* (c. 922; *A Treatise on the Small-Pox and Measles*, 1848), which is the first clinical account of smallpox. In this work he describes the types of human bodies most susceptible to each disease, the season in which each disease most often occurs, and the varied symptoms indicating the approaching eruption of smallpox and measles. These symptoms included fever, back pain, nausea, anxiety, itching in the nose, and nightmares.

Because al-Rāzī believed that these diseases were caused by fermentation of the blood, his remedy was purification of the blood. The therapeutic measures he employed were based on his readings of the ancient Greeks and his own clinical trials. He devised two different approaches to treatment: to counteract the disease with antidotes such as camphor mixtures, purgatives, bloodletting, and cooling with cold sponges or baths; and to effect a cure with heat, especially steam, to stimulate the eruption of pustules and hasten healing. The choice of treatment depended on the degree of fever and the patient's general condition. Bloodletting, which was a common practice, he recommended using with caution and not on the very young, the very old, or those with a weak constitution. Al-Rāzī also developed detailed measures for preventing secondary effects from these diseases, such as damage to the eyes, ears, and throat and scarring of the skin.

Possessing an extensive knowledge of pharmacology and therapeutics, al-Rāzī claimed to have acquired much valuable information from women healers and herbalists in his own country and from his travels to Syria, Palestine, Egypt, and Muslim Spain. Other medieval physicians added little to his vast knowledge of drugs. His drug therapy was similar to contemporary practice in that dosage was based on age and weight. Drugs with which he was acquainted included nux vomica, senna, cam-

Ninteenth century engraving of Persian physician and alchemist, al-Rāzī, in his laboratory in Baghdad. (Hulton|Archive at Getty Images)

phor, cardamom, sal ammoniac, and arrack as well as other alcoholic drinks. He used oils, powders, infusions, syrups, liniments, plasters, suppositories, compresses, and fumigations. His diligent search for drugs of therapeutic value and his methods of clinical observation laid the foundation on which future physicians would build.

Al-Rāzī's extensive medical and pharmacological knowledge is contained in his most important work, *al-Kitāb al-hāwī fiʿl ṭibb* (c. 930; the comprehensive book), a twenty-four-volume encyclopedia that summarized the medical knowledge of the time, that is, the knowledge of the Greeks, Persians, Indians, and Arabs. It was completed posthumously by his students. First translated into Latin in 1279, it was repeatedly printed from 1486 onward under the title *Continens Medicinae* and exercised considerable influence in the Latin West. Medieval Muslim knowledge of anatomy and physiology was limited by the Qurʾānic prohibition against dissection of the human body. Thus, most information on anatomy and surgery in *al-Kitāb al-hāwī fiʿl ṭibb* was drawn from Greeks such as Galen and Hippocrates. Al-Rāzī provided numerous descriptions of his own surgical procedures, however, including those for intestinal obstructions, various forms of hernia, vesical calculi, tracheotomy, and cancer. In treating cancer, he stressed that there should be no surgical removal of cancerous tissue unless the entire cancer could be removed.

Much of al-Rāzī's philosophical thinking can be gleaned from two of his treatises on ethics: *Kitāb al-ṭibb al-rūḥānī* (c. 920; *The Book of Spiritual Physick*, 1950) and *Sīrat al-faylasūf* (c. 920; *The Philosopher's Way of Life*, 1926). He propounded egalitarian views, rejecting a contemporary argument that humans can be stratified according to innate abilities. Rather, he believed that all people possess the capacity to reason and do not need the discipline imposed by religious leaders. The latter he accused of deception, and the miracles of prophets he regarded as trickery. His critical attitude toward religious authority carried over to the established dogmas of science. Only by questioning and testing received knowledge, he argued, could there be continuing progress in science.

Al-Rāzī asserted that he did not accept Aristotle's philosophy and that he was a disciple of Plato, with whom he shared certain ideas on matter; his egalitarianism, however, was antithetical to Plato's political ideas. Al-Rāzī's attitude toward animals was also part of his ethics. He believed that only carnivores and noxious animals such as snakes should be killed, for he endorsed the doctrine of transmigration, according to which a soul may pass from an animal to a person. Killing an animal set the soul on a path of liberation, while al-Rāzī maintained that only souls occupying human bodies should be liberated. Toward the end of his life, al-Rāzī became blind from cataracts. He reportedly rejected surgery, remarking that he had seen too much of the world already. Some biographers have argued that his interest in alchemy contributed to his blindness; others ascribed it to his excessive consumption of beans. He died around 925 in abject poverty, having given all of his wealth to his impoverished patients.

Significance

Al-Rāzī's antireligious attitude and his interest in alchemy caused other Muslim intellectuals to criticize his work and question his medical competence. To his credit, his principal work on alchemy, *Kitāb al-asrār wa-sirr al asrra* (c. 916; the book of secrets), which was translated into Latin in 1187 (*De spiritibus et corporibus*), was a chief source of chemical knowledge through the fourteenth century. Later, more talented medieval physicians such as Moses Maimonides found fault with his philosophy but not with his medicine. As Aristotelians they were intolerant of his disavowal of Aristotle and his readiness to accept empirical evidence that upset established doctrines. It was in his insistence on rigorous scientific research and valid evidence, however, that al-Rāzī anticipated the position of modern medicine. Moreover, as a conscientious practitioner who stressed qualitative medicine—devising the best therapy, based on an evaluation of the patient's physical and mental condition—he set high standards for physicians and paved the way for modern medical practice.

As a result of his many achievements—the application of chemistry to medical treatment, the earliest study of smallpox and other epidemiological studies, the elaboration of medical ethics and scientific trials, the invention of the seton for surgery—al-Rāzī secured the historical reputation of the medieval Muslim Arab world as the primary center of science and medicine. His Muslim predecessors introduced clinics, hospitals, and pharmacies, but al-Rāzī established more rigorous ethical, clinical, and scientific standards, free from dogmatic prejudices, which foreshadowed those of modern science. For that reason, al-Rāzī's portrait is one of only two portraits of Muslim physicians (the other being that of Avicenna) that were hung long ago in the great hall of the School of Medicine at the University of Paris as permanent testimony to the West's debt to the science of medieval Islam.

—*Kathleen K. O'Mara*

Further Reading

Amundsen, Darrel W., ed. *Medicine, Society, and Faith in the Ancient and Medieval Worlds*. Baltimore: Johns Hopkins University Press, 1996. Covers the connections between medicine and religious faith, canon law on medical practice, medical ethics, and more

Bakar, Osman. *The History and Philosophy of Islamic Science*. Cambridge, England: Islamic Texts Society, 1999. Discusses questions of methodology, doubt, spirituality and scientific knowledge, the philosophy of Islamic medicine, and how Islamic science influenced medieval Christian views of the natural world.

Browne, Edward G. *Arabian Medicine*. Westport, Conn.: Hyperion Press, 1983. A brief text that contains separate sections on al-Rāzī's life, writings, influence, and pharmacological contributions. Index.

Campbell, Donald E. H. *Arabian Medicine and Its Influence on the Middle Ages*. 1926. Reprint. Vol. 1. New York: AMS Press, 1973. Focuses on medieval Muslim contributions to medical history and contains a sympathetic section on al-Rāzī.

Gordon, Benjamin L. *Medieval and Renaissance Medicine*. New York: Philosophical Library, 1959. A readily available, 843-page volume containing a summary of al-Rāzī's career and a concise summary of his clinical work in the chapter on smallpox. Bibliography.

Hitti, Philip K. *History of the Arabs*. 10th ed. New York: St. Martin's Press, 1974. Still the best and most available text with extensive coverage of the ʿAbbāsid period. Contains a discussion of al-Rāzī's work within the context of ʿAbbāsid scientific and literary accomplishments. Illustrations, genealogical tables, maps, and bibliographical references.

Huff, Toby E. *The Rise of Early Modern Science: Islam, China, and the West*. 2d ed. New York: Cambridge University Press, 2003. Provides a strong cross-cultural background for the rise of science and medicine in the Middle East, Asia, and the West. Includes illustrations, a bibliography, and index.

Martin, Richard C., Mark R. Woodward, and Dwi S. Atmaja. *Defenders of Reason in Islam: Mutazilism from Medieval School to Modern Symbol*. Boston: Oneworld, 1997. Examines Mutazilism, the belief in the primacy of reason over theological teachings, in Islam during the Middle Ages and through the twentieth century. Bibliography, index.

Rāzī, al-. *The Spiritual Physick of Rhazes*. Translated by Arthur J. Arberry. London: John Murray, 1950. An excellent example of al-Rāzī's thinking, this slender volume provides clinical information and treatment advice on various issues such as alcoholism, anxiety, and mendacity.

_______. *A Treatise on the Small-Pox and Measles*. Translated by William Alexander Greenhill. London: Sydenham Society, 1848. A translation of the classic work, the volume provides an excellent example of al-Rāzī's medieval Muslim thinking, scientific methodology, and medieval Muslim thought in general.

Stroumsa, Sarah. *Freethinkers of Medieval Islam: Ibn al-Rāwandī, Abū Bakr al-Rāzī and Their Impact on Islamic Thought*. Boston: Brill, 1999. Discusses the contradiction inherent to the brilliance ascribed to so-called free or radical thinkers in Islam, such as al-Rāzī, and their marginalization by historians of Islamic thought. Bibliography, index.

See also: Pietro d'Abano; Alhazen; Arnold of Villanova; al-Ashʿarī; Avicenna; Jacqueline Félicie; Guy de Chauliac; Hārūn al-Rashīd; Abū Mūsā Jābir ibn Ḥayyān; Moses Maimonides; Trotula.

Related articles in *Great Events from History: The Middle Ages, 477-1453*: 786-809: Reign of Hārūn al-Rashīd; 809: First Islamic Public Hospital; c. 1010-1015: Avicenna Writes His *Canon of Medicine*; c. 1150: Moors Transmit Classical Philosophy and Medicine to Europe.

RAZIYA

Fifth sultan of Delhi (r. 1236-1240)

Raziya seized the throne of the Delhi sultanate from her incompetent predecessor. She exercised sovereignty as long as she commanded the support of a faction of the ruling elite. When that support was withdrawn, she was overthrown and killed.

BORN: Date unknown; place unknown
DIED: probably October 13, 1240; Kaithal (now in India)
ALSO KNOWN AS: Raziyya; Razia; Radiyya; Raziyyatuddīn
AREA OF ACHIEVEMENT: Government and politics

EARLY LIFE

Raziya (rah-ZEE-yuh) was the daughter of Iltutmish (r. 1211-1236), a sultan of Delhi. A Central Asian Turk of the Ilbari tribe, Iltutmish was sold into slavery by resentful kinsmen, was taken to Bukhara, and there was purchased by a master who had him instructed in the tenets of Islam and in the skills of a warrior. Subsequently, he was sold as a military slave (*mamlūk*) to Quṭ al-Dīn Aybak, a celebrated *mamlūk*-commander who became the first Delhi sultan (r. 1206-1210). At his master's death and after a brief reign by Aybale's son, Ārām Shāh, who proved to be incompetent, Iltutmish replaced him on the throne, eliminating rivals and consolidating his hold over much of northern India. Like all great *mamlūk*-commanders who clawed their way up the ladder of power, Iltutmish found it impossible to found a permanent dynasty, although for thirty years after his death, the Delhi throne was occupied by three sons, a daughter, and a grandson. Iltutmish, however, considered only his daughter, Raziya, worthy of succeeding him.

Before her accession, not much is known about Raziya. Her mother, styled Turkan Khatun, may have been the daughter of Quṭ al-Dīn Aybak, the former sultan, and this bloodline may explain the support that Raziya enjoyed from her father's *mamlūks*, despite her gender. She would have grown up secluded in the women's quarters of the palace, but Iltutmish held her in high esteem, had encouraged her to interest herself in state affairs, and wanted to designate her as his heir. In addition, it is known that she intoned the Qurʾān correctly, a feat unusual among Central Asian Turks, but one that would have impressed a religious scholar such as Minhāj Sirāj Jūzjānī, the chronicler of her reign.

LIFE'S WORK

At Iltutmish's death, his eldest son, Ruknuddin Firūz Shāh (r. 1236), succeeded him. The new sultan immediately embarked on a course of extravagance and dissipation, abandoning Delhi for his pleasure palace at Kilokhri, a few miles away. The conduct of affairs was left to his mother, Shāh Turkan, an Indian concubine who now sought to pay off old scores, executing several of the late sultan's wives, including any who were pregnant, thus eliminating potential rivals to her son. Likewise, she ordered first the blinding and then the killing of Iltutmish's youngest son, although his other sons escaped her vengeance. She also tried to seize and kill Raziya, but the latter escaped as a result of a popular uprising of supporters who stormed the palace and took Shāh Turkan prisoner. Ruknuddin returned to Delhi only to discover that his high-ranking *mamlūks* had gone over to Raziya and that she had already been proclaimed sultan. Ruknuddin was seized and imprisoned and was executed shortly afterward.

Because of her gender, Raziya's rise to sultan was unusual. In Islamic tradition, there was nothing comparable to the contemporary Christian coronation ceremony, but the loyal Turkish *mamlūks* would have immediately taken the oath of allegiance (*bayʾat*) to Raziya. Then, on the first Friday after the *coup d'état*, probably in the Quwwat al-Islam ("might of Islam") mosque, close to her father's grave, her name would have been read in the *khutba* (prayers invoking God's blessing on the ruler) for the first time. This, together with the minting of coins with the new ruler's name and title, constituted the formal "proofs" of sovereignty. The wording used on that occasion is not recorded, but Jūzjānī, who every week for four years read the *khutba* in her name, may have replicated the wording in the phrase he used when writing his account of her reign: "The Sultan, Praiseworthy [*raziya*] in the Eyes of the World and of the Faith, the Daughter of the Sultan." Significantly, a surviving coin of 1236-1237 from Lakhnawti in Bengal, proclaims: "The Great Sultan, Illustrious [*jalalat*] of the World and of the Faith, Queen [*malikat*], Daughter of the Sultan Iltutmish." Clearly, she wished to remind her subjects that she was her father's daughter.

No sooner was Raziya on the throne than some of those who had supported her candidacy, not satisfied with the offices, titles, and revenue assignments (*iqta*) they had received, mutinied. Through devious intrigues aimed at dividing the rebels, Raziya managed to surmount this crisis. A treacherous vizier was driven into exile, summary executions were performed, and at least one rebel head was brought back to Delhi as a trophy.

One event that added to Raziya's prestige was the submission of the Karakhitan warlord who had seized control of Bengal, but who was anxious to be left undisturbed with his ill-gotten gains. Raziya, pleased not to have to deal with insubordination from that quarter, sent him a canopy of state and ceremonial banners and symbols of sovereignty (but in this instance delegated ones), which stressed her authority as donor and his as loyal recipient. This event led Jūzjānī to remark that the whole realm was obedient to her from Lakhnawti to Diwal (from Bengal to Sind), an illusion, however, on his part.

The shuffling of great officeholders with the object of reinforcing loyalty was crucial for any sultan, but in this Raziya was not wholly successful. Because a woman was not expected to lead her troops into battle, the office of sultan's military deputy (*na'ib-i lashgar*) was of critical importance. In 1237, she appointed to that office Quṭ al-Dīn Ḥasan ibn ʿAlī, an experienced *malik* (lord or king) who had ties with the Ghūrid past and who had ranked third in seniority at Iltutmish's court. The remote fortress of Ranthanbor had been captured by Iltutmish in 1226, but perhaps sensing the fragility of Raziya's rule, a Rājput army was now besieging it. About 1237-1238, Quṭ al-Dīn Ḥasan ibn ʿAlī was sent to relieve it. He drove off the besiegers, entered the fortress, dismantled its defenses, and evacuated the beleaguered garrison. This was the one major military achievement of the reign, although because Quṭ al-Dīn was not a Turkish *mamlūk*, his triumph probably caused resentment among the latter rank and file.

Another sensitive office was that of *amir-hajib* (military chamberlain), which determined who had access to the sultan. Here, Raziya chose most unwisely, appointing a senior *mamlūk*, Ikhtiar al-Dīn Aytegin, who proceeded to undermine her authority surreptitiously. After he had helped to destroy her, he endeavored to repeat his role under her successor and younger brother, Bahrām Shāh (r. 1240-1242), who swiftly procured his assassination.

Another appointment, which proved disastrous because it deeply offended the Turkish *mamlūks*, was that of an Abyssinian slave, Jamāl al-Dīn Yakut, to the office of *amir-i akhur* (master of the horse). As with the appointment of Quṭ al-Dīn Ḥasan ibn ʿAlī, Raziya may have made this appointment as a ploy to build up an alternative power base to the Turkish *mamlūks*. If so, it backfired, not least because it coincided with Raziya's unpopular decision to abandon wearing women's clothing for a male tunic and headdress and, instead of governing indirectly from the harem, to appear in public.

During the winter of 1239-1240, Raziya was compelled to lead an army into Punjab to put down a revolt. She returned to Delhi in triumph in the spring of 1240, but in her absence, the governor of Tabarhindh, Ikhtiar al-Dīn Altuniya, encouraged by the treacherous Aytegin, rebelled. In April, 1240, Raziya marched against Tabarhindh, but while her troops were besieging the town there was a mutiny in her camp. Yaqut was assassinated, Raziya was arrested, and besiegers and besieged joined forces. Meanwhile, in Delhi, a *coup d'état* engineered by Aytegin placed Bahrām Shāh on the throne.

This last development angered Altuniya. who was holding Raziya captive in the Tabarhindh fort. He promptly married her, and together they set off for Delhi to restore her to power. In October, 1240, their forces were intercepted and defeated near Kaithal by her brother's supporters, and both were taken and killed probably on October 13.

Jūzjānī states that she was killed by Hindus, local villagers, or camp followers preying on battlefield fugitives, but the fourteenth century Moroccan traveler to Delhi, Ibn Baṭṭūṭah, heard a more specific account of her death that may embody a genuine oral tradition. In this account, Raziya, dressed as a man and fleeing from the slaughter, begged a crust of bread from a cultivator tilling his field. Exhausted, she then lay down and slept. The cultivator, noticing a tunic embroidered with jewels beneath her outer garments, killed her and stripped the body, and then buried it. After attempting to sell the jew-

India's Muʿizzī Slave Sultans, 1206-1290

Reign	*Ruler*
1206-1210	Quṭ al-Dīn Aybak
1210-1211	Ārām Shāh
1211-1236	Iltutmish
1236	Ruknuddin Firūz Shāh
1236-1240	Raziya
1240-1242	Bahrām Shāh
1242-1246	Masʿūd Shāh
1246-1266	Maḥmūd Shāh
1266-1287	Balban Ulugh Khān
1287-1290	Kay Qubādh
1290	Kayūmarth

els in a nearby market, he was arrested and tortured and then confessed. A local police officer went to where she had been killed, disinterred and washed the body, had it wrapped in a shroud, and reburied it in the same place, which, according to Ibn Baṭṭūṭah, became a pilgrimage center. In Old Delhi, however, within the Turkoman Gate and near the Kalan mosque, is an enclosure with two unmarked stones traditionally supposed to mark the graves of Raziya and a sister, whose name is unknown.

Perhaps the best assessment of her rule was that made by the chronicler Jūzjānī, who was also a Muslim judge (*qadi*) in her service. As a ruler, he described her as prudent, just, and generous, an upholder of justice, the protector of her subjects, a patron of learned men, and endowed with all the attributes of kingship save one: She was not born a man.

Jūzjānī is the only contemporary source for Raziya's reign. Later accounts derive from his narrative but are modified to reflect differing points of view. There is scant surviving numismatic and epigraphic material. Modern Indian novelists and filmmakers have presented Raziya as a romantic and exotic heroine, but there is no basis for this view in the historical record. Ethnically, Raziya was of Central Asian Turkish descent and physically may have resembled a modern Uzbek or Kazakh woman. No description survives, but the fact that she apparently needed assistance in mounting her horse suggests that she may have been short. She was certainly accustomed to handling weapons, which implies physical strength, but this too is a surmise.

Significance

Raziya is a unique figure in medieval Muslim history. From time to time, circumstances led to women ruling on behalf of a minor or a dead kinsman, and under the Seljuk Turks and the Mongol Il-Khans, considerable latitude was given to widows, mothers, and daughters to act as surrogate rulers. However, Raziya's case was different, because despite the turmoil of the four years of her reign, she was recognized by a substantial portion of the ruling elite of the sultanate as being the de jure as well as the de facto ruler.

—*Gavin R. G. Hambly*

Further Reading

Jackson, Peter. *The Delhi Sultanate*. New York: Cambridge University Press, 1999. A very detailed study of the early sultanate period (1210-1400), emphasizing politics and warfare, with careful scrutiny of the source material. Addresses the reign of Sultan Raziya in a broader context. The maps are outstanding.

________. "Sultan Radiyya bint Iltutmish." In *Women in the Medieval Islamic World*, edited by Gavin R. G. Hambly. New York: St. Martin's Press, 1998. This scholarly essay provides a thoughtful summary of the essential facts relating to Sultan Raziya's career.

Juzjani, Siraj-i Minhaj. *Tabakat-i Nasiri*. Translated by H. G. Raverty. 2 vols. 1881. Reprint. Calcutta, India: Asiatic Society, 1995. The only truly contemporary account of Sultan Raziya's reign, by a writer who knew her personally. All later chronicles are virtually paraphrases, with some embroidering of the facts.

Wink, André. *Al-Hind: The Making of the Indo-Islamic World*. Vol. 2. Leiden, Netherlands: E. J. Brill, 1997. This volume, covering the eleventh to thirteenth centuries, perfectly complements Jackson's monograph, while ranging far beyond the northern frontiers of the Delhi sultanate. Excellent maps.

See also: Harṣa; Kōken; Sorghaghtani Beki; Queen Tamara; Wu Hou.

Related articles in *Great Events from History: The Middle Ages, 477-1453*: 690-705: Reign of Empress Wu; 1206-1210: Quṭ al-Dīn Aybak Establishes the Delhi Sultanate; 1236-1240: Reign of Raziya; 1299: ʿAlāʾ-ud-Dīn Muḥammad Khaljī Conquers Gujarat.

RICHARD I
King of England (r. 1189-1199)

Although Richard has not gone down in history as a particularly good king, he was the epitome of the literary medieval knight—brave, skilled, and chivalrous.

BORN: September 8, 1157; Beaumont Palace, Oxford, England
DIED: April 6, 1199; Châlus, the Limousin, Duchy of Aquitaine, France
ALSO KNOWN AS: Richard the Lion-Hearted
AREAS OF ACHIEVEMENT: Government and politics, military

EARLY LIFE

Richard I was the third son of Henry II and Eleanor of Aquitaine, two historical giants of the era. Tall, with blue eyes and golden hair, he inherited from his mother a sensitivity for music and poetry that made him very popular with the troubadours. His real interest, however, was warfare, and it was because of his great valor that he was called "the Lion-Hearted." He was plunged into the game of international politics very early, when at the age of three he was betrothed to Louis VII's daughter Alice. When he was eleven, he rendered homage to Louis for his mother's duchy of Aquitaine, and in 1172, he was formally installed as duke at Poitiers. A year later, he joined his brothers, the younger Henry and Geoffrey of Brittany, in a revolt against their father, which ended only after Henry II had invaded Aquitaine twice to subdue his rebellious son. Richard was soon forgiven, however, and reinstated in his duchy.

From 1175 to 1181, Richard's reputation as a warrior grew steadily as he was forced to crush a series of rebellions in Aquitaine. He skillfully razed castles and drove some nobles from the land while forcing others such as the count of Toulouse to render homage. Richard's growing power and influence and the prospect of an independent Aquitaine alarmed his brother Henry. When Richard refused to acknowledge Henry's claim to Aquitaine, another family war ensued. Henry invaded Aquitaine and enjoyed some success before the king came to Richard's aid. The war ended abruptly with the younger Henry's untimely death in 1183.

Richard was now heir to England and Normandy, but his father wanted him to give up Aquitaine to his younger brother John. Once again, Richard refused to accede to this request and a new civil war was begun. Although a temporary compromise was arranged on November 18, 1188, at Bonmoulins, France, in the presence of Henry and the French king Philip II, Richard threw his support to Philip and acknowledged him as overlord for all of his Continental possessions. In the struggle that followed, Henry was chased from Le Mans to Chinon, where the father, who had reigned for thirty-five years, was forced to recognize the son as his successor on July 4, 1189. Henry II died two days later.

LIFE'S WORK

Two years before Richard assumed the English crown came the news that Saladin had decisively defeated the Christians at the Battle of Hattin. This proved to be the turning point in Richard's life. He took the Cross almost immediately and, since a crusade was an expensive undertaking, he began to raise money in various ways. He sold castles, manors, earldoms, and archbishoprics, and he declared that he would even have sold London itself if he had been able to find an acceptable buyer.

Richard embarked on the Third Crusade with Philip II in the summer of 1190. Although the two kings had once been close friends, they spent most of the trip quarreling. They parted company in Sicily in the spring of 1191.

Richard I. (Library of Congress)

Philip sailed directly to Palestine, but Richard took a more circuitous route and conquered Cyprus, whose ruler had abducted his fiancé after her ship had been wrecked along the coast. After matters had been settled on Cyprus, Richard went on to the Holy Land, arriving in the summer of 1191 in time to join Philip in the siege of Acre. Once again, however, the two kings quarreled, which made the conduct of war difficult. Eventually, the city surrendered and Philip went home, but Richard remained and was able to work out a truce with Saladin that allowed Christians access to Jerusalem. The Third Crusade would prove to be the crowning achievement of Richard's reign and would contribute greatly to his image as a chivalrous knight.

PLANTAGENET KINGS OF ENGLAND, 1154-1399

Reign	*Monarch*
1154-1189	HENRY II (with ELEANOR OF AQUITAINE, r. 1154-1189)
1189-1199	RICHARD I THE LION-HEARTED
1199-1216	JOHN I LACKLAND
1216-1272	HENRY III
1272-1307	EDWARD I LONGSHANKS
1307-1327	EDWARD II (with ISABELLA OF FRANCE, r. 1308-1330)
1327-1377	EDWARD III (with PHILIPPA OF HAINAUT, r. 1327-1369)
1377-1399	RICHARD II

In the meantime, news of John's intrigues in Normandy and England had reached Richard, who resolved to return home as quickly as possible. He left in October of 1192, but a storm wrecked his ship and forced him to take a more dangerous route through Germany, where he had many enemies. Although traveling incognito, he was recognized and captured by the duke of Austria's men, who turned him over to the emperor to be held for ransom. It was difficult, but Richard's faithful ministers set about the task of raising the astronomical sum of 150,000 marks, approximately five times the annual income of the English government. By March of 1194, Richard was back in England.

This was only Richard's second appearance in the country he supposedly ruled and, like the first, his stay was very brief. After raising the requisite capital, Richard was off to new military enterprises on the Continent. He would devote the last five years of his life to a meaningless war with Philip II. Although the war accomplished little, it was during this period that Richard's interest in military engineering peaked, as attested by the construction of the magnificent fortress of Château Gaillard. Richard could not content himself, however, with building castles. In 1199, his adventurous spirit involved him in an insignificant battle for a treasure trove with one of his own vassals. He was wounded by an arrow, and a few days later, he died. At his own request, he was buried in the Church of Fontevrault next to his father.

SIGNIFICANCE

Richard the Lion-Hearted was an enigmatic figure, a curious mixture of bad and good. In his own day, he was hailed as a great warrior and a Christian prince. Recent scholarship, however, depicts him as a rebellious son and brother, a neglectful husband, and a bad king. To some degree, both characterizations are correct. It was a violent age and Richard was probably justified in resisting his father and brothers' attempts to take his inheritance, especially the Aquitaine. Relations with his father never improved significantly, but Richard later repented of his behavior, and he was quick to forgive John for his machinations of 1193-1194. He was always on good terms with his mother, from whom he acquired an interest in poetry and music. Richard was a romantic figure, but he was not a romantic man. He contrived a flimsy political excuse to break off his engagement with Alice, and although he later married Berengaria of Navarre, he spent little time with her.

If the measure of a good king is time spent in the kingdom, then Richard was, indeed, a very bad king. He reigned ten years and spent only about six months in England. It is also true that he exploited the country's resources to finance his many wars. Richard's behavior might be explained by the fact that he was not thoroughly English. Also, he knew that his father had created an efficient administrative machine that would function capably in his absence. Richard's chief problem was his obsession with battle and adventure, which left him precious little time for anything else. Yet it was this same obsession that would enable him to become one of the most romantic and chivalrous figures in history.

—*Larry W. Usilton*

FURTHER READING

Appleby, John. *England Without Richard*. Ithaca, N.Y.: Cornell University Press, 1965. A good chronological survey of England minus its ruler during this period. The author makes excellent use of original materials.

Brundage, James. *Richard Lion Heart*. New York: Charles Scribner's Sons, 1974. Primarily concerned with Richard's participation in the Third Crusade, which was probably the greatest event of his reign. A critical study that portrays Richard as a vain, arrogant, and rapacious warrior.

Gillingham, John. *Richard I*. New Haven, Conn.: Yale University Press, 2002. Richard is seen in a sympathetic light, as more than a warrior; he was also the capable ruler of the duchy of Aquitaine. The author also attempts to refute the notion that Richard was homosexual.

Kelly, Amy. *Eleanor of Aquitaine and the Four Kings*. Cambridge, Mass.: Harvard University Press, 1950. This is an interesting study of Richard's mother and her relationships with four of the great figures of the twelfth century, taking a novelistic approach.

Norgate, Kate. *England Under the Angevin Kings*. 2 vols. 1887. Reprint. New York: Haskell House, 1969. Concerned with the rise of the Angevin house in ninth century Anjou through the early years of John's reign. Two chapters are devoted exclusively to Richard's reign.

_______. *Richard the Lion Heart*. New York: Russell and Russell, 1924. This older biographical study has many enduring qualities. Approximately half the book is devoted to the Third Crusade.

Reston, James, Jr. *Warriors of God: Richard the Lionheart and Saladin in the Third Crusade*. New York: Knopf, 2002. This history of the Third Crusade presents Richard as a complex and at times brutal figure, and it discusses his homosexuality. Saladin, by contrast, is depicted as a sophisticated political leader.

Trindade, Ann. *Berengaria: In Search of Richard the Lionheart's Queen*. Dublin: Four Courts Press, 1999. Based on medieval chronicles and administrative records, the story of the lonely life of the woman whom Richard married on the way to the Third Crusade. A fascinating look at women and the role of the Papacy during Richard's time.

Turner, Ralph V., and Richard R. Heiser. *The Reign of Richard Lionheart: Ruler of the Angevin Empire, 1189-1199*. Upper Saddle River, N.J.: Pearson Education, 2000. Two academics view Richard's achievements as a military leader and administrator from the geopolitical perspective of the Angevin Empire, using original French and English sources.

Warren, W. L. *Henry II*. Berkeley: University of California Press, 1973. This biography of Richard's father treats the youth's life up to his father's death in 1189.

See also: Eleanor of Aquitaine; Henry II; King John; Alexander Neckam; Philip II; Saladin.

Related articles in *Great Events from History: The Middle Ages, 477-1453*: 1154-1204: Angevin Empire Is Established; 1189-1192: Third Crusade.

Richard II

French-born king of England (r. 1377-1399)

Seeking to overcome his powerful uncles who dominated English government before he reached majority, Richard II harshly asserted his royal powers and became the second English monarch to be deposed by his subjects.

Born: January 6, 1367; Abbey of St. André, Bordeaux (now in France)

Died: February, 1400; Pontefract Castle, Yorkshire (now in West Yorkshire), England

Also known as: Richard of Bordeaux

Area of achievement: Government and politics

Early Life

Richard of Bordeaux was born the second son of Joan, "the Fair Maid," countess of Kent, and the Black Prince, Edward, prince of Wales, the eldest son of King Edward III. Richard remained in Bordeaux until January, 1371, when he traveled to England with his ailing father. Little is known about Richard's early years or his education as a crown prince of England. During his youth, it is likely that he became familiar with the workings of a princely court, acquired a basic education from his tutors, and enjoyed the companionship of his older brother, Edward, and his two half brothers, Thomas Holland, earl of Kent, and John Holland, earl of Huntingdon, born of his mother's previous marriage.

A series of deaths, which ultimately brought the crown to this younger son of the Black Prince in 1377, punctuated Richard's childhood. In 1371, his older brother, Prince Edward, died at the age of seven. Five years later, Richard's father died, predeceasing his own father by a year. In 1377, the great Plantagenet warrior and patriarch King Edward III died after many years of illness, during which his son, John of Gaunt, duke of Lancaster, had controlled the government. This death left the ten-year-old Richard heir to the throne as the oldest surviving male heir of Edward III's oldest son.

As the new king of England, crowned on July 16, 1377, Richard did not actually exercise autonomous authority. He ruled with the guidance of several noblemen and the help of his mother, until her death in 1385. The regency, which lasted until Richard declared himself of age and capable of rule in 1389, established both the character and the problems of the young king's reign. Joan and the noblemen formed a council that represented a variety of political viewpoints and set itself the task of leading the country in Richard's name. The twelve-person council was dominated by two of Richard's paternal uncles, John of Gaunt and Thomas Woodstock, duke of Gloucester. As a result of the leadership vacuum created by the last years of the dying Edward III and the government of the regency council manipulated by the uncles of the boy king, England lacked a single, strong leader. Learning from the early years of his reign, the tall, slender, graceful, boyish-looking, and often moody Richard II attempted to become the strong and absolute monarch he thought England needed and wanted.

Richard II. (Library of Congress)

Life's Work

When Richard ascended the throne in 1377, England was at war with France. The regency council summoned Parliament in 1377, 1378, and 1380 in order to raise tax revenues for the war effort. Since 1347, when the plague decimated the English population and upset the economic functioning of the country, the fiscal systems of the Crown had been unbalanced. Attempting to fight a war for the French throne with irregular or uncertain human and financial resources forced the Crown to request that the Parliament assess new and greater taxes on a kingdom that had difficulty paying them. In the fourth parliament of Richard's reign, the new poll tax was adopted. It was a fixed assessment on individuals, rather than a proportional tax on incomes.

The poll tax of 1380, which many landlords paid by demanding new exactions from their peasants, resulted in the Peasants' Revolt of 1381 (also known as Wat Tyler's Rebellion). The rioting peasant mob objected to the heavy financial burden of the taxes. Led by John Ball and Wat Tyler, the angry crowd marched to London, destroying estates of royal councillors along the way. The rioters demanded to meet with the king, a request that was finally granted. While only fourteen years old, the king received the loud complaints of the peasants about taxes, the maladministration of justice, and the unfairness of landlords and indicated his willingness to implement reforms. At one of these meetings, Tyler was killed by some of the king's guards and the rebellion suddenly ended. Although Richard did not play a major role in quashing the uprising, it became clear to him during the revolt that his people truly held him in high esteem. He was perceived as an individual who could not only lead the country but also solve its problems.

With his maturation and his marriage to Anne of Bohemia on January 14, 1382, Richard gradually became a more confident ruler. He increasingly made his ideas and opinions known to the regency council. Richard's outspokenness contributed to a dangerous division of the council into a faction of his supporters and an opposing one that leaned toward Richard's uncle, John of Gaunt (father of Henry Bolingbroke, the future Henry IV). In July, 1386, John sailed off to Portugal in an attempt to conquer the kingdom of Castile for England and himself.

His departure initially relieved the factional tensions on the regency council, but the manipulative Gloucester soon began to dominate it. Gloucester, attempting to build his own base of power, incited Parliament, which had convened on October 1, 1386, in order to raise money for an anticipated French invasion, to attack the wasteful manner in which Richard and his supporters spent parliamentary revenues. Gloucester went so far as to request that Parliament be given the records of the deposition of King Edward II from 1327, so that the members could learn how to rid themselves of a "bad" king who ruled with corrupt advisers. Richard viewed Gloucester's maneuvers as treasonous but did not dare to arrest him. Instead, Richard began to gather an army that would give him the power to silence Gloucester and his rapidly growing party of critics. Throughout 1387, however, Gloucester's own military support outnumbered and outmaneuvered Richard's. Capitulating to Gloucester and the other four "lords appellant" (among whom numbered Henry IV), Richard returned to London, called a meeting of Parliament for February, 1388, and surrendered to his uncle Gloucester's domination. With this "Merciless Parliament," Gloucester directed impeachment proceedings against many of the king's supporters and advisers, some of whom were executed, banished, or imprisoned by order of the Parliament.

Shattered and weak, Richard accepted the domination of his uncles despite his declaration in May, 1389, that he could rule the kingdom on his own. In August, 1389, Richard requested that John of Gaunt return from his unsuccessful campaign against Castile and negotiated truces with all of England's foreign enemies. Accepting the outcome of the 1388 purge for the moment, Richard led England into a short-lived era of peace. From 1388 to 1397, the kingdom was prosperous, Parliament was pleased with the low level of taxation, and Richard became accustomed to self-rule, even under his uncles' shadows. This period was marred only by Queen Anne's death on June 7, 1394. As Anne and Richard had produced no heirs, Richard needed to marry again. In July, 1395, King Charles VI of France, wishing to negotiate a permanent peace treaty, offered his eldest daughter, the seven-year-old Isabella, to Richard as a symbol of their friendship. Isabella and Richard were married on November 4, 1395, at Calais.

Although cowed by the events of 1387 and 1388, Richard ultimately obtained his revenge: On July 8, 1397, the king ordered the arrests of Gloucester; Thomas Arundel, archbishop of Canterbury; and Thomas Beauchamp, earl of Warwick, all of whom had participated in the impeachment of Richard's supporters during the Merciless Parliament of 1388. Richard charged them all with treason, and in September, 1397, Parliament found them guilty. Warwick was sentenced to exile on the Isle of Man, while Arundel was banished from the kingdom. Gloucester, who was found guilty posthumously, had been smothered by his captors early in September, on orders of the king.

From September, 1397, until September, 1399, Richard ruled with a striking determination. He was ruthless and developed policies that were at once incoherent and absolute. For example, he announced his intention to punish several counties that had not supported him from 1387 to 1388 by exacting a heavy fine, yet he did not state when he would collect the fine, creating great financial uncertainty and emphasizing his absolute royal arbitrariness. Perhaps his riskiest act was the banishment of both his supporter Thomas Mowbray, duke of Norfolk and earl of Nottingham, and Henry Bolingbroke, duke of Hereford and earl of Derby, as a settlement of a quarrel between the two regarding an alleged conspiracy against the king. When John of Gaunt died on February 3, 1399, Richard greedily seized his property and prevented Bolingbroke from receiving his inheritance. This royal seizure of land created much dissatisfaction among the nobility who thought that the king had overstepped his authority.

While Richard was on a military campaign in Ireland during the summer of 1399, Bolingbroke seized the opportunity to return from his banishment and demand his inheritance. Although he landed in England with fewer than one hundred soldiers, he quickly won the support of Parliament and nearly every nobleman in the kingdom. Politically and militarily more powerful than the king, Bolingbroke demanded that Richard abdicate his throne. On September 29, 1399, Richard agreed to resign his crown. The following day, Parliament assembled and deprived Richard of his crown because of his "crimes and cruelties." With the throne vacant, Parliament crowned Bolingbroke Henry IV, king of England and Wales. Richard, now Henry's prisoner, was taken first to the Tower of London and then to Pontefract Castle in Yorkshire, where he was allegedly murdered in February, 1400.

SIGNIFICANCE

Although Richard II's reign was brief and riddled with political machinations and murders, it provides vivid illustrations of the problems confronting a late medieval monarch and of the constitutional development of England. Richard's struggle with his domineering uncles—

powerful noblemen in their own right—and the Parliament, which they manipulated, reveals that the title "king" was not always enough to ensure a monarch's ability to rule according to his desires. By the end of the Middle Ages, Parliament and the nobility challenged and limited the monarch's ability to rule. It was this tug-of-war between his own desires and the various demands of his subjects that made Richard's task of ruling England so difficult.

For Richard, the consequences of this power struggle were fatal, regardless of whether it was a result of a flaw in his character, as William Shakespeare portrays it, or a result of a desire to exercise royal authority against traitors, as Richard himself saw it. For England, however, Richard's reign witnessed the firm establishment of the constitutional concept that subjects can, in many ways, respond to an abusive king. During the later Middle Ages, subjects more frequently made public complaints about the state of the kingdom and English parliaments had begun to restrain the king by refusing to provide him with funds to pursue his policies. With the deposition of Richard II, noblemen and Parliament demonstrated their ability and willingness to use more dramatic means to resist royal encroachments on the legal and property rights of Englishmen. Over the next three centuries, the struggle for the control of England by subjects and Parliament, on one hand, and the monarch seeking to utilize a "divinely inspired" power, on the other, resulted in the permanent constitutional limitation of royal power.

—*David M. Bessen*

FURTHER READING

Bennett, Michael. *Richard II and the Revolution of 1399*. Stroud, England: Sutton, 1999. Overview of Richard from age ten to his downfall, from a psychological as well as political perspective.

Costain, Thomas B. *The Last Plantagenets*. New York: Doubleday, 1962. A popular and anecdotal account of the reigns of English kings from Richard II through Richard III, with much emphasis on the character and personality of the rulers.

Dodd, Gwilym, ed. *The Reign of Richard II*. Charleston, S.C.: Tempus, 2000. A collection of essays offering new insights into Richard's reign.

Fowler, Kenneth. *The Age of Plantagenet and Valois: The Struggle for Supremacy, 1328-1498*. New York: Putnam, 1967. A well-illustrated and informative book about England and France during the Hundred Years' War. The book surveys the causes and the course of the conflict, as well as providing descriptions of the social context and the nature of the war itself.

Goodman, Anthony, and James Gillespie, eds. *Richard II: The Art of Kingship*. New York: Oxford University Press, 1999. An international group of scholars reassesses Richard's reign in the light of the way English kingship and related institutions were evolving during the Middle Ages.

Hilton, Rodney. *Bond Men Made Free: Medieval Peasant Movements and the English Rising of 1381*. New York: Methuen, 1977. The standard modern account of the Peasants' Revolt of 1381, set in the context of the late fourteenth century and the economic crisis caused by the Black Death and the Hundred Years' War. The book also surveys the general history of peasant revolts in the Middle Ages.

Holmes, George. *The Later Middle Ages, 1272-1485*. New York: W. W. Norton, 1962. A survey of the High Middle Ages in England, providing a balanced overview of social, ecclesiastical, and political history, in addition to a brief history of the Wars of the Roses.

Saul, Nigel. *Richard II*. New Haven, Conn.: Yale University Press, 1999. Examines the monarch and his rule, characterized by feuding and dissention. Illustrated.

SEE ALSO: John Ball; Edward III; Henry IV (of England); Wat Tyler.

RELATED ARTICLES in *Great Events from History: The Middle Ages, 477-1453*: 1347-1352: Invasion of the Black Death in Europe; May-June, 1381: Peasants' Revolt in England; 1387-1400: Chaucer Writes *The Canterbury Tales*.

COLA DI RIENZO
Italian ruler

Though his reign as tribune of Rome was short-lived, Rienzo put in place genuine reforms that effectively broke the power of nobles and barons who had been plundering the city in the manner of warlords.

BORN: 1313; Rome (now in Italy)
DIED: October 8, 1354; Rome
ALSO KNOWN AS: Nicola di Lorenzo (given name)
AREA OF ACHIEVEMENT: Government and politics

EARLY LIFE

Little is known about the early life of Cola di Rienzo (RYEHNT-soh). The anonymous fourteenth century biography to which modern sources are much indebted concentrates mostly on Rienzo's meteoric rise to power and his rule as tribune of Rome. Though scant, evidence suggests that he was born the son of a poor innkeeper and his wife in a Roman slum in 1313. Because his mother was dying while he was still a small boy, Rienzo was brought by his father to relatives in the town of Anagni, where he was reared.

Like so many great men and women, Rienzo exhibited a love of learning early in his life. He was a zealous youth who read avidly Livy's history of Rome, acquainted himself with the classical poets Vergil and Horace, and patterned his own rhetorical style on the works of Cicero. Exactly how Rienzo gained access to these writings and exactly who these relatives in Anagni were to have afforded the boy the opportunity for such study are matters that remain unresolved. It is clear, however, that by the time he was twenty years old, Rienzo had returned to Rome a master of classical literature.

At this time, the dawn of the Renaissance, Rome was a virtual armed camp. The Papacy—a unifying force of medieval society—had abandoned the city in 1305, when the new pope, Clement V, a Frenchman, determined to make the town of Avignon his seat of government. For more than seventy years, this small village in the Rhone River valley was the center of Western Christendom. Meanwhile, Rome itself was left as political carrion. Two great families, the Colonna and the Orsini, ruled as medieval barons. Living in their fortified estates, they plundered at will like gangsters. The city was dangerous, falling into decay. Marble from the ancient public buildings was taken as booty. The air was rank from the surrounding Campagna di Roma, a morass that in summer bred the plague. Cattle and pigs grazed in the streets, and beggars were everywhere.

Into this setting of urban rot and political chaos, Rienzo returned sometime in the early 1330's. Rienzo married the beautiful daughter of a notary, and he became a public notary himself, soon gaining the reputation for being a clever, efficient, and honest public servant.

For the next decade, Rienzo pursued the modest duties of his office. He also spent time studying the ancient Roman inscriptions, talking to the peasants, perfecting his knowledge of Latin and the classics, and above all becoming deeply imbued with the glories of the past, when Rome was the center of Western civilization.

LIFE'S WORK

This deep love for the Roman past had become a guiding principle for Rienzo. He dreamed of making Rome the supreme city it had once been. Inspired by a brief popular uprising in 1339 that had failed for lack of papal support, Rienzo was convinced that the first step in bringing Rome out of its desperate condition was to gain the support of the pope, whose influence was indispensable. The pope could raise an army in those days, and the Church's territorial and political claims rivaled those of the Holy Roman Empire. Although he resided in Avignon, the new pope, Clement VI, would claim Rome as part of his traditional see. Rienzo aligned himself with those men in Rome who saw that the pope should be coaxed into declaring a jubilee for 1350, thus making Rome a commercial and cultural locus for travelers, pilgrims, and all other Christians. In 1342, having persuaded the Romans that only he could sell Clement on the idea, Rienzo left Rome, alone, for Avignon.

There, in 1343, Rienzo secured a papal audience. He denounced the noble oppressors of Rome and sought the pontiff's favor with such stunning rhetoric that Clement—himself a scholar and orator—was deeply impressed by the young notary. In Avignon, Rienzo also became acquainted with the famous poet and Humanist Petrarch, whose work was ushering in a new literary movement. Having been appointed to the papal staff, Petrarch, like Clement, was struck by Rienzo's eloquence. He was to become an enduring supporter of Rienzo and at this time took him into the papal court, introducing him to influential and powerful men. Rienzo stayed at the court for more than a year, but in 1344, he returned to Rome, having been given the office of papal notary, a steady income, and an entrée into the political fabric of his city.

For the next three years, Rienzo, now financially secure, continued to engage in scholarship. Though genuine, his studies were only a temporary resort; he was waiting for an opportunity to fulfill his dream of bringing Rome to greatness. Meanwhile, he gathered about him loyal supporters, men who were impressed with his learning and shared his dream.

Rienzo's opportunity arose in 1347, with one of those events in which chance and natural ability conjoin, shaping a turning point in the career of a great man. In pursuit of his studies, Rienzo happened on a bronze plate virtually buried among the debris of a rebuilt church. As he began to decipher the timeworn inscription, he discovered that he had unearthed the original text of the Lex Regia, the ancient law by which the rights of the Roman people were transferred to Vespasian, who ruled the Roman Empire from 69 to 79 C.E. Though the law was well known and had been the subject of academic discussions throughout the Middle Ages, Rienzo saw his discovery of the plate as an opportunity to give his own interpretation on the law. In his best rhetorical style, he called a public meeting and read the law, indicting the barons, the members of the aristocratic families who were in control of city government, as subversives.

When the leaders of these families, the Orsini and the Colonna, left Rome on business, taking with them their militia, Rienzo saw the time as ripe. Gathering his own forces, he organized an uprising in May, 1347, and quickly took power. Speaking before the assembled populace, he denounced the nobles and proclaimed Rome free of their tyranny. Showing the lack of tact for which he was famous, Rienzo declared himself tribune of Rome—a title redolent of ancient honor—and installed as his partner in government the pope's vicar, the bishop of Orvieto, thus preempting any military intervention by the pope by showing deference to papal authority.

For the next seven months, Rienzo was the master of Rome. He had broken the power of the barons and now put forth a new constitution that contained several notable reforms, among them the dismissal and punishment of all corrupt judges and the establishment of civil pro-

Depiction of Cola di Rienzo vowing revenge for the death of his brother, from a painting by William Holman Hunt. (Hulton|Archive at Getty Images)

grams protecting the poor and the weak. Rienzo also initiated a program of taxation and trade that gave Rome a fiscal stability it did not have under the barons.

Rienzo's next move was to make Rome the acknowledged capital of the Italian peninsula, as it had once been the center of the Western world. To this end, he arranged to give himself a triumph, a magnificent procession through the city to the steps of the capitol, where he would be crowned. Designed to evoke the ancient Roman custom in which a great leader would be carried through the streets in glory, Rienzo's triumph was more than a sop to his vanity: It was a dramatic rite, a political symbol of Roman sovereignty. Rome's preeminence was promoted by scores of letters that Rienzo, as tribune, addressed to major Italian cities, urging them to forge informal alliances with Rome; such letters always showed tact and diplomacy so as not to incite either the emperor or the pope.

Yet Rienzo's effective rule was to be short-lived. The opulence and pomp with which he played the role of tribune—his triumph culminating in a lavish feast reminiscent of the decadent caesars—scandalized many of his loyal followers. In addition, Rienzo's complete humiliation of the barons, his cruelty and severity in dealing with them, made him enemies among those relatives of the barons who held powerful positions in the papal court—including Cardinal Orsini.

By September, 1347, the pope's vicar arrived in Rome with orders to plumb Rienzo's true fealty to the Holy See. Distrustful of Rienzo's pledges of obedience, the cardinal legate called for the popular leader's immediate resignation. The pope, meanwhile, had already issued an edict of excommunication against him. Bereft of any appeal and facing pressure from the barons, Rienzo resigned his tribunate on December 15, 1347.

Abandoned, Rienzo fled to Naples, where he sought aid from King Louis. Yet the Black Death, which was then ravaging the city, forced Louis to leave, and Rienzo saw the last of his allies withdraw from Italy. Fearing death—either from the papal forces or from the plague—Rienzo fled once again, this time to the mountains of central Italy, where he joined an order of Franciscan monks. The Franciscans accepted Rienzo as a kindred spirit, for they had called for a purging of the impurities of the Church (as Rienzo had sought to cleanse the civil government of its abuses). He stayed in this mountain retreat for about a year, returning briefly to Rome in his Franciscan robes before fleeing to Prague, where he hoped to persuade the emperor, Charles IV, to support his cause.

Charles, however, was not disposed to help Rienzo when such aid might antagonize the pope. The emperor wished to maintain a balance between the papal jurisdiction and his own attempts to consolidate his power. Rienzo was a threat to that balance, and Charles thus kept him imprisoned for several years, forestalling any commitments to the pope. In 1351, the pope's envoys officially ordered the extradition of Rienzo, and Charles released him to the papal authorities. In Avignon once again, this time as prisoner, Rienzo was to be tried for heresy when Clement VI died in 1352. The new pope was Innocent VI, whose administration, seeking reforms, believed that it could use Rienzo as a stabilizing force in the chaos of Roman politics. Through Rienzo, the Papacy hoped to regain jurisdiction over Rome.

Reinstated, Rienzo again rode into Italy, this time as a senator in support of the pope. After months of rebuilding friendships and raising money, Rienzo took control of the city in September, 1354. His time, however, had clearly passed. Those years of absence had irrevocably lost for him any hold on the civil government. The irascible barons had regrouped, and the economy of the city had once again fallen prey to mismanagement. Unable to raise enough money to pay his mercenaries, who had formed the largest portion of his army, Rienzo imposed taxes on food, wine, and salt. Prompted by the Colonna family, a mob stormed Rienzo's palace. On October 8, 1354, they dragged him to the steps of the capitol and murdered him, hanging him from his feet for two days while children threw stones at his corpse. The following year, Innocent VI absolved all persons involved in the assassination of Rienzo.

Significance

Rienzo's career can be evaluated from several points of view. To some historians, he was a dictator, a proto-Fascist whose self-glorification helped to bring him down. To others, such as Victorian novelist Edward Bulwer-Lytton (1803-1873) and the composer Richard Wagner (1813-1883), each of whom treated Rienzo as the subject of a major work, the popular leader was a hero, a patriot sacrificed on the altar of freedom. Yet Rienzo's career is more clearly understood in the broader context of fourteenth century European history—a period of economic stagnation and political divisiveness, when the Church was struggling to remain whole in spite of an "expatriated" Papacy and an enervating secularism.

Rienzo viewed himself as a dreamer, and his apologists, such as Petrarch, commended his patriotism in support of his dreams. Yet his ambition for Rome, and for himself, was of necessity thwarted by the political and social turbulence that signaled the end of the Middle

Ages and the dawn of the Renaissance. Last, his devotion to classical studies certainly puts him in the position of harbinger of the new age.

—*Edward Fiorelli*

FURTHER READING

Collins, Amanda. *Greater than Emperor: Cola di Rienzo and the World of Fourteenth Century Rome.* Ann Arbor: University of Michigan Press, 2002. This biography of Rienzo focuses on his power and the environment in which he governed. Bibliography and index.

Cosenza, Mario Emilio. *Francesco Petrarca and the Revolution of Cola di Rienzo.* Chicago: University of Chicago Press, 1913. A seminal source, discussing Rienzo's concept of a united Italy and the political thought of Petrarch. Drawn largely from the letters of Rienzo and Petrarch, the study concludes that both men were centuries ahead of their time.

The Life of Cola di Rienzo. Translated by John Wright. Toronto: Pontifical Institute of Mediaeval Studies, 1975. The anonymous fourteenth century biography that is the primary source of information on Rienzo. Contains an excellent introduction by the translator, who provides a concise historical background of the period and the various critical views of Rienzo's character.

Musto, Ronald G. *Apocalypse in Rome: Cola di Rienzo and the Politics of the New Age.* Berkeley: University of California Press, 2003. A biography of Cola di Rienzo that describes his role as tribune. Bibliography and index.

Petrarca, Francesco. *The Revolution of Cola di Rienzo.* 3d ed. New York: Italica Press, 1996. A translation of Petrarch's letters and the letters of Cola di Rienzo as well as from the Church's archives. The introduction by Ronald G. Musto provides valuable information on the letters and Rienzo. Bibliography and index.

SEE ALSO: Charles IV; Petrarch.

RELATED ARTICLES in *Great Events from History: The Middle Ages, 477-1453*: c. 1320: Origins of the Bubonic Plague; 1347-1352: Invasion of the Black Death in Europe; May 20, 1347-October 8, 1354: Cola di Rienzo Leads Popular Uprising in Rome; c. 1350-1400: Petrarch and Boccaccio Recover Classical Texts.

ROLLO

Norwegian-born count of Rouen (911-c. 932)

Rollo established the Norman Dynasty—made up of Scandinavians who settled the lower Seine Valley—after signing an agreement with Charlemagne to protect the region. The Normans under William the Conqueror eventually invaded England in 1066.

BORN: c. 860; present-day Norway
DIED: c. 932; Rouen, Normandy (now in France)
ALSO KNOWN AS: Rolf; Rou; Rollon; Hrolfr
AREA OF ACHIEVEMENT: Government and politics

EARLY LIFE

Rollo (RAHL-oh), probably a son of the Norse earl of Möre, was born in Scandinavia at the height of the Viking raids on the entire coastline of Western Europe, including the British Isles. Most of what is known about Rollo's early life is based on legend or superstition. Among these tales is one that suggests that he joined the journeys of the Swedes into Russia in his early years. Another has him taking part in a conspiracy against the Norwegian king Harold Fairhair. According to the legend, the king broke up the conspiracy, and Rollo was sentenced to banishment. Whatever the initial impetus, Rollo became part of the wave of Scandinavian raiders that terrorized Western Europe in the ninth and tenth centuries.

Although the conditions that prompted this assault on Christianized Western Europe by men dedicated to pagan beliefs are not well established, it is probable that overpopulation in Scandinavia, attributed by some writers to the common Norse practice of polygamy, was the chief cause. Another factor was the development of a new type of ship, the clinker-built, low-draft vessel sometimes called a dragon ship. The legends of the Vikings are closely bound up with such ships, which figure prominently in medieval portrayals of the Vikings. Possession of these craft enabled the Vikings to sail out to sea instead of hugging the shore, allowing them to range over all the Atlantic coastline of Europe and eventually as far west as Iceland, Greenland, and North America.

LIFE'S WORK

Rollo appears to have left the ancestral home in the early 880's. Some legends suggest he went to England, others that he may have gone to Ireland. For whatever reason, he went either directly or indirectly to the coast of France, where he quickly became the leader of the Viking band located along the lower Seine River. The Vikings had been conducting raids up the Seine as far as Paris since 845, but the earlier raids had ended with the Vikings sailing back down the river and retreating to Scandinavia. In the early 850's, however, instead of returning to Scandinavia, the Viking bands wintered on the lower Seine, conducting intermittent raids into the surrounding countryside. In 876, another raiding party advanced on Paris but was persuaded to leave when the Frankish king offered a ransom. Still, ransom sufficed only to induce the Vikings to retreat to the lower Seine. It was there that Rollo joined them around 885 and became their leader.

Engraved depiction of the treaty made between Charles VI, left, and Rollo. (F. Pease)

Under Rollo, the Vikings resolved on another attack on Paris. After an intermittent siege of the city lasting some two years, the Frankish ruler, Charles the Fat, bought off the band, which retired to the lower Seine Valley around Rouen. There, the Viking camp was gradually converted to a colony, joined by new immigrants from Scandinavia after 887.

Many legends accumulated around Rollo at this time. One is that he was so tall that he was unable to ride a horse because his long legs easily reached the ground when he was mounted. The Vikings, when asked to name their lord, were said to have replied to their questioners, "We have no lord, for we are all equal." They apparently regarded Rollo not as their lord but simply as their leader in battle.

From their camp on the lower Seine, the Vikings under Rollo staged regular raids into the surrounding countryside. Although the Vikings were unable to capture the town of Chârtres when they besieged it in 887, the Frankish king was unable to oppose them effectively. They were able to find many areas where they could collect booty, mostly from the monasteries that dotted the countryside. It was at this time that the popular prayer arose: "From the fury of the Northmen, dear Lord, deliver us."

Increasingly, in all parts of Western Europe, the Vikings no longer sailed again for home after a successful raid but instead remained in settlements along the coast. New bands joined the older ones, adding more fighters to the group. Until the middle of the following century, a continuous surge of men and even some women built up the population of the Viking settlements along the coast of France. Similar settlements occurred in Scotland, Ireland, and England; in England, the English king, Alfred the Great, finally reached an agreement in 878 that effectively turned over the northwestern part of the country to the Scandinavians.

The assaults of the Vikings reflected not only the ethnic differences between the Vikings and the Franks (the inhabitants of the France of the time) but also the religious differences. The Franks had been Christians for more than three centuries; the Vikings, by contrast, worshiped a collection of gods headed by Odin or Wotan. Many of the targets of the Viking raiders were monasteries, not only because more portable booty was to be collected there but also because the monasteries represented and symbolized a religion the Vikings did not respect.

Moreover, in those turbulent years, religion was one of the principal means rulers had to pacify their subjects. From the days of Charlemagne, who was crowned emperor of a renewed Roman empire in Western Europe in 800, the rulers had used the advance of Christianity as both a justification for imperial expansion and a means of keeping control of the lands conquered. Charlemagne had pushed Christianity into northern Germany, into lands bordering Scandinavia; some authorities believe that the threat of Christianity sparked the earliest Viking raids.

By concentrating on the monasteries as the objects of their raids, the Vikings undermined the authority of the Christian rulers of the Franks and captured the wealth that many monasteries had acquired during the preceding centuries. Unable to rely on the network of monasteries created by his predecessors, the Frankish ruler, Charles the Fat, lasted but three years on the throne and was replaced by one of the powerful nobles who had defended Paris effectively against the Viking assault. After five years of civil war, another Charles, Charles the Simple, won the throne. He was no more able than his predecessors to hold off the Vikings, and in 911, he conceived of another policy to deal with the Vikings: signing a treaty with them that made them, in effect, the defenders of the lower Seine Valley against future Viking assaults.

Although the precise terms of the Treaty of St.-Clair-sur-Epte between Rollo and Charles the Simple were not recorded (or, if they were, the records have not survived), it is fairly clear that the agreement envisaged ceding to Rollo and his followers responsibility for the defense of the lower Seine Valley. Rollo was made count of Rouen and of Evreux (the title of duke of Normandy was first acquired by his grandson, although it is commonly applied to him) and agreed to be baptized as a Christian, an event that apparently occurred the following year, in 912. It may also have been agreed that Rollo would marry a daughter of Charles named Gisela. According to legend, Charles required Rollo to kiss his foot as a demonstration of subordination. Rollo refused to do so and assigned the task to a member of his entourage. This bold Viking, so the story goes, seized the king's foot and lifted it up before kissing it, so that the king fell backward. True or not, the story illustrates Rollo's unwillingness to accept subordination to anyone.

Although Rollo had agreed to be baptized a Christian, it is doubtful that he took his conversion seriously. His followers continued to raid the parts of France not consigned to his responsibility as count of Rouen. He is reported on his deathbed to have required his men to make a typical sacrifice to the pagan gods of the Norse, along with the rites of Christian burial. He also adhered to the marriage rites of his people, taking as his wife a daughter of one of the local Viking bands named Poppa. Poppa was the mother of William, who was to succeed Rollo as count of Rouen at his death.

Yet although he retained much of the Norse culture into which he was born, Rollo seized on his new responsibility to create the beginnings of an administrative system that became the hallmark of the Normans, as the Scandinavian inhabitants of the area around Rouen came to be called. Reversing one previous policy of the Vikings, he began the restoration of the monasteries his men had so wantonly destroyed. Particularly around Rouen itself, he rebuilt the church and used his control of the archbishops of his new possession to maintain his authority. He built fortresses along his border and assigned them to followers on whose allegiance he could count. He effectively played politics among the many contenders for political power in the France of his day, and for his allegiance to the Carolingian ruler, he won the addition to his holdings of land around Bayeux, to the west of Rouen.

Rollo died, probably in Rouen, around 932; he was buried in the Rouen cathedral. He was succeeded by his son, William Long-Sword, whom he had associated with himself in managing his realm for several years. In the years following Rollo's death, Normandy quickly became absorbed into the prevailing Frankish culture, until little survived of the Scandinavian origins of the Normans. Despite vicissitudes, the family of Rollo retained control of Normandy for several centuries. Rollo's great-great grandson was William the Conqueror, the duke of Normandy who seized England in 1066.

SIGNIFICANCE

Despite his origin in a society dedicated to vandalizing neighboring countries, Rollo revealed that, properly engaged, the Norse who became the Normans had constructive political skills of a high order, especially noteworthy in that turbulent time. Normandy under Rollo and his descendants was almost always at peace, whatever might be the state of affairs elsewhere in the land that was to become modern France. In some respects, he set the stage for the feudalism that was to become the primary method of providing a minimal degree of government in an age when military prowess was the mark of leadership. Rollo, and his successors, used the alliance between the Church and the secular authorities most successfully as a means of preserving peace.

—*Nancy M. Gordon*

FURTHER READING

Bates, David. *Normandy Before 1066*. New York: Longman, 1982. Emphasizes the distinctive features of Norman society, distinguishing them from those of Norman England.

Chibnall, Marjorie. *The Normans*. Malden, Mass.: Blackwell, 2000. Part of the Peoples of Europe series. The author briefly explores the life of the Normans in the medieval period, including their emergence as a distinct people in Normandy, their conquest and settlement of lands such as England, and more. Brief bibliography and index.

Crouch, David. *The Normans: The History of a Dynasty*. London: Hambledon and London, 2002. Explores the history of the Norman Dynasty and the dukes of Normandy. Illustrations, bibliography, and index.

Dudo of St. Quentin. *History of the Normans*. Translated by Eric Christiansen. Rochester, N.Y.: Boydell Press, 1998. The first English translation, with introduction and notes by the translator, of a work written around 1015. A partly fictionalized history of the Normans, which follows the trials and tribulations of Rollo's "family." Language might be difficult for beginning readers, but the text discusses why certain words are used in their respective ways.

Haskins, Charles Homer. *The Normans in European History*. New York: Ungar, 1959. The classic account in English, first published in 1915, of the Normans and their place in European history. The chapters deal with successive developments in the Norman role, chiefly in England; the first two chapters serve as general background.

Jones, Gwyn. *A History of the Vikings*. Rev. ed. New York: Oxford University Press, 1984. Although the Vikings in Normandy constitute only a small part of the whole story of the Viking expansion, Rollo can best be approached by reading about the Vikings in general.

Mawer, Allen. "The Vikings." In *The Cambridge Medieval History*. Vol. 3. New York: Cambridge University Press, 1929. Old text but still useful for hard-to-find information about Rollo. A look at chapter 13, as well as chapters 3 and 4, will introduce Rollo and help set the stage for his accomplishments within the context of the Frankish kingdom.

Shopkow, Leah. *History and Community: Norman Historical Writing in the Eleventh and Twelfth Centuries*. Washington, D.C.: Catholic University of America Press, 1997. A critical evaluation of the writers on whom historians depend for accounts of the achievements of Rollo and his successors. Since there are virtually no contemporary accounts of Rollo, a critical view of the writers of subsequent accounts is vital to knowing about him.

SEE ALSO: Alfred the Great; Charlemagne; Leif Eriksson; William the Conqueror.

RELATED ARTICLES in *Great Events from History: The Middle Ages, 477-1453*: 850-950: Viking Era; 878: Alfred Defeats the Danes; 11th-12th centuries: First European-Native American Contact; October 14, 1066: Battle of Hastings; 1169-1172: Normans Invade Ireland.

RUDOLF I
Holy Roman Emperor (r. 1273-1291)

Rudolf, as the first of his family to achieve eminence, founded a dynasty that was to remain one of the most important royal families in Europe for more than six centuries.

BORN: May 1, 1218; Limburg-im-Breisgau (now in Germany)
DIED: July 15, 1291; Speyer (now in Germany)
ALSO KNOWN AS: Rudolf of Habsburg
AREA OF ACHIEVEMENT: Government and politics

EARLY LIFE

Until the age of fifty-five, when events were to raise him to the German throne as king of the Romans, Rudolf I was a relatively insignificant noble in northern Switzerland. His family originated in Alsace, near Mulhouse, and his lands included areas of Swabia, Alsace, and Switzerland that lie in modern southern Germany, eastern France, and northwestern Switzerland. He oversaw these possessions from Habichtsburg (goshawk's castle) in Aargau Canton. As was usual at the time, the family name was taken from the castle, and Habichtsburg came to be known as Habsburg. This area became so important to the Habsburgs as the site of their origin that Emperor Francis-Joseph I tried to buy it from the Swiss just before World War I. The Swiss refused, as they considered themselves well rid of the Habsburgs. In fact, Switzerland still celebrates its national holiday on August 1, which is the anniversary of the day in 1291 when news of the death of Rudolf I arrived.

Until his election, Rudolf had been quite active in disputes with the bishop of Basel and other quarrels within Switzerland. In 1254, he had been involved in a crusade against the Prussian Slavs and had gained a good reputation as a military leader. Although all this sounds impressive, he was actually rather unimportant in comparison with several other German nobles who controlled more land and were more powerful. He ranked only as a count in the feudal hierarchy.

Despite his comparatively low status, or rather because of it, he was elected to the throne in 1273. The reasons for this apparently extraordinary election are to be found in the conditions prevailing in Europe after the fall of the Hohenstaufen imperial dynasty in the middle of the thirteenth century. The trouble had begun with Emperor Frederick II. Although Frederick was a Hohenstaufen, his interests were in Sicily and Italy. In fact, he had never been to Germany before his election in 1212. His absence from Germany and his involvement in a feud with the Papacy over control of Italy meant that the German nobles were free to strengthen their own territories and establish their independence from imperial control. The situation continued to deteriorate under Frederick's successors; between 1250 and 1272, there was a succession of weak emperors, some of whom never entered Germany. The German nobles believed that it was in their interest to perpetuate this situation because it afforded them opportunities to increase their personal power. They very willingly exchanged support for one imperial candidate or another in return for concessions, such as control of cities, the right to collect tolls, and grants of land.

It also appeared to be in the interest of various foreign powers to prevent the election of a strong emperor. The French, in particular, were interested in obtaining territory in Alsace, Lorraine, Burgundy, and other areas west of the Rhine River that were controlled by the emperor. The English were usually interested in opposing French ambitions, and the Papacy was interested in these struggles as well as in increasing its temporal power in Italy. Moreover, some popes were very eager to see a new crusade to the Holy Land. Opposing foreign powers championed candidates who would further their causes, and there were often two claimants, each of whom maintained that he had been elected. The results were minor wars and a state of near anarchy within Germany.

With the death of the latest nominal ruler, Richard of Cornwall, in 1272, Pope Gregory X determined that something had to be done to change the situation. He was primarily alarmed at the growing power of France. There had been suggestions from the French that the king of France should be made Holy Roman Emperor, since France was the most powerful country in Europe and could do most for the position. The Papacy was not interested in having an emperor who was too strong or too independent of the pope. With the territorial encroachments by France into Germany becoming increasingly bold, Gregory feared that France would soon be too powerful to resist. He therefore threatened the electors with a candidate of his own choice if they did not elect a suitable German noble. The German aristocracy did not want a strong emperor, so they turned to someone who posed little threat to their independence.

LIFE'S WORK

Rudolf's main ambition from the beginning of his reign in 1273 was to acquire as much land as possible for himself and to establish a hereditary monarchy for his descendants. He was always willing to sacrifice some abstract imperial right or some advantage in a distant part of the empire in return for recognition of the hereditary principle or for territorial additions to his own possessions.

His first task was to defeat the powerful nobles who questioned his election to the throne. Soon after he was elected, the Diet of Speyer gave him the authority to take back all the imperial lands that had been usurped by nobles during the previous twenty-five years. He was unable to carry out any general plans he might have had to confiscate such lands for his own use, because he was too dependent on the support of nobles who controlled them. The authorization did, however, give him an excuse to proceed against some of his most dangerous enemies.

The most important of these enemies was Otakar II, king of Bohemia. Otakar had not been allowed to vote in the election of Rudolf and had other grievances, but his real motive for rebellion was the desire to be elected emperor himself. Rudolf laid siege to Vienna in 1276 and quickly obtained the surrender of Otakar. As punishment, Otakar was dispossessed of many of his lands, including Austria. Vienna thus became the new seat of Rudolf and remained the Habsburg capital until the twentieth century. Otakar received assistance from some of his Slav dependents and resumed his opposition to Rudolf in 1278. He was killed after one of the ensuing battles, and the major threat to Rudolf ended. After the defeat of Otakar, Rudolf's position was stronger, and he granted fewer exceptions to the prohibition against nobles retaining imperial lands.

The defeat of Otakar was the key event in establishing Rudolf's credibility. He was not directly challenged afterward, although there were numerous threatening incidents in addition to the usual refusal of individual knights and nobles to recognize his authority. There were, for example, several impostors who claimed to be either Frederick I Barbarossa or Frederick II, despite the fact that

Rudolf I receives news of his election as emperor. (Library of Congress)

HABSBURG MONARCHS

Reign	*Ruler*
1273-1291	RUDOLF I
1298-1308	Albert (Albrecht) I
1314-1325	Frederick of Habsburg (co-regent)
1438-1439	Albert II
1440/52-1493	Frederick III
1493/08-1519	Maximilian I
1519-1558	Charles V (last to be crowned as Holy Roman Emperor)
1558-1564	Ferdinand I
1564-1576	Maximilian II
1576-1612	Rudolf II
1612-1619	Matthias
1619-1637	Ferdinand II
1637-1657	Ferdinand III
1658-1705	Leopold I
1705-1711	Joseph I
1711-1740	Charles VI
1740-1742	Interregnum
1742-1745	Charles VII (Wittelsbach-Habsburg)
1745-1765	Francis I (Lorraine)
1745-1780	Maria Theresa (empress consort; queen of Hungary, 1740; empress dowager, 1765)

Note: Slashes are preceded by year of ascendancy as German king and followed by year of ascendancy as Holy Roman Emperor; otherwise, beginning of range indicates beginning of both offices.

both had been dead for many years. The legend persisted that one or the other of them was not dead, but merely sleeping, and would return in an hour of need. In 1285, Rudolf had one of the most significant of these impostors, Dietrich Holzschuh, burned at the stake. The impostors were a real threat, because they could become focal points for revolt. Rudolf's execution of Holzschuh demonstrated that he was able to deal with such threats.

Rudolf's power and prestige grew to such an extent that he was able to field a large and impressive army against Otto IV, Count Palatine of Franche-Comté. This rebel count had conspired with the king of France to gain independence from the empire. His scheme failed in 1289 with the arrival of the imperial army, and Rudolf was left firmly in control.

Although Rudolf had been elected and had shown that he could exercise power, he was never crowned Holy Roman Emperor by the pope. Gregory X promised to perform the ceremony on several occasions but died before he could carry out his promise. One of his successors, Pope Nicholas III, was less cooperative. The negotiations between him and Rudolf over this issue are an indication of how weak the empire had become and how far Rudolf was willing to go to secure the succession of his family. In return for the imperial crown, Rudolf was prepared to give up all the historic claims by previous emperors to territory in Italy. He also recognized the temporal superiority of the pope. These great concessions produced no results, as death intervened again. Nicholas died in 1280, before the negotiations were complete, and, in 1287, the death of Pope Honorius IV prevented the coronation. By the time arrangements had been made with the new pope, Nicholas IV, Rudolf himself was too ill to make the journey to Rome. When he died, he still had not received the imperial crown. Without recognition as emperor, he could not have his son crowned king of Rome during his own lifetime; thus, Rudolf could never ensure the royal succession of his family.

The second feature of Rudolf's reign was his determination to increase his family's territorial holdings and pass them on to his sons. Soon after taking the defeated Otakar's lands, Rudolf made the acquisition permanent by naming his eldest son, Albert, duke of Austria and Styria. He attempted to extend his influence to the east by marrying the fourteen-year-old Isabella of Burgundy himself in 1284. Apparently, he hoped to carve out another duchy for his younger son, Rudolf, in Burgundy or Swabia. He also married his daughter to Wenceslaus II of Bohemia in a continuing effort to establish as many dynastic ties with important families as possible.

Clearly, the object of these maneuvers was to obtain recognition of his younger son as his successor to the throne. It appeared that he might succeed in that ambition, as a significant number of nobles agreed to recognize Rudolf's son as legitimate successor if Rudolf were crowned Holy Roman Emperor. With the death of the younger Rudolf in 1289, at the age of twenty, these hopes were dashed. The elder Rudolf's recent marriage had produced a third son, Johann, but he was still a baby, so the only remaining hope was his oldest son, Albert. In the eyes of most German nobles, Albert was too strong to be a safe king. His father had been too successful at acquiring territory for him. As usual, the German nobles preferred someone who was less of a threat to their independence.

By 1291, Rudolf's health was so bad that he was unable to make the trip to Rome to receive the imperial crown from the hands of the pope. In any case, there seemed little point in such an exercise after the death of the younger Rudolf. He considered abdicating in favor of Albert, but he had first to obtain recognition of Albert as his successor from the nobles. To that end, he called a diet at Frankfurt-am-Main in May, 1291. As expected, the nobles were unwilling to recognize Albert, and Rudolf left the diet for Speyer, where he wanted to be buried alongside previous emperors. He died there on July 15.

SIGNIFICANCE

Although Rudolf I was willing to trade privileges and concessions for recognition of his authority and for advantages to his family, he did maintain order throughout most of Germany and restore much of the lost prestige of the crown. He used force successfully when necessary, as shown by his campaigns against Otakar of Bohemia and Otto of Burgundy. The appearance of military prowess, his ability to deal with the complaints of cities and nobles, and his forceful suppression of insurrections gained a higher degree of respect for the throne than had existed for the past forty years.

Nevertheless, Rudolf was unable to accomplish any lasting constitutional changes that would alter the course of German history. The pattern of weak central authority and strong nobles that was to prevent the emergence of a German state on the model of France or England had been set. Without a hereditary monarch, those elected to the throne were mainly interested in gaining what they could for their families rather than strengthening the monarchy itself. In other words, in a feudal age when family meant everything, unless the monarchy could be seen as a family possession it would remain secondary in the policy of any king. Rudolf was no exception to this general pattern. He was able to restore something of the crown's prestige, but his gains in power were traded away by his successors in return for support for their election.

—*Philip Dwight Jones*

FURTHER READING

Barraclough, Geoffrey. *The Origins of Modern Germany*. New York: W. W. Norton, 1984. This volume is probably the best English-language discussion of Rudolf in the context of his times.

Crankshaw, Edward. *The Habsburgs: Portrait of a Dynasty*. New York: Viking Press, 1971. A readily available, popularized account of the Habsburgs, from Rudolf to the twentieth century. Many illustrations, including contemporary pictures of Rudolf. With anecdotes about his military campaigns.

Eyck, Frank. *Religion and Politics in German History: From the Beginnings to the French Revolution*. New York: St. Martin's Press, 1998. An analysis of how Germanic peoples preserved links with classical civilization through their ability to assimilate other cultures and peoples, from their alliances with eighth century popes through the Reformation and Counter-Reformation. The initial bond between the Germanic rulers and popes turned to conflict as the Papacy gained power. Tables, maps, bibliography, index.

Heer, Friedrich. *The Holy Roman Empire*. New York: Praeger, 1968. Translated from the German edition of 1967. Rudolf receives some attention in this account of the development of the Holy Roman Empire.

Jeep, John M., et al., eds. *Medieval Germany: An Encyclopedia*. New York: Garland, 2001. An A-Z encyclopedia that addresses all aspects of the German- and Dutch-speaking medieval world from 500 to 1500. Entries include individuals, events, and broad topics such as feudalism and pregnancy. Bibliographical references, index.

Moore, Robert Ian. *The First European Revolution, c. 970-1215*. Malden, Mass.: Blackwell, 2000. According to the publisher, "a radical reassessment of Europe from the late tenth to the early thirteenth centuries [arguing that] the period witnessed the first true 'revolution' in European society," supported by transformation of the economy, family life, political power structures, and the rise of the non-Mediterranean cities. Bibliography, index.

Wilks, Michael J. *The Problem of Sovereignty in the Later Middle Ages: The Papal Monarchy with Augustinus Triumphus and the Publicists*. New York: Cambridge University Press, 1963. This work provides a context for Rudolf, focusing on the relations between king and nobles.

SEE ALSO: Frederick I Barbarossa; Frederick II; Otto I.

RELATED ARTICLES in *Great Events from History: The Middle Ages, 477-1453*: August 10, 955: Otto I Defeats the Magyars; c. 960: Jews Settle in Bohemia; November 15, 1315: Swiss Victory at Morgarten over Habsburg Forces.

JALĀL AL-DĪN RŪMĪ
Muslim poet

Rūmī was the leading poet of Sufism, the eponymous founder of the still-active Maulawiyah Sufi order, and a direct inspiration for almost all subsequent Gnostic writing in the Islamic world.

BORN: c. September 30, 1207; Balkh (now in Afghanistan)
DIED: December 17, 1273; Konya, Asia Minor (now in Turkey)
ALSO KNOWN AS: Maulāna; Mawlānā
AREAS OF ACHIEVEMENT: Literature, religion and theology

EARLY LIFE

Jalāl al-Dīn Rūmī (juh-LAHL uhl-DEEN REWMEE), also known as Maulānā (our master), was born in Balkh, a major eastern city in what is now Afghanistan. His father, a well-known Sufi preacher and scholar, moved his family from Balkh across Iran and into Turkey shortly before (and perhaps in anticipatory fear of) the Mongols' devastating westward incursion into the Islamic world. Nishapur (now in Iran), the home of ʿAṭṭār (c. 1142-c. 1220), the leading Sufi poet before Rūmī, fell to the Mongols in 1219-1220. A generation later, in 1258, Hülegü, Genghis Khan's grandson, overran the Islamic capital of Baghdad and ended the caliphate.

Rūmī's family settled in Konya, in Turkish Anatolia, a region then called Rum, from which the poet later got the name "Rūmī," by which he is best known in the West. Rūmī studied the Qurʾān, religious sciences, and literature. He was expert in Arabic, but Persian was to be his literary language. When his father died, Rūmī, then twenty-three or twenty-four and married, assumed his position as a teacher in a religious school in Konya. Also at this time, Rūmī began further study of Sufi doctrine and further initiation into Sufi practice with Burhan al-Dīn Muhaqqiq, a former pupil of Rūmī's father. Burhan al-Dīn died in 1239 or 1240, by which time Rūmī was being referred to as "shaykh," the title indicating his standing as a Sufi mentor with students and followers.

To this point in his life, Rūmī was presumably an orthodox Sufi and had demonstrated no special interest in poetry or in music and dance as vehicles for or accompaniments to religious devotion and expression of faith. All this was to change in the fall of 1244, when he met a peripatetic and charismatic Sufi called Shams al-Dīn of Tabrīz (d. c. 1247). Rūmī felt mystical love for Shams of Tabrīz, who introduced the latter to wholehearted love as the true Sufi's requisite attitude and who became Rūmī's chief "sun" and source of illumination. Rūmī had apparently found in Shams the image of the Divine Beloved, a focus that would inspire the rest of his life. The intensity of the relationship caused Rūmī to begin to express himself in Persian lyric verse and to find special meaning and joy in music and dance.

The attraction of Shams for Rūmī and the former's influence on the latter did not please Rūmī's family and students. Presumably as a result of verbal abuse, perhaps including threats, Shams suddenly left Konya without telling anyone of his plans. This event brought Rūmī great sorrow and inspired the composition of Sufi verse lamenting the separation of lover from beloved. Nearly two years later, after hearing that Shams was in Syria, Rūmī sent his older son to bring the wandering dervish back to Konya.

The reunion of the two Sufis inspired Rūmī to compose further Sufi poems, this time on the union of lover and beloved. Yet again, however, some of Rūmī's followers and family members were vexed at Shams's presence in their community and his hold on Rūmī. Shams disappeared for good in late 1248 (reportedly murdered by Rūmī's son and disciples). Rūmī was again inconsolable and set out for Syria to find his mystical guide and beloved. The poet gradually came to realize, however, that the spirit of Shams was with him, that his poems were really Shams's voice. He consequently chose "Shams" as his own nom de plume.

LIFE'S WORK

Rūmī's life after the disappearance of Shams became as creative and inspirational as that of any literary-religious figure in history. He composed the bulk of the much-loved and inimitable Sufi lyrics in Persian that constitute the *Dīwan-i Shams-i Tabrīz* (*Selected Poems from the Dīwani Shamsi Tabriz*, 1898). The following is an especially appreciated example of these lyric poems, in a version by Reynold Nicholson, Rūmī's foremost Western editor and translator:

> This is love: to fly heavenward,
> To rend, every instant, a hundred veils.
> The first moment, to renounce life;
> The last step, to fare without feet.
> To regard this world as invisible,
> Not to see what appears to one's self.

"O heart," I said, "may it bless thee
To have entered the circles of lovers,
To look beyond the range of the eye,
To penetrate the windings of the bosom."

Not long after Shams's disappearance, Rūmī entered into a Sufi relationship with another man in whom he saw something of Shams. Called Sālah al-Dīn Zarkub, this man was reportedly illiterate and also not to the liking of Rūmī's other disciples. Nevertheless, Rūmī dedicated some poems to Sālah al-Dīn (who died in 1258), and Rūmī's eldest son married the latter's daughter. After Sālah al-Dīn's death, Rūmī became interested in a disciple of his called Chalabī Husamuddin Ḥasan, of whom Shams had presumably thought highly. Rūmī and Husamuddin lived together for ten years, and it was the latter who prevailed on Rūmī to compose a didactic and inspirational Sufi verse guide for his disciples. Thus began Rūmī's most famous work, called *Mathnawī-i maʿnawī* (*The Mathnawi*, 1926-1934), which grew into some twenty-six thousand Persian couplets and is an encyclopedic compendium of Sufi lore, combining anecdotal narratives, didactic commentary, and passages best described as ecstatic reflections and outbursts.

Mathnawī-i maʿnawī begins with the most famous metaphorical representation of the human condition in Middle Eastern literature. In Talat S. Halman's translation, the passage reads,

Listen to the reed, how it tells its tales;
Bemoaning its bitter exile, it wails:
Ever since I was torn from the reed beds,
My cries tear men's and women's hearts to shreds.
Let this separation slit my sad breast
So I can reveal my longing and quest.
Everyone is my friend for his own part,
Yet none can know the secrets of my heart.
The flames of love make the reed's voice divine;
It is love's passion that rages in the wine.
The reed cries with the lovers who fell apart,
It rends the chest and tears open the heart.
Nothing kills or cures the soul like the reed;
Nothing can crave or console like the reed.

For Rūmī, then, the proper life is the mystic's quest through dedication to love to return to the original condition of proximity to God, the Divine Beloved. *Mathnawī-i maʿnawī* offers Rūmī's vision through precept and anecdote for the life lived for love. The work is not formally structured or unified; rather, the poet proceeds as inspiration strikes him, often inspired by verbal association to mystical association. He may have composed large parts of it extemporaneously or orally, with Husamuddin transcribing passages. According to tradition, Rūmī composed or recited some tales while dancing around a column at his school.

Rūmī died in December, 1273, before finishing *Mathnawī-i maʿnawī*, which stops in the middle of a tale in book 6. His death was cause for great mourning in Konya, where his mausoleum is still visited yearly by thousands of pilgrims.

Husamuddin thereafter assumed leadership of Rūmī's disciples. At his death in 1283 or 1284, Sultan Walad, Rūmī's eldest son, became their leader and organized them into a formal Sufi order called the Maulawiyah (or Mawlawis), for Rūmī's title; its members are now known throughout the world as the whirling dervishes. Sultan Walad also composed a spiritual biography of his father in verse.

Significance

Collections of Jalāl al-Dīn Rūmī's sermons, letters, and sayings have survived. It is his chief works, *Dīwan-i Shams-i Tabrīz* and *Mathnawī-i maʿnawī*, however, which put him in the first rank of Persian poets and which make him the chief poetic voice of Sufism in history.

In Persian poetry, Rūmī's intensity of feeling and sure sense of rhythm give him a place in classical Persian *ghazal* poetry alongside his contemporary Saʿdi (1200-1291), the supreme technical virtuoso of the Persian *ghazal* (short ode verse), and Hafiz (c. 1320-1389 or 1390), the master of ambivalent lyric expression in the *ghazal*. At the same time, as a master of the Persian quatrain, Rūmī stands at the opposite end of the thematic spectrum from Omar Khayyám (1048?-1123?), whose verses question the very existence of God and the immortality of the human soul.

Rūmī also stands apart from the mainstream of classical Persian poets because he was not involved with the court system of patronage. He apparently had good relations with rulers in Anatolia, because of which he was able to be of great service to the poor and needy. Whereas the majority of Persian poets praised kings and mundane beloveds, however, Rūmī praised God and his Divine Beloved, and felt no attraction to temporal power or material wealth.

In addition, as knowledgeable as Rūmī was in the craft of Persian poetry, he had little patience for technically and rhetorically correct verse, but concentrated mainly on the development of rhythms that would complement his message. His passionate love of God was filtered through his creativity into a unique Persian style of musical, expressive, spontaneous verse, combining his heartfelt views, his deepest feelings, his abundant knowledge and experience, and his feel for the everyday. The following verses, translated by Annemarie Schimmel, exhibit Rūmī's recognition of the spontaneity of his art, which may sometimes not withstand prolonged scrutiny for theological content or technical niceties of verse:

> My poetry resembles Egyptian bread:
> When a night passes over it you cannot eat it anymore.
> Eat it at this point when it is fresh
> Before dust settles on it!

If Rūmī was not a professional Persian poet in a conventional sense, he was also not a philosopher or theologian. His special place as a religious thinker and Sufi does not depend on originality or complexity of thought, but on his intense personal and artistic dedication to his convictions and his ability through word and deed to communicate those views to others. Among the themes that surface in his verse are a sense of God's transcendence, a perception of nature as offering a hint of God, and a concept of humankind as the highest creatures, who, beyond body, soul, and mind, possess deeper spirits that partake of divine revelation. Prophets and saints are special in this respect because God speaks through them. In death, humans will be absorbed into God, but some residue of the individual may remain. Still, though these elements of a theological system can be extracted from Rūmī's writings, Rūmī is not to be appreciated as a systematic thinker; he is to be experienced as an inspired man of great vitality, virtue, and love, whose writings attest the nobility of the human spirit.

—*Michael Craig Hillmann*

FURTHER READING

Barber, David. "Rūmī Nation." *Parnassus: Poetry in Review* 25, nos. 1-2 (2001): 176-209. Explores several modern translations of Rūmī's work and argues that his complex poetry has been oversimplified and even distorted by scholars and others.

Halman, Talat S. "Jalāl al-Dīn Rūmī: Passions of the Mystic Mind." In *Persian Literature*, edited by Ehsan Yarshater. Albany, N.Y.: Bibliotheca Persica, 1988. An engaging, sympathetic portrait with stylish translations from Rūmī's poetry. Another essay in this volume, "Lyric Poetry," provides background and context for appreciating Rūmī's achievements as a poet.

Keshavarz, Fatemeh. "'How Sweetly with a Kiss Is the Speech Interrupted': Rūmī's Poetics of Silence." In *Reading Mystical Lyric: The Case of Jalāl al-Dīn Rūmī*. Columbia: University of South Carolina Press, 1998. Discusses the more than thirty-five thousand verses written by Rūmī that celebrate silence, or, more specifically, the absence of speech. Compares Rūmī's thoughts on silences with those in the work of Samuel Beckett, Søren Kierkegaard, and Ludwig Wittgenstein. Bibliography, index.

Lewis, Franklin. *Rūmī, Past and Present, East and West: The Life, Teachings and Poetry of Jalāl al-Dīn Rūmī*. Boston: Oneworld, 2000. A comprehensive study of Rūmī's life and times, using primary sources by and about Rūmī to draw pictures of his legacy and to discuss his continuing significance. Looks also at *Selected Poems from the Dīwani Shamsi Tabriz*, Rūmī's children, Rūmī and the Muslim and Western worlds, mythology, and media representation. Maps, bibliography, index.

Rūmī, Jalāl al-Dīn. *The Mathnawí of Jalālu'ddin Rūmī*. Translated and edited by Reynold A. Nicholson. Vols. 2, 4, 6. 1926-1934. Reprint. London: Luzac, 1972. A complete scholarly verse translation of Rūmī's most important poetic work. Bibliography.

_______. *Mystical Poems of Rūmī*. Translated by Arthur J. Arberry. Chicago: University of Chicago Press, 1974. Bibliography.

_______. *Mystical Poems of Rūmī, Second Selection*. Translated by Arthur J. Arberry. Chicago: University of Chicago Press 1991. These two volumes contain translations of four hundred of Rūmī's shorter poems. Bibliography.

_______. *Tales from "The Masnavi"* and *More Tales from "The Masnavi."* Translated by Arthur J. Arberry. 1961-1963. Reprint. Surrey, England: Curzon Press, 1993. Prose retellings of two hundred anecdotal stories from *The Mathnawi*. Bibliography.

Schimmel, Annemarie. *As Through a Veil: Mystical Poetry in Islam*. 1982. Reprint. Boston: Oneworld, 2001. Five densely annotated essays (originally lectures) titled "The Development of Arabic Mystical Poetry," "Classical Persian Mystical Poetry," "Maulana Rūmī and the Metaphors of Love," "Mystical Poetry in the Vernaculars," and "Poetry in Honor of the Prophet." The author demonstrates the centrality of Rūmī to all subsequent Sufistic literary expression. The chapter on Rūmī reviews his life, suggests a chronology of his lyrics, and describes images and symbols for love in his verse.

_______. *The Triumphal Sun: A Study of the Works of Jalāloddin Rūmī*. 1978. Reprint. Albany: State University of New York Press, 1993. The standard study by the leading Rūmī scholar, with emphasis on Rūmī's poetic vocabulary and thought. Includes extensive quotations from Rūmī's works and a comprehensive bibliography.

Wines, Leslie. "The Poet of Love and Tumult." In *Rūmī: A Spiritual Biography*. New York: Crossroad, 2000. This chapter in a brief text places Rūmī's spiritual and love poetry in a Western, modern context, including his commercialization. Part of the Lives and Legacies series. Bibliography, index.

SEE ALSO: Firdusi; Hafiz; al-Ḥallāj; al-Jāḥiẓ; Omar Khayyám; Saʿdi; Tamerlane.

RELATED ARTICLES in *Great Events from History: The Middle Ages, 477-1453*: 637-657: Islam Expands Throughout the Middle East; 1010: Firdusi Composes the *Shahnamah*; 1273: Sufi Order of Mawlawīyah Is Established.

RURIK

Scandinavian-born politician

According to tradition, Rurik established Kiev Rus, the first Russian state, and founded the ruling House of Rurik, which endured until 1598. He is still politically significant, both as the creator of an exemplary nondespotic government and as the inspiration for the controversial Norman Theory, which claims that Russia's very existence as a nation is the result of the political and military activities of Germanic peoples.

BORN: Ninth century; Scandinavia
DIED: 879; probably in the vicinity of Novgorod, Russia
ALSO KNOWN AS: Hrorekr; Rorik; Ryurik
AREAS OF ACHIEVEMENT: Government and politics, military

EARLY LIFE

The specific circumstances of the childhood of Rurik (ROOR-ihk) are not clear, and much has to be inferred from the earliest surviving Russian annalistic literature, *Povest vremennykh let* (c. 1113; *The Russian Primary Chronicle*, 1930). *The Russian Primary Chronicle* and the *Nestor Chronicle* describe him as a Varangian "rus" ("beyond the sea"). Furthermore, *The Russian Primary Chronicle* calls the Rus a particular kind of Varangian; identifies Varangians with Swedes, Northmen, Angles, and Goths; and describes a failed attempt by the Varangian Rus from 859 to 862 to control Slavic tribes and trade routes in northwestern Russia. Finally, it notes that when Rurik entered Russia (sometime after 862), he brought in a large retinue of fellow Russes. This information places him in the broad context of the Viking expansionism of the early Middle Ages and suggests that he was a prominent Scandinavian war leader.

The Carolingian government had dealings with a Rorik of Jutland (b. 800) who may have been Rurik. If that conjecture is correct, he was born in Friesland of Danish parents; served as a vassal of Charlemagne's son, Louis the Pious; was baptized, perhaps as a requirement of that vassalage; and lost his lands in 843 at the Treaty of Verdun, when the Carolingian Empire was partitioned among Louis's three sons. In evident response to his loss of status, Rorik then became a Viking adventurer, leading large-scale raids into England, the Rhineland, and northern France, and along the Elbe.

Within a few years, his disruptive tactics were rewarded; in order to exert some control over him and raise a barrier against other Vikings, the Carolingian emperor Lothair I offered him successive fiefs in Friesland and Jutland. Rorik then disappeared from Western view for a time and, given the inexact nature of contemporary evidence, could have transferred his attentions to the eastern Baltic during the 860's.

The argument that Rurik was indeed Rorik of Jutland is disputable, for it is based on inconclusive evidence such as the similarity of names; the prominence, successes, and large followings of both personages; and the fact that Rorik became inactive in Western affairs at roughly the same time that Rurik appeared in Eastern records. Yet the parallels are instructive, even though the issue is unlikely to be resolved satisfactorily; the fluctuations in their fortunes would have been quite similar, and they both typified the restless, aggressive Viking war leaders of the 800's to the 1000's.

LIFE'S WORK

The Russian Primary Chronicle is both clear and succinct about Rurik's role in Russian history. After the

Varangian incursion of 859-862 was repelled, the mostly Slavic tribes in the region were unable to establish peaceful relations with one another. Accordingly, they appealed to their former opponents for help: "Our whole land is great and rich," they are reported to have said, "and there is no order in it. Come to rule and reign over us." They then selected Rurik and his younger brothers, Truvor and Sineus, who migrated to Russia with their relatives and "all the Russes." Initially, Rurik ruled only in Novgorod (which previously had been Slavic but which became a Varangian city), while his brothers controlled Izborsk to the west and Beloozero to the east. On their deaths, however, he assumed sole authority and assigned cities to his followers. Finally, within his lifetime, subordinates of Rurik campaigned down the Dnieper River and broke the control of the Volga-based nomadic Khazars over Kiev, the embryonic state's future capital. Thus, to the authors of *The Russian Primary Chronicle*, Rurik stands as the maker of the original Russian state and the founder of its earliest dynastic family, the Rurikides.

Modern scholarship has demonstrated that the traditional accounts of Russia's origins are chronologically unreliable and heavily propagandistic. In the first place, even the earliest authors of the texts that compose *The Russian Primary Chronicle* were far removed in time from the described events. Second, the texts were repeatedly reworked during the copying process, producing multiple variants. Finally, their authors were always obliged to advance the political interests of the ruling family—and their immediate rulers were always Rurikides.

Nevertheless, when these texts are bolstered by supplementary information from Carolingian, Byzantine, and ʿAbbāsid sources, much can be gleaned from them. By the ninth century, evidently, the Slavic and Finnish tribes along the Dvina, the Volkhov, and the Dnieper Rivers had developed a network of fortified posts to facilitate trade with Byzantium. The wealth generated by that expanded trade in furs and slaves attracted unwelcome attention; Asiatic Khazars from the Volga region and Vi-

Depiction of the funeral of Rurik. (F. R. Niglutsch)

kings from the Baltic both tried to dominate the riverine trade routes of western and northwestern Russia. The Vikings under Rurik and his fellow Russes won that competition. They probably first came as raiders (the "expulsion" of 862), then as mercenaries (the later "invitation"), and finally as conquerors and settlers (the transformation of Novgorod into a Varangian city, the assigning of other cities to Varangian supporters, and the securing of the Dnieper trade route as far south as Kiev).

Numerous Viking chieftains of the age followed those opportunistic tactics, winning control of a shifting hodgepodge of territories from the Netherlands to southern Italy. Few, though, were as fortunate as Rurik and his successors, who rapidly became accepted as native rulers, transferred their ethnic identity as Russes to the whole of their subject population, and presided over the flowering of a remarkably advanced and prosperous state, the Confederation of Kievan Rus.

That success was the result of extremely shrewd political choices made by Rurik and his immediate successors in the transition period before their political legitimacy was generally accepted. Because they were a minority in their newly conquered lands, the first Rurikides cooperated with one another, forming a hierarchic network of intercity alliances. An individual Rurikide ruled over his city as a prince (*knigz*) but acknowledged the overlordship of the grand duke (the *velikii knigz*—literally, the "high prince"), who was, after Rurik's death, supposed to be his closest male descendant.

Moreover, the Rurikides were able to defuse potential opposition within those cities by developing a system of shared power. Although they represented the monarchical principle, they also consulted their armed retainers through an institution known as the *boyar dunia* and the general population through a popular assembly known as the *veche*. Thus, by admitting aristocratic and democratic elements into policy making, the Rurikides gave every important segment of their society a sense of participation and involvement. Eventually, that politically inspired solidarity replaced the tribal divisions that made Russia susceptible to outside conquest in the first place. It also promoted increased trade with Byzantium and, through Scandinavian connections, expanded that trade into Northern and Western Europe.

Rurik's successes attracted intense interest throughout Scandinavia and as far west as Iceland, and early Rurikide armies were frequently bolstered by the influx of immigrant Viking war bands. That additional manpower, combined with the effective integration of native forces into the military and the large accumulations of gold and silver generated by intensifying trade connections between the Baltic and Black Seas, allowed them to expand their political base throughout the northwestern river systems and down the Dnieper into the Russian steppe. Within Rurik's own lifetime, the emerging state of Kiev Rus promised to replace the declining Carolingian Empire as the most powerful and prosperous European state after the Byzantine Empire. Before the next century was over, his successors had accomplished that feat.

RULERS OF KIEVAN RUS, C. 862-1167

Reign	*Ruler*
c. 862-879	RURIK
879-912	Oleg
912-945	Igor
945-964	SAINT OLGA (regent)
964-972	Svyatoslav I
972-980	Yaropolk
980-1015	VLADIMIR I (with ANNA)
1015-1019	Sviatopolk I
1019-1054	Yaroslav
1054-1073	Iziaslav
1073-1076	Svyatoslav II
1076-1078	Iziaslav (restored)
1078-1093	Vsevolod
1093-1113	Sviatopolk II
1113-1125	Vladimir II Monomakh
1125-1132	Mstislav
1132-1139	Yaropolk
1139-1146	Vyacheslav
1146-1154	Iziaslav
1149-1157	Yuri I Dolgoruky
1154-1167	Rostislav

SIGNIFICANCE

Over the general course of Russian history, Rurik was best known as the creator of the earliest Russian state and the founder of its ruling dynasty. Since the eighteenth century, however, his historical importance has transcended that traditional role. In the first place, the Rurikides of the Kievan period served as Russia's outstanding example of nondespotic rulers of a dynamic, prosperous state; increasingly, nationalist historians could cite Rurikide policies in order to condemn retrograde characteristics of later rulers in succeeding historical periods. This had a telling effect; when compared to the oppression of the Mongol khans in the 1300's and 1400's or the arbitrary rule of Muscovite czars such as Ivan IV, the era of

Kiev Rus took on the aura of a golden age. The democratic role of the *veche* and the interclass cooperation typical of city governance in Kiev Rus were also used for political purposes because they stood in stark contrast to the dictatorial behavior of the later Romanovs and their authoritarian communist successors.

Finally, Rurik became the center of a bitter nationalistic dispute between Germans and Russians known as the Norman Controversy. Initially inspired by information provided by *The Russian Primary Chronicle*, German Normanist historians maintained that the Russian state owed its existence, and its very name, to the presence and activities of Germanic peoples. Russian anti-Normanists claimed that Rurik's influence was vastly inflated in the annalistic texts, that the word Rus (or Rhos) was of indigenous origin, and that Kiev Rus was an exclusively Slavic creation.

The issue is not completely resolved; archaeological excavations corroborate textual evidence of a Scandinavian presence in northwestern Russia in the 800's, but further work is needed to establish its full extent. Nevertheless, current scholarly opinion has accepted the historic importance of Rurik, despite his semilegendary status. Recent works on early Russia have gravitated toward a modified Normanist position, holding that in creating Kiev Rus, Rurik and his successors accelerated, named, and put a distinctive stamp on a process that had, in a tentative fashion, already begun.

—*Michael J. Fontenot*

FURTHER READING

Davidson, H. R. Ellis. *The Viking Road to Byzantium*. London: Allen and Unwin, 1976. A work that covers the founding and growth of Kiev Rus, its economic bases, and its cultural characteristics. Illustrations, bibliography, and index.

Duffy, James P., and Vincent L. Ricci. *Czars: Russia's Rulers for More than One Thousand Years*. New York: Facts On File, 1995. A bibliographical account of the history of Russian rulers, including Rurik. Two chapters explore Rurik and "the birth of a nation," and the "end" of Rurik and troubled times. Illustrations, maps, bibliography, index.

Dukes, Paul. *A History of Russia: Medieval, Modern, Contemporary, Circa 882-1996*. 3d ed. Durham, N.C.: Duke University Press, 1998. Part 1 introduces medieval Russia and the construction and then collapse of Kiev (882-1240). Extensive bibliography and an index.

Evans, John L. *The Kievan Russian Principality, 860-1240*. Gaithersburg, Md.: Associated Faculty Press, 1981. A short overview of Kiev Rus, with a useful discussion of Soviet historiography. Includes an index and a short bibliography.

Franklin, Simon, and Jonathan Shepard. *The Emergence of Rus, 750-1200*. New York: Longman, 1996. A comprehensive work on Kiev Rus. Places Rurik and his successors in the general context of the Viking eastward expansion. Maps, extensive bibliography, list of genealogies, and excellent index.

Mazour, Anatole G. *Modern Russian Historiography*. Rev. ed. Westport, Conn.: Greenwood Press, 1975. Contains an excellent discussion of the origins of the Norman Controversy, a good bibliography, and a comprehensive index.

Obolensky, Dimitri. *Byzantium and the Slavs*. Crestwood, N.Y.: St. Vladimir's Seminary Press, 1994. Surveys Slavic relations with the Byzantine Empire in the Middle Ages. Includes a chapter on "Russia's Byzantine Heritage." Bibliography, map, index.

Roesdahl, Else. *The Vikings*. 2d ed. Translated by Susan M. Margeson and Kirsten Williams. New York: Penguin Books, 1998. Provides a solid, meticulous survey of Viking activities, with a chapter on Kiev Rus and its relations with Byzantium. Includes maps, illustrations, an extensive bibliography, and indexes.

Zenkovsky, Serge A., ed. and trans. *Medieval Russia's Epics, Chronicles, and Tales*. 2d ed. New York: Dutton, 1974. Contains key excerpts from the *Chronicle* along with an excellent analysis of Kiev Rus documentary material. Includes illustrations, a glossary, and a brief chronology.

SEE ALSO: Saint Alexander Nevsky; Anna, Princess of the Byzantine Empire; Charlemagne; Genghis Khan; Kublai Khan; Queen Tamara; Vladimir I.

RELATED ARTICLES in *Great Events from History: The Middle Ages, 477-1453*: 740: Khazars Convert to Judaism; 843: Treaty of Verdun; 850-950: Viking Era; 988: Baptism of Vladimir I; July 15, 1240: Alexander Nevsky Defends Novgorod from Swedish Invaders.

Saʿdi
Persian writer

Saʿdi's literary works, particularly his worldly-wise and entertaining classics, The Orchard *and* The Rose Garden, *have made him one of the leading writers of Iran, where he is fondly known as Shaykh Saʿdi or simply the Shaykh.*

Born: c. 1200; Shīrāz, Persia (now in Iran)
Died: c. 1291; Shīrāz
Also known as: Shaykh; Mosharrif al-Dīn ibn Moṣliḥ al-Dīn (possible original name)
Area of achievement: Literature

Early Life

Like the expedient morality of his writings, the facts of the life of Saʿdi (sah-DEE) are difficult to pin down. Much information about him is available but untrustworthy; most of it tends to be legendary or to come from autobiographical passages in his writings, where Saʿdi indulged the common human impulse to invent or correct oneself and in addition needed to make his stories fit his points (though not all do). As one of his characters puts it, "a man who has seen the world utters much falsehood." Moreover, G. M. Wickens, one of his translators, warns that "Saʿdi is most often portrayed with shrewd and subtle features, enlivened by a wicked, enigmatic smile." The intermingling of fact, fiction, and uncertainty about Saʿdi leaves his biography undependable but ontologically correct because his main point is that one can never "know" oneself, anybody else, or anything with certainty.

Not even Saʿdi's real name is certain. The best opinion is that his true name was Mosharrif al-Dīn ibn Moṣliḥ al-Dīn or some variation of this (sometimes with "Abdullah" or "Saʿdi Shirazi" tacked on). Saʿdi is a *takhallus* (pen name) taken from the rulers of Fārs Province during Saʿdi's lifetime—Saʿd ibn Zangi, his son Abū Bakr ibn Saʿd, and his grandson Saʿd ibn Abū Bakr. In Persian, which uses the Arabic alphabet, the name Saʿdi contains an ayn, a separate sound or tightening of the throat for which there is no exact equivalent in English. To indicate this pronunciation, the name is sometimes transliterated as "Saadi."

Saʿdi was born in Fārs Province, a southern region whose ancient name, Persis, the early Greeks extended to all Iran (which was thus known in the West until recently as Persia). As this etymology suggests, Fārs Province has played a central role in Iranian history, and such was especially the case during Saʿdi's lifetime. Saʿdi's father was a minor official at the court of the provincial ruler, Saʿd ibn Zangi. When Saʿdi's father died, Saʿd ibn Zangi assumed responsibility for the young Saʿdi's care and education. After schooling in Shīrāz, Saʿdi attended Nizamiya College in Baghdad, then perhaps the world's best educational institution. According to some accounts, Saʿdi spent his time there carousing and having a good time. In the *Bustan* (1257; *The Orchard*, 1882), Saʿdi says that he had a teaching fellowship requiring hours of instructional drudgery. In any case, he apparently had the opportunity for an excellent education, even if he was not himself cut out for the academic life.

Following his university studies, Saʿdi entered on the second of three main periods in his life, each of which represented a drastic change. He now began a period of wandering and adventure that, by the standard accounts, lasted for some thirty years. What motivated him to take to the road is not known, but it could have been any of a number of things—his desire to leave university life, the appeal of roaming, the influence of the dervishes or Sufis, or the approach of the conquering Mongol hordes. The Mongols, known as "the Scourge of Islam," were then devastating whole territories, leaving mountains of skulls piled up outside burned cities. In strange ways, Saʿdi's fate intertwined with theirs, much as his achievement stands in opposition to what they represented. If the Mongols caused him to flee, they thereby brought about the period of wandering that constituted his real education and the source of his wisdom.

Life's Work

Saʿdi's travels ranged throughout the Muslim lands, including Iran, Iraq, Syria, Anatolia (now Turkey), Palestine, Egypt, and other parts of North Africa. He visited the holy city of Mecca in Arabia numerous times. Sometimes he stayed with or traveled in the company of dervishes, members of the mystical Sufi fraternal orders, then at their height in the Islamic world. It is possible that he joined one of the Sufi orders for a time, even if his easygoing, skeptical temperament was not really compatible with Sufi discipline and emotionalism (ecstasy induced by various practices—such as chanting or whirling—to celebrate an all-embracing love). He did enjoy the singing, dancing, and company. Wandering about as a mendicant dervish also enabled him to travel more safely and to get handouts and hospitality, sometimes by preaching sermons that were good practice for writing his great didactic works.

His travels were naturally not without incident and occasionally perilous adventure. For example, in the *Gulistan* (1258; *The Rose Garden*, 1806), Saʿdi says that he was captured in Palestine by Christian Crusaders and put to work digging moats. What most offended him about the experience was that the other prisoners in his work gang were "infidels" (or "Jews," depending on the translation); unfortunately, Saʿdi displays the typical Muslim bigotry of his time. Eventually, a friend from Aleppo came by, recognized Saʿdi, and ransomed him from the Crusaders for ten dinars. Then the friend gave his daughter to Saʿdi in marriage, along with a dowry of one hundred dinars. His new wife proved so mean, however, that soon Saʿdi was wishing himself back among the Christians and Jews. When she pointedly reminded him of how her father had saved him, Saʿdi replied that it had cost her father only ten dinars to ransom him from the Crusaders but a hundred dinars to marry him to her. Later Saʿdi might have married another woman in Arabia, where they had a child who died. There is no indication of what happened to either woman or that either returned with him to Iran; it is possible that he left them both behind.

Outside Muslim territory, Saʿdi seems to have traveled in Armenia and possibly India, though his travel in India has been disputed. In *The Orchard*, Saʿdi tells how he got into trouble in India over religion. While watching a temple crowd worship an idol, he commented on the crowd's superstition to a friend. The friend, who turned out to be a believer himself, angrily got up and denounced Saʿdi to the crowd, which became ugly. Saʿdi saved himself by pretending to be an ignorant foreigner eager to learn more about their worship. The head Brahman instructed Saʿdi by making him spend all night with the statue, and the next morning the statue rewarded Saʿdi and other worshipers by raising its hands in salute. Apologizing and kissing the statue, Saʿdi claimed to be convinced, but a few days later he slipped behind the scenes and caught the Brahman operating levers that raised the statue's hands. Saʿdi says that he killed the Brahman by throwing him down a well and dropping a rock onto his head. Then Saʿdi got out of India as fast as he could.

Such incidents might have helped persuade Saʿdi, sometime during the 1250's, to enter his third major phase—to return to Shīrāz and take up a life of seclusion and writing. In addition, as his introduction to *The Rose Garden* shows, Saʿdi was impelled by a feeling (although he had already established a literary reputation by then) that he had wasted his life and accomplished nothing of importance. Saʿdi's retreat also coincided with another Mongol invasion of the eastern Muslim world, which could have lent urgency to his feelings by threatening both him and the world he knew. He was relatively safe, however, in Fārs Province, whose ruler, Abū Bakr ibn Saʿd, had made peace with the Mongols by submitting and paying tribute before the province was invaded. Around the time Saʿdi finished writing *The Orchard* and *The Rose Garden*, the Mongols (in January, 1258) devastated Baghdad, the center of Muslim culture for the previous five centuries, and killed its one and a half million inhabitants. Saʿdi mourned the occasion in a famous lament.

If the Islamic world had suffered a crushing blow, Saʿdi's fortunes dramatically improved. *The Orchard* and *The Rose Garden* found an eager audience. Numerous copies were made and circulated, and Saʿdi's literary fame spread. Abū Bakr ibn Saʿd invited him to come and stay in the court, but Saʿdi graciously declined the offer, content to live out his years in his "rose garden." After finishing his masterpieces, Saʿdi lived on for some thirty more years, aware of his gradually diminishing literary powers but already venerated by his country folk as "the Shaykh" (wise old man). He died sometime in the early 1290's, probably in 1291.

SIGNIFICANCE

While admiring Saʿdi as a wise old man, his Victorian translators and editors were distressed by his casual acceptance of pederasty and by his *khabisat* (obscene poetry and prose). Readers today might be more offended by his bigotry, especially toward Jews and blacks, and by his numerous *qasidas* (long poems of fulsome praise for patrons or rulers). These offending features illustrate some of the more obvious cultural barriers that stand in the way of Westerners reading Saʿdi with full understanding. More subtle barriers are posed by the allusions, imagery, and play with language, some of which cannot be translated.

Yet in his own country Saʿdi has been revered for more than seven centuries. He has entered the culture and become part of the language, much like Shakespeare in the English-speaking world. Only the Qurʾān has been quoted more in Iran than Saʿdi, even if some Iranians now consider him old-fashioned. The British were acting on the right instincts when, during the colonial period, they adopted *The Rose Garden* as a Persian text for training civil servants going to India (Persian was the official language of the Moguls, who ruled parts of India before the British arrived). Anyone hoping to understand the Iranians, and indeed other groups in the Islamic world, could hardly find a better place to begin than with Saʿdi. Few writers have so thoroughly defined a culture as Saʿdi, both as the culture existed in the past and as it still to some extent persists.

Although Saʿdi's *qasidas*, *ghazals* (love poems), and *rubáiyát* (quatrains) are relatively unknown to Westerners, *The Orchard* and *The Rose Garden* remain his main works and the most accessible ones. Both works are in the Eastern didactic tradition (not entirely unknown in the West), combining literary, folk, and religious elements. *The Orchard*, written in verse (the *mathnavi* or rhymed couplet form), is a bit more serious and formal than the lighter, looser *The Rose Garden*, written in prose and verse (mostly quatrains). *The Rose Garden* might consist of leftovers from *The Orchard*, since both works are blends of stories, anecdotes, homilies, maxims, and folk sayings purportedly illustrating the virtues or moral topics of the chapter headings (for example, "On Love, Intoxication, and Delirium," "The Morals of Dervishes," "On the Advantages of Silence"). The easy but artful mixture of material tends to grow on the reader, as does Saʿdi's slightly warped approach to life. After all, who can resist an author who makes the scorpion say, "What renown do I have in summer that I should also come out in winter?"

—*Harold Branam*

FURTHER READING

Arberry, A. J. *Classical Persian Literature*. Richmond, Surrey, England: Curzon Press, 1994. One of the leading introductions, originally published in 1958, to Iran's greatest period of literature (ninth through fifteenth centuries). The chapter on Saʿdi gives an excellent idea of his range. Includes generous quotations of his lyrical poetry in translation, a bibliography, and an index.

Levy, Reuben. *An Introduction to Persian Literature*. New York: Columbia University Press, 1969. Another good introduction to the literature of Iran, concentrating on the classical period. Includes useful information on the historical setting and Persian verse forms. Saʿdi is covered in a separate chapter with Hafiz, another writer from Shīrāz. Map, bibliography.

Saʿdi. *The "Gulistan": Or, Rose Garden of Saʿdi*. Translated by Edward Rehatsek. 1888. Reprint. New York: Putnam, 1965. An excellent English translation by a nineteenth century Hungarian who traveled to India. Brief bibliography.

_______. *Morals Pointed and Tales Adorned: The "Bustan" of Saʿdi*. Translated by G. M. Wickens. Buffalo, N.Y.: University of Toronto Press, 1974. An excellent English translation, in verse, with a brief but good introduction and a brief bibliography.

Zand, Michael I. *Six Centuries of Glory: Essays on Medieval Literature of Iran and Transoxania*. Translated by T. A. Zalite. Moscow: Nauka, 1967. A compact work examining Iran's classical period of literature from a Communist point of view. The brief but interesting essay on Saʿdi comments on his treatment of social issues.

SEE ALSO: Firdusi; Hafiz; al-Jāḥiẓ; Omar Khayyám; Jalāl al-Dīn Rūmī.

RELATED ARTICLES in *Great Events from History: The Middle Ages, 477-1453*: 637-657: Islam Expands Throughout the Middle East; 1010: Firdusi Composes the *Shahnamah*; 1248-1254: Failure of the Seventh Crusade; 1273: Sufi Order of Mawlawīyah Is Established.

SALADIN
Sultan of Syria (r. 1174-1193)

In a period of disunity in the Muslim world, Saladin conquered and unified warring factions. As sultan of Syria, Saladin defeated King Richard I of England in the Third Crusade and drove the Christian rulers from Jerusalem.

BORN: 1138; Tikrīt, Mesopotamia (now in Iraq)
DIED: March 4, 1193; Damascus (now in Syria)
ALSO KNOWN AS: Al-Malik al-Nāṣir Ṣalāḥ al-Dīn Yūsuf ibn Ayyūb ibn Shadi
AREAS OF ACHIEVEMENT: Government and politics, religion and theology, military

EARLY LIFE

Saladin (SAHL-ehd-ehn), as he has been known since his own time, learned diplomacy at his father's knee. Born in the town of Tikrīt on the banks of the Tigris River, Saladin was the third of eight children of the Kurdish Najm al-Dīn Ayyūb. Ayyūb had risen to prominence in the decade before Saladin's birth in the service of the Seljuk Empire and was ruler of Tikrīt. As an ethnic outsider, Ayyūb had developed administrative skills that made him useful to his overlord, but he was also ambitious for wealth and power. After performing a favor for a rival leader, Ayyūb was forced—on the very night of Saladin's birth—to flee Tikrīt with his family. Despite this episode, Ayyūb's status as an outsider made him a logical compromise candidate for later positions in an atmosphere of jealousy and intrigue; later, Saladin would be elevated for similar reasons.

Ayyūb became governor of Baalbek, in Syria, and it was here that Saladin spent his childhood. Like many other well-born youths of his era, Saladin became an accomplished horseman and hunter—lion and gazelle were favored prey—and he learned hawking. He was a highly skilled polo player. Following the accepted educational program for young ruling-class men, Saladin studied the Qur'ān and learned poetry, grammar, and script. He spoke Kurdish, Arabic, and probably Turkish. Also, in his early years, he drank wine.

Saladin early followed his father and brothers in a military career. His brother Shāhān Shāh fought in the Second Crusade and was killed in 1148. During this period, Ayyūb attained leadership of Damascus, and even before his brother's commander, Sultan Nureddin (d. 1174), conquered that city, Saladin became a member of Nureddin's military establishment.

When he was only fourteen, Saladin had his own fief, and at sixteen, he had considerable property holdings. He may have had a wife by this time, according to some historians, but others say there is no evidence of his marriage before age thirty.

At the beginning of his military career Saladin was posted near Nureddin in Aleppo, but at age eighteen he became a deputy in Damascus, responsible for administrative and judicial matters. There Saladin cultivated a love for the fairness and impartiality of Qur'ānic law, and he rendered judgments with loyalty and compassion. When he found that his chief accountant was dishonest, Saladin resigned his position and returned to Nureddin as an aide-de-camp.

Their close relationship led to a turning point for Saladin, one of importance to the entire Islamic world for a century: He was sent to Egypt, a major battleground of Islam in the Middle Ages. There he gained his vision for unification of the Muslim world and expulsion of the Christian Crusaders.

LIFE'S WORK

The Muslim world was rent by religious differences. The Seljuk caliphate, ruled by Nureddin, was of the more liberal Sunni sect and had its seat of power in Baghdad. The Fāṭimid caliphate of Egypt, which had embraced the more orthodox Shia sect, was a volatile agglomeration with weak rulers. Like a splinter between them was the Latin kingdom, a Christian stronghold along the eastern Mediterranean coast, ruled by Amalric I (r. 1163-1174). Nureddin believed that if Amalric were able to join forces with the Byzantine emperor to conquer Egypt, the whole Islamic world would be threatened. The stakes were great: Rich trade routes to Asia, religious and educational centers, and plentiful agricultural lands could be lost.

Saladin, as one of Nureddin's principal advisers, helped plan three Syrian invasions of Egypt between 1164 and 1169 to conquer the Fāṭimid caliphate. During part of this period, Amalric had a treaty to defend Cairo against Syrian invaders. Saladin's first command came at Alexandria, where he was in charge of one thousand men under difficult conditions. After a short time back in Damascus, Saladin returned on Nureddin's orders to Egypt after the Fāṭimid alliance with Amalric broke down.

Saladin had grave misgivings about returning to Egypt, in part because he distrusted the motives of his powerful uncle Shirkuh, who was leading the return. The political situation there was dangerous and unstable. When Shirkuh suddenly died, however, Saladin was well placed to assume Shirkuh's place as vizier of Egypt commanding Nureddin's forces there; in this case, he was the compromise candidate among many factions.

Now thirty years old, Saladin drew strength from Qurʾānic exhortations to fulfill God's purpose. Saladin, like Nureddin, was pious. He kept little money, acting instead as custodian for the whole Muslim community; the proper function of wealth, he believed, was to further the aims of Islam. Both men saw stable leadership in Egypt as a key to preserving Muslim unity. Still, Nureddin was suspicious when Saladin insisted on autonomy to do this—including lessened payments of tribute. Not only did Saladin have military bases on the Egyptian front, but he also had to fight political battles at his rear.

Saladin consolidated power in Egypt by getting rid of Fāṭimid commanders and substituting loyalists; uprisings continued in the provinces for some years, but finally Fāṭimid rule was abolished. Saladin then built up the military and raided nearby areas. His strength was growing just when Ayyūb, Nureddin, and Amalric died in quick succession. Both Nureddin's and Amalric's successors were young boys; thus, both kingdoms were weakened.

Saladin swore fealty to al-Ṣāliḥ, Nureddin's successor, but quickly moved to consolidate the empire under his own rule, citing the need for a unified Islam. He struck quickly at the Frankish kingdom, taking a string of small towns, but the important town of Aleppo did not fall and remained a refuge for al-Ṣāliḥ. Mosul, too, was a holdout, but with other victories Saladin became sultan of Syria, succeeding Nureddin.

The Damascus-Cairo axis was all-important to Saladin as he set out on a *jihad* (holy war) to drive the Franks from the region. After 1176, he undertook major public works and religious and educational projects in Egypt, but at the same time he needed military action to convince his critics that the *jihad* was not a fraud merely intended to further his personal power.

After a serious reverse at the strategic outpost of Ascalon, he quickly returned to the attack. Angered by the Franks' breaking of a truce, Saladin was successful against them in southern Lebanon, and he consolidated troops from Syria and Egypt in order to destroy the fort at Jacob's Mill. In capturing Frankish defenses, Saladin often destroyed them so they could not be recaptured. He hoped to win strategic territory in Mesopotamia as a base from which to move against Christian-held Jerusalem, his ultimate target.

With the death of young al-Ṣāliḥ in 1180, Saladin had to contend with more Muslim infighting. Aleppo finally surrendered to Saladin, and eventually Mosul did too. Struggling with a serious illness, the conqueror tried to fix the succession among some of his seventeen sons. He managed, however, to recover.

The Latin Kingdom, on the brink of civil war, was rocked when Saladin's forces captured the walled city of Hattin, along with many Frankish leaders. The Christian defenses were weakened, and Jerusalem surrendered after a two-week siege.

Saladin's troops became tired and were not easily disciplined; the European forces were regrouping for a Third Crusade, led by Richard I (the Lion-Hearted) of England. Muslim-held Acre, after a long siege, was fi-

Saladin. (Library of Congress)

SALADIN AND THE BEGINNING OF THE AYYŪBID SULTANATE

Reign	*Ruler*
1138	Birth of Yūsuf ibn Ayyūb (Saladin)
1147-1169	Second Crusade
1147-1174	Mahmud Nur al-Din (Nureddin) reigns in Aleppo and Damascus (Syria)
1169	Saladin and uncle Shirkuh return to Egypt; death of Shirkuh
1171	Last Fāṭimid caliph dies
1174-1193	Saladin reigns in Egypt and Syria
1180's	Saladin begins to divide succession among sons
1183	Damascus and Aleppo fall to Saladin
1186-1196	al-ʿAfḍal Nūr al-Dīn rules Damascus
1187	Jerusalem falls to Saladin
1189	Third Crusade begins
1191	Acre falls to to Richard I
1192	Richard retreats; end of Third Crusade
1193	Death of Saladin; empire divided
1202-1204	Fourth Crusade

nally given up in 1191. Yet the cost was high for the Crusaders, and Richard did not want to be gone too long from England.

The final confrontation between Saladin and Richard came in July, 1192. After a day of prayer, Saladin and his troops were ready to face the Crusaders as they poised for an attack on Jerusalem. Suddenly, the Crusaders withdrew. Saladin attributed the retreat to divine intervention, but military historians say that Richard had decided to attack Egypt instead. Such an attack, however, was not undertaken. The Third Crusade was over.

Saladin retired to Damascus to spend time with his wives and children. In the winter of 1193, he rode out in bad weather to meet a group of pilgrims returning from Mecca. He became ill and died a short while later at age fifty-five, penniless by choice.

Saladin's title, al-Malik al-Nāṣir, or "strong to save the faith," was appropriate in his lifetime. Within a hundred years of his death, however, the many tensions beneath the Muslims' surface unity split apart what Saladin had accomplished.

SIGNIFICANCE

Saladin stands out in Western accounts of the Middle Ages because his beliefs and actions reflected supposedly Christian characteristics: honesty, piety, magnanimity, and chivalry. Unlike many Muslim rulers, he was not cruel to his subordinates; Saladin believed deeply in the Qurʾānic standard that all men are equal before the law. He set a high moral tone; for example, he distributed war booty carefully to help maintain discipline in the ranks.

As an administrator, Saladin demonstrated great vision. He altered the tax structure in Egypt and elsewhere to conform to Qurʾānic instructions, and he supported higher education. It was his vision—together with luck and military skill—that enabled him to begin a quest for Muslim unification that would bear fruit many years later.

The failure of Saladin's empire to survive him was a result of factors beyond his control: polygamy and the lack of primogeniture. The inevitable fighting for political inheritance caused ruptures again and again in the Muslim world.

—*Nan K. Chase*

FURTHER READING

Ehrenkreutz, Andrew S. *Saladin*. Albany: State University of New York Press, 1972. Presents details of Saladin's early life and of his first years in Egypt not included elsewhere. A chapter on Saladin in historical perspective gives a dissenting view—highly critical—concerning his efficacy as a leader. Detailed bibliography.

Gibb, Hamilton A. R. *The Life of Saladin*. Oxford, England: Clarendon Press, 1973. A short account of Saladin's life, this densely footnoted book is based on two famous accounts of Saladin by men who knew him. There is no discussion of his fiscal or administrative policies. Bibliography.

_______. *Saladin: Studies in Islamic History*. Edited by Yusuf Ibish. Beirut: Arab Institute for Research and Publishing, 1974. Collection of some of the author's earlier articles and chapters, including material on the caliphate, the Ayyubids, and Saladin's military career and translations of contemporary chronicles. Bibliography, index.

Hindley, Geoffrey. *Saladin*. New York: Barnes and Noble Books, 1976. General biography traces Saladin's rise to power. Emphasis on historical context. Many fine illustrations of desert locations and artifacts of the era. Bibliography, index, notes on sources.

Hodgson, Marshall G. *The Expansion of Islam in the Middle East*. Vol. 2 in *The Venture of Islam*. Chicago: University of Chicago Press, 1974. This seminal work places the dynamic of Islamic culture in the world context. Glossary of terms and names, bibliography (which includes coverage of visual arts), maps, and timetables.

Jubb, Margaret. *The Legend of Saladin in Western Literature and Historiography*. Lewiston: Edwin Mellen Press, 2000. Traces early hostile views and later views of Saladin that turned more positive. Also considers the legends surrounding his life, such as knighthood and influential French predecessors. Bibliography, index.

Lane-Poole, Stanley. *Saladin: All-powerful Sultan and the Uniter of Islam*. New York: Cooper Square Press, 2002. This is the forerunner of other modern biographies of Saladin, first published under a different title in 1898, and draws extensively on original chroniclers; includes discussions of major campaigns. Illustrations, map, bibliography, index.

Lev, Yaacov. *Saladin in Egypt*. Boston: Brill, 1999. An exploration of Saladin's time in Egypt and his rise to power there. Also considers the fall of the Fāṭimids. Part of the Medieval Mediterranean series. Bibliography, index.

Lyons, Malcolm Cameron, and D. E. P. Jackson. *Saladin: The Politics of the Holy War*. New York: Cambridge University Press, 1997. Explores Saladin in the context of the Crusades and his administrative, diplomatic, and political power. Uses Arabic texts and documents, some before unpublished and some from Saladin's court, as resources. Maps, bibliography, index.

Newby, P. H. *Saladin in His Time*. 1963. Reprint. London: Phoenix Press, 2001. A concise and readable account of the Muslim and Christian background to Saladin's accomplishments. Presents major battles and Saladin's methods of government. Contains convenient map of the Middle East around 1170. Bibliography, index.

Reston, James, Jr. *Warriors of God: Richard the Lionheart and Saladin in the Third Crusade*. New York: Knopf, 2002. This history of the Third Crusade presents Saladin as a sophisticated political leader. Richard is depicted as a complex and at times brutal figure.

SEE ALSO: Baybars I; Lalibela; Melisende; Richard I; Geoffroi de Villehardouin.

RELATED ARTICLES in *Great Events from History: The Middle Ages, 477-1453*: 969-1171: Reign of the Fāṭimids; 11th century: Expansion of Sunni Islam in North Africa and Iberia; 1077: Seljuk Dynasty Is Founded; c. 1120: Order of the Knights Templar Is Founded; 1147-1149: Second Crusade; 1189-1192: Third Crusade; 1225-1231: Jalāl al-Dīn Expands the Khwārizmian Empire; April, 1291: Fall of Acre, Palestine.

SALIMBENE

Italian religious leader and biographer

A wandering Franciscan friar, priest, preacher, and writer, Salimbene met and wrote about the most important figures of his age—popes, emperors, kings, and prelates—as well as ordinary people and their daily lives.

BORN: October 9, 1221; Parma (now in Italy)
DIED: c. 1290; Montefalcone (now in Italy)
ALSO KNOWN AS: Balian de Adam (given name); Ognibene de Adam
AREA OF ACHIEVEMENT: Literature

EARLY LIFE

Salimbene (sahl-eem-BEHN-ay) was born Balian de Adam in Parma, in northern Italy. His father, Guido de Adam, was a handsome and gallant Crusader who headed a wealthy, well-connected bourgeois family that aspired to nobility. In his *Cronica* (1282-1288; *The Chronicle of Salimbene de Adam*, 1986, commonly known as the *Chronicle*), Salimbene recounts a revealing story about his infancy. In 1222, a powerful earthquake shook northern Italy. The baptistry of Parma, which stood next to the de Adam house, seemed about to collapse on the house. Salimbene's mother grabbed her two daughters and carried them to safety but left her baby boy in his cradle at home. After he learned later about this incident, Salimbene could never trust his mother's love. She had rejected him for his sisters, he believed, but God had saved him. As a result, Salimbene's attitude toward his family was ambivalent, guarded, and emotionally distant. Moreover, he was at odds with his father, whose worldly desires for his son clashed with Salimbene's more reserved temperament. On February 4, 1238, when he was only sixteen years old, Salimbene renounced his prospects of material success and entered the Franciscan order. Angered, Guido never forgave his son and tried in both devious and violent ways to snatch Salimbene away from the order. Salimbene remained a Franciscan, however—traveling to such places as Lyon, Troyes, Paris, Sens, Geneva, Bologna, Genoa, Modena, and Ravenna; on his travels in Genoa, in 1248, he was ordained a priest. He was dubbed "Salimbene" (meaning "good move" or "good leap") by an elderly friar who took issue with the boy's nickname, Ognibene ("all good"), regarding it as an affront to God; "Salimbene" commemorated the young man's wise move away from the worldly and toward the monastic life.

Salimbene soon found a new family and new, otherworldly hopes in the Franciscans (or Friars Minor or Minorites). Saint Francis of Assisi had founded his Order of Friars Minor in 1209 and provided its rule and more guidance in his testament. After the death of Saint Francis, his order split into the Spirituals, who strictly followed his rule and testament and idealized poverty, and the Conventuals, who compromised with what they saw as social and human realities and rejected the ideal of poverty. Both Spirituals and Conventuals found their inspiration in Francis's spirituality but differed about how best to realize the saint's religious vision. Salimbene admired the Franciscan Spirituals and men such as John of Parma and Hugh of Digne. He despised the politician Elias of Cortona and Frederick II.

LIFE'S WORK

Shortly after entering the Franciscan order, Salimbene came under the influence of the writings of Joachim of Fiore (c. 1135-1202), a saintly hermit and Cistercian abbot of Calabria whose prophecies influenced medieval thought tremendously. Joachim taught that history consists of three ages corresponding with the three aspects of the Trinity. The first age, that of God the Father, had ended with the new dispensation of Jesus Christ. The second age, that of the Son, would soon end with the new dispensation of the Holy Spirit, forty-two generations, or 1260 years, from the birth of Christ. In 1260 would begin an age of perfection, peace, and freedom, which Joachim termed the Sabbath of the Faithful under Christ the king, and a new religious order.

The thirteenth century was perhaps the greatest medieval century, the age of Gothic architecture and Scholasticism, but it was also a time of troubles, with deadly conflict between the Papacy and the Hohenstaufen, civil wars in Italy between the Guelphs and the Ghibellines, heresy, persecution, the decline of the Crusades, and the new menace of the Mongol invasions. This seemed to many to be the time of troubles that Joachim had predicted would occur immediately before the millennium, and the Franciscans to be the new religious order that would officiate at the Sabbath of the Faithful. Joachism appealed to the finest, holiest men of the time, but also to many of the worst sort, who used prophecy as pretext for gross indecency and wild radicalism.

Shortly after the fatal year 1260 had passed without the Joachist apocalypse, Salimbene began his life's work. He had been a Joachist but later would write, "After the death of Frederick II [the Antichrist figure to the Joachists] and the passing of the year 1260, I completely abandoned Joachimism and, from now on, I intend to believe only what I can see." From about 1262 until 1288, the disillusioned Salimbene compiled his *Chronicle*, writing its final draft at Reggio and Montefalcone between 1282 and 1288. Salimbene remained interested in Joachist prophecy as a philosophy of history and futurist orientation, but he loathed the literal-minded Joachism of vulgar heretical millenarians. Often in his *Chronicle*, Salimbene remarks on events that occurred exactly as Joachim of Fiore had foretold but stresses that he saw them "with my own eyes." His objective as a chronicler was not to discover signs of the Last Days but instead to hold up a mirror to his age.

Salimbene was a keen observer of the human comedy. His *Chronicle* is an affectionate album of candid verbal portraits of thirteenth century humanity. In it, Salimbene gently reveals human foibles and contradictions between people's self-images and real characters. He writes, for example, of a Dominican friar who was so puffed up with self-importance that when he had a haircut he demanded that friars collect the clippings as holy relics, of a star-bedazzled nun who is so entranced by the beautiful singing of the musical friar Vita of Lucca that she jumps out of her convent window to follow him on tour but breaks her leg in the fall, and of the bizarre and cruel scientific experiments that Frederick II performed on human subjects.

Like the Florentine poet Dante, the Parmesan chronicler Salimbene had the gift of presenting the telling detail—the anecdote, saying, gesture, mannerism, or incident that reveals, by a sort of epiphany, the essential character of its subject. Salimbene captured the vicious hypocrisy of the millenarianist heresiarch Gerard Segarelli, who claimed to be like Christ, lying in a manger and shamelessly sucking the breasts of an obliging maiden. The *Chronicle* also contains Salimbene's copious biblical quotations and commentary, as well as curious trivia that some squeamish translators have deleted as extraneous or undignified.

Salimbene's principal activity in the Franciscan order was writing chronicles, histories, and treatises. He wrote a history of the Roman Empire; miscellaneous chronicles; *XII scelera Friderici imperatoris* (c. 1248; the twelve calamities of the Emperor Frederick); books on Joachim's prophecies regarding the Franciscan and Dominican orders; works on the correspondences between the lives of Christ and Saint Francis of Assisi, on Elisha, and on Pope Gregory X; and many other treatises. None of these other works is extant except Salimbene's "Book of the Prelate," attacking Elias of Cortona, which he incorporated in his *Chronicle*.

Salimbene traveled widely in France and Italy, conversing, collecting tales, and pausing here and there, sometimes for a few years, to write. He wandered more extensively than the usual friar and was taken to task once by the minister general of his order for being a gadabout. Salimbene's wanderlust seems to have been the outgrowth of innocent curiosity and amiability, however, and he was a good and loyal Franciscan who was intrigued by Joachism, not a revolutionary chiliast. The atrocities wrought by Frederick II were bearable if indeed he was Antichrist, as the Joachists held, and the tribulation would usher in the happy Sabbath of the Faithful. Ominous portents, such as the Mongol invasions and setbacks in the Holy Land and at Constantinople, could be rendered understandable, given a Joachist interpretation. In his own order, Salimbene admired the saintly Spiritual John of Parma and loathed the political realist and opportunist Elias of Cortona. Although Salimbene regarded Joachism as illuminating historically and true figuratively, he prudently dissociated himself from the Joachist movement within the Franciscan order. His fondness for Joachism and the Spirituals is nevertheless clear.

Salimbene died at Montefalcone, probably in 1290; the last entry in his *Chronicle* is dated 1288. The *Chronicle* remained virtually unknown until its publication in several scholarly editions in the nineteenth century. G. G. Coulton's English translation in 1906 brought Salimbene to the attention of a wider audience. The *Chronicle*'s charm, vividness, wit, candor, humanity, and range of observations make the work indispensable reading for all serious students of medieval civilization. Coulton called Salimbene's *Chronicle* "the most remarkable autobiography of the Middle Ages," historian Maurice Keen called it "perhaps the best gossip of the Middle Ages," and other medievalists have appropriately used the superlatives "greatest" and "finest" to describe this unique, wonderful, charming work.

SIGNIFICANCE

Salimbene was an amiable and loquacious itinerant Franciscan friar who chronicled the history of his contemporary Italy and France. His lively sketches of people, great and lowly, reveal their characters, foibles, human nature, and details of everyday life and popular culture. His *Chronicle* is a valuable historical source. He recounts the conflict in the Order of Friars Minor after the death of Saint Francis, the influence of Joachism, the struggle between the Papacy and the Hohenstaufen, and other momentous events, as well as matters of everyday life.

—*Terence R. Murphy*

FURTHER READING

Brentano, Robert. *Two Churches: England and Italy in the Thirteenth Century*. 1968. Reprint. Berkeley: University of California Press, 1988. Contains illuminating comparison and contrast between Salimbene and his older contemporary the English Benedictine historian Matthew Paris (c. 1200-1259).

Cohn, Norman. *The Pursuit of the Millennium: Revolutionary Millenarians and Mystical Anarchists of the Middle Ages*. Rev. ed. New York: Oxford University Press, 1970. Contains a provocative discussion of medieval chiliasm; important cultural and social background in chapters on Joachim of Flora, Frederick II, and the Flagellants; and examination of other matters relevant to Salimbene's literary flirtations with millenarianism. Cohn argues the controversial thesis of continuity between medieval chiliasm and modern totalitarianism.

Moorman, John. *A History of the Franciscan Order from Its Origins to the Year 1517*. 1968. Reprint. Chicago: Franciscan Herald Press, 1988. The standard history of the medieval Friars Minor. Many citations of Salimbene. Essential for the Franciscan context.

Reeves, Marjorie. *The Influence of Prophecy in the Later Middle Ages: A Study in Joachimism*. 1969. Reprint. Notre Dame, Ind.: University of Notre Dame, 1993. A magisterial study of medieval and Renaissance attitudes toward the future stimulated by the prophetic writings of Joachim of Fiore. A preface has been added to the new edition.

Saggau, Elise, ed. *True Followers of Justice: Identity, Insertion, and Itinerancy Among the Early Franciscans*. St. Bonaventure, N.Y.: The Franciscan Institute, 2000. A general work on the spirituality of the early Franciscan friars, especially in regard to itinerancy.

Salimbene. *The Chronicle of Salimbene de Adam*. Translated and edited by Joseph L. Baird, Giuseppe Baglivi, and John Robert Kane. Binghamton, N.Y.: Medieval and Renaissance Texts and Studies, 1986. A magnificent scholarly edition of Salimbene's *Chronicle*, unabridged in translation, with exemplary critical apparatus and important commentary.

_______. *From Saint Francis to Dante: A Translation of All That Is of Primary Interest in the Chronicle of the Franciscan Salimbene, 1221-1288*. Translated and edited by G. G. Coulton. 2d rev. ed. Philadelphia: University of Pennsylvania Press, 1972. A reprint of Coulton's 1907 edition, with a new introduction by Edward Peters. Heavily edited and abridged, a hodgepodge of translated passages, paraphrase, commentary, and illustrative passages from other chronicles. Passages that the Victorian Coulton regarded as too racy are provided in Latin in an appendix. Although superseded by the edition of Baird et al., this volume is of value where the better edition is unavailable.

SEE ALSO: Dante; Saint Francis of Assisi; Frederick II; Joachim of Fiore.

RELATED ARTICLES in *Great Events from History: The Middle Ages, 477-1453*: April 16, 1209: Founding of the Franciscans; 1217-1221: Fifth Crusade; 1227-1230: Frederick II Leads the Sixth Crusade; 1248-1254: Failure of the Seventh Crusade.

ŚAṄKARA

Hindu philosopher and religious leader

Śaṅkara, the preeminent philosopher of medieval India, founded the Advaita school of philosophy, which asserts the oneness of the individual soul (ātman) and the universal soul (Brahman). Through public disputations, numerous writings, and the founding of several monasteries in strategic locations, he revived and defended the intellectual foundations of Vedism against the threats of Buddhism and Brahmanic ritualism.

BORN: c. 700; Kālaḍi (now in Kerala, India)
DIED: c. 750; Himalayas
ALSO KNOWN AS: Samkara; Shankara; Śaṅkarācārya
AREAS OF ACHIEVEMENT: Philosophy, religion and theology

EARLY LIFE

Śaṅkara (SHUHN-kuh-ruh), also known by his honorific name as Śaṅkarācārya, was born into a Nambudiri Brahman (Hindu priestly class) family in southwest India. Biographies of the philosopher were composed hundreds of years later based on oral traditions, anecdotes, and legends. Some scholars believe that Śaṅkara lived from c. 700 to c. 750; others believe he lived from 788 to 820. The most anyone can state with any degree of certainty is that Śaṅkara lived a relatively short life, probably around thirty-two years, within the period between 650 and 800.

Books on Śaṅkara's life, most of which were originally written in Sanskrit, freely mix facts with legends, seeking to glorify him as a saint or even as an incarnation of the god Śiva. For example, it is stated that his parents Śiva guru and Aryamba had remained childless for many years. When they prayed for a child at the Vadakkunathan temple in the nearby town of Trichur, Śiva appeared in the form of light and entered Aryamba's womb, granting her wish for a child. Because of the mythical framework within which Śaṅkara's life has been portrayed, books on his life are more hagiographies than biographies. What follows is a summary of what is commonly regarded as historically accurate.

Śiva guru died when Śaṅkara was five or six years old, leaving the burden of raising the young boy to his mother, Aryamba. As was expected of young Brahman boys of the time, Aryamba entrusted her son to an experienced teacher for instruction in the Vedas, *Sastras*, and other Hindu classics. At age sixteen, when he completed the required course of studies and returned home, he was faced with a choice that all young Brahman men of the time needed to make: Either get married and become a householder and priest (as most preferred) or become a *sannyāsin*, an itinerant monk, and leave home to lead a spiritual life. Against the wishes of his mother and other relatives, Śaṅkara opted to become a *sannyāsin*. He did, however, promise his mother to return home and perform her funeral rites when she died.

LIFE'S WORK

When he left home, Śaṅkara's immediate goal was to find a guru (spiritual preceptor) from whom to receive further instruction in the classics and to prepare himself to lead the life of a successful ascetic. After traveling far and wide, he met a holy man named Govindapada, the disciple of the famous Vedāntist Gauḍapāda, at a hermitage on the banks of River Narmada in central India. Impressed by the young aspirant's intelligence, background, character, and determination, Govindapada agreed to accept him as his disciple. From Govindapada, Śaṅkara learned the basic principles of Advaita (nondualism):

Brahman is pure consciousness.
This *ātman* is *Brahman*.
Thou art that.
I am *Brahman*.

Govindapada initiated Śaṅkara into the Paramahamsa order of *sannyāsins*, requiring the highest degree of austerity and renunciation, and encouraged him to develop the Advaita system by reinterpreting the Upaniṣads (c. 1000-c. 200 B.C.E.), the *Brahmasūtra* of Bādarāyana, and the *Bhagavadgītā* (c. 200 B.C.E.-200 C.E.; *The Bhagavad Gita*, 1785).

After he was thoroughly grounded in Advaita, Śaṅkara started to undertake a pilgrimage throughout the land, visiting all the traditional centers of learning, including Varanasi, Gaya, Ajodhya, Indraprastha (now Old Delhi), Badari, Kailasa, and Kasmira (Kashimir) and engaging the leaders of various Hindu sects in public disputations. The tradition at the time was for scholars to present and discuss their point of view in front of large audiences, especially in conjunction with festive occasions. Local rulers also used to sponsor public disputations for both the erudition of the public and entertainment of learned audiences. Public disputations at that time were refereed events, and it would be agreed on in advance that the loser would become the disciple of the winner. Taking advantage of all such opportunities, Śaṅkara challenged the leaders of various established sects, argued with them, and won them over to his point of view.

Śaṅkara's travels around the Indian subcontinent are typically described as a *digvijaya* (conquest of the land), evoking the specter of a regal victory parade. His journey from one cultural center to another was apparently nothing short of a spiritual conquest of the land, winning an increasingly large following for himself. The imagery of a victory parade is even more significant when one considers that a journey of this kind traditionally culminated in a ceremony in which the victor was seated in the Sarvajna Pitha (seat of omniscience) in Kasmira. Śaṅkara was finally installed in the Sarvajna Pitha as the undisputed scholar of the time. Because of his vast erudition, fame, and success as a scholar, Śaṅkara was also conferred the title *acarya*, or great teacher. Furthermore, Śaṅkara's victory in every philosophical disputation eventually won him the title *jagadguru*, or teacher of the world.

The debate with Mandanamisra is often cited as the most famous of all Śaṅkara's public debates and underscores his skills as a debater, his depth of knowledge, and his passion as a Vedāntist. Mandanamisra was a very famous and learned Brahman, belonging to the Mimamsa school, who lived in a city called Mahismati on the northern bank of the Narmada River. Śaṅkara decided to debate him because of his fame as a scholar and a staunch defender of Brahmanic ritualism. Śaṅkara first surprised Mandanamisra by dropping in on him exactly when he was getting ready to perform a ritual sacrifice. After initial exchanges of witticisms and insults, Mandanamisra agreed to a public debate with Śaṅkara, and Mandanamisra's wife, Bharati, who was also a very learned person, agreed to serve as the referee.

According to traditional accounts, the debate lasted eighteen days. They began by agreeing on the authority of the Vedas, and both of them demonstrated their mastery of the classic texts by extensive quotes, explanation of their intricate meanings, and references to authorities. At every turn, through carefully constructed arguments, Śaṅkara established, to Bharati's satisfaction, that all scriptures ultimately teach the superiority of the way of knowledge over the way of ritualism. He insisted that the main teaching of the Vedas is that Brahman alone is real and *ātman* is identical with Brahman. Convinced that rituals serve only a subordinate role in one's quest for salvation and that the superior path to salvation is knowledge of Brahman itself, Mandanamisra finally yielded and accepted Śaṅkara's discipleship.

Śaṅkara's biographers also note that at the end of his victorious journeys, hearing about his mother's ill health, Śaṅkara returned home to perform her final rites as he had promised. Although he was a *sannyāsin*, he insisted on conducting his mother's funeral rites, a privilege reserved only to priests. After the cremation of her body, he traveled north and died in a cave in an unknown location as *sannyāsins* of the time preferred to end their life.

During his pilgrimages, Śaṅkara not only engaged in public disputations but also wrote many works. Although more than three hundred works are attributed to him, most of them are not considered authentic. His most important work is the *Brahmasūtrabhāsya* (early eighth century; *The Vedānta Sūtras of Bādarāyana with the Commentary of Samkara*, 1890-1904), a commentary on Bādarāyana's *Brahmasūtra*, which is considered a major document of the Vedānta school. He also wrote commentaries on twelve principal Upaniṣads and *The Bhagavad Gita*. These three commentaries constitute the canon of the Advaita system. He also wrote a commentary on Patañjali's *Yogasūtra*. His other works include *Upadesa-sāhasrī* (early eighth century; *A Thousand Teachings*, 1949) and *Vivekachudamani* (early eighth century, authorship questionable; *The Crest Jewel of Wisdom*, 1890).

Śaṅkara's commentaries on the classical Indian texts are among the densest Indian philosophical treatises. He consistently teaches that knowledge of Brahman, the absolute, is the one sure path to final release from the cycle of transmigration and that *ātman*, one's true self, is identical with Brahman. He insists that realization of these fundamental truths, contained in the Upaniṣads and the Vedas, constitutes both the means and the end of the human striving for salvation. The philosophical problem of explaining the distinction between Brahman and the consciousness of individual self is resolved by his famous theory of *māyā* (illusion) and *avidyā* (nescience), concepts that are very complex in their details. Nevertheless, Śaṅkara's Advaita system remains the most dominant school of Indian thought.

One of Śaṅkara's lasting legacies is the establishment of several monasteries and centers of learning known as Mathas in various parts of India. It is difficult to ascertain how many of these Mathas were actually founded by him. Four of the most famous Mathas that claim their origin in Śaṅkara are Dwaraka (Sadaramatha, west), Sringeri (Sringerimatha, south), Puri (Govardhanamatha, east), and Badarinatha (Jyotirmatha, north). Interestingly, these are located in the four regions of India, symbolizing the claim that Śaṅkara was the unquestionable teacher for all of India. Śaṅkara is said to have appointed four of his most trusted disciples—Padmapada, Sureshwara, Hastamalaka, and Trotaka—to head these Mathas. The successors of these monastic heads eventually assumed the title of *Śaṅkarācārya* to claim their lineage to Śaṅkara himself.

Significance

The significance of Śaṅkara's spiritual conquest of the intellectual landscape of India is enormous and explains why Indian philosophers and theologians hold him in such a high regard even today. The eighth century saw many threats to the dominance of Hinduism. Two of these major threats were the spread of Buddhism, which openly rejected the traditions of Brahmanism, and the splintering of Hinduism into competing sects. Buddhists taught the importance of spiritual enlightenment and self-conquest through asceticism for attaining liberation from *saṃsāra* (the cycle of birth and rebirth). They rejected the spiritual value of Brahmanism with its mindless devotion to *dharma* (duty) and elaborate ritualism.

Śaṅkara felt it was necessary to counter Buddhism on philosophical grounds while incorporating some of its insights. He agreed with the Buddhists that wearing a sacred thread and a tuft of hair or performing sacrifices did not ensure salvation. In fact, because of his critical stance toward Brahmanic ritualism, his opponents sometimes criticized him as a disguised Buddhist. However, he was a Hindu reformer who accepted what was valuable in the Buddhist rejection of ritualism and sought to revive what he saw as the original teachings of Vedānta.

Śaṅkara attempted to face the second threat—the growing divisions within Hinduism—by reviving its intellectual vitality and correcting the errors of the leaders of various sects through public discourses. His opponents included Saivites, Vaisnavites, Saurites, Saktas, and Kapalikas. By prevailing over these competing philosophical systems, he sought to establish Advaita Vedānta as representing the true Vedic tradition. Although there are many Hindus who belong to other sects and competing interpretations of the Vedas and Upaniṣads are still in existence, Śaṅkara's Advaita Vedānta dominates the Indian philosophical landscape.

—*Mathew J. Kanjirathinkal*

Further Reading

Bader, Jonathan. *Conquest of Four Quarters: Traditional Accounts of the Life of Sankara*. New Delhi, India: Aditya Prakasan, 2000. Bader critically examines the principal hagiographies of Śaṅkara and provides a framework for understanding the cultural context in which the Śaṅkara story is told.

Chenkner, William. *A Tradition of Teachers: Sankara and the Jagadgurus Today*. Delhi, India: Motilal Banarsidas, 1983. Chenkner provides valuable insights into Śaṅkara's life and work by placing him in India's classical tradition of itinerant gurus. He also focuses on the special relationship between teacher and student in the context of Indian tradition.

Madugula, I. S. *The Acarya Sankara of Kaladi: A Story*. Delhi, India: Motilal Banarsidas, 1985. Although the author does not try to separate historical facts from legends, Madugula's work weaves the story of Śaṅkara with his teachings in an interesting and highly readable manner.

Mayeda, Sengaku. *A Thousand Teachings: The "Upadesasahasri" of Sankara*. New York: State University of New York Press, 1992. In this new edition and translation of one of Śaṅkara's original works, Mayeda presents an excellent introduction to the life and works of Śaṅkara in a fashion that is easily understood by the general reader.

Mudugal, G. S. *Advaita of Sankara, a Reappraisal: Impact of Buddhism and Samkhya on Sankara's Thought*. Delhi, India: Motilal Banarsidas, 1975. Mudugal presents a very useful discussion to help understand the competing intellectual positions against which Śaṅkara developed the Advaita system.

SEE ALSO: Rāmānuja.

RELATED ARTICLES in *Great Events from History: The Middle Ages, 477-1453*: c. 710: Construction of the Kāilaśanātha Temple; 788-850: Śaṇkara Expounds Advaita Vedānta; 1193: Turkish Raiders Destroy Buddhist University at Nalanda; c. 1380: Compilation of the Wise Sayings of Lal Ded.

SAXO GRAMMATICUS

Danish scholar, historian, and writer

Saxo Grammaticus, Denmark's most prominent medieval scholar and its first national historian, wrote one of the earliest chronicles of Danish legend and history. The only great writer of Latin prose in Denmark before the Reformation, Saxo is the most important source of information about early Danish literature and history.

BORN: c. 1150; probably Zealand, Denmark
DIED: c. 1220; place unknown
AREAS OF ACHIEVEMENT: Historiography, literature

EARLY LIFE

The meager details known of the life of Saxo Grammaticus (SAK-soh gruh-MA-tuh-kuhs) have been gleaned from his own history and from the writings of others. Since the accuracy of the external accounts is questionable, however, Saxo himself remains a scholarly mystery.

Based on careful research, scholars have concluded that Saxo was born into a noble family on the island of Zealand in Denmark. If the thirteenth century Zealand chronicle's mention of a Saxo Longus (the Tall) alludes to the historian, height is the only physical characteristic known about him. Saxo himself tells his readers that his grandfather and father served as soldiers in the army of Valdemar I, who reigned from 1157 to 1182.

It is from other, much later, sources that the name Grammaticus (the Lettered) arises. The fourteenth century Jutland chronicle is the first to assign Saxo the title. The writer of his epitome (1431) and the first edition of his work both retain the reference. This surname apparently refers to Saxo's conspicuous scholarship and elaborate style of Latin composition.

Saxo's complex Latin sentences have led scholars to conjecture that his education must have been meticulous, for in his day Latin was the language of the learned. Saxo was no doubt educated in the three major areas of grammar, dialectic, and rhetoric. His stories, literary allusions, and themes suggest that he studied the classics and Vergil's poetry, as well as such authors as Livy, Martianus Capella, Plato, Cicero, Boethius, and Valerius Maximus. He may also have had formal training in law. He seems to have been slightly familiar with spoken Icelandic and marginally acquainted with German. He may have gone to Paris to complete his education, or perhaps to Germany or England.

Scholars have also debated Saxo's profession. Saxo describes himself as one of the retinue of Absalon, archbishop of Lund from 1179 to 1201, but fails to say what services he actually performed, no doubt assuming that his readers would understand. Sven Aggesen, a slightly older contemporary, mentions Saxo as his *contubernalis* (literally, tent mate), but Sven's exact meaning is unclear because he may have meant anything from a military comrade to a fellow member of Absalon's retinue. In his will, Absalon mentions a clerk by the name of Saxo, but even if this reference is to Saxo Grammaticus (and it has been debated), scholars are uncertain whether this designation was applied to clerics or to laymen. To add to the confusion, the first edition of Saxo's work lists him as "sometime Head" of the cathedral church at Roskilde. One scholar has even suggested that he may have been Absalon's official historian. Such uncertainty has divided scholars; some believe that he was a monk serving as the archbishop's secretary, and some argue that he was a secular clerk. What is certain, and what Saxo himself tells his readers, is that his patron, Absalon, encouraged him to record in Latin the history of Denmark, the work for which Saxo is famous.

LIFE'S WORK

In *Gesta Danorum* (1514; *The History of the Danes*, 1894, 1980-1981), sometimes called *Historia Danica*, Saxo traces the lives of the Danes and their kings from their eponymous founder, Dan, to 1187 and Gorm III. The composition of the text occupied him from about 1185 until 1208; he spent from about 1208 until his death revising it and writing the preface.

Saxo had many reasons for composing *The History of the Danes*. His primary purpose, stated in the first sentence of his preface, was to glorify his country, then approaching the zenith of its political influence. Aware of Vergil's glorification of Rome, Saxo was eager to present his country folk with a similar monument to their own great past and recent accomplishments. Furthermore, the appearance of his history some fifty years after Denmark's civil war (1147-1157) was designed to reconcile peoples only lately reunified. Comments on his fellow Danes reveal that he also hoped to civilize his country and to provide evidence of its rich culture to the rest of the world.

Saxo did not use only one source for his history. He drew on ancient epic poems, folktales, popular tradition, inscriptions, lists of Danish kings, and oral lays of Denmark. He also borrowed from Icelandic sagas and Norse mythology. Some scholars have even recognized borrowings from Russian stories in the early books. For contemporary history, Saxo's chief source was probably his mentor, Absalon. Saxo also borrowed from foreign colleagues, directly quoting Dudo, Saint Bede the Venerable, and Paul the Deacon, all medieval historians. He may also have known of Jordanes, Gregory of Tours, Wittekind, Helmold, Giraldus Cambrensis (Gerald de Barri), and Geoffrey of Monmouth. It is clear that Saxo reworked everything he borrowed in order to shed greater glory on Denmark.

In literary style, Saxo again made use of others, this time pagan Latin authors of the Silver Age and of late antiquity. Justin and Curtius Rufus were important to him. Martianus Capella provided the Latin meters he used. His favorite author, however, was Valerius Maximus. Saxo's writing, characterized by moralizing and artificial cleverness, imitates the pointed style of Silver Age Latin.

Saxo's style, in fact, is another point of contention among scholars. Some say the style is vigorous and compelling; others accuse him of pomposity. Some find him biased against the early kings, Norwegians, Germans, and Swedes, and prejudiced in favor of Icelanders and Zealanders. Others argue that far from being naïve and uncritical, he contrived to use his stories to give meaning to the ancient past as the precedent for his glorious contemporary Denmark. Still others have discovered an elaborate four-part division to *The History of the Danes:* Books 1 to 4 deal with the world before Christ, books 5 to 8 discuss the period up to Denmark's conversion to Christianity, books 9 to 12 examine the growth of the new Church, and books 13 to 16 tell of events after the Church is firmly established. Another scholar has shown that Saxo inserts a visit to the Underworld halfway through his history, much as Vergil did in the *Aeneid* (c. 29-19 B.C.E.; English translation, 1553).

The story of most interest to students of English literature in Saxo's chronicle has to do with how a Danish prince named Amleth wreaked vengeance on his uncle for the murder of his father. This tale represents the earliest known form of the plot of William Shakespeare's *Hamlet* (pr. c. 1600-1601), and Saxo was the first to set it down in writing. All the evidence indicates that Saxo's tale is not literary fiction but a literary reworking of a Danish oral legend dating from at least the tenth century. Saxo expanded it with details of the story known in Iceland.

Though many scholars have admired his pioneer achievements, Saxo has also been sharply criticized for his Latin style, his naïve recounting of fables and fantasies, and even his choice of Latin as a linguistic medium. Historians have found little of value in the first nine books and have disputed the historic reliability of the later ones.

Yet Saxo has left his mark on literature and history for a number of reasons. First, *The History of the Danes* exemplifies the literary renaissance of the twelfth century. Saxo's chronicle is one of only two important sources for this period, the other being the account of Sven Aggesen. The latter's history of Denmark, however, is inferior to Saxo's in its scope, its Latin, and its literary background, and thus is of less importance. Prior to Saxo, Danish heroic poetry had been preserved only by oral tradition. Many of the tales in *The History of the Danes* are unrecorded elsewhere. Some of Saxo's sources are known only through allusions in his work. Consequently, mythologists and folklorists are indebted to Saxo for his preservation of all of these.

Saxo may have had little effect on his own time. His work was not immediately popular; in fact, it was mostly forgotten for three hundred years, surviving only in an epitome and a few manuscripts. The epitome reveals that Saxo's writing was considered to be difficult to comprehend. In the early sixteenth century, however, Christiern Pedersen, canon of Lund and Denmark's greatest Humanist, prepared a manuscript of Saxo that was published in 1514 in Paris by the renowned printer Jodocus Badius Ascensius. The Renaissance writers were greatly interested in Saxo. As a consequence, editions of Saxo became popular, and libraries throughout Europe boasted copies of his history. Desiderius Erasmus praised Saxo's force of eloquence. One of François de Belleforest's translations of Saxo is generally considered to have been Shakespeare's immediate source for *Hamlet*. Shakespeare himself may have had some knowledge of Saxo's work.

Saxo's work is now known almost completely from the first printed version. No complete manuscript survives. The most important fragment, four quarto leaves on parchment with fifteen lines to a page, is from Angers. Notes and corrections on these pages have been argued to have been written by Saxo's own hand or by the hand of one of his scribes.

Saxo's death probably occurred about 1220. Evidence in his history shows that he died before he completed the revision of his work.

Significance

Saxo was ideally suited to write the history of Denmark. He was well educated in the ways of the Church, in the language and literature of the Romans, and in the culture and literature of his native land, and he used all these resources to praise his people. Like Absalon, Saxo favored a strong, nationalistic monarchy, with the king controlling the legislative, military, and ecclesiastical branches. Through his *History of the Danes* he was able to emphasize the Church's—and especially Absalon's—importance in national reunification. His knowledge of Latin and the genre of the medieval history allowed him to choose a medium ideal for his purpose of tracing the royal family to the founding of the kingdom, much as Vergil had done in the case of Caesar Augustus in the *Aeneid*. By showing the king to be one with his country folk, Saxo hoped to reconcile hostile factions of people and to instill national pride. Though he despised all foreign influence and praised ancient Norse ideals, Saxo was so well versed in the literary culture of his age that he could construct a work using a Latin (and therefore foreign) framework and intertwine cultural and literary features from other peoples with his own country's heritage. In this way he hoped to create a work that would place Denmark among the learned civilizations of the world.

Medieval scholars and historians have also benefited from Saxo's history. Because Saxo chose to borrow from many different sources, many of which no longer exist, mythologists and students of folklore have a clearer picture of the evolution, transmission, and migration of certain legends and sagas. Students of Shakespeare gain a deeper appreciation of *Hamlet* through the story of Amleth. Finally, Saxo reveals important information about his own time, observations that would have been lost to subsequent generations if not for *The History of the Danes*.

—*Joan E. Carr*

Further Reading

Benoit-Dusausoy, Annick, and Guy Fontaine, eds. *History of European Literature*. Translated by Michael Wooff. New York: Routledge, 2000. A critical history of European literature, with chapters on Saxo, Shakespeare, and dozens of others.

Dumézil, Georges. *From Myth to Fiction: The Saga of Hadingus*. Translated by Derek Coltman. Chicago: University of Chicago Press, 1973. The introduction provides a clear synopsis of Saxo's life. Though the book deals with only one personage from *The History of the Danes*, the arguments also provide insight into other Saxonian legends.

Hansen, William F. *Saxo Grammaticus and the Life of Hamlet: A Translation, History, and Commentary*. Lincoln: University of Nebraska Press, 1983. The main part of the book is concerned with Saxo's style and the story of Hamlet. Significant parts also deal with Saxo's entire work. The general reader will find the text informative and easy to read. Includes useful notes, bibliography, and index. Illustrated.

Lausten, Martin Schwarz. *A Church History of Denmark*. Translated by Frederick H. Cryer. Burlington, Vt.: Ashgate, 2002. Provides a comprehensive survey of the history of the church in Denmark—a topic critical to Saxo's own *History*—from Viking paganism to the Viking contact with Christians and Christian culture abroad, and from the Christian conversion in the tenth century to the present. Includes a bibliography and an index.

Mitchell, P. M. *A History of Danish Literature*. 2d ed. New York: Kraus-Thomson Organization, 1971. A reproduction of the Angers fragment is included in this volume. The author places Saxo in perspective with the other writers of Danish literature. Appropriate for the general reader. Illustrations and an extensive bibliography.

Oakley, Stewart. *A Short History of Denmark*. New York: Praeger, 1972. Though Saxo is not treated extensively, the author puts him in historical perspective. Contains illustrations, an index, and suggestions for further reading.

Saxo Grammaticus. *The First Nine Books of the Danish History of Saxo Grammaticus*. Translated by Oliver Elton. Edited by Frederick York Powell. 1894. Reprint. Nendeln, Liechtenstein: Kraus, 1967. Footnotes in the introduction will help mainly the specialist. Footnotes in the text of the translation will be more valuable to the general reader.

_______. *The History of the Danes*. Translated by Peter Fisher. Edited by Hilda Ellis Davidson. 2 vols. 1979-1980. Reprint. Rochester, N.Y.: D. S. Brewer, 1996. The translation is lively and eminently readable. The introductions in both volumes will be extremely helpful for the general reader and the more advanced researcher. Summarizes Saxo's life, his place in Danish literature, the history of his text, and the history of scholarship on his work. Useful bibliography.

Taylor, Marion A. *A New Look at the Old Sources of Hamlet*. Paris: Mouton, 1968. The author deals only with Saxo's story of Hamlet but is conscientious in showing more than Danish and Roman influence. The footnotes are fairly specialized. The bibliography, however, will be of some use to the general reader.

SEE ALSO: Saint Bede the Venerable; Boethius; Jean Froissart; Geoffrey of Monmouth; Gregory of Tours; Snorri Sturluson; Valdemar II.

RELATED ARTICLES in *Great Events from History: The Middle Ages, 477-1453*: 731: Bede Writes *Ecclesiastical History of the English People*; 1373-1410: Jean Froissart Compiles His *Chronicles*.

SEI SHŌNAGON

Japanese writer and poet

Sei Shōnagon wrote The Pillow Book*, one of the most significant literary works of Japan's Heian period and an important primary source of information about life in the Japanese imperial court in the tenth century.*

BORN: 966 or 967; place unknown
DIED: c. 1013; possibly near Kyoto, Japan
AREA OF ACHIEVEMENT: Literature

EARLY LIFE

No direct biographical or historical records about Sei Shōnagon (say shoh-nah-gohn) have survived; information is fragmentary or conjectural about her life before and after her service at the imperial court, and about possible relationships, marriages, or children. Hints are embedded in her work *Makura no sōshi* (c. 994-c. 1001; *Pillow Book*, 1929; best known as *The Pillow Book of Sei Shōnagon*, 1967, or *The Pillow Book*) and in comments by contemporaries, especially her literary rival, Murasaki Shikibu.

Sei Shōnagon was born into the Kiyohara family, descendants of the Emperor Temmu (r. 673-686) and a family of some distinction, although by Shōnagon's lifetime, its influence was primarily literary. Her father, mentioned only once in her work, was Kiyohara no Motosuke, provincial governor of Higo, a poet whose work appears in several imperial anthologies, a scholar, and one of the compilers of *Gosen wakashū* (951; later collection of poetry). Her great-grandfather, Fukuyabu, was also a celebrated poet. Sei Shōnagon was apparently raised in a literary family, and evidence in her work points to an education in Japanese and Chinese literature. About her childhood and early years, there is no information.

Even Shōnagon's name is something of a mystery: *Sei* is the Sinified reading of *kiyo*, the first character of her family name, and *Shōnagon* represents an honorary title, "lesser or minor counselor." The combination was commonly used to refer to ladies of the imperial court and may have been given to her because a male relation held the title of *shōnagon*. Shōnagon's given name may have been Nagiko.

In 983, Sei Shōnagon may have married a government official named Tachibana no Norimitsu; the union may have produced a son, Norinaga. Certainly, Tachibana no Norimitsu is mentioned in *The Pillow Book*, but its translator, Ivan Morris, thinks it unlikely that Shōnagon was married to him, although the pair may have had an amorous relationship. The relationship or marriage did not survive; one legend about Shōnagon is that she then entered a relationship with another man. Although no specifics are provided, *The Pillow Book* contains evidence that Shōnagon had other intimate relationships, some of which were pleasant, others regrettable.

LIFE'S WORK

Sometime between 990 and 994, Sei Shōnagon entered court service as a lady-in-waiting or attendant to Empress Sadako (also known as Teishi), a consort of Emperor Ichijō (r. 986-1011) and the daughter of the powerful Fujiwara Michitaka. It appears that for at least half a decade, Sadako and her circle—including Shōnagon—shaped the arts and culture at the court. Shōnagon was a favorite of Sadako, a status that the writer repaid through her unabashed devotion to the empress. When Michitaka died, his position as a power broker was taken by his uncle and political enemy, Michinaga, whose daughter Akiko (or Shōshi) first became a concubine to the emperor and then later supplanted Sadako as favored consort. Despite Sadako's waning influence at court, Shōnagon remained with her mistress until Sadako died in childbirth near the end of 1000.

Some scholars believe that after leaving the court, Shōnagon married Fujiwara no Muneyo, who became governor of Settsu Province, and that she had a daughter, Koma no Myōbu. No definitive information is available on the remaining years of Sei Shōnagon's life; however, a number of legends have persisted to this day. One tradition claims that she died impoverished and alone; another says that she entered a convent. One scholar suggests that she probably died at Tsukinowa, a suburb of what is now Kyoto, where her father owned a residence. The geographical distribution and prevalence of legends about Shōnagon suggest that she had the means to travel after leaving the court.

The Pillow Book reveals some facets of the personality of Shōnagon, who apparently was a highly intelligent, acutely observant, and well-informed woman whose position as Sadako's lady-in-waiting afforded unparalleled access to the activities, opinions, attitudes, and concerns of the Heian aristocracy. The book introduces a witty writer who takes pleasure in words and in the language and imagery of poetry, a flamboyant woman who revels in celebrations and festivals and in court pageantry and protocol. Shōnagon's sensitivity to beauty shines through descriptions of the natural charms of her surroundings, in delineations of colors and textures in clothing, and in notes about harmonious design elements in homes and public buildings. Especially obvious is Shōnagon's joy in being a member of the court. She adored the imperial family, especially the empress Sadako, and was a favored member of the empress's inner circle.

Murasaki Shikibu, a contemporary of Shōnagon and the author of *Genji monogatari* (c. 1004; *The Tale of Genji*, 1925-1933), was not among Shōnagon's admirers. In her diary, Murasaki complained that Shōnagon had an excessively good opinion of herself—in translation, the criticism is variously rendered "conceit and arrogance" or "self-satisfaction." Murasaki was introspective and philosophical, and her dislike of the gregarious and showy Shōnagon is not surprising. In general, the criticism should be read as an opinion from a rival whose personality was decidedly different. There may, however, be a germ of truth in Murasaki's description of Shōnagon.

Scholars and readers who are charmed by the elegance and cleverness of *The Pillow Book* are frequently taken aback by Shōnagon's intolerance for those whom she considered beneath her, socially, economically, or intellectually. She writes of women "who are of no more value than a roof tile" and complains that it is annoying "to be disturbed by a herd of common people." Comments such as these are not uncommon; however, although her elitism is discomfiting, contemporary readers must remember that Shōnagon was a product of her upbringing and historical milieu; her values mirrored those of the courtiers around her.

Although she wrote both prose and poetry, Shōnagon is celebrated for *The Pillow Book*. Probably begun around 994 while Shōnagon was in Sadako's service, the work was completed sometime after the writer left the court, possibly around 1001. *The Pillow Book* is significant in Japanese literature, praised for its linguistic purity, celebrated for its variety, and still widely read more than a thousand years after its composition.

The greatest Heian period (794-1185) literature flowered during the late tenth and early eleventh centuries, the years under Emperor Ichijō, during which Sei Shōnagon and Murasaki Shikibu served successive consorts at the imperial court. Dominated by the great Fujiwara family, those years were noted for their cultural and artistic achievements, for tremendous literary production, and for the development of new genres and literary subjects. The major writers of Ichijō's reign were women, including Izumi Shikibu, hailed as the era's greatest poet; Murasaki Shikibu, known for her diary and *The Tale of Genji*; and Sei Shōnagon.

Evidence in *The Pillow Book* suggests that its existence was known, and the creation of manuscripts many centuries later speaks to the work's enduring popularity.

So iconic was *The Pillow Book* in the ensuing centuries that a fourteenth century artist created the *Makura no sōshi e-maki*, a scroll ornamented with scenes and events from Shōnagon's book.

The Pillow Book consists of more than three hundred entries (the number varies among manuscripts) covering the years Shōnagon spent at court. As the only work of its kind surviving from the Heian period, *The Pillow Book* is not only a literary masterpiece but also a vast resource for cultural historians interested in the court of a Heian emperor.

The title of Shōnagon's work may not have been of her choosing. The term "pillow book" was commonly used at the time for an informal journal containing jottings and observations composed in solitude. These books were kept private, probably in small drawers built into wooden pillows, hence the label. Because *The Pillow Book* consists of pieces, apparently composed spontaneously and irregularly, it is impossible to determine—except for some fifty dateable sections—when and in what order the entries were written. Extant manuscripts from long after Shōnagon's death disagree on the arrangement of the various sections in the book.

Several early texts of *The Pillow Book* exist, but none of them dates back to Shōnagon's lifetime. As later revisions or editions, these manuscripts vary in the placement of Shōnagon's entries; yet whatever the order, they each fit into one of several fairly distinct categories: essays on a variety of subjects, essays on emotions and feelings, short observations and musings, and autobiographical vignettes that reveal not only Shōnagon's life at court but also fragments about her life before she entered Sadako's service.

Among the prose forms represented in *The Pillow Book* are short tales, personal narratives, reflections, anecdotes, descriptions of nature, character sketches, vignettes, standard diary entries, prose poems, and commentaries. Also included are sixteen poems, although most scholars agree that Shōnagon's genius lay in her facility and deftness with prose forms, and that her poetry is, at best, pedestrian. Topics covered in *The Pillow Book* vary tremendously, appearing random and haphazard; Shōnagon writes about chance encounters, amorous intrigues, politics, ceremonies, festivals, fashion, men, penmanship, and food. She comments on serious subjects: class and gender relations, court attitudes and values, social hierarchies, and the shape of life in her aristocratic universe. Yet she is also playful and informal, describing the emperor playing his flute, lovers' visits, and the origins of names. She illuminates the lives of women—those of her class and those below her—their activities, cosmetics, clothing, apartments, pastimes, and even their faces. Her descriptions of the natural world—trees, birds, flowers, even insects—are delicate and painterlike.

A striking feature of *The Pillow Book* are 164 delightfully personal lists interspersed throughout the work. Shōnagon enumerates the hateful or depressing, the annoying or awkward; she details the elegant, adorable, splendid, or rare. She lists "Poetic Subjects," "Things That Arouse a Fond Memory of the Past," "Things Without Merit," and "Things That Give a Pathetic Impression." Some lists are brief, with two or three items; others are extensive and detailed. The lists are quirky, always engaging and revelatory of Shōnagon's personality and thoughts.

SIGNIFICANCE

Through *The Pillow Book*, Sei Shōnagon influenced the development of the genre known as *zuihitsu* (literally "following the pen"), an anthology or miscellany whose elements lack a formal arrangement and that has an air of spontaneity and of having been composed on the inspiration of the moment. *The Pillow Book* opens a window into a medieval Japanese royal court, revealing glimpses of the human beings behind historical personages such as Emperor Ichijō and his consort Sadako.

—*E. D. Huntley*

FURTHER READING

Keene, Donald. *Seeds in the Heart*. New York: Columbia University Press, 1999. Keene's excellent overview of early Japanese literature includes a chapter on *The Pillow Book* and useful bibliographies for further study.

Miner, Earl, Hiroko Odagiri, and Robert E. Morrell. *The Princeton Companion to Classical Japanese Literature*. Princeton, N.J.: Princeton University Press, 1985. Covering the earliest times to the mid-nineteenth century, this volume is an extensive overview of the development of Japanese literature, with sections on literary history, major authors, literary terms, and essential cultural and historical information.

Morris, Ivan. *The World of the Shining Prince: Court Life in Ancient Japan*. 1964. Reprint. New York: Kodansha International, 1994. Morris's book is probably the best single introduction to the world of Heian Japan in which Sei Shōnagon wrote and flourished.

Putzer, Edward. *Japanese Literature: A Historical Outline*. Tucson: University of Arizona Press, 1973. This work provides an overview of Japanese literature from its earliest years to World War II, through translations or adaptations of work by Japanese scholars. The section on Heian literature is adapted from Japanese scholar Abe Akio.

Sarra, Edith. *Fictions of Femininity: Literary Inventions of Gender in Japanese Court Women's Memoirs*. Stanford, Calif.: Stanford University Press, 1998. Explores how four Heian memoir writers, including Sei Shōnagon, create identities for themselves in their prose. The analysis of each work asks two questions: how the memoir functions as a literary piece and how it reflects the author's negotiations with Heian society's ideas about women and writing.

Sei Shōnagon, *The Pillow Book of Sei Shōnagon*. Translated by Ivan Morris. 1967. Reprint. New York: Columbia University Press, 1991. This is the standard, complete translation of *Makura no sōshi*, including the lists that have captivated readers. Features a useful introduction as well as genealogical tables, maps, and floor plans.

See also: Fujiwara Michinaga; Murasaki Shikibu; Nijō.

Related articles in *Great Events from History: The Middle Ages, 477-1453*: 794-1185: Heian Period; c. 800: *Kana* Syllabary Is Developed; c. 1001: Sei Shōnagon Completes *The Pillow Book*; c. 1004: Murasaki Shikibu Writes *The Tale of Genji*.

Sergius I

Patriarch of Orthodox Christian Church (610-638)

As head of the Orthodox Christian Church, Sergius I made a major if unsuccessful effort to resolve the vexing Monophysite controversy by advancing the Monothelete doctrine. At the same time, he became the loyal and invaluable partner of Emperor Heraclius, helping him save the Byzantine Empire in a time of dire crisis.

Born: Date unknown; place unknown

Died: December 9, 638; Constantinople, Byzantine Empire (now Istanbul, Turkey)

Also known as: Patriarch Sergius of Constantinople

Areas of achievement: Religion and theology, government and politics

Early Life

Virtually no information is available regarding the early life of Sergius. He is said to have been Syrian in origin. He is recorded as holding the office of dean of the clergy of Hagia Sophia, the cathedral of Constantinople, and was also in charge of the church's ministries of charity at the time of the death of the patriarch Thomas in 610. Sergius was chosen to succeed to the patriarchal chair himself at this point.

His elevation came in a period of upheaval, strain, and crisis, in both immediate and long-range terms. He was enthroned during the reign of the bloody usurper Emperor Phocas, against whom a revolt was brewing. More broadly, he assumed the status of ecumenical patriarch—prelate of the Byzantine Empire's capital and one of the five great ecclesiastical leaders recognized as partners in the rule of the larger Christian community—during a time when the Christian world was torn by continuing doctrinal dissent. Various positions in the debate over the understanding of Christ's nature as both a divine and a human being had become identified with divergent cultural traditions and political loyalties as well as spiritual commitments. Fiercely held dissident beliefs among the inhabitants of certain regions of the empire posed political as well as theological problems, threatening the loyalty of those regions. Whether, left to his own impulses, Sergius would have developed the doctrinal positions that he came to espouse cannot be known, but his career as patriarch was to force him to develop them.

Life's Work

Sergius became patriarch of Constantinople while the tyrant Phocas was fighting to retain the throne he had won by rebellion and murder in 602. Sergius was barely installed when Heraclius, son of the exarch (viceroy) of Africa, sailed to Constantinople at the head of a fleet in the autumn of 610 to lead the uprising against Phocas. With the help of dissidents in the city, Phocas was overthrown and executed, and Heraclius was acclaimed as his successor, reigning until 641. On October 5, 610, Sergius presided over not only the coronation of Heraclius but also his marriage to Eudoxia.

The patriarch was soon drawn into a close understanding and partnership with the new emperor, a relationship that was not to be without its tensions and trials. After less than two years of marriage, Heraclius was shattered by the loss of Eudoxia, her weak health undermined further by bearing two children. In his bereavement, Heraclius was urged by his mother to take as his second wife the intelligent and devoted Martina. Several objections to such a union were immediately raised: Martina was ambitious, she was twenty-three years younger than Heraclius, and she was his niece—the daughter of his own sister. This last fact prompted outrage and indignation on the part of populace and clergy alike. Sergius is reported to have attempted personally to dissuade the emperor from this plan, but Heraclius became determined to take Martina as his wife. Apparently judging it best not to destroy what must have become an important trust between prelate and sovereign, Sergius capitulated and performed the marriage a year or so later.

Trust and supportive understanding were needed between Sergius and Heraclius as the emperor had to deal with the mounting crises that faced the empire. While the Turkish Avars ravaged the Balkan provinces, the Persians to the east had begun a program of systematic conquest of imperial territories. In 611, they invaded Syria-Palestine, and their bloody conquest of Jerusalem in 614 was carried out as a calculated humiliation of the Christian faith. Between 616 and 620, the Persians went on to conquer Egypt, and their armies began to penetrate Asia Minor and threaten the approaches to the capital.

With shattered military forces and rapidly dwindling resources, Heraclius seemed paralyzed, despite his best efforts to cope, and must at times have felt despair. It is reported that, by 619, the emperor had decided to withdraw from Constantinople and to transfer his residence to the safer distance of Carthage, from which he might launch a counteroffensive. It is said that, in response, Sergius confronted the emperor on behalf of the panic-stricken citizens of the capital and compelled him to swear a public oath that he would not abandon Constantinople. Historically accurate or not, this story does seem to reflect an understanding reached between Sergius and Heraclius in a time of crisis. For his part, Sergius agreed that the impoverished state should be allowed to draw on the vast wealth of the Church, at least as a loan, to replenish its depleted coffers. With these new funds, Heraclius was able to finance the recruitment and training of a new and expanded military force to meet the Persian menace.

Meanwhile, Sergius had already been working to assist the emperor in other ways. The demoralizing speed with which the Persians had been conquering Syria-Palestine and Egypt pointed out the added urgency of a problem that had long undermined the stability and loyalty of those regions under the empire: the large popular adherence there to the Christological heresy known as Monophysitism—the doctrine of the single (divine) nature of Christ—which had been condemned by the Council of Chalcedon in 451 but still remained attractive to many. As patriarch, Sergius was pledged to uphold the Chalcedonian doctrine of the two natures of Christ. Though past attempts at bridging the gap between the two positions had failed, Sergius recognized the desperate need to try again if the empire's population was to be restored to unity. Moreover, if the report is true that his own parents had been Monophysites of the Syrian Jacobite church, he must have been able to understand the heretical position well.

Sergius therefore drew on some earlier theological arguments to propose a compromise: a doctrine that bypassed the issue of one or two natures and stressed the concept of a single motivating energy (*energeia*), "one activity and one will," in Christ. Apparently, the emperor approved this doctrine of "monoenergism" as one with which both Monophysites and dyophysite Chalcedonians might agree. From about 618, Sergius began a round of contacts with prelates and theologians around the empire, finding much support and encouragement from them. This theological olive branch, as a basis for sectarian pacification and reunion among dissident populations, was as important as the Church's financial support for Heraclius's struggle to save the empire.

On April 4, 622, all was ready, and Sergius presided with the emperor over a solemn ceremony of public consecration to the new enterprise—one that later generations in Western Europe would hail as a veritable crusade on behalf of the Christian faith, as much as a political and territorial counteroffensive. Crossing to Asia Minor, Heraclius began his initial campaigns with great success. His route took him into the areas of the Caucasus and Armenia, where Monophysite doctrine was strong, so that discussions of the monoenergist doctrine were important components of the emperor's efforts to win allies and recruits for his military operations.

In the midst of the emperor's campaigns, the Persians persuaded the Avars to attack Constantinople as a countermeasure to distract Heraclius. Though repeatedly bribed by tributes to keep the peace, the greedy Avars were only too glad to mount a ferocious and determined siege of the capital, beginning on June 29, 626. Heraclius had entrusted the command of the city in his absence to able civil and military officials, under the general supervision of Sergius himself, and the emperor's confidence in them was not tested as he boldly decided not to end his campaigning to return to the besieged city, as the Persians had hoped. To Sergius in particular fell the task of keeping up the spirit of resistance during this trial. In this he succeeded: The Avars were repulsed and abandoned the attack by August 8, amid stories that the Virgin Mary herself had intervened miraculously to drive off the pagan attackers. Sergius led celebrations of joy and thanksgiving, and this deliverance of Constantinople is still commemorated in one of the most famous hymns of the Greek Orthodox liturgy, the great Akathistos hymn. Indeed, it was once thought that the entire hymn dated from this event, perhaps being a composition of Sergius himself; it is now known that the bulk of it was the work of Romanos the Melode of a century earlier, but the prologue, with its explicit reference to the Virgin's intervention against the Avars to save her city, was apparently an addition dating from this episode of 626.

Vindicated by the deliverance of Constantinople, Heraclius renewed his campaigning, and, within the next two years, brought the Persian kingdom to its knees. In September, 628, Heraclius was welcomed back to the capital as a victorious hero, and at some time thereafter he ceremonially restored to Jerusalem the True Cross that had been carried off by the Persians. As part of his restoration of imperial government in the recovered territories, Heraclius continued to promote the doctrinal compromise developed by Sergius. It met with mixed receptions. Among its most determined opponents were the aged and dogmatic Palestinian monk Sophronius and the brilliant young theologian Maximos (later to become known as "the Confessor"). Sergius strove to convince them by theological arguments, and, in his correspondence with the bishop of Rome, he was able to win qualified acceptance from Pope Honorius I. In the process, the wording of the compromise doctrine began to shift to the concept of Christ having a single will (*thelēma*) rather than a single energy: hence the doctrine's eventual label of Monothelism.

The quest for religious unity acquired new urgency as the areas of greatest sectarian dissent became the target of unexpected and sudden onslaughts of the Arabs, who between 634 and 636 effectively destroyed the empire's capacity to control Syria-Palestine. Sophronius himself was elected patriarch of Jerusalem in 634, amid the scramble, and used his position to renew opposition to the Monothelete doctrine. Its failure to win back popular loyalty in Syria-Palestine and the apparent collaboration of the dissidents with the tolerant conquerors made the emperor and patriarch only more anxious to use it to save Egypt from the same fate, as well as to silence the opposition of Chalcedonian loyalists. With help from his advisers, Sergius drew up a doctrinal statement, or *ekthesis*, formally propounding the dogma of the One Will of Christ and forbidding further debate over the one or two natures. It was finally approved by Heraclius and issued about October, 638. This *ekthesis* was Sergius's last service to his emperor. In early December of that year, the old patriarch died, leaving the struggle to his heirs.

Significance

The year of Sergius's death witnessed the deaths of several other central figures in the religious controversy. In March, 638, shortly after negotiating the capitulation of Jerusalem to the Arabs, the adamant Sophronius had died. Pope Honorius I died in October, about the time the *ekthesis* was promulgated. Despite the ruthless Monothelete policies of Cyrus, the patriarch of Alexandria, Egypt remained unreconciled, and it soon submitted to the Arab invasion of 639-641. Broken and disillusioned, the aged Heraclius died in February, 641. Sergius's Monothelete doctrine was subsequently repudiated by Rome and, after decades of bitter ecclesiastical strife, it was abandoned by the imperial government at the sixth ecumenical council in 681, though some support for it survived in the provinces.

The failure of Monothelism should not, however, tarnish Sergius's achievement. His formulation was the product of a sincere desire to end religious controversy, of a flexible and pragmatic theological learning, and of a noble spirit of service to his church and faith. It must be placed also in the context of Sergius's service to sovereign and people, including his supreme moments of glory in supporting Heraclius and in leading the defense of Constantinople in 626. In a tradition in which the patriarch was often either the subordinate or the opponent of the emperor, Sergius was one of the few prelates to be a genuine partner to his sovereign and to make the theoretical harmony between Church and state in Byzantium actually work.

—*John W. Barker*

Further Reading

Bury, J. B. *A History of the Later Roman Empire: From Arcadius to Irene (395 A.D. to 800 A.D.).* 2 vols. New York: Macmillan, 1889. Outdated in its coverage of the early seventh century, but includes a still-useful treatment of the ecclesiastical history of the period, including the career of Sergius.

Every, George. *The Byzantine Patriarchate, 451-1204.* 1962. Reprint. 2d ed. New York: AMS Press, 1980.

This very general survey is useful for its broad perspective, even though it includes only a few pages on the epoch of Sergius.

Frend, W. H. C. *The Rise of the Monophysite Movement: Chapters in the History of the Church in the Fifth and Sixth Centuries*. Cambridge, England: Cambridge University Press, 1972. Written by a leading historian of the early Christian church and its heretical movements, this is an excellent treatment of this particular sectarian controversy. The latter part of its final chapter gives an excellent account of the doctrinal efforts of Sergius.

Hussey, J. M. *The Orthodox Church in the Byzantine Empire*. Oxford, England: Clarendon Press, 1986. A volume in the Oxford History of the Christian Church series, this book covers the time span from the early seventh century through 1453. The treatment of Sergius's era is brief but useful and set in good context.

Kaegi, Walter E. *Heraclius: Emperor of Byzantium*. New York: Cambridge University Press, 2003. A thorough overview of Heraclius's life and times. Includes an extensive bibliography and an index.

Ostrogorsky, George. *History of the Byzantine State*. Translated by Joan Hussey. Rev. ed. New Brunswick, N.J.: Rutgers University Press, 1969. Though now showing its age, still the most comprehensive one-volume treatment of the Byzantine Empire's history and institutions, from the early fourth through the mid-fifteenth century, with an excellent perspective on the sixth century era in general.

Stratos, Andreas N. *Byzantium in the Seventh Century*. 5 vols. Translated by Marc Ogilvie-Grant and Harry T. Hionides. Amsterdam: Adolf M. Hakkert, 1968-1980. The opening volumes (of six in the original Greek version, five in the English translation) of a remarkably comprehensive study of seventh century Byzantium. These volumes cover the age of Heraclius, including the career of Sergius. Displays great admiration and sympathy for Sergius.

Whittow, Mark. *The Making of Byzantium, 600-1025*. Berkeley: University of California Press, 1996. A history of the Byzantine Empire and the Orthodox Church. Maps, bibliography, and index.

SEE ALSO: Heraclius; Justinian I; Theodora.

RELATED ARTICLES in *Great Events from History: The Middle Ages, 477-1453*: 630-711: Islam Expands Throughout North Africa; 637-657: Islam Expands Throughout the Middle East; 726-843: Iconoclastic Controversy; 1054: Beginning of the Rome-Constantinople Schism.

SAINT SERGIUS I

Italian pope (687-701)

During his time as pope, Sergius greatly strengthened relations between Rome and the churches in the Anglo-Saxon west and maintained the western church's independence from the emperors of Constantinople. He introduced the Agnus Dei into the Mass and was responsible for the restoration and embellishment of churches throughout Rome.

BORN: 635; Palermo, Sicily (now in Italy)
DIED: September 8, 701; Rome (now in Italy)
AREA OF ACHIEVEMENT: Religion and theology

EARLY LIFE

The father of Sergius (SAHR-jee-uhs), a merchant named Tiberius, migrated from the Syrian town of Antioch to Sicily. It was on this island, in the town of Palermo, that the young Sergius received his early education. Little else is known of this part of his life, except that he journeyed to Rome and entered the priesthood under the papacy of Adeodatus II. During his training for the priesthood, Sergius revealed an enthusiasm for music and was allowed to study under the head cantor. His interest in music would persist throughout his papacy. In either 682 or 683, he was ordained by Pope Leo II and became the titular priest of the town of Santa Susanna, located on the Quirinal. As a priest he developed a reputation for his love of saying Mass in the catacombs, a practice that, though once common, had become rare by his time. In 687, Pope Conon died after a long illness, and a bitter struggle for the papal successor ensued. It was out of this struggle that the humble priest from Santa Susanna emerged as leader of the Church.

LIFE'S WORK

While Pope Conon was still on his deathbed, his archdeacon Paschal had offered a bribe of one hundred pounds of gold to the new Byzantine imperial exarch John Platyn, in order to guarantee the papal chair for himself. John Platyn was at Ravenna at the time and proved to be more than obliging in this request. When the pope finally died, Platyn managed to secure the nomination of Paschal for the papal succession. Platyn was successful in this because the faction that nominated Paschal was composed of officials whom Platyn himself had earlier appointed to govern Rome.

Such treachery would probably have passed unnoticed and Paschal would have become pope had not a larger rival faction nominated the archpriest Theodore as Conon's successor. That created a stalemate. In fact, the opposing factions barricaded themselves in separate parts of the Lateran Palace, each refusing to back down. The group backing Theodore occupied the interior section of the Lateran Palace that contained the private apartments of the pope, while the group backing Paschal occupied the exterior sections.

In the midst of this turmoil, a meeting of leading civic authorities, army officers, and clergy was held in the Palatine Palace with the aim of selecting a third candidate to break the deadlock. The priest of Santa Susanna was unanimously chosen by this group to become the pope. On the nomination of Sergius, the gates of the Lateran were stormed and the rival groups ousted. When Sergius himself entered the palace, Theodore immediately renounced his pretensions to the throne. Paschal, too, renounced his designs and recognized the legitimacy of Sergius, but he did so grudgingly and only under compulsion. In fact, Paschal continued with his machinations against Sergius and offered more money to John Platyn if the latter would come to Rome and overturn the election.

Platyn went secretly to Rome. Probably to the surprise of Paschal, however, Platyn gave his approval to Sergius when he realized that the installment in power had been carried out regularly and enjoyed massive popular support. Unfortunately, Platyn demanded of Sergius the money that had been promised him by Paschal. Sergius refused—on the grounds, first, that he had not been partner to any such deal and, second, that he simply did not have the money. Nevertheless, Platyn insisted on being paid, and Sergius offered to pledge as payment the candelabra and crowns that stood in front of the altar of Saint Peter. This offer did not satisfy Platyn, and

Saint Sergius I. (Library of Congress)

he refused to permit Sergius to be consecrated until the money had actually been raised and paid. Sergius relented, paid Platyn, and was finally consecrated on December 15, 687. Paschal continued, however, to intrigue against the new pope until he was finally arraigned, deprived of the position of archdeacon, and imprisoned. Paschal remained unrepentant and died in prison five years later.

The first noteworthy act of Sergius in his position as leader of the Catholic Church was of a housekeeping nature. He had the remains of Leo the Great moved from their relatively inconspicuous burial ground and housed in a newly constructed ornate tomb in the basilica.

The reign of Pope Sergius I was primarily noteworthy for his refusal to endorse the Second Trullan Synod (also known as the Quinisext Council), called in 692 by the Eastern Roman emperor Justinian II. This meeting, of more than two hundred bishops of the eastern church, was convened by Justinian II with the ostensible purpose of supplementing the work of the Fifth (held in 553) and Sixth (held in 680) general councils. However, though the Trullan Synod legislated for the entire Church, only one bishop of the west was present, and the 102 disciplinary and ritual canons enacted by the council were actually motivated by a degree of hostility toward and defiance of the western church.

The canons banned practices that were established in the west (such as the celibacy of the clergy and fasting on Saturdays in Lent), ignored western canon law, and reestablished the Twenty-eighth Canon of Chalcedon, which granted patriarchal status to Constantinople (second only to Rome). The latter canon had been vigorously and continuously resisted by Rome. Representatives of the pope in Constantinople were forced to sign the acts of the council, and in the year after the synod Justinian II sent the canons to Sergius for his signature and approval. Sergius not only refused to sign the acts, he even refused to let them be read out loud. Justinian II responded by arresting two of the pope's councillors stationed in Constantinople and by sending the commandant of his personal bodyguard, Zacharias, to Rome to arrest Sergius and bring him back to Constantinople.

Zacharias arrived in Rome to an extremely inhospitable welcome. Before Zacharias's arrival, Sergius had appealed to the exarch for assistance, and troops were sent from Ravenna to Rome. Though Zacharias managed to corner the pope in the Lateran, he in turn became the hunted. The troops from Ravenna, aided by the Pentapolis and Roman citizens, stormed the Lateran and pursued Zacharias. The commandant of the bodyguard fled in terror from his pursuers and ended up hiding under Sergius's bed in the papal apartments. Sergius was then forced to plead with the people for the life of Zacharias, who was arrested and forced to leave the city. This humiliating defeat for Justinian II would have precipitated serious consequences for Sergius, but the former was himself deposed within two years by Leontius. The major result of the incident was that it served to deepen the existing gulf between the eastern and western churches. Since that time, the only response of the Papacy to the Trullan Synod has been tacit approval of the canons for the eastern church.

Sergius promulgated relations of an entirely different ilk with the western church. The first major event in the papacy of Sergius concerning the western churches occurred in 689 on the vigil of Easter. On that date he baptized Caedwalla, the once-pagan king of the West Saxons. Caedwalla, "the strong-armed," had been converted the year before by Saint Wilfrid, whereupon he abandoned his kingship and made the royal pilgrimage to Rome. Caedwalla died only ten days after his baptism by Sergius, who ordered the remains of this notable convert to be buried on the grounds of Saint Peter's itself.

Another well-known Englishman who visited Sergius was the abbot Aldhelm, who was later appointed bishop of Sherburne by Sergius. Aldhelm was the founder of Malmesbury Abbey and had visited Sergius in order to gain a charter of privilege for the abbey. The charter, which placed the monasteries of Malmesbury and Frome under the immediate jurisdiction of Rome, was granted by Sergius and greatly fortified the power of Rome over the English churches. Sometime around 700, Sergius ordered Saint Wilfrid to be restored to the See of York as bishop. Sergius also approved of the appointment of Brithwald, as the successor of Saint Theodore, to be bishop of Canterbury.

Connections between Rome and England were further strengthened by Sergius when he authorized the missionary work to the Continent of Saint Willibrord. Willibrord had trained at the monastery of Saint Wilfrid in Ireland and went as a missionary in 691 to Frisia, a country that lay between the Rhine and the Elbe. After four successful years in that country he was sent to Rome and was consecrated bishop of the Frisians by Sergius. Inspired by the achievements of Willibrord, Sergius sent Saint Chilian and Saint Swibert to do further missionary work in Germany.

Toward the end of his tenure as pope, Sergius was active in rectifying the schism of Aquileia. This schismatic group, in existence since the condemnation of the "Three Chapters" by Vigilius in 553, consisted of a collection of suffragan bishops under the leadership of the patriarch of Aquileia, in northern Italy. To bring about a rectification of the schism, the king of the Lombards, Cunibert, invited the schismatic bishops to a synod at Pavia. The council was an overwhelming success, and the renegade sect was brought back into the Catholic fold. After the reunion, Sergius commanded that all the works of the schismatic sect be burned to ward off the possibility of ideological contamination.

During the closing days of Sergius's reign, monks were sent to him by Saint Ceolfried from the monasteries of Saint Peter and Saint Paul (of Wearmouth in England) to secure yet another charter for English monasteries. The pope gave his approval to the monasteries and, more important, learned from these men of the great erudition of their fellow monk Bede. Bede would later become known as the greatest historian of early England. Sergius later requested Bede's presence in Rome to help solve certain problems. Unfortunately, Sergius died shortly afterward and Bede never made the pilgrimage.

Sergius's early musical talent was not wasted during his reign as pope. An alumnus of the Schola Cantorum, he was an accomplished singer. Most important, he was responsible for the introduction of the singing of the Agnus Dei into the Mass. He also introduced the practice of making processions to the various churches on the feasts of the Virgin Mary (the Nativity, the Annunciation, the Purification, and the Assumption).

Throughout his tenure as pope, Sergius was active in restoring the churches of Rome, including Saint Peter's, Saint Paul's, and his own church of Santa Susanna. He is reported to have discovered a small silver box hidden in the sacristy of Saint Peter's that contains a portion of the "true cross," embedded on a jeweled cross. This relic is used in the feast of the Exaltation of the Cross, initiated by Sergius himself.

Significance

Sergius died in 701 and was buried in Saint Peter's. The cult of his sainthood began shortly after his death, and his life is celebrated by Catholics on September 8. During his lifetime, he developed a reputation for exceptional piety. Though Sergius was ineffective in bringing the eastern and western churches together, he was important in extending the influence of the Church in the west, especially in England. In addition, he was successful in helping to bring about an end to the schism that had split the church of Italy. Most important, however, was his successful resistance to the attempts of the eastern emperors to achieve hegemonic control of the Church.

It has often been argued that the popes of this time acquired temporal power through the strength of their own vaulting ambitions. This claim is clearly false where Sergius is concerned. He could hardly have been ambitious to become pope in the first place; indeed, one almost gets the impression that he became pope against his will.

—*Mark Stephen Pestana*

Further Reading

Coppa, Frank J., ed. *Encyclopedia of the Vatican and Papacy.* Westport, Conn.: Greenwood Press, 1999. An encyclopedia of the popes. Lists antipopes and ecumenical councils. Bibliography and index.

Duffy, Eamon. *Saints and Sinners: A History of the Popes.* 2d ed. New Haven, Conn.: Yale University Press, 2001. A general history of the popes, with information on Saint Sergius I.

Mann, Horace K. *The Lives of the Popes in the Early Middle Ages.* Vol. 2. Reprint. Wilmington, N.C.: Consortium Books, 1980. Contains a chapter devoted to the life of Sergius. Very important for an understanding of the general era in which Sergius lived and of the lives of the popes who came immediately before and after him.

Ullmann, Walter. *A Short History of the Papacy in the Middle Ages.* 1972. Reprint. New York: Routledge, 2003. A general study by the foremost authority in the field. Focuses primarily on the Papacy, very little on individual popes. Good discussion of the influence of the Papacy throughout Europe. Enormous bibliography.

See also: Saint Bede the Venerable, Saint Patrick.

Related articles in *Great Events from History: The Middle Ages, 477-1453*: 596-597: See of Canterbury Is Established; 726-843: Iconoclastic Controversy; 735: Christianity Is Introduced into Germany.

SHŌTOKU TAISHI

Japanese regent

As regent for his aunt, Empress Suiko, Shōtoku is credited with strengthening the central government, solidifying the rule of the imperial family, and transforming Japan's civilization through adoption of Confucian and Buddhist institutions and values.

BORN: 574; Yamato, Honshu, Japan
DIED: April 8, 622; Yamato, Honshu, Japan
ALSO KNOWN AS: Umayado no Miko (Prince Umayado)
AREAS OF ACHIEVEMENT: Government and politics, religion and theology

EARLY LIFE

Little is known about the life of Shōtoku Taishi (shoh-toh-koo ti-shee); what is recorded is more legend than fact. The *Nihon shoki* (compiled 720 C.E.; *Nihongi: Chronicles of Japan from the Earliest Times to A.D. 697*, 1896; best known as *Nihon shoki*) describes stages and events in Shōtoku's life, beginning with a wondrous birth. His mother, the empress-consort, was walking near the imperial stables when she suddenly gave birth. Shōtoku was "able to speak at once and grew up so wise that he could listen to and understand ten men's petitions simultaneously and decide their cases without error."

Son of Emperor Yōmei (r. 585-587), Shōtoku rose to eminence in a time of intense political rivalry among several clans. Among these, the Yamato clan, claiming divine descent, was accepted as the imperial line by the fifth century, while the Soga and the Mononobe contended for the position closest to the throne. Interwoven with their political strife were disagreements over a newly arrived faith, Buddhism.

In 552, according to the *Nihon shoki*—some sources have it as early as 538—the king of Paekche in Korea sent the emperor an image of Buddha along with scriptures and a letter recommending the worship of Buddha to bring blessings and prosperity on Japan. He had a two-fold reason for his action: As a devoted Buddhist, he wanted to propagate Buddhist teachings, and as a ruler faced with powerful enemies, he hoped for an alliance with Japan.

The Japanese court was favorable to the new religion, but it asked the other clans for advice regarding its final acceptance or rejection. (In his youth, Shōtoku studied under a Korean Buddhist monk as well as a Confucian scholar, which indicates of the court's openness to foreign culture.) The Soga and Mononobe took opposite sides in the ensuing dispute. Under its chieftain, Soga Umako, the Soga and its allies defeated the Mononobe in battle and, by 587, Buddhism's status in Japan was secure. It would become a major vehicle for Soga Umako and Shōtoku in their joint efforts to strengthen Japan politically and culturally.

LIFE'S WORK

Soga Umako placed his niece Suiko (r. 593-628) on the throne and arranged that she appoint Shōtoku regent. Shōtoku married Umako's daughter, thus cementing an already close relationship. According to the *Nihon shoki*, Shōtoku "had general control of the government, and was entrusted with all the details of the administration." For almost thirty years, the two men collaborated to establish a strong central government.

Nihon shoki, written at a time when the Soga were out of favor and power, credits Shōtoku with major achievements between 593 and 622. In book 22, two political moves by Shōtoku are listed: initiation of a twelve-cap system of court ranks and authorship of the Seventeen Article Constitution. The twelve-cap system was an innovation in that, at least theoretically, offices would be based on personal merit rather than on privileged class. In actuality, the new system, begun in 603, was primarily a means of distinguishing ranks by means of different cap patterns and colors. Shōtoku was concerned with creating a well-developed bureaucracy, dependent on the emperor's will. Lineage remained very important in obtaining office, however, as it would well into the twentieth century.

Historians disagree over authorship of the Seventeen Article Constitution. Nevertheless, the *Nihon shoki* states that in 604 Shōtoku prepared the constitution as the fundamental law of the land. It was a set of moral and political principles, combining Buddhist and Confucian concepts and values. As did Buddhism, Confucianism came to Japan through Korea—long a channel of Chinese culture to Japan.

In the fourth century, around 368-369, Japanese troops had invaded Korea, establishing a colony, Mimana, on the southern tip of the peninsula. In addition to the colony, three Korean states vied for dominance from the fourth to the seventh century: Silla, Paekche, and Koguryŏ. Silla gradually overthrew its rivals—Mimana in 562, Paekche in 663, and Koguryŏ in 668—unifying Korea. The flow of refugees to Japan was at its height during the seventh century. Korean and Chinese immigrants brought with them continental culture, contributing many skills and much wealth to Japanese clans wherever they settled.

During the Sui Dynasty (581-618), China was seen by Japan's leaders as a powerful nation, highly developed politically and culturally. Even pre-Sui, Chinese histories record Japanese missions to China. Although there had been missions during the first and second centuries, these remained sporadic, unlike the more sustained ones of the seventh through the ninth centuries. Clan chiefs were eager to select Chinese ideas and institutions that would strengthen the imperial line and their own power within the socioeconomic hierarchy. Umako and Shōtoku further believed that adopting Chinese institutions would help unify Japan and raise its cultural level. During Shōtoku's regency, at least three embassies were sent to China—in 600, 607, and 608. The Sui emperor responded with an embassy in 608. Japan was aiming not only at emulating China but also at becoming its equal.

Chinese influence is readily apparent in the Seventeen Article Constitution. Its first three articles give basic principles of government, and the remaining fourteen give practical guidelines for efficient functioning of the government: Value harmony, revere the "Three Treasures" (Buddha, the law, the monks), obey imperial commands, behave decorously, deal impartially with all cases, chastise the evil and encourage the good, fit the right man to the office, attend court early and retire late, observe good faith with one another, cease from wrath and learn from others, deal out sure reward and punishment, let the government alone levy taxes, attend to functions if you are an official, avoid envy, prefer public good to private, employ the people in [forced] labor at seasonable times, and consult with others on important matters.

Buddhism is specifically mentioned only in the second article. Shōtoku, although devoutly Buddhist, turned to Confucian models for guidance in reorganizing the government. Confucianism stressed cultivation of virtue and dedication to public service. These and other Confucian ideals are clearly evident in all the articles—especially articles 1, 2, 4, 9, 10, 14, 15, and 17. Some of the articles, however, are more revelatory than others about the conditions that faced Shōtoku as he began his reform. For example, articles 12, 14, and 16 address abuses prevalent at the time: arbitrary taxation by clan lords, jealousy among officials, and the corvée (forced labor). Overall, the constitution aimed at subduing the clans under the throne and unifying the nation.

MAJOR PERIODS IN JAPANESE HISTORY, 538-1912

Dates	*Period*
538-710	Asuka
710-794	Nara
794-1185	Heian
1185-1333	Kamakura
1333-1336	Kemmu Restoration
1336-1392	Nanboku-cho
1336-1573	Muromachi
1476-1615	Sengoku (Warring States)
1573-1603	Azuchi-Momoyama
1603-1867	Tokugawa (Edo)
1868-1912	Meiji

SIGNIFICANCE

Perhaps Shōtoku Taishi was, as some historians claim, a puppet of Soga Umako. Nevertheless, he is revered by the Japanese as a wise ruler who unified the nation, opened direct relations with China, and, by importing continental civilization, raised Japan's civilization to new heights. In particular, Shōtoku's promotion of Buddhism—through sponsorship of temples and temple schools, study of the scriptures, and advancement of the arts—gave Japan a rich spiritual as well as artistic foundation for future development. This borrowing from and imitation of Chinese civilization would continue into the late ninth century. Fifteen missions were sent to Tang China (T'ang; 618-907) between 630 and 838.

Aided by Soga Umako, Shōtoku Taishi led Japan to a higher political and cultural plane than it had attained before his regency. A strong central government now curbed clan rivalries, and the expansion of Buddhist thought and art enriched all areas of life. The Taika reforms, begun in 645, would continue Shōtoku's policy to bring all people directly under the power of the throne, united politically and spiritually.

—*S. Carol Berg*

FURTHER READING

Aston, W. G., trans. *Nihongi: Chronicles of Japan from the Earliest Times to A.D. 697*. 1896. Reprint. Tokyo: Charles E. Tuttle, 1972. The standard translation of one of the earliest works of Japanese history. Provides details about the life of Shōtoku Taishi and the impact of his reforms.

De Bary, William Theodore, et al., comps. *Sources of Japanese Tradition*. 2d ed. Vol. 1. New York: Columbia University Press, 2001. Contains complete reprints of the Seventeen Article Constitution as well as other important documents relating to Shōtoku Taishi's life.

Reischauer, Edwin O. *Japan: The Story of a Nation*. 4th ed. New York: McGraw-Hill, 1990. A concise history of Japan from its beginnings to 1973. Chapter 2, "The Adoption of the Chinese Pattern," is most useful. Includes an excellent bibliography.

Sansom, George. *A History of Japan to 1334*. Vol. 1. Stanford, Calif.: Stanford University Press, 1958. This study begins with the origins of the Japanese and ends with the Mongol invasions. Chapter 3, "The Yamato State," is the most helpful. Includes a very good bibliography and helpful footnotes.

Tamura, Yoshio. *Japanese Buddhism: A Cultural History*. Translated by Jeffrey Hunter. Tokyo: Tuttle, 2001. A detailed assessment of the cultural implications and historical development of Japanese Buddhism from the introduction of the faith to modern times, including details of Shōtoku Taishi's life and his place in the development of the Buddhist religion in Japan.

Varley, H. Paul. *Japanese Culture*. 4th ed. Honolulu: University of Hawaii Press, 2000. Intended for the general reader, this study covers religion, philosophy, and the arts, and connects cultural with political and institutional trends. Includes an excellent bibliography.

SEE ALSO: Suiko.

RELATED ARTICLES in *Great Events from History: The Middle Ages, 477-1453*: 5th or 6th century: Confucianism Arrives in Japan; 538-552: Buddhism Arrives in Japan; 593-604: Regency of Shōtoku Taishi; 607-839: Japan Sends Embassies to China; 645-646: Adoption of *Nengo* System and Taika Reforms; 701: Taihō Laws Reform Japanese Government; March 9, 712, and July 1, 720: Writing of *Kojiki* and *Nihon Shoki*.

SIGER OF BRABANT

French philosopher and theologian

By combining his mastery of Latin Averroistic philosophy with his intention to remain loyal to the institution and doctrines of the Roman Catholic Church, Siger was able to help clarify the enduring questions concerning the relationship of philosophy to theology and of reason to revelation.

BORN: c. 1235; probably duchy of Brabant (now in Belgium)

DIED: c. 1282; Orvieto, Tuscany (now in Italy)

ALSO KNOWN AS: Siger de Brabant

AREAS OF ACHIEVEMENT: Philosophy, religion and theology

EARLY LIFE

Most of the details of the life of Siger of Brabant (see-zhay uhv brah-bahn), especially his early life, appear to be irretrievably lost. He was born probably in or near the region of Brabant, in what is modern Belgium. Beyond a few sketchy facts, however, historians can only speculate.

Scholars suppose that his academic training was typical for his day. Siger's education began with the *trivium*, which consisted of introductory instruction in grammar, dialectic, and rhetoric. Such studies were designed not only to aid the student in speaking sense plainly and compellingly but also in speaking it beautifully. This course of study typically was followed by the *quadrivium*, which consisted of instruction in mathematics, music, geometry, and astronomy.

Sometime between 1255 and 1260, Siger seems to have studied at the University of Paris in the faculty of arts. There he developed the philosophical prowess on which his reputation chiefly rests. Also, most of the important events in his turbulent academic career occurred there. Significantly, Siger and the works of Aristotle made their way into the university at almost the same time. In those days, the university was agitated by the ancient Greek works of philosophy and science that, by means of Arab commentators and commentaries, were enjoying new prominence in the Latin-speaking world of Western intellect. Because these writings offered conclusions that were apparently well conceived and well reasoned, and because these conclusions occasionally stood at odds with Christian orthodoxy, conflict ensued.

Scholars had various responses to the problem of what relationship should exist between the newly emerging Greek thought and Christian theology. On the left were those called "the secular Aristotelians," who pursued their philosophical studies without regard to Christian doctrine. On the right were the orthodox Roman Catholic theologians such as Thomas Aquinas and his mentor, Albertus Magnus. They believed that, if properly understood, reason and revelation could not conflict. If ever they appeared to conflict, an error could be presumed either in one's philosophizing or in one's theologizing, or both. To them, because all truth came from God, and because God could not lie, truth admitted no contradictions. With such reasonings, the secularists were unconcerned. As will be seen, Siger would assume a position between the two sides and, from those two sides, would receive the severest forms of opposition, especially after the works of Aristotle were officially admitted to the university's course of study and curricular adjustment became necessary.

After approximately five years of university study, Siger received his degree. He studied at, was graduated from, and later taught at a university wracked by internal dissent.

Life's Work

Siger joined the faculty of arts in the mid-1260's. Even though (unlike many of his colleagues) he never went on to join the theological faculty, he acted as a loyal son of the Church. Despite the fact that many of his philosophical propositions stood in opposition to received dogma, and despite the fact that he was condemned twice for erroneous teaching, Siger remained, at least in his own views, a faithful Roman Catholic.

Siger's doctrinal deviations are centered on four major ideas. First, unlike traditional views that pictured God as Creator, Siger viewed God as the *primum mobile* (or first mover). That is, God's role in making the world was not to create it *ex nihilo* (out of nothing) but to shape it, or form it, out of a preexisting yet shapeless matter. This matter was independent of God, not created by God, and was eternal. God's role was to move on the matter in such a way as to shape it, not to create it. Hence, he is the first mover.

Second, as a correlative of the previous premise, Siger believed in an eternal cosmos. To him, not only was matter eternal, but so also was the world it constituted. By this Siger did not mean to say that the world is now like it always has been. The world changes; it always has changed and it always will change. Yet, of the various changes through which the world has passed, the change from nonexistence to existence, or the change from existence back to nonexistence, was not among them. To Siger, the world was eternal.

Third, Siger advocated monopsychism, or the belief that the intellect that all humans share is the same and unitary. It is one and indivisible throughout the human race. It alone survives death. Thus, the phenomenon of individuality is a temporary epiphenomenon. It will prove a meaningless and unenduring contortion of personality on the face of an underlying and undying world soul. Put differently, the world soul (or world mind), not humans themselves, is immortal. The soul (or what appears to be the soul) is not one person's—much less does it constitute a human being. The individual intellect returns to the world intellect when a person dies.

Fourth, Siger advocated what is often, but mistakenly, termed "the double truth theory." Genuine "double-truthism" holds that two propositions, one philosophical and one theological, could be opposites and could both be true. This Siger did not believe. Although he did affirm that what is true for reason may not necessarily be true for faith, he did not let the two ideas stand as equal opposites. When philosophical ideas and theological doctrines collided, Siger would give the palm to faith. Thus, whereas thinkers such as Thomas Aquinas believed that good theology and good philosophy could not conflict, Siger believed that they could. When they did, they were not considered to be both true and opposites. They were reconciled by sacrificing philosophy to theology.

For many churchmen, that sacrifice was not enough. They pressed Siger for further explanation. Siger's response was two-sided. First, Siger said that when he taught such ideas to his students he was not affirming that they were absolutely true, only that Aristotle and other philosophers affirmed them. Second, Siger professed to approach his work solely from the standpoint of reason. He said that human reason, while useful, was fallible, and that its conclusions, though perhaps philosophically unassailable, were provisional. Thus, Siger attributed these heretical ideas to past thinkers, on one hand, and to the occasionally undependable workings of the human intellect, on the other. This defense, he believed, would exonerate him; it did not.

In 1270, Siger was condemned by Étienne Tempier, bishop of Paris, for his unacceptable Averroistic doctrines. In spite of this condemnation, however, Siger and the other Averroists on the faculty of arts continued to teach their heterodox opinions in private. In 1272 they were prohibited from dealing with any theological matters. When this measure failed, all private teaching was banned.

In 1277, Siger was condemned again in an official denunciation of 219 heretical ideas, most of which were attributed to Siger and to Boethius of Dacia. As a result, Siger was summoned to appear before Simon du Val, the inquisitor of France. He refused to appear and protested his innocence on all charges. He then appealed to the pope for protection and relief and fled to Rome. Siger never returned to Paris from his self-imposed exile in Italy. He died in about 1282, in Orvieto, where he is thought to have been assassinated by his insane secretary.

SIGNIFICANCE

Some thinkers are important not for the conclusions they reach but for the questions they raise and the issues and conflicts that swirl around them. Siger is such a thinker. The history of Western thought has been punctuated by the persistent repetition of conflict between the advocates of faith and those of reason. Because such thinkers deal with ultimate concerns, and because opposing viewpoints on such questions are vigorously advanced and vigorously opposed, the conflict that surrounds them is varied and intense. In other words, Siger of Brabant's life is proof, if proof is needed, that ideas have consequences.

For Siger those consequences were often difficult and eventually tragic. Furthermore, not even at his death did the turmoil surrounding him come to a close. Both the philosophers and the theologians thought him a martyr. To the philosophers, he was a twice condemned and brutally murdered champion of philosophical and academic freedom. The theologians, by contrast, point to the tradition that late in life Siger recanted his unorthodox philosophical views and was converted to the beliefs of Thomas Aquinas. That, they argue, is the reason Dante was able not only to place Siger in Paradise but also to make him the recipient of Thomas's lavish praise. That also is the reason he died, they say. His secretary, a convinced Averroist, did not wish to see Siger exercise his considerable talents on behalf of Thomism, and he killed him to prevent it. That the two sides both claimed Siger for their own is eloquent testimony to his significance, at least to his contemporaries.

—*Michael E. Bauman*

FURTHER READING

Copleston, Frederick. *Medieval Philosophy: Augustine to Scotus*. Vol. 2 in *A History of Philosophy*. New York: Image Books, 1985. The chapter "Latin Averroism: Siger of Brabant," though brief and little concerned with the details of Siger's life, is a useful and erudite account of some of the salient aspects of his thought as seen against its historical background.

Gilson, Étienne. *Dante and Philosophy*. Translated by David Moore. Reprint. Gloucester, Mass.: P. Smith, 1968. Part of chapter 4, "The Symbolism of Siger of Brabant," along with the sections "Concerning the Averroism of Siger of Brabant" and "Concerning the Thomism of Siger of Brabant," constitutes one of the most complete and insightful delineations in English of Siger's thought. Author's treatment is well balanced, well informed, and thoroughly documented.

Gonzalez, Justo L. *From Augustine to the Eve of the Reformation*. Vol. 2 in *A History of Christian Thought*. Rev. ed. Nashville, Tenn.: Abingdon Press, 1987. The chapter "Extreme Aristotelianism" is a lucid and useful account of Siger's ideas, especially with regard to their theological implications.

Hyman, Arthur, and James J. Walsh, eds. *Philosophy in the Middle Ages: The Christian, Islamic, and Jewish Traditions*. 2d ed. Indianapolis, Ind.: Hackett, 1983. In a twelve-page chapter entitled "Siger of Brabant," the editors provide a brief and informative account of Siger's life and thought and of the intellectual milieu in which he lived. They also reproduce an earlier translation of Siger's "Question on the Eternity of the World."

McInerny, Ralph. *Aquinas Against the Averroists: On There Being Only One Intellect*. West Lafayette, Ind.: Purdue University Press, 1993. Discusses Aquinas's philosophy in the light of other medieval thinkers, including Siger, opposed to his work. Includes a bibliography and an index.

Marenbon, John, ed. *Medieval Philosophy*. New York: Routledge, 1998. Surveys thinkers of the Middle Ages, with a chapter on Siger and the Paris Faculty of Arts. Another chapter, "The Intellectual Context of Later Medieval Philosophy: Universities, Aristotle, Arts, Theology," contextualizes the debates of Siger's time.

Marrone, Steven P. *The Light of Thy Countenance: Science and Knowledge of God in the Thirteenth Century*. 2 vols. Boston: Brill, 2001. Volume 1 discusses attempts by thirteenth century scholars to reconcile and adapt the tradition of Augustinian-inspired theology with an emerging Aristotelian-inspired science.

Wippel, John F. *Mediaeval Reactions to the Encounter Between Faith and Reason*. Milwaukee, Wis.: Marquette University Press, 1995. Explains for general readers, especially students new to philosophy, the debates on the question of faith and reason between "radical Aristotelians," including Siger, and theologians committed to faith always above reason. Includes an extensive bibliography.

See also: Peter Abelard; Saint Albertus Magnus; Averroës; Jean Buridan; Dante; John Duns Scotus; William of Ockham; Thomas Aquinas; William of Auvergne; William of Auxerre.

Related articles in *Great Events from History: The Middle Ages, 477-1453*: 907-960: Period of Five Dynasties and Ten Kingdoms; c. 950: Court of Córdoba Flourishes in Spain; c. 1150: Moors Transmit Classical Philosophy and Medicine to Europe; c. 1265-1273: Thomas Aquinas Compiles the *Summa Theologica*.

Sima Guang

Chinese statesman, historian, and poet

Sima Guang was a scholar, statesman, and poet who compiled the Zizhi tongjian, *one of the outstanding works in Chinese historiography. He was also a significant political figure in the Northern Song Dynasty.*

Born: 1019; Xia, Hunan Province, China
Died: 1086; Bian Lian, Hunan Province, China
Also known as: Ssu-ma Kuang (Wade-Giles)
Areas of achievement: Literature, historiography, government and politics

Early Life

Sima Guang (suh-mah gwahng) was intensively educated in the Confucian classics and influenced by the historical writings of Gao Jun (Kao Chün) and the commentaries of the *Zuozhuan* (fifth century B.C.E.; *Tso chuen*, 1872). Early in his life, he developed a passion for historical studies that motivated him to read widely. He completed his education in 1038, passed the civil service examinations, and moved rapidly into public office.

From 1038 to 1060, Sima Guang established a distinguished and productive record in a variety of high positions. An excellent writer and speaker, he built a reputation as a fiscal conservative, opposing high taxes and extravagance in public office. He was firmly committed to the Confucian emphasis on the correct understanding of the past as a guide to proper life and preparation for service to the state, and, as a consequence, he served to promote the growth of schools and academies in Song China. Sima Guang is frequently represented as a hero in Chinese children's books. This reputation stems from his having saved a young friend from drowning by breaking the water tank into which the child had fallen.

Life's Work

It is as one of China's greatest historians that Sima Guang is most remembered. In 1064, he presented to Emperor Yingzong (Yang-tsung; r. 1064-1067) a chronological table of Chinese history from its origins to the beginnings of the Song Dynasty. His purpose was to organize the scattered records and existing information into a convenient and manageable form. Two years later, he presented the emperor with a chronicle of the history of the Warring States (475-221 B.C.E.), which he titled the *Tongzhi* (comprehensive record). The emperor was so impressed with this work that he gave Sima Guang a mandate to compile the records of all the emperors, rulers, and ministers before the Song Dynasty. Two distinguished scholars were appointed to assist in the work.

In 1067, Sima Guang was directed to read his work in the emperor's presence. The emperor titled it *Zizhi tongjian* (1084; comprehensive mirror for aid in government) and wrote a preface that would later be included with the completed work.

At approximately the time Sima Guang began his historical project, the celebrated reformer Wang Anshi rose to power as literary councillor, vice grand councillor, and, in 1070, grand councillor. The two acquaintances were philosophically opposed to each other and had vigorously debated their differences on national policies. When Wang Anshi's reform program received imperial support from 1070 to 1085, Sima Guang emerged as the leader of the opposition to Wang's sweeping reforms. His vigorous opposition forced Sima out of government during this period. He retired to Luoyang with a comfortable sinecure and dedicated himself to his historical endeavor.

Between 1070 and 1084, Sima Guang directed the collection and writing of his great history. He began with a chronological outline of the 1,362 years of Chinese history preceding the Song Dynasty. Next, he had all available sources, family records, biographies, anecdotes, document collections, inscriptions, dynastic histories, and literary works reviewed and cited in the outline in the appropriate places. From this outline he created what he called the "long draft." If the cited accounts all agreed, the draft was so written; if there were varying interpretations, the most logical explanation was used with the conflicting accounts noted and an explanation offered as to the inclusion or exclusion of the account.

Sima Guang then began the process of summarizing and reducing the text to the most essential details. He reduced the long draft (originally several hundred manuscript rolls) to 294 rolls. As each phase of the project was finished, it was presented to the emperor. In 1084 the final work, along with a thirty-roll outline and a thirty-roll examination of the differences between the sources, was completed. This work was the first of its kind in the discipline of historiography and one of the most significant efforts in world history.

The inherent disadvantages of the chronicle nature of the project were overcome, in large measure, by subsequent works. In the twelfth century, a scholar, Yuan Shu (Yüan Shu), rewrote the history by tracing 239 topics from beginning to end, creating the first topical history in the Chinese experience. Also in the twelfth century, the philosopher Zhu Xi completed a digest of the *Zizhi tongjian*, selecting the most significant historical events included and developing them in narrative fashion so as to convey the moral lessons of history from the Confucian perspective. According to many historians, it is unfortunate that it was Zhu Xi's version of the history that became the most widely used in China, resulting in a moralism that stifled intellectual life for some time.

Sima Guang's work brought a new emphasis to Chinese dynastic history, fitting it into the cyclical idea of history that had emerged with Sima Qian in the Han Dynasty. Sima Guang interpreted the rise and fall of dynasties as a part of an established rhythm but was of the opinion that wise leaders could learn from past cycles and make moral choices that would extend the life of the dynasty. This perspective led Sima Guang to assume the leadership of the conservative opposition to Grand Councillor Wang Anshi and his reform program. The fierce power struggle between these two brilliant scholars developed into one of the most famous political conflicts in Chinese history.

The reign of Emperor Shenzong (Shen-tsung; r. 1068-1085) coincided with Wang Anshi's reform program and Sima Guang's writing of the *Zizhi tongjian*. It had been the emperor's support for Wang that had driven Sima Guang to his scholarly efforts. In the third month of 1085, however, the emperor died and was succeeded by his ten-year-old son, Zhezong (Che-tsung; r. 1086-1101). The young emperor's grandmother, Xuan Ren (Hsuan Jen), was appointed to act as his regent. Opposed to many of Wang's reforms and impressed with the *Zizhi tongjian*, she immediately called Sima Guang to the capital. In the fourth month of 1085, the famous historian made a triumphant return to power. He was determined to eliminate all Wang's programs, which were, in his view, the result of wrong ideas. Within a year, Sima Guang had rescinded every one of Wang's reform measures. Boards and agencies were abolished, supporters of Wang were transferred out of the capital, and laws were canceled. Nearly every trace of Wang's reforms was removed. Wang Anshi was a southerner and a reformist; Sima Guang was a northerner and a conservative: The struggle was both philosophical and political.

Wang Anshi lived until 1086, long enough to see his reform program destroyed. Five months later, Sima Guang, having achieved his desire to rescind Wang's program, died in Bian Lian. From every account, his funeral was a national event. The emperor and empress dowager attended, all routine business in the capital city was suspended for the day, and memorial services were conducted in all parts of the country.

Although the two factional leaders were gone, the struggle continued long after their deaths. With every subsequent change of leadership, the battle lines were redrawn. Liberal forces would restore Wang Anshi's reforms, then conservatives would call up the image and history of Sima Guang and rescind them again. For years, the two men and their supporters were alternately defamed and restored. This inability to maintain a steady course may have significantly weakened the Song Dynasty and contributed to its decline.

SIGNIFICANCE

Sima Guang was one of the outstanding historians of China. He is important because of the critical intelligence used in the examination and evaluation of sources, the understanding and development he contributed to the historical process, the great skill he demonstrated in narration, the preservation and organization of early Chinese records that he accomplished, and the enormous scope of *Zizhi tongjian*, which many consider the finest single historical work in Chinese history. Sima Guang sought to develop history as a means of understanding the present. He is deserving of a prominent place in the history of China and in the writing of history in general.

—*Frank Nickell*

FURTHER READING

De Bary, William Theodore, Irene Bloom, and Wing-tsit Chan, comps. *Sources of Chinese Tradition*. 2d ed. New York: Columbia University Press, 1999-2000. Contains several passages from the writings of Sima Guang with editorial analysis of not only his work but also that of other historians and political leaders of the Song Dynasty.

De Crespigny, Rafe, trans. *To Establish Peace: Being the Chronicle of Late Han for the Years 189-220 A.D. as recorded in chapters 59 to 69 of the "Zizhi tongjian" of Sima Guang*. Canberra, Australia: Faculty of Asian Studies, Australian National University, 1996. A partial translation of Sima Guang's major work.

Hymes, Robert P., and Conrad Schirokauer, eds. *Ordering the World: Approaches to State and Society in Sung Dynasty China*. Berkeley: University of California Press, 1993. A collection of papers on the state and society in China during the Sung Dynasty. Bibliography and index.

Liu, James T. C. *Reform in Sung China: Wang An-shih (1021-1086) and His New Policies*. Cambridge, Mass.: Harvard University Press, 1959. A careful analysis of the reform program of Wang Anshi with reference to the philosophical differences between Wang and his antagonist Sima Guang.

Meskill, John Thomas. *Wang An-shih: Practical Reformer?* 1963. Reprint. Boston: Heath, 1967. A study of Wang Anshi and his reform program.

Williamson, H. R. *Wang An-shih: A Chinese Statesman and Educationalist of the Sung Dynasty*. 2 vols. 1935-1937. Westport, Conn: Hyperion, 1973. A detailed biography of Wang Anshi. Places great emphasis on Sima Guang. Williamson effectively develops the power struggle between the two and includes quotations from their correspondence and debate.

SEE ALSO: Wang Anshi.

RELATED ARTICLE in *Great Events from History: The Middle Ages, 477-1453*: 1069-1072: Wang Anshi Introduces Bureaucratic Reforms.

CLAUS SLUTER

Dutch sculptor

Sluter's innovations in creating individually distinct and expressively sculptured figures brought to Western art a new realism. Credited with bridging the late Gothic and the early Renaissance in northern Europe, Sluter and his name are synonymous with the Burgundian school of sculpture.

BORN: c. 1340-1350; probably Haarlem, Holland (now in the Netherlands)

DIED: c. 1405-1406; Dijon, Burgundy (now in France)

AREA OF ACHIEVEMENT: Art

EARLY LIFE

Many details of the life of Claus Sluter (klaoos SLEW-tuhr) have been lost, as have many of the sculptures he created. What is known of his early life is that he was born in Haarlem, and around 1379 or 1380, he moved to Brussels. Some historians believe that while in Brussels, Sluter created the sculpture for the porch of the Brussels Town Hall. Dated around 1380, the Brussels sculpture, a set of seated prophets, resembles some of the sculpture Sluter created at Champmol, Dijon, later in the decade. The figures at Brussels reveal traces of individualization, the quality that would distinguish Sluter's art. Up to this time, figures depicted with individually distinct characteristics, although slightly detectable at the time, were unusual in Europe. Sculptural figures were generally solemnly posed and rigid, presenting abstract representations rather than individual characterizations. Personal details such as hair, beards, and clothing were stylized in formal patterns rather than depicted naturally.

Sculpture was also usually subordinated to the architecture it was intended to decorate, confined within the niches in which it was enclosed or barely distinguished from the columns on which it was mounted. After sculptors completed their work, statues were provided with personal details by painters. This polychromatic process was the common artistic practice through Sluter's time and continued well into the sixteenth century. As for the figures on the Brussels Town Hall, historians hesitate to attribute them to Sluter because of scanty evidence. In addition, although the sculptures reveal qualities of individual expression, Sluter did not single-handedly introduce sculptural realism. The work that he would complete in the next two decades, however, would more than any other sculpture contribute to its development. The Town Hall sculpture, therefore, regardless of attribution, provides early examples from which to study Sluter's development. The sculpture reveals the degree to which Sluter developed his own style in contrast to his early work and that of his contemporaries.

Life's Work

In 1385, Sluter went to Dijon, the center of the duchy of Burgundy. Rich and prosperous, the duchy of Burgundy was the source of one of the great ages of artistic patronage, promoting the most talented architects, sculptors, stained-glass designers, illuminators, and painters from all over Europe. Sluter worked for the court of Philip the Bold, the duke of Burgundy. Philip was a brother to Jean de France, the duke of Berry, and to Charles V, the king of France. The three projects that have established Sluter's reputation were commissioned by Philip the Bold for the monastery he founded, the Chartreuse of Champmol.

Arriving at Philip's court, Sluter worked as the head sculptor under another artist, Jean (Hennequin) de Marville. Marville had designed the architectural and iconographic scheme for the Champmol portal when he died in 1389. Sluter, now responsible for completing the project, created the six figures adorning the portal—the Virgin and Child, flanked by a kneeling duke and duchess (Philip and Margaret), and Saint John the Baptist and Saint Catherine. Canopies frame each figure except for those of the Virgin and Child, whose canopy, now missing, was decorated with angels bearing the instruments of the Passion. The corbels on which Saint John and Saint Catherine stand depict two prophets reading a manuscript. The corbels bearing Philip and Margaret are decorated with shield bearers (the same figures that are said to resemble the statues on the Brussels Town Hall).

The composition of the Virgin and Child in the center pillar, or *trumeau*, flanked by propitiating prophets and patrons, is traditional. Sluter's modeling of the figures is far from traditional, however, as the bodies suggest movement, and their faces evoke emotion. The canopies or niches no longer frame the figures, which are positioned so that they turn toward the Virgin holding Christ. Saint John and Saint Catherine, about to kneel, emphasize the inward movement; each knee points to and breaks the space occupied by Philip and Margaret.

The movement and unity of the scene are enhanced by Sluter's modeling of the drapery. The figures' clothes fall into heavy diagonal folds, and the natural breaks in the clothes suggest the movement of these robust figures. As the folds of the Virgin's garb emphasize her swayed pose, the diagonals of her robes meet just above her left hip, on which the Christ child rests, suggesting Mary's efforts to secure him. The viewer's eye is now focused on the heavily draped figure of Christ, the thematic and visual center of the scene. The visual and iconographic play continue as Christ is visually distracted, looking up at the angels who carry the instruments of Passion, the symbols of Christ's eventual suffering. Sluter provided these figures with individual gestures, depicting them with realistic facial features and expressions. This personalized treatment, particularly of Philip and Margaret, was exemplary of the new change in sculpture. The faces are not abstractions or idealized portraits but individual representations. Their solemn expressions are suitable for the emotions that the religious scene demands. Yet Sluter also provided the mundane details revealed in the faces—furrowed brows, wrinkled eyes, pursed mouths, and even double chins.

Sluter's next project was entirely his own, a Calvary scene built in the center of a well in the cloister of the Chartreuse. The sculpture is unquestionably the dominant interest in the structure, also known as the Well of Moses. A large hexagonal base provides the structure for the central and slightly larger-than-life sculptures of six Old Testament figures—Moses, Isaiah, Daniel, Zechariah, Jeremiah, and David. Each figure, broad-shouldered and heavily modeled, dwarfs the niches and columns and gives the impression that if it were not affixed, it could descend from the pedestal. Angels with varied expressions of grief fly above the Old Testament figures. Their spreading wings support the cornices on which once stood the Calvary scene—the Virgin, Saint John, and Saint Mary Magdalene surrounding Christ on the Cross. Only a fragment remains of this scene—the head and torso of Christ, which are now in the museum of Dijon.

As is the tradition for religious sculpture, the Old Testament figures are identified symbolically. Each carries a scroll with a text that relates the story of the death of Christ. Breaking with tradition, however, Sluter individualized each figure, which provided distinct physiognomies. Moses possesses a stern, fixed expression, suggesting his anger at the sight of the Jews worshiping the golden calf. Zechariah, with a despondent look suggesting his rejection by his people, bows his head and avoids the viewer's gaze. Jeremiah and David are sunk in meditation; each is modeled with deeply defined brows that encircle closed eyes. Daniel and Isaiah twist to see and hear each other from around one of the corners of the base, presumably to discuss the advent of Christ, who is traditionally portrayed. Thorns pierce Christ's brow, and the spear's wound scars his left side. His nearly emotionless face is outlined by finely detailed long hair and beard; his eyes and mouth are gently closed, portraying the divine man recently crucified.

The architectural plan of Sluter's final project, the tomb of Philip the Bold at Champmol, was established during Marville's time. The style was once again traditional. The recumbent figure of the duke is mounted on a black marble slab, and two angels kneel at his head. An open gallery runs along the base of the tomb, and within its niches, forty figures form a procession mourning the duke's death. Although some of the figures were completed after his death following his design, all the sculpture is attributed to Sluter. The duke's figure was badly damaged in 1791 and poorly restored in the nineteenth century. The figures in mourning, however, are well preserved and reveal the culmination of Sluter's development. Ten choirboys, clergy, and thirty mourners weave in and out of the niches, creating an undulating effect around the tomb. Unlike the larger-than-life stature of the sculpture from the Well of Moses, these figures are in miniature, no higher than two feet. Each figure maintains a strikingly fresh pose, and individual gestures rather than detailed facial expressions create the emotional and dramatic effect. Some figures hold their hands in silent prayer or clench them to their chests. With dramatic effect, the hands are highlighted against finely modeled flowing robes, which were perhaps shaped to hint at the position of the hands folded beneath them.

This dramatic and natural rendering of drapery, always Sluter's trademark, creates excitement in the play between the physical features the viewer sees and those covered by or partially glimpsed through the gowns and robes. Only a hand protrudes from beneath the flowing robes of one mourner; in another, the eyes are hidden and only the lower half of a solemn face appears. Some figures are completely covered, the grief expressed through the swayed or bent figure whose shape underneath can only be guessed.

Sluter died in late 1405 or early 1406, before he completed the tomb. His nephew, Claus de Werve, finished the project in 1410, and historians have no doubt that he closely followed Sluter's plans. Overall, the tomb reveals the high point of Sluter's technique. Its monumentality is achieved not by mere stature and size but by subtle and minimal suggestion of individual movement and expression.

Significance

In creating sculptures expressive of human qualities, whether personal emotions or bodily movements, Sluter broke the stylized and static quality of sculpture that was common in the Middle Ages. His work influenced much of the sculpture of the first half of the fifteenth century throughout northern Europe, France, Germany, and the Low Countries, and extended as well into Spain and Switzerland (through the efforts of his assistants). Sluter is often compared to the great Italian masters Donatello and Jacopo della Quercia, who were also transitional figures whose work contributed or led to the high development of Renaissance sculpture.

Sluter's work helped to establish the independence of sculpture from architecture and painting. No longer would sculpture provide merely the ornament for buildings; it could well be the center of interest, as it would become in the Renaissance. Sculpture, too, could provide the dramatic unity and realism found in painting. Given the realism achieved by Sluter and later sculptors, polychroming would be unnecessary to provide realistic and naturalistic detail. Sluter demonstrated how sculptures attained their own beauty and interest.

Sluter also influenced the development of painting in northern Europe; in particular, his work opened the way for the development of realistic portraiture. While credited with directly or indirectly influencing the work of some of the most important painters—the master of Flémalle, Rogier van der Weyden, and Konrad Witz—Sluter's most direct influence was on Jan van Eyck, who worked for the Burgundian court in the generation following Sluter's death. Sluter is noted as having inspired van Eyck's interest in painting lifelike compositions that created the three-dimensional effect of sculpture. Indeed, van Eyck and Sluter played similar roles in the development of a basic tenet of Western art: Each, through close attention to detail, created the illusion of reality through his art.

—*Steven P. Schultz*

Further Reading

Cartellieri, Otto. *The Court of Burgundy.* Translated by Malcolm Letts. 1929. Reprint. New York: Barnes and

Noble Books, 1972. In a narrative style, this work recreates the political and artistic flavor of the fourteenth and fifteenth century Burgundian court. Chapter 2 focuses on Sluter as Philip the Bold's favorite sculptor and vividly describes Sluter's life and work at the Champmol monastery. Includes photographs of sculpture.

David, Henri. *Claus Sluter.* Paris: P. Tisné, 1951. An examination of the artist in French that provides very fine photographic plates of Sluter's sculptures.

Forsyth, William H. *The Entombment of Christ: French Sculptures of the Fifteenth and Sixteenth Centuries.* Cambridge, Mass.: Harvard University Press, 1970. Chapter 5, "Burgundy," explores the history of the duchy of Burgundy and Sluter's lasting influence in French sculpture—well beyond his death and the demise of the political power and independence of Burgundy.

Gardner, Arthur. *Medieval Sculpture in France.* 1931. Reprint. New York: Kraus, 1969. Historical background of the duke of Burgundy's artistic efforts at Champmol, featuring Sluter's work. Excellent description and photographs of individual sculptures.

Male, Emile. *Religious Art in France: The Late Middle Ages, a Study of Medieval Iconography and Its Sources.* Translated by Marthiel Mathews. Edited by Harry Bober. Princeton, N.J.: Princeton University Press, 1986. Written by one of the most eminent historians of medieval art. Provides an analysis of the iconography of the Well of Moses.

Marks, Richard. "Sculpture in the Duchy and County of Burgundy, c. 1300-1500." *Connoisseur* 194 (March, 1977): 154-163. Accounts for the rise of Burgundian sculpture to its primary place among French schools. Explains influence of Netherlandish carvers, notably Sluter. Provides very good photographs and descriptions of sculpture and discusses background to the rise of the duchy of Burgundy's power and influence in Europe.

Morand, Kathleen. *Claus Sluter: Artist at the Court of Burgundy.* Austin: University of Texas Press, 1991. Discusses Sluter and his artistic work at the court of Burgundy and art patronage in Burgundian France. Includes illustrations, a map, a bibliography, and an index.

Stratford, Neil. *Studies in Burgundian Romanesque Sculpture.* 2 vols. London: Pindar Press, 1998. A study of the artistic realm so greatly influenced by Sluter. Includes illustrations, a bibliography, and an index.

SEE ALSO: Donatello; Jan van Eyck and Hubert van Eyck; Jacopo della Quercia; Rogier van der Weyden.

RELATED ARTICLE in *Great Events from History: The Middle Ages, 477-1453*: c. 1410-1440: Florentine School of Art Emerges.

SNORRI STURLUSON

Icelandic historian

Snorri preserved the myths, poetry, history, and culture of the early Germanic people of Iceland. In doing so, he created an original literature of permanent significance and renown for himself as one of the foremost authors of the Middle Ages.

BORN: 1178 or 1179; Hvamm, Iceland
DIED: September 22, 1241; Reykjaholt, Iceland
AREAS OF ACHIEVEMENT: Historiography, literature

EARLY LIFE

Snorri Sturluson (SNAWR-ee STUR-luh-suhn) was the son of Sturla Thortharson, a shrewd and ambitious landholder who had acquired wealth and power through incessant legal feuds with neighboring farmers and through other devious manipulations of the law. Snorri's mother, Guthńy, was the daughter of Bothvar Thortharson, who was descended from the famed warrior-poet Egill Skallagrímsson. After a legal settlement between his father and Jón Loptsson, the most powerful chieftain in Iceland, Snorri was taken (at age three) to live at Oddi, Jón's family estate in southern Iceland, as a foster son. Oddi had been for several generations the center of Iceland's highest culture and functioned as an informal school for clerics as well as for the study of law, history, Latin, and skaldship (poetry). Snorri thus spent his formative years in an atmosphere that engendered a respect for learning and culture and that provided him with a thorough knowledge of law, history, and skaldship.

Snorri's father died in 1183, and his mother, a woman of extravagant tendencies, soon squandered Snorri's patrimony. Snorri thus lacked the means to establish himself in a society in which wealth was important. He remained at Oddi after the death of Jón Loptsson in 1197 and seems to have remained there for several years following his marriage in 1199 to Herdís, daughter of Bersi the Rich. The marriage appears to have been arranged solely for money—a marriage typical of the chieftain class in medieval Iceland. Following the death of his father-in-law, Snorri inherited and moved to Bersi's estate at Borg, which was also the ancestral homestead of the saga-hero Egill Skallagrímsson, Snorri's distant relative. Thus, through marriage and inheritance of extensive properties, Snorri went from being penniless to being a very rich young man, but his desire for money, power, and fame was unsatisfied. In 1206, he left his wife and their son and daughter in Borg and moved to Reykjaholt, an estate more glamorous and famous. Within a few years, Snorri had greatly increased his fortune and stature. One evidence of his standing is the fact that he was twice elected to the influential post of "lawspeaker" for the Althing, the Icelandic high court. Because laws in Iceland were not originally written, the lawspeaker's duty was to preserve them by memory and to pronounce the letter of the law in doubtful cases. Given the litigious nature of Icelandic society, a lawspeaker had numerous opportunities for enriching himself through unscrupulous dealings and subtle manipulations of the law, opportunities of which Snorri fully availed himself.

It must be noted, however, that Snorri was in many ways merely a product of his time. The Sturlung Age (mid-twelfth century to the fall of the Commonwealth in 1262), so named because of the predominance of Snorri's family, was a time of great moral corruption, licentiousness, turbulence, and bloodshed. *Sturlunga saga* (*Sturlunga Saga*, 1970-1974), written by Snorri's nephew Sturla Thortharson in the thirteenth century, gives a particularly unflattering portrait of Snorri in his willingness to exploit enmities for personal gain; his disregard for friendship, kinship, or alliance; and his seeming indifference to questions of right and wrong. Historians have wondered to what extent Snorri's early poverty and the influence of his foster father, Jón, contributed to Snorri's character. Certainly Snorri's avarice and thirst for power appear as serious character flaws, but the mystery is that they are so ironically inconsistent with the character and personality that readers sense in his writings. Beyond doubt, however, is that Snorri's avarice led to an increasing immersion in feuds and legal quarrels that did not always turn out to his financial advantage, which made him many enemies and which led ultimately to his violent death. Before that grim ending, however, Snorri did achieve one of his life's goals. Through successful lawsuits, advantageous marriages for his children, and a liaison with the country's wealthiest woman (Hallveig Ormsdóttir), he became, like his foster father before him, the wealthiest, most powerful man in Iceland.

Life's Work

Nevertheless, Snorri had another goal in life, beyond wealth and power. He desired fame as a *skald* (poet), something best achieved through recognition at royal courts. He had composed poems to the rulers of Norway even before he set sail for the Norwegian court in 1218, and on one occasion he was rewarded with the gift of a sword, a shield, armor, and an invitation to visit. Little is known of Snorri's first trip to Norway except that he attached himself to Earl Skúli, regent for King Haakon Haakonarson, who was then a boy of thirteen. Snorri was given lavish gifts and the title of baron, and he was charged with a major diplomatic mission: to settle disputes between Icelandic and Norwegian merchants and to persuade the Icelanders to become subjects of the Norwegian crown. On his return, Snorri did nothing to advance the royal cause, but he did write a poem, no longer extant, in honor of Earl Skúli and King Haakon (*Háttatal*, 1223). Presumably, it was during this period of his life, between 1220 and 1235, that Snorri wrote the major works for which he has been universally recognized and which secured his lasting fame: *Snorra Edda* (c. 1220-1230), translated as *The Prose Edda* (partial translation, 1916, 1954; full translation, 1987), and *Heimskringla* (c. 1230-1235; *The Heimskringla: Or, Chronicle of the Kings of Norway*, 1844).

Snorri's *The Prose Edda* is a handbook for the composition of skaldic poetry, which in the twelfth century was doubly jeopardized: by the Church, which frowned on the pagan mythology contained in the *kenningar* (that is, the unique system of paraphrasis and metaphor used by skaldic poets), and by the dancing ballads, or songs, which were becoming popular. Even the noblemen who were frequently honored in skaldic verse began expressing a preference for a simple, less oblique poetry. *The Prose Edda* was Snorri's attempt to preserve an intellectual and poetic tradition that was vanishing. It demonstrates his love for and his thorough knowledge and mastery of this difficult, esoteric art. *The Prose Edda*, in addition to a prologue, has three parts. "Haattatal" (list of meters) consists of one hundred two stanzas in one hundred different "meters," composed in honor of Haakon and Earl Skúli (this poem is not, however, the one dedicated in 1223 to Haakon and Skúli). "Skáldskaparmál" (poetic diction) records a number of old tales about gods, giants, dwarfs, and heroes to illustrate the two primary technical devices of skaldic poetry: *heiti* (poetic names) and *kenningar* (poetic circumscriptions). "Gylfaginning" (the deluding of Gylfi) presents a comprehensive survey of Old Norse mythology; it is on this section that the reputation of *The Prose Edda* chiefly rests. Gylfi, king of Sweden, comes in disguise to the citadel of the gods to learn their secrets. Finding three of them—known as High, Equally High, and Third—sitting on the high seat, Gylfi proceeds to ask them questions concerning the origin of the world, the gods, and the end of the world. In response, the gods recite classic tales that present the complete cycle of Northern mythology, from the birth of the universe to the destruction of the cosmos (Ragnarok) and its rebirth. Besides being an indispensable compendium of Scandinavian mythology, "The Deluding of Gylfi" reveals Snorri's mastery of the art of storytelling. The stories are told with a charm, sophistication, and satiric wit rare in any age and that only a natural storyteller can command. To placate the Church (Iceland had accepted Christianity around 999), Snorri included in his work a disclaimer about the veracity of his pagan stories ("Christians . . . must not believe in pagan gods or that these tales are true in any . . . way"), but he succeeds in bringing the stories and the gods to life. In the end, however, the myths are revealed as a delusion: Gylfi heard a loud crash; looking around, he saw that there was no citadel, nothing but a level plain. Thus, the myths were a heathen deception that temporarily deluded Gylfi and that has continued to delude readers.

The *Heimskringla* is indisputably Snorri's greatest achievement. It begins with the Swedish kings of legendary times and chronologically follows the dynasty across to Norway to the year 1177. Actual history begins with Halfdan the Black, who ruled in the first half of the ninth century, and with Halfdan's son Harald I Hårfager (Fairhair), the first king of Norway, who ruled from 872 to 930. Each king is given a saga, but the saga of the royal saint of Norway, Olaf (King Olaf II, r. 1015-1030), is Snorri's masterpiece, both in its extended consideration (some three hundred pages) and in its quality.

Snorri has been praised as being a more realistic and critical historian than his predecessors—with the exception of Ari the Learned, whose work Snorri knew and admired. (Ari is the only one of his sources that Snorri mentions by name in his foreword.) To appreciate Snorri as historian, something of his methods and assumptions must be taken into consideration. In part, he used written sources (only some of which survive), but he also made important use of oral literature—folktales, tales told by wise people, and particularly skaldic poems, which he regarded as his most trustworthy source. The idea of relying on poetry as a source for history appears ludicrous to a modern historian, but for a historian of a preliterary age, poetry may be the only source available. Some modern commentators have conceded that skaldic poetry's rigid form and meter render it less subject to corruption than other forms of oral literature. Snorri presents his own argument for skaldic veracity in his foreword.

> At the court of King Harald [Fairhair] there were skalds, and men still remember their poems and the poems about all the kings who have since his time ruled in Norway; and we gathered most of our information from what we are told in those poems which were recited before the chieftains themselves. . . . We regard all that to be true which is found in those poems about their expeditions and battles. It is [to be sure] the habit of poets to give highest praise to those princes in whose presence they are; but no one would have dared to tell them to their faces about deeds which all who listened, as well as the prince himself, knew were only falsehoods and fabrications. That would have been mockery, . . . not praise.

In what is sometimes called *The Separate Saga of St. Óláfr*, which is part of the *Heimskringla*, Snorri reminds readers that one of the functions of the skald was to be a truthful recorder of events: Olaf called his skalds to be important witnesses at his final battle at Stiklestad.

It is Snorri's own concern with truth and realism that makes "Saint Olaf's Saga" a masterpiece. He rejects much of the tendentious, hagiographic tradition associated with Saint Olaf, ignoring some of the early miracles and rationalizing others. Snorri presents a man of complex psychological shadings, a man who was a ruthless Viking and an ambitious king, who nevertheless became a saint as he gradually faced the painful trials at the end of his life. Snorri's objectivity allows readers to understand and appreciate the motives of those who opposed Olaf as well as Olaf's own view. His superb dramatic gift brings a host of characters to life, while his narrative skillfully interweaves complicated stories of internal politics with the king's saga. It is this incorporation of epic tradition with high standards of historical truthfulness that has caused some scholars, such as Lee M. Hollander, to assert that Snorri bears favorable comparison with Thucydides, the great Greek historian.

> Considering the great disparity in general culture and intellectual advancement between his [Snorri's] times and Periclean Greece we may marvel all the more at Snorri's

> genius. His work is unique in European historiography in presenting us with a continuous account of a nation's history from its beginnings in the dim prehistoric past down into the High Middle Ages.

In many ways, Snorri Sturluson's own death seems as fateful and tragic as any about which he wrote. Like many of his subjects, Snorri came to grief partly because of bad political judgment and partly because of character flaws. During his second journey to Norway (1237-1239), he failed to seek out King Haakon and spent his time instead with Earl Skúli, who was now the king's enemy. Rumors circulated that Skúli had in a secret ceremony made Snorri an earl and that Skúli planned a revolt against the king. The king issued a ban on travel from Norway, but Snorri in open defiance sailed to Iceland, at least partly in hope of recovering some property his own relatives had seized. Haakon then sent a letter to Snorri's estranged son-in-law, Gissur Thorvaldsson, ordering that Snorri be brought to Norway or that he be killed, because he had committed high treason. Because of Snorri's avarice and treatment of his relatives, Gissur and his followers chose to surprise Snorri the night of September 22, 1241, at Reykjaholt and kill him rather than deliver him to the king. Ironically, the king claimed Snorri's properties and thus gained the foothold in Iceland that he needed. Twenty-three years after Snorri's death, Iceland was subjugated to the Norwegian crown; the country remained under a foreign ruler until the Republic was proclaimed in 1944.

Significance

Snorri's life seems in many ways a paradigm of the vices and virtues of the Sturlung Age. He was energetic, astute, imaginative, well learned, and a leader. Yet these qualities were vitiated by the controlling passion of greed, which according to Snorri's nephew Sturla in *Sturlunga Saga* led directly to his death. So great is the discrepancy between Sturla's depiction of Snorri and the Snorri who readers encounter in his writings, that some have doubted that Snorri could be the author of *The Prose Edda* or the *Heimskringla* or *Egils saga* (c. 1222-1230; *Egil's Saga*, 1893), which computer-aided scholarship has tended to ascribe to him. Given the remoteness of the times and the scant evidence that survives, such questions will inevitably continue to be the focus of scholarly debate, as will the question of whether Snorri should be revered chiefly as historian or as literary stylist. In the meantime, the *Heimskringla* has become a kind of national bible for Norwegians, who found inspiration in it for their nineteenth and twentieth century struggle for national emancipation, and *The Prose Edda* remains an invaluable, delightfully readable sourcebook of northern mythology and culture.

—*Karen A. Kildahl*

Further Reading

Bagge, Sverre. *Society and Politics in Snorri Sturluson's Heimskringla*. Berkeley: University of California Press, 1991. Explores the social and political life of Iceland as Snorri presents it in the *Heimskringla*. Includes an extensive bibliography and an index.

Ciklamini, Marlene. *Snorri Sturluson*. Boston: Twayne, 1978. A complete discussion of Snorri's life and writings. Includes summaries and a detailed literary analysis of all Snorri's works with a view to placing them in the context of medieval European culture.

Einarsson, Stefán. *A History of Icelandic Literature*. New York: American-Scandinavian Foundation, 1957. Provides a succinct summary of Snorri's life and achievements and comprehensive background material on twelfth and thirteenth century literature and life. Extensive survey of saga literature.

Eskeland, Ivar. *Snorri Sturluson: A Biography*. Translated by Pat Shaw. Oslo: Grøndahl Dreyer, 1993. A brief biography of Snorri. Includes a bibliography and an index.

Hallberg, Peter. *The Icelandic Saga*. Translated by Paul Schach. Lincoln: University of Nebraska Press, 1962. An introductory work that provides a lucid overview of the Sturlung Age as portrayed in *Sturlunga Saga*. Contains a summary and interpretation of *Egil's Saga*. Discusses theories of origin and composition and the significance of saga literature.

Ross, Margaret Clunies, ed. *Old Icelandic Literature and Society*. New York: Cambridge University Press, 2000. Examines the literature of Iceland in the Middle Ages, including the literature of myth, romance, and religion, and medieval Iceland's poetry, sagas, social institutions, belief systems, and more. Also provides a bibliography and an index.

Snorri Sturluson. *Heimskringla: History of the Kings of Norway*. Translated by Lee M. Hollander. Reprint. 1964. Austin: University of Texas Press, 1991. In addition to the most readable translation of Snorri's major work, the translator offers an introduction to Snorri's life and times filled with valuable insights and information and written in a way that seems to belie the immense scholarship it required. Probably the best introduction to Snorri's life and work.

Turville-Petre, Gabriel. *Origins of Icelandic Literature.* 1953. Reprint. Oxford, England: Clarendon Press, 1975. Examines the uses that Snorri made of some of his sources to illustrate the skald's imaginative and creative genius. Accepts the theory that Snorri was the author of *Egil's Saga.*

Zaleski, Carol, and Philip Zaleski, eds. *The Book of Heaven: An Anthology of Writings from Ancient to Modern Times.* New York: Oxford University Press, 2000. Presents Snorri's "The Deluding of Gylfi," from *The Prose Edda.* Includes an index.

SEE ALSO: Jean Froissart; Geoffrey of Monmouth; Gregory of Tours; Saxo Grammaticus.

RELATED ARTICLE in *Great Events from History: The Middle Ages, 477-1453*: 1373-1410: Jean Froissart Compiles His *Chronicles.*

SORGHAGHTANI BEKI

Mongolian princess

Sorghaghtani Beki orchestrated the election of her son Mongke to rule the Mongol Empire, leading to the dominance of the line of Tolui, her husband and the son of Genghis Khan, over the other family branches of Genghis Khan.

BORN: late 1100's; central Mongolia
DIED: February or March, 1252; place unknown
ALSO KNOWN AS: Sorqoqtani; Sorkaktani; Sorghaqtani; Sorghagtani
AREAS OF ACHIEVEMENT: Government and politics, religion and theology

EARLY LIFE

Sorghaghtani Beki (sor-GAHG-tah-nee beh-kee) began her life as the niece of Toghrïl Khan, the ruler of the Kereit tribal confederation, which dominated much of central Mongolia in the twelfth century. Very little is known about her early life; however, she and her sisters, Ibaka (the eldest) and Bek-tutmish Fujin (the middle child), played an important role in later Mongolian politics as wives of leading figures within the Mongol Empire (1204-1260).

In the latter part of the twelfth century, as her uncle strove to dominate Mongolia, at first in alliance with Temüjin (later known as Genghis Khan) and then against him, warfare became a constant in the Mongolian steppes. In 1203, hostilities between Genghis Khan and Toghrïl increased to the point that they engaged in open conflict. Although Sorghaghtani's uncle initially defeated the Mongols, Genghis Khan regrouped his forces and defeated the Kereit in a surprise attack.

With this defeat and after the death of Toghrïl in hiding, the Kereit were absorbed into the Mongols. Customarily, the daughters and relatives of the defeated rulers were given to loyal followers of the victor as wives, and Sorghaghtani and her sisters were no exception. Ibaka went to Jurchedei, one of Genghis Khan's generals, and Bek-tutmish Fujin was given to Jochi, the eldest son of Genghis Khan. Tolui, Genghis Khan's youngest son, received Sorghaghtani Beki as his wife in 1203. Most of what is known about this Kereit princess occurred after 1203.

LIFE'S WORK

Sorghaghtani's most important role in the Mongol Empire occurred later in her life. Her husband, Tolui, a great general in his own right, died in 1233. Although it has not been proven conclusively, some scholars believe that because Tolui did not succeed Genghis Khan after the latter's death although he did serve as regent until his brother Ogatai ascended the throne, Sorghaghtani became embittered against the new khan. If this is true, after Tolui's death she never openly displayed it.

After the death of her husband, she never remarried. This was somewhat unusual as often the widowed wives of nobility remarried a brother or other relative of the husband. Ogatai, the emperor, attempted to arrange a marriage between Sorghaghtani Beki and his son (and future emperor) Güyük. This marriage would have cemented a relationship between the families of Tolui and Ogatai and lessened the chance of conflict over the matter of succession to the throne. Indeed, had the marriage taken place, the disputes and civil wars that later marred the Mongol Empire may never have happened. Sorghaghtani Beki, however, declined the offer and chose to devote herself solely to the upbringing of her children. Considering the careers of her sons, it was a most fortuitous choice, as she became a great influence on their lives.

As a Nestorian Christian, Sorghaghtani Beki exposed her children to Christianity. Although none of her sons, Mangu, Hülegü, Kublai, and Arigböge, converted to Christianity, they demonstrated respect for it as well as for other religions. This was due to the influence of their mother. Sorghaghtani Beki, while a Nestorian Christian, also provided funds to Muslims to establish mosques and madrasas (religious schools). Furthermore, she also cultivated relationships among Daoist and Buddhist monks in China. In part, her actions among the Buddhists and Daoists were because she held large tracts of land in Hebei Province of China. Although it increased her support among her Chinese subjects, her display of favor to the Buddhists or Daoists was also because of a general belief in tolerance of all religions, a belief her sons would later display.

In addition, Sorghaghtani also encouraged the education of her children. Although her late husband, Tolui, had been a great warrior and an exceptional general, Sorghaghtani Beki realized the value of education in addition to martial prowess. Thus she procured the services of a Uighur Turk who educated her sons to read and write in Mongolian. Her actions were exceptional, as the Mongolian language had only recently adopted an alphabet after the defeat of the Naiman in 1204, on the orders of Genghis Khan.

Most of the sources, particularly the Persian ones, display Sorghaghtani Beki as a pillar of society. During the regency of Toregene, the wife of Ogatai, many of the sources recorded that she never veered from the *yasa* (thought to be the law code of Genghis Khan although no one has found conclusive evidence of its contents) and continually promoted the interests of the empire over the interests of individual princes and ministers. Of course, much of this depiction must be viewed with great scrutiny as the authors in question, Juvaini and Rashīd al-Dīn, served princes descended from her. In the case of Juvaini, he was an official in the administration of her son Hülagü, the first Il-Khan of Persia, and Rashīd al-Dīn served Ghazan, her great grandson.

These authors portrayed Toregene, Ogatai's wife and the regent after his death, as a vile and corrupt woman who constantly was involved with misconduct. Their statements condemned her for carrying out her ambitions of personal vengeance and elevating her son Güyük to the throne. Ogatai had nominated another son, Shiremun, from a different wife as his successor. On the other hand, these authors portrayed Sorghaghtani as promoting the interests of the empire. She did later encourage her eldest son Mangu to pursue the throne after Güyük's death. However, when it came to Güyük's election in 1246, Sorghaghtani Beki, along with her sons, placed her considerable influence behind Güyük. Thus, Sorghaghtani was never portrayed as a schemer or a detriment to the Mongol court.

These sources must be read with caution as their bias in favor of Sorghaghtani is apparent. Nonetheless, when compared with the regent Toregene or the regent who presided after Güyük's death in 1248, his wife, Oghul Qaimish, Sorghaghtani remains unblemished. A wide variety of sources describe both Toregene and Oghul Qaimish as vile and corrupt. Sorghaghtani, although she perhaps did not receive the attention she deserved, remained considerably less influenced by politics and greed than Toregene and Oghul Qaimish.

The court historians were not alone in their assessment of Sorghaghtani. Other chroniclers throughout the empire also marveled at her qualities. In addition, Western travelers such as Giovanni da Pian del Carpini, an emissary from Pope Innocent IV, remarked on her exceptional intelligence and noted that only Borte, the mother of Genghis Khan, held more respect among the Mongols than Sorghaghtani.

Her political acumen came to the fore during the period after Güyük's death. Although she publicly supported Güyük's election, Sorghaghtani carefully cultivated alliances with the other princes of the Mongol Empire. She alerted Batu Khan, the ruler of the Golden Horde (consisting of much of what is now western Russia and the Ukraine), when Güyük assembled an army to march against Batu in 1248. This matter stemmed from a rivalry between the two princes during the Mongol invasion of Europe in 1240. Batu abstained from the election of Güyük, excusing himself by claiming illness. Güyük, however, died en route, and potential civil war was averted.

With Güyük's death, his wife, Oghul Qaimish, came to power. Despite numerous attempts to arrange a *quriltai*, or council, to elect a new khan, Oghul Qaimish stalled the process so that she could remain in power. The court historians remarked extensively on the corruption of power and of officials during her regency and noted the justness of Sorghaghtani Beki's character.

As time passed, Sorghaghtani continued to work and built numerous political alliances with not only the Mongol princes but also ministers of state who increasing became dissatisfied with the precarious nature of Oghul Qaimish. Thus in 1251, a council was held in which the majority of Mongol princes and generals elected Mangu, Sorghaghtani's eldest son, as the khan of the Mongol Empire.

Although Sorghaghtani died in the winter of 1252, not long after Mangu was elected, the ascendancy of her family drastically altered the balance of power in the empire. A purge quickly eliminated many of the line of Ogatai and Chagatai, two brothers of Sorghaghtani's late husband Tolui. Thus with Mangu on the throne, his brother Hülagü received orders to finish the conquest of the Middle East, while Kublai and Mangu marched south to fight the Song Dynasty (Sung; 960-1279) in China.

Mangu died in 1259, which led to a conflict between Kublai and his brother Arigböge for the crown. Kublai ultimately won; however, the Mongol Empire essentially split apart. Nevertheless, Sorghaghtani's sons, Kublai and Hülagü, established control and set up empires in East Asia and the Middle East, respectively, while other grandsons of Genghis Khan ruled over Central Asia and much of what is now Russia and the Ukraine.

SIGNIFICANCE

Due to the relative equality among genders among the Mongols, Sorghaghtani's contributions are noteworthy not because she was a woman but because she was an exceptional person in general. Unlike women in other societies at the time, the Mongol women had opportunities to influence the course of government, and they often did. Because of her involvement in politics, Sorghaghtani changed the ruling house of the Mongol Empire. Furthermore, her involvement in supporting various religious establishments despite being a Nestorian Christian herself ensured that religious tolerance was a cornerstone of the Mongol Empire. Her actions greatly influenced her sons, all of whom played significant roles in the course of the empire's history. With her wide range of activities and influence, there is little wonder why so many chroniclers and travel accounts consistently remarked on the quality of her character and her exceptional intelligence.

—*Timothy May*

FURTHER READING

Allsen, Thomas T. *Mongol Imperialism*. Berkeley: University of California Press, 1987. Considers the rise and rule of Mangu, the son of Sorghaghtani, and has a useful description of Sorghaghtani's role.

Dawson, Christopher, ed. *The Mongol Mission: Narratives and Letters of the Franciscan Missionaries in Mongolia and China in the Thirteenth and Fourteenth Centuries*. Translated by a nun of Stanbrook Abbey. London: Sheed and Ward, 1955. A collection of travel accounts during the reign of Güyük and Mangu that have anecdotes pertaining to Sorghaghtani.

Grousset, René. *The Empire of the Steppes: A History of Central Asia*. Translated from the French by Naomi Walford. New Brunswick, N.J.: Rutgers University Press, 1970. A classic history of Central Asia with a lengthy section on the Mongols. Although somewhat outdated, it remains a useful introduction to the period in which Sorghaghtani lived.

Juvaini, ʿAla-ad-Din ʿAta-Malik. *The History of the World-Conqueror*. Edited and translated by John A. Boyle. 2 vols. Seattle: The University of Washington Press, 1997. As one of the most important sources on the Mongol Empire, Juvaini's history relates several important events pertaining to Sorghaghtani.

Morgan, David. *The Mongols*. Oxford, England: Basil Blackwell, 1986. Perhaps the best introduction to the Mongol Empire. Morgan pays considerable attention to the role of the female nobility in the empire as well as the trend of religious tolerance.

Ratchnevsky, Paul. *Genghis Khan: His Life and Legacy*. Translated by Thomas Nivison Haining. Cambridge, England: Blackwell, 1992. Although a biography of Genghis Khan, there are a few notes pertaining to Sorghaghtani's life before she married Tolui.

Rossabi, Morris. *Khubilai Khan: His Life and Times*. Berkeley: University of California Press, 1988. This is an excellent biography of Sorghaghtani's son, Kublai. Rossabi also devotes a section to his mother's life and her influence on him.

SEE ALSO: Genghis Khan; Kublai Khan.

RELATED ARTICLES in *Great Events from History: The Middle Ages, 477-1453*: 960: Founding of the Song Dynasty; 960-1279: Scholar-Official Class Flourishes Under Song Dynasty; 1204: Genghis Khan Founds Mongol Empire; 1271-1295: Travels of Marco Polo.

Stefan Dušan

King of Serbia (r. 1331-1355)

The greatest king of medieval Serbia, Stefan Dušan extended his kingdom's borders at the expense of the Byzantine Empire. He successfully defended Serbia against its enemies, promulgated an important law code, and was crowned czar of the Serbs and the Greeks in 1346.

Born: 1308; central Serbia
Died: December 20, 1355; near Prizren, Serbia
Also known as: Stefan Uroš IV; Stephen Dushan; Stephen Uroš
Areas of achievement: Government and politics, law, military

Early Life

Stefan Dušan (DEW-shahn) was the son of Stefan Uroš III Dečanski and his first wife, Theodora. He was born during the reign of his grandfather, the Serbian king Stefan Uroš II Milutin (r. 1282-1321), who was successfully waging war with the Byzantine Empire and expanding Serbian rule in the Balkans. Dušan's father was the governor of the maritime provinces of Serbia on the Adriatic coast, but he rebelled against Milutin and tried to seize royal power. The revolt was unsuccessful and Dečanski was captured and subsequently blinded by Milutin to make him unfit for succession. Around 1314, Dečanski was sent into exile to Constantinople with his wife and young son. For nearly seven years, Dušan lived in the imperial capital, where he received an excellent education and came to understand and appreciate Byzantine government and traditions. These were to be important influences on his later policy.

About 1320, Dušan's father and grandfather were reconciled, and the family returned to Serbia. The following year, Milutin died, and Dečanski made a successful bid for the throne. He claimed that his blindness had been miraculously cured (other sources suggest that he had always been able to see a little but had hidden that fact), and the Serbian nobility accepted him from among three claimants as their new king. At an assembly in January, 1322, Dečanski was crowned by Serbian archbishop Nikodim, and Dušan was proclaimed coregent or junior king (in Serbian, *mladi kralj*). The exact significance of this title is difficult to determine, but it may have been partly based on reservations that the nobility expressed about Dušan's father. From the beginning of Dečanski's reign, Dušan played an important role in the kingdom. He was appointed to govern the crucial region of Zeta, in what is now Serbia and Montenegro, and he participated actively in several important military campaigns. The most crucial of these was against the Bulgarians and resulted in a great Serbian victory at Velbužd (now Kjustendil) on July 28, 1330. This battle established Serbian control over Macedonia and became the foundation on which Dušan's later Balkan hegemony was based.

In the aftermath of the Battle of Velbužd, the Serbian nobility revolted against Dečanski. They resented his cautious and pacific policy, especially toward Byzantium. There may also have been conflict between Dušan and his father, either from natural rivalry or because the nobility influenced Dušan. The son marched against the king and captured him on August 21, 1331. Early in September, Dušan was crowned king. His father was subsequently murdered and eventually canonized by the Orthodox Church. Before Dušan could embark on the great work that justified posterity in calling him Serbia's greatest medieval ruler, he had to suppress a revolt in Zeta, probably based on provincial bitterness felt by the local nobility, who did not achieve the degree of influence over the new king that they had expected. By the end of 1332, Dušan's position was secure.

Life's Work

The major focus of Dušan's foreign policy was the Byzantine Empire. Before he could begin the process of further territorial expansion to the south into the Greek lands of the Byzantine Empire, however, he had first to consolidate relations with Bulgaria and his other neighbors. During the spring of 1332, Dušan signed a peace treaty with the new Bulgarian ruler, Czar Ivan Alexander. Throughout his reign, Dušan was able to count on good relations with Bulgaria and to rely on there being no Byzantine-Bulgarian alliance directed against Serbia. To the north, Dušan adopted a two-part policy toward Charles I (Charles Robert of Anjou; r. 1308-1342), king of Hungary, and toward his son and successor, Louis the Great, king of Hungary and Poland (r. 1342-1382 and 1370-1382). On one hand, Dušan's stance was militarily defensive, and he prevented Hungary from pursuing its territorial interests south of the line of the Sava and Danube Rivers. On the other hand, he was diplomatically aggressive, forcing the Angevin rulers of Hungary to protect their other European interests rather than focusing on Serbia. Dušan was also careful not to antagonize Bosnia to the northwest and the powerful maritime city

PRINCES AND CZARS OF SERBIA, 1168-1459

Reign	*Ruler*
1168-1169	Tichomir Great Prince
1169-1196	Stefan I Nemanja
1180	Serbian independence
1180-1196	Instability
1196-1228	Stefan II
1228-1234	Stefan III Radoslav
1234-1243	Stefan IV Vladislav
1243-1276	Stefan Uroš I
1276-1282	Stefan Dragutin
1282-1321	Stefan Uroš II Milutin
1321-1331	Stefan Uroš III Dečanski
1330	Battle of Velbužd: Serbia controls Macedonia
1331-1355	STEFAN UROŠ IV DUŠAN
1345	Dušan assumes title czar of Serbia
1349	Dušan's law code promulated
1355-1371	Stefan Uroš V the Weak
1371	Dynastic collapse
1371-1389	Stefan Lazar I (prince)
1389	Battle of Kosovo: defeat by Ottomans
1389-1427	Stefan Lazar II Lazarevich (despot)
1396	Serbia is an Ottoman vassal state
1427-1456	George Brankovich
1456-1458	Lazar III Brankovich
1458-1459	Helene Palaeologina (regent)
1459	Annexation by Turkey

of Dubrovnik on the Adriatic Sea. Though Serbia had territorial interests and claims in this region, especially the district of Hum, which it had lost during the reign of Dečanski, Dušan chose not to pursue these. He correctly judged that the support of the nobility for any ventures in this area was lacking. In 1333, he reached a settlement with Dubrovnik, which brought substantial revenues to the Serbian royal treasury. In the following year, he concluded an agreement with Bosnia. To the east, the north, and the northwest, therefore, Dušan was assured of peace and had a free hand to pursue his southern policy.

In the spring of 1334, the Serbian king launched an attack into the Byzantine territory of Macedonia. Dušan's efforts achieved early successes, in part through the help of the Byzantine general Syrgiannes, who was the governor of the region and who had earlier revolted against Emperor Andronicus III Palaeologus (r. 1328-1341). The Serbian army captured several important fortified cities, but the campaign ended when Syrgiannes was killed and the Byzantines mounted a counteroffensive. In a peace treaty signed on August 26, 1334, a compromise was reached. The Serbs withdrew, but the Byzantines confirmed many of their conquests. The border established between the two states at this time was nearly identical to the modern border between Serbia and Montenegro and Greece.

The next phase of Dušan's southward expansion came following the death of Andronicus III in 1341. Quarrels over the succession in the Byzantine Empire brought the empire near to civil war. One of the leading parties was John VI Cantacuzenus (r. 1347-1354), who had been Andronicus III's leading general and close adviser but whose own ambitions had been shunted aside in 1341. He led his army to Serbia to seek Dušan's support in ousting his opponents in Constantinople.

An agreement was forged between the two in July, 1342, in which the Serbs expected to be rewarded with imperial territory. Dušan invaded southern Macedonia and also captured large portions of Albania. After early cooperation that benefited both sides, the alliance between Dušan and Cantacuzenus dissolved over conflicting interests. The Serb advance in the Balkans continued, however, and by the end of 1345, Dušan controlled all Macedonia, except Thessaloniki, east to the straits of Chrysopolis. In the following three years, Dušan added to his empire, conquering Epirus and the region of Thessaly from the Byzantine Empire. These conquests extended his control south to the Gulf of Corinth.

Even before these successes, Dušan had changed his title. After 1343, he called himself king of Serbia, of Albania, of the Coast (that is, the Dalmatian coast), and of the Greeks. Late in 1345, he began to style himself czar, the Slavonic equivalent of emperor. To reflect this enhanced status, he arranged for the archbishop of Serbia to be raised to the rank of patriarch, and then, in April, 1346, Dušan was himself crowned czar of the Serbs and the Greeks. In his next years, the czar turned his attention primarily to consolidating and administering his royal lands and his multiethnic empire.

To regularize practice, he introduced a system of titles and ranks that he modeled on the Byzantine structure of government. He also reorganized the imperial chancery, again using the Byzantine model. His greatest achievement, however, was the law code that was prepared at his direction during the late 1340's. It was promulgated by a council in Dušan's capital of Skoplje in 1349. It consisted of 201 articles that specialized in public and criminal matters. It did not deal with issues of civil legislation, which were addressed in other ways. In general, the code reflected Dušan's great reliance on his nobility as a base of political support for the monarchy, for it significantly enhanced their authority over lands and villages given them as fiefs. Byzantine elements may be found in the code, especially in matters relating to the church, but it was primarily based on previous Serbian practice and codes. The code was modified slightly in 1353 or 1354.

In his last years, Dušan's relations with the imperial court in Constantinople worsened. Emperor John V Palaeologus (r. 1341-1391) and his coruler, Cantacuzenus (Dušan's former ally), sought to recover parts of Macedonia. By allying themselves with Turkish auxiliaries, the Byzantine rulers defeated Dušan in 1352. In retaliation, the Serbian czar planned an invasion of Byzantium; he was most likely preparing for an expedition that would reach Constantinople itself when he unexpectedly died in December, 1355. As his successor he left his son Stefan Uroš V, who was, however, unable to maintain Dušan's accomplishments.

SIGNIFICANCE

One measure of the magnitude of Stefan Dušan's territorial expansion is the fact that he doubled Serbia's size and conquered the parts of Macedonia and the south that his predecessors had either not been able to annex or had not even attempted to acquire. During his reign, he was able to transform his position from that of a semipuppet placed on the throne by a rebellious nobility into that of a strong and effective ruler whom later centuries remembered as "Dušan the mighty." His military and territorial successes were, however, not his only claim to be regarded as the greatest of medieval Serbia's rulers. His legislative skill, his administrative reforms, and his law code also contribute to this reputation.

Another measure of Dušan's greatness is found in the fact that his attention was by no means limited narrowly to Serbian affairs. He developed cordial ties with Popes Clement VI (1342-1352) and Innocent VI (1352-1362) in Avignon with two policies in mind. First, he was sympathetic to the possibility of Church reunion between Latin West and Orthodox East, especially since the patriarch of Constantinople had anathematized Dušan and the Serbian church after 1346. Second, he needed support from the west against the Ottoman Turks. They had significantly expanded their empire in Anatolia (now Turkey) during the early part of the fourteenth century and in 1354 had established themselves in Europe by conquering Gallipoli. Dušan recognized them as a danger not only to Serbia but also to all Christians, whether Catholic or Orthodox. He hoped to be named to head a great crusade against the Turks. That he thought he might be able to use such a campaign also to conquer Constantinople and establish his rule there is clear from some of his preliminary negotiations with the Venetians.

All these ambitions came to naught. Within twenty years of Dušan's death, Serbia had been reduced to a territorial extent smaller than when he had ascended the throne. In the Battle of Kosovo on June 15, 1389, Serbia was decisively defeated by the Ottomans, who were thereby firmly established in the Balkans. Nevertheless, Dušan may fairly be credited with having fundamentally established the predominance of the Serbian state in the region. This accomplishment was, in subsequent generations, to be an important and enduring fact of Balkan history.

—*Paul W. Knoll*

FURTHER READING

Cox, John K. *The History of Serbia*. Westport, Conn.: Greenwood Press, 2002. This comprehensive history of the Serbian region includes a chapter on "The Splendor of Medieval Serbia."

Dinič, M. "The Balkans, 1018-1449." In *The Cambridge Medieval History*, edited by Joan M. Hussey. Vol. 4. Cambridge, England: Cambridge University Press, 1966. Based solidly in nineteenth and twentieth century Balkan scholarship, this reliable study treats Dušan's reign in the context of both Balkan history and Byzantine relations with the region. The treatment of Dušan's law code is superficial, but political and diplomatic details are reliable. The analysis of the fate of Dušan's empire is particularly good.

Dušan, Stefan. "The Code of Stephan Dušan." Translated by Malcolm Burr. *Slavonic and East European Review* 28 (1949-1950): 198-217, 516-539. A full translation of the text of the czar's law code, originally issued in 1349. The English rendering is fluid and readable, and there are helpful annotations of technical terms and obscure references.

Fine, John V. A. *The Late Medieval Balkans: A Critical Survey from the Late Twelfth Century to the Ottoman Conquest*. Ann Arbor: University of Michigan Press, 1987. An authoritative study on all aspects of Balkan history in the era covered in its subtitle. Two long chapters are devoted to the period of Dušan's life and rule. They are particularly good with regard to social conditions in Serbia and to Serbia's relations with its

Balkan neighbors. This work contains one of the very few presentations of Serbian-Albanian relations.

Pavlowitch, Stevan K. *Serbia: The History of an Idea*. New York: New York University Press, 2002. A history focused on Serbia as an idea that persisted even through its border changes and through its temporary "nonexistence." Includes significant discussion of medieval Serbian rulers and their relationship to the Church.

Soulis, George Christos. *The Serbs and Byzantium During the Reign of Tsar Stephen Dušan (1331-1355) and His Successors*. Washington, D.C.: Dumbarton Oaks Library and Collections, 1984. The most thorough study in English of Dušan's career. The focus is on Serbian-Byzantine relations, but this is treated broadly enough to include detailed analysis of other aspects of the czar's foreign policy. One chapter is devoted to Dušan's internal policy in his conquered Byzantine lands, and there is a full discussion of the law code of the czar.

_______. "Tsar Stephen Dušan and Mount Athos." *Harvard Slavic Studies* 2 (1954): 125-139. A specialized study that focuses on the monastic communities of the arm of the Chalcidian peninsula that is dominated by Mount Athos. Dušan sought the support of the monastic groups on Mount Athos for the creation of a Serbian patriarch and his own eventual coronation as czar. He was, in addition, a patron of considerable importance for several of the monasteries. An important work for understanding Dušan's ecclesiastical policy.

SEE ALSO: Basil the Macedonian; János Hunyadi.

RELATED ARTICLES in *Great Events from History: The Middle Ages, 477-1453*: 963: Foundation of the Mount Athos Monasteries; 1040-1055: Expansion of the Seljuk Turks; 1054: Beginning of the Rome-Constantinople Schism; 1167: Foundation of the Nemanjid Dynasty; 1305-1417: Avignon Papacy and the Great Schism; June 28, 1389: Turkish Conquest of Serbia.

KING STEPHEN

King of England (r. 1135-1154)

Stephen was king of England and duke of Normandy during a period of civil war and anarchy. His monarchy, described by a contemporary chronicler as "nineteen long winters in which Christ and his saints slept," became a period of anarchy during which Stephen was unable to sustain the peace created by Henry I.

BORN: c. 1097; place unknown

DIED: October 25, 1154; Dover, Kent, England

ALSO KNOWN AS: Stephen of Blois; count of Mortain; count of Boulogne

AREA OF ACHIEVEMENT: Government and politics

EARLY LIFE

Stephen of Blois was the third son of Stephen, count of Blois and Chartres, and Adela, daughter of William the Conqueror. Count Stephen died in 1102, at Ramlah in Palestine, and the children were reared by their mother. The eldest son, William the Incompetent, received minor fiefs in France. The bulk of the family's patrimony fell to the second son, Theobald IV the Great, who, in 1125, succeeded to the rich province of Champagne, making him one of the most important tenants in Northern France.

Stephen, following a traditional pattern of younger, landless sons, was sent to the court of a relative to make his fortune. In his case the relative was his uncle, Henry I, king of England (1100-1135) and duke of Normandy (1106-1135). Stephen first appears in the records of Henry's court in 1113, by which time the king had made him count of Mortain. This gave Stephen important fiefs in England and Normandy and marked him as one of the famous "new men" whom Henry used as the linchpins of his government. Stephen was further enriched in 1125, when Henry married Stephen to Matilda, heiress to the county of Bolougne. Bolougne, independent but linked to Normandy, was a gateway to the wealthy cloth trade of Flanders. It provided Stephen with important links to England's commercial center in London and to the Flemish community in Kent.

Henry I ruled long and well and was much praised by chroniclers as a keeper of peace and a lion of justice. His only legitimate son, however, had died in a shipwreck in 1120, and Henry had only a daughter, Matilda (also called Maud or "the empress" because of her former marriage to the Emperor Henry V of Germany), to succeed him. Recognizing the difficulties of female succession, the king, in 1126, asked all of his magnates to swear an oath of fealty to her. Stephen, who was gaining a reputation as a chivalrous man, contested with Henry I's illegitimate son, Robert, earl of Gloucester, for the honor of swearing first.

This attempt to secure the succession was a gamble. When Matilda was married to Geoffrey Plantagenet, count of Anjou, the ceremony of the oaths was repeated, probably because Anjou was the ancient enemy of Normandy, and Henry I wanted his barons to reaffirm their commitment to his daughter. The oaths were repeated one more time, after a temporary estrangement between Matilda and Geoffrey. Henry I clearly recognized that his daughter might easily face a disputed succession, and so he attempted to coopt all opposition.

The plan might have worked, but late in 1135, Geoffrey, impatient that Henry had not surrendered some Norman castles promised by the terms of his marriage with Matilda, made war against the king. In the midst of this conflict, on December 1, 1135, Henry I died. The succession problem became a crisis: Henry I's plan was that Matilda would succeed him, but now Matilda was invading Normandy. To remain loyal to Henry's scheme would have required allying with an invader, and to repel the invader would have meant disloyalty to the king. Normandy was in chaos, and there was no clear successor to the dead king, so on December 22 some of the leading men of the duchy met with Count Theobald of Blois to offer him the throne, but the meeting broke up when a messenger brought the astonishing news that Stephen had already been crowned.

Nineteenth century engraving of King Stephen. (Library of Congress)

LIFE'S WORK

Stephen's coronation came in part from his own dash and bravery and in part from circumstance. Geoffrey's invasion led many, Stephen most obviously, to believe that their oaths to Matilda were now superseded by events. Stephen's contacts with southeastern England gave him a place to land, and his commercial ties brought the Londoners over to his side. Finally, his younger brother, Henry of Blois, whom Henry I had also enriched, making him abbot of Glastonbury and bishop of Winchester, secured the essential support of the treasurer and other officials of the central government and persuaded the archbishop of Canterbury to crown and anoint Stephen.

For the first two years of his reign, Stephen was able to defeat or defer his opposition. Matilda's supporters had to attend Stephen's court or risk banishment to a political wilderness. Stephen did not, however, inspire the confidence that Henry I had. He besieged the castle of one baron who did not recognize his claims, but then, against the advice of his brother, let the rebels go. This created an implacable enemy who now sought safety with Geoffrey of Anjou and indicated to other dissidents that Stephen lacked the backing for strong action. Moreover, the act antagonized his brother.

More mistakes followed. Stephen attempted to neutralize the influence of Earl Robert of Gloucester, Matilda's half brother, whose vast lands in England and Normandy made him one of the most powerful men in the kingdom. He limited Robert's lordship over some strategic castles and apparently was behind a plot to kidnap him. This alienated the earl without really damaging him and again showed other barons that Stephen could not discipline his own vassals.

The magnates of Stephen's reign had grown up at the court of Henry I and had become accustomed to a style of government that included swift justice and evenhanded patronage. Stephen seemed capable of neither: He was partial and unpredictable, severe to the weak and mild to the strong. This quality was fatal, for barons unable to obtain favor at Stephen's court had a ready-made alternative in the person of Matilda.

In 1138, Robert of Gloucester defected to Matilda, the first of the great barons to do so. He drew with him several other followers, in both England and Normandy, who now repudiated Stephen. So began the Anarchy, a civil war that would last to the end of the reign.

To meet the threat Stephen reorganized his government. His first decision was to diminish the power of the church in general, and his brother, Henry of Blois, in particular, for to fight a war required the allegiance of the secular baronage, whose ambitions were balked by a powerful and influential cadre of ecclesiastics. Stephen first prevented Henry's elevation to archbishopric of Canterbury, signaling the end of the close cooperation between the brothers that had made Stephen king. Next he took more drastic steps. At the head of the administration was the family of Bishop Roger of Salisbury: Roger acted as a justice and supervisor; Roger's nephews, the bishops of Lincoln and Ely, were officials in both the judicial and financial administration of the realm; and another relative, rumored to be Roger's son, served as Stephen's chancellor. In 1139, the king fabricated charges against them all and had them arrested—a flagrant breach of church law. He seized their castles and lands and released them only when threatened with church sanctions, but their power was broken. Stephen attained no decisive advantage by these maneuvers, however, and he cost himself church support. At best he managed to maintain his position in the civil war; the defections of 1138 and 1139 had not been followed by further rebellions.

On February 2, 1141, at the Battle of Lincoln, Stephen was captured by his enemies, and it appeared that Matilda had triumphed: Henry of Blois, acting as papal legate, recognized her authority on behalf of the Church. Stephen's queen, however, kept resistance alive in the southeast—another legacy of Stephen's long association with Bolougne and the commercial centers of England. With the help of the citizens of London, Stephen's queen was able to drive the empress west and then surrounded Matilda's forces at Winchester. Earl Robert of Gloucester, commanding the rear guard of Matilda's armies, was captured on September 14. Though negotiations, mediated by Henry of Blois, began at once, the rival parties could agree to no more than a simple exchange, the king for the earl.

The events of 1141 were in fact decisive, but in Normandy, not in England. There Geoffrey of Anjou continued his campaigns, and by 1142, he had taken most of the duchy up to the south bank of the Seine. Stephen was too busy to mount an expedition to Normandy. He had been there only once as king, in 1137, while both William the Conqueror and Henry I, knowing the importance of the duchy, had spent half their reigns there. Thus, Count Geoffrey's conquest of Normandy was opposed only on a local level and only with the resources at hand; given Geoffrey's determination, the results were entirely predictable.

Thus, in the mid-1140's, events in England drifted. Stephen, secure in the east, tried to advance against Matilda's outposts in central England. Robert of Gloucester, Matilda's viceroy, established a stable government in the southwest. There were frequent clashes—Matilda narrowly escaped capture at Oxford, and had to flee, dressed in white, across the frozen Thames—but nothing broke the stalemate. In 1147, Earl Robert of Gloucester died, and the following year Matilda, having lost her most able captain, retired to Normandy. Still the Angevin resistance in England did not collapse. Stephen was too powerful to lose England but not powerful enough to break the rebels.

Normandy was different, for late in 1144, Geoffrey captured the citadel at Rouen, and formally took control of the entire region. This had far-reaching implications for England as well. Many barons, especially the most important ones, had estates in both England and Normandy; in fact, the Norman lands, though usually smaller in extent, were often more important, for they represented the ancestral, patrimonial holdings of the family. If they remained loyal to Stephen, they would certainly lose their Norman possessions, while if they renounced him, they could keep their Norman lands and there was always the chance that they would triumph in England. In consequence, there began a slow erosion of Stephen's support in England, a trend that would become decisive by the early 1150's.

The additional dilemma facing Stephen was his growing estrangement from the Church. In the 1140's, the king intervened in increasingly heavy-handed ways to secure control of ecclesiastical appointments, attempting, for example, to promote a candidate of his own choosing to the archbishopric of York. This was dangerous even for a strong and secure monarch; for Stephen, unable to conquer even his domestic opposition, it was a grave mistake. Stephen needed the Church to secure the fortunes of his own dynasty, for only the Church could sanction the accession of his son. He hoped to have his son crowned before the succession became an issue, but the archbishop of Canterbury, displaying a surprising autonomy, refused to comply: succession to the Anglo-Norman realm remained an open issue.

The stalemate was finally broken in 1150 by events in Normandy. There Geoffrey of Anjou abdicated in favor of his son, Henry. Henry Plantagenet was a young man of seventeen, who had already visited England twice, once at the head of a small military expedition. Though he was half Angevin, he was also half Norman, so he inherited little of the hostility that had been directed against his father. Henry had skill and ambition, and, over the next several years, he added a vast collection of resources: In 1151, Geoffrey died, and Henry inherited the counties of Anjou and Maine; in 1152, he married Eleanor, heiress of Aquitaine, and added her vast French fiefs to his own. He was, by this time, by far the most important man in France, with holdings that eclipsed those of the French king. In 1153, he sailed to England to claim the last portion of his inheritance.

Stephen's reign effectively ended with Henry of Anjou's arrival, though the king lived for another year. Henry and Stephen met for battle three times, yet the magnates would not fight: They had already arranged a series of truces among themselves, and now they imposed a similar program on their leaders. Stephen's son Eustace clearly saw the drift of events and attempted to draw Henry into battle, but Eustace was ineffective in his plots and unable to turn events to his own advantage. He died in August, of grief, some said.

Eustace had been the last obstacle to peace. Stephen did not wish to fight on behalf of his other son, nor could he have enlisted any significant support for such a plan. Stephen and Henry established the Treaty of Winchester, proclaimed on November 6, 1153. By its terms, Stephen was to remain king for the rest of his life, and Henry of Anjou would succeed him.

Stephen's last year as king was uneventful. He made a circuit of his kingdom, visiting places that had not welcomed him for fifteen years, showing himself in pomp and regal splendor. In the fall, Stephen contracted a fever, from which he died on October 25, 1154. He was buried in the abbey at Feversham, which he had founded, next to his queen and Eustace. Henry of Anjou was crowned King Henry II at Westminster Abbey on December 9.

SIGNIFICANCE

Stephen was a weak monarch in an age that had grown accustomed to strong leadership. The government established by Henry I relied on careful royal supervision and a steady and politic touch, something Stephen did not give and did not have. He came to the throne in a crisis, but he did not have the qualities needed in a twelfth century king. Rather than settling that crisis, his elevation prolonged it, and he proved to be the last of the Norman kings. With Henry II a new dynasty, the Plantagenets, came to power.

In some ways, Stephen was an attractive man. He had been a good and trusted vassal of Henry I, and he was popular at court—his elevation would have been impossible without that. Even in the Anarchy, his enemies admitted that he was kind and pleasant, refusing, for example, to execute a hostage whose father had reneged on his pledge: Stephen took the boy out and played a game with him instead. Except for the last weeks of 1135, however, he was irresolute, listening to too much counsel or not enough. He had energy but no sure direction. In settled and peaceful times, Stephen might have managed, but in settled and peaceful times, Stephen would not have become king. The conflicts that allowed his accession prevented his success.

England suffered during the Anarchy. In some places there was widespread devastation, the product of armies, foragers, plunderers. Churches, which had fewer defenses than castles, were often the target of attacks, and some were invaded and used as outposts by warriors. Even where the physical damage was small, the institutions of central government were sundered from the locales. In some cases the techniques of government were nearly forgotten, and in others they were turned to serve the purposes of local strongmen. The centralized and codified government of Henry II was in many respects a reaction to the Anarchy, and he wished Stephen's reign to be remembered as no more than an unpleasant interlude between the strong government of his grandfather and his own.

—*Joseph W. Leedom*

FURTHER READING

Bradbury, Jim. *Stephen and Matilda: The Civil War of 1139-1153*. Stroud, England: Sutton, 1996. Focuses on the war and its battles, weapons, and fortifications.

Cronne, H. A. *The Reign of Stephen*. London: Weidenfeld and Nicolson, 1970. Focuses on the whole of Anglo-Norman society and less on the individual claimants to the throne. Material on the baronage is especially good.

Crouch, David. *The Reign of King Stephen, 1135-1154*. New York: Longman, 2000. At nearly four hundred pages, a sweeping overview of Stephen and the civil war, politics, and institutions of the time. Illustrations, maps, appendices, bibliography, index.

Davis, R. H. C. *King Stephen*. 1967. 2d ed. London: Longman, 1977. One of the best biographies of Stephen. Argues that the problems of the reign were caused by the "disinherited," men who had lost their lands under the earlier Norman kings. The Anarchy was an attempt by the magnates to secure recognized rights of inheritance.

Dunn, Diana, ed. *War and Society in Medieval and Early Modern Britain*. Liverpool, England: Liverpool University Press, 2000. A collection of essays that includes a consideration of civil war and peace during Stephen's reign and earls and earldoms during his rule.

Gesta Stephani. Translated and edited by K. R. Potter and R. H. C. Davis. Oxford, England: Clarendon Press, 1976. An important narrative source for the reign and possibly the only source for parts of the reign. The author, perhaps Bishop Roger of Bath, changed his allegiances in the late 1140's, and the shift in perspective helps clarify the weakening of Stephen's rule.

King, Edmund. *The Anarchy of King Stephen's Reign*. New York: Oxford University Press, 1994. Covers the power struggle between Stephen and Matilda, the Anarchy, and how the monarchy survived.

Matthew, Donald. *King Stephen*. New York: Hamgledon and London, 2002. A rare attempt to see Stephen in a generous light. The author argues that Stephen's reputation survives largely through testimony of hostile witnesses.

SEE ALSO: Christina of Markyate; David I; Eleanor of Aquitaine; Henry I; Henry II; William the Conqueror.

RELATED ARTICLES in *Great Events from History: The Middle Ages, 477-1453*: October 14, 1066: Battle of Hastings; 1147-1149: Second Crusade; 1154-1204: Angevin Empire Is Established.

STEPHEN I

King of Hungary (r. 997-1038)

Stephen I zealously spread the Christian faith to his largely pagan people, taking a great interest in the welfare of the poorest of his subjects and establishing numerous churches and monasteries both at home and abroad to place Christianity at the center of Hungarian life.

BORN: 975; Esztergom, Hungary
DIED: August 15, 1038; Alba Regia (now Székesfehérvár), Hungary
ALSO KNOWN AS: Saint Stephen; Vajk; Vaik; István
AREAS OF ACHIEVEMENT: Religion and theology, government and politics

EARLY LIFE

Stephen was born with the name of Vajk at Esztergom, Hungary, to Géza, the fourth duke of the Hungarians, and Sarloth (or Sarolta). Stephen was baptized by the renowned missionary to the Hungarians, Saint Adalbert, bishop of Prague, the man responsible for converting his father to Christianity. Adalbert educated young Stephen in the mysteries of the Christian faith, a religion with few Hungarian adherents. Stephen was also strengthened in the faith by his tutor, Count Theodatus, whose piety mirrored that of Adalbert. Together these men impressed on Stephen that by taking Christianity as its guide, a pagan and therefore ungodly nation could be transformed into a nation dedicated to peace and inner harmony.

Both Adalbert and Theodatus believed that Stephen had the potential to lead his country by applying Christian principles, and great time and effort were therefore given to his education. When Géza died in 997, Stephen became duke and assumed leadership of the state and its army. An able military leader who deplored bloodshed and prayed that his soldiers would not harm the enemy, Stephen made peace with neighboring states. By establishing a peaceful relationship with others, Stephen was able to make missionary work, which he had seen Adalbert doing in Hungary, his chief preoccupation. He gathered a band of itinerant ministers of the gospel to preach to anyone who would listen to their message. In their company, Stephen traveled extensively throughout his dukedom, proclaiming God's liberation of humankind through Jesus's death on the cross at Jerusalem. Such proclamations, Stephen hoped, would convert the pagans to Christianity and free them from their bondage to superstition and fear.

Stephen's efforts in converting the masses to Christianity were so successful that a number of pagan chieftains were angry with him and discussed making war on Stephen's entourage. The most important of these chieftains, Koppány, took action and attacked Stephen's forces at the town of Veszprém. Stephen's army, though badly outnumbered by Koppány's forces, was able to rout and kill many pagan troops. Koppány was captured and executed, thus ending the most serious threat to Stephen's attempt to impose his religion on unbelievers. In celebration of this impressive victory, Stephen founded a monastery, which became widely known throughout Christendom as Martinsberg, in honor of Saint Martin. Subsequently, Stephen invited many holy men from surrounding countries not only to visit but also to live permanently at Martinsberg and help him establish the Christian religion as the nation's singular faith.

LIFE'S WORK

As a result of his victory against Koppány, Stephen was crowned king of Hungary. Moreover, the title he bore was not merely "king" but "apostolic majesty." To his subjects, he became known as Stephen, the apostle of Hungary. He was crowned on August 15, 1000, by Pope Sylvester II. The pope admired Stephen's dedication to the Vatican and included him among the preferred monarchs, on whom many favors were bestowed. At the time of his coronation, Stephen dedicated his kingdom to Mary, the Blessed Virgin, the patroness of Hungary, and made veneration of her a centerpiece of the Catholic faith in that country.

As king, Stephen took his high office seriously and worked from the outset of his reign to change Hungary into a humane, Christian kingdom where the dignity of the individual was of central importance. He created a new constitution, which survived into the twentieth century, that advocated and promoted Christian standards of conduct and provided for punishment of those who violated the strictures. At Alba Regia, Stephen built a great church that was to serve as the burial place of all Hungarian kings and a center of national religious life. He built another imposing monastery, named for Saint Peter and Saint Paul, in the city of Buda, and created the Church of Saint Stephen in Rome near the inn he constructed for Hungarian pilgrims. Under his guidance, many smaller churches and monasteries were established throughout Hungary.

In a politically significant move, Stephen married Gisela, sister of the German king and emperor-to-be, Henry II, known as Saint Henry. Henry was an administrative genius who divided his German territory into counties to be administered by people he appointed. By so doing, he made certain that the provinces were ruled by the monarchy rather than the often-rapacious local gentry. Applying these ideas and others given to him by Henry II, Stephen did much to bring order to his kingdom, which added to his popularity. In near-total control of the kingdom, Stephen was not only able to make pagan religious observances and practices illegal but was also empowered to put an end to the lawlessness that had been the hallmark of pre-Christian Hungary. Murder, robbery, assault, and other crimes were punished severely, and impiety and acts against the newly established church received ferocious punishment.

On a few occasions, Stephen had to resort to the threat of warfare in order to safeguard his kingdom from incursions by neighboring states. One marauder who brought his army into Hungary was Stephen's cousin, the prince

Stephen I. (Library of Congress)

ÁRPÁD KINGS OF HUNGARY, C. 896-1301

Reign	*Ruler*
d. 907	ÁRPÁD
d. 947	Zsolt
d. 972	Taksony
997	Géza
997-1038	SAINT STEPHEN (ISTVÁN) I
1038-1041	Peter Orseleo
1041-1044	Samuel
1044-1046	Peter (second rule)
1047-1060	Andrew I
1060-1063	Béla I
1063-1074	Salamon
1074-1077	Géza I
1077-1095	SAINT LÁSZLÓ (LADISLAS) I
1095-1116	Kalman
1116-1131	Stephen II
1131-1141	Béla II
1141-1162	Géza II
1162-1163	László II
1163-1172	Stephen III
1163-1165	Stephen IV
1172-1196	Béla III
1196-1204	Imre
1204-1205	László III
1205-1235	Andrew II
1235-1270	Béla IV
1270-1272	Stephen V
1272-1290	László IV
1290-1301	Andrew III

of Transylvania, who, after being defeated in battle, divested of his lands, and taken prisoner, was released unharmed on the condition that he allow Christianity to be preached in his domain. Stephen's kingdom was also confronted by Bulgarian forces, who mysteriously retreated without fighting, which Stephen attributed to his prayers to God for protection against bloodshed. In general, however, Stephen ruled over a tranquil kingdom that was unblemished by large-scale war or threats of war. His constitution, which guaranteed the rights of citizens, proved to be a sound basis for a society, for Hungary flourished under its protection. Stephen was well loved by his people, who regarded him as an ideal monarch.

The latter part of Stephen's reign, however, was marred by personal tragedy. All of his children died of various conditions, including his much-relied-on eldest son, Emeric (Imre), who had greatly assisted Stephen in governing the kingdom. After the death of Henry, Stephen again had to contend with the possibility of war, this time the invasion of Hungary by the Germans under Henry's successor, Conrad II. Stephen was said to have again prayed to God that there would be no conflict, and, as in the past, the invader did an about-face and retreated to its territory. No blood had been spilled. This seeming miracle added to Stephen's reputation as a saintly king who had a close relationship with God.

At the end of his life, Stephen was the object of a murder plot created by knights who wanted to usurp his power. The plot was not carried out because the man who was to strike the killing blow against Stephen fell to his knees and begged the king's forgiveness. He was forgiven, but his fellow conspirators were executed. Stephen, reminded by this murder attempt that his life was coming to a close, commended his kingdom to the care of the Virgin Mary and was then given the last rites of the Catholic Church. He died on August 15, 1038, having reigned over Hungary for a remarkable forty-one years. His remains were enshrined by request of Saint László I, the king of Hungary (r. 1077-1095), within the latter's own chapel at Buda. Stephen was later canonized by Pope Benedict IX.

SIGNIFICANCE

Stephen I was a ruler who did much for his country during his long and relatively peaceful period of rule. One of his most illustrious achievements from a historical perspective was that he created the nation of Hungary from an assortment of miniature states. Without Stephen's unifying genius and the guidance from Henry II, Hungary may have remained a divided nation or fallen under the sway of more powerful neighboring states. As an administrator, Stephen devised a fair, comprehensive, and consistent constitution that endured for many centuries. As an apostle, he succeeded in spreading Christianity throughout his kingdom. Not only did Stephen preach Christian ideals, but he also put them in practice in his daily life, even to the extent of washing the feet of the poor people whom he invited to his palace. His unusual degree of sympathy for the poor helped make him a widely popular and beloved king.

Stephen is perhaps most important as a source of national pride for Hungarians during the past ten centuries, for he was one of the most humane, resourceful, and brave monarchs of his time. His humility, love of peace, hatred of impiety, and compassion for the least fortunate members of society make him one of history's most admirable figures.

—John D. Raymer

Further Reading

Engel, Pál. *The Realm of St. Stephen: A History of Medieval Hungary, 895-1526*. Translated by Tamás Pálosfalvi. Edited by Andrew Ayton. New York: I. B. Tauris, 2001. A comprehensive study of the history of Hungary during the time of Stephen through the sixteenth century. Explores the economic, social, political, cultural, and military history of the Magyars. Written especially for readers with little or no knowledge of the region and time period. Maps, tables, bibliography, index.

Englebert, Omer. *The Lives of the Saints*. Translated by Christopher Freemantle and Anne Freemantle. New York: D. McKay, 1951. A good summary of how Stephen extended the power of the Catholic Church in Europe, especially Eastern Europe, where the Church felt it needed to assert its authority.

Head, Thomas, ed. *Medieval Hagiography: An Anthology*. New York: Garland, 2000. Presents a collection of biographical sketches about Stephen. Includes an introduction by the editor, a guide to further reading, and a general bibliography.

Hoyt, Robert S. *Europe in the Middle Ages*. 3d ed. New York: Harcourt Brace Jovanovich, 1976. Discusses Stephen's successes as short-lived, destroyed by the inept kings who followed him. Illustrations, bibliography, index.

Kosztolnyik, Z. J. *Hungary Under the Early Árpáds, 890's to 1063*. Boulder, Colo.: East European Monographs, 2002. A historical survey of the House of Árpád, which includes Stephen as king. Discusses the early years of the Magyars, their migrations and settlement patterns, military campaigns, and more. Genealogical tables, maps, bibliography, index.

Lázár, István. *Hungary: A Brief History*. Translated by Albert Tezla. 6th ed. Budapest: Corvina Press, 2001. Presents a brief but concise history of Hungary, from its beginnings during the days of Árpád (Stephen's predecessor) through the twentieth century. Maps, index.

Lendavi, Paul. *The Hungarians: A Thousand Years of Victory in Defeat*. Translated by Ann Major. Princeton, N.J.: Princeton University Press, 2003. Comprehensively traces the history of the Hungarians from the Magyars' entry into the Carpathian region in the 890's to the end of the Cold War in the late twentieth century. Includes a summary, maps, chronology, bibliography, and an index.

Poulet, Dom Charles. *A History of the Catholic Church*. Edited by Sidney A. Raemers. 2 vols. St. Louis, Mo.: B. Herder, 1941-1943. Vol. 1 presents a still-useful and solid discussion of Stephen's struggles and ultimate victory against pagans and paganism. Bibliography.

Thurston, Herbert, and Donald Attwater, eds. *Butler's Lives of the Saints, Complete Edition*. 1956. Reprint. Vol. 3. Westminster, Md.: Christian Classics, 1990. Extensive discussion of how Stephen I made Hungary a thoroughly Christian country, with special emphasis on his saintly character and his application of the Christian virtues to his dealings with the poor and disenfranchised. Bibliography.

Watkins, Dom Basil, ed. *The Book of Saints: A Comprehensive Biographical Dictionary*. 7th rev. ed. New York: Continuum, 2002. An informative assessment of the major accomplishments of Stephen I that places him within the context of the Europe of his time. Brief bibliography.

See also: Árpád; Saint Elizabeth of Hungary; Henry II the Saint; Saint László I; Sylvester II.

Related articles in *Great Events from History: The Middle Ages, 477-1453*: c. 850: Development of the Slavic Alphabet; 890's: Magyars Invade Italy, Saxony, and Bavaria; August 10, 955: Otto I Defeats the Magyars; November, 1330: Basarab Defeats the Hungarians; 1442-1456: János Hunyadi Defends Hungary Against the Ottomans.

SU DONGPO

Chinese poet and scholar

One of China's most famous poets and scholars, Su Dongpo was also an important government official during the Song Dynasty. He figured prominently in the political controversies surrounding the attempted imposition of state capitalist programs.

BORN: December 19, 1036; Meishan, Sichuan Province, China

DIED: July 28, 1101; Changzhou, China

ALSO KNOWN AS: Su Tung-p'o (Wade-Giles); Su Shi (Pinyin), Su Shih (Wade-Giles)

AREAS OF ACHIEVEMENT: Government and politics, literature, scholarship art

EARLY LIFE

Su Dongpo (sew dahng-poh), born Su Shi, was the eldest son of an upper-class, landowning family living in the western part of Sichuan during the Song Dynasty (Sung; 960-1279). His clan was one of the most distinguished literary families in the history of China. He, his father, Su Xun (Su Hsün), and his younger brother, Su Zeyou (Su Tse-yu), all were famous scholars and government officials. In the eleventh century, Sichuan Province produced a high percentage of scholar-officials, noted for their cosmopolitan prose and poetry. Su Dongpo grew up in a cultured, sophisticated home that prepared its sons to take imperial civil service examinations. Success in these exams would guarantee for the family official positions and access to wealth and power.

Su Dongpo and his brother Su Zeyou were both brilliant students. Lifelong friends, their careers in scholarship and government were inextricably linked. Their personalities were different but complementary: Su Zeyou was serious, stable, and cautious, whereas Su Dongpo was impetuous, volatile, and excitable. They stayed in continuous contact with each other, even when their official duties separated them by hundreds of miles, communicating in poetry at least monthly throughout their lives.

In 1056, the brothers went to Kaifeng in northern China to take the imperial exams. This city was the metropolis of China, cloaked in imperial grandeur. The wealth, talent, and beauty of the nation centered on the court. The brothers were not dazzled by the city's splendor, however, and passed the exams with high honors. Su Dongpo's main examination essay, which developed the principle of simplicity and leniency in the administration of a country, caught the attention of the imperial examiner and the emperor himself. On April 14, 1057, at the age of twenty, Su Dongpo was officially designated a *jinshi* (the highest ranking academic honor), second in a class of 388 successful candidates. He thus achieved instant fame and recognition as one of the leading scholars of China. Normally he would have entered immediately into government service, but his mother died during the examinations and he had to go into a compulsory period of twenty-seven months of mourning. He already was known as a literary genius, however, and he emerged from the mourning ready to assume his public life.

LIFE'S WORK

Su Dongpo's life was notable for three reasons. First, he was a brilliant, if somewhat impetuous, scholar-bureaucrat who figured prominently in the political disputes of the early Song Dynasty. Because he took controversial stances on important issues, he frequently found himself in serious conflict with his bureaucratic superiors and opponents. Second, he was one of China's most gifted poets and literary figures. His contemporaries compared him to China's greatest men of letters, and succeeding generations have continued to honor his genius. He was equally versatile in prose and poetry, writing in a beautiful classical style. He experimented with a common form of poetry, the *ci*, which had been previously confined to love songs composed in cabarets, and turned it into a vehicle for discourse on Buddhist and Daoist philosophy. Third, he developed a theory of calligraphy and painting resembling modern impressionism. The purpose of painting, according to Su Dongpo, was to paint the inner spirit rather than the form of an object. The painting should reflect not only the spirit of the object but also the artist's inner essence.

In the early phase of his career, from 1062 to 1079, he achieved fame as both a government bureaucrat and a poet. After a brief posting as a minor provincial official, he returned to the capital (Kaifeng) in 1064. Thereafter, he and his brother were swept into the center of a political storm surrounding the efforts of the statesman Wang Anshi (1021-1086) to reform Chinese government and society.

To most of its inhabitants, the Song Dynasty seemed peaceful, prosperous, and humane. China had agricultural wealth, busy commercial cities, and great public works such as canals, walls, and roads. Beneath the surface, however, lay chronic national difficulties. Barbarian tribes in the north and west constantly threatened invasion, forcing the Song to maintain large armies, which overtaxed the imperial treasury. Despite the country's apparent productivity, the government rarely had sufficient revenues to meet its obligations. It was clear to many officials, if not the majority, that fundamental reform was necessary to save the dynasty. Yet the questions of the shape the reforms should take and who should lead them caused acrimonious bureaucratic conflicts.

Between 1069 and 1077, Wang Anshi served as the chief imperial adviser and initiated institutional reforms designed to change fundamental fiscal, economic, and bureaucratic practices. First, he instituted state capitalist schemes to increase government revenues. One such program, for example, provided government loans to farmers at an actual interest rate of 30 percent. Second, he levied numerous new taxes. Finally, he established methods of registration to regiment and control the people. The *baojia* system, for example, organized the people into groups of ten and sixty, from which able-bodied men were called up for military training and duty. Although these reforms seemed capable of resolving some of the government's fiscal woes, the methods by which they were implemented alarmed Su Dongpo and his colleagues.

In essence, Su Dongpo contended that Wang's methods were too authoritarian and resulted in exploitation of commoners by arbitrary central officials. Su Dongpo risked his career by writing a nine-thousand-word letter to the emperor in June, 1071, criticizing Wang's reforms, which had been authorized by the emperor. He was particularly concerned about the farm-loan program. Participation in this was supposedly voluntary, but in order to please Wang, provincial and local bureaucrats frequently forced peasants to take out loans even if they did not need them. When Wang's critics noted this fact, he had them demoted or removed from office. Su Dongpo's letter argued that, contrary to what the emperor had been told, public opinion was solidly against Wang. He reminded the emperor that his power derived from the people and that he ignored their will at his peril. Unfettered dissent, he claimed, was vital to the health of the government. The emperor did not take his advice, however, and demoted Su Dongpo from the capital to the Hangzhou area, where he served as governor of three cities between 1071 and 1080. Eventually, in 1076, Wang was forced out of office, but the doctrinal disputes fired by his reform continued to plague Su Dongpo and China for the remainder of the Song era.

The years Su Dongpo spent in the Hangzhou area saw his greatest activity as a poet. His distaste for the internecine political squabbles in the capital drove him to seek solace in his poetry, in which he explored the beauties of nature and the highest reaches of the human spirit. By this time, Su Dongpo had assumed his mature temperament and appearance. From his portraits, he had a muscular build, stood 5 feet, 8 inches (173 centimeters) in height, and had a dominating face with prominent cheekbones and an imposing forehead. He wore a long, tapering mandarin beard and regarded the world through wide-set, brilliant eyes. His chief personality fault was his propensity to speak his mind too freely among people who had no loyalty to him.

He loved the Hangzhou area and wrote such beautiful poetry about it that he has been regarded ever since as the city's poet laureate. It was there, between 1071 and 1074, that he mastered and transformed the *ci* form of poetry. This poetic form had originated in houses of entertainment (disguised brothels) in which female entertainers sang songs arranged in such a way that each succeeding line contained a definite number of syllables. In time, the *ci* became an honorable form of literary expression. Su Dongpo took the lead in transforming the *ci* from love poetry to a vehicle fit to express the highest sentiments of the human spirit. He freed the *ci* from its sentimentality and infused it with power and grace.

Yet the poet's life was not untouched by strife in these years, for political disputes about Wang Anshi's reforms continued to rage and Su Dongpo could not ignore them. He wrote numerous poems of protest satirizing the government officials. He did not overtly criticize the Song leadership or advocate rebellion, but his subtle satire thoroughly annoyed his enemies. In all, his poetry, whether *ci* or protest, crackles with life and depth. Eventually, in 1079, he was impeached for his veiled attack on officialdom, and he was exiled in 1080 to a small, poor town near Hankou on the Yangtze. By then, however, he had proved his administrative skills, saving the city of Suchou from a disastrous flood in 1077 by building huge dikes, and ruling equitably over a series of districts. His literary reputation and his commitment to virtue were also well established.

The next period of his life, from 1080 to 1093, continued this pattern of official success followed by degradation and demotion. During his periods of demotion and exile, he studied Buddhist and Daoist philosophy, which profoundly shaped his writing and thinking. He was one of the first Confucian scholars to incorporate these ideas into the official philosophy and he played a leading role in creating neo-Confucian philosophy, which dominated Chinese life into the twentieth century.

Between 1084 and 1093, Su Dongpo's party was in power at the capital, and he rose to the post of secretary to the emperor. Nevertheless, he managed eventually to lose his job because his propensity to attack corruption even within his own party gained for him many enemies.

He remained close to the seat of power, however, until a new emperor ascended the throne in the autumn of 1093 and Su Dongpo's enemies regained power. Thereupon, he was again dismissed from office and was eventually exiled to the far southern island of Hainan, from which he returned only in time to die in July of 1101. This last phase of his career, from 1094 to 1101, was the saddest time of his life.

SIGNIFICANCE

The Song Dynasty was noted for its versatile intellectuals, and Su Dongpo stands out as one of the most prominent. His position in history is secured by his poems and prose and by his courageous stand for his political and ethical principles. Although he was a respected patriot and hero, his life provides a study of national degeneration through factional strife. His party's clash with Wang Anshi set in motion the forces that undermined the dynasty, as ineffective, corrupt administrators controlled the dynasty and sapped its vitality.

He is best remembered, however, as a poet, writer, and artist. He incorporated Buddhist philosophy into Confucianism and was the central figure in the formulation of the theory of "literati painting" as a coherent body of doctrine. His fundamental contention was that a painting should be a revelation of the nature of the artist who painted it, and of his mood and feelings at the moment of creation. Under the influence of Buddhism, Su Dongpo delved into problems of the mind and the universe. He believed that nature was spiritually alive and that an artist should catch that inner spirit in painting. The essence of things had to be seized by the eye and the imagination. To paint a fish, for example, the artist must imagine swimming with it in the water and share its reactions to current and storm. Only then could he paint the salmon leaping the rapids. Su Dongpo's theories informed the Chinese approach to painting thereafter.

Su Dongpo ranks as one of China's greatest poets, painters, and prose writers. He also was an able administrator, containing floods, building causeways, and struggling against bureaucratic corruption. He was one of China's greatest men of letters as well as a great man of action.

—*Loren W. Crabtree*

FURTHER READING

Bi, Xiyan. *Creativity and Convention in Su Shi's Literary Thought*. Lewiston, N.Y: Edwin Mellen Press, 2003. An examination of Su Dongpo's literary works. Bibliography and index.

Chaffee, John W. *The Thorny Gates of Learning in Sung China*. New York: Cambridge University Press, 1985. Su Dongpo, like his scholar-bureaucrat friends and enemies, entered China's governmental elite through the examination system. This book provides a social history of the examinations and details Su Dongpo's experience with them, as both a student and a chief examiner.

Egan, Ronald C. *Word, Image, and Deed in the Life of Su Shi*. Cambridge, Mass.: Harvard University Press, 1994. Egan covers the life of Su Dongpo and his literary output as well as his philosophy, political activities, painting, and calligraphy. Contains translations of many of his poems.

Fuller, Michael Anthony. *The Road to East Slope: The Development of Su Shi's Poetic Voice*. Stanford, Calif.: Stanford University Press, 1990. An examination of the poetry of Su Dongpo. Bibliography and indexes.

Grant, Beata. *Mount Lu Revisited: Buddhism in the Life and Writings of Su Shih*. Honolulu: University of Hawaii Press, 1994. An examination of Buddhism and its influence on Su Dongpo as revealed in his writings and life.

Lin Yutang. *The Gay Genius: The Life and Times of Su Tungpo*. New York: John Day, 1947. This classic biography of Su Dongpo is clearly written and is based on original Chinese sources. Lin feels a strong attraction for Su Dongpo but presents a balanced account of his life and ideas. An indispensable source.

Su Dongpo. *Selected Poems of Su Tung-p'o*. Translated by Burton Watson. Port Townsend, Wash.: Copper Canyon Press, 1994. A collection of poems by Su Dongpo, with some commentary. Bibliography.

SEE ALSO: Li Bo; Li Qingzhao; Ouyang Xiu; Sima Guang; Wang Anshi.

RELATED ARTICLE in *Great Events from History: The Middle Ages, 477-1453*: 1069-1072: Wang Anshi Introduces Bureaucratic Reforms.

Suger

French abbot

As abbot of Saint-Denis, Suger rebuilt the abbey church according to principles that make him the founder of the Gothic style. As lover of peace, order, and political harmony, Suger defined and popularized the centralizing and peacekeeping mission of the Capetian monarchy, increasing its prestige and assisting its rise to dominance in medieval France.

Born: 1081; Saint-Denis, near Paris, France
Died: January 13, 1151; Saint-Denis
Areas of achievement: Architecture, government and politics, religion and theology

Early Life

Suger (sew-zhehr) was born of villein parentage in or near Saint-Denis, just outside the city of Paris. He entered the monastery as a student in 1091; one of his fellow pupils, who became his lifelong friend and patron, was Louis Capet, afterward King Louis VI (Louis the Fat). Suger was an outstanding student, practical and efficient as well as intelligent. He described himself as "small and frail," but he was also energetic and untiring. He was amiable and discreet, with a talent for peacemaking; he was also an enthusiastic defender of the privileges and prestige of his own monastery. In 1106, he was made secretary to abbot Adam.

Saint-Denis was a royal monastery, and many of the kings of France were buried there. It possessed relics of the Passion of Christ and of Saint Dionysius, the apostle of France, but much of its prestige came from the belief, historically untrue, that this Saint Dionysius was identical with Dionysius the Areopagite, the disciple of Saint Paul mentioned in Acts 17:34. (A further misunderstanding, which was to have important consequences, was the belief that Dionysius was the author of a mystical treatise, now known to be an anonymous composition of the fifth century and referred to as Pseudo-Dionysius, proclaiming the manifestation of God to human beings in the form of light.) The king and his entourage often lodged at the monastery, allowing the abbot and his staff proximity to the center of royal politics.

In 1109, the monastery obtained from the king the right to hold the famous Lendit fair, to which merchants came from great distances; during the event, the monastery displayed its relics to crowds of pilgrims, and the fair became an important religious as well as commercial occasion.

In 1107, Suger was made provost of one of the monastery's dependent houses in Normandy; there he saw firsthand both Norman experiments in church architecture and the efficient organization of the duchy under Duke Henry Beauclerc (who was also King Henry I of England), the most effective feudal overlord of the time. In 1118, he was sent by King Louis on the first of a series of missions to the Papal court. The Investiture Controversy between the Papacy and Emperor Henry V had turned into open warfare, and the king of France was a strong supporter of the Papacy. Suger was in Rome in 1122 when this conflict was at last resolved by the agreement known as the Concordat of Worms; it was there that he received the news that the monks of Saint-Denis had elected him abbot on the death of Adam, a position he held until his death in 1151. He did not return to France at once but spent several months visiting pilgrimage churches in Italy. Pope Calixtus II summoned him to the papal court again in order to make him a cardinal but died before Suger reached Rome. His future was to lie with the royal rather than the Papal court.

Life's Work

The first great crisis of Suger's career came in 1124, when the emperor, seeking vengeance for the French king's support of the Papacy, invaded France. Louis convened an assembly of clerics and lay magnates at Saint-Denis and there, in an elaborate ceremony organized by Suger, took from the altar the banner of Saint Dionysius and formally declared himself a vassal of the saint. He then appealed to the assembled dignitaries to join him in defense of the Church and the realm. This appeal succeeded even among barons who were the king's rivals, and the appearance of Louis and his vassals in arms persuaded the emperor, who had anticipated no such united opposition, to depart without giving battle.

In gratitude for the saint's support during the invasion of 1124, the king gave the monastery entire control of the Lendit fair. Suger hoped to make Saint-Denis a major pilgrimage center during the season of the fair; in this he was successful, and the church rapidly became overburdened by the crowds of pilgrims coming to see the relics. He devised an ambitious program of rebuilding, using the profits from the fair; he also reorganized the estates of the abbey to make them more profitable, replacing customary fixed rents by a percentage of the annual yield and encouraging more intensive agriculture.

Suger. (Hulton|Archive at Getty Images)

Suger's intention to rebuild the church took shape soon after 1124, but actual work did not begin until 1137. Two factors, in addition to his close attendance on the king, seem to have been responsible for the delay. One was a reaffirmation of his own sense of religious mission. Suger had long been an admirer of Saint Bernard of Clairvaux and had come under increasing pressure from Bernard to reform Saint-Denis on Cistercian principles. The monastery's wealth and the crowds of courtiers and pilgrims had eroded much of its discipline and made the traditional monastic life almost impossible. There is a famous letter of Bernard's in which he sneers at an unnamed abbot whom he had seen riding in state with sixty horsemen attending him; this is usually taken as a denunciation of Suger, intended to shame him into reform, but it may well have been aimed instead at his predecessor Adam, whose sense of religious vocation seems to have been less intense than Suger's. In 1127, Suger undertook the reform of the monastery, reaffirming the Benedictine rule but stopping short of imposing the full rigors of Cistercian discipline. This task occupied much of his time for the next several years.

In 1137, Louis VI died and was succeeded by his son Louis VII, a young man of hotter temperament, who wanted independence from his father's policies and advisers. Suger lost his influence at court until harsh experience proved that he was indispensable. In the meantime, he began the building campaign that was to revolutionize medieval architecture.

After centuries of decay, destruction, and restoration, disappointingly little of Suger's building remains today; what does remain, however, as interpreted from his own writings, allows one to understand the magnitude of his achievement. The western front of Saint-Denis, the first part of the work to be undertaken, is still Norman in appearance; there is an unprecedented rose window, however, flooding the interior with light, and the architectural elements are arranged to emphasize the central doorway, identified by an inscription as the gate of Heaven. The church, built according to rule in harmonious proportion, is a model of the kingdom of heaven. Church architecture was said to have an anagogical purpose, guiding the beholder by visible signs to the perception of divine reality. This purpose becomes more explicit in the choir at the east end of the church, a theological treatise in architecture putting into practice the mystical vision of Pseudo-Dionysius. The cross-ribbed vault and pointed arch, both of which had been known to the Normans but not combined by them, are employed together for the first time to allow a maximum of height with a minimum of masonry, dissolving the walls and filling the space with stained glass; the interior columns radiate from a central point to avoid obstructing the light entering through the windows.

The divine light, according to Pseudo-Dionysius, does not appear directly to human beings; rather, it shines "through a veil" of created objects. Suger therefore made his windows translucent, not transparent. Some are plain gray (grisaille); others are brightly colored "sermons in glass" illustrating biblical passages important to Dionysian theology.

Suger then decided to rebuild the nave in the same style as the choir, but the pace of construction slowed in 1147 when Louis VII decided to take part in the Second Crusade. Suger attempted to dissuade him, arguing that his absence would be used by the barons as an opportunity for violence and plunder. He could not, however, change the king's mind. Instead, Louis appointed him regent, and Suger was effectively ruler of France for two years during the king's absence. He governed firmly, suppressing a baronial revolt aimed at deposing the absent king. When Louis returned in 1149, his crusade a humiliating failure, he gave Suger the title "father of his country" in recognition of his services. Though approaching seventy, Suger determined to renew the Crusade himself, financing it out of the revenues of Saint-Denis, but he died before he could embark for the East.

SIGNIFICANCE

Suger wrote four books, which are the principal sources for the knowledge of his career and policies. His biographies of Louis VI and Louis VII (the latter unfinished) are masterpieces of medieval biography, but there is no complete English translation of either. Two others, *De rebus in administratione sua gestis* (the accomplishments of his administration) and *De liber alter de consecratione ecclesiae Sancti Dionysii* (*Abbot Suger on the Abbey Church of St. Denis and Its Art Treasures*, 1946), are accounts of his career as abbot and of the rebuilding of the church. Although he shows considerable modesty in writing about himself, one would occasionally like to see him through someone else's eyes. There is no doubt, however, that he is one of the founding fathers of the medieval French monarchy. The kings might on their own have pursued some of the policies that he advocated; there is no evidence, however, that they had considered them, perceived them clearly, or would have followed them systematically. Suger encouraged the kings to take seriously the promise of their coronation oath to protect the poor and the helpless and to do justice; he urged them to invite the barons themselves to seek justice at the king's court in return for accepting the obligations of vassalage. He saw in the ties of lord and vassal an orderly framework within which disputes could be resolved by conciliation rather than violence: An ordered hierarchical society was the earthly image of the kingdom of heaven.

The impact of his other great achievement, the architecture of Saint-Denis, was even more widely felt than his political artistry. The Gothic style spread rapidly from Saint-Denis to Paris, inspiring the larger-scale use and refinement of its techniques in the great Cathedral of Notre Dame and then around the Île de France (at Chartres, for example) and elsewhere, sometimes as the official style of the French monarchy, sometimes as an advance messenger glorifying French culture by its own intrinsic merits. Suger was buried in Saint-Denis, but his tomb was desecrated during the French Revolution. In one sense, however, every Gothic cathedral is his monument, and his work makes him the medieval figure whose influence is most widely felt and most highly visible today.

—*Robert I. Willman*

FURTHER READING

Burckhardt, Titus. *Chartres and the Birth of the Cathedral*. Translated by William Stoddart. Bloomington, Ind.: World Wisdom Books, 1996. A look into the architectural history of the Gothic cathedral of Chartres. Includes illustrations, plans, a bibliography, and an index.

Crosby, Sumner McKnight. *The Royal Abbey of Saint-Denis: From Its Beginnings to the Death of Suger, 475-1151*. Edited by Pamela Z. Blum. New Haven, Conn.: Yale University Press, 1987. Discusses the construction history of Saint-Denis, including Suger's building campaigns, as revealed by archaeological investigation. Indispensable for tracing the fate of Suger's work through centuries of neglect, vandalism, and overenthusiastic restoration.

Gelernter, Mark. *Sources of Architectural Form: A Critical History of Western Design Theory*. New York: St. Martin's Press, 1995. Surveys architectural form in the history of design, including a chapter discussing scholasticism as well as the "shift from the secular to the divine" in medieval architecture theory.

Grant, Lindy. *Abbot Suger of St-Denis: Church and State in Early Twelfth-Century France*. New York: Longman, 1998. Discusses the state of the Church and government in the time of Suger. Includes illustrations, maps, plans, a bibliography, and an index.

Hallam, Elizabeth M., and Judith Everard. *Capetian France, 987-1328*. 2d ed. New York: Longman, 2001. A study of the Capetian Dynasty in medieval France. Includes an extensive bibliography and an index.

Kessler, Herbert L. *Spiritual Seeing: Picturing God's Invisibility in Medieval Art*. Philadelphia: University of Pennsylvania Press, 2000. Discusses the mysterious power of particular images, in this case the images of medieval art. Provides a chapter that looks at Suger's stained-glass windows at Saint-Denis.

Male, Émile. *Religious Art in France, the Thirteenth Century: A Study of Medieval Iconography and Its Sources*. Princeton, N.J.: Princeton University Press, 1984. Still one of the great classics of art history, this volume, originally published in 1902, initiated the modern study of Gothic art as theologically programmed visual sermons. Analyzes the themes of Saint-Denis's sculpture and stained glass in relation to those of other Gothic churches.

Panofsky, Erwin. *Abbot Suger on the Abbey Church of Saint-Denis and Its Art Treasures*. 2d ed. Princeton, N.J.: Princeton University Press, 1979. A translation of Suger's account of his building campaigns, with a long introduction considered the starting point for the study of Gothic architecture as an expression of religious symbolism.

_______. *Gothic Architecture and Scholasticism*. New York: Meridian Books, 1957. An elaboration and expansion of the ideas contained in the author's earlier work, relating Suger's intellectual and religious objective at Saint-Denis to the planning and execution of other Gothic buildings. Makes clear the systematic and deliberate connection between Scholastic philosophy and Gothic architecture as logical, ordered intellectual systems.

Petit-Dutaillis, Charles. *The Feudal Monarchy in France and England from the Tenth to the Thirteenth Century*. London: Routledge and Kegan Paul, 1936. A comparative study of the two major feudal monarchies and the influence of Norman feudalism on both. There is considerable attention to the lessons Suger drew from his Norman experience, which he urged the king of France to apply within his own territories.

Von Simson, Otto. *The Gothic Cathedral: Origins of Gothic Architecture and the Medieval Concept of Order.* 3d ed. Princeton, N.J.: Princeton University Press, 1988. Provides two long chapters on Suger, one on his career and one on the rebuilding of Saint-Denis. Emphasizes the intellectual consistency between Suger the statesman and Suger the builder. The definitive work on Suger's church as an embodiment of the ideas of Pseudo-Dionysius, and on the influence of Saint-Denis on other major French Gothic buildings.

SEE ALSO: Alcuin; Arnolfo di Cambio; Saint Bernard of Clairvaux; Filippo Brunelleschi; Charlemagne; Henry I; Andrea Orcagna.

RELATED ARTICLES in *Great Events from History: The Middle Ages, 477-1453*: 532-537: Building of Hagia Sophia; 685-691: Building of the Dome of the Rock; 781: Alcuin Becomes Adviser to Charlemagne; c. 950: Court of Córdoba Flourishes in Spain; 11th-12th centuries: Building of Romanesque Cathedrals; 1147-1149: Second Crusade; c. 1150-1200: Development of Gothic Architecture; c. 1410-1440: Florentine School of Art Emerges.

SUIKO

Japanese empress (r. 593-628)

The first female monarch of Japan, Suiko presided over reforms of the bureaucracy and the first known attempts to compile a history of Japan. Her reign saw the compilation of a blueprint for a far-reaching modernization process, the Seventeen Article Constitution. She was also instrumental in lending support to Buddhism.

BORN: 554; Yamato (now Nara Prefecture), Japan
DIED: April 15, 628; Yamato (now Nara Prefecture), Japan
ALSO KNOWN AS: Suiko Tennō
AREA OF ACHIEVEMENT: Government and politics

EARLY LIFE

According to the *Nihon shoki* (compiled 720 C.E.; *Nishongi: Chronicles of Japan from the Earliest Times to A.D. 697*, 1896; best known as *Nihon shoki*), an early chronicle of Japan, the future empress Suiko (sew-ee-koh) was the daughter of Emperor Kimmei (r. 539-571) and his consort Kitashi Hime. At the time of Suiko's birth, nothing predestined her eventual rise to the pinnacle of power in Yamato, the center of a loose confederation of clans ruled by her father. Most significantly, her gender appeared to exclude her from high office. Although archaeology has unearthed ample evidence for the existence of female rulers in various regions of archaic Japan, and later Japanese chronicles describe the exploits of powerful women before Suiko, officially there was no precedent for a woman to be accorded the title of "great king" in her own right.

Very little is known about her life before she ascended the throne at the age of thirty-nine in 593. The historicity of the few anecdotes related in the official chronicles is highly questionable, and her role in the imperial family has been the object of much speculation. It is clear, however, that she was at once a product of and a facilitator for the consolidation of the dynasty that continues to occupy the throne of Japan to this day. According to the official version of dynastic history as fixed in the early eighth century records, Suiko's father, Kimmei, was the twenty-ninth in a line of sovereigns of Japan that claimed direct descent from the sun goddess Amaterasu. Suiko's paternal grandfather Keitai (r. 507-531) is acknowledged by many historians as the first verifiable historical emperor of Japan (other historians begin with Kimmei) and might have been the actual founder of the dynasty.

Suiko's mother came from the powerful Soga clan. The head of this clan, Soga Iname (d. 570) was not only the chief minister but also the father of two consorts of Kimmei. Both women gave birth to future occupants of the throne and their consorts, thus enhancing the fortune of the Soga clan. It appears that Suiko's designated role was to help solidify the power of the dynasty by becoming the consort of her own half brother, Emperor Bidatsu (r. 572-585) in 576. This endogamous marital arrangement was perhaps one way to exclude the possibility of other powerful in-laws usurping the power of the dynasty or that of the Soga clan. Many, if not all, of Suiko's aunts, sisters, and half sisters appear to have shared a similar fate.

Suiko thus makes her first appearance in the official chronicles as empress not in her own right but rather as "queen consort" of her half brother, Emperor Bidatsu. Beyond that fact, very little is known about her early life. Even Bidatsu himself was overshadowed in the imagination of later chroniclers by his powerful chief minister Soga Umako (d. 626), who also happened to be Suiko's uncle. Umako was the quintessential king maker. During his tenure, he installed no less than four sovereigns, starting with Bidatsu and ending with his niece Suiko.

It is impossible to ascertain exactly what Suiko's role was after the death of her husband in 585. The throne passed first to her full brother, who reigned as Yōmei (r. 585-587) for two years, and then, in 587 to her cousin, Emperor Sushun (r. 587-592). Although all historians agree that the real power behind the throne was Soga Umako, some believe that the person on the throne was actually none other than Suiko herself, with Yōmei and Sushun as mere puppets whose role was elevated by later chroniclers. Such a scenario would explain why she emerged as an acceptable candidate for the position of sovereign in 592; she simply had the expertise.

Furthermore, Suiko appears to have been a neutral candidate at a time when a preponderance of princes of the blood might have led to succession disputes and perhaps even dynastic war. The throne had fallen vacant because of the untimely and violent death of Emperor Sushun in 592. Later chroniclers made no secret of the fact that the assassination was the work of Sushun's chief minister (and uncle) Soga Umako, although the motive behind the deed is less clear. Having literally gotten away with murder, Umako proceeded to promote the candidacy of his niece Suiko, a cousin, sister, widow, daughter, and granddaughter of previous emperors. Umako prevailed, and Suiko was ceremonially installed as the thirty-third sovereign ruler of Japan in early 593.

Life's Work

Suiko's reign as the first officially recognized female monarch of Japan lasted for an astonishing thirty-six years, until her death at age seventy-four in 628. She outlived not only the man who had put her on the throne, Soga Umako, but also the person who more than anybody else contributed to making her reign an unqualified success—Prince Shōtoku (574-622). In almost all subsequent histories, it is Shōtoku who is credited with the great innovations undertaken during Suiko's long reign. The official chronicle relates that on ascending the throne, the empress entrusted all matters of state to the prince, her nineteen-year-old nephew and a son of Emperor Yōmei. Shōtoku was subsequently recognized as the creative genius behind a modernization drive unparalleled in history, and to this day, textbooks and scholarly works alike describe his role in detail while Suiko is hardly mentioned at all.

Although it might be impossible to determine the exact nature of Suiko's role as empress because of the rather limited written evidence available, research has revealed an image of Suiko that goes beyond that of a mere figurehead. Shōtoku's appointment as prince regent would have acted as a check on the power of chief minister Soga Umako, thus enhancing Suiko's position as empress. Given the experience Suiko had on ascending the throne, she probably did choose the person who would be entrusted with carrying out the policies she intended to promote. Most likely, neither Empress Suiko nor Prince Regent Shōtoku could have accomplished so much without the presence and help of the other.

Suiko apparently realized that the Japan of her day was increasingly becoming part of an East Asian region dominated by recently reunified China. The two greatest cultural imports from the Asian mainland, the Chinese writing system and Buddhism, had been introduced in the fifth and sixth centuries respectively. Unsurprisingly, Suiko is often portrayed as a great sponsor of Buddhism.

MAJOR EMPERORS OF THE ASUKA PERIOD, 539-715

Reign	*Ruler*
539-571	Kimmei
572-585	Bidatsu
585-587	Yōmei
587-592	Sushun
593-628	SUIKO (f)
629-641	Jomei
642-645	Kōgyoku (f)
645-654	Kōtoku
655-661	Saimei (f)
661-672	Tenji
672	Kōbun
673-686	Temmu
686-697	Jitō (f)
697-707	Mommu
707-715	Gemmei (f)

Note: (f) indicates an empress.

Her Soga relatives were early supporters, her brother Yōmei is considered the first Japanese monarch to have embraced the new religion, and Prince Shōtoku's commentaries on Buddhist scripture survive to this day. The state sponsorship of Buddhism has often been interpreted as an attempt to curtail the independence of aristocratic clans who defined themselves as descendants of gods from the native Shintō pantheon. Ironically, the imperial dynasty was also such a clan, believed to have descended from the sun goddess Amaterasu.

To ensure the political future of the dynasty, Suiko took important steps toward turning the court into an institution. In 600, Suiko sent the first official Japanese embassy to China, then ruled by the Sui Dynasty (581-618). In her messages to the Chinese emperor, she referred to herself as *tennō*, a "heavenly sovereign," and called her country Nippon, or "land of the rising sun." She thus pioneered the use of both terms, which are used to this day. The ensuing diplomatic relationship with China led Suiko and her court to realize that if Japan were to stand its ground as an independent power, learning and applying the principles of Chinese administration and statecraft were of utmost importance. The two most basic principles to emulate were centralization of power in the hands of the imperial institution and administration of the realm through a bureaucracy. Suiko's actions throughout her reign show that she was committed to achieving just that kind of modernization.

In 603, construction began at a new palace site in Oharida just south of the present-day city of Nara. Its layout was closely modeled after the ideal plan for a monarch's palace found in the Chinese classics. The imperial palace grounds occupied the north-central part of a larger rectangle. A central north-south axis provided a pivot for the symmetrical layout of buildings on either side. The site was thus designed to symbolize harmony and equilibrium, values that were to prevail in all political affairs.

That same year, Suiko introduced a new ranking system for courtiers. Henceforth, people close to the emperor were to be assigned twelve ranks named after the six cardinal Confucian virtues (virtue, benevolence, propriety, loyalty, justice, and knowledge) with a junior and senior grade for each. Unlike earlier ranking systems, this new hierarchy worked on a strictly individual basis. Ranks could not be inherited, and promotion and demotion occurred at the discretion of the monarch. Although historians have cast some doubt on the actual implementation of this system in Suiko's day, it remains the first attempt on record to impose a bureaucratic ranking order not based on clan membership.

Perhaps the single most important document to come out of Suiko's long reign was the Seventeen Article Constitution of 604. Though attributed to Shōtoku Taishi, it is reasonable to assume that Suiko had at least some hand in compiling this document. The "constitution" was a general blueprint for the building of a Chinese-style polity centered on the imperial court. The text is full of references to Confucianism and Buddhism, drawing cosmological parallels between nature and society and exhorting officials to uphold the quintessentially moral order in which the king commands and the minister obeys. The Seventeen Article Constitution is the oldest extant Confucian text in Japan.

Later in her reign, in 624, Suiko created the first government agency to oversee the proliferating new religion of Buddhism. Her interest in Buddhism had been longstanding; an apocryphal anecdote has her intervening on behalf of Buddhist clerics at the tender age of sixteen. As empress, Suiko had managed to make Buddhism an integral part of courtly society; her patronage of this religion culminated in the construction of a huge 16-foot (5-meter) bronze statue of Buddha in 608.

Suiko died in 628, having outlived her erstwhile mentor Soga Umako and her protégé Shōtoku Taishi. It would take seventeen more years of bloody intrigues and Soga domination of court affairs before her visionary plans were finally put into practice in the Taika reforms of 645.

SIGNIFICANCE

The reforms of 645, based largely on what Suiko and Shōtoku had envisioned earlier in the century, created the Japanese state. Ironically, the turmoil surrounding the inauguration of these reforms apparently also cost later generations a priceless glimpse into the realities of Suiko's reign. Later chronicles reveal that the two earliest histories ever to be compiled in Japan were destroyed in a fire in 645. These two histories had been compiled by Soga Iruka and Shōtoku Taishi at the behest of Suiko in 620. The compilation of such dynastic histories is in itself a significant step toward institutionalization. With Suiko's reign as the culminating point, such an account would have provided priceless details about this remarkable historical figure.

Suiko's achievements as empress make her significant beyond the mere fact that she was the first woman to occupy the throne of Japan. Her efforts to reorganize the court and make it the viable center of a well-structured polity put her among the ranks of the true founders of Japan.

—*Ronald K. Frank*

FURTHER READING

Barnes, Gina. *China, Korea, and Japan: The Rise of Civilization in East Asia*. London: Thames and Hudson, 1993. Includes an analysis of pre- and proto-historic Japan, emphasizing connections with the mainland.

Martin, Peter. *The Chrysanthemum Throne: A History of the Emperors of Japan*. Honolulu: University of Hawai'i Press, 1997. A collection of short biographical sketches of all emperors and empresses. Not a scholarly work.

Mulhern, Chieko I., ed. *Heroic with Grace: Legendary Women of Japan*. Armonk, N.Y.: M. E. Sharpe, 1991. Includes two chapters on all empresses of Japan. A valuable source of information on the question of female rulership.

Piggott, Joan R. *The Emergence of Japanese Kingship*. Stanford, Calif.: Stanford University Press, 1997. Contains a chapter on Suiko, the most complete treatment of the subject available in English.

SEE ALSO: Kōken; Shōtoku Taishi.

RELATED ARTICLES in *Great Events from History: The Middle Ages, 477-1453*: 5th or 6th century: Confucianism Arrives in Japan; 538-552: Buddhism Arrives in Japan; 593-604: Regency of Shōtoku Taishi; 607-839: Japan Sends Embassies to China; 645-646: Adoption of *Nengo* System and Taika Reforms; 701: Taihō Laws Reform Japanese Government; March 9, 712, and July 1, 720: Writing of *Kojiki* and *Nihon Shoki*.

SUNDIATA

Mandingo founder of Mali (r. 1235-1255)

Founder of the thirteenth century empire of Mali in the western Sudan, Sundiata became the unifying cultural figure for the Mandingo peoples of West Africa.

BORN: c. 1215; near the confluence of the Niger and Sankarani Rivers, Kingdom of Kangaba (now in Guinea)

DIED: c. 1255; near Niani, Kingdom of Mali (now in Guinea)

ALSO KNOWN AS: Son-Jara; Soundiata; Sun-Jata; Sundjata; Sunjata; Mari Jata; Mārī Diāṭa

AREA OF ACHIEVEMENT: Government and politics

EARLY LIFE

Sundiata (soon-DYAH-tah) is mentioned in written sources by medieval Arabs, but his life is best known from the oral epic poetry of his descendants, the Mandingo peoples of West Africa. That poetry, sung by hereditary performers commonly known as griots (or as *jeli* or *djeli* in Mandingo), is filled with contradictory and mythical accounts of Sundiata's life and deeds. While many details of this tradition must be dismissed as exaggerated, a biographical sketch of the historical Sundiata emerges from the griot's song.

Great attention is given to names and their meanings in Mandingo epics, where names may vary in form from region to region and version to version. Sundiata's name, for example, is alternately spelled Soundiata, Sundiata, Son-Jara, and Sun-Jata. According to various interpretations, *sundjata* means Prince Lion or Thief Lion. In the Arabic sources, he is known as Mari Jata, or Lord Lion. Association with the lion gives Sundiata the power and authority of this beast, which is considered both physically and spiritually powerful in Mandingo culture. Other names in the tradition illustrate a similar variation and significance.

Genealogies are also important for the Mandingo. The oral tradition of Sundiata associates his lineage with Islam and with certain families, such as the Konnatés, Keitas, and Kondés, who are still prominent in the modern Mandingo world. Thus, Sundiata's father, whose name is usually given as some variation on Maghan Kon Fatta, or Fatta Magan, the Handsome, can trace his ancestry back to the African Bilali, companion of the Prophet Muḥammad and one of the first converts to Islam. The immediate predecessor of Sundiata's father is sometimes said to have been the first Muslim ruler of the area and a maker of a *hajj*, or pilgrimage to Mecca. Through his mother, Sugulun, Sundiata is related to the Kondés and associated with traditional African religious beliefs, such as fetishism and animism.

Sundiata's father was a local ruler in the Mandingo heartland on the border between the modern nations of Guinea and Mali. He took Sugulun as one of his several wives. She is described in the tradition as a deformed or ugly woman from the region of Du (Do) near the modern city of Ségou, Mali. Sundiata, born about 1215, is usually said to have been a younger son of his father but his mother's firstborn.

In his infancy and childhood, Sundiata was a weak and crippled youth who did not walk until an advanced age and showed little promise. The death of his father during this period left the lame Sundiata and his foreign mother vulnerable to the scorn and mistreatment of his older half brothers. At the same time, his whole family suffered from the cruel oppression of Sumanguru Kanté, king of the Susu, near modern Bamako, at whose hands all Sundiata's elder brothers are said to have been killed or defeated in battle. As a teenager, Sundiata left his home to escape either the dangers of family rivalry or, perhaps, Sumanguru. After a period of wandering, he was a guest of Tunkara, who was the king of Mema, a Soninke state located on the border of modern Mauritania and Mali.

LIFE'S WORK

In the late twelfth and early thirteenth centuries, West Africa experienced a severe population upheaval and political fragmentation caused by the waning of the power of Wagadu. Located on the borders of the Sahara Desert, Wagadu is often identified with the great empire of ancient Ghana. This major movement of peoples, often called the Soninke dispersion, included the migration of the Susu from Ghana—where the ancestors of their ruler, Sumanguru, were said to have been members of the slave class. As the strongest king in the region, Sumanguru took advantage of the power vacuum, according to Arabic sources, by attacking Ghana and reducing it to slavery around 1203. He then moved to subdue the region to the south, including Sundiata's homeland. In this conflict, Sumanguru defeated Sundiata's older half brother Dankaran, who then sought refuge in the region of Kissidougou in Guinea, where many inhabitants still claim descent from him.

Sumanguru's ruthlessness and cruelty is illustrated in the tradition by two crimes, the theft of Sundiata's griot and the abduction of the wife of his own nephew, Fa Koli. Both these actions galvanized opposition to Sumanguru, encouraged Fa Koli to break with his uncle, and sent some Mandingo to seek the help of the exiled Sundiata.

From exile, Sundiata organized an army against Sumanguru. His allies included Fa Koli and Fran Kamara, from the mountainous Fouta Djallon region of modern Guinea. Sundiata's sister, Sukulung Kulukang, is also thought to have played an important role in her brother's war by marrying Sumanguru and robbing state secrets from her husband. Around 1235, Sundiata's army defeated the forces of Sumanguru, and Sumanguru himself is said to have disappeared mysteriously in the hills near Koulikoro. After this victory, many Susu refugees fled to the region of modern Sierra Leone, where their descendants still live.

Following the defeat of Sumanguru, Sundiata oversaw a great gathering of the clans at Ka-ba, the traditional center of the Mandingo world. There each chief swore allegiance to Sundiata as *mansa*, or king, and was granted authority over his own province. For the first time, the various Mandingo peoples were organized under one head; this assembly is thus considered to mark the beginning of the ancient empire of Mali. About this time, Sundiata also established a new capital for his empire, probably near modern Niani, Guinea. This city was well known to medieval Arab travelers and was inhabited for several hundred years. Its exact location, however, remains the subject of scholarly debate.

Sundiata's position in West Africa's great religious conflict between Islam and animism is uncertain. The Arabic sources consistently refer to Sundiata as a Muslim, but in the oral tradition, he exhibits both Islamic and animistic features. As a result, some twentieth century scholars have referred to Sundiata as an animist, while others consider him a champion of Islam against fetishism.

Around 1240, Sundiata led a successful military expedition against the weakened power of Ghana and incorporated this kingdom into his growing empire. During his reign, Sundiata may also have begun a policy of commercial and political expansion along the Gambia River. After the defeat of Sumanguru, Tira Makhang, Sundiata's greatest general, is said to have gone as far west as the Gambia and to have founded several towns in that area.

In his later years, Sundiata apparently led no military campaigns but pursued the life of a farmer, a noble occupation that has remained for centuries the mark of a free Mandingo warrior. There are several versions of his death, many mythical in nature. The most common tale is that he was accidentally killed by an arrow at a festival held in his capital city. In Mandingo oral tradition, the deaths of great men are usually shrouded in mystery, but cult shrines in Sundiata's memory have long existed along the Sankarani River near Niani.

Sundiata founded not only an empire but also a dynasty. According to Arab sources, Sundiata was succeeded by his son Mansa Uli, who is said to have made a *hajj* in or around the years 1260-1277. Since succession from brother to brother rather than from father to son is not unusual in Mandingo culture, Uli was followed in succession by each of his two brothers. Sundiata's greatest descendant was Mansa Mūsā, who reigned from 1312 to 1337 and whose pilgrimage to Mecca was so spectacular that word of it reached even contemporary Europeans. Members of the Keita family, as descendants of Sundiata, continued to rule in this region for centuries after his death. The first president of modern Mali, Modibo Keita, was also a member of this important family.

SIGNIFICANCE

Sundiata was a great military leader and conqueror. His victories over Sumanguru and Ghana mark the beginning of the Malian Empire, which, at its height in the fourteenth century, stretched from Senegal and the Gambia on the Atlantic Ocean to Gao and Es-Souk on the Sahara Desert and controlled the gold and salt trade across the desert. The empire of Mali lasted until the fifteenth century, when its authority was replaced by the Songhai of Gao, under the leadership of Sonni (or Sunni) ʿAlī. The Mandingo heartland and Sundiata's capital of Mali remained independent until a Bambara prince seized the region in about 1670.

As founder of the empire of Mali, Sundiata is known as the father of the Mandingo world. His military conquests and policy of political expansion began the great geographic growth of the Mandingo, who form a major cultural and linguistic group in modern West Africa. As the victor over the ruthless Sumanguru, Sundiata is considered by the Mandingo to have been their first great liberator and champion of the oppressed.

Sundiata has continued to serve as a major unifying element in Mandingo culture. His genealogy has established a system of kinship and interfamily obligations on which Mandingo society has operated for centuries. For example, the ancient conflict between Sundiata and Sumanguru still affects relationships between their descendants, the Keitas and the Kantés. The religious ambiguity of Sundiata, who can be seen as both animist and Muslim in the oral tradition, reflects West Africa's tendency toward religious assimilation. Through the oral poetry linked with Sundiata's name, the Mandingo, who live in wide areas of modern Mali, Senegal, the Gambia, and Guinea, have managed to preserve an intense sense of cultural cohesion over great spatial and temporal distances.

—*Thomas J. Sienkewicz*

FURTHER READING

Conrad, David C., ed. *Epic Ancestors of the Sunjata Era: Oral Tradition from the Maninka of Guinea*. Illustrated by Mohamed Chejan Kromah and Sidiki Doumbia. Madison, Wis.: African Studies Program, University of Wisconsin, 1999. Includes map, illustrations, bibliographical references.

Fage, J. D. *A History of West Africa: An Introductory Survey*. 4th ed. New York: Cambridge University Press, 1969. A standard history of the region with specific discussion of the rise of the empire of Mali and the life of Sundiata. Several excellent maps are included as well as a useful annotated bibliography arranged according to period.

Innes, Gordon. *Sunjata: Three Mandika Versions*. London: University of London, 1974. This publication contains three versions of the story of Sundiata from The Gambia in the original Mandingo with parallel English translation, introduction, and explanatory notes.

Johnson, John William. *The Epic of Son-Jara: A West African Tradition*. Bloomington: Indiana University Press, 1986. An English translation of an oral performance of the epic transcribed under careful ethnographic conditions. Includes an excellent introduction to Mandingo culture and epic poetry, explanatory notes, genealogical charts, illustrations, and an extensive annotated bibliography.

_______. *The Epic of Sun-Jata According to Magan Sisòkò*. Bloomington, Ind.: Bloomington Folklore Publications Group, 1979. An oral performance of

Sunjata is here translated and annotated. The singer of this version is the son of the performer of Johnson's 1986 variant. Many notes found in this version are repeated word for word in the 1986 text.

Laye, Camara. *The Guardian of the Word*. New York: Vintage Books, 1984. This literary reworking of the epic by an important Guinean author was first published in French in 1978. One map is included.

Levtzion, Nehemia. *Ancient Ghana and Mali*. New York: Methuen and Co., 1973. This detailed history of the area pays particular attention to the rise of the empire of Mali and its founder and includes a good summary of the oral tradition of Sundiata's life along with a comprehensive bibliography.

Niane, Djebril T. "Mali and the Second Mandingo Expansion." In *UNESCO General History of Africa*. Vol. 4, *Africa from the Twelfth to the Sixteenth Centuries*. Paris: UNESCO, 1984. Part of an excellent universal history of Africa, this article analyzes the history of the empire of Mali, the life of Sundiata, and the archaeological evidence for his capital at Niani with maps and photographs of sites and archaeological finds.

_______. *Sundiata: An Epic of Old Mali*. Translated by G. D. Pickett. London: Longmans, Green and Co., 1965. An eminent scholar of early Mali, publishing this literary version of the epic at the time of the African independence movement, introduced the epic into the mainstream of Western literature. A map and some explanatory notes are included in this English translation of Niane's French adaptation of the oral epic.

Pageard, Robert. "Soundiata Keita and the Oral Tradition." *Présence africaine* 8 (1961): 53-72. An essay review of Niane's book in the English edition of this periodical with a highly politicized but thorough analysis of the oral tradition of Sundiata.

Suso, Bamba, and Banna Kanute, eds. *Sunjata: Gambian Versions of the Mande Epic*. Translated and annotated by Gordon Innes with the assistance of Bakari Sidibe, edited with a new introduction and additional notes by Lucy Duran and Graham Furniss. London: Penguin, 1999. A reprint of the English translations published in 1974 by London's School of Oriental and African Studies as *Sunjata*.

Wisniewski, David. *Sundiata: Lion King of Mali*. New York: Clarion Books, 1992. Designed for young readers, the story of Sundiata, who overcame physical and social obstacles to rule Mali. Illustrated.

SEE ALSO: ʿAbd al-Malik; Ibn Baṭṭūṭah; Ibn Khaldūn; al-Idrīsī; Damia al-Kāhina; Lalibela; Mansa Mūsā; Ṭāriq ibn-Ziyād.

RELATED ARTICLES in *Great Events from History: The Middle Ages, 477-1453*: 1230's-1255: Reign of Sundiata of Mali; 1324-1325: Mansa Mūsā's Pilgrimage to Mecca Sparks Interest in Mali Empire.

SURYAVARMAN II

Khmer king (r. 1113-1150)

Suryavarman II increased the territory of Khmer by capturing areas from neighboring Vietnam, Laos, and Thailand, and he built a temple to Viṣṇu, Angkor Wat, which symbolized his power as a god-king.

BORN: Date unknown; Kingdom of Khmer (now in Cambodia)

DIED: 1150; Kingdom of Khmer (now in Cambodia and Vietnam)

AREAS OF ACHIEVEMENT: Government and politics, warfare and conquest, architecture

EARLY LIFE

Little is known about the birth and early life of Suryavarman II (soor-yuh-VAWR-muhn). He came to power through a military coup. A stele recovered by M. Jules Harmand in Bat Than, a small village on the Mekong River in Laos, portrays Suryavarman II's battle with the royal army and shows him jumping onto the king's elephant and killing his great-uncle, Dharanīndravarman I (r. 1107-1112).

Suryavarman II was related through a sister to Dharanīndravarman I and his predecessor Jayavarman VI (r. 1080-c. 1107). Succession in the Khmer kingdom was not necessarily hereditary; however, kings usually asserted legitimacy by claiming a blood link back to Jayavarman II (c. 770-850, r. 802-850), who is generally credited with being the king who consolidated and created an identity for the Angkor kingdom. The name Angkor comes from the Khmer word *Nokhor* and the Sanskrit *nagara*, or city. When Suryavarman II seized power, the capital of the kingdom was well established at Angkor city, which symbolized the power and the architectural grandeur of the Khmer kingdom. The suffix *varman* attached to the names of Khmer kings means "protector or armor."

Suryavarman II was the seventeenth king in a long line of twenty-three identified Khmer rulers whose kingdoms were located along the Mekong River and the Tonle Sap Lake and the Tonle Sap River in the Indochina peninsula. Through wars and agreements, the kingdom of Angkor encompassed at various times areas now known as Cambodia, Laos, and parts of Thailand, Vietnam, China, and Myanmar (Burma.) During the period of the Angkor kingdom (804-1432), boundaries grew or constricted as a result of military campaigns.

Suryavarman II received the endorsement of Divākarapandita, a priest-minister who had served Udayādityavarman II (r. 1050-c.1066) and Harsavarman III (r. 1066/1077-1080) and had consecrated Dharanīndravarman I, who reigned for five years before his overthrow by his great-nephew. Divākrapandita was a learned priest or *pandita* (pundit) and under Suryavarman II was rewarded by symbols of power: a gold palanquin and two peacock-feather fans with gold handles. Kings, who were able to gain power through military effort, required the participation of the priestly class to legitimize their rule.

The Khmer had contact with India through trade since 350 B.C.E., and local rulers adopted the Sanskrit language and incorporated the gods from the Hindu pantheon into their worship of ancestral divinities. The king served as an intermediary between the people and the gods. The installation of Suryavarman II in 1113 as a transmogrified form of the *linga*, the phallic emblem of Śiva, took place in a temple in the capital city of Angkor, which was a city of about a million people. Jayavarman II had instituted the cult of the *devaraja*, or the god-king. Jayavarman and succeeding kings, including Suryavarman II, installed a stone *linga* in each royal temple. The *linga* represented the male procreative power and was identified with the Hindu god Śiva. The *Śivalingam* became a visual representation of the creative power of the king, who was seen as the reincarnation of Śiva on Earth. Thus, Suryavarman II legitimized his rule.

The cult of the *devaraja* gave the kingdom a sense of solidarity and unity of purpose for five centuries. The kings did not rule by just being a god; he was the apex of a vertical society. The social order had defined layers of relationships based on class, status, and role relationships. Jayavarman II appointed one of the men of a leading Khmer family as the high priest. This office was hereditary and had the task of installing each king. The temples functioned as repositories of wealth and culture and also were centers of worship, learning, and political power. The priestly class may have been as large as 300,000 during Suryavarman II's reign. Priests were the only ones able to compose the poetry that extolled the king and to consult the religious manuscripts, written on palm leaves and housed in the temples. Monks and priests served as advisers to the king and often were appointed as officials at all levels of government. The high priest would perform ceremonies to reestablish that the essence of the new king had entered into the *linga*, thus continuing the cult of the *devaraja*, the god-king.

LIFE'S WORK

Suryavarman II served as the commander in chief of the military, the court of last appeal, and the god whom citizens were expected to worship. A king could choose which major god of the Hindu pantheon, either Śiva, Viṣṇu, or Brahma, he wished to represent. Suryavarman II chose to patronize Viṣṇu, but he also permitted offerings to be made to Śiva and to the Buddha. Early in his reign, work was begun on a temple, Angkor Wat, which would serve as a temple, an observatory, and a tomb for Suryavarman. The temple was not completed until after his death in 1150. The temple housed a now lost gold statue of Viṣṇu, which was installed in July, 1131, and which may have commemorated Suryavarman II's thirty-third birthday.

Angkor Wat, a World Heritage site, took some fifty thousand workers and thirty-seven years to complete. The temple has five lotus-bud towers linked by galleries. The temple is 200 feet (65 meters) high and is surrounded by a moat, which is 200 yards (200 meters) wide. The moat was linked to reservoirs and canals and was an important part of the complex irrigation system that sustained the cultivation of rice, the main cereal crop for a growing population. The temple was constructed from sandstone cut from quarries some 25 miles (40 kilometers) away and transported by river barges to the building site.

The bas-relief functions as a tapestry and tells stories from Khmer history and Hindu legends. The sculptures on the walls of the third outermost gallery depict Suryavarman II and his court. The king, larger than life, is seated on a wooden throne and is receiving four of his ministers. Fourteen parasols, five large fans, and four flywisks, the symbols of his power, surround him. The king wears an elaborate crown and pectoral. His wealth is depicted in the ear ornaments, anklets, armlets, and bracelets that he wears. Later scenes depict the king seated on an elephant that wears a jeweled headdress. His royal priest and military generals, also on elephants, accompany him. Rows of troops, some wearing helmets with deer-head images, are at his service. Royal archers wear loincloths and tight short-sleeved jackets. The elevation of the sacred fire and the presence of the orchestra of trumpets, drums, conches, and a drum herald the king's entrance. Parasols, flywisks, fans, and banners again announce his presence. In front of his elephant is a standard of Viṣṇu riding Garuda. Women of the court are carried on palanquins. Suryavarman II was not monogamous and most likely had several wives and many concubines.

Chandler and Mabbett observe that no checks existed over the exercise of royal power save for a "notion of religious morality" and the ever-possible rebellion by regional rivals. The kingdom did not maintain a standing army but instead relied on the lords in the provinces to enforce conscription and raise a force to either defend or expand the holdings of the kingdom. Suryavarman II had come to power by using a network of families. The king could ingratiate these families by giving them honors and land. In return, they gave their support and often their daughters to the king. Mutual trust and the patronage held the kingdom together.

Written reports by a Chinese traveler, Zhou Daguan (Chou Ta-kuan), show that by the thirteenth century, the holdings of these families had evolved into administrative units and were the equivalents of provinces. Over the years, a sizeable bureaucracy developed in order to collect taxes, usually in the form of grain or commodities such as honey and wax. This bureaucracy extended into the villages in which officials functioned as village elders to carry out the tasks of local government and the king's wishes. Temple inscriptions indicate that these men collected taxes and witnessed land transactions. Others were inspectors and oversaw temple property, temple dues, and the management of religious foundations. Still others managed the administration of forced labor, which was given as a tax for the construction of roads, irrigation projects, temples, and buildings used by the royal family.

Suryavarman II served as the final court of appeal and presided over a system of lower courts. Khmer kings used case law, which was recorded on palm leaves. The king could not invent the law, but he was the final appeal. Legal terms such as case, plaintiff, proof, and sentence were borrowed from Indian terminology. Legal texts from India were known in the Khmer kingdom, and judicial procedures also used ordeals similar to those used in India to determine guilt or innocence. Fines, amputations, flogging, and torture were meted out to those shown to be guilty. The five major crimes included murdering a priest, theft, drunkenness, adultery with the wife of one's master, and being an accessory to any of these crimes. Citizens could also bring lawsuits against each other. How corrupt or fair the judicial system was cannot be determined.

Suryavarman II had expansionist plans and sought to extend the Khmer empire through trade and war. He was most successful in commerce and reopened the China market. He was the first king in three hundred years to send embassies to China in 1116 and 1120 and in 1128 to the court of the Chinese emperor Gaozong (Kao-tsung; r. 1127-1162). Such alliances also served to keep the Chinese from forging alliances with the enemies of the Khmer kingdom.

After conquering several Champa states (in the southeast coast of Vietnam), Suryavarman II sent troops in 1128 and 1132 to control the Annamite kingdom of Dai Viet (Vietnam). The king launched a two pronged attack on the kingdom of Dai Viet. Troops went over land through Laos, while Suryavarman's navy of seven hundred junks attacked the coastal areas of the Gulf of Tonkin. He asked the king of Champa for assistance, but in 1137 after the Champa forces made an alliance in 1136 with the Annam, Suryavarman II invaded Champa. He captured the capital of Vijaya and installed his brother-in-law, Prince Harideva, on the Champa throne. The Champa fought back, and Suryavarman had to make a partial retreat, but the Khmers remained in control of Northern Champa for the next thirty years.

Suryavarman II also went west to occupy the Haripunjaya Kingdom, one of the Mon tribal states in Thailand. In 1150, Suryavarman again invaded Annam after the Champa had killed Prince Harideva in 1149, but his army was decimated by fever while it traveled through jungle mountains to reach Tongking. Suryavarman died in 1150 either during or after the retreat from Annam.

Significance

Suryavarman II presided over the Angkor empire at the height of its military and diplomatic power. His ambitious building program included not only what is generally regarded as the highest achievement of Khmer temple architecture, Angkor Wat, but also Preah Pithu, Chansay Tevoda, and Thommanon, which were other temples in the Angkor region.

—Fran J. Hassencahl

FURTHER READING

Audic, John. *Angkor and the Khmer Kingdom.* London: Robert Hale, 1972. Audic presents a reader-friendly text. He criticizes the building of Angkor Wat as extravagant and exhaustive of the resources of the Khmer Empire.

Higham, Charles. *The Civilization of Angkor.* Berkeley: University of California Press, 2001. Useful maps, a glossary of terms, and great pictures add to this overall history of Angkor. Higham makes good use of studies of Angkor published outside the United States.

Mabbett, Ian, and David Chandler. *The Khmers.* Oxford, England: Blackwell, 1995. Mabbett and Chandler provide a historical context and provide a discussion of the scholarship on *devaraja*, the god-king cult.

Mannikka, Eleanor. *Angkor Wat: Time, Space, and Kingship.* Honolulu: University of Hawaii Press, 2000. The black-and-white and color photographs and Mannikka's text walk the reader through the architectural features of Angkor Wat and Khmer art.

Murray, Stephen O. "A Thirteenth Century Imperial Ethnography." *Antropology Today* 10 (October, 1994): 15-18. Murray compares the impressions of Chinese visitors about the Khmer armies with the depictions of the military in the bas-relief on the buildings in Angkor.

Peang-Meth, Abdulgaffar. "Understanding the Khmer: Sociological-Cultural Observations." *Asian Survey* 31 (May, 1991): 442-455. Peang-Meth draws on Hinduism and Buddhism to explain how the Khmer people could be cruel warriors and also peaceful and compassionate people.

Pym, Christopher. *The Ancient Civilization of Angkor.* New York: Mentor Books, 1968. Pym provides a detailed discussion of the construction of Angkor Wat and daily life in the kingdom.

SEE ALSO: Taizong; Wu Hou.

RELATED ARTICLES in *Great Events from History: The Middle Ages, 477-1453*: 802: Founding of the Khmer Empire; 982: Le Dai Hanh Invades Champa; 1323-1326: Champa Wins Independence from Dai Viet.

SYLVESTER II

Frankish pope (999-1003)

Sylvester II, known earlier as Gerbert, was an outstanding teacher whose brilliant pedagogy and ideas contrasted sharply with the cultural darkness of his age, ideas that predated the Humanists and scientists of the Renaissance. Also, he furthered papal-imperial cooperation during his short but significant pontificate.

BORN: c. 945; Aurillac, Aquitaine, West Frankish Kingdom (now in France)

DIED: May 12, 1003; Rome, Papal States (now in Italy)

ALSO KNOWN AS: Gerbert d'Aurillac; Gerbert of Aurillac

AREAS OF ACHIEVEMENT: Education, philosophy, religion and theology, government and politics, astronomy, mathematics, medicine

EARLY LIFE

Sylvester II, who was given the name Gerbert at birth, was born to poor parents in Aurillac, which was then part of the late Carolingian West Frankish kingdom. He was educated in grammar at the Benedictine monastery near his birthplace by the monk Raymond, under whose teaching he developed a thorough knowledge and appreciation of Latin literature. Gerbert may himself have taken monastic vows, and he certainly would have spent his life in obscurity if he had not come to the attention of Count Borrell of Barcelona, the Carolingian ruler of the Spanish march (a border region), who visited Gerbert's monastery in 967. Raymond, by then abbot, asked Borrell to take Gerbert with him to Spain to continue his education, for schools there were regarded as superior to those in Aquitaine. During the next three years, Gerbert studied in Christian Spain with Bishop Hatto of Vich and may have come in contact with Arabic learning. He became particularly expert in mathematics.

About 971, Borrell took Hatto to Rome in an effort to have Vich raised to the level of an archbishopric. Gerbert accompanied them, and he was introduced to Pope John XIII, who was impressed with his mathematical skills. The pope, who was closely allied with the Holy Roman Empire, brought Gerbert to the attention of Emperor Otto I, called "the Great." This marked an important moment in Gerbert's career; henceforth he was to have very close association with the imperial family, which came from Saxony. Otto I appointed Gerbert to teach students at the imperial court, including his son and successor, the eventual Otto II.

Gerbert was not satisfied, however, for—as he told the emperor—he would rather learn what he did not know (that is, philosophy) than teach what he did. In 972, Gerbert met Archdeacon Gerann of Reims, a well-known philosopher, at the imperial court. With the emperor's permission, Gerbert returned to France with Gerann to study logic (dialectic), while also teaching the archdeacon mathematics. Gerbert quickly surpassed his teacher in philosophy. His accomplishments attracted the attention of Archbishop Adalbero of Reims, who in 973 appointed him to direct the cathedral school. This appointment initiated the most fruitful period of Gerbert's life.

LIFE'S WORK

For a decade, Gerbert taught brilliantly at Reims. His reputation extended throughout Europe, and his successful efforts to gather together a first-rate library at the school ensured that in subsequent generations Reims would continue to be an important cultural center. From the numerous letters Gerbert left, one can follow the process by which he obtained copies of the best books available on each subject he taught. His knowledge and appreciation of the work of classical authors, especially Cicero, was extensive.

Sylvester II. (Library of Congress)

One of the most important aspects of Gerbert's educational accomplishment was that he taught all seven of the courses in the *trivium* and the *quadrivium*, the two groups of three and four subjects that together constituted the seven liberal arts of medieval education. None in his own day and few in subsequent generations could match this pedagogical omnicompetence. Gerbert began with grammar, which he defined as "the art of explaining the poets and historians and speaking and writing correctly." Next came the teaching of dialectic, beginning with introductory works and commentaries by Porphyry and Boethius, then using more advanced works by Aristotle, Cicero, and Boethius. These constituted all the treatises on logic available in Gerbert's day and represented a standard of accomplishment not to be matched for a century and more. In the teaching of rhetoric, Gerbert made sure that his students understood both the wisdom and the style of the ancient and Christian authors whose works were studied, so that they would be prepared for an active life.

The four subjects of the *quadrivium* were taught with both textbooks and visual aids. In arithmetic, Gerbert himself wrote two works (completing a third after he became pope) and made use of the abacus for computational purposes. He was probably the first in Western Europe to make use of an early form of Arabic numerals (actually Hindu-Gobar numerals) from one to nine, without the use of the zero. It is possible that Gerbert had picked up an imperfect knowledge of these numerals while studying in Spain—not from direct contact with the Arabs, but from secondary contacts with merchants and the like.

Gerbert's teaching of music was done in such a way as to emphasize the practical and mathematical aspects of the subject. He utilized a monochord with a sliding bridge, which could be positioned so as to create all the overtones from the root note, thus showing the mathematical qualities and relationships of sounds. One of his students implies in his description of Gerbert's teaching that a symbol was placed over each note on manuscript music corresponding to the position of that note on the monochord; thus, each pupil could pick out melodies without Gerbert's help. To present geometry, Gerbert also wrote a textbook of his own. It emphasized classical elements from Euclid's work as filtered through Boethius, but it drew also on the surveying methods of the Romans. Little is known about the details of Gerbert's actual teaching of this subject.

It was in the teaching of astronomy that Gerbert was at his best and was most creative. He was familiar with a variety of astronomical hypotheses, but he opted for the geostatic theories of the Roman authority Pliny, probably on the pragmatic grounds of simplicity. To teach the principles of astronomy, Gerbert constructed a celestial globe, made of polished wood covered with horsehide, on which were marked the poles, the celestial circles, and the constellations of the Northern and Southern hemispheres. He also constructed an intricate planetarium, in which the planets were mechanically moved, and at least two complex viewing instruments that allow modern viewers to conclude that his astronomy not only was theoretical but was based on observation as well.

The range of Gerbert's interests extended beyond the curriculum of the arts. He had a solid acquaintance with medical literature, was familiar with scientific and astrological literature in the Islamic world, and wrote a philosophical treatise that dealt with issues beyond those treated in the study of dialectic. In his learning and his teaching, he had no equal in his time.

It was perhaps this reputation that aroused the jealousy of another well-known teacher, Otric of Magdeburg. After sending one of his own students to spy on Gerbert's teaching, Otric accused him of a pedagogical error relating to the relationship between the disciplines, which was of considerable importance in the constructing of an educational curriculum. The dispute was important enough and the personalities sufficiently well known that the matter was eventually referred to the imperial court of Otto II. After an extended debate, recorded in the careful notes taken by Gerbert's pupil Richer, the emperor decided the issue in favor of his former teacher, Gerbert, who returned to Reims with many imperial gifts.

In 983, the emperor further rewarded Gerbert by appointing him abbot of the famous monastery at Bobbio. Even though he continued to teach there, he was unhappy, for local disputes and controversies distracted him. Bobbio was a monastery where corruption had been particularly extensive, and Gerbert's efforts at reform met aggressive resistance. After the death of Otto II on December 7, 983, Gerbert returned to his school in Reims. There, however, he was unable to resume his teaching career, instead becoming involved in political disputes between the French and imperial parties. He was elected archbishop of Reims in 991, but the circumstances were irregular and he was opposed by the new Capetian Dynasty in France. Gerbert returned to Italy, where he was dependent on the favor of Emperor Otto III, to whom he was close. Otto named Gerbert archbishop of Ravenna in 998. A year later, when the incumbent pope suddenly died, Gerbert was elected his successor, taking the pontifical name Sylvester II.

This choice was significant, for it consciously looked back to the pontificate of the first Sylvester, pope at the time of the first Christian emperor, Constantine. Between this fourth century pair, there was supposed to have been close cooperation; Gerbert and his youthful patron Otto (born 980) intended their era to be one of papal-imperial partnership. Despite this ideal and despite some concrete steps to bring about a period of perfect peace, the reality proved to be different. Otto died prematurely in January, 1002, and Sylvester followed him less than a year and a half later.

Even if Sylvester and Otto had lived longer, it is doubtful that their goal could have been accomplished. Despite the appearance of equal partnership, the Papacy was in reality a subordinate element. Sylvester and his predecessors had, for the most part, been puppets to an imperial policy predicated on theocratic assumptions. Sylvester had a sharply circumscribed sphere of independent action. Even in the city of Rome itself, he was closely controlled by the emperor, who modeled himself on the Byzantine tradition of the superiority of the state over the church (caesaropapism).

Practically the only act Sylvester undertook during his pontificate that was even slightly at variance to imperial policy was in his relations with Poland and Hungary. Otto III was a close friend of Duke Bolesław of Poland (nicknamed "Chrobry"—the brave) and had gone to

Gniezno in 1000 to worship with the Polish duke at the shrine of the martyred Bohemian missionary Adalbert of Prague and to establish an archiepiscopal see for Poland at Gniezno. There had also been some talk at that time of a royal crown for Bolesław. The emperor clearly conceived that his goal of a sanctified Christian commonwealth was predicated on Germany, the Papacy, and the Western Slavs, especially the Poles. (Indeed, there is a contemporary manuscript illustration that shows Otto being waited on by three figures labeled *Germania*, *Romania*, and *Sclavinia*.) Sylvester, however, was more inclined to reward the Hungarians for their recent conversion to Christianity. The crown that had been intended for Poland was instead given by him in 978 to Stephen I of Hungary. While Otto could not object, for the Hungarians were fully deserving, Sylvester's initiative was not precisely what he intended.

Significance

For the most part, however, Sylvester was a pliant pontiff who did not challenge imperial authority. It was to be another three-quarters of a century before the Papacy would emerge as an independent force. In other respects, Sylvester's pontificate was characterized by a high moral tone, which was reflected in his efforts to eliminate simony (the buying and selling of Church offices), and by an administrative efficiency that set a standard for decades to come. His numerous extant letters clearly reflect these concerns. Yet despite these accomplishments, Sylvester's importance does not lie in the history of his pontificate. It rests instead on his pre-papal career as Gerbert.

As the leading scholar and educator of his time, Gerbert shone with a brilliance all the more bright because of the way he contrasted with the darkness of his age. In the larger picture of medieval and European civilization and culture, he does not seem to merit the reputation for learning he possessed in his own day. One should not forget, however, that he established a tradition that continued. His pupil Richer was in turn the teacher of figures whose importance and influence extended into the generation that brought about the cultural revival known as the medieval Renaissance or the Renaissance of the twelfth century.

In his own time, Gerbert's accomplishments were so astonishing to his contemporaries they could explain him only by resorting to legends. Some medieval chroniclers, for example, told stories about Gerbert having stolen a book of magic while in Spain, having conjured up the Devil, having sold his soul to gain knowledge and power, and—at his death—telling his servant to cast his body into the street to let the Devil "have the service of my limbs . . . for my mind never consented to that oath." All of this reflects the awe in which Gerbert, the peasant boy who became pope, was held.

—*Paul W. Knoll*

Further Reading

Dales, Richard C. *The Intellectual Life of Western Europe in the Middle Ages*. 2d ed. New York, Brill, 1992. The author clearly and thoroughly analyzes Gerbert's teaching and his philosophical thought, and the chapter that treats tenth century developments is especially well done. Includes a bibliography and index.

Duckett, Eleanor Shipley. *Death and Life in the Tenth Century*. Ann Arbor: University of Michigan Press, 1967. An excellent study of the politics, culture, and religious life of the period. Explores major figures, including Sylvester, against the background of their times. Effectively describes Sylvester's relations with the three Ottos and analyzes his teaching and cultural influence.

Evans, G. R. *Fifty Key Medieval Thinkers*. New York: Routledge, 2002. A collection of brief biographies, including that of Gerbert and Boethius. Provides a bibliography and index.

Ferzoco, George, and Carolyn Muessig, eds. *Medieval Monastic Education*. New York: Leicester University Press, 2000. A survey of the history of monastic education during the Middle Ages. Focuses mostly on England but does include generalized discussion of religious education during Gerbert's time.

Lattin, Harriet. *The Peasant Boy Who Became Pope: Story of Gerbert*. New York: Henry Schuman, 1951. A biography based on primary sources. The author traces the political issues in which Sylvester was involved.

Pekonen, Osmo. "Gerbert of Aurillac: Mathematician and Pope." *Mathematical Intelligencer* 22, no. 4 (Fall, 2000). Discusses Gerbert's significance as a mathematician, especially his reputed introduction of Arabic numerals into Europe.

Poole, Austin Lane. "Germany: Henry I and Otto the Great" and "Germany: Otto II and Otto III." In *The Cambridge Medieval History*, edited by J. B. Bury. 2d ed. Vol. 3. New York: Cambridge University Press, 1968. A detailed treatment of the larger picture of European and imperial politics in which Sylvester was involved. Especially good at showing the policies and ambitions of the Saxon emperors. The relations between the Ottos and Sylvester are traced carefully.

Sylvester II, Pope. *The Letters of Gerbert, with His Papal Privileges as Sylvester II.* Translated by Harriet Lattin. New York: Columbia University Press, 1961. A fluid translation of 264 extant letters fully reflecting the intellectual, educational, political, and religious interests and activities of Sylvester.

Taylor, Henry Osborn. *The Mediaeval Mind: A History of the Development of Thought and Emotion in the Middle Ages.* 4th ed. 2 vols. Cambridge, Mass.: Harvard University Press, 1966. The author's chapter on Gerbert contains a good treatment of the dispute with Otric and a fine analysis of Gerbert's philosophical works.

White, Lynn T., Jr., ed. "Symposium on the Tenth Century." *Medievalia et Humanistica* 9 (1955): 3-29. Focuses on the vitality and dynamism of the tenth century. Various aspects of the period are treated, but Gerbert receives special attention within the context of learning. His contributions in astronomy are well treated and placed within the European astronomical tradition.

SEE ALSO: Boethius; Saint Fulbert of Chartres; Otto I; Stephen I.

RELATED ARTICLES in *Great Events from History: The Middle Ages, 477-1453*: c. 950: Court of Córdoba Flourishes in Spain; 987: Hugh Capet Is Elected to the French Throne; c. 1025: Scholars at Chartres Revive Interest in the Classics; c. 1100: Arabic Numerals Are Introduced into Europe; 1275: First Mechanical Clock.

al-Ṭabarī
Arab historian

The premier historian of the first century of the Islamic Empire and a renowned commentator on Qurʾānic tradition, al-Ṭabarī established a model of universal history and a corpus of religious tradition crucial to the development of later Islamic theology and scholarship.

Born: c. 839; Āmol, Tabaristān (now in Iran)
Died: 923; Baghdad (now in Iraq)
Also known as: Abū Jaʿfar Muḥammad ibn Jarīr al-Ṭabarī (full name)
Areas of achievement: Historiography, religion and theology

Early Life

Al-Ṭabarī (ahl-tah-BAHR-ee) was born to a moderately wealthy family. He demonstrated all the traits of a child prodigy and began formal study at an extremely early age. Legend has it that he memorized the entire Qurʾān by the time he was seven. Al-Ṭabarī's father, realizing the extent of his son's talents and the limitations of his hometown, provided financial support for the travel so crucial to a broad education in those days.

After visiting centers of learning in northern Iran, al-Ṭabarī, while still a teenager, set out for Baghdad in hopes of studying under the great Muslim jurist Aḥmad ibn Ḥanbal, who, unfortunately, died just before al-Ṭabarī's arrival in the city. Nevertheless, the youth remained briefly in Baghdad and also visited the important traditional Iraqi Muslim centers of Basra and Al-Kūfa. There followed a trip to Syria to study Hadith, the traditions attributed to Muḥammad. Al-Ṭabarī also spent some time in Egypt before returning to Baghdad around 872, where he would pass the remaining half century of his long life as an increasingly renowned scholar, teacher, and writer.

Al-Ṭabarī's Baghdad career was one of modest means and stupendous productivity. Despite his family's largesse in providing travel money in his early life, al-Ṭabarī endured what some have described as a life of extreme poverty in Baghdad. There is a story that he was once reduced to selling the sleeves of his shirt in order to buy bread. To some extent, al-Ṭabarī placed himself in these dire straits by rejecting several lucrative offers of government posts and commissions. His independence may have helped free him from official drudgery, making possible his voluminous literary output. Some early writers claim that al-Ṭabarī customarily wrote or copied forty manuscript pages each day.

There was, however, one brush with politics and notoriety. After breaking with the uncompromising literalism of Hanbali religious law, al-Ṭabarī attempted to form his own school of Muslim jurisprudence. This enterprise brought a pro-Hanbali mob to his door and required police intervention to ensure his safety. Little of the nature of al-Ṭabarī's legal essays is known, since these works are among a considerable number of his writings that have been lost. (Some scholars have concluded that his proclivity for iconoclastic thinking and the catholic nature of his works—a quality that probably made them less attractive to specialists—may have been responsible for the disappearance of so much of his output.)

Life's Work

Al-Ṭabarī's career spanned many fields of study, including history and Qurʾānic commentary, poetry, lexicography, grammar, ethics, mathematics, and medicine. He was an unparalleled collector of Hadith, devoting most of his early years to gathering and copying material wherever he went. His commentary on the Qurʾān was the first to bring together sufficient material from different regions of Islam to make it a standard work, on which later generations of commentators could draw. Even for modern scholars, al-Ṭabarī is an important source of information on Qurʾānic tradition. Although he was concerned with the structure and syntax of oral traditions, al-Ṭabarī seldom introduced his own conclusions or opinions on religious or historical questions.

The most important surviving work of al-Ṭabarī is his world history, *Taʾrīkh al-rusul wa al-mulūk* (872-973; *The History of al-Ṭabarī*, 1985-1999, 39 vols.). It is an enormous work; a late nineteenth century edition fills thirteen volumes, and numerous authorities assert that in its final form *Taʾrīkh al-rusul wa al-mulūk* was ten times that long. (Some scholars, however, doubt this claim, noting that the language of the work does not lead one to suspect large amounts of missing material or any sort of abridgment, and that, in any case, a work of such dimensions would have been beyond the capacity of a single person in the ninth century.)

The History of al-Ṭabarī is more than simply a history of Islam. By al-Ṭabarī's time, Islam was a vast aggregation of civilizations and cultures, and the work considers the pre-Islamic history of many of them. It begins with a history of the patriarchs, prophets, and rulers from early Semitic cultures, followed by a history of Persia and Iraq during the Sāsānid period (third to seventh centuries). Then comes the era of Muḥammad and the first four caliphs (570-661), the Umayyad Dynasty in Damascus (661-750), and, finally, the ʿAbbāsid period in Baghdad. The coverage stops in 915.

The style of the annals changes from a somewhat disconnected narrative for pre-Islamic times to a yearly chronology of events for the Muslim era. The source material came from both oral traditions and written accounts. Throughout *The History of al-Ṭabarī*, a connected narrative is sacrificed in the interest of compiling accounts of the same events from a variety of sources. Not surprisingly, the work is full of contradictions. In declining to make judgments between variant accounts, al-Ṭabarī may perhaps be subject to criticism from modern historians. On the other hand, *The History of al-Ṭabarī* provides an unsurpassed record of primary sources on given events, to be winnowed by later scholars.

In a supplement, al-Ṭabarī provides biographical information on most of his informants, evidently to aid the reader in discerning the true versions of events. This method is closely related to the early Muslim technique of testing the veracity of Hadith by examining the character and known biographies of individuals who transmit them. Early Muslim legists used this system to determine authentic Hadith and to arrive at a codified Muslim system of law. Al-Ṭabarī does the same, or rather invites the reader to exercise such discretion, by providing the necessary data.

The structure of al-Ṭabarī's historical work, confusing though it may be to a general reader, is especially helpful for scholars, since there is relatively little trustworthy material on the first century of Muslim history, a century in which Islam grew from a local system in western Arabia into a monumental imperial organization. Most other Arabic sources on this period, in fact, were produced much later, after religious and political divisions had led to civil war and competitive dynasties in Islam. Many Islamicists regard these later histories, which are far more interpretive and judgmental than al-Ṭabarī's annals, as untrustworthy because their information often was selected for political or sectarian ends. It is unfortunate that *The History of al-Ṭabarī* deals mainly with Iraq and Iran and has only scant material on Syria, center of the area ruled by the Umayyad Dynasty, or other parts of the Muslim west.

Many later Muslim historians emulated al-Ṭabarī's method of presentation. They not only depended heavily on his work for the early period but also often extended the annalistic coverage into their own eras. As a result, numerous "Tabariesque" works that recount Islamic history, and often events in other civilizations, were produced into the early thirteenth century. Some of these historians attempted to reconcile variant accounts in al-Ṭabarī's annals, and they occasionally supply additional information of which al-Ṭabarī himself apparently was not aware.

The value of *The History of al-Ṭabarī* as a universal history, not a record of Islamic developments only, is evident in the fact that it was translated into Persian shortly after it was completed.

SIGNIFICANCE

Al-Ṭabarī's voluminous collections of Qurʾānic and Hadith commentary are crucial to the modern understanding of the evolution of Muslim thought in its formative period. He epitomizes the early Muslim practice of seeking exemplary truth and Qurʾānic exegesis through a careful examination of genealogical and historical components. Though a traditionalist in this sense, al-Ṭabarī also represents a break in the Islamic tradition of regarding history as a simple dichotomy between the pre-Islamic "days of ignorance" and the era of Muḥammad and his community, or between Muslims and non-Muslims. He took a major step toward the development of world history by transcending these early limitations in the Muslim worldview. Al-Ṭabarī also appreciated the importance of source preservation and criticism. His career was that of a pioneer on the road that would lead to modern historical scholarship. No other early Muslim historian would be so widely imitated by students and successors.

—*Ronald W. Davis*

FURTHER READING

Butler, Alfred Joshua. *The Treaty of Miṣr in Ṭabarī: An Essay in Criticism*. Oxford, England: Clarendon Press, 1913. Reprinted as an addendum to the author's *The Arab Conquest of Egypt and the Last Thirty Years of the Roman Dominion* (Oxford: Clarendon Press, 1978). A brief essay concerning the sources used by al-Ṭabarī in forming his account of the Arab conquest of Egypt. Focuses on the textual problems presented by such early materials. Brief bibliography and index.

Dahmus, Joseph. *Seven Medieval Historians*. Chicago: Nelson-Hall, 1982. Contains an excellent synopsis of the career and intellectual antecedents of al-Ṭabarī. The discussion incorporates some lengthy translated passages of his work as illustrative material. Bibliography, index.

Dodge, Bayard, ed. and trans. *The Fihrist of al-Nadīm: A*

Tenth-Century Survey of Muslim Culture. 2 vols. New York: Columbia University Press, 1970. Contains a brief biography of al-Ṭabarī in traditional Muslim form, also listing some of the scholars associated with him, by a tenth century chronicler. A good example of biographical treatment at the time, it provides a sense of the intellectual environment in which al-Ṭabarī lived and worked. Bibliography.

Donner, Fred M. *Narratives of Islamic Origins: The Beginnings of Islamic Historical Writing*. Princeton, N.J.: Darwin Press, 1998. A study of the early years (around the seventh century) of Islamic historiography. Extensive bibliography, index.

Hodgson, Marshall G. S. *The Venture of Islam: Conscience and History in a World Civilization*. Vol. 1. Chicago: University of Chicago Press, 1974. This volume includes one of the best descriptions in English of al-Ṭabarī's methods and technique, exemplified by his account of the murder of the caliph ʿUthmān in 656. Shows how the study of history and that of Qurʾān and Hadith intermingle in al-Ṭabarī's thought. Bibliography, index.

Marin, Elma, trans. *The Reign of al-Muʿtasim (833-842)*. New Haven, Conn.: American Oriental Society, 1951. This book, volume 35 in the American Oriental series, includes a rare translation into English of a small portion of al-Ṭabarī's annals.

Robinson, Chase F. *Islamic Historiography*. New York: Cambridge University Press, 2003. An introduction to the writing of history in Arabic, with a focus on the sociopolitical functions of historiography from the eighth to the sixteenth century. Written especially for those with little or no background in Islamic history or in Arabic. Bibliography, index.

Tayob, Abdelkader I. "Ṭabarī on the Companions of the Prophet: Moral and Political Contours in Islamic Historical Writing." *Journal of the American Oriental Society* 119, no. 2 (April-June, 1999). An examination of an early motif in the writing of Islamic history, that of the status and roles of the Prophet's companions. Shows how al-Ṭabarī considers the companions' involvement as moral, and not political, beings.

SEE ALSO: Aḥmad ibn Ḥanbal; Avicenna; al-Ghazzālī; Ibn Khaldūn; al-Masʿūdī; Muḥammad; Yaqut.

RELATED ARTICLES in *Great Events from History: The Middle Ages, 477-1453*: c. 610-632: Muḥammad Receives Revelations; 872-973: Publication of *The History of al-Ṭabarī*; 1377: Ibn Khaldūn Completes His *Muqaddimah*.

TAIRA KIYOMORI

Japanese military leader

A warrior who rose to power in the last years of aristocratic government in Japan, Taira Kiyomori used political connections and the marriages of his daughters to control the imperial court. Shortly after his death, his family was destroyed, marking the most dramatic rise and fall of a family in Japanese history.

BORN: 1118; Japan

DIED: March 21, 1181; Heian-kyō (now Kyoto), Japan

AREAS OF ACHIEVEMENT: Government and politics, military

EARLY LIFE

Taira Kiyomori (ti-rah kee-yoh-moh-ree) was the son of the great warrior Taira Tadamori, whose military family had formed an alliance with retired emperors at the Japanese court. Both sides prospered from this alliance as the aristocratic Fujiwara family, which had dominated imperial government for generations, declined in power.

Actually, there is some doubt about Kiyomori's parentage on both sides. He may have been the son of the emperor Shirakawa (r. 1073-1087, cloistered r. 1086-1129), who asked that Tadamori rear him as a warrior. His mother was said to be Lady Gion, a favorite mistress of Shirakawa. She was apparently very pious, for she commissioned costly Buddhist services, but little is known about her influence or the early training of the young Kiyomori. Imperial patronage helped gain for him important appointments and governorships in southwest Japan and the Inland Sea. These areas were important sources of revenue, because trade with the Song Dynasty (Sung; 969-1279) in China flowed through their harbors, many of which Kiyomori developed.

In twelfth century Japan, the aristocratic court in the imperial capital of Kyoto retained its prestige, but real power had fallen into the hands of warrior clans in the provinces. Some of these warriors realized that their ignorance of classical learning and lack of refined taste made them inferiors in the eyes of the nobility. The Ise branch of the Taira (the name can also be read Heike or Heishi) was particularly aware of this problem, as it was based near the capital. Kiyomori's reputed father, Tadamori, took an interest in cultivating the arts and gained the favor of the court, including influential women. His rise in rank and privilege was a result of his provincial power base and successful currying of favors at the court. When Tadamori died in 1153, Kiyomori was ready to take his place.

LIFE'S WORK

Kiyomori led his family to its peak of power in the 1170's, but his stubborn temperament also created many enemies who would crush the Taira family in 1185. He played a central but unsuccessful role in the transition from aristocratic to warrior rule in medieval Japan.

When Kiyomori took over the leadership of his powerful family in 1153, a complicated power structure existed in Japan. Retired emperors appointed a share of the country's provincial governorships in return for protection of their private estates, and Taira estate managers profited from this imperial patronage system. Kiyomori was able to strengthen his influence at the court during two brief but important factional struggles.

The first was the Hōgen disturbance of 1156. Kiyomori and Minamoto Yoshitomo defended Go-Shirakawa (r. 1155-1158, cloistered r.1158-1192) against a coup attempt by the abdicated emperor Sutoku (r. 1123-1142) and Minamoto Tameyoshi. Yoshitomo was less generously rewarded than Kiyomori, so he attempted to rectify this slight in another coup attempt (Heiji disturbance) in 1159 directed against Go-Shirakawa, who was then a retired emperor, and Kiyomori. Unfortunately for the Minamoto warrior clan, Kiyomori was able to crush their uprising and make himself dominant as a member of the most powerful military family at the court.

Because he now had military control of the capital and court, Kiyomori was able to place Taira family members and supporters in many important posts for the next twenty years. Until he finally crushed all opposition to his position in 1179, however, there was an uneasy sharing of power with Go-Shirakawa, his former sponsor. In fact, Japanese scholar Ishimoda Sho has argued that in sharing authority, Go-Shirakawa had the upper hand until 1179 and that Kiyomori, far from being in control of Japan, had yet to emerge as the clear ruler even of Kyoto.

It is clear that Kiyomori continued to receive official appointments from the retired emperor, continuing the patron-client relationship. For his part, Go-Shirakawa was able to build up a huge landed base to support the imperial family. Facing no real military threat from the defeated Minamoto or other warrior clans, Kiyomori could have seized complete power, but he preferred to work within the old system of court alliances, marrying his daughters into the aristocracy and leaving the influential Fujiwara family their hereditary posts.

In 1160, Kiyomori received the rank of imperial adviser, and he was appointed to the grand council of state. He also was given the office of chief police commissioner in the capital. None of these positions had ever been held by a warrior from the provinces, and the nobility resented his rise to prominence. As Kiyomori placed his sons and followers in more and more official posts, nearly all political factions turned against him in the 1170's. Plots were frequent as hostility toward the perceived arrogance of the Taira clan grew. Kiyomori had suffered an illness in 1168, and that, or a lack of discretion, led him to abandon the delicate compromise at the court.

In 1177, discontent surfaced in a plot by several of Go-Shirakawa's followers. The incident was precipitated by the assignment of a military title coveted by one of Go-Shirakawa's advisers to Kiyomori's heir, Shigemori. This Shishigatani affair, named after the valley in which the conspiracy was hatched, was revealed by one of Kiyomori's spies. Kiyomori rebuked his former patron, Go-Shirakawa, replaced high officials with Taira clansmen, seized Fujiwara land, and executed many of his enemies.

Despite the ruthlessness of Kiyomori's suppression of the Shishigatani plot, opposition to his control continued to grow. In 1179, his enemies and Go-Shirakawa sought to take advantage of two misfortunes that befell the Taira house. Kiyomori's daughter, who had married into the Fujiwara family to gain control of their land, died. The retired emperor seized the land. Only two months later, Kiyomori's heir, Shigemori, also died, and Echizen Province was confiscated.

It appeared that the court was getting out of control, so once again Kiyomori ordered his troops into the capital in December, 1179. He placed Go-Shirakawa under house arrest, dismissed all officials opposed to his rule, and appointed his kinsmen in their place. Although Kiyomori's personal power was greatly enlarged by the takeover of the capital, his actions destroyed the fragile balance of court power and threatened the economic and political interests of major Kyoto institutions, including the powerful monasteries.

In 1180, discontent surfaced yet again when Prince

Mochihito, a son of Go-Shirakawa who had been passed over for succession, joined with Minamoto Yorimasa and several temples to overthrow the Taira. They were soon pursued by Taira troops to the banks of the Uji River, where Yorimasa, an ally of Kiyomori in the 1150's, committed *seppuku* (ritual suicide) within the grounds of a peaceful temple. Mochihito was also killed, but his call to arms against the Taira had reached the eastern provinces of Japan, where Minamoto Yoritomo, a son of Yoshitomo who was spared by Kiyomori in 1160, gathered around him a powerful military alliance. Mochihito's move marked the beginning of the Gempei War (1180-1185), which ended with the Minamoto (Genji) destroying the Taira in 1185.

Kiyomori's last years were therefore ones of danger and growing animosity to his rule. He had to rely on an army of informers and spies and was surrounded by troops at all times. To help forestall further plots, Kiyomori moved the court to his base at Fukuhara (modern Kōbe) in late 1180, but he was forced to return the court to Kyoto after six months. Not long after the return to Kyoto, Kiyomori took to his deathbed, dying of a fever on March 21, 1181. His last request was not for a Buddhist service but rather that Yoritomo be killed and his head be placed on his tomb. Kiyomori's own death was not mourned by the court, and the official histories do not treat him sympathetically.

His son Munemori, a man of limited abilities, was left in charge, but the days of Taira power were already numbered. Early in 1180, Kiyomori's grandson had become the emperor Antoku. Kiyomori was fond of the infant and hoped that he would perpetuate the Taira line, but he was destined to die a tragic death, one that is deeply ingrained in the Japanese mind through the classic war epic that depicts the military defeat of the Taira by the revived Minamoto clan, the *Heike monogatari* (c. 1240; *The Tale of the Heike*, 1918-1921).

This work is Japan's greatest medieval war chronicle, and it tells of the Minamoto victories that drove the Taira from the capital in 1183 and forced them away from their base of power in the Inland Sea in 1184. The clan was destroyed in 1185 with the drowning of the young emperor Antoku (r. 1180-1185) in the last stand of the Taira in the famous sea Battle of Dannoura.

Then and now *The Tale of the Heike* is a reminder that those who flourish are destined to fall, a Buddhist message regarding the impermanence of things. In the opening paragraph of the epic, Kiyomori's fate is predicted: "The brave and violent man—he too must die away in the end, like a whirl of dust in the wind."

Significance

Although Taira Kiyomori is not treated with sympathy in *The Tale of the Heike*, he played an important role in the transition from aristocratic court government in Japan to the warrior rule of the Kamakura (1185-1333) and later periods. Kiyomori at first ruled in cooperation with Go-Shirakawa, but his nepotism and provincial origins were resented and finally resisted by a court full of pride but with little real power beyond tradition.

The continuing prestige of that tradition was what attracted Kiyomori to the court and caused him to create a military coalition centered in Kyoto. His very success in gaining control over official positions and adopting the values of the court may have separated him from his warrior followers in the provinces. In any case, it was the resurrected Minamoto clan, led by Minamoto Yoritomo, that represented the new power of the provincial warrior class that would rise and destroy Kyoto-centered political authority in Japan.

Much has been written by court officials about the errors of Kiyomori and his character defects, yet the message that comes down through the ages is a tragic tale of the impermanence of glory. It was not only the Taira clan that perished in 1185 but also the last vestiges of the Heian court-dominated society and most of the refined aristocratic values that the aristocratic age embodied. Perhaps the greatest tragedy of Kiyomori and his clan was that they were crushed in the transition from one great period of Japanese history to the next.

—*Richard Rice*

Further Reading

Hall, John W., and Jeffrey P. Mass, eds. *Medieval Japan: Essays in Institutional History*. 1974. Reprint. Stanford, Calif.: Stanford University Press, 1988. Eleven essays and an epilogue by scholars of medieval Japan. The chapters on *insei* (retired emperor) government by G. Cameron Hurst and on the emergence of the Kamakura government by Mass provide insights on Kiyomori.

Hurst, G. Cameron. *Insei: Abdicated Sovereigns in the Politics of Late Heian Japan, 1086-1185*. New York: Columbia University Press, 1976. An important study of the institution of *insei*, who made the important decisions of state. Retired emperors such as Go-Shirakawa could ignore the sitting emperor (often an infant) and establish channels of imperial government. Chapter 7 analyzes the complicated relationship between Kiyomori and Go-Shirakawa.

Mass, Jeffrey P. *Warrior Government in Early Medieval*

Japan: A Study of the Kamakura Bakufu, Shugo, and Jitō. New Haven, Conn.: Yale University Press, 1974. Analysis of how power shifted from the court to local power bases of warrior clans. Mass argues that until 1179 Kiyomori shared power and benefits with his patron, the retired emperor Shirakawa.

_______. *Yoritomo and the Founding of the First Bakufu*. Stanford, Calif.: Stanford University Press, 1999. Revisionist work stressing Yoritomo's conservatism and the slow implementation of his system.

_______, ed. *Court and Bakufu in Japan: Essays in Kamakura History*. New Haven, Conn.: Yale University Press, 1982. Nine articles consider the development of feudal institutions in Japan following the demise of the Taira.

Morris, Ivan. *The Nobility of Failure*. 1975. Reprint. New York: Penguin Books, 1980. A highly readable survey of failed heroes in Japanese history. Chapter 5 deals with Minamoto Yoshitsune.

Sansom, George. *A History of Japan to 1334*. Vol. 1. Stanford, Calif.: Stanford University Press, 1958. A classic study of early Japanese history that is still valuable for its lucid style, although many of the details and interpretations have been revised by later studies. Contains a chapter on Kiyomori that discusses his character, the Shishigatani affair, the dangers of monastic armies, and Kiyomori's enemies.

The Tale of the Heike. 2 vols. Translated by Hiroshi Kitagawa and Bruce T. Tsuchida. Tokyo: Tokyo University Press, 1975-1977. A careful translation of *Heike monogatari*, Japan's greatest war chronicle. This thirteenth century epic culminates in the three battles that destroyed the Taira. It is the most important source for Nō drama, and its tales are found in Kabuki and puppet theater, as well as modern film and television.

_______. Translated by Helen Craig McCullough. Stanford, Calif.: Stanford University Press, 1988. A translation of the famous war epic by a respected scholar of classical Japanese. Contains an introduction by the translator.

Yoshitsune: A Fifteenth-Century Japanese Chronicle. Translated by Helen Craig McCullough. Stanford, Calif.: Stanford University Press, 1966. A translation and introduction to a medieval war tale that depicts the life of the most famous figure of his time, Minamoto Yoshitsune, who defeated the Taira and was in turn killed by his brother Yoritomo.

See also: Ashikaga Takauji; Fujiwara Michinaga; Minamoto Yoritomo.

Related articles in *Great Events from History: The Middle Ages, 477-1453*: 792: Rise of the Samurai; 794-1185: Heian Period; 858: Rise of the Fujiwara Family; 1156-1192: Minamoto Yoritomo Becomes Shogun; 1219-1333: Hōjō Family Dominates Shoguns, Rules Japan; 1336-1392: Yoshino Civil Wars.

Taizong

Chinese emperor (r. 627-649)

The second ruler of the Tang Dynasty, Taizong consolidated his regime through administrative reorganization and centralization, codification of laws, extension of hegemony over domestic enemies and menacing foreign powers, stabilization of commerce, and cultivation of the arts. Throughout East Asia, his regime is regarded as the exemplar of civic order and military might.

Born: January 23, 599; Wohong County, Shaanxi Province, China

Died: May, 649; Chang'an, Shaanxi Province, China

Also known as: T'ai-tsung (Wade-Giles); Li Shimin (given name, Pinyin), Li Shih-min (given name, Wade-Giles); Tang Taizong (Pinyin), T'ang T'ai-tsung (Wade-Giles)

Area of achievement: Government and politics

Early Life

Taizong (ti-tsahng), born Li Shimin, was the second son of the first Tang emperor, Gaozu (Kao-tsu, r. 618-626). A member of the influential Dou clan, his mother was equally aristocratic, having been reared in the northern court of an imperial uncle.

Because his father's reign did not begin until Li Shimin was seventeen, he was reared without special preparations. He received an upper-class Confucian education, exposing him to historical and classical learning. Buddhist beliefs, important to his family, were also passed on to him, and he persisted in observance of Buddhist rituals. His northern frontier upbringing centered on development of the martial arts—pertinent training in view of the political rivalries, rebellions, and warfare that marked Chinese history after the imperial unity of the Han and the Jin Dynasties shattered.

Traditional accounts of Li Shimin stress his youthful military prowess. While an adolescent, he accompanied his father and brothers on campaigns against the Turks. Apparently, he was a superb presence: forceful, histrionic, imperious in bearing, and awesome in his rages—qualities requisite for survival in a northern frontier family of landholding, fighting aristocrats.

Ruthless cunning characterized Li Shimin's responses to the conniving of his eldest brother, Li Jiancheng (Li Chien-ch'eng), the heir apparent to the Tang throne, and his younger brother, Li Yuanji (Li Yüan-chi), who supported the crown prince. Reacting decisively to these fraternal plots, to which his father, in some measure, acquiesced, he ambushed and killed his brothers at the gate of the capital city, Chang'an. Li Shimin then humiliated his father, the emperor, constraining him to abdicate after designating him as heir to the Tang throne in January, 627. Taizong would reign for twenty-three years, a period that, at the outset, he named *Zhengua*, the reign of "true vision."

Engraved depiction of Taizong departing for his campaign against the Tartars. (F. R. Niglutsch)

LIFE'S WORK

Taizong endeavored to mark his rule with an indelible personal style. Unlike most educated Chinese, he was preeminently a rationalist. The shaping of human destiny, in his view, was the consequence of human actions and not the uncertain result of magical rituals, superstitions, or intractable mandates of heaven. Unlike his predecessors, he developed his own role as a leader whose initiatives or failures would be evaluated by history rather than by spirits or gods. To this end, the advice he sought, his consultations with officials, and the manner in which he arrived at decisions were open and carefully recorded. Anxious to place his imprimatur on his times, he was capable of sublimating his convictions the better to ensure the approbation of those around him and to avoid the risk of historical rebuke or misjudgment. For much of his reign, he acted out a drama of which he perceived himself to be the principal author. If Taizong's style deemphasized the accomplishments of previous reigns, while exaggerating claims for his own, his problems nevertheless were immense and his assaults on them were impressive, often unprecedented.

Once renowned for his military prowess, after assuming power he affected the role of the humble scholar, anxious to remedy his lack of administrative skills. By virtue of his high intelligence and inexhaustible energies, however, he swiftly reordered imperial administration and soon evidenced increasing confidence in his mastery of administrative affairs. Officials, like himself, were expected to be continuously accessible. He valued their frank criticisms and strove to convince them that they had a share in policymaking, thus in improving the lot of the people—those to whom he and his officials were ultimately responsible.

Confucian frugality marked the early years of his reign. Public works were curtailed or abandoned in order to lessen the burdens of corvée labor and of taxation. Though he had been an ardent hunter, he forbade great formal hunts, principally because, like military maneuvers, they were expensive and destructive of property. Similarly, he at first restrained the elaborate construction of palaces. Such measures brought him wide popularity.

Selection of his chief ministers brought him great respect. He valued ability and dedication over personal compatibility. Wei Zheng (Wei Cheng) and Wang Gui (Wang Kuei), two of Taizong's principal ministers, for example, had served against him with the slain crown prince. Generally, he sought to minimize nepotism and, despite exceptions, preferred his own appointments to the continuation of inherited ministers. A notable deviation from this preference was the installation of his brother-in-law, Zhangsun Wuji (Chang-sun Wu-chi), as vice president for the department of state affairs. Zhangsun Wuji remained the emperor's confidant throughout his reign, despite allegations of excessive influence, and was entrusted with a codification of Tang laws and with settlement of the future question of succession to the throne.

The appointment of Fang Xuanling (Fang Hsuanling), who for thirteen years helped direct the department of state affairs, was another splendid ministerial choice. A practical man of affairs, though intellectually precocious, Fang, an easterner from Shandong, brought many of the emperor's former enemies from the east into high office. In company with Du Ruhui (Tu Ju-hui), scion of a famed northwestern clan of officials, Fang developed a brilliantly balanced executive administration respected for its efficiency and fairness. Similarly, the humorless Confucian moralist Wei Zheng (Wei Cheng), a southerner and former enemy of the emperor, was chosen for his diplomatic skills and served superbly in negotiations with external opponents of the regime.

Appointments of this caliber not only brought singular talents into Taizong's service but also lent geographical breadth and social cohesion to the government. Fearless critics were made integral parts of policymaking and administration. Aided by such experts, Taizong reordered and consolidated administrative changes begun by his father. Where Gaozu, however, had greatly increased the number of government positions to increase his patronage support, Taizong reduced them. China was divided into ten *dao*, or circuits, which were overseen by imperial commissioners. In tightening and centralizing authority, Taizong, through his ministerial galaxy, also attempted an upgrading of provincial bureaucracies by special education in law, calligraphy, and civil administration—establishing the School of the Sons of State, the School of Calligraphy, and the Superior School—and by means of rigorous examinations. Endemic under his father's regime, bribery and corruption were substantially diminished or made disreputable.

Isolated on the north central Chinese frontier, Taizong, like his father, was ringed by real and potential enemies with their own bases of political and social power. Therefore, he gave priority to centralization of authority, through combinations of diplomatic and military action. The broad geographical representation of his officials, their obvious contributions to Tang policy, plus their cultivation by the emperor, drew many of his enemies' followers under his rubric. Establishment of more than six hundred provincial militias led by loyal aristocrats or solid citizens contributed to this process of ensuring the ascendancy of Chang'an over neighboring regions, without necessity of quartering alien troops and without the imposition of financial burdens on local populations.

The reunification of China was Taizong's most formidable objective. Not since the Han Dynasty had China been united, although the Sui and Qin rulers, and Taizong's own father, had taken steps in that direction. While Taizong consolidated his own authority, he initially sought détentes with menacing neighbors, but direct military actions were unavoidable. In 630, when the collapse of the khanate of the Eastern Turks eliminated his most dangerous foreign rivals and opened a political vacuum along the northern frontier, he seized the chance for expansion. Whereas his father had been obliged to declare himself a vassal of the Eastern Turks, Taizong so effectively defeated them that the new khan acknowledged his vassalage to the Tang, dramatically altering the Asian power equilibrium for half a century.

The Western Turks, however, had grown stronger with the collapse of the Eastern Turks, dominating a vast stretch from the Great Wall to the western borders of Sāsānian Persia and from Kashmir in the south to the Altai Mountains in the north. Using "barbarians" to control "barbarians" and exploiting their internal dissensions, Taizong defeated them in the 640's, liberating the Silk Road from China to the Western world and extending his hegemony over most of Central Asia. Subsequently, he added the oasis states and eventually nearly

MAJOR RULERS OF THE TANG DYNASTY, 618-907

Reign	*Ruler*
618-626	Gaozu (Li Yuan)
627-649	TAIZONG
650-683	Gaozong
684	Zhonggong
684-690	Ruizong
690-705	Wu Hou
705-710	Zhongzong
710-712	Ruizong
712-756	Xuanzong
756-762	Suzong
762-779	Daizong
779-805	Dezong
805	Shunzong
805-820	Xianzong
820-824	Muzong
824-827	Jingzong
827-840	Wenzong
840-846	Wuzong
846-859	Xuanzong
859-873	Yizong
873-888	Xizong
888-904	Zhaozong
904-907	Aizong

all states in the Tarim basin, either through military occupation or by accepting their tribute.

Bitter opposition by his chief ministers worried about military expenditures as well as the employment of Chinese troops among foreigners did not alter Taizong's imperial ambitions. The powerful and expansive Tibetan state, which eventually he defeated in battle, he allied to the Tang by marriage. By 646, he had also crushed and received the submission of the chief Turkish tribes in northern Sinkiang. Anxious to redeem his father's failures, he found pretexts for the reconquest of Koguryŏ (now in Korea) in 644, although in this venture he succeeded no better than his predecessors.

Such attempts at grandeur curtailed prosperity at home. Commerce was made safe and flourished. Although Taizong was unable to solve some major agricultural problems, he sought to prevent the growth of large estates, partly to maintain revenues and partly to increase peasant proprietorships. Although an effervescence of fine arts and letters awaited Taizong's successors, historical scholarship, long neglected, prospered under his aegis. Directed by Wei Zheng and Fang Xuanling, histories of the Liang, Chen (Ch'en), Qi (Ch'i), Zhou (Chou), and Sui Dynasties were begun in the 630's. Work on the Northern Wei recommenced after 636 and a fresh history of the Qin (Ch'in) was completed by 646. Although they promoted Taizong's historical prejudices about his own regime, these works nevertheless proved invaluable to subsequent generations. In spite of neo-Confucian pressures on him to extirpate Buddhism, Taizong reformed aspects of the religion's relationships to the state and, though publicly observing its rituals, tried to meliorate criticisms by bringing it under official control.

Undeniably the quality of Taizong's regime degenerated in the latter years of his reign. He became arrogant, self-satisfied, and spendthrift. He relapsed into extravagant palace building, indulged in memorializing his horses and dogs, rediscovered the delights of expensive and destructive hunts, and shaped major policies contrary to ministerial advice. In addition, efforts to extend his fiscal system throughout his realms were aborted; despite numerous battles and lengthy sieges, Koguryŏ escaped incorporation; and his own succession was mismanaged. Debilitated by a disease incurred during his campaigns in Koguryŏ and thereafter dependent on the heir apparent, Taizong died in May, 649, in his capital, Chang'an.

SIGNIFICANCE

The weaknesses of Taizong's rule are easily listed because they were few and natural. Expansions of his fiscal system failed, and a larger proportion of the population than ever before eluded taxation; the growth of landed estates slowed but did not cease; codifications and revisions of the law remained incomplete; state-sponsored historical scholarship tended to exaggerate the emperor's attainments; Confucians who wanted Buddhism eradicated saw it merely controlled; the emperor's foreign policy burdened the nation's manpower and resources and the Korean adventure failed; and finally, his personal virtues degenerated.

His weaknesses or failures, however, were but the obverse of Taizong's great achievements in the face of immense difficulties. He consolidated a precarious Tang rule, carrying to fruition initiatives of his father. He brilliantly rationalized China's administrative system both formally and stylistically. Ministerial selections based on talents and character brought the highest capacities to bear in governance, discouraging sycophancy and venality. Emphasis on the emperor as the people's servant set a high tone for the times and for future generations. His ideal of service was enhanced by legal codifications, as was his restoration of China's historical record. Subordination of Buddhist influences to those of the state, while keeping an open arena for other religions, was important for China's spiritual and intellectual needs. Combinations of astute diplomacy and decisive military action against opponents brought the Chinese domestic tranquillity and prosperity. Finally, his virtual reunification of China restored an important part of China's heritage.

Taizong's regime represents an unprecedented high point in Chinese history. It approximated the Confucian ideal of *wu* and *wen:* a harmonious combination of civil order and military strength. It was a regime centered on securing the people's welfare. For later generations, Wu Jing's *Zhenguan zhengyao* (705; important principles of government from the Zhenguan period) embodied the wisdom accumulated by Taizong and his ministers, and Li Jing's *Li Weigong wendui*, also compiled after his death, summarized the military strategies of the emperor and his principal general, Li Jing. Both works have continued to be reminders throughout Asia of the principles of wise and effective government.

—*Clifton K. Yearley and Kerrie L. MacPherson*

FURTHER READING

Benn, Charles D. *Daily Life in Traditional China: The Tang Dynasty.* Westport, Conn.: Greenwood Press, 2002. An examination of the social life and customs of the Tang Dynasty in which Taizong lived. Bibliography and index.

Bingham, Woodbridge. *The Founding of the T'ang Dynasty: The Fall of Sui and Rise of T'ang, a Preliminary Survey.* 1941. Reprint. New York: Octagon Books, 1975. Concentration is on the fall of the Sui Dynasty; of Tang rulers, only Gaozu is examined. The study identifies the period's important problems. Useful appendices.

Capon, Edmund. *Tang China: Vision and Splendour of a Golden Age*. London: Macdonald Orbis, 1989. A study of the civilization of China during the Tang Dynasty. Illustrations, bibliography, and index.

Fitzgerald, Charles P. *Son of Heaven: A Biography of Li Shih-min, Founder of the T'ang Dynasty.* 1933. Reprint. Taipei: Ch'eng Wen, 1970. A classic biography of Taizong.

McMullen, David. *State and Scholars in T'ang China*. New York: Cambridge University Press, 1988. An examination of learning and scholarship during the Tang Dynasty. Bibliography and index.

Pulleyblank, Edwin G. *Essays on Tang and Pre-Tang China*. Burlington, Vt.: Ashgate, 2001. These essays focus on the history of the Tang Dynasty and deal with the period just before it. Bibliography and index.

Sen, Tansen. *Buddhism, Diplomacy, and Trade: The Realignment of Sino-Indian Relations, 600-1400*. Honolulu: University of Hawaii Press, 2003. An examination of the relations between China and India in the Tang and Song Dynasties. Bibliography and index.

Twitchett, Denis Crispin. *The Writing of Official History Under the Tang*. New York: Cambridge University Press, 1992. A look at the writing of official histories, which flourished under Taizong. Bibliography and index.

Wechsler, Howard J. *Mirror to the Son of Heaven: Wei Cheng at the Court of T'ang T'ai-tsung*. New Haven, Conn.: Yale University Press, 1974. Wechsler looks at the relationship between Taizong and Wei Zheng. Bibliography and index.

SEE ALSO: Xuanzang; Yan Liben.

RELATED ARTICLES in *Great Events from History: The Middle Ages, 477-1453*: 618: Founding of the Tang Dynasty; 629-645: Pilgrimage of Xuanzang; 690-705: Reign of Empress Wu; 845: Suppression of Buddhism; 960: Founding of the Song Dynasty; 960-1279: Scholar-Official Class Flourishes Under Song Dynasty.

QUEEN TAMARA

Georgian queen (r. 1184-1212)

Queen Tamara ruled the Transcaucasian kingdom of Georgia during the height of its medieval cultural development, the period of the composition of the Georgian national epic, The Knight in the Panther's Skin.

BORN: 1159; Kingdom of Georgia (now Republic of Georgia)
DIED: 1212; Kingdom of Georgia (now Republic of Georgia)
ALSO KNOWN AS: T'amar; Tamar
AREA OF ACHIEVEMENT: Government and politics

EARLY LIFE

Queen Tamara (tuh-MAW-ruh) was the daughter of Giorgi III of the Bagrationi Dynasty of kings. Giorgi III was the grandson of David the Builder, one of the greatest kings of the Transcaucasian kingdom of Georgia, located between the Greater and Lesser Caucasus, two ranges of mountains running from the Black Sea to the Caspian Sea. Western Georgia, or Imerti, was known in classical times as Colchis, and eastern Georgia, or Kartli, was known as Iveria, or Iberia, not to be confused with the Iberian peninsula of Western Europe.

Giorgi III had no sons and wanted his only daughter Tamara to succeed him, but there was no existing tradition for a ruling queen in Georgia. Anticipating resistance and determined to establish her right to the throne, he had her crowned as his coruler in 1178. He had a special coin struck showing both his and his daughter's names. It is significant that in the Georgian language Queen Tamara is always referred to by the same title, *mepe*, used for a male ruler, rather than the title usually used for the queen consort of a king.

LIFE'S WORK

On the death of her father in 1184, Tamara assumed the throne in her own right as ruler of the kingdom of Georgia. As her father had anticipated, she faced intense resistance from the powerful noble families, who formed a council known as the *darbazi* to force their wishes on the monarch. The Georgians can point with some pride to the fact that the formation of this body predates by some twenty-five years the Magna Carta, which allowed the English barons to form Parliament, although the *darbazi* did not become a permanent political tradition as the English Parliament did. In many ways, the council of Georgian nobles had more in common with the Fronde, the group of rebellious French nobles who sought to wrest control away from the monarchy in the early reign of Louis XIV and produced no lasting parliamentary tradition.

Such was the nobles' power in the early part of Tamara's reign that they were able to force her to make Mikel Mirianisdze, the patriarch of the Georgian Orthodox Church, her primary adviser and to demote her military commander in chief, Qubasar. The nobles also forced her to marry Yuri, son of Andrei Bogolyubsky, prince of Rostov-Suzdal, one of the principalities of Kievan Rus, the pre-Tatar Russian state. In Georgia, Yuri was known as Giorgi Rusi, Giorgi being the Georgian equivalent to the Russian Georgi-Yegor-Yuri group of names and Rusi literally meaning "the Russian." Although Prince Yuri was a successful military commander and won several important battles against Georgia's hostile Muslim neighbors, he was also an unfaithful husband who preferred the company of slave concubines to that of his wife.

Tamara did not acquiesce peacefully to these demands, although she had to bide her time to overturn some of the more onerous ones. After the death of Mikel Mirianisdze, she obtained a divorce from Yuri and sent him back home to Kievan Rus. Tamara then married David Soslan, an Ossetian prince who had been raised in the Georgian court. By him she had a son and a daughter, both of whom would subsequently rule Georgia. When the rebellious nobles tried to restore Yuri in 1191, Tamara successfully put down the attempted revolt with the aid of the royalist Mkhargrdzeli (Zakarid) family, who subsequently lent their military skills to expand her realm.

Internal dissension was not the only threat Tamara faced. Beyond the borders of Georgia lay several strong Muslim nations that regularly sought to invade and conquer the Christian kingdom. In 1195, Tamara's armies defeated the Azeri commander Abū Bakr at the Battle of Shamkhor. In 1199, Tamara retook the traditionally Georgian town of Ani, which she gave to the Mkhargrdzelis as a reward for their faithfulness to her. During 1203 to 1204, her forces fought significant battles in the area of Basian, defeating Rukn al-Dīn, sultan of Rum, and subsequently annexed Dwin, Shamkhor, and Ganjak.

At its height, Queen Tamara's empire stretched throughout the Transcaucasus, including territory that would become modern Armenia and Azerbaijan as well as what would become the modern Republic of Georgia. The later period of

Queen Tamara's reign became known as the golden age of medieval Georgia. The establishment of strong commercial centers brought trade wealth to a nation that already possessed rich soil and a favorable climate.

As a result, Georgia underwent an outburst of literary and artistic culture. It was during this period that Shota Rustaveli composed *Vepkhistkaosani* (twelfth century; *The Knight in the Panther's Skin*, 1968) a lengthy narrative poem dealing with heroic themes of knight errantry. Very little is known about Rustaveli. His name merely means "man from Rustavi," and Georgia has several towns by this name, so he cannot be definitely connected with the modern-day Rustavi downstream of Tbilisi on the Mtkvari River. Tradition makes Rustaveli a courtier hopelessly in love with Queen Tamara and suggests that he may have ultimately retired to a monastery. However, no evidence exists to confirm or deny these legends.

Queen Tamara donated generously to the Church and particularly to the various monasteries, which were important centers of learning. She funded the second phase of the building of the Vardzia cave-complex monastery in the mountains not far from the modern Turkish border. This religious community had originally been established by her father and is said to have gotten its name from one of her childish escapades while accompanying her father on an inspection of the early work.

One particularly famous icon, the Khakhuli Theotokos (Virgin Mary as Mother of God) in the Gelati monastery, has an interesting legend surrounding the precious stones that adorn it. Supposedly, Queen Tamara was preparing for Divine Liturgy when she was told that an elderly woman was begging for alms outside the door of her chamber. Wanting to finish weaving precious stones into her long hair, the queen ordered the woman to wait outside. When Tamara emerged, the old woman had vanished without a trace. At that moment, Tamara realized that she had turned aside the Lord God himself, who had taken this guise to test her hospitality. In shame, Tamara took the royal headband that had been the cause of her delay and placed it on the icon of the Virgin Mary, where it has remained to modern times.

Queen Tamara died in 1212. She was succeeded by her son, Giorgi IV Lasha (the Resplendent), who ruled from 1212 to 1223, when the Mongol invasion cut short his reign and he was killed in battle. He was succeeded briefly by his sister, but she was forced to flee ahead of the invading horde. Most scholars believe that Tamara was buried in one of the niches in the crypt of the Gelati monastery, which had been established by David the Builder as an intellectual redoubt against Turkish invasion. Literary sources contemporary to her quote her as having commanded that her remains be taken to Gelati as the land of her ancestors, and there given an honorable grave. However, as many as seven other putative grave sites have been identified for Queen Tamara, including one in Zhibiana, one of the four subsettlements of Ushguli, the highest continuously inhabited village in Europe. Archaeologists have been excavating the church under one of the two tall Svanetian watchtowers that folk tradition identify as the summer and winter residences of Queen Tamara in Upper Svaneti.

SIGNIFICANCE

Tamara was one of the greatest monarchs of feudal Georgia and one of the most warmly remembered. She was canonized (made a saint) by the Georgian Orthodox Church. Her feast day is May 14 (May 1 in the Julian Calendar, which is retained for purposes of religious observances in the Eastern Orthodox churches), and she is regarded as a healer of infirmities. In the modern Republic of Georgia, Tamara has remained one of the most common names given to girls, and many families bear the surname Tamarashvili, one of the few instance of the usually patronymic *-shvili* suffix being used with a woman's name.

Throughout the modern Republic of Georgia, one can find archeological sites associated with Queen Tamara, some genuine, others not. For example, one large cavern in the Uplis-Tsikhe cave village near Gori is known as the Tamara Hall, although there is no evidence that Queen Tamara herself lived there, only that it was reserved as a royal residence. In addition, there is a ruin on the slopes of Mount Kazbek called Tamara's Castle, which is thought by modern scholars to have been the work of David the Builder, but is associated in local folklore with a different Queen Tamara, unrelated to the beloved Tamara of the Georgian golden age. This legendary queen was supposed to be an evil temptress whose fondest amusement was to seduce handsome travelers for a night of pleasure, only to have them executed the following morning.

The art of the period is greatly treasured by the modern Georgian people. Most prized is Rustaveli's masterpiece, *The Knight in the Panther's Skin*, which has come to be regarded as the national epic and has greatly affected Georgian literature. Many Georgians can recite lengthy passages of the poem. Georgian scholars have created a scholarly journal devoted entirely to the study of Rustaveli and his poem.

—*Leigh Husband Kimmel*

FURTHER READING
Allen, W. E. D. *A History of the Georgian People: From the Beginning Down to the Russian Conquest in the Nineteenth Century.* New York: Barnes and Noble, 1971. This overview of pre-Russian Georgian history includes a fair amount of information on the reign of Queen Tamara but does not include information that has been gained since the fall of the Soviet Union.
Eastmond, Anthony. *Royal Imagery in Medieval Georgia.* Philadelphia: Pennsylvania State University Press, 1998. A study of artifacts relating to the kings and queens of Georgia, with a fair amount of information on images of Queen Tamara and their importance in the society of the time.
Rosen, Roger. *Georgia: A Sovereign Country of the Caucasus.* Hong Kong: Odyssey, 1999. A travel guide that includes information about Queen Tamara in relation to archeological sites in modern Georgia.
Suny, Ronald Grigor. *The Making of the Georgian Nation.* Bloomington: Indiana University Press, 1994. Although its focus is primarily on the post-Soviet republic, this book includes an overview of earlier Georgian history, including the era of Queen Tamara.

SEE ALSO: Kublai Khan; Raziya.
RELATED ARTICLES in *Great Events from History: The Middle Ages, 477-1453*: 1077: Seljuk Dynasty Is Founded; 1204: Genghis Khan Founds Mongol Empire; 1236-1240: Reign of Raziya; 1271-1295: Travels of Marco Polo.

TAMERLANE
Turkic military leader and conqueror

Tamerlane combined extraordinary military talent with strong administrative leadership to create the first large independent Central Asian state to throw off the domination of the Mongols. In the process, he altered the regional balance of power and revived Central Asia's main cities as international trading and cultural centers.

BORN: 1336; Kesh, near Samarqand, Transoxiana (now in Uzbekistan)
DIED: 1405; Otrar, near Chimkent, Turkistan, Central Asia (now Shymkent, Kazakhstan)
ALSO KNOWN AS: Timur; Timur Lenk; Timurlenk; Tamberlaine; Tamburlaine; Timour
AREAS OF ACHIEVEMENT: Warfare and conquest, government and politics, patronage of the arts

EARLY LIFE

Aḥmed ibn ʿArabshāh, captured by Tamerlane (TAHM-uhr-layn) at Damascus in 1401, later composed a generally critical history about him, entitled *Kitāb ʿajāʾib al-maqdūr fī akhbār Tīmūr* (1410; *Tamerlane: Or, Timur the Great Amir,* 1936). Writing soon after the death of Tamerlane, the historian described him as a brave, big-hearted youth friendly with the sons of the viziers, main advisers to the ruler at court. Contemporaries and later Central Asians called the formidable ruler Timur or Timur Lang (Timur the Lame), from which Europeans derived the form Tamerlane. His skeleton, found buried at Samarqand below a royal mausoleum, the Gur-e Amir, showed his damaged right leg attached to a tall, sturdy frame.

Tamerlane's Barlas tribal origin sharply defined his outlook and behavior. Like the other nomadic tribesmen of the region, he virtually lived and usually fought on horseback. Habits of nomadic life kept the youth from any inclination toward ease and settled existence. Emulating the former Mongol masters of the area, Tamerlane displayed a distaste for urban residence. Migratory life also probably accounted for the almost ceaseless campaigning he undertook, starting from young adulthood. In his early years, aggressive opposition repeatedly drove Tamerlane into retreat with only a handful of followers.

LIFE'S WORK

By the time Tamerlane reached the age of twenty-four, however, he had begun to acquire a reputation as an effective chieftain. He became prince of the Barlas clan in 1360 and continued to expand his influence during the next decade. Within Central Asia, he repeatedly had to fight the deadly rivals who held Khwārizm, just south of the Aral Sea, and the nomadic Moghuls (then called Jata or Jattah) of the plains and mountain passes east of Transoxiana. In his drive to ascendancy, he sanctioned the killing of his superior, the emir Ḥusayn of Transoxiana, and then married the emir's widow. This royal link improved Tamerlane's political position and added the honorific *gurakan* (son-in-law of the ruler's family) to the new leader's title. At Balkh in 1370, he took the throne of Central Asia.

Tamerlane's idea of his natural domain apparently encompassed the subregions of Transoxiana, Khorāsān, Afghanistan, Turkistan, Iran, and the Transcaucasus, in whose Karabakh region he preferred to pass the winter. These areas served the Chaghatay and other tribal warriors as summer and winter pasturage. Within that periphery, his settled subjects found irrigable lands for farming and safe routes for travel.

Perhaps the most salient feature of Tamerlane's leadership was his ability to employ the mobile military might of the Turkic Chaghatay tribes to build a state. With this tribal support, Tamerlane checked internal opposition. From Samarqand, his splendid capital, the Central Asians thrust into Kashgar (several times from the 1370's to the 1390's), southern Russia (1395), Delhi (1398), Baghdad and Damascus (1401), and the environs of Ankara (1402). After widespread destruction, enslaving, and plundering, however, they remained in none of these places. Unlike earlier conquerors of the same region, such as Alexander the Great and Genghis Khan (whose relative Tamerlane proudly but on tenuous grounds claimed to be), Tamerlane chose not to colonize or govern these distant lands.

Tamerlane. (Library of Congress)

In campaigns north of the Caspian and Aral Seas, Tamerlane's forces routed the vast armies of the Golden Horde, commanded by Toktamish Khan. Two great battles in 1391 and 1395, along with numerous lesser skirmishes, broke the hold of the Golden Horde. For some one hundred years, these offensive victories gave Central Asia a defense against the incursions of nomads north of Transoxiana. Equally significant, Tamerlane's success released the Russians from the tight grip imposed by the Mongols' Tatar successors, who had been centered at Sarai, near the great bend in the Volga River.

The emir spoke both the Turkic and Persian languages of Central Asia, but he never learned to read or write. To overcome this handicap and to satisfy his keen interest in history, he established the post of official reader of manuscripts (*qissakhan*). Despite his illiteracy, the conqueror learned the Qurʾān and Islamic teachings so well from his spiritual counselors that he could discuss controversial points of dogma with them. Later historians, including Ibn ʿArabshāh, accused him of ruthlessly using religion for political purposes. In Syria, opponents regarded Tamerlane and his Central Asian forces as zealous Shīʿites, whereas in parts of Iran, Shīʿite defenders knew him to be a devout Sunni. He demonstrated his merciless commitment to Islamic doctrine when he drove into India. There, his troops slaughtered Hindus by the thousands as a pious act in response to the commandment to convert or kill infidels. Had his planned invasion of the Far East run its course, non-Muslims there might have suffered a similar fate.

In 1405, Tamerlane initiated a campaign directed toward China. Pushing eastward from his capital, he had scarcely reached Turkistan (regarded then as stretching beyond the Syr Darya River) when he died, not in combat but from illness. His successors fell to struggling for power in clashes that soon diminished Timurid authority and territory.

SIGNIFICANCE

Tamerlane's principal achievement fulfilled what he considered to be the normal responsibilities of a sovereign: to establish and maintain a large, secure, prosperous state and to embellish it with artistic and cultural institutions of the highest quality. At the heart of his empire, Samarqand, Bukhara, Herāt, and smaller cities were graced with large numbers of talented intellectuals, artisans and artists, theologians and teachers, many of them foreigners, for whom Tamerlane served as a demanding patron. The civilization under the Timurid Dynasty that Tamerlane founded set the highest standards in western Asia in literary composition, miniature painting, and historiography.

Great architectural monuments of the fourteenth and early fifteenth centuries still demonstrate his accomplishment in such fields. The most magnificent of the structures designed and built by Tamerlane's order served religious purposes. A grand mosque rose in his birthplace, Kesh, and another, dedicated to a favorite wife, Bibi Khanum, in Samarqand. Tamerlane's architects constructed a huge mausoleum in Yasi, Turkistan, to honor the sainted Ahmed Yesevi (d. 1166), a Turkish poet and mystic.

Politically, the durability of the state of Tamerlane and his successors was determined by certain factors characteristic of medieval Central Asia. Political power at that time was founded primarily on the military might of the nomadic tribesmen; at the same time, these tribes posed the greatest threat to a ruler. Tamerlane was able to bring the tribes under his control by replacing the potentially dangerous tribal chieftains with individuals personally loyal to him. As long as this practice was maintained, the stability of the state was assured. No one of his successors, however, could completely command the loyalty of these factions, and the unity of the realm gradually broke up during the century following Tamerlane's death. Despite this factionalism, Samarqand continued to flourish as a great cultural center under the Timurid Dynasty until it was overrun by the Shaybanid Uzbeks at the beginning of the sixteenth century. Tamerlane's longest-lasting legacy was the Turkic literary language called Chaghatay, which emerged during his rule and supplanted Persian. It survived as the primary language of the literary arts in Central Asia down to the twentieth century.

—*Edward Allworth and William McCabe*

Further Reading

Barthold, Vasilii V. *Four Studies on the History of Central Asia.* Translated by V. Minorsky, and T. Minorsky. 3 vols. Leiden, The Netherlands: E. J. Brill, 1962-1963. A history of Turkistan and Semirechie that also discusses the origins of the Timurid state and the lives of Tamerlane and his successors, emphasizing his grandson Ulugh Beg. Also covers the history of the Turkmens. Illustrations, notes, index, chronological table.

Blair, Sheila S. and Jonathan M. Bloom *The Art and Architecture of Islam 1250-1800.* New Haven, Conn.: Yale University Press, 1994. An important scholarly study that explores the art and architecture of the Islamic world from 1250 to 1800. Chapter 4 discusses Tamerlane's Bibi Khanum mosque in Samarqand.

Grousset, Rene. *The Empire of the Steppes: A History of Central Asia.* Translated by Naomi Walford. New Brunswick, N.J.: Rutgers University Press, 1970. A general chronological history of the Eurasian Plains empires through the eighteenth century. Chapter 11 surveys the history of Tamerlane's conquests and the fate of his successors. Based on fifteenth and sixteenth century histories, with little analysis provided. Maps, bibliography, index.

Howorth, Henry H. *History of the Mongols, from the Ninth to the Nineteenth Century.* 1876-1927. Reprint. 4 vols. New York: B. Franklin, 1964. Vol. 2 discusses Toktamish, khan of the Golden Horde, perhaps Tamerlane's most formidable adversary. Genealogical tables, maps, and extensive index.

Ibn Arabshah, Ahmed. *Tamerlane: Or, Timur, the Great Amir.* Translated by J. H. Sanders. 1936. Reprint. Lahore, Pakistan: Progressive Books, 1976. A translation of the medieval historian's account of Tamerlane's life. Written after the emir's death, it is based on the works of earlier historians and on Ibn Arabshah's own experience. The author took a very negative view of Tamerlane's actions. Appendices give a conversion table for the Islamic calendar and a list of tribal names. There is also a chronological table of the main events in Tamerlane's career.

Ibn Khaldūn. *Ibn Khaldūn and Tamerlane: Their Historic Meeting in Damascus, 1401 A.D.* Translated by Walter J. Fischel. Berkeley: University of California Press, 1952. A short work supplemented with many explanatory remarks and notes. It gives Ibn Khaldūn's account of his meeting with Tamerlane during a siege at Damascus, and of his later service with the emir. Bibliography.

Jackson, Peter, and Laurence Lockhart, eds. *The Cambridge History of Iran.* Vol. 6, *The Timurid and Safavid Periods.* Cambridge, England: Cambridge University Press, 1986. Contains chapters devoted to the history of Tamerlane and his successors. Analyses also of science, religion, architecture, other arts, and literature in the period, primarily in Iran. Many explanatory notes, a long bibliography, and thorough index.

Lamb, Harold. *Tamerlane: The Earth Shaker.* New York: Robert M. McBride, 1928. A readable history tracing Tamerlane's life from his rise to power until his death. Written in the style of a historical novel, based on nineteenth century interpretations of primary and secondary sources. There is some discussion of Tamerlane's world, but Lamb slips into an uncritical use of primary documents. Illustrations, maps, bibliography, and index.

Manz, Beatrice Forbes. *The Rise and Rule of Tamerlane.* New York: Cambridge University Press, 1999. A scholarly study of Tamerlane as a nomadic conqueror and a successful political leader and administrator. Discusses state formation, tribal politics, tribal relations with central government, and struggles for succession. Bibliography, index.

Meddicott, J. A., and D. M. Palliser, eds. *The Medieval State.* Rio Grande, Ohio: Hambledon Press, 2000. A history of the idea of the state in the Middle Ages. Includes a chapter on Tamerlane's political power and his empire. Illustrations, maps, bibliography, index.

Timur, the Great. *The Mulfuzat Timury.* Translated by Charles Stewart. London: J. Murray, 1830. This work purports to be Tamerlane's autobiography. Some historians have doubted its authenticity. Scholars, especially in Central Asia, however, continue to refer to it as a source for the study of Tamerlane's life. May be difficult to locate.

SEE ALSO: Alp Arslan; Genghis Khan; Ibn Khaldūn; Maḥmūd of Ghazna; Mehmed II; Osman I.

RELATED ARTICLES in *Great Events from History: The Middle Ages, 477-1453*: 956: Oğhuz Turks Migrate to Transoxiana; 1130: Karakitai Empire Established; 1381-1405: Tamerlane's Conquests; 1399-1404: Tamerlane Builds the Bibi Khanum Mosque.

TANCRED

Norman Crusader and military leader

Through his leadership and political sense, Tancred contributed greatly to the success of the First Crusade, spreading Christian influence and establishing a firm Christian presence in the Near East that lasted for decades.

BORN: c. 1078; place unknown
DIED: December 12, 1112; Antioch, Syria (now Antakya, Turkey)
ALSO KNOWN AS: Tancred of Hauteville
AREA OF ACHIEVEMENT: Military

EARLY LIFE

Very little is known about the formative years of Tancred (TAN-krehd). He was the son of Odo the Good Marquis and Emma, the daughter of Robert Guiscard. Tancred first appeared prominently in southern Italy when his uncle, Bohemond I of Taranto, and grandfather, Guiscard, led the Norman conquest of southern Italy. They established Tancred as a lord there just as Pope Urban II called for Christian knights to crusade against the Muslims in the Holy Land.

According to Tancred's chronicler, Ralph of Caen, the young knight grappled with the dilemma of being a Christian knight; knightly warfare seemed at odds with God's commandments. While the Church preached Christian pacifism, young Tancred had to survive as a knight in a violent world. Pope Urban recognized this problem as well. He solved the knight's dilemma by granting remission of all sins and declaring that killing Muslims while liberating the Holy Land was favorable in God's eyes. With this problem solved, Tancred "was aroused, his powers grew, his eyes opened, his courage was born. For before . . . his mind was divided, uncertain whether to follow in the footsteps of the Gospel or the world."

LIFE'S WORK

With the growing passion of Urban's crusade spreading quickly throughout Christendom, Bohemond had little difficulty convincing Tancred to accompany him on the First Crusade. In September, 1096, Tancred set out with his uncle and Guiscard for the Holy Land. On their way to Constantinople, the Crusaders terrorized Jews. Tancred failed to see a difference between the Muslims who occupied the Holy Land and the Jews, who he believed had executed Christ. He frequently held Jews hostage, usually for a ransom of thirty pieces of silver. Considering Tancred's financial situation, he badly needed the money to pay the men under his command. Bohemond sponsored Tancred financially, but Tancred was still responsible for his own men. The expense of going on crusade was enormous, even by the standards of the 1090's.

Tancred quickly gained a reputation as a valiant, fearless leader who harbored intense ambitions. He recognized the potential power, fame, and wealth that a successful campaign could bring to a young knight. On arrival in Constantinople, he refused to take the oath of allegiance to Byzantine emperor Alexius I Comnenus, who had originally requested Christian forces from the west to help stave off Muslim encroachment into the Byzantine Empire. After the fall of Nicaea in 1097, Tancred led a raiding force into Cilicia and captured Tarsus, Ardana, Misis, and Iskenderun. It was a spectacular campaign; however, Baldwin, the brother of Godfrey of Bouillon and later count of Edessa, ordered Tancred to abandon his diversionary conquests and return to the main body for the assault on Antioch and Jerusalem. Beginning in October, 1097, the assault on Antioch quickly turned into a lengthy siege. Tancred commanded the western section of the siege line, gaining a reputation for his ruthless treatment of the enemy. He was known to have personally decapitated Turkish prisoners and had their heads sent to the bishop of Le Puy as a tithe payment. Antioch finally fell in June, 1098. The Turks abandoned the city, but they were not fast enough to escape the wrath of the Christians. A frenzied slaughter ensued as Tancred and his men chased down the fleeing Turks, killing hundreds.

Tancred joined Raymond of Toulouse on the march to Jerusalem only after Raymond offered him a large gift of cash. The fact that Tancred was bribed to continue the crusade indicated the growing divisions among the crusade leadership. Power and greed were already getting in the way of this most Christian undertaking. Along the way, Tancred captured Bethlehem, showing his own ambition for power and land. When Jerusalem fell in mid-July, 1099, Tancred plundered the temple area mercilessly, taking a small fortune for himself. After he received much criticism from several clergymen, notably Arnulf, the chaplain of Robert of Normandy, Tancred gave some of his booty to the Church.

Tancred was now a major player in the First Crusade. His loyalty was desired and even necessary as internal division rocked the crusading army. Granted the title "prince of Galilee," Tancred offered his services to Godfrey of Bouillon when the latter was elected the first Latin leader of Jerusalem.

Tancred continued his sideshow campaigns of conquest, but he failed in attempts to take Jaffa, Haifa, and Tiberias. On the death of Godfrey of Bouillon in 1100, Baldwin took control of Jerusalem. Still smarting from Baldwin's cold treatment of him in Cilicia, Tancred tried to gain the new king's favor by continuing campaigns in Galilee. By 1101, they had apparently settled their differences, but no friendship blossomed between the two ambitious knights.

When Tancred's uncle Bohemond was captured in 1101, Tancred took his place as regent of Antioch. The new regent retook Cilicia, perhaps to spite Baldwin, and captured Laodicea. Bohemond returned in 1103 and again became regent of Antioch, leaving his nephew Tancred with little in the way of money and land. To make matters worse for Tancred, Bohemond thought that his nephew had been much too slow in securing his uncle's release from the Turks. Bohemond forced Tancred to return much of the land he had conquered as regent, leaving Tancred with only a few small castles.

The year 1104 brought another strange twist to Tancred's career when Bohemond returned to Europe to gain support for a war against Alexios. Tancred was again named regent. He defeated the Turks again and joined forces with William Jordan, count of Cerdagne, who had his eyes on the county of Tripoli. For several years, Tancred attempted conquests in Syria and Palestine. He died in Antioch on December 12, 1112.

Significance

Tancred exemplifies the problems of the First Crusade. He overcame the basic dilemma of being a Christian knight and sought fame and fortune in the conquest of the Holy Land. He slaughtered Jews and Turks alike. He quickly became a major player in the internal intrigue among the crusade's leaders, who often turned on one another for personal gain.

Tancred did ensure a strong Christian presence in northern Syria for several decades. He is portrayed in Torquato Tasso's epic poem *Gerusalemme liberata*, but the account is mostly fictionalized. He is also glorified in a number of plays, mostly written in the seventeenth century.

—*William Allison*

Further Reading

Foss, Michael. *People of the First Crusade*. New York: Arcade Publishing, 1997. Covers the history of the First Crusade with an emphasis on individual personalities, including Tancred.

France, John. *Victory in the East: A Military History of the First Crusade*. Cambridge, England: Cambridge University Press, 1994. A military history of the First Crusade that emphasizes the leadership, the siege of Antioch, and the divisions among the crusading knights.

Hill, John Hugh, and Laurita Lyttleton Hill. *Raymond IV, Count of Toulouse*. Syracuse, N.Y.: Syracuse University Press, 1962. The standard biography on Raymond, with frequent reference to Tancred.
Nicholson, Robert Lawrence. *Tancred: A Study of His Career and Work in Their Relation to the First Crusade and the Establishment of the Latin States in Syria and Palestine*. 1940. Reprint. New York: AMS Press, 1978. A biography of Tancred, based on Nicholson's doctoral dissertation.
Riley-Smith, Jonathan. *The First Crusade and the Idea of Crusading*. Philadelphia: University of Pennsylvania Press, 1986. A well-rounded history of the First Crusade, focusing on the religious and economic nature of the campaign.
Yewdale, Ralph Bailey. *Bohemond I, Prince of Antioch*. Princeton, N.J.: Princeton University Press, 1924. One of the few biographies of Tancred's uncle.

SEE ALSO: Bohemond I; Urban II.
RELATED ARTICLES in *Great Events from History: The Middle Ages, 477-1453*: November 27, 1095: Pope Urban II Calls the First Crusade; 1147-1149: Second Crusade.

ṬĀRIQ IBN-ZIYĀD

Berber-Muslim conqueror of Spain

By decisively defeating the Visigoths in Spain in July of 711, Ṭāriq ibn-Ziyād destroyed the Visigothic monarchy and began the Muslim conquest of the Iberian Peninsula.

BORN: Before 700; possibly Algeria
DIED: c. 720; place unknown
ALSO KNOWN AS: Tarik ibn Zeyad
AREA OF ACHIEVEMENT: Warfare and conquest

EARLY LIFE

Little is known of the early life of Ṭāriq ibn-Ziyād (TAH-rihk ihb-n zi-YAHD). It is often said that his mother was Berber and his father Arab. This would suggest his birth in North Africa, but at least one scholar has argued for Persian origins. Arabic sources consider him a Berber. There is a tradition in some Muslim histories that his mother was related to the Berber leadership that resisted Arab conquest. The Algerian government named one of its fleet of ferries after him, considering him to be one of the nation's famous native sons. He is often referred to as the "freedman" or "former slave" of Mūsā ibn Nuṣayr, but the nature of his servitude is uncertain. This situation may be due to conditions of capitulation of the town in which he was living at the time it was conquered. Most of what is known of his subsequent life is based on a very few contemporary documents and on Muslim histories written several generations later.

LIFE'S WORK

In the early 700's, Mūsā ibn Nuṣayr, commanding the Arab armies of Islam, broke Berber resistance in Northwest Africa and then became governor of the region. Following traditional Arabic practice, he continued to assimilate conquered peoples by confirming their local rights in return for their acceptance of the new religion and military service. Ṭāriq ibn-Ziyād appears first as a soldier in Mūsā's service and later as commander of his vanguard, as Mūsā moved into Morocco, took Tangier, and then led several expeditions into the interior. About 708, Mūsā garrisoned Tangier exclusively with Berber soldiers and named Ṭāriq ibn-Ziyād governor of the city. The only Arabs present in Tangier were a handful left to teach the Berbers the tenets of Islam. Feeling himself comfortable in his control of the territory, Mūsā ordered a reconnaissance of the southern Spanish coast. There were several intelligence-gathering expeditions, but no decisive action was taken until an exploratory party under Ṭarīq ibn Malik landed in Spain in 710 and returned with tales of easy booty.

In the late spring of 711, Ṭāriq, still governor of Tangier, was ordered to follow up on this earlier report and to land in Spain. There he was to await reinforcements or return to Morocco as the situation might warrant. Ṭāriq landed near Gibraltar (which now bears his name: Jabal Ṭāriq, or Ṭāriq's Rock) with about 1500 mostly Berber troops. A lack of appropriate vessels and uncooperative currents made the crossing from Tangier a slow one, possibly taking place over a period of several days and done mostly at night to avoid detection. Once across, Ṭāriq burned his ships to encourage his men to remain in Spain and established a garrison near Gibraltar, having met little resistance. He is reported to have had little or no cavalry. Ṭāriq did not take much military action in the more than a month's time between his arrival at Gibraltar and his meeting with the forces of Roderick, king of Spain, in the summer. Ṭāriq might have been waiting for the Spanish forces to come to him in territory with which he was already familiar. There is also a tradition that holds that Ṭāriq acted on his own initiative in crossing to Spain, without consulting Mūsā, who had returned to Ifriqiya (essentially, modern Tunisia). If this is true, it may help to explain Mūsā's later treatment of Ṭāriq at Toledo.

Spain at this time was ruled by Roderick, newly elected king of the Visigoths. The recent nature of Roderick's election and the civil wars that ensued because of it made the kingdom particularly vulnerable. It is also probable that this civil unrest gave rise to the tradition that Julian, count of the southern marches—feeling himself aggrieved by the king—invited the Muslims to help his cause and even guided some of Ṭāriq's forces. When the king received news of Ṭāriq's landing, he was in the far north putting down a Basque rebellion and was obliged to call off this action abruptly, gather such forces as he could, and march to the far south to meet the invading troops.

In July of 711, the forces of Ṭāriq and Roderick met in the Battle of the Guadalete (also known as the Barbate and the Wadi Bakka), at an as yet undetermined site on the Guadalete River not far from Gibraltar. Here Ṭāriq thoroughly defeated the much larger Visigothic army. Desertions from Roderick's troops and the Visigoths' unfamiliarity with Muslim tactics were major factors in Ṭāriq's victory.

Finding victory easy, Ṭāriq advanced inland, his forces increased by a continual flow of deserters from the Visigothic army. He gradually increased his cavalry by taking enemy mounts as booty after each battle. He met his stiffest resistance at Ejica later in 711. There elements of the Visigothic army regrouped under new leadership in a second attempt to remove the invaders.

After this victory, Ṭāriq, apparently realizing the weakness of the Visigothic state, divided his forces into four groups, sending one each to Malaga, Granada, and Córdoba. At Córdoba Ṭāriq's lieutenant applied a tradi-

Engraved depiction of Ṭāriq ibn-Ziyād presenting his conquests to Mūsā. (F. R. Niglutsch)

tional Muslim practice: Terms of surrender were offered and refused. When the city later surrendered, the male population was executed and the women were enslaved. Ṭāriq himself led the fourth body of troops to Toledo, the Visigothic capital, which surrendered without a fight in 712. There is a tradition which says that Toledo was abandoned by the Visigothic nobility, leaving it in the hands of the recently disenfranchised Jewish population. This population now opened the city gates to possible deliverers.

In 713, Ṭāriq was joined near Toledo by Mūsā, who had with him about eighteen thousand mostly Arab troops, including cavalry. Mūsā had become jealous of Ṭāriq's continued successes and was annoyed by his not following instructions to wait for reinforcements. Fresh from his own successes in southwestern Spain, Mūsā now humiliated Ṭāriq, ordering him flogged and beating him with his own sword. With Ṭāriq at his side, Mūsā now executed many of the Visigothic nobles who had returned to Toledo, this presumably to reduce further the Visigothic leadership and the possibility of rebellion. With Mūsā's arrival in Spain, Ṭāriq therefore became a secondary figure in the conquest of the peninsula.

Mūsā and Ṭāriq wintered at Toledo and from there they rode together, taking Guadalajara and Alcalá de Henares before entering the valley of the Ebro River. There Zaragoza, Huesca, and a number of other towns fell to them. At Zaragoza Mūsā again applied the consequences of not accepting terms of surrender that were earlier used at Córdoba.

While in the vicinity of Zaragoza in the spring of 714, Mūsā received a summons from the Umayyad caliph, al-Walīdī I, to report to Damascus as soon as possible to give an account of his actions. He had earlier been accused of financial improprieties, which may have contributed to his recall. He was also instructed to take Ṭāriq with him. Because of this summons and because they were encountering increasing resistance, Mūsā and Ṭāriq turned west, subduing sections of León, Asturias, and Galicia.

At this time Ṭāriq issued a warrant for the arrest of Pelagius (or Pelayo), an important former official in the Visigothic court who would emerge several years later as the victor at the Battle of Covadonga, the first serious setback for the Arabs in Spain. Mūsā took the higher regions, leaving Ṭāriq to subdue several towns in the Duero River Valley before they both turned south and left Spain in the winter of 714. Another consideration for ending further conquests may have been Mūsā's fear that his Arab forces, spread from Tunisia to the Ebro River, were now stretched to their limit. As proof of their achievements, the two leaders took some Visigothic prisoners as well as considerable treasure. Mūsā left his son Abd al Aziz as governor in his absence.

The caliph al-Walīdī I died within a few weeks of Mūsā and Ṭāriq's arrival in Damascus, and Mūsā fell foul of the new, short-lived caliph Sulaymān (r. 715-717). Mūsā and Ṭāriq had some differences over aspects of the administration of Spain and Mūsā was humiliated, ending his days in poverty, reputedly on his way to Mecca. His and Ṭāriq's achievements in Spain were denigrated as the next caliph, ʿUmar II (r. 717-720), considered abandoning the Iberian Peninsula altogether. Sulaymān had briefly considered Ṭāriq as Mūsā's replacement as governor of Spain, but rivalry between Arabs and Berbers and fear of Ṭāriq's following the same independent line of action as before quashed this plan. Ever since the conquest of Egypt, the caliphs had been reluctant to commit large numbers of Arab troops to the conquest and maintenance of the western territories. At about this time, a tax collector for part of Iraq named Ṭāriq ibn-Ziyād is reported; he may be the same person. However, the conqueror of Spain is not heard of after 720—that is, after the reign of Caliph ʿUmar II.

SIGNIFICANCE

Ṭāriq's actions in spearheading the Muslim conquest of Spain altered significantly the future course of Spanish and Portuguese history. His decisive defeat of King Roderick and the speed with which he then took Toledo, the royal capital, probably went far toward preventing any serious regrouping of forces or rebellion on the part of the Visigoths. His decision to follow through after his initial victory forced the hand of his superior to act while the Muslims had the advantage.

His military tactics were typical of those of the early Arab conquests in that they involved extended, unsupported military maneuvers deep into enemy territory. These tactics would be continued by his successors as the Arabs invaded Aquitaine and the France's Rhone Valley. Ṭāriq himself also represents a common use of clients or conquered peoples in the Arab expansion in the first centuries of Islam.

—St. John Robinson

FURTHER READING

Collins, Roger. *The Arab Conquest of Spain, 710-797*. London: Blackwell, 1994. The only work to focus specifically on the eighth century in Spain, it is particularly valuable for its evaluation of original sources and of the problems posed in documenting the period of Ṭāriq's activity.

_______. *Early Medieval Spain: Unity and Diversity, 400-1000.* New York: St. Martin's, 1983. A broad study of the shift from Roman to Arab dominance in Spain, it contains a very detailed study of the conquest and its immediate aftermath.

Kennedy, Hugh. *Muslim Spain and Portugal: A Political History of Al-Andalus.* Menlo Park, Calif.: Addison-Wesley, 1997. Though a general survey of the Muslim period, it contains valuable and detailed information on the period of the conquest.

Taha, Abdulwahid Dhanun. *The Muslim Conquest of North Africa and Spain.* New York: Routledge, 1989. One of relatively few serious histories of this topic by a modern Arab scholar which is also readily available in English. The work relies heavily on Arabic sources, most of which date from several generations after the fact. This allows the author to provide very detailed, if somewhat unsubstantiated, accounts of the conquest.

Wolf, K. B. *Conquerors and Chroniclers of Early Medieval Spain.* Translated Texts for Historians, Vol. 9. Liverpool: Liverpool University, 1990. One of the more accessible translations of four major Latin chronicles of the Visigothic and early Muslim periods. Contains texts and useful essays on each.

SEE ALSO: ʿAbd al-Malik; Ibn Baṭṭūṭah; Ibn Khaldūn; al-Idrīsī; Damia al-Kāhina; Lalibela; Mansa Mūsā; Sundiata.

RELATED ARTICLES in *Great Events from History: The Middle Ages, 477-1453*: c. 610-632: Muḥammad Receives Revelations; 630-711: Islam Expands Throughout North Africa; 685-691: Building of the Dome of the Rock; April or May, 711: Ṭārik Crosses into Spain; October 11, 732: Battle of Tours; 1048: Zīrids Break from Fāṭimid Dynasty and Revive Sunni Islam; 1062-1147: Almoravids Conquer Morocco and Establish the Almoravid Empire; 1230: Unification of Castile and León.

THEODORA

Byzantine empress (r. 527-548)

Theodora used her privileged position as consort of the great Byzantine emperor Justinian I to administer the complex political machinery of an empire. An empress in more than title, she took an active part in political decision making and social reform, was sympathetic to the rights of women, and succeeded in defending the religious rights of the persecuted Monophysites against the Orthodox majority in the early Christian era.

BORN: c. 497; Constantinople, Byzantine Empire (now Istanbul, Turkey)

DIED: June 28, 548; Constantinople

AREAS OF ACHIEVEMENT: Government and politics, women's rights, religion and theology

EARLY LIFE

The girl who would grow up to become Empress Theodora (thee-uh-DOHR-uh), the most famous of the Byzantine empresses, was born to a family of poor circus performers in Constantinople probably in 497. The Greek Byzantines shared with the Latin Romans a love for the circus, which included chariot racing, athletic contests, and various types of animal acts. The Hippodrome, or racetrack, was the colorful center of a turbulent area of Constantinople frequented by every social class and nation from beggar to emperor, barbarian to Byzantine Greek; this was the setting for Theodora's earliest experiences, and it was there that her father Acacius worked as a bearkeeper in the employ of the "Green" circus faction. The circus factions were groups that organized and supported the competing teams of charioteers and athletes. They performed a rudimentary political function as well, in that they became the focus of various popular allegiances.

Theodora's father died when she was four or five, leaving her destitute mother to provide for herself and her three young daughters. Because the bearkeeper had worked for the Greens, the mother turned to them for help, hoping to obtain her husband's old job for her new husband. In an effort to win favor, she coached her daughters to perform and beg in a graceful manner, thinking thus to melt the hearts of the crowd; however, the attempt was unsuccessful. She and the children were ridiculed, and it was the rival faction, the Blues, who came to the family's rescue. The future empress would never forget, nor forgive, the humiliation of the episode and the cruelty of the Greens.

Theodora's older sister Comito began to perform as an actress several years after these events; at the time, the

Theodora, third from left, stands with attendants in this photograph of a mosaic. (Library of Congress)

profession was held in very low esteem, particularly for women. Actresses were treated as no better than prostitutes and were forbidden to marry men of the upper classes. There were few other careers available to women, however, and the tough world of the Hippodrome provided a ready-made audience for female entertainers. Like her older sister, Theodora was attractive, and she began to accompany her sister on the stage, where her lively antics, quick wit, and physical beauty brought her popular success. She also soon won fame for less refined talents, such as her willingness to disrobe in public and perform obscene acts. In time, she became a notorious courtesan, according to the *Anecdota* (c. 550; *Secret History of the Court of the Emperor Justinian*, 1674) of Procopius of Caesarea, the contemporary historian on whom most modern information about Theodora is based. (The *Anecdota* was discovered in the Vatican library more than a millennium after its original appearance.) According to Procopius, there was no limit to the extent of her perversions and scandalous behavior, which he describes in lascivious detail. However, Procopius intensely disliked both Emperor Justinian and Theodora, which may explain his scurrilous and probably biased account of the empress's behavior.

Around 520, Theodora disappeared for a time from Constantinople in order to accompany a lover, Hecebolus, to Cyrene in North Africa, where he had just obtained a position as governor. They soon quarreled, however, and she found herself alone and destitute. She made her way to Alexandria, Egypt, a major center of civilization within the Byzantine Empire and across the Mediterranean Sea from Constantinople. There she apparently met Timothy, the patriarch of Alexandria, and Severus, the patriarch of Antioch, two of the five leaders of Christendom at the time. Both men had suffered persecution because they believed in the Monophysite (unitary) nature of Christ, a belief recently termed heretical by the Orthodox Church. Both treated her with kindness, which she remembered with gratitude for the rest of her life. She seems to have experienced a sort of religious conversion that changed her life such that, when she returned in 522 to Constantinople, she took up a modest but honest livelihood spinning wool, forsaking the theater and her former life.

LIFE'S WORK

It was not long after her return to Constantinople that Theodora met Justinian, nephew of the emperor and heir apparent to the throne of Byzantium. Justinian, fifteen years her senior and a supporter of the Blues circus faction, fell deeply in love with her, and they soon began living together in the Palace of Hormisdas. Although Justinian showered Theodora with love and expensive gifts, he also wished to marry her. This was contrary to current law, which forbade marriage between a patrician and an actress. Although the current empress Euphemia was implacably opposed to the marriage, having herself risen from lowly estate to achieve royal status, her timely death and the compliance of Justinian's uncle, the emperor Justin I, enabled the couple to wed in 525. Thus it came about that the daughter of a bearkeeper and the son of a peasant were to become the next emperor and empress of the powerful and vast Byzantine commonwealth.

Two years passed between the marriage and the assumption of the throne, which gave Theodora time and seasoning for the important role she would play as empress and co-ruler with her husband. She learned court etiquette, observed and discerned the centers of political power, and formed alliances with key palace players. By April, 527, when Justinian was formally crowned in the palace, Theodora had transformed herself into an empress worthy of the throne of Byzantium.

As a ruler, Justinian is remembered as a codifier of Roman law. He wished as well to restore the divided Roman empire, of which the Byzantine state was the eastern branch, to its former unified and exalted position. To do this, however, he was obliged to wage numerous long and costly wars. Predictably, the taxes levied against the population to finance these projects were a source of popular resentment, which reached a climax in 532 when the circus factions, including the Blues whom Justinian had previously supported, united against him in the Hippodrome. Justinian's attempt to quell the rebellion, known as the Nika Riots after the war cry *nika* (victory) chanted by the populace, only exacerbated the anger of the crowd, which then proceeded to destroy many of the principle public buildings and churches of the city and threatened the royal palace itself. Theodora is credited with stiffening Justinian's resolve in putting down the rioters, at least thirty thousand of whom were subsequently massacred by Justinian's military general Belisarius (c. 505-565). She also insisted on the execution of Hypatius, a nephew of the former emperor who had been crowned by the rioters.

Theodora also eventually prevailed against one of the men, John of Cappadocia, who had been a focus of popular antipathy and a cause of the rebellion. This man, promoted to praetorian prefect in 531 and a genius at raising the money to finance Justinian's wars, was known for his coarseness and brutality as well as for his contempt for the empress. Theodora used her palace connections and her capacity for intrigue to bring about John of Cappadocia's fall from favor and ultimate exile.

Contemporary accounts reveal Theodora as thoroughly accustomed to a life of luxury and opulence. She was famed for her beauty, which even her prime detractor Procopius acknowledged. She reveled in elaborate jewelry and extravagant costume, and she insisted on observance of all the intricacies of court etiquette and ceremony. According to Procopius, she slept many hours a day, spent hours on personal adornment, and enjoyed rich food. The most famous surviving portrait of her is from a mosaic in the Church of San Vitale in Ravenna, Italy, where she is depicted just a few years before her death. This shows her as a slender woman of elegance, with large eyes and a fine complexion.

Besides enjoying the splendors of court life, however, Theodora was also deeply engaged in religious issues. She was a source of support and even refuge for members of the often-persecuted Monophysite sect. Theodora is perhaps best known for her activity in the founding of many churches, among which was the Church of Saints Sergius and Bacchus in Constantinople. The most notable ecclesiastic foundation of the reign of Justinian and Theodora, however, was the rebuilding and redesign of Hagia Sophia, the Church of Holy Wisdom, in Constantinople, shortly after its destruction in the Nika Riots. Later in her life, one of Theodora's chief plans was to install as pope of Rome a candidate who would be positively inclined toward the Monophysites. Thus, on the death of Pope Agapetus in 536, she struck a bargain with a Roman deacon named Vigilius that in return for her support of his candidacy to the papacy, he would accede to her wishes regarding the Monophysites. When instead a rival claimant, Silverius, was installed as pope, Theodora engineered his deposition in favor of Vigilius. However, Theodora's hopes that the new pope would prove to be her puppet turned out to be unfounded. Once ensconced in the Holy See, Vigilius refused to recognize the legitimacy of the Monophysites.

Although in modern terms Theodora probably would not be considered a feminist, relying as she did on her husband's position and on palace intrigue to achieve her goals, it is nevertheless noteworthy that Theodora did take measures to help women at a time when there were

BYZANTINE EMPERORS: JUSTINIAN LINE, 518-610

Reign	*Emperor*
518-527	Justin I
527-548	THEODORA
527-565	JUSTINIAN I THE GREAT
540	Khosrow I sacks Antioch
565-578	Justin II
578-582	Tiberius II Constantinus
582-602	Maurice
602-610	Phocas (non-Justinian)

few institutional means to do so. She was instrumental in promulgating laws that improved the legal status of actresses, ensured inheritance rights for females, and protected prostitutes from exploitation by pimps and brothel-keepers. Both her sisters, in spite of their early careers as actresses, married men of high rank in the Byzantine Empire. By the time of her death, presumably from cancer, in 548, Theodora had succeeded in improving the lot of many distressed women.

SIGNIFICANCE

Theodora, a woman who shared the real political power of the Byzantine throne with her emperor husband, was an early example of women's ability to make political and social change in a complex society. Theodora's achievements in the realm of social legislation, religious tolerance, and Realpolitik show her to have been well in advance of her time in many respects.

—*Gloria Fulton*

FURTHER READING

Bridge, Antony. *Theodora: Portrait in a Byzantine Landscape*. 1978. Reprint. Chicago: Academy Chicago, 1993. A well-written and somewhat idealized portrayal of Theodora. Maps, bibliography, and index.

Browning, Robert. *Justinian and Theodora*. Rev. ed. New York: Thames and Hudson, 1987. A scholarly and readable account of the reign of Justinian and Theodora. Depicts historical events as they appeared to the emperor and empress.

Calkins, Robert G. *Medieval Architecture in Western Europe: From A.D. 300 to 1500*. New York: Oxford University Press, 1998. Explores the history of Western European architecture of the Middle Ages, including the buildings inspired by Justinian and Theodora. Illustrations, extensive bibliography, index.

Cameron, Averil. *Procopius and the Sixth Century*. Berkeley: University of California Press, 1985. Discussion of the Byzantine historiographer Procopius, on whose *Secret History* much of the modern knowledge of Theodora is based. Chapter 5 is devoted to Theodora and discusses the question of Procopius's reliability as a historian in the light of his obvious dislike of her.

Diehl, Charles. *Theodora: Empress of Byzantium*. Translated by Samuel R. Rosenbaum. New York: Frederick Ungar, 1972. A classic account of Theodora by a noted historian. The somewhat romanticized conception of Theodora has influenced later scholarship.

Evans, James Allan. *The Age of Justinian: The Circumstances of Imperial Power*. New York: Routledge, 1996. Scholarly treatment of power structures of the Justinian period.

_______. *The Empress Theodora: Partner of Justinian*. Austin: University of Texas Press, 2002. A brief look at the life of Theodora and her role as empress. Maps, bibliography, index.

Garland, Lynda. *Byzantine Empresses: Women and Power in Byzantium, A.D. 527-1204*. New York: Routledge, 1999. Explores the history of the empresses of the Byzantine Empire, including a chapter on Theodora. Map, extensive bibliography, index.

McCash, June Hall, ed. *The Cultural Patronage of Medieval Women*. Athens: University of Georgia Press, 1996. A study of the female benefactors of the arts and of culture during the Middle Ages. Includes a chapter on Theodora's role in cultural patronage. Extensive bibliography and an index.

Norwich, John Julius. *Byzantium: The Early Centuries*. New York: Alfred A. Knopf, 1994. An account of the social and political panorama of the Byzantine Empire, from the founding of Byzantium by Constantine the Great through the eighth century. Chapters 9 to 12 cover the reign of Justinian and Theodora.

Procopius. *The Anecdota: Or, Secret History*. Vol. 6 in *Procopius*. Translated by H. B. Dewing. Cambridge, Mass.: Harvard University Press, 1960-1962. The original source for much of the historical knowledge about Theodora, written by a contemporaneous historian.

SEE ALSO: Amalasuntha; Saint Irene; Justinian I.

RELATED ARTICLES in *Great Events from History: The Middle Ages, 477-1453*: 529-534: Justinian's Code Is Compiled; 532-537: Building of Hagia Sophia; 726-843: Iconoclastic Controversy.

THEODORIC THE GREAT
Hungarian-born king of the Ostrogoths (r. 474-526)

For a third of a century, Theodoric gave Italy strong, stable governance and its longest period of peace and prosperity in more than a century. His promotion of Roman ideals of justice and civic virtue led to the preservation of Roman law, administration, learning, and urban life. These formed the groundwork for the structure of medieval Italian society.

BORN: c. 454; Pannonia (now primarily in Hungary)
DIED: August 30, 526; Ravenna (now in Italy)
ALSO KNOWN AS: Theodoricus
AREAS OF ACHIEVEMENT: Government and politics, law

EARLY LIFE

Theodoric the Great (thee-oh-DOHR-ihk) was the eldest son of Theodemir, a warrior king of the Ostrogoths. The family traced its ancestry back to a legendary Ostrogothic king, Amal, who lived around the year 200. In the late fifth century, the Amal kingship was shared by three brothers—Valamir, Vidimir, and Theodemir—but the Ostrogoths lived under the domination of the Hunnish king Attila (r. 434-453). After Attila died, the Amal kings revolted, defeating the Huns in 454. News of the victory supposedly reached Theodemir's home on the day of Theodoric's birth, considered an auspicious sign for the new prince. The Ostrogoths then moved westward into the Roman province of Pannonia (now western Hungary, eastern Austria, and Slovenia). They entered into a treaty with the Eastern Roman emperor Leo I (r. 457-474), pledging to defend the Roman frontiers in return for financial subsidies.

When Theodoric was about seven years old, the subsidies failed to arrive. After the Ostrogoths raided a nearby Roman province, the alliance was renewed, the subsidies paid, and peace restored. Yet young Theodoric was taken to Constantinople as a hostage to assure the future good behavior of the Ostrogoths. For ten years, he lived in the imperial palace under the protection of Emperor Leo I. Not much is known of Theodoric's life or education during this decade. He almost certainly learned to speak Latin, still the official language of the government, and possibly some Greek. He must have observed the dynamics of imperial court politics and the character of late Roman society.

In 471, Leo sent the young prince home to his royal father with rich presents. Theodoric immediately won fame by leading a war party to seize the city of Singidunum (now Belgrade) from the Sarmatians, who had recently taken it from the Romans. The victorious general was hailed as a true Amal king, and the conquered city was kept under Ostrogothic control.

In 473, famine forced the Ostrogoths to abandon Pannonia. Theodemir and his son marched south from Singidunum, eventually laying siege to Thessalonica, one of the most important cities in the Greek world. The Roman government was forced to renew the peace with the Goths and to agree to their resettlement in Roman territory. In return, the Goths undertook the defense of the lower Danube frontier as federates of the Roman Empire. Shortly after, Theodemir died, and Theodoric assumed sole rule at about age twenty.

During the next fourteen years, Theodoric was a key player in the game of Roman Balkan politics. Residing in the fortress city of Novae on the lower Danube, he supervised defense of the nearby Roman frontier. When Emperor Zeno (r. 474-491) was temporarily overthrown by a rival, Theodoric intervened to restore him to power. Later, Theodoric had to contend with treachery from Zeno, as well as opposition from a rival Ostrogothic army not related to his own royal tribesmen. After much fighting, diplomacy, and shifting of loyalties, Theodoric triumphed, and peace with the emperor was restored. He again resumed military defense of the Roman frontier.

In 483, Theodoric was named master of soldiers, and in 484, he was appointed consul, the most prestigious office in the empire. Yet the peace was frequently broken, as the Ostrogoths continued plundering the provinces whenever supplies were short. While Theodoric continued to live at Novae, his warriors sought adventure and loot where they could. In these circumstances, it is likely that Theodoric developed his plan to invade Italy to ensure his people a permanent home.

LIFE'S WORK

The main achievement of Theodoric was to create a Romano-Gothic regime that brought more than thirty years of peace, prosperity, cultural revival, and some justice to the peoples of Italy.

In 488, Theodoric was elevated to the rank of patrician and commanded by Emperor Zeno to march into Italy and overthrow Odoacer, the German general who had overthrown the last Western Roman emperor in 476 and then ruled Italy. Theodoric, with his tribal army, was to rule in Italy until Zeno's arrival. The emperor may have thought that the Goths were less dangerous to him in Italy than in the Eastern Empire. Both Theodoric and Zeno recognized Italy to be a Roman province—and Theodoric to be a military subordinate of the Roman emperor. Yet the Gothic general was essentially the hereditary king of a warrior nation. He is sometimes called "king" in Byzantine sources, but that seems to have been a courtesy title for any Germanic war leader who signed a formal contract with the Romans to provide military services for pay.

Invading Italy in 489, Theodoric won a series of hard-fought battles against Odoacer's armies. A central factor in the 476 coup had been the demand of Odoacer's soldiers that they be given landed estates in Italy as recompense for their defense of the country. When the demand was refused by the Roman government, Odoacer had seized power and distributed *tertia* (thirds) of large Roman estates among his followers.

Following Odoacer's surrender in 493, Theodoric murdered him at a banquet in his palace in the old imperial capital at Ravenna. Theodoric then distributed the *tertia* of the estates previously held by Odoacer's soldiers to his own faithful troops. Those whose lands were not seized paid a special tax to the Gothic treasury. While the military affairs of the new regime were the exclusive province of the Ostrogoths, the civil affairs of Italy continued to be directed by Roman administrators. The senate continued to govern in Rome, and local Roman councils governed in the cities. Roman law prevailed in all cases in which both litigants were Romans; a Gothic court heard cases if one litigant was non-Roman. Among themselves, the Goths maintained their own national legal customs.

Theodoric maintained the capital in Ravenna, although he also kept royal palaces in Pavia and Verona, areas where many Goths had settled, whence they could be mobilized quickly to defend the frontiers of Italy. Other groups were settled thinly throughout the Italian peninsula, where they provided local garrisons for police and defense purposes. The number of Goths under Theodoric's command in 490 has been variously estimated at 40,000 to 100,000, of whom one-quarter were full-time soldiers. Because Italy had a population of several million, the Goths did not constitute an overwhelming addition to its total population and yet were enough to give it adequate order and defense.

One problem for Theodoric was that he and the Goths were considered heretics by orthodox Christians. As Arians, they denied the orthodox Christian doctrine of the Trinity. Theodoric's solution was to practice religious toleration. He was particularly insistent on protecting Jews from religiously inspired violence. When a schism arose as a result of a disputed papal election, he refused at first to decide the case, ultimately granting legal recognition to the candidate elected first and with the most votes. At a later time, he refused to sit in judgment on a pope accused by his enemies of adultery. He insisted that the matter be decided by a council of bishops. Yet he was frequently persuaded to change his policies through the influence of saintly bishops acting as defenders of the weak or persecuted.

Under the Ostrogothic regime, new buildings were constructed and older monuments and public works restored. The king and the bishops took the lead in this work and were helped to some extent by senatorial aristocrats. In 500, Theodoric celebrated the tenth year of his rule in the city of Rome with traditional games, ceremonies, and distribution of gifts. The walls of the imperial city were repaired, as was the principal road leading south, the Appian Way. The old imperial palace on the Palatine Hill was renovated. At his capital in Ravenna, he restored the broken aqueduct and repaired the imperial

Theodoric the Great. (Hulton|Archive at Getty Images)

KINGS OF THE OSTROGOTHS, 474-774

Reign	Ruler
474-526	THEODORIC THE GREAT
526-534	Athalaric
534-536	Theodahad (with AMALASUNTHA)
536-540	Vitiges (Witiges)
540	Theodobald (Heldebadus)
541	Eraric
541-552	Totila (Baduila)
552-553	Teias
553-568	Roman domination (Byzantine emperor Justinian I)
568-774	Lombard domination
774	Frankish conquest

palace. He also built a new church, now called St. Appollinare Nuovo, richly decorated with brilliant mosaics on its walls and inlaid gold plates on its roof. Other palaces and baths were built in Pavia and Verona.

Public offices were still the goal of ambitious Romans seeking power and social prestige. The Gothic king occasionally reached out beyond the local Roman aristocracy to Romans from the Eastern Empire or even to fellow Goths for appointees to high civil offices, but mostly he relied on the local elites. The king also intervened in the traditional imperial task of organizing relief during local famines and promoted reclamation work in the Pontine Marshes south of Rome and in the plain north of Spoleto.

Theodoric's foreign policy was successful in defending Italy from invasions and in expanding Ostrogothic control over the strategic approaches to Italy from beyond the mountains to the north, west, and east. Through prudent diplomacy, limited military interventions, and Amal dynastic marriages with the ruling Visigothic, Frankish, Burgundian, Vandal, and Thuringian royal families, Theodoric sought peace and unity among the Germanic peoples ruling the former Western Roman Empire. He expanded the areas of his direct rule from Italy eastward to the Danube River and westward to the lower Rhone River. Theodoric's de facto rulership in Italy was recognized by successive Eastern Roman emperors: Zeno, Anastasius I (r. 491-518), and Justin I (r. 518-527). Theodoric, in turn, recognized the right of Roman imperial sovereignty over Italy by nominating consuls each year and notifying the Eastern emperor for his approval.

Only in the last three years of his life were Theodoric's political relations with Emperor Justin and the neighboring Germanic kings suddenly shaken by events beyond his control. In 522, his son-in-law and heir Eutharic died, leaving an infant son as heir to Theodoric's realm. An older grandson, Sigeric, heir as well to the Burgundian kingship, was murdered the same year. Theodoric's alliances with both Vandals and Thuringians also broke down because of dynastic changes. When the Roman emperor Justin began a systematic persecution of Arians within his realm, it seemed a calculated challenge to Theodoric, who responded with threats against the Catholics of Italy. In the midst of this crisis, Theodoric was persuaded that two of the highest Roman officials in his regime, Symmachus and Boethius, were plotting against him with the Eastern Roman emperor. In 525, both were executed, probably without a fair trial. Theodoric, aged and seeing his life's work unraveling around him, died the following year.

He designated his ten-year-old grandson, Athalaric (r. 526-534), as his heir, under the regency of the boy's mother, Amalasuntha (r. 534-535). Within a decade, Athalaric was dead and his mother forced to open negotiations with Justin, bringing about the Gothic-Byzantine war that ravaged Italy in the mid-sixth century and ultimately led to the destruction of the Ostrogothic nations.

SIGNIFICANCE

The principal policies Theodoric the Great used in governing Italy were already in place during the rule of his predecessor Odoacer: religious toleration, cooperation with the local Roman aristocracy, Germanic control of all military power, respect for the existing Roman law and political institutions, and efforts to seek legitimacy from the Eastern Roman emperor.

Like most Goths, Theodoric was an Arian Christian, a heretic in the eyes of his Catholic Roman subjects. Following a policy of religious toleration and avoiding interference in the religious quarrels that beset the orthodox Christian church in his time, Theodoric managed to defuse the religious disputes in Italy. He won the cooperation of the Roman aristocracy by allowing it to govern the city of Rome and hold the higher civil offices. He also sustained the customary operations of Roman law. Theodoric believed that the best way to govern the two peoples under his control was by respecting their cultural distinctiveness and leaving to each as wide an area of autonomy as seemed compatible with Gothic military supremacy.

Theodoric's sense of justice was famous in a society in which litigation was frequently used as a weapon of oppression by the powerful. The king used Gothic special agents called *saiones* to investigate injustices, supervise special projects, and exercise the royal will against recalcitrant bureaucrats. Taxes were collected with efficiency and greater fairness than before. Commerce, manufacturing, and reconstruction were encouraged, and famine relief was effectively organized.

Theodoric also demonstrated the greatest respect for Roman culture and encouraged the efforts of such Roman intellectuals as Boethius, Symmachus, and Cassiodorus to preserve and promote the Greek scientific and philosophical learning among the Latin-speaking population of Italy. Cassiodorus wrote a history of the Goths, now lost, which served as the principal source of a later history of the Goths by Jordanes. Boethius's textbooks on Greek arithmetic, geometry, music, and Aristotelian logic became the basis for the curriculum of the medieval Latin schools. Boethius's father-in-law, Symmachus, supported a revival of Neoplatonic philosophy, and Boethius's last work, *De consolatione philosophiae* (523; *The Consolation of Philosophy*, late ninth century), is considered the finest expression of Greek humanistic philosophy of late classical civilization and was very influential in the early medieval schools. Symmachus also patronized many poets, rhetoricians, and the Latin grammarian Priscian, whose works were authoritative for medieval Latin scholars. This intellectual revival, so important for the future direction of European culture, would have been impossible without the personal patronage and atmosphere of peace and stability provided by the great Ostrogothic ruler.

Although Theodoric's heretical Arian religious views and his brutal execution of both Symmachus and Boethius have tempered the enthusiasm of some historians for his judgment and moral excellence, even the hostile Byzantine historian Procopius treated the king with respect.

When the armies of Justin invaded Italy after Theodoric's death, the Goths put up stiff resistance and received considerable support from their Roman subjects. The Gothic-Byzantine wars devastated Italy and ended what most Italians later looked back on as the last good times their country would see for the next two centuries. Nevertheless, the reign of Theodoric allowed the structure of Roman society to survive the fall of the empire and become the foundation for the new, vibrant, and creative Italy of the Middle Ages.

—*Joseph R. Peden*

FURTHER READING

Amory, Patrick. *People and Identity in Ostrogothic Italy, 489-554*. New York: Cambridge University Press, 1997. A well-researched and well-argued examination of Italian Gothic culture of the fifth and sixth centuries. Argues for a new understanding of the racial and cultural makeup of the so-called barbarians, as well as a new understanding of their role in the fall of Rome.

Bark, William. "The Legend of Boethius' Martyrdom." *Speculum* 21 (1946): 312-317. The author argues that Boethius and Symmachus should not be viewed as Catholics martyred for their faith, victims of Theodoric's alleged sudden outburst of religious prejudice. He believes it much more plausible that both were guilty of treasonable acts designed to undermine the Ostrogothic regime.

Burns, Thomas S. *A History of the Ostrogoths*. Bloomington: Indiana University Press, 1984. An extensive synthesis of the history and culture of the Ostrogoths, using original documentary and archaeological and modern monographic sources. The focus is the Ostrogoths' culture and achievements—from their first mention in Roman records of the third century to their extinction as a nation in the sixth century. The author uses a mixed chronological and topical approach. References to Theodoric are scattered throughout the text. Illustrations, bibliography, index, maps, and dynastic tables.

Chadwick, Henry. *Boethius: The Consolations of Music, Logic, Theology, and Philosophy*. Oxford, England: Clarendon Press, 1981. A masterful study of the career and literary works of the greatest intellectual of the court of Theodoric. The first chapter describes the revival of Greek classical learning in the West stimulated by the Roman statesman Symmachus, his son-in-law Boethius, and others under the patronage of Theodoric. Later chapters deal with Boethius's literary and philosophical works. Examining the causes that led to Theodoric's brutal execution of both men, the author finds religious as well as political reasons for the sudden reversal of favor. Bibliography, index.

Duckett, Eleanor S. *The Gateway to the Middle Ages: Italy*. Ann Arbor: University of Michigan Press, 1961. A rich portrait of the cultural life of the leading intellectuals of Theodoric's Gothic-Roman Italy. After an introduction to broader historical events, the author offers two chapters on Boethius and Cassiodorus and another chapter on two historians, Ennodius and Jordanes. The interaction of each with Theodoric is emphasized throughout the text. Bibliography, index.

Jones, A. H. M. "The Constitutional Position of Odovacar and Theodoric." *Journal of Roman Studies* 52 (1962): 126-130. Lack of clear evidence has made the exact constitutional relationship between Theodoric and the Eastern Roman emperors a matter of controversy among historians. Argues that both Odoacer and Theodoric were no more than typical Germanic kings without formal status under Roman law.

La Rocca, Cristina, ed. *Italy in the Early Middle Ages, 476-1000*. New York: Oxford University Press, 2002. Ten chapters by historians and archaeologists integrate new archaeological findings to examine medieval Italy's regional diversities, rural and urban landscapes, organization of public and private power, ecclesiastical institutions, manuscript production, and more. Illustrations, maps, bibliography, index.

Moorhead, John. *Theodoric in Italy*. New York: Oxford University Press, 1992. This study of Theodoric's reign focuses on the relationship between the Goths and the Romans. It details both the difficulties and the consequences of their partial unification within Theodoric's empire.

O'Donnell, James J. *Cassiodorus*. Berkeley: University of California Press, 1979. A top official in the government of Theodoric, Cassiodorus collected a book of official letters, *Variae*, which are a principal source for the history of the Ostrogothic ruler. His history of the Goths, now lost, was the basic source used by the later historian of the Goths, Jordanes. The author has made a detailed study of Cassiodorus's life and works; chapters 2 and 3 focus on Cassiodorus's role as a courtier of Theodoric the Great.

Schutz, Herbert. *The Germanic Realms in Pre-Carolingian Central Europe, 400-750*. New York: P. Lang, 2000. An important complement to the other texts on this list, this work examines the Italian Goths from the point of view of Germanic history, rather than from a Roman historical perspective.

Thompson, E. A. *Romans and Barbarians: The Decline of the Western Empire*. Madison: University of Wisconsin Press, 1982. In chapter 4, the author discusses the Ostrogothic conquest of Italy and its consequences, the popularity of the government of Theodoric, and the constitutional character of the regime with respect to the Roman imperial government in Constantinople. He also compares the Ostrogothic regime with its predecessor, headed by Odoacer.

SEE ALSO: Amalasuntha; Boethius; Cassiodorus; Justinian I; Odoacer; Priscian; Theodora.

RELATED ARTICLES in *Great Events from History: The Middle Ages, 477-1453*: 524: Imprisonment and Death of Boethius; 529-534: Justinian's Code Is Compiled.

THEOLEPTUS OF PHILADELPHIA

Nicean writer and teacher

As a spiritual writer, dynamic speaker, and respected teacher among medieval Greeks, Theoleptus played a major role in preventing the reunion of the Roman Catholic and Greek Orthodox churches. He also was influential in promoting Hesychasm, a mystical form of prayer and meditation.

BORN: c. 1250; Nicaea (now İznik, Turkey)
DIED: c. 1326; Philadelphia (now Alasehir, Turkey)
AREA OF ACHIEVEMENT: Religion and theology

EARLY LIFE

Theoleptus (THEE-ah-LEHP-tuhs) was born into a Christendom that was divided, long before the sixteenth century Reformation. Differences between the Latin Christianity of the West and the Greek Christianity of the East were long-standing. In the sixth century, the *Filioque* controversy had begun. The Western church, believing that the Christian Church could grow and unfold in time, and trusting in reason and the intellect, added this word to the Nicene Creed of the second century: "Credo . . . in Spiritum Sanctum . . . qui ex Patre Filioque procedit" (I believe . . . in the Holy Spirit . . . who proceeds from the Father and the Son). The Eastern church, believing the Christian Church to be fixed and immutable, and relying on tradition and mysticism, insisted that the Holy Spirit proceeded only from the Father and that this doctrine had been upheld by the early Church fathers. Theologians of the West desired a more precise definition of the Godhead, while those of the East saw such a quest as producing legalistic interference. The *Filioque* doctrine had become entrenched in the West by the eighth century, but the Eastern church continued to oppose it and to claim true orthodoxy for its interpretation.

In addition to the *Filioque* issue, there were other doctrinal and liturgical differences. The Western church eventually came to forbid marriage of the clergy, while the East continued to allow it. The West forbade divorce; the Eastern church, never having completely cut its ties to the state, viewed marriage as a civil contract and tolerated divorce under certain conditions. The West had teachings on Purgatory, while in the East such things were thought to be unknowable. The Western church used cold water and unleavened bread in the celebration of the Eucharist, while the Eastern church used warm water and leavened bread.

All these matters reflected the deepest division, which centered on the question of authority: Would Rome or Constantinople lead Christianity? In 1054, a Western cardinal laid on the altar of Hagia Sophia in Constantinople a decree excommunicating the patriarch of Constantinople. The next day, the patriarch expelled the papal legate, and a schism between the two churches resulted. While Latin churches and monasteries in the East continued to maintain contact with local Orthodox bishops, the Western church increasingly came to view Constantinople as rigid and decadent, and the Eastern church came to see Rome as careless and arrogant.

The Crusades, which began in 1095 and which brought a massive Western presence into the Byzantine world, steadily reinforced these differences. During the Fourth Crusade (1202-1204), the Greeks, hating their emperor, Alexius III Angelus, for taking orders from Western Crusaders and the pope, resisted the emperor. Crusaders then overthrew Alexius; sacked, pillaged, and raped in Constantinople; made Baldwin, count of Flanders, the Eastern Roman emperor; and divided Asia Minor among ten rulers and four national groups. This situation did not last; still, the Crusades, and particularly the events of 1204, served to solidify the differences between the Roman West and the Greek East.

During the latter half of the thirteenth century, when Theoleptus was a young man, the Eastern emperor, Michael VIII Palaeologus (r. 1259-1282), sought reconciliation with the Western powers, for he feared the power of the encroaching Turks. He was joined by Patriarch John XI Becchus (1275-1282) and certain other powerful Orthodox clergymen. The majority of the Orthodox clergy and people, however, remembering centuries of differences and the abuses of the Crusades, opposed such a reunion. Theoleptus would join the latter.

Life's Work

Reconciliation between the Roman and Byzantine churches was accomplished at the Second Council of Lyon in 1274. Opening on May 2, it was presided over by Pope Gregory X and attended by more than five hundred prominent Western clergymen, making it the largest ecclesiastical gathering since the Second Lateran Council of 1139. The Greek delegation, which did not arrive until June 24, consisted of Germanus, a representative of the patriarch of Constantinople; Theophanus, archbishop of Nicaea; the chancellor; and two high officials of the Eastern Empire. The Greek delegation also brought a letter of support signed by five hundred Greek clergymen. Nevertheless, most prominent Orthodox clergymen boycotted the council.

The council agreed on July 26, at its fourth session, to a plan of reconciliation. The council agreed to the *Filioque* doctrine—a determination that had been made even before the Greek delegation arrived on June 24. The reunion plan also upheld Western teachings on marriage of the clergy, Purgatory, and the celebration of the Eucharist. Finally, the plan called for the supremacy of the Roman pope in all disputes. Virtually every area of dispute was decided in favor of the Western teaching, and the Greek delegation accepted these decisions.

Shortly after the council's pronouncements had been promulgated, Theoleptus, an Orthodox church deacon, openly repudiated the council's stance. With the support of the majority of Orthodox clergy, he began to organize opposition to the decrees, principally in Bithynia, in northwestern Asia Minor near Constantinople. His polemics resulted in his excommunication by the patriarch of Constantinople, and Emperor Michael VIII Palaeologus imprisoned and mistreated him. After his release in 1275, Theoleptus left the wife whom he had only recently married, abandoned the diaconate, and retired as a monk to Mount Athos in northeastern Greece, near the city of Thessalonica.

Mount Athos was a center of monasticism. Here Theoleptus practiced a form of prayer and spirituality known as Hesychasm, from the Greek word *hēsychia* (quiet). An early form of Hesychasm had been practiced by certain Greeks who had called for a solitary life and withdrawal from the world. At Mount Athos, Theoleptus was a student of Nicephorus the Athonite, who taught a variation on Hesychasm that did not require withdrawing into the wilderness. Under Nicephorus, Theoleptus learned a profound silence and spiritual vigilance brought about by fixing the eyes on the middle of the body, controlled breathing, and concentrating on a litany known as the "Jesus prayer." These disciplines elevated the mind from the world and human passions and were believed to result in an intuition of God in the form of light. Theoleptus's writings on Hesychasm exerted a profound influence on the fourteenth century Hesychast and contemplative Saint Gregory Palamas (1296-1359). Theoleptus remained at Mount Athos, first as a student and later as a spiritual teacher, for ten years, and his reputation grew throughout the Byzantine world.

With the 1282 accession of Andronicus II Palaeologus as Eastern Roman emperor and of Gregory II Cyprius (1241-1290) in 1283 as patriarch of Constantinople, the antiunionists among the Greeks once again gained ascendancy. To Theoleptus's satisfaction, the Council of Lyon' decrees and union with the West were repudiated. Because of his earlier opposition to reunion and his reputation as a spiritual leader at Mount Athos, Theoleptus was made archbishop of Philadelphia in 1285. Philadelphia, in southeastern Asia Minor, eighty miles east of the port city of Smyrna (now İzmir), had been Christian since apostolic times. It was the titular see of the province of Lydia, but during the fourteenth century its jurisdiction came to extend over other neighboring sees as well. Theoleptus would be the spiritual leader here for at least thirty-five years, until his death; he did, however, frequently depart to spend long periods in Constantinople.

As archbishop of Philadelphia, Theoleptus was once again thrust into controversy. He wrote a blistering attack against the Orthodox clergy who had followed the unionist patriarch John XI Becchus. He even turned on the new patriarch, Gregory II. Gregory actually had wanted unity, but without a complete surrender to Western doctrines. In opposition to the Western *Filioque* doctrine—that the Holy Spirit proceeds from the Father and the Son—the Orthodox followed Photius's teaching regarding the "eternal progression" of the Holy Spirit from the Father alone and the "emission in time" by the Son.

Gregory, seeing a need for delineating a clearer, more permanent relationship between the Father and the Son, attempted a compromise. In a tome written in 1285, Gregory proposed the "eternal manifestation" of the Spirit by the Son. After the publication of this treatise, Theoleptus and many other Orthodox clergy refused to mention Gregory's name during the enactment of the liturgy; later, however, Theoleptus pronounced Gregory orthodox, after the latter disavowed certain passages in the 1285 tome. Nevertheless, Gregory ultimately pleased no one; he came to be denounced by unionists and antiunionists alike, including Theoleptus, whose renewed attack was instrumental in persuading the emperor and a church synod to remove Gregory from the office of patriarch in 1289.

In 1303, Theoleptus reportedly helped to rally the residents of Philadelphia against a Turkish siege of the city, at a time when many bishops were deserting their sees because of the Turkish threat. The city would change hands many times between the eleventh and fourteenth centuries, succumbing permanently to the Turks—under Sultan Bayezid I's leadership (r. 1389-1402)—in 1390; at that time, it was renamed Alasehir.

On the death in 1308 of John Palaeologus, son of Emperor Andronicus II, Theoleptus became spiritual adviser to his widow, the empress Irene, daughter of Nicephorus Chumnus. Widowed at sixteen, after four years of marriage, she entered a convent in Constantinople under the name Eulogia. Theoleptus was the spiritual director of this convent and also of an adjacent monastery. In about 1320, Eulogia's parents requested of Theoleptus that they be allowed to be near their daughter. Nicephorus Chumnus was permitted to enter the monastery, and her mother joined Eulogia's convent. Not long afterward, Theoleptus died, and it was Nicephorus who presented the funeral oration, which has been preserved as a valuable summary of Theoleptus's life. A generation after Theoleptus's death, Eulogia would take part in theological controversies against Gregory Palamas.

In his final years, Theoleptus is supposed to have skillfully defended Hesychasm against the attacks of one its most virulent critics, Barlaam the Calabrian (c. 1290-c. 1350), a pro-Western Italo-Greek monk, theologian, and bishop. Because Barlaam first appeared as a teacher at the Imperial University in Constantinople in 1326, many believe that Theoleptus lived until that year. According to Nicephorus Chumnas, however, Theoleptus died shortly after 1320. In any case, Barlaam ridiculed Hesychasm, calling its practitioners *omphalopsychoi* (men with their souls in their navels). The written and oral debates of Barlaam with the monks of Mount Athos after the death of Theoleptus (in the 1330's and 1340's) actually helped bring Hesychasm into prominence.

SIGNIFICANCE

Centuries before the Reformation, the most serious division in the medieval Church was the one that separated the church of Rome from the church of Constantinople. Theoleptus of Philadelphia played a major role during the late thirteenth and early fourteenth centuries in opposing, reversing, and keeping reversed the reunion of the Roman Catholic and Greek Orthodox churches.

Despite the centuries of division, the Orthodox were much closer to Rome dogmatically than were the individualistic Protestant sects that arose later. Paradoxically, Theoleptus actually spent his life upholding sacramentalism and the ideal unity of the Christian Church. According to Theoleptus, Christ never intended anything less than one faith, one doctrine, and one Church, united under him. Theoleptus conceived of the monastic Hesychast life as having a prophetic mission to benefit the whole world, not merely as a means of individual salvation.

Theoleptus was a dynamic religious writer and orator, a charismatic teacher and spiritual leader, and a composer of hymns. Almost all of his works remain unedited. Despite his importance, his name is rarely mentioned even in histories of the Eastern (Byzantine) Empire or of the Greek Orthodox church. Scholars in the English-speaking world would do well to give attention to this influential teacher.

—*John J. Hunt*

FURTHER READING

Geanakoplos, Deno John. *Emperor Michael Palaeologus and the West, 1258-1282: A Study in Byzantine-Latin Relations.* 1959. Reprint. Hamden, Conn.: Archon Books, 1973. A helpful work on the character of the Eastern emperor who sought reunion with the West. Chapter 2, "The Ecclesiastical Union of Lyons," contains an excellent summary of East-West differences, although it does not mention Theoleptus. Well annotated and indexed, good bibliography.

Hero, Angela Constantinides, ed. *The Life and Letters of Theoleptos of Philadelphia.* Brookline, Mass.: Hellenic College Press, 1994. Surveys Theoleptus's significant work toward the spiritual formation of the Eastern Orthodox church. Also discusses Empress Irene. Greek text with English translation and commentary. Bibliography, index.

Hughes, Philip. *The Church in Crisis: A History of the General Councils, 325-1870.* Garden City, N.Y.: Hanover House, 1961. While it does not contain information on Theoleptus, this work is a clear and concise description of the important Second General Council of Lyon in 1274, which reunited the Latin West and Orthodox East after more than two centuries of division. It was his repudiation of this council that gave Theoleptus historical importance. Bibliography, index.

Le Guillou, M. J. *The Spirit of Eastern Orthodoxy.* Translated by Donald Attwater. New York: Hawthorn, 1962. This concise monograph introduces the reader to the "church outside the Church," that is, the Byzantine (Orthodox) heritage in Christendom. Chapters 7 and 8 focus on the estrangement between Rome and the Orthodox churches of the East, concentrating on the two largest churches, the Greek and Russian Orthodox. Select bibliography.

Meyendorff, John. *A Study of Gregory Palamas.* Translated by George Lawrence. 1964. Reprint. Crestwood, N.Y.: St. Vladimir's Seminary Press, 1998. This work centers on the renowned contemplative Gregory Palamas, who was influenced by Theoleptus in the practice of Hesychasm and who was a spokesman for conservative Orthodoxy. There are numerous references to Theoleptus but only about four or five total pages of information on him, which appear mostly in chapter 1. Brief bibliography and an index.

Pavlikianov, Cyril. *The Medieval Aristocracy on Mount Athos: The Philological and Documentary Evidence for the Activity of Byzantine, Georgian, and Slav Aristocrats and Eminent Churchmen in the Monasteries of Mount Athos from the Tenth to the Fifteenth Century.* Sofia, Bulgaria: Center for Slavo-Byzantine Studies, 2001. A study of the literary and documentary evidence of the activities of the ruling elite of Mount Athos during Theoleptus's time.

Runciman, Steven. *The Great Church in Captivity: A Study of the Patriarchate of Constantinople from the Eve of the Turkish Conquest to the Greek War of Independence.* London: Cambridge University Press, 1968. Chapter 4, "The Church and the Churches," is an excellent description of the differences between Latin West and Greek East just before and during the time of Theoleptus, although Theoleptus himself is only briefly mentioned. Bibliography and thorough index.

Sinkewicz, Robert E., trans. *The Monastic Discourses: Theoleptos of Philadelphia.* Toronto: Pontifical Institute of Mediaeval Studies, 1992. A critical examination of Theoleptus's theological writings during his monastic life. English and Greek text on facing pages. Bibliography, index.

SEE ALSO: ʿAbd al-Malik; Charlemagne; John of Damascus; Theophanes the Confessor.

RELATED ARTICLES in *Great Events from History: The Middle Ages, 477-1453*: 532-537: Building of Hagia Sophia; 726-843: Iconoclastic Controversy; 963: Foundation of the Mount Athos Monasteries; 1054: Beginning of the Rome-Constantinople Schism; 1204: Knights of the Fourth Crusade Capture Constantinople; 1248-1254: Failure of the Seventh Crusade.

THEOPHANES THE CONFESSOR
Byzantine historian, scholar, and monk

Theophanes the Confessor was a historian and monk whose chronicle, Chronographia, *is for modern scholars the main source for the history of the Byzantine Empire from about 600 to 813.*

BORN: c. 752; Constantinople, Byzantine Empire (now Istanbul, Turkey)
DIED: c. 818; island of Samothrace, Greece
AREAS OF ACHIEVEMENT: Historiography, monasticism

EARLY LIFE

Theophanes (thee-AHF-uh-neez) was born to a wealthy family. At the time of his birth, the Byzantine Empire was mired in what is now called the Iconoclastic Controversy. The iconoclasts were Christians who believed that all religious art was idolatry and therefore should be destroyed. (The characteristic religious artform of East Christian churches is the icon, hence the name iconoclasts, or icon breakers.) Those who defended the use of religious art were called iconodules (icon servers) or iconophiles (icon lovers). At the time of Theophanes' birth, the imperial government was sympathetic to the iconoclasts, and iconophiles were being persecuted. Theophanes' parents were secret iconophiles. As he grew up, Theophanes followed their lead in concealing his iconophile sympathies; as a result, he held a number of government posts under Emperor Constantine V Copronymus (r. 741-775). After Constantine's death, government policy changed; iconoclasm ceased to enjoy official support. Theophanes could now openly reveal his iconophilism. He became a monk and founded a monastery near Constantinople, the capital of the Eastern Roman Empire.

LIFE'S WORK

Theophanes' importance lies principally in his authorship of *Chronographia* (c. 810-815), a chronicle covering the history of the Eastern Roman Empire to August, 813. Theophanes undertook this project at the suggestion of a friend, George Syncellus. George had written a chronicle that began with the creation of the world and continued through the beginning of the reign of the Roman emperor Diocletian (r. 284-305). When he learned that he was dying, George requested that Theophanes complete the chronicle down to their own day, and Theophanes agreed.

The *Chronographia* is marred by Theophanes' extremely negative depiction of people with views other than his own. He disliked Muslims and hated iconoclasts. His attitude toward the iconoclasts is understandable, for he and his family had suffered under their rule. Still, two of the most important iconoclastic emperors, Leo III (r. 717-741) and Constantine V, had been mighty generals who won great victories over the Arabs, Bulgars, and Slavs. The empire owed its survival to them.

Theophanes also made some errors in the chronology of his *Chronographia*. Today, virtually the entire world uses the Christian or common era system of dating, which dates everything before or after the approximate year Jesus Christ was born. In Theophanes' time, this system was just coming into use, and he used it only occasionally and incorrectly, because he was not completely familiar with it. Eastern Christians and Jews most often used the *annus mundi* system (dating things from the year of the Creation), a system Jews still employ for religious purposes. In addition to the *annus mundi*, Theophanes dated events by the indiction, a fifteen-year cycle originally used by the imperial government for reassessment of property for tax purposes. From September, 610 (the Byzantine year began on September 1), through August, 773, except for the years between 715 and 725, Theophanes' *annus mundi* and the indiction were one year out of synchronization.

Yet another major problem with the *Chronographia* lies in its format. A chronicle is not a true history, but rather a year-by-year record of events. Because of its structure, a chronicle cannot give a proper account of events such as long wars that stretch over more than one year. A great Roman historian, Cornelius Tacitus, deliberately used a modified chronicle format for one of his books, *Ab excessu divi Augusti* (c. 116; *Annals*, 1793). In general, however, sophisticated historians avoid writing chronicles.

Theophanes, however, was neither sophisticated nor well educated. He lived in a time when the Byzantine Empire was fighting for its very life on three fronts. In the East, it was engaged in a great struggle with Muslim Arabs, who had already wrested Syria, Palestine, and North Africa (including Egypt) from the empire. In 717, the Arabs had besieged Constantinople with a huge army and fleet. This attack endangered the existence not only of the Eastern Roman Empire but indeed of Western civilization itself, for if the capital had fallen, the Arabs would have swept on into Europe. Emperor Leo III, however, managed to turn back the Arab armies and fleets. In the last year of his reign, he inflicted a second humiliating defeat on the Arabs at Acroïnum, deep in Asia Minor (now eastern Turkey). The second threat to the Byzantines came from the Balkan peninsula. There, a people known as the Bulgars (ancestors of the modern Bulgarians) had seized much territory and were making their way toward Constantinople. Leo's son, Constantine V, fought several wars with the Bulgars and eventually brought them to a standstill. Other barbarian tribes, mostly Slavs, were also roaming about the Balkans, causing considerable damage. Finally, there was occasional warfare in Italy, the original homeland of the Romans, where the empire still had a few outposts, mostly in the south.

These terrible wars caused many changes in the Byzantine Empire. For example, in 600, the empire had been dominated by large estates called *latifundia*. Worked by slaves or tenant farmers, each estate grew one or two crops which were then sold on the open market for cash. By 800, however, the *latifundia* seem to have largely disappeared; by then, the agricultural scene was characterized by small family farms. Moreover, many cities disappeared, and the populations of those that survived declined. Finally, because the constant wars were a severe drain on the empire's resources, most schools closed and intellectual activity came to an almost complete halt. Thus, although Theophanes' parents could afford the best possible education for their son, he was not well trained by the standards of two centuries before or a century after his own day, when the empire was stronger and there were more schools.

Theophanes' work was used by all later Byzantine historians. Years after Theophanes died, his work was continued by a group of writers who are collectively known as Theophanes Continuatus (the Continuator of Theophanes); these writers were better historians than Theophanes himself. By the end of the ninth century, the empire had grown much stronger; schools reopened, and learning once again began to flourish. About fifty years after Theophanes died, the *Chronographia* was translated into Latin by Anastasius, a librarian who was one of the few Western scholars at the time to know Greek. As a result, Theophanes' work influenced not only the historians of the later Byzantine or Eastern Roman Empire but those of medieval Western Europe as well, for Latin was the language of all educated Western Europeans in the Middle Ages.

Theophanes' later life was not happy. After 800, iconoclasm revived briefly. Emperor Leo V (r. 813-820), one of the last of the iconoclastic rulers, exiled Theophanes because of his position regarding icons. Already in poor health, Theophanes died in exile on the Aegean island of Samothrace around the year 818, probably of some kind of kidney disease. Theophanes is revered as a saint by both the Roman Catholic and the Greek Orthodox churches.

SIGNIFICANCE

Today, many historians call the period from about 600 to 800 the Dark Age of the Eastern Roman Empire. Few Greek sources survive from this period. Therefore, scholars must frequently use the writings of Arab historians to piece together the story of what was happening in the Eastern Roman Empire at this time. Theophanes' *Chronographia* is thus a precious document, despite its many flaws. Without it, even less would be known about the Byzantine Empire during two centuries when it was undergoing profound political, social, economic, and cultural changes as a result of the wars it fought. Even the Latin translation of the *Chronographia* by Anastasius is useful. Anastasius used manuscripts that are now lost; consequently, his translation of Theophanes' work contains a few scraps of information that are not included in extant Greek manuscripts of the work.

—*Martin Arbagi*

FURTHER READING

Guenther, Alan M. "The Christian Experience and Interpretation of the Early Muslim Conquest and Rule." *Islam and Christian Muslim Relations* 10, no. 3 (October, 1999). Examines the accounts of Islam and of Arab expansion by historians around the eighth century, including the chronicles of Theophanes.

Ostrogorsky, George. *History of the Byzantine State*. Translated by Joan Hussey. Rev. ed. New Brunswick, N.J.: Rutgers University Press, 1969. Chapters 2 and 3 are most important for those interested in Theophanes and his time. Each chapter starts with a section on the sources for the period covered by that chapter. Especially interesting comments on the chronological errors found in the *Chronographia*.

Theophanes. *The Chronicle of Theophanes Confessor: Byzantine and Near Eastern History, A.D. 284-813*. Translated by Cyril Mango and Roger Scott. New York: Oxford University Press, 1997. A translation that also provides an excellent introduction to Theophanes' *Chronographia*.

_______. *Chronographia: A Chronicle of Eighth Century Byzantium*. Translated by Anthony R. Santoro.

Gorham, Maine: Heathersfield Press, 1982. This translation includes only the entries from September, 717, to August, 803. Includes an excellent set of full-color maps.
Treadgold, Warren. *A History of the Byzantine State and Society*. Stanford, Calif.: Stanford University Press, 1997. A lucid depiction of political, military, cultural, and religious contexts for Theophanes' life and work.
Vasiliev, A. A. *History of the Byzantine Empire, 324-1453*. 2 vols. 2d rev. ed. Madison: University of Wisconsin Press, 1964. With extensive notes and bibliography, this account of the Eastern Roman state discusses political, dynastic, social, literary, scholarly, and artistic events and achievements.
Whittow, Mark. *The Making of Byzantium, 600-1025*. Berkeley: University of California Press, 1996. A history of the formation of the Byzantine Empire. Maps, bibliography, and index.

See also: Jean Froissart; Hārūn al-Rashīd; Saint Irene; Michael Psellus.

Related articles in *Great Events from History: The Middle Ages, 477-1453*: 630-711: Islam Expands Throughout North Africa; 637-657: Islam Expands Throughout the Middle East; April or May, 711: Ṭārik Crosses into Spain; 726-843: Iconoclastic Controversy; 786-809: Reign of Hārūn al-Rashīd; 1373-1410: Jean Froissart Compiles His *Chronicles*.

Thomas à Kempis

Dutch-German ecclesiastic and writer

Thomas is credited by most historians with writing The Imitation of Christ, *the most important piece of devotional literature produced by the late medieval pietistic movement called the* devotio moderna *and one of the most influential religious works in history. Some scholars claim that this work has been more widely read than any Christian work other than the Bible.*

Born: 1379; Kempen, the Rhineland (now in Germany)

Died: August 8, 1471; monastery of St. Agnietenberg, near Zwolle, Bishopric of Utrecht (now in The Netherlands)

Also known as: Thomas Hammerken; Thomas Hammerlein; Thomas Hemerken

Area of achievement: Religion and theology

Early Life

Thomas Hammerken of Kempen, better known as Thomas à Kempis (ah KEHM-puhs), was born in 1379 to a blacksmith named John Hemerken and his wife, Gertrude, who ran a school for children and apparently began her son's education. In 1392, at the age of thirteen, Thomas left his family to attend the chapter school in Deventer. That town was home to a number of the Brethren of the Common Life, followers of an ascetic religious movement known as the *devotio moderna* (modern devotion), founded between 1374 and 1384 by Gerhard Groote (1340-1384) and most prominent in Holland, the Rhineland, and central Germany. Thomas did not come to Deventer because of the movement, however, and—contrary to a common misconception—he never became a member of the Brethren. Still, he accepted the ideals of the *devotio moderna*, was befriended by Groote's successor, Florentius Radewyns (c. 1350-1400), and lived in a hostel that the Brethren owned. When he left the school in Deventer in 1399, on the verge of adulthood, he was well versed in Latin and knew some philosophy, though little of theology.

Thomas was reared at the end of the catastrophic fourteenth century, which brought to Europe famine, the Black Death (bubonic plague), economic disruption and decline, the Hundred Years' War (1337-1453), conflicts between inept monarchs and greedy aristocrats, and popular uprisings, such as the French Jacquerie and the English Peasants' Revolt. There were also disturbing problems within a church increasingly politicized during the Middle Ages. Its image suffered greatly between 1305 and 1376, when the Papacy was transplanted from Rome to Avignon and lay mired in corruption, and even more so when there ensued in 1378 a papal schism, with two rival (French and Italian) popes and then, from 1409 to 1417, three. Meanwhile, the upper clergy's wealth aroused criticism, while the reforming orders of recent centuries—the Cistercian monastics and the Dominican and Franciscan friars—had lost much of their original vitality. Disillusioned with ecclesiastics and demoralized by disasters that some attributed to God's wrath toward the Church, many Europeans clamored for reform or sought spiritual consolation outside ordinary avenues. Yet conciliarist reformers failed to replace the pope with a council, and the challenge that John Wyclif and Jan Hus posed to the Church's worldliness and to fundamental doctrines about revelation, the sacraments, and papal authority, the Church branded as heresy.

The *devotio moderna* avoided that stigma, despite its resemblance to an earlier generation of ascetic—and often heretical—spiritualists, the Beghards and Beguines. Its founder, Groote, the well-educated son of a wealthy cloth merchant, was loyal and orthodox. Following a serious illness in 1372, he lived for a time in a monastery near Arnhem belonging to the austere eremitic order of Carthusians, whose asceticism he adopted (although he did not become a monk). In 1374, he donated a house he had inherited in Deventer to a group of religious women who became known as the Sisters of the Common Life, and over the next decade a similar group of Brethren emerged. Both groups devoted themselves to a common life of poverty, chastity, and obedience, although they took no formal vows and belonged to no established order. In 1387, however, some adherents of the *devotio moderna* known as the Windesheim congregation adopted and rigorously observed the rule of the Augustinian canons. Thomas's older brother, John, became prior of St. Agnietenberg, one of the order's houses near Zwolle. In 1399, Thomas visited him there and became a monk, though he was not invested until 1406. Ordained a priest in 1413 or 1414, Thomas served unsuccessfully as procurator and subprior before moving on—with better results—to a career as a copyist, preacher, and writer of hymns and treatises. Aside from being exiled with his fellow monks to Ludingakerk from 1429 to 1431 and a brief stint in Mariaborn, he remained at St. Agnietenberg for the rest of his life.

Life's Work

As is illustrated above, the particulars of Thomas's long life (he died at the age of ninety-two) are well known, something that often cannot be said for much less obscure figures in medieval history. The only important exception is the mistaken notion that he was one of the Brethren, when in fact he was a monk for his entire adult life. Whereas a Brother or Sister of the Common Life might abandon with comparative ease the life of poverty, chastity, and obedience, Thomas's vows were formal and permanent, though in any case, he showed little inclination to return to the world once he had left it. Contemporary observers reveal that the adult Thomas, described as of medium build and dark complexion, was quiet by nature and most fond of reading, study, and contemplation. Indeed, the great value of a life of prayerful, meditative, monastic devotion is a theme found throughout his work. Even the limited involvement of the Brothers and Sisters of the Common Life in the ordinary world—which must have seemed particularly wicked to a monk living at the end of the fourteenth century and the beginning of the fifteenth—was more than Thomas wanted.

Given that the basic facts about Thomas's life are clear, it is ironic that the most important part of his life's work—his authorship of *Imitatio Christi* (c. 1427; *The Imitation of Christ*, c. 1460-1530)— is the one most subject to doubt and controversy. Ever since the fifteenth century, there have been those who question whether Thomas is, in fact, the author of *The Imitation of Christ*. His authorship is accepted by the late R. R. Post in *The Modern Devotion: Confrontation with Reformation and*

Thomas à Kempis. (Hulton|Archive at Getty Images)

Humanism (1968), generally considered the definitive work on the *devotio moderna*. Post notes, however, that claims have been made on behalf of a number of writers, often along essentially nationalistic lines. For a long time many French scholars favored Jean de Gerson (also known as Jean Charlier), the reform-minded chancellor of the University of Paris at the beginning of the fourteenth century, although by the twentieth century such claims had diminished. A number of Italians have suggested Giovanni Gersen (whose name, Post observes, is suspiciously like Jean de Gerson's); it is impossible, however, to prove even the existence of this man, who was supposedly abbot of Santo Stefano, a Benedictine monastery in Vercelli in northern Italy. The Belgians, Dutch, and Germans have generally accepted that Thomas wrote *The Imitation of Christ*, but a vocal minority has given credit instead to the founder of the *devotio moderna*, Gerhard Groote. Since the 1920's the application of textual criticism has given renewed vigor to the debate, with various scholars supporting Groote, Giovanni Gersen, and Gerard Zerbolt (one of the Brethren associated with Radewyns in Deventer), although Thomas is still the most commonly accepted author.

Thomas was in any case quite a prolific writer, producing biographies of Groote, Radewyns, and other important figures in the *devotio moderna*, as well as a number of devotional works—although none of the others was of the quality of *The Imitation of Christ*. In fact, it is the obvious superiority of the latter that has led some to doubt that Thomas wrote it, while his extensive work as a copyist has been used to suggest that he merely transcribed someone else's book (even a manuscript dated to 1441, written in Thomas's own hand and containing *The Imitation of Christ* and nine other treatises, is unsigned). It is doubtful whether the question will ever be settled to everyone's satisfaction. Yet regardless of the controversy about the author's identity, it is the attribution of *The Imitation of Christ* to Thomas that has lifted him out of obscurity, and—more generally—it is that work which has made the *devotio moderna* as influential as it has been since the fourteenth century. Thus, if Thomas's authorship is accepted—as it is here—*The Imitation of Christ* must be treated as the centerpiece of his life's work. (Conversely, if his authorship should ever be decisively disproved, Thomas's other work will merit considerably less attention from historians.)

The Imitation of Christ is actually not one treatise, but four, the first of which appeared no later than 1424, while all were completed by 1427. Thomas evidently never intended that the four treatises be seen as a unit, and indeed, in the century after their appearance, they were not always found together or in the same order as in more recent editions. Yet despite some differences among the four—and especially between the first three and the fourth—the treatises have several elements in common. As Post notes, all were written for monastics who shared Thomas's contemplative lifestyle, a rather narrow group. Thus it was not the author's purpose to address the concerns of the general populace, of adherents of the *devotio moderna* as a whole, of the secular clergy, or even of all the regular clergy (monks and nuns). That is not to suggest, however, that Thomas dealt with matters unfamiliar to other monastics or followers of the *devotio moderna* or that what he had to say could not be appreciated outside his small intended audience. In fact, notwithstanding his exhortation to despise the things of the world, Thomas's urgings that men seek comfort, consolation, and security in the love of God, the friendship of Jesus, and a turning to the inner self, or spirit, struck a responsive chord among many of his contemporaries living in the world, as they have for subsequent generations.

A common "weakness" of the treatises is that the author gives them almost no theological foundation: These are not learned works. Yet this unscholarly quality, at the same time, is one of the strengths of *The Imitation of Christ*, for it is the simplicity of Thomas's explication of Christian virtues and practices that has attracted so many readers to his work. In the sometimes frightening conditions of the fifteenth century, Thomas's straightforward, inspirational prose met the needs of many individual believers much more immediately and directly than the complex arguments of theologians or even the Latin liturgy of the local parish church, which they might understand only partially. All the treatises, particularly the first three, encourage the *contemptus mundi* (contempt for the world) associated with traditional medieval monasticism, in which the regular clergy sought to escape the temptations and sinfulness of the world by living in isolation from it. Yet while the monastic life was not an option that most of Thomas's contemporaries considered, a significant number shared his disdain for the vanities of the world, while his emphasis on remaining pure in heart is one of the central ideals of Christianity, in or out of the monastery. Another pervasive characteristic of the treatises is Thomas's disregard for secular learning, which at times seems rather anti-intellectual (although he encourages respect for the "wise").

The first treatise admonishes its readers to lead a more spiritual life by reading the Bible, the church fathers, and other holy works, by praying and meditating, by being humble in the presence of greater wisdom and obedient to authority, and by contemplating the life and holy sacrifice of Christ, as well as the reader's own life, sinful nature, and impending judgment by God. In the second treatise, Thomas concentrates on the inner life—self-examination and self-knowledge, being at peace with oneself and accepting life's adversity, seeking the friendship of Christ and the comfort of God, and willingly following the way of the Cross. The longer third treatise stresses disregard of worldly desires, temporal honor, and the opinions of men, while emphasizing the need to accept humbly God's will and Christ's example, trusting not one's own wisdom and virtue. Unlike the first three treatises, the fourth deals explicitly with sacramental life, focusing on the Eucharist, the sacrament most frequently received by all medieval Christians (some weekly or even daily) and by no means limited in importance to monastics alone.

SIGNIFICANCE

The overall significance of the *devotio moderna* outside its own age has been much debated. Post contends that its impact on Christian Humanism and the Reformation was at most very slight. Yet while Post's account of the *devotio moderna* is considered to be in most respects the ultimate authority, other historians have discerned a substantially greater degree of influence on such figures of the Reformation era as the Christian Humanist Desiderius Erasmus and the first great Protestant reformer, Martin Luther. Nor does it seem mere coincidence that pietism, asceticism, and mysticism of the type espoused by Thomas à Kempis and the Brethren remained characteristic of religious movements in the Low Countries and Germany, the heartland of the *devotio moderna*, during the Reformation and even into the Enlightenment. (Thomas and other followers of the *devotio moderna*, however, did not aspire to the ecstatic union with God sought by some late medieval and early modern mystics.)

Much more apparent, however, and thus less controversial, is the continuing importance of *The Imitation of Christ* from the fifteenth century onward. It is still widely read by Catholics and Protestants alike and is one of the most important devotional works available to modern readers. The translation of the entire work into English took some time. The first English version, done by an anonymous translator in 1460, and the first English edition, produced in 1502 by William Atkinson of the University of Cambridge, included only the first three books. The fourth was finally rendered in English in 1503 by, interestingly enough, Margaret Beaufort, the mother of the English king Henry VII (who reigned from 1485 to 1509). Thereafter, there were numerous editions containing all four treatises, the most important being that compiled in 1530 by Richard Whitford of Queens' College, Cambridge. This edition enjoys much the same status with regard to others in English as the King James Version of the Bible does relative to later English translations of the Scriptures. Like the King James Bible, it is thought to have been so widely read as to have had a formative influence on the modern English language. There have, however, been many other English versions of *The Imitation of Christ* in print in modern times, a testimony to the book's continuing significance.

The Imitation of Christ has been translated into many languages; in fact, the bulk of scholarship that it has generated is found in non-English works (notably French, German, and Italian). Regardless of what tongue is spoken by its readers, the continuing popularity of this work is remarkable. Although written by a comparatively obscure adherent of a religious movement smaller and less organized than many others in the late medieval and early modern period, and directed not to Christian society as a whole or even all monastics but limiting its intended audience to monks whose lifestyle was primarily contemplative, it remains relevant to generation after generation. The work of Thomas à Kempis thus surpasses in longevity not only that of Gerhard Groote and Florentius Radewyns but also that of more famous figures of medieval Christianity.

—*William B. Robison*

FURTHER READING

Creasy, William C. Introduction to *The Imitation of Christ*, by Thomas à Kempis. Macon, Ga.: Mercer University Press, 1989. Creasy provides a useful introduction to his modern translation of Thomas's most famous work, reminding readers that the intellectual life was not an invention of the modern age and tracing Thomas's influence on later theologians and devotional writers.

Grendler, Paul. "Form and Function in Italian Renaissance Popular Books." *Renaissance Quarterly* 46, no. 3 (Autumn, 1993): 451ff. Seeking what made popular literature popular, Grendler compares the content and audience of four fifteenth and sixteenth century works, including Thomas's *The Imitiation of Christ*.

Hyma, Albert. *The Christian Renaissance: A History of the "Devotio Moderna."* 1924. Reprint. Hamden, Conn.: Archon Books, 1965. Unique among English-language works in that it rejects Thomas as author of

The Imitation of Christ in favor of Zerbolt. It asserts perhaps more strongly than any work in any language that the *devotio moderna* was the source of all religious reform in the sixteenth century, whether manifested in Christian Humanism, Protestantism, or the Catholic Reformation.

Montmorency, J. E. G. de. *Thomas à Kempis: His Age and Book*. New York: G. P. Putnam's Sons, 1906. Reprint. Port Washington, N.Y.: Kennikat Press, 1970. A still-useful English-language biography of Thomas. Places Thomas and the *devotio moderna* in a wider historical framework, taking into account the very uneasy time in which both emerged. Montmorency examines the debate about authorship up to the beginning of the twentieth century, although he prematurely declares it at an end—with Thomas the author. He also discusses in detail the structure of *The Imitation of Christ* and examines its content in the context of medieval Christianity as a whole.

Oakley, Francis. *The Western Church in the Later Middle Ages*. Ithaca, N.Y.: Cornell University Press, 1978. Contains a chapter on modes of piety, which gives considerable attention to the *devotio moderna* and Thomas. This book is useful in relating both to other aspects of late medieval religious history, including the problem of order, doctrine and theology, heresy, reform movements, and spirituality. Oakley for the most part follows Post in his interpretation of the *devotio moderna* and Thomas's career.

Oberman, Heiko A. *Masters of the Reformation: The Emergence of a New Intellectual Climate in Europe*. Translated by Dennis D. Martin. New York: Cambridge University Press, 1981. Contains a chapter on the *devotio moderna*, although Oberman, unfortunately, has relatively little to say about Thomas and *The Imitation of Christ*. With regard to the impact of the movement and Thomas on the Reformation, Oberman accepts the position taken by Post that it was slight.

Ozment, Steven E., ed. *The Reformation in Medieval Perspective*. Chicago: Quadrangle Books, 1971. Although not concerned primarily with Thomas or the *devotio moderna* as a whole, this book nevertheless examines the connection between late medieval reform movements and the Reformation, giving some attention to the influence of Thomas on subsequent reformers. Some of the authors featured here—Gerhard Ritter, Bernd Moeller, and so on—see a greater influence than Post, who is also represented in this collection.

Post, R. R. *The Modern Devotion: Confrontation with Reformation and Humanism*. Leiden, Netherlands: E. J. Brill, 1968. The essential English-language work on the *devotio moderna* and Thomas, all the more important because it discusses in considerable detail the very extensive non-English scholarly literature on both subjects and thus deals comprehensively with the controversies about the movement's influence on the Reformation and the authorship of *The Imitation of Christ*. Although he regards Thomas as the most likely author, Post examines in depth the earlier attempts to give credit for the work to Jean de Gerson, Giovanni Gersen, and Groote, as well as more recent scholarship. Devotes only one chapter to Thomas, but makes reference to his work in discussing various aspects of the *devotio moderna* and offers very valuable commentary on *The Imitation of Christ*.

See also: Jan Hus; John Wyclif.

Related articles in *Great Events from History: The Middle Ages, 477-1453*: 1305-1417: Avignon Papacy and the Great Schism; 1377-1378: Condemnation of John Wyclif; 1414-1418: Council of Constance; July 6, 1415: Martyrdom of Jan Hus.

Thomas Aquinas

Italian saint and philosopher

By adapting pagan philosophy as a handmaiden to Christian doctrine, Thomas created both a magisterial systematization of medieval Catholic faith and a philosophical system with implications for ethics, law, psychology, semantics, and the nature of reason itself.

Born: 1224 or 1225; Roccasecca, near Naples, Kingdom of Sicily (now in Italy)
Died: March 7, 1274; Fossanova, Latium, Papal States (now in Italy)
Also known as: Tommaso d'Aquino; Saint Thomas Aquinas; Doctor Communis; Doctor Angelicus
Areas of achievement: Religion and theology, philosophy

Early Life

Thomas Aquinas (uh-KWAY-nuhs), also known as Tommaso d'Aquino, was the youngest son of Count Landulf (Landolfo) of Aquino and his second wife, Donna Theodora of Naples, who was descended from Norman nobility. Landulf, along with his older sons, had been employed as a soldier by Emperor Frederick II to defend Sicily from the Papal States to the north. Thomas was born in the family castle near the old city of Aquino in 1224 or 1225 (the testimony from Thomas's first biographers is conflicting). When he was five, he was taken to the nearby Benedictine monastery of Monte Cassino; there he received his early religious instruction. Hostilities between Frederick II and the pope had calmed for the moment, and it is thought that Thomas's parents hoped that their son would one day become an abbot. The feudal system brought little prospect of family stability; perhaps Thomas's eventual clerical influence would provide for the future.

The emperor was excommunicated in 1239. In return, he threatened Monte Cassino; most of the monks there were sent into exile. That year, Thomas returned to his parents, who sent him to the *studium generale* (later to become the university) in Naples, a school that had been founded by the emperor in 1224 to compete with similar church institutions. Frederick welcomed the introduction of Islamic as well as Christian scholarship into his university. Thomas's studies included logic, grammar, natural philosophy, and metaphysics, and it was probably at Naples that he began his first serious study of Aristotle. Portions of Aristotle's works were being translated from the Greek, making their way into the Latin West often accompanied by interpretations of Arabic scholars, most notably the twelfth century Islamic philosopher Averroës.

It was an age of ferment: Intellectually, the new learning, especially Aristotle's teaching on the eternity of the world, threatened Christian doctrine. Politically and militarily, with the continued clash of secular and ecclesiastical powers, the old feudal order was coming to an end.

At Naples, Thomas was drawn to the Order of Preachers, the Dominicans, founded in France in 1216 by Saint Dominic. The Dominicans taught obedience and poverty (and thus the begging of alms), as did the Franciscan order (founded by Saint Francis of Assisi less than a decade earlier), but the Dominicans also put special emphasis on the life of study, preaching, and teaching. The order penetrated many of the universities of Western Europe, opening study houses devoted to theology and philosophy. Though reared to appreciate the Benedictine cycle of prayer, worship, sleep, and manual labor, Thomas found the new order better suited to his temperament.

His decision to join the Dominicans in 1244 was not without controversy. His mother, now a widow, persuaded Thomas's older brothers to abduct and imprison him until he changed his mind. There is a story, perhaps based in fact, that when his brothers brought a prostitute into Thomas's cell to break his resolve, he picked up a burning stick from the fire and drove her from the room. Taken to Roccasecca, Thomas remained steadfast, and after about a year of detention, he was permitted by his family to join his Dominican brothers at the University of Paris in 1245. His novitiate was under the tutelage of the German Dominican theologian Saint Albertus Magnus.

An early biographer notes that in 1248 Thomas joined Albert in Cologne and a new *studium generale* there, where Thomas was often referred to as the "dumb ox." This sobriquet did not pertain to his intelligence, but to his massive physique: Though Thomas was a bit taller than his peers, he was corpulent, slow of movement, quiet, and often withdrawn. Yet Albert saw deeper; his mentor remarked that the bellowing of this ox would be heard throughout the world.

Life's Work

On Albert's recommendation, Thomas returned to the University of Paris in 1252 to prepare for his degree in theology. Not yet thirty years of age, Thomas would have little more than two decades of life remaining. In that time, he was to produce an enduring systematization of the Catholic faith, numerous commentaries on the works of Aristotle, liturgical works, and polemical pieces.

Already he was discussing theological issues in public disputations and lecturing on the era's standard theological textbook, *Sententiarum libri IV* (1148-1151; *The Books of Opinions of Peter Lombard*, 1970; better known as *Sentences*) of Peter Lombard. The "sentences," or opinions, were collected from church fathers and medieval theologians and arranged by doctrines. Book 1, for example, treated God; book 2, the Fall of Man. Theology students, "bachelors of the Sentences," tried to harmonize the varying viewpoints and elucidate the fine points; nuance was everything. Thomas's own *Scriptum super "Libros sententiarum"* (1252-1256; English translation, 1923) joined more than a thousand other commentaries. The structure of Thomas's book was derived from the oral tradition of the public disputation. The master would employ his students in framing theological arguments, both pro and con, with debate sometimes lasting six or eight hours. The master then met in private with his students, analyzing the arguments and formulating a written version of the dispute. Many of Thomas's theological works are based on the form of the disputation and thus were not intended for lay audiences. In the multiplicity of distinctions and definitions, Thomas's writings exemplified a Scholastic style popular during the Middle Ages but stigmatized in later eras as hollow and pedantic.

Thomas Aquinas. (Library of Congress)

In 1256, Thomas obtained his license to teach theology at the university. For three years thereafter, he continued to lecture, primarily on the Gospel of Matthew, and to participate in public disputations. During this time, he began work on a theological guidebook for Dominican missionaries as they engaged in disputes with Muslims, Jews, and heretical Christians in North Africa and Spain. This treatise, the *Summa contra gentiles* (c. 1258-1264; English translation, 1923), was completed after he returned to Italy to lecture at the papal court in 1261. In 1265, he left Orvieto and Pope Urban IV for a two-year stay in Rome. While he was in Rome, teaching Dominican students, Thomas began his masterwork, *Summa theologiae* (c. 1265-1273; *Summa Theologica*, 1911-1921). He finished the first part, on God's existence and attributes, during his stay at the papal court of Clement IV in Viterbo, Italy, from 1267 to 1268. Here Thomas was apparently associated with William of Moerbeke, a Flemish Dominican who was working on more accurate translations of Aristotle than those that had come to the West via the Arabic. In 1268 or 1269, Thomas was sent back to the University of Paris for his second tenure as a professor—and found himself in the midst of a seething controversy.

Masters and students at the university had become fascinated not only with the speculative works of Aristotle but also with those of his Arab interpreter Averroës. Though at least nominally a Muslim, Averroës taught, contrary to Islam and certainly to Christianity, that there was a fundamental duality between reason and faith. That is, philosophy might conclude that the world existed from eternity (as Aristotle did), while faith might speak of Creation. Both assertions, though contradictory, would be "true" in their own realm. Averroës also brought into question the nature of the soul and, using Aristotle's writings, concluded that it was doubtful that each individual had a separate, immortal soul, as the Church taught. In 1266, the Latin Averroist Siger of Brabant had begun to popularize Averroës's understanding of Aristotle and to

MAJOR WORKS BY THOMAS AQUINAS

Date	*Work*
1252-1256	*Scriptum super "Libros sententiarum"*
c. 1258-1264	*Summa contra gentiles*
c. 1265-1273	*Summa theologiae*

attract disciples among the university's faculty. Thomas plunged into dispute with Siger, attempting to argue that Averroës had misinterpreted Aristotle on matters of the soul and that though the eternity of the world might be a reasonable conclusion of science, such a conclusion was not absolute. Faith supplemented or fulfilled reason (not contradicting it) by teaching the Creation.

Nevertheless, Thomas was caught in the middle. When radical Averroism was officially condemned in 1270, Thomas's own reliance on Aristotle's reasoning was also brought into question. Thomas was criticized by the followers of Saint Augustine's more mystical Platonism, who claimed that human reason had been hopelessly compromised in the Fall. Although Thomas condemned the doctrine of double truth (believing, apparently mistakenly, that Siger and others were teaching it), he did maintain that natural reason can discover certain fundamental theological truths by studying the effects of God's working in the universe—thus the celebrated five proofs for God's existence. Reason, however, can take humans only so far. Grace completes nature by revealing what cannot be learned from reason—for example, that God is Triune. There are not two truths here: Because God is responsible for both reason and revelation, the two can never be contradictory. Thomas sought to separate Aristotle from his heterodox interpreters but at the same time was forced to defend his own use of the philosopher.

In the first three years of his return to the University of Paris, Thomas finished both the first and second sections of part 2 of *Summa Theologica*, dealing with happiness, virtue, sin, law, and grace and, in the second section, with specific moral questions. It is said that Thomas sometimes employed four secretaries at a time to take his dictation and that he would often dictate in his sleep. One story has Thomas sitting next to King Louis IX at a banquet. Completely forgetting himself, Thomas lifted his head from a trance, banged his hand on the table, and called for his secretary to dictate some prize answer to Christian heretics.

In 1272, Thomas returned to Naples to set up a Dominican study house at the university there. His attention was also given to completing part 3 of the *Summa Theologica*, on the person and work of Christ. Yet on December 6, 1273, three months before his death, he put aside his writing, explaining that all he had written seemed as straw and that he could not continue. It is not known whether Thomas suffered a stroke or received a mystical vision or whether his faculties simply collapsed as a result of overwork. In 1274, he was summoned to attend a church council at Lyon. In poor health to begin with, he found himself unable to complete his journey after he struck his head on a tree or branch that had fallen in the road. He stopped at his niece's castle near Fossanova; a few weeks later, he was taken to the nearby Cistercian monastery, where he died on March 7, 1274.

Though Thomas never completed the *Summa Theologica*, a supplement drawn from his earlier work was added to round out the presentation. In its two million words, the *Summa Theologica* contains more than five hundred questions, twenty-six hundred articles, and ten thousand objections and replies. The prolific Thomas had produced more than one hundred other works as well.

Though in 1277 an official church body in Paris condemned some 219 theological propositions that included twelve held by Thomas, by 1319, inquiries had begun concerning Thomas's possible canonization. Thomas Aquinas was canonized a saint in 1323 (the Paris condemnation concerning his teachings was canceled in 1325), and in 1567, he was named doctor of the Church, his works sanctioned as a repository of orthodoxy.

SIGNIFICANCE

For the Roman Catholic Church, the thirteenth century was a time of synthesis. The writings of Aristotle and other ancients posed a new challenge to the Christian tradition, as did the influx of teachings from the Muslim world. It was the abiding passion of Thomas's life to integrate faith and reason, exploring systematically the teachings of the Church by taking natural reason as far as it might go and supplementing it with the reasonableness of revelation. To him, the Christian faith was both reasonable and rationally defensible.

Aristotle supplied many of the categories by which the nature and content of theology might be profitably organized. The philosopher maintained that the world was purposive, and Thomas adopted this idea of a final cause. Thomas also used Aristotle's conception of matter and form, and act and potentiality, in formulating his *Summa Theologica*. Moreover, although Thomas disputed with the Augustinians, he also adapted Neoplatonism for his purposes, much as he did Aristotelianism. Creation was ordered in a kind of chain of being, with humans occupying a unique place, sharing earthly existence with other creatures but also possessing the capacity of receiving the vision of God after death and thus complete happiness. Critics have called the *Summa Theologica* the capstone of passionless Scholasticism, the last gasp of medieval society in its effort to hold the world together by outmoded categories. Others have called Thomas an elitist who preferred order to freedom, citing his description of women as naturally inferior to men, his preference for monarchy, and his attitude toward Jews as examples of his outmoded beliefs. In response, twentieth century Thomists have attempted to demonstrate that certain historically conditioned positions should not invalidate Thomas's method or his insights and that Thomistic thought can be modified in favor of freedom, human rights, and democracy. Through Jacques Maritain in France and Mortimer Adler in the United States, generations of intellectuals have been introduced to the thought of Thomas Aquinas. Thomas's influence in theology has diminished since the Catholic Church ceased to promulgate Thomism after the Second Vatican Council ended in 1965; yet his contribution to philosophy as an interpreter of Aristotle continues to be widely recognized.

—*Dan Barnett*

Further Reading

Davies, Brian. *Aquinas*. New York: Continuum, 2002. A biography of Thomas Aquinas that covers his approaches to God, theories of being and existence, and his views of the problems of evil, among other topics. Bibliography and index.

_______, ed. *Thomas Aquinas: Contemporary Philosophical Perspectives*. A collection of essays on the philosphy of Thomas Aquinas. Includes essays on matter and actuality, realism, natural reason, freedom, and being and goodness. Bibliography.

Finnis, John. *Aquinas: Moral, Political, and Legal Theory.* New York: Oxford University Press, 1998. An examination of Thomas's contributions to political and social science. Looks at the saint's views on freedom, reason, and human goods; human rights; fulfilment and morality; the state; and humans' origin and end. Bibliography and indexes.

Gilson, Étienne. *Thomism: The Philosophy of Saint Thomas Aquinas*. Translated by L. K. Shook and Armand Maurer. 6th ed. Toronto: Pontifical Institute of Mediaeval Studies, 2002. A classic and scholarly treatment of Thomas as philosopher and theologian. Chapters fall under the headings of God, Nature, and Morality. The book contains a comprehensive bibliography of Thomas's works with descriptive details.

Kreeft, Peter. *A Summa of the Summa: The Essential Philosophical Passages of Saint Thomas Aquinas' "Summa Theologica."* San Francisco: Ignatius Press, 1990. An explanation of the philosophy of Thomas's *Summa Theologica*. Index.

Kretzmann, Norman, and Eleonore Stump, eds. *The Cambridge Companion to Aquinas*. New York: Cambridge University Press, 1993. Topics covered include Thomas's philosophy, his relation to Aristotle and Jewish and Islamic thinkers, philosophy of mind, ethics, law and politics, and biblical commentary and philosophy. Bibliography and index.

Nichols, Aidan. *Discovering Aquinas: An Introduction to His Life, Work, and Influence*. Grand Rapids, Mich.: William B. Eerdmans Publishing, 2003. A biography of Thomas Aquinas that looks at his life and work as well as his legacy. Index.

Pasnau, Robert, and Christopher Shields. *The Philosophy of Aquinas*. Boulder, Colo.: Westview Press, 2004. A study of Thomas that concentrates on his contributions to the field of philosophy. Index.

Stump, Eleonore. *Aquinas*. New York: Routledge, 2003. A look at the philosophy of Thomas by a well-known scholar.

See also: Saint Albertus Magnus; Alexander III; Saint Anselm; Averroës; Avicenna; Saint Bonaventure; Saint Dominic; John Duns Scotus; Gregory the Great; Louis IX; Andrea Orcagna; John Pecham; Raymond of Peñafort; Siger of Brabant; Vincent of Beauvais; William of Auvergne; William of Moerbeke; William of Saint-Amour.

Related articles in *Great Events from History: The Middle Ages, 477-1453*: 1100-1300: European Universities Emerge; c. 1150: Moors Transmit Classical Philosophy and Medicine to Europe; c. 1250-1300: Homosexuality Criminalized and Subject to Death Penalty; c. 1265-1273: Thomas Aquinas Compiles the *Summa Theologica*; November 18, 1302: Boniface VIII Issues the Bull *Unam Sanctam*; c. 1310-1350: William of Ockham Attacks Thomist Ideas.

Trotula
Italian physician and writer

Author of a respected treatise on women's disease and childbirth, Trotula was influential in the field of women's medicine for nearly five hundred years.

Born: Eleventh century; place unknown
Died: c. 1097; Salerno (now in Italy)
Also known as: Trotula of Salerno; Trotula di Ruggiero (full name); Trota; Trocta
Area of achievement: Medicine

Early Life

For most of the twentieth century, the facts of the life of Trotula (TROT-yew-luh) seemed clear enough. Many scholars believed that Trotula lived in Salerno, Italy, in the eleventh century. Her full name was Trotula di Ruggiero, and her family was wealthy, but no other information was known about her birth and childhood. Salerno, the center of medical knowledge in medieval Europe, was the site of several world-famous hospitals and spas. The city also had the Western world's first medical school, which welcomed women as students and instructors. Trota, known as *magistra mulier sapiens* (wise woman teacher), was a physician and teacher there, specializing in women's health and childbirth. Her husband, John Platearius, was another physician at the school. They were the parents of two sons, Matteo or Mattias, who also studied medicine, and Johannes the Younger. Trotula was the author of several medical textbooks, alone and in collaboration with her husband.

Tracing the life history of medieval figures is always difficult, because few records were kept and fewer have survived to the present. Scholars have concluded that there was no factual evidence for what they thought they knew about Trotula, and the most significant details of her life came into question. There was a historical figure named Trotula di Ruggiero, but she may not have been the same Trotula or Trota who interests scholars of the history of medicine. Trota the medical practitioner may have been an illiterate though knowledgeable midwife, or a practicing physician and teacher. She may have been the first female professor of medicine, or one of many *mulieres saleritanae* (ladies of Salerno) teaching in the same period. There may not have been women studying and practicing in Salerno at all. Although many sources give 1097 as the year of Trotula's death, others say she was born in that year, and still others find no record. Most intriguingly, Trotula may have been a man—or may not have existed at all.

Life's Work

Interest in the historical figure of Trotula stems from several Italian manuscripts about medicine, gynecology, and obstetrics, attributed variously to Trotula, or Trocta, or Trota. The two most important of these manuscripts are *De passionibus mulierum ante, in, et post partum* (on the diseases of women before, during, and after childbirth), a compendium in sixty brief chapters of medical information pertaining to the special health issues of women, and *Practica secundum Trotam* (practical medicine according to Trotula), a larger work of a more general nature. Both appear to have been written during the late twelfth century or perhaps as late as the middle of the thirteenth. At this time, medicine in Italy flourished, in part because of an influx of learning from the Arab world, but was still greatly influenced by Christian conceptions of woman as the embodiment of Eve, and therefore fallen, weak, and shameful.

The manuscripts attributed to Trotula are collections of treatments for menstruation, conception, pregnancy, and childbirth in addition to medical advice of a more general kind, such as remedies to lighten freckles, treat snakebite, or cure bad breath. The author of *De passionibus mulierum* gathered much information that was commonly known at the time and also proposed some revolutionary ideas. For example, Trotula was unusual in claiming that some failures to conceive were caused by physical problems in men. Further, she advocated for the use of drugs to make labor less painful, in opposition to religious teaching that women were ordained to suffer through childbirth.

The manuscripts reveal that medieval medical knowledge contained a great deal of what would today be considered mere quackery, as well as advice that strikes people in the twenty-first century as sensible and modern. Typical of the first type is a treatment for a woman who is too fat to conceive: She should be anointed with cow dung mixed with wine and placed in a steam bath a few times a week. A powder made from the testicles of a pig, mixed with wine and drunk, will also guarantee conception. Midwives are instructed to say a specific prayer as they cut an umbilical cord and tie it off with a string from a stringed instrument. They must also take note that the length of a grown man's penis is directly proportional to the length of umbilical cord that was left attached when he was born. Worms may be lured out of a person's ears with a cored apple. Interestingly, Trotula explains month by month how a fetus develops and states that life begins during the eighth month.

Some of Trotula's advice is similar to that of the holistic healers practicing almost a thousand years later. She urges physicians to examine their patients thoroughly and to be good listeners. She recommends various herbs to calm nerves and ease pain, as well as exercise, a balanced diet, good hygiene, avoidance of stress, aromatic massage, and a cheerful outlook.

Instructions for a normal delivery are given, as well as contingency plans for breech birth and stillbirth. Trotula appears to be unique in explaining how to sew up perineal tears suffered in childbirth and also offers advice about avoiding the tearing. Several of the chapters discuss ways to bring on menstruation when it has stopped; presumably these are instructions for abortion. There is also advice for a woman who is no longer a virgin but who would like to appear as one, including various ways to tighten the vaginal muscles. She warns against the practice of rubbing ground glass on the vagina to produce a simulation of the blood of first intercourse.

The Trotula manuscripts were written in Latin, the language of science and learning in Europe in the eleventh and twelfth centuries. At that time, manuscripts were copied out by hand and translated and revised freely. Because the information in the manuscripts attributed to Trotula was considered complete and reliable, it was distributed widely. A collection called the *Trotula* became the standard work on medieval women's medicine; it consisted of three short works on conditions and treatments of women and on cosmetics. Dozens of medieval copies of these works are located today in libraries and special collections throughout Europe, some in Latin, and others in Dutch, French, Irish, English, and other languages. Many of these manuscripts give credit to Trota, or Trocta, as the source of the information; others have the title *Trotula* (Little Trota), from which an author's name is inferred.

The work is mentioned in many other writings from the late twelfth through the fifteenth centuries, and gradually the name Trota or Trotula entered the public consciousness as the most important source of information about women's medicine. One indication of Trotula's fame is found in Geoffrey Chaucer's *The Canterbury Tales* (1387-1400), in which a passing mention of medical advice from "Dame Trot" demonstrates that his audience could be expected to know the reference.

As the manuscript was copied and revised through the centuries, editors tended to make small notes explaining the source of the material. Gradually, a biography for the author evolved, based on imperfect knowledge and memory, and more works were attributed to her. Through the fourteenth, fifteenth, and most of the sixteenth centuries, Trotula's identity as a female medical specialist in Salerno was accepted without question. By the mid-1500's, however, it was no longer the case that women were allowed to study at universities or to practice medicine, and Trotula's identity came under question. With no biographical evidence beyond the fact that the author *must* have been a man, a parallel tradition grew up claiming that Trotula was the pseudonym of a male writer. At the end of the sixteenth century, editions of the *Trotula* gave the author's name as Eros, attributing the work to a man.

This compendium was thought for almost four hundred years to be the work of a single author—the woman Trotula or perhaps the man Eros—but is now acknowledged as three independent works by three authors. As demonstrated in 1985, only the middle section is in fact by Trotula, and this author may or may not be the same Trotula to whom other manuscripts are attributed.

SIGNIFICANCE

For four hundred or more years, the manuscripts attributed to Trotula represented the state of the art in gynecology and obstetrics in Europe. Copied in Latin and the common languages of several countries, these manuscripts were the standard reference works for midwives and physicians. Although the original manuscripts no longer exist, and their author or authors cannot be verified, and although much of the medicine described in the manuscripts has been supplanted with new knowledge and practice, the *Trotula* was the single most important collection of information about women's medicine in medieval Europe and provides a wealth of historical and sociological information. In addition, many (though not all) of the treatments recommended in the Trotula manuscripts were genuinely new and appropriate, making it possible for physicians to enhance and save lives.

The question as to whether Trotula was indeed a woman is probably not ultimately solvable. For some scholars, a female Trotula is evidence of an earlier golden age of women's education and medicine, and the claims that the author could not have been a woman are evidence of masculine denial of women's accomplishments. To others, attribution to a female author points to political, rather than scholarly, motivation. It remains for philologists to examine the surviving manuscripts and attempt to unravel the truth not only about Trotula but also about the sexual politics that have shaped theories about her over the centuries.

—Cynthia A. Bily

FURTHER READING

Benton, John F. "Trotula, Women's Problems, and the Professionalization of Medicine in the Middle Ages." *Bulletin of the History of Medicine* 59 (1985): 30-53. An important study, the first to use evidence in the manuscripts themselves to demonstrate that the pieces collected in the *Trotula* were written by three different authors and that much of what was believed about Trotula's biography could not be substantiated.

Green, Monica H. "In Search of an 'Authentic' Women's Medicine: The Strange Fates of Trota of Salerno and Hildegard of Bingen." *Dynamis* 19 (1999): 25-54. Green is the foremost scholar of medieval gynecology and the *Trotula*. Here she sorts through the sources of information and misinformation published about Trotula's life and clarifies what can and cannot be verified.

_______, ed. and trans. *The Trotula: A Medieval Compendium of Women's Medicine*. Philadelphia: University of Pennsylvania Press, 2001. Green's lengthy introduction to this edition presents the most complete discussion of the work—and of Trotula and the other authors—available.

Hughes, Muriel Joy. *Women Healers in Medieval Life and Literature*. 1943. Reprint. Freeport, N.Y.: Books for Libraries Press, 1968. Devotes much of the chapter "Medieval Midwives" to Trotula, making the case that she was a knowledgeable and successful midwife in Salerno.

Riddle, John M. *Contraception and Abortion from the Ancient World to the Renaissance*. Cambridge, Mass.: Harvard University Press, 1992. Brief discussion of the *Trotula*'s advice about birth control, and a portrait of Trotula from a medieval manuscript.

SEE ALSO: Pietro d'Abano; Arnold of Villanova; Jacqueline Félicie; Guy de Chauliac; Moses Maimonides; Paul of Aegina; al-Rāzī.

RELATED ARTICLES in *Great Events from History: The Middle Ages, 477-1453*: 809: First Islamic Public Hospital; c. 1150: Moors Transmit Classical Philosophy and Medicine to Europe.

WAT TYLER

English reformer and rebel leader

Wat Tyler led a popular uprising, which, though suppressed, speeded the end of serfdom and focused the attention of the English people on the importance of personal freedom.

BORN: Fourteenth century; England
DIED: June 15, 1381; Smithfield, near London, England
AREA OF ACHIEVEMENT: Social reform

EARLY LIFE

Nothing is known about Wat Tyler's early life, and even his occupation has been questioned. Some scholars follow the lead of the medieval French historian Jean Froissart, who reported in his *Chroniques de France, d'Engleterre, d'Éscose, de Bretaigne, d'Espaigne, d'Italie, de Flandres et d'Alemaigne* (1373-1410; *The Chronycles of Englande, Fraunce, Spayne . . .* , 1523-1525 better known as *Chronicles*) that Tyler had been a soldier in France; others even believe that he was an adventurer or a highwayman, placed by chance in a position of leadership. However, the early chroniclers were representatives of the establishment, and their assessment of Tyler's character reflects their prejudices. Such later antiestablishment writers as Thomas Paine, author of *The Rights of Man* (1791-1792), were just as biased. Paine thus accepted without question the identification of Wat, or Walter, Tyler as a Deptford tiler, or roofer, who killed a tax collector for taking liberties with his daughter. Such an incident did occur; however, the hero was John Tyler, a man who in fact was from Dartford, not Deptford. Wat Tyler was probably also a tiler, just as his name would suggest. Such an opinion is supported by the fact that members of that craft were heavily involved in the uprising. Less prosperous than other artisans, they had reason to be unhappy with their lot, and as they were constantly moving from place to place, they could easily rally followers.

As for his place of residence, there is ample proof that Wat Tyler was not from Maidstone, in Kent, as some have said, but from Essex, probably from Colchester. There he would surely have known John Ball, a priest excommunicated for his stand against oppression. It has been said that Ball was the soul and voice of the Peasants' Revolt and Wat Tyler its sword.

LIFE'S WORK

Tyler appeared on the stage of history on June 7, 1381, when he became the leader of the Peasants' Revolt, and he departed from it just eight days later, on June 15, when he was killed in the presence of King Richard II. However, it is not improbable that popular leaders like Tyler had been planning the uprising for some time, for widespread discontent had been building in England for several decades. In rural areas, the shortage of labor as a result of the Black Death had persuaded serfs and free workers alike that they were essential to society and deserved better treatment. In the cities, artisans and the unskilled were increasingly resentful of their exploitation by merchants. Ordinary Englishmen resented being conscripted for service in foreign wars and taxed to support a corrupt government. When Parliament in 1380-1381 passed a poll tax to be collected from every adult in England, rebellion ensued; despite the name, the revolt was not limited to peasants but also included serfs, free laborers, artisans, clerks, friars, and even merchants.

Although some scholars believe that the uprising was spontaneous, the fact that it broke out at approximately the same time in so many different areas of England suggests that it may have been well planned. In any case, it erupted on May 30, 1381, when a hundred men drove the king's commissioner out of Brentwood, Essex. Within a couple of days, Essex and Kent were in arms. On June 5, men gathered at Dartford began a march toward Maidstone. Wat Tyler may have been among the Essex men who made this journey. Certainly he was at Maidstone, for it was there on June 7 that the assembled captains named him their leader. Thereafter, Tyler served both as the military commander of the rebels and their spokesperson when at last they met with the king.

The qualities that made Wat Tyler a good leader—his intelligence, his strength of personality, and his talent for organization, with which he is credited even by those writers most hostile to his cause—soon became evident. It took just two days for Tyler to shape his army and move on to Canterbury, where his troops sacked the castle of the archbishop, Simon Sudbury, who was also the chancellor of England. The rebels destroyed tax documents, freed prisoners, and executed several men they considered traitors. Tyler then consolidated his control by leaving some of the local recruits to hold the town thus brought under the rebels' control.

Scene depicting the death of Wat Tyler. (H. Bricher)

Tyler was undoubtedly responsible for coordinating the two contingents, that from Essex and his own from Kent, so that they arrived outside London at the same time. By June 12, there were sixty thousand men encamped outside the city, and more were on the way. Moreover, although the mayor of London, Sir Thomas Walworth, was determined to resist, many Londoners were sympathetic with the rebels, as one of Walworth's emissaries admitted in a secret meeting with Tyler.

From the beginning, the insurgents had insisted that they were loyal to the young king and wished only to clear out the traitors who surrounded him. Realizing that he was probably the only person who could placate the rebels and persuade them to disperse, Richard finally agreed to meet with them. On June 13 and on the two days that followed, the king issued forth from the Tower of London, where he had taken refuge, and met with Tyler in front of the thousands under the rebel leader's command.

At the first of these meetings, there was no negotiation at all. Richard had proceeded by barge to the Greenwich shore, but when the men on the bank began to shout threats at those close to the king, someone in the royal party ordered the boats back to the Tower. Interestingly, Tyler's men did not fire a single arrow. Their restraint may have been because of the monarch's presence, but more probably, it indicates how well Tyler could control his men.

After a vague document sent by the king to the rebels was summarily rejected, a second meeting was set up. On Friday, June 14, Richard rode out to Mile End, where Tyler and his men were waiting. The king immediately agreed to the rebels' demands—including the abolition of serfdom, freedom to trade and negotiate, and amnesty for the rebels—and even promised to hand over those on their list of traitors for suitable punishment.

However, the rebels were already in London, burning palaces and beheading those they blamed for their misfortunes. More bloodshed ensued, along with widespread looting. Whether Tyler himself led a gang of arsonists and murderers, as his enemies charged, or whether he attempted to restrain his men will never be known. It is a matter of record that some men were put to death for looting. At any rate, by the time of the meeting on Saturday morning, June 15, Richard was ready to halt the uprising, whatever the cost.

Armed only with a dagger and accompanied by just one of his men, Tyler rode out to talk with the king. There are many different accounts of what happened then. Some say that Tyler grew unmannerly toward the monarch and that he picked a quarrel with one of the king's retainers and attacked him. However, others insist that Tyler was merely naïve, treating the monarch as a friend, and that he reacted to an insult as any man would, not suspecting that it was all part of a carefully orchestrated plot. Certainly, Tyler did draw his dagger, but he was immediately surrounded, then stabbed by Walworth and another of the king's men. Tyler managed to break away, and he spurred toward his men crying "treason," but before he could reach them, he fell to the ground and died. Tyler's men were thrown into confusion; when the king came toward them and asked them to disperse, they obeyed. Later, Walworth sought out Tyler's body, cut off his head, and bore it off on his lance, presumably to persuade the insurgents that the rebellion was finished. After the usual executions, those in power assumed that it all could be forgotten.

SIGNIFICANCE

Though Tyler's background, his character, and his motivations will always remain matters for conjecture, there is no doubt that though John Ball may have provided the ideology of the Peasants' Revolt, Tyler was responsible for its phenomenal success. However, a protest is one thing; formulating a new society is quite another. Realistically, when Wat Tyler died, his movement had done as much as it could do. His rural followers were on the road home, where they had families to support and crops to tend. His Londoners were tired of bloodshed. Soon all he would probably have had left were those who thrived on disorder, over whom he probably would have had little control.

Nevertheless, Tyler left his mark on history. One must credit him for so ordering his forces that their uprising was far less violent than most similar rebellions, such as the French Jacquerie movement (also a peasants' revolt) of 1358. Moreover, although those who held the power in England became even more repressive after the revolt, there were signs that the people had been heard. For example, the idea of a general poll tax was dropped, and before long laborers were being permitted to negotiate their own wages. It is also thought that the fear of another revolt hastened the end of serfdom. Perhaps Tyler's most important legacy, however, is an intangible one. After the uprising of 1381, never again could the English people be persuaded that they had no value. From this time on, they would raise their voices demanding personal freedom—and, like Wat Tyler, they would die for it if necessary.

—*Rosemary M. Canfield Reisman*

Further Reading

Dobson, R. B. *The Peasants' Revolt of 1381*. London: Macmillan, 1970. A collection of documents presenting contemporary accounts of the Peasants' Revolt, as well as later interpretations of its significance. Each selection is preceded by a commentary. Numerous references to Tyler are accessible through an excellent index. Extensive bibliography.

Dunn, Alastair. *The Great Rising of 1381: The Peasants' Revolt and England's Failed Revolution*. Stroud, Gloucestershire, England: Tempus, 2002. Novelistic rendition of the uprising. Color illustrations, bibliography, index.

Fryde, E. B. *Peasants and Landlords in Later Medieval England: c. 1380-c. 1525*. New York: St. Martin's Press, 1996. A social history of rural England during the century that led up to the Tyler uprising and beyond. Illustrations, bibliography, indexes.

Hill, Douglas, comp. *The Peasants' Revolt: A Collection of Contemporary Documents*. 1968. Reprint. Amawalk, N.Y.: Jackdaw, 1998. A study guide accompanies facsimile reproductions of a map, a pamphlet, and transcripts.

Hilton, R. H. *Bond Men Made Free: Medieval Peasant Movements and the English Rising of 1381*. 1973. Reprint. New York: Routledge, 1988. A section on the medieval economic system, explaining why it made revolt almost inevitable, is followed by a detailed account of the events of 1381. It is argued that while the peasants failed to achieve most of their aims, their vision of freedom changed the direction of British society.

Hilton, R. H., and T. H. Aston. *The English Rising of 1381*. Cambridge, England: Cambridge University Press, 1984. Included in this collection are essays on urban rebellion, both in England and in the rest of Europe, as well as on the more familiar subject of unrest among peasants. Though there are only a few references to Tyler, the volume contains helpful background information.

Justice, Steven. *Writing and Rebellion: England in 1381*. Berkeley: University of California Press, 1994. Examines six texts by rebels in the uprising, which, the author argues, demonstrate a cohesive insurgent ideology.

Lindsay, Philip, and Reg Groves. *The Peasants' Revolt: 1381*. 1950. Reprint. Westport, Conn.: Greenwood Press, 1974. An admirable volume, written in a vivid, dramatic style but evidencing the most painstaking research and evaluation of historical evidence. Tyler is seen as a brilliant leader, not the oaf or rogue that aristocratic writers of his own time liked to think him. Illustrations and bibliography.

Oman, Charles. *The Great Revolt of 1381*. 1906. Reprint. London: Greenhill, 1989. A detailed narrative by an early scholar whose opinions are quoted, though not always seconded, by serious students. Includes two helpful maps and a number of appendices containing records, statistics, and documents.

Tuchman, Barbara W. *A Distant Mirror: The Calamitous Fourteenth Century*. New York: Alfred A. Knopf, 1978. Sees the Peasants' Revolt as an expression of a growing passion for personal freedom, influenced by the preaching of men such as John Wyclif and John Ball. Tyler is pictured as a demagogue, power-crazed and increasingly violent, whose death came in consequence of his own rashness. The author's comparison of the English uprising to Continental rebellions is of particular interest.

See also: John Ball; Edward III; Jean Froissart; Richard II; John Wyclif.

Related articles in *Great Events from History: The Middle Ages, 477-1453*: 1337-1453: Hundred Years' War; May-June, 1381: Peasants' Revolt in England.

ʿUmar I
Muslim caliph (r. 634-644)

ʿUmar pursued territorial expansion of Islam through military conquest following indecisive moves by his predecessor Abū Bakr. He also helped to institutionalize early Islamic forms of government, and he developed systems of compensation and accountability for military members.

Born: c. 586; Mecca, Arabia (now in Saudi Arabia)
Died: November 3, 644; Mecca
Also known as: ʿUmar ibn Khaṭṭāb (full name); ʿUmar al-Farouq; al-Faruk; Farooq
Areas of achievement: Warfare and conquest, military, government and politics, religion and theology

Early Life

The historical importance of ʿUmar I (EW-mahr), second of the four Rashidun (rightly guided) caliphs in Islam, began well before the death of Prophet Muḥammad in 632. During the formative years of Muḥammad's prophetic message, individual decisions to convert to Islam played a more important role than kinship associations in forming the original *ummah*, or community of believers. One might have thought that most of Muḥammad's supporters would have come from his own clan of Hashim, or from other important Qurayshi tribal families, including members of the second key Meccan clan, the Umayyads. In fact, the Qurayshis held quite divided opinions of Muḥammad's claim to the cloak of true prophecy.

The kinship status of ʿUmar ibn Khaṭṭāb's mother, who was a member of the wealthy (and—from Muḥammad's point of view, arrogant) Makhzūmī clan, may have numbered him naturally among the opponents of a religious call that emphasized equality within a new "classless" religious community. Although the youthful Makhzūmī clan member ʿUmar was not a strident critic of Muḥammad, his decision to convert (by tradition in the fifth year of the Prophet's mission) seems to have marked an important turning point: ʿUmar's influence as a high ranking Meccan went with him into the fledgling ranks of a Muslim community that would, within a few years, need identifiable potential for various forms of leadership. His eventual role as Muḥammad's second successor (caliph) would show how valuable such leadership would be.

Until 634, however, ʿUmar's role would be to declare himself among the first ranks of Muḥammad's companions, or *ashab*. The title *ashab*, limited to only a handful of early converts, ranks among the highest of the original founders of the Islamic community. It may have been the presence of ʿUmar and a few other highly respected individuals in the circle around Muḥammad that led to a growing number of converts. This did not suffice, however, to convince more Meccans to join the Muslim community. In fact, the possibility of open persecution was rising. To protect his religious community, in 620 (marking year one, or 1 A.H., of the Islamic *Hijrah* calendar) Muḥammad called on the *ashab* to emigrate to the neighboring town of Yathrib, which later became known as the city of the Prophet, or Medina. This flight seemed to be the only way to build a larger Islamic community free from the danger of Meccan opponents.

Until the successful return of the Muslims to Mecca in 630, traditional accounts emphasize the importance of political abilities of Muḥammad and his companions in establishing alliances with various supportive clans in Medina and using these alliances to make the Islamic community into a potential military force. Indeed the organization of military forays (marking traditional small scale victories and some failures) against the Meccans must have been one of ʿUmar's chief responsibilities at this time. Little direct evidence of his role emerges, however, until Muḥammad's death in 632. With this came the need to select a successor to the Prophet of God, or Khalīfah Rasūl Allāh, not as a divinely inspired leader but as a respected and responsible leader of the Muslim community. The first such selection, which seems to have been based on Muḥammad's own preference, led to the appointment of Abū Bakr, an elder among the companions, and Muḥammad's father-in-law. At first Abū Bakr had to meet the challenge of protecting the community from its enemies and potential backsliders among recently converted Arab tribes (the so-called Wars of Apostasy inside the Arabian Peninsula itself). Some raids by Muslims into the Byzantine and Sāsānian domains beyond traditional tribal borders did occur, even during Abū Bakr's short caliphate.

Life's Work

It fell to ʿUmar I, the second caliph, to transform these military efforts into real expansionary campaigns. The terms of his accession to the caliphate merit some discussion, since his was apparently the last succession to be accepted without dissension from emergent subgroups in the Islamic community.

AFTER MUḤAMMAD: THE ORTHODOX CALIPHS, 632-661

Reign	Caliph
632-634	Abū Bakr
634-644	ʿUMAR I
644-656	ʿUthmān ibn ʿAffān
656-661	Alī ibn Abī Ṭālib

Whereas Abū Bakr had essentially been chosen by the immediate circle of Prophet companions and was recognized for his close ties with Muḥammad, ʿUmar's succession in 634 contained early seeds of disappointment that ʿAlī, the Prophet's cousin and son-in-law, did not garner enough support for the post. Potential divisions over the question of caliphal succession generally, and ʿAlī's hereditary claim to leadership of the Islamic community in particular, would surface openly soon after ʿUmar's assassination in 644.

In the meantime, the second caliph's rapid escalation of the first territorial conquests made by Abū Bakr (first the Persian-held al-Hīrah in Iraq in 633, and then Byzantine Syria, or Palestine, in 634) created military momentum that would reinforce ʿUmar's position politically. Muslims often cite the defeat of the Byzantines at the Battle of the Yarmūk (a tributary of the Jordan River) in 636 as the first great victory that would leave most of Syria open to almost unopposed advance by Arab armies. By that date, ʿUmar's generals had already scored a victory in 635 at al-Qādisīyah, near Najaf in Iraq, and prepared to cross the Euphrates River to expel the Persians from their capital at Ctesiphon. When the capital city was taken, the Persian shah retreated with his army into the mountains leading into Iran.

Soon it was apparent that Caliph ʿUmar would have to act to consolidate these new holdings in the name of the Islamic community. This meant introducing at least some semi-institutionalized government structures before calling on Arab tribesmen to continue their conquests.

The first indication of ʿUmar's skill as a governing leader was the innovative construction of totally new garrison towns (*misr*), initially in Al-Kūfa, near the site of al-Qādisīyah, then in Basra near the head of the Persian Gulf. Each *misr* was designed to keep Arab military forces under close surveillance while their generals (appointed by ʿUmar) dispatched tribe members further into zones of fighting to receive new Arab elements to replace them. The *amsar* (plural for *misr*) physically isolated Arab Islamic warriors from already existing towns in Syria and Iraq.

The garrison camp-town principle was soon applied in another conquest, this time in Egypt, where the garrison of Fusṭāt (possibly the earliest Islamic site on the edge of what is now Cairo) would apply the name *misr* to the entire country.

When Islamic armies reached Egypt (under a somewhat independently minded general ʿAmr ibn al-ʿAs) and prepared to advance westward across North Africa (a process that led a combined Arab and Berber army to the Straits of Gibraltar in a little more than sixty years), ʿUmar was incited to introduce another new key institution of governance. ʿUmar instituted the *diwan*, roughly translated as muster sheet, which was a tribal listing that named each Arab clan (and its individual members) serving in the ranks of the caliph's armies. The *diwan* was developed apparently to keep track of lengths of service and involvement in specific campaigns and battles to determine appropriate compensation, including clan rights to seizure of booty. This "payroll" system provided a formal structure for what might otherwise have become uncontrollable plundering by individuals or rival tribal clans.

Probably the most significant military victories under ʿUmar's banners involved pursuit of the Persians into Iran, where, at al-Qādisīyah in 636 and Nahāvand in 642, the last Sāsānian king, Yazdegerd III (r. 632-651), met defeat and fled from the important city of Hamadān toward Iran's distant northeastern province of Khorāsān. This left open to Arab advance the mountain passes leading from Hamadān to the rich city of Eşfahān in Fārs province. Although Yazdegerd was able to find refuge, he was eventually betrayed and assassinated in 651. Ironically, the defeated Persian shah outlived ʿUmar by more than six years. The second caliph, who by the early 640's had preferred to adopt the title Amir al-Muʾminin (commander of the faithful), was assassinated during his return from his second pilgrimage to Mecca. His assassin was a disgruntled Persian slave named Feroz.

SIGNIFICANCE

Aside from the unexpectedness of the violent end to his life, ʿUmar's sudden passing created a succession dilemma that would affect the entire future of the caliphate specifically and Islam in general. Some have said he had already appointed a council of Islamic notables to elect the next caliph; others claim that the council emerged spontaneously when the community learned of ʿUmar's sudden death. Two of its five members, Abū Ṭālib (d. 619) and ʿUthmān ibn ʿAffān (d. 656), were related to the Prophet through marriages to Muḥammad's blood kin. In the case of his cousin ʿAlī, this marriage tie was very close, involving a union with Muḥammad's daughter, Fāṭimah. Instead of selecting ʿAlī, the council settled on the aristocratic but otherwise not well qualified ʿUthmān, who would lead the Muslim community until he, too, was assassinated, in 656. This time the mortal blow was dealt by unruly military contingents unhappy with the application of the pay schedules and promotion system developed by ʿUmar. Whatever the cause of the rebellion, ʿUthmān's death allowed ʿAlī to rise to the position of caliph—something he definitely expected at the time of ʿUmar's demise. Not too many years would pass, however, before ʿAlī would be murdered by opponents of what might be called "in-house" nominations to the office of caliph.

The significance of these events happening so soon after ʿUmar's passing is key: The era of consensus around the charismatic figures of the first two caliphs clearly was coming to a close. The longer term significance of this loss of consensus would be institutionalized, as the partisans of ʿAlī (Shiat ʿAlī, or Shias) broke off from the main line of support for the orthodoxy (Sunnism) that Caliph ʿUmar had tried to engender as a bond uniting all Muslims.

—*Byron D. Cannon*

Further Reading

Chaudri, Rashīd Ahmad. *ʿUmar Farooq*. Islamabad, Pakistan: Islam International, 2001. Provides a recent example of Pakistani views of the traditional origins of Islam and ʿUmar's key role in Arab conquests and government organization of a multinational community.

Majdalawi, Faruq. *Islamic Administration Under Omar ibn al Khaṭṭāb*. Amman, Jordan: Majdalawi Press, 2002. A privately published translation of the author's doctoral dissertation in Arabic. Like Chaudri's text above, this work is mainly useful for showing recent trends in Islamic reconsideration of well-known topics drawn, in almost all cases, from traditional sources.

Sadi, Abdullah Jaman Said. *Fiscal Policy in the Islamic State: Its Origins and Contemporary Relevance*. Translated by Ahmad al-Anani. Newcastle, England: Lyme Books, 1986. Because of ʿUmar's key contributions to Islamic fiscal conceptions and practices, this study of the institutions he founded is of both general and particular interest.

Shamsul-Ulama Allama Shibli Numani. *Omar the Great: The Second Caliph of Islam*. Translated by Maulana Zafar Ali Khan. 2 vols. Lahore, Pakistan: M. Ashraf, 1961-1962. This is a translation of a traditionally oriented biography of ʿUmar. The original work seems to have been published posthumously in 1943 and 1957.

Tritton, A. S. *The Caliphs and Their Non-Muslim Subjects: A Critical Study of the Covenant of ʿUmar.* 1930. Reprint. London: F. Cass, 1970. This study documents ʿUmar's endeavors to deal administratively with non-converted subjects of the Islamic state, both in terms of guarantees of religious practice and fiscal responsibilities. Bibliography.

See also: ʿAbd al-Malik; al-Ḥasan al-Baṣrī; Heraclius; Muḥammad.

Related articles in *Great Events from History: The Middle Ages, 477-1453*: c. 610-632: Muḥammad Receives Revelations; 630-711: Islam Expands Throughout North Africa; August 15-20, 636: Battle of Yarmūk; 637-657: Islam Expands Throughout the Middle East.

UNKEI
Japanese sculptor

During the Kamakura period, Unkei established a new style of Buddhist sculpture that reflected the ascendency of the warrior culture in Japan.

BORN: c. 1150; probably Nara, Japan
DIED: 1223; probably Nara, Japan
AREA OF ACHIEVEMENT: Art

EARLY LIFE

Unkei (ewn-kay) is the best-known sculptor in Japanese history. He was active in the early Kamakura period and was the son of Kōkei, who was probably a fifth-generation descendant of Jōchō, another influential Japanese sculptor. The date of Unkei's birth is uncertain; nevertheless, scholars have speculated that it was around 1150, based on the birth date of his eldest child, Tankei, in 1173. Although there is no literary record of his early life, it is likely that Unkei was an apprentice to his father, who was chief sculptor of the Kei school (also called the Nara school) during the last half of the twelfth century. The Kei school, which began in 1096 with Jōchō's grandson, Raijo, had developed in Nara, Japan's oldest permanent capital, centering on the Kōfukuji (Kōfuku temple).

During the late twelfth century, the In and En schools (also known as the Kyoto schools) were prosperous in Kyoto and enjoyed aristocratic patronage. These two schools dominated the sculptural arts, preserving the traditional Jōchō style as their noble patrons desired. Unfortunately, this tradition was becoming overly refined in detail and was no longer fresh and vivid as it had been under Jōchō. It was degenerating into a formalistic imitation.

To counter this stagnation, the Kei school attempted to create a new style, one based on the more realistic expression found in art during the latter part of the Nara period (710-784). Being less involved in important art commissions than the Kyoto schools were and thus freed from the constraints of aristocratic taste, the Kei school was allowed to establish a distinctive manner. Kōkei promoted this movement, and his son Unkei completed the innovation by creating the Kamakura style.

The Amida triad in the Chōgakuji (Chōgaku temple) in Nara, sculpted in 1151, was one of the early experimental works, possibly made by Raijo's son, Kōjo. A monumental effort, it attempted to defeat the mannerism of the traditional Jōchō style by returning to the classic, naturalistic style of the latter Nara-period sculpture and adding a new technique: the creation of crystal eyes called *gyokugan*, which gave statues an increased realism.

Unkei's Buddha Dainichi at the Enjōji (Enjō temple) in Nara is one of the sculptures that seem to follow the style seen in the Chōgaku-ji triad. The Dainichi was made in 1176 and is the earliest of Unkei's extant works. The inscription on the pedestal states that the image was made by "true apprentice of Kōkei, Unkei." This inscription is usually interpreted by scholars to mean that Unkei was the son and disciple of Kōkei. Unkei, probably in his mid-twenties, appears to have carved the Buddha under the guidance of his father. The image's rounded cheeks and chin, wide, high knees, and strong articulation of folds reflect a sense of youthfulness. A high topknot and crystal eyes clearly follow the Chōgaku-ji Amida. Overall, the Dainichi retains the grace of the traditional Jōchō style, but Unkei's youthful vigor, seen in this image, indicates his future brilliant career.

LIFE'S WORK

Unkei lived during a time of social and political revolution in which power shifted from the aristocracy to the warrior class. In 1192, Minamoto Yoritomo, the leader of the Minamoto clan, which replaced the Taira clan, established its military government (*bakufu*) in Kamakura in eastern Japan. Prior to this action, Nara's most disastrous event had occurred during the war between the two clans: the destruction of the Tōdaiji and Kōfukuji, two important temples, in 1180. The Kei school sculptors contributed their full energy to the reconstruction of the two temples.

Unkei's association with the warrior class began during this period. The Kei school needed powerful support in the new era because the Kyoto and Kei schools were in conflict over the right to reconstruct the Kōfukuji. According to the historical record *Azuma kagami* (twelfth century; mirror of the east), the sixth-generation descendant of Jōchō went to eastern Japan and made the temple images for Minamoto Yoritomo in 1185. Scholars are still debating whether Unkei actually went to the eastern region. Nevertheless, after having been invited by two important politicians of the Kamakura *bakufu*, he made the images for two eastern Japanese temples.

In 1186, Unkei carved the images of the Ganjōjuin temple in the prefecture of Shizuoka. Yoritomo's father-in-law, Hōjō Tokimasa, commissioned the project, praying for the success of his northeastern expedition. The images consisted of an Amida, a Fudō, and a Bishamonten; the flanking bodhisattvas of the Amida do not remain. Four inscribed wooden tablets from each figure of the Fudō and Bishamonten prove the images to be Unkei's works.

In 1189, following the Ganjōjuin images, Unkei worked for the Jōrakuji (Jōraku temple) in the prefecture of Kanagawa. The statues to be made were an Amida, a Fudō, and a Bishamonten. The patron was Wada Yoshimori, another important figure of the Kamakura *bakufu*. Inscribed tablets were also found in each of these statues. They state that these icons were made by Unkei with the help of ten *shōbusshi* (minor sculptors).

Both sets of temple images share common features: iconography, inscribed wooden tablets, and style. This style, which is characterized by a rough, massive body and complicated drapery folds, is dissimilar to his most important works, such as the Enjōji Dainichi and Hokuendō Miroku. Thus, the statues were not identified as Unkei's work until all the inscribed tablets were found.

By his mid-thirties, Unkei still had not acquired any honorable titles and the roughness and wildness of the Jōrakuji and Ganjōjuin images were probably the results of one of his experiments in negating the aristocratic sense of beauty. These *bakufu* commissions were perfect opportunities for him to express himself artistically without any restrictions. Such a trend is particularly noticeable in the Ganjōjuin figures.

In the Ganjōjuin Amida, the work's massiveness and the triangular shape of the drapery on the leg, which is also seen in the Chōgakuji Amida, seem to derive from early Heian period (794-1185) sculpture. Deeply undulating folds and the preaching mudra (symbolic position of the hands) are often found in work of the Nara period. Unkei's image is an extension of the Chōgakuji Amida and shows his study of the classical sculpture. Moreover, the power of the later Amida exceeds that of the classical figures, and its realism appeals strongly to the viewer. The realistic facial expressions and movements of the Fudō and Bishamonten also seem to reflect the warrior class's taste and Unkei's interpretation of the people in the eastern region. The wild impression was reduced and became more organized in the later Jōrakuji images.

Unkei perhaps went back to the Kōfukuji and Tōdaiji reconstruction project after his commissions at Jōrakuji. He was awarded the Buddhist rank of *hōgen* (eyes of law) in 1195 for his work at Tōdaiji. The Kei school, which was treated less favorably than the Kyoto schools in the Kōfukuji project, was given great opportunities to work on the Tōdaiji by the monk Chōgen (one of the men in charge of the restoration) and Yoritomo. While working at Tōdaiji, Unkei acquired the position of chief sculptor for the Tōji (Tō temple) in Kyoto.

The works for Tōji were arranged by Mongaku, a monk who was closely associated with Yoritomo. Unkei's relationship with the warrior class was further strengthened by his ties to Mongaku. Unkei also worked on the images for Mongaku's temple, Jingoji. Through these works, Unkei learned more about early Heian sculpture; this influence appears in his later images.

In 1202, Unkei made a small Fugen bodhisattva for the regent Konoe Motomichi. This commission indicates that Unkei was finally being favored by the courtiers of Kyoto. During this period, Unkei's studio was located in Kyoto, and he was commissioned by both warriors and aristocrats. His success led to the prosperity of the Kei school.

Two of Unkei's masterpieces, the giant devas at the Tōdaiji South Gate, were made in 1203 with the help of Kaikei in approximately seventy days. The statues, nearly 28 feet (9 meters) high, present the essence of Kamakura sculpture. The expressions of rage, stances of the bodies, and flowing movements of the costumes are vigorous and tense.

The deities also display perfect studio work. Unkei, Kaikei, and two other *daibusshi* (major sculptors) made the statues in collaboration with sixteen *shōbusshi* (minor sculptors). Because of the statues' similarities, it is almost impossible to distinguish any one sculptor's techniques. Although the *A-gyō* (statue with an open mouth) can be ascribed to Kaikei because of the inscribed names inside it, the two statues were conceived by one person, probably Unkei. Unkei's ability to lead and the organized studio system of the Kei school made this high degree of stylistic consistency possible. Also in 1203, Unkei was promoted to the highest rank, *hōin* (seal of law), and Kaikei was awarded the *hokkyō* (bridge of law) rank.

Several years later, with his sons and other Kei school sculptors, Unkei began to work on his last project for Kōfukuji. Of these images, the Buddha Miroku and the monks Muchaku and Seshin remain in the Hokuendō hall of the temple. The Miroku, which was finished around 1212, presents a more mature style than the earlier Ganjōjuin and Jōrakuji figures; this maturity is particularly noticeable in the Buddha's gentle, stable form and slenderness. The massive portrait statues of Muchaku and Seshin demonstrate Unkei's dedication to a more realistic technique, as may be seen in the heavy robes with their roughly carved folds, the static postures, the three-dimensional forms, and the sensitive movement of the hands. Despite this realism, like all Buddhist icons, these statues capture a spiritual truth as well: They represent the eternal truth in the human figure and move the viewer's soul with their ponderous, serious forms.

In his later years, Unkei is known to have worked primarily for the Kamakura *bakufu*. Despite his activity, however, no works remain extant after the Kōfukuji Hokuendō images. He is believed to have died in 1223.

Significance

From the end of the Heian period to the early part of the Kamakura period (1185-1333) was a time of disturbance. The decline of the aristocrats and the rise of the warrior class required a new type of art. Quickly responding to this need, Unkei and other Kei school artists created a new style whose strong, masculine, realistic features were suitable to the taste of the new powers in the land. This realism was also a comment on the sculptors of Nara who had merely tolerated their inferior position. Unkei not only achieved a powerfully innovative individual style but also raised the social status of the entire Kei school with his great insight and leadership.

Historically, Japanese sculpture has almost always made rapid progress under intense foreign influence, particularly from China. Contrary to this trend, starting with the conversion of Jōchō's pure Japanese style, Unkei brought Japanese sculpture to fruition by recapturing the sculptural qualities of classic Japanese works and adding to this legacy a new realism.

—*Yoshiko Kainuma*

Further Reading

Harris, Victor, and Ken Matsushima. *Kamakura: The Renaissance of Japanese Sculpture, 1185-1333*. London: British Museum Press, 1991. The catalog from an exhibition of the British Museum, the Agency for Cultural Affairs, Tokyo, and the Japan Foundation featuring sculpture in the Kamakura period.

Horomitsu, Washizuka, et al. *Enlightenment Embodied: The Art of the Japanese Buddhist Sculptor, Seventh to Fourteenth Centuries*. Translated and edited by Reiko Tomii and Kathleen M. Fraiello. New York: Agency for Cultural Affairs, Government of Japan, and Japan Society, 1997. This catalog of an exhibition at the Japan Society Gallery in 1997 features Buddhist art.

Kuno, Takeshi, ed. *A Guide to Japanese Sculpture*. Tokyo: Maruyama, 1963. Useful for a survey of the major trends in the history of Japanese sculpture. Contains a helpful glossary and charts.

Mori, Hisashi. *Japanese Portrait Sculpture*. Translated by W. Chie Ichibashi. Tokyo: Kodansha International, 1977. Discusses the history of portrait sculpture from the Nara to the Kamakura period. Useful for its references to the statues of Muchaku and Seshin.

_______. *Sculpture of the Kamakura Period*. Translated by Katherine Eickmann. New York: John Weatherhill, 1974. A good source covering the full range of Kamakura sculpture; pays special attention to the social and historical background.

Morse, Anne Nishimura, and Nobuo Tsuji, eds. *Japanese Art in the Museum of Fine Arts, Boston*. 2 vols. Boston: The Museum, 1998. This catalog of Buddhist art in the Museum of Fine Arts, Boston, presents a wide array of art, including painting, sculpture, Nō masks, robes, and paintings from the Kano and Rimpa schools.

Nishikawa, Kyōtarō, and Emily J. Sano. *The Great Age of Japanese Buddhist Sculpture, A.D. 600-1300*. Fort Worth, Tex.: Kimbell Art Museum, 1982. The catalog of an exhibition of Japanese Buddhist sculpture at the Kimbell Art Museum.

Stanley-Baker, Joan. *Japanese Art*. Rev. ed. New York: Thames and Hudson, 2000. A general work on Japanese art. Chapter 5 focuses on the Kamakura and Muromachi periods, covering the period in which Unkei worked.

See also: Jōchō.

Related articles in *Great Events from History: The Middle Ages, 477-1453*: 538-552: Buddhism Arrives in Japan; 792: Rise of the Samurai; 1156-1192: Minamoto Yoritomo Becomes Shogun; 1175: Hōnen Shōnin Founds Pure Land Buddhism.

Urban II

French pope (1088-1099)

By practicing a quiet, astute diplomacy, Urban II laid the foundation for papal supremacy within the medieval Church in Europe and lifted the Papacy to the leadership of Western Christendom during the High Middle Ages.

Born: c. 1042; Châtillon-sur-Marne, France
Died: July 29, 1099; Rome (now in Italy)
Also known as: Odo of Lagery; Otto of Lagery; Otho of Lagery; Eudes of Lagery
Areas of achievement: Government and politics, religion and theology

Early Life

Urban II was born Odo in Châtillon-sur-Marne, France. Most scholars place his birth in the year 1042, others as early as 1035. Odo came from a knightly family. His father was Eucher, the lord of Lagery.

From the beginning of his education, Odo was destined to play a role in the reform movement that swept through the Church during the eleventh and twelfth centuries. He began his education for the clergy in the cathedral school at Reims, in northeastern France. There, he studied under Saint Bruno, a canon of the cathedral and master of the school, who later founded the strict Carthusian order of monks.

Odo's character and administrative talents were recognized early by his superiors at Reims. He rose rapidly through the ranks. He served as canon and around 1055 was appointed archdeacon of the cathedral church. Perhaps following the example of his former teacher, Saint Bruno, Odo sought the more disciplined atmosphere of the monastery. Sometime between 1067 and 1070, he entered the famous monastery of Cluny, just north of Lyon, in central France.

Cluny was the birthplace and incubator of the reform movement. From Saint Hugh, leader of the order during Odo's tenure at Cluny, he learned the art of diplomacy that was to serve him so well later as one of the three reform popes to come out of Cluny. Again, Odo's talents were recognized and appreciated. In 1076, he was appointed prior of the monastery. In 1078, Pope Gregory VII, himself a former monk from Cluny, asked Hugh, then the abbot of Cluny, to send some monks to work under him at Rome. Odo was one of those sent in 1079 or 1080.

Gregory VII appointed Odo cardinal-bishop of Ostia. From then until Gregory VII's death in 1085, Odo served as one of his closest advisers. Although he remained close to the pope, Odo occasionally was sent on important missions as papal legate (1082-1085) to France and Germany. During one mission to Germany, Odo was held prisoner (1083-1084) by Emperor Henry IV, the chief opponent of the reform movement in the Church. So closely were Odo and Gregory VII in agreement on the principles and goals of the reform program that, prior to his death, Gregory VII recommended Odo as his successor.

Life's Work

On the death of Gregory VII, the cardinals chose as his successor Victor III, also a monk from Cluny. Although Odo opposed Victor III's election, the new pontiff bore him no malice. Indeed, as Victor III lay dying, he chose Odo as his successor. Victor III's choice, and that of Gregory VII, was honored by the cardinals when they met on March 12, 1088, at Terracina, south of Rome. There Odo was unanimously elected pope and took the name Urban II.

The circumstances surrounding Urban II's election exemplified the issues and problems that preoccupied his reign. The cardinals had to meet outside Rome, in Terracina, because Rome was occupied by the antipope Clement III, who enjoyed the support of Henry IV. Indeed, Urban spent most of his reign outside Rome, establishing the legitimacy of his election, upholding the authority of the pope within the reformed Church, and defending the independence of the Church against the claims of the imperial party.

From the beginning of his reign, Urban II affirmed and pursued the reform policies of Gregory VII. He held a council at Melfi in southern Italy in September, 1089. There, he renewed Gregory VII's decrees against simony, clerical marriage, and lay investiture. He also anathematized both Henry IV and Clement III, an act he repeated several times during his reign. If Urban II agreed in principle with Gregory VII, however, his pursuit of reform was very different.

Urban II was in many ways different from his illustrious predecessor. Contemporary sources describe him as a tall, handsome, bearded man whose speech was eloquent and learned. In his relationships with friend and foe alike, he was friendly, gentle, and always courteous. The fact that he chose to pursue his goals through persuasion rather than direct confrontation did not mean that he was weak. Always uncompromisingly committed to the principles of reform, he cautioned church authorities to exercise reason in their implementation.

As a skillful diplomat, Urban II had few equals. He saw clearly that to maintain the program of reform begun by Gregory VII, it was necessary to win the support of the secular princes. To do so, he chose not to press the exaggerated claims to political sovereignty made by Gregory VII and instead emphasized the spiritual leadership of the Papacy. To combat Henry IV in Germany, Urban II allied himself with Matilda of Canossa, countess of Tuscany. He arranged a marriage (1089) between the forty-three-year-old countess and the seventeen-year-old Welf V, duke of Bavaria, whose father had been deposed by Henry IV. By astute diplomacy, in 1093, Urban II was able to attract Henry IV's son, Conrad, to the alliance with Matilda and Welf V.

Urban II was rewarded for diplomatic maneuvers. In 1093, he was able to enter Rome, and on Easter, 1094, he sat on the papal throne for the first time. His entry into the Lateran Palace was achieved by "diplomacy." The governor of the Lateran Palace offered to surrender it in exchange for a bribe supplied by a wealthy abbot. The event signaled the defeat of Henry IV's ambitions in Italy and, with them, those of Clement III.

Urban II exhorts his listeners to participate in the First Crusade. (Library of Congress)

Throughout his struggle with Henry IV, Urban II never ceased in his efforts to reform Church government. His efforts were directed at increased centralization. His goal was a papal monarchy modeled after that of the secular princes. The role of the College of Cardinals, founded in 1059, was transformed. The cardinals henceforth had authority to excommunicate secular and ecclesiastical lords and to decide disputed episcopal elections. As with the king's council in England and France, the College of Cardinals became the pope's supreme advisory body, participating in the highest levels of Church government.

As the cardinals became a more integral part of the administrative structure of Church government, political duties distracted them from their traditional religious functions. These were increasingly assigned to chaplains. Thus, Urban II gave birth to the papal chapel, which, like the new role of the College of Cardinals, was modeled after the chapels at the courts of the secular kings.

Similarly, Urban II reorganized papal finances and the papal secretariat. He chose Cluny as the model for the former and appointed a monk from Cluny as the first treasurer, or *camerarius*. Many scholars believe that Urban II's creation of the papal treasury (called a camera) was one of his most important innovations in Church government.

Nothing demonstrated Urban II's success in enhancing the position of the Papacy more than his initiation of the Crusades. His call, at the Council of Clermont

THE CRUSADES, 1095-1270

Crusade	*Dates*	*Leaders*	*Destination*
First	1095-1099	URBAN II, Bohemond I, Raymond IV	Nicaea, Dorylaeum, Antioch, Jerusalem
Second	1147-1149	Eugenius III, Bernard of Clairvaux, Louis VII, Conrad III	Outremer, Iberian Peninsula, Damascus
Third	1189-1192	Gregory VIII, Richard I, Philip II, Frederick I Barbarossa	Acre, Arsuf
Fourth	1202-1204	Innocent III, Enrico Dandolo	Zara, Constantinople
Fifth	1217-1221	Innocent III, Honorius III, Andrew II, John of Brienne	Damietta in Egypt
Sixth	1227-1230	Honorius III, Frederick II	Sidon, Tyre, Acre, Jerusalem
Seventh*	1248-1254	Louis IX	Damietta and Mansurah in Egypt
Eighth**	1270	Louis IX	Tunis

*Sometimes known as the Eighth Crusade
**Sometimes known as the Ninth Crusade

in 1095, for a crusade to rescue the Holy Land from the clutches of the Seljuk Turks was one of the key events of the Middle Ages. It was in part a culmination of efforts by Urban II to restore the unity between the Western and Eastern churches fragmented since the schism of 1054.

Soon after his election as pope, Urban II opened negotiations with the Eastern Christians. He met with ambassadors from the Byzantine court at the Council of Melfi in 1089. There, in their presence, he lifted the ban of excommunication against the Emperor Alexius I. Another embassy from Alexius visited Urban II in 1090. It may be assumed that at these and other possible meetings, Alexius's desire for Western military aid against the Turks and Urban II's desire for unity between the two churches were discussed.

By March, 1095, Urban II felt secure enough to call the first great council of his reign at Piacenza, north of Rome. Ambassadors from Constantinople were present and may have addressed the assembly. For the first time, Urban II called on the Christian knights of Western Europe to go to the aid of the Eastern Christians. It was at the Council of Clermont in Auvergne, France, in November, 1095, however, that the effectual call went out—and the call was heard.

Some thirteen archbishops, two hundred bishops, more than ninety abbots, and thousands of nobles and knights assembled before Urban II at Clermont. It was the moment of triumph not only for Urban II but also for the reformed Church. Standing before the crowd on a specially constructed platform in an open field, Urban II, with all of his eloquence, called on the knighthood of Western Christendom to embark on an armed pilgrimage to Jerusalem. When he finished speaking, the crowd spontaneously broke out with shouts of "God wills it."

Following Clermont, Urban II continued to preach the Crusade at subsequent synods and councils, while consolidating his control of the Church. A group of Crusaders stopped off at Rome on their way to the Holy Land and drove the antipope, Clement III, from the city. Clement retired to his archbishopric of Ravenna. Jerusalem fell to the first wave of Crusaders on July 15, 1099. Urban II never heard of the victory. He died two weeks later, on July 29, in Rome.

SIGNIFICANCE

The Council of Clermont was the crowning achievement of Urban II's reign. His speech before the assembled ecclesiastical and secular lords has been ranked with the great orations of history. At Clermont, the pope supplanted the Holy Roman Emperor as the leader of Western Christendom. Historians often view the Crusades as Europe's first imperialistic venture and note that economic greed played a key motivational role. In the context of the High Middle Ages, however, the Crusades were, above all, a religiously motivated pilgrimage. The Crusades brought unity to Western Christendom and elevated the pope to the moral leadership of Europe for the next two centuries.

It may be argued, however, that the Crusades eventually undermined papal leadership in European affairs. Renewed contact between Western Europe and the Levant awakened forces that had been dormant in Europe since the fall of the Roman Empire in the fifth century. The Renaissance of the fourteenth and fifteenth centuries, the scientific revolution of the fifteenth and sixteenth centuries, and the rise of the secular nation-state were all stimulated by the Crusades. Each in its own way contributed to the eventual fragmentation of the Church in the West and the loss of papal leadership in Europe.

Urban II's greatest achievement lay in his creation of the Papal Curia (papal court). By giving the Church a monarchical form of government, complete with an administrative structure modeled after the courts of the kings of England and France, Urban II placed the Papacy on an equal footing with the secular monarchs. As with the courts of the kings, the papal court was henceforth both a central administration and a court of law. The power and influence of the pope has waxed and waned since Urban II's reign, but the Papal Curia he founded has only grown stronger.

—*Paul R. Waibel*

FURTHER READING

Barraclough, Geoffrey. *The Medieval Papacy*. New York: W. W. Norton, 1979. Discusses Urban II's role as a reform pope. Particularly helpful for understanding his contributions to the construction of the papal monarchy. Emphasizes Urban II's pontificate as a turning point in the history of the medieval Church.

Bull, Marcus. "The Pilgrimage Origins of the First Crusade." *History Today* 47, no. 3 (March, 1997). The author explores Urban II's speech at Clermont and then traces the Crusades from their start as a Christian pilgrimage to a holy war.

Bury, J. B., ed. *Contest and Empire*. Vol. 5 in *The Cambridge Medieval History*, edited by C. W. Previté-Orton and Z. N. Brooke. New York: Cambridge University Press, 1968. Chapter 2, "Gregory VII and the First Contest Between Empire and Papacy," discusses the reform movement within the Church and the accompanying clash with imperial interests. Urban II's role in initiating the First Crusade is examined in chapter 7, "The First Crusade."

Cowdrey, H. E. J. *Popes and Church Reform in the Eleventh Century*. Burlington, Vt.: Ashgate/Variorum, 2000. A study on the topic of Church reform and renewal in medieval times.

Krey, August C. *The First Crusade: The Accounts of Eye-Witnesses and Participants*. Gloucester, Mass.: Peter Smith, 1958. This source is of particular value not only for its factual content but also for its ability to communicate a sense of participation. Urban II's role in summoning the First Crusade is presented through the words of those present.

Mourret, Fernand. *Period of the Later Middle Ages*. Vol. 4 in *A History of the Catholic Church*. St. Louis, Mo.: B. Herder, 1947. Chapter 6, "From the Death of St. Gregory VII to the Death of Urban II (1085-99)," discusses Urban II's reign as pope, emphasizing his struggle to reform the Church and defend its independence from imperial control.

Phillips, Jonathan. "Who Were the First Crusaders?" *History Today* 47, no. 3 (March, 1997). Looks at the history of the First Crusade and Crusaders, including Urban II and his role.

Riley-Smith, Jonathan. *The First Crusaders, 1095-1131*. New York: Cambridge University Press, 1997. The story of the First Crusade, including recruitment, preparation, preaching, the holy war, and the return. Includes an appendix listing the Crusaders, illustrations, maps, and index.

Runciman, Steven. *The First Crusade and the Foundation of the Kingdom of Jerusalem*. Vol. 1 in *A History of the Crusades*. New York: Cambridge University Press, 1985. One of the best histories of the Crusades. Provides an in-depth understanding of the background and course of the First Crusade. In addition to Urban II's role, the author provides some information about his early life and election to the papacy.

Somerville, Robert, and Stephan Kuttner. *Pope Urban II, the Collectio Britannica, and the Council of Melfi (1089)*. New York: Clarendon Press, 1996. Part II introduces the council, presents its history in the context of canon law, and comments on the papal letters.

SEE ALSO: Alp Arslan; Saint Anselm; Bohemond I; Gregory VII; Henry IV (of Germany); Matilda of Canossa; Tancred.

RELATED ARTICLES in *Great Events from History: The Middle Ages, 477-1453*: 726-843: Iconoclastic Controversy; 1040-1055: Expansion of the Seljuk Turks; 1054: Beginning of the Rome-Constantinople Schism; 1077: Seljuk Dynasty Is Founded; November 27, 1095: Pope Urban II Calls the First Crusade; 1248-1254: Failure of the Seventh Crusade; 1305-1417: Avignon Papacy and the Great Schism.

Valdemar II
King of Denmark (r. 1202-1241)

Valdemar II was a warrior, lawgiver, builder, and Crusader. He extended Danish control over North Germany, Scandia, and Estonia, leaving to his successors the dream of an empire extending over the Baltic Sea.

Born: May 9, 1170; Denmark
Died: March 28, 1241; Vordingborg, Denmark
Also known as: Valdemar the Victorious; Waldemar I
Areas of achievement: Government and politics, warfare and conquest

Early Life

Valdemar II's father, Valdemar I (1157-1182), had brought to an end the long struggles between the Church and Crown for dominance in the north of Europe. Working with Absalon, the archbishop of Lund, he began a crusading program that secured internal peace through external expansion, occupying the military talents of potentially rebellious nobles in defeating Wendish (Slavic peoples of eastern Germany) pagans on the Mecklenburg coast and islands and seizing Scandia (the southern part of modern Sweden), while establishing royal authority inside the kingdom. His defeat of the Wendish pirates made possible the rapid expansion of agriculture, the foundation of towns, and the growth of international trade. He secured his mainland conquests by wedding his sons, Canute (Knut) and Valdemar, to daughters of the Welf prince, Henry the Lion, duke of Saxony.

Canute VI (1182-1202) continued this program, with his brother Valdemar's help, by occupying Mecklenburg, Holstein, and the archbishopric of Hamburg-Bremen. Canute was not a modern nationalist. He paid little attention to the ethnic origin of his subjects, and since his Danish-speaking subjects were hardly numerous enough to settle on the underpopulated mainland coast, the principal beneficiaries of his policies were German fishermen, peasants, burghers, and petty nobles. With Canute's encouragement, they founded towns, exploited the herring grounds, and traded in Gotland, Livonia (modern Latvia), and Russia. Canute's Wendish vassals introduced Germans into their lands in such numbers as to change the ethnic composition of Mecklenburg. Canute relied greatly on his vigorous younger brother, Valdemar, because he himself was too weak to lead armies in the field. Consequently, when Canute died childless at a relatively young age, Valdemar came to the throne well prepared for his duties and confident of his ability to continue the dynasty's program.

Life's Work

The political situation in 1202 was extremely favorable for Valdemar. The Holy Roman Empire was in political turmoil: Pope Innocent III was playing the Welf and Hohenstaufen factions against each other, encouraging the weaker of the two parties to continue its efforts to secure the throne. Valdemar intervened in the North, replacing some local rulers and rewarding others, thus consolidating his empire in Germany while winning papal thanks for his contributions to the Church's cause. Afterward, neither the Welf emperor, Otto IV, nor the Hohenstaufen, Frederick II, dared attack him. Frederick even confirmed his rights to the lands north of the Elbe in a Golden Bull.

Valdemar's policies on the mainland were not uniformly successful. His decision to send his sister, Ingeborg, to marry Philip II of France was an embarrassing debacle. His decision to release Valdemar of Schleswig from prison cost him years of conflict in Hamburg-Bremen. He seemed, however, to have the golden touch in the Baltic.

Valdemar envisioned extending his rule over all the still-pagan shores of the eastern sea—over Pomerania, Prussia, Kurland (Courland), Livonia, and Estonia. His first step came in 1202, in his approval of the crusading mission of Bishop Albert to Riga in Livonia in return for recognition of Valdemar's overlordship. In 1206, Valdemar himself led a force to Oesel, the largest of the Estonian islands, to intimidate the fierce pirates there. In 1210, he raided Samland in Prussia. Still, he had to secure peace in North Germany before he could take a major force to the east. Peace came in 1215, followed quickly by the news that Bishop Albert's Crusaders were making such rapid headway in Livonia that they would soon overstep the agreed northern boundary of their conquests; moreover, they were refusing to recognize Valdemar as overlord.

In 1219, Valdemar sailed with a great army to Estonia. The overawed tribesmen surrendered so quickly that Valdemar became careless about his personal safety. When attacking natives penetrated right into the royal tent, they killed Valdemar's newly appointed bishop of Estonia and missed the king only because his modest clothing gave little clue as to his status. Valdemar, fighting courageously

VALDEMAR KINGS OF DENMARK, 1157-1241

Reign	*Ruler*
1157-1182	Valdemar I the Great
1182-1202	Canute IV (VI) the Pious
1202-1241	VALDEMAR II THE VICTORIOUS

at the head of his Danish, German, and Wendish vassals, crushed the uprising, built a castle at Reval (Tallinn) and went home determined to humble Bishop Albert's unruly Crusaders. He brought home the Dannebrog, the distinctive red banner with a white cross, which, as legend tells it, had fallen from heaven to encourage his Crusaders at a critical moment and which became the Danish standard.

A similar lapse of attention in May of 1223 cost Valdemar greatly. He invited Count Henry (Heinrich) of Schwerin to accompany him hunting on the island of Lyø. A few years earlier, Henry's brother had given a daughter as wife to Valdemar's eldest son. Though the couple died soon after their wedding, Valdemar was claiming half of Schwerin as the dowry. Henry, desperate to avoid this debt, kidnapped Valdemar and his eldest son—who had been made joint king in 1218—and imprisoned them in Dannenberg.

Papal threats failed to move Count Henry, who understandably feared Valdemar's revenge. Henry organized a coalition of local nobles and prelates that defeated Valdemar's allies in 1225, then expelled the Danish appointees to office and divided the spoils. Meanwhile, the news of Valdemar's fall had precipitated a rebellion in Estonia that was crushed by Livonian Crusaders, who henceforth occupied that land. Henry was then in a position to ransom the king for a large sum and his promise to surrender all territorial claims in North Germany. Valdemar retained control of Rügen and Estonia.

Valdemar sought to recover his losses by force of arms but was defeated on July 22, 1227, at Bornhöved, after which he abandoned his hopes of a mainland empire. He retained Estonia by diplomacy, through the Treaty of Stenby, in 1238.

The king contented himself with domestic affairs, particularly law reform. His codification of Jutland law was completed only a few days before his death in 1241. His children by Richza of Saxony and Margarete of Bohemia died before him. His sons by Berengaria of Portugal each, in turn, became king; Eric from 1241 to 1250, Abel from 1250 to 1252, and Christopher from 1252 to 1259. Their mutual hatred disrupted the kingdom and brought an end to the hard-won unity and internal peace of the Valdemar era.

SIGNIFICANCE

The age of the Valdemars, from 1157 to 1241, was the most glorious era of Danish medieval history. For a short period, brilliant churchmen and monarchs ended the endemic civil wars, expanded trade, created a great empire, built churches and cathedrals, and established the kingdom on a hereditary basis.

Denmark profited greatly from the long era of internal peace and stability. The population grew steadily and more land was brought under cultivation. This provided the taxes and tithes that built palaces, cathedrals, and churches.

The king abandoned the common levy for raising troops, relying instead on prominent warriors and rich farmers, who were freed from taxation in return for serving as royal officials and mounted troops. These knights soon became a new nobility. Though bound to the king by an oath, in time they tended to work more for their own interests than those of the monarchy.

Another enduring accomplishment of the period was securing the safety of international trade across the Baltic Sea. Merchants from the Holy Roman Empire sailed east under Danish protection. Although Lübeck owed its rise to prominence to Valdemar II's policy of supporting merchants against local nobles, the merchants naturally chafed against any tax or interference in their affairs. Consequently, Lübeck joined Count Henry's coalition and made a significant contribution at the Battle of Bornhöved in 1227. The citizens' subsequent alliances with other growing mercantile communities were forerunners of the Hanseatic League. Valdemar's successors were to wage long wars against Lübeck and the League in an effort to re-create his Baltic empire, but with equal lack of ultimate success.

Valdemar II was a great warrior and an effective administrator, especially when he had the services of gifted vassals and churchmen. His self-confidence led him to be somewhat careless about his personal safety and less than thoughtful about the long-term results of his policies. His failure to instill brotherly love among his sons serves well to illustrate his shortcomings as man and ruler. Similarly, he failed to make the nobles more concerned for their country than for themselves or to reconcile his mainland subjects to Danish rule. These shortcomings were not made good by successors who modeled themselves on him.

—*William L. Urban*

FURTHER READING

Birch, J. H. S. *Denmark in History.* Westport, Conn.: Greenwood Press, 1975. This standard survey summarizes adequately the insights of the many historians who publish in Danish and German.

Christiansen, Eric. *The Northern Crusades.* New ed. New York: Penguin Books, 1997. Good background to the Wendish and Estonian Crusades, the origins of the Hanseatic League, and the long contest for hegemony over the Baltic Sea.

Jones, Prudence, and Nigel Pennick. *A History of Pagan Europe.* New York: Routledge, 1997. A survey of the history of pagans and paganism in Europe, against which Valdemar struggled in his realm of the Baltics. Includes a bibliography and index.

King, Wilson. *Chronicles of Three Free Cities: Hamburg, Bremen, Lübeck.* New York: E. P. Dutton, 1914. A dated romantic history, but timeless good reading. Includes some color illustrations and a map.

Lauring, Palle. *A History of Denmark.* Translated by David Hohnen. Copenhagen: Host and Son, 1986. This is the seventh edition of a highly respected general survey.

Lewis, Archibald Ross, and Timothy J. Runyan. *European Naval and Maritime History, 300-1500.* Bloomington: Indiana University Press, 1990. A survey written for the general reader on the rich maritime and shipping history of the European Middle Ages, including the Baltic region during the time of Valdemar. Includes maps and a bibliography.

Urban, William L. *The Baltic Crusade.* Chicago: Lithuanian Research and Studies Center, 1994. This volume describes the situation in the Holy Roman Empire before and after 1200, which made Valdemar's empire possible. There are detailed descriptions of Valdemar's policies, his Crusades to Estonia, and his kidnapping and fall.

SEE ALSO: Frederick II; Henry the Lion; Innocent III; Margaret of Denmark, Norway, and Sweden; Philip II; Saxo Grammaticus.

RELATED ARTICLES in *Great Events from History: The Middle Ages, 477-1453*: 850-950: Viking Era; c. 1150-1200: Rise of the Hansa Merchant Union; 1228-1231: Teutonic Knights Bring Baltic Region Under Catholic Control; June 17, 1397: Kalmar Union Is Formed.

LORENZO VALLA

Italian philosopher

By means of his careful scholarship, Valla helped legitimize Renaissance Humanism, reorganize philosophical methodology, and expose certain prevalent Roman Catholic beliefs and practices to critical scrutiny, thus helping to prepare the way for the rise of Protestantism.

BORN: 1407; Rome, Papal States (now in Italy)

DIED: August 1, 1457; Rome, Papal States (now in Italy)

ALSO KNOWN AS: Laurentius Vallensis (Latin name)

AREAS OF ACHIEVEMENT: Religion and theology, philosophy

EARLY LIFE

Few important details have survived concerning the early life of Lorenzo Valla (VAHL-lah), one of the greatest of the Italian Renaissance Humanists. It is known that he was born to a pious, upper-class family that traced its roots back to Piacenza, in the Italian Alps. The advantages he enjoyed by birth were magnified by his education, for Valla was extremely fortunate in his instructors, sitting at the feet not only of Vittorino da Feltre, one of the premier scholars at the University of Rome, but also Leonardo Bruni, who taught Valla Latin, and Giovanni Aurispa, who taught him Greek. Under their tutelage Valla became a superb linguist. He became so proficient, in fact, that he often was commissioned by the pope for official translations. Ironically, the same linguistic proficiency that brought him papal attention and commendation would eventually call forth the pope's ire.

While still in his early twenties, Valla was appointed to the chair of eloquence at the University of Pavia, an appointment that required him to teach rhetoric, Latin, and Greek. It was during his tenure at Pavia that Valla, in 1431, was ordained a Roman Catholic priest.

The same year he was ordained, Valla published *De voluptate* (1431), later revised under the title *De vero bono* (1433; *On Pleasure*, 1977). In it, he searches for the highest human good. This search is conducted as a comparative exposition, in dialogue form, between Leonardus, Antonius, and Nicolaus, Valla's imaginary representatives of Stoicism, Epicureanism, and Christianity, respectively. According to Leonardus, the highest human good is moral virtue, which must be pursued at all costs, even the cost of one's life and happiness, if need be. Antonius counters this assertion by identifying pleasure (which he closely ties to utility), as the highest good. Nicolaus, whose views are probably to be seen as Valla's own, says that Christanity is the highest good because it combines the best of Stoicism and Epicureanism without any of their shortcomings. To him, whoever serves God gladly does best (that is, has virtue) and is happiest (that is, has pleasure). To Nicolaus, Christianity is our glad service for God and, because it is, it is the highest human good.

Valla's service at the University of Pavia lasted for about three years until, in 1433, his public letter attacking a notable local jurist aroused such a tempest that he was forced to resign his academic post. For the next three years, in true Renaissance fashion, he followed the ancient peripatetic model for scholars, moving from Pavia to Milan, to Genoa, and to Mantua, before settling finally in Naples, where he became private secretary to King Alfonso, a post from which he rose to public prominence.

LIFE'S WORK

At about the same time that Valla enlisted in the service of the king, he published *De libero arbitrio* (c. 1436; *On Free Will*, 1948), an influential work that examines the relationship between divine foreknowledge and election, on the one hand, and human free will and responsibility, on the other. It also examines the relationship between reason and religion. In it, Valla argues that human beings cannot shun their responsibility to do good and they cannot blame God for their shortcomings, as if he were the cause of their evil and not they themselves. To Valla, because God is omniscient, he knows what a person will do even before he or she does it. That person, nevertheless, cannot say that God caused the action, because prior knowledge is not a cause. The verb "to know" is an intransitive verb. That is, it has no external effect. Simply to know that one will deposit money in one's bank account will neither make one richer nor cause the deposit to occur. Only going to the bank and leaving money in the account can do that, and that is a human responsibility. It also is something one is free to do or to leave undone. The fact that God knows what will happen does not alter the action or relieve a person of the responsibility to get it done, nor does it vitiate the freedom to do so. Thus, divine foreknowledge and human freedom are compatible concepts. Infallible prediction is not the same as predeterminism.

Valla goes on to explain that while the human mind can comprehend such difficult problems and even offer plausible solutions to them, religion is not reducible merely to reason. Some things in religion exceed reason's grasp. As a pious Renaissance Humanist, Valla believed that religion, rhetoric, and reason form a hierarchy. Religion, so to speak, is king; rhetoric is queen, and reason is their servant. Thus, while good theology and good philosophy are complementary, religion takes precedence over reason. Valla is not opposed to philosophy. He is opposed to bad philosophy and to philosophy that does not keep to its proper place or role. God's revelation is understandable to reason, but it is not subject to reason. Reason is subject to it.

At about the same time that Valla published *On Free Will*, he began work on what was perhaps his most popular work, *Elegantiae linguae latinae* (1444). This book is Valla's effort to restore Latin usage to its ancient purity, a purity he believed was lost at the hands of medieval Latinists, whom he called "barbarians." This book, therefore, is a Humanist handbook on how to achieve graceful style and verbal precision. Because it was the first great effort at Humanistic philology, it was the first work to place the study of Latin usage on a somewhat scientific basis. It soon became the standard textbook for Humanists interested in verbal accuracy and verbal art.

Dialecticae disputationes (c. 1439) is Valla's attempt to restore and restructure medieval philosophy by rearranging its arguments. In this book, Valla tried to simplify logic and to rearrange it according to the discipline of rhetoric. By allying philosophical clarity with rhetorical flourish, Valla was trying to teach scholars not only how to speak sense (logic) but also how to speak sense beautifully and compellingly (rhetoric). Reason (ratio) must be combined with eloquence (oratio). Valla, in other words, tried to modify the prevailing Aristotelianism of his day by showing that metaphysical truth could be clarified by linguistic criticism, literary analysis, and rhetorical emphasis. To Valla, Aristotle's philosophical language was unsound. *Dialecticae disputationes* is Valla's effort to correct this shortcoming with a philosophy that was rhetorically a better description of reality.

Easily Valla's most sensational work, *De falso credita et ementita Constantini donatione declamatio* (1440; *The Treatise of Lorenzo Valla on the Donation of Constantine*, 1922), revealed the fraudulent nature of the document on which medieval popes based their claim for political and military power. Written while he was still in the pay of King Alfonso (an adversary of the pope), and probably written at the king's suggestion, this book resulted in Valla's trial on charges of heresy, a trial that was stymied by the king's intervention. The spurious Donation of Constantine, supposedly written by the ancient Roman emperor himself, gave the entire western region of the Empire to Pope Sylvester because the pope allegedly had cured the emperor of leprosy. As a result, Constantine withdrew himself and his court from Rome to Constantinople because he did not feel worthy to live in the same city as such a holy man as Sylvester. In gratitude for his healing, the emperor granted the pope political and military charge over the west.

Valla's critical analysis, both linguistic and historical, overturned the integrity of the document. By means of his own philological expertise, Valla showed that this document could not have been written in the fourth century, as it purports to have been. Instead, by exposing many of its anachronisms, he showed it to be an eighth century forgery, perhaps from Paris. Thus, while he was not the first to question this document's authenticity—Dante and John Wyclif had done so before him—he was the first to establish his objection on the basis of sound historical and linguistic judgment.

Having to some extent debunked papal claims to civil power, Valla next took aim at traditional Roman Catholic piety. *De professione religiosorum* (1442; on monastic views) is his effort to prove that religious people, such as priests, monks, and nuns, are not necessarily the best. Ostensibly a dialogue between Frater, a traditional Roman Catholic, and Lorenzo, whose views represent Valla's own, this book is a courageous and outspoken challenge to prevalent views on Christian life. In it, Valla denies, as the Protestant reformers do later, that any special spiritual status attaches to members of the clergy or of the religious orders. To Valla, all Christians are on equal footing. One must not be called religious simply because one has taken vows. Vows, he believes, are worthless if one does not lead a godly life. If one can lead a godly life without vows, why are they necessary? True sanctity comes from being acceptable to God, not to one's ecclesiastical superiors. Vows, in fact, are inimical to spirituality because virtue begins with pious inner attitudes, not obedience to external rules. On this point Valla believed the laity actually to be superior because when they obey they do so out of their own good will, not because of pressure imposed on them from the outside. In addition to vows, Valla opposes the exaltation of poverty. To be wealthy, he said, is not the same as being sinful, nor is being poor synonymous with being pious. Christ taught us to be poor in spirit, not poor in goods. The monkish practice of giving all one's money to the poor so that one too may become a beggar is, to Valla, a perversion of Christianity, which is faith in Christ and love to God and humanity.

In 1448, Valla left the service of King Alfonso in order to assume the dual role of apostolic secretary to Pope Nicholas V and professor at the University of Rome, tasks that allowed him plenty of time to engage in scholarly pursuit. That he was employed by the pope, even after the attack on the Donation of Constantine was published, is a tribute to the pope's tolerance, to his confidence in himself and his office, and to Valla's prestige and worth as a scholar.

Valla's final major work, one published posthumously by Desiderius Erasmus, was his *Adnotationes in Novum Testamentum* (1505). This book deals with the Latin translation of the Bible (the Vulgate) in the light of Valla's knowledge of Greek. In it, he attempts to correct some of the Vulgate's mistakes, which he evaluated on grammatical, stylistic, and philosophical grounds. The first assesses the strict accuracy of the Vulgate's vocabulary and syntax, the second how well the Vulgate captured the eloquence and power of the original, and the third how fully the philosophical and theological content have been preserved. It was by these tests, Valla believed, that one could best aid the cause of theological restoration and the recovery of the fundamentals of Christianity. After nearly a decade in Rome, Valla died, in 1457, after suffering an unidentified illness.

Significance

Valla was one of the most original and influential scholars of the Italian Renaissance. His work demonstrates most clearly the effect that accurate historical perspective and careful literary analysis could have on the various fields of knowledge, especially theology and philosophy. In that light, he was one of the leading critical minds of his age. He succeeded in establishing the new study of philology as a respectable and useful academic discipline.

Thus, Valla was a groundbreaker and a pioneer. His work served as a guide and inspiration for later Humanists such as Erasmus, who also desired to restore theology by means of the humanities. Valla also enjoyed a measure of success in reorganizing philosophical inquiry by freeing it from the control of medieval Scholastic methods. In this he anticipated later European thinkers such as Peter Ramus. By Protestants such as Martin Luther, Valla was considered a theological forerunner and a kindred spirit. Like them, he believed that faith was the basis of Christian living, not any external actions. Like them, he also denied the spiritual superiority of the monastic lifestyle, and he attacked the validity of some papal claims to authority. It is wrong, nevertheless, to see Valla as a Protestant. Although he was a protesting Catholic, he was not a Protestant. He never thought of himself as outside the Roman fold. Whenever he differed from the Church, he considered himself not un-Catholic, but "more orthodox than the orthodox."

—*Michael E. Bauman*

Further Reading

Ginzburg, Carlo. *History, Rhetoric, and Proof.* Hanover, N.H.: University Press of New England for Brandeis University Press/Historical Society of Israel, 1999. Contains a chapter on Lorenzo Valla and the Donation of Constantine. Bibliography and index.

Lorch, Maristella De Panizza. *A Defense of Life: Lorenzo Valla's Theory of Pleasure*. Munich: W. Fink, 1985. A look at the belief's of Valla regarding pleasure, as expressed in his *De vero falsoque bono*. Bibliography and index.

Mack, Peter. *Renaissance Argument: Valla and Agricola in the Traditions of Rhetoric and Dialectic*. New York: E. J. Brill, 1993. An examination of rhetoric and dialectic that analyzes Valla's philosophy and his contribution to logic, among other topics. Works described are Valla's *Repastinatio dialecticae et philosophiae* and Rodolphus Agricola's *De inventione dialectica*. Bibliography and index.

Monfasani, John. *Language and Learning in Renaissance Italy: Selected Articles*. Brookfield, Vt.: Variorum, 1994. A look at Valla's contributions to language as well as at learning and scholarship in Renaissance Italy. Bibliography and indexes.

Trinkaus, Charles. *In Our Image and Likeness: Humanity and Divinity in Italian Humanist Thought*. 2 vols. Chicago: University of Chicago Press, 1970. Chapter 3, "Lorenzo Valla: Voluptas et Fruitio, Verba et Res," is a well-documented, closely argued, seventy-page account of Valla's moral and religious thought. Trinkaus traces several key motifs through Valla's most important books, from which, in his footnotes, he quotes at length in the original Latin.

_______. "Lorenzo Valla on the Problem of Speaking About the Trinity." *Journal of the History of Ideas* 57 (January, 1996): 27. The author examines Valla's application of humanistic theology to the Christian doctrine of the Trinity, the diastrous result of the "Repastinatio dialectice et philosophie." He cites Augustine's discussion of the three members of the Trinity.

Valla, Lorenzo. *The Treatise of Lorenzo Valla on the Donation of Constantine*. Translated by Christopher B. Coleman. Toronto: University of Toronto Press in association with the Renaissance Society of America, 1993. A translation of *De falso credita et ementita Constantini donatione declamatio*. Includes analysis and biographical material on Valla.

See also: Leonardo Bruni; Dante; Nicholas V.

Related article in *Great Events from History: The Middle Ages, 477-1453*: 1440: Donation of Constantine Is Exposed.

Jean de Venette

French friar and writer

A friar who wrote a chronicle recording the political and social events of northern France between 1340 and 1368, Jean captured the sense of urgency and distress of the times in which he lived, while criticizing those whom he thought to be at least partially responsible for the time's troubles.

Born: 1307 or 1308; probably the village of Venette, near Compiègne, France

Died: 1368 or 1369; probably Paris, France

Areas of achievement: Religion and theology, monasticism, literature, government and politics

Early Life

Some details of the life of Jean de Venette (zhahn duh vay-neht) can be gleaned from references in his chronicle and the records of the Paris convent in which he lived much of his adult life. He wrote that he was seven or eight years old when the famine of 1315 struck Europe, indicating that he was born in 1307 or 1308, most likely in the provincial village of Venette, northeast of Paris, on the banks of the Oise River. Of peasant stock, Jean was reared in the rolling and fertile countryside of northern France. In the years following the famine of 1315, it is probable that Jean, having shown interest and promise, began his formal education, learning the basics of reading and writing Latin at a local monastery. In all likelihood, he was the only individual from his village to acquire training beyond the memorization of prayers and psalms that the parish priest might have provided.

At some point, probably in his teens, Jean decided to devote his life to the Church and joined the order of Carmelite friars. The Carmelites, also known as the White Friars for their white cloaks, had originated in Palestine, where in the twelfth century groups of hermits lived on the slopes of Mount Carmel, having dedicated their lives to prayer. Members of the group soon migrated to Western Europe, and, in 1250, Pope Innocent IV formally recognized the order and approved their constitution. Each friar pledged to devote himself to prayer, preaching, and study and to live a humble beggar's life in the urban centers of Europe. Rejecting the accumulation of property, the convents of Carmelites shared their meager resources and preached to townspeople about charity, humility, and the simple life of Christ. Jean's early years as a Carmelite have escaped the records of history, but in the 1320's or 1330's he joined the Parisian convent of Carmelites on the Place Maubert and studied theology at the University of Paris. After studying theology for several years, he became a master of theology; by 1339, he had become the prior, or head, of the Paris Carmelite convent.

Life's Work

As prior of a Carmelite convent in the capital city of France, Jean likely had many official duties to fulfill, such as running his own convent and inspecting the smaller convents in towns near Paris. He held this post until 1342, when the Carmelites selected him as the head of the order of the province of France, a post that he apparently held until his death. Despite his official duties, which undoubtedly consumed much time, Jean developed an interest in past events and historical accounts. He stressed the importance of historical study to the younger friars and likely enlisted their aid in collecting evidence and stories about the history of the Carmelite order. In 1360, Jean compiled this information in a brief history of the order from its legendary founding by Elijah until the mid-twelfth century, when two English barons brought to Europe some Carmelite hermits from Palestine.

Jean's historical avocation further appears in *Chronicon* (*The Chronicle of Jean de Venette*, 1953), a book better known than the history of the order itself. The chronicle, which describes events from 1340 to 1368, contains many eyewitness accounts and tidbits of news that Jean received in Paris or on his travels to other convents throughout northern France. The chronicle's narrative—like most medieval chronicles—consists of entries for each of the years recorded by the author. In these yearly summaries, Jean wrote of weather conditions; political events; military campaigns, victories, and defeats; the wartime condition of the cities, villages, and countryside of France; and the social conflicts present in the France of his day. While parts of the book appear to have been written on a day-to-day basis, most of the Latin manuscript was written after Jean had spent some time reflecting on the dramatic events of the mid-fourteenth century.

Throughout the text of the chronicle, Jean's sensitivity and humaneness are apparent. Coming from peasant stock, he understood the hardships and sufferings of peasants during times of war, famine, and plague and was clearly proud of the endurance and fortitude of his social class. As one who dedicated himself to a life of humility, he was sharply critical of the fourteenth century French nobility, whom he perceived as lax, vain, and impotent. Jean particularly criticized the aristocracy for their inability to protect the French from the English during the repeated invasions of the Hundred Years' War. Unlike many medieval chronicles or historical accounts, Jean's history comes alive with feeling, giving his audience the sense that Jean was often in the middle of the events he describes or was at least deeply concerned about their outcome.

Jean's history has a stately unity in that it begins and ends in years when Jean reported that a comet was observed in the skies above France. Despite this astronomical coherence, the years between 1340 and 1368 were years of social and political turmoil in the kingdom. Beginning in 1340, when the English king, Edward III, crossed the English Channel and invaded France to claim the throne that had belonged to his grandfather, Jean described a world that was increasingly unstable. He noted in 1340, for example, that men were beginning to wear unbecoming clothes and garments that were so short as to be indecent. Noblemen, except those of royal blood, grew their beards long and seemed to lose their courage in battle. Far from being prudish, Jean was seeking from the very beginning of his chronicle to provide an explanation for France's having nearly succumbed to English conquest in the 1350's and 1360's. Throughout the 1340's, Jean described the English military successes and depicted the incredible hardship that confronted the common people of France. Not only was the war difficult to endure when grain fields were trampled or set afire, but the king also seemed unable to protect his subjects from the depredations of his officials, who continuously levied taxes and altered the currency so that coins did not retain their true value. While the commoners thought that they were contributing their hard-earned pennies to the French war effort, Jean cynically and angrily noted that nobles and knights used the funds for their own pleasures, such as gambling.

The Black Death (the bubonic plague) struck the kingdom in 1347 and ushered in a new era, in which, according to Jean, children developed only twenty or twenty-two teeth, instead of the normal thirty-two. Jean thought that humans had become more covetous and brawling, suing one another at every turn. Despite the vast mortality of the plague, however, the war between England and France continued, adding to the fear and suffering of those devastating years. In 1354, a nighttime political assassination ushered in new calamities for the French: With the murder of a leading royal official by Charles of Navarre, the son-in-law of King John, civil war erupted in the kingdom. On the heels of this tragedy followed the English capture of King John himself on the battlefield at Poitiers in 1356. With the king a captive in England, the states general attempted to provide some order in the kingdom, but its efforts were in vain, as noblemen utterly refused to cooperate with the representatives of the towns. In the ensuing confusion, aristocrats sought to exploit their subjects and refused to defend France from further English attacks. It seemed to many that the noblemen, who were charged with the responsibility of protecting the realm from its enemies, had severely neglected their duty. Revenge came when the exploited peasants rose up and slaughtered hundreds of these dissolute aristocrats. Seeking justice, the peasants became overzealous in their vengeance; they were then overpowered by noblemen who brutally restored a semblance of order.

Throughout the account of the calamities that befell France in the 1350's, Jean displayed not only his human sensitivity but also a deep love for his homeland. In 1359, when he wrote about the destruction of the region surrounding Compiègne, Jean emotionally described how vines were left unpruned and rotting, how the fields were not plowed or sown, how no hens called to their chicks, and how robbers and thieves freely wandered from village to village carrying off whatever they could find. The reader senses Jean's love of France and his recognition that France had the potential to be a great and rich kingdom, if only the noblemen responsible for its defense and protection would fulfill their duties. This attitude, prevalent among townspeople and peasants through the later 1350's, not only captured the frustration created by years of military misfortune but also condemned the upper classes for their corrupt lifestyle, their self-centeredness, and their exploitive greed.

Jean's sentiments about his kingdom and society, however, were not limited to sorrow and condemnation. In his accounts of the mid-1360's, after the captive King John's death in London and the accession of Charles V, Jean recorded the gradual process of reestablishing order and peace in France. After some lengthy negotiations, truces were arranged between the royal adversaries, the civil war between Charles of Navarre and the king ended, and noblemen began once again to fulfill their social role as the kingdom's protectors. Throughout these final annual accounts, Jean reflected the tentative hopefulness of his times and glorified the recently established Valois Dynasty, which had the opportunity to create a powerful and peaceful France.

Significance

Although Jean de Venette was clearly a dedicated friar and capable administrator within the order of Carmelites, he is best known for his chronicle of the mid-fourteenth century. While the veracity of a chronicle cannot always be judged from the distance of several hundred years, it is clear that Jean's writing has great historical value. Arising from the peasantry, Jean was an individual who understood and appreciated the value of learning and writing in an age when illiteracy was predominant. Using his skills, he recorded the passage of time, the events, the pleasures, and the tragedies of his era. Unlike many dry, emotionless records of the Middle Ages, however, Jean's work comes alive, reflecting his personality, his ideas, his dreams for France, and his moral judgment of the French people.

This living work offers the historian a special opportunity to comprehend the mentality of the fourteenth century. Understanding the war-weariness of France and the frustration of the lower classes provides a perspective that corrects the overly romantic idealization of the Middle Ages as a time of knights in shining armor performing feats to please ladies. Instead, Jean reveals a population gravely concerned about the fate of the kingdom and hopeful for the return of peace and order. Within Jean's writing, the reader can glimpse patriotic stirrings that were to give France a powerful cohesiveness in later centuries.

—*David M. Bessen*

Further Reading

Fowler, Kenneth. *The Age of Plantagenet and Valois: The Struggle for Supremacy, 1328-1498*. New York: Putnam, 1967. A beautifully illustrated book that covers the origins of the Hundred Years' War, its key battles, and the political and social changes the French and English kingdoms experienced.

Froissart, Jean. *The Chronicle of England, France, Spain, Etc*. Edited by Ernest Rhys. London: J. M. Dent and Sons, 1927. A chronicle of the fourteenth century and the Hundred Years' War. Incorporates English evidence and gives the reader a slightly different perspective on the international conflict.

Jotischky, Andrew. *The Carmelites and Antiquity: Mendicants and Their Pasts in the Middle Ages*. New York: Oxford University Press, 2002. Explores the history of the Carmelites, including the Carmelite habit, defending the tradition, Carmelite theology in the 1300's, and the development of a historical narrative.

Kooper, Erik, ed. *The Medieval Chronicle: Proceedings of the First International Conference on the Medieval Chronicle*. Atlanta: Rodopi, 1999. A collection of essays on the significance of the medieval chronicle in the history of literature of the time. Includes bibliographical references.

_______. *The Medieval Chronicle II: Proceedings of the Second International Conference on the Medieval Chronicle*. Atlanta: Rodopi, 2002. A second collection of essays from a subsequent conference on the medieval chronicle.

Lawrence, C. H. *Medieval Monasticism: Forms of Religious Life in Western Europe in the Middle Ages*. London: Longman, 1984. This survey of monasticism provides basic information on the monastic movement throughout the Middle Ages, including a chapter on the friars and mendicants such as the Carmelites.

Perroy, Edouard. *The Hundred Years' War*. Translated by D. C. Douglas. New York: Capricorn Books, 1965. A good survey of the late medieval conflict between the kings of England and France. This book describes not only the military conflict between the kingdoms but also the social upheavals in France caused by Charles of Navarre's civil war and the plague.

Seward, Desmond. *A Brief History of the Hundred Years' War: The English in France, 1337-1453*. London: Robinson, 2003. A valuable adjunct to an understanding of the complicated period of struggle between France and England, with attention to the Burgundian faction. A clear, historical overview of a most difficult subject. Includes illustrations and maps.

Tuchman, Barbara W. *A Distant Mirror: The Calamitous Fourteenth Century*. New York: Alfred A. Knopf, 1978. A very readable book that not only uses Jean's chronicle as one of its sources but also carefully explains the political and social turmoil experienced by France during the 1340's and 1350's.

Venette, Jean de. *The Chronicle of Jean de Venette*. Translated by Jean Birdsall. Edited by Richard A. Newhall. New York: Columbia University Press, 1953. An excellent English-language edition of the chronicle, this volume contains a good introduction to the life and times of Jean and copious explanatory notes on the complexities of the fourteenth century.

See also: Edward III; Jean Froissart; Innocent IV; John Pecham; William of Saint-Amour.

Related articles in *Great Events from History: The Middle Ages, 477-1453*: April 16, 1209: Founding of the Franciscans; 1337-1453: Hundred Years' War; August 26, 1346: Battle of Crécy; 1347-1352: Invasion of the Black Death in Europe; 1373-1410: Jean Froissart Compiles His *Chronicles*.

GIOVANNI VILLANI
Italian historian

In his Chronicle, *Villani conveyed an empirical account of the Italian communes and laid the foundation for a historiography based on human will and action.*

BORN: c. 1275; Florence (now in Italy)
DIED: 1348; Florence
AREA OF ACHIEVEMENT: Historiography

EARLY LIFE

Giovanni Villani (joh-VAHN-nee veel-LAH-nee) was born into a wealthy merchant family in Florence. It may be assumed that Villani, like most sons of merchants, went to a grammar school to learn Latin and then to another school to learn computation on the abacus. Thereafter, he most likely apprenticed with a merchant firm, perhaps the Peruzzi company, with which his name was first associated. He served as an agent and partner in this great merchant banking house in Flanders off and on from 1300 to 1307. From his intimate knowledge of the affairs of Philip IV, it has been conjectured that he had contact with the French royal court. In Florence, international trade and banking were integrally linked, and at some point, Villani entered the guild of bankers. He witnessed and contributed to Florence's golden age of commerce when the city served as Europe's banker and one of its chief centers of trade. After 1308, Villani continued to act as a representative of the Peruzzi, but he was no longer a formal partner. In 1322, Villani became a member of the rival merchant company of the Buonaccorsi. His participation in the Buonaccorsi firm reflects his independence, for he appears to have been one of the principal partners, which would have required a sizable investment.

LIFE'S WORK

In a manner similar to that of other Florentine merchants, Villani served abroad in his early adulthood and accumulated knowledge and wealth. He thus possessed the leisure and experience to participate in the Florentine Republic from 1316 to 1341. In addition to numerous minor offices, including responsibility for coining money and for the city walls, Villani held the position of prior, the most prestigious and powerful in the Florentine government, in 1316, 1321-1322, and 1328. Though he apparently never fathered children, he married twice, his second wife being from the wealthy family of the Pazzi. This marriage into the highest echelon of Florentine society and his political offices best indicate Villani's social prominence in the city of Florence.

In 1338, Villani's economic and social fortunes suffered a disastrous blow that affected the entire Florentine merchant community. In that year, the Buonaccorsi suffered bankruptcy, as did the Bardi and Peruzzi companies. Villani was sent to the infamous Florentine prison, the Stinche, for his debts, and he never recovered his wealth or prestige. From 1342 to 1343, the Florentines experimented with rule by a dictator, which led to a more popular government composed of new citizens, many of them from the Florentine countryside. Villani held no offices after 1341 and felt alienated from the rule of the new governors. In his history of Florence, he frequently criticized these newcomers for their presumption and political ineptitude. Villani died in 1348 from the plague while describing in his history the devastating power of that terrible disease.

The fame of Villani derives from his *Croniche fiorentine* (*Chronicle*, 1896). The Italian edition was completed by F. G. Dragomanni in four volumes dated 1844 to 1845, though it has never been fully translated into English. Villani informs the reader that he was stimulated to write his history of Florence while on a pilgrimage in Rome for the Great Jubilee of 1300. Excited by the ancient monuments and the great deeds of Roman heroes and stirred by the belief that Florence was the daughter of Rome, Villani determined to memorialize the numerous accomplishments of his native city. On the basis of internal evidence, critics have judged that he began to write in the 1320's or even as late as the 1330's. He probably did conceive of writing the history in 1300, beginning to accumulate materials then or soon thereafter. He also may have sketched the chief events of the period of Florentine political conflict from 1301 to 1304, which he knew at first hand. It was only in 1322, however, that he began to treat Florentine history fully. From that year until his death, Villani appears to have written contemporaneously with the events and to have recorded all the important occurrences that came into his purview. In the 1330's or early 1340's, he decided on the overall form of the work, to which he added chronicles of the final years.

The *Chronicle* is composed of twelve books, with the first six dealing primarily with events before Villani's lifetime. In the broadest analysis, Villani's *Chronicle* remains in the tradition of medieval histories because it places the events of fourteenth century Florence within a universal history that begins with the Tower of Babel as a dispersal of Adam's descendants. In the first book, Villani narrates the history of Rome intertwined with the mythical origins of Florence and its rival to the north, the small hilltop town of Fiesole. This Etruscan town was to serve Villani as the source of enmity and social conflict within Florence, a conflict that could be overcome only through the triumph of Roman virtues implanted within the Florentines by Julius Caesar's founding. Books 2 through 6 center on Florence's dealings with the two great medieval superpowers, the Roman Empire and the Papacy. Villani claimed that Charlemagne had refounded the city after the Gothic king Totila had destroyed it; Villani believed that Florence was to play an important role within the divine order by participating with the Papacy in the Guelph alliance.

Villani drew heavily from Roman and Christian legends as well as from a number of thirteenth and early fourteenth century Florentine chronicles. From the latter, he took a knowledge of specific events and the ideology of Florence's preeminent place in Christendom and Christian history. Utilizing these earlier chronicles and his personal observations, Villani in books 7 through 12 recounted the history of Florence through 1348. Here he demonstrated an empirical knowledge of both the daily political and social life of his town and the larger political questions that troubled all Europe.

Villani structured his narration of events on the belief that history has several meanings. His history frequently illustrates the working out of divine judgment as sinful figures eventually come to earthly punishments after a season of success. Thus, God's will finds expression in historical time, often through the use of one historical personage to punish another. God's justice, however, triumphs in the world only to be tested again through another people's or individual's vices. Villani sought a confirmation of religious and moral beliefs in the events of history: In his chronicle, history is a stage for the conflict of moral forces and, insofar as historical individuals represent states and institutions, political forces.

Villani also recounted fully the round of natural events, particularly unusual storms, eclipses, and portents. The Florentine chronicler often explained the behavior of individuals and natural phenomena by the movement of comets, stars, and planets. Moreover, the devil and Providence play important roles in the *Chronicle* by influencing both human decisions and the natural world. Next to these irrational explanations of behavior, however, are rational analyses of human will, thought, and act. At times these analyses are integrated with an intimate knowledge of the natural environment to yield a convincing explanation of human character and events. Villani is best and justly known for his empirical description of the world of the Florentine merchant of the fourteenth century. Historians have thoroughly explored his chronicle for information on Florentine life in the fourteenth century, in part because he describes it in intimate detail. His chapter on Florence in 1336-1338 demonstrates a statistical frame of mind. As one of the first demographers, he judged the size of the city's population; the number of adult males, foreigners, nobles, and knights; the number of males and females born each year; and the number of students in grammar schools, schools of computation with the abacus, and schools of Latin and logic. He noted the number of churches, ab-

Sculpture of Giovanni Villani. (Library of Congress)

beys, and parishes along with the names of their priests and friars. He celebrated the guilds, especially those of merchants and bankers, noted the number of members and shops, and estimated their output. He focused particularly on the achievements of the Florentine cloth industry. Though scholars have suggested that he exaggerated the number of shops and the amount of cloth they produced, Villani's account enables the reader to gain a sense of the complexity of cloth manufacturing and sale in a premodern city. He describes in considerable detail the amount of food brought into the city in 1280 and notes the quantities of wine, grain, cows, sheep, goats, pigs, and melons.

Villani initiated a family practice of writing chronicles. Soon after his death in 1348, Villani's brother, Matteo, took up the craft of writing history. Matteo continued many of Giovanni's practices, including an emphasis on morality (perhaps heightened in the new history because of the depression resulting from the Black Death), a chronological ordering of events, and a penchant for detailed description. Matteo's history of Florence also was ended by the plague when in 1363 he succumbed to the disease. Matteo's son Filippo continued the family tradition of writing history; he wrote one book that narrated the events of 1364.

Significance

Villani's *Chronicle* should be judged as the best expression of the writing of Italian history in the Middle Ages, combining two qualities of medieval historiography. In common with the chronicles of monasteries and towns, it recounts in vivid detail the events that the chronicler believed deserved attention, from natural events to human accomplishments and viciousness. His chronicle also places these events within a divine ordering of nature and history. Villani could have borrowed this providential view of history from a variety of sources, but he ultimately draws it from the church fathers, particularly Saint Augustine.

Within these traditional qualities, Villani began several novel practices that came to fruition in Italian Renaissance history writing. Particularly significant was his close analysis of political motivation, a focus that came to be one of the hallmarks of Renaissance historiography. His explanations of human character and values often are complete and convincing, undermining his supernatural and magical explanations and rendering them superfluous. It is important to note, however, that his history does not demonstrate the influence of classical rhetoric, which added structure and a more complex awareness of audience to the histories of the Italian Renaissance Humanists.

—*James R. Banker*

Further Reading

Armstrong, Lawrin D. *Usury and Public Debt in Early Renaissance Florence: Lorenzo Ridolfi on the Monte Comune*. Toronto: Pontifical Institue of Mediaeval Studies, 2003. This work, which includes a translation of Lorenzo Ridolfi's *Tractatus de usuris*, examines the role of debt in Florentine society and, in so doing, sheds light on the circumstances in which Villani found himself.

Brucker, Gene A. *Florence, the Golden Age, 1138-1737*. Berkeley: University of California, 1998. A general work that looks at Florence during its most powerful years and later decline and provides background material for understanding Villani. Includes information on the economy, politics, the Church, and daily life. Bibliography and index.

Holmes, George. *Florence, Rome, and the Origins of the Renaissance*. New York: Oxford University Press, 1986. Looks at the conditions that existed in Florence and Rome and led up to the Renaissance. Bibliography and index.

Villani, Giovanni. *Villani's "Chronicle": Being Selections from the First Nine Books of the "Chroniche fiorentine" of Giovanni Villani*. Translated by Rose E. Selfe. 2d ed. London: Constable, 1906. A translation of selected chapters of the *Chronicle* through 1321. Though the selections were intended to aid in understanding Dante's *La divina commedia* (c. 1320; *The Divine Comedy*, 1802), they convey a good sense of the general ordering of the history of Florence in the medieval period and in the age of the great poet.

See also: Alfonso X; Saint Bede the Venerable; Leonardo Bruni; Giovanni da Pian del Carpini; Cassiodorus; Jean Froissart; Gregory of Tours; Hrosvitha; Joachim of Fiore; Michael Psellus; Saxo Grammaticus; Snorri Sturluson; Theophanes the Confessor; Vincent of Beauvais.

Related articles in *Great Events from History: The Middle Ages, 477-1453*: c. 1320: Origins of the Bubonic Plague; 1347-1352: Invasion of the Black Death in Europe.

Geoffroi de Villehardouin

Burgundian historian and military leader

Villehardouin wrote an original history of the Fourth Crusade, La Conquête de Constantinople, *the first known prose history—on any topic—in French, and also played a significant role in organizing and conducting the Crusade.*

Born: c. 1150; near Bar-sur-Aube, Burgundy (now in France)
Died: c. 1213; possibly Greece
Areas of achievement: Historiography, literature, warfare and conquest

Early Life

Geoffroi de Villehardouin (zhaw-frwah deh vee-luh-ahr-dwahn), who was in all likelihood the son of Villain I de Villehardouin, was born to a family whose earlier history is virtually unknown. While little information exists about Villehardouin's youth, it seems that by 1172, the year that his name was entered on a list of the vassals of the count of Champagne, he was already married and had children. The surviving records suggest that Villehardouin married twice and that he had, in all, five children.

In 1185, Villehardouin became marshal of Champagne, which means that he assumed specific domestic and military responsibilities at a high level. In addition to overseeing the care of all the horses of his suzerain, Count Henry II of Champagne, Villehardouin's charge included the supervision of the military service and remuneration of the count's vassals. In time of war, Villehardouin's duty as marshal was to follow his overlord into battle, in the forefront of the army. Villehardouin may have done just that in 1190, when Henry left for the Holy Land to join in the Third Crusade, but there is no historical evidence establishing this as fact. While versed in Latin, theology, and music, Henry had little interest in works of literature written in the vernacular. It is quite possible, therefore, that Villehardouin's lack of enthusiasm for the courtly ideal, as later reflected in the generally sober style of his historical writing, was conditioned by the count's literary tastes.

Life's Work

Villehardouin achieved distinction both as a leader and as a historian of the Fourth Crusade. Unhappily, this dual distinction was to a certain degree tarnished by the abortive outcome of the Crusade itself, which, setting out to liberate the Holy Land from the Muslims, was diverted to the assaulting, capturing, and looting of Christian cities, such as Zadar on the Dalmatian coast and Constantinople, the capital of the Byzantine Empire. Furthermore, Villehardouin's largely positive account of the expedition fueled the suspicion that he was primarily concerned with justifying his decisions and those of his fellow commanders rather than exposing the errors and the dubious motivations. In the final analysis, however, Villehardouin's achievement both as a participant in and as a chronicler of the Fourth Crusade proved to be outstanding.

Along with his new suzerain, Count Thibaut III of Champagne, Villehardouin became a Crusader in November, 1199, responding to the appeal launched the previous year by Pope Innocent III. From the outset, Villehardouin's role in the Fourth Crusade was prominent. He and Conon de Béthune, the celebrated poet, were among six envoys who went to Venice in February, 1201, in order to negotiate for the transportation of the Crusaders to the Holy Land. Subsequently, on the death on May 24, 1201, of Thibaut, it was again Villehardouin who assumed an active role in the search for Thibaut's replacement. Indeed, at the Council of Soissons in June, 1201, Villehardouin argued in favor of Boniface of Montferrat as the new commander in chief of the Crusaders and saw his personal choice ratified.

After the Crusaders had captured Constantinople on July 17, 1203, and restored Emperor Isaac II Angelus, who had been deposed by his brother, Alexius III Angelus, Villehardouin was designated the spokesperson among the four representatives sent to meet with the emperor. Villehardouin was charged with reminding the latter of the political and financial obligations that the emperor's son, young Alexius, had assumed when he had asked for the Crusaders' help for his father. Villehardouin's mission proved successful, and on August 1, 1203, the young Alexius was crowned coemperor, becoming Alexius IV. Later, however, because their fraternization with a Latin army of Crusaders had angered their Greek constituents, Isaac II Angelus and Alexius IV no longer seemed disposed to respect the agreement to provide monetary assistance to the Crusaders. In November, 1203, Villehardouin was again among envoys dispatched to the coemperors to convince them to honor their commitments.

Following the second conquest of Constantinople on April 13, 1204—in the course of which the Crusaders put to flight the usurper Alexius Ducas Murtzuphlus, who had strangled Alexius IV and seized power as Alexius V

(Isaac II Angelus having died shortly before his son, apparently from a stroke)—an opportunity was afforded Villehardouin to display his skills as a conciliator. A dispute having arisen between the new emperor of Constantinople, Count Baldwin of Flanders, and Boniface of Montferrat over the kingdom of Thessalonica, Villehardouin brought about a face-saving truce by blaming the dispute on the bungling of the disputants' advisers. Emperor Baldwin then agreed to give Thessalonica to Boniface.

In 1205, with the Greeks in open revolt and the Bulgars and Vlachs invading the Crusaders' strongholds, circumstances developed that permitted Villehardouin to display his military prowess. After Baldwin had laid siege to Adrianople and had in turn been attacked by King Ioannitsa of the Vlacho-Bulgarian state, Count Louis of Blois was killed, on April 14, 1205, when he unwisely left the main detachment of the Crusaders to pursue the enemy's Cuman archers. Baldwin himself was captured in this engagement, having followed Louis. Villehardouin halted the disorderly retreat of the Crusaders, reassembled them into a fighting unit—despite the constant harassment of the Bulgars—and effected an orderly withdrawal. Yet Villehardouin could not single-handedly stem the tide of military reverses. On September 4, 1207, Boniface was killed in an ambush by the Bulgars, thus dramatically marking, at least as far as Villehardouin was concerned, the official and tragic conclusion of the ill-fated Fourth Crusade.

Beyond being a trusted ambassador, an adroit conciliator, and an effective, courageous military commander, Villehardouin was also a chronicler of the momentous events of the Crusade. The portrait of Villehardouin the historian, however, is far more complex than that of Villehardouin the Crusader.

Villehardouin's work, written after 1207, was entitled, in full, *L'Histoire de Geoffroy de Villehardouyn, mareschal de Champagne et de Roménie: De la conqueste de Constantinople par les barons Français associez aux Vénitiens, l'an 1204* (1584; *The Chronicle of Geoffry de Villehardouin, Marshal of Champagne and Romania, Concerning the Conquest of Constantinople, by the French and Venetians, Anno MCCIV*, 1829; also known as *Memoirs of the Crusades*, 1908). More commonly known by the modernized French title *La Conquête de Constantinople*, Villehardouin's account seems at first glance designed not only to chronicle the deflection of the Fourth Crusade from its intended objective but also to justify that deflection. Thus the historian notes that the decision on the part of the Crusaders to help the Venetians invest Zadar—which was taken on November 24, 1202—in return for the transportation of the crusading army to the Holy Land was inevitable: The defection of so many Crusaders had made it impossible to pay the Venetians as originally agreed, and the Zadar diversion was a way of removing the debt. Villehardouin does not reveal, however, that he and other leaders of the Crusade had erred in their estimate of the number of Crusaders needing transportation and had thus contracted for an excessive quantity of ships. Because, of the estimated 33,500 men, only one-third actually appeared in Venice, even without the defections the error of calculation would still have loomed large.

At the same time, Villehardouin appears overly bent on justifying his choice of Boniface of Montferrat as leader of the Crusade on the basis of the latter's having possessed the chivalric qualities of nobility, piety, generosity, loyalty, and courage. Villehardouin does not indicate that Boniface had a definite familial and political stake in the Crusade. His brother Conrad had kept Saladin out of Tyre in 1187; married Isabel, heiress to the kingdom of Jerusalem; and thought of himself as king to the end of his life, when he was assassinated in 1192. Another brother, Renier, had married Maria, the daughter of Emperor Manuel I Comnenus of Constantinople, in 1180, and had been given Thessalonica. When, after the second conquest of Constantinople, Boniface demanded the kingdom of Thessalonica, it was therefore much more than a sudden whim. Indeed, another medieval French historian of the Fourth Crusade took stern and critical note of Boniface's private motives: In 1216, Robert de Clari accused the commander in chief of opportunism and hypocrisy in his book *Li Estoire de chiaus qui conquisent Coustantinoble de Robert de Clari, en Aminois, chevalier* (1868; *The Conquest of Constantinople*, 1936).

As for the initial conquest of Constantinople, Villehardouin again seems to have wanted to put the best possible construction on this additional attack on a Christian city. He maintains that the capture of Constantinople not only brought to an end the cruel reign of Alexius III Angelus and allowed the restoration to power of the dispossessed Isaac II Angelus and the future Alexius IV but also guaranteed that the new imperial authority would pledge fidelity to Rome and also support the Crusade. Villehardouin does not report that, beyond Boniface's personal stake in the matter as noted above, there was the special interest of the Venetians themselves. Having pressed for the move against Zadar because it had been a Venetian vassal state until lured away by King Béla III of Hungary in 1186, Venice encouraged the assault on Constantinople because that city had long persecuted Venetian residents. Moreover, Constantinople had favored the Genoese and the Pisans, commercial competitors of the Venetians, in part by levying huge taxes on the latter. Finally, if the doge (duke, or chief magistrate) of Venice, Enrico Dandolo, was half blind, it may have been because of the barbarity of his Greek "hosts."

Nevertheless, one must recognize that Villehardouin's failure to discuss the whole range of motives behind the diversion of the Fourth Crusade was neither demonstrably intentional nor substantially distortive. He appears genuinely to have believed that the leaders of the Crusade had no choice but to divert it from its original destination, given the circumstances. Villehardouin might be faulted for having overestimated the number of ships needed to transport the Crusaders. On the other hand, the majority of his actions seem to have been based on much more than narrowly partisan considerations. For example, the choice of Boniface as commander in chief, whatever his vested interest, was sound: He was widely recognized as one of the most accomplished men of his time, being a proven warrior who had fought against Saladin and a patron of the arts who encouraged troubadours at his court. Moreover, before deciding on him, Villehardouin and others had approached two other candidates, the duke of Burgundy and the count of Bar-le-Duc.

As for the involvement of the Venetians, it had become common practice to seek maritime transportation to the Holy Land, in the light of the extended and complicated overland route. Although the Venetians were not exactly enamored of Byzantium, there is no evidence that, beyond seeking a fair financial return for their services, they actually conspired to steer the Crusaders away from the announced objective. Villehardouin's obvious respect for their organizational acumen, nautical skill, and courage did not appear suspect at a time when Venice was at the height of its prestige as a great maritime and commercial power. Even the portrait of the doge, admittedly epic, was not incompatible with the fame and glory of the aged but admired Dandolo.

If a more balanced view of the political and military realities of Villehardouin's time shows his history to be a worthy achievement in substantive terms, so a fair analysis of the work's place in the formal evolution of French historiography shows it to be a worthy achievement in stylistic terms. It is clear that Villehardouin's work owes much to the epic tradition of narration, as evidenced not only by the use of conventional techniques of anticipation, recapitulation, and transition, but also, and more fundamentally, by the attribution of legendary traits to the heroes of his narrative. In a manner reminiscent of the portrait of Charlemagne in the famous twelfth century medieval epic *Chanson de Roland* (*Song of Roland*, 1880), the doge of Venice is characterized as *preuz* (valiant), *sages* (wise), and *vigueros* (vigorous) despite his years; his feats in the first Battle of Constantinople are attended by miraculous occurrences, as when the defenders of the city fled before this fearless brandisher of the standard of Saint Mark. Similarly, by its heroic loneliness, the death of Boniface—with which, significantly, Villehardouin chose to end his work—recalled that of Roland in the *Song of Roland*, without the subsequent redress of the situation featured in the medieval epic.

Yet in spite of being clearly indebted to the epic style, *La Conquête de Constantinople* broke new historical ground. Though primarily interested in the grand lines of strategy and combat, the historian, in dealing with specific events, often strove for the factual accuracy characteristic of the best Latin historical tradition, availing himself of eyewitness accounts when his own perspective—generally that of a direct participant—was inadequate. More significant still, Villehardouin chose to write his history in French prose, not in poetry. His work would be, in fact, the first known prose history in French. The nature of Villehardouin's prose, moreover, is itself remarkable for its straightforwardness, sobriety, and simplicity—qualities highlighted by a third-person narrative judiciously combined with moments of direct speech and marked by a more systematic use of the past tense than was typical of the epic style. In short, however great the temptation to be thoroughly partisan, Villehardouin appears, more often than not, to have made a real effort to move from fact to fact without rhetorical digressions—much in the manner of the modern historian.

If it is known that Villehardouin wrote *La Conquête de Constantinople* after 1207, that is practically all that is known about his last years. He is thought to have died between 1212 and 1218, at a site unknown.

Significance

Villehardouin's skill in negotiating with the Venetians, his success in getting his personal choice approved as commander in chief of the Fourth Crusade, and his actions to avert total disaster after the failure of the siege of Adrianople testify amply both to the importance of his role in the organization of the Crusade and to the extent of his influence in determining its orientation and outcome. As a historian, however, Villehardouin's impact was perhaps even more impressive. With no known model to guide him, he composed a history in French prose that represented such a high standard of achievement that it would be matched only on rare occasions before the seventeenth century.

—*Norman Araujo*

Further Reading

Andrea, Alfred J, ed. *Contemporary Sources for the Fourth Crusade*. Boston: Brill, 2000. Explores the varied sources that documented the Crusade, including Innocent III and the Soissons council. Includes a bibliography and an index.

Bartlett, W. B. *An Ungodly War: The Sack of Constantinople and the Fourth Crusade*. Stroud, Gloucestershire, England: Sutton, 2000. Surveys the Crusade, its "misguided idealism," the massive physical destruction of Constantinople, and the killing of thousands of its people. Includes maps and other illustrations, a bibliography, and index.

Beer, Jeanette M. A. *Villehardouin: Epic Historian*. Geneva: Librairie Droz, 1968. An insightful study of Villehardouin's stylistic technique, with particular attention given to his antecedents, the role in his work of biblical references, the influence on him of the Latin historical tradition, and his employment of devices drawn from the medieval French epic. Includes vocabulary appendices and a bibliography.

Godfrey, John. *1204: The Unholy Crusade*. New York: Oxford University Press, 1980. The author places the Crusade within the broader framework of relations existing at the time between Constantinople and Western Europe, on the one hand, and Constantinople and Islam, on the other. Intended primarily for the general reader.

Kooper, Erik, ed. *The Medieval Chronicle: Proceedings of the First International Conference on the Medieval Chronicle*. Atlanta: Rodopi, 1999. Includes an essay comparing Villehardouin's and others' historiographical approaches to chronicling the Fourth Crusade.

Mango, Cyril, ed. *The Oxford History of Byzantium*. New York: Oxford University Press, 2002. A detailed history of Byzantium, including the period of the Crusades. Also contains appendices on "hierarchies, pilgrimage, commerce, and monasticism."

Morris, Colin. "Geoffroy de Villehardouin and the Conquest of Constantinople." *History* 53 (1968): 24-34. The author systematically and informatively compares what is known about the Fourth Crusade with Villehardouin's account.

Queller, Donald E., and Thomas F. Madden. *The Fourth Crusade: The Conquest of Constantinople, 1201-1204*. 2d ed. Philadelphia: University of Pennsylvania Press, 1997. Adopts a Western European rather than Byzantine perspective on the Crusade. Includes maps, an extensive bibliography, and an index.

Villehardouin, Geoffroi de, and Jean de Joinville. *Memoirs of the Crusades*. Translated by Sir Frank Marzials. Reprint. Westport, Conn.: Greenwood Press, 1983. This work contains English translations of the chronicles of Villehardouin and Jean, sire of Joinville, preceded by an introduction that discusses the chronicles from the standpoint of their political and literary importance. In the section on Villehardouin, the translator also provides a helpful summary of the earlier Crusades.

See also: Charlemagne; Enrico Dandolo; Innocent III; Saladin.

Related articles in *Great Events from History: The Middle Ages, 477-1453*: 1189-1192: Third Crusade; 1204: Knights of the Fourth Crusade Capture Constantinople; May 29, 1453: Fall of Constantinople.

VINCENT OF BEAUVAIS

French scholar and historian

Vincent compiled the most comprehensive encyclopedia of the Middle Ages, encompassing natural science, history, theology, philosophy, and the liberal and mechanical arts.

BORN: c. 1190; Beauvais, Oise, France
DIED: 1264; Beauvais, Oise, France
AREAS OF ACHIEVEMENT: Historiography, scholarship, education, literature

EARLY LIFE

Very little is known about Vincent of Beauvais (boh-vay), except for his association with the court of the French king Louis IX and inferences that can be drawn from his writings. He never refers to his birthplace, but he often shows a familiarity with people and events in Beauvais. No record of his birth exists, and the approximate dates commonly given for it (usually between 1190 and 1200) stem partly from the assumption that he must have been a fairly young man when he became a member of the newly formed Order of Preachers, the Dominicans, in about 1220.

According to some sources, Vincent was based at the Dominican House on rue St. Jacques in Paris and studied at the University of Paris in the 1220's. He probably participated in the founding of the Dominican House in Beauvais in 1228-1229, perhaps in keeping with the Dominican custom of sending members of the order back to their hometowns to establish convents. It was during this period of his life in Beauvais that he came to the attention of Louis IX because of his early work on the compendium of knowledge that finally became the *Speculum majus* (1244, revised 1256-1259).

LIFE'S WORK

Although Vincent did not receive an official appointment from Louis IX until about 1246, when he was made lector of the royally founded Cistercian abbey at Royaumont (not far from Beauvais), he was probably in correspondence with the king in the early 1240's concerning his compendium, and he received royal encouragement and financial support for some of the copying and research on that immense project. The first version of the *Speculum majus* seems to have been finished and ready for the king by 1244. From the time of his appointment at Royaumont, however, Vincent was intimately involved with the royal family, which was often in residence there. He became a kind of educational director for the king's children (although he did not tutor them himself), and in 1260, he wrote, at the commission of the queen, a work on the education of princes, *De eruditione filiorum nobilium* (on the instruction of nobly born children). When one of the royal children, the dauphin Louis, died in 1260, Vincent wrote *Epistola consolatoria super morte filii* (letter of consolation on the death of his son), a personal consolation to the king. In the preface to this letter, Vincent mentions that he has preached before the king, a comment that offers further evidence of the respect he was shown by the royal family.

Vincent of Beauvais is chiefly remembered, however, for his tremendous three-volume encyclopedia, the *Speculum majus*. This work was begun probably in the 1230's and went through several stages before the revised version (covering material up to 1250) was made available sometime between 1256 and 1259. The Dominican emphasis on intellectual endeavors no doubt nurtured Vincent's desire to provide an all-inclusive reference book for the learned, but he devised the specific rationale and organization for the work, even though he presented himself as no more than an extractor of the wisdom of others. He saw the work as an aid to memory amid the bewildering abundance of materials one would have to consult to answer questions of theology, natural science, or history. He was a selector and arranger of knowledge, not an original thinker.

Nevertheless, what he produced was a monumental and influential treatise in three parts: the *Naturale*, the *Historiale*, and the *Doctrinale* (dealing, respectively, with the elements of nature, human acts, and the arts and sciences). The common purpose of these three parts (later editions added a spurious fourth book, the *Morale*) was to enable the readers more easily to observe, admire, and imitate the best in human wisdom up to that time; in other words, Vincent wanted to provide materials not only for intellectual instruction but also for moral improvement. The *Naturale* uses the six days of creation in Genesis as the basis of its organization, dealing with all aspects of the relationships among God, humans, and nature. This line of thought leads into the next book, the *Historiale*, which through the account of fallen humans' experiences shows the need for redemption through Jesus Christ. This redemption can be applied to humans, however, by the process of education, and thus the arts and sciences discussed in the *Doctrinale* (*doctrina* means "instruction") serve to pull humans out of the error imposed by sin and into the natural, uncorrupted knowledge of God's world.

With this emphasis on the value of human wisdom, the *Speculum majus* is one of the marvels of thirteenth century Scholasticism, ranking in its own way with the clearly more profound work of Saint Thomas Aquinas in his *Summa theologiae* (c. 1265-1273; *Summa Theologica*, 1911-1921). Although Vincent did not share Thomas's exalted view of Aristotle, he did, like Thomas, show the usefulness of non-Christian sources of knowledge and affirmed the power of intellect to participate in the process of salvation.

Vincent's comments in the prologue to the *Speculum majus* indicate that he was a humble, unpretentious man, not bred to expectations of greatness. He wanted only to present the best of what others had said in the most usable form. When he wrote his smaller books of instruction, they were all commissioned, not volunteered. His last known work was *De morali principis institutione* (1263; of the order of moral principles for rulers), which he was entreated to write by Louis IX. An active and honored old man, Vincent died the next year after completing this book, his work assured of distribution through the patronage of his king, whom he had served as instructor, preacher, and friend.

SIGNIFICANCE

Vincent was the most comprehensive of the medieval encyclopedists, going beyond the efforts of such others as Saint Isidore of Seville (c. 560-636), Lambert of St. Omer (*Liber floridus*, c. 1120), and Bartholomeus Anglicus (*De proprietatibus rerum*, c. 1230-1240; English translation, c. 1495). Vincent's authority was recognized well into the Renaissance. His treatment of the legends of Alexander the Great was the most extensive in the Middle Ages, and his lives of the saints and his other moral stories were drawn on or recommended by such well-known writers as Guillaume de Lorris and Jean de Meung in their *Le Roman de la rose* (c. 1230; *The Romance of the Rose*, 1914-1924), Jacob of Voragine (*Golden Legend*, late thirteenth century), Geoffrey Chaucer ("The Monk's Tale," late fourteenth century), and Christine de Pizan (various texts, early fifteenth century); even Sir Walter Ralegh, in *The History of the World* (1614), mentions Vincent as a source. The *Speculum majus* fell into disrepute as an emerging scientific age began to require more critical methods for ascertaining and presenting what purported to be facts, but Vincent's work remains an astounding intellectual feat and a monumental record of what medieval Europeans of the mid-thirteenth century regarded as their basic body of knowledge.

—*Elton D. Higgs*

FURTHER READING

Aerts, W. J., E. R. Smits, and J. B. Voorbij, eds. *Vincent of Beauvais and Alexander the Great: Studies on the "Speculum Maius" and Its Translations into Medieval Vernaculars*. Gröningen, The Netherlands: Egbert Forsten, 1986. A collection of essays, mostly on translations of Vincent's version of the Alexander story. The first two essays offer views of the Cistercian roots of the form, purpose, and function of the *Speculum majus* and of the probable chronology of the development of its parts.

Dominguez, Cesar. "Vincent of Beauvais and Alfonso the Learned." *Notes and Queries* 45, no. 2 (June, 1998): 172-173. A brief note discussing the arrival of Vincent's encyclopedia in Spain.

Gabriel, Astrik L. *The Educational Ideas of Vincent of Beauvais*. Notre Dame, Ind.: University of Notre Dame Press, 1962. An excellent survey of Vincent's work, with special emphasis on his ideas on education. Thorough footnotes. Contains outlines of major works and a generous number of translated quotations.

Taylor, Henry Osborn. *The Mediaeval Mind: A History of the Development of Thought and Emotion in the Middle Ages*. 2 vols. Cambridge, Mass.: Harvard University Press, 1966. Volume 2 discusses the relationship between Vincent's *Historiale* and the statuary at Chartres Cathedral and outlines and comments on the whole *Speculum majus*.

Tobin, Rosemary Barton. *Vincent of Beauvais' "De eruditione filiorum nobilium": The Education of Women*. New York: P. Lang, 1984. A look at Vincent's *De eruditione* as it relates to girls' and women's education. Includes a bibliography and an index.

_______. "Vincent of Beauvais' Double Standard in the Education of Girls." *History of Education* 7 (1978): 1-5. An exposition of the distinction made in Vincent's *De eruditione filiorum nobilium* between programs of education for boys and those for girls. Shows that girls' education is primarily moral, with the emphasis on preservation of chastity, whereas boys' education stresses intellectual development.

_______. "Vincent of Beauvais on the Education of Women." *Journal of the History of Ideas* 35 (July, 1974): 485-489. Disputes the claim that Vincent's comments on women's education are more liberal than others of his time, concluding that Vincent's ideas on the education of women are quite consonant with other opinions in the thirteenth century.

Ullman, Berthold Louis. "A Project for a New Edition of Vincent of Beauvais." *Speculum* 8 (July, 1933): 312-326. In the context of demonstrating the need for a new edition of the *Speculum majus*, the author surveys what is known about Vincent and his work. Enumerates major figures influenced by the encyclopedia.

SEE ALSO: Saint Albertus Magnus; Averroës; Roger Bacon; Henry de Bracton; Saint Dominic; John Duns Scotus; Saint Isidore of Seville; Louis IX; Paul of Aegina; Rabanus Maurus; al-Rāzī; Thomas Aquinas; Yaqut.

RELATED ARTICLES in *Great Events from History: The Middle Ages, 477-1453*: c. 1010-1015: Avicenna Writes His *Canon of Medicine*; c. 1025: Scholars at Chartres Revive Interest in the Classics; 1100-1300: European Universities Emerge; c. 1150: Moors Transmit Classical Philosophy and Medicine to Europe; c. 1265-1273: Thomas Aquinas Compiles the *Summa Theologica*; 1403-1407: *Yonglo Dadian* Encyclopedia Is Compiled.

PHILIPPE DE VITRY

French writer and musician

Vitry, whose reputation as a musician and poet was well known among his contemporaries, is remembered as the author of the treatise Ars nova. *Vitry proposed a solution to notational problems that was adopted in France and Italy in the fourteenth century.*

BORN: October 31, 1291; Vitry, Champagne, France
DIED: June 9, 1361; Meaux, France
ALSO KNOWN AS: Philippus de Vitriaco
AREAS OF ACHIEVEMENT: Music, literature

EARLY LIFE

Philippe de Vitry (fee-leep deh vee-tree) was born in one of six towns named Vitry in the province of Champagne. His father was a member of the royal chancellery. In 1322, Vitry became an officer in the French royal household, where he served as clerk and secretary to Charles IV in Paris.

Before the twentieth century, it had been generally believed that Vitry was a musician and poet who had largely developed his skills through individual instruction and private study. Modern scholarship, however, suggests that Vitry studied at the Sorbonne and was one of the important intellectuals of his day, with interests ranging from music to mathematics. Petrarch, who met Vitry at the Avignonese court and who described him as an active seeker of truth and a great philosopher, was one among many prominent contemporaries who held Vitry in high esteem.

LIFE'S WORK

Vitry maintained his connection with the royal court throughout his life; in addition to serving Charles IV, he served Philip VI and Duke Jean of Normandy in the capacity of secretary. His association with Duke Jean was to prove particularly helpful. While in his service, Vitry performed various functions and participated in at least one military campaign. He was in the service of the duke in 1350, when the duke became Jean II of France. Vitry made several diplomatic journeys to the papal court at Avignon on behalf of Jean II. In addition to his royal posts, Vitry held several ecclesiastical offices during his life; he was canon of Soissons and archbishop of Brie. In 1351, Pope Clement VI, acting on Jean II's recommendation, appointed Vitry bishop of Meaux, a position he held until his death, in 1361.

Vitry's most significant work is a treatise on music entitled *Ars nova* (1320; English translation, 1961). There is some disagreement about the exact date of the manuscript, but the most widely accepted date is 1320, which means that Vitry would have been twenty-nine years old at the time of its completion. His treatise, which proposed a new theory of mensural notation, was actually a response to the generally perceived shortcomings of the older Franconian notational system that was used in the late thirteenth century.

Composers during this time pushed the older system beyond its limits, as they began to compose music using shorter note values than could be accommodated by the old Franconian system. The common compositional practice in use at that time dictated that the old notational system be revised or a new one be devised to allow the composer greater rhythmic flexibility. Vitry's system, as outlined in *Ars nova*, was not the only solution proposed, but it was the one that ultimately prevailed.

There are several innovative features in Vitry's treatise.

He recognized the minim as the newest and shortest note value and added it to the maxim, long, breve, and semibreve already found in the older Franconian system. Thus, it became possible to notate shorter note values in a systematic way. Also, the notation and usage of the minim in compositions exerted a strong influence on overall notational practice, for, as increased usage of the minim came to be realized, the *tactus*, or unit of beat, slowed down and rendered the larger note values, such as maxims and longs, impractical in actual use. Further, Vitry held that any note longer than the minim could be reduced to two or three shorter notes of equal value—for the first time placing duple meter on an equal footing with triple meter.

Before the fourteenth century, triple meter was regarded as perfect, the number three being symbolic of the Trinity and thus constituting a perfection. Duple meter was regarded as imperfect and was used sparingly. That began to change in the early fourteenth century, and Vitry was actively involved in effecting this change.

The practical effect of Vitry's system was to identify four commonly used mensurations. To assist the performer and to reduce the possibility of confusion as to which mensuration to apply, Vitry introduced the idea of time signatures to indicate mode—the relationship between long and breve—and time—the relationship between breve and semibreve. Time signatures were not widely used until the last quarter of the fourteenth century. Vitry also describes coloration in his treatise, the practice of using red ink notes to indicate changes in mensuration or value from those designated by the standard black notes.

Vitry enjoyed a substantial reputation as a musician, particularly as a composer and most especially as a composer of motets. Fourteen motets are attributed to him. Five of the motets are found in the *Roman de Fauvel* (romance of Fauvel), a beautiful manuscript dating from around 1316 and containing thirty-three polyphonic motets. The other nine motets are found in the *Ivrea codex*, a manuscript containing a variety of sacred and secular compositions and dating from about 1360.

Vitry's innovations are notable. His compositions reveal an extended range for the voices, and the added fourth voice to be found in the later motets reflects his increased interest in sonority. Vitry's motets also reveal one of the first uses of isorhythm, an important fourteenth century technique of repeating the same rhythm with different notes.

Isorhythm involved the *cantus prius factus*, a previously made melody, and was initially associated with the tenor voice, where the previously made melody was usually found. It featured the separation of the two elements always associated with melody: the pitch sequence of a given melody, which was called the color, and the rhythm pattern superimposed on that melody, which was called a *talea*. Once having been viewed separately, it was then possible to combine the color and *talea* in a variety of configurations. The color and *talea* could coincide or the two could be placed in a ratio; for example, two statements of one would be made equal to three of the other. The technique was a means of providing coherence to the composition. While Vitry's creation of this technique cannot be irrefutably documented, the procedure, which was a logical outgrowth of the old repeated rhythm patterns commonly found in the tenors of thirteenth century clausulae (or ornamented cadences), was quite frequently used by him, as it was by some of his contemporaries. The principle was extended and came to be applied to the other voices as well.

Another compositional device found in Vitry's motets, but not unique to him, is the use of hocket. Hocket was quite popular with French composers of the late thirteenth and the fourteenth century. The device consisted of the rapid alternation of notes between a pair of voices, each voice sounding and resting in turn. The desired result was a hiccuping effect.

SIGNIFICANCE

Vitry enjoyed a substantial reputation as a composer, theorist, poet, statesman, and ecclesiastic during his own lifetime. As a poet, he was as well known and respected for the excellence of the Latin and French texts of his motets as he was for the composition of the music itself.

The paucity of Vitry's musical output remains a puzzle, particularly in view of the fact that most of the extant motets and treatises for which he is known were completed while he was still a young man. It appears that Vitry's responsibilities and interests led him in other directions during the mature part of his life.

Even so, it is clear that his impact on the musical milieu of his time was significant, particularly with respect to the *Ars nova* treatise, which served to intensify the already long-standing concern about the proper use of music in church. Pope John XXII, in reaction to the treatise and the swelling tide of support for it, issued a bull in 1324 condemning the effect on sacred music of the new rhythmic procedures advocated by Vitry. While it would be a mistake to credit Vitry as the sole initiator and leader of the rhythmic and notational reform occurring in the fourteenth century, his was a prominent role.

—*Michael Hernon*

Further Reading

Butterfield, Ardis. *Poetry and Music in Medieval France: From Jean Renart to Guillaume de Machaut*. New York: Cambridge University Press, 2002. Explores the world of poets, musicians, and composers in the time of Vitry, looking at topics such as song combined with performance and poetry and the sources of songs. Includes an extensive bibliography and an index.

Faulkner, Quentin. *Wiser than Despair: The Evolution of Ideas in the Relationship of Music and the Christian Church*. Westport, Conn.: Greenwood Press, 1996. A study of the Church's powerful influence on the making of music, including in medieval Europe. Provides a chapter called "Ecclesiastical Authority in Theory and Practice," and includes a bibliography and an index.

Fuller, Sarah. "A Phantom Treatise of the Fourteenth Century? The *Ars Nova*." *Journal of Musicology* 4 (1985-1986): 23-50. Presents the original view that Vitry did not write a definitive treatise entitled *Ars nova*. The author questions whether certain manuscripts traditionally attributed to Vitry were actually his and suggests that colleagues and students actually created a teaching tradition based on Vitry's concepts.

Hoppin, Richard. *Medieval Music*. New York: W. W. Norton, 1978. Provides an excellent survey of medieval music from chant to the music of the early fifteenth century. One chapter is devoted solely to the French *Ars nova* and the innovations of Vitry. Also contains a discussion of isorhythm and important manuscript sources.

Plantinga, Leon. "Philippe de Vitry's *Ars Nova:* A Translation." *Journal of Music Theory* 5, no. 2 (1961): 204-223. A translation from the single complete manuscript source of the *Ars nova*. Some variant readings have been used and are so noted.

Reaney, Gilbert. "*Ars Nova* in France." In *Ars Nova and the Renaissance, 1300-1540*, Vol. 3 in *The New Oxford History of Music*, edited by Egon Wellesz. London: Oxford University Press, 1966. An excellent overview of the forms and composers of fourteenth century France. Contains information about major composers, such as Vitry and Guillaume de Machaut. Also contains some information about less-known composers of the period.

Sanders, Ernest Helmut. "The Early Motets of Philippe de Vitry." *Journal of the American Musicological Society* 28, no. 1 (1975): 24-45. An identification and careful study of motets composed by Vitry as a young man.

_______. "Philippe de Vitry." In *New Grove Dictionary of Music and Musicians*, edited by Stanley Sadie. 6th ed. Vol. 20. New York: Macmillan, 1980. Provides important biographical information. Vitry's theoretical writings and compositions are carefully discussed. A listing of Vitry's compositions is provided at the end; includes citations of sources in which the compositions are found, listings of modern editions containing the works cited, as well as some brief commentary. Excellent bibliography.

See also: Adam de la Halle; Boethius; Guido Cavalcanti; Charles IV; John Dunstable; Guido d'Arezzo; Hildegard von Bingen; Hrosvitha; Francesco Landini; Guillaume de Machaut; Johannes de Muris; Pérotin; Petrarch.

Related article in *Great Events from History: The Middle Ages, 477-1453*: 1305-1417: Avignon Papacy and the Great Schism.

Vladimir I

Grand prince of Kiev (r. 980-1015)

Vladimir expanded the territorial base of Kiev, the first Russian state, to unite the East Slavs and Finno-Baltic peoples into a large nation. He linked the cultural fortunes of the Rus with the Byzantine world by his conversion of the East Slavs to Orthodox Christianity in 988.

Born: c. 956; Kiev, Kievan Rus (now in Ukraine)
Died: July 15, 1015; Berestova, near Kiev
Also known as: Vladimir Svyatoslavich; Vladimir, Saint; Vladimir the Great; Vladimir Veliky; Valdamar; Volodimer; Volodymyr
Areas of achievement: Government and politics, warfare and conquest, religion and theology

Early Life

Born in Kiev sometime after 950, Vladimir Svyatoslavich was the son of Malusha and Svyatoslav I, grand prince of Kiev. Svyatoslav, as prince of Novgorod, had fought bravely against the Khazars, Volga Bulgars (Huns), and Viatichi. He later fought against the Byzantines and the Bulgarians of southern Europe. Although Vladimir's grandmother, grand princess and later saint Olga, had converted to Christianity in Constantinople around 957, the principality remained pagan, as did her son, Svyatoslav. When he died in 971, civil wars erupted as his sons fought over the succession to the throne. Yaropolk, prince of Kiev, defeated Oleg and compelled Vladimir to flee to Scandinavia. For a short time, Yaropolk united Novgorod and Kiev. Vladimir, however, recruited Viking armies, which liberated Novgorod and then Polotsk from Yaropolk's governance. Rogvold, the ruler of Polotsk, allowed his daughter, Ragneda, to marry Vladimir. Then Vladimir marched on Kiev, forcing his brother to flee. Soon after, Yaropolk died. Vladimir forged a new union of Novgorod and Kiev with the help of Scandinavian and Novgorodian forces. To maintain this empire, however, a common religious bond was required; thus the new grand prince considered a new religion for the nation.

Life's Work

Early in his reign, Vladimir considered the adoption of a new pagan cult to unify the realm. He had already created a pagan pantheon of gods, using regional cults in conjunction with the state cult of Perun. He soon realized, however, that the pagan cult could have little impact on the frontiers of the state. There were missionaries from Rome, Constantinople, the Volgan Islamic Bulgars, and the Jewish Khazars. Vladimir's grandmother Olga had been baptized in Constantinople, and there is evidence of Christian settlements in various parts of Rus.

Chroniclers relate the famous story of emissaries sent to investigate the various religions and the discussions the grand prince had with each of them. There is undoubtedly some truth to the account of the prince's aversion to the abstinence from drink and the practice of circumcision among the Jews and Muslims as well as to his particular attraction to the beauty of the Byzantine liturgy over that of the Roman and his aversion to the "foul-smelling" Islamic mosques. Yet it seems that the close political and economic ties between Kiev and Constantinople were decisive, as was the prince's apprehension of submitting to the central authority of Rome. His proposed marriage to the Byzantine emperor's sister, Anna, surely was another factor. The early chroniclers do not hesitate to reveal that the adoption of Byzantine Orthodoxy in 988 was a state decision enforced on the community of Kiev, whose people were marched to the Dnieper River for baptism. Nor was there any doubt that the new church organization would be tied to the prince, whose elevation was invariably blessed by the clergy.

Vladimir is remembered for building the Kievan empire and expanding it in nearly all directions. His early concerns were toward the south and east, where the state was frequently attacked by nomads from the steppes. The internecine warfare that preceded his reign weakened the frontier defenses; thus, Vladimir began offensive operations. He began a number of expeditions against the Viatichi, forcing them into dependence on Kiev in 981-982; he then did the same against the Radimichi in 984, thus uniting all the eastern Slavic peoples. Next he subdued the Volga Bulgars, descendants of the Huns, and the Khazars, their overlords. Making alliances with some Turkic tribes, Vladimir compelled the Bulgars to accept Kievan suzerainty over almost the entire Volga area, although his lieutenant Dobrynia told him that people who wore boots, as did the Bulgars, would never submit. Later campaigns in 994 and 997 were designed to reassert Kiev's control. The Khazar tribes, no longer the powerful empire of old, were weakened by the regime of Khorezm and so fell before Vladimir's armies in 985. As a result, the Black Sea port of Tmutarakan, with its link to the Volga, fell into Kievan hands. Vladimir also strengthened his presence in Sarkel, a former Khazar stronghold taken by Svyatoslav in 965. These successful operations in the east and southeast were supplemented by the grand prince's construction of a chain of fortifications in the southeast to check the raids of the Petchenegs. Divided into eight hordes, the Petchenegs sometimes wandered within a day's march of Kiev itself. The forts at the rivers Desna, Oster, Trubezh, Sula, and Stugna were constructed in 988-989. Staffed by northerners, who sometimes resented service in the south, the forts in the steppes were linked by stockades and entrenchments. These measures enabled Vladimir to contain the nomad threat.

The seizure of Tmutorakan was a delicate matter, however, since that city was also within the influence of the Byzantine Empire. In 988, therefore, Vladimir sent a bodyguard of six thousand Varangian warriors to aid Basil II to quell a rebellion. This force was the origin of the famed Varangian Guard in Constantinople. When Basil refrained from sending his sister to Vladimir, however, an angry prince attacked the Byzantine port of Chersonesus. Soon after, the emperor sent Anna to marry Vladimir in Chersonesus and recognized the Kievan presence in the Black Sea.

Meanwhile, Vladimir paid attention to the lands to the north and west as well. In the borderlands between Kiev and Poland lived many peoples of uncertain ethnic identity; in 981, the Kievan forces moved to incorporate these regions within the state. This action did not cause irreparable damage to Kievan-Polish relations, since Vladimir's son Svyatopolk married the daughter of King Bolesław I Chrobry (r. 1000-1025) early in the next century. Polish missionaries were even allowed to cross Kievan territory to preach to the Petchenegs, although little is known about the success of that mission. Vladimir also maintained friendly relations with Stephen I of Hungary and Udalrich of Bohemia. Troubles began with Poland only late in his reign, when Svyatopolk was suspected of trying to turn over his appanage of Turov-Pinsk to his father-in-law. When Vladimir imprisoned his son in 1012, the Poles invaded the Kievan state, supported by Petchenegs and Germans. The war continued after Vladimir's death in 1015, and three years later, Poland had regained the borderlands lost to Vladimir earlier.

Early in his reign, Vladimir sent Dobrynia to be *posadnik* of Novgorod. His mission was to defend the northern borders. Under Dobrynia, Novgorod paid two thousand *grivny* each year to Kiev as tribute and another one thousand to cover its defense expenses. Novgorod often sent troops to the southern reaches but with increasing reluctance. In 988, Dobrynia was replaced by Vladimir's son Vycheslav, himself later replaced by another son, Yaroslav, later called "the Wise." In 1014, Yaroslav rebelled against the grand prince's financial exactions, an event that foreshadowed a new round of fratricidal warfare when Vladimir died in 1015.

Less is known of Vladimir's internal policies except for the matter of religion. By allying with the upper class, whose sons were the first students in his new religious schools, he provided its members with important posts in his newly created bureaucracy. By suppressing tribal boundaries, Vladimir set up a network of new administrative centers in Polotsk, Novgorod, Turov, Rostov, Murom, Vladimir, and Tmutorakan with his own sons and *druzhiny* as chieftains. He adopted the administrative organizations called the "hundreds" and "thousands" from tribal military practices, making their officers princely officials. Tribal leaders were treated lavishly and used by the grand prince within his administrative structure, as were many elders of the towns. Vladimir

Vladimir I. (F. R. Niglutsch)

RULERS OF KIEVAN RUS, C. 862-1167

Reign	*Ruler*
c. 862-879	RURIK
879-912	Oleg
912-945	Igor
945-964	SAINT OLGA (regent)
964-972	Svyatoslav I
972-980	Yaropolk
980-1015	VLADIMIR I (with ANNA)
1015-1019	Sviatopolk I
1019-1054	Yaroslav
1054-1073	Iziaslav
1073-1076	Svyatoslav II
1076-1078	Iziaslav (restored)
1078-1093	Vsevolod
1093-1113	Sviatopolk II
1113-1125	Vladimir II Monomakh
1125-1132	Mstislav
1132-1139	Yaropolk
1139-1146	Vyacheslav
1146-1154	Iziaslav
1149-1157	Yuri I Dolgoruky
1154-1167	Rostislav

freely used Varangian mercenaries from the north; once, when they threatened to pillage Kiev, he simply sent them on an offensive mission to Constantinople. Vladimir also preceded Yaroslav's famed Russian law code by adopting the principle of fixed fines in the court of justice to replace the dependence on blood feuds and vengeance. This unusual policy was not influenced by churchmen, who even had to convince him that it was proper to execute robbers. To support the construction of a new cathedral, Vladimir introduced the collection of the tithe, a Western church practice. The metropolitan of Kiev, Ilarion (1051-1054), noted that Vladimir often consulted with the bishops on matters of state and security.

SIGNIFICANCE

The religion adopted by Vladimir was to strengthen the princely class, to combat the centrifugal movements within the state, and to abet the state's need for ties to the West. Most important was the fact that Vladimir's decision to choose the Orthodox faith meant the adoption of an entire culture, replete with the artistic tradition of icon painting, Byzantine architecture, monasticism, religious education, legal principles, and other patterns of thought. It is worth noting that one feature was absent from the legacy of the Byzantine Empire—namely, the interest in theological speculation. Several modern authorities argue that Vladimir and the Kievan Rus were so entranced by the beauty of Orthodoxy that tampering with doctrinal formulations was thought to be tampering with perfection. Another modern analysis holds that the Russians were not really converted to Christianity so much as they overlaid a veneer of Christianity over a pagan base.

The extent to which Vladimir himself was converted is also disputed. Chroniclers make frequent mention of his weekly feasts, wherein he invited *druzhiny* and others to dine at court, while servants would distribute food to the poor in the streets. Notice is also made of his newfound aversion to capital punishment and the cessation of his harem. He continued to exercise little restraint in warfare, however, allowing his soldiers to pillage at will—the usual custom of the time.

It is strange to discover some Western elements in Vladimir's religious policies. Reference was made earlier to the introduction of the Western tithe to support the grand prince's designs for a church. In the matter of ecclesiastical law, Vladimir gave the Church a broad charter of immunity from civil law—so broad that it included many persons dependent on the Church and even those without the protection of clan or class. The Church's own jurisdiction included not only moral and liturgical matters but also family disputes and inheritances. Such a situation corresponds more to Western than to Greek practices.

Unlike his Kievan predecessors, who were chiefly concerned with defending the frontiers, Vladimir wanted to expand those frontiers; consequently, he took an active interest in European affairs. To each of his twelve sons, Vladimir left a principality. His son Yaroslav of Novgorod eventually was to succeed him in Kiev. Vladimir was canonized two centuries after he died.

—*John D. Windhausen*

FURTHER READING

Cross, Samuel Hazzard, and Olgerd P. Sherbowitz-Wetzor, eds. and trans. *The Russian Primary Chronicle*. Cambridge, Mass.: Medieval Academy of America, 1953. This work contains the translation of "Povest vremennykh let" (compiled c. 1113), the principal annals of Vladimir's era.

Fedotov, George P. *Kievan Christianity*. Vol. 1 in *The Russian Religious Mind*. Cambridge, Mass.: Harvard University Press, 1946. A classic exploration of the historical roots of Russian Orthodoxy and its relations with the state by a writer who combines scholarship with beautiful prose.

Fennell, John. *A History of the Russian Church: To 1448*. London: Longman, 1995. A volume on the life of the early Russian church that also contains considerable detail concerning the ties between Byzantium and the early Russian metropolitans.

Franklin, Simon, and Jonathan Shepard. *The Emergence of Rus: 750-1200*. New York: Longman, 1996. This book examines the medieval origins and development of the Slavic peoples of Eastern Europe, focusing on Scandinavian, Byzantine, and barbarian influences. Includes an important chapter on the period from 960 to 1015 and Vladimir's role in expanding and shoring up the power structure in Kiev. Maps, extensive bibliography, list of genealogies, and excellent index.

Grekov, Boris D. "The Reign of Prince Vladimir Svyatoslavich." In *Kiev Rus*, translated by Y. Sdobnikov. Moscow: Foreign Languages, 1959. The most noted work by a Soviet scholar on the Kievan era of Russian history. Argues that paganism yielded to Christianity because the former was a tribal religion whereas the latter was essentially class oriented.

Grunwald, Constantin de. "Saint Vladimir." In *Saints of Russia*, translated by Roger Capel. New York: Macmillan, 1960. A concise, intelligent account of Vladimir's life, drawing on many Nordic sources and stressing his Scandinavian ties. Argues that the conversion of the Kievan people took place in 990.

Kluchevsky, Vasily O. *A History of Russia*. Translated by C. J. Hogarth. 5 vols. New York: Russell and Russell, 1960. An entertaining analysis by a great Russian historian. Though sparing of detail on Vladimir's career, it contains well-considered judgments on the grand prince's milieu.

Korpela, Jukka. *Prince, Saint, and Apostle: Prince Vladimir Svjatoslavič of Kiev, His Posthumous Life, and the Religious Legitimization of the Russian Great Power.* Wiesbaden, Germany: Harrassowitz, 2001. This ingenious study examines how Vladimir has been described and represented in Russia since his death. It looks at how the image of Vladimir was used to support and even legitimate several rulers of Russia, especially Ivan the Terrible.

Vernadsky, George. *Kievan Russia*. New Haven, Conn.: Yale University Press, 1948. The standard account of Vladimir's reign by a well-respected scholar whose discussion of the grand prince is still unchallenged.

Volkoff, Vladimir. *Vladimir, the Russian Viking*. Woodstock, N.Y.: Overlook Press, 1985. The first full-scale, twentieth century biography of the grand prince. This account is interesting, faithful to detail, and imaginatively constructed. Includes an index, maps, illustrations, and a select bibliography.

See also: Anna, Princess of the Byzantine Empire; Olaf I; Saint Olga; Rurik; Stephen I.

Related articles in *Great Events from History: The Middle Ages, 477-1453*: 740: Khazars Convert to Judaism; c. 850: Development of the Slavic Alphabet; 850-950: Viking Era; 976-1025: Reign of Basil II; 988: Baptism of Vladimir I.

William Wallace
Scottish military leader

With a combination of valor, ferocity, and tenacity, William Wallace galvanized the Scottish will to rise against English invaders and thus sparked the Scots' determination to be an independent nation once again.

Born: c. 1270; Ellerslie (now Elderslie), near Paisley, Ayrshire, Scotland
Died: August 23, 1305; London, England
Also known as: William Walays; Sir William Wallace; William Wallensis
Area of achievement: Military

Early Life

William Wallace was born the second son of a little-known knight, Sir Malcolm Wallace. Although the Wallaces of Ayrshire were an old, landed family, they were not prominent; moreover, as the second son, William would not have inherited his father's title or lands. This untitled second son of an obscure knight, with no apparent hopes for prominence or fame, would become Scotland's greatest national hero.

Despite his fame, Wallace remains to a large extent shrouded in mystery. Many details of his life are little more than conjecture and supposition derived from the works of chroniclers who wrote a century or more after Wallace's death. Also complicating Wallace's story are the fear and animosity he provoked in the English historians of the period, who demonized Wallace, his motives, and his deeds. Thus, records of his life, and especially of his early years, are sketchy and often inaccurate. The best modern biographers freely admit the likely inaccuracy of the early sources.

What is clear, however, is that the young Wallace's boyhood benefited from the social, political, and financial security characterizing the reign of Scotland's King Alexander III, who ruled from 1249 to 1286. During these early years, Wallace probably led a comfortable, peaceful life as the son of a knight, perhaps receiving a rudimentary formal education at the hands of local monks and an uncle who was a priest. More important to history, the young Wallace doubtless practiced and trained during this period with his older brother, Malcolm, in the martial arts of the day, including horsemanship and weaponry.

Wallace's destiny—to lead Scottish patriots against English invaders—had its roots in his early military training. From contemporary descriptions, including those of armorers, it is known that Wallace was a large, powerful man. In an age when foot soldiers averaged only slightly more than 5 feet (152 centimeters) in height, William Wallace reportedly stood nearly 6 feet, 6 inches (183 centimeters) tall. Neither was he lanky: Numerous witnesses describe him as being brawny, well-proportioned, muscular, and handsome. He was, in short, a giant of a man in his time; an armor-clad Wallace, mounted on a huge warhorse and wielding a six-foot-long claymore battle sword, would have presented a terrifying prospect to opponents.

Wallace may have prepared to pursue a life in the church, but that possibility faded as Scotland drifted closer to a civil war within its borders and a defensive war against King Edward I of England. By the time Wallace was twenty, Scotland was essentially under English occupation. Two incidents made the conflict personal for him. In the first incident, his father, Sir Malcolm Wallace, was killed in a skirmish with English troops in 1291. In the second incident, Wallace was provoked into a fight with the brash son of the constable of Dundee Castle. Insulted and enraged by the abusive behavior, Wallace drew his dirk and killed his tormentor.

From this period on, Wallace would be an outlaw, hunted and feared by the English but admired by many of his fellow Scots. Even after gaining fame in the next several years, he would never again know peace in his short life.

Life's Work

From 1291, the young William Wallace, twenty or twenty-one years old, found himself thrust into conflict that revealed the worst of nobles. The aristocratic Scottish Guardians intrigued against one another, variously aligning themselves with Edward of England when it suited their personal ambitions, and then defying their loyalty to the English king when doing so served their purposes. At the same time, English troops, including mercenaries and frequently disgruntled Welsh and Irish conscripts, ranged freely over Scotland from their garrisons and stockaded camps. Abuses against civilians abounded, and for the most part, the Scottish nobles showed no interest in redressing these abuses. Little can be known for certain about Wallace's life during this period except that he lived the life of an outlaw, moving constantly, avoiding the English when possible and intermittently confronting the invaders with lethal ferocity.

In 1296, Edward I himself led a campaign in southern Scotland and humiliated the ineffectual claimant to the

Scottish throne, John de Baliol. In the same year, Wallace engaged local soldiers in the village of Ayr. After killing several of them, he was overpowered and thrown into a dungeon, where he was slowly starved. Apparently in a coma, Wallace was presumed dead, and his body was discarded. He was nursed back to health by sympathetic villagers. Recovered, Wallace attracted several local comrades-in-arms and began his systematic, deadly fight against the hated English and their Scottish sympathizers.

As his supporters grew in number, his attacks broadened. Early in 1297, Wallace, by then with as many as fifty men, revenged his father's death by ambushing the knight responsible, along with a retinue of soldiers. He was no longer merely an outlaw but a local military leader who had struck down a number of Edward's knights and fighters. William Wallace had become the king's enemy.

Although most of Scotland was in Scottish hands by August, 1297, Edward (nicknamed "Longshanks") had such confidence in his veteran commanders and battle-tested soldiers that he sailed for Flanders. The size of the English army left its leaders confident, and when Wallace and his coleader, Sir Andrew de Moray, marched their forces toward Stirling Castle, a stronghold of vital importance, the English commanders were confident that the upstart Scots would retreat or surrender. The Scots not only declined the terms but also sent a defiant rebuke.

Wallace and de Moray were both in their twenties. Neither could claim exalted status, and their aristocratic enemies had as yet little real respect for their burgeoning roles as national, not merely local, military commanders. Wallace, the man to whom the Scots chiefly rallied, was disparaged by the English leaders as a "thief." Nevertheless, under Wallace, the Scots—commoners and knights, not nobles—coalesced into a spirited army consciously fighting for their liberty. Where Scotland's nobles had capitulated and bargained, Wallace's army of patriots remained steadfast.

At the Battle of Stirling Bridge on September 11, 1297, Wallace demonstrated that he was not only a charismatic leader and warrior but also a brilliant tactician. The English were lured into a rash advance and slaughtered; English fatalities approached five thousand. Never before had a Scottish army so triumphed over an English aggressor. The youthful but grimly determined Wallace had dispelled the myth of the invincibility of Edward's experienced army. Young Wallace succeeded brilliantly where his aristocratic betters had utterly failed.

Victory over the formidable English army at Stirling Bridge enhanced Wallace's fame and enthusiastic support throughout Scotland. Late in 1297 or early in 1298, Wallace was knighted. Recent scholarship suggests that the nobleman knighting Wallace was probably the earl of Carrick, who would become better known as Robert Bruce. In many ways, Wallace was a necessary precursor for Bruce, who would be crowned king of Scotland (King Robert) on March 25, 1306.

Ironically, Bruce's family claims to the Scottish throne placed him politically at odds with Wallace, who remained loyal to the now-exiled king, John de Baliol. Yet, acknowledging Wallace's meteoric rise to power, Bruce would later refer to him as Lord William Wallace. In any case, by early spring of 1298, the newly knighted Sir William Wallace also ruled as official regent, or guardian, of Scotland. In less than six years, this remarkable young warrior had risen from obscurity to one of the most important positions in the realm.

Wallace's acclaim, however, was short-lived. By March, 1298, Edward had initiated plans for another invasion of Scotland, intending to crush Wallace and all others daring to assert Scotland's independence. The English army entering Scotland may have numbered almost ninety thousand. On July 22, 1298, near Falkirk, Edward

William Wallace. (Library of Congress)

attacked the much smaller Scottish army. Although vastly outnumbered, Wallace's disciplined troops withstood the initial charges of the English. Decimated by longbowmen able to dispatch numerous arrows over great distances, and deserted at a crucial moment by their nobles' cavalry, the stalwart Scottish army was at last overwhelmed. As many as ten thousand Scots may have been killed; with the bloodied remnant of his army, Wallace retreated into the thick woods. Soon thereafter, he relinquished his guardianship of Scotland. With his defeat went Scotland's apparent hopes of independence.

In the following years, Wallace seems to have returned to his earlier tactics of engaging the English on a smaller scale, using hit-and-run guerrilla tactics in a war of attrition. Guided by his patriotism and unwavering hatred of the English, Wallace continued to serve his country selflessly. Along with several of his loyal supporters, Wallace apparently sailed to France on a diplomatic mission to seek support from King Philip IV; in 1303, however, the Treaty of Paris effectively ended hostilities between England and France.

The treaty's ratification also allowed Edward to focus his attention on the Scots, who continued to resist the English. Wallace was singled out; Edward's order was for Wallace, unlike the Scottish nobles, to surrender unconditionally. Edward took personal charge of the Scottish campaign of 1304.

Stirling Castle fell to the English in July of 1304. Wallace, still denigrated by Edward's officers as an outlaw, was hunted down. By refusing to acknowledge Wallace as a worthy opponent from another country's army, the English could officially regard Wallace as a mere traitor. Thus, unlike the relatively lenient sanctions imposed on the Scottish nobles, the terms offered Wallace were unconditional—an ominous message from such a vindictive king as Edward.

Captured at last—by a Scottish knight in service to the English king—Wallace was brought to London in August, 1305. Denied status as a captured soldier, Wallace endured a mock trial and was sentenced to a traitor's death. Dragged through the streets of London, he was humiliated, tortured, hanged, drawn, and quartered on August 23, 1305. Edward ordered Wallace's quartered body dispatched to four locations in Scotland and on the English border, to be hung in public view. His severed head was impaled on a pike and displayed on London Bridge. Edward believed that he had at last broken the Scots' spirit. He was wrong. With Wallace's barbarous execution, he had in fact made the Scots' popular military leader a martyr.

Significance

William Wallace sought neither the glory nor the hardship that distinguished his short life. Thrust into the complex conflicts of late thirteenth century Scotland, Wallace accepted the roles his leadership and personal valor brought him. A violent man living in a violent age, he was intransigent in his resistance to the English invaders, implacable in his war against them. A ferocious, powerful warrior, he rarely granted quarter to English captives, nor did he ask any of his English enemies. Unlike the conniving Scottish nobles, Wallace never sought personal fame or benefited from it, and he never accrued wealth or lands. Late twentieth century scholars describe Wallace as an anomaly, a historical figure who truly lived his life by an inviolable code of honor. Yet for all his self-sacrifice and brilliance as a military leader, Wallace's greatest achievement was his inspiration to his fellow Scots: to claim their own liberty and to be willing to die for it. His story became an Academy Award-winning feature film, *Braveheart* (1995), starring Mel Gibson as Wallace.

—*David Pitre*

Further Reading

Barrow, G. W. S. *Kingship and Unity: Scotland, 1000-1300*. Toronto: University of Toronto Press, 1981. Offers a broad social history of William Wallace's Scotland. Includes an annotated bibliography and a helpful "chronological table" appendix.

Fisher, Andrew. *William Wallace*. 1986. Reprint. Edinburgh: John Donald, 2002. Synthesizes numerous sources into a concise factual biography. The author strives to be judicious in separating the legend from the man. Includes a lengthy bibliography.

Gray, D. J. *William Wallace: The King's Enemy*. London: R. Hale, 1991. Chronicles Wallace's life and times, profiling him as a medieval freedom fighter. Bibliographic references, index.

Mackay, James. *William Wallace: Brave Heart*. Edinburgh: Mainstream, 1995. Sympathetic toward Wallace and the Scottish struggle for independence, Mackay's biography offers both accessibility to the facts and thorough research. Includes a select bibliography.

Mitchison, Rosalind. *A History of Scotland*. New York: Methuen, 1982. Chapter 3, "The War of Independence," provides a brief but invaluable discussion of Wallace's Scotland and the explosive political issues that brought Wallace—and Robert Bruce—to the forefront of the conflict. Includes a list of important dates, maps, and a lengthy annotated bibliography.

Morton, Graeme. *William Wallace: Man and Myth.* Stroud, England: Sutton, 2001. A Scottish historian deconstructs the myth of Wallace, fully examining contemporary sources.

Reese, Peter. *Wallace: A Biography.* Edinburgh: Canongate, 1996. Detailed look at the life and times of Wallace, with illustrations, maps, bibliographic references, and index.

Scott, Ronald McNair. *Robert the Bruce: King of Scots.* Edinburgh: Canongate, 1982. Part 1 of Scott's book provides an excellent discussion of the Scottish struggle for independence from 1295 to 1306, the period of Wallace's heroic achievements. Among others, Wallace is placed within this historical context.

Young, Alan, and Michael Stead. *In the Footsteps of William Wallace.* Stroud, England: Sutton, 2002. Wallace's story is accompanied by photographs and maps of historic sites.

See also: Robert Bruce; Edward I; Edward II.

Related article in *Great Events from History: The Middle Ages, 477-1453*: June 23-24, 1314: Battle of Bannockburn.

Walther von der Vogelweide

German poet

Walther von der Vogelweide was the greatest lyric poet of the German High Middle Ages; his writings set high standards of artistic quality in the genre of the courtly love lyric as well as that of political poetry.

Born: c. 1170; probably lower Austria (now in Germany)
Died: c. 1230; near Würzburg, Bavaria
Area of achievement: Literature

Early Life

Few details are known regarding the life of Walther von der Vogelweide (WAHL-thuhr fuhn dehr VOH-guhl-vi-duh). He was born within the area of Austria and was in Vienna around 1190 at the court of the Babenberg rulers. At the death of his sponsor, Duke Frederick, in 1198, he wandered around Austria in search of another wealthy patron. He resided at various royal courts and finally settled in Würzburg at the court of Emperor Frederick II, from whom he received a small stipend in 1220. Only one document exists that testifies to his life: a note that he was given money by Wolfger, bishop of Passau, in 1203 in order to purchase a winter coat. He is depicted in a colorful illumination (from the famous *Manessische Handschrift* manuscript) as the "king of poets," in a pose described in one of his most famous poems.

Walther was born toward the end of the period of the German High Middle Ages, when the culture and art of the royal courts were at their zenith. Courtly society was highly codified and stratified; hierarchies of rank and authority were carefully observed. This period was the legendary age of chivalry and knightly virtues, an era whose ideal knight combined the bravery of the Germanic warrior with the spiritual discipline of Christianity. The knights were a class of soldiers who pledged fealty to a lord and were in attendance at his court when not engaged in battle or a crusade. Since many were literate, they were devoted to the arts of song and the lyric.

The knightly caste had strict rules of conduct that promoted certain primary social virtues. Honor, loyalty, and discipline were important qualities of the warrior who served a lord in battle. Mildness and steadfastness of character and moderation in all behavior were social and psychological virtues that complemented as well as moderated the more aggressive qualities of the soldier. The goals of a knight were threefold: to attain worldly honor, material wealth, and, above all, the blessings of God.

Knights who were in attendance at a court often practiced devotion to a noblewoman of higher station (*Minnedienst*); the knight who undertook such a commitment dedicated all of his heroic efforts to his lady and composed in her honor highly stylized love poetry (*Minnesang*). This idealized love was thought to be a spiritual exercise that would ennoble the soul of the knight. If the knight were dutiful in his service to the lady, she might grant him the favor of a glance or a nod.

Because Walther both incorporated and transcended the conventions of the courtly love lyric in many of his poems, a closer look at the genre and its history is in order. The tradition of the love lyric in Germany was determined primarily by foreign influences, descending from the older cultural heritage of Arabic love poetry by way

In this depiction of a competition between minstrels at the court of Hermann of Thuringia in 1207, Walther von der Vogelweide, standing on right wearing the laurel leaves of the winner, gestures to the loser, Henry of Ofterdingen, who kneels at the feet of Hermann's wife. (F. R. Niglutsch)

of the Moorish invasion of Spain and then subsequently from the Provençal area of France, where the tradition of Latin love poetry remained and where the ideals of knighthood also flourished. Provençal poetry reached its high point around 1100 in the songs of the troubadour. Prominent poets of the French tradition were Bertrand de Born, William of Poitou, and Bernard de Ventadour.

These Provençal poets devoted themselves and their poetry to an unreachable ideal, to the honor of a married lady of the court—which therefore (usually) excluded the possibility of physical love—and this striving for the ideal in attitude and behavior ennobled their souls. Love expressed to a young, unmarried woman was discouraged. The earlier Christian tradition of love poetry dedicated to the Virgin Mary is here also an obvious influence. Because this love service to the married woman was extremely passionate, in spirit at least, the affairs of the knight and his chosen lady were closely watched by others of the court. Secret meetings between the lovers were presumed by all, and such a clandestine rendezvous was a perennial theme in much of the poetry. The *alba*, or morning song, for example, celebrated the awakening of the two lovers after a night of secret passion. They were usually outdoors and romantically awakened by the singing of a bird. These motifs became highly stylized and were part of the poet's standard lyric repertoire.

The German reception of the French tradition of courtly poetry began in northern Germany and the Low Countries (by way of northern France) in the realistic love lyrics of Heinrich von Veldeke. From there, it was transmitted to the Rhineland area in the works of Friedrich von Hausen and to Middle Germany in the poetry of Heinrich von Morungen. These early German poets gave fresh inspiration to the conventions of the genre, writing lyrics that captured the passion and intensity of this spiritualized love experience in naturalistic imagery. By way of northern Italy, the tradition came to Austria, and at the Babenberg court in Vienna, the love lyric attained a high degree of formal stylization. The poet Reinmar von Hagenau (from the Franco-German area of

Alsatia) produced poems in a folklike style and wrote of the sadness and melancholy longing of the lovers rather than the intensity and energy of their passion. The social prohibitions that denied the natural consummation of the love relationship had eventually produced an experience that was more form or gesture than content. This shift in theme toward the introspective suggests the waning of the genre. Reinmar was the major influence at the Babenberg court and was Walther's teacher. The German tradition of the love lyric became highly conventionalized and artificial at this stage. Numerous writers of lesser talent than Reinmar and Walther merely imitated the particulars of the style and form without entering into the original spirit of its early poets.

The impossibility of intimate union with the idealized lady gave rise to a variant of the courtly love genre, called "common love" (*niedere Minne*). This was a love lyric dedicated to the young and accessible girls of the local villages rather than the unapproachable, idealized ladies of the court. It was a poetry that celebrated the joys of reciprocal love and the simple village life, free of the formal and codified rules of courtly society. Its imagery was that of rural life and the simple pleasures of the village community. The rise of the common-love school again suggests that the tradition of the courtly love lyric had exhausted its thematic and stylistic possibilities.

The medieval courtly love lyric eventually devolved into a mere formal exercise during the fourteenth century, the period of the "master song" (*Meistergesang*). The meistersingers imitated the style of masters such as Walther in a mechanical and highly formalized manner. Singing schools (*Singschulen*), structured much like guilds, were organized in towns, and strict rules for composition were established. Competitions were held in which judges counted the syllables and assessed the rhymes in each line. Michel Beheim, a weaver, was one of the more famous meistersingers of the period.

Life's Work

Walther's career thus spanned the zenith and the decline of the courtly love genre. His poetry shunned the artificiality and conventionality so prominent in the works of others. His language and imagery were natural, spontaneous, and vital. Poems such as "Sô die Bluomen ûz dem Grase dringent" ("When the Flowers Spring out of the Grass") celebrate in natural images of spring the physical as well as the inner spiritual beauty of the beloved lady. In many of his texts, Walther questions the nature of the courtly love experience itself. Love is not the stylized and formal gestures of favor granted by the revered lady of the court of the dutiful knight, but the harmony of two hearts in delighted union. The poem "Saget mir ieman, waz ist Minne?" ("What Is Loving?"), for example, rejects the unequal relationship between a woman placed on an idealized pedestal and a subservient man kneeling before her. Love, Walther suggests, is a natural relation of equality between two lovers that enriches both participants. Consequently, Walther also composed poetry in the vein of the common love style. In texts such as "Herzeliebes Frouwelin" ("Dear Young Woman") and "Nemt, Frouwe, disen Kranz" ("Take, Young Woman, This Wreath"), as well as the well-known poem "Unter der Linden" ("Under the Linden-Tree"), he described the natural passions of the simple girl and his reciprocal affection for her.

Walther lived during a period of great political turmoil, and in many of his poems he gave voice to his concerns. After the death of Emperor Frederick I Barbarossa in 1190, conflicts ensued among the royal houses of the Guelphs and the Waiblingen. The Guelphs sought to assume leadership from the Hohenstaufen Dynasty. Frederick II, son of Barbarossa, was finally crowned as emperor in 1220. This was also the era in which church and state vied for political hegemony in Europe, a conflict that extended over most of the thirteenth century. Walther was distressed at the loss of harmony and unity that had marked the earlier years of the Hohenstaufen empire. In many of his poems, he praised his German homeland, lauding its beautiful women, its landscapes, and its brave knights and chivalry. In his best-known poem, "Ich saz uf eine Steine" ("I Was Sitting upon a Rock"), he laments the violence and discord that had disrupted the land. He fears that the knightly ideals of honor, wealth, and God's blessings are threatened by the conflicts he sees around him. Unfortunately, the gradual process of disintegration within his beloved empire continued long after his death. The Hohenstaufen Dynasty came to an end in 1268 with the execution of Conradin in Naples.

Significance

If Johann Wolfgang von Goethe was the lyric genius of Germany's second golden age of literature (during the eighteenth century), then Walther von der Vogelweide was certainly the greatest genius of its first great era, during the Middle Ages. His poetry achieved a splendid union of form and content. He was able to infuse the conventions of the courtly love lyric with a freshness and vitality unequaled by others of his generation. His imagery is distinguished by a keen sense of realism combined with a genuine poetic sensibility. His love for his homeland, his concern for its future, and his egalitarian attitudes suggest a warm-spirited individual able to look beyond the parochial concerns that marked so many of his contemporaries.

If it can be said that the literary production of a society is the highest expression (in linguistic terms) of its values and ideals, then Walther's place in the history of German culture and civilization is assured. In certain respects, the tradition of the courtly love lyric manifested European (and especially Germanic) society's attempt to harmonize the virtues of two distinct cultural traditions, that of the strong and fearless tribal warrior and that of the humble Christian whose strength lay not in the physical but in the spiritual domain. As the foremost poet of this tradition, one who both epitomized and transcended its limits, Walther left a legacy that will continue to be examined by future generations.

—*Thomas F. Barry*

FURTHER READING

Garland, Henry, and Mary Garland. *Oxford Companion to German Literature*. 2d ed. Oxford, England: Oxford University Press, 1986. Encyclopedic reference work with brief but informative section on Walther. Contains several important bibliographic references.

Heinen, Hubert. "Lofty and Base Love in Walther von der Vogelweide's 'So die bluomen' and 'Aller werdekeit.'" *The German Quarterly* 51 (1978): 465-475. Treats Walther's concept of love; includes quotations in German and English, notes, and bibliography.

O'Connell Walshe, Maurice. *Medieval German Literature*. Cambridge, Mass.: Harvard University Press, 1962. A good history of literature in the Middle Ages that contains a substantial section on Walther. Also includes a bibliography.

Reinhardt, Kurt Frank. *Germany: Two Thousand Years*. Milwaukee: Bruce, 1950. A very useful history of German civilization with a section on medieval culture, history, and literature including a discussion of Walther. Contains a bibliography.

Scheibe, Fred Karl. *Walther von der Vogelweide: Troubadour of the Middle Ages*. New York: Vantage Press, 1969. A good brief introduction to Walther's life and poetry that also surveys the reception of his works and lists English translations. Contains a bibliography.

Sullivan, Robert G. *Justice and the Social Context of Early Middle High German Literature*. New York: Routledge, 2001. A history of the Holy Roman Empire hinging on an examination of High German literature and its authors' focus on social, political, and spiritual issues during a time of transformation. Bibliographical references, index.

SEE ALSO: Gottfried von Strassburg; Hartmann von Aue; Wolfram von Eschenbach.

RELATED ARTICLES in *Great Events from History: The Middle Ages, 477-1453*: After 1000: Development of Miracle and Mystery Plays; c. 1025: Scholars at Chartres Revive Interest in the Classics; c. 1100: Rise of Courtly Love; 1100-1300: European Universities Emerge; 1136: Hildegard von Bingen Becomes Abbess; c. 1180: Chrétien de Troyes Writes *Perceval*; c. 1306-1320: Dante Writes *The Divine Comedy*; c. 1350-1400: Petrarch and Boccaccio Recover Classical Texts.

Wang Anshi

Chinese statesman and writer

A writer and statesman during the Northern Song Dynasty, Wang Anshi introduced sweeping reforms in government, affecting particularly the state financial system and the bureaucracy.

Born: 1021; Linchuan (now in Jiangxi Province), China
Died: 1086; Chianning (now Nanjing), China
Also known as: Wang An-shih (Wade-Giles)
Area of achievement: Government and politics

Early Life

Wang Anshi (wahng ahn-shih) was born in south-central China in an area noted as a center of tea producers and merchants. His family first prospered in farming, although on a small scale, but later generations produced scholars, several holding the *jinshi*, or doctorate, degree. Wang's father was a minor official who served in a variety of local government posts. His family thus instilled in Wang traditional Confucian values of education and of government service.

In 1042, Wang earned a doctorate, and for the next eighteen years, he served in local government posts. His experience, especially a year spent as a district magistrate, gave him insight into the conditions of the poor in the countryside and of the workers in the growing urban centers. His experience with incompetent bureaucrats led him, in 1058, to present to Emperor Renzong (Jen-tsung; 1022-1063) a memorial, the basis of his later reform proposals. In it, Wang showed how a well-trained, well-controlled bureaucracy could serve as the chief tool in bringing about a Confucian moral society.

Wang urged, among other things, that the emperor give highest consideration to the character and ability of candidates for government office. Further, he suggested "a prolonged period of probation as the best method of testing the appointees." Wang, as chief justice of the circuit for one year, noted the scarcity of competent government employees and saw the need for securing capable officials. It was a theme he would repeat following his appointment to the court a few years later. No action was taken on his ideas at the time, but Wang's reputation as a scholar grew, and after 1060, he was called to the capital, where he served in a number of minor posts that brought him access to the emperor.

Life's Work

In 1067, Wang Anshi became governor of Nanjing, from where the new emperor, Shenzong (Shen-tsung; r. 1068-1085), summoned him to court in early 1069. Wang was made second privy councillor, with responsibility for general administration. The emperor supported Wang's reform measures, which began to be implemented in 1069. Opposition built to the reforms, but the emperor reaffirmed Wang by appointing him first privy councillor in 1071, adding to Wang's prestige and power.

At the time Wang rose to eminence, the Song Dynasty (Sung; 960-1279) was experiencing heavy financial strains as a result of an enlarged military budget and the increase of great estates with their tax-evading landowners. Government income had fallen substantially by 1065. Northern barbarian tribes were a constant threat, and a sizable professional army to contain them proved very costly. The military alone accounted for close to 80 percent of the government revenue.

Along with financial distress, the dynasty, having become more centralized than at any previous time, suffered from the inertia of an inflexible bureaucracy. Officials were often divided over policies, and factionalism prevented easy resolutions. Most bureaucrats were traditionalists whose positions were threatened by Wang's reforms. Scholar-statesmen such as Ouyang Xiu (Ou-yang Hsiu; 1007-1072), Sima Guang (Ssu-ma Kuang; 1019-1086), and Han Wei (1017-1098) led the antireform forces, leading to Wang's resignation, briefly, in 1074.

Wang's reforms, known as the New Policies, covered several areas, all of them aiming at the creation—or restoration—of a Confucian moral society. Wang cast his reforms with continuity as well as change in mind. He argued that change was necessary because "the present system of administration is not in accordance with the principles and ideas of the ancient rulers." He was, therefore, advocating a return to the principles of a golden age. The reforms were intended to shape the behavior of the people and the bureaucracy, bringing about fundamental changes in political and social institutions.

The New Policies' areas were planning of state finance, state financing for farmers, state revenue and maintenance (for example, transportation and distribution of tribute items, a graduated cash tax, collective police duties, an equitable land tax), national defense, currency reform, trade expansion, and education and civil service (establishment of more prefectural schools, training in specialized fields such as law or military science, and emphasis on problem solving in the examination system). The majority of these New Policies tried to deal realistically with the problems of tax burden and state finance. However, their success would depend on a competent bureaucracy.

The core of Wang's reforms was an improved bureaucracy. He advised the emperor to "search for and make use of the talented men who are capable of reviving the regulatory system of the ancient kings" before attempting to establish the regulatory systems for the country. The Song Dynasty paid great respect to scholar-officials, some of whom were exempt from taxes and service to the state. Many scholars, however, especially those not stationed in the capital, received low pay and few privileges; morale therefore was low. Wang increased their salaries in the hope of raising morale and lessening corruption. Idealistic himself, Wang maintained high standards and demanded them of other scholar-officials as well. His criticism of what he considered an ill-prepared and impractical bureaucracy brought heated rejoinders, while his thinking on state finance was an additional irritation to many conventional Confucians, who held a laissez-faire philosophy in the areas of business and industry.

Wang believed that the state could increase revenue by increasing productivity, primacy being given to agricultural productivity. He attacked the production of luxury goods, and extravagance in general. He reminded the emperor that "the good ruler maintains an economical standard in public life, extravagance being recognized as a great evil" and urged punishment for those producing articles of luxury. Wang wanted to force workers back into the fields so that "as more land is brought under cultivation, there will be no lack of food." To this end, Wang introduced state farming loans to rescue farmers from moneylenders, thereby enabling the farmers to keep their land. He also favored heavier taxation on merchants than on farmers.

Wang wanted the government to restrain and limit the powerful monopolizing families and to use its authority vigorously to aid the poor. He did not advocate revolution, the overthrow of the gentry and large landlords; rather, he feared that a peasant uprising would occur if poverty were not alleviated. Yet such reforms as remission of corvée (compulsory labor), a graduated land tax, and cheaper credit alienated large landowners, moneylenders, and merchants. They joined forces with conservative bureaucrats to condemn Wang and his program, forcing his resignation in 1074.

Although Wang returned to court in early 1075, his position was considerably weaker than before. The emperor was less open to his counsel, and previous supporters turned against him. Wang retired permanently in 1076. His reforms continued in effect until the death of Emperor Shenzong in 1085. Thereafter, they were gradually rescinded, although a brief revival of his system occurred between 1093 and 1125.

Major Rulers of the Northern Song Dynasty, 960-1126

Reign	*Ruler*
960-976	Taizu (Zhao Kuangyin)
976-997	Taizong
998-1022	Zhenzong
1022-1063	Renzong
1064-1067	Yingzong
1068-1085	Shenzong
1086-1101	Zhezong
1101-1125	Huizong
1125-1126	Qinzong

Significance

Many historians, assessing Wang's reforms, view him as a champion of small or middle landowners and small businesses. At the least, his efforts showed an interest in the broader sectors of society. In the long run, however, these efforts failed. A principal cause of this failure was Wang's inability to develop a dedicated and trustworthy official corps. Additionally, his opponents, in and out of government, succeeded in portraying him as a radical—and not truly Confucian at all. Sima Guang, leader of the opposition until his death in 1086, accused Wang of being self-satisfied and opinionated and of setting his own ambition above the nation's interests; he added that Wang was impractical as well.

Wang did, however, have his defenders. Several decades after Wang's death, a Confucian philosopher, Liu Xiongshan (Liu Hsiang-shan; 1113-1192), praised him as a man of "heroic mould and will." He attributed the failure of the New Policies to the intransigence of both Wang and his opponents, each side failing to make the necessary compromises. Certainly, Wang lacked sufficient tact to win over the traditionalists. At times, he was more theoretical than practical in political matters. Nevertheless, the New Policies did improve the financial situation for a time, and, as some twentieth century historians hold, perhaps Wang's reforms, as much as any other factor, enabled the Song Dynasty to last another half century after his death.

Several of Wang's reforms, such as the militia organization—the *baojia* system—and the graduated land tax, would be revived by later dynasties. His measures were not without defect. Still, as the centuries passed, aspects of them gained more approval, and Wang's reputation rose accordingly.

—*S. Carol Berg*

Further Reading

De Bary, William Theodore, Irene Bloom, and Wing-tsit Chan, comps. *Sources of Chinese Tradition*. 2d ed. New York: Columbia University Press, 1999-2000. Contains translations of documents by and about Wang Anshi and his New Policies. Brief essays in each section. Several documents cover aspects of Song society in general, giving a good framework for Wang's reforms. Index.

Fairbank, John King, Edwin O. Reischauer, and Albert M. Craig. *East Asia: Tradition and Transformation*. Rev. ed. Boston: Houghton Mifflin, 1989. Chapter 6 is most pertinent. Contains an overall analysis of the Song Dynasty with a brief but good summary of Wang Anshi's reforms. Index, maps, and illustrations.

Hymes, Robert P., and Conrad Schirokauer, eds. *Ordering the World: Approaches to State and Society in Sung Dynasty China*. Berkeley: University of California Press, 1993. A collection of papers on the state and society in China during the Sung Dynasty. Bibliography and index.

Lee, Thomas H. C. *Government Education and Examinations in Sung China*. New York: St. Martin's Press, 1985. An analysis of the civil service examinations and bureaucracy systems of the Song Dynasty. Index.

Liu, James T. C. *Reform in Sung China: Wang An-shih (1021-1086) and His New Policies*. Cambridge, Mass.: Harvard University Press, 1959. A careful analysis of the reform program of Wang Anshi with reference to the philosophical differences between Wang and his antagonist Sima Guang.

Meskill, John Thomas. *Wang An-shih: Practical Reformer?* 1963. Reprint. Boston: Heath, 1967. A study of Wang Anshi and his reform program.

Roberts, J. A. G. *A Concise History of China*. Cambridge, Mass.: Harvard University Press, 2003. Contains a chapter on the Song and Yuan Dynasties with a section on Wang Anshi's reforms.

See also: Ouyang Xiu; Sima Guang.

Related articles in *Great Events from History: The Middle Ages, 477-1453*: 960: Founding of the Song Dynasty; 960-1279: Scholar-Official Class Flourishes Under Song Dynasty; 1069-1072: Wang Anshi Introduces Bureaucratic Reforms; 1115: Foundation of the Jin Dynasty.

Wang Kŏn

Korean king (r. 918-943)

Wang Kŏn founded the Koryŏ Dynasty, which reunited the Korean peninsula and became the first Korean state to successfully integrate all the peoples living on the peninsula.

Born: 877; Songak (now Kaesŏng, North Korea)

Died: 943; Kaegyŏng (now Kaesŏng, North Korea)

Also known as: Wang Geon; T'aejo (posthumous title)

Areas of achievement: Government and politics, warfare and conquest

Early Life

Wang Kŏn (wang guhn) was born in Songak, a prefecture in central Korea that was part of the Silla kingdom. His family, which had settled there several generations before, had become de facto leaders of the prefecture. They relied partly on maritime trade for their wealth and power.

Nothing is known about Wang Kŏn's childhood and adolescence. According to a twelfth century mythological account, his rise to power was preordained. The account traces the origin of the Wang clan to a semidivine ancestor, who descended from Mount Paektu, the sacred mountain also associated with Tangun, the mythical ancestor of the Korean race. After settling in Songak, the Wang clan was further enhanced through intermarriage with the daughter of a dragon king and a Chinese emperor. In 876, the geomancer-monk Tosŏn (827-898) instructed Wang Kŏn's father, Wang Yong, on using and adapting the geomantic conditions of Songak to prepare for the future ruler, Wang Kŏn, whose birth Tosŏn predicted.

In actuality, scholars believe that Wang Yong benefited from the collapse of the Silla Dynasty (668-935), which enabled him to build his own power base. The Silla kings had once ruled more than two-thirds of the Korean peninsula from their capital in Kyŏngju. However, their power gradually eroded during the ninth century, as local strongmen became more and more independent. In the last decade of the ninth century, two independent states broke away from Silla: Later Paekche (900-936) in the southwest and Later Koguryŏ state (also known as T'aebong).

In 898, Kungye moved his capital to Songak and appointed Wang Kŏn as his chief military commander. Wang Kŏn was entrusted with consolidating and expanding the frontiers of the new state. He carried out this duty with great zeal and ability. Over the next twenty years, he was engaged in numerous land and sea battles with Kyŏn-hwŏn, the king of Later Paekche. Wang Kŏn was especially successful in establishing naval superiority: He established a naval base in Naju, in the southwestern corner of the peninsula, from which he controlled the western sea coast. About 910, in an attempt to drive Wang Kŏn out of Naju, Kyŏn-hwŏn sent a large fleet to recapture the city but was defeated in a major naval battle, in which Wang Kŏn used a surprise attack to set fire to the enemy fleet.

Although Wang Kŏn was loyal to Kungye, signs of a rift became apparent at an early stage. In 905, Kungye moved his capital out of Kaesŏng, and from then on, Kungye and Wang Kŏn avoided each other. According to the official histories, written to justify Wang Kŏn's actions, Kungye became increasingly tyrannical, gradually becoming insane. Everyone rallied behind Wang Kŏn and begged him to become the new ruler. Wang Kŏn finally relented and took the throne in 918, when he proclaimed the Koryŏ Dynasty (918-1392).

LIFE'S WORK

After assuming the title of king of Koryŏ at the age of forty-one, Wang Kŏn still had a long way to go to establish the authority of his new dynasty. Final reunification would be achieved only in 936, and at his death in 943, centralized government control still did not reach most local areas.

In spite of his military successes against Later Paekche, Wang Kŏn's military power was limited; he set about consolidating the new dynasty by concluding alliances with the town heads and castle lords who controlled major cities and regions. These alliances were often forged through marriage ties: Wang Kŏn married no less than twenty-nine times, each of his spouses belonging to an important regional family. While this promoted wider recognition of the dynasty, it also proved a liability, especially when it came to choosing a successor, as each family would vie to place one of its own on the throne.

At the time of his succession, his authority was far from universal in the territory he inherited from Kungye, which stretched from the upper Han River in the south to the Taedong River in the north. He had to overcome several rebellions and only gradually won the allegiance of regional strongmen. This process of internal consolidation diverted Wang Kŏn's attention from dealing with his rival states, Silla and Later Paekche. A stalemate developed with Later Paekche, as neither side took any major military initiative.

Kyŏn-hwŏn tried to lure Wang Kŏn into a trap by turning his attention to Silla. Weakened by centuries of infighting among the royal clan, the Silla court had lost control over all but the Kyŏngju basin. Still, it commanded considerable symbolic authority, and Wang Kŏn was keen to obtain the mantle of legitimacy from the Silla Dynasty. Therefore, while trying to win over regional commanders nominally loyal to Silla, he also professed his loyalty to Silla and acted as its protector. When Kyŏn-hwŏn sacked Kyŏngju in 927 and installed a puppet king, Wang Kŏn was forced to lead a force of five thousand deep into Silla territory to save the dynasty but was routed by Kyŏn-hwŏn and barely escaped with his life. After this defeat, another stalemate arose between Koryŏ and Later Paekche.

Wang Kŏn's patience in winning over the old Silla elite finally paid off in 935 when the last Silla ruler abdicated and submitted to Wang Kŏn, thus transmitting his mandate to the new dynasty. In the same year, Kyŏn-hwŏn suffered a major setback when his elder sons, angry at being passed over for succession, rebelled and imprisoned their father. He escaped, however, and sought refuge with Wang Kŏn, who welcomed him and used the dissent at his enemy's court to his advantage. In 936, he finally defeated the last forces of Later Paekche, his enemy of forty years, in the Battle of Ilsŏn-gun, thus unifying all but the northernmost part of the peninsula.

Wang Kŏn was a skillful military strategist and an astute political leader. After making his conquests, his biggest task was to present himself as the legitimate ruler of all the Korean people. To this end, he created a persona that appealed to the various regional sensibilities and relied on a variety of ideologies.

First, Wang Kŏn chose a name for the dynasty that reclaimed the inheritance of an ancient state: Koryŏ was simply an alternative spelling for Koguryŏ. At its peak, between c. 300 and its defeat by combined Silla-Tang forces in 668, the state of Koguryŏ had covered a vast area, consisting of much of present-day Manchuria and the northern and central part of the Korean peninsula. Silla managed to integrate only part of the former Koguryŏ territory and never claimed its people as part of Silla. Wang Kŏn, on the other hand, was keen to integrate the remnants of the ancient Koguryŏ state, particularly Parhae, founded by Koguryŏ renegades in 698 in the area now known as Manchuria. However, his ambitions were thwarted when Parhae was overrun by the Khitan in 926. Despite this setback, Wang Kŏn made recovery of the ancient Koguryŏ heartland an official policy, which set Koryŏ on a collision course with the Khitan, the effective rulers of these lands.

Identification with Koguryŏ apparently was done primarily for territorial purposes. There were no attempts to favor people of Koguryŏ descent. Indeed, Koryŏ looked up to the Silla heritage and sought to integrate officials who had worked for the Silla court. Wang Kŏn's policy was to integrate peoples from all the former Korean states. Symbolically, this was expressed in the integration of the former ruling clans: Remnants of the Silla, Parhae, and Later Paekche royal families were all welcomed by Wang Kŏn, and some of the family members were integrated into the Wang clan through marriage. An exception was made for Later Paekche, however. In his political testament, he warned his successors never to trust people from this area. This statement seems to have sown the seeds of a long-standing discrimination against people from the southwest, which continues to this day.

Wang Kŏn also invoked the mandate of heaven theory (heavenly authorization of rule) to justify his kingship. He was careful to make his actions and persona fit with this theory, according to which a person endowed with the right character and moral fiber will resonate with the cosmic order, producing signs in the natural world that he is fit to rule. This explains why Koryŏ historiography is so keen to portray Kungye as an evil ruler who has lost that mandate, and why Wang Kŏn took so much care to receive the mandate from the last Silla ruler rather than to simply usurp it. He also tailored his policies to conform with those of the Chinese dynastic founders: He granted amnesties, alleviated the people's tax burdens, and took measures to stimulate agriculture.

Besides the mandate of heaven, Wang Kŏn appealed to more popular ideologies to support his dynasty, notably geomancy and Buddhism. In the Korean reinterpretation of geomantic principles, the natural flow of *ki* (energy) through the earth was connected with the peninsular geography and the mythical importance of Mount Paektu. All the positive energy was thought to originate from Mount Paektu and diffuse via the mountain ridges that ran down the peninsula. Kaegyŏng, as the capital of Koryŏ became known, was situated at the end of one of those ridges, tapping directly into the positive energy. Wang Kŏn was also a keen supporter of Buddhism, notably of the Sŏn (Zen) school. The Sŏn school not only was the most vibrant religious force of the time, but its temples also were established across the peninsula and were important religious, intellectual, and economic centers

MAJOR RULERS OF THE KORYŎ DYNASTY, 918-1392

Reign	*Ruler*
918-943	T'aejo (WANG KŎN)
944-945	Hyejong
946-949	Chŏngjong
949-975	Kwangjong (Wang So)
975-981	Kyŏngjong (Wang Yu)
981-997	Sŏngjong (Wang Ch'i)
997-1009	Mokshong
1009-1031	Hyŏngjong
1031-1034	Tokjong
1034-1046	Chŏngjong
1046-1083	Munjong (Wang Hwi)
1083	Sunjong
1083-1094	Sŏnjong
1094-1095	Hŏnjong
1095-1105	Sukjong
1105-1122	Yejong I
1122-1146	Injong I (Wang Hae)
1146-1170	Ŭijong
1170-1197	Myŏngjong
1197-1204	Sinjong
1204-1211	Hŭijong
1211-1213	Kangjong
1214-1259	Kojong I
1260-1274	Wŏnjong
1274-1308	Ch'ungugŏl Wang
1308-1313	Ch'ungsŏn Wang
1313-1330	Ch'ungsuk Wang
1330-1332	Ch'unghye Wang
1332-1339	Ch'angsuk Wang
1339-1344	Ch'unghye Wang
1344-1348	Ch'ungmok Wang
1348-1351	Ch'ungjŏng Wang
1351-1394	Kongmin Wang
1374-1388	U (Sin-u)
1389	Sinch'ang
1389-1392	Kongyang Wang

with strong ties to local society. By patronizing Sŏn monks and inviting them to his court, Wang Kŏn was able to spread an image of himself as a humane ruler and devout Buddhist in the local societies in which the Sŏn monks were based.

Wang Kŏn died at the age of sixty-six, exhausted after conducting nearly forty years of continuous warfare. He left behind a kingdom that was still beset by internal contradictions, and it was up to his successors to build institutions of state and a more sophisticated government structure that could recruit people to administer the country. He failed to secure a stable succession, as his designated successor proved unable to fend off rival siblings. Only after a bloody succession struggle and equally bloody purges among the elites who had supported Wang Kŏn's rise to power was King Kwangjong (r. 949-975), another son of Wang Kŏn, able to secure the dynasty.

SIGNIFICANCE

Wang Kŏn laid the foundations of a dynasty that lasted nearly five centuries, from 918 to 1392. He was, in effect, the first known dynastic founder among the Korean people and the first to achieve true unification. Previous peninsular states had all evolved from tribal societies and never quite shook off the constraints of these local origins. Although the Silla Dynasty unified most of the peninsula, it consistently excluded anyone not belonging to the Kyŏngju-based Kim clan from power. Wang Kŏn managed to take over the best elements of Silla culture, but through the judicious use of geomancy, Confucianism, and Buddhism, he created a culture with which various elite groups could identify.

Despite the remarkable longevity of the Koryŏ Dynasty, its kingship was inherently weak. Wang Kŏn had initially tried to create an empire, using his own reign titles and calendar, but in the end, he chose to become vassal to China. Although vassal status was largely symbolic, it meant that he could not find sufficient support for his position internally. Though his policies of reconciliation and alliance laid the foundations of a unified state, he had to make too many compromises to achieve a strong centralized leadership.

—*Sem Vermeersch*

FURTHER READING

Duncan, John. *The Origins of the Chosŏn Dynasty*. Seattle: University of Washington Press, 2000. Analyzes the descent groups that monopolized political power in the Koryŏ period. Contains a useful introduction on the political system of early Koryŏ.

Hurst, Cameron G., III. "'The Good, the Bad and the Ugly': Personalities in the Founding of Koryŏ." *Korean Studies Forum* 7 (1981): 1-27. Still the only work in a Western language that contains reliable biographies of the main actors in the founding of Koryŏ.

Kang, Hugh H. W. "The First Succession Struggle of Koryŏ, in 945: A Reinterpretation." *Journal of Asian Studies* 36, no. 3 (1977): 411-428. A detailed study of the factors that led to the violent succession struggles after Wang Kŏn's death.

_______. "Wang Kŏn and the Koryŏ Dynastic Order." *Han'guk Munhwa* 7 (1986): 161-175. Highlights the Confucian elements in Wang Kŏn's legitimation strategy.

Rogers, Michael. "*P'yŏnnyŏn T'ongnok:* The Foundation Legend of the Koryŏ State." *Journal of Korean Studies* 4 (1982-1983): 3-72. A detailed study of the geomantic discourse and legends that served to mythologize the Wang royal lineage.

SEE ALSO: Kōken; Shōtoku Taishi; Taizong; Wu Hou.

RELATED ARTICLES in *Great Events from History: The Middle Ages, 477-1453*: 668-935: Silla Unification of Korea; 918-936: Foundation of the Koryŏ Dynasty.

Wang Wei

Chinese poet

A major Tang poet, Wang Wei left a body of some 370 poems that can be considered authentic; his much-admired nature poetry accounts for his preeminence in Chinese literature. A highly skilled musician and an unusually competent government official, he was credited with founding the Southern school of landscape painting.

Born: 701; District of Qi, Taiyuan Prefecture, Shanxi Province, China
Died: 761; Chang'an, Jingzhao Prefecture, China
Areas of achievement: Literature, art, music, government and politics

Early Life

Not much is known about the early life and education of Wang Wei (wahng way). He was the eldest child of a family of aristocratic, middle-level officials. Wang Wei's father, Wang Chulian (Wang Ch'u-lien), despite his middle-official rank, belonged to the powerful Taiyuan Wang clan, and Wang Wei's mother belonged to the prominent Boling Cui clan. Wang and Cui were among the "seven great surnames" (*qi xing*) and wielded much political power.

Wang Wei was a prodigy and evidently had the typical Confucian literary education, which prepared him for the civil service examinations. He began to compose poetry at the age of nine and also showed talent in painting, calligraphy, and music. At the age of fifteen, he went to the capitals of Luoyang and Chang'an to prepare himself for the examinations and was warmly welcomed at the courts of the imperial princes, especially that of Prince Qi (Ch'i, or Li Fan), the younger brother of the emperor. Known for his court poetry and ability to play *pipa* (Chinese guitar), Wang Wei was an immediate success at court, where he shrewdly made important social and literary contacts.

Having taken first place in the provincial examination, he became qualified to take the metropolitan examination. In 721, he was among the thirty-eight successful candidates for the *jinshi* degree out of the several thousand who attempted it. As a result, he was soon appointed one of the court's associate secretaries of music. His future looked bright.

Life's Work

Nevertheless, at this time, Wang Wei's position as a literatus came to overshadow his background as an aristocrat. When the empress Wu Hou usurped the throne in 690, she initiated a conflict between the aristocracy and the literati by rejecting hereditary privilege in favor of the examination system for choosing high officials. Although Emperor Xuanzong (Hsüan-tsung, r. 712-756) had revived the hereditary privilege after ascending the throne in 712, he remained suspicious of political intrigues and kept a watch on the princes. Soon after Wang Wei assumed his official position at the court of Prince Qi, the prince was suspected of conspiring against his brother. In 722, the emperor responded by breaking up the princely entourages. Wang Wei was charged with an indiscretion (allowing the performance of a forbidden dance). In 723, he was dismissed from court, demoted, and banished to the distant district of Jizhou (Chi-chou; now in Shandong Province), thus beginning the early period of his literary development.

Wang Wei served in Jizhou until 727, when he began a period of travel in the eastern provinces. These travels frequently provided inspiration for poems that are unusual in their perspectives. During his travels, Wang Wei made the acquaintance of Daoist and Buddhist masters and frequented their retreats. He also made important political friendships during his exile. His friendship with Pei Yaoqing (P'ei Yao-ch'ing), the prefect of Jizhou, led to his introduction to the outstanding statesman and brilliant poet Zhang Jiuling (Chang Chiu-ling), the powerful imperial minister.

About 730, Wang Wei's wife died. He never remarried and chose to remain celibate the rest of his life, beginning a serious study of Chan Buddhism with the Chan master Zuoguang (Tso-kuang). At this time, he also discovered his own poetic voice. In 733, he returned to Chang'an. Now his acquaintance with Zhang Jiuling paid off, for this powerful and highly ethical man sponsored his reentry into politics. In 734, Emperor Xuanzong appointed him "reminder on the right" (*youshiyi*). True to his Confucian ideal, Wang Wei was in public service once again, thus ending his first stage of poetic development.

As reminder on the right, Wang Wei reminded the emperor of overlooked or forgotten matters. Such a position required much tact and subtle diplomacy; apparently Wang Wei was equal to it, for he maintained his position and continued to advance. Nevertheless, he found Xuanzong's new ministry dangerous. Although the triumvirate included Zhang Jiuling and Pei Yaoqing, the third member was the ambitious Li Linfu. Zhang Jiuling and Pei Yaoqing had both risen to positions of power through the examination system; they were literati. Li Linfu, however, was an aristocrat and a member of the imperial clan that supported hereditary privilege: Conflict was inevitable. When Zhang Jiuling was banished and Pei Yaoqing demoted in 737, Wang Wei also was in danger. Nevertheless, he survived, although he temporarily became investigating censor (*jian cha yushi*) of Hexi, a post on the northwest frontier in the province of Liangzhou (modern Gansu). Here he assisted the military governor, Cui Xiyi (Ts'ui Hsi-i), from 737 until 738, when Cui's forces were defeated by the Tibetans and the general was killed. Although not technically an exile, Wang Wei's frontier assignment gave Li Linfu time to consolidate his power without undue interference. He became a virtual dictator when the elderly emperor, preoccupied with his consort, Yang Guifei (Yang Kuei-fei), began to allow him a free hand in public affairs.

When Wang Wei returned to Chang'an in 738, he was promoted to palace censor (*dianzhong shiyu shi*). In 740, he was sent to the south to supervise the provincial examinations, returning to the capital and continuing his steady advancement. At about this time, he seems to have acquired his famous Wangchuan estate, which was located in the foothills of the Zhongnan Mountains, some 30 miles (48 kilometers) south of Chang'an; the estate was to prove important to his life and to his painting and poetry. About 750, his mother died, and he withdrew from court for the customary period of mourning, a little more than two years. On his return to Chang'an in 752, Wang Wei was appointed secretary of the civil office (*lilu langzhong*), which obliged him to nominate, examine, and evaluate civil officials. In 754, he became grand secretary of the imperial chancellery (*jishizhong*), which represented a more prestigious rank. The following year, however, any further advance was abruptly curtailed by the onslaught of the An Lushan rebellion, which dispersed the entire court.

The years from 734 to 755 may be considered Wang Wei's middle period, his most productive and significant literary period. It includes his poem written to Zhang Jiuling after the latter's exile to Xingzhou in 739 and the frontier poems inspired by his military experience at Heshi. There are also such outstanding court poems as "Zeng cong di si ku yuan wai Qiu" ("Given to My Paternal Cousin, Military Supply Officer Qiu"), "Feng he sheng zhi zhongyangjie zai chen ji chun chen shang shou ying zhi" ("Written at Imperial Command to Harmonize with His Majesty's Poem, 'On the Double Ninth Festival the Ministers and Assembled Officials Offer Their Wishes for Longevity'"), and "Datong dian sheng yu zhi Long Chi shang yu qing yun; bai guan gongdu; sheng en bian si yan yue gan shu ji" ("At Datong Hall a Jade Iris Grew, and There Were Auspicious Clouds by Dragon Pond; the Hundred Officials Observed [These Phenomena] Together; Imperial Kindness Bestowed a Banquet with Music, so I Dared to Write on This Occasion"). The first court poem expresses Wang Wei's desire to withdraw from politics and celebrates the peace and serenity of reclusion. The latter two, however, celebrate imperial power. Finally, this period includes many fine Buddhist and nature poems, the latter often showing Daoist influences.

During the 740's and early 750's, Wang Wei apparently spent much of his time on his Wangchuan estate. It is evident that he enjoyed this place immensely. His best-known companion was his friend Pei Di (P'ei Ti), a minor poet and official, who shared in the composition of the masterly "Wangchuan ji" ("Wang River Collection"). Together they treated a series of topics whose order was determined simply by the geographical layout of the landscape. Wang Wei's continuous scroll on which he depicted the same twenty landscapes is no longer extant, but copies of it give a viewer some sense of what he must have done.

When Li Linfu died in 752, he was replaced by Yang Guozhong (Yang Kuo-chung), who, although a man of little merit, was a relative of the emperor's consort, Yang Guifei. When the frontier general An Lushan rebelled in 755 and attempted to overthrow the emperor, Xuanzong was caught unprepared. Fearing an attack on Chang'an, he and his court fled at night to Sichuan. Some officials, however, remained behind, including Wang Wei.

Having almost immediately occupied Luoyang, the rebels then attacked Chang'an. Wang Wei attempted to join the emperor but was captured by the rebels. Although he pretended physical disability in an effort to escape having to serve the rebel government, he did not succeed and faced execution. Because An Lushan had been previously impressed with his abilities, however, he was imprisoned instead in the Pudi Monastery. Later he was compelled to collaborate with the rebel government.

Meanwhile, when Xuanzong learned that his son had fled to Shaanxi in northwest China, he abdicated. His son proclaimed himself Emperor Suzong (Su-tsung, r. 756-762) and organized Uighur forces to help him overcome the rebels. After An Lushan was killed and Chang'an was recaptured toward the end of 757, the new emperor and his court returned to the capital.

Debate now raged on what to do with the collaborators. Two of the emperor's ministers urged that they be killed; a third, Li Xian (Li Hsien), argued that the instability of the military and political situation demanded selective clemency. Most of the collaborators were punished by death, flogging, or banishment. Because of his brother's intercession and of a poem he had written from the monastery during the rebel occupation, however, Wang Wei was pardoned by the emperor. Wang Wei was then reinstated in the official ranks as vice president of the grand secretariat of the crown prince (*taizi zhongyun*) and later became its president. After again serving briefly as grand secretary of the imperial chancellery (*jishizhong*), in 759, he was advanced to the highest position he ever attained, that of assistant secretary of state on the right (*shuangshu yucheng*).

Despite this honor, it appears that toward the end of his life Wang Wei became disheartened and increasingly inactive. He seldom stayed at his Wangchuan estate but lived mostly just outside the capital. He wrote no more nature poems and, on returning home from work, spent his leisure hours reading Buddhist sutras. Lonely, old, weak, and with poor eyesight, he petitioned the emperor to recall his brother, Wang Jin (Wang Chin), to court so the two could be near each other. The emperor did so, and Wang Jin was appointed grand counselor of the emperor on the left (*zuosan jichang shi*). Wang Wei wrote a memorial thanking the emperor for his kindness; it is dated the fourth day of the fifth month of 761. Wang Wei died in the same year and was buried on his Wangchuan estate.

Wang Jin survived Wang Wei to become a chief minister under the next emperor. The new emperor, who was fond of poetry, asked Wang Jin if enough of Wang Wei's poems had survived to make a collection for presentation to the throne. The poems that were extant, out of the several thousand written, were gathered together by Wang Jin and presented to the emperor in 763.

The years 756-761 may be considered Wang Wei's late period. The poems written during this time reflect his loneliness, his struggles with the infirmities of old age, and his growing awareness of death. In 756, as a prisoner of the rebels in the Pudi Monastery, awaiting a doubtful fate, Wang Wei was surprised by a visit from his friend Pei Di, who somehow had managed to slip into the monastery. Pei Di brought news of the outside world, especially about the behavior of the Pear Garden musicians when forced to celebrate the rebel victory. This event inspired Wang Wei to write a poem. Shortly thereafter, he addressed a poem directly to Pei Di. These two poems exemplify the poet's ability to identify with both the recluse and the government official. At the time he wrote the poem about the Pear Garden musicians, Wang Wei could not have dreamed that it would play an important part in his rehabilitation and restoration, resulting in a pardon from the emperor and in his return to office.

Wang Wei's gratitude for the emperor's clemency is shown by his poem "Ji meng youzui xuan fu fei gong fu gan sheng en qie shu bi yi jian xin xu shi jundeng zhugong" ("Having Received Pardon for My Offense and Been Returned to Office, Humbly Moved by Imperial Kindness, I Write My Lowly Thoughts and Present Them to My Superiors"). Written in 758, the poem celebrates a return to the old order of stability and brilliance and predicts an even more glorious reign.

Significance

Wang Wei was the most prominent poet of his time. He knew the rigorous conventions of the court poetry of the Early Tang, but he reacted against them and made his own way, becoming the premier capital poet, one who could hew to the rules and then go beyond them. Nevertheless, for centuries he has been best known as a nature poet. Indeed, he was a master at portraying tranquil landscapes, and he often composed such poems when he was away from court. Commonly admired for their concrete images and visual immediacy, they display at the same time an intuitive sense of the unreality of sensory experience. Such an impression is frequently supported by statements of a philosophical or religious character.

Wang Wei was politically a Confucian who dabbled in Daoism and who loved the Buddhist Way, and he studied for years under a Chan master. When away from court, he burned incense, practiced Chan meditation, and loved to associate with Buddhist and Daoist monks. His commitment to Buddhism inspired many of his poems.

As a poet Wang Wei was independent, daringly experimental, and original. He strove always for simplicity, integrity, and spiritual truth. Although interested in perception, he was concerned not with what the eye saw but with what the mind intuited, with the inner spirit of things. His own emotion was always restrained. His poetry is wide in scope both thematically and stylistically. His contributions to the development of genre by his treatment of the quatrain, which depended on proper closure, and his personal handling of the couplet were of major importance.

Wang Wei's influence on later Chinese poets began early. It is evident in the work of the later eighth century minor poets Liu Zhangqing (Liu Chang-ch'ing)—whose poetry was written late in his life—and Wei Yingwu (Wei Ying-wu). The great practitioners of the new *shiyu* poetry of the Northern Song Dynasty (Sung; 960-1126)—

Ouyang Xiu (Ou-yang Hsiu), Wang Anshi, and above all Su Dongpo (Su Tung-p'o)—looked to Wang Wei as their model. Indeed, it was Su Dongpo who elevated Wang's reputation as a painter to equal his reputation as a poet. He was also responsible for a remark about one of Wang's poems that, taken out of context and misinterpreted by others, led to his false reputation as the "painter-poet." This misunderstanding in turn led to the aesthetic ideal that a good poem was a "painting-poem" (*huashi*). Two prominent poets of the Qing Dynasty (Ch'ing; 1644-1911)—Wang Shizheng (Wang Shih-cheng) and Shen Deqian (Shen Te-ch'ien)—who were also critics formulated their poetic theories out of their admiration for Wang Wei's poetry. Wang Shizheng held that genuine poetry amounted to the immediate embodiment of spiritual inspiration in words. Shen Deqian, a fine teacher of Chinese prosody, held that the technical proficiency of Wang Wei proved him the greatest of all Chinese poets.

—*Richard P. Benton*

Further Reading

Seth, Vikram, trans. *Three Chinese Poets: Translations of Poems by Wang Wei, Li Bai, and Du Fu*. Boston: Faber and Faber, 1992. A collection of poems by Du Fu, Li Bo, and Wang Wei. Commentary provides useful information.

Wagner, Marsha L. *Wang Wei*. Boston: Twayne, 1982. Part of the Twayne World Authors series, this scholarly, well-written account of Wang Wei's life provides a balanced, perceptive appraisal of his contributions as poet, painter, and government official. Includes fine translations.

Wang Wei. *Laughing Lost in the Mountains: Poems of Wang Wei*. Translated by Tony Barnstone, Willis Barnstone, and Xu Haixin. Hanover, N.H.: University Press of New England, 1991. Translations of selected poems of Wang Wei. A critical introduction provides information on the poet and his works. Bibliography and index.

_______. *Poems of Wang Wei*. Translated by G. W. Robinson. Baltimore: Penguin Books, 1973. Fluid translations of 127 poems, with a brief introduction.

_______. *The Poetry of Wang Wei: New Translations and Commentary*. Translated by Pauline Yu. Bloomington: Indiana University Press, 1980. This study provides excellent, scholarly translations and notes as well as knowing critical appraisals of Wang Wei's poems.

See also: Du Fu; Li Bo; Li Qingzhao; Ouyang Xiu; Su Dongpo; Wang Anshi.

Related articles in *Great Events from History: The Middle Ages, 477-1453*: 581: Sui Dynasty Reunifies China; 618: Founding of the Tang Dynasty; 690-705: Reign of Empress Wu; 755-763: Rebellion of An Lushan; 907-960: Period of Five Dynasties and Ten Kingdoms.

Wenceslaus

King of Bohemia (r. 1378-1419)

Wenceslaus encouraged the development of a Czech national consciousness, but through his incompetence and hesitation he also contributed to the weakening of central authority in Germany and Bohemia.

Born: February 26, 1361; Nuremberg (now in Germany)

Died: August 16, 1419; Prague, Bohemia (now in Czech Republic)

Also known as: Wenceslaus IV; Wenceslas IV; Wenzel; Václav

Area of achievement: Government and politics

Early Life

In the early 1300's, the counts of Luxembourg added to their titles and territories the kingdom of Bohemia, the march of Brandenburg, and the duchy of Silesia. The dynasty's high point came under the father of Wenceslaus (WEHN-seh-slaws), Holy Roman Emperor Charles IV (r. 1355-1378), one of the greatest rulers of European history. He presided over a Bohemian golden age, transforming Prague into a major center of Gothic civilization as well as a political capital for both Bohemia and the empire.

Charles's eldest son, Wenceslaus, was born in the important imperial city of Nuremberg. He grew up in the creative atmosphere of Prague, where his father crowned him Wenceslaus IV, king of Bohemia, at the age of three. He received the best education, becoming fluent in German, Czech, and Latin. According to the chroniclers, his father often had Wenceslaus attend court, where the emperor taught his royal son both pragmatic politics and honorable justice. Hoping also to secure his son's succession in the empire, Charles approached the seven electoral princes. They decided who would become the next "king of the Romans" in Germany, who then could be crowned Holy Roman Emperor by the pope in Rome. Emperor Charles's prestige led to the young Wenceslaus's election as king in 1376.

Yet the brilliance of Charles IV's later years hid serious weaknesses in imperial Germany. The crown had lost much prestige, with power slipping away into the hands of territorial princes such as the duke of Bavaria and the archbishop of Cologne. Tensions were rising between the princes and both the towns and the petty nobles. In Bohemia itself, Charles faced growing opposition from nobles who wanted both to resist royal power and to dominate the growing independent-minded towns and restless free peasants. Finally, just before his death, Charles faced the Great Schism of the Papacy. In 1378, two popes, one in Rome and the other in Avignon in southern France, each claimed to be the rightfully elected pontiff of the Christian Church in the West.

Engraved sigillum, or seal, containing the likeness of Wenceslaus. (Library of Congress)

LIFE'S WORK

On Charles IV's death on November 29, 1378, many expected the young Wenceslaus to continue his father's successes. A slender, handsome youth, he had an easy affability, even playfully mimicking members of his court. His interest in culture led him to continue his father's patronage of the arts. Likewise, he expanded the University of Prague and support for its students. Unusual for a king, he liked to disguise himself and go among everyday people, for whom he retained affection throughout most of his reign.

Rather than building on his father's success and generally good reputation, however, Wenceslaus became renowned for his failure to govern. Some authorities blame this incompetence on certain negative aspects of his character. His worst enemies have even portrayed him as a monster, surpassing even the legendary excesses of the Roman emperor Nero. While such a view is clearly exaggerated, Wenceslaus did alienate friends with a mercurial temperament that could spark sudden rages. Instead of showing diligence in his royal duties, moreover, he indulged his passions for hunting and alcohol. Sometimes called Wenceslaus "the lazy," he regularly avoided tough decisions.

Additionally, the Luxemburger family contributed strongly to Wenceslaus's failures. His inheritance from his father left him politically enfeebled, since many territories and titles went to other relatives. Indeed, he inherited only Bohemia and Silesia. A half uncle received Luxembourg proper. His half brother Sigismund, the later emperor (r. 1433-1437), got Brandenburg, with its electoral vote, as well as the kingdom of Hungary through an arranged marriage. Nephews gained other important border provinces around Bohemia, giving them influence with the local nobility. Even worse, these family members would often pursue their own interests, rather than those of the Luxembourg dynasty, the German empire, or the Bohemian kingdom.

Still, Wenceslaus's early years seemed promising. In his first imperial diet, he united support behind the Roman pope, who encouraged him to come to Rome for the imperial coronation. Wenceslaus also arranged the marriage of his sister Anne with King Richard II of England (r. 1377-1399), who lent money to Wenceslaus to finance the trip. Wenceslaus never bothered to go to Rome to be crowned emperor, however, so he remained weak and dependent on the electoral princes. Challenging his authority, the cities of the empire began to ally themselves together formally in leagues to protect themselves from the continual warfare. Although Wenceslaus successfully promulgated an imperial peace, or Landfriede, in 1383 and again in 1389, he wound up unable to appease either the princes or the towns.

He withdrew into Bohemia, where he quarreled with the archbishop of Prague in 1393. Reputedly, he even took part in the torture of several clerics, killing John of Pomuk, the general vicar, and dumping his body in the Vltava River. Years later, after the victim was canonized as Saint John of Nepomuk, his veneration promoted the Counter-Reformation, elevating him to be the new patron saint of Bohemia. In Wenceslaus's own time, this heinous act spurred the nobility into an alliance with both Luxemburger relatives and the Austrian Habsburgs. On May 8, 1394, this *fronde*, or noble conspiracy, even arrested the king. Surprisingly, Wenceslaus's youngest brother, John, duke of Görlitz (north of Bohemia), came to his defense, briefly pursuing the captors and their prisoner into Upper Austria.

Following the protests of the Roman pope and the princes in Germany, the nobles released Wenceslaus on August 1. The conflict continued, however, as Wenceslaus tried to delay, buy off one side or another, and outmaneuver his eager relatives, including John, who turned against him before his death in 1396. Finally, his half brother Sigismund and his nephew Jobst, margrave of Moravia, forced Wenceslaus to agree to terms that gave the nobles control of many royal prerogatives.

After a long absence from Germany, Wenceslaus tried at an imperial diet in 1397 to promote a territorial peace for Franconia. His failure there, together with an increasing disaffection by and rivalry with the princes, led an organized opposition to remove him from power. On August 20, 1400, the electoral princes deposed him, citing him for not resolving the papal schism and not preserving the empire's peace. The next day, they elected Rupert III, elector of the palatinate, as king (r. 1400-1410). Fortunately for Wenceslaus, Rupert lacked the power to force him to renounce his title. Unfortunately, however, Wenceslaus's own relatives yet again became his opponents. When Wenceslaus impetuously planned to go to Rome for the imperial coronation, he made his half brother Sigismund regent. Sigismund promptly took the king prisoner on March 6, 1402. Jobst came to Wenceslaus's defense, as did some of the cities and nobility, but Wenceslaus had to escape on his own from imprisonment in Vienna on November 11, 1403. After further conflicts with the Bohemian nobles, Wenceslaus bought their support by handing over still more of his royal authority. The king's effective rule was thereafter largely confined to his own personal lands.

A new problem arose at the University of Prague, where some professors were adopting the reforming ideas of the famous English theologian John Wyclif, whose writings the church had declared heretical. Wyclif called for a purified church hierarchy, especially demanding that priests ought to live a more simple and virtuous life. When the rector of the university, who was German, successfully banned Wyclif's teachings there in 1403, he angered the large number of Czech supporters of those ideas. One native professor, Jan Hus, soon became the leading exponent of church reform in Bohemia, inspiring followers known as Hussites.

Theology was not the only controversy at the university. At the same time, the Bohemian professors had also been encouraging a new nationalistic frustration against the dominance of "foreigners." The university administration had originally been divided into four "nations"—the Czechs and three different kinds of Germans—each with one vote on important issues. In 1409, Wenceslaus tried to reassert his royal title, gaining support from France at the price of recognizing the Avignon pope. When the university's three nations of Germans resisted this proposition, Wenceslaus retaliated. With the Kutná Hora decree, the voting rights switched from three to one favoring the Germans to a system that favored the Czechs. In protest, many Germans left to found a new university in Leipzig, and the University of Prague took on a national, Bohemian character. Further, the remaining Bohemians more effectively championed Hus and his reforms. Wenceslaus's subsequent policies toward the Hussites vacillated; his general toleration allowed them to flourish, while his occasional restrictions were ineffective.

Meanwhile, the divisions in Europe deepened. The Council of Pisa in 1410 elected yet another new pope, although the Avignon and Roman pontiffs both refused to resign. The death of King Rupert then required a new royal election in Germany. Wenceslaus tried both to assert his claim to the royal title and to support his nephew Jobst and half brother Sigismund, both of whom were elected. Thus three popes competed to govern the church, while three kings claimed to rule Germany. Jobst's death after three and a half months led the electors to unite on Sigismund, who promised to support Wenceslaus's expedition to Rome to be crowned emperor.

While Wenceslaus continued to put off any such trip, the initiative was gained by Sigismund. Under his patronage, the Council of Constance (1414-1418) convened to end the papal schism. Additionally, it summoned Hus for examination concerning heresy, arrested him (despite the safe conduct guaranteed by Sigismund), and burned him alive at the stake. Back in Bohemia, supporters of the martyred Hus thereupon openly defied church and council. By December, 1416, Wenceslaus finally rejected most accommodations with the Hussites and joined the archbishop in restricting them, but by then it was too late. In 1419, Wenceslaus's enforcement of the papal order placing Catholic priests back into parishes unleashed rioting in Prague, as well as the first defenestrations—the defiant tossing of government officials out of windows. Hiding from decision and responsibility, Wenceslaus died of a stroke on August 16, 1419. Thereafter, Bohemia dissolved into civil war and rebellion.

Significance

Perhaps no monarch could have completely mastered the difficulties facing Christendom, Germany, and Bohemia around 1400. In addition, Wenceslaus was certainly not the vicious tyrant portrayed by some critics. Ultimately, though, his indecision and inaction harvested a destructive course of events. The German monarchy under his successor Sigismund continued its precipitous decline. Moreover, the Hussite revolution convulsed Bohemia for most of the next century. Consequently, the Czechs gained increasing national and cultural independence from the German empire, although more in spite of Wenceslaus than inspired by him.

—*Brian A. Pavlac*

Further Reading

Betts, R. R. *Essays in Czech History*. London: Athlone Press, 1969. A collection of scholarly, readable articles, mostly about persons and events contemporary with Wenceslaus. Includes a select bibliography of works cited and other works by the author.

Bradley, J. F. N. *Czechoslovakia: A Short History*. Edinburgh: Edinburgh University Press, 1971. In the context of a general, national history, the author surveys clearly and in some depth the failures of Wenceslaus that led to the Hussite revolution.

Klassen, John Martin. *The Nobility and the Making of the Hussite Revolution*. New York: Columbia University Press, 1978. A detailed, complex examination of the Bohemian nobles and both their conflict with Wenceslaus's royal authority and their divisions on religious reform issues. Includes a helpful map, appendices of noble families, and a bibliography.

Newcomer, James. *The Grand Duchy of Luxembourg: The Evolution of Nationhood, 963 A.D. to 1983*. Lanham, Md.: University Press of America, 1984. This history of the grand duchy of Luxembourg over a thousand-year period includes discussions of the counts who became rulers of Bohemia.

Spinka, Matthew. *John Hus: A Biography*. Princeton, N.J.: Princeton University Press, 1968. A standard biography of the religious reformer, although the king is only of secondary importance. Also features photographs, a map, and a select bibliography of primary and secondary sources.

Stejksal, Karel. *European Art in the Fourteenth Century*. Translated by Till Gottheinerová. London: Octopus Books, 1978. The many color illustrations, including contemporary portraits of Wenceslaus, present the rich cultural milieu of the Bohemia of Charles IV. The text mostly focuses on artistic achievements and includes time lines and a map.

Teich, Mikuláš, ed. *Bohemia in History*. New York: Cambridge University Press, 1998. This anthology includes essays on medieval Bohemia and Moravia, Bohemian culture under Charles IV, and the Hussite movement.

See also: Charles IV; Jan Hus; Richard II; John Wyclif; Jan Žižka.

Related articles in *Great Events from History: The Middle Ages, 477-1453*: 735: Christianity Is Introduced into Germany; 1305-1417: Avignon Papacy and the Great Schism; 1377-1378: Condemnation of John Wyclif; July 15, 1410: Battle of Tannenberg; 1414-1418: Council of Constance; July 6, 1415: Martyrdom of Jan Hus.

Rogier van der Weyden
Flemish painter

One of the greatest of the fifteenth century Flemish painters, Rogier influenced other painters of the Christian altarpiece, stylistically and tonally, and dominated northern European painting throughout the period.

Born: 1399 or 1400; Tournai, France (now in Belgium)
Died: June 18, 1464; Brussels (now in Belgium)
Also known as: Roger de La Pasture
Areas of achievement: Art, religion and theology

Early Life

Although Rogier van der Weyden (roh-gee-ur van dur VI-duhn) was presumably born in the French-speaking, southern region of the Netherlands, there is no specific knowledge of his ethnic background. Indeed, scholarly controversy continues to surround his life and his work. No single painting by him is confirmed by his signature, and the documentary evidence is also very slight. It is known that one Rogier van der Weyden entered an apprenticeship with the painter Robert Campin in 1427 in Tournai and fulfilled his service, getting his patent as master in 1432. However, the facts are complicated by the name Rogier van der Weyden appearing on Tournai documents in 1426, already denoted a master.

It may be that Rogier had been previously trained in another trade, perhaps sculpture, because the modeling in his paintings has distinct affinities to that art, which has led to speculation that his father might have been a sculptor. He also seems to have come to his apprenticeship as a painter relatively late in life; there is evidence that he had a son, eight years old in 1435, which suggests that he must have been married sometime in the mid-1420's.

Even his apprenticeship to Campin is conjectural. Stylistically, his work is very close to that of Campin, and it is presumed that he is the "Rogelet de le Pasture" who was taken into training by Campin. If so, he was the son of Henry de le Pasture, whose family can be traced back in Tournai as far as 1260. Whatever the truth may be concerning his early years, he was, by 1436, firmly established in Brussels, married to a Brussels native, Elisabeth Goffaerts, and employed as the official town painter.

Life's Work

The three most important Flemish painters of the late Gothic period are Jan van Eyck, the Master of Flémalle, and Rogier van der Weyden. Jan van Eyck has emerged in the long run as the most admired of the three, but that was not the case in the fifteenth century. In truth, Rogier had considerably more influence on other contemporary painters than either of the other two. The difficulty in speaking of his career, however, lies in the peculiar fact that there is no work clearly identified as an example of his early career as a painter. Only the great works of his maturity (although the greatest, his *The Descent from the Cross*, may be fairly early) are extant, a situation that has produced one of the most interesting scholarly puzzles in art history: Where are the works of his early career?

Like van Eyck, Rogier was primarily a painter of altarpieces—that is, paintings specifically ordered to be hung above the altar used in Roman Catholic churches to celebrate the Mass. They tend, as a result, to be large and connected to a specific church, and their original function was religious rather than aesthetic. The twentieth century preference for van Eyck's works over the paintings of Rogier is directly related to the fact that van Eyck, who is often credited with developing, sometimes with inventing, oil painting, anticipated Renaissance Humanist realism in his works. There is some slight influence of his work in Rogier, but Rogier seems deliberately to eschew the splendid technical leap forward into recording the real world in favor of the more static representation of humans and nature that characterized the medieval style. Rogier refused to abandon the last stages of Gothic art; thus, Rogier's work was not only distinct from that of van Eyck but also more popular in his own century.

The painter Rogier seems to resemble most is the Master of Flémalle, the shadowy figure whose altarpieces seem to have been produced in the 1430's. Touches of van Eyckian naturalism and a close relationship to Rogier's mature works distinguish the Master's painting. The Master's identity remains a mystery, but it is often suggested that he was an associate of Rogier's master, Robert Campin, or that he was, in fact, Campin. There is also an intriguing suggestion that the very paintings ascribed to the Master of Flémalle are Rogier's missing early work—that is, that Rogier is, in short, the Master of Flémalle, or at least the creator of some of the paintings now identified with the master. Given the present lack of signed works and limited documentation, the question falls into the slippery area of style, technique, and connoisseurship, in which the eye of the critic dominates. Aside from the historical importance of the question, and the rather piquant nature of the problem, the arguments themselves cut to the heart of the nature of Rogier as a painter.

It is believed that much of Rogier's work has been lost. He produced a major work for the Brussels town hall, four variations on the theme of justice, but it was lost in a fire in 1695. There exist, however, several examples of his work as an altarpiece painter and some of his portraits that clearly show why he had such a long and prosperous career, not only as a painter but also as the head of a busy workshop. His best and most popular work is *The Descent from the Cross*, displayed at the Prado Museum in Madrid. It features all those aspects of his talent that not only distinguished him from van Eyck but also established him as the most influential painter of his time in the Netherlands. The subject is the common one of the lifting of the dead Christ from the Cross; yet where other painters of van Eyckian inclination might try to portray this scene with some sense of the physical, realistic surrounding of the act of pity and awe, Rogier packs ten figures into a flat, shallow niche that reminds one of the tomb itself—with the figures spread out (though densely impinging one another) in a line across the front, similar to a sculptural frieze. The fall of the draperies and the sharply contorted poses are Gothic; yet the colors are bright and hard, almost enamelized, and the faces are charged by Rogier's greatest gift, the ability to convey a sense of spiritual suffering.

There is in Rogier not only a mannered, stylized way with composition, structures, and nature (all of which run contrary to van Eyck's warm naturalism) but also a capacity to express emotions, usually spiritual, which are quite beyond anything attempted by van Eyck. Rogier's work as a portrait painter (the lovely *Portrait of a Woman* is a good example) draws back from the particulars of realism into a kind of introverted world of religious dream.

Scholars surmise that Rogier made a trip to Italy, perhaps in 1450, and that he must have visited both Florence and Rome. His *Entombment* in the Uffizi shows that he was not entirely obdurate in his approach to his art because it shows signs of the influence of Fra Angelico. Further, his *Madonna with Four Saints* in Frankfurt, which contains in its panels the Florentine coat of arms, contains elements of the Italian *sacra conversazione*.

Rogier's career seems to have prospered from beginning to end, and his large studio employed a group of painters who carried on in his style a type of altar painting that was to dominate during the late medieval period in the Netherlands. Rogier died in Brussels in June of 1464.

Significance

If van Eyck is the twentieth century's painter of choice for the late Gothic period, then Rogier, with his stiffer, somewhat monumental seriousness and lyric, almost mystic intensity was the choice not only of the public but also of the painters who came to maturity in the same period. Rogier's way of telling the eternal story, ascetically restrained, physically desiccated (although in glowing color), was deeply admired and unabashedly imitated. It was as if Rogier read the sensibility of the age and knew that people still clung to the old imperatives, subordinating the particular and the individual to the general and the idealized; he knew that society was not yet ready to break with the safety of the collectivized, Church-centered world of religious submission to the mystery of Christianity.

The inclination today is to read Rogier's paintings through the strangely vibrant colors, the ambiguous intensities of the portrait heads, and to find his stylized draperies, his dispositions of the human body, as somewhat quaint in their Gothic awkwardness. Yet an understanding of what Rogier was doing and when he was doing it allows for a deeper appreciation of his greatness as a painter, of the imploded power, the sonority, and the graceful, dramatic timelessness of his best work.

—*Charles H. Pullen*

Further Reading

Acres, Alfred. "The Columba Altarpiece and the Time of the World." *Art Bulletin* 80, no. 3 (September, 1998). A scholarly article that focuses on the oft-neglected or understudied theme of time in art, in this case the time theme expressed in Rogier's Columba altarpiece. Also mentions the work of Jan van Eyck and the details of other Rogier altarpieces. Includes extensive footnotes.

De Vos, Dirk. *The Flemish Primitives: The Masterpieces*. Princeton, N.J.: Princeton University Press, 2002. A historical look at several Flemish master painters, including Rogier and van Eyck. Includes mostly color illustrations, a map, and a bibliography.

Friedländer, Max J. *Early Netherlandish Painting: From Van Eyck to Bruegel*. New York: Phaidon Press, 1967. This popular volume contains a chapter on Rogier, in addition to helpful chapters on van Eyck and the painting of the period in general.

_______. *Early Netherlandish Painting: Rogier van Weyden and the Master of Flémalle*. Translated by Heinz Norden. Brussels: Éditions de la Connaissance, 1967. A scholarly work delightfully and reasonably written and thoroughly accessible to the general reader. Not only does the author deal with the mystery of Rogier and the master, but he also handles the entire career and makes pertinent assessments of Rogier's style and influence.

Fuchs, R. H. *Dutch Painting*. New York: Oxford University Press, 1978. A popular, well-illustrated history of painting in the Netherlands region. Chapter 1 is a simple and direct discussion of the period in which Rogier worked.

Lane, Barbara G. *The Altar and the Altarpiece: Sacramental Themes in Early Netherlandish Painting*. New York: Harper and Row, 1984. The problem of fully understanding the quality of Rogier's work, given the limited knowledge and understanding of the deeply religious sensibility, is met with care, attention, and careful argument in this short book. Rogier's work figures substantially in the text.

Panofsky, Erwin. *Early Netherlandish Painting: Its Origins and Character.* 2 vols. 1953. Reprint. New York: Harper and Row, 1971. By a master of iconography, intriguing essays on how to read the secret language of the religious painting.

Warburg, Aby. *The Renewal of Pagan Antiquity: Contributions to the Cultural History of the European Renaissance*. Translated by David Britt. Los Angeles: Getty Research Institute for the History of Art and the Humanities, 1999. A huge collection by one of the most influential art historians of the twentieth century. Text includes the 1903 essay "Rogier van der Weyden's Entombment in the Uffizi." Includes illustrations, maps, an extensive bibliography, and an index.

See also: Fra Angelico; Arnolfo di Cambio; Cimabue; Donatello; Duccio di Buoninsegna; Jan van Eyck and Hubert van Eyck; Giotto; Pietro Lorenzetti and Ambrogio Lorenzetti; Simone Martini; Masaccio; Andrea Orcagna; Philip the Good; Nicola Pisano and Giovanni Pisano; Jean Pucelle; Claus Sluter.

Related article in *Great Events from History: The Middle Ages, 477-1453*: c. 1410-1440: Florentine School of Art Emerges.

Widukind

Westphalian chieftain

As a pivotal military and spiritual leader of the Saxons in their numerous struggles against the expanding Frankish empire, Widukind organized several pagan rebellions that repeatedly forced Charlemagne to reestablish his supremacy within the region of Saxony.

Born: Eighth century; probably Saxony (now in Germany)
Died: c. 807; place unknown
Also known as: Wittekind
Areas of achievement: Government and politics, warfare and conquest

Early Life

The name Widukind (VEE-doo-kihnt) first appears in history texts as the leader of a rapidly growing Saxon uprising in Westphalia in approximately 774. Unlike other Saxon military leaders, Widukind refused to accept baptism and take an oath of allegiance to the Frankish empire of Charlemagne. Widukind refused to submit at the Diet of Paderhorn, a council called by Charlemagne in 777 to announce that Saxony was being forcibly annexed into the Frankish realm. Frankish accounts indicate that when Widukind realized that immediate opposition to the Franks was not feasible, he took refuge to the north in Denmark, under the protection of his brother-in-law, Sigfrid the Dane. The Danes were a race barely familiar to the Franks at the time, but they would later have an important influence on how rapidly and smoothly Charlemagne would be able to expand his empire. Charlemagne's subjugation of the north would prove more difficult than his conquest of the south because there existed no natural barriers to prevent his adversaries from retreating. Widukind and his followers were thus able to withdraw from battles that could have ended the "Saxon wars" years earlier.

Life's Work

Believing that further Saxon uprisings could be controlled by his remaining troops, Charlemagne led a large portion of his army across the western Pyrenees in an attempt to invade Spain. After Basque armies forced his retreat back to Aquitaine, Charlemagne was informed that Widukind had organized the Saxons into waging a war of revenge. The Saxons sought vengeance for acts of destruction carried out by Charlemagne's soldiers such as the burning of the Irminsul, or Igdrasail, a sacred tree that stood at Eresburg and was important to Saxon worship.

Scene depicting the baptism of Widukind. (F. R. Niglutsch)

By rekindling Saxon pride and love of independence, Widukind led his Danish allies into fierce invasions of the middle Rhine region from Deutz to Anderach, notably ravaging the town of Hesse.

The Saxons' devastation and plundering resulted in the slaughter of Catholic priests, the rebuilding of pagan temples, and an organized refusal to pay tribute money. When Widukind's armies threatened the township of Fulda, the monks working as missionaries there were forced to flee, carrying with them the remains of Saint Boniface. A Frankish army later defeated the Saxons at Laisa and was successful in restoring some order among the Saxons, again forcing Widukind to flee to Denmark. Yet when Charlemagne, again believing the Saxons to have been subdued, left to invade other regions, Widukind again returned, this time successfully inciting the Wend tribes to join him.

Subsequent invasions saw Widukind direct a larger portion of the Saxon forces directly against Catholic churches and priests, exerting enough military power to force Willihad, first bishop of Bremen, to flee to Rome and temporarily abandon his missionary work in the area. A furious Charlemagne again returned to the swamps and forests of Saxony, forcing Widukind to flee one last time into Denmark. During his final retreat, Widukind was successful in convincing the armies of the northern Elbe district and the Frisians to join his next revolt.

The familiar pattern of Westphalia being put to "fire and sword," with Saxons fleeing the avenging Franks, soon repeated itself for the final time. Charlemagne embarked on a well-orchestrated plan designed to forever suppress the threat of further Saxon uprisings. While Charlemagne continued to enforce the practices of Catholicism, this time he also founded Frankish villages and monasteries and organized the country into divisions, making it much easier for his appointed nobles to govern and control the rebels.

In 780, Charlemagne ordered a council at which all of Saxony was divided into missionary territories, with each territory placed under the religious instruction of a group of monks from Austrasia. The eventual goal of these divisions was to combine secular and religious political control and to entice Saxon chieftains to submit by enabling them to hold public office.

The theory that limited empowerment of local Saxon leaders would prevent the organization of further rebellions proved to be effective, and other Crusaders would employ it in the future. Generous rewards were given to those who cooperated with and assisted in further Frankish conquests. A strict Saxon code of law was established and publicly proclaimed to deal with any rebel attempts to revert to paganism; the death penalty was given to those who, for example, refused water baptism, failed to conform to disciplines handed out by appointed religious and political leaders, or refused to fast during Lent. Several thousand pagans were baptized, and Charlemagne himself may have assisted in large baptismal ceremonies in the rivers Elbe and Ocker. It remains controversial, however, whether the numerous conversions claimed by the empire were the result of military threats or real devotion to the Catholic faith. As planned, however, the baptisms and confessions of faith did serve to make further Saxon rebellions more serious crimes; the Saxons were now confessed Catholics, making further insurrections a crime of apostasy.

In response to this most organized and formal spread of the Catholic empire to date, Widukind convinced the northern tribes to participate in his final revolt. He returned from Denmark to Saxony to convince many former pagans to join him, and many ritually washed off their enforced baptisms. Historical accounts relate that Widukind surprised and annihilated a large Frankish army at Suntel on the river Weser in approximately 782, causing Charlemagne to retaliate with the most severe reprisals he had ever inflicted. Most accounts relate that Charlemagne ordered all rebel leaders to be taken to a prisoner-of-war camp at Verden on the river Aller, where an estimated four thousand or more Saxon prisoners were beheaded in 785.

Angry Saxons under Widukind's leadership attempted to avenge the mass executions, but they were forced to flee; they held out in dense and almost impassable forests and marshes before they were eventually defeated. Many theories have been proposed as to why and how Widukind's armies were finally defeated, with the most accepted explanation being that Widukind's earlier lack of success in uniting more of the Saxon nation under his command probably had a negative influence on the level of organization he was able to achieve once Saxony was united under him. Unlike the Bavarians, the Saxons had never before united politically, making their decentralized society more difficult to control. Some historians have argued that Widukind's biggest military error was enlisting tribes such as the non-Teutonic Sorbs as allies, which probably created some race-related antagonism that weakened his forces. Charlemagne's strategy included the removal of Saxon peasants and the resettling of them in other lands. This scattering contributed to Widukind's inability to organize the tribes that united under him, created internal feuding, and eventually resulted in the eradication of the Saxon culture.

Widukind's public life and religious beliefs following Charlemagne's last defeat of the Saxons will probably remain forever unclear. What is well documented is that Widukind lived at least twenty years following Charlemagne's decisive final victories but did not play a leadership role in any later military struggles. It is also clear that Charlemagne greatly desired to convert Widukind and his followers to the Catholic faith and to announce to medieval Europe that the pagan leader had surrendered and joined the empire. Some historical records state that Widukind, Aboin, and several other chieftains peacefully joined Charlemagne's later campaigns and were water baptized at the imperial camp at Attigny in Champagne. Charlemagne may have served as godfather at this baptism, at which Widukind may have finally acknowledged that the "god of Charlemagne was greater than Odin."

Regardless of what actually occurred, Charlemagne convinced Rome that Widukind would no longer be leading further Saxon opposition, and a general feast of thanksgiving was ordered by the Papacy. Legends of subsequent events conflict, with some accounts indicating that Widukind became a great builder of churches and even was officially recognized as a Catholic saint. Other accounts relate that Charlemagne gave Widukind the title duke of the Saxons and that he died in battle attempting to convert other former pagans to Catholicism. Other reports imply that Widukind spent the rest of his life imprisoned in a monastery. Enger, near Herford in Westphalia, is often reported to be Widukind's place of burial, with a gravestone and life-size figure of him having been built there sometime in the twelfth century. What is often called "Widukind's reliquary" is probably a work of the ninth or tenth century, years after legends about Widukind's later life had been circulated. Some history books state that Mathilde, second wife of King Henry I of Germany, was a member of Widukind's family line.

Significance

Widukind was an influential military and spiritual leader in the Saxons' long struggle against the Franks for independence and freedom to practice their faith. Although Saxon culture was extirpated by Charlemagne, the extended conflict between his empire and Widukind's followers instilled a dislike for the Franks in Saxon descendants that continued for several centuries.

—*Daniel G. Graetzer*

FURTHER READING

Brooke, Christopher Nugent Lawrence. *The Saxon and Norman Kings*. New York: Macmillan, 1963. An often referenced text covering the history of the Saxon rulers (449-1066) and the Norman rulers (1066-1154) of England, with essays on several aspects of medieval and Anglo-Saxon civilization.

Eyck, Frank. *Religion and Politics in German History: From the Beginnings to the French Revolution*. New York: St. Martin's Press, 1998. An analysis of how Germanic peoples preserved links with classical civilization through their ability to assimilate other cultures and peoples, from their alliances with eighth century popes through the Reformation and Counter-Reformation. The initial bond between the Germanic rulers and popes turned to conflict as the Papacy gained power. Tables, maps, bibliography, index.

Harper-Bill, Christopher. *Anglo-Norman Studies 29*. Rochester, N.Y.: Boydell & Brewer, 1997. A descriptive work on medieval civilization and the history of Frankish society.

Hines, John. *Anglo-Saxons from the Migration Period to the Eighth Century: An Ethnographic Perspective*. Rochester, N.Y.: Boydell & Brewer, 1997. Describes land settlement, archaeoethnology, and social history in early medieval Europe.

John, Eric. *Re-assessing Anglo-Saxon England*. New York: St. Martin's Press, 1997. A history text on the Anglo-Saxon period that challenges several common beliefs regarding the era.

MacDonald, Fiona. *The World in the Time of Charlemagne*. New York: Silver Burdett Press, 1998. An excellent examination of Europe in the time of Widukind, with emphasis on the history of continental Europe.

Schutte, G. *Our Forefathers, the Gothonic Nations: Manual of the Ethnography of the Gothic, German, Dutch, Anglo-Saxon, Frisian, and Scandinavian Peoples*. 2 vols. Translated by J. Young. New York: Gordon Press, 1977. Provides several interesting perspectives on the ethnography of individuals with Gothic, German, Dutch, Anglo-Saxon, Frisian, or Scandinavian backgrounds.

Stenton, F. M. *Anglo-Saxon England*. Oxford, England: Clarendon Press, 1971. A thorough history of the Anglo-Saxon period. Extensive bibliography.

SEE ALSO: Saint Boniface; Charlemagne; Otto I.

RELATED ARTICLES in *Great Events from History: The Middle Ages, 477-1453*: 754: Coronation of Pépin the Short; 781: Alcuin Becomes Adviser to Charlemagne; 878: Alfred Defeats the Danes.

WILLIAM OF AUVERGNE

French philosopher

William was the first European medieval scholar to attempt to integrate Aristotelian philosophy and Christian theology. He encouraged the growth of philosophy as a discipline distinct from theology and paved the way for the great synthesis of faith and reason of the later Middle Ages.

BORN: c. 1190; Aurillac, Auvergne, France
DIED: March 30, 1249; Paris, France
ALSO KNOWN AS: William of Paris; William of Alvernia
AREAS OF ACHIEVEMENT: Philosophy, religion and theology

EARLY LIFE

The exact date of birth of William of Auvergne (oh-vehrn-yuh) is unknown, as are most of the facts about his early life. Scholars have assumed that he was born around 1190 because in 1225 he was teaching theology at the University of Paris, a privilege not usually granted to those below the age of thirty-five. A legend suggests that his parents were poor: As a child, William was begging one day on the street, where a woman offered him some money if he would promise never to become a bishop. Perhaps William had a sense of his own destiny, for he declined the offer.

Regardless of whether he was prescient, rich, or poor, he must have shown enough intellectual promise to be sent to school, though where or when is unknown. In the Middle Ages, almost all elementary instruction was given in cathedral or monastic schools, and it was expected that most students would become candidates for the priesthood. William not only was ordained but also went to the University of Paris, the most prestigious school of higher learning in France. By 1223, he was a cathedral priest, or canon, of the Cathedral of Notre Dame, and was probably already teaching at the university.

In the early thirteenth century, the basic intellectual assumptions of the academic world were undergoing a rapid process of change, and William was to become an important part of this transformation. Until shortly before William went to Paris, most of the works of the Greek philosopher Aristotle had been unavailable to the Christian scholars of Europe. After the fall of the Western Roman Empire in 476, Europe had been virtually cut off from the more affluent and cultured Eastern Roman Empire, and much of the heritage of Greek philosophy that had been passed to the Romans was lost. In the disruption that followed Rome's fall, the decline of the towns and the disappearance of secular schools left most education in the hands of the only well-organized institution that remained intact, the Church. While the flickering lamp of civilization was kept alight in the monasteries, it was necessarily colored by the viewpoint of religious faith. Thus for several centuries, philosophy, which then included all forms of inquiry about the universe, was taught as a part of Christian theology and remained firmly anchored to the views articulated by Saint Augustine early in the fifth century.

In the Augustinian universe, the knowledge of God obtained through the revelation of the Gospels and maintained in its purity by the Church was seen as inherently superior to the knowledge gained through reason and the senses. These faculties existed, in fact, simply to help human beings understand the revelation in which they already believed. Following Augustine, medieval philosophers had attempted to explain the phenomena of the world around them within a framework limited by such tenets of faith as God, his creation, and the Resurrection. This effort was seen as the whole purpose of Christian philosophy; ideas or observations that contradicted the structure of faith, as it had been revealed in the Bible and by the Church fathers, were rejected as heresy.

Starting in the late twelfth century, however, the works of the Greek philosophers, particularly Aristotle, began to filter once more into Europe through Arabic translations and commentaries from Islamic Spain. As they were gradually translated into Latin, these works revealed a whole new (or, rather, very old) world of pre-Christian explanations of the universe based solely on the use of reason. At first, the Church attempted to stamp out the Greek ideas, and, in 1228 and 1231, Pope Gregory IX condemned the use of Aristotle's ideas by the faculty at the University of Paris. Since Aristotle had addressed nearly every area of knowledge, however, the curiosity of the scholars could not be suppressed for long, and William was among the first to attempt to integrate Aristotelian ideas into Christian philosophy.

Life's Work

That William was a man of some prominence and ability, even early in his career, is evidenced by his appointments, in 1224 and 1225, to papal commissions assigned to investigate monasteries in need of reform. He was also, apparently, quite ambitious, as his actions following the death of Bartholomaeus, bishop of Paris, in 1227 demonstrate. Church law provided that the canons of Notre Dame were to elect a new bishop, subject to papal approval. If the canons were not essentially unanimous in their choice, the right of selection would revert to the pope. On April 10, 1228, the canons elected a candidate, but only by a slim majority. William proclaimed that the election was invalid and threatened to appeal the decision to Rome. The other canons, not wishing to lose their autonomy in the matter, accordingly held another election, but William was still unsatisfied and complained to Pope Gregory. The result was that William himself was appointed to the position, in which he remained for the rest of his life.

Though he is remembered today as a philosopher, among his contemporaries William was known primarily for his activities as bishop of Paris. In fact, he was largely unknown to all but a few of the great philosophers who followed him, and Thomas Aquinas, John Duns Scotus, and William of Ockham seem not to have been familiar with his writings. Only Roger Bacon briefly mentions William, and even Bacon's brief note of praise seems more connected with William the bishop than with William the philosopher.

During William's tenure as prelate, the University of Paris was gradually gaining its independence from the Church. Because it had evolved out of the cathedral school of Notre Dame, the university remained under the jurisdiction of the bishop of Paris. By the early thirteenth century, however, it had become a largely autonomous body, governed not by the laws of the city or the kingdom but by its own teachers (called "masters") and students. The immunity of the university from either royal or municipal control set a precedent for other universities and became the basis of the centuries-long conflicts between "town and gown" which can still occasionally be seen.

The only check on the often highly disruptive behavior of students and teachers was the bishop, who was himself often a former student and master. Nevertheless, both faculty and scholars chafed under even this usually sympathetic form of control and worked to end it.

William's relations with the university got off to an inauspicious start, for a famous strike of masters and students occurred in the spring of 1229. In February, the students had begun a riot in the course of celebrating the annual Carnival, and, after complaints from many citizens, royal troops were sent in to quell the disturbance. The resulting bloodshed outraged both masters and students, who demanded that William obtain redress from the king for this violation of their immunity. When William either refused or was unable to do anything, the students and faculty suspended all classes and dispersed to other cities. In response, William brought in some Dominican friars as substitutes; the striking masters appealed to the pope, who ordered William to reinstate the strikers. In addition, the pope created a commission to investigate the matter, which was decided in favor of the university. Masters and students then returned to Paris in triumph.

From this point onward, William seems to have been much more cautious in dealing with the university, and he frequently convoked the masters to seek their advice on issues which, technically, he could have decided on his own authority. The masters remained unsatisfied, though, and they demanded that William relinquish to them the authority to grant teaching licenses. The dispute over this issue, which dragged on from 1238 to 1245, may have arisen as a response to William's action in 1229, or it may simply have been part of the more general demand of the university for complete autonomy. The problem was not finally resolved until an agreement was drawn up, under pressure from Pope Innocent IV, among the masters, the university chancellor, and William.

Attempting to restrain the excesses of the university was not William's only function as bishop. In the Middle Ages, the Church was deeply involved in secular politics, and aside from his many purely religious duties, William was often called on to play a role in affairs of state as the French representative of the Papacy. In 1231, for example, he acted in this capacity in peace negotiations between France and England, and in 1229, he was even asked to provide Pope Gregory IX with troops in a war against the Holy Roman Emperor, Frederick II. William sent money instead.

William also typifies the anti-Semitism of the Middle Ages, for he was responsible for the public condemnation and burning of the Talmud in June, 1242. Some four years previously, a converted Jew named Nicholas had compiled a list of heretical and anti-Christian doctrines contained in the Talmud and sent them to the pope. Gregory wrote to William for advice, and the bishop recommended that strong measures be taken to suppress the Jewish sacred books. A papal bull (proclamation) was thus issued in 1240 through William as the papal representative ordering civil and ecclesiastical authorities to enter all French synagogues and confiscate copies of the Talmud. When the Jews understandably complained, a joint investigation by the royal and episcopal authorities into the contents of the Talmud resulted in its public incineration.

Despite such a busy schedule, William found time to write more than twenty treatises of varying lengths, most of which were to form a monumental *Magisterium divinale sive sapientale* (on divine or philosophical wisdom), which was completed about 1240. William's objective was to cover the whole field of theology and metaphysics and to answer questions of physics, logic, morals, and law through the application of reason, as well as through the learning of the past. In the *Magisterium divinale sive sapientale*, as well as in his other works, William shows that his attitude toward the newly rediscovered ideas of Aristotle is respectful without being slavish. While the Church authorities had only recently condemned these ideas, many of the students and masters of Paris had gone to the opposite extreme of accepting them almost as if they were revealed truth. William preferred to follow a middle course: Whenever Aristotle presented a philosophical doctrine that disagreed with Christian belief, William would declare it erroneous, but rather than simply appeal to tradition or authority, he would then go on to attempt to show by argument why the doctrine was incorrect.

Although William often disagreed with positions taken by Aristotle, he knew that Christians could not ignore them. To attempt to dismiss Aristotle or reject his ideas without analyzing them, said William, would be ridiculous. He went even further, offering the nearly revolutionary advice that, in matters of philosophy, only philosophers should be consulted. While this may appear to suggest that William had adopted the modern view that philosophy is quite distinct from religion, his purpose was in fact theological: The theologian could only overcome the arguments of pagan philosophy by himself becoming a philosopher. In this view, he foreshadows the reasoning of Thomas Aquinas.

For example, Aristotle had argued that the world was

eternal and therefore uncreated. This idea contradicts the Christian belief that God created the world. In his treatise *De Universo* (c. 1247; *The Universe of Creatures*, 1998), William not only gives the reasons behind Aristotle's point of view but also improves on Aristotle's arguments—after which he refutes them by using elaborate and systematic proofs. Thus despite his willingness to accept some of Aristotle's views and methods of argument, William remains in the tradition of Augustine, using philosophy as the handmaiden of faith.

William died on March 30, 1249, of unknown causes, and he was buried in the Abbey of St. Victor. Though his relationship with the university was bumpy, he was apparently loved as a witty and eloquent preacher, an outstanding master of theology, and a conscientious servant of the Church.

Significance

William of Auvergne stands, unfortunately, in the shadows of his great successors. Because he took on Aristotle piecemeal rather than developing a coherent system and because his writing is often obscure and extremely complex, he has been largely ignored except by a few specialists in the field of medieval philosophy. Yet among these authorities, his achievement is very much respected. He is seen as a transitional figure, perhaps even a pioneer whose acceptance of some Aristotelian ideas paved the way for Saint Albertus Magnus and Thomas Aquinas, but whose rejection of the Aristotelian system as a whole also led to the anti-Aristotelian viewpoint of Saint Bonaventure. As the first of the great thirteenth century philosophers, his views might be symbolized as the twelfth century meeting the thirteenth, sympathetically, but not uncritically.

Because William appears to have had little direct influence on his successors, it is fair to ask how he can be considered historically important. Perhaps this question can be answered best if attention is turned more directly on his career as a teacher and bishop of Paris. Influence need not always be a matter of showing a direct relationship between two events, people, or sets of ideas; it can also be indirect and subtle. As a teacher and philosopher, William undoubtedly had some kind of effect on each of his students. His congenial reception of new ideas allowed those ideas to be discussed, debated, and further developed. He realized the importance, if not all the implications, of the rediscovery of Aristotle, and he knew that the Church could not and should not simply attempt to ignore the tools of logic and reason that Aristotle offered. William insisted, in fact, that they be used to strengthen Christian faith. In this way, he made a positive contribution, not only to medieval philosophy but also to the freedom of inquiry that was, and is, the essence of the university.

—*Thomas C. Schunk*

Further Reading

Bréhier, Émile. *The History of Philosophy: The Middle Ages and the Renaissance*. Translated by Wade Baskin. Chicago: University of Chicago Press, 1965. Considered a classic summary of medieval and Renaissance philosophy. Includes a section on William that concentrates on his doctrine of Being and the way in which it relates to Aristotle and Avicenna.

Copleston, Frederick. *A History of Philosophy*. 9 vols. New York: Image Books, 1985. Part of an extremely well-written series by a prominent Jesuit philosopher. Volume 2, *Medieval Philosophy: Augustine to Scotus*, emphasizes the importance of William as a transitional figure and offers the view that William foreshadows not only Thomas Aquinas and Bonaventure but also John Duns Scotus. A clear introduction, not only to William but to the entire field of medieval philosophy.

Gilson, Étienne. *History of Christian Philosophy in the Middle Ages*. New York: Random House, 1955. An authoritative and scholarly work and a standard reference. Covers the entire period from the earliest Christian philosophers to the beginning of the fourteenth century.

Kretzmann, Norman, Anthony Kenny, and Jan Pinborg, eds. *The Cambridge History of Later Medieval Philosophy: From the Rediscovery of Aristotle to the Disintegration of Scholasticism, 1100-1600*. New York: Cambridge University Press, 1982. An immense compilation by many scholars, this work is organized topically. Contains several brief comparative discussions of William but no separate section.

Leff, Gordon. *Medieval Thought: St. Augustine to Ockham*. Baltimore: Penguin Books, 1965. An excellent, brief introduction to medieval philosophy that divides the era into three periods, each with an introduction that offers helpful general comments. Includes a concise section on William. Especially useful for those with no background in philosophy.

McInerny, Ralph M. *Philosophy from St. Augustine to Ockham*. Vol. 2 in *A History of Western Philosophy*. Notre Dame, Ind.: University of Notre Dame Press, 1970. A very good text for those new to philosophy. Several chapters of background information on related topics help provide a solid context. Includes a separate section on William with a very clear analysis of his theory of Being.

Marrone, Steven P. *The Light of Thy Countenance: Science and Knowledge of God in the Thirteenth Century.* 2 vols. Boston: Brill, 2001. Volume 1 discusses attempts by thirteenth century scholars to reconcile and adapt the tradition of Augustinian-inspired theology with an emerging Aristotelean-inspired science.

_______. *William of Auvergne and Robert Grosseteste: New Ideas of Truth in the Early Thirteenth Century.* Princeton, N.J.: Princeton University Press, 1983. A full-length, scholarly study of William's philosophy, which is discussed in great depth and detail. The author considers William a philosopher of the first rank and of great historical importance. Analyzes William's work from the standpoint of the method by which truth can be perceived.

Moody, Ernest A. "William of Auvergne and His Treatise *De Anima*." In *Studies in Medieval Philosophy, Science, and Logic: Collected Papers, 1933-1969.* Berkeley: University of California Press, 1975. Contains fourteen chapters by a renowned historian of medieval philosophy. The chapter on William is a significant biographical source.

Teske, Roland J. "William of Auvergne." In *A Companion to Philosophy in the Middle Ages*, edited by Jorge E. Gracia and Timothy B. Noone. Malden, Mass.: Blackwell, 2003. The author discusses the life and work of William in the context of Middle Ages philosophy.

_______. "William of Auvergne on the Relation Between Reason and Faith." *Modern Schoolman* 75, no. 4 (May, 1998): 279-291. Argues that there are two strains evident in William's *Magisterium divinale sive sapientale*, one committed to philosophizing through faith and grace the other to philosophizing through reason.

See also: Peter Abelard; Saint Albertus Magnus; Saint Anselm; Averroës; Avicenna; Boethius; Saint Bonaventure; Jean Buridan; John Duns Scotus; al-Ghazālī; Gregory IX; Alexander Neckam; Nicholas of Autrecourt; William of Ockham; Thomas Aquinas; Vincent of Beauvais; William of Auxerre; William of Saint-Thierry.

Related articles in *Great Events from History: The Middle Ages, 477-1453*: c. 950: Court of Córdoba Flourishes in Spain; c. 1025: Scholars at Chartres Revive Interest in the Classics; 1100-1300: European Universities Emerge; c. 1150: Moors Transmit Classical Philosophy and Medicine to Europe; c. 1310-1350: William of Ockham Attacks Thomist Ideas.

William of Auxerre

French philosopher

William was one of the first European medieval scholars to use the methods of philosophy to answer theological questions. He ranks as a pioneer in the growth of Scholasticism and the centuries-long attempt to harmonize Aristotelian philosophy with the theology of Saint Augustine.

Born: c. 1150; Auxerre, Bishopric of Auxerre (now in France)

Died: November 3, 1231; Rome (now in Italy)

Areas of achievement: Religion and theology, philosophy

Early Life

As is true of most medieval intellectuals, virtually nothing is known of the origins or early career of William of Auxerre (oh-seer). Because it was customary in the twelfth century for young men planning for an academic life to enter the university at age thirteen or fourteen, he had probably already begun his studies by that age. The University of Paris, where William was to spend nearly all of his life, was Europe's most renowned center of learning, especially in the areas of theology and philosophy. A new student typically spent six years studying the seven liberal arts—grammar, rhetoric, logic (the *trivium*); and arithmetic, geometry, astronomy, and music (the *quadrivium*)—which had been inherited from the ancient world. The arts as a whole were often referred to as "philosophy." Following this generalized preparation, the scholar could become a teacher of the arts himself or begin specialized studies in theology, law, or medicine.

The greatest minds of the time chose theology, which was by far the most rigorous and respected discipline. That was natural because the university itself was an outgrowth of the cathedral school of Notre Dame de Paris and was still under the jurisdiction of the Church. Though many were never ordained as priests, students of the university were regarded as "clerics" and were subject to the discipline of the chancellor, an official of the cathedral.

After six years of attending lectures on the Bible and selected works of theology, the student received the baccalaureate and was then himself required to lecture for two years on two books of the Bible. After several more years of study, the apprentice teacher engaged in several "disputations," theological debates judged by a member of the faculty. If he successfully completed these tasks, the student was awarded the doctorate and, at age thirty-four, was allowed to teach theology. It is known that William made it through this arduous course, for by 1189 hewas already famous as a "master" (professor) of theology.

LIFE'S WORK

The thirteenth century was an age of intellectual ferment, particularly at the University of Paris. The university itself owed its existence to the revival of learning that had begun after about the year 1000. The gradual rediscovery of the literature of the pre-Christian world had increasingly challenged the relatively simple and dogmatic faith of the earlier Middle Ages, and scholars had begun to use the tools of logic to justify and explain their Christian beliefs and doctrine. By the end of the twelfth century, a flood of translations of the works of the Greek philosopher Aristotle as well as commentaries on him by Islamic philosophers such as Avicenna had begun to arrive in Paris from Moorish Spain. Aristotle's wide-ranging intellect had applied itself to virtually every area of human knowledge, from the creation of the universe and the nature of the soul to the proper structure of a logical argument. It was obvious that Aristotle was a genius, yet, as a pagan, he had arrived at conclusions and insights that often conflicted with the accepted doctrine of the Church.

From throughout Europe, scholars came to Paris to study the "new" learning; thus the cathedral school had expanded to become practically a separate institution, the university. By the time of William, famous medieval scholars such as Peter Abelard and Peter Lombard had been developing for more than a century the techniques of intellectual inquiry that would later be called Scholasticism. The Scholastic approach involved the solution of an intellectual problem by posing it as a question, such as "Is the universe eternal?" The medieval scholar would respond to the question by juxtaposing answers derived from the Bible, or works of the Church fathers, to those offered by philosophy or reason, often as supplied by Aristotle. By constructing such a back-and-forth argument, called the "dialectic," the scholar hoped to reconcile the two positions, thus allowing reason to support faith. While Scholasticism clearly fostered a considerable amount of intellectual ingenuity, it later got a bad reputation because its practitioners always deferred to established authority, whether that of the Church or of the philosophers, rather than venturing to observe the real world or setting up empirical experiments. The reasoning of the Scholastics became increasingly abstract, and they often dealt with issues that were fantastically irrelevant. (The most famous of these is the old question, "How many angels can dance on the head of a pin?")

While it may seem strange today that the great intellectuals of the Middle Ages spent so much time trying to "marry" what now are considered the distinctly separate fields of philosophy and theology, the attempt itself represented a tremendous advance over the thinking of the early Christian period and the early Middle Ages, when many Church authorities had disparaged the use of reason, insisting that, should philosophy and faith disagree, philosophy must always give way. Many of the Church fathers had actually regarded study of the ancient authors as pernicious and sinful—one of the reasons that Aristotle's works had largely disappeared until the period of the Crusades. The efforts of the Scholastics to make philosophy and theology work together demonstrated that the processes of reason and logic had once again become respectable.

By the time of William, those works of Aristotle which had become available had themselves already gained the status of authority and threatened to dethrone Church doctrine, at least as far as many of the students at the university were concerned, as the basis of theology. In the eyes of the Church authorities, this threat was so dangerous that, in 1215, when the basic statutes of the university were drawn up, the papal legate (representative) at Paris prohibited the teaching of those works of Aristotle that dealt with "natural philosophy," meaning science. This decree apparently had little effect, for in 1231 Pope Gregory IX felt compelled to create a commission of three scholars to study and "correct" the works of Aristotle, so that they could be used at the university without contradicting Church doctrine.

The head of the commission was William, who had by this time become famous both as a theologian and as a churchman. During the reign of Pope Honorius III (1216-1227), William had become archdeacon of Beauvais, a powerful and influential office, as well as a proctor of the University of Paris. In the latter capacity, he presented the interests of the university to the papal court at Rome; he had been sent there by King Louis IX in the spring of 1230 to advise the new pope, Gregory IX, on how to resolve a strike of teachers and students that had begun the year before. The bishop of Paris, William of Auvergne, had failed to end the strike and may even have exacerbated the situation by bringing in Dominican friars to replace the striking teachers.

The strike had arisen out of a student riot that had occurred during the Shrove Tuesday festivities of February, 1229. Townsmen had requested the intervention of royal troops to quell this drunken rampage, and several students were killed in the ensuing melee. When demands by both students and masters for compensation went unsatisfied, the scholars voted to strike and return to their homes. By the time William of Auxerre left for Rome, however, the original issue had been subsumed in more general conflicts that had been brewing between the Church and the university for several years. The arts faculty, in particular, resented Church hostility toward their growing acceptance of Aristotle, and the university faculty as a whole had long been seeking policy-making autonomy from the Church.

The pope now believed that his personal intervention was necessary, but he was unsure of the best course of action. William of Auxerre, who seems to have been a peaceful individual of very even temperament, apparently helped to craft Gregory's conciliatory response, which not only ordered the university authorities to reinstate the strikers but also promised to set up a commission to investigate the issues involved, including the position of Aristotle in the curriculum of the university. While the ban of 1215 on Aristotle's works on natural philosophy was maintained, it was only provisional, to be held until the papal commission had an opportunity to investigate Aristotle's works. Nowhere was it suggested that the use of Aristotelian logic to examine and analyze philosophical or theological questions be discontinued. Faculty and students returned triumphantly to Paris, regarding the papal decree as an academic bill of rights.

Unfortunately, the commission never really started work, probably because William of Auxerre died on November 3, 1231, only seven months after he was appointed to it. Why the pope did not appoint a successor is unclear: Possibly the commission had already decided that the effort to expurgate such a large and popular body of work would be impossible. The ban was allowed to expire without having much effect, and the process of attempting to reconcile philosophy and theology continued, leading eventually to the brilliant synthesis of Thomas Aquinas later in the thirteenth century.

William of Auxerre himself contributed to this process in a work that had a considerable amount of influence on his contemporaries, *Summa super quattuor libros sententiarum*, usually known as *Summa aurea* (golden summation), written between 1215 and 1220. This was a commentary on the compilation of Christian teachings created by Peter Lombard in a series of four books used as basic texts in the fifth and sixth years of theological training at the university. Lombard had used the dialectic to address many questions of theology, but a host of new issues had been occasioned by the influx of translations of Aristotle and the Arabian philosophers. It was common practice among Scholastics of the twelfth and thirteenth centuries to write commentaries on earlier works regarded as authoritative and to bring them up to date, but *Summa aurea* is outstanding in that it not only looks back at the pre-Aristotelian framework of theology but also comes to grips with some of the new questions addressed by Aristotle.

While the core of William's view of the relationship between reason and faith is derived from Saint Augustine and is therefore completely traditional, William also shows how some of the philosophy of Aristotle can be put to the service of Christian theology. Pre-Aristotelian Scholastics, for example, had discussed the nature of God and the Trinity at great length without ever seeing the need to prove God's existence. That, they believed, was self-evident, a matter of faith not to be questioned. Yet Aristotle, in *Metaphysica* (fourth century B.C.E.; *Metaphysics*, 1801) and other works, had attempted to understand the natural world around him by making direct observations and reasoning about them. Because God was not directly perceivable with the senses, Aristotle maintained that the answer to the question of his existence was unknowable. *Summa aurea* marks a break with the past because William addresses such questions and seeks to answer them with philosophical reasoning: He proves the existence of God, for example, by using the philosopher Avicenna's argument for the necessity of what was called a "prime cause," meaning an agency of creation from which everything else must ultimately originate.

In similar fashion, *Summa aurea* deals with problems such as natural law, free will, the nature of the soul, and the definition of virtue—issues seen by William's predecessors only in theological terms. William, however, often uses the tools of Aristotelian logic to substantiate the traditional answers of faith. Thus he asks, as Aristotle had, if the universe is eternal, but he disagrees with Aristotle's affirmative answer; since the universe was created by God, William reasons that it cannot have always existed. His general approach is thus to ask some of the questions that Aristotle's works necessitate but to use both reason and faith to prove the truth of the beliefs of the past. At the same time, though, William is inconsistent; he is often satisfied simply to repeat the doctrines of his predecessors, and he creates no new comprehensive system or approach to theological thinking. *Summa aurea* is, therefore, a work of transition, one that points the way to the future but is firmly rooted in the past.

Significance

William of Auxerre was the first medieval theologian to acknowledge explicitly the arguments of the philosophers, but he mixed them indiscriminately with those of earlier theologians. Yet even his reliance on the past seemed to foreshadow the views of his better-known successors, for he insisted that theology is an "art" or "science"—rather than a simple matter of blind faith—because it argues from principles, even if these principles are themselves articles of faith. Further, he insisted that philosophy can be useful to theologians because they can use it to prove the articles of faith.

Such an argument, if offered today, might seem hopelessly backward, for science (philosophy) and religion (theology) have become completely separate; the idea of using logic to prove what faith believes appears to be a paradox. William of Auxerre's viewpoint may be viewed more sympathetically, however, if the context is considered. He was arguing for the validity and existence of philosophy against many who believed that all such approaches to knowledge should be suppressed. The university was a religious establishment; as an important member of the theological faculty, he could not, unlike some of the faculty in the arts, hope to escape intellectually the consequences of his position. In encouraging the integration of Aristotle into the teaching of theology, he demonstrated a courage and an open-mindedness, as well as an intellectual originality, which helped to make the University of Paris a bastion of academic freedom and intellectual growth. Until recently, the originality of William and his contemporaries and immediate successors, such as Philip the Chancellor and William of Auvergne, was largely ignored because these pioneers in religious philosophy did not attempt to create an entirely new system of thought. It is only now being realized by historians of medieval philosophy that the achievements of the great Scholastics who followed later, such as Thomas Aquinas and William of Ockham, were possible only because William of Auxerre was instrumental in clearing the path.

—*Thomas C. Schunk*

Further Reading

Copleston, Frederick. *A History of Philosophy.* 9 vols. New York: Image Books, 1985. Part of an extremely well-written series by a prominent Jesuit philosopher. Volume 2, *Medieval Philosophy: Augustine to Scotus*, includes an informative discussion of the development of the University of Paris in its early years, as well as its curriculum, teaching methods, and student life during this period. Contains a short discussion of William and *Summa aurea*.

Gilson, Étienne. *History of Christian Philosophy in the Middle Ages.* New York: Random House, 1955. An authoritative and scholarly work in the field and still a standard reference, this work includes a thorough set of notes on nearly every philosopher of the period, including William, and works by or related to each. Covers the entire period from the earliest Christian philosophers to the beginning of the fourteenth century.

Haren, Michael. *Medieval Thought: The Western Intellectual Tradition from Antiquity to the Thirteenth Century.* 2d ed. Buffalo, N.Y.: University of Toronto Press, 1992. An excellent, brief summary that assumes a good deal of background on the reader's part. Contains one of the few discussions of any length on the views of William expressed in *Summa aurea* on specific questions.

Kretzmann, Norman, Anthony Kenny, and Jan Pinborg, eds. *The Cambridge History of Later Medieval Philosophy: From the Rediscovery of Aristotle to the Disintegration of Scholasticism, 1100-1600.* New York: Cambridge University Press, 1982. An immense compilation by many scholars, organized topically, this study contains several brief comparative discussions of William but no separate section. Has a pronounced emphasis on English philosophers. Primarily useful as a reference, particularly for its outstanding bibliography.

Leff, Gordon. *Medieval Thought: St. Augustine to Ockham.* Baltimore: Penguin Books, 1965. An excellent, brief introduction to medieval philosophy. Divides the era into three periods, each with an introduction that offers helpful general comments. Notes the tran-

sitional role of William and the place of *Summa aurea* in the development of Scholasticism. Especially useful for those with no background in philosophy.
McInerny, Ralph M. *Philosophy from St. Augustine to Ockham*. Vol. 2 in *A History of Western Philosophy*. Notre Dame, Ind.: University of Notre Dame Press, 1970. A very good text for those new to philosophy. Well organized by prominent scholars. Several chapters of background information on related topics help to provide a solid context.
Marrone, Steven P. *The Light of Thy Countenance: Science and Knowledge of God in the Thirteenth Century*. 2 vols. Boston: Brill, 2001. Volume 1 discusses attempts by thirteenth century scholars to reconcile and adapt the tradition of Augustinian-inspired theology with an emerging Aristotelean-inspired science.
Zupko, Jack. "William of Auxerre." In *A Companion to Philosophy in the Middle Ages*, edited by Jorge J. Gracia. Malden, Mass.: Blackwell, 2003. The author discusses the life and work of William in the context of Middle Ages philosophy.

SEE ALSO: Peter Abelard; Saint Albertus Magnus; Saint Anselm; Averroës; Avicenna; Boethius; Saint Bonaventure; Jean Buridan; John Duns Scotus; al-Ghazzālī; Gregory IX; Louis IX; Alexander Neckam; Nicholas of Autrecourt; William of Ockham; Siger of Brabant; Thomas Aquinas; Vincent of Beauvais; William of Auvergne; William of Saint-Thierry.

RELATED ARTICLES in *Great Events from History: The Middle Ages, 477-1453*: c. 950: Court of Córdoba Flourishes in Spain; c. 1025: Scholars at Chartres Revive Interest in the Classics; 1100-1300: European Universities Emerge; c. 1150: Moors Transmit Classical Philosophy and Medicine to Europe; c. 1310-1350: William of Ockham Attacks Thomist Ideas.

WILLIAM OF MOERBEKE

Flemish scholar and philosopher

Along with many translations of classical works by other authors, William provided Europe with its first Latin translations from the Greek of Aristotle's major works.

BORN: c. 1215; Moerbeke, near Ghent, Flanders (now in Belgium)

DIED: c. 1286; Corinth, Greece

ALSO KNOWN AS: Guillaume de Moerbeke (French name)

AREA OF ACHIEVEMENT: Philosophy

EARLY LIFE

William of Moerbeke (MEWR-behk-eh) was Flemish, born near Ghent, then in the duchy of Brabant, in about 1215. Innocent III had just recognized the Dominican order at the Fourth Lateran Council. William entered the Dominican priory in Ghent, where his education began. Later, he studied in Paris and Cologne, where he probably knew Albertus Magnus, one of the great teachers of the century. The fact that William was a Neoplatonist reflected the dominant intellectual climate of both Paris and Germany; Albertus Magnus and his students, such as Ulrich of Strasbourg and the greatest of the medieval mystics, Meister Eckhart, were also Neoplatonists. Significantly, William contributed to this spirit of mysticism with his translation of Proclus, finished in 1268, which became the basis of Christian humanism. William joined the papal court of Urban IV, who patronized William and encouraged his translations. This support, which came at the beginning of the 1260's, marked the beginning of William's astoundingly productive career as a Greek translator.

The enthusiasm of the Europeans for classical Greek works, particularly Aristotle, during the thirteenth century was overwhelming. The establishment of the Latin Empire in Constantinople in 1205 drove this enthusiasm because of the easy access to Greek manuscripts it provided. Pope Innocent III encouraged the translation of these works into Latin. King Philip II of France founded a school in Paris for the purpose of teaching Latin to Byzantines residing in his country. Roger Bacon, the great medieval scientist, wrote a Greek grammar. The revival of Aristotle, in particular, led to renewed interest in science and a more accurate perspective on classical philosophy.

No one did more to reinforce this interest in the classics than William of Moerbeke and Robert Grosseteste, the two who did most of the translations from Greek into Latin. The effect of the translations was revolutionary, and Moerbeke was the hero of this effort. Only Gerard of

Cremona, a great Arab-Latin translator of the twelfth century, matched William's productivity and range of material translated.

LIFE'S WORK

At the same time, also at the papal court, William met Thomas Aquinas, who became his lifelong friend and who urged him to revise the existing Arab-to-Latin Aristotelian texts and to translate previously unknown ones coming into Europe from Byzantium. Thomas believed that the direct translations would give European scholars, such as himself, a clearer understanding of Aristotle's philosophical intentions. The pope also wished to use the direct translations to curb Averroism (named after the Spanish-Muslim philosopher Averroës), which conveyed Aristotle with Neoplatonic and Islamic overtones and was unacceptable—in part because of the strong undercurrent of superstition that ran through the Arabic texts.

Between 1260 and 1278, William revised and translated all Aristotle's major works, which were written from 335 to 323 B.C.E.: the *Politica* (*Politics*, 1598)—unknown even to the Arabs—*Metaphysica* (*Metaphysics*, 1801), *Physica* (*Physics*, 1812), and a number of his other works. William translated some of Plato's dialogues as well as works by Galen, Hippocrates, Archimedes, Hero of Alexandria, Simplicius, and Alexander of Aphrodisias. The *Politics* was picked up quickly by both the Church and the state as a system of governance and a justification for the authority that each wished to exercise over the other.

In 1260, the pope sent William to Dominican priories, first in Thebes and then in Nicaea. As a result, William traveled widely throughout the Greek world, becoming even more proficient in Greek. In 1265, Pope Clement IV called William back to the papal court to serve as his confessor and chaplain. He held this position through the reigns of five additional popes. Papal confidence in William is further exemplified by the fact that he represented Pope Gregory X at the 1274 Second Council of Lyon called to reform the Church and to promote the reunion of the Eastern and Western halves of Christendom, for an optimistic attitude had been encouraged by the political existence of the Latin Empire. Having spent time in the East, William understood the Greek church better than many and was deeply committed to that reunion—a hope that was to remain unfulfilled.

Pope Nicholas III appointed him archbishop of Corinth on April 9, 1278. That same year, William finished his translation of Aristotle's *Poetics*. The last eight years of William's life were spent in Corinth, where he continued to translate until his death around 1286.

SIGNIFICANCE

Most of William's translations made their way into European libraries through their use by the Dominicans, especially Thomas Aquinas, who used William's translations of Aristotle to construct his *Summa theologiae* (c. 1265-1273; *Summa Theologica*, 1911-1921), the epitome of the medieval synthesis of reason and faith. In addition, and as important, William's translations of other Greek authors opened the door to classical learning, especially in the sciences, that had been unknown or unavailable to Western scholars for centuries. The undeniable force of Aristotle's influence on the thirteenth century mind owed much of its vitality to the translations completed by William. The interest stimulated by these works intensified the impact of Aristotelian philosophy on medieval society and, by extension, on the whole intellectual tradition of Western civilization. William of Moerbeke stands as an indispensable component in the development of that tradition.

—*Shirley F. Fredricks*

FURTHER READING

Crombie, A. C. *Medieval and Early Modern Science*. 2 vols. 2d ed. Cambridge, Mass.: Harvard University Press, 1963. Details William's translations of classic texts. An excellent introduction to the history of science. The book is highly readable and contains an excellent bibliography.

Durant, Will. *The Age of Faith*. Vol. 4 in *The Story of Civilization*. New York: Simon and Schuster, 1950. Good reading and an excellent source for little-known facts about William's life. This long work contains an extensive index, a standard bibliography, and a detailed table of contents.

Heer, Friedrich. *The Intellectual History of Europe*. New York: Doubleday, 1968. An excellent analysis of the development of Western thought. In Volume 1, William is described as a crucial figure in the shaping of the medieval mind. This is a long, detailed study, and the sources must be culled from copious notes.

_______. *The Medieval World: Europe 100-1350*. Translated by Janet Sondheimer. New York: New American Library, 1964. While this book does not discuss the work of William specifically, it is one of the best available historical surveys of the High Middle Ages. It is interpretive and provocative in tone and topical in arrangement, and it covers the standard medieval subjects. It includes chapters on intellectualism in the universities and the intellectual warfare in Paris, much of which centered on the works of Aristotle.

Knowles, David. *The Evolution of Medieval Thought*. Edited by D. E. Luscombe and C. N. L. Brooke. 2d ed. New York: Longman, 1988. An excellent presentation of the philosophical and theological development of the Middle Ages, including the significance of William's translations in this development. A synthetic work of notable merit. Bibliographic essay.

Leff, Gordon. *Medieval Thought: St. Augustine to Ockham*. Baltimore: Penguin Books, 1965. An easily understood description of the development of medieval thought, stressing the influence of William's translations on the medieval mind.

Marías, Julián. *History of Philosophy*. Translated by Stanley Appelbaum and Clarence C. Strowbridge. New York: Dover, 1967. A detailed survey that includes some information about William but is more important for giving the reader an understanding of the major philosophical problems of the age.

See also: Saint Albertus Magnus; Averroës; Roger Bacon; Innocent III; Philip II; Siger of Brabant; Thomas Aquinas.

Related articles in *Great Events from History: The Middle Ages, 477-1453*: c. 1025: Scholars at Chartres Revive Interest in the Classics; 1054: Beginning of the Rome-Constantinople Schism; c. 1150: Moors Transmit Classical Philosophy and Medicine to Europe; November 11-30, 1215: Fourth Lateran Council; c. 1265-1273: Thomas Aquinas Compiles the *Summa Theologica*.

William of Rubrouck

Dutch geographer

William provided the first accurate account of the geography of Central Asia and its people, the Mongols. He thus helped to fill in a symbolic blank space on the map of Asia and opened up a new era of exploration.

Born: c. 1215; Rubrouck, Flanders (now in the Netherlands)
Died: c. 1295; place unknown
Also known as: Willem van Ruysbroeck; Wilhelmus Rubruquis
Areas of achievement: Geography, exploration

Early Life

The life of William of Rubrouck (REW-brewk) remains shrouded in mystery despite scholarly efforts to shed light on it. He appears on the stage of history between May, 1253, and August, 1255, the period during which he undertook a journey to the court of the Great Khan in Mongolia. Except for a brief stay in Paris during the late 1250's or early 1260's, nothing is known about his life before or after his historic journey.

Scholars assume that William was from the village of Rubrouck in Flanders, the northeasternmost corner of what is now the Netherlands. The date of his birth is unknown, though some historians place it as early as 1215. Similarly, the year and place of his death are unknown, though it is assumed that he was still alive when Marco Polo returned from his journey to China in 1295.

Nothing is known of William's educational background. When Louis IX commissioned him to go to Mongolia, William was a Franciscan friar serving at the king's court. The saintly Louis IX was fond of the mendicant (begging) orders of monks and so surrounded himself with friars. William's own narrative of his journey provides the only insight into his learning and character. Though the work is not written in the best Ciceronian Latin, the author reveals himself as a keen observer, one who was able to sift the relevant from the irrelevant and thus provide Europe with its first truly reliable information about the geography and peoples of inner Asia.

William reveals himself as a bold, even daring adventurer. The brazenness with which he preached the Christian faith shocked his Mongolian hosts, whose religious tolerance no doubt puzzled and angered William. He records in his narrative that several times the Great Khan urged him to be more diplomatic in his debates with Muslims, Buddhists, shamanists, and Nestorians. Fear that William was disrupting the religious peace may have been one reason that the Great Khan ordered him to return to his home.

Life's Work

It was only his journey to Mongolia that lifted William of Rubrouck from obscurity onto the pages of history.

Hence, a discussion of his life's work must focus on a period of roughly twenty-eight months.

William and Louis IX had similar yet different motives for a mission to Mongolia (Tartary). William's motives were primarily religious; Louis's motives were a mixture of religious and political. William was apparently deeply moved by reports of the plight of German slaves of the khan of the Golden Horde (Russia and Kazakhstan). The Germans were Catholics, and William felt burdened to go and minister the sacraments to them. He was encouraged by rumors that some of the Mongol rulers had already accepted, or were on the verge of accepting, Christianity.

Louis IX, noted for his piety, was similarly influenced by the rumors that certain of the khans were Christians. He was also encouraged, however, by the prospects of an alliance with the Mongols against the Muslims in the Middle East. Louis hoped to learn something about the intentions of the Mongol armies in Syria. Thus, he was persuaded to overcome his reluctance to send William. William was not to travel as an accredited envoy of the French king, however, but as a Christian missionary seeking permission to settle, found a mission, and preach the Gospel among the Mongols. Louis gave William a letter addressed to Prince Sartach, an alleged Christian and eldest son of Batu, ruler of the Golden Horde, requesting that William be given safe conduct and permission to preach.

William was commissioned by Louis IX in the spring of 1252, while Louis was resident in Acre, Palestine, following a disastrous crusade in Egypt. From Acre, William journeyed to Constantinople, where he preached in the church of Hagia Sophia on Palm Sunday, 1253. On May 7, 1253, he departed from Constantinople on the first leg of his historic journey.

William's party consisted of four individuals. With William there was a fellow Franciscan, Bartholomew of Cremona. Bartholomew was later to remain at the court of the Great Khan and become the first Catholic missionary to die in the East. There was also a clerk to look after the gifts Louis was sending and an interpreter, who proved unreliable.

William and his party reached Sartach's camp at Sarai, where the Volga River empties into the Caspian Sea, on July 31. During the three days he remained with Sartach, William learned that the Mongol prince was neither a Christian nor really interested in religious matters. Sartach ordered William to proceed to the court of his father, Batu Khan. Batu was encamped near Saratov, on the upper reaches of the Volga River, in present-day southwest Russia.

Batu in turn sent William on to Mangu, the Great Khan himself, and provided two Nestorian Christian guides for the journey. They reached Mangu's encampment on the northeastern slopes of the Altai Mountains on December 27, 1253. They were treated courteously by Mangu, though he remained suspicious of William's true motives.

In the spring of 1254, Mangu returned to his capital at Karakorum, capital of the vast Mongol Empire. William and his party went with him and remained at Karakorum until July, when Mangu ordered him to return home. William was regularly questioned by Mangu's ministers, who apparently were never fully convinced that he was not an ambassador. Because he insisted that he was only a Christian missionary, he did not have the right to request an audience with the Great Khan; William had to wait for Mangu to summon him.

During his stay at Karakorum, William was housed with Nestorian monks. From time to time, Mangu himself arranged for disputations between William and representatives of the various religions of his subjects. Mangu was obviously very proud of the Mongols' tradition of religious toleration. William noted that the khan was careful not to show any preference for any one religion; he diplomatically spread his patronage equally among Buddhists, Daoists, shamanists, Muslims, and various Christian sects and attended all of their important ceremonies. William's dogmatic advocacy of his own Christian faith offended Mangu, apparently leading to Mangu's decision to send William back to Europe.

William departed Karakorum in July, 1254. He carried with him a letter from Mangu to Louis IX, calling on the great lords and priests of Europe to go to Karakorum and do homage to the Great Khan. On June 16, 1255, he arrived in Cyprus, where he was disappointed to find that Louis IX had returned to France. Though he desired to go to Paris and report personally to Louis IX, he was ordered by his provincial vicar to return to Acre, where he became a lecturer in theology. This turn of events was fortuitous, for it forced William to write a narrative of his journey. All in all, William had traveled some ten thousand miles, much of it on horseback over harsh terrain.

SIGNIFICANCE

William of Rubrouck's narrative of his journey provided a wealth of information for Europeans. His geographical revelations restored knowledge that had been lost to Western Europeans since the fall of the Roman Empire in the West (in 476). He confirmed that the Caspian Sea was in fact an inland sea. He was the first European to recognize that Cathay was "Seres," the mythical city where ancient and medieval Westerners believed silk originated.

William was also the first European to describe an Asian city. Though he found Karakorum less impressive than Paris, what he described was a metropolitan capital of a vast, pluralistic empire. Not only did he note the existence in Karakorum of twelve Buddhist, Daoist, and shamanist temples, two Muslim mosques, and one Nestorian church, but he also provided the first descriptions of the religious rites and practices of those religions.

Karakorum was a meeting place of the various Asiatic peoples ruled over by the Mongols. William observed and recorded their lifestyles, folklore, and customs. He was the first person to make Chinese writing known to Europeans. By his description of Karakorum and its varied residents, William dispelled the traditional belief that Asian cities contained palaces made of gold and precious gems. In the same way, his observations of Central Asia laid to rest the popular belief that the area was inhabited by mythical monsters.

After his return, William served as lecturer in theology at Acre. Perhaps as a result of the intervention of Louis IX, William was given permission by his vicar to return to Paris in the late 1250's or early 1260's. There he met the English scientist and philosopher Roger Bacon, a fellow Franciscan. Much of William's narrative was incorporated by Bacon in his *Opus majus* (1267; English translation, 1897-1900), which he acknowledges was written with William's help.

In a subsequent study, published in the mid-1260's, Bacon recorded the formula for gunpowder. Modern scholars believe that Bacon had obtained the formula from William, who in turn had learned of it while in Karakorum. Thus, William of Rubrouck's legacy was a mixed one. On one hand, he opened up to Europeans a whole new world. On the other hand, he may well have given Europe gunpowder, thus helping usher in the era of modern warfare.

—*Paul R. Waibel*

FURTHER READING

Chambers, James. *The Devil's Horsemen: The Mongol Invasion of Europe*. Rev. ed. London: Cassell, 1988. Provides a survey of the Mongolian invasion of Europe in an expanded edition. Several clear maps help the reader locate geographical and battle sites mentioned in the text. Includes a summary of William's journey and places it in historical context.

Dawson, Christopher, ed. *Mission to Asia*. 1955. Reprint. Buffalo, N.Y.: University of Toronto Press, 1992. Originally published as *The Mongol Mission*, provides the text of William's narrative in a very readable translation. The author's lengthy introduction includes all that is known about William and his mission. William's journey is placed in historical context with the other thirteenth century journeys of exploration to Mongolia.

Martels, Zweder von, ed. *Travel Fact and Travel Fiction: Studies on Fiction, Literary Tradition, Scholarly Discovery, and Observation in Travel Writing*. New York: E. J. Brill, 1994. Discussion focuses on the technique and history of travel writing, and includes a chapter on the "perception and prejudices" of William during his travels to the Mongol Empire. Includes a bibliography and an index.

Nederman, Cary J. *Worlds of Difference: European Discourses of Toleration, c. 1100-c. 1550*. University Park: Pennsylvania State University Press, 2000. Explores the idea and practice of religious tolerance during medieval times. Includes an introductory chapter, "Beyond Intolerance: Sources and Sites of Medieval Religious Dispute" and another chapter discussing William, "Negotiating the Tolerant Society: The Travail of William of Rubruck."

Olschki, Leonardo. *Marco Polo's Asia*. Translated by John A. Scott. Berkeley: University of California Press, 1960. Though this study focuses on Marco Polo, it also deals with Polo's predecessors, including William. It is a scholarly discussion of the European discovery of Asia.

Peden, Alison. "The Medieval Antipodes." *History Today* 45, no. 12 (December, 1995). A brief article on the medieval preconceptions and misconceptions—influenced by both science and theology—about the so-called edges of the known world. Mentions William's journey to Asia.

Prawdin, Michael. *The Mongol Empire: Its Rise and Legacy*. Translated by Eden Paul and Cedar Paul. New York: Free Press, 1967. Especially helpful for a discussion of the Great Khan's religious tolerance. Includes maps and a genealogical table.

Ruysbroek, Willem van. *The Mission of Friar William of Rubruck: His Journey to the Court of the Great Khan Möngke, 1253-1255*. Translated by Peter Jackson. 1900. Reprint. London: Hakluyt Society, 1990. This is still the most authoritative English translation of William's narrative. The text is accompanied by rich explanatory footnotes, maps, and an itinerary of William's journey. An introduction provides an excellent summary of Europe's relations with the Mongols in the thirteenth century and the background to William's journey.

SEE ALSO: Roger Bacon; Genghis Khan; Prince Henry the Navigator; Ibn Baṭṭūṭah; al-Idrīsī; Louis IX; al-Masʿūdī; Tamerlane; Yaqut.

RELATED ARTICLES in *Great Events from History: The Middle Ages, 477-1453*: Mid-9th century: Invention of Gunpowder and Guns; 1204: Genghis Khan Founds Mongol Empire; April 16, 1209: Founding of the Franciscans; c. 1320: Origins of the Bubonic Plague; 1325-1355: Travels of Ibn Baṭṭūṭah; September 8, 1380: Battle of Kulikovo; 1381-1405: Tamerlane's Conquests.

WILLIAM OF SAINT-AMOUR

French theologian

William opposed the papal and royal support of the newly created Franciscan and Dominican orders in Europe, laying foundations for opposition to the Papacy and papal authority seen in later Protestantism and in Gallicanism, a movement started in France in 1407.

BORN: c. 1200; Saint-Amour, Jura, Kingdom of Arles (now in France)
DIED: September 13, 1272; Saint-Amour
AREA OF ACHIEVEMENT: Religion and theology

EARLY LIFE

At the beginning of the thirteenth century, there were two clergies, seculars and regulars. The seculars served in the world (hence their name) as bishops and parish pastors; the regulars, on the other hand, submitted themselves to a regimen (from the Latin word *regula*) and lived as monks in a monastery or as members of a cathedral chapter. Many of the regulars were ordained and able to serve the sacraments, but ideally they restricted their use of these powers to their fellow regulars. William of Saint-Amour (san-tah-mewr) accepted this bipartite arrangement from his earliest school days and chose for himself the way of the seculars.

Probably given his basic education in the arts at Saint-Amour and Mâcon, William attended the University of Paris as a secular cleric, a subdeacon. He received in the course of his career the incomes of several ecclesiastical positions: By 1228, he was canon of Beauvais and rector of the church of Guerville, and in 1247, he was given the pastorate (though William was not an ordained priest) of the parish of Granville in the diocese of Coutances. These earnings supported William in his career as a master (teacher) at Paris. William distinguished himself by becoming one of the few persons of his age to take three advanced degrees, in liberal arts (1228), in canon law (1238), and in theology (c. 1250).

No doubt William was established as a young student-teacher when his university welcomed the Franciscans (in 1228) and the Dominicans (in 1231) into the Paris academic community. At first, William may have shared the popular esteem for these friars (from the Latin *fratres*, "brothers"), who exhibited admirable evangelical zeal. Officially recognized by the Papacy only a generation earlier, the friars were the most conspicuous ecclesiastical innovation of the thirteenth century. They operated outside the ordinary ecclesiastical hierarchy, preaching, serving sacraments, and performing various other services directly under the auspices of the pope. At Paris, as well as at other universities, both orders set up independent houses of study and recruited their students from their own outlying provincial schools. In time, however, the zeal of these newcomers attracted converts from the secular staff and student body of the university. Moreover, other orders imitated the friar convents. Consequently, by 1254, only three of the fifteen chairs of theology at the University of Paris were still occupied by seculars, and there was considerable sentiment among the remaining seculars in favor of halting further encroachment by the friars. Also, out in the parishes of France, secular priests and bishops had begun to resent the intrusion of the friars into their traditional spheres of ministry. Accordingly, one of the three remaining secular theologians emerged to provide brief but powerful leadership to the campaign against the friars—a campaign that brought on him the condemnation of both Louis IX, known as Saint Louis, the king of France, and Pope Alexander IV. This man was William of Saint-Amour.

LIFE'S WORK

William argued that there was no biblical support for the mendicant orders. The bishops properly base their existence on the Apostles, and priests rightly trace their authority back to the seventy-two disciples commissioned by Christ. Similarly, deacons (such as William himself), and those in other minor orders, find biblical precedent for their ministry in the "helpers" who assisted the Apostles. Monks present no problem because they simply reside in monasteries and seek after perfection, as Jesus directed those who "would be perfect." Yet where is the scriptural foundation for friars? William found none. The friars, in his view, were neither fish nor fowl. They could not be regarded as true seculars or as true regulars.

Further, William even claimed to have discovered biblical warnings to beware of the friars and to repulse them as heretics. Saint Paul prophesied that in the "last days" there would be corrupt men, proud and treacherous, who would "make their way into households and capture weak women, burdened with sins." Such are the friars, according to William. They steal their way into the consciences of laypersons, hear their confessions, and absolve them without episcopal authority. They abduct the faithful parishioners away from the sheepfold. They build on other men's foundations, contrary to the precepts of Paul. They beg for their living, even though the Apostle commands manual labor. They are like the abominable Egyptian magicians Jannes and Jambres, who, according to medieval legend, were brothers (*fratres*). In short, friars lead students and faithful laity away from their proper bishops and teachers and therefore away from Christ.

By such arguments, William launched against the friars a polemic that went beyond simple criticism of friarly misbehavior. He called for the virtual suppression of both orders. At first glance, this argument appears motivated wholly by self-interested defense of traditional privileges. On close examination, however, it is clear that William was echoing the antipapal sentiments of the entire secular ecclesiastical hierarchy, which believed itself subverted from above. Could the pope justly send legions of friars, loyal only to himself, across diocesan boundaries, alongside long-established parish churches, and into the universities, to compete with the duly ordained and installed resident clerics? This century saw papal power greatly extended (for example, in taxation and legal review). This period was the age of "papal monarchy," when even kings were sometimes punished by excommunication and their lands subjected to the interdict. Thus William and his secular allies, in their attack on the friars, were protesting the papal assertion of *plenitudo potestatis* (fullness of power), first articulated by Pope Innocent III in 1198 and augmented throughout the 1200's.

The pope, the king, and the friars took offense at such criticism. In their view, Christendom was in need of renewal and reform, and the best corrective measure consisted in an evangelical "end run" around the vested interests of the complicated and complacent secular hierarchy. The friar movement, as they saw it, met the spiritual needs of parishioners long starved by poorly educated priests and absentee bishops. In the parishes, the Franciscans and Dominicans were usually the best preachers; in the universities, they were often the best teachers. At Paris, for example, Thomas Aquinas (a Dominican) and Bonaventure (a Franciscan) countered William's views. If William was distinguished for nothing else, he may be remembered as the man who was opposed by these scholars, both later canonized as saints and certainly the greatest theologians of the century.

This controversy between William's party and the friars lasted from 1250 to 1257. It passed through two phases. First, from 1250 to 1254, there were some encouraging developments for the seculars, and consequently they had some confidence that their side would prevail. Then, from 1255 to 1257, the contest turned in favor of the friars. The death of Pope Innocent IV in 1254 and his replacement by Alexander IV was the principal factor in this shift.

Innocent was originally disposed to favor the friars and had in fact ordered the secular masters to readmit the friar-masters as full members of the Paris theological faculty (in 1253 the seculars had ordered the friar-masters to confine their teaching to their own convents and friar-students). Innocent was alarmed, however, by the publication of a sensationalist Franciscan book, *Introductorius in evangelium aeternum* (1254; introduction to the everlasting Gospel), that made extravagant predictions of a coming Age of the Spirit in which the traditional structure of the Church would be dismantled. This writing did not reflect the sober judgment of the majority of the friars, but it was an effective pretext for William to secure papal support for the seculars. Thus, on November 21, 1254, the pope placed extensive restrictions on the ministries of the friars. This victory was to be short-lived, however, as Innocent died a few weeks later. Seculars at Paris lamented his passing and mockingly attributed his death to the influence of Dominican intercessions. Thus the seculars sang in the streets, "From the prayers of the Dominicans, good Lord deliver us." On December 22, 1254, Alexander annulled the decree of his predecessor and restored the privileges of the friars. Alexander, because he had been the cardinal-protector of the Franciscans before his elevation, could be relied on to support his own friar-dependents unreservedly.

William's party, undaunted, continued to disallow the

readmittance of the friar-masters into the Paris faculty of theology. Thomas Aquinas, as a consequence, was forced to await his licensure to teach. (When Thomas eventually gave his inaugural lecture, in 1256, he and his audience had to be protected by soldiers of Louis IX.) The bishops of Orléans and Auxerre, under directives from the Papacy, began proceedings in 1255 to bar William and his followers from the consolation of the Sacraments. However, in the summer of that year, William successfully defended himself in the episcopal courts of Mâcon and Paris, and at Paris, he was supported by a sympathetic audience of four thousand clerics. Moreover, in October, the secular masters sought to annul the pope's directives, and thereby cancel their status of excommunication, by dissolving the university—and they threatened to leave the university altogether. Alexander obdurately insisted that they submit to him. In December, he instructed the chancellor of the university to license only those faculty who observed his pronouncement and demanded that William and his partisans be deprived of their teaching positions.

Throughout 1256, the dispute increasingly came to center on William himself. In the spring and early summer of that year, William composed in rapid succession three drafts of his best-known work, *De periculis novissimorum temporum* (1256; on the dangers of the last times), the third of which passed into the hands of king and pope.

In August, Alexander ordered the examination of *De periculis novissimorum temporum* by a commission that was dominated by the great Dominican biblical scholar, and William's rival at Paris, Hugh of Saint-Cher. The university, for William's defense, sent three theologians, the university rector, and a master of arts. Before this delegation arrived, however, the commission found the treatise to be scandalous and pernicious. Thus, by the time the seculars entered Rome, Alexander had condemned the treatise, and William and his supporters argued his case in vain. All other seculars at length submitted to the pope, but William stood alone and recalcitrant. In the winter of 1257, in ill health, William went into exile (by order of the king), where he remained despite numerous attempts by his colleagues at Paris to have his sentence overturned. He was later allowed to return to his native Saint-Amour, where he remained until his death in 1272. While in forced retirement, he composed his *Collectiones catholicae et canonicae scripturae* (1266; collections of Catholic and canonical writings), an extensive final warning to the Church to beware of the mounting dangers introduced by the friars.

SIGNIFICANCE

Some scholars have dismissed William as an ultraconservative, a mere crank, who stood against the most progressive developments of the thirteenth century. Others have seriously suggested that William's biblical interpretation—that the "last days" were at hand—was actually a sophisticated farce designed to mock similar biblical exegeses by the more radical friars. Both views, however, are inaccurate. William is better understood as an early representative of the antipapal cause that reached its height in later centuries. Most striking is William's biblical interpretation of Church ministry, an exegesis that he certainly intended to be taken seriously, in which the thirteenth century clerical hierarchy is judged in the light of its apostolic first century antecedents. One can see here a precedent for the scriptural exegeses of John Wyclif (in the fourteenth century) and Martin Luther (in the sixteenth century). Indeed, Wyclif acknowledged his debt to William.

It is a matter of historical record that William's caricatures of the friars proved immensely popular. William was warmly remembered by many of his students and fellow clergy, and his rhetoric made its way into later literature. The poet Rutebeuf (fl. 1245-1285) vigorously defended William against both pope and king, whom he disparaged as Judases. Jean de Meung, author of the last part of *Le Roman de la rose* (c. 1230; *The Romance of the Rose*, 1914-1924), devoted some thousand verses to praise of William and his ideas and depicted the friars by the type "False Semblance." William Langland, in the fourteenth century, portrayed the friars as "Doctor Friar Flatter," alias "Father Creep-into-Houses." Sixteenth century Protestants blessed William's memory and printed (in 1530) his *De periculis novissimorum temporum*. Perhaps there was even a dim echo as late as the eighteenth century, when Edmund Burke satirized the French radicals as "praters [who] effect to carry back the clergy to that primitive evangelical poverty."

—*Larry C. Watkins*

FURTHER READING

Bolton, Brenda. *Innocent III: Studies on Papal Authority and Pastoral Care*. Brookfield, Vt.: Variorum, 1995. Discusses papal primacy and authority as articulated by Pope Innocent III, to which William was deeply opposed. Includes a bibliography and an index.

Dawson, James D. "William of Saint-Amour and the Apostolic Tradition." *Mediaeval Studies* 40 (1978): 223-238. Argues that William gave new meaning to the ancient ideal of apostolic tradition and therefore was one of the inventors of the primitive first century ideal that later would be used as a weapon against the Church.

Douie, D. L. *The Conflict Between the Seculars and the Mendicants at the University of Paris in the Thirteenth Century.* London: Blackfriars, 1954. A brief but comprehensive survey of the controversy between the seculars and the friars.

_______. "St. Bonaventura's Part in the Conflict Between Seculars and Mendicants at Paris." In *S. Bonaventura, 1274-1974*, edited by J. G. Bougerol. Vol. 2. Rome: Collegio S. Bonaventura Grottaferrata, n.d. Examines the controversy from 1252 to 1270 with special regard to the role of the Franciscan friar Saint Bonaventure. William figures prominently in this essay, which ends with observations regarding the implications of the controversy for the development of the medieval Papacy.

Lambert, Malcolm D. *Franciscan Poverty: The Doctrine of the Absolute Poverty of Christ and the Apostles in the Franciscan Order, 1210-1323.* London: Society for Promoting Christian Knowledge, 1961. An extensive study of the idea of poverty as conceived by Saint Francis of Assisi and developed by his order until the papacy of Pope John XXII in the fourteenth century. Contains illuminating insights on the practical problems faced by the Franciscans and on the hostility they encountered from the seculars. Includes index.

Leff, Gordon. *Paris and Oxford Universities in the Thirteenth and Fourteenth Centuries: An Institutional and Intellectual History.* New York: John Wiley and Sons, 1968. A good introduction to the background of the friar-secular controversy.

Rosewein, Barbara H., and Lester K. Little. "Social Meaning in the Monastic and Mendicant Spiritualities." *Past and Present* 63 (May, 1974): 4-32. This article provides insight into the social and economic factors that augmented the spirituality of the friars. Notes the differences between the older Benedictines and the thirteenth century friars.

Traver, Andrew. *The Opuscula of William of Saint-Amour: The Minor Works of 1255-1256.* Münster, Germany: Aschendorff, 2003. A study of four of William's Latin texts in the context of the history and criticism of literature on the friars. Includes a bibliography and index.

_______. "Secular and Mendicant Masters of the Faculty of Theology at the University of Paris, 1505-1523." *Sixteenth Century Journal* 26, no. 1 (Spring, 1995). Looks at the relationship between the mendicants and the University of Paris faculty of theology in the early Renaissance period. Although the article's time period follows that of William, the discussion is still useful as an examination of the tensions between the friars and the seculars.

SEE ALSO: Saint Bonaventure; Boniface VIII; Saint Francis of Assisi; Jan Hus; Innocent III; Innocent IV; Louis IX; William of Ockham; Thomas Aquinas; John Wyclif.

RELATED ARTICLES in *Great Events from History: The Middle Ages, 477-1453*: March 21, 1098: Foundation of the Cistercian Order; c. 1175: Waldensian Excommunications Usher in Protestant Movement; April 16, 1209: Founding of the Franciscans; c. 1265-1273: Thomas Aquinas Compiles the *Summa Theologica*; November 18, 1302: Boniface VII Issues the Bull *Unam Sanctam*; 1305-1417: Avignon Papacy and the Great Schism; c. 1310-1350: William of Ockham Attacks Thomist Ideas; 1377-1378: Condemnation of John Wyclif; 1414-1418: Council of Constance; July 6, 1415: Martyrdom of Jan Hus.

WILLIAM OF SAINT-THIERRY

French monk and theologian

William of Saint-Thierry, whose name is forever linked with that of Saint Bernard of Clairvaux, was one of the greatest of twelfth century monks, mystics, and theologians of the spiritual life. His writings on love, monastic friendship, and the Trinity were particularly influential.

BORN: c. 1085; Liège, Lower Lorraine (now in France)
DIED: September 8, 1147 or 1148; Signy Abbey, Diocese of Reims, France
AREAS OF ACHIEVEMENT: Religion and theology, monasticism

EARLY LIFE

William of Saint-Thierry (san-tyehr-ee) was born in Liège of noble parentage; nothing else is known about his family. While still young, he left Liège, probably for Reims, where, it is thought, he studied between 1105 and 1115. Little is known with certainty about William's early life and education, but his writings give evidence of a good education.

Having decided to become a Benedictine monk, William joined the abbey of Saint-Nicaise of Reims, probably in 1113. Saint-Nicaise was a monastery of good reputation, and every indication is that from the beginning William practiced the monastic life with great seriousness and commitment. The quiet of the monastic cloister allowed him time for study of the Church fathers, especially the works of Saint Augustine, Saint Ambrose, Saint Hilary of Poitiers, Boethius, and Gregory the Great. His growing reputation for learning and strictness of life led to his election in 1119 or 1120 as abbot of Saint-Thierry, northwest of Reims.

Saint-Thierry was a well-endowed monastery, and much of William's time was taken with administration of the monastic properties. At the time he became abbot, Saint-Thierry was not as well known as the abbey of Saint-Nicaise. William's success in temporal administration and the spiritual guidance of the community, together with the respect accorded to his writings, was soon to make it one of the preeminent monasteries in the Benedictine order.

LIFE'S WORK

If William was not already a priest by the time he became abbot of Saint-Thierry, at some unknown time he was so ordained. During his first three years as abbot, he wrote *De natura et dignitate amoris* (c. 1119-1128; *On the Nature and Dignity of Love*, 1956). This work envisioned the monastic life as a continuation of the communal life practiced at Jerusalem by the Apostles (see Acts 2:42-47 and 4:32-35), the goal of which was unity of mind from which love flows. For William, the monastery was a school of love. His interest in the contemplative life is also evident in another work from this period, *De contemplando Deo* (c. 1119-1128; *On Contemplating God*, 1955). As it was to turn out, these earliest of his writings were, along with his last two works, *Epistola ad fratres de Monte-Dei* (1144; *The Golden Epistle of Abbot William of St. Thierry*, 1930) and *Vite prima Bernardi abbatis* (c. 1147; *Saint Bernard of Clairvaux: The Story of His Life*, 1960), to have a significant influence on later generations. Yet these earliest two works were circulated in the thirteenth century under Saint Bernard's name.

William found the burdens of his position as abbot hard to bear. He was shy and sensitive, and commanding others did not come easily. Increasingly through the 1120's, he was troubled by the criticisms made by Saint Bernard regarding the Cluniac form of Benedictinism, the usages of which had been adopted by William's own monastery. He had first met Bernard, who followed a stricter Cistercian reading of the Rule of Saint Benedict, in 1118. About 1125, Bernard addressed to William a pair of sharply written satirical works that created much controversy, for although on certain points Bernard was conciliatory, he persisted in many of his criticisms of the Cluniacs, hitherto the most influential monastic order, as lax and fond of luxury. Perceiving the justice of much of Bernard's criticism, William gave his approval to the work and subsequently cited it in some of his own writings. Beyond this, he became active in reform of his order in the province of Reims.

William had made journeys to Saint Bernard's monastery at Clairvaux for spiritual conversation, and by 1124, he told Bernard that he wished to resign his abbacy and move to Clairvaux. Bernard advised against it. For the time being, William accepted this advice and remained at Saint-Thierry, governing and writing.

In 1128, Bernard sent William a new work addressing the issues of grace and free will, asking for his criticism. In response, William composed *De sacramento altaris* (c. 1128; *On the Sacrament of the Altar*, 1970). This book on the meaning of the Eucharist is one of the first devoted solely to this subject. Probably about this time, William also began other works, for the most part dependent on his extensive knowledge of the Latin fathers, but with some use, through the Latin translation by Rufinus, of the Greek Christian writer Origen (c. 185-c. 254). Although both earlier and later Origen had fallen and was to fall under censure, in the twelfth century, he was fairly widely read, and William was to adopt themes from Origen in several treatises. It is likely that many of the works of this period, including the *Meditativae orationes* (c. 1128-1135; *The Meditations*, 1954), were only begun at Saint-Thierry and were finished after William had moved to Signy.

The idea of becoming a Cistercian had never been abandoned by William, and in 1135 he resigned his abbacy and, as a simple monk, joined the new Cistercian monastery of Signy, also in the diocese of Reims. There followed a time of trial and self-doubt. William never had been particularly robust, and it may be that the very sparse diet of the Cistercians, who subsisted for the most part on bread and vegetables, weakened him further. In addition, doubts grew that he had made the right choice. He became so ill that he almost died. He remained frail even after recovering and was thereafter exempted from the daily manual labor practiced by most Cistercians.

He returned to his writing. The *Expositio super cantica canticorum* (c. 1135-1138; *Exposition on the Song of Songs*, 1970) became a main preoccupation; in this work, William elaborated his teaching on humans as images of God and as possessing, as Augustine had taught, memory, intellect, and will. Beginning in 1138, there arose a controversy whose repercussions were felt all across Europe. Certain of Peter Abelard's teachings had been condemned as early as 1121, but only in the mid-1130's did some of his later writings come into William's possession. William was outraged at what he took to be Abelard's contempt for tradition. He immediately took the attack and called Abelard's abuses to Bernard's attention. By 1140, the latter had seen to it that Abelard was condemned by Rome.

Abelard might have been condemned, but the issues he raised concerning the relation of faith and reason—of the role of reason in speaking of the things of God—remained. Like many others, William tried his hand at addressing these issues. Two works have been preserved, *Speculum fidei* (1140; *The Mirror of Faith*, 1959) and *Aenigma fidei* (1144; *The Enigma of Faith*, 1974). These works both treat the problem of how humans know God; *The Mirror of Faith* is virtually an exposition of the theological virtues of faith, hope, and love, and *The Enigma of Faith* centers on the Trinity. William elsewhere attacked what he took to be a tendency of theologians such as William of Conches to undermine the unity of the Trinity, a theme taken up in *The Enigma of Faith*.

William gained a wide readership in the twelfth century (and even more in the thirteenth) from a work intended for hermits, *The Golden Epistle*. In about 1144, he had visited the recently founded Carthusian Charterhouse of Mont-Dieu, a community of hermits, also in the diocese of Reims. After William returned to Signy, his gift to the hermits was a long epistle on the eremitic life. Like other of his works, this was to suffer at the hands of later medieval editors, who reshaped what had originally been a long letter into a formal treatise on the solitary life, eventually attributed to Saint Bernard.

William felt old and tired, but he had one final work to write: *Saint Bernard of Clairvaux*. Death intervened before he could finish, and he left the tale told only through about 1130. He died on September 8, 1147 or 1148, and was buried in his own cloister at Signy.

SIGNIFICANCE

William of Saint-Thierry stands at the center of the twelfth century monastic impulse toward solitude, austerity, and contemplation. The movement of his life was from the less strict practices of Cluny to the more demanding life of the Cistercians, with an interest toward the end in the even more austere eremitic life of the Carthusians. Linked forever with his almost lifelong friend, Saint Bernard of Clairvaux, whose life he was writing at the time of his death, William was not the public figure that Bernard was. Although very much involved in monastic reform and always attentive to the threat of heresy, for the most part William lived a quiet life of solitude, a life of meditation and writing. It is here that his importance lies.

The revival of learning occurring all across Europe in the twelfth century had many aspects. One of these was an exploration of the reliability and limits of human reason, especially in understanding the nature of God. William considered that many of the scholars of the rapidly growing cities of his day were too audacious in speaking of God and too careless in abandoning established terminology for new ideas. His own interest lay elsewhere, in mystical theology, especially in elaborating for monks the manner in which, through love, the human soul becomes receptive to salvation and to God—indeed, in a certain sense becomes like God, who is Love.

At one level, William was one of the most conservative theologians of his day, siding with Saint Bernard against innovators such as Abelard and William of Conches. William of Saint-Thierry disliked the application of dialectic to theology: Better than the new Scholasticism was the prayer and contemplative theology of the church fathers, who attempted to reach God more by love and desire than by intellect and saw all understanding of God as rooted in love. In another sense, William can be said to evince a rather modern sensibility in his perception of inner peace and joy as signs of God's grace and consolation. The main point is that, by returning to the Church fathers, William often recaptured ancient insights and expressed them in a contemplative synthesis built around access to God through love. This he offered as an alternative to the growing Scholastic attempt to turn theology into a science whose main instrument was intellect.

—*Glenn W. Olsen*

Further Reading

Anderson, John D. Introduction to *The Enigma of Faith*, translated by John D. Anderson. Vol. 3 in *The Works of William of St. Thierry*. Washington, D.C.: Consortium Press, 1974. This volume corrects several errors repeated in many descriptions of William's life and downplays William's knowledge of the Greek Church fathers.

Bell, David N. *The Image and Likeness: The Augustinian Spirituality of William of St. Thierry*. Kalamazoo, Mich.: Cistercian Publications, 1984. This is an informed, full-length study of William's spirituality and theology. The biographical comments in the introduction are sound. Includes an extensive bibliography and indexes.

Brooke, Odo. *Studies in Monastic Theology*. Kalamazoo, Mich.: Cistercian Publications, 1980. This volume discusses William's theology.

Déchanet, Jean Marie. *William of St. Thierry: The Man and His Work*. Translated by Richard Strachan. Spencer, Mass.: Cistercian Publications, 1972. This biography is sometimes uncritical and sometimes overly speculative in advancing points of view for which there is little evidence. Its final chapter, however, gives a useful survey of previous scholarship.

Evans, G. R., ed. *The Medieval Theologians*. Malden, Mass.: Blackwell, 2001. Chapter 9 considers the theology of William and Bernard as part of a "medieval Renaissance." Includes a bibliography and an index.

Gilson, Étienne. *The Mystical Theology of Saint Bernard*. Translated by A. C. Downes. 1940. Reprint. Kalamazoo, Mich.: Cistercian Publications, 1990. A great work by one of the best twentieth century historians of medieval thought. Its fifth appendix, "Notes on William of St.-Thierry," gives an excellent outline of William's thought, clearly placing it in the Augustinian tradition.

Renevey, Denis. *Language, Self and Love: Hermeneutics in the Writings of Richard Rolle and the Commentaries on the Song of Songs*. Cardiff: University of Wales Press, 2001. A critical look at commentaries on William's *Song of Songs*.

See also: Peter Abelard; Saint Benedict of Nursia; Saint Bernard of Clairvaux; Boethius; Saint Fulbert of Chartres; Gregory the Great; Hildegard von Bingen; Joachim of Fiore; Suger.

Related articles in *Great Events from History: The Middle Ages, 477-1453*: 590-604: Reforms of Pope Gregory the Great; c. 700-1000: Heavy Plow Helps Increase Agricultural Yields; 963: Foundation of the Mount Athos Monasteries; March 21, 1098: Foundation of the Cistercian Order; 1100-1300: European Universities Emerge; c. 1150: Moors Transmit Classical Philosophy and Medicine to Europe; c. 1200: Scientific Cattle Breeding Developed.

WILLIAM THE CONQUEROR
King of England (r. 1066-1087)

Through his conquest of the English at the Battle of Hastings in 1066, William made it possible for his Anglo-Norman successors to develop a strong feudal monarchy that flourished for several centuries.

BORN: c. 1028; Falaise, Normandy (now in France)
DIED: September 9, 1087; Rouen, Normandy
ALSO KNOWN AS: William I
AREAS OF ACHIEVEMENT: Government and politics, military

EARLY LIFE

Very little is known about William the Conqueror's childhood, though it is reasonable to assume that he spent his infancy in the care of his mother. William was the bastard son of Duke Robert I and Herleve, the daughter of a tanner. On his father's side, William was the descendant of Vikings who had settled Normandy in the early tenth century. He was destined to become one of the greatest figures in European history. Because of his illegitimate birth, there is no reason to believe that Robert had any special plans for the youth. Robert, however, died in 1035 while returning from a pilgrimage to Jerusalem, and William, age seven, was proclaimed duke.

William's birth and youth made it inevitable that his position would be challenged by ambitious nobles of the realm. There can be no doubt that he grew up in difficult times, and many of those closest to the young duke, including four successive guardians, died violently. Undoubtedly, these tumultuous years left an indelible mark on his young mind, which, in years to come, would manifest itself in a stern, repressive manner of ruling and various acts of cruelty. In 1047, William faced his first major crisis as discontent in western Normandy crystallized into a great revolt. Fortunately, William had the support of his liege lord, King Henry I of France, who crushed the revolt in the Battle of Val-ès-Dunes near Caen.

LIFE'S WORK

The Battle of Val-ès-Dunes was a significant event because it temporarily put an end to the anarchy of the realm, and in a sense, it marked the close of William's minority. In the years that followed, William's stature as a baronial leader and warrior grew rapidly. In his twenties, William was physically imposing. He was almost 6 feet (183 centimeters) in height, with long arms and legs. His chroniclers spent much time extolling his great physical strength and military prowess.

In the years after Val-ès-Dunes, William increased his power in various ways. In 1053, he married Matilda, daughter of the count of Flanders, which was a politically advantageous alliance. Matilda, for her part, proved to be a good companion and duchess, an invaluable supporter who, on occasion, ruled Normandy in her husband's absence. Unfortunately, the union aroused the ire of both the Church, which feared consanguinity, and William's lord, King Henry of France. Relations deteriorated rapidly after the king formed an alliance with Geoffrey Martel, count of Anjou, one of William's enemies. Henry and Geoffrey twice invaded Normandy, but William, now an accomplished warrior, defeated them decisively in battles at Mortemer in 1054 and Varaville in 1058. These battles, for all practical purposes, allowed William to become independent of his former lord. Thereafter, William assumed the offensive, waging war with Anjou and seizing the district of Maine. In 1060, both Henry and Geoffrey died, allowing William to turn his attention to other matters.

That which now commanded his attention was the rather chaotic state of affairs in England. William first became interested in the English throne when he visited Edward the Confessor's court in 1051 and supposedly was named as his heir. William's hopes were further strengthened when, in 1064, Harold Godwinson, the most powerful of the English earls, was shipwrecked and captured in Normandy. In exchange for his freedom, Harold took an oath to support William's candidacy for the crown on Edward's death. When Edward died in 1066, however, the Anglo-Saxon Witan chose Harold as his successor. Harold refused to honor his oath, and William prepared for war.

An invasion of England was an enormous task that required both diplomatic and military preparations. In addition to building a fleet, William began to gather mercenaries who were interested in both adventure and booty. Estimates of William's army, once assembled, range from five thousand to twenty-five thousand men. William also sought the support of the Papacy as an aid in recruiting and to lend an aura of legitimacy to the whole operation. England, he reasoned, must be liberated from Harold, who was an oath-breaker. The pope sent a consecrated banner, and William prepared to launch his holy mission.

William, however, could not at first catch a favorable wind to cross the channel. While he waited, his allies, Harold Hardrada, king of Norway, and Tostig, the English king's exiled brother, invaded northern England. Harold Godwinson marched north and scored a decisive victory at Stamford Bridge. In the meantime, the winds changed and William crossed to an unopposed southern shore. Harold, in a much-debated move, marched his battle-weary troops rapidly southward and two weeks later, on October 14, faced William's troops at Hastings. In one of the most important battles in English history, William, adroitly using mounted warriors, defeated the English, who fought on foot. With Hastings, William had control of England, but there was much work still to be done. William moved slowly, but inexorably, toward London, devastating much of the countryside as he terrorized the English. He took London with little opposition and was crowned King William I at Westminster on Christmas Day.

England did not at once come under William's rule. In the years that followed, there were many revolts that were crushed swiftly and with great savagery. There were uprisings in Northumbria, Dorset, Cornwall, Somerset, and elsewhere. In the north, William found it necessary to devastate large areas with fire and sword; the Durham and Yorkshire region did not recover from William's depredations until the next century. Once the sparks of rebellion were doused, Norman castles featuring an enclosed mound surmounted by a wooden or stone tower were built throughout the country to keep the peace.

William the Conqueror. (Library of Congress)

By 1071, William had sufficiently pacified the countryside and could turn his attention to domestic reform. The lands of those who opposed him were confiscated and given to his loyal supporters. Each of his vassals, in turn, owed a certain number of knights for the fiefs they held. These were important elements of Norman feudalism. The Norman *magnum concilium*, or Great Council, replaced the Anglo-Saxon Witan as the governing body of the realm from which evolved a smaller advisory body called the *curia regis*. All the great lords of the realm, lay and ecclesiastical, were required to attend the meetings of the Great Council.

The last fifteen years of William's reign were relatively uneventful. He was the undisputed king of England and duke of Normandy, the most powerful figure in northern Europe. Yet various parts of his empire were always on the verge of fresh rebellion. He was frequently harried by the Scots and the restive nobility of both Maine and Anjou. Within his family, the only serious threat came from his eldest son, Robert, who, aided by the king of France and on one occasion by his mother, Matilda, frequently stood in opposition to his father. In 1087, William, old and corpulent, invaded the French Vexin, a region that existed between central Normandy and the royal domain around Paris. He was thrown from his horse and mortally injured. He was carried to Rouen, where he died on September 9. On his deathbed, he made arrangements for the division of his kingdom. Normandy would pass to Robert, but his successor in England was William, called Rufus.

Significance

William the Conqueror's life lends credence to the idea that great persons shape history. With some difficulty, he rose above his ignoble beginnings as the bastard son of Duke Robert I to become the greatest warrior and administrator of his age. If the Battle of Hastings had never occurred, William's accomplishments between 1047 and 1060 would have earned for him a certain measure of fame. The rebellious nobles of his duchy were subjugated while offensives led by powerful enemies were turned back. As a result, he was able to create a far larger

NORMAN KINGS OF ENGLAND, 1066-1189

Reign	*Monarch*
1066-1087	WILLIAM I THE CONQUEROR
1087-1100	William II Rufus
1100-1135	HENRY I BEAUCLERC
1135-1154	Stephen (Norman)
1154-1189	HENRY II (Plantagenet line begins)

and wealthier kingdom in northern Europe from which to launch his invasion of England.

The year 1066 is perhaps the most familiar date in English history. In that year, William gathered his army, crossed the channel, and conquered England. Yet he never regarded himself as a mere conqueror—rather, as the rightful successor to the English throne. His approach was, at times, conciliatory, and to that end he retained many features of English administration and society. The courts of the shire, for example, were retained, while the life of the peasantry was not significantly changed.

While William could be magnanimous, he could also be quite harsh, especially to those who opposed him. When the residents of Alençon reminded him of his bastardy, he cut off the hands and feet of thirty-two of them. The many revolts after Hastings may have forced William to become more tyrannical and even avaricious. The introduction of Norman feudalism provided him with both knights and castles to tame an unruly land, while Normans and Norman administrative agencies replaced those of the English. William so completely brought England under his control that in 1086, one year before his death, he was ready to inventory his great wealth. The results were incorporated into the Domesday Book (1086), also called the Domesday Survey, which serves as an invaluable record of baronial and peasant holdings. In church affairs, he was equally dominant. Although he supported and promoted the growth of the Church in both Normandy and England through the appointment of wise counselors such as Lanfranc, he made it very clear that he was not subservient to the pope and that the ecclesiastics of his realm held their positions at his pleasure. In sum, William the Conqueror left no doubt that he was supreme in things both temporal and spiritual.

—*Larry W. Usilton*

FURTHER READING

Bradbury, Jim. *The Battle of Hastings*. Stroud, England: Sutton, 1998. Focuses on the tactics and strategies of the battle and discusses the battle in the context of European military events of the eleventh century.

Brooke, Christopher. *From Alfred to Henry III, 871-1272*. New York: Norton, 1969. Provides a brief sketch of William's life from his accession as duke of Normandy in 1035 until his death in 1087. It is especially good for the beginning student.

_______. *The Saxon and Norman Kings*. 3d ed. Malden, Mass.: Blackwell, 2001. Provides two brief chapters on William, the Norman conquest, and his sons. It is informal in style and at times even entertaining. A select bibliography lists some of the better primary and secondary sources on the subject.

Corbett, W. J. "The Development of the Duchy of Normandy and the Norman Conquest of England." In *The Cambridge Medieval History*, edited by J. R. Tanner et al. Vol. 5. New York: Cambridge University Press, 1926. This is a chapter from still one of the best multivolume surveys of the period. It treats succinctly the chief events of William's life, Hastings, and the aftermath.

Douglas, David C. *William the Conqueror: The Norman Impact upon England*. Berkeley: University of California Press, 1964. A scholarly work that provides a wealth of information about William's life and especially the many ways in which England was affected by the conquest. Includes a good bibliography.

Freeman, Edward A. *The History of the Norman Conquest of England: Its Causes and Results*. 5 vols. Reprint. New York: AMS Press, 1977. A classic, originally published 1867-1879, with which all students of English history should be familiar. Argues that the Norman conquest did not significantly alter Anglo-Saxon institutions.

Haskins, C. H. *Norman Institutions*. 1919. Reprint. New York: F. Ungar, 1960. A still-useful work that argues that one must take a look at Norman roots before understanding the full impact of the conquest.

Riley, Brent A., and Joe Bageant. "William from Bastard to Conqueror." *Military History* 19, no. 1 (April, 2002). Discusses William's ancestors, his often-mentioned physical characteristics, and his skills as a warrior and a terrorizer of enemies. Includes a map and illustrations.

Stenton, F. M. *Anglo-Saxon England*. 3d ed. Oxford, England: Clarendon Press, 1989. This text is the result of many years of specialized work and has been well received by the scholarly community. Several chapters are devoted to William.

Van Houts, Elisabeth. "The Norman Conquest Through

European Eyes." *English Historical Review* 110, no. 438 (September, 1995). Looks at the coverage of William's conquest of England in the European press, condemns the rational for extreme Norman violence during the conquest, and analyzes the resultant reform of the English Church.

Walker, David. *The Normans in Britain*. Cambridge, Mass.: Blackwell, 1995. An overview of the Anglo-Norman period in England, Scotland, Ireland, and Wales, beginning with the Battle of Hastings.

See also: Canute the Great; Edward the Confessor; Ethelred II, the Unready; Harold II.

Related articles in *Great Events from History: The Middle Ages, 477-1453*: October 14, 1066: Battle of Hastings; 1086: Domesday Survey.

Władysław II Jagiełło and Jadwiga

King of Poland (r. 1386-1434) and Queen of Poland (r. 1384-1399)

Jagiełło and Jadwiga's marriage brought about the unification of Lithuania and Poland and the conversion of the Lithuanian people from paganism to the Roman Catholic faith.

Władysław II Jagiełło

Born: c. 1351; place unknown

Died: June 1, 1434; Gródek Jagielloński, near Lwów, Poland (now Gorodok, near Lviv, Lithuania)

Also known as: Ladislaus II; Jogaila

Jadwiga

Born: 1373 or 1374; place unknown

Died: July 17, 1399; place unknown

Also known as: Hedvig; Hedwig

Areas of achievement: Government and politics, diplomacy, religion and theology, military

Early Lives

Władysław II Jagiełło (LAD-ihs-lahs or vlah-DIH-slahf yah-GEHL-oh) was the eldest son of Algirdas (also known as Olgierd), the grand duke of Lithuania, by his second marriage. Though Jagiełło's mother, Juliana of Tver, taught him Ukrainian and pushed him toward her Russian Orthodox Church and a Russian marriage, Jagiełło took after his cautious pagan father in most respects, even in the unusual practice of refusing to drink alcoholic beverages. Algirdas had shared power in Lithuania with his brother, Kęstutis, who had governed the western half of the country and fended off the eastern march of the Teutonic Knights and Kings Casimir the Great (r. 1333-1370) and Louis the Great, king of Hungary and Poland (r. 1342-1382 and 1370-1382). Algirdas had ruled over central Lithuania and the Russian dependencies.

Algirdas's death in 1377 precipitated a struggle between the sons of the two marriages. Jagiełło and his brothers overcame those rivals and, in 1382, they fought their uncle, Kęstutis, through secret alliances with the Teutonic Knights in which the brothers promised to convert the Lithuanians to the Roman Catholic Church. They found themselves in trouble, however, when Kęstutis's son, Vytautas, escaped to the Teutonic Knights and persuaded the Crusaders that he would be more likely to carry out his promises than Jagiełło. Soon, the baptized Vytautas threatened Jagiełło's hold on Lithuania so seriously that in 1385 Jagiełło looked abroad for help.

The kingdom of Poland was undergoing a serious crisis. Casimir the Great had expanded its frontiers to the east, but after his death in 1370 he left the country without a legitimate male heir. The crown had gone to Louis the Great, who was not in a position to defend Poland well. Confronted by the Turkish advance into the Balkans and in poor health, Louis ruled Poland through Hungarian and Silesian favorites. When Louis died in 1382, it appeared that foreigners would continue to dominate Poland, because his two young daughters were promised to prominent German princes.

Jadwiga (yahd-VEE-gah), the daughter who became queen in 1384, had been married while still a child to Wilhelm von Habsburg. In 1385, young Wilhelm came to Kraków to urge his childhood playmate to consummate their marriage before the Polish bishops could arrange an annulment. The Polish nobles and clergy meanwhile looked hurriedly for an alternative bridegroom. The austere, clean-shaven, seemingly compliant Lithuanian grand duke was their choice.

Lives' Work

The Treaty of Krewo, August 14, 1385, provided for Jagiełło to marry Jadwiga, for the conversion of the Lithuanian people, and for a dynastic union of the two states. Jadwiga was persuaded by the Polish bishops to marry the short, quiet, balding stranger, who would be known as her consort. She held the title "rex," and her advisers saw to it that Jagiełło's powers were strictly limited. The marriage does not seem to have been a love match (despite what has been written in nineteenth century Romantic novels), and only one child, a daughter, was born, in 1399. (Jadwiga died in childbirth, and the baby girl died three days later.)

The marriage took place on February 14, 1386, in Kraków. The following year, on February 1, Jagiełło established a bishopric in Vilnius, his Lithuanian capital, and possibly wrote the "Our Father and the Apostles' Creed" in Lithuanian and led the converts in their first recitation. There were too few Lithuanian-speaking priests to make a great impact on the mass of the population, but that was perhaps just as well: The sincere pagans and the many Russian Orthodox believers were consequently left in peace until the new church was well established.

Jagiełło, meanwhile, had made his peace with Vytautas by promising to give him Kęstutis's lands. Failing to live up to that promise, he later had to fight Vytautas and the Teutonic Knights again—but without Polish help. Poland had lived in almost unbroken peace with the Teutonic Knights since the Treaty of Kalisz in 1343, and Jadwiga (supported strongly by her advisers) did not want war with them. Consequently, Jagiełło ultimately gave Vytautas all Lithuania, rescuing only a claim to ultimate sovereignty and a promise of help against the Mongols in the Ukraine, where Jadwiga's advisers had wanted Jagiełło to employ his talents all along.

The turning point in all Jagiełło's relationships came in 1399. Jadwiga's strong, independent personality had expressed itself largely in acts of piety and in curbing her husband's ambitions. Her death in childbirth made Jagiełło king in name and in fact. Vytautas, routed by the Mongols in pitched battle, pled for Polish help and two years later formally acknowledged Jagiełło as his overlord.

In all these endeavors, Jagiełło had not demonstrated outstanding military skill. Instead, he was a master diplomat, a cautious but skillful politician, and a clever manipulator of personal and national weaknesses. Slowly, he made himself master of Poland, favoring that section of Polish nobility that had encouraged him to take the formal title of Władysław II, thus linking himself to Władysław I's lifelong efforts to recover Pomerelia (West Prussia) from the Teutonic Knights.

War with the Teutonic Knights came in 1410. On the battlefield of Tannenberg (Stębark), Jagiełło and Vytautas thoroughly crushed the grand master's army. Afterward, Jagiełło's brilliant statecraft isolated his enemy and, by forcing the knights to hire mercenaries year after year, drained their strength. In 1422, his armies laid Prussia to waste so thoroughly that the grand master renounced his last claims on Lithuanian territory. Jagiełło failed to recover Pomerelia, but his successors did so in the Thirteen Years' War (from 1454 to 1466), with the aid of West Prussian burghers and secular nobles.

Jagiełło restored royal authority over Masovia, rees-

RULERS OF POLAND, 1333-1516

Reign	*Ruler*
1333-1370	CASIMIR III THE GREAT
1370	End of the Piast Dynasty
1370-1382	Ludvik I the Great (Louis of Anjou)
1382-1384	Confederation of Radom and civil war
1384-1399	QUEEN JADWIGA
1385	Treaty of Krewo
1386-1434	WŁADYSŁAW II JAGIEŁŁO and JADWIGA
1410-1411	War with Teutonic Knights, Battle of Tannenberg and Peace of Thorn
1433	Charter of Kraków (grants rights to nobles)
1434-1444	Władysław (Vladislav) III
1444-1447	Instability; Poland united with Lithuania
1447-1492	Casimir IV
1454-1466	Thirteen Years' War: Poles defeat Teutonic Order, gain access to the Baltic in the Second Peace of Thorn
1471-1516	Vladislav Jagiełło (son of Casimir IV) king of Bohemia and then Hungary
1492-1501	John Albert I
1496	Statute of Piotrkow (Poland's Magna Carta)

tablished control over the southeastern provinces, and worked closely with the Hussites in Bohemia to weaken German power along the Polish border. In 1433, Jagiełło and Vytautas confirmed the dynastic union of their states and defined the constitutional rights of the nobles of Poland and Lithuania, a major step toward limiting royal authority. Further steps came through concessions to Archbishop Oleśnicki.

Last, when Jagiełło's fourth wife produced two long-awaited sons (Władysław and Casimir), the king was unable to secure their succession without sacrificing more royal prerogatives. His authority over Lithuania was even weaker. Even though he frustrated Vytautas's ambitions to become king, Jagiełło was unable to secure the country for his own brother on Vytautas's death in 1430. After Jagiełło died, Vytautas's brother, Sigismund, won the struggle for power, and regents ruled in Poland on behalf of the nobility and clergy.

SIGNIFICANCE

When Władysław II Jagiełło defeated the Teutonic Knights, it was the most brilliant moment in Polish military history between 1200 and the victory of John III Sobieski (r. 1674-1696) over the Turks in 1683—at least from the point of view that prevailed after Poland had been divided among its neighbors. There is a tendency among an oppressed and divided people to simplify history and to remember and honor those moments when the country was militarily triumphant. This tradition has been a disservice to other glorious periods of Polish history and culture, and it has led to considerable distortion and romanticizing of the activities of Jagiełło and Jadwiga. Nationalist historians and novelists gave these figures all the virtues, their enemies all possible vices.

Lithuanians have always had an ambiguous attitude toward Jagiełło. They gave their real love to Vytautas, whose relationship with Jagiełło was rarely warmer than cautious mistrust. The Lithuanian attitude is most evident in nationalist analyses of the Battle of Tannenberg. The extreme Lithuanian point of view is that Jagiełło merely attended masses and prayed for victory, while Vytautas devised the brilliant feigned retreat that caused the Teutonic Knights to break their lines and open the way for the Polish attack. The extreme Polish view is that the Germans drove the Lithuanians from the field, so that victory was a result of Jagiełło's inspiring leadership and Polish courage alone. Germans have traditionally disliked Jagiełło, because his victory in Prussia dimmed the only brightness in their declining Holy Roman Empire. A recent change in this attitude reflects the disappearance of the generations that expected historical interpretations to support nationalistic aspirations.

Jadwiga was a strong figure in her lifetime, but she made only a small impression on the historical record. In contrast, no one questions that Jagiełło was one of the great Polish monarchs. Although he was unable to reverse the decline of royal authority, for a short period he restored the unity of the kingdom and defeated or frustrated all enemies. Moreover, he extended Roman Christianity to Lithuania, founded the Jagiellonian University in Kraków (with a legacy from Jadwiga), and established a dynasty that lasted until 1572.

—*William L. Urban*

FURTHER READING

Christiansen, Eric. *The Northern Crusades: The Baltic and the Catholic Frontier, 1100-1525*. Minneapolis: University of Minnesota Press, 1980. The description of the Crusades of the Teutonic Knights from Prussia and Livonia provides helpful background to Jagiełło's conversion. Concise, witty, and well-written.

Davies, Norman. *God's Playground: A History of Poland*. 2 vols. New York: Columbia University Press, 1982. A well-written, scholarly account of medieval Polish history.

Evans, Geoffrey Charles. *Tannenberg: 1410-1914*. London: Hamilton, 1970. This volume, which describes Jagiełło's great victory, is strictly focused on military concerns. It predates archaeological work on the battlefield, thus providing important scholarship.

Halecki, Oskar. *Borderlands of Western Europe: A History of East Central Europe*. New York: Ronald Press, 1952. This work is the standard English-language survey of medieval Poland, Lithuania, and Russia. It has particularly strong coverage of the religious controversies.

Jasienica, Pawel. *Jagiellonian Poland*. Translated by Alexander Jordan. Miami, Fla.: American Institute of Polish Culture, 1978. A well-recommended history of the dynasty that covers Jagiełło. This work is a translation from a standard text used in Poland.

Longworth, Philip. *The Making of Eastern Europe: From Prehistory to Postcommunism*. 2d ed. New York: St. Martin's Press, 1997. This comprehensive history begins with contemporary times and moves backward in time in each successive chapter. The Jagiellons are discussed in the chapter on the cultural and religious tensions of 1352-1526.

Lukowski, Jerzy, and Hubert Zawadski. *A Concise History of Poland*. New York: Cambridge University

Press, 2001. A general introduction to Polish history. Includes a chapter on Jagiellonian Poland.

Reddaway, W. F., et al., eds. *The Cambridge History of Poland*. 2 vols. Cambridge, England: Cambridge University Press, 1950. This set remains a solid, useful work on the history of Poland.

See also: Casimir the Great; Jan Hus; Jan Žižka.

Related articles in *Great Events from History: The Middle Ages, 477-1453*: 1228-1231: Teutonic Knights Bring Baltic Region Under Catholic Control; July 15, 1410: Battle of Tannenberg; 1414-1418: Council of Constance.

Wolfram von Eschenbach

German poet

In the era of the High Middle Ages, Wolfram was a master in the tradition of the courtly epic; his works constitute one of the high points of the narrative writing produced during this first golden age of German literature.

Born: c. 1170; probably Eschenbach bei Ansbach, Franconia (now in Germany)

Died: c. 1217; probably Eschenbach bei Ansbach, Franconia

Area of achievement: Literature

Early Life

As is the case with many medieval figures, little is known about the life of Wolfram von Eschenbach (WOHL-fruhm fuhn EHSH-ehn-bahk). He probably was born and likely also died in the town of Eschenbach bei Ansbach and was a Frankish knight in the service of the count of Wertheim. He was married, had a child, and possessed a modest estate. His grave in the Frauenkirche of Eschenbach was unmarked and has become lost over the centuries. He was well read but received no formal education, felt close to the common people, and was deeply committed to the ideals of Christianity.

He lived during the reign of the Hohenstaufen Dynasty—its most notable ruler being Frederick I Barbarossa. It was the age of the Crusades and feudalism. European knighthood was in full bloom, especially in France, England, and Germany. The knights were the bearers of a culture that centered on the courts of the liege lords to whom they had sworn fealty. During a period when Christianity was in competition with the secular domain for political and cultural hegemony, the ethos of knighthood constituted an attempt to merge religious and profane values.

The courtly culture of the time was a formative influence on Wolfram and his writings. The knightly code of behavior was guided by a number of prominent formal virtues, some of which had descended from older Germanic tribal codes. Honor (*êre*) was foremost and meant that the knight would do nothing in thought or action to disgrace himself or the order of knighthood before God and the king. The courtly culture was concerned with proper form, and a knight's appearance before the world was of the greatest importance. Loyalty (*triuwe*) meant that the knight kept his oath of allegiance to his liege lord. Discipline (*zucht*) indicated that the knight must maintain his proper knightly attitude on the battlefield and in court. Moderation (*mâze*) suggested that he must avoid all extremes and maintain his formal bearing. A knight's goals in life were threefold: to own property (such as an estate), to maintain his honor before his peers, and to strive for God's blessing. As a landed knight, Wolfram was committed to the values of his class, and they are evident in his works. A deeply religious man, he regarded the institution of knighthood as a manifestation of God's will on earth.

The High Middle Ages was also the period of the formalized institution of courtly love (*Minnedienst*). Although occasional sexual liaisons undoubtedly occurred, courtly love was not an erotic affair but a form of spiritualized service in which the knight pledged his loyalty and honor to the defense of a lady of the court and thereby believed himself ennobled. The knight's adoration of his lady was most often manifested in the writing of love poetry (*Minnesang*). Wolfram did write some poetry, although he is not known primarily for this type of literary production.

Life's Work

Wolfram's greatest achievements were in the genre of the courtly heroic epic. Before turning to his individual works, a few words about this form of literature might be in order. The literary models for the German courtly epic came primarily from France in the *chansons de geste*, tales of great heroic deeds, such as the *Chanson de Roland* (c. 1100; *Song of Roland*), and especially in the tales of knightly glory that were associated with the legendary King Arthur and his Round Table. The French writer Chrétien de Troyes, who lived toward the end of the twelfth century, had given classic form to the genre with his Arthurian epics, and his works were an important influence on later German authors.

Wolfram's most famous text was his courtly epic *Parzival* (c. 1200-1210; English translation, 1894), which consists of sixteen sections and was handed down in more than eighty manuscript versions and fragments. The text is written in rhymed couplets, the form characteristic of medieval German narrative poetry. It is based on Chrétien's *Perceval: Ou, Le Conte du Graal* (c. 1180; *Perceval: Or, The Story of the Grail*, 1844), stories surrounding the legendary chalice that was held by Christ at the Last Supper and was used by the disciple Joseph to catch Christ's blood. Wolfram's version is the story of the young and naïve Parzival in his quest for the Holy Grail and for his true relationship to God and knighthood. Parzival serves as a literary representative of his social class.

Since his father, the heroic knight Gachmuret, had been killed on a crusade, Parzival's mother, Herzeloyde, rears her son alone in a secluded wood so that he might be saved from the worldly fate of his father. One day, however, the young boy, unfamiliar with the ways of the world, does meet three knights who advise him to go to the court of King Arthur. Since it was then believed that a knight's noble nature was inborn, Parzival's true heroic heritage is awakened, and he leaves his mother, who dies, in order to pursue his dream of becoming a knight at Arthur's court. There he kills the Red Knight Ither and is instructed in the ways of courtly behavior by Gurnemanz. He is told to be humble and modest and not to ask too many questions.

Wolfram von Eschenbach. (Hulton|Archive at Getty Images)

After becoming betrothed to the beautiful Condwiramurs, he journeys to the Grail Castle, whose lord, Amfortas, lies suffering from a terrible wound. Naïvely following the advice he has received, Parzival does not ask Amfortas about his suffering, and he is told that he shows no pity for his fellowman. Discouraged, he leaves Condwiramurs and Arthur's circle and sets forth into the world, resenting God, who he believes has abandoned him. Parzival shows here that he lacks faith in God's wisdom, and such religious despair is considered a major sin within Christian thought.

Parzival wanders in despair for four years and finally comes on Trevrezent, the brother of Amfortas and the uncle whom he has never known. From Trevrezent, he learns that his mother has died—as well as the secret of Amfortas's wound. He is instructed in the meaning of sin, grace, and faith in God's plan and comes to realize that his rejection of God was a result of his rage and pride. No longer naïve in the ways of God and humankind, Parzival finally attains an inner peace. He leaves his uncle and engages in combat with a strange knight who turns out to be his friend Gawain. They return to Arthur's court, but Parzival longs for Condwira-

MAJOR WORKS BY WOLFRAM VON ESCHENBACH

Date	*Work*
c. 1200	*Lieder*
c. 1200-1210	*Parzival*
c. 1212-1217	*Willehalm*
c. 1217	*Titurel* (*Schionatulander and Sigune*)

murs and the Grail and once more sets out on a journey. He again engages in combat with an unknown knight, Feirefiz, who is his own half brother. They travel back to Arthur's court, where it is announced that Parzival is to be king of the Grail Castle. He is also reunited with his love, Condwiramurs. Having finally attained worldly glory and God's blessing, Parzival spends the remainder of his life committed to serving others in God's name.

Parzival serves as a kind of Everyman figure. His individual destiny describes the road to ideal knighthood and is, broadly speaking, an idealized vision of the path of medieval education. As a boy he is an "innocent," unwise in the ways of the world, but he eventually attains a prowess in battle that defines his social status within the hierarchy of the court. He is on his way to reaching the three goals of the Christian knight (worldly honor, wealth, and God's blessing) but must embark on an arduous journey in order to attain them. These ideals are symbolized by the Grail Castle, a union of secular values (knighthood) and religious faith (the guarding of the sacred chalice). His seeming lack of human compassion (not asking about Amfortas's wound) and his rejection of God during his years of self-imposed exile are symbolically illustrative of the difficulties the individual Christian knight would face in achieving the goals of his station.

Wolfram clearly indicates the Christian idea that despite people's good intentions, sin and guilt are an inevitable result of human existence. Parzival's battles with strange knights who turn out to be friends (Gawain) or relatives (Feirefiz) suggest his "blindness" to those around him. His education must be directed at learning to recognize the truths of his faith and his society: that of the spirit (faith and the acceptance of God's will) and that of his class (learning how to conduct himself properly within courtly society). Parzival's eventual appointment as king of the Grail Castle indicates that he finally does become the ideal knight. His journey moves him from the ignorance and naïveté of childhood to the wisdom and salvation of adulthood.

Wolfram worked on several other epics that remained uncompleted. In *Titurel* (c. 1217; *Schionatulander and Sigune*, 1960), he tells the tragic love story of Sigune and Schionatulander, two of the characters who had appeared briefly in the *Parzival* text. This tale reflects the influence of the courtly love lyric tradition and its idealization of the love experience. Wolfram had also composed some poetry in this genre. In *Willehalm* (c. 1212-1217; English translation, 1977), written during his old age, he narrates the story of William of Toulouse and his battles against the heathen Saracens. This work owes its plot elements to the tradition of the heroic epic with its descriptions of battles and the bravery of the knights who fought them. Its theme focuses on the differences between the Christian and heathen worlds.

SIGNIFICANCE

Along with Gottfried von Strassburg and Hartmann von Aue, Wolfram von Eschenbach is one of the greatest writers in the genre of the courtly epic, and his place within world literature is certain. His works indicate a talented artist with a well-developed sense of humor and fantasy, a visual and highly symbolic narrative style, and a deep concern with Christian values and the ideals of knighthood.

His *Parzival* is one of the few great epics of the German Middle Ages. This tale of its hero's struggles to attain honor before his courtly peers, as well as the grace of God, presents a vision of ideal knighthood but is universal in its appeal. Such themes certainly relate to the individual's experience in the modern world as well as to the life of the medieval man. Whatever their historical time or belief, all human beings must seek at some point in their lives to balance the spiritual and the material, or social, sides of existence.

The story of Parzival's journey through life, his learning of his own strengths and weaknesses as well as the ways of God and the world, has represented in certain respects a model of the maturation of the exemplary individual. This kind of narrative has become, in its later manifestations, a genre in itself, the so-called novel of education (*Bildungsroman*), in which the inner and outer development of the protagonist from youth through adulthood serves as the central theme of the text. Johann Wolfgang von Goethe's *Wilhelm Meisters Lehrjahre* (1795-1796; *Wilhelm Meister's Apprenticeship*, 1825) and Thomas Mann's *Der Zauberberg* (1924; *The Magic Mountain*, 1927) are later examples of this genre. Wolfram's *Parzival* stands at the beginning of this tradition.

—*Thomas F. Barry*

Further Reading

Green, Dennis H. *The Art of Recognition in Wolfram's "Parzival."* New York: Cambridge University Press, 1982. Scholarly analysis of *Parzival*.

Hanlin, Todd C. "Wolfram von Eschenbach." In *Critical Survey of Poetry*, edited by Philip K. Jason. 2d rev. ed. Pasadena, Calif.: Salem Press, 2003. A six-page entry on Wolfram that covers his life and provides analysis of his most significant works.

Hasty, Will, ed. *A Companion to Wolfram's "Parzival."* Columbia: Camden House, 1999. Essays provide analysis of the popular vernacular work as well as social and cultural context.

Hutchins, Eileen. *Parzival: An Introduction*. 1979. Reprint. London: Temple Lodge, 1992. Filled with spiritual wisdom and artistic beauty, *Parzival* is one of the greatest works of world literature. A basic introduction, accessible to students, to the story and its moral significance.

Jones, Martin, and Timothy McFarland, eds. *Wolfram's "Willehalm": Fifteen Essays*. New York: Camden House, 2001. Jones, a senior lecturer in German at King's College, London, and McFarland, a retired senior lecturer in German at University College, London, provide fifteen essays on Wolfram's epic of the Christian-Muslim conflict, placing it in historical and literary context and elucidating the epic's main themes, characters, and techniques.

Poag, James F. *Wolfram von Eschenbach*. New York: Twayne, 1972. A useful introduction with quotations in both English and German. Contains index and bibliography.

Sivertson, Randal. *Loyalty and Riches in Wolfram's "Parzifal."* New York: P. Lang, 1999. A reinterpretation of *Parzival* as the presentation of a conflict in medieval knighthood between the fight for abstract ideals and service for material gain. The author argues that Wolfram's epic defends feudal values that were in a state of decline. Compares works by Chrétien de Troyes and others.

Sullivan, Robert G. *Justice and the Social Context of Early Middle High German Literature*. New York: Routledge, 2001. A history of the Holy Roman Empire hinging on an examination of High German literature and its authors' focus on social, political, and spiritual issues during a time of transformation. Bibliographical references, index.

Weigand, Hermann J. *Wolfram's "Parzival."* Ithaca, N.Y.: Cornell University Press, 1969. General but very good introduction to Wolfram's text by a noted scholar. Contains bibliographic references and index.

See also: Gottfried von Strassburg; Hartmann von Aue; Walther von der Vogelweide.

Related articles in *Great Events from History: The Middle Ages, 477-1453*: After 1000: Development of Miracle and Mystery Plays; c. 1025: Scholars at Chartres Revive Interest in the Classics; c. 1100: Rise of Courtly Love; 1100-1300: European Universities Emerge; 1136: Hildegard von Bingen Becomes Abbess; c. 1145: Prester John Myth Sweeps Across Europe; c. 1180: Chrétien de Troyes Writes *Perceval*; c. 1306-1320: Dante Writes *The Divine Comedy*; c. 1350-1400: Petrarch and Boccaccio Recover Classical Texts.

Wu Hou

Chinese empress (r. 690-705)

Wu Hou, known for her ruthlessness, rose from the position of courtier to became the only woman to rule as empress of China in her own name; she was perhaps the most powerful leader in the world during her lifetime. She was a patron of Buddhism and attempted to elevate the position of women in China.

Born: 625; Chang'an (now Xi'an), Shaanxi Province, China

Died: December 16, 705; Chang'an (now Xi'an), Shaanxi Province, China

Also known as: Wu Zhao (given name), Wu Chao (Wade-Giles); Wu Zetian (Pinyin), Wu Tse-t'ien (Wade-Giles)

Areas of achievement: Government and politics, art, religion and theology

Early Life

The future empress Wu Hou (wew-hoh) of China was born as Wu Zhao into a politically well-connected family in the early years of the Tang Dynasty (T'ang; 618-907). The young woman was selected at an early age to become a minor concubine of the emperor Taizong (T'ai-tsung; r. 627-649). Her father, Wu Shihou (Wu Shih-hou), was a supporter of Gaozu (Kao-tsu, r. 618-626), the first emperor of the Tang, and it was only natural that Wu Shihou's support would be rewarded by the inclusion of his daughter Wu Zhao in the royal court. Later, Wu Zhao would leverage this privileged position; she would plot and intrigue to eventually usurp the throne and eventually rule in her own name.

During Taizong's reign, China reached what was probably the height of its success and power. Taizong's many military reforms led to a consolidation of Chinese power throughout Central Asia and as far north as Korea. Further expansion south into Vietnam and Tibet continued throughout his reign, but periodic uprisings in Yunnan prevented China from achieving full control of the southern region.

The large military expansion was made possible by brilliant financial and economic development, most notably through the issue of new coinage, the *Kaiyuan tongbao*, which became an accepted currency from Vietnam to Japan, and virtually everywhere along the Silk Road to Persia. The new trade coinage not only facilitated trade but also greatly eased the burden of tax collection, permitting the imperial coffers to overflow. Under the watchful Chinese military along the main trade routes of the Silk Road, brigandage was curtailed, and merchants could make the trek from Byzantium to China confident of their security.

The beginnings of trouble for Taizong may have been his failure to manage his own success. The *pax sinica* of the Tang Dynasty greatly stimulated international trade, created a rapidly expanding middle class, and initiated a flowering of cultural arts. This meant that the state had few problems to occupy its time. Therefore, the palace turned inward, and the emperor spent more time engaging in idle pursuits with concubines in the harem than dealing with state affairs. This enabled the courtiers to dominate state politics, a trend that would plague the Tang Dynasty and eventually lead to its downfall.

Life's Work

Wu Zhao's rise to the throne began when she became a minor concubine during the latter years of Taizong's reign. The latter stages of the emperor's reign were marked by dissipation and degeneracy. It is possible that Taizong knew only tangentially of Wu Zhao, as his late years were preoccupied with the selection of a suitable heir. The emperor had more than fourteen sons and numerous daughters, but his favorite sons were effeminate, homosexual, or otherwise unsuitable for the throne. Perhaps in dejection, Taizong finally placed the young and weak Li Zhi (Li Chih), known as Gaozong (Kao-tsung; r. 650-683), on the throne. The controversial choice would place Wu Zhao into a position to seize power.

Gaozong was a poor choice for leader of the world's largest empire. Weak and indecisive, he often turned to his court for decisions of policy. He was also preoccupied with creating his own heir. His first wife, the empress Wang, had failed to give birth to a son. Wu Zhao, however, had become a concubine of Gaozong and had given birth to a son. When Wu Zhao gave birth to a daughter who died, she blamed the empress Wang for the infant's death. The emperor believed Wu Zhao's accusation. The empress Wang was not immediately deposed, but she and a concubine who had given birth to a son were later accused of plotting against the emperor and were imprisoned and eventually executed. Wu Zhao was elevated to the emperor's side as empress.

Wu Zhao quickly became the true power behind the throne. Gaozong, untrained by Taizong for the emperorship, was never able to make decisions for himself or to function as emperor. He was further incapacitated by a stroke in 660, which left him inarticulate and partially paralyzed—an event that consolidated Wu Zhao's power. She quickly created her own branch of the imperial secret police, which then began investigating, framing, and murdering her rivals.

The palace plots and intrigues were able to take place because of a continuing rise in living standards and economic power in China. Wu Zhao's decision to undertake a major military operation in Korea ended with China annexing the peninsula, and major defeats of Sāsānid and Turkish forces consolidated Chinese control over Central Asia. The overall economic prosperity allowed people to concern themselves with arts and religion. Buddhism, which advocated a search for personal enlightenment rather than pursuit of worldly concerns, became increasingly dominant. Wu Zhao was a Buddhist and became an active patron of the religion, while acting to suppress imperial Confucianism, at least in part because of its male supremacist worldview.

After the death of Gaozong at the end of 683, Wu Zhao placed her third son, Li Zhe (Li Che) on the throne in 684, where he would rule as Zhongzong (Chung-tsung; r. 684). However, she realized he would be difficult to control and, within six weeks, replaced him with her fourth son, Li Dang (Li Tang), who became Emperor Ruizong (Jui-tsung, r. 684-690), a puppet emperor. During the year, a failed attempt to assassinate Wu Zhao was the impetus for her to sentence to death nearly half of the imperial family. Virtually all the members of the aristocracy and imperial court as well as high-ranking officials and nobility were replaced by officials loyal to Wu Zhao alone. Under the veil of Ruizong's rule, Wu Zhao reigned supreme.

To begin building support for her sole reign, Wu Zhao actively strove to elevate the place of women, founding a branch of the imperial library to write biographies of famous and influential women. Styling herself Wu Zetian, the sage mother blessed by heaven, she ordered Daoist temples to incorporate statues of the sage mother of the philosopher Laozi (Lao-tzu; 604-sixth century B.C.E.) to generate favorable publicity for a female ruler. She had two of her own daughters inducted into the Lingpao canon of the Daoist faith. Although this may have been primarily to keep her daughters cloistered until she arranged a suitable marriage rather than from a true devotion to Daoism, Wu Zetian's reign was marked by the construction of numerous Daoist temples, and it is clear that she was a patron to Daoists as well as Buddhists.

The Buddhist religion had become increasingly popular in China since the return of the monk Xuanzang (Hsüan-tsang) from India with Buddhist texts in 645. Taizong himself had granted Xuanzang a temple in Chang'an, and the religion spread quickly among both nobles and peasants. Recognizing the potential of using popular Buddhist support, Wu Zetian commissioned a project developing massive Buddhist caves at Longmen (south of Luoyang, Henan Province). The site had been carved out as a Buddhist shrine more than one hundred years earlier, but under Wu Zetian, the shrine would reach eminent status as one of the principal places of Buddhist worship. The main feature of the site is the colossal 57-foot (17-meter) statue of Maitreya, the Buddha of the future, whose facial features were styled after those of Wu Zetian. Construction at the caves began in 673, and the site grew to contain more than 1,300 caves and 100,000 statues. Longmen was named a United Nations Educational, Scientific, and Cultural Organization (UNESCO) World Heritage site.

In addition to Longmen, Wu Zetian was a major patron for the temple of Famensi (the open doorway temple) in modern-day Fufang, Shaanxi Province. The discovery of a *sarira*, or reliquary of the Buddha, at the site during archaeological excavation has led Sinologist Roderick Whitfield to speculate that some of the objects uncovered may have been interred by Wu Zetian herself. Notable among the findings was a small monk's robe, about doll sized, covered with stylistic white clouds. These clouds may be reflective of the *Bai hua jing* (white cloud sutra), a Buddhist text that was "discovered" by the monk Xue Huaiyi. The sutra became a critical text supporting the legitimacy of Wu Zetian's reign; her translator interpreted the text as proclaiming that a female ruler with Wu Zetian's qualities would appear on the earth and that this ruler would be the reincarnation of Maitreya, the future Buddha. During the time the Maitreya spent on the earth, the texts indicated that there would be bountiful harvests and that people would not suffer illnesses.

To propagate the text, Buddhist temples in honor of Maitreya were established throughout the empire. The main carving of the Longmen Maitreya began after the discovery of this text. The Buddhists "discovered" several auspicious omens in 690. In view of this development, Ruizong abdicated, and Wu Zetian went through the imperial rituals to become empress. Her first action changed the dynastic title from Tang to Zhou, proclaiming a new era of the universal ruler.

Wu Zetian ultimately turned her back on ruling and occupied most of her time with a pair of young lovers, the Zhang brothers, who grew to be bullies in the court and openly corrupt. By 705, Wu Zetian's hold on power had grown weak, and she could not prevent the assassination of the Zhang brothers. She abdicated in favor of Zhongzong, placing him on the throne for the second time. Bereft of power and with few friends, she died not long after her abdication. After her death, Wu Zetian was interred beside Gaozong in the Qianling Mausoleum, north of modern Xi'an.

Significance

The upward climb of Wu Hou (her posthumous name) bears striking similarity to the rise of Theodora, wife of the Byzantine emperor Justinian (r. 527-565). Theodora had been an exotic dancer, an actress, a Monophysite Christian, and probably a prostitute before becoming the wife of Justinian. Justinian, who in his early years was marked by indecision, was pushed to strength by Theodora's impassioned speech to him during the Nika revolt of 532. The event strengthened Justinian's resolve and encouraged him to rule ably. Thus, Wu Hou and Theodora both played a strong role in politics, and their rise was anathema to the upper classes. Although Wu Hou ultimately was able to rule in her own name, Theodora was never recognized as augusta—or empress—in her own right, as Justinian realized that this would push the nobility too far.

Modern Chinese historians often view the reign of Wu Hou as that of a brutal and depraved usurper, but they agree that she certainly changed the perception of the strength and position of women in Chinese society. After Wu Hou's reign, no woman in China would ever rule in her own name, although many women would wield real power behind the scenes. The Buddhist caves, temples, and statues created as a result of Wu Hou's patronage of Buddhism are a lasting legacy, providing examples of the art and architecture of Tang China.

—*Jason D. Sanchez*

Further Reading

Jiang, Cheng An. *Empress of China, Wu Ze Tian*. Monterey, Calif.: Victory Press, 1998. A young adult work that presents Wu Hou in a favorable light.

McCune, Evelyn. *Empress*. New York: Ballantine, 1994. A work of historical fiction, this is nevertheless a well-researched and enjoyable piece that romanticizes some of the details of Wu Hou's life.

Paludan, Ann. *Chronicles of the Chinese Emperors*. London: Thames and Hudson, 1993. Paludan's popular account of the rulers of China contains good biographical and bibliographic material but is more suitable for the layperson rather than the serious academic, who will want to use the standard Chinese imperial biographies.

Paul, Diana. "Empress Wu and the Historians." In *Unspoken Worlds: Women's Religous Lives in Non-Western Cultures*, edited by Nancy Falk and Rita Gross. New York: Harper and Row, 1980. A concise examination of the treatment of Wu Hou by various historians.

Tian, Hengyu. *Wu Zetian: The Mighty Woman Sovereign of China*. Hong Kong: Asiapac Books, 1997. Not strictly a scholarly work, Tian's book nevertheless serves as a fine introduction to the debate on whether Wu Hou was a wicked or good ruler.

See also: Taizong.

Related articles in *Great Events from History: The Middle Ages, 477-1453*: 618: Founding of the Tang Dynasty; 629-645: Pilgrimage of Xuanzang; 690-705: Reign of Empress Wu; 845: Suppression of Buddhism; 907-960: Period of Five Dynasties and Ten Kingdoms; 960: Founding of the Song Dynasty.

JOHN WYCLIF

English philosopher and theologian

Wyclif's ideas became the rallying point for demands for religious reform in England and influenced the Hussite movement in Bohemia, preparing the way for the Reformation. Wyclif's emphasis on the authority of Scripture and the priesthood of the believer inspired the first translation of the entire Bible into English.

BORN: c. 1328; Wyclif-on-Tees, Yorkshire, England
DIED: December 31, 1384; Lutterworth, Leicestershire, England
ALSO KNOWN AS: John Wycliffe; John Wiclif
AREAS OF ACHIEVEMENT: Religion and theology, philosophy

EARLY LIFE

Little is known about the early years of John Wyclif. His family was of the lesser aristocracy; they held the manor and living of Wiclif in Richmond, in the lands of John of Gaunt, the duke of Lancaster. Wyclif entered Oxford sometime around 1345. There is little evidence and much conjecture concerning his career at the university. Three different colleges claim Wyclif as a student: Queen's, Merton, and Balliol. It is known that he took his first degree in the arts, and sometime between 1356 (when he might have become a probationary fellow at Merton) and 1360, he became a regent master in the arts at Balliol.

Wyclif resigned his mastership at Balliol in 1361 and was instituted to the collegiate living of Fillingham in Lincolnshire. It is almost incontestable that he had advanced to the priesthood by then. In 1363, he was granted a license from the bishop of Lincoln to absent himself from Fillingham to return to Oxford; his new course of study was in theology. It appears that Wyclif took a bachelor of divinity degree about 1369. In 1368, he had been granted another license from his bishop for nonresidency at Fillingham and then in the same year exchanged that living for the parish of Ludgershall, which was closer to Oxford.

Wyclif obtained his master of theology degree by December, 1373. Shortly thereafter, probably with John of Gaunt's sponsorship, he entered the king's service. While in royal service, Wyclif was appointed to the English deputation, which met at Bruges with papal representatives to negotiate the outstanding differences between England and Rome. On April 7, 1374, King Edward III presented him with the rectory of Lutterworth in Leicestershire, which he was to hold until his death.

LIFE'S WORK

During his Oxford years, Wyclif had established himself as a significant voice in the philosophical debates of his time. Central to these debates was the ongoing opposition between realism and nominalism; in this context, "realism" denotes a belief in the reality of essences independent of the temporally existing objects of perception. Wyclif was an unabashed realist at a time when nominalism was growing increasingly dominant, but had he restricted himself to this issue, narrowly defined, he would not have occasioned controversy outside university circles. As he developed the theological implications of his metaphysics, however, Wyclif entered the public arena with a vengeance, for his was a time in which theological and political issues were inextricably intertwined.

Wyclif came to maturity during the so-called Babylonian Captivity of the Church, the period from 1305 to 1378 when the Papacy was based in Avignon instead of Rome and successive popes were controlled by the French throne. (Wyclif lived to see the beginning of the Great Schism, the period from 1378 to 1417 during which there were rival popes, one at Avignon and one at Rome.) Throughout the fourteenth century, the prestige of the Papacy was low, corruption was widespread, and calls for clerical reform were commonplace. Wyclif's developing views, however, went far beyond most of these criticisms, for they rested on a radical redefinition of the Church itself.

In keeping with his metaphysical distinction between unchanging universals and temporal particulars, Wyclif distinguished the true Church from the visible Church. The true Church consists of those and only those who, before the beginning of time, were elected by God. Because it is God's choice alone that determines membership, the priesthood of the visible Church cannot claim to initiate individuals into or exclude them from the true Church.

Wyclif thus shifted authority from the Church hierarchy to the Bible, which he regarded as the sole rule of faith and practice—a shift with historic consequences, to be fully realized in the Reformation. Wyclif held that every one of those elected by God was a priest. He noted that the New Testament did not distinguish between priests and bishops, and that they, as church officials, should be honored only because of their character. He implored them to set a good example for their flock through their personal lives. Sincerity in worship, he argued, was of more value than form or ritual; indeed, elaboration and formalization of worship services might hinder true worship. He urged that the Bible be translated into the English vernacular so that the priests could better include scriptural passages in their sermons. He argued that the Scriptures were the supreme authority and that priests and bishops should be familiar with them; he urged priests to stress the exposition of biblical passages rather than the recounting of fables, miracles, and saints' lives. He also insisted that even unlettered and simple men could understand the Scriptures and should study them.

Clearly, Wyclif's patron, John of Gaunt, an antipapist, was alert to the political implications of Wyclif's views, as spelled out in 1376 in public readings of his treatise *De civili dominio* (1376-1377). In this work Wyclif argued that all temporal ecclesiastical ownership is God's and that God's granting of the use of the property was conditional on the holder rendering faithful service. A stated corollary was that if an ecclesiastical holder continually misused his holdings, he could be stripped of them by the secular power. Wyclif maintained that individual popes might err; he even considered worldly popes to be heretics and suggested that as such they should be removed from office. He also stated that the Papacy was not necessary for the administration of the Church.

His public preaching of these ideas caused English ecclesiastical attention to focus on him as he gained increasing popular support for his views. Bishop Courtenay of London and Archbishop Sudbury of Canterbury forced his appearance before a Convocation held at St. Paul's, London, in February, 1377. This proceeding against him ended, however, without Wyclif being molested or condemned when John of Gaunt's retainers disrupted the inquiry and removed him. It is obvious that Wyclif enjoyed great aristocratic support at this time.

Within months of the St. Paul's confrontation, Pope Gregory XI issued five papal bulls that condemned eighteen errors found in Wyclif's pronouncements. The Papacy urged, but did not command, the arrest of the Oxford don. The king died, the archbishop delayed, and the university would not condemn. Wyclif allowed himself to be placed under house arrest in Black Hall. He refused to appear again at St. Paul's, but he did face the bishops at Lambeth Palace in 1378. His popular support was now perhaps at its greatest; he had significant political support, and his trial produced nothing more than an innocuous warning to him.

The year 1378, however, was also the initial year of the Great Schism. The spectacle of two popes locked in conflict was for Wyclif an infuriating one, and he became even more critical of the Church. He demanded thorough reform of the Church: that it be stripped of its endowments and that these be distributed to the poor; that ecclesiastical temporal holdings be given to the king and the other secular lords; that ecclesiastics surrender all temporal offices and that these henceforth be held only by laymen (Wyclif complained that the secular hierarchy labored more in the king's business than they labored with the cure of the souls—he proposed that the bishops' wealth be stripped from them and that they be confined solely to spiritual ministration); that the Church surrender all of its judicial administration to the royal courts (he was especially critical of the use of archdeacons within the ecclesiastical courts, because so often the archdeacons were aliens); and that all pastors should preach from

John Wyclif. (Library of Congress)

the Gospels and be dependent on their flock for their sustenance and clothing. Wyclif denounced the monks and the friars for their vast holdings and was especially critical of the monasteries' use of lay brethren to do the physical labor. He additionally attacked the friars for setting bad examples that influenced the religious life of the laymen (he charged that they had reduced the sacrament of confession to a farce and that they twisted the words of the Bible out of their true meaning).

It was Wyclif's attack on the doctrine of transubstantiation, however, that became the focus of the ecclesiastical hierarchy's attention and caused a second examination of his opinions. While affirming that Christ was in some manner present in the bread and the wine of the Mass, Wyclif denied the orthodox belief of the miracle of the Mass as defined in the doctrine of transubstantiation. In 1380, by a vote of seven to five, a committee of Oxford doctors condemned Wyclif's statements as being heretical. Shortly thereafter Wyclif left Oxford and retired to his parish at Lutterworth. Another committee was summoned to Blackfriars, London, in May of 1382. It examined twenty-four of Wyclif's conclusions and found ten to be heretical and the other fourteen to be merely erroneous. Two of Wyclif's most ardent Oxford followers felt the fury of the Blackfriars Synod: Philip Repingdon was forced to recant his belief in Wyclif's opinions, and Nicholas of Hereford fled to Rome for safety. Wyclif himself, however, remained at Lutterworth unmolested by the English church.

At Lutterworth, his works became yet more polemical. In addition to completing a series of theological writings in Latin, he wrote a series of English sermons. He was summoned to Rome in 1382 but cited his incapacity to travel because of a stroke, a justified excuse for it left him partly paralyzed. During 1383, Wyclif's scorn for the temporal involvement of the Church intensified because of the crusade into Flanders led by Henry Despenser, bishop of Norwich. A second severe stroke struck Wyclif as he was hearing Mass at Lutterworth on December 28, 1384. He died three days later and, not having been excommunicated, was buried in consecrated ground.

After his death, the force of the Church effected its way. In 1410, his works were publicly burned at Prague and at Oxford. In 1415, the Council of Constance (1414-1418) ordered his remains to be dug up and scattered to the four winds. In 1428, Richard Fleming, bishop of Lincoln, actually carried out this loathsome operation: He dug up the bones of Wyclif, burned them, and cast them into the River Swith.

SIGNIFICANCE

Assessments of Wyclif's influence are sometimes clouded by exaggerated claims. Such claims are not needed to establish his contributions, which stand on their own merit. It is sometimes alleged, for example, that Wyclif's theories were responsible for fomenting the Peasants' Revolt of 1381. Yet, while some of his prescriptions for ecclesiastical reform overlapped with the ideas spread by the "poor priests" who helped to instigate the revolt, that movement was sparked mainly by economic and social concerns, not religious ones.

Wyclif is also frequently credited with having made the first translation of the entire Bible into English. While this claim is in error—there is little evidence that Wyclif himself undertook any of the translation work—his influence in this area was indeed significant. It is incontestable that the first full translation of the Bible into English was made by followers of Wyclif as a direct result of his emphasis on the authority of Scripture and the priesthood of the believer. The first Wyclifite translation, produced in 1380, was marred by an attempt to reproduce Latin word order in English. In 1384, however, Wyclif's secretary, John Purvey, produced a much-revised translation that is notable for the idiomatic freshness of its English.

Wyclif's writings, influential in England during his lifetime but soon lost to the public eye, had their greatest direct impact in Bohemia, where the martyr Jan Hus, an ardent follower of Wyclif, helped to prepare the way for the Reformation. Through Hus, Wyclif had a significant impact on Martin Luther and others among the great reformers.

—*Dale E. Landon*

FURTHER READING

Dahmus, Joseph H. *The Prosecution of John Wyclyf.* New Haven, Conn.: Yale University Press, 1952. A revisionary work on Wyclif that is an indispensable corrective to Workman's standard biography. It investigates the most crucial aspects of Wyclif's public life. Valuable interpretation of Wyclif's distance from the "poor priests" and the Lollards.

Kenny, Anthony. *Wyclif.* Oxford, England: Oxford University Press, 1985. This slim volume in the Past Masters series offers an excellent introduction to Wyclif's life and thought. The author places greater emphasis on Wyclif's philosophical concerns than is found in most studies.

_______, ed. *Wyclif in His Time*. Oxford, England: Clarendon Press, 1986. This work features the 1984 Wyclif commemorative lectures at Balliol by Anne Hudson, Gordon Leff, and Maurice Keen and several other articles by Wyclif specialists. Valuable for several issues concerning Wyclif.

Lahey, Stephen E. *Philosophy and Politics in the Thought of John Wyclif.* New York: Cambridge University Press, 2003. Part of the Cambridge Studies in Medieval Life and Thought series, presents Wyclif's philosophical and political ideas. Bibliography, index.

Long, John D. *The Bible in English: John Wycliffe and William Tyndale*. Lanham, Md.: University Press of America, 1998. Considers the lives and sacrifices of Wyclif and William Tyndale, addressing their roles in translating the Latin Vulgate and the New Testament, respectively.

McFarlane, K. B. *John Wycliffe and the Beginnings of English Nonconformity.* New York: Macmillan, 1953. The author proposes that Wyclif's excesses and those of his disciples made reform disreputable and thus drove it "underground." Follows the view that Wyclif and the Lollards were closely linked.

Robson, John A. *Wyclif and the Oxford Schools*. Cambridge, England: Cambridge University Press, 1961. A valuable examination of Wyclif's philosophical and theological development. Concentrates on his early years at Oxford and the philosophers and theologians whose writings influenced Oxford thought.

Workman, Herbert B. *John Wyclif: A Study of the English Medieval Church*. 2 vols. Oxford, England: Clarendon Press, 1926. The standard biography of Wyclif, still useful but in many respects outdated.

See also: Pietro d'Abano; Peter Abelard; Saint Dominic; Edward III; Jan Hus; Joan of Arc; Margery Kempe; Lady Alice Kyteler; William of Ockham; Marguerite Porete; Thomas à Kempis; Lorenzo Valla; Jan Žižka.

Related articles in *Great Events from History: The Middle Ages, 477-1453*: 1305-1417: Avignon Papacy and the Great Schism; c. 1310-1350: William of Ockham Attacks Thomist Ideas; July 2, 1324: Lady Alice Kyteler Is Found Guilty of Witchcraft; 1377-1378: Condemnation of John Wyclif; 1414-1418: Council of Constance; July 6, 1415: Martyrdom of Jan Hus.

XIA GUI

Chinese painter

Together with Ma Yuan, Xia Gui formed the Ma-Xia school of painting, which was extremely influential in the subsequent development of landscape painting in China and Japan.

BORN: c. 1180; Qiantang (now Hangzhou), Zhejiang Province, China
DIED: 1230; Hangzhou, Zhejiang Province, China
ALSO KNOWN AS: Hsia Kuei (Wade-Giles)
AREA OF ACHIEVEMENT: Art

EARLY LIFE

Known as the younger contemporary of painter Ma Yuan (c. 1165-c. 1225), Xia Gui (sheeah gwee) served the Southern Song emperors Ningzong (Ning-tsung; r. 1195-1224) and Lizong (Li-tsung; r. 1225-1264). Little information exists about Xia Gui's life. It is known that, like Ma Yuan, Xia received the Golden Girdle honor from the court and was artist-in-attendance at the imperial palace in Hangzhou. Unlike Ma, however, who came from northwestern China, Xia was apparently born very close to the capital, and Chinese art critics intimate that Xia received imperial honors earlier in his life than did Ma.

Hangzhou had become the capital in 1126, when an alliance between the Chinese of the Northern Song (Sung; 960-1127) and the Tungusic Jurchen turned sour, and North China fell to the Jurchen. The Northern Song rulers fled to the Yangtze and settled into what was, at the time, an unimposing provincial capital situated at the mouth of the Zhe estuary. The imperial court apparently chose the town in part because it was easier to defend against "barbarians" but also because of the beauty of its location. Hangzhou is surrounded by scenic hills and lies just east of what is perhaps China's most attractive lake, Hu.

In keeping with the generally favorable climate for commerce that characterized the Northern Song period, trade continued to flourish during the Southern Song era (1127-1279). As a consequence, Hangzhou grew into a bustling trade center and by the middle of the thirteenth century had a population of more than half a million people. It also became what many consider to be China's most beautiful city, with scenic canals winding through the town. The wealthy led luxurious lives, living in multistoried villas replete with servants, gardens, and amenities brought to China from all over the globe. Scholars, poets, and painters lived near or within the court, and the favored professionals led fairly comfortable lives, with fancy titles and imperial stipends. Undoubtedly, Xia was one of the favorite artists of the Southern Song court, and like Ma Yuan, he chose subject matter that reflected his lifestyle and that of his patrons. Many of his paintings are found on fans, album leaves, and silk scrolls. Like Ma Yuan, Xia used ink and slight traces of color on silk. He often depicted night scenes of China's elite enjoying the scenic splendors of Hangzhou or diverting themselves with pleasant pastimes.

This idyllic situation was, however, somewhat deceiving, as the Chinese during the Southern Song chafed at the fact that North China was in barbarian hands. After 1234, the situation grew progressively worse, as the Jurchen Dynasty, known as the Jin, succumbed to the Mongol successors of Genghis Khan. From 1234 on, as the Mongol Empire continued to expand, the threat to the Southern Song was never really far from the minds of China's literati, and Hangzhou exhibited an almost *fin de siècle* atmosphere. Xia's paintings, perhaps even more than those of Ma Yuan, reflected a sense of impending change. Whereas Ma was a northerner who had moved to the imperial court in the south and was therefore strictly a courtier, Xia was a native of Zhejiang Province, presumably with a less sophisticated background.

LIFE'S WORK

Although less is known about Xia Gui than about Ma Yuan (and fewer of Xia's paintings are extant), in many ways, Xia revealed more of himself through his art than did Ma. In fact, Xia went beyond Ma in exploring new avenues of self-expression. Like Ma, Xia used the ax-stroke technique of painting mountains, generally attributed to the great Northern Song painter Li Tang (Li T'ang). This technique has been likened to hacking out the angular features and crevices of the rocks with the side of a brush. Xia also adopted Ma's tendency to emphasize one corner of his painting, though not nearly to the degree that Ma did.

Xia's paintings tend to be much simpler and yet more emotional than those of Ma. Whereas Ma tended to be elegant and subdued, Xia exhibited what one could almost call humility in his work. Perhaps Xia was deferring to Ma's age; perhaps the difference in style merely reflects Xia's humbler background. It is equally possible, however, that Xia Gui held different Daoist beliefs and avoided the occasional vanities that appear in Ma Yuan's paintings. As scholar Max Loehr has pointed out, in Xia Gui's paintings,

> the dramatically bent and twisted pines of the Ma school are replaced by less conspicuous types of deciduous trees; . . . Ma's architecture gives way to rustic abodes. . . . Even Hsia's figures appear to be humbler folk than Ma's aristocratic types.

Chinese critics have suggested that Xia was clearly more expressive than Ma and that the former's paintings had a greater sense of urgency and passion. Moreover, it appears that Xia was less interested in humans than in nature, and, like nature, Xia could exhibit changing moods, even within one work.

In some of Xia's works, for example, one may find a soft setting of mountains bathed in an evening mist, while a lone fisherman's boat drifts gently in a quiet stream. As with Ma, the empty spaces become as important as the painted areas, for the viewer is expected to determine, using his own imagination, whether these are clouds, rain, or a mystical Daoist-Chan void. In such paintings, there is economy without affectation, subtlety without mannerism, and a sense of peace. In other works, Xia seems anxious to show flux and movement by suggesting ominous possibilities. Here, there is distortion, asymmetry, and passionate uncertainty. Trees are larger than they should be, the rocks seem ready to fall, mountains vie with one another, and the water is turbulent and uninviting. These works are a reminder that fall and winter, in providing the eternal changes of life, do not always do so in a gentle fashion. In keeping with this genuinely Daoist understanding of nature's vagaries, there are some works by Xia that suggest transitional stages, in which serenity lies juxtaposed to passion. Always, however, as yin is to yang, one is in ascendancy while the other is subordinated and therefore lies in the background.

As with Ma, Chinese explanations of Xia's motifs range from the poetical-philosophical to the dreary political. Again, Xia may have been reacting to the circumstances north of the Southern Song Empire. If this was so, however, it is far less pronounced than in Ma's works. It may be that Xia felt less compelled to reflect the court's political sentiments in his paintings than did Ma. Xia's family did, however, enjoy imperial patronage, and at least one of his sons, Xia Sen, was also a court painter. Only a few of Xia Sen's paintings have survived, and little is known about him.

In the United States, works attributed to Xia Gui can be found in the Boston Museum of Fine Art, the Freer Gallery, the Metropolitan Museum in New York, and galleries in Cleveland, Fort Worth, Indianapolis, Kansas City, and San Francisco. Unfortunately, some of these are probably forgeries, copied from the originals during the Ming (1368-1644) or early Ching (Ch'ing; 1644-1912) dynasties. Because of the great Japanese admiration for Xia, which began during the Ashikaga period (Muromachi; 1336-1573), many more of his works are located throughout Japan. In particular, several private Japanese galleries have excellent examples of Xia's work. The Beijing and Taipei palace museums also have fine collections by Xia Gui.

SIGNIFICANCE

During several centuries subsequent to the fall of the Southern Song Dynasty in 1279, Xia Gui, together with Ma Yuan, suffered the stigma of having labored for a weak and ultimately supine imperial court. Furthermore, Chinese critics labeled the two as being leaders of the so-called northern school of painters, which the critics considered substantially inferior to the southern, or proper, school. This was not as much a criticism of their style as it was a suggestion that gentlemen-scholars do not paint for a living but rather pursue art only as a hobby to complement scholarship. Another reproach that later critics aimed at the two, although perhaps more at Ma than at Xia, was that they were academic painters whose technique could be learned. This criticism, however, misses the mark, for there is no question that the totality of a Xia painting is unique, and its spirit defies imitation.

Much like Ma Yuan, Xia Gui drew on existing styles and techniques. In addition to the aforementioned ax-stroke and one-cornered methods, Xia used the squeezed-brush technique to paint mountains, and his water was of the fighting-water style. The sum total of his work, however, marks him not merely as one of the two luminaries of the influential Ma-Xia school but also as one of the dominant figures in Chinese landscape painting. Xia's greatest influence, however, may not have been on subsequent Chinese painters, but rather on numerous schools of Japanese art. Initially, during the Ashikaga shogunate, the works of Ma Yuan were more in demand in Japan than were those of Xia. By the time of Nōami (1397-1494), however, a definite shift had occurred, and Xia Gui had become a legendary figure among Japanese artists. Several of his techniques were of great importance in the development of Japanese painting from the late fifteenth century through the Tokugawa shogunate (1603-1867). To this day, Xia's paintings are greatly admired by Japanese collectors.

By the middle of the Ming Dynasty (1368-1644), there was already substantial praise for Xia Gui among Chinese art critics. The considerable interest in Xia shown by the Japanese and, more recently, by Western critics has led to an even greater admiration of Xia in China itself, and Chinese critics today are rightfully proud of this great artist.

—*Hilel B. Salomon*

FURTHER READING

Barnhart, Richard M., et al. *Three Thousand Years of Chinese Painting*. New Haven, Conn.: Yale University Press, 1997. The chapter "The Five Dynasties and the Song Period (907-1279)" discusses the Ma-Xia painters. This oversize book includes beautiful color plates and a helpful glossary.

Cahill, James. *Chinese Painting*. New York: Rizzoli International, 1977. Contains a chapter devoted to Ma Yuan, Xia Gui, and Ma Lin, with examples of their work.

_______. *An Index of Early Chinese Painters and Paintings: T'ang, Sung, and Yuan*. Berkeley: University of California Press, 1980. Contains a lengthy list of paintings attributed to Xia Gui that are located in museums and private collections.

Fong, Wen C., and James Watt. *Possessing the Past: Treasures from the National Palace Museum, Taipei*. New York: The Metropolitan Museum of Art, 1996. Informative discussions of the Ma-Xia school and its artists, especially in the chapter on the Imperial Painting Academy of the Song Dynasty. Beautifully illustrated with examples of paintings by the Ma-Xia artists.

Lee, Sherman. *Chinese Landscape Painting*. 1954. Reprint. Cleveland, Ohio: Cleveland Museum of Art, 1962. Contains examples of Xia's art, together with a brief critique of his technique.

Loehr, Max. *The Great Painters of China*. New York: Harper and Row, 1980. Contains a very brief sketch of Xia Gui's life and an excellent discussion of his technique. Also has several photographs of Xia's paintings.

Sullivan, Michael. *The Arts of China*. 4th ed. Berkeley: University of California Press, 1999. Contains a brief passage about Ma Yuan and Xia Gui with examples of their work.

SEE ALSO: Ma Yuan; Yan Liben.

RELATED ARTICLE in *Great Events from History: The Middle Ages, 477-1453*: c. 1190-1279: Ma-Xia School of Painting Flourishes.

XUANZANG

Chinese monk and religious leader

Xuanzang provided the Chinese with their first reliable informational about India, translated many classical Buddhist texts into the Chinese language, and founded the Weishi school of Chinese Buddhism.

BORN: c. 602; Luoyang, Henan Province, China

DIED: 664; Chang'an (now Xi'an), China

ALSO KNOWN AS: Hsüan-tsang (Wade-Giles); Chen Yi (given name, Pinyin), Ch'en I (Wade-Giles); Tang Sanzang (Pinyin), T'ang San-tsang (Wade-Giles); Tipiṭaka Master; Master of the Law

AREAS OF ACHIEVEMENT: Religion and theology, exploration, literature, monasticism

EARLY LIFE

Xuanzang (shewan-tsahng) was raised in a family of scholars and civil servants. One grandfather had been president of the Imperial College of Beijing. Xuanzang's immediate family, nevertheless, was poor because his father, Chen Hui, refused to serve as an official of the Sui Dynasty (581-618), presumably because he did not want to be associated with a dictatorial and corrupt regime that had a reputation for exploiting poor peasants. Although Xuanzang was educated in the classical Confucian tradition, he was greatly influenced by his brother who became a Buddhist monk and an outstanding scholar of the Buddhist scriptures.

At the age of thirteen, Xuanzang left home and entered a monastery. Initially, he became a monk as a means of securing a livelihood. Once there, however, he approached the study of the sutras with great dedication. By the time he was fifteen, he was recognized as a knowledgeable scholar in the Mahāyāna (or "great vehicle") school of Buddhism, which taught that boddhisattvas (people who had reached enlightenment but postponed nirvana to aid others) who would help individuals find enlightenment. Because the last years of the Sui Dynasty saw terrible famine and civil war, Xuanzang was forced to move south to live in Sichuan Province, where he studied the theories of Hīnayāna (or "small vehicle") Buddhism, which taught that each person must seek enlightenment without assistance.

With a fervent desire to learn to distinguish between truth and falsehood, Xuanzang went to various cities in China to study with several of the great Buddhist masters. He was increasingly troubled by the apparent contradictions and discrepancies among the alternative schools of thought. Not satisfied with the answers of the Chinese masters, he resolved to make a pilgrimage to India to study and meditate in the same places in which the Buddha had lived and worked. He also hoped to find and bring back as many sacred texts of Buddhism as possible, thereby establishing "true and genuine" interpretations of the Buddhist religion. He looked forward to sitting at the feet of the masters of Buddhist thought in India. He was inspired by the example of Faxian (Fa-hsien), a monk who had traveled to India two centuries earlier.

Taizong (T'ai-tsung; r. 627-649), the powerful emperor of the recently established Tang Dynasty (T'ang; 618-907), refused to grant Xuanzang a travel permit to leave China. However, the stubborn monk was determined to make the voyage. To prepare for the mountainous journey, he reportedly piled up tables and chairs to simulate mountains and practiced jumping from one pile to another. Monks observing his strange behavior wondered why he was jumping on furniture rather than meditating and reciting the sutras.

LIFE'S WORK

In 629, a reoccurrence of famine conditions provided Xuanzang with the opportunity to travel westward. Joining hundreds of hungry refugees, he traveled along the Silk Road, crossing dry deserts and snowy mountains. His guide tried to murder him, and numerous times, he almost died of hunger and thirst. The Chinese police caught and detained him in the Taklimakan Desert. Initially, they planned to send him back to China, but when Xuanzang insisted that he would rather die than return, the commanding officer, a devout Buddhist, finally agreed to let him continue his pilgrimage. To avoid police outposts, Xuanzang took detours that were extremely treacherous.

After traveling more than a thousand miles (sixteen hundred kilometers), Xuanzang stopped at the oasis center of Turfan, on the northern edge of the Taklimakan Desert. The king of Turfan, impressed with the monk's learning, insisted that he stay and work as a teacher in the village. The king allowed him to leave only after he threatened a hunger strike. The king then gave him some money and letters of introduction to help him obtain safe passage through the various kingdoms along the way to India.

Traveling by horse, by camel, and by foot, Xuanzang next visited the oasis centers of Kucha, Aksu, and Kashgar (modern-day Kashi). He continued through the Turugart Pass and the towns of Tokmak, Tashkent, and Samarqand. He then headed eastward across the Hindu Kush Mountains of modern-day Afghanistan and Pakistan, until he entered Kashmir in northwest India. He then sailed down the Ganges River until he reached the holy places in and around Nepal in which the Buddha had lived. He was about five thousand miles (eight thousand kilometers) from his home in Xi'an, and his voyage had lasted a little more than two years. For the next several months, Xuanzang visited the holy sites and fervently meditated. He also began the difficult task of learning to read and communicate in the Sanskrit language.

During his twelve-year stay in India, Xuanzang spent much of his time at the Buddhist monastery at Nalanda, which at the time was the greatest center of Buddhist learning in the world. At Nalanda, he studied under a saintly monk named Silabhadra, whose mystical Buddhism would profoundly influence his thought. He also studied Hinduism and other Indian religious traditions. Both monks and laypeople in India learned to respect his scholarship and dedication of purpose. In several theological debates, he argued in favor of the Mahāyāna point of view. One debate lasted eighteen days. His disciples reported that he was victorious.

After a few years at Nalanda, Xuanzang made a long excursion to visit the extremities of India. He sailed to the city of Calcutta and then traveled along the eastern coast as far south as Madras. He wanted to visit the island of Sri Lanka, but conditions of civil war and famine made it impossible for him to go there. Next he crossed over the Indian mainland to Bombay, finally returning to Nalanda. During his trip, he collected Buddhist scriptures and had discussions with ascetic hermits. On more than one occasion, he had visions and other mystical experiences.

As his reputation for scholarship and piety spread far and wide, the powerful king of northern India, Harṣa, became his patron. Harṣa wanted him to stay in India but finally agreed to let him return to China in 643. Because the king provided him with considerable financial assistance, Xuanzang's return to China was not nearly as difficult as his earlier voyage to India. He took with him twenty-two horses loaded with some 520 cases of Buddhist texts, relics, and religious images. Because the return trip was not illegal, he was able to take a more direct route than the way he came.

When Xuanzang arrived at the Tang capital of Xi'an in 645, he had been gone about sixteen years. By this time, the Tang government had managed to establish conditions of relative stability and prosperity, especially when compared with the violence and poverty of the latter years of the Sui Dynasty. Xuanzang received an enthusiastic welcome. Emperor Taizong, was so impressed with his accounts of the lands of the west that he offered him a position as a high official. Xuanzang declined the offer, for he was determined to devote the his life to translating, writing, and meditating.

At the request of the emperor, Xuanzang agreed to write about the cultures and politics of the lands he had visited. The work he produced, *Datang xiyouji* (c. 650; *Buddhist Records of the Western World*, 1884), has long been recognized as one of the great classics of Chinese literature. It provides information about Xuanzang's life in India and during his travels and is one of the major sources of information about the medieval history of China, Central Asia, and especially India. Archaeologists frequently carry the work with them when working on digs. All educated Chinese have heard about the travels of Xuanzang through historical and fictional works. Hundreds of novels, stories, and plays have been written about his search for truth and enlightenment, including the popular *Xiyouji* (c. 1570-c. 1580, oldest surviving edition, 1592; *Journey to the West*, 1977-1983) by Wu Cheng'en, in which a magical monkey king helps Xuanzang.

Xuanzang brought back almost six hundred Buddhist texts from India. For the rest of his life, he diligently worked at translating these texts from Sanskrit into Chinese, eventually translating about seventy-three of them. The difficult work of translation allowed Xuanzang to become an outstanding authority on the Buddhist scriptures called the *Tipiṭaka* (compiled c. 250 B.C.E.; English translation in *Buddhist Scriptures*, 1913), or "three baskets," so that he was named the Tipiṭaka Master. Because these scriptures were commonly called the law, some Buddhist writers refer to him as the Master of the Law.

By the time of his return to China, Xuanzang was firmly committed to the mystical school of Indian thought known as Yogācāra. In essence, this school held that the material world does not really exist but is simply a representation of the mind. In China, the doctrine was called *weishi* (meaning "consciousness only"). Xuanzang maintained that it accurately expressed the Buddha's authentic teachings, providing a true path for individuals to find enlightenment and escape the cycle of birth and rebirth. He translated and compiled a collection of essential writings about the topic, *Cheng weishi lun* (659; English translation, 1973).

Xuanzang's scholastic and idealistic approach to Buddhism had only limited appeal to the pragmatic Chinese people, and other approaches seemed more compatible with their religious and philosophical concerns. For this reason, the *weishi* school almost disappeared from China within a century after Xuanzang's death. However, his Japanese disciple, Dōshō, carried the *weishi* doctrine to Japan, where it was called Hossō and became the most influential school of Japanese Buddhism during the seventh and eighth centuries.

During his last years, Xuanzang continued to work in Xi'an under the patronage of the Tang emperors. To house Xuanzang's collection of Buddhist works, Emperor Gaozong (Kao-tsung, r. 650-683) in 652 built the Wild Goose Pagoda, which still survives as a landmark of Chinese architecture. As Xuanzang's health deteriorated, he told his followers that his work was finished, so that there was no need for him to stay any longer. Just before his death in 664, his followers reported that he mumbled that everything was illusionary, concluding, "Unreality itself is unreal." After he died, the emperor honored his memory by canceling all of his audiences for three days.

SIGNIFICANCE

Xuanzang was an outstanding explorer, writer, translator, and thinker. His pilgrimage to India was unquestionably one of the great epic voyages of the ancient world, and his descriptive account of the pilgrimage is widely acknowledged as one of the most important primary sources of the period. By translating numerous Buddhist writings from India, he greatly enriched Chinese thought. His translations also helped preserve many works that might have otherwise perished. Although his *weishi* school of Buddhism has never attracted large numbers of adherents, it is nevertheless recognized as one of the important currents of Buddhist thought.

—*Thomas Tandy Lewis*

FURTHER READING

Bernstein, Richard. *Ultimate Journey: Retracing the Path of an Ancient Buddhist Monk Who Crossed Asia in Search of Enlightenment*. New York: Alfred A. Knopf, 2001. A noted journalist discusses both his own experiences and those of Xuanzang in the same places.

Ch'en, Kenneth. *Buddhism in China*. Princeton, N.J.: Princeton University Press, 1964. A readable and helpful historical account that includes a concise summary of Xuanzang's career.

Devahuti, D. *Unknown Hsuan-Tsang*. New York: Oxford University Press, 2001. A collection of English translations of Xuanzang's translations into Chinese, with commentary and a biographical sketch.

Grousset, René. *In the Footsteps of the Buddha*. Translated by J. A. Underwood. London: Routledge and Sons, 1932. Rev. ed. New York: Grossman Publishers, 1971. A very interesting and scholarly biography that places Xuanzang in the context of Tang history and Buddhist philosophy, with excellent illustrations.

Hui-li. *The Life of Hiuen-Tsiang*. Translated by Samuel Beal. Westport, Conn.: Hyperion Press, 1911. Written by one of Xuanzang's students soon after his death, this is an important primary source for obtaining information about the man and his religious ideas.

_______. *The Life of Hsüan-tsang*. Translated by Li Yung-hsi. Beijing: Chinese Buddhist Association, 1959. Although perhaps difficult to locate, this is a readable, direct translation of the biography written by Hui-li. Paperback edition includes reproductions of a traditional painting of Xuanzang and a fourteenth century woodcut showing him translating scriptures. Limited footnotes assist in identifying ancient place-names with modern counterparts.

Waley, Arthur. *The Real Tripitaka and Other Pieces*. London: Allen and Unwin, 1952. An interesting biography of medium length that emphasizes Xuanzang's religious ideas.

Watters, Thomas. *On Yuan Chwang's Travels in India*. New York: AMS Press, 1971. A scholarly discussion of the places that Xuanzang visited, containing very little about his ideas.

Wriggins, Sally. *Xuanzang: A Buddhist Pilgrim on the Silk Road*. Boulder: Westview Press, 1996. A well-written biography that incorporates modern scholarship, with detailed endnotes, bibliography, index, glossary, and many illustrations. Highly recommended.

Wu Cheng'en. *The Journey to the West*. 4 vols. Translated by Anthony C. Yu. Chicago: University of Chicago Press, 1977. A famous sixteenth century folk novel known as *Monkey*, which was inspired by Xuanzang's voyage and experiences in India.

SEE ALSO: Harṣa; Taizong.

RELATED ARTICLES in *Great Events from History: The Middle Ages, 477-1453*: 618: Founding of the Tang Dynasty; 629-645: Pilgrimage of Xuanzang.

YAN LIBEN
Chinese painter

Yan Liben introduced a new sense of realism to portrait painting, a genre that he did much to develop during the period of the Tang Dynasty.

BORN: c. 600; Wannian, Shaanxi Province, China
DIED: 673; Siking (now Xi'an), Shaanxi Province, China
ALSO KNOWN AS: Yen Li-pen (Wade-Giles)
AREA OF ACHIEVEMENT: Art

EARLY LIFE

Yan Liben (yehn lee-behn) was born to a distinguished family of artist-officials. His father, Yan Pi (Yen P'i), was a famous Sui Dynasty (581-618) painter, calligrapher, and official, holding the title vice director of construction. Apparently, Yan Pi spent much time with his two sons, Lide (Li-te; c. 580-656) and Liben, training them in art and calligraphy. Liben's older brother, Lide, rose to become president of the board of public works and held the title grand architect during the early years of the Tang Dynasty (T'ang; 618-907).

The first half of the Tang Dynasty is generally considered to be one of the two most glorious periods in Chinese history, the other being the Western Han (206 B.C.E.-23 C.E.). During the period between 618 and 750, the Tang rulers were committed patrons of the arts as well as conquerors who expanded China's frontiers. By the end of the seventh century, the Chinese empire was one of the largest in world history. During the second half of the seventh century, moreover, the capital city, Siking (modern Xi'an), would become the most cosmopolitan city of its day and one of the most sophisticated cities of all time.

The first ruler, Li Yuan—known to posterity as Gaozu (Kao-tsu, r. 618-626)—rose to power primarily through the efforts of his young son, Li Shimin (Li Shih-min). The Li had been a powerful aristocratic family that had served the Sui but later joined in the rebellion against them. Led by Shimin, the Li family succeeded in ending the Sui Dynasty and eliminating other potential claimants to the Chinese throne. Just when it appeared that Li Yuan was about to choose a son other than Shimin to succeed him, the emperor suddenly became ill and died, and Shimin quickly ascended the throne in 627. Though his reign was relatively brief, ending in 649, it was an active and rich period in Chinese history, and Taizong (T'ai-tsung; r. 627-649), as Shimin would be called posthumously, is considered to have been one of the brightest and most capable rulers in Chinese history.

Even before becoming emperor, Li Shimin, who was then prince of Qin (Ch'in), surrounded himself with numerous scholars, poets, and painters, perhaps in anticipation of his ascension to the Dragon Throne. One of the people whom the future Taizong called on to serve him was the young Yan Liben. In 626, Yan was commissioned to paint a picture of eighteen famous scholars who had gathered at the prince's palace five years before. Although a scroll titled *The Eighteen Scholars at the Palace of Qin* bearing Yan's name is in the Taipei Palace Museum, most scholars agree that it is probably a Song Dynasty copy. The original was good enough to establish Yan Liben as one of China's greatest portrait artists, with his speciality being the depiction of famous historical personages. In 642, for example, he was assigned to paint the official portraits of twenty-four meritorious officials, and these were then placed in a "hall of fame" situated in the palace. With these and several other works, Yan established himself as China's first truly great portraitist.

LIFE'S WORK

Of the paintings by Yan Liben that have survived, the most famous is probably the series depicting thirteen Chinese emperors, beginning with Han Wendi (Wen-ti, r. 180-157 B.C.E.) and ending with Sui Yangdi (Yang-ti, r. 604-617 C.E.). Located in the Chinese collection of the Boston Museum of Fine Arts, the first six that have survived are probably later copies, but the last seven are generally acknowledged to be by Yan himself. Clearly, Yan was able to capture the unique personalities of each of his subjects. Moreover, his limited use of color and his technique for drawing faces and setting them up with appropriate backgrounds established the guidelines for such painting in China. Many Chinese, Japanese, and Western art critics consider the *Scroll of the Emperors* to be among the greatest masterpieces in all Chinese art history.

Not all of Yan Liben's works were devoted to historical portraiture. Although none of these works has survived, he painted Buddhist and Daoist subjects with such great mastery that the catalogs of imperial art holdings during the period of the Northern Song (Sung; 960-1126) mention numerous selections with religious motifs by Yan Liben. Another subject matter apparently popular with Yan was the depiction of tributary missions from "barbarian" lands. During the apogee of the Tang Dynasty (the years between 625 and 755), foreigners from all over the world came to China bearing tribute to the throne. These "exotics" came with great pomp and circumstance to Siking, bringing with them native goods. The "barbarians" would offer some of the goods to the emperor but would also trade other wares in Siking and other Chinese cities. On one occasion, on the request of Taizong in 635, Yan painted a lion brought as a tribute from Sogdiana. Several copies of barbarian-related paintings by Yan are located in the Beijing and Taipei palace museums. The tribute missions were important to the Tang emperors not so much because of any economic benefits the Chinese rulers would derive but more as a testament to the claim that the Chinese emperor ruled everyone "under Heaven." Yan's paintings were, therefore, valuable visual recordings of such events, and the Chinese ruler clearly prized them.

Taizong may have treated Yan Liben well, but there was no question that the artist was still not much more than a servant to the throne. On one occasion, it is said that while Yan was sweating and dirty, in the midst of painting, Taizong peremptorily summoned him to sketch an unusual bird that had settled onto a lake in front of the emperor. Perhaps because of this incident, Yan is reputed to have lamented that he was known "only by painting as if I were a menial." He is said to have discarded his brushes in anger and counseled his sons not to pursue an artistic career. Recently, pointing to his later honors, scholars have expressed doubt regarding the accuracy of this anecdote. The fact is, however, that Chinese intellectuals made the distinction between scholars who painted as a hobby and those who did so for a living, with the latter class suffering in reputation. Unquestionably, most of Yan's paintings were in fact court-commissioned works, and it may be that Yan was embarrassed by this.

Despite his purported chagrin, one of Yan's greatest achievements is still another commissioned work. The earliest and probably best example of funerary sculpture in China is that of a set of bas-reliefs of Taizong's six chargers that was based on Yan's sketches. The Tang emperor was particularly fond of horses, and it is likely that he commissioned Yan to make a drawing of his horses to serve as the design for subsequent carving. Most art critics are in agreement that the reliefs are based on Yan's drawings; thus, he can be credited with originating the finest stone sculpture work of the Tang. Four of the horses are in the Shaanxi Provincial Museum at Xi'an; the other two are at the University of Pennsylvania Museum in Philadelphia. It may also be that Yan painted some of the murals for Taizong's mausoleum, but they are now lost. That Yan's work was well received can be inferred from the fact that Yan himself is buried not far from the emperor's tomb at Zhaoling (Chao-ling).

If Yan was humiliated by Taizong's use of him principally as a painter, then he must have been more satisfied during the period after Taizong's death in 649. Under the nominal rule of Emperor Gaozong (Kao-tsung; r. 650-683)—in actuality power lay in the hands of Empress

Detail of Portraits of Thirteen Emperors, *attributed to Yan Liben.* (Corbis)

Wu—Yan rose to important official positions. In 656, on the death of his brother, Yan Lide, Liben became president of the board of public works. Although this position did not carry with it much political power, it certainly was beyond the reach of all but a few of China's scholar-official elite. In 668, Yan Liben became prime minister of the right (there were two prime ministers at the time), and in 670, he was appointed secretary general of the secretariat. It is possible, however, that despite these honors, the stigma of being a "commissioned painter" never quite left Yan, for a saying of that time derided the minister of the left as being incompetent and the minister of the right as getting his job through the use of "cinnabar and blue."

In 673, Yan Liben died and was buried with the highest possible honors, obtaining the posthumous title of *wen zhen*, or "true scholar." As noted above, his burial in the vicinity of Taizong's tomb is an indication that he was highly respected by Empress Wu. Such honors were enough to guarantee wealth and prestige to the Li family for several generations, but none of his children or grandchildren enjoyed any particular fame. Perhaps they had heeded Yan's admonition against pursuing a career in art. The legacy of Yan, however, has endured and grown.

Significance

Yan Liben was one of the great luminaries of the culturally resplendent Tang Dynasty. Perhaps in order to downplay the Tang imperial family's Turkic and therefore "barbarian" origins, the imperial court tended to be a very active sponsor of the arts. Being great patrons of Chinese culture may have been an attempt to compensate somehow for such questionable heritage. During the early years, however, such support was not without limitations. The Tang rulers—in particular Taizong—handled Chinese artists and poets as if they were hirelings who were at the beck and call of the Dragon Throne. This must have rankled men of great artistic ability, and no doubt Yan must at least on occasion have felt maligned and insulted.

One wonders, however, whether Yan's scholarship alone would have been enough to earn for him the very high official positions he attained. At the time he was being rewarded with such honors, the Chinese court, under Empress Wu's prodding, was moving increasingly toward a very rationalized system of bureaucracy, one which rewarded scholarship and knowledge of the Confucian classics. There is no record or even indication that Yan was subjected to rigorous civil service examinations. One can therefore assume that Yan arose to his position primarily by virtue of his reputation as an artist. Being a commissioned painter, therefore, led to a career success that few other painters in Chinese history would enjoy.

It was court sponsorship that enabled Yan to paint and develop his unique style of portraiture, a style that would be emulated but not equaled by subsequent Chinese portrait painters. In several cases, it was also court action hat guaranteed that his works would survive. What the artist's sensitivity could not well endure, his admirers, and those who are grateful that Yan's works are still extant, can understand and forgive.

—*Hilel B. Salomon*

Further Reading

Cahill, James. *T'ang, Sung, and Yuan*. Vol. 1 in *An Index of Early Chinese Painters and Paintings*. Berkeley: University of California Press, 1980. Contains a lengthy list of paintings and other works by Yan Liben that are held in museums and private collections. Includes a twelve-page bibliography.

Loehr, Max. *The Great Painters of China*. New York: Harper and Row, 1980. Contains an excellent account of Yan Liben's career together with several photographs of paintings and works that are attributed to him. Includes an index and a bibliography.

Sirén, Osvald. *The First Millennium: Early Chinese Painting*. Vol. 1 in *Chinese Painting: Leading Masters and Principles*. 1956. Reprint. New York: Hacker Art Books, 1973. This volume, by a leading historian of Asian art, contains a glowing assessment of Yan's work. Illustrated, with a bibliography.

Sullivan, Michael. *The Arts of China*. 4th ed. Berkeley: University of California Press, 1999. An overview of Chinese history that covers Yan Liben.

Waley, Arthur. *An Introduction to the Study of Chinese Painting*. 1958. Reprint. New York: AMS, 1979. Excellent discussion of Yan Liben and his impact on Chinese art. The volume contains forty-nine plates. Brief bibliography.

See also: Ma Yuan; Taizong; Xia Gui.

Related articles in *Great Events from History: The Middle Ages, 477-1453*: 618: Founding of the Tang Dynasty; 690-705: Reign of Empress Wu; c. 1190-1279: Ma-Xia School of Painting Flourishes.

YAQUT

Muslim historian and geographer

A major compiler of geographical, historical, and ethnographic information, Yaqut was the first Muslim scholar to use an encyclopedic organization for his material. His work gives modern scholars the most comprehensive insight on the state of knowledge in the thirteenth century Islamic world.

BORN: 1179; possibly Greece or Ḥamāh (now in Syria)
DIED: 1229; Aleppo (now in Syria)
ALSO KNOWN AS: Yakut; Yaqut ibn ʿAbdallah al-Rumi; Yaqut ibn ʿAbdallah al-Hamawi
AREAS OF ACHIEVEMENT: Historiography, geography, education

EARLY LIFE

Yaqut (yaw-KUHT) was born of Greek parents. He is known by two different sobriquets indicative of uncertainty about his origins: al-Rumi (the Roman or the Byzantine) and al-Hamawi, in reference to his claimed place of birth in Ḥamāh. Yaqut's early life was one of slavery in the service of a prominent merchant in Ḥamāh. (The name Yaqut means "ruby"; slaves often received names of gems or other precious objects.) Slavery in medieval Islam, however, did not necessarily imply the dire fate usually assumed by Westerners. Yaqut's master quickly recognized his servant's scholarly inclinations and gave him a solid, practical education, whereupon he became the merchant's personal secretary for several years.

Yaqut and his merchant master moved to Baghdad around 1199. According to some sources, Yaqut married in Baghdad and fathered several children. When Yaqut reached his majority, however, his master, rather than endowing him with property and a place in the family inheritance order—gestures expected in the middle-class culture of the time—released Yaqut from his service. Forced to make his own way in the world, Yaqut took to wandering, copying and selling manuscripts for a living.

Yaqut's travels took him first to Oman and the island of Qeshm at the mouth of the Persian Gulf, where he appears to have attempted some merchant ventures. He was seen in Tabrīz, in northwestern Iran, in 1213. During the next two years, he traveled through Egypt, Palestine, and Syria. In 1215, in Damascus, Yaqut ran afoul of politics. At this time, he was a follower of the Kharijites, a fervently democratic, almost anarchist movement that violently rejected the idea of a caliphate based on descent from Muḥammad. The Kharijites argued that the caliph could be anyone, even a non-Arab (which is to say, from among the great majority of Muslims), and that selection should be based strictly on merit.

Yaqut's Kharijite views did not sit well in Damascus, and he became embroiled in a fierce public quarrel that forced him to flee the city with the police on his heels. He withdrew all the way to the important library center of Marw in northeastern Iran, where he spent the next two years combing libraries. By 1218, Yaqut had reached the city of Khiva (now Khwārizm), south of the Aral Sea. There, hearing of the impending advance of Genghis Khan and the Mongols, he decided to beat a hasty retreat back to Iraq.

LIFE'S WORK

The scholarly fame of Yaqut rests principally on two works, the better known of which is his geographical dictionary *Kitāb muʿjam al-buldān* (1224, 1228; partially translated as *The Introductory Chapters of Yaqut's "Muʿjam al-buldān,"* 1959). The manuscript comprises some four thousand pages, with an introductory section discussing various theories of the nature of the world, followed by more than fourteen thousand entries. The second work is a dictionary of learned scholars, *Muʿjam al-udabaʾ* (*Yaqut's Dictionary of Learned Men*, 1907-1913), which covers about twenty-seven hundred manuscript pages and includes about one thousand biographical sketches.

Yaqut completed the first draft of *Kitāb muʿjam al-buldān* in Mosul in 1224 and the final version in Aleppo in 1228. The work is of particular significance because Yaqut was one of the last scholars in medieval Islam to have access to libraries east of the Caspian Sea—many of which were in long-established intellectual centers—before the Mongol invasions of that region that resulted in the loss of large amounts of material. Yaqut acknowledges in his introductory remarks that it was the intellectual environment of Marw that inspired him to write the work, which affords an unrivaled synopsis of what was known about the world, its structure, and its place in the cosmos, in the twilight of caliphal times.

Kitāb muʿjam al-buldān is a much more organized study than some of its rambling predecessors in the broad fields of history, geography, and ethnography. The entries are arranged alphabetically, and most follow a consistent internal structure in which historical, cultural, and scientific material on each location is discussed and evaluated. Particularly with respect to cosmography and related questions about the nature of the earth, Yaqut often presents conflicting theories developed by earlier scholars.

Yaqut was more a compiler than a synthesizer of knowledge. He lived at a time when most of the creative impulse of Islamic culture in its youth had been spent, and scholars contented themselves with assembling the enormous mass of information gathered by preceding generations. In composing *Kitāb muʿjam al-buldān*, Yaqut worked without official patronage or, indeed, much encouragement of any kind, a circumstance that explains his numerous caustic comments on the state of scholarship in Syria.

The introductory portions of *Kitāb muʿjam al-buldān* represent a mix of Greek and Islamic learning. The cosmographical schemes show heavy Hellenistic influence. On other matters, Yaqut made extensive use of his Muslim predecessors. His material on oceanography, for example, comes almost verbatim from the writing of the eleventh century scholar al-Bīrūnī, who flourished in the lands east of the Caspian. References on eastern Asia derive from the tenth century historian al-Masʿūdī. Many of Yaqut's primary sources, however, have been lost or remain undiscovered.

Yaqut's Dictionary of Learned Men is among several such compilations from various periods in medieval Islam that provide valuable data not only on individual scholars and intellectuals but also on the general state of learning and the scholarly environment in those times.

After his return from Khiva, Yaqut spent the remainder of his life in Mosul and in Aleppo. It is said that in later life he was in a position to offer financial assistance to the widow and children of his former master, who had been left destitute.

Significance

Kitāb muʿjam al-buldān has been acclaimed as one of the most complete and comprehensive statements of geographical knowledge to survive from medieval Islam. Muslim scholars from later generations utilized it extensively. Many Arabic editions, some of them abridged, have appeared. Western scholars have also made extensive use of the work and in some cases have attempted to reconstruct the histories of whole periods or regions based on its authority.

Yaqut's work is a valuable artifact of the knowledge of his age and, as such, has assisted scholars of Asia in identifying and, in some cases, eventually tracking down surviving manuscripts of authors once known only through his references. As new manuscripts are discovered, they generally confirm Yaqut's accuracy of reference and breadth of learning.

—*Ronald W. Davis*

Further Reading

De Slane, Baron MacGuckin, ed. and trans. *Ibn Khallikan's Biographical Dictionary.* 1871. Reprint. 4 vols. New York: Johnson Reprint, 1961. Vol. 4 contains a traditional biography of Yaqut, describing some of the influences on his career and his various activities. A good example of traditional biographical treatment of the figure. Bibliography.

Donner, Fred M. *Narratives of Islamic Origins: The Beginnings of Islamic Historical Writing.* Princeton, N.J.: Darwin Press, 1998. A study of the early years (around the seventh century) of Islamic historiography. Extensive bibliography, index.

Elahie, R. M. *The Life and Works of Yaqut ibn ʿAbd Allāh al-Hamawi.* Lahore, Pakistan: Punjab University Press, 1965. A biographical sketch together with some translated passages. One of the few sources on Yaqut in English.

Khalidi, Tarif. *Arabic Historical Thought in the Classical Period.* New York: Cambridge University Press, 1994. Traces the history of Muslim historiography during Yaqut's time, especially its focus on the documentation of scholars, scholarship, and learned society. Quotes historians and historical texts of the time period. Bibliography, index.

Robinson, Chase F. *Islamic Historiography.* New York: Cambridge University Press, 2003. An introduction to the writing of history in Arabic, with a focus on the sociopolitical functions of historiography from the eighth to the sixteenth century. Written especially for those with little or no background in Islamic history or in the Arabic language. Bibliography, index.

Rosenthal, Franz. *A History of Muslim Historiography.* 2d rev. ed. Leiden, the Netherlands: E. J. Brill, 1968. A broad survey covering such topics as the Muslim concept of history, the forms of Muslim historiography—such as annals and genealogies—and the wide-ranging topics addressed by Muslim historians (from astrology to political science). The frequent references to Yaqut as a source attest his importance, but no extended study of individual historians or their works is included. Bibliography.

Yaqut. *The Introductory Chapters of Yaqut's "Muʿjam al-buldān."* Translated and annotated by Wadie Jwaideh. Leiden, the Netherlands: E. J. Brill, 1959.

Virtually the only readily available source of Yaqut in English. An exhaustively annotated translation of the portion of Yaqut's text that lays out his cosmographical scheme. The introductory section is an excellent example of his dependence on Greek paradigms and his methods of citation of earlier Muslim writers. Bibliographical footnotes.

SEE ALSO: Pietro d'Abano; Roger Bacon; al-Bīrūnī; Genghis Khan; Ibn Khaldūn; Saint Isidore of Seville; al-Masʿūdī; al-Ṭabarī; Vincent of Beauvais; William of Rubrouck.

RELATED ARTICLES in *Great Events from History: The Middle Ages, 477-1453*: 872-973: Publication of *The History of al-Ṭabarī*; c. 950-1100: Rise of Madrasas; 1100-1300: European Universities Emerge; c. 1150: Moors Transmit Classical Philosophy and Medicine to Europe; 1377: Ibn Khaldūn Completes His *Muqaddimah*; 1399-1404: Tamerlane Builds the Bibi Khanum Mosque.

YO FEI

Chinese military leader

The Chinese general Yo Fei was killed in prison by members of his own government during a war against an external army. Since that time, he has been hailed as a symbol of patriotic resistance to foreign invaders.

BORN: 1103; Tangyin, Henan Province, China
DIED: December 29, 1141; Hangzhou, Zhejiang Province, China
ALSO KNOWN AS: Yue Fei (Pinyin), Yüeh Fei (Wade-Giles)
AREAS OF ACHIEVEMENT: Warfare and conquest, military

EARLY LIFE

One of the exemplary heroes of Chinese civilization is Yo Fei (yoh fay), also known as Yue Fei. The many myths and legends surrounding his life make it difficult to see the real man, and not much is known of his early life. Modern biographers accept that his father, Yo He (Yo Ho), was a farmer of modest wealth. The family property was damaged by a flood when Yo Fei was an infant, and his mother narrowly escaped with her child by floating to safety in a large water jar.

Although he did not pursue a career in the civil service, Yo Fei was apparently well educated by his father in the literary, historical, and military classics. The discipline and dedication of the young student and devoted father can be seen in the formation of an impressive writing style, evidenced by the extant specimens of his calligraphy. In addition to his scholarly interests, the young Yo Fei had unusual physical strength and became highly skilled in archery, swordsmanship, and the use of the lance.

At age nineteen, Yo chose the military route to prominence when he volunteered to serve in a special force that sought to seize Beijing from the Khitan state (Liao Dynasty; 907-1125) in the northeast. Although the campaign failed in its objective, Yo was impressed with the great city to the north and remained with his commander, Liu Jia (Liu Chia), in what amounted to police action on the frontier between their Song regions and the Khitan, a federation of nomadic Mongolian tribes. During this campaign, Yo demonstrated a remarkable military skill, which prompted many tales of courage and daring. Before the end of his nineteenth year, however, as a result of his father's death, he returned home to attend to the needs of his mother and family. During the four years that he remained with his family, 1122-1126, one foreign invader replaced another in China. In 1123, the Jurchen from Manchuria overthrew the Khitan with some assistance from the Song. This move was soon recognized as an error, and the Song withdrew southward, establishing the Southern Song Dynasty (Sung; 1127-1279) and seeking to hold the area north of the Yangtze River to the Huai River. This action resulted in a fierce and extended war between the Song and the Jurchen and prompted Yo Fei's return to military service.

LIFE'S WORK

From his return to the field in 1126 until his death in 1141, Yo Fei occupied a prominent place in the military history of the Southern Song Dynasty. Personality conflicts among the ambitious officers complicated the command system, however, and for a brief period Yo moved out of the official army to become the commander of an independent army unit on the frontier. Eventually, he would return to the ranks and establish an army that enjoyed a wide and prestigious reputation for its spirit, discipline, and striking power. Under his leadership, his

MAJOR RULERS OF THE SOUTHERN SONG DYNASTY, 1127-1279

Reign	*Ruler*
1127-1162	Gaozong
1163-1190	Xiaozong
1190-1194	Guangzong
1195-1224	Ningzong
1225-1264	Lizong
1265-1274	Duzong
1275-1275	Gongdi
1276-1278	Duanzong
1279	Bing Di

army was reported to have never suffered a defeat. According to his grandson, Yo built his army on the following principles: careful selection, careful training, justice in rewards and punishments, clear orders, strict discipline, and community of both pleasure and toil. Yo was widely known for sharing with his troops the fortunes and misfortunes of war. He slept where they slept, ate what they ate, and inflicted a fair but severe justice. On one occasion he sentenced his son to be decapitated for permitting his horse to stumble during military exercises. His son was spared only by the pleadings of the other generals.

Yo's early education led him to welcome scholars and civilians to his various camps. He reportedly sought their advice and used them to relate tales of past military heroics to the troops. A portion of his spare time was spent in the writing of poetry and music, some of which survives as early symbols of Chinese nationalism and patriotism. His goal was a unified China under an emperor who would be a scholar, warrior, and statesman; undoubtedly, he saw himself in that role. With the confidence of success behind him, Yo went so far as to recommend to Emperor Gaozong (Kao-tsung; r. 1127-1162) that he seek to meet that ideal more effectively. From 1129 to 1134, Yo Fei's army operated in the valley of the Yangtze River and on the frontier between the Southern Song Dynasty and the Jurchen, who were now identified as the Jin Dynasty (Chin; 1115-1234). This period was marked by Yo Fei's struggles against independent military units similar to those he had previously commanded and by general frontier lawlessness. In 1134, Yo was named regional commandant and directed a number of major campaigns against the Jin and their Qi (Ch'i) buffer state, which had been established between themselves and the Southern Song. Here he achieved his greatest military reputation, directing large forces and coordinating with other armies to drive forcefully into northern China, his target being Beijing. The rallying cry of the campaign—"Give us back our rivers and mountains!"—came from one of his poems, an expression that remains symbolic as a cry of Chinese nationalism.

It may have been Yo's great successes, however, that contributed to his downfall and death. The campaign of 1140 proved especially effective, with his army driving far north into Jin areas along the Yellow River. This invasion encouraged the Jin to establish negotiations with the government of the Southern Song, an opportunity that the latter seemed eager to pursue if for no other reason than to slow the successes of an ambitious and powerful general. While the army was in the field, a treaty was concluded that provided for the withdrawal of the Song army from the Jin areas in the north. Emperor Gaozong had decided on retrenchment rather than restoration. This decision may have been motivated by the fact that the Jin were holding the emperor's older brother captive; should the army of Yo Fei have proven too successful, the emperor would probably have been forced to surrender his throne. The emperor used his chief councillor, Qin Gui (Ch'in Kuei), to negotiate a settlement with the Jin that effectively made the Southern Song a vassal state of the Jin. Yo had little choice except to withdraw or lose his command. The army pulled back but protested what was widely regarded as a traitorous peace. As a result of this protest, a number of leading generals, Yo Fei included, were removed from military command and relocated to civilian posts. Loyal subordinate officers objected to this action, and rumors of plots began to emerge, including one alleged plan by Yo's principal lieutenant, Zhang Xian (Chang Hsien), and Yo's son Yo Yun, which resulted in their arrest and public execution. Yo Fei was himself soon identified as having been a party to the rumored plot and was imprisoned. On December 29, 1141, he was murdered.

SIGNIFICANCE

Although the details of Yo Fei's death are obscure, the traditional account relates that the arrangements for his murder were included in the negotiations and agreement between the Jin and Qin Gui. The Chinese therefore universally view Qin Gui as the quintessential traitor, while Yo Fei is depicted as the ideal patriot and national hero. Late nineteenth and early twentieth century groups that organized to oppose foreign exploitation of China took his name as the symbol of their cause. As the Chinese depend heavily on models, imitation, and precedent to teach, Yo Fei has been an enduring subject, combining those values that are so much a part of Confucian China: discipline, courage, loyalty to parents, self-sacrifice, harmony with one's community members, intense dedication to vocation, scholarship, and strength. Yo Fei is the subject of numerous plays, novels, and poems, and there are many temples that stand in celebration of his defense of his country. He remains a powerful symbol of Chinese nationalism and resistance to foreign invaders.

—*Frank Nickell*

FURTHER READING

Franke, Herbert, and Hok-lam Chan. *Studies on the Jurchens and the Chin Dynasty*. Brookfield, Vt.: Ashgate, 1997. An examination of the rise of the Jurchens, against whom Yo Fei battled. Bibliography and index.

Hartman, Charles. "The Making of a Villain: Ch'in Kuei and Tao-hsueh." *Harvard Journal of Asiatic Studies* 58, no. 1 (June, 1998): 59-88. An analysis of Qin Gui's role as reputed executioner of Yo Fei and the myths that have arisen around him.

Kuhn, Anthony. "Age-Old Nationalist Hero Gets a Demotion in China: Beijing Decides That a Twelfth Century General Long Revered for His Loyalty Is No Longer PC." *The Los Angeles Times*, January 28, 2003, p. A3. Discusses the reasons that China removed Yo Fei from its list of national heroes.

Rodzinski, Witold. *The Walled Kingdom: A History of China from Antiquity to the Present*. 2d ed. London: Fontana, 1991. Contains an excellent chapter on the Song Dynasty and the northern invaders. Briefly discusses Yo Fei's role in the wars between the Song and the Jin and the significance of Yo's historical image.

Tillmann, Hoyt Cleveland, and Stephen H. West, eds. *China Under Jurchen Rule: Essays on Chin Intellectual and Cultural History*. Albany: State University of New York Press, 1995. A study of the Jin Dynasty that examines, among other topics, its conflict with the Song Dynasty. Bibliography and index.

SEE ALSO: Genghis Khan.

RELATED ARTICLES in *Great Events from History: The Middle Ages, 477-1453*: 936: Khitans Settle Near Beijing; 1115: Foundation of the Jin Dynasty; 1153: Jin Move Their Capital to Beijing.

YONGLO

Chinese emperor (r. 1402-1424)

Combining traditional Chinese and Mongol ideas of imperial rule, Yonglo brought the Ming Dynasty to its height, making it notable for the caliber of its ministers, internal improvements, support of the arts, and domestic stability.

BORN: May 2, 1363; Chianning (now Nanjing), China
DIED: August 5, 1424; Beijing, China
ALSO KNOWN AS: Yung-lo (Wade-Giles); Zhu Di (Pinyin), Chu Ti (Wade-Giles); Wen Di (Pinyin), Wen Ti (Wade-Giles); Chengzu (Pinyin, temple name), Ch'eng-tsu (Wade-Giles)
AREA OF ACHIEVEMENT: Government and politics

EARLY LIFE

Zhu Di, who on ascension to the throne in 1402 took the reign name Yonglo (yoong-loh, meaning "eternal joy") and later received the temple name Chengzu (Ch'eng-tsu; "completing ancestor"), was born in the Imperial Palace in Nanjing. He was the fourth son of Zhu Yuanzhang (Chu Yüan-chang), also known as Hongwu (r. 1368-1398), who was shortly to become the first Ming emperor, and a Korean palace concubine. A northerner and a commoner whose family background included lower-class Yangtze artisans and Huai River (northern Anhui Province) tenant farmers, Zhu Yuanzhang had emerged from a background of abysmal poverty, seeking refuge for a time in a Buddhist monastery, where he received a rudimentary education. Subsequently, he lived by his wits, eventually establishing a rebel power base in his northern home district. Before he was forty, by adroit selection of comrades and great military skill, he became the master of Han lands along the Yangtze, successfully expelled the Mongols (thus causing the collapse of the Yuan Dynasty, 1279-1368), and seized power.

Zhu Di's early years were shaped by his father's sometimes savage efforts to found and stabilize what he designated as the Ming, or "brilliant," Dynasty (1368-1644). Conscious of the internal dynastic rivalries of his Yuan predecessors, Zhu Di's father centralized authority in his own hands, maintained the loyalty of ministers and other officials by frequent bloody purges, and dispatched all of his sons to separate princely fiefs, except the heir apparent.

As prince of Yan, Zhu Di ruled over Beijing, not then the capital, and the region surrounding it. It was essentially a northern border post, and although the princes were not entrusted with civil administration, they were responsible to their father for the military security of their regions. Meanwhile, they were further educated both by members of the military aristocracy and by Confucian scholars. Nevertheless, military exigencies proved the dominant formative influence, for Zhu Di spent much of his early life in military campaigns and earned his initial reputation from them.

A carved lacquer box from the Ming Dynasty, created during the reign of Yonglo. (Corbis)

Placed in command in 1390 and again in 1391, he led notable expeditions against the Mongols, who—although previously defeated by his father—were not quiescent. Following his father's massive purges of allegedly subversive nobles and military officials during the early 1390's, designed further to concentrate power in his own hands, Zhu Di, as a result of the shakeup, was given command over all troops within his fiefdom, along with generous subsidies of land and grain, a substantial administrative staff, and a body of princely guards. Thus, Zhu Di developed a powerful base for himself in a northern region, a region not only preferred by his father but also considered by most Chinese to be the heart of their civilization.

The final years of his father's reign were peaceful ones. Zhu Di's last victorious patrol north of the Great Wall was in 1396, and thereafter, there was a general stacking of arms. Still, the problem of succession was seriously unsettled when Zhu Di's father died in June, 1398. The chief difficulty, as he himself had feared, was the power of Zhu Di and the other princes, whom—with prospects of their plotting in mind—he had previously banned from attending his funeral.

Twenty-one, gentle, scholarly, and eager to profit from his elders' excesses, the dead emperor's grandson and heir Jianwen (Chien-wen, r. 1399-1402) nevertheless immediately sought to impose his authority over his uncles, the princes. Five of the leading princes were systematically stripped of their support, and another died, leaving Zhu Di the oldest survivor, the most dangerously situated strategically, and the most popular and powerful.

Seeking to isolate Zhu Di, Jianwen and his advisers hoped to provoke him into a rebellion they believed they could crush. Overconfident, they rashly sent a force against Zhu Di in the summer of 1399 that Zhu Di ambushed and destroyed. Declaring that he was merely trying to liberate the new emperor from bad advisers, Zhu Di, as the prince of Yan, took to the field, and for the next three years, civil war raged in North China, essentially a conflict between north and south.

Notwithstanding serious handicaps, Zhu Di maintained himself against imperial forces, generally defeated them, and, in January of 1402, was able to commence precarious drives south across the Huang River toward the Yangtze River, Suzhou, and Nanjing. In July, 1402, Nanjing capitulated. The emperor and empress purportedly died in the blaze of the Imperial Palace, and the northern rebel, the prince of Yan, assumed the Ming throne.

LIFE'S WORK

Hongwu, the first Ming emperor, was forty when, as a rebel, he seized the throne; Yonglo was thirty-nine and, like his father, a rebel destined to rule for about two decades. A large, strong, active man, Yonglo profited from his physical presence, his military reputation, and his capacity for ruthless action, and in these respects, he also resembled his father. Yet he evinced a greater confidence, more control of his temper, and a more sensitive ability to work effectively with subordinates.

Nevertheless, Yonglo's reign opened with a bloody purge of Jianwen's supporters. He reduced the remaining princes to mere figureheads and precluded any future threats to the stability of government from imperial family members or from within either the civil or the military establishment. Inevitably, this meant a further concentration of power in his own hands, but it was precisely that which permitted a resumption of the sounder policies of his predecessors and encouraged the return of stability within the empire.

Because his own power base had always been in the north, Yonglo transferred the capital from Nanjing to Beijing in 1407, gradually leaving only the heir apparent and his entourage in Nanjing. Beiping Province was transformed into a metropolitan area and given a functional importance as the seat of government that was confirmed when it was officially designated the capital in 1421. The recovering Mongols also lent impetus to Yonglo's shift of power to Beijing. To counter their perpetual menace, he made Beiping Province the mainstay of his northern, hence major, defense system. After 1407, therefore, both personal predilection as well as security considerations kept him continuously based in his new capital.

Relocation northward brought substantial logistical problems. Previous establishment of sizable mercantile colonies along the northern frontier, plus his predecessors' upgrading of regional agriculture, meant that the transport of grain by sea around the Shandong Peninsula—for generations a costly expedient because of losses from pirates, rebels, and weather—had become unnecessary. The presence of officials and the growing military establishment in the Beiping metropolitan area required new, assured avenues of supply.

To develop these avenues, Yonglo mobilized the Yangtze naval command to reinstitute sea transport of the capital's grain supplies while simultaneously reconstructing inland waterways that were inadequate or had fallen into desuetude. His minister of works, Song Li (Sung Li), and Chen Xuan (Ch'en Hsüan), the Yangtze commander who had surrendered to Yonglo in 1402, began reconstruction of the Grand Canal, which had silted so badly that it was unnavigable. A system of forty-seven locks was brilliantly engineered so that after 1415, grain shipments could be delivered directly into the Huang River, precluding further perilous sea journeys around Shandong and ensuring the capital's sustenance.

Yonglo dealt with potentially menacing or factious neighbors by resorting both to diplomacy and to force. In the north, he was able to extend indirect Chinese influence by successfully wooing Jurchen tribesmen, who, although previously under Mongol influence, had by 1402 come more under the influence of Korea. Offering them commercial inducements and incorporating them into Ming militia units, he brought them under Chinese overlordship by 1415. In addition, Mongols who had been settled between the Great Wall and the Liao River while retaining their own chieftains were encouraged to assimilate to Chinese organization; others, such as the Urianghad Mongols, were rewarded for having served as Yonglo's cavalry by a grant of independence within the Beiping regional military organization. Still other such tribes were relocated farther in the interior under Chinese supervision.

More important were the menacing remnants of the Yuan Dynasty's forces composed of Eastern Mongols, or Tatars, and the Western Mongols, or Oirats. Because far to the west, Tamerlane had conquered much of the Middle East, Syria, and parts of India, the great danger to Yonglo was Tamerlane's potential for deploying various of these Mongol peoples against him. Indeed, Tamerlane

MAJOR RULERS OF THE MING DYNASTY, 1368-1644

Reign	*Ruler*
1368-1398	Hongwu (Zhu Yuanzhang)
1399-1402	Jianwen (Zhu Yunwen)
1402-1424	YONGLO (Zhu Di)
1424-1425	Hongxi
1426-1435	Xuande
1436-1449	Zhengtong
1450-1457	Jingtai
1457-1464	Tianshun
1465-1487	Chenghua
1488-1505	Hongzhi
1506-1521	Zhengde
1522-1567	Jianjing
1567-1572	Longqing
1573-1620	Wanli
1620	Taichang
1621-1627	Tianqi
1628-1644	Chongzhen

had been preparing such a campaign when, fortunately for Yonglo, he died in 1405. Taking no chances, however, Yonglo personally led forces beyond the Great Wall into the Gobi Desert in attempts to keep various Mongol chieftains, particularly the Tatar Arughtai, divided and off balance.

Northern frontiers solicited no more of his attention than did those to the south. Since the 1370's, Annam had been rent by dynastic quarrels that by Yonglo's ascension involved his government. Annamese refugees in China urged Yonglo to intervene in the restoration of their legitimate ruler, and in anticipation of Chinese interference, Le Qui-ly, the Annamese usurper, launched spoiling attacks along China's southern border. Chinese envoys dispatched to seek a peaceful solution to the problem in 1406 were murdered.

Retaliating, Yonglo, from bases in Guangxi and Yunnan, invaded Annam, crushed the opposition, and, failing to discover an acceptable replacement for Le Qui-ly, absorbed Annam as a new Chinese province in 1407. Thousands of well-educated Annamese, many of them possessing superior knowledge about firearms, were brought into the employment of Yonglo's government. Such actions did not stabilize the situation, and not even the best Chinese administrative and military talents could prevent the outbreak of guerrilla resistance, the deterioration of China's position, and, after Yonglo's death, the loss of the province.

Despite his background, events make it clear that Yonglo preferred the extension of Chinese influence through diplomacy, commerce, and other peaceful means. After years of tensions between his father and a Japan torn by political tumults, Yonglo was pleasantly confronted by the new Ashikaga shogunate, which had reunified Japan in 1392 and which sought amicable relations. In 1403, Japanese plenipotentiaries arrived in Beijing to announce that the shogun recognized himself as a subject of Yonglo and was eager for close commercial relations. These were sanctioned the following year, with the result that Japanese fleets were permitted periodic visitations to Ningbo to trade and deliver tribute. The shogun even hunted down Japanese pirates who for generations had scourged the Chinese boat traders and delivered them for punishment to Beijing. Such idyllic conditions dissipated with the succession of a new shogun in 1408, and thereafter relations cooled. The new shogun rejected a tributary position and ignored the pirates' return to their enterprises.

Two of Yonglo's remarkable eunuchs acted as emissaries and spread his influence into other parts of Asia. Beginning in 1403, when several fleets were sent to ports in Southeast Asia and Javanese and southern Indian ports, an unprecedented extension of China's naval activities commenced. A number of expeditions were led by Hou Xian (Hou Hsien), who had previously journeyed to Tibet and Nepal, and by the famed Muslim admiral (also a eunuch) Zheng He (Cheng Ho), who had been in Yonglo's service since he was a boy. Between them, Hou and Zheng, often with great fleets, tens of thousands of personnel, and vessels of immense size (440 feet, or 135 meters, in length; 186 feet, or 57 meters, in beam), traveled to thirty-seven countries, including a number on Africa's west coast, on Zanzibar, and along the Persian Gulf.

These voyages were indisputably profitable in terms of tribute, commerce, and the emperor's prestige. Occasionally these voyages encouraged the use of Chinese force: the suppression of pirates in Sumatra, intervention in a Javanese civil war, the capture of a hostile Ceylonese ruler for imprisonment in Beijing, and assistance to local rulers in quelling domestic rebellions. However, they were mostly peaceful and instructive, exotic adventures that lasted from 1403 until Yonglo's death, although the indefatigable Zheng He continued voyaging after 1424.

After a vigorous reign generally marked by domestic stability and prosperity, Yonglo died in the autumn of 1424 as the result of an illness contracted on a campaign waged north of the Great Wall against Mongol tribesmen.

SIGNIFICANCE

Yonglo's two decades of rule consolidated Ming power. In many ways, his reign was the apogee of the Ming Dynasty. He persisted in concentrating authority in his own hands, thus ensuring continuation of an absolutism characteristic of his father, the dynasty's founder. Yonglo was, however, less barbarous. There were fewer sanguinary purges during his reign, and a stabler environment developed in which his ministers could work more effectively. By relying heavily on eunuchs and military officers to implement his initiatives, he permitted the civil service to function somewhat apart and to cohere around Confucian principles: to recruit and indoctrinate through the *jinshi* examination system and to serve according to it, thus allowing it to evolve its own institutional ideology and esprit.

In part, these developments account for the unusual official longevity of Yonglo's secretaries and ministers in their posts. There were two vitally important long-term consequences of these conditions. First, in a positive sense, the civil service was rendered more capable of removing from the emperor the daily burdens of administering justice, handling financial problems, and attending to the routines of governing. Second, in the process of assuming such responsibilities, the civil service became—although not during Yonglo's regime—a powerful political force that was able to control and even thwart emperors.

Without question, Yonglo's military and diplomatic actions aggressively secured China's borders, even extending them somewhat, while establishing China's presence throughout Asia and parts of the Middle East in an unprecedented fashion. In the fifteenth century, no other power could claim influence over such vast areas and numerous populations. The immediate import of this was domestic security and tranquillity. China ceased for a time to be torn by dynastic successions, warlords, powerful rebellions, and governmental incompetence. Inevitably, after Yonglo's death, there was an erosion of some achievements: Annam fought its way out of the Ming grasp, Japan's shoguns withdrew from their subjection to Beijing, and the several major Asian tribes to the north, west, and southwest remained actual or potential menaces and kept Ming borders in constant jeopardy.

More lasting was Yonglo's consolidation of the Yuan absolutism that had characterized the rule overthrown by his father with an evolving Confucian, or scholars', bureaucracy. Together, they defined much of the character of Chinese government for centuries.

—*Clifton K. Yearley and Kerrie L. MacPherson*

FURTHER READING

Antony, Robert J. *Like Froth Floating on the Sea: The World of Pirates and Seafarers in Late Imperial South China*. China Research Monographs 56. Berkeley, Calif.: Institute of East Asian Studies, 2003. An examination of the pirates in South China during the Ming and Qing Dynasties.

Brook, Timothy. *The Confusion of Pleasure: Commerce and Culture in Ming China*. Berkeley: University of California Press, 1998. A look at the role of commerce during the Ming Dynasty. Illustrations, maps, bibliography, and index.

Chan, Hok-lam. *China and the Mongols: History and Legend Under the Yuan and Ming*. Brookfield, Vt.: Ashgate, 1999. An examination of the Yuan and Ming Dynasties' relations with the Mongols. Index.

Dreyer, Edward L. *Early Ming China: A Political History, 1355-1435*. Stanford, Calif.: Stanford University Press, 1982. Scholarly and eminently readable, this volume is one of the most extensive English-language studies of its subject. Detailed notes, an excellent annotated bibliography, a standard character list, and a very useful index.

Levathes, Louise. *When China Ruled the Seas: The Treasure Fleet of the Dragon Throne, 1405-1433*. New York: Oxford University Press, 1996. Describes the life and activities of Zheng He as well as conditions in the Ming Dynasty during his lifetime. Illustrations, maps, bibliography, and index.

Menzies, Gavin. *1421: The Year China Discovered the Americas*. New York: William Morrow, 2003. A somewhat controversial treatment of Zheng He's travels that suggest that his ships reached the Americas. Illustrations, maps, bibliography, and index.

Ptak, Roderich. *China and the Asian Seas: Trade, Travel, and Visions of the Others (1400-1750)*. Brookfield, Vt.: Ashgate, 1998. An examination of the explorations of Zheng He and the trade in which the Chinese engaged. Bibliography and index.

Tsai, Shih-shan Henry. *The Eunuchs in the Ming Dynasty*. Albany: State University of New York Press, 1996. A study of how the eunuchs were used during the Ming Dynasty. One chapter focuses on Ming maritime activities. Illustrations, maps, bibliography, and index.

_______. *Perpetual Happiness: The Ming Emperor Yongle*. Seattle: University of Washington Press, 2001. A study of the reign of Yonglo, Zheng He's supporter, and its place within the Ming Dynasty.

SEE ALSO: Tamerlane; Zheng He.

RELATED ARTICLES in *Great Events from History: The Middle Ages, 477-1453*: 1153: Jin Move Their Capital to Beijing; 1368: Establishment of the Ming Dynasty; 1397: Publication of the Laws of Great Ming; 1403-1407: *Yonglo Dadian* Encyclopedia Is Compiled; 1405-1433: Zheng He's Naval Expeditions.

Zeami Motokiyo
Japanese dramatist

A great actor and a great dramatist, Zeami was also an outstanding teacher of acting and a theoretician of theatrical aesthetics. He established the Nō form of drama, which has survived to modern times.

Born: 1363; Near Nara, Japan
Died: 1443; Kyoto, Japan
Areas of achievement: Theater, literature

Early Life

Little is known of the birth and early life of Zeami Motokiyo (zay-ah-mee moh-toh-kee-yoh). His great-grandfather was the lay priest Keishin, Kamajima Kagemori, the lord of the fief of Asada in Iga Province. Zeami was the son of Kan'ami, an actor, playwright, teacher, and leader of the Yamato *sarugaku* troupe. His mother was Yasaburō Ukikujo, the daughter of a priest who was the lord of the fief of Obata. At a tender age, Zeami was put into the hands of Yasburō Katsukiyo, the leader of the Konparu troupe, to be trained as an actor.

During the late 1360's and early 1370's, Kan'ami's genius began to be recognized, and he and his troupe became very popular in Kyoto and its environs. Soon Zeami was acting on the stage with his father, and the precocious youngster was attracting unusual attention. In 1374, the troupe gave a performance at the Daigoji (a Buddhist temple southeast of the capital) that was witnessed by Ashikaga Yoshimitsu (1358-1408), who had become a *shōgun* (generalissimo, or military dictator) at the age of ten. Almost seventeen years old and already an important patron of the arts, Yoshimitsu was amazed and enchanted by the beauty, charm, and talent of the eleven-year-old Zeami. As a result, the shogun became Zeami's patron, as well as his friend and companion.

Yoshimitsu's affection for Zeami was so openly displayed that some of the court nobility (*kuge*) were annoyed. They were particularly critical of the military nobility (*daimyō*) for trying to please the shogun by giving expensive presents to Zeami. Their objection to the intimate relationship between Yoshimitsu and the boy actor was not, as one might suppose, to any homoerotic possibilities in it but simply to Zeami's low-class status as a commoner and an actor.

Ironically, Zeami was actually the descendant of feudal lords of the Ōta clan and of royal blood. This family of *daimyō* had descended from Minamoto Yorimasa (1106-1180), who was famous both as a poet and as a warrior. The Minamoto branch had descended from Sadazumi-shinno (874-916), the son of the emperor Seiwa (r. 858-876). It had produced the three shogun families of Minamoto, Ashikaga, and Tokugawa. Kan'ami, however, had deliberately kept his family line secret from Yoshimitsu when he had founded his *sarugaku* dramatic troupe.

At least one old aristocrat was not repelled by the mixing of social classes at the court: the poet Nijō Yoshimoto, who proved an enthusiastic admirer of the young actor. A letter exists in which Yoshimoto expresses his delight in the company of Zeami, referring to him, however, by the name Fujiwaka, which had been conferred on him by Yoshimoto himself:

> Should Fujiwaka have time, please bring him over with you once again. The entire day was wonderful, and I quite lost my heart. A boy like this is rare—why look at his *renga* and court kickball [*kemari*], not to mention his own particular art! Such a charming manner and such poise! I don't know where such a marvelous boy can have come from.

In the same year (1378), the retired emperor Sukō, who had reigned at Kyoto from 1348 to 1351, was informed of a *renga* session held at Yoshimoto's residence in which Zeami was a participant. As host, Yoshimoto would produce the first two lines of a proposed five-line poem. As guest, Zeami was obliged to produce the final three lines and link them to the first two. The emperor recorded his opinion of Zeami's skill in his diary, stating that the boy's linkages were "inspired" and copying a pair of the poems the two composed as examples. However inspired Zeami's linkages may have been, they show that he understood thoroughly the rules for *renga* compositions and sought to adhere strictly to them. This contest between a common teenager and a senior court noble required much self-confidence and poise on Zeami's part.

In 1384, Kan'ami died at the age of fifty-one. Zeami, who was then twenty-one, was obliged to assume the responsibility of the leadership of the Kanze troupe.

Life's Work

As leader of the Kanze *sarugaku* troupe, Zeami proved highly successful. Although he lost an important supporter with the death of Yoshimoto in 1388, he retained the patronage of Yoshimitsu. The first documented reference to Zeami—he was then known as Kanze Saburo—as an adult performer occurred in 1394, when it was said that he gave a performance during Yoshimitsu's pilgrimage to Nara. In 1399, he gave two performances, both witnessed by Yoshimitsu. From 1400 to 1402, Zeami wrote his first treatise on the aesthetics of Nō, *Fūshi-kaden* (also known as *Kadensho*; English translation, 1968), which purported to transmit the teachings of his father. In this work, he introduced the concept of *ka*, or *hana*, literally meaning "flower." In his aesthetics, however, the symbol of the flower referred to the freshness and charm evoked by the actor's performance. Zeami followed the lead of Kan'ami, who had chosen his stage name by selecting the first character of the name of the bodhisattva Kanzeon. Zeami selected the second character of the same name. The sound of this character was unvoiced as "se," but according to tradition, Yoshimitsu advised Zeami to voice the sound as "ze"; therefore, his name became Zeami instead of Seami.

Yoshimitsu had abdicated the shogunate in 1395 in favor of his son Yoshimochi, who was then nine years old. Nevertheless, he continued to rule under the title of prime minister. Even when a year or so later, he had his head shaved and became a bonze at Tojiin, a Buddhist temple of the Shingon sect, he still ruled from the splendid palace at Kitayama, which the people called Kinkakuji, or Golden Temple. During an emperor's visit there in 1408, a *sarugaku* performance was given in which the Kanze troupe no doubt took part. Not long after this performance, Yoshimitsu died, at the age of fifty. Zeami lost the powerful ruler who had been his friend and patron for so long.

Although Zeami faced competition for the shogun's favor from other acting troupes, he and his Kanze players fared well during most of Yoshimochi's rule (1395-1423). In 1422, at the age of fifty-nine, Zeami retired as leader of the Kanze troupe. He immediately took Sōtō Zen vows to become a lay Buddhist priest. His gifted son Kanze Motomasa succeeded his father as the leader of the Kanze troupe. At this time, also, Konparu Zenchiku (1405-1468) must have married one of Zeami's daughters. Actor, playwright, and critic, he was to become a model son-in-law to the aging Zeami. It should be recalled that Zeami had a connection with the Konparu troupe as a young child, a tie that no doubt accounted for his daughter's marriage to Zenchiku.

On the death of Yoshimochi, Yoshikazu (ruled 1423-1425) and then Yoshinori (ruled 1429-1441) became shogun. With the advent of Yoshinori's shogunate, Zeami and his sons began to be treated badly. In 1429, Yoshinori sponsored a grand *sarugaku* performance at the Kasakake Riding Grounds. Two Kanze troupes participated in this competition against two other troupes. This performance was odd in that it was done in the style of Tōnomine, the mounted characters riding live horses and wearing real armor. Motomasa and Zeami in some way displeased and angered Yoshinori. Not long afterward, the shogun retaliated. He ordered that both of them be excluded from the Sentō Imperial Palace, which was the residence of the retired emperor. No sooner had they been banned from the palace than On'ami, the son of Zeami's brother Shirō, began to perform there. In addition, in 1430, Motomasa had the musical directorship at the Kiyotaki shrine taken from him. It was then conferred on On'ami. Motomasa was now apparently forced from the capital. He retired to Ōchi, in the province of Yamato.

Zeami's troubles continued. Later in 1430, his second son, Motoyoshi, who had been acting with the Kanze troupe, became discouraged with his career as an actor, apparently believing himself lacking in talent. He thereupon retired and took Buddhist orders. Worst of all for Zeami was the death of Motomasa in 1432. It seems probable that Motomasa had been banished from the capital because of suspected ties with the southern dynasty. Perhaps fear for his life made him retire to the protection of the lord of Ōchi. Shortly before his death, he gave a performance at the Tennokawa shrine, not far from Yoshima, where the southern dynasty had established its court. Following his performance, he said a prayer and left a mask at the shrine. Afterward, he died in the province of Ise, possibly the victim of murder. Zeami not only grieved for his dead son but also worried that no one would carry on the Nō tradition and the subtle art he had made of it.

Perhaps as important as any political factors that might have made Yoshinori reject Zeami and his sons was the refusal of Zeami to recognize the shogun's favorite as Motomasa's legitimate successor. Yoshinori was deficient in elegant, stylish knowledge (*yabo*). He lacked the connoisseurship (*tsū*) required to appreciate the kind of artistry practiced by Zeami. Before he became shogun, his favorite theatrical performer had been Enami. After Enami died in 1424, Yoshinori supported On'ami, because he liked the demoniac plays he regularly presented. Demoniac plays depended more on realistic miming than on symbolically significant acting, dancing, and words. Zeami rejected demon characters altogether in his Nō drama. Furthermore, he rigidly opposed On'ami's becoming leader of the Kanze school and refused to turn over the Kanze secret treatises to him, giving them to his son-in-law Konparu Zenchiku instead. On'ami considered himself a legitimate member of the Kanze school. He had chosen his stage name by selecting the third syllable of the Kanzeon name, just as Kan'ami had taken the first and Zeami the second. Zeami once stated that the Kan'ami-Zeami artistic line had been brought to an end with Motomasa's death, and, in his short treatise *Kyakuraika* (1433; the flower of returning), Zeami was even more adamant on this point. Zeami's opposition to Yoshinori's will must have angered the shogun considerably. Despite Zeami's resistance, On'ami eventually became leader of the Kanze school.

At any rate, in 1434, Yoshinori banished Zeami (then seventy-one years old) to Sado, a large island on the west coast of Japan that for years had been a place of exile for important personages. How long he lived on Sado and when he returned to the mainland—if he did return—is unknown. It is certain that he was exiled for at least two years, for he left a record of his exile in *Kintōsho* (1436; the book of the golden isle). This work consists of eight pieces meant to be recited and sung in the Nō style, and their formal character keeps the reader at some distance from Zeami's personal experience. He discloses no bitterness over his fate and views himself as part of the tradition of the personages who had also been exiled on Sado. Toward the end of his collection, he even adopts a hopeful and lighthearted tone. One tradition affirms that Zeami sent this collection to his friend Ikkyū (Sōjun), a notable Renzai Zen Buddhist priest and poet in Chinese, for editing. Ikkyū, also a friend of Konparu Zenchiku, is said to have given Zeami's pieces to the emperor, who was so impressed by them that he pardoned Zeami. If this legend is true, then Zeami probably returned to the mainland about 1437. According to this tradition, he died in Kyoto in 1443; others place his death on Sado Island.

Zeami had a high reputation as an actor in his time, but his acting method and style can only be imagined from his plays. As a playwright, he excelled. Not only are his plays well received in modern time but they are also superior in literary value to other extant Nō plays. Although some ninety Nō dramas have been attributed to Zeami, only about twenty can be specifically identified as his; about thirty-five others, however, can be considered almost certainly his. Occasionally Zeami did adapt the plays of others to suit his own purposes. Also, the sources of Nō plays were strictly conventional, and the playwrights typically chose material from specific classic Japanese narratives (which often included poems), as well as from certain ancient Chinese and Japanese verse.

Typical of those plays that are specifically identified as Zeami's or which can reasonably be considered his are *Aridōshi*, *Ashikari* (*The Reed Cutter*, 1970), *Atsumori* (English translation, 1921), *Aya no tsuzumu* (*The Damask Drum*, 1921), *Izutsu* (*Well-curb*, 1955), *Kinuta* (*The Clothbeating Block*, 1960), *Matsukaze* (*The Wind in the Pines*, 1960), and *Semimaru* (English translation, 1970).

Practically nothing was known of Zeami's important contributions to aesthetics until the beginning of the twentieth century. Between 1908 and 1909, Yoshida Tōgo discovered sixteen of Zeami's critical treatises. He published these as *Nōgaku koten: Zeami jūrokubushū* (1909; "Zeami's Sixteen Treatises," 1941-1942). In 1945, Kawase Kazuma discovered seven additional Zeami texts, which he published as *Tōchū Zeami nijūsambushū* (prologue to Zeami). Two of these texts are spurious, and one is fragmentary. A more accurate version of one of these, *Shūgyoku tokka* (finding gems and gaining the flower), was discovered in 1956, and a full version of the partial text, *Go on* (five sounds), was published in 1963. In 1984, J. Thomas Rimer and Yamazaki Masakazu published an excellent English translation of seven of Zeami's better-known texts that treat the essentials of acting.

Zeami used the term "flower" (*ka*, or *hana*) as one of his central concepts and "mystical beauty" (*yūgen*) as another. By *hana*, he meant the effect the actor ought to have on his audience. By *yūgen*, he meant the ideal beauty the actor ought to exude from within himself. *Yūgen* would be evident in the grace of his movements, in the elegance of his clothing, and in the gentleness of his voice. The word Nō literally meant "ability" or "talent." As a dramatic form, Nō grew out of both *dengaku*, or field music, and *sarugaku*, or comic entertainment, to become *sarugaku no nō*, or Nō. There are two types of *sarugaku:* Nō, drama that combines acting, dancing, and singing, and *kyōgen*, an improvised comic drama with some singing and dancing. Nō employs a stylized literary language; *kyōgen* uses colloquial language. The actors in Nō wear masks, but in *kyōgen*, they do not. In Nō, the characters are supernatural beings, famous men and women of the Heian period, and celebrated warriors. In *kyōgen*, the characters range from *daimyō* and their followers to monks, thieves, artisans, and peasants.

It was Zeami who developed Nō in a direction different from the *sarugaku* of his father, Kan'ami. He avoided the confrontation of two characters and developed dramatic tension from the anguished self-examination of one. He developed an economy of presentation that amounted to asceticism, since it was a transposition of aesthetic values through the medium of secularized Buddhism. His critical treatises were designed to pass on his tradition to his heirs. To Zeami, art was a way toward human perfection.

SIGNIFICANCE

Building on his father's work, Zeami Motokiyo revolutionized Nō drama. He made it respectable, an entertainment for the elite. He also pointed the way to its perfection. The idea of *yūgen* figured more prominently in his Nō than in Kan'ami's. The severe training that Zeami demanded of his students derived from the "difficult practice" of secularized Zen Buddhism as opposed to the "easy practice" of Pure Land Buddhism—burning incense, prayer, recitation of the Buddha's name, and reading of scripture—so popular with the masses. This difficult practice required discipline, asceticism, composure of body and mind through silent meditation, and the disappearance of the self. It appealed to the samurai class. Zeami replaced the traditional heroes of the masses with the warrior heroes—Atsumori, Tadanori, Yorimasa—or with the classical figures of Heian court culture.

In addition to his fine plays, Zeami left critical treatises both on the aesthetics of Nō and on the art of acting. Although he inherited the affective-aesthetic poetics of Ki no Tsurayuki's preface to the *Kokin Wakashū* (c. 905; also known as *Kokinshū*; English translation, 1970), with Tsurayuki's terms *kokoro* (heart), *tane* (seed), and *kokoba* (words), he went beyond Tsurayuki's idea that Japanese poetry takes the human heart as its seed, or effecting cause. Zeami held that in Nō the seed was artistic performance (*waza*). In Nō performance, the *yūgen* (mystic beauty) issued from the human heart and produced the *hana* (flower). Zeami replaced Kan'ami's *monomane*, or realistic miming, with the idea of the actor fulfilling a role by intuitive feeling and artistic acting.

Nō survives in present-day Japan, and even the Kanze school is still existent (a Nō performance in modern times, however, is much slower than it was in the medieval era). Nevertheless, some 250 plays constitute the present repertoire. There are god plays, warrior plays, woman plays, lunatic plays, revenge plays, and some other kinds. Further, Nō has influenced twentieth century Western drama, most notably through the works of William Butler Yeats and Ezra Pound.

—*Richard P. Benton*

FURTHER READING

Brandon, James, ed. *The Cambridge Guide to Asian Theater.* Cambridge, England: Cambridge University Press, 1993. Comprehensive overview of traditional Asian theater forms.

De Bary, William Theodore, et al., comps. *Sources of Japanese Tradition.* 2d ed. Vol. 1. New York: Columbia University Press, 2001. Includes excellent translations of important Zeami treatises, such as "On Attaining the Stage of *Yugen*," "On the One Mind Linking All Powers," "The Nine Stages of No in Order," and "The Book of the Way of the Highest Flower."

Hare, Thomas Blenman. *Zeami's Style: The Noh Plays of Zeami Motokiyo.* Stanford, Calif.: Stanford University Press, 1986. Superb study of Zeami's career and artistic contributions.

Keene, Donald, ed. *Nō: The Classical Theatre of Japan.* Palo Alto, Calif.: Kodansha International, 1966. An authoritative, substantial study of Nō drama. With photographs by Kaneko Hiroshi.

_______. *Twenty Plays of the Nō Theatre.* New York: Columbia University Press, 1970. Includes good translations of Zeami's work.

Ortolani, Benito. *The Japanese Theater: From Shamanistic Ritual to Contemporary Pluralism.* Rev. ed. Princeton, N.J.: Princeton University Press, 1995. Standard text for traditional and contemporary Japanese theater forms.

Terasaki, Etsuko. *Figures of Desire: Wordplay, Spirit Possession, Fantasy, Madness, and Mourning in Japanese Noh Plays.* Ann Arbor: Center for Japanese Studies, University of Michigan, 2002. An analysis of six plays attributed to Kan'ami and Zeami. Bibliography and index.

Thorndike, Arthur H., III. *Six Circles, One Dewdrop: The Religio-Aesthetic World of Komparu Zenchiku.* Princeton, N.J.: Princeton University Press, 1993. Includes translations of Zenchiku's theoretical work and an extensive commentary.

Zeami, Motokiyo. *Kadensho.* Translated by Sakurai Chuichi, Hayashi Shuseki, Satoi Rokuro, and Miyai Bin. Kyoto: Sumiya Shinobe Publishing Institute, 1968. One of Zeami's most influential treatises.

_______. *On the Art of the Nō Drama: The Major Treatises of Zeami.* Translated by J. Thomas Rimer and Yamazaki Masakazu. Princeton, N.J.: Princeton University Press, 1984. Excellent translations of nine of Zeami's treatises that deal with the essentials of acting.

SEE ALSO: Ashikaga Takauji.

RELATED ARTICLES in *Great Events from History: The Middle Ages, 477-1453*: 538-552: Buddhism Arrives in Japan; 792: Rise of the Samurai; 1156-1192: Minamoto Yoritomo Becomes Shogun; 1175: Hōnen Shōnin Founds Pure Land Buddhism; 1219-1333: Hōjō Family Dominates Shoguns, Rules Japan; 1336-1392: Yoshino Civil Wars; c. 1360-1440: Kan'ami and Zeami Perfect Nō Drama.

ZHENG HE
Chinese explorer

An imperial eunuch, Zheng He commanded the Ming Dynasty's voyages of exploration in the early fifteenth century, sailing farther than any person in history at that time.

BORN: c. 1371; Kunyang, Yunnan Province, China
DIED: between 1433 and 1436; possibly Calicut, India
ALSO KNOWN AS: Cheng Ho (Wade-Giles); Ma Sanbao (given name, Pinyin), Ma San-pao (Wade-Giles)
AREA OF ACHIEVEMENT: Exploration

EARLY LIFE

Zheng He (jehng heh) was born into a Muslim family surnamed Ma (a Chinese transliteration of Muḥammad). Although little is known about his family, it apparently had a tradition of foreign travel and adventure because both his father and grandfather made the traditional Muslim pilgrimage to Mecca.

In Zheng He's day, Yunnan was a frontier region heavily populated by non-Chinese (principally Tibeto-Burman) ethnic groups. Formerly a loose confederation of tribal states known as Nanzhao, Yunnan had been conquered by the Mongols in the thirteenth century during their invasion of China. The cities of Yunnan had a thin veneer of Chinese culture, but the civilization of the countryside remained essentially non-Chinese.

At the beginning of the Ming Dynasty (1368-1644), Chinese generals campaigned in Yunnan to wrest control of the area from the Mongols. The founder of the Ming, Zhu Yuanzhang (Chu Yüan-chang), also known as Hongwu (Hung-wu), sent about 300,000 troops under the control of a redoubtable commander in chief named Fu Youde (Fu Yu-te) to subdue the region. In the process, Fu recruited eunuchs (castrated males) into the service of the new dynasty.

Eunuchs were employed at the Chinese court to manage internal palace affairs, particularly those of the emperor's harem. Despite the opposition of the imperial bureaucracy, eunuchs frequently exerted remarkable power in Chinese politics. Because most emperors lived in seclusion from the outside world, they relied on the eunuchs to bring them information and to advise them on matters of state. At times in Chinese history, eunuchs usurped effective control of the government from the emperor and his bureaucracy. Although this was not particularly true of the emperors Zheng He served, his rise to power does illustrate the influence eunuchs have frequently enjoyed in Chinese history.

Zheng He became a eunuch in 1381, when he was about ten years old. He was assigned to the emperor's fourth son, Zhu Di (Chu Ti), who eventually became the third Ming emperor and ruled under the reign title of Yonglo (Yung-lo; r. 1402-1424). Zheng He's long service with Zhu Di earned him access to wealth and power. A huge, commanding man—his family records claim that he was 7 feet (210 centimeters) tall, with a waist 5 feet (152 centimeters) in circumference, glaring eyes, and a stentorian voice—he distinguished himself as a warrior in Zhu Di's armies, particularly in campaigns against the Mongols from 1393 to 1397. He played a key military role in Zhu Di's rebellion and usurpation of the throne and thus became one of the emperor's most powerful advisers.

During the climactic battle in Nanjing (Nanking) that toppled the emperor Jianwen (Chien-wen) and brought Zhu Di to the throne, the Ming palace area was burned and the deposed emperor apparently escaped. The fate of the deposed emperor remains a mystery, for he was never seen again. Zhu Di (by then known as Yonglo), seeking to complete his conquest by finally eliminating Jianwen, sent one of his trusted advisers throughout China in search of the former emperor and dispatched Zheng He on seven maritime expeditions to the "western ocean" (a term used to denote South and Southeast Asia).

LIFE'S WORK

Zheng He's voyages were the most spectacular maritime expeditions China ever launched. They began in 1405 and continued until 1433. During this period of twenty-eight years, Zheng He directed seven voyages that visited some thirty-seven countries and reached as far as Aden at the southeastern end of the Red Sea and the east coast of Africa. Zheng He was the driving force behind these expeditions, which ceased with his death.

Zheng He was promoted to the position of director of eunuch affairs and was granted the surname Zheng in 1404, just before he was appointed commander in chief of the first expedition. In comparison with the early European voyages of exploration, Zheng He's expeditions were gigantic. His largest ships measured 440 feet (134 meters) long and 186 feet (57 meters) wide, the medium-sized ships measured 370 by 150 feet (113 by 46 meters), and the battleships, which were equipped with cannon, measured 180 by 68 feet (55 by 21 meters). Some of the vessels had four decks and watertight compartments.

(In contrast, Christopher Columbus's largest ship, the *Santa Maria*, was less than 80 feet, or 24 meters, long.) Each of the voyages carried more than twenty thousand men.

Chinese sources offer two reasons for the launching of these expensive expeditions. First, Yonglo wanted to trace the whereabouts of the deposed emperor, who might have fled into Southeast Asia. Although this may have been one of the reasons for the first expedition, it apparently was not the primary impetus, for Zheng He made few efforts to search for Jianwen. The succeeding voyages, which ranged as far as Africa, obviously were not mounted in order to search for the former emperor. It is more likely that Yonglo authorized the voyages to demonstrate China's power and prestige to the world. Unlike the later Europeans, the Chinese were not exploring the world in search of commercial gain, for they did not believe that the non-Chinese could offer them products, ideas, or institutions that could equal their own. Believing that he was the son of heaven in control of all people on Earth, the Ming emperor sought to gain the allegiance of as many nations as he could. Paradoxically, then, it appears that the Chinese launched Zheng He's voyages, one of the most costly operations in history, for nonmaterialistic reasons.

It was the case, however, that the Chinese, particularly in the southeastern part of the country, had for centuries been engaged in overseas trade. As population pressures increased, they sailed abroad with Chinese products and returned with exotic goods of various kinds. Overseas trade proved extremely profitable, and consequently many southeastern seaports flourished. The migration of Chinese merchants to various parts of Southeast Asia began long before the Ming Dynasty. Seamanship improved with each succeeding generation, so that when Yonglo ordered the mounting of his huge expeditions, Zheng He could readily recruit his officers and crewmen. Moreover, the Chinese had perfected shipbuilding techniques and navigation skills to the level that they could undertake massive voyages of exploration. Their ships could travel as fast as six knots per hour, and their knowledge of the compass permitted accurate navigation. Therefore, Zheng He could lead seven huge and highly successful expeditions that nearly led to the Chinese discovery of Europe.

Zheng He's first voyage left the central coast of China in the summer of 1405 with a twenty-seven-man crew and 62 large and 255 small vessels carrying cargoes of silk, embroidered goods, and other such products. The colossal fleet called at Champa (the southeast coast of modern-day Vietnam) and fought to clear the strategic Strait of Malacca of the powerful Chinese pirates who had plagued the area for decades. Zheng He's victory over the pirates made passage through the straits safe and enhanced Ming prestige in Southeast Asia.

The second voyage left China in the fall of 1407 and eventually reached Calicut on the southwestern coast of India. Zheng He extended imperial gifts and greetings to the ruler of Calicut, who had frequently sent gifts to the Chinese emperors. On the return leg of the voyage, Zheng He called on Siam and Java, where he intervened in Javanese politics and established a ruler friendly to the Ming.

The third voyage began in September, 1409, and lasted until June, 1411. It again visited Calicut but traveled onward to Siam, Malacca, Sumatra, and Ceylon, where Zheng He defeated a Ceylonese king and carried out extensive trade. The fourth voyage took 27,670 men and sixty-three large vessels far beyond India to the Maldives, Hormuz, and Aden. As a consequence of this journey, nineteen countries sent tributary missions to the Ming capital at Nanjing. During the fifth voyage, from 1417 to 1419, Zheng He escorted the envoys of these missions home. Zheng He brought strange and exotic animals, such as giraffes, ostriches, zebras, and leopards, back with him to China. The sixth voyage, lasting from 1421 to 1422, also reached Aden and the east coast of Africa. Before a seventh expedition could be launched, Zheng He's patron, Yonglo, died, and opponents of the voyages recommended that they be abandoned. Eventually, however, the final Zheng He voyage left China in late 1431 and returned in July of 1433. It once again visited the Arabian peninsula, including Mecca, and eastern Africa. Zheng He is believed to have died between 1433 and 1436; one source maintains that he died early in 1433 at Calicut and was later buried in Nanjing.

Not much is known about Zheng He's private life. He may have had an adopted son, and he made his permanent home in Nanjing. He undoubtedly retained his Islamic faith, which facilitated his interchanges with the Muslim states of Southeast Asia, Africa, and Arabia, but he was interested in Buddhism and Chinese folk religion. He was a man of unique power and influence. To have led so many massive expeditions would have required a rare combination of navigational, managerial, and diplomatic skills.

SIGNIFICANCE

Zheng He's achievements mark him as one of the great explorers of all time. His organizational and command skills were extraordinary. He established firm contacts with nearly forty countries in the "western ocean," and he provided China with detailed geographical information about the outside world. The commercial contacts he initiated continued even though the Ming government terminated the large-scale voyages after his death.

The Ming did not continue the voyages for three reasons. First, the costs were extremely high and did not result in significant economic gains. Second, dangers on China's northern and western frontiers, where the Mongols and other Central Asians threatened the Ming, distracted Chinese attention from overseas adventures. Third, and most important, the Chinese saw little need to explore areas outside the "Middle Kingdom." They believed China was a superior civilization that did not need to go overseas to propagate Chinese beliefs. Others could come to China to learn, but the Chinese had no desire to convince outsiders of the efficacy of their beliefs and institutions. Moreover, most Chinese believed they were economically self-sufficient and needed no foreign goods. Thus, even though Zheng He's voyages were spectacular, they were by no means essential to Chinese life and were discontinued as abruptly as they began.

In 1497, only sixty-four years after Zheng He's last expedition, Vasco da Gama reached India, thus inaugurating the era of European imperialism in Asia and reversing the direction of exploration. If the Chinese had continued Zheng He's efforts—establishing permanent bases, maintaining their sea power, and founding a vast empire—it is possible that the course of world history would have been altered profoundly. China might have "discovered" Europe. Instead, Europeans "discovered" China, Ming sea power declined, and Portugal created vast maritime empires. China remained landlocked, and its failure to develop seafaring capabilities eventually invited European imperialism.

Zheng He's expeditions were important in their own right, as they established patterns of Chinese diplomacy and trade as far as the coasts of Arabia and Africa and momentarily stimulated China's commerce. In the final analysis, however, the voyages remain a Chinese historical aberration, a trip down a blind alley, because the Chinese did not continue their explorations. Still, historians will continue to wonder how world history might have been different if Zheng He, the Chinese Columbus, had been succeeded by an equally adventurous voyager.

—*Loren W. Crabtree*

FURTHER READING

Antony, Robert J. *Like Froth Floating on the Sea: The World of Pirates and Seafarers in Late Imperial South China.* China Research Monographs 56. Berkeley, Calif.: Institute of East Asian Studies, 2003. An examination of the pirates in South China (encountered by Zheng He) during the Ming and Qing Dynasties.

Levathes, Louise. *When China Ruled the Seas: The Treasure Fleet of the Dragon Throne, 1405-1433.* New York: Oxford University Press, 1996. Describes the life and activities of Zheng He as well as conditions in the Ming Dynasty during his lifetime. Illustrations, maps, bibliography, and index.

Menzies, Gavin. *1421: The Year China Discovered the Americas.* New York: William Morrow, 2003. A somewhat controversial treatment of Zheng He's travels that suggest that his ships reached the Americas. Illustrations, maps, bibliography, and index.

Ptak, Roderich. *China and the Asian Seas: Trade, Travel, and Visions of the Others (1400-1750).* Brookfield, Vt.: Ashgate, 1998. An examination of the explorations of Zheng He and the trade in which the Chinese engaged. Bibliography and index.

Tsai, Shih-shan Henry. *The Eunuchs in the Ming Dynasty.* Albany: State University of New York Press, 1996. A study of how the eunuchs were used during the Ming Dynasty. One chapter focuses on Ming maritime activities. Illustrations, maps, bibliography, and index.

_______. *Perpetual Happiness: The Ming Emperor Yongle.* Seattle: University of Washington Press, 2001. A study of the reign of Yonglo, Zheng He's supporter, and its place within the Ming Dynasty.

SEE ALSO: Marco Polo; Xuanzang; Yonglo.

RELATED ARTICLES in *Great Events from History: The Middle Ages, 477-1453*: 1271-1295: Travels of Marco Polo; 1368: Establishment of the Ming Dynasty; 1397: Publication of the Laws of Great Ming; 1405-1433: Zheng He's Naval Expeditions.

ZHU XI

Chinese scholar

Through writings and educational activities, Zhu Xi reformulated Confucianism. His work helped Confucianism regain intellectual ascendancy over Buddhism and Daoism, establishing basic Confucian orientations for centuries and influencing East Asian culture.

BORN: October 18, 1130; Youxi, Fujian Province, China
DIED: April 23, 1200; Jianyang County, Fujian, China
ALSO KNOWN AS: Chu Hsi (Wade-Giles)
AREAS OF ACHIEVEMENT: Philosophy, government and politics

EARLY LIFE

The early years of Zhu Xi (jew shee) were dominated by the uncertainty in the wake of the loss of northern China to Jurchen conquerors and the reestablishment of the Song Dynasty in the south in 1128. His father, Zhu Song (Chu Sung), after protesting against peace talks, was sent to a local post in Fujian; his fortunes continued to decline to the point that he even lost his position as sheriff of Youxi shortly before Zhu Xi's birth there in 1130. In the traditional pattern of accounts of great scholars, biographers have presented Zhu Xi as a precocious child, with exceptional interest in metaphysics, filial piety, and classical scholarship. Zhu Xi claimed that by the time he was nine, he was determined to become a Confucian sage.

In 1140, Zhu Song's second term of governmental service ended because of his continued opposition to the peace party. Having studied with disciples of the brothers Cheng Hao and Cheng Yi, he devoted three years to teaching his son; on his deathbed, he entrusted Zhu Xi to three neighboring scholars. Five years after his father's death, Zhu Xi passed the national civil service examinations at the age of eighteen, which was about half the average age of successful candidates that year. During these early years, Zhu Xi suffered much grief; in addition to his father, two brothers and two of the three neighboring scholars who taught him died. These deaths may have contributed to Zhu Xi's fascination with Buddhism and Daoism during his teens as well as his sense of mission as a survivor. He was apparently of good health, in spite of complaints beginning in his mid-fifties about unspecified illnesses and foot ailments.

Beginning in 1153 and lasting for five years, Zhu Xi held his first government position as a registrar in Tongan County in Fujian, where he concentrated on reforming the management of local taxation and police, upgrading educational standards, and drafting codes for decorum and ritual. After leaving that post, he enjoyed his first sinecure appointment as overseer of a mountain temple; such honorary positions provided him with the leisure to study and write.

An invasion by the Jurchen, which renewed debate about foreign policy, provoked Zhu Xi into submitting memorials to the emperor in 1162 and 1163. In those memorials and the resulting audience with the emperor, he followed his father's lead in criticizing peace advocates. To Zhu Xi, war to liberate northern China was the only moral course of action. Although appointed a professor at the military academy, he resigned on hearing that the government was making peace. Returning home to Fujian, he repeatedly declined office until 1178. Yet he remained active in local affairs, such as emergency famine relief.

During the 1150's and 1160's, Zhu Xi continued to evolve intellectually. His teacher Li Tong convinced him to abandon Buddhism and Daoism and led him to a definitive embrace of Confucianism by the time he was twenty-eight. During the 1160's, he accepted as standard the teachings of the Cheng brothers; moreover, his exchange of letters with Zhang Shi about the cultivation of the mind in action and tranquillity demonstrated that by 1169, nearing age forty, Zhu Xi had attained intellectual maturity in his interpretation of Confucianism.

LIFE'S WORK

Although he repeatedly declined many offices during his remaining thirty years, Zhu Xi's political career was eventful. In 1178, he was appointed a prefect in Jiangxi, where he concentrated on preventing famine and improving education. In addition to lecturing advanced students at least once every five days, he reestablished the once-flourishing White Deer Hollow Academy. Under Zhu Xi's leadership, the academy became an educational model that endured for almost seven centuries. The next post he assumed was as a regional superintendent in Zhejiang, where he was in charge of famine relief. In addition to establishing community granaries and other relief measures, he toured the countryside to ferret out corrupt and incompetent officials. Impeaching several county and prefectural heads—including Tang Zhongyou, who was a relative of the prime minister—Zhu Xi aroused such controversy that he resigned from office after serving for roughly a year.

The indictment of a noted scholar whose Confucianism differed from Zhu Xi's added to the controversy about the *dao xue* (learning of the true way) tradition, which was rooted in the teachings of the Cheng brothers. In his memorials to the emperor, Chu expounded on the need for government officials to follow the ethical principles of this tradition if they were to reform themselves and provide for the welfare of the people. Resentment at court toward such advice hindered his career, but he did serve as prefect of Zhangzhou, Fujian (from 1190 to 1191), and of Tanzhou, Hunan (1194), where he continued his educational and community service reforms.

In 1194, Zhu Xi was summoned to court to be a lecturer to the emperor but was so outspoken that he was dismissed and returned to Fujian after spending only about forty days as a member of the emperor's court. Soon the officials whom he had criticized launched a purge of political opponents and an attack on *dao xue* for being "false learning." Although every major intellectual of the day was implicated in this attack, Zhu Xi was the leading figure whose teachings were proscribed. Zhu Xi died in 1200, still in official disfavor, but several thousand people dared to attend his funeral. Indeed, he was regarded by many of the literati of the era as a martyr and a symbol of the Confucian scholar defending ethical principles against arbitrary exercise of governmental power. Soon the political climate improved, and he was exonerated. Later, in 1241, the government honored him with a place in Confucian temples.

Although he held office for only nine years, Zhu Xi contributed significantly to reform of educational and community institutions and family rituals. Nevertheless, his reputation rests primarily on his scholarship. Over the course of forty years, he wrote a series of commentaries on the Four Books, and these commentaries best demonstrate his agenda. The Four Books are Confucius's *Lunyu* (later sixth-early fifth centuries B.C.E.; *The Analects*, 1861), Mencius's *Mengzi* (first transcribed in the early third century B.C.E.; English translation in *The Confucian Classics*, 1861; commonly known as *Mengzi*), the *Da Xue* (fifth-first century B.C.E.; *The Great Learning*, 1861), and the *Zhong yong* (written c. 500 B.C.E.; *The Doctrine of the Mean*, 1861). Although some earlier *dao xue* masters had focused on these four works, Zhu Xi was the first to make them explicitly the pedagogical foundation of all Confucian studies. In his series of commentaries on these books, he corrected the mistakes of earlier Confucians and established what he considered to be the true interpretation of these crucial texts. Zhu Xi reinterpreted other classics as well and directed a rewriting of the standard history of China in order to subject historical issues to ethical judgments.

Zhu Xi's writings and activities aimed at building a community among Confucian scholars. Joining with Lü Zuqian (Lü Tsu-ch'ien; 1137-1181), he compiled the *Jin si lü* (1175; *Reflections on Things at Hand*, 1967) as a primer to direct Confucian learning based on statements by earlier *dao xue* masters. In 1175, he began having disagreements with Lu Jiuyuan (Lu Chiu-yüan) about the relative priority of erudition and intuition of essential virtues as a basis for the Confucian way of life. In the 1180's, Zhu Xi was challenged by Chen Liang (Ch'en Liang), who had a utilitarian idea of using results to define virtues and a historicist penchant for regarding the Dao as having evolved with temporal and spatial changes. To Zhu Xi, Lu Jiuyuan followed the mistakes of Chan Buddhists in concentrating too exclusively on personal enlightenment and reducing normative patterns to aspects of the mind. Chen Liang pursued social and political achievement at the expense of ethical training; moreover, historicism devalued the constancy of ethical norms, according to Zhu Xi.

These Confucians did agree on a wide range of political and philosophical issues; moreover, they shared a sense that scholars needed to be part of a community with a sharper awareness of Confucian traditions. Although Lu Jiuyuan more often reached beyond scholars directly to the masses and Chen Liang directed his comments mostly to scholar-officials, Zhu Xi had a clearer educational pedagogy; hence, although he concentrated more on the literati and sought to reach the masses through them, his educational work and his work for the community reached the largest audience.

Zhu Xi was arguably the most systematic philosopher, with the broadest scope of interests in traditional China; moreover, he sought to apply his philosophical understanding to all areas of inquiry: Each thing had an inherent pattern (order or principle) that should be investigated and placed in the context of its relation to the universal order. Although he made careful observations of diverse things, the subject of Zhu Xi's inquiry was essentially Confucian ethical thought and action.

Significance

The scope of Zhu Xi's scholarship and the power of his intellect joined with his contributions to education, community unity, and ritual bonding within the family to make him the most influential scholar after Confucius in China. Even if they disagreed with his restructuring of the tradition, Chinese scholars have been unable to ignore his writings and terms of discourse. From 1313 to 1905, his commentaries on the Four Books were decreed to be the standard interpretation and the authority of the civil service examinations.

Later emperors, far more autocratic than the ones he personally admonished, observed the popularity of Zhu Xi among the literati and discovered that aspects of his philosophy of inherent pattern and his effort to build a Confucian community could be appropriated to enhance intellectual orthodoxy as well as hierarchical social and political order. Appealing to both literati and rulers in traditional Korea and Japan, Zhu Xi has also had more influence than any other Chinese thinker since the third century B.C.E. on various areas of culture in those countries. Although he has been blamed by modern-day intellectuals and political reformers for much of the oppressiveness in East Asian cultures, some since the 1960's have increasingly emphasized positive impacts of his legacy on philosophy, education, and ethics.

—*Hoyt Cleveland Tillman*

FURTHER READING

Chan, Wing-tsit. *Chu Hsi: Life and Thought*. Hong Kong: Chinese University Press, 1987. Essays survey the history of Zhu Xi's impact on China, Korea, Japan, Europe, and the United States. Special attention is given to changing attitudes toward Zhu Xi in the twentieth century. Chan has done more than anyone else to introduce Zhu Xi's philosophy in the English language. Includes bibliography and index.

_______, ed. *Chu Hsi and Neo-Confucianism*. Honolulu: University of Hawaii Press, 1986. An international collection of essays by thirty-one senior scholars covers diverse areas of Zhu Xi's philosophy but emphasizes his metaphysics. The volume is especially noteworthy for including most of the major twentieth century Chinese and Japanese historians of Chinese thought. One essay relates Zhu Xi's life to his philosophy, and several evaluate his influence on later generations in East Asia. Includes an index.

Chu Hsi. *Further Reflections on Things at Hand*. Translated by Allen Wittenburn. Lanham, Md.: University Press of America, 1991. Selections from several of Zhu Xi's works, arranged by topic. Wittenburn's commentary is complex but good on outlining the wide range of Zhu Xi's ideas.

Chu Hsi, and Lu Tsu-ch'ien. *Reflections on Things at Hand: The Neo-Confucian Anthology*. Translated by Wing-tsit Chan. New York: Columbia University Press, 1967. A translation of a fundamental work that gave direction to neo-Confucianism.

Gardner, Daniel K. *Chu Shi and the "Ta-hsüeh": Neo-Confucian Reflection on the Confucian Canon*. Cambridge, Mass.: Harvard University Press, 1986. In addition to an original annotated translation based on Zhu Xi's writings, Gardner provides a study of the *Da xue* text, its history through the Song, and the reasons Zhu Xi found the text so philosophically compelling. Includes annotations, bibliography, index, and the Chinese text.

Liu Shu-hsien. *Understanding Confucian Philosophy Classical and Sung-Ming*. Westport, Conn.: Greenwood Press, 1998. A discussion of the development of Confucian thought from the viewpoint of a contemporary neo-Confucian. The section on Zhu Xi is very good on the development of Zhu Xi's ideas and the philosophical problems he faced and provides critical commentary on the views of current scholars studying the philosopher.

Tillman, Hoyt Cleveland. *Confucian Discourse and Chu Hsi's Ascendancy*. Honolulu: University of Hawaii Press, 1992. This is a study of what is conventionally known as "neo-Confucianism" (Confucian discourse), ranging chronologically from the mid-twelfth to the mid-fourteenth century. Thus Zhu Xi is seen in dialogue with his predecessors, contemporaries, and disciples.

_______. *Utilitarian Confucianism: Ch'en Liang's Challenge to Chu Hsi*. Cambridge, Mass.: Harvard University Press, 1982. In addition to analyzing the issues between Chen Liang and Zhu Xi, this study also surveys the evolving intellectual and political environment during the eleventh and twelfth centuries. The lives and personal relations of the two principals are also discussed. Includes bibliography and index.

SEE ALSO: Ouyang Xiu.

RELATED ARTICLES in *Great Events from History: The Middle Ages, 477-1453*: 960: Founding of the Song Dynasty; 960-1279: Scholar-Official Class Flourishes Under Song Dynasty; 1115: Foundation of the Jin Dynasty; 1130: Birth of Zhu Xi; 1368: Establishment of the Ming Dynasty.

JAN ŽIŽKA
Bohemian general

Žižka's innovations in military organization and weapons, mobile artillery in particular, were directly responsible for the success of the Hussite revolution. They also spelled the end of the medieval system of mounted knights.

BORN: c. 1360; Trocnov, Bohemia (now in Czech Republic)
DIED: October 11, 1424; Přibyslav, Bohemia (now in Czech Republic)
ALSO KNOWN AS: John Ziska
AREAS OF ACHIEVEMENT: Warfare and conquest, science and technology, military, religion and theology

EARLY LIFE

Jan Žižka (yahn ZHISH-kaw) was born in Trocnov, Bohemia. Trocnov was only a few miles north of the border of what is now Austria. The region south of Trocnov was populated and controlled mostly by Germans. Žižka was thus brought up in an essentially bilingual culture. Žižka meant "one-eyed" and was a nickname derived from his early loss of an eye. His family was poor, and Žižka was apparently reared in the royal court, gaining military experience in its service.

From about 1380 to 1392, Žižka's activities are a mystery, except that he was apparently the royal hunter in the town of Zahorany near the royal castle of Orlik for Wenceslaus IV. About 1405 Žižka returned to his homeland. Sometime during this period, he left the king's service to fight as a mercenary in one of the guerrilla bands employed by barons who sided with either the Bohemians or the Moravians in their protracted struggle. In 1409, King Wenceslaus pardoned Žižka for his renegade military adventures, and Žižka was soon fighting with Jan Sokol of Lamberg for the Polish king against the Teutonic Knights. From this campaign Žižka derived considerable valuable military experience.

The court register of Prague's New Town (Nove Mesto, established in the mid-fourteenth century) reveals that Žižka bought a house there in 1414. Two years later, he sold this house and bought another one closer to the king's residence, at the same time apparently assuming some official position in the city palace. It is quite probable that during these years Žižka met Jan Hus and heard him preach.

Hus became dean of the faculty of arts at the university in Prague in 1401, and in the same year, he began an outstanding career preaching at Bethlehem Chapel. In many ways, he was a follower of John Wyclif, and in 1408 he was censured for ignoring an order from cathedral officials to reject a list of forty-five articles drawn up from Wyclif's writings. Hus's continued defense of Wyclif and defiance of the Church led to his being burned at the stake in 1415. A similar fate met Jerome of Prague the next year.

These events created a furor. Hus approved of the custom of administering Holy Communion in both forms—wine as well as bread—as expressed in the phrase *sub utraque specie*, and soon after Hus's death, many nobles and university men took up the custom in what became known as the Utraquist revolt. By 1420, they were also demanding punishment for simony, freedom to preach the Word of God, and a halt to the venality rampant among priests and monks. These three points, along with the demand for both forms of Communion, became known as the Four Articles of Prague. Thus, the Hussite revolt can be seen as a precursor to the Reformation.

LIFE'S WORK

After an angry crowd threw the members of the Prague council out of the council building's windows in 1419, King Wenceslaus accepted a new council made up of Hussites. He died shortly thereafter. It is at that time that Žižka entered the complicated political and religious maneuvering, often in the service of the Taborites.

The Taborites were a radical, chiliastic (apocalyptic) sect who took their name from the biblical Mount Tabor. In November, 1419, when various Taborite groups approached Prague, several were ambushed by royalist supporters. Then Žižka took up arms for the Taborites and led them in capturing the royal castle, the Vyšehrad.

Following this triumph, Žižka left Prague to settle in Pilsen as the resident Hussite leader; in February, 1420, he received a call for help from Tabor (the home community of the Taborites). Thus, in late March, 1420, Žižka set out with a small group and twelve wagons, armed with cannon, determined to assist the Taborites against the royalists. When his forces were ambushed in the village of Sudomer, Žižka led them to a stunning victory over superior numbers and thereby kept radical Hussitism alive in the Tabor community. Žižka was soon elected one of the four captains of the Taborites, and during this period he carried out many terrorist campaigns against both castles and towns. He was also instrumental in building up the defenses around Tabor.

In the aftermath, King Sigismund of Hungary (Wenceslaus's half brother) in 1420 led a military force against Prague; the Hussites quickly mustered an army to meet him. Žižka was called back to Prague, where he trained and commanded a force that completely routed Sigismund's men. Important to Žižka's success against Sigismund was the placement of his war wagons in a quadrangle surrounded by a moat. The decisive battle was fought on July 14, 1420, on the hill of Vitkov near New Town, where Žižka defeated a huge army that outnumbered the Hussites four or five to one.

The struggle between the royalists and the Hussites continued for several more years, with Žižka winning numerous important engagements; by the autumn of 1420, the Taborites of the south had become a potent national faction, which often disagreed with the moderate Utraquists in Prague. By the spring of 1421, the Hussites were in command of Hradčany Castle, forcing the Utraquists to sign an armistice on May 21.

The ceaseless haggling over theological and ecclesiastical issues soon brought Žižka back into combat, however, and in June, 1421, while directing an assault on the castle at Bor, Žižka was hit in his remaining eye by an arrow and blinded permanently. Nevertheless, his greatest victories were yet to come. He helped drive the Misnians out of Bohemia, and he purified the Taborite faith of what he considered the evil influence of Martin Houska, a Moravian priest, and his heretical teachings about the Eucharist. Žižka also defeated in pitched battle the Adamite wing of the Taborites. The Adamites were radicals who taught that one should succumb completely to one's impulses, leading to nudity, the prohibition of marriage, and group orgies. Žižka's campaign against them in October, 1421, finished the Adamite movement. Of his military conquests after his blindness, his defeat of Sigismund at Kutná Hora in December, 1421, and his victory at the Battle of Malesov on June 7, 1423, stand out.

Žižka's death came in October, 1424, when he fell ill—perhaps of the plague—during the siege of Přibyslav. After his death, his followers called themselves "orphans" in acknowledgment of their bereavement.

SIGNIFICANCE

Much of Jan Žižka's fervor was generated by his dedication to the Four Articles of Prague. He strongly supported the third of the articles—that which deprived monks and priests of their accumulation of earthly possessions—and he even more strongly supported the fourth.

> All mortal sins and especially those that are committed publicly, as well as other disorders offending against the Law of God, shall be properly and sensibly prohibited and punished in each estate by those who have the authority to do so; and . . . evil and slanderous rumors about this country [shall] be cleansed away, thus insuring the general welfare of the Bohemian kingdom and Nation.

A long list of sins accompanied this article. Laypersons were condemned for adultery, gluttony, and the like, while the members of the clergy were called to task for simony, selling indulgences, and taking money for saying Mass, as well as for whoring, brawling, and many other faults. For the many pious Christians such as Žižka, this list of human failings threatened the foundation of God's Kingdom: Žižka clearly saw himself as a "severe avenger" (as he was described in the inscription to a sixteenth century portrait of him) whose duty it was to purify the church membership. According to Frederick G. Heymann, Žižka regarded himself as

Jan Žižka. (Library of Congress)

> the legitimate prosecutor, judge, and executor in implementing the Fourth Article. He never had any doubt that this was his office, that he was fully authorized by God and Christ, as was any true Christian with enough power on his hands, to destroy the deadly sins wherever he met them.

This conception explains the ruthlessness of many of Žižka's actions.

Žižka's success as leader of the Taborite military force can hardly be overestimated. The strategy that produced his enormous successes was his deployment of his wagons, and these were his major contribution to military science. Their use made obsolete the medieval style of military combat with mounted knights. In addition, Žižka's deployment of his peasant warriors surpassed in discipline and flexibility any previous approach to military tactics. Finally, when Žižka mounted guns on his wagons, he created his own field artillery, an invention that proved to be psychologically as well as materially devastating to his enemies.

—*Frank Day*

FURTHER READING

Durant, Will. "The Western Slavs: 1300-1517." In *The Story of Civilization*. Vol. 6. New York: Simon and Schuster, 1957. This chapter gives an excellent, succinct overview of the period, with sections on Bohemia, Jan Hus, and the Bohemian Revolution. A good introductory essay.

Fudge, Thomas A. *The Magnificent Ride: The First Reformation in Hussite Bohemia*. Brookfield, Vt.: Ashgate, 1998. Traces the social, political, and ideological events surrounding the Hussite movement in Bohemia. Includes a discussion of the role of Žižka and two other warriors, Prokop and Rohac, in the reformation.

Heymann, Frederick G. *John Žižka and the Hussite Revolution*. Princeton, N.J.: Princeton University Press, 1955. A detailed, five-hundred-page study of Žižka and the Hussites. Especially good at clarifying the role of the Taborites in the Hussite revolution and explaining what the Taborites meant to Žižka. The military campaigns are recounted in detail.

Holmes, George. *Europe, Hierarchy and Revolt, 1320-1450*. 2d ed. Malden, Mass.: Blackwell, 2000. Includes chapters on the Avignon and Roman papacies, the Great Schism, and the Hussite movement, and several maps.

Kaminsky, Howard. *A History of the Hussite Revolution*. Berkeley: University of California Press, 1967. A lengthy scholarly study with an excellent bibliography. There are frequent references to Žižka, and the discussion of the Taborite movement is very good.

Klassen, John M. *Warring Maidens, Captive Wives, and Hussite Queens: Women and Men at War and at Peace in Fifteenth Century Bohemia*. New York: Columbia University Press, 1999. A useful text for broadening one's understanding of the cultural effects of the revolution that Žižka helped bring about. Examines the changing roles of women in fifteenth century bohemia. The author argues that women gained more freedom from traditional roles as men came to respect those dissident women working to resist women's oppression and subordination.

Urbanek, R. "Jan Žižka, the Hussite." *Slavonic Review* 8 (December, 1924): 272-284. A glowing survey of Žižka's career written for his quincentenary. Traces the key events in Žižka's life.

SEE ALSO: Jan Hus; Wenceslaus; John Wyclif.

RELATED ARTICLES in *Great Events from History: The Middle Ages, 477-1453*: c. 1175: Waldensian Excommunications Usher in Protestant Movement; 1228-1231: Teutonic Knights Bring Baltic Region Under Catholic Control; 1305-1417: Avignon Papacy and the Great Schism; 1377-1378: Condemnation of John Wyclif; July 15, 1410: Battle of Tannenberg; July 6, 1415: Martyrdom of Jan Hus.

Rulers and Dynasties

Major world leaders during the period covered in *Great Lives from History: The Middle Ages, 477-1453* are listed below, beginning with the Roman Catholic popes and followed by rulers of major nations or dynasties, alphabetically by country. Within each country section, rulers are listed chronologically. Rulers whose names appear in SMALL CAPITAL LETTERS are covered in separate essays within these volumes. It is important to note that name spellings and regnal dates vary among sources, and that variations do not necessarily suggest inaccuracy. For example, dates when leaders took power may not match dates of coronation, and the names by which leaders have been recorded in history may represent given names, epithets, or regnal names. Date ranges and geographical borders of nations and dynasties vary, given the complexities of politics and warfare, and the mere fact that "nations" (a concept not clearly defined until modern history) evolved over time from competing and allied principalities, particularly in the post-Roman Empire millennium conventionally called the "Middle" Ages. Hence, not every civilization, dynasty, principality, or region can be covered here; we have, however, attempted to provide lists of those rulers for those countries most likely to be studied in general and area history courses that address the period 477-1453. Where dynasties, houses, or lines extended somewhat beyond these chronological "borders," full lists are included for continuity.

Contents

Popes and Antipopes

Asterisked (*) names indicate popes who have been sainted by the Church. Names appearing in square brackets [ ] are antipopes.

Term	*Pope*
440-461	*Leo I the Great
461-468	*Hilarius
468-483	*Simplicius
483-492	*Felix III
492-496	*Gelasius I
496-498	Anastasius II
498-514	*Symmachus
498-505	[Laurentius]
514-523	*Hormisdas
523-526	*John I
526-530	*Felix IV
530-532	Boniface II
530	[Dioscursus]
533-535	John II
535-536	*Agapetus I

Term	*Pope*
536-537	*Silverius
537-555	Vigilius
556-561	Pelagius I
561-574	John III
575-579	Benedict I
579-590	Pelagius II
590-604	*GREGORY I THE GREAT
604-606	Sabinian
607	Boniface III
608-615	*Boniface IV (Adeodatus I)
615-618	*Deusdedit
619-625	Boniface V
625-638	Honorius I
638-640	Vacant
640	Severinus
640-642	John IV
642-649	Theodore I
649-655	*Martin I
655-657	*Eugene I
657-672	*Vitalian
672-676	Adeodatus II
676-678	Donus
678-681	*Agatho
682-683	*Leo II
684-685	*Benedict II
685-686	John V
686-687	Conon
687	[Theodore II]
687-692	[Paschal I]
687-701	*SAINT SERGIUS I
701-705	John VI
705-707	John VII
708	Sisinnius
708-715	Constantine
715-731	*Gregory II
731-741	*Gregory III
741-752	*Zachary
752-757	Stephen II
757-767	*Paul I
767	[Constantine]
767	[Philip]
767-772	Stephen III
772-795	Adrian I
795-816	*Leo III
816-817	Stephen IV
817-824	*Paschal I
824-827	Eugene II
827	Valentine
827-844	Gregory IV
844	[John VIII]
844-847	Sergius II
847-855	*Leo IV
855-858	Benedict III
855	[Anastasius III]
858-867	*NICHOLAS I THE GREAT
867-872	Adrian II
872-882	John VIII
882-884	Marinus I
884-885	*Adrian III
885-891	Stephen V
891-896	Formosus
896	Boniface VI
896-897	Stephen VI
897	Romanus
897	Theodore II
898-900	John IX
900-903	Benedict IV
903	Leo V
903-904	Christopher
904-911	Sergius III
911-913	Anastasius III
913-914	Lando
914-928	John X
928	Leo VI
929-931	Stephen VII
931-935	John XI
936-939	Leo VII
939-942	Stephen IX (VIII)
942-946	Marinus II
946-955	Agapetus II
955-963	John XII
963-964	Leo VIII
964	Benedict V
965-972	John XIII
973-974	Benedict VI
974-983	Benedict VII
983-984	John XIV
983-984	Boniface VII
985-996	John XV
996-999	Gregory V
996-998	[John XVI]
999-1003	SYLVESTER II
1003	John XVII
1003-1009	John XVIII
1009-1012	Sergius IV
1012-1024	Benedict VIII
1012	[Gregory VI]
1024-1033	John XIX
1033-1045	Benedict IX
1045	Sylvester III
1045-1046	Gregory VI (John Gratian Pierleoni)
1046-1047	Clement II (Suitgar, count of Morslegen)
1048	Damasus II (Count Poppo)
1049-1054	*LEO IX (Bruno of Egisheim)

Term	*Pope*
1055-1057	Victor II (Gebhard, count of Hirschberg)
1057-1058	Stephen IX (Frederick of Lorraine)
1058	Benedict X (John, count of Tusculum)
1058-1061	Nicholas II (Gerhard of Burgundy)
1061-1073	Alexander II (Anselmo da Baggio)
1061-1064	[Honorius II]
1073-1085	*GREGORY VII (Hildebrand)
1080-1100	[Clement III]
1086-1087	Victor III (Desiderius, prince of Beneventum)
1088-1099	URBAN II (Odo of Lagery)
1099-1118	Paschal II (Ranieri da Bieda)
1100-1102	[Theodoric]
1102	[Albert]
1105	[Sylvester IV]
1118-1119	Gelasius II (John Coniolo)
1118-1121	[Gregory VIII]
1119-1124	Callixtus II (Guido, count of Burgundy)
1124-1130	Honorius II (Lamberto dei Fagnani)
1124-1130	[Celestine II]
1130-1143	Innocent II (Gregorio Papareschi)
1130-1138	[Anacletus II (Cardinal Pierleone)]
1138	[Victor IV]
1143-1144	Celestine II (Guido di Castello)
1144-1145	Lucius II (Gherardo Caccianemici)
1145-1153	Eugene III (Bernardo Paganelli)
1153-1154	Anastasius IV (Corrado della Subarra)
1154-1159	ADRIAN IV (Nicolas Breakspear)
1159-1181	ALEXANDER III (Roland Bandinelli)
1159-1164	[Victor IV]
1164-1168	[Paschal III]
1168-1178	[Calixtus III]
1179-1180	[Innocent III (Lando da Sessa)]
1181-1185	Lucius III (Ubaldo Allucingoli)
1185-1187	Urban III (Uberto Crivelli)
1187	Gregory VIII (Alberto del Morra)
1187-1191	Clement III (Paolo Scolari)
1191-1198	Celestine III (Giacinto Boboni-Orsini)
1198-1216	INNOCENT III (Lothario of Segni)
1216-1227	Honorius III (Cencio Savelli)
1227-1241	GREGORY IX (Ugo of Segni)
1241	Celestine IV (Goffredo Castiglione)
1243-1254	INNOCENT IV (Sinibaldo Fieschi)
1254-1261	Alexander IV (Rinaldo di Segni)
1261-1264	Urban IV (Jacques Pantaléon)
1265-1268	Clement IV (Guy le Gros Foulques)
1268-1271	Vacant
1271-1276	Gregory X (Tebaldo Visconti)
1276	Innocent V (Pierre de Champagni)
1276	Adrian V (Ottobono Fieschi)
1276-1277	John XXI (Pietro Rebuli-Giuliani)
1277-1280	Nicholas III (Giovanni Gaetano Orsini)
1281-1285	Martin IV (Simon Mompitie)

Term	*Pope*
1285-1287	Honorius IV (Giacomo Savelli)
1288-1292	Nicholas IV (Girolamo Masci)
1294	*Celestine V (Pietro Angelari da Murrone)
1294-1303	BONIFACE VIII (Benedict Caetani)
1303-1304	Benedict XI (Niccolò Boccasini)
1305-1314	Clement V (Raimond Bertrand de Got)
1316-1334	John XXII (Jacques Duèse)
1328-1330	[Nicholas V (Pietro di Corbara)]
1334-1342	Benedict XII (Jacques Fournier)
1342-1352	Clement VI (Pierre Roger de Beaufort)
1352-1362	Innocent VI (Étienne Aubert)
1362-1370	Urban V (Guillaume de Grimord)
1370-1378	Gregory XI (Pierre Roger de Beaufort, the Younger)
1378-1389	Urban VI (Bartolomeo Prignano)
1378-1394	[Clement VII (Robert of Geneva)]
1389-1404	Boniface IX (Pietro Tomacelli)
1394-1423	[Benedict XIII (Pedro de Luna)]
1404-1406	Innocent VII (Cosmto de' Migliorati)
1406-1415	Gregory XII (Angelo Correr)
1409-1410	[Alexander V (Petros Philargi)]
1410-1415	[John XXIII (Baldassare Cossa)]
1415-1417	Vacant
1417-1431	Martin V (Ottone Colonna)
1423-1429	[Clement VIII]
1424	[Benedict XIV]
1431-1447	Eugene IV (Gabriele Condulmero)
1439-1449	[Felix V (Amadeus of Savoy)]
1447-1455	Nicholas V (Tommaso Parentucelli)
1455-1458	Calixtus III (Alfonso de Borgia)
1458-1464	Pius II (Enea Silvio Piccolomini)
1464-1471	Paul II (Pietro Barbo)
1471-1484	Sixtus IV (Francesco della Rovere)
1484-1492	Innocent VIII (Giovanni Battista Cibò)
1492-1503	Alexander VI (Rodrigo Borgia)
1503	Pius III (Francesco Todeschini Piccolomini)
1503-1513	Julius II (Giuliano della Rovere)
1513-1521	Leo X (Giovanni de' Medici)
1522-1523	Adrian VI (Adrian Florensz Boeyens)
1523-1534	Clement VII (Giulio de' Medici)
1534-1549	Paul III (Alessandro Farnese)
1550-1555	Julius III (Giovanni Maria Ciocchi del Monte)
1555	Marcellus II (Marcello Cervini)
1555-1559	Paul IV (Gian Pietro Carafa)
1559-1565	Pius IV (Giovanni Angelo de' Medici)
1566-1572	Pius V (Antonio Ghislieri)
1572-1585	Gregory XIII (Ugo Buoncompagni)
1585-1590	Sixtus V (Felice Peretti)
1590	Urban VII (Giambattista Castagna)
1590-1591	Gregory XIV (Niccolò Sfondrato)
1591	Innocent IX (Giovanni Antonio Facchinetti)
1592-1605	Clement VIII (Ippolito Aldobrandini)

Term	*Pope*
1605	Leo XI (Alessandro de' Medici)
1605-1621	Paul V (Camillo Borghese)
1621-1623	Gregory XV (Alessandro Ludovisi)
1623-1644	Urban VIII (Maffeo Barberini)
1644-1655	Innocent X (Giovanni Battista Pamphili)
1655-1667	Alexander VII (Fabio Chigi)
1667-1669	Clement IX (Giulio Rospigliosi)
1670-1676	Clement X (Emilio Altieri)
1676-1689	Innocent XI (Benedetto Odescalchi)
1689-1691	Alexander VIII (Pietro Ottoboni)
1691-1700	Innocent XII (Antonio Pignatelli)
1700-1721	Clement XI (Giovanni Francesco Albani)
1721-1724	Innocent XIII (Michelangelo Conti)
1724-1730	Benedict XIII (Pierfrancesco Orsini)
1730-1740	Clement XII (Lorenzo Corsini)
1740-1758	Benedict XIV (Prospero Lambertini)
1758-1769	Clement XIII (Carlo Rezzonico)
1769-1774	Clement XIV (Giovanni Ganganelli)
1775-1799	Pius VI (Giovanni Angelo Braschi)
1800-1823	Pius VII (Barnaba Gregorio Chiaramonti)
1823-1829	Leo XII (Annibale della Genga)
1829-1830	Pius VIII (Francesco Saverio Castiglioni)
1831-1846	Gregory XVI (Bartolomeo Cappellari)
1846-1878	Pius IX (Giovanni Mastai-Ferretti)
1878-1903	Leo XIII (Gioacchino Pecci)
1903-1914	Pius X (Giuseppe Sarto)
1914-1922	Benedict XV (Giacomo della Chiesa)
1922-1939	Pius XI (Achille Ratti)
1939-1958	Pius XII (Eugenio Pacelli)
1958-1963	John XXIII (Angelo Roncalli)
1963-1978	Paul VI (Giovanni Battista Montini)
1978	John Paul I (Albino Luciani)
1978-	John Paul II (Karol Wojtyla)

AFRICA. *See* EGYPT, ETHIOPIA

AMERICAS

SOME MAJOR MAYA KINGS OF TIKAL

The Maya, who occupied the region of Central America from the Yucatán to Guatemala, maintained several centers in the region, but one, Tikal, recorded in Mayan glyphs a line of kings for nearly eight hundred years, roughly corresponding to the Classic Period now considered by scholars to be the height of Mayan civilization. The list below is from Chronicle of the Maya Kings and Queens, *by Simon Martin and Nikolai Grube (New York: Thames and Hudson, 2000).*

Reign	*Ruler*
c. 90-150	Yax Ehb Xook (First Step Shark)
c. 307	Siyaj Chan K'awiil I
d. 317	Ix Une Balam (Baby Jaguar)
d. 359	K'inich Muwaan Jol
360-378	Chak Tok Ichaak I (Great Jaguar Paw)
378-404	Nuun Yax Ayiin I (Curl Snout)
411-456	Siyaj Chan K'awiil II (Stormy Sky)
458-c. 486	K'an Chitam
c. 486-508	Chak Tok Ich'aak II
c. 511-527	Kaloomte' B'alam
537-562	Wak Chan Ka'awiil
c. 593-628	Animal Skull
c. 657-679	Nuun Ujol Chaak
682-734	Jasaw Chan K'awiil I
734-746	Yik'in Chan K'awiil
768-794	Yax Nuun Ayiin II
c. 800	Nuun Ujol K'inich
c. 810	Dark Sun
c. 849	Jewel K'awiil
c. 869	Jasaw Chan K'awiil II
c. 900	End of Mayan Classic Period

INCAS (PERU)

Reign	*Ruler*
c. 1200	Manco Capac I
?	Sinchi Roca
?	Lloque Yupanqui
?	Mayta Capac
?	Capac Yupanqui
?	Inca Roca
?	Yahuar Huacac
?	Viracocha
1438-1471	Pachacuti
1471-1493	Topa
1493-1525	Huayna Capac
1524-1532	Huáscar
1525-1533	Atahualpa
1532-1533	Spanish conquest (Pizzaro)
1533	Manco Capac II
1544-1561	Sayri Tupac
1561-1571	Titu Cusi
1571	Tupac Amaru I

BOHEMIA. *See also* HUNGARY, POLAND

Reign	*Ruler*
921-929	Václav (Wenceslaus)
929-967	Boleslav I (Přemyslid)
967-999	Boleslav II
1000-1012	Fratricidal warfare
1012-1037	Oldrich
1037-1055	Bretislav I

Reign	Ruler
1055-1061	Instability
1061-1091	Vratislav II
1092-1125	Vladislav (Władysław) I
1125-1140	Instability
1140-1173	Vladislav (Władysław) II
1173-1198	Instability
1198-1230	Přemysl Otakar I
1230-1253	Václav (Wenceslaus) I
1253-1278	Přemysl Otakar II
1278-1305	Václav (Wenceslaus) II
1305-1306	Václav (Wenceslaus) III
1306	End of the Přemyslid Dynasty
1306-1307	Rudolf of Habsburg
1307-1310	Jindrich (Heinrich or Henry)
1310-1346	Jan (John) of Luxembourg
1346-1378	Charles or Karel I (Emperor Charles IV)
1378-1419	VÁCLAV (WENCESLAUS) IV
1419-1437	Sigismund
1438-1439	Albert of Austria
1440-1457	Ladislas V of Hungary
1458-1471	Jiri (George Podiebrad)
1471-1516	Vladislav Jagiełło (Władysław or Ladislas VI of Hungary)
1516-1526	Ludvik (Louis II of Hungary)
1526-1564	Ferdinand I; Bohemia under Habsburg rule

BULGARIA

EARLY BULGARIA

Reign	Czar
c. 681-701	Asparukh
c. 701-c. 718	Tervel
c. 718-750	Sevar
750-762	Kormesios
762-763	Vinekh
762-763	Teletz
763	Umar
763-765	Baian
765	Tokt
c. 765-777	Telerig
c. 777-c. 803	Kardam
c. 803-814	Krum
814-815	Dukum
814-816	Ditzveg
814-831	Omurtag
831-836	Malamir (Malomir)
836-852	Presijan
852-889	BORIS I
865	Boris converts to Christianity
889-893	Vladimir
893-927	Simeon I the Great
927-969	Peter I
969-972	Boris II
971	Bulgaria conquered by John I Tzimisces
971-1018	Dissolution, instability
1018	Basil II annexes Bulgaria to Macedonia

ASEN LINE

Reign	Czar
1186	Bulgarian Independence
1186-1196	John I Asen
1196-1197	Peter II Asen
1197-1207	Kalojan Asen
1207-1218	Boril
1218-1241	John II Asen
1242	Mongol invasion
1242-1246	Kaloman I
1246-1257	Michael II Asen
1257-1258	Kaloman II
1257-1277	Constantine Tich
1277-1279	Ivalio
1278-c. 1264	Ivan Mytzes
1279-1284?	John III Asen
c. 1280	Terter takeover

TERTER LINE

Reign	Czar
1280-1292	George I Terter
1285	Mongol vassal
1292-1295/8	Smilech
1295/8-1298/9	Caka (Tshaka)
1298/9-1322	Theodore Svetoslav
1322-1323	George II

SHISHMANS

Reign	Czar
1323-1330	Michael III Shishman
1330-1331	John IV Stephan
1331-1371	John V Alexander
1355-1371	John Sracimir
1360-1393	John VI Shishman
1385-1396	Decline
1396	Ottoman conquest

BYZANTINE EMPIRE

Reign	Emperor or Empress
330-337	Constantine I the Great
337-361	Constantius
361-363	Julian the Apostate

Reign	*Emperor or Empress*
363-364	Jovian
364-378	Valens
379-395	Theodosius I the Great
395-408	Arcadius
408-450	Theodosius II
450-457	Marcian
457-474	Leo I the Great
474	Leo II
474-475	Zeno
475-476	Basiliscus
476-491	Zeno (restored)
491-518	Anastasius I
518-527	Justin I
527-548	THEODORA
527-565	JUSTINIAN I THE GREAT
565-578	Justin II
578-582	Tiberius II Constantinus
582-602	Maurice
602-610	Phocas
610-641	HERACLIUS
641	Constantine III and Heracleonas
641-668	Constans II Pogonatus
668-685	Constantine IV
685-695	Justinian II Rhinotmetus
695-698	Leontius
698-705	Tiberius III
705-711	Justinian II (restored)
711-713	Philippicus Bardanes
713-715	Anastasius II
716-717	Theodosius III
717-741	Leo III the Isaurian (the Syrian)
741-775	Constantine V Copronymus
775-780	Leo IV the Khazar
780-797	Constantine VI
797-802	SAINT IRENE
802-811	Nicephorus I
811	Stauracius
811-813	Michael I
813-820	Leo V the Armenian
820-829	Michael II the Stammerer
829-842	Theophilus
842-867	Michael III the Drunkard
867-886	BASIL I THE MACEDONIAN
886-912	Leo VI the Wise (the Philosopher)
912-913	Alexander
913-919	Constantine VII Porphyrogenitus (Macedonian)
919-944	Romanus I Lecapenus (Macedonian)
944-959	Constantine VII (restored)
959-963	Romanus II (Macedonian)

Reign	*Emperor or Empress*
963	Basil II Bulgaroktonos (Macedonian)
963-969	Nicephorus II Phocas (Macedonian)
969-976	John I Tzimisces
976-1025	Basil II (restored)
1025-1028	Constantine VIII (Macedonian)
1028-1034	Zoë and Romanus III Argyrus (Macedonian)
1034-1041	Zoë and Michael IV the Paphlagonian (Macedonian)
1041-1042	Zoë and Michael V Calaphates (Macedonian)
1042	Zoë and Theodora (Macedonian)
1042-1050	Zoë, Theodora, and Constantine IX Monomachus (Macedonian)
1050-1055	Theodora and Constantine IX (Macedonian)
1055-1056	Theodora (Macedonian)
1056-1057	Michael VI Stratioticus
1057-1059	Isaac I Comnenus
1059-1067	Constantine X Ducas
1067-1068	Michael VII Ducas (Parapinaces)
1068-1071	Romanus IV Diogenes
1071-1078	Michael VII Ducas (restored)
1078-1081	Nicephorus III Botaniates
1081-1118	Alexius I Comnenus
1118-1143	John II Comnenus
1143-1180	Manuel I Comnenus
1180-1183	Alexius II Comnenus
1183-1185	Andronicus I Comnenus
1185-1195	Isaac II Angelus
1195-1203	Alexius III Angelus
1203-1204	Isaac II (restored) and Alexius IV Angelus
1204	Alexius V Ducas
1204-1205	Baldwin I
1206-1222	Theodore I Lascaris
1222-1254	John III Vatatzes or Ducas
1254-1258	Theodore II Lascaris
1258-1261	John IV Lascaris
1259-1282	Michael VIII Palaeologus
1282-1328	Andronicus II Palaeologus
1328-1341	Andronicus III Palaeologus
1341-1376	John V Palaeologus
1347-1355	John VI Cantacuzenus (usurper)
1376-1379	Andronicus IV Palaeologus
1379-1391	John V Palaeologus (restored)
1390	John VII Palaeologus (usurper)
1391-1425	Manuel II Palaeologus
1399-1412	John VII Palaeologus (restored as coemperor)
1425-1448	John VIII Palaeologus
1449-1453	Constantine XI Palaeologus
1453	Fall of Constantinople to the Ottomans

CHINA

SUI DYNASTY

Reign	Ruler
581-604	Wendi
604-617	Yangdi
618	Gongdi

TANG DYNASTY

Reign	Ruler
618-626	Gaozu (Li Yuan)
627-649	TAIZONG
650-683	Gaozong
684	Zhonggong
684-690	Ruizong
690-705	Wu Hou
705-710	Zhongzong
710-712	Ruizong
712-756	Xuanzong
756-762	Suzong
762-779	Daizong
779-805	Dezong
805	Shunzong
805-820	Xianzong
820-824	Muzong
824-827	Jingzong
827-840	Wenzong
840-846	Wuzong
846-859	Xuanzong
859-873	Yizong
873-888	Xizong
888-904	Zhaozong
904-907	Aizong

LIAO DYNASTY

Reign	Ruler
907-926	Abaoji (Taizu)
926-947	Deguang (Taizong)
947-951	Shizong
951-969	Muzong
969-982	Jingzong
982-1031	Shengzong
1031-1055	Xingzong
1055-1101	Daozong
1101-1125	Tianzuodi

WESTERN LIAO DYNASTY

Reign	Ruler
1125-1144	Dezong
1144-1151	Empress Gantian
1151-1164	Renzong
1164-1178	Empress Chengtian
1178-1211	The Last Ruler

JIN DYNASTY

Reign	Ruler
1115-1123	Aguda (Wanyan Min; Taizu)
1123-1135	Taizong (Wanyan Sheng)
1135-1149	Xizong
1150-1161	Wanyan Liang, king of Hailing
1161-1190	Shizong
1190-1209	Zhangzong
1209-1213	Wanyan Yongji, king of Weishao
1213-1224	Xuanzong
1224-1234	Aizong
1234	The Last Emperor

NORTHERN SONG DYNASTY

Reign	Ruler
960-976	Taizu (Zhao Kuangyin)
976-997	Taizong
998-1022	Zhenzong
1022-1063	Renzong
1064-1067	Yingzong
1068-1085	Shenzong
1086-1101	Zhezong
1101-1125	Huizong
1125-1126	Qinzong

SOUTHERN SONG DYNASTY

Reign	Ruler
1127-1162	Gaozong
1163-1190	Xiaozong
1190-1194	Guangzong
1195-1224	Ningzong
1225-1264	Lizong
1265-1274	Duzong
1275-1275	Gongdi
1276-1278	Duanzong
1279	Bing Di

YUAN DYNASTY. *See also* MONGOL EMPIRE

Reign	Ruler
1279-1294	KUBLAI KHAN (Shizu)
1294-1307	Temür Oljeitu (Chengzong)
1308-1311	Khaishan (Wuzong)
1311-1320	Ayurbarwada (Renzong)
1321-1323	Shidelbala (Yingzong)
1323-1328	Yesun Temür (Taiding)
1328-1329	Tugh Temür (Wenzong Tianshundi)
1329	Tugh Khoshila (Mingzong)
1329-1332	Tugh Temür (Wenzong)
1333-1368	Toghon Temür (Shundi)
1368	Ming Dynasty begins: Hongwu

MING DYNASTY

Reign	*Ruler*
1368-1398	Hongwu (Zhu Yuanzhang)
1399-1402	Jianwen (Zhu Yunwen)
1402-1424	YONGLO (Zhu Di)
1424-1425	Hongxi
1426-1435	Xuande
1436-1449	Zhengtong
1450-1457	Jingtai
1457-1464	Tianshun
1465-1487	Chenghua
1488-1505	Hongzhi
1506-1521	Zhengde
1522-1567	Jianjing
1567-1572	Longqing
1573-1620	Wanli
1620	Taichang
1621-1627	Tianqi
1628-1644	Chongzhen

DENMARK. *See also* NORWAY, SWEDEN

Reign	*Ruler*
588-647	Ivar Vidfamne
647-735?	Harald I Hildetand
735-750?	Sigurd I Ring (poss. 770-812)
c. 750	Randver
850-854	Horik I
c. 854-?	Horik II
c. 860-865	Ragnar Lobrok
865-873	Sigurd II Snogoje
873-884	Hardeknut I
884-885	Frodo
885-889	Harald II
c. 900-950	Gorm
c. 950-985	Harald III Bluetooth
985-1014	Sweyn I Forkbeard
1014-1019	Harald IV
1019-1035	CANUTE I (III) THE GREAT
1035-1042	Hardeknut
1042-1047	Magnus the Good
1047-1074	Sweyn II
1074-1080	Harald V Hen
1080-1086	Canute II (IV) the Holy
1086-1095	Olaf IV the Hungry
1095-1103	Eric I the Evergood
1103-1134	Niels Elder
1134-1137	Eric II
1137-1146	Eric III
1146-1157	Sweyn III
1147-1157	Canute III (V) Magnussen
1157-1182	Valdemar I the Great
1182-1202	Canute IV (VI) the Pious
1202-1241	VALDEMAR II THE VICTORIOUS
1241-1250	Eric IV
1250-1252	Abel
1252-1259	Christopher I
1259-1286	Eric V
1286-1319	Eric VI
1320-1326	Christopher II
1326-1330	Instability
1330-1332	Christopher II (restored)
1332-1340	Instability
1340-1375	Valdemar III
1376-1387	Olaf V (or II; IV of Norway)
1380	Unification of Denmark and Norway
1376-1412	MARGARET I OF DENMARK, NORWAY, AND SWEDEN
1397	Unification of Norway, Denmark, and Sweden
1412-1439	Eric VII (III of Norway, XIII of Sweden)
1439-1448	Christopher III
1448-1481	Christian I of Oldenburg
1481-1513	Hans/John (II of Sweden)
1513-1523	Christian II
1523	Kingdoms of Denmark and Norway joined, Sweden separate

EGYPT

After the rise of Islam in the seventh century, Egypt was Islamicized and came under the control of a succession of emirs and caliphs.

ṬULUNID EMIRS

Reign	*Ruler*
868-884	Aḥmad ibn Ṭūlūn
884-896	Khumārawayh
896	Jaysh
896-904	Hārūn
904-905	Shaybān
905	Recovered by Abbasids

IKHSHIDID EMIRS

Reign	*Ruler*
935-946	Muḥammad ibn Ṭughj al-Ikhshīd
946-961	Unūjūr
961-966	ʿAlī
966-968	Kāfūr al-Lābī (regent)
968-969	Aḥmad
969	Fāṭimid conquest

Fāṭimid Caliphs in Egypt

Reign	Ruler
975-996	al-ʿAzīz
996-1021	al-Ḥākim
1021-1036	al-Zahīr
1036-1094	al-Mustanṣir
1094-1101	al-Mustadī
1101-1130	al-Amīr
1130-1149	al-Ḥāfiz
1149-1154	al-Zafīr
1154-1160	al-Fāʾiz
1160-1171	al-ʿAdīd

Ayyūbid Sultans

Reign	Ruler
1169-1193	Saladin
1193-1198	al-ʿAzīz Imad al-Dīn
1198-1200	al-Mansūr Naṣīr al-Dīn
1200-1218	al-ʿAdil I Sayf al-Dīn
1202-1204	Fourth Crusade
1217-1221	Fifth Crusade
1218-1238	al-Kāmil I Nāṣir al-Dīn
1227-1230	Sixth Crusade
1238-1240	al-ʿAdil II Sayf al-Dīn
1240-1249	al-Ṣāliḥ II Najm al-Dīn
1249-1250	al-Muʿaẓẓam Tūrān-Shāh Ghiyāt al-Dīn
1248-1254	Seventh (or Eighth) Crusade
1252	Cairo seized by Mamlūks

Mamlūk Sultans

Baḥrī Line (Mongol, then Turkish)

Reign	Ruler
1252-1257	Aybak al-Turkumānī
1257-1259	ʿAlī I
1259-1260	Quṭuz al-Muʿizzī
1260-1277	Baybars I (defeats Mongols 1260)
1277-1279	Baraka (Berke) Khān
1279	Salāmish (Süleymish)
1279-1290	Qalāʾūn al-Alfī
1290-1293	Khalīl
1291	Fall of Acre
1293	Baydarā (?)
1293-1294	Muḥammad I
1294-1296	Kitbughā
1296-1299	Lāchīn (Lājīn) al-Ashqar
1299-1309	Muḥammad I
1303	Earthquake destroys Pharos lighthouse
1309-1310	Baybars II al-Jāshnakīr (Burjī)
1310-1341	Muḥammad I
1341	Abū Bakr
1341-1342	Kūjūk (Küchük)
1342	Aḥmad I
1342-1345	Ismāʿīl
1345-1346	Shaʿbān I
1346-1347	Ḥājjī I
1347-1351	al-Ḥasan
1351-1354	Ṣāliḥ
1354-1361	al-Ḥasan
1361-1363	Muḥammad II
1363-1377	Shaʿbān II
1377-1382	ʿAlī II
1382	Ḥājjī II
1389-1390	Ḥājjī II

Burjī (Circassian) line

Reign	Ruler
1382-1398	Barqūq al-Yalburghāwī
1399-1405	Faraj
1405	ʿAbd al-ʿAzīz
1405-1412	Faraj (second rule)
1412	al-Mustaʿīn
1412-1421	Shaykh al-Maḥmūdī al-Ẓāhirī
1421	Aḥmad II
1421	Ṭāṭār
1421-1422	Muḥammad III
1422-1438	Barsbay
1438	Yūsuf
1438-1453	Chaqmaq (Jaqmaq)
1453	ʿUthmān
1453-1461	Ināl al-ʿAlāʾī al-Ẓāhirī
1461	Aḥmad III
1461-1467	Khushqadam
1467	Yalbay
1467-1468	Timurbughā
1468-1496	Qāyit Bay al-Ẓāhirī
1496-1498	Muḥammad IV
1498-1500	Qānṣawh I
1500-1501	Jānbulāṭ
1501	Ṭūmān Bay I
1501-1516	Qānṣawh II al-Ghawrī
1516-1517	Ṭūmān Bay II
1517	Ottoman conquest

ʿAbbāsid Caliphs of Egypt

Unlike the earlier ʿAbbāsid line (see Islamic Caliphs, below), these were ʿAbbāsid figureheads in place under the Mamlūks.

Reign	Ruler
1261	Aḥmad al-Mustanṣir
1261-1302	Aḥmad al-Ḥākim I (Aleppo 1261-1262, Cairo, 1262-1302)
1302-1340	Sulaymān al-Mustakfī I
1340-1341	Ibrāhīm al-Wāthiq I
1341-1352	Aḥmad al-Ḥakīm II
1352-1362	Abū Bakr al-Muʿtaḍid I
1362-1377	Muḥammad al-Mutawakkil I
1377	Zakariyyāʿal-Muʿtaṣim

Reign	*Ruler*
1377-1383	Muḥammad al-Mutawakkil I
1383-1386	ʿUmar al-Wāthiq II
1386-1389	Zakariyyāʿal-Muʿtaṣim
1389-1406	Muḥammad al-Mutawakkil I
1406-1414	Sulṭān
1412	ʿAbbās or Yaʿqūb al-Mustaʿīn
1414-1441	Dāwūd al-Muʿtaḍid II
1441-1451	Sulaymān al-Mustakfī II
1451-1455	Ḥamza al-Qāʿim
1455-1479	Yūsuf al-Mustanjid
1479-1497	ʿAbd al-ʿAzīz al-Mutawakkil II
1497-1508	Yaʿqūb al-Mustamsik
1508-1516	al-Mutawakkil III
1516-1517	Yaʿqūb al-Mustamsik
1517	Ottoman conquest

ENGLAND

Reign	*Ruler (House)*
802-839	EGBERT (Anglo-Saxon/Wessex)
839-856	Æthelwulf (Anglo-Saxon/Wessex)
856-860	Æthelbald (Anglo-Saxon/Wessex)
860-866	Æthelbert (Anglo-Saxon/Wessex)
866-871	Ethelred (Æthelred) I (Anglo-Saxon/Wessex)
871-899	ALFRED THE GREAT (Anglo-Saxon/Wessex)
899-924	EDWARD THE ELDER (Anglo-Saxon/Wessex; with sister ÆTHELFLÆD)
924-939	Æthelstan (Anglo-Saxon/Wessex)
939-946	Edmund the Magnificent (Anglo-Saxon/Wessex)
946-955	Eadred (Anglo-Saxon/Wessex)
955-959	Eadwig (Edwy) All-Fair (Anglo-Saxon/Wessex)
959-975	Edgar the Peaceable (Anglo-Saxon/Wessex)
975-978	Edward the Martyr (Anglo-Saxon/Wessex)
978-1016	ETHELRED (ÆTHELRED) II THE UNREADY (Anglo-Saxon/Wessex)
1016	Edmund II Ironside (Anglo-Saxon/Wessex)
1016-1035	CANUTE (KNUD) THE GREAT (Dane)
1035-1040	Harold I Harefoot (Dane)
1040-1042	Harthacnut (Dane)
1043-1066	EDWARD THE CONFESSOR (Saxon/Dane)
1066	HAROLD II (Saxon/Dane)
1066-1087	WILLIAM I THE CONQUEROR (Norman)
1087-1100	William II Rufus (Norman)
1100-1135	HENRY I BEAUCLERC (Norman)
1135-1154	Stephen (Norman)
1154-1189	HENRY II (Norman/Plantagenet; with ELEANOR OF AQUITAINE, r. 1154-1189)
1189-1199	RICHARD I THE LION-HEARTED (Plantagenet)
1199-1216	JOHN I LACKLAND (Plantagenet)
1216-1272	HENRY III (Plantagenet)
1272-1307	EDWARD I LONGSHANKS (Plantagenet)
1307-1327	EDWARD II (Plantagenet; with ISABELLA OF FRANCE, r. 1308-1330)
1327-1377	EDWARD III (Plantagenet; with PHILIPPA OF HAINAUT, r. 1327-1369)
1377-1399	RICHARD II (Plantagenet)
1399-1413	HENRY IV (Lancaster)
1413-1422	HENRY V (Lancaster)
1422-1461	Henry VI (Lancaster)
1461-1470	Edward IV (York)
1470-1471	Henry VI (Lancaster)
1471-1483	Edward IV (York, restored)
1483	Edward V (York)
1483-1485	Richard III Hunchback (York)
1485	Tudor line begins: Henry VII

ETHIOPIA

The evidence for the succession of Ethiopian rulers is debated by scholars; here, the regnal dates reflect primarily the order of succession and vary widely among sources.

EARLY KINGS

Reign	*Ruler*
c. 320-350	Ezana
c. 328-370	Shizana
c. 356	Ella Abreha
?	Ella Asfeha
?	Ella Shahel
474-475	Agabe
474-475	Levi
475-486	Ella Amida (IV?)
486-489	Jacob I
486-489	David
489-504	Armah I
504-505	Zitana
505-514	Jacob II
c. 500-542	Ella Asbeha (Caled)
542-c. 550	Beta Israel
c. 550-564	Gabra Masqal
?	Anaeb
?	Alamiris
?	Joel
?	Israel
?	Gersem I
?	Ella Gabaz
?	Ella Saham
c. 625	Armah II

Reign	*Ruler*
?	Iathlia
?	Hataz I
?	Wazena
?	Za Ya'abiyo
?	Armah III
?	Hataz II
?	Gersem II
?	Hataz III

ZAGWE DYNASTY

Reign	*Ruler*
c. 1137-1152	Mara Tekle Haimanot
c. 1152-1181	Yimrehane-Kristos
c. 1181-1221	LALIBELA
c. 1221-1260	Na ʿakuto La ʿab
c. 1260-1270	Yitbarek (Yetbarek)
1270	Solomonid Dynasty begins; reign of Yekuno Amlak

SOLOMONID DYNASTY

Reign	*Ruler*
1270-1285	Yekuno Amlak
1285-1294	Solomon I
1294-1297	Bahr Asgad
1294-1297	Senfa Asgad
1297-1299	Qedma Asgad
1297-1299	Jin Asgad
1297-1299	Saba Asgad
1299-1314	Wedem Arad
1314-1344	Amade Tseyon I
1344-1372	Newaya Krestos
1372-1382	Newaya Maryam
1382-1411	Dawit (David) I
1411-1414	Tewodros (Theodore) I
1414-1429	Isaac
1429-1430	Andrew
1430-1433	Takla Maryam
1433	Sarwe Iyasus
1433-1434	Amda Iyasus
1434-1468	Zera Yacob (Constantine I)
1468-1478	Baeda Mariam I
1478-1484	Constantine II
1494	Amade Tseyon II
1494-1508	Na'od
1508-1540	Lebna Dengel (David II)
1540-1559	Galawedos (Claudius)
1543	Battle of Lake Tana (defeat of Muslims)

FRANKISH KINGDOM AND FRANCE

The Merovingians and Carolingians ruled different parts of the Frankish kingdom, which accounts for overlapping regnal dates in these tables. The term "emperor" refers to rule over what eventually came to be known as the Holy Roman Empire.

THE MEROVINGIANS

Reign	*Ruler (Principality)*
447-458	Merovech
458-481	Childeric I
481-511	CLOVIS I (with CLOTILDA, r. 493-511)
511	Kingdom split among Clovis's sons
511-524	Chlodomer (Orléans)
511-534	Theodoric I (Metz)
511-558	Childebert I (Paris)
511-561	Lothair I (Soissons 511-561, all Franks 558-561)
534-548	Theudebert I (Metz)
548-555	Theudebald (Metz)
561	Kingdom split among Lothair's sons
561-567	Charibert I (Paris)
561-575	Sigebert I (Austrasia)
561-584	Chilperic I (Soissons)
561-592	Guntram (Burgundy)
575-595	Childebert II (Austrasia 575-595, Burgundy 593-595)
584-629	Lothair II (Neustria 584, all Franks 613-629)
595-612	Theudebert II (Austrasia)
595-613	Theodoric II (Burgundy 595-612, Austrasia 612-613)
613	Sigebert II (Austrasia, Burgundy)
623-639	Dagobert I (Austrasia 623-628, all Franks 629-639)
629-632	Charibert II (Aquitaine)
632-656	Sigebert III (Austrasia)
639-657	Clovis II (Neustria and Burgundy)
656-673	Lothair III (Neustria 657-673, all Franks 656-660)
662-675	Childeric (Austrasia 662-675, all Franks 673-675)
673-698	Theodoric III (Neustria 673-698, all Franks 678-691)
674-678	Dagobert II (Austrasia)
691-695	Clovis III (all Franks)
695-711	Childebert III (all Franks)
711-716	Dagobert III (all Franks)
715-721	Chilperic II (Neustria 715-721, all Franks 719-720)
717-719	Lothair IV (Austrasia)
721-737	Theodoric IV (all Franks)
743-751	Childeric III (all Franks)

The Carolingians

Reign	*Ruler*
687-714	Pépin II of Heristal (mayor of Austrasia/Neustria)
714-719	Plectrude (regent for Theudoald)
719-741	Charles Martel (the Hammer; mayor of Austrasia/Neustria)
747-768	Pépin III the Short (mayor of Neustria 741, king of all Franks 747)
768-814	Charlemagne (king of Franks 768, emperor 800)
814-840	Louis the Pious (king of Aquitaine, emperor)
840-855	Lothair I (emperor)
843	Treaty of Verdun divides Carolingian Empire into East Franks (Germany), West Franks (essentially France), and a Middle Kingdom (roughly corresponding to Provence, Burgundy, and Lorraine)
843-876	Louis II the German (king of Germany)
843-877	Charles II the Bald (king of Neustria 843, emperor 875)
855-875	Louis II (emperor)
877-879	Louis II (king of France)
879-882	Louis III (king of France)
879-884	Carloman (king of France)
884-887	Charles III the Fat (king of France, emperor 881)
887-898	Odo (Eudes; king of France)
887-899	Arnulf (king of Germany 887, emperor 896)
891-894	Guy of Spoleto (Wido, Guido; emperor)
892-898	Lambert of Spoleto (emperor)
893-923	Charles III the Simple (king of France)
915-923	Berengar I of Friuli (emperor)
923-929?	Robert I (king of France)
929-936	Rudolf (king of France)
936-954	Louis IV (king of France; Hugh the Great in power)
954-986	Lothair (king of France; Hugh Capet in power 956)
986-987	Louis V (king of France)

The Capetians

Reign	*Ruler*
987-996	Hugh Capet
996-1031	Robert II the Pious
1031-1060	Henry I
1060-1108	Philip I the Fair
1108-1137	Louis VI the Fat
1137-1179	Louis VII the Younger (with Eleanor of Aquitaine, r. 1137-1180)
1179-1223	Philip II Augustus
1223-1226	Louis VIII the Lion
1223-1252	Blanche of Castile (both queen and regent)
1226-1270	Louis IX (Saint Louis)
1271-1285	Philip III the Bold
1285-1314	Philip IV the Fair
1314-1316	Louis X the Stubborn
1316	Philip, brother of Louis X (regent before birth of John I and during his short life)
1316	John I the Posthumous
1316-1322	Philip V the Tall
1322-1328	Charles IV the Fair

Valois Dynasty, Main Branch

Reign	*Ruler*
1328-1350	Philip VI the Fortunate
1350-1364	John II the Good
1364-1380	Charles V the Wise
1380-1382	Louis I of Anjou (regent for Charles VI)
1380-1422	Charles VI the Well-Beloved
1422-1461	Charles VII the Victorious
1461-1483	Louis XI
1483-1484	Anne de Beaujeu (regent for Charles VIII)
1483-1498	Charles VIII the Affable

Valois-Orléans Branch

Reign	*Ruler*
1498-1515	Louis XII, the Father of His People

Valois-Angoulême Branch

Reign	*Ruler*
1515-1547	Francis I
1547-1559	Henry II
1559-1560	Francis II
1560-1563	Catherine de Médicis (regent for Charles IX)
1560-1574	Charles IX
1574-1589	Henry III (King of Poland, 1573-1574)
1589	Bourbon Dynasty begins: Henry IV (Henry III of Navarre)

GERMANIC TRIBES. *See also* **HOLY ROMAN EMPIRE**

In the fifth and sixth centuries, Europe was invaded from the east by several "barbarian" tribes from eastern Europe and Central Asia, including the Visigoths, who inflicted the earliest damage on Rome in the late fourth and early fifth centuries; the Burgundians, from central and northeastern Europe; the Vandals, who eventually settled in Spain and North Africa; the Suevi, who made their way to the north of Spain and finally fell to the Visigoths; the Alans, a non-Germanic steppe tribe from Iran who, along with the Suevi and the Visigoths, overran Gaul (France) and the Iberian Peninsula; and the Franks (see Frankish Kingdom and France, above), who occupied most of Gaul during the later Roman Empire and were the only of these early tribes to survive. The Franks would evolve into the Merovingian and Carolingian lines, and by the ninth century they dominated Europe. Below is a list of some of the Germanic tribes and tribal leaders before and during the Frankish period. The region known today as Germany was initially occupied by these tribes and then came under the subjugation of the Frankish Merovingians and Carolingians. In 962, the Holy Roman Empire came into existence and held sway over Germany for nearly a millennium (see Holy Roman Empire, below). Not until the late nineteenth century did the nation-state of Germany come into existence.

ALEMANNI (OR ALAMANNI)

The Alemanni occupied Swabia.

Reign	*Ruler*
c. 536-554	Leuthari
c. 536-554	Butilin
d. c. 539	Haming
c. 570-587	Leutfred I
588-613	Uncilen
d. 613	Gunzo
c. 615-639	Chrodebert
c. 640-673/95	Leutfred II
c. 700-709	Godefred
d. c. 712	Huocin
d. c. 712	Willehari
c. 720-730	Lanfred I
c. 737-744	Theodobald
d. 746	Nebi
746-749	Lanfred II
791-799	Gerold
799-806	Isenbard
After 806	Annexed by the Franks

BAVARIANS

The Bavarians occupied a region approximating present-day Bavaria.

Reign	*Ruler*
508-512	Theodo I
512-537	Theodo II
537-565	Theodo III
537-567	Theodobald I
550-590	Garibald I
590-595	Grimwald I
591-609	Tassilo I
609-630	Agilulf
609-640	Garibald II
640-680	Theodo IV
680-702	Theodo V
702-715	Theodobald II
702-723	Grimwald II
702-725	Theodobert
702-730	Tassilo II
725-737	Hubert
737-748	Odilo
748-788	Tassilo III
After 788	Annexed by Franks

BURGUNDIANS

The Burgundians occupied central and southeastern France.

Reign	*Ruler*
c. 407	Gebicca
407-434	Gundahar/Gondikar/Gunther
434-473	Gundioc/Gunderic
443-c. 480	Chilperic I
473-486	Gundomar I
473-493	Chilperic II
473-501	Godegisel
473-516	Gundobad
516-524	Sigismund
524-532	Gudomar II
532	Frankish conquest

FRANKS

The Franks initially occupied the area now known as the Netherlands and northern France, and they eventually dominated Europe. See Frankish Kingdom and France, above.

LOMBARDS

The Lombards occupied northern Italy.

Reign	*Ruler*
565-572	ALBOIN
573-575	Celph
575-584	Unstable
584-590	Authari
590-591	Theodelinda
591-615	Agilulf
615-625	Adaloald

Reign	Ruler
625-636	Arioald
636-652	Rotharis
652-661	Aribert I
661-662	Godipert
662-671	Grimoald
671-674	Garibald
674-688	Bertharit
688-700	Cunibert
700-701	Liutpert
701	Raginpert
701-712	Aribert II
712-744	Liutprand
744-749	Rachis of Friuli
749-756	Aistulf of Friuli
756-774	Desiderius
774	Frankish conquest

OSTROGOTHS

The Ostrogoths migrated from the east into the Balkans and Italian peninsula.

Reign	Ruler
474-526	THEODORIC THE GREAT
526-534	Athalaric
534-536	Theodahad (with AMALASUNTHA)
536-540	Vitiges (Witiges)
540	Theodobald (Heldebadus)
541	Eraric
541-552	Totila (Baduila)
552-553	Teias
553-568	Roman domination (Byzantine emperor Justinian I)
568-774	Lombard domination
774	Frankish conquest

SUEVI

The Suevi migrated from the east into northern Spain.

Reign	Ruler
409-438	Hermeric
428-448	Rechila
439	Mérida
441	Seville
448-456	Rechiar
452	Peace with Romans
456	Visigoths defeat Rechiar
456-457	Aioulf
457-460	Maldras
460-c. 463	Richimund
460-c. 465	Frumar
c. 463-?	Remisund
c. 500-550	Unknown kings
c. 550-559	Carriaric
559-570	Theodemar
561	Catholic
570-582	Miro
582-584	Eboric
584-585	Andeca
After 585	Visigoth conquest

VANDALS

The Vandals migrated west into southern Spain and northern Africa.

Reign	Ruler
c. 406-428	Gunderic
428-477	Gaiseric
477-484	Huneric
484-496	Gunthamund
496-523	Thrasamund
523-530	Hilderic
530-534	Gelimer
After 534	Roman overthrow

VISIGOTHS

The Visigoths migrated west into southwestern France.

Reign	Ruler
395-410	Alaric I
410-415	Athaulf (Ataulfo)
415	Sigeric
415-417	Wallia
417-451	Theodoric I
451-453	Thorismund
453-466	Theodoric II
466-484	Euric I
484-507	Alaric II
508-511	Amalaric
511-526	Theodoric the Great
526-531	Amalaric
531-548	Theudes
548-549	Theudegisel
549-554	Agila
554-567	Athanagild
567-571	Theodomir
571-572	Leuva (Leova) I
572-586	Leuvigild
586-601	Reccared I
601-603	Leova II
603-610	Witterich
610-612	Gundemar
612-621	Sisebut (Sisebur)
621	Reccared II
621-631	Swintilla (Suinthila)
631-636	Sisenand
636-640	Chintila
640-642	Tulga
642-653	Chindaswind

Reign	Ruler
653-672	Recdeswinth
672-680	Wamba
680-687	Euric (Erwig) II
687-702	Egica (Ergica)
702-709	Witiza
709-711	Roderic (Rodrigo)
711	Overthrown by Umayyads
718	Christian Kingdom of Asturias

HOLY ROMAN EMPIRE

Although some sources consider the Holy Roman Empire to have begun with Otto I's coronation in 962, others date the Empire's beginning as early as Charlemagne's consolidation of the Franks and his coronation as emperor of the Frankish Empire in 800. The term "Sacrum Romanum Imperium" (Holy Roman Empire) dates to 1254, the use of the term "Holy Empire" to 1157, and the term "Roman Empire" to 1034 (reign of Conrad II). "Roman emperor" was applied to Otto I during his reign; however, Charlemagne also used the term to refer to his own reign. The concept of a "Holy" Roman Empire goes back to the beginning of the Byzantine Empire and the reign of the first Christian Roman emperor, Constantine the Great. Hence, the concept of this political entity can be considered to have evolved incrementally over time. The practice of papal coronation to legitimate the emperor began with Otto I. Regnal dates are therefore often listed as beginning with the date of coronation. However, the German kings who became Holy Roman Emperors frequently asserted their de facto power earlier as rulers of West Frankia (France), East Frankia (essentially Germany), and/or Italy (roughly the northern portion of modern Italy). In the table below, where a date of ascension to the West Frankish (French), East Frankish (German), Middle Frankish (Lorraine south to Italy), or other throne is different from that to Emperor, the former date is set before a slash and the date of assuming the rule of the Empire falls after the slash. Asterisks indicate that the monarch was not formally crowned at Rome by the pope, a practice that officially ended with Frederick II, although Charles V was last to be crowned outside Rome.

Reign	Emperor (House)
768/800-814	CHARLEMAGNE (Carolingian)
814/813-840	Louis I the Pious (Carolingian)
840/817-855	Lothair I (Carolingian)
840-876	LOUIS II THE GERMAN (Carolingian; first king of East Franks only)
840/875-877	CHARLES II THE BALD (Carolingian)
855/850-875	Louis II of Italy (Carolingian)
877-881	Empire unstable
876/881-888	Charles III the Fat (Carolingian)
888-891	Viking and Arab incursions
891	Italian line begins
888/891-894	Guy (Guido, Wido) of Spoleto (Italian)
894/892-898	Lambert of Spoleto (Italian, co-emperor)
888/896-899	Arnulf (East Frankish)
899/901-905	Louis III of Provence (Carolingian, deposed)
905/915-924	Berengar I of Friuli (Italian)
911-918	*Conrad
919	Saxon line begins
919-936	*Henry I the Fowler (Saxon)
936/962-973	OTTO I (Saxon): crowned in 962 by Pope John XII; the Empire no longer lays claim to West Frankish lands (essentially France), but now is basically a union of Germany and northern Italy.
973/967-983	Otto II (Saxon)
983/996-1002	Otto III (Saxon)
1002/14-1024	HENRY II THE SAINT (Saxon)
1024	Franconian/Salian line begins
1024/27-1039	Conrad II (Franconian/Salian)
1039/46-1056	Henry III (Franconian/Salian)
1056/84-1106	HENRY IV (Franconian/Salian)
1077-1080	*Rudolf of Swabia
1081-1093	*Hermann (of Luxemburg)
1093-1101	*Conrad (of Franconia)
1106/11-1125	Henry V (Franconian/Salian)
1125	Franconian/Salian line ends
1125/33-1137	Lothair II (duke of Saxony)
1138	Hohenstaufen line begins
1138-1152	*Conrad III (Hohenstaufen)
1152/55-1190	FREDERICK I BARBAROSSA (Hohenstaufen)
1190/91-1197	Henry VI (Hohenstaufen)
1198-1208	*Philip of Swabia (Hohenstaufen)
1208/09-1215	Otto IV (married into Hohenstaufens)
1215/20-1250	FREDERICK II (Hohenstaufen): Last emperor crowned at Rome.
1246-1247	*Henry Raspe
1247-1256	*William of Holland
1250-1254	*Conrad IV
1254-1273	Great Interregnum
1257-1272	*Richard of Cornwall (rival, Plantagenet)
1257-1273	*Alfonso X of Castile (rival)
1273-1291	*RUDOLF I (Habsburg)
1292-1298	*Adolf of Nassau
1298-1308	*Albert (Albrecht) I (Habsburg)

Reign	*Emperor (House)*
1308/11-1313	Henry VII (Luxembourg)
1314/28-1347	Louis IV of Bavaria (Wittelsbach)
1314-1325	*Frederick of Habsburg (co-regent)
1346/55-1378	CHARLES IV (Luxembourg): Changes the name to the Holy Roman Empire of the German Nation as France begins to assert power; Charles abandons the Empire's French and Italian claims, and the history of the Holy Roman Empire and Germany are now basically the same.
1349	*Günther of Schwarzburg
1378-1400	*Wenceslaus (Luxembourg; deposed)
1400	*Frederick III (of Brunswick)
1400-1410	*Rupert of the Palatinate (Wittelsbach)
1410-1411	*John (of Moravia)
1410/33-1437	Sigismund (Luxembourg)
1438-1439	*Albert II (Habsburg)
1440/52-1493	Frederick III (Habsburg)
1493-1519	*Maximilian I (Habsburg)
1519-1558	*Charles V (Habsburg, last to be crowned as emperor, outside Rome)

HUNGARY. *See also* BOHEMIA, POLAND

Reign	*Ruler*
c. 896-907	ÁRPÁD
d. 947	Zsolt
d. 972	Taksony
997	Géza
997-1038	SAINT STEPHEN (ISTVÁN) I
1038-1041	Peter Orseleo
1041-1044	Samuel
1044-1046	Peter (second rule)
1047-1060	Andrew I
1060-1063	Béla I
1063-1074	Salamon
1074-1077	Géza I
1077-1095	SAINT LÁSZLÓ (LADISLAS) I
1095-1116	Kalman
1116-1131	Stephen II
1131-1141	Béla II
1141-1162	Géza II
1162-1163	László II
1163-1172	Stephen III
1163-1165	Stephen IV
1172-1196	Béla III
1196-1204	Imre
1204-1205	László III
1205-1235	Andrew II
1235-1270	Béla IV
1270-1272	Stephen V
1272-1290	László IV
1290-1301	Andrew III (end of the Árpád line)
1301-1304	Wenceslaus (Václav) II
1304-1308	Otto I of Bavaria
1305-1306	Wenceslaus (Václav) III
1306	End of the Přemlysid line
1306-1310	Instability
1310-1342	Károly (Charles Robert) I
1342-1382	Lajos (Louis) I
1382-1395	Maria
1387-1437	Sigismund
1438-1439	Albert II of Habsburg
1440-1444	Ulászló I (Władysław III, Poland)
1444-1457	László (Ladislas) V
1458-1490	Matthias (Matyas) Corvinus

INDIA

FIRST CĀLUKYA DYNASTY

Reign	*Ruler*
543-566	Pulakeśin I
c. 566-597	Kīrtivarman I
598-610	Maṇgaleśa
610-642	Pulakeśin II
655-680	Vikramāditya I
680-696	Vinayāditya
696-733	Vijayāditya
733-746	Vikramāditya II
747-757	Kīrtivarman II

PALLAVAS

Reign	*Ruler*
c. 550-575	Simhavarman (some sources give c. 436)
c. 575-600	Simhavishnu
c. 600-630	Mahendravarman I
c. 630-668	Narasiṃhavarman I Mahāmalla
c. 668-670	Mahendravarman II
c. 670-700	Paramesvaravarman I
c. 695-728	Narasiṃhavarman II
c. 728-731	Paramesvaravarman II
c. 731-796	Nandivarman
750-770	Gopāla
770-810	Dharmapāla
810-850	Devapāla
854-908	Narayanpāla
c. 988-1038	Māhipāla I
c. 1077-1120	Rāmapāla
1143-1161	Madanpāla

SECOND WESTERN CĀLUKYA DYNASTY

Reign	*Ruler*
973-997	Taila II
997-1008	Saṭyaśraya
1008-1014	Vikramāditya I
1014-1015	Ayyana
1015-1042	Jayasimha I
1043-1068	Someśvara I
1068-1076	Someśvara II
1076-1126	Vikramāditya VI
1127-1135	Someśvara III
1135-1151	Jagadhekamalla II
1151-1154	Taila III
1155-1168	Bijjala
1168-1177	Someśvara IV
1177-1180	Saṇkama II
1180-1183	Āhavamalla
1183-1184	Singhana
1184-1189/90	Someśvara IV

GURJARA-PRATIHĀRA DYNASTY

Reign	*Ruler*
c. 730-c. 756	Nāgabhaṭa I
n.d.	Devaraja
c. 778-c. 794	Vatsarāja
c. 794-c. 833	Nāgabhaṭa II
c. 836-c. 885	Mihira Bhoja I
c. 890-c. 910	Mahendrapāla I
c. 914-?	Mahipāla
n.d.	Mihira Bhoja II
n.d.	Vinayakapāla
c. 946-c. 948	Mahendrapāla II
c. 948-c. 960	Devapāla
c. 960-?	Vijayapāla
n.d.	Rājyapāla
c. 1018-c. 1027	Trilocanapāla

THE CŌLAS

Reign	*Ruler*
c. 850-c. 870	Vijayālaya
871-907	Āditya I
907-955	Parāntaka I
956	Arinjayā
956	Parāntaka II
956-969	Āditya II
969-985	Madhurantaka Uttama
985-1014	Rājarāja I
1014-1044	Rājendracōla Deva I
1044-1052	Rājadhirāja I
1052-1060	Rājendracōla Deva II
1060-1063	Ramamahendra
1063-1067	Virarājendra
1067-1070	Adhirājendra
1070-1122	Rājendra III
1122-1135	Vikrama Cōla
1135-1150	Kulottuṇga II Cōla
1150-1173	Rājarāja II
1173-1179	Rājadhirāja II
1179-1218	Kulottuṇga III
1218-1246	Rājarāja III
1246-1279	Rājendra IV

DELHI SULTANATE

Muʿizzī Slave Sultans

Reign	*Ruler*
1206-1210	Quṭ al-Dīn Aybak
1210-1211	Ārām Shāh
1211-1236	Iltutmish
1236	Ruknuddin Firūz Shāh
1236-1240	RAZIYA
1240-1242	Bahrām Shāh
1242-1246	Masʿūd Shāh
1246-1266	Maḥmūd Shāh
1266-1287	Balban Ulugh Khān
1287-1290	Kay Qubādh
1290	Kayūmarth

Khaljī Dynasty

Reign	*Ruler*
1290-1296	Jalāl-ud-Dīn Fīrūz Khaljī
1296-1316	ʿALĀʾ-UD-DĪN MUḤAMMAD KHALJĪ
1316	ʿUmar Shāh
1316-1320	Mubārak Shāh
1320	Khusraw Khān Barwārī

Tughluq Dynasty

Reign	*Ruler*
1320-1325	Tughluq I (Ghiyās-ud-Dīn)
1325-1351	Muḥammad ibn Tughluq
1351-1388	Fīrūz III
1388-1389	Tughluq II (Ghiyās-ud-Dīn)
1389-1390	Abū Bakr
1390-1394	Nāṣir-ud-Dīn
1394	Sikandar I (Humayun Khān)
1394-1395	Maḥmūd II
1395-1399	Nuṣrat
1401-1412	Maḥmūd II (second rule)
1412-1414	Dawlat Khān Lōdī

Sayyid Dynasty

Reign	*Ruler*
1414-1421	Khiḍr
1421-1434	Mubārak II
1434-1443	Muḥammad IV
1443-1451	ʿĀlām

Lodi Dynasty

Reign	*Ruler*
1451-1489	Bahlūl
1489-1517	Sikandar II
1517-1526	Ibrāhīm II
1526	Moghul Dynasty begins: Bābur

Iran (Persia). *See also* Islamic Caliphs, Ottoman Empire, Seljuk Empire

Later Sāsānian Empire

Reign	*Ruler*
309-379	Shāpūr II
379-383	Ardashīr II
383-388	Shāpūr III
388-399	Barham (Varahran) IV
399-421	Yazdegerd (Yazdgard) I
421-439	Barham (Varahran) V
439-457	Yazdegerd (Yazdgard) II
457-459	Hormizd III
459-484	Peroz
484-488	Valash
488-496	Kavadh I
496-498	Zamasp
499-531	Kavadh I (restored)
531-579	Khosrow (Khusro or Chosroes) I
579-590	Hormizd IV
590-628	Khosrow (Khusro or Chosroes) II
628	Kavadh II
628-629	Ardashīr III
629-630	Boran
630-632	Hormizd V and Khosrow III
633-651	Yazdegerd (Yazdgard) III
651	Islamic conquest
651-656	ʿUthmān ibn ʿAffān
656-661	Alī ibn Abī Ṭālib
661-750	Umayyad caliphs (*see* Islamic Caliphs)
750-821	ʿAbbāsid caliphs (*see* Islamic Caliphs)

Later Iranian Dynasties

Dates	*Dynasty*
821-873	Tāhirid Dynasty (in Khorāsān, northeastern Persia)
c. 866-c. 900	Ṣafārrid Dynasty
c. 940-1000	Sīmjūrid Dynasty (in Khorāsān)
945-1055	Būyid Dynasty (western Iran)
977-1186	Ghaznavid Dynasty (in Khorāsān, Afghanistan, northern India)
999-1211	Qarakhanid Dynasty (Transoxania)
c. 1038	Seljuks take power (*see* Seljuk Empire)
1153-1231	Khwārezm-Shāh Dynasty (in Khwārezm, northeastern Iran)
c. 1231	Mongol invasion
1256-1353	Il-Khanid (Mongol) Dynasty
1353-1393	Mozaffarid Dynasty
1393-c. 1467	Timurid Dynasty
c. 1467-1500	Turkmen/Ottoman incursions
1501-1736	Safavid Dynasty

Ireland: The High-Kings

Reign	*Ruler*
379-405	Niall Noígillach of the Nine Hostages
405-428	Dathi (Nath) I
429-463	Lóeguire MacNéill
456-493	Saint Patrick converts Irish
463-483	Ailill Motl MacNath I
483-507	Lugaid MacLóeguiri O'Néill
507-534	Muirchertach MacErcae O'Néill (Muiredach)
534-544	Tuathal Máelgarb MacCorpri Cáech O'Néill
544-565	Diarmait MacCerbaill O'Néill
565-566	Domnall MacMuirchertaig O'Néill and Forggus MacMuirchertaig O'Néill
566-569	Ainmere MacSátnai O'Néill
569-572	Báetán MacMuirchertaig O'Néill and Eochaid MacDomnaill O'Néill
572-581	Báetán MacNinnedo O'Néill
581-598	Aed MacAinmerech O'Néill
598-604	Aed Sláine MacDiarmato O'Néill
598-604	Colmán Rímid MacBáetáin O'Néill (rival)
604-612	Aed Uaridnach MacDomnaill O'Néill
612-615	Máel Cobo MacAedo O'Néill
615-628	Suibne Menn MacFiachnai O'Néill
628-642	Domnall MacAedo O'Néill
642-658	Conall Cóel MacMáele Cobo O'Néill and Cellach MacMáele Cobo O'Néill
656-665	Diarmait MacAedo Sláine O'Néill and Blathmac MacAedo Sláine O'Néill
665-671	Sechnussach MacBlathmaic O'Néill
671-675	Cenn Fáelad MacBlathmaic O'Néill
675-695	Finsnechtae Fledach MacDúnchada O'Néill
695-704	Loingsech MacOengus O'Néill
704-710	Congal Cinn Magir MacFergus Fánat O'Néill
710-722	Fergal MacMáele Dúin O'Néill
722-724	Fogartach MacNéill O'Néill
724-728	Cináed MacIrgalaig
724-734	Flaithbbertach MacLoingsig O'Néill
734-743	Aed Allán MacFergal O'Néill
743-763	Domnall Midi O'Néill
763-770	Niall Frossach MacFergal O'Néill
770-797	Donnchad Midi MacDomnaill Midi O'Néill
797-819	Aed Oirdnide MacNéill Frossach O'Néill
819-833	Conchobar MacDonnchado Midi O'Néill
833-846	Niall Caille MacAedo Oirdnide O'Néill

Reign	*Ruler*
846-862	Máel Sechnaill MacMáele Ruanaid O'Néill
862-879	Aed Findliath MacNéill Caille O'Néill
879-916	Flann Sionna MacMáele Sechnaill O'Néill
916-919	Niall Glúndubh MacAedo Findliath O'Néill
919-944	Donnchad Donn MacFlann O'Néill
944-950	Ruaidrí ua Canannáin (rival)
944-956	Congalach Cnogba MacMáel Mithig O'Néill
956-980	Domnall MacMuirchertaig O'Néill
980-1002	Máel Sechnaill MacDomnaill O'Néill
1002-1014	Brian Bóruma MacCennétig and Brian Boru
1014-1022	Máel Sechnaill MacDomnaill O'Néill (restored)
1022-1064	Donnchad MacBrian
1064-1072	Diarmait MacMáil na mBó
1072-1086	Toirdelbach O'Brien
1090-1121	Domnall MacArdgar O'Lochlainn O'Néill
1121-1135	Toirrdelbach MacRuaidrí na Saide Buide ua Conchobair (Turlogh)
1141-1150	Toirrdelbach MacRuaidrí na Saide Buide ua Conchobair (Turlogh)
1150-1166	Muirchertach MacNéill MacLochlainn (Murtagh)
1166-1175	Ruaidrí MacToirrdelbaig (Rory O'Connor)
1175-1258	Henry II of England claims title Lord of Ireland
1258-1260	Brian Catha an Duin
1260-1316	English rule restored
1316-1318	Edward de Bruce
1318	English rule restored
1801	Act of Union: Ireland is joined with Britain

ISLAMIC CALIPHS. *See also* IRAN, OTTOMAN EMPIRE, SELJUK EMPIRE, SPAIN

ORTHODOX (SUNNI) CALIPHS, 632-661

Reign	*Caliph*
632-634	Abū Bakr
634-644	ʿUMAR I
644-656	ʿUthmān ibn ʿAffān
656-661	Alī ibn Abī Ṭālib

THE UMAYYAD CALIPHS, 661-750

Reign	*Caliph*
661-680	Muʾāwiyah I (Muʾāwiyah ibn Abī Sufyna)
680-683	Yazīd I
683	Muʾāwiyah II
684-685	Marwān I
685-705	ʿABD AL-MALIK
705-715	al-Walīd I
715-717	Sulaimān
717-720	ʿUmar II
720-724	Yazīd II
724-743	Hishām
743-744	al-Walīd II
744	Yazīd III
744	Ibrāhīm
744-750	Marwān II

THE ʿABBĀSID CALIPHS, 750-1256

Reign	*Caliph*
750-754	Abū al-ʿAbbās al-Saffāḥ
754-775	al-Manṣūr
775-785	al-Mahdī
785-786	al-Hādī
786-809	Hārūn al-Rashīd
809-813	al-Amīn
813-833	al-Maʾmūn (Maʾmūn the Great)
833-842	al-Muʿtaṣim
842-847	al-Wathīq
847-861	al-Mutawakkil
861-862	al-Muntaṣir
862-866	al-Mustaʿin
866-869	al-Muʿtazz
869-870	al-Muqtadī
870-892	al-Muʿtamid
892-902	al-Muʿtaḍid
902-908	al-Muktafī
908-932	al-Muqtadir
932-934	al-Qāhir
934-940	al-Rāḍī
940-944	al-Mustaqfī
946-974	al-Mutī
974-991	al-Tāʾiʿ
991-1031	al-Qadir
1031-1075	al-Qāʾim
1075-1094	al-Muqtadī
1094-1118	al-Mustazhir
1118-1135	al-Mustarshid
1135-1136	al-Rashīd
1136-1160	al-Muqtafī
1160-1170	al-Mustanjid
1170-1180	al-Mustadī
1180-1225	al-Nāṣir
1225-1226	al-Zāhir
1226-1242	al-Mustanṣir
1242-1256	al-Mustaʿṣim

FĀṬIMID CALIPHS, 909-1171

Reign	*Caliph*
909-934	al-Mahdī
934-945	al-Qāʾim
945-952	al-Manṣūr

Reign	*Caliph*
952-975	al-Muʿizz
975-996	al-ʿAzīz
996-1021	al-Ḥākim
1021-1036	al-Zahīr
1036-1094	al-Mustanṣir
1094-1101	al-Mustadī
1101-1130	al-Amīr
1130-1149	al-Ḥāfiz
1149-1154	al-Zafīr
1154-1160	al-Fāʾiz
1160-1171	al-ʿAdīd

Italy

The Italian peninsula was occupied by a number of fiefs and principalities during the better part of the millennium that made up the Middle Ages. These included Lombardy in the north, the Papal States in the center, and various duchies, margavates, and republics, including Sardinia, Benevento, Spoleto, Modena, Milan, Tuscany, Parma, Montferrat, and independent centers of trade such as Venice and Genoa. Only those early rulers who dominated the area are listed below; thereafter, the northern part of the peninsula was primarily under the power of the Carolingians (see Frankish Kingdom and France), the Holy Roman Emperors (see Holy Roman Empire, above), and the Papacy (see Popes and Antipopes, above). In the south, Naples and Sicily dominated. Thus, during the millennium 476-1453, the Italian Peninsula was a complex of ever-shifting jurisdictions, of which only the more prominent rulers are listed below.

Barbarian Rulers

Reign	*Ruler*
476-493	Odoacer
493-526	Theodoric
526-534	Athalaric
534-536	Theodatus (Theodahad)
536-540	Vitiges (Witiges)
540-541	Theodobald (Heldebadus)
541	Eraric
541-552	Totila
552-553	Teias

Byzantine (East Roman) Rule

Reign	*Ruler*
518-527	Justin I
527-565	Justinian I

Lombards (northern Italy)

Reign	*Ruler*
565-572	Alboin
573-575	Celph
575-584	Unstable
584-590	Authari
590-591	Theodelinda
591-615	Agilulf
615-625	Adaloald
625-636	Arioald
636-652	Rotharis
652-661	Aribert I
661-662	Godipert
662-671	Grimoald
671-674	Garibald
674-688	Bertharit
688-700	Cunibert
700-701	Liutpert
701	Raginpert
701-712	Aribert II
712-744	Liutprand
744-749	Rachis of Friuli
749-756	Aistulf of Friuli
756-774	Desiderius
774-888	Frankish conquest, subsumed under Carolingian Empire

Kingdom of Italy

Reign	*Ruler*
888-891	Berengar I of Friuli
891-894	Guy of Spoleto (Guido, Wido)
894-896	Lambert of Spoleto
896-899	Arnulf, King of Germany
899-905	Louis III
905-922	Berengar I of Friuli (restored)
922-933	Rudolf II
933-947	Hugh of Arles
947-950	Lothair II of Arles
950-961	Berengar II of Ivrea
961	Conquest by Otto I; Italian peninsula divided among Holy Roman Empire, Papacy, and other principalities until unification in 1861

Naples and Sicily

Reign	*Ruler (Line)*
1042-1046	William Iron Arm (Norman)
1046-1051	Drogo (Norman)
1051-1057	Humphrey (Norman)
1057-1085	Robert Guiscard (Norman)
1071-1101	Roger I (Norman)
1101-1154	Roger II of Sicily (Norman; king in 1130)
1154-1166	William I (Norman)
1166-1189	William II the Good (Norman)

Reign	*Ruler (Line)*
1190-1194	Tancred of Lecce (Norman)
1194	William III (Norman)
1194-1197	Henry VI (Hohenstaufen)
1197-1250	FREDERICK II (Hohenstaufen)
1250-1254	Conrad IV (Hohenstaufen)
1250-1266	Manfred (Hohenstaufen)
1267-1268	Conradin (rival)
1266-1285	Charles I of Anjou (Angevin)
1282	Sicily and Naples split

SICILY

Reign	*Ruler*
1282-1285	Pedro III of Aragón
1285-1296	James II of Aragón
1296-1337	Frederick II (or I)
1337-1342	Peter II
1342-1355	Louis
1355-1377	Frederick III (or II) the Simple
1377-1401	Mary
1390-1409	Martin the Younger
1395-1410	Martin (I) the Older Aragón
1412-1416	Ferdinand I Sicily & Aragón
1416-1458	Alfonso V of Aragón (Naples and Sicily)
1458-1479	John II
1479-1516	Ferdinand II

NAPLES

Reign	*Ruler*
1285-1309	Charles II (Angevin)
1309-1343	Robert Ladislas (Angevin)
1343-1382	Joanna I (Angevin)
1382-1386	Charles III (Angevin)
1386-1414	Ladislas (Angevin)
1414-1435	Joanna II (Angevin)
1416-1458	Alfonso V of Aragón (Naples and Sicily)
1458-1494	Ferdinand I (Naples)
1494-1516	Alfonso II (Naples)
1495-1496	Ferdinand II (Naples), French occupation

VISCONTIS (GENOA)

Reign	*Ruler*
1310-1322	Matteo Visconti
1322-1328	Galeazzo I
1328-1339	Azzo
1339-1349	Lucchino
1349-1354	Giovanni
1354-1355	Matteo II and Bernabò
1354-1378	Galeazzo II
1378-1402	Gian Galeazzo II
1402-1447	Filippo Maria

SFORZAS (GENOA)

Reign	*Ruler*
1450-1466	Francesco Sforza
1466-1476	Galeazzo Maria
1476-1494	Gian Galeazzo
1494-1500	Ludovico
1500-1512	[Louis XII of France]
1512-1515	Massimiliano
1521-1535	Francesco Maria

DOGES OF VENICE

Reign	*Doge*
727-738	Orso (Ursus) Ipato
742, 744-736	Teodato (Deusdedit) Ipato
756	Galla Gaulo
756-765	Domenico Monegaurio
765-787	Maurizio I Galbaio
787-802	Giovanni and Maurizio II Galbaio
802-811	Obelerio Antenorio
808-811	Beato
811-827	Angello Partecipazio
827-829	Giustiniano Partecipazio
829-836	Giovanni I Partecipazio
836-864	Pietro Tradonico
864-881	Orso I Badoer (I Partecipazio)
881-888	Giovanni Badoer (II Partecipazio)
887	Pietro I Candiano
888-912	Pietro Tribuno
912-932	Orso II Badoer (II Partecipazio)
932-939	Pietro II Candiano
939-942	Pietro Badoer (Partecipazio)
942-959	Pietro III Candiano
959-976	Pietro IV Candiano
976-978	Pietro I Orseolo
978-979	Vitale Candiano
979-991	Tribuno Menio (Memmo)
991-1009	Pietro II Orseolo
1009-1026	Ottone Orseolo
1026-1030	Pietro Centranico (Barbolano)
1030-1032	Ottone Orseolo (second rule)
1032-1043	Domenico Flabianico
1043-1070	Domenico Contarini
1070-1084	Domenico Silvio (Selvo)
1084-1096	Vitale Falier
1096-1101	Vitale I Michiel (Michel)
1101-1118	Ordelafo Falier
1118-1129	Domenico Michiel
1129-1148	Pietro Polani
1148-1155	Domenico Morosini
1155-1172	Vitale II Michiel
1172-1178	Sebastiano Ziani
1178-1192	Orio Mastropiero (Malipiero)
1192-1205	Enrico Dandolo

Reign	*Doge*
1205-1229	Pietro Ziani
1229-1249	Giacomo Tiepolo
1249-1253	Marino Morosini
1253-1268	Reniero Zeno
1268-1275	Lorenzo Tiepolo
1275-1280	Jacopo Contarini
1280-1289	Giovanni Dandolo
1289-1311	Pietro Gradenigo
1311-1312	Marino Zorzi
1312-1328	Giovanni Soranzo
1328-1339	Francesco Dandolo
1339-1342	Bartolomeo Gradenigo
1343-1354	Andrea Dandolo
1354-1355	Marino Falier
1355-1356	Giovanni Gradenigo
1356-1361	Giovanni Dolfin
1361-1365	Lorenzo Celsi
1365-1368	Marco Corner
1368-1382	Andrea Contarini
1382	Michele Morosini
1382-1400	Antonio Venier
1400-1413	Michele Steno
1414-1423	Tommaso Mocenigo
1423-1457	Francesco Foscari
1457-1797	Doges continue to rule Venice
1797	Venice Falls to Napoleon Bonaparte

JAPAN

ASUKA PERIOD

Reign	*Ruler*
539-571	Kimmei
572-585	Bidatsu
585-587	Yōmei
587-592	Sushun
593-628	SUIKO (empress)
629-641	Jomei
642-645	Kōgyoku (empress)
645-654	Kōtoku
655-661	Saimei (empress)
661-672	Tenji
672	Kōbun
673-686	Temmu
686-697	Jitō (empress)
697-707	Mommu
707-715	Gemmei (empress)

NARA PERIOD

Reign	*Ruler*
707-715	Gemmei (empress)
715-724	Genshō (empress)
724-749	Shōmu
749-758	Kōken (empress)
758-764	Junnin
764-770	Shōtoku (Kōken, empress)
770-781	Kōnin
781-806	Kammu

HEIAN PERIOD

Reign	*Ruler*
781-806	Kammu
806-809	Heizei
809-823	Saga
823-833	Junna
833-850	Nimmyō
850-858	Montoku
858-876	Seiwa
876-884	Yōzei
884-887	Kōkō
887-897	Uda
897-930	Daigo
930-946	Suzaku
946-967	Murakami
967-969	Reizei
969-984	En'yu
984-986	Kazan
986-1011	Ichijō
1011-1016	Sanjō
1016-1036	Go-Ichijō
1036-1045	Go-Suzaku
1045-1068	Go-Reizei
1068-1073	Go-Sanjō
1073-1087	Shirakawa (cloistered, 1086-1129)
1087-1107	Horikawa
1107-1123	Toba (cloistered, 1129-1156)
1123-1142	Sutoku
1142-1155	Konoe
1155-1158	Go-Shirakawa (cloistered, 1158-1192)
1158-1165	Nijō
1165-1168	Rokujō
1168-1180	Takakura
1180-1185	Antoku

FUJIWARA REGENTS

Some Fujiwara were regents more than once or for more than one emperor. The position of sessho indicates regency for an underage emperor; that of kampaku, regency for an adult emperor.

Reign	*Regent (position)*
866-872	Fujiwara Yoshifusa (sessho)
872-884	Fujiwara Mototsune (sessho)
884-891	Fujiwara Mototsune (kampaku)
930-941	Fujiwara Tadahira (sessho)

Reign	Regent (position)
941-949	Fujiwara Tadahira (kampaku)
967-969	Fujiwara Saneyori (kampaku)
969-970	Fujiwara Saneyori (sessho)
970-972	Fujiwara Koretada (sessho)
973-977	Fujiwara Kamemichi (kampaku)
977-986	Fujiwara Yoritada (kampaku)
986-990	Fujiwara Kaneie (sessho)
990	Fujiwara Kaneie (kampaku)
990-993	Fujiwara Michitaka (sessho)
993-995	Fujiwara Michitaka (kampaku)
995	Fujiwara Michikane (kampaku)
996-1017	FUJIWARA MICHINAGA (kampaku)
1016-1017	FUJIWARA MICHINAGA (sessho)
1017-1020	Fujiwara Yorimichi (sessho)
1020-1068	Fujiwara Yorimichi (kampaku)
1068-1075	Fujiwara Norimichi (kampaku)
1075-1087	Fujiwara Morozane (kampaku)
1087-1091	Fujiwara Morozane (sessho)
1091-1094	Fujiwara Morozane (kampaku)
1094-1099	Fujiwara Moromichi (kampaku)
1106-1107	Fujiwara Tadazane (kampaku)
1107-1114	Fujiwara Tadazane (sessho)
1114-1121	Fujiwara Tadazane (kampaku)
1121-1123	Fujiwara Tadamichi (kampaku)
1123-1129	Fujiwara Tadamichi (sessho)
1129-1142	Fujiwara Tadamichi (kampaku)
1142-1151	Fujiwara Tadamichi (sessho)
1151-1158	Fujiwara Tadamichi (kampaku)
1158-1165	Fujiwara Motozane (kampaku)
1165-1166	Fujiwara Motozane (sessho)
1166-1173	Fujiwara Motofusa (sessho)
1173-1179	Fujiwara Motofusa (kampaku)
1184	Fujiwara Moroie (sessho)

KAMAKURA PERIOD AND KEMMU RESTORATION

Reign	Ruler
1183-1198	Go-Toba
1198-1210	Tsuchimikado
1210-1221	Jintoku
1221	Chukyo
1221-1232	Go-Horikawa
1232-1242	Shijō
1242-1246	Go-Saga
1246-1260	Go-Fukakusa
1260-1274	Kameyama
1274-1287	Go-Uda
1287-1298	Fushimi
1298-1301	Go-Fushimi
1301-1308	Go-Nijō
1308-1318	Hanazonō
1318-1339	Go-Daigo

KAMAKURA SHOGUNATE

Reign	Shogun
1192-1199	MINAMOTO YORITOMO
1202-1203	Minamoto Yoriie
1203-1219	Minamoto Sanetomo
1226-1244	Kujo Yoritsune
1244-1252	Kujo Yoritsugu
1252-1266	Prince Munetaka
1266-1289	Prince Koreyasu
1289-1308	Prince Hisaaki
1308-1333	Prince Morikuni

HŌJŌ FAMILY

Reign	Regent
1203-1205	Hōjō Tokimasa
1205-1224	Hōjō Yoshitoki
1224-1242	Hōjō Yasutoki
1242-1246	Hōjō Tsunetoki
1246-1256	Hōjō Tokiyori
1256-1264	Hōjō Nagatoki
1264-1268	Hōjō Masamura
1268-1284	Hōjō Tokimune
1284-1301	Hōjō Sadatoki
1301-1311	Hōjō Morotoki
1311-1312	Hōjō Munenobu
1312-1315	Hōjō Hirotoki
1315	Hōjō Mototoki
1316-1326	Hōjō Takatoki
1326	Hōjō Sadaaki
1327-1333	Hōjō Moritoki

MUROMACHI PERIOD

Emperors: Southern Court

Reign	Ruler
1318-1339	Go-Daigo
1339-1368	Go-Murakami
1368-1383	Chōkei
1383-1392	Go-Kameyama

Ashikaga Pretenders: Northern Court

Reign	Ruler
1336-1348	Komyō
1348-1351	Sukō
1351-1371	Go-Kogon
1371-1382	Go-En'yu

Later Emperors

Reign	Ruler
1382-1412	Go-Komatsu
1412-1428	Shōkō
1428-1464	Go-Hanazono
1464-1500	Go-Tsuchimikado
1500-1526	Go-Kashiwabara

Reign	*Ruler*
1526-1557	Go-Nara
1557-1586	Ogimachi

ASHIKAGA SHOGUNATE

Reign	*Shogun*
1338-1358	ASHIKAGA TAKAUJI
1359-1368	Ashikaga Yoshiakira
1368-1394	Ashikaga Yoshimitsu
1395-1423	Ashikaga Yoshimochi
1423-1425	Ashikaga Yoshikazu
1429-1441	Ashikaga Yoshinori
1442-1443	Ashikaga Yoshikatsu
1449-1473	Ashikaga Yoshimasa
1474-1489	Ashikaga Yoshihisa
1490-1493	Ashikaga Yoshitane
1495-1508	Ashikaga Yoshizumi
1508-1521	Ashikaga Yoshitane (second rule)
1522-1547	Ashikaga Yoshiharu
1547-1565	Ashikaga Yoshiteru
1568	Ashikaga Yoshihide
1568-1573	Ashikaga Yoshiaki

KINGDOM OF JERUSALEM

The Christian rulers of Jerusalem were ushered in by the First Crusade and essentially were ushered out after the last Crusade.

Reign	*King*
1095-1099	First Crusade
1099-1100	Godfrey of Boulogne (or Bouillon)
1100-1118	Baldwin I of Boulogne
1118-1131	Baldwin II of Le Bourg
1131-1153	MELISENDE
1131-1143	Fulk V of Anjou
1143-1162	Baldwin III
1147-1149	Second Crusade
1162-1174	Amalric I
1174-1183	Baldwin IV the Leper
1183-1186	Baldwin V
1185-1190	Sibylla
1186-1192	Guy of Lusignan
1189-1192	Third Crusade
1190-1192	Conrad of Montferrat
1192-1197	Henry of Champagne
1192-1205	Isabella I
1197-1205	Amalric II
1202-1204	Fourth Crusade
1205-1210	Maria of Montferrat (regent)
1210-1225	John of Brienne
1210-1228	Isabella (Yolanda) II
1217-1221	Fifth Crusade
1225-1228	FREDERICK II
1227-1230	Sixth Crusade
1228-1254	Conrad IV Hohenstaufen
1244	Fall of Jerusalem
1248-1254	Seventh (or Sixth) Crusade
1254-1268	Conradin Hohenstaufen
1268-1284	Hugh III
1268-1284	Charles of Anjou (rival)
1270	Eighth (or Seventh) Crusade
1284-1285	John I
1285-1306	Henry I of Jerusalem (II of Cyprus)
1291	Fall of Acre to the Mamluks

KOREA

UNIFIED SILLA DYNASTY

Reign	*Ruler*
661-681	Munmu Wang
681-692	Sinmun Wang
692-702	Hyoso Wang
702-737	Sŏngdŏk Wang
737-742	Hyosŏng Wang
742-765	Kyŏngdŏk Wang
765-780	Hyesong Wang
780-785	Sŏndŏk Wang
785-798	Wŏnsŏng Wang
798-800	Sosŏng Wang
800-809	Aejang Wang
809-826	Hŏndŏk Wang
826-836	Hŭngdŏk Wang
836-838	Hŭigang Wang
838-839	Minae Wang
839	Sinmu Wang
839-857	Munsŏng Wang
857-861	Hŏnan Wang
861-875	Kyŏngmun Wang
875-886	Hŏn'gang Wang
886-887	Chŏnggang Wang
887-896	Queen Chinsŏng
897-912	Hyogong Wang
912-917	Pak Sindŏ Wang
917-924	Kyŏngmyŏng Wang
924-927	Kyŏngae Wang
927-935	Kyŏngsun Wang

KORYŎ DYNASTY

Reign	*Ruler*
918-943	T'aejo (WANG KŎN)
944-945	Hyejong
946-949	Chŏngjong
949-975	Kwangjong (Wang So)

Reign	Ruler
975-981	Kyŏngjong (Wang Yu)
981-997	Sŏngjong (Wang Ch'i)
997-1009	Mokshong
1009-1031	Hyŏngjong
1031-1034	Tokjong
1034-1046	Chŏngjong
1046-1083	Munjong (Wang Hwi)
1083	Sunjong
1083-1094	Sŏnjong
1094-1095	Hŏnjong
1095-1105	Sukjong
1105-1122	Yejong I
1122-1146	Injong I (Wang Hae)
1146-1170	Ŭijong
1170-1197	Myŏngjong
1197-1204	Sinjong
1204-1211	Hŭijong
1211-1213	Kangjong
1214-1259	Kojong I
1260-1274	Wŏnjong
1274-1308	Ch'ungugŏl Wang
1308-1313	Ch'ungsŏn Wang
1313-1330	Ch'ungsuk Wang
1330-1332	Ch'unghye Wang
1332-1339	Ch'angsuk Wang
1339-1344	Ch'unghye Wang
1344-1348	Ch'ungmok Wang
1348-1351	Ch'ungjŏng Wang
1351-1394	Kongmin Wang
1374-1388	U (Sin-u)
1389	Sinch'ang
1389-1392	Kongyang Wang

Yi Dynasty

Reign	Ruler
1392-1398	Yi T'aejo
1398-1400	Chŏngjong
1400-1418	T'aejong
1418-1450	Sejong
1450-1452	Munjong
1452-1455	Tanjong
1455-1468	Sejo
1468-1469	Yejong
1469-1494	Sŏngjong
1494-1506	Yŏnsan Gun
1506-1544	Chungjong
1544-1545	Injong
1546-1567	Myŏngjong
1567-1608	Sŏnjo
1592-1598	Japanese invasions of Korea
1910	End of the Yi Dynasty

Macedonia

Reign	Ruler
867-886	Basil I
886-912	Leo VI the Wise
886-913	Alexander
913-959	Constantine VII Porphyrogenitus
919-944	Romanus I Lecapenus
944-945	Stephen & Constantine
959-963	Romanus II
963-969	Nicephorus II Phocas
963-1025	Basil II Bulgaroctonus
969-976	John I Tzimisces
976-1028	Constantine VIII
1028-1034	Romanus III Argyrus
1028-1050	Zoë Porphyrogenita
1034-1041	Michael IV the Paphlagonian
1041-1042	Michael V Calaphates
1042-1055	Constantine IX Monomachus
1042-1056	Theodora Porphyrogenita
1056-1057	Michael VI Stratioticus
1057-1059	Isaac I Comnenus

Moldavia

Reign	Ruler
1352-1353	Dragosh
1354-1358	Sas
1359	Balc
1359-1365	Bogdan I Founder
1365-1373	Latcu
1373-1375	Costea
1375-1391	Petru I al Mushatei
1391-1394	Roman I
1394-1399	Stephen I
1399-1400	Ologul (Iuga)
1400-1432	Alexander the Good
1432-1433	Ilias (Elias)
1433-1447	Stephen II
1435-1442	Ilias (Elias)
1444-1445	Petru II
1447-1448	Roman II
1448-1449	Ciubar
1449	Alexandrel
1449-1451	Bogdan II
1451-1452	Petru Aron
1452-1454	Alexandrel
1454-1455	Petru Aron
1455	Alexandrel
1455-1457	Petru Aron
1457-1504	Stephen III the Great
1504-1517	Bodgan III the Blind

Reign	Ruler
1517-1527	Shtefanita
1527-1538	Petru Raresh
1538	Ottoman conquest
1546-1551	Ilias (Elias)
1551-1552	Stephen IV
1552	Ioan Joldea
1552-1561	Alexandru Lapushneanu
1561-1563	Despot Voda (Iacob Basilikos Heraklides/ Eraclid)
1562	Ilias (Elias)
1563-1564	Sephen Tomsha
1564-1568	Alexandru Lapushneanu
1568-1572	Bogdan Laprushneanu
1572-1574	Ion Voda (John the Terrible)
1574-1577	Petru Schiopul (the Lame)
1577	Ioan Potcoava
1579-1582	Iancu Sasul
1592-1595	Aron the Terrible
1595	Stefan Razvan
1595-1600	Ieremia Moghila
1600	Ottoman control
1600	Michael II the Brave

MONGOL EMPIRE. *See also* CHINA: YUAN DYNASTY

Reign	Ruler
1206-1227	GENGHIS KHAN
1227-1229	Tolui (regent, son of Genghis Khan)
1229-1241	Ogatai Khan
1241-1246	Toregene (regent, wife of Ogatai)
1246-1248	Güyük
1248-1251	Oghul Qaimish (regent, wife of Güyük)
1251-1259	Mongu
1259-1260	Arigböge (regent, brother of Mongu and Kublai)
1260-1294	KUBLAI KHAN

NORWAY. *See also* DENMARK, SWEDEN

Reign	Ruler
680-710	Olaf the Tree Hewer
710-750	Halfdan I
750-780	Oystein (Eystein) I
780-800	Halfdan II White Legs
800-810	Gudrod the Magnificent
810-840	Olaf Geirstade
840-863	Halfdan III the Black
863-872	Civil war
872-930/33	Harald I Fairhair
933-934	Erik I Bloodaxe
934-961	Hákon I the Good
961-970	Harald II Grayfell
970-995	Earl (Jarl) Hákon
995-1000	OLAF I TRYGGVASON
1000-1015	Erik I
1016-1028	SAINT OLAF II HARALDSSON
1028-1035	CANUTE THE GREAT
1035-1047	Magnus I the Good
1047-1066	Harald III Hardrada
1066-1069	Magnus II
1069-1093	Olaf III the Peaceful
1093-1103	Magnus III the Barefoot
1103-1122	Oystein (Eystein) II
1103-1130	Sigurd I the Crusader
1130-1135	Magnus IV the Blinded
1130-1136	Harald IV Gillechrist
1136-1155	Sigurd II
1136-1161	Inge I
1142-1157	Oystein (Eystein) III
1161-1162	Hákon II
1163-1184	Magnus V
1184-1202	Sverre Sigurdsson
1202-1204	Hákon III
1204-1217	Inge II
1217-1263	Hákon IV
1263-1281	Magnus VI
1281-1299	Erik II Magnusson
1299-1319	Hákon V
1320-1343	Magnus VII (II of Sweden)
1343-1380	Hákon VI
1376-1387	Olaf IV (V of Denmark)
1380	Unification of Norway and Denmark
1380-1410	MARGARET I OF DENMARK, NORWAY, AND SWEDEN
1397	Unification of Norway, Denmark, and Sweden
1412-1439	Erik III (VII of Denmark, XIII of Sweden)
1439-1448	Christopher (III of Denmark)
1448-1481	Christian I of Oldenburg
1481-1513	Hans/John (II of Sweden)
1513-1523	Christian II
1523	Kingdoms of Denmark and Norway joined, Sweden separate

OTTOMAN EMPIRE. *See also* IRAN, ISLAMIC CALIPHS, SELJUK EMPIRE, SPAIN

Reign	Sultan
1281/88-1326	OSMAN I
1326-1360	Orhan I
1360-1389	Murad I
1389-1402	Bayezid I
1402-1421	Mehmed I
1421-1444	Murad II

Reign	Sultan
1444-1446	MEHMED II
1446-1451	Murad II (second rule)
1451-1481	MEHMED II (second rule)
1453	Ottomans take Constantinople
1481-1922	Ottoman Empire continues
1912-1918	Balkan Wars
1918-1922	Mehmed VI (last Ottoman sultan)

POLAND

Reign	Ruler
962-992	Mieszko I
992-1025	Bolesław I the Brave
1025-1034	Mieszko II
1034-1037	Instability
1037-1058	Casimir I the Restorer
	Instability
1058-1079	Bolesław II
1079-1102	Władysław (Vladislav or Ladislas) I
1102-1106	Zbigniev (rival to brother Bolesław III)
1102-1138	Bolesław III
1138-1146	Instability following Bolesław III's division of Poland into five principalities
1146-1173	Bolesław IV
1173-1177	Mieszko III
1177-1194	Casimir II
1194-1227	Leszek I
1227-1279	Bolesław V
1228-1288	Instability: arrival of Teutonic Knights followed by Mongol incursions
1288-1290	Henry Probus
1290-1296	Przemyslav II (crowned 1295)
1297-1300	Instability
1300-1305	Wenceslaus (Vacław) I
1306-1333	Władysław I (Vladislav IV, Lokietek)
1333-1370	CASIMIR III THE GREAT
1370	End of the Piast Dynasty
1370-1382	Ludvik I the Great (Louis of Anjou)
1382-1384	Confederation of Radom and civil war
1384-1399	QUEEN JADWIGA
1386-1434	WŁADYSŁAW II JAGIEŁŁO
1410-1411	Battle of Tannenberg and Peace of Thorn
1434-1444	Władysław (Vladislav) III
1444-1447	Instability; Poland united with Lithuania
1447-1492	Casimir IV
1454-1466	Poles defeat Teutonic Order, gain access to the Baltic in the Second Peace of Thorn
1471-1516	Vladislav Jagiełło (son of Casimir IV) king of Bohemia and then Hungary
1492-1501	John Albert I
1496	Statute of Piotrkow (Poland's Magna Carta)

PORTUGAL

Reign	Ruler
1093-1112	Henry of Burgundy, count of Portugal
1112-1185	AFONSO I (count of Portugal 1112-1139, king 1139-1185)
1185-1211	Sancho I
1211-1223	Afonso II
1223-1245	Sancho II
1245-1279	Afonso III
1279-1325	Diniz (Denis)
1325-1357	Afonso IV
1357-1367	Peter I
1367-1383	Ferdinand I
1385-1433	John I of Avis
1433-1438	Edward I
1438-1481	Afonso V
1481-1495	John II
1495-1521	Emanuel I
1521-1557	John III
1557-1578	Sebastian I
1578-1580	Cardinal Henry
1580-1598	Philip I of Portugal (Philip II of Spain)
1598-1621	Philip II of Portugal (Philip III of Spain)
1621-1640	Philip III of Portugal (Philip IV of Spain)
1640	Revolt of Portugal

RUSSIA

PRINCES OF KIEVAN RUS

Reign	Ruler
c. 862-879	RURIK
879-912	Oleg
912-945	Igor
945-964	SAINT OLGA (regent)
964-972	Svyatoslav I
972-980	Yaropolk
980-1015	VLADIMIR I (with ANNA, PRINCESS OF THE BYZANTINE EMPIRE)
1015-1019	Sviatopolk I
1019-1054	Yaroslav
1054-1073	Iziaslav
1073-1076	Svyâtoslav II
1076-1078	Iziaslav (restored)
1078-1093	Vsevolod
1093-1113	Sviatopolk II
1113-1125	Vladimir II Monomakh
1125-1132	Mstislav
1132-1139	Yaropolk
1139-1146	Vyacheslav
1146-1154	Iziaslav

Reign	Ruler
1149-1157	Yuri I Dolgoruky
1154-1167	Rostislav

PRINCES OF VLADIMIR

Reign	Ruler
1169-1174	Andrei I Bogolyubsky
1175-1176	Michael
1176-1212	Vsevolod III
1212-1217	Yuri II
1217-1218	Constantin
1218-1238	Yuri II (restored)
1238-1246	Yaroslav II
1240	Mongol conquest
1246-1247	Svyatoslav III
1248-1249	Michael
1249-1252	Andrei II
1252-1263	SAINT ALEXANDER NEVSKY
1264-1271	Yaroslav III of Tver
1272-1276	Vasily
1276-1281	Dmitry
1281-1283	Andrei III
1283-1294	Dmitry (restored)
1294-1304	Andrei III (restored)
1304-1319	Saint Michael of Tver
1319-1326	Yuri III of Moscow
1326-1327	Alexander II of Tver
1328-1331	Alexander III

PRINCES OF MOSCOW

Reign	Ruler
1263-1303	Daniel
1303-1325	Yuri III
1328-1341	Ivan I
1341-1353	Simeon
1353-1359	Ivan II
1359-1389	Dmitry Donskoy
1389-1425	Vasily I
1425-1462	Vasily II
1462-1505	Ivan III the Great
1480	Fall of the Golden Horde
1505-1533	Vasily III
1533	Ivan IV the Terrible becomes first czar of Russia

SCOTLAND

Reign	Ruler
404-420	Fergus
420-451	Eugenius II
451-457	Dongardus
457-479	Constantine I
479-501	Congallus
569-606	Aldan
606-621	Eugenius III
646-664	Ferchard II
664-684	Mulduinns
684-688	Eugenius V
688-699	Eugenius VI
699-715	Eugenius VII
715-730	Mordachus
730-761	Etfinus
761-767	Interregnum
767-787	Solvatius
787-819	Achaius
819-824	Dongallus III
824-831	Dongal
831-834	Alpine
834-854	Kenneth
854-858	Donald V
858-874	Constantine II
874-893	Gregory
893-904	Donald VI
904-944	Constantine III
944-953	Malcolm I
953-961	Gondulph
961-965	Duff
965-970	Cullen
970-995	Kenneth II
995-1005	Grimus
1005-1034	Malcolm II
1034-1040	Duncan I
1040-1057	Macbeth
1057-1058	Lulach
1058-1093	Malcolm III
1093-1094	Donaldbane
1094	Duncan II
1094-1097	Donaldbane (second rule)
1097-1107	Edgar
1107-1124	Alexander I
1124-1153	DAVID I
1153-1165	Malcolm IV
1165-1214	William I the Lion
1214-1249	Alexander II
1249-1286	Alexander III
1286-1290	Margaret
1290-1292	Interregnum
1292-1296	John Baliol
1296-1306	Interregnum
1306-1329	ROBERT I THE BRUCE
1329-1371	DAVID II
1371	Ascendancy of Robert II, House of Stuart
1371-1390	Robert II
1390-1406	Robert III

Reign	*Ruler*
1406-1437	James I
1437-1460	James II
1460-1488	James III
1488-1513	James IV
1513-1542	James V
1542-1567	Mary
1567-1625	James VI
1625	Joined with England

SELJUK EMPIRE. *See also* IRAN, ISLAMIC CALIPHS, OTTOMAN EMPIRE, SELJUK EMPIRE

GREAT SULTANS

Reign	*Sultan*
1037-1063	Toghrïl Beg
1063-1072/73	ALP ARSLAN
1073-1092	Malik Shāh I
1092-1093	Maḥmūd I
1093-1104	Berk Yaruq (Barkyaruk, Barkiyarok)
1104-1105	Malik Shāh II
1105-1117	Muḥammad Tapar
1117-1157	Aḥmad Sanjar (Sinjar)

SULTANS OF IRAQ

Reign	*Sultan*
1105-1118	Maḥmūd Tapar
1118-1131	Maḥmūd
1131-1132	Dāʿūd (Dawd)
1132-1135	Toghrïl I
1135-1152	Masʿūd
1152-1153	Malik Shāh
1153-1159	Muḥammad
1159-1161	Sulaimān Shāh
1161-1177	Arslan Shāh
1177-1194	Toghrïl II

SELJUK SULTANS OF ANATOLIA/RUM

Reign	*Sultan*
1077-1066	Sulaimān Shāh
1092-1107?	Qïlïch (Kilij) Arslan I
1107?-1116	Malik Shāh I
1116-1156	Masʿūd I
1156-1192	Qïlïch (Kilij) Arslan II
1192	Malik Shāh II
1192-1196	Kai Khusrau (Khosrow, Khosru, Khusraw) I
1196-1204	Suleiman II
1203-1204	Qïlïch (Kilij) Arslan III
1204-1210	Kai Khusrau I (second rule)
1210-1219	Kai Kāʾūs I
1219-1236	Kai Qubād (Kobadh) I
1236-1246	Kai Khusrau II
1246-1259	Kai Kāʾūs II
1248-1264	Qïlïch (Kilij) Arslan IV
1249-1257	Kai Qubād (Kobadh) II
1264-1283	Kai Khusrau III
1283-1298	Masʿūd II
1298-1301?	Kai Qubād (Kobadh) III
1303-1308	Masʿūd II (second rule)

SELJUK SULTANS OF SYRIA

Reign	*Sultan*
1078-1094	Tutush
1095-1113	Riḍwān (Damascus)
1098-1113	Duqaq (Aleppo)
1113-1114	Alp Arslan
1114-1117	Sultan Shāh

SULTANS OF KIRMĀN (KERMAN)

Reign	*Sultan*
1041-1073	Qāvurt (Qawurd)
1073-1074	Kirmān (Kerman) Shāh
1074-1085	Sultan Shāh
1085-1097	Turān Shāh I
1097-1101	Īrān Shāh
1101-1142	Arslan Shāh I
1142-1156	Muḥammad I
1156-1170	Toghrïl Shāh
1170-1175	Bahrām Shāh
1170-1177	Arslan Shāh II
1175-1186	Muḥammad Shāh II
1177-1183	Turān Shāh II

SERBIA

Reign	*Ruler*
1167-1196	Stefan I Nemanja
1180	Serbian independence
1180-1196	Instability
1196-1228	Stefan II
1228-1234	Stefan III Radoslav
1234-1243	Stefan IV Vladislav
1243-1276	Stefan Uroš I
1276-1282	Stefan Dragutin
1282-1321	Stefan Uroš II Milutin
1321-1331	Stefan Uroš III Dečanski
1331-1355	STEFAN UROŠ IV DUŠAN

Reign	*Ruler*
1355-1371	Stefan Uroš V the Weak
1371	Dynastic collapse
1371-1389	Stefan Lazar I (prince)
1389	Battle of Kosovo, defeat by Ottomans
1389-1427	Stefan Lazar II Lazarevich (despot)
1396	Ottoman vassal state
1427-1456	George Brankovich
1456-1458	Lazar III Brankovich
1458-1459	Helene Palaeologina (regent)
1459	Annexed by Turkey

SPAIN. *See also* **PORTUGAL**

The Iberian Peninsula now occupied by Spain and Portugal was a turbulent region during the Middle Ages, a place where numerous cultures clashed, notably Christianity and Islam but also a broad and ethnically diverse group of peoples, from the Suevi and Visigoths of the seventh century through the Berbers and Islamic peoples in the south. Through most of the Middle Ages the region saw a succession of fluctuating principalities in the north—primarily Asturias, Galicia, Aragón, Navarre, León, and Castile, while in the south Islam held sway from the eighth century to the time of Columbus's voyage to the Americas in 1492. In that year the Reconquista concluded with the Fall of Granada, and Christianity claimed the peninsula. In 1516, the Kingdom of Spain united all former kingdoms, with the exception of Portugal, into one Kingdom of Spain.

MAJOR ISLAMIC RULERS

Córdoba's Umayyad Caliphs (emirs until 929)

Reign	*Ruler*
756-788	ʿAbd al-Raḥmān I (emir)
788-796	Hishām I (emir)
796-822	al-Hakam I (emir)
822-852	ʿAbd al-Raḥmān II (emir)
852-886	Muḥammad I (emir)
886-888	al-Mundhir (emir)
888-912	ʿAbd Allāh (emir)
912-961	ʿABD AL-RAḤMĀN III AL-NĀṢIR
961-976	al-Hakam II al-Mustanṣir
976-1008	Hishām II al-Muayyad
1008-1009	Muḥammad II al-Mahdī
1009	Sulaimān al-Mustaʿīn
1010-1013	Hishām II (restored)
1013-1016	Sulaimān (restored)
1016-1018	Alī ben Hammud
1018	ʿAbd al-Raḥmān IV
1018-1021	al-Qasim
1021-1022	Yaḥyā
1022-1023	al-Qasim (restored)
1023-1024	ʿAbd al-Raḥmān V
1024-1025	Muḥammad III
1025-1027	Yaḥyā (restored)
1027-1031	Hishām III
1031	End of Umayyads; dissolution of Umayyad Spain into small states

After the Umayyads, Turbulence: Some Major Rulers

Reign	*Ruler*
1031-1043	Jahwar ibn Muḥammad ibn Jahwar
1043-1058	Muḥammad ar-Rashīd
1058-1069	ʿAbd al-Malik Dhu's-Siyādat al-Manṣur
1069	ʿAbbādid conquest
1085	Toledo falls to León and Castile; Christian Reconquista begins

Almoravid Sultans (Spain and North Africa)

Reign	*Ruler*
1061-1107	Yūsuf ibn Tāshufīn
1086	Entry into Spain; Alfonso VI defeated at Zallāqa
1107-1142	ʿAlīx ibn Yūsuf
1142-1146	Tāshufīn ibn ʿAlī
1146	Ibrāhīm ibn Tāshufīn
1146-1147	Isḥāq ibn ʿAlī
1147	Almohad conquest

Almohad Caliphs (Spain and North Africa)

Reign	*Ruler*
1130-1163	ʿABD AL-MUʾMIN
1163-1184	Abū Yaʿqūb Yūsuf
1184-1199	Abū Yūsuf Yaʿqūb al-Manṣūr
1199-1213	Muḥammad ibn Yaʿqūb
1212	Christians defeat Almohads at Las Navas de Tolosa
1213-1224	Yūsuf II Abū Yaqūb
1224	ʿAbd al-Wāḥid Abū Muḥammad
1224-1227	ʿAbd Allāh Abū Muḥammad
1227-1232	Idrīs I ibn Yaʿqūb
1227-1235	Yaḥyā Abū Zakariyyāʿ
1228-1229	Retreat from Spain
1232-1242	ʿAbdul-Wāḥid ibn Idrīs I
1242-1248	ʿAlī ibn Idrīs I
1248-1266	ʿUmar ibn Isḥāq
1266-1269	Idrīs II ibn Muḥammad
1269	End of Almohad domination in North Africa

Naṣrid Sultans of Granada

Reign	*Ruler*
1232-1273	Muḥammad I al-Ghālib (Ibn al-Aḥmar)
1273-1302	Muḥammad II al-Faqīh
1302-1309	Muḥammad III al-Makhlūʿ

Reign	Ruler
1309-1314	Naṣr
1314-1325	Ismāʿīl I
1325-1333	Muḥammad IV
1333-1354	Yūsuf I al-Muʾayyad
1354-1359	Muḥammad V al-Ghani
1359-1360	Ismāʿīl II
1360-1362	Muḥammad VI al-Ghālib (El Bermejo)
1362-1391	Muḥammad V al-Ghani (restored)
1391-1392	Yūsuf II al-Mustahgnī
1392-1408	Muḥammad VII al-Mustaʿīn
1408-1417	Yūsuf III an-Nāṣir
1417-1419	Muḥammad VIII al-Mustamassik (al-Ṣaghīr, El Pequeño)
1419-1427	Muḥammad IX al-Ghālib (al-Aysar, El Zurdo)
1427-1429	Muḥammad VIII al-Mustamassik
1429-1432	Muḥammad IX al-Ghālib
1432	Yūsuf IV, Abenalmao
1432-1445	Muḥammad IX al-Ghālib
1445	Muḥammad X al-Aḥnaf (El Cojo)
1445-1446	Yūsuf V (Aben Ismael)
1446-1447	Muḥammad X al-Aḥnaf
1447-1453	Muḥammad IX al-Ghālib
1451-1455	Muḥammad XI (El Chiquito)
1454-1464	Saʿd al-Mustaʿīn (Ciriza, Muley Zad)
1462	Yūsuf V (Aben Ismael)
1464-1482	ʿAlī (Muley Hácen)
1482-1483	Muḥammad XII al-Zughūbī (Boabdil, El Chico)
1483-1485	ʿAlī (Muley Hácen)
1485-1490	Muḥammad ibn Saʿd al-Zaghal
1486-1492	Muḥammad XII al-Zughūbī (Boabdil, El Chico)
1492	Conquest by Castile and Aragón, end of Islamic Spain

NON-ISLAMIC AND CHRISTIAN RULERS

Asturias and Galicia

Reign	Ruler
718-737	Pelayo
737-739	Favila
739-757	Alfonso I the Catholic
757-768	Fruela I
768-774	Aurelio
774-783	Silo
783-788	Mauregato
788-791	Vermundo I
791-842	Alfonso II the Chaste
842-850	Ramiro I
850-866	Ordoño I
866-910	Alfonso III the Great
910	Subsumed by León

Navarre

Reign	Ruler
840-851	Inigo Arista
905-925	Sancho Garces
925-970	Garcia Sanchez I
970-994	Sancho Abarca
994-1000	Garcia Sanchez II
1000-1035	Sancho III the Great
1035-1054	Garcia IV
1054-1076	Sancho IV
1076-1094	Sancho Ramirez
1094-1134	Subsumed under Aragón, Castile, León; reemerges with reduced territory
1134-1150	Garcia V Ramirez
1150-1194	Sancho VI
1194-1234	Sancho VII
1234-1253	Teobaldo I of Champagne
1253-1270	Teobaldo II
1270-1274	Henry I
1274-1305	Juana I
1305-1316	Luis (Louis)
1316-1322	Philip V the Tall
1322-1328	Charles I
1328-1349	Juana II
1349-1387	Charles II the Bad
1387-1425	Charles III the Noble
1425-1479	Blanca & John
1479	Leonor
1479-1481	Francis Febo
1481-1512	Catalina
1512-1516	Ferdinand of Navarre (Ferdinand II)
After 1516	Subsumed under Spain

León

Reign	Ruler
910-914	Garcia
914-924	Ordoño II
924-925	Fruela II
925-930	Alfonso IV the Monk
930-950	Ramiro II
950-956	Ordoño III
956-967	Sancho I the Fat
967-982	Ramiro III
982-999	Vermundo II
999-1028	Alfonso V the Noble
1028-1037	Vermundo III
1038-1065	Fernando
1065-1070	Sancho II
1070-1072	Sancho III
1072-1109	Alfonso VI (king of Castile)
1109-1126	Urraca (married to Alfonso I of Aragón)
1126-1157	Alfonso VII
1157-1188	Ferdinand II
1188-1230	Alfonso IX

Reign	Ruler
1230-1252	Saint Fernando III
1252	Subsumed under Castile

Castile

Reign	Ruler
1035-1065	Ferdinand I
1065-1072	Sancho II
1072-1109	Alfonso VI
1109-1157	Castile joins with León
1157	Castile restored as separate principality
1157-1158	Sancho III
1158-1214	Alfonso VIII
1214-1217	Henry I
1217-1252	Saint Ferdinand III
1252	Castile rejoins with León
1252-1284	ALFONSO X (emperor)
1284-1295	Sancho IV
1295-1312	Ferdinand IV
1312-1350	Alfonso XI
1350-1369	Peter the Cruel
1369-1379	Henry II
1379-1390	John I
1390-1406	Henry III
1406-1454	John II
1454-1474	Henry IV
1474-1504	Isabella I
1492	Fall of Granada, end of Reconquista
1504-1516	Juana the Mad (d. 1506) & Philip I of Habsburg
1516	Formation of Kingdom of Spain

Aragón

Reign	Ruler
1035-1063	Ramiro I
1063-1094	Sancho Ramirez
1094-1104	Pedro I
1104-1134	Alfonso I (co-ruled León and Castile, 1109-1126)
1134-1137	Ramiro II
1137	Union with County of Barcelona
1137-1162	Petronilla
1162-1196	Alfonso II
1196-1213	Pedro II
1213-1276	JAMES I THE CONQUEROR (under regency to 1217)
1276-1285	Pedro III
1285-1291	Alfonso III
1291-1327	James II
1327-1336	Alfonso IV
1336-1387	Peter IV
1387-1395	John I
1395-1410	Martin I
1412-1416	Ferdinand I
1416-1458	Alfonso V
1458-1479	John II
1479-1516	Ferdinand II (Ferdinand V of Castile/Spain, Ferdinand of Navarre)
1516	Formation of Kingdom of Spain: Carlos I (Emperor Charles V)

SWEDEN. *See also* **DENMARK, NORWAY**

Reign	Ruler
647-735?	Harald Hildetand
735-750?	Sigurd Ring
750-794?	Ragnar Lodbrok
?	Eystein Beli
794-804	Björn Järnsida
804-808	Erik II (to 870?)
808-820	Erik III
820-859	Edmund I
860?-870	Erik I (poss. Erik II)
870-920	Björn
920-930	Olaf I Ring
?	Erik IV
930-950	Erik V
950-965	Edmund II
965-970	Olaf II
970-995	Erik VI the Victorious
995-1022	Olaf III Skötkonung
1022-1050	Anund Jakob Kolbrenner
1050-1060	Edmund III
1066-1067	Erik VII (VIII)
1066-1070	Halsten
1066-1080	Inge I Elder
1080-1083	Blot-Sven
1083-1110	Inge I Elder
1110-1118	Filip Halstensson
1118-1125	Inge II Younger
1125-1130	Magnus Nielsson
1130-1156	Sverker I Elder
1156-1160	Sain Erik IX
1161-1167	Charles VII
1167-1196	Knut I
1196-1208	Sverker II Younger
1208-1216	Erik X
1216-1222	John I
1222-1229	Erik XI
1229-1234	Knut II the Long
1234-1250	Erik XI
1250-1275	Valdemar
1275-1290	Magnus I
1290-1320	Berger
1320-1365	Magnus II (VII of Norway)
1356-1359	Erik XII

Reign	*Ruler*
1364-1389	Albert
1389-1412	MARGARET I OF DENMARK, NORWAY, AND SWEDEN
1397	Unification of Norway, Denmark, and Sweden
1412-1439	Erik XIII (VII of Denmark, III of Norway)
1439-1448	Christopher (III of Denmark)
1448-1481	Christian I of Oldenburg
1481-1513	Hans/John II
1513-1523	Christian II
1523-1560	Gustav I Vasa
1560-1568	Erik XIV
1568-1592	Johan/John III
1592-1604	Sigismund
1604-1611	Carl/Charles IX
1611-1632	Gustav II Adolph
1632-1654	Christina
1654-1660	Charles X
1660-1697	Charles XI
1697-1718	Charles XII (Madman of the North)
1718-1720	Ulrika
1730-1751	Frederick (landgrave of Hesse)
1751-1771	Adolphus Frederick
1771-1792	Gustav III
1792-1809	Gustav IV Adolph
1809-1818	Charles XIII
1814	Sweden and Norway joined
1818-1844	Charles XIV
1844-1859	Oscar I
1859-1872	Charles XI
1872-1907	Oxcar II
1905	Norway separates
1907-1950	Gustav V
1950-1973	Gustav VI Adolph
1973-	Karl/Charles XVI Gustaf

VIETNAM: INDEPENDENT GOVERNMENTS

Dates	*Government*
939-965	Ngo Dynasty (NGO QUYEN, founder)
968-980	Dinh Dynasty
980-1009	Le Dynasty
1009-1225	Ly Dynasty
1225-1400	Tran Dynasty
1400-1407	Ho Dynasty
1428-1789	Le Dynasty

WALACHIA

Reign	*Ruler*
c. 1290	Founded by Radu Negru (Ralph the Black)
c. 1290-1310	Tihomir
c. 1330-1352	Ioan Basarab I
1352-1364	Nicholas Alexander
1364-1377	Vladislav I Vlaicu
1377-1383	Radu I
1383-1386	Dan I
1386-1418	Mircea the Old
1417	Ottomans assert control
1394-1397	Vlad I
1418-1420	Michael I
1420-1431	Dan II
1421, 1423	Radu II the Poor
1431-1436	Alexander I
1436-1442	Vlad II Dracul
1442	Mircea
1442-1443	Basarab II
1443	Vlad II Dracul
1447	János Hunyadi (prince of Transylvania, 1441-1456, and regent of Hungary, 1446-1456)
1447	Petru II
1447	Radu II the Poor
1447	Vlad II Dracul
1447-1448	Vladslav II
1448	Vlad III Tepesh the Impaler
1448-1449	Petru II
1448-1456	Vladslav II
1456-1462	Vlad III Tepesh the Impaler
1462-1475	Radu I cel Frumos
1473, 1474-75	Basarab Laiota
1476	Vlad III Tepesh the Impaler
1476-1477	Basarab Laiota
1477-1481	Basarab Tepelush
1481	Vlad Calugarul
1481-1482	Basarab Tepelush
1482-1495	Vlad Calugarul
1495-1508	Radu II cel Mare the Great
1508-1509	Mihnea cel Rau
1509-1510	Mircea
1510-1512	Vlad cel Tinar
1512-1521	Neagoe Basarab
1521	Teodosie
1521	Vlad (Dragomir Calugarul)
1522-1529	Radu III de la Afumati
1523-1524	Radu IV Badica
1523-1525	Vladislav III
1529-1530	Moise
1530-1532	Vlad Inecatul
1532-1535	Vlad Vintila
1535-1545	Radu Paisie
1541-1546	Petru Raresh
1545-1552	Mircea Ciobanul
1552-1553	Radu Ilie

Reign	*Ruler*
1553-1554	Mircea Ciobanul
1554-1557	Patrascu cel Bun (the Kind)
1558-1559	Mircea Ciobanul
1559-1568	Petru cel Tinar
1568-1574	Alexander II
1574	Vintila
1574-1577	Alexander II
1577-1583	Mihnea Turcitul
1583-1585	Petru Cercel
1585-1591	Mihnea Turcitul

Reign	*Ruler*
1591-1592	Stephen Surdul
1592-1593	Alexander cel Rau
1593-1601	Michael II the Brave
1596	Michael unites Walachia, Moldavia, and Transylvania, shaking off Ottoman control
1594	Petru Schiopul (the Lame)
1595-1600	Ieremia Moghila
1601-1611	Radu VII (IV) Serban
1611	Ottoman control reasserted
1859	Joins Moldavia to form Romania

Great Lives from History

The Middle Ages

477 - 1453

Chronological List of Entries

The arrangement of personages in this list is chronological on the basis of birth years (where known; other vital years appear where birth year is unknown). All personages appearing in this list are the subjects of articles in *Great Lives from History: The Middle Ages, 477-1453*; those personages treated in two-person articles are Saint Cyril and Saint Methodius, Jan van Eyck and Hubert van Eyck, Pietro Lorenzetti and Ambrogio Lorenzetti, Nicola Pisano and Giovanni Pisano, and Władysław II Jagiełło and Jadwiga.

Fifth Century

Priscian (5th cent.-6th cent.)
Saint Patrick (between 418 and 422-March 17, 493)
Odoacer (c. 435-about March 15, 493)
Dionysius Exiguus (latter half of 5th cent.-first half of 6th cent.)
Saint Brigit (c. 450-Feb. 1, 525)
Theodoric the Great (c. 454-Aug. 30, 526)
Clovis (c. 466-Nov. 27, 511)
Saint Clotilda (c. 474-June 3, 545)
Āryabhaṭa the Elder (c. 476-c. 550)
Boethius (c. 480-524)
Saint Benedict of Nursia (c. 480-c. 547)
Justinian I (probably May 11, 483-Nov. 14, 565)
Cassiodorus (c. 490-c. 585)
Amalasuntha (c. 495-April 30, 535)
Theodora (c. 497-June 28, 548)

Sixth Century

Alboin (6th cent.-572)
Khosrow I (c. 510-579)
Gregory of Tours (Nov. 30, 539-Nov. 17, 594)
Gregory the Great (c. 540-March 12, 604)
Fredegunde (c. 550-597)
Khadīja (c. 554-619)
Suiko (554-April 15, 628)
Saint Isidore of Seville (c. 560-April 4, 636)
Muḥammad (c. 570-June 8, 632)
Shōtoku Taishi (574-April 8, 622)
Heraclius (c. 575-Feb. 11, 641)
ʿUmar I (c. 586-Nov. 3, 644)
Harṣa (c. 590-c. 647)
Brahmagupta (c. 598-c. 660)
Taizong (Jan. 23, 599-May, 649)
Yan Liben (c. 600-673)

Seventh Century

Cædmon (early 7th cent.-c. 680)
Xuanzang (c. 602-664)
Saint Hilda of Whitby (614-Nov. 17, 689)
Paul of Aegina (c. 625-c. 690)
Wu Hou (625-Dec. 16, 705)
Saint Sergius I (635-Sept. 8, 701)
Sergius I (d. Dec. 9, 638)
al-Ḥasan al-Baṣrī (642-728)
ʿAbd al-Malik (c. 646-Oct., 705)
Damia al-Kāhina (c. 650-c. 702)
Saint Bede the Venerable (672 or 673-May 25, 735)
John of Damascus (c. 675-Dec. 4, 749)

Saint Boniface (c. 675-June 5, 754)
Charles Martel (c. 688-Oct. 22, 741)
Abū Ḥanīfah (c. 699-767)
Ṭāriq ibn-Ziyād (before 700-c. 720)
Śaṅkara (c. 700-c. 750)

Eighth Century

Widukind (8th cent.-c. 807)
Wang Wei (701-761)
Li Bo (701-762)
An Lushan (703-757)
Du Fu (712-770)
Rābiʿah al-ʿAdawiyah (c. 717-801)
Kōken (718-770)
Abū Mūsā Jābir ibn Ḥayyān (721-815)
Alcuin (c. 735-May 19, 804)
Charlemagne (April 2, 742-Jan. 28, 814)
Saint Irene (c. 752-Aug. 9, 803)
Theophanes the Confessor (c. 752-c. 818)
Hārūn al-Rashīd (Feb., 766-March 24, 809)
Egbert (c. 770-839)
Kōbō Daishi (July 27, 774-April 22, 835)
al-Jāḥiẓ (c. 776-868)
al-Khwārizmī (c. 780-c. 850)
Rabanus Maurus (c. 780-Feb. 4, 856)
Aḥmad ibn Ḥanbal (Dec., 780-July, 855)

Ninth Century

Ratramnus (early 9th cent.-c. 868)
Rurik (9th cent.-879)
Louis the German (c. 804-Aug. 28, 876)
Dhuoda (c. 805-c. 843)
Basil the Macedonian (812 or 813-Aug. 29, 886)
Nicholas the Great (c. 819/822-Nov. 13, 867)
Charles the Bald (June 13, 823-Oct. 6, 877)
Saint Methodius (c. 825-April 6, 884)
Saint Cyril (c. 827-Feb. 14, 869)
Boris I of Bulgaria (830-May 15, 907)
al-Ṭabarī (c. 839-923)
Alfred the Great (849-Oct. 26, 899)
Árpád (c. 850-907)
al-Ḥallāj (c. 858-March 26, 922)
al-Battānī (858-929)
Saint Ludmilla (c. 860-Sept. 15, 921)
Rollo (c. 860-c. 932)
al-Rāzī (c. 864-925)
Æthelflæd (c. 870-June 12, 918)
Edward the Elder (870?-July 17, 924)
al-Ashʿarī (873 or 874-935 or 936)
Wang Kŏn (877-943)
al-Masʿūdī (c. 890-956)
Saint Olga (890-969)
ʿAbd al-Raḥmān III al-Nāṣir (Jan., 891-Oct. 15, 961)
Ngo Quyen (c. 898-944)

Tenth Century

Otto I (Nov. 23, 912-May 7, 973)
Hrosvitha (c. 930/935-c. 1002)
Firdusi (932/941-between 1020 and 1025)
Abul Wefa (June 10, 940-July 15, 998)
Sylvester II (c. 945-May 12, 1003)
Vladimir I (c. 956-July 15, 1015)
Gershom ben Judah (c. 960-c. 1028)
Saint Fulbert of Chartres (c. 960-April 10, 1028)
Anna, Princess of the Byzantine Empire (March 13, 963-1011)
Alhazen (965-1039)
Sei Shōnagon (c. 966 or 967-1013)
Fujiwara Michinaga (966-Jan. 3, 1028)
Olaf I (c. 968-Sept. 9, 1000)

Eleventh Century

Twelfth Century

MATHEMATICS

MEDICINE

MILITARY

MONASTICISM

MUSIC

Geographical Index

Personages Index

Subject Index

All personages appearing in boldface type in this index are the subjects of articles in *Great Lives from History: The Middle Ages, 477-1453*; those personages treated in two-person articles are Saint Cyril and Saint Methodius, Jan van Eyck and Hubert van Eyck, Pietro Lorenzetti and Ambrogio Lorenzetti, Nicola Pisano and Giovanni Pisano, and Władysław II Jagiełło and Jadwiga.